Fundamentals of
Human Neuropsychology

Fundamentals of
Human Neuropsychology

Fifth Edition

Bryan Kolb
Ian Q. Whishaw

University of Lethbridge

WORTH PUBLISHERS

A Series of Books in Psychology

Editors:

Richard C. Atkinson
Gardner Lindzey
Richard F. Thompson

On the front cover is a contemporary carved mask (Daydreamer) created by Robert B. Jackson of the Gitskan nation, a Northwest Coast tribe of British Columbia, Canada. Narrative masks, such as this one, have associated stories or songs that document historical and personal events passed down through families by oral tradition using dance, narrative, and song. In Jackson's mask, each side of the face displays a different expression: surprise on the right and understanding on the left. Not only do certain regions of the brain control facial expression, but each hemisphere makes a special contribution to facial expression and each side of the face reflects the contribution of the contralateral hemisphere. (Mask carving by R. B. Jackson of Sky Clan Arts. <www.village.hazelton.bc.ca>. Photo courtesy of the Inuit Gallery of Vancouver Ltd., photography by Kenji Nagai.)

Senior Sponsoring Editor: Laura Pople
Executive Marketing Manager: Renée Altier
Development Manager: Mimi Melek
Development Editors: Moira Lerner, Barbara Brooks
Art Development Coordinator: Danielle Storm
Senior Project Editor: Georgia Lee Hadler
Line Editor: Patricia Zimmerman
Art Director: Barbara Reingold
Text and Cover Design: Lissi Sigillo
Layout Design: Lee Ann Mahler
Production Manager: Sarah Segal
Illustration Coordinator: Bill Page
Illustrations: J/B Woolsey Associates
Photo Research Manager: Patricia Marx
Photo Editor: Nigel Assam
Supplements and Media Editor: Graig Donini
Composition: Compset Inc.
Printing and Binding: R. R. Donnelley and Sons

Library of Congress Control Number: 2003100573

ISBN: 0-7167-5300-6 (FAN: 9780716753001)

Printed in the United States of America
Third printing

Worth Publishers
41 Madison Avenue
New York, NY 10010

http://www.worthpublishers.com

Brief Contents

Contents

Part II Cortical Organization

Part IV Higher Functions

Part V Plasticity and Disorders

CHAPTER 27

Psychiatric and Related Disorders 723

CHAPTER 28

Neuropsychological Assessment 751

Preface

When we embarked on *Fundamentals of Human Neuropsychology* in 1977, we could not imagine how much the field would change in the next 25 years. An exciting development in neuropsychology has been the use of neuroimaging as a research tool, and we have increased the emphasis on neuroimaging in this new edition in a variety of ways. First, an entire chapter deals with neuroimaging technology, bringing together all the major techniques for studying the living brain in one place. Second, we feature a "Snapshot" of imaging in each of the core neuropsychology chapters (Chapters 8 through 27) and in Chapters 6 and 7. Third, when appropriate we include tables summarizing neuroimaging findings on different topics, such as cerebral asymmetry and frontal-lobe function. Fourth, discussions of neuroimaging studies naturally led to the incorporation of more cognitive neuroscience. As basic neuroscientists, however, our emphasis remains on the neural mechanisms underlying relations between brain and behavior, rather than on cognitive theories that more naturally belong in textbooks dealing with cognitive neuroscience.

Another major feature of this edition is a completely new illustration program. We, in conjunction with John Woolsey, with whom we have collaborated in the past, developed an expansive and, we believe, exceptional set of illustrations that, hand in hand with our words, describes and illuminates the world of the brain. The illustrations in every chapter are consistent and reinforce one another, with a second color being used to great advantage.

Readers familiar with earlier editions of *Fundamentals* will find other changes, too. The chapters forming Part V have been reorganized and reintegrated to better correspond with the direction in which the field has been going. In particular, Chapters 23 and 25 focus on brain plasticity, which has become an area of intense experimental interest. Furthermore, every chapter in the book has been thoroughly revised with an emphasis on what we judged to be major advances since 1995.

Although other textbooks have appeared in the past 25 years, none is like *Fundamentals* in one important dimension. To us, neuropsychology is the bridge between psychology and neuroscience. It thus must include extensive consideration of anatomy and physiology as well as cognitive, experimental, and clinical psychology. The book is still divided into parts in accord with this philosophy. Part I provides the background information for those who are new to the brain. A new chapter has been added, Chapter 6 (on drugs), because we have found that students have a particular interest in how drugs work and how they can be used therapeutically. Parts II, III, and IV provide the core of information that forms the basis of a course in neuropsychology. This organization makes *Fundamentals* different from other books in that we consider the relations between brain and behavior by first focusing on the general organization of the cerebral hemispheres (Part II) and anatomy (Part III) and then on psychological functions (Part IV). As basic behavioral neuroscientists, we strongly believe that a solid grounding in understanding the anatomical and physiological organization of the cerebral hemispheres is essential to understanding behavior and the brain. Part V considers brain plasticity and disorders of the brain and provides useful supplementary reading materials not only for advanced (or senior) courses but also for interested students.

We feel that many chapters can be read at many levels, depending on the reader's sophistication in the neurosciences. We find that beginning students have little interest in history, for example, but, as their interest in certain problems increases, they find historical or other theoretical information more relevant.

As in the past, we must say that we are deeply indebted to those who have written us with advice and comments on how to improve the book. Of course, the improvements are due to their help, and the errors are attributable solely to us. We are grateful to Pamela Brouillard, Robert Flint, Jr., Stuart Hall, Nancy Squires, Carol Seger, Neil Watson, and Arturo Hernandez for their feedback. We are indebted to David Boles, Gabriele Leonard, Michael Peters, and Michael Petrides. Sam Weiss, a biochemist who has discovered the power of behavioral analysis, and Robert Sutherland arranged for us to have electronic access to dozens of journals that we could not otherwise obtain, which proved to be invaluable. Elzabeth Hudson and Richard Tees provided welcome assistance in finding information regarding the native mask that is the front cover image. Many provided original illustrative material that made a real difference in the quality of the illustrations, for which we and John Woolsey are grateful.

We also must thank the staff at Worth Publishers and W. H. Freeman and Company for their patience and assistance. The earlier editions of this book did not undergo editorial development, and the developmental editors provided a fresh perspective to two authors who perhaps had become too familiar and comfortable with the material and organization of the book. We want to thank especially Barbara Brooks, Moira Lerner, Mimi Melek, and Patty Zimmerman, who were relentless in insisting on changes that much improved the book; they have our thanks and admiration, especially for times when we were less than generous in return. Project editor Georgia Lee Hadler once again organized the final editing and layout and once again did an excellent job. We also wish to acknowledge our sponsoring editors, Jessica Bayne and Laura Pople, and our production manager, Sarah Segal, for their enthusiasm and support of yet another attempt to get things right! Finally, we must express our continuing gratitude to W. Hayward (Buck) Rogers, formerly with W. H. Freeman and Company, who had the foresight to agree to publish *Fundamentals* in 1978—a time at which no other major publisher believed there was such a field as neuropsychology. There is, and 25 years later it is alive and well.

BRYAN KOLB AND IAN Q. WHISHAW

Fundamentals of
Human Neuropsychology

The Development of Neuropsychology

In Sophocles' (496–406 B.C.) play *Oedipus the King,* Oedipus finds his way blocked by the Sphinx, who threatens to kill him unless he can answer this riddle: "What walks on four legs in the morning, two legs at noon, and three legs in the evening?" Oedipus replies, "A human," and is allowed to pass, because a person crawls as an infant, walks as an adult, and uses a cane when old. The Sphinx's riddle is the riddle of human nature, and as time passes Oedipus comes to understand that it has a deeper meaning: "What *is* a human?" The deeper question in the riddle confounds Oedipus and remains unanswered to this day. The object of this book is to pursue the answer in the place where it should be logically found: the brain.

The term *neuropsychology* in its English version originated quite recently, in part because it represented a new approach to studying the brain. According to Daryl Bruce, it was first used by Canadian physician William Osler in his early-twentieth-century textbook, which was a standard medical reference of the time. It later appeared as a subtitle to Canadian psychologist Donald O. Hebb's 1949 treatise on brain function, *The Organization of Behavior: A Neuropsychological Theory.* Although Hebb neither defined nor used the word in the text itself, he probably intended it to represent a multidisciplinary focus of scientists who believed that an understanding of human brain function was central to understanding human behavior. By 1957, the term had become a recognized designation for a subfield of the neurosciences. Heinrich Kluver, an American investigator into the neural basis of vision, wrote in the preface to his *Behavior Mechanism in Monkeys* that the book would be of interest to neuropsychologists and others. (Kluver had not used the term in the 1933 preface to the same book.) In 1960, it appeared in the title of a widely read collection of writings by American psychologist Karl S. Lashley—*The Neuropsychology of Lashley*—most of which described rat and monkey studies directed toward understanding memory, perception, and motor behavior. Again, *neuropsychology* was neither used nor defined in the text. To the extent that they did use the term, however, these writers, who specialized in the study of basic brain function in animals, were recognizing the emergence of a subdiscipline of investigators who specialized in human research and would find the animal research relevant to understanding human brain function.

Today, we define **neuropsychology** as the study of the relation between human brain function and behavior. Although neuropsychology draws information from many disciplines—for example, anatomy, biology, biophysics, ethology, pharmacology, physiology, physiological psychology, and philosophy—its central focus is the development of a science of human behavior based on the function of the human brain. As such, it is distinct from **neurology,** which is the diagnosis of nervous system injury by physicians who are specialists in nervous system diseases, from **neuroscience,** which is the study of the molecular basis of nervous system function by scientists who mainly use nonhuman animals, and from **psychology,** which is the study of behavior more generally.

Neuropsychology is strongly influenced by two traditional foci of experimental and theoretical investigations into brain function: the **brain hypothesis,** the idea that the brain is the source of behavior; and the **neuron hypothesis,** the idea that the unit of brain structure and function is the neuron. This chapter traces the development of these two ideas. We will see that, although the science is new, its major ideas are not.

The Brain Hypothesis

People knew what the brain looked like long before they had any idea of what it did. Very early in human history, hunters must have noticed that all animals have a brain and that the brains of different animals, including humans, although varying greatly in size, look quite similar. Within the past 2000 years, anatomists began producing drawings of the brain and naming some of its distinctive parts without knowing what function the brain or its parts performed. We will begin this chapter with a description of the brain and some of its major parts and will then consider some major insights into the functions of the brain.

What Is the Brain?

Brain is an Old English word for the tissue that is found within the skull. Figure 1.1 shows a typical human brain as oriented in the skull of an upright human. The brain has two relatively symmetrical halves called **hemispheres,** one on the left side of the body and one on the right. Just as your body is symmetrical, having two arms and two legs, so is the brain. If you make your right hand into a fist and hold it up with the thumb pointing toward the front, the fist can represent the position of the brain's left hemisphere within the skull.

Taken as a whole, the basic plan of the brain is that of a tube filled with fluid, called **cerebrospinal fluid** (CSF). Parts of the covering of the tube have bulged outward and folded, forming the more complicated looking surface structures that initially catch the eye. The most conspicuous outer feature of the brain consists of a crinkled tissue that has expanded from the front of the tube to such an extent that it folds over and covers much of the rest of the brain. This outer layer is known as the **cerebral cortex** (usually referred to as just the cortex). The word *cortex*, which means "bark" in Latin, is aptly chosen both because the cortex's folded appearance resembles the bark of a tree and because its tissue covers most of the rest of the brain, just as bark covers a tree.

The folds of the cortex are called **gyri,** and the creases between them are called **sulci** (*gyrus* is Greek for "circle" and *sulcus* is Greek for "trench"). Some large sulci are called fissures, such as the **longitudinal fissure** that divides the two hemispheres and the **lateral fissure** that divides each hemisphere into halves (in our fist analogy, the lateral fissure is the crease separating the thumb from the other fingers).

The cortex of each hemisphere is divided into four lobes, named after the skull bones beneath which they lie. The **temporal lobe** is located at approximately the same place as the thumb on your upraised fist. The lobe lying immediately above the temporal lobe is called the **frontal lobe** because it is located at the front of the brain. The **parietal lobe** is located behind the frontal lobe, and the **occipital lobe** constitutes the area at the back of each hemisphere.

The cerebral cortex comprises most of the **forebrain,** so named because it develops from the front part of the tube that makes up the embryo's primitive brain. The remaining "tube" underlying the cortex is referred to as the **brainstem.** The brainstem is in turn connected to the **spinal cord,** which descends down the back in the vertebral column. To visualize the relations between these parts of the brain, again imagine your upraised fist: the folded fingers represent the cortex, the hand represents the brainstem, and the arm represents the spinal cord.

This three-part division of the brain is conceptually useful evolutionarily, anatomically, and functionally. Evolutionarily, animals with only spinal cords preceded those with brainstems, which preceded those with forebrains. Likewise, in prenatal development, the spinal cord forms before the brainstem, which forms before the forebrain. Functionally, the forebrain mediates cognitive functions; the brainstem mediates regulatory functions such as eating, drinking, and moving;

(B)

Your right hand, if made into a fist, represents the positions of the lobes of the left hemisphere of your brain.

Frontal lobe (fingers)   Parietal lobe (knuckles)

Temporal lobe (thumb)   Occipital lobe (wrist)

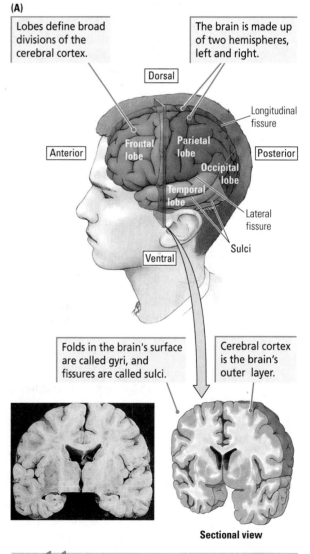

(A)

Lobes define broad divisions of the cerebral cortex.

The brain is made up of two hemispheres, left and right.

Dorsal

Longitudinal fissure

Anterior

Frontal lobe   Parietal lobe   Posterior

Occipital lobe

Temporal lobe

Lateral fissure

Ventral

Sulci

Folds in the brain's surface are called gyri, and fissures are called sulci.

Cerebral cortex is the brain's outer layer.

Sectional view

Figure 1.1 (A) This representation of the human brain shows its orientation in the head. The visible part of the intact brain is the cerebral cortex, a thin sheet of tissue folded many times and fitting snugly inside the skull. (B) Your right fist can serve as a guide to the orientation of the brain and its lobes. (Glauberman/Photo Researchers.)

and the spinal cord is responsible for sending commands to the muscles. Neuropsychologists commonly refer to functions of the forebrain as being higher functions because they include thinking, perception, and planning. The regulatory and movement-producing functions of the brainstem and spinal cord are thus sometimes referred to as lower-level functions.

How Is the Brain Related to the Rest of the Nervous System?

The brain and spinal cord in mammals such as ourselves are protected by bones: the skull protects the brain, and the vertebra protect the spinal cord. Because they are both enclosed within this protective covering, the brain and spinal cord together are called the **central nervous system** or CNS. The central nervous system is connected to the rest of the body through **nerve fibers,** some of which carry information away from the CNS and some of which bring information to it. These fibers constitute the **peripheral nervous system,** or PNS.

The fibers that bring information to the CNS are extensively connected to sensory receptors on the body's surface, to internal body organs, and to muscles, enabling the brain to sense what goes on in the world around us and in our body. These fibers are organized into **sensory pathways,** collections of fibers that carry messages for specific sensory systems, such as hearing, vision, and touch. Using information gathered by the various sensory receptors and sent to the brain over these pathways, the brain constructs its current images of the world, its memories of past events, and its expectations about the future. The **motor pathways** are the groups of fibers that connect the brain and spinal cord to the body's muscles. The movements produced by motor pathways include the eye movements that you are using to read this book, the hand movements that you make while turning the pages, and the posture of your body as you read. Motor pathways also influence movements in the muscles of your internal organs, such as the beating of your heart, the contractions of your stomach, and the raising and lowering of your diaphragm, which inflates and deflates your lungs. The pathways that control these organs are a subdivision of the PNS called the **autonomic nervous system.**

The Brain Versus the Heart

Since earliest times, people have puzzled over how behavior is produced. Their conclusions are preserved in the historical records of many different cultures. Among the oldest surviving recorded hypotheses are those of two Greeks, Alcmaeon of Croton (ca. 500 B.C.) and Empedocles of Acragas (ca. 490–430 B.C.). Alcmaeon located mental processes in the brain and so subscribed to what is now called the *brain hypothesis;* Empedocles located them in the heart and so subscribed to what could be called the *cardiac hypothesis.*

The relative merits of those two hypotheses were debated for the next 2000 years. For example, among Greek philosophers, Plato (427?–347 B.C.) developed the concept of a tripartite soul (nutritive, perceptual, and rational) and placed its rational part in the brain because that was the part of the body closest to the heavens. Aristotle (384–322 B.C.) had a good knowledge of brain structure and realized that, of all animals, humans have the largest brain relative to body size. Nevertheless, he decided that, because the heart is warm and active, it is the source of mental processes, whereas the brain, because it is cool and inert, serves as a radiator to cool the blood (actually, it turns out that the blood cools the brain). He interpreted the large size of the human brain as evidence that our blood is richer and hotter than that of other animals and so requires a larger cooling system.

Early Greek and Roman physicians, such as Hippocrates (ca. 460–377 B.C.) and Galen (A.D. 129–ca. 199), influenced by their clinical experience, described aspects of the brain's anatomy and argued strongly for the brain hypothesis. Before becoming the leading physician in Rome, Galen spent 5 years as a surgeon to gladiators and witnessed some of the behavioral consequences of brain damage. He went to great pains to refute Aristotle, pointing out that not only did brain damage impair behavior but the nerves from the sense organs go to the brain and not to the heart. He also reported on his experiences in attempting to treat wounds to the brain or heart. He noted that pressure on the brain causes cessation of movement and even death, whereas pressure on the heart causes pain but does not arrest voluntary behavior.

Although we now accept the brain hypothesis, the cardiac hypothesis has left its mark on our language. In literature, as in everyday speech, emotion is frequently ascribed to the heart: love is symbolized by an arrow piercing the heart; a person distressed by unrequited love is said to be heartbroken; an unenthusiastic person is described as not putting his or her heart into it; an angry person says, "It makes my blood boil."

Descartes: The Mind–Body Problem

Simply knowing that the brain controls behavior is not enough; the formulation of a complete hypothesis of brain function requires knowing *how* the brain controls behavior. Modern thinking about this question began with René Descartes (1596–1650), a French anatomist and philosopher. Descartes replaced the Platonic concept of a tripartite soul with a single soul that he called the **mind.** Described as nonmaterial and without spatial extent, the mind, as Descartes saw it, was different from the body. The body operated on principles similar to those of a machine, but the mind decided what movements the machine should make. Descartes was impressed by machines made in his time, such as those of certain statues that were on display for public amusement in the water gardens of Paris. When a passerby stopped in front of one particular statue, for example, his or her weight would depress a lever under the sidewalk, causing the statue to move and spray water at the person's face. Descartes proposed that the body is like these machines. It is material and thus clearly has spatial extent, and it responds mechanically and reflexively to events that impinge upon it (Figure 1.2).

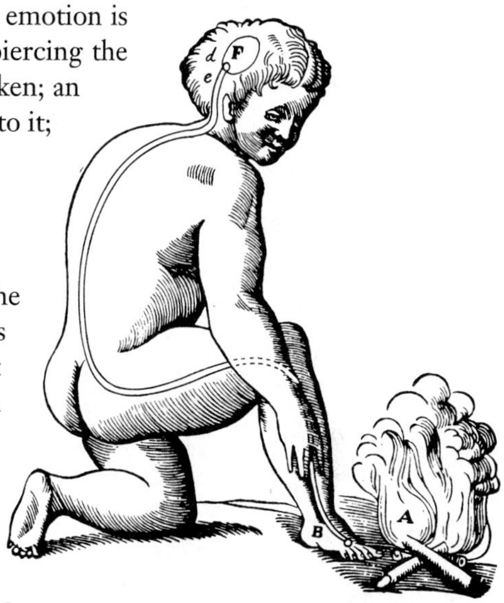

The position that mind and body are separate but can interact is called **dualism,** to indicate that behavior is caused by two things. Descartes's dualism originated what came to be known as the **mind–body problem:** for Descartes, a person is capable of being conscious and rational only because of having a mind, but how can a *nonmaterial* mind produce movements in a *material* body? To understand the problem, consider that, in order for the mind to affect the body, it would have to expend energy, adding new energy to the material world. The creation of new energy would violate a fundamental law of physics. Thus, dualists who argue that the two interact causally cannot explain how. Other dualists

Figure 1.2 The concept of a reflex action originated with Descartes. In this very mechanistic depiction of how he thought physical reflexes might work, heat from the flame causes a thread in the nerve to be pulled, releasing ventricular fluid through an opened pore. The fluid flows through the nerve, causing not only the foot to withdraw but also the eyes and head to turn to look at it, the hands to advance, and the whole body to bend to protect it. Descartes applied the reflex concept to behaviors that would today be considered too complex to be reflexive, whereas behavior described as reflexive today was not conceived of by Descartes. (From Descartes, 1664.)

avoid this problem by reasoning either that the mind and body function in parallel without interacting or that the body can affect the mind but the mind cannot affect the body. These dualist positions allow for both a body and a mind by sidestepping the problem of violating the laws of physics. Other philosophers called **monists** avoid the mind–body problem by postulating that the mind and body are simply two words for the same thing and both are either material or nonmaterial. Most neuropsychologists are materialists and hold that the terms *mind* and *brain* are two different ways of describing the same object. Clearly, it would be difficult to be a neuropsychologist who is a nonmaterialist, because such a person would believe that there are no physical things to study.

In addition to being a dualist, Descartes ascribed functions to different parts of the brain. He located the site of action of the mind in the **pineal body,** a small structure in the brainstem. His choice of this structure was based on the logic that the pineal body is the only structure in the nervous system not composed of two bilaterally symmetrical halves and moreover that it is located close to the ventricles. His idea was that the mind in the pineal body controlled valves that allowed cerebral spinal fluid to flow from the ventricles through nerves to muscles, filling them and making them move. For Descartes, the cortex was not functioning neural tissue but merely a covering for the pineal body. People later argued against Descartes's hypothesis by pointing out that, when the pineal body was found to be damaged, there were no obvious changes in behavior. Today the pineal body is thought to take part in controlling seasonal rhythms.

In proposing his dualistic theory of brain function, Descartes also proposed that animals did not have minds and so were only machinelike. The inhumane treatment of animals, children, and the mentally ill was justified on the grounds that they did not have minds by some followers of Descartes. For them, an animal did not have a mind, a child developed a mind only when about 7 years of age and able to talk and reason, and the mentally ill had "lost their minds." Misunderstanding Descartes's position, some people still argue that the study of animals cannot be a source of useful insight into human neuropsychology. Descartes himself, however, was not so dogmatic. Although he proposed the idea that animals and humans are different with respect to having a mind, he also suggested that the idea could be tested experimentally. He proposed that the key indications of the presence of a mind are the use of language and reason. He suggested that, if it could be demonstrated that animals could speak or reason, then such demonstration would indicate that they have minds. As we will note later on, some lines of research in modern experimental neuropsychology are directed toward the comparative study of animals and humans with respect to these abilities.

Darwin and Materialism

By the mid–nineteenth century, another theory of the brain and behavior was taking shape. This was the modern perspective of **materialism**—the idea that rational behavior can be fully explained by the working of the nervous system, without any need to refer to a nonmaterial mind. This perspective had its roots in the evolutionary theories of two English naturalists, Alfred Russell Wallace (1823–1913) and Charles Darwin (1809–1892).

Wallace and Darwin independently arrived at the same conclusion—the idea that all living things are related. Darwin arrived at the idea much earlier than Wallace did but failed to publish his writing at that time. So that both could receive credit for the idea, their papers were presented together before the Linnaean Society of London in July 1858. Darwin elaborated further on the topic in *On the Origin of Species by Means of Natural Selection*, published in 1859.

Both Darwin and Wallace looked carefully at the structures of plants and animals and at animal behavior. Despite the diversity of living organisms, they were struck by the number of similarities and common characteristics. For example, the skeleton, muscles, internal organs, and nervous systems of humans, monkeys, and other mammals are remarkably similar. These observations supported the idea that living things must be related, an idea widely held even before Wallace and Darwin. But more importantly, these same observations led to the idea that the similarities could be explained if all animals evolved from a common ancestor.

Darwin argued that all organisms, both living and extinct, are descended from some unknown ancestor that lived in the remote past. In Darwin's terms, all living things are said to have **common descent.** As the descendants of that original organism spread into various habitats through millions of years, they developed structural and behavioral adaptations that suited them for new ways of life. At the same time, they retained many similar traits that reveal their relatedness to one another. The brain is one such common characteristic found in animal species. It is an adaptation that emerged only once in animal evolution. Consequently, the brains of living animals are similar because they are descendents of that first brain. Furthermore, if animals are related and their brains are related and if all behavior of nonhuman animals is a product of their brains, then all human behavior must also be a product of the brain.

Some people reject the idea that the brain is responsible for behavior, because they think it denies the teaching of their religion that there is a nonmaterial soul that will continue to exist after their bodies die. Others regard the biological explanation of brain and behavior as being neutral with respect to religion. Many behavioral scientists with strong religious beliefs see no contradiction between those beliefs and using the scientific method to examine the relations between the brain and behavior.

Experimental Approaches to Brain Function

Philosophical and theoretical approaches to brain function do not require physical measures of the brain or experimental methods for testing hypotheses. Those methods belong to science. Beginning in the early 1800s, scientists began to test their ideas about brain function by examining and measuring the brain and by developing methods to describe behavior quantitatively (so that researchers could check one another's conclusions). In this section, we will describe a number of influential experimental approaches to the study of brain function and some of the important neuropsychological ideas that resulted from them.

Localization of Function

Philosophers who argue that the mind controls behavior see "the mind" as indivisible. In their view, theories that subdivide brain function cannot possibly be correct. You may have heard statements such as "most people use only 10% of their brains," or "he put his entire mind to the problem." Both sayings suggest that the brain or mind does its work as a unified whole. Nevertheless, most victims of brain damage find that some behavior is lost and some survives, suggesting that different parts of the nervous system have different functions. In the nineteenth century, physiologists perplexed by such observations would often puzzle over the symptoms of brain damage and then speculate about how the observations could be consistent with a holistic notion of the mind.

The first general theory to present the idea that different parts of the brain had different functions was the phrenological theory of German anatomist Franz Josef Gall (1758–1828) and his partner Johann Casper Spurzheim (1776–1832). Gall and Spurzheim made a number of important discoveries in neuroanatomy that alone give them a place in history. They proposed that the cortex and its gyri were functioning parts of the brain and not just coverings for the pineal body. They supported their position by showing through dissection that a large pathway called the **pyramidal tract** leads from the cortex to the spinal cord, suggesting that the cortex sends instructions to the spinal cord to command movement of the muscles. As they dissected the pathway they noted that, as it travels along the base of the brainstem, it forms a large bulge, or pyramid, on each side of the brain. Because the tract travels from the cortex to the spinal cord, it is also called the **corticospinal pathway.** Thus, not only did they propose that the cortex was a functioning part of the brain, they also proposed that it produced behavior through the control of other parts of the brain and spinal cord through this pathway. They also recognized that the two symmetrical hemispheres of the brain are connected by another large pathway called the **corpus callosum** and thus could interact with each other.

Gall's behavioral ideas began with an observation made in his youth. He is reported to have been annoyed by students with good memories who achieved excellent marks but did not have an equivalent ability for original thinking. According to his recollection of those days, the students with the best memories had large, protruding eyes. Using this crude observation as a starting point, he developed a general theory of how the brain might produce differences in individual abilities into a theory of brain function called **localization of function.** For example, Gall proposed that a well-developed memory area of the cortex located behind the eyes could cause the eyes to protrude.

Gall and Spurzheim then began to collect instances of individual differences and relate them to other prominent features of the head and skull. They proposed that a bump on the skull indicated a well-developed underlying cortical gyrus and therefore a greater capacity for a particular behavior; a depression in the same area indicated an underdeveloped gyrus and a concomitantly reduced faculty (Figure 1.3). Thus, just as a

(A)

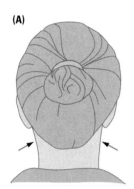

(B)

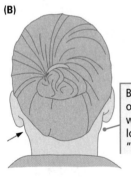

Bumps in the region of the cerebellum were thought to locate the brain's "amativeness" center.

Figure 1.3 According to phrenologists, depressions (A) and bumps (B) on the skull indicate the size of the underlying area of brain and thus, when correlated with personality traits, indicate the part of the brain controlling the trait. Gall, examining a patient (who because of her behavior became known as "Gall's Passionate Widow"), found a bump at the back of her neck that he thought located the center for "amativeness" in the cerebellum. French physiologist Pierre Flourens refuted this hypothesis by removing a dog's cerebellum to show that the chief purpose of the cerebellum is to coordinate movement. As phrenology (Spurzheim's name for the theory) grew in popularity, bumps and depressions that were not even adjacent to the brain were interpreted as being signs of behavioral and personality traits—as was the case with amativeness. (After Olin, 1910.)

person with a good memory had protruding eyes, a person who had a high degree of musical ability, artistic talent, sense of color, combativeness, or mathematical skill would have a large bump in other areas of the skull. Figure 1.3B shows where they located the trait of amativeness (sexiness). A person with a bump there would be predicted to have a strong sex drive, whereas a person low in this trait would have a depression in the same region.

Gall and Spurzheim identified a long list of behavioral traits that were borrowed from English or Scottish psychology. Each trait was assigned to a particular part of the skull and, by inference, to the underlying part of the brain. Figure 1.4 shows the resulting map that they devised. Spurzheim called the study of the relation between the skull's surface features and a person's faculties **phrenology** (*phren* is a Greek word for "mind"). The map of the relation between brain functions and the skull surface is called a phrenological map.

Gall and Spurzheim went to considerable effort to gather evidence for their theory. As Gall described it, he devoted himself to observation and waited patiently for nature to bring her results to him. Thus, in developing his idea of the carnivorous instinct, Gall compared the skulls of meat- and plant-eating animals, collecting evidence from more than 50 species, including a description of his own lapdog. His studies of human behavior included accounts of a patricide and a murderer, as well as descriptions of people who delighted in witnessing death or torturing animals or who historically were noted for cruelty and sadism. He also examined the skulls of 25 murderers and even considered evidence from paintings and busts.

Interestingly, Gall placed no emphasis on evidence from cases of brain damage, even though he is credited with giving the first complete account of a case in which left frontal brain damage was followed by loss of the ability to speak. The patient was a soldier who had had a sword pierce his brain through the eye. Note that, on the phrenological map in Figure 1.4, language is located below the eye. Yet Gall felt that this type of finding was not evidence per se but rather confirmation of a finding that was already established by the phrenological evidence.

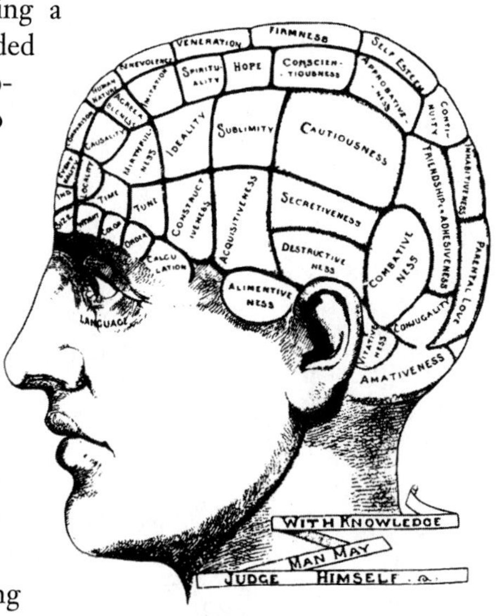

Phrenology was seized on by some people as a means of making personality assessments. They developed a method called **cranioscopy,** in which a device was placed around the skull to measure the bumps and depressions there. These measures were then correlated with the phrenological map to determine the person's likely behavioral traits. Cranioscopy invited quackery and thus, indirectly, ridicule by association. Because most of its practitioners produced extremely superficial personality analyses, the entire phrenological endeavor was eventually brought into disrepute. There were other problems intrinsic to the theory. For example, the faculties described in phrenology—characteristics such as faith, self-love, and veneration—are impossible to define and to quantify objectively. The phrenologists also failed to recognize that the superficial features of the skull reveal little about the underlying brain. The outer skull does not mirror even the inner skull, much less the surface features of the cortex.

A historical remnant from the phrenology era is that the lobes of the cortex are named after the bones of the skull; for example, the lobes in the front of the

Figure 1.4 Originally, Gall's system identified putative locations for 27 faculties. As the study of phrenology expanded, the number of faculties increased. This drawing shows the location of faculties according to Spurzheim. Language, indicated in the front of the brain (below the eye), actually derived from one of Gall's case studies. A soldier had received a knife wound that penetrated the frontal lobe of his left hemisphere through the eye. The soldier lost the ability to speak. That case represented the first comprehensive report of speech loss following left frontal damage.

cortex are called frontal lobes and those on the side are called temporal lobes after the respective overlying bones. Additionally, despite the failure of scientific attempts to correlate appearance with various aspects of behavior, it is not uncommon to hear people accord virtues to others on the basis of their physical appearance. Readers might ask themselves how accurate they would be if asked to judge intelligence on the basis of photographs. Social psychologists have found that, when university students are asked to make such judgments, the rule that they apply to the task is, "Beauty equals intelligence." In fairness to Gall, we must note that his science attempted an actual physical measurement. His conclusions were inaccurate in part because he did not test his hypotheses with experiments, a method that was to come into general use only much later.

Recovery of Function

French physiologist Pierre Flourens (1794–1867) is generally credited with the demolition of phrenology. Flourens disagreed with Gall and Spurzheim's correlation of bumps and depressions with behavior, but he did not use argument alone to decide whose ideas were most accurate. He developed the method of controlled laboratory experiments. He was not, however, above using ridicule as well, as the following story from his book *Comparative Psychology* shows:

> The famous physiologist, Magendie, preserved with veneration the brain of Laplace (a famous French mathematician). Spurzheim had the very natural wish to see the brain of a great man. To test the science of the phrenologist, Mr. Magendie showed him, instead of the brain of Laplace, that of an imbecile. Spurzheim, who had already worked up his enthusiasm, admired the brain of the imbecile as he would have admired that of Laplace. (Krech, 1962)

Flourens's experimental method consisted of removing parts of the brains of animals to study the changes produced in their behavior. He removed a small piece of cortex and then observed how the animal behaved and how it recovered from the loss of brain tissue. In essence, he created animal models of humans who had received injury to a part of the brain by a blow to the head or by having the skull pierced by a missile. To search for different functions in the cortex, he varied the location from which he removed brain tissue.

Flourens found that, after he removed pieces of cortex, animals at first moved very little and neglected to eat and drink, but with time they recovered to the point at which they seemed normal. This pattern of loss and recovery held for all his cortex experiments, seeming to refute the idea that different areas of the cortex had specialized functions. He did find that parts of the brainstem had specialized functions. For example, he found that the brainstem is important for breathing, because animals suffocated if it was damaged. He also found that the cerebellum, a part of the brainstem, coordinates locomotion. Gall had proposed that the cerebellum was the location of "amativeness" (see Figure 1.3).

Flourens's experiments furnished neuropsychologists with a number of new ideas. A strict Cartesian, even to the point of dedicating his book to Descartes, Flourens invested the cortex with the properties that Descartes had ascribed to the mind, including the functions of will, reason, and intelligence. Today, we recognize that the cortex is indeed central to most cognitive functions. Another key contribution was the discovery that, after damage to a part of the brain, substantial behavioral recovery could be expected. A central area of investigation in neuropsychology today is the paradox of how a behavior recovers even after the area of the brain thought to be central to the behavior has been damaged. Flourens used these findings to argue, however, that the cortex worked as a whole. For example, recovery from a cortical injury was possible because the remaining cortex could do the same things that the missing cortex had done and so could take over. Flourens's studies were mainly cursory descriptions of changes in the motor behavior of animals, however, and so he has been criticized because he was not really able to adequately test the idea that different regions of the cortex had different functions.

Localization and Lateralization of Language

A now-legendary chain of observations and speculations led to the discovery that really launched the science of neuropsychology, the localization of language. On 21 February 1825, a French physician named Jean Baptiste Bouillaud (1796–1881) read a paper before the Royal Academy of Medicine in France in which he argued from clinical studies that certain functions *are* localized in the neocortex and, specifically, that speech is localized in the frontal lobes, in accordance with Gall's beliefs and opposed to Flourens's beliefs. Observing that acts such as writing, drawing, painting, and fencing are carried out with the right hand, Bouillaud also suggested that the part of the brain that controls them might possibly be the left hemisphere. Physicians had long recognized that damage to a hemisphere of the brain impaired movement of the opposite side of the body. Why, he asked, should people not be left-brained for the movements of speech as well? A few years later, in 1836, Marc Dax read a paper in Montpellier, France, about a series of clinical cases demonstrating that disorders of speech were constantly associated with lesions of the left hemisphere. Dax's manuscript received little attention, however, and was not published until 1865, when it was published by his son.

Although neither Bouillaud's nor Dax's work had much effect when first presented, Ernest Auburtin, Bouillaud's son-in-law, took up Bouillaud's cause. At a meeting of the Anthropological Society of Paris in 1861, he reported the case of a patient who lost the ability to speak when pressure was applied to his exposed frontal lobe. Auburtin also gave the following description of another patient, ending with a promise that other scientists interpreted as a challenge:

> For a long time during my service with M. Bouillaud I studied a patient, named Bache, who had lost his speech but understood everything said to him and replied with signs in a very intelligent manner to all questions put to him. This man, who spent several years at the Bicetre [a Parisian mental asylum], is now at the Hospital for Incurables. I saw him again recently and his disease has progressed; slight paralysis has appeared but his intelligence is still unimpaired, and speech is wholly abolished. Without a doubt this man will soon die. Based on the symptoms that he presents we have diagnosed softening of the anterior lobes. If, at autopsy, these lobes are found to be intact, I shall renounce the ideas that I have just expounded to you. (Stookey, 1954)

Paul Broca (1824–1880), founder of the society, attended the meeting and heard Auburtin's challenge. Five days later he received a patient, a Monsieur Leborgne, who had lost his speech and was able to say only "tan" and utter an oath. He had paralysis on the right side of his body but in other respects seemed intelligent and normal. Broca recalled Auburtin's challenge and invited Auburtin to examine Tan, as the patient came to be called. Together they agreed that, if Auburtin was right, Tan should have a frontal lesion. Tan died on 17 April 1861, and the next day Broca submitted his findings to the Anthropological Society (this submission is claimed to be the fastest publication ever made in science). Auburtin was correct, the left frontal lobe was the focus of Tan's lesion. By 1863, Broca had collected eight more cases similar to Tan's and stated:

> Here are eight instances in which the lesion was in the posterior third of the third frontal convolution. This number seems to me to be sufficient to give strong presumptions. And the most remarkable thing is that in all the patients the lesion was on the left side. (Joynt, 1964)

As a result of his studies, Broca located speech in the third convolution (gyrus) of the frontal lobe on the left side of the brain (Figure 1.5). Thus, he accomplished two feats. He demonstrated that language was localized; thus different regions of the cortex could have specialized functions. He also discovered something new: functions could be localized to a side of the brain, a property that is referred to as **lateralization.** Because speech is thought to be central to human consciousness, the left hemisphere is frequently referred to as the dominant hemisphere, to recognize its special role in language. In recognition of Broca's contribution, the anterior speech region of the brain is called **Broca's area,** and the syndrome that results from its damage is called **Broca's aphasia** (from the Greek *a,* for "not," and *phasia,* for "speech").

An interesting footnote to this story is that Broca did not do a very careful examination of Tan's brain. Broca's anatomical analysis was criticized by French anatomist Pierre Marie, who reexamined the brains of Broca's first two patients, Tan and a Monsieur Lelong, 25 years after Broca's death. Marie pointed out in his article titled "The Third Left Frontal Convolution Plays No Particular Role in the Function of Language" that Lelong's brain showed general nonspecific atrophy, common in

(A)

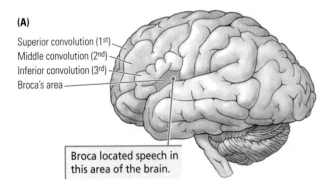

Superior convolution (1st)
Middle convolution (2nd)
Inferior convolution (3rd)
Broca's area

Broca located speech in this area of the brain.

(B)

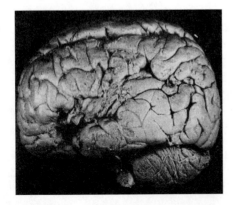

Figure 1.5 (A) A sketch of the lateral view of the left hemisphere of the brain showing the superior, middle, and inferior convolutions (gyri) of the frontal lobes. The convolutions are also referred to as the first, second, and third. Broca's area is located in the posterior third of the inferior convolution. (B) A photograph of the left hemisphere of the brain of Leborgne ("Tan"), Broca's first aphasic patient. (Part B from the Musee Dupuytren; courtesy of Assistance Publique, Hospitaux de Paris.)

senility, and that Tan had additional extensive damage in his posterior cortex that may have accounted for his aphasia. Broca had been aware of Tan's posterior damage but concluded that, whereas the posterior damage contributed to his death, the anterior damage had occurred earlier, producing his aphasia. The question of the extent to which specific functions are localized within the brain is still being explored today, as we shall see.

Sequential Programming and Disconnection

Broca's description of aphasia as a condition resulting from left frontal lesions made the following two-part argument: (1) a behavior, such as language, is controlled by a specific brain area; and (2) destroying the area selectively destroys the behavior. People who interpreted Broca's findings in this way are called strict localizationists. Many other scientists began to find that other regions of the brain had localized functions and to interpret their findings in this way. The first notable scientist to dissent was German anatomist Carl Wernicke (1848–1904). Wernicke was aware that the part of the cortex that receives the sensory pathway, or projection, from the ear—and is thus called the auditory cortex—is located in the temporal lobe, behind Broca's area. He, therefore, suspected a relation between the functioning of hearing and speech, and he described cases of aphasic patients with lesions in this auditory projection area that differed from those described by Broca.

For Wernicke's patients, (1) there was damage in the first temporal gyrus; (2) there was no contralateral paralysis (Broca's aphasia is frequently associated with paralysis of the right arm, as described for Tan); (3) the patients could speak fluently, but what they said was confused and made little sense (Broca's patients could not articulate, but they seemed to understand the meaning of words); and (4) although the patients were able to hear, they could not understand or repeat what was said to them. Wernicke's finding that the temporal lobe also was implicated in language disproved the strict localizationists' view that language was localized to a part of the frontal lobe. Temporal lobe aphasia is sometimes called fluent aphasia, to emphasize that the person can say words. It is more frequently called **Wernicke's aphasia,** however, in honor of Wernicke's description. The region of the temporal lobe associated with the aphasia is called **Wernicke's area.**

Wernicke also provided the first model for how language is organized in the left hemisphere (and the first modern model of brain function). It hypothesizes a programmed sequence of activities in Wernicke's and Broca's language areas (Figure 1.6). Wernicke proposed that auditory information is sent to the temporal lobes from the ear. In Wernicke's area, sounds are turned into sound images or ideas of objects and stored. From Wernicke's area, the ideas can be sent through a pathway called the arcuate fasciculus (from the Latin *arc*, for "bow," and *fasciculus*, for "band of tissue," because the pathway arcs around the lateral fissure as shown in Figure 1.6) to Broca's area, where the representations of speech movements are retained. From Broca's area, instructions are sent to muscles that control movements of the mouth to produce the appropriate sound. If the temporal lobe were damaged, speech movements could still be mediated by Broca's area, but the speech would make no sense, because the person would be unable to monitor the words. Because damage to Broca's area produces loss of speech movements without the loss of sound

(A) Wernicke's model on a chimpanzee brain

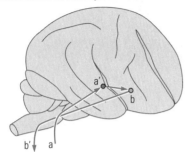

(B) Wernicke's model on a human brain

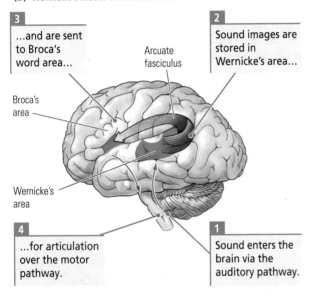

3 ...and are sent to Broca's word area...

Arcuate fasciculus

2 Sound images are stored in Wernicke's area...

Broca's area

Wernicke's area

4 ...for articulation over the motor pathway.

1 Sound enters the brain via the auditory pathway.

Figure 1.6 (A) Wernicke's 1874 model shows how language is organized in the brain. Sounds enter the brain through the auditory pathway *(a)*. Sound images are stored in Wernicke's area *(a')* and are sent to Broca's word area *(b)* for articulation through the motor pathway *(b')*. Lesions along this route *(a–a'–b–b')* could produce different types of aphasia, depending on their location. Curiously, Wernicke drew all his language models on the right hemisphere and not the left, which is the dominant hemisphere for language, as Wernicke believed. Also curious is that he drew the brain of an ape, which could not speak, as Wernicke knew. (B) Geschwind's model of the neurology of language shows the regions of the cortex involved in human speech. Although the model was a useful summary when published, more recent PET data have shown it to be limited in explanatory value. (Part A after Wernicke, 1874.)

images, Broca's aphasia is not accompanied by a loss of understanding.

Wernicke also predicted a new language disorder, although he never saw such a case. He suggested that, if the arcuate fibers connecting the two speech areas were cut, disconnecting the areas but without inflicting damage on either one, a speech deficit that Wernicke described as **conduction aphasia** would result. In this condition, speech sounds and movements would be retained, as would comprehension, but speech would still be impaired because the person would not be able to judge the sense of the words that he or she heard uttered. Wernicke's prediction was subsequently confirmed. Wernicke's speech model was updated by American neurologist Norman Geschwind in the 1960s and is now sometimes referred to as the Wernicke-Geschwind model.

Wernicke's idea of disconnection was a completely new way of viewing some of the symptoms of brain damage. It proposed that, although different regions of the brain have different functions, they are interdependent in that, to work, they must receive information from one another. Thus, just as cutting a telephone line prevents two people from speaking and so prevents them from performing a complex action such as concluding a business deal, cutting connecting pathways prevents two brain regions from communicating and performing complex functions. Using this same reasoning, French neurologist Joseph Dejerine (1849–1917) in 1892 described a case in which the loss of the ability to read (alexia, meaning "word blindness," from the Greek *lexia*, for "word") resulted from a disconnection between the visual area of the brain and Wernicke's area. Similarly, Wernicke's student Hugo Liepmann (1863–1925) was able to show that an inability to make sequences of movements (apraxia, from the Greek *praxis*, for "movement") resulted from the disconnection of motor areas from sensory areas. Disconnection is an important idea because it predicts that complex behaviors are built up in assembly-line fashion as information collected by sensory systems enters the brain and travels through different structures before resulting in an overt response of some kind. Furthermore, the disconnection of structures by cutting connecting pathways can result in impairments that resemble those produced by damaging the structures themselves.

Electrophysiological Confirmation of Localization

Although many researchers were excited by the idea of the localization of function, others voiced equally strong objections, largely because they still believed in the indivisibility of the mind. A new approach was developed for using electrical stimulation to study the brain, and it, too, supported the idea of functional localization. This new technique consisted of placing a thin insulated wire, an electrode, onto or into the cortex and passing a small electrical current through the uninsulated tip of the wire, thus exciting the tissue near the electrode tip.

In 1870, Gustav Theodor Fritsch (1838–1929) and Eduard Hitzig (1838–1907) described the new technique in an extraordinary paper, "On the Electrical Excitability of the Cerebrum." Hitzig may have derived the idea of stimulating the cortex from an observation that he made while dressing the head wound of a soldier in the Prussian war: mechanical irritation of the soldier's brain caused twitching in the contralateral limbs. Working in Hitzig's bedroom, the two colleagues performed successful experiments with a rabbit and then a dog in which they showed that stimulating the cortex electrically could produce movements. Furthermore, not only was the neocortex excitable, it was selectively excitable. Stimulation of the frontal lobe produced movements on the opposite side of the body, whereas stimulation of the parietal lobe produced no movement. Stimulation of restricted parts of the frontal lobe elicited movement of particular body parts—for example, neck, forelimb, and hind limb (Figure 1.7)—which suggested that the cortex possesses **topographic representations** of the different parts of the body. Fritsch and Hitzig summarized their interpretation of these findings in the paper's conclusion:

> Furthermore, it may be concluded from the sum of all our experiments that, contrary to the opinions of Flourens and most investigators who followed him, the soul in no case represents a sort of total function of the whole cerebrum, the expression of which might be destroyed by mechanical means in toto, but not in its individual parts. Individual psychological functions, and probably all of them, depend for their entrance into matter or for their formation from it, upon circumscribed centers of the cerebral cortex. (Fritsch and Hitzig, 1960)

The first experiment in which the electrical stimulation of a human cortex was formally reported was performed in 1874 by Roberts Bartholow (1831–1904) in Cincinnati. Mary Rafferty, a patient in his care, had a cranial defect that exposed a part of the cortex in each hemisphere. The following extract is from Bartholow's report:

> Observation 3. *To test faradic reaction of the posterior lobes.* Passed an insulated needle into the left posterior lobe so that the non-insulated portion rested entirely in the substance of the brain. The other insulated needle was placed in contact with the dura mater, within one-fourth of an inch of the first. When the circuit was closed, muscular contraction in the right upper and lower extremities ensued, as in the preceding observations. Faint but visible contraction of the left orbicularis palpebrarum [eyelid], and dilation of the pupils, also ensued. Mary complained of a very strong and unpleasant feeling of tingling in both right extremities, especially in the right arm, which she seized with the opposite hand and rubbed vigorously. Notwithstanding the very evident pain from which she suffered, she smiled as if much amused. (Bartholow, 1874)

Bartholow's publication caused a public outcry and he was forced to leave Cincinnati. Researchers today believe that he probably stimulated the brainstem, not the cortex, because his account says the electrodes were inserted

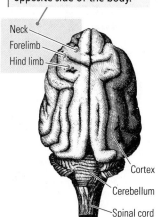

Electrical stimulation of the frontal lobe at various points produced movements on the opposite side of the body.

Neck
Forelimb
Hind limb

Cortex
Cerebellum
Spinal cord

Figure 1.7 Drawing of the brain of a dog from Fritsch and Hitzig (1870). The areas from which movements of the opposite side of the body were evoked with electrical stimulation are restricted to the frontal cortex. Note that the dog's cortex does not completely cover the brainstem; so the cerebellum can be seen.

about an inch into the brain tissue. The cortex is only a few millimeters thick. Nevertheless, he had demonstrated that the electrical-stimulation technique could be used with a conscious person, who could then report the subjective sensations produced by the stimulation. (The pain that Mary was reported to have suffered was not caused by stimulation of pain receptors in the brain—because there are none—but was probably evoked by a part of the brain that normally receives pain messages from other parts of the body.)

Subsequent research clarified that the movements produced by cortical stimulation were transmitted along a pathway from the cortex to the spinal cord through the pyramidal tract, the pathway that Gall had described nearly a 100 years earlier. David Ferrier (1843–1928), an English physiologist, refined the stimulation technique and duplicated Fritsch and Hitzig's results in many other animals, including primates. The primate studies were especially important because they provided a stepping stone for the construction of similar maps in humans. The technique was adopted by Wilder Penfield (1891–1976) at the Montreal Neurological Institute in Montreal, Canada, for identifying functional areas in human patients who were undergoing elective brain surgery for epilepsy or brain tumors. The maps that he made of a patient's cortex helped guide the surgery.

Hierarchical Organization of the Brain

When Fritsch and Hitzig made their historical discovery that stimulation of restricted parts of the neocortex resulted in specific movement, they concluded that the cortical area evoking a given movement was necessary and sufficient for producing that movement. The experiments performed by Friedrich L. Goltz (1834–1902) in 1892 were intended specifically to test this idea.

Goltz argued that, if a part of the neocortex had a function, then removal of the cortex should lead to a loss of that function. He made large lesions in three dogs, removing the cortex and a good deal of underlying brain tissue, and then studied the dogs for 57 days, 92 days, and 18 months, respectively, until the dogs died. The dog that survived for 18 months was studied in the greatest detail. After the surgery, it was more active than a normal dog. Its periods of sleep and waking were shorter than normal, but it still panted when warm and shivered when cold. It walked well on uneven ground and was able to catch its balance when it slipped. If placed in an abnormal posture, it corrected its position. After hurting a hind limb on one occasion, it trotted on three legs, holding up the injured limb. It was able to orient to touches or pinches on its body and snap at the object that touched it, although its orientations were not very accurate. If offered meat soaked in milk or meat soaked in bitter quinine, it accepted the first and rejected the second. It responded to light and sounds, although its response thresholds were elevated.

In sum, removal of the cortex did not appear to completely eliminate any function, though it seemed to reduce all functions to some extent. This demonstration appeared to be a strong argument against the localization of function and even to cast doubt on the role of the cortex in behavior. We will see, however, that a new theory of brain function was able to resolve the seemingly irreconcilable difference between Fritz and Hitzig's conclusions and Goltz's.

The fundamental disagreement between Goltz and those whom his experiments were intended to contradict was resolved by the **hierarchical organization** concept of brain function proposed by English neurologist John Hughlings-Jackson (1835–1911). Hughlings-Jackson thought of the nervous system as being organized in a number of layers arranged in a functional hierarchy. Each successively higher level would control more complex aspects of behavior but do so through the lower levels. Often Hughlings-Jackson described the nervous system as having three levels: the spinal cord, the brainstem, and the forebrain. But equally often he assigned no particular anatomical area to a given level. He had adopted the theory of hierarchy from philosopher Herbert Spencer's argument that the brain evolved in a series of steps, each of which brought animals the capacity to engage in new behaviors. Spencer in turn derived his idea from Charles Darwin, who had proposed that animals evolved from simple to more complex forms. What Hughlings-Jackson did with Spencer's theory, however, was novel. He suggested that diseases or damage that affected the highest levels would produce *dissolution*, the reverse of evolution: the animals would still have a repertoire of behaviors, but the behaviors would be simpler, more typical of an animal that had not yet evolved the missing brain structure.

If the logic of this argument is followed, it becomes apparent how the results from Goltz's experiments can be reconciled with those of his opponents. Goltz's dogs were "low level" dogs. They were able to walk and to eat but, had food not been presented to them (had they been required to walk to find food), they might have failed to take the necessary action and starved. Under the experimental conditions, the walking did not serve a useful biological function. Hughlings-Jackson's concepts allowed the special role of the cortex in organizing purposeful behavior to be distinguished from the role of lower-level brain areas in supporting the more elementary components of behavior.

Hughlings-Jackson applied his concepts of hierarchical organization to many other areas of behavior, including language and aphasia. It was his view that every part of the brain functions in language, with each part making some special contribution. The relevant question was not where language is localized but what unique contribution is made by each part of the cortex. Hughlings-Jackson was ahead of his time—so much so, in fact, that his ideas are central to the way in which we now think about brain function. We now recognize that functions are localized in one sense but are also distributed over wide areas of the brain in another sense. An expression sometimes used today to encompass Hughlings-Jackson's idea is that behaviors are organized in **distributed systems.**

The Neuron Hypothesis

After the development of the brain hypothesis, that the brain is responsible for all behavior, the second major influence on modern neuropsychology was the development of the neuron hypothesis, the idea that the nervous system is composed of discrete, autonomous units, or neurons, that can interact but are not physically connected. In this section, we will first provide a brief description of the cells of the nervous system, and then we will describe how the neuron hypothesis led to a number of ideas that are central to neuropsychology.

Nervous System Cells

The nervous system is composed of two basic kinds of cells, **neurons** and **glia** (a name that comes from the Greek word for "glue"). The neurons are the functional units that enable us to receive information, process it, and produce actions. The glia help the neurons out, holding them together (some *do* act as glue) and providing other supporting functions. In the human nervous system, there are about 100 billion neurons and perhaps 10 times as many glial cells. (No, no one has counted them all. Scientists have estimated the total number by counting the cells in a small sample of brain tissue and then multiplying by the brain's volume.)

Figure 1.8 shows the three basic parts of a neuron. The neuron's core region is called the **cell body.** Most of a neuron's branching extensions are called **dendrites** (Latin for "branch"), but the main "root" is called the **axon** (Greek for "axle"). Neurons have only one axon, but most have many dendrites. Some small neurons have so many dendrites that they look like garden hedges. The dendrites and axon of the neuron are extensions of the cell body, and their main purpose is to extend the surface area of the cell. The dendrites of a cell can be a number of millimeters long, but the axon can extend as long as a meter, as do those in the pyramidal tract that extend from the cortex to the spinal cord. In the giraffe, these same axons are a number of meters long.

Understanding how billions of cells, many with long, complex extensions, produce behavior is a formidable task, even with the use of the powerful instrumentation available today. Just imagine what the first anatomists with their crude microscopes thought when they first began to make out some of the brain's structural details. But insights into the cellular organization did follow. Through the development of new, more powerful microscopes and techniques for selectively staining tissue, good descriptions of neurons emerged. By applying new electronic inventions to the study of neurons, researchers began to understand how axons conduct information. By studying how neurons interact and by applying a growing body of knowledge from chemistry, they discovered how neurons communicate and how learning takes place.

The Neuron

The earliest anatomists who tried to examine the substructure of the nervous system found a gelatinous white substance, almost a goo. Eventually it was discovered that, if brain tissue were placed in alcohol or formaldehyde, water would be drawn out of the tissue, making it firm. Then, if the tissue were cut into thin sections, many different structures could be seen.

Early theories described nerves as hollow, fluid-containing tubes; however, when the first cellular anatomist, Anton van Leeuwenhoek (1632–1723), examined nerves with a primitive microscope, he found no such thing. He did mention the presence of "globules," which may have been cell bodies. As micro-

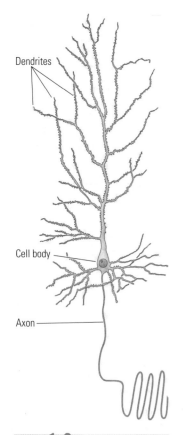

Dendrites

Cell body

Axon

Figure 1.8 The major parts of a neuron include the dendrites, the cell body, and the axon.

scopes improved, the various parts of the nerve came into ever sharper focus, eventually leading Theodor Schwann, in 1839, to enunciate the theory that cells are the basic structural units of the nervous system, just as they are for the rest of the body.

An exciting development in visualizing cells was the introduction of staining, which allows different parts of the nervous system to be distinguished. Various dyes used for staining cloth in the German clothing industry were applied to thinly cut tissue with various results: some selectively stained the cell body, some stained the nucleus, and some stained the axons. The most amazing cell stain came from the application of photographic chemicals to nervous system tissue. Italian anatomist Camillo Golgi (1843–1926) in 1875 impregnated tissue with silver nitrate (one of the substances responsible for forming the images in black-and-white photographs) and found that a few cells in their entirety—cell body, dendrites, and axons—became encrusted with silver. This technique allowed the entire neuron and all its processes to be visualized for the first time. Golgi never described how he had been led to his remarkable discovery.

Microscopic examination revealed that the brain was nothing like an amorphous jelly; rather, it had an enormously intricate substructure with components arranged in complex clusters, each interconnected with many other clusters. How did this complex organ work? Was it a net of physically interconnected fibers or a collection of discrete and separate units? If it were an interconnected net, then changes in one part should, by diffusion, produce changes in every other part. Because it would be difficult for a structure thus organized to localize function, a netlike structure would favor a holistic, or "mind," type of brain function and psychology. Alternatively, a structure of discrete units functioning autonomously would favor a psychology characterized by localization of function.

In 1883, Golgi suggested that axons, the longest fibers coming out of the cell body, are interconnected, forming an axonic net. Golgi claimed to have seen connections between cells, and so he did not think that brain functions were localized. This position was opposed by Spanish anatomist Santiago Ramón y Cajal (1852–1934), on the basis of the results of studies in which he used Golgi's own silver-staining technique. Cajal examined the brains of chicks at various ages and produced beautiful drawings of neurons at different stages of growth. He was able to see a neuron develop from a simple cell body with few extensions to a highly complex cell with many extensions (Figure 1.9). He never saw connections from cell to cell. Golgi and Cajal jointly received the Nobel Prize in 1906; each in his acceptance speech argued his position on the organization of neurons, Golgi supporting the nerve net and Cajal supporting the idea of separate cells.

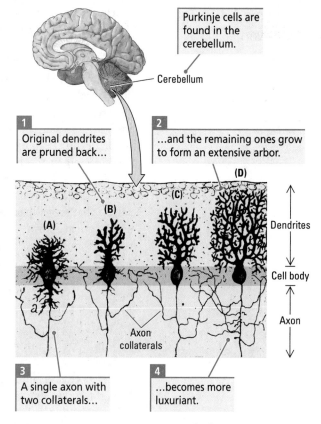

Purkinje cells are found in the cerebellum.

Cerebellum

1 Original dendrites are pruned back...

2 ...and the remaining ones grow to form an extensive arbor.

(A) (B) (C) (D)

Dendrites

Cell body

Axon

Axon collaterals

3 A single axon with two collaterals...

4 ...becomes more luxuriant.

Figure 1.9 Successive phases (A–D) in the development of branching in a type of neuron called a Purkinje cell as drawn by Ramón y Cajal (1937).

On the basis of Cajal's work on nerve cells, the expression *neuron hypothesis* has come to describe the idea that neurons are not physically connected through their axons. Images produced by electron microscopes in the twentieth century fully support this hypothesis.

Information Conduction

We have mentioned early views that suggested a hydraulic flow of liquid through nerves into muscles (reminiscent of the way that filling and emptying changes the shape and hardness of a balloon). Such theories have been called **balloonist theories.** Descartes espoused the balloonist hypothesis, arguing that a fluid from the ventricles flows through nerves into muscles to make them move (see Figure 1.2). English physician Francis Glisson (1597–1677) in 1677 made a direct test of the balloon hypothesis by immersing a man's arm in water and measuring the change in the water level when the muscles of the arm were contracted. Because the water level did not rise, Glisson concluded that no fluid entered the muscle (bringing no concomitant change in density). Johan Swammerdam (1637–1680) in Holland reached the same conclusion from similar experiments on frogs, but his manuscript lay unpublished for 100 years. (We have asked students in our classes if the water will rise when an immersed muscle is contracted. Many predict that it will.)

The impetus to adopt a theory of electrical conduction in neurons came from an English scientist, Stephen Gray (1666–1736), who in 1731 attracted considerable attention by demonstrating that the human body could conduct electricity. He showed that, when a rod containing static electricity was brought close to the feet of a boy suspended by a rope, a grass-leaf electroscope (a thin strip of conducting material) placed near the boy's nose would be attracted to the boy's nose. Shortly after, Italian physicist Luigi Galvani (1737–1798) demonstrated that electrical stimulation of a frog's nerve could cause muscle contraction. The idea for this experiment came from his observation that frogs' legs hanging on a metal wire in a market twitched during an electrical storm. In 1886, Joseph Bernstein (1839–1917) developed the theory that the membrane of a nerve is polarized (has a positive charge on one side and a negative charge on the other) and that an electric potential can be propagated along the membrane by the movements of ions across the membrane. Many of the details of this ionic conduction were worked out by English physiologists Alan Hodgkin (1914–1988) and Andrew Huxley (1917–), who received the Nobel Prize in physiology in 1963. Their explanation of how neurons conduct information will be more fully described in a later chapter.

As successive findings refuted the hydraulic models of conduction and brought more dynamic electrical models into favor, hydraulic theories of behavior also were critically reassessed. For example, Viennese psychiatrist Sigmund Freud (1856–1939) had originally envisioned the biological basis of his theory of behavior, with its three levels of id, ego, and superego, as being a hydraulic mechanism of some sort. Although conceptually useful for a time, it had no effect on concepts of brain function, because there was no evidence of the brain functioning as a hydraulic system.

Connections Between Neurons As the Basis of Learning

Even though neurons are independent structures, they must influence one another. Charles Scott Sherrington (1857–1952), an English physiologist, examined how nerves connect to muscles and first suggested how the connection is made. He applied an unpleasant stimulation to a dog's paw, measured how long it took the dog to withdraw its foot, and compared that rate with the speed at which messages were known to travel along axons. According to Sherrington's calculations, the dog took 5 milliseconds too long to respond. Sherrington theorized that neurons are connected by junctions, which he called **synapses** (from the Greek word for "clasp"), and that additional time is required for the message to get across the junction. The results of later electron microscopic studies were to confirm that synapses do not quite touch the cells with which they synapse. The general assumption that developed in response to this discovery was that a synapse releases chemicals to influence the adjacent cell. In 1949, on the basis of this principle, Donald Hebb proposed a learning theory stating that, when individual cells are activated at the same time, they grow connecting synapses or strengthen existing ones and thus become a functional unit. He proposed that new or strengthened connections, sometimes called Hebb or plastic synapses, are the structural bases of memory. Just how synapses are formed and change is a vibrant area of research today.

Modern Developments

Given the nineteenth-century advances in knowledge about brain structure and function—the brain and neuron hypotheses, the concept of the special nature of cortical function, and the concepts of localization of function and of disconnection—why was the science of neuropsychology not established by 1900 rather than after 1949, when the word *neuropsychology* first appeared? There are several possible reasons. In the 1920s, some scientists still rejected the classical approach of Broca, Wernicke, and others, arguing that their attempts to correlate behavior with anatomical sites were little more sophisticated than the attempts of the phrenologists. Then two world wars disrupted the progress of science in many countries. In addition, psychologists, who traced their origins to philosophy rather than to biology, were not interested in physiological and anatomical approaches, directing their attention instead to behaviorism, psychophysics, and the psychoanalytical movement.

A number of modern developments have contributed to the emergence of neuropsychology as a distinct scientific discipline: neurosurgery; psychometrics (the science of measuring human mental abilities) and statistical analysis; and technological advances, particularly those that allow a living brain to be imaged.

Neurosurgery

Wilder Penfield and Herbert Jasper, pioneers in brain surgery, have provided a brief but informative history of neurosurgery. They note that anthropologists have found evidence of brain surgery dating to prehistoric times: neolithic

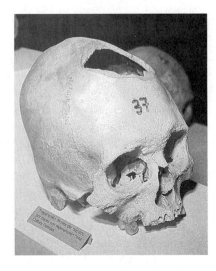

skulls that show postsurgical healing have been found in Europe (Figure 1.10). Similar skulls were left by the early Incas of Peru. It is likely that these early peoples found surgery to have a beneficial effect, perhaps by reducing pressure within the skull when an injured brain began to swell up. Hippocrates gave written directions for **trephining** (cutting a circular hole in the skull) on the side of the head opposite the site of an injury as a means of therapeutic intervention to relieve pressure from a swelling brain. Between the thirteenth and nineteenth centuries, a number of attempts were documented, some of which were quite successful, to relieve various symptoms with surgery.

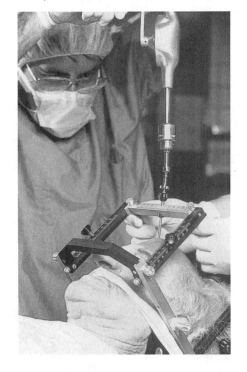

The modern era in neurosurgery began with the introduction of antisepsis, anesthesia, and the principle of localization of function. In the 1880s, a number of surgeons reported success with operations for the treatment of brain abscesses, tumors, and epilepsy-producing scars. Later, the Horsley-Clarke "stereotaxic device" was developed for holding the head in a fixed position (Figure 1.11). This device immobilizes the head by means of bars placed in the ear canals and under the front teeth. A brain atlas is then used to localize areas in the brain for surgery. Local anesthetic procedures were developed so that the patient could remain awake during surgery and contribute to the success of the operation by providing information about the effects of localized brain stimulation.

The development of neurosurgery as a practical solution to some types of brain abnormality in humans had an enormous influence on neuropsychology. In animal research, the tissue-removal, or lesion, technique had been developed to the point that it became one of the most important sources of information about brain–behavior relations. Research on the human brain, however, was minimal. Most information came from patients with relatively poorly defined lesions—blood-vessel damage that included the brainstem, as well as the cortex, or brain-trauma lesions that were diffuse and irregular. And human patients often lived for years after injury; so histological localization (localization of structures on a microscopic level) was not possible. (Recall Pierre Marie's criticism of Broca's description of Tan's lesion.) Neurosurgery provided a serendipitous solution. The surgical removal of cortical tissue in humans was as localized as the tissue removal in animal experiments. The surgeon would draw a map of the lesion, sometimes after stimulating the surrounding tissue electrically to discover the exact extent of the damages. As a result, good correlations were obtained between focal lesions in the brain and the changes in behavior that resulted from the lesions. Information about behavior obtained from patients who have undergone surgery is very useful for diagnosing the causes of problems in other patients. For example, if tissue removal in the temporal lobes is found to be related to subsequent memory problems, then people who develop memory problems might also have injury or disease of the temporal lobes.

Psychometrics and Statistical Evaluation

The first experiments to measure individual differences in psychological function were made by an astronomer, Friedrich Wilhelm Bessel, in 1796. Bessel had become curious about the dismissal of an assistant at the Greenwich observatory near London for always being a second or so slower than his superior in observing stars and setting clocks. Bessel began a study of reaction time and found quite large variations among people. Individual differences were very much a part of Gall and Spurzheim's phrenology but, unlike their idea of localization of function, this aspect of their research attracted little interest.

The question raised by such observations is, How do we explain individual differences? Charles Darwin's cousin Francis Galton (1822–1911) maintained a laboratory in London in the 1880s, where he gave subjects three pennies to allow him to measure their physical features, perceptions, and reaction times with the goal of finding individual differences that could explain why some people were superior in ability to others. Galton's elegant innovation was to apply the statistical methods of Adolphe Quetelet (1796–1874), a Belgian statistician, to his results and so rank his subjects on a frequency distribution, the so-called bell-shaped curve (a graphical representation showing that some people perform exceptionally well, some perform exceptionally poorly, and most fall somewhere in between on almost every factor measured). This innovation was essential for the development of modern psychological tests. It seems fitting that Galton's work was directed to describing individual differences, because Darwin's evolutionary theory of natural selection required that individual differences exist. To Galton's surprise, the perceptual and reaction time differences that he measured did not distinguish between the people he was predisposed to think were average and those he thought were eminent.

French biologist Alfred Binet (1857–1911) came up with a solution to Galton's problem of identifying who would perform poorly on a test. In 1904, the minister of public instruction commissioned Binet to develop tests to identify retarded children so that they could be singled out for special instruction.

In collaboration with Theodore Simon, Binet produced what is now known as the 1905 Binet-Simon scale, designed to evaluate judgment, comprehension, and reason, which Binet thought were essential features of intelligence. The tests were derived empirically by administering questions to 50 normal 3- to 11-year-old children and some mentally retarded children and adults. The scale was revised in 1908; unsatisfactory tests were deleted, new tests were added, and the student population was increased to 300 children aged 3 to 13 years. From the tests, a **mental level** was calculated, a score attained by 80% to 90% of normal children of a particular age. In 1916, Lewis Terman in the United States produced a version of the Stanford-Binet test in which the **intelligence quotient** (IQ)—mental age divided by chronological age times 100—was first used. He set the average intelligence level to equal IQ 100.

Hebb first gave IQ tests to brain-damaged people in Montreal, Canada, in 1940, with the resultant surprising discovery that lesions in the frontal lobes—since Gall's time considered the center of highest intelligence—did not decrease IQ scores. Lesions to other main areas not formerly thought to be implicated in "intelligence" did reduce IQ scores. This counterintuitive finding revealed the utility of such tests for assessing the location of brain damage and effectively created a bond of common interest between neurology and psychology. Many of the clever innovations used for assessing brain function in various patient populations are strongly influenced by intelligence-testing methodology. The tests are brief, easily and objectively scored, and standardized with the use of statistical procedures. In addition, neuropsychologists use the IQ test to assess patients' general level of competence; many other tests that they administer are IQ-like in that they are rapidly administered paper-and-pencil tests. Although certain applications of "mental testing" are liable to criticism, even harsh critics concede that such tests have appropriate uses in neuropsychology. In turn, mental tests are continually being modified in light of new advances in neuropsychology.

Advances in Technology

Because advances in technology have been numerous and because we will consider the most important of them later on, we will not describe individual technological advances here. Instead, we offer Flourens's often-repeated observation that "methods give the results," which was his argument in advocating the experimental method over Gall's anecdotal, merely confirmatory approach. It was repeated by Fritsch and Hitzig when they overthrew Flourens's dogma concerning the mind and the cortex. Progress in science requires advancements in theory and methodology, but it also depends on improvements in technology. In fact, in response to the question of why papers on methods are those most cited in science, one wag declared that you cannot conduct an experiment with a theory. Only through technological advance could the internal structure of neurons be visualized, their electrical activity recorded, and their biochemical activity analyzed and modified. Only through technology can the processes of disease, degeneration, and regeneration in the nervous system be understood. In fact, methodology and results are often so intimately linked that they cannot be dissociated. Technological advances provide new opportunities to review old and well-established ideas, and old and well-established ideas should be thrown into the mill of technological innovation for confirmation or modification.

An important current area of technological advance is brain imaging, of which there are a variety of methods. All of them take advantage of the ability of computers to reconstruct images of the brain. The images describe regional differences in structure or function, electrical activity, cell density, or chemical activity (such as the amount of glucose that a cell is using or the amount of oxygen that it is consuming). Whereas once the neurologist and the psychologist administered time-consuming batteries of tests to patients to locate the site of brain injury, brain-imaging techniques quickly provide a picture of the brain and the injury. The use of such techniques does not mean that neurologists and neuropsychologists are no longer needed. Individual assessments of patients are still required for treatment and research. Moreover, individual brains can be surprisingly different, and so it is difficult to predict what job a given brain region does for a given person.

Brain-imaging methods are important in another way, too. Some imaging techniques can reveal changes in the brain at the very moment a task is being performed or learned or both. The imaging methods thus provide a new and extremely powerful research tool for investigating how the brain produces behavior and changes with experience.

Summary

This chapter has sketched the history of two formative ideas in neuropsychology: (1) the brain is the organ of the mind and (2) the cell is its functional unit. The chapter has also examined some early ideas of how the brain functions. Early scientists argued about whether each specific brain function—language for example—is localized in a particular part of the brain or whether many different brain areas participate to produce the function. The conclusion was that brain functions are localized and require the participation of a number of different brain areas as well. Extensive damage in the cortex was found to leave surprisingly complex functions intact. The theory of hierarchical organization accounted for this observation by proposing that the brain evolved in steps, with each step adding a new level of complexity to behavior. The brain is composed of cells, and neurons are its functional units. Neurons are autonomous but can work in conjunction through existing synapses or by forming new synapses.

Studies of human surgical patients with well-localized brain lesions, improvements in the use of statistics to develop and interpret behavioral tests, and the continuing development of technology have all provided new ways of evaluating favored theories.

Although this chapter has focused on the history of the current science of neuropsychology, the history presented is selective. Many important people and interesting stories have been omitted. We wish nevertheless to leave the reader with the thought that to know history is to be able to replicate it, to advance it, and even to confound sphinxes with it.

References

Bartholow, R. Experimental investigation into the functions of the human brain. *American Journal of Medical Sciences* 67:305–313, 1874.

Beach, F. A., D. O. Hebb, C. T. Morgan, and H. W. Nissen. *The Neuropsychology of Lashley.* New York, Toronto, and London: McGraw-Hill, 1960.

Benton, A. L. Contributions to aphasia before Broca. *Cortex* 1:314–327, 1964.

Brazier, M. A. B. The historical development of neurophysiology. In J. Field, H. W. Magoun, and V. E. Hall, Eds. *Handbook of Physiology*, vol. 1. Washington, DC: American Physiological Society, 1959.

Broca, P. Sur le siege de la faculte du langage articule. *Bulletin of the Society of Anthropology* 6:377–396, 1865.

Broca, P. Remarks on the seat of the faculty of articulate language, followed by an observation of aphemia. In G. von Bonin, Ed. *The Cerebral Cortex.* Springfield, IL: Charles C. Thomas, 1960.

Bruce, D. On the origin of the term "Neuropsychology." *Neuropsychologia* 23:813–814, 1985.

Clark, E., and C. D. O'Malley. *The Human Brain and Spinal Cord.* Berkeley and Los Angeles: University of California Press, 1968.

Descartes, R. *Traite de l'Homme.* Paris: Angot, 1664.

Eccles, J. C. *The Neurophysiological Basis of Mind: The Principles of Neurophysiology.* Oxford: Clarendon Press, 1956.

Finger, S. *Origins of Neuroscience.* New York: Oxford University Press, 1994.

Flourens, P. Investigations of the properties and the functions of the various parts which compose the cerebral mass. In G. von Bonin, Ed. *The Cerebral Cortex.* Springfield, IL: Charles C. Thomas, 1960.

Fritsch, G., and E. Hitzig. On the electrical excitability of the cerebrum. In G. von Bonin, Ed., *The Cerebral Cortex.* Springfield, IL: Charles C. Thomas, 1960.

Geschwind, N. *Selected Papers on Language and Brain.* Dordrecht, Holland, and Boston: D. Reidel, 1974.

Goltz, F. On the functions of the hemispheres. In G. von Bonin, Ed. *The Cerebral Cortex.* Springfield, IL: Charles C. Thomas, 1960.

Gould, S. J. *The Mismeasure of Man.* New York: Norton, 1981.

Head, H. *Aphasia and Kindred Disorders of Speech.* London: Cambridge University Press, 1926.

Hebb, D. O. *The Organization of Behavior: A Neuropsychological Theory.* New York: Wiley, 1949.

Hebb, D. O., and W. Penfield. Human behavior after extensive bilateral removals from the frontal lobes. *Archives of Neurology and Psychiatry* 44:421–438, 1940.

Hughlings-Jackson, J. *Selected Writings of John Hughlings-Jackson*, J. Taylor, Ed., vols. 1 and 2. London: Hodder, 1931.

Joynt, R. Paul Pierre Broca: His contribution to the knowledge of aphasia. *Cortex* 1:206–213, 1964.

Kluver, H. *Behavior Mechanisms in Monkeys.* Chicago: University of Chicago Press, 1933, 1957.

Krech, D. Cortical localization of function. In L. Postman, Ed. *Psychology in the Making.* New York: Knopf, 1962.

Olin, C. H. *Phrenology.* Philadelphia: Penn Publishing, 1910.

Penfield, W., and H. Jasper. *Epilepsy and the Functional Anatomy of the Human Brain.* Boston: Little, Brown, 1954.

Ramón y Cajal, S. *Recollections of My Life.* Cambridge, MA: MIT Press, 1989.

Rothschuk, K. E. *History of Physiology.* Huntington, NY: Robert E. Krieger, 1973.

Stookey, B. A note on the early history of cerebral localization. *Bulletin of the New York Academy of Medicine* 30:559–578, 1954.

Wernicke, C. *Der aphasische Symptomenkomplex.* Breslau, Poland: M. Cohn and Weigert, 1874.

Young, R. M. *Mind, Brain and Adaption in the Nineteenth Century.* Oxford: Clarendon Press, 1970.

chapter *2*

Origins of the Human Brain and Behavior

A badger recounts the story that God created all animals as embryos and called them before his throne, offering them the changes that they desired. They opted for specialized adult features, claws, teeth, hoofs, antlers, and so forth. But the human embryo, trusting God's judgment, accepted the way it was made. The creator was delighted and said that it would therefore remain an embryo until buried but would dominate the other animals, walk upright, and feel sorrow and feel joy. (White, 1958)

The embryo who walks upright belongs to the primate order, a group of animal families that includes lemurs, tarsiers, monkeys, and apes, all having diverged from a common ancestor. The primate order is shown in Figure 2.1 in the form of a **cladogram,** a graph that shows the relative time of origin of

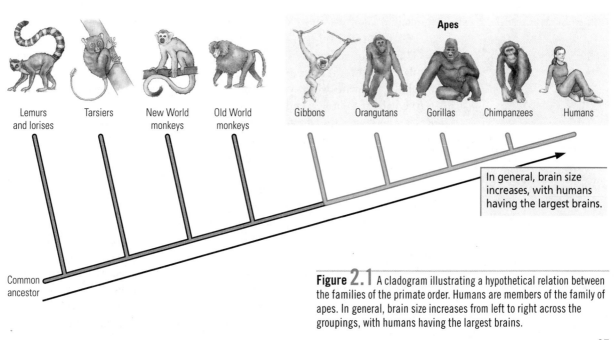

In general, brain size increases, with humans having the largest brains.

Figure 2.1 A cladogram illustrating a hypothetical relation between the families of the primate order. Humans are members of the family of apes. In general, brain size increases from left to right across the groupings, with humans having the largest brains.

27

various closely related groups. Primates have excellent vision, including color vision and eyes positioned in the front of the face to enhance depth perception, and they use this excellent vision to deftly guide their hand movements. Female primates usually produce only one infant per pregnancy, and they spend a great deal more time caring for their young than most other animals do.

In the past 5 million to 8 million years, the embryo that walked upright diverged from its ancestral ape lineage, acquiring a number of characteristics that distinguished it from other apes. It was taller, and there was less difference in height between males and females. It was bipedal, had long legs, and was such a great traveler that its descendents populated every habitable continent. Changes in hand structure allowed the skilled use of tools. Changes in tooth structure and a massive reduction in jaw size facilitated the consumption of a more varied diet. Its brain underwent an unmatched evolution in size, increasing to about five times its original volume.

Although the purpose of this book is to describe the functions of the human brain as we know it today, an important clue to understanding the brain of modern humans is to consider its origins and the evolutionary forces that sculpted it. In this chapter, we shall examine the evolutionary history of this special brain.

Species Comparison

Why Study Nonhuman Animals?

Many people draw a sharp distinction between the study of the human brain and behavior and the study of nonhuman animals. They assume that both human neuroanatomy and human cognitive processes (that is, thinking) differ fundamentally from those of other animals. After all, humans talk, read, write, and do all sorts of things that monkeys and rats do not.

This line of reasoning is wrong. Human and chimpanzee bodies are very similar, their brains are very similar, and their behavior is very similar. Thus, psychologists who work with chimps and other apes assume that the things learned about them are applicable to the human brain and to human behavior. Researchers also find that comparisons with more distantly related species, such as rats or cats and even slugs and fruit flies, are very informative. The behavior of the rat is extremely complex. Most structures of the rat brain are much like those of the human brain, and many aspects of neocortical function in laboratory rats are remarkably similar to those of humans. Slugs are especially useful for studying how neurons interconnect to produce behavior because their nervous systems are relatively simple. Fruit flies are useful for studying the genetic basis of behavior because many generations of flies can quickly be produced in the laboratory.

In emphasizing the utility of interspecies comparisons, we are not saying that other animals are merely little people in fur suits. We are emphasizing, rather, that the similarities between humans, monkeys, rats, and other animals suggest that the study of other animals can make an important contribution to an understanding of human behavior–brain relations. Behavior–brain comparisons across species provide information that would be difficult to obtain from the study of a single species, even one as interesting as humans. Additionally, the behavior–brain relations of other animals are interesting in themselves, as bird watchers, pet owners, and naturalists will confirm.

Questions That Can Be Addressed by Using Nonhuman Animals

What questions can be addressed through the study of nonhuman species? There are three primary lines of neuropsychological research in animals: (1) studies directed toward understanding the basic mechanisms of the brain, (2) studies designed to produce models of human neurological disorders, and (3) studies that aim to describe the phylogenetic (evolutionary) development of the brain. We shall consider each of them separately in the following paragraphs.

One purpose of cross-species comparisons in neuropsychology is to arrive at an understanding of the basic mechanisms of brain function. For example, the eye, a very complex organ for detecting light, takes different forms in different species. Thus, fruit flies and mammals have eyes that appear to have little in common. Although their apparent differences were taken as evidence that the eye evolved a number of times, the results of recent studies of the genes responsible for coding information about how the eye should develop suggest that the same genes are implicated in all species. According to Hetzer-Egger and coworkers, a gene called *Pax* may be responsible for eye development in all seeing animals, suggesting a much closer relationship between apparently very diverse kinds of animals than had been suspected previously. Similarly, very similar genes, called homeobox genes, take part in body segmentation in both fruit flies and humans. Thus, segmentation of the human nervous system into the spinal cord, brainstem, and forebrain is produced by genes first discovered in fruit flies. The differences in structure of the eye and the nervous system in different animal species are the products of slight alterations, called **mutations,** in genes and in the way the products of those genes interact with the products of other genes.

The second goal of comparative work is to produce models of human neurological disorders. The aim is to produce the disorder, then manipulate numerous variables to understand the cause, and ultimately formulate a treatment. For example, **Parkinson's disease** is associated with aging in humans and can affect as many as 1% of the population older than 65 years of age. The symptoms include rigidity that impedes voluntary movement, balance problems, and tremors of the hands and limbs. The cause of Parkinson's disease is unknown, and there is no cure. Thus, scientists have three goals in finding treatments: to prevent the disease, to slow its progression once it has occurred, and to treat the symptoms as the disease progresses. Models have been developed in the mouse, rat, and monkey to seek the causes of this abnormal behavior and to find treatments. The animals are substitutes for humans, because similar principles are assumed to underlie the emergence and treatment of the disorder in humans and nonhumans alike.

The third rationale for using nonhuman species is to provide a description of how the mammalian brain and behavior evolved. Studying the evolutionary

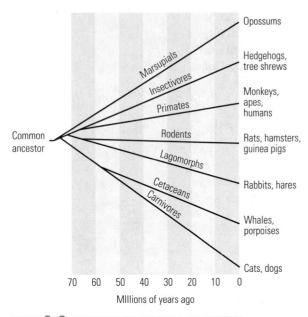

Figure 2.2 A phylogenetic tree showing the probable times of origin and affinities of the orders of mammals most commonly studied in comparative psychology and neuropsychology. Note that all contemporary species are the same evolutionary age. (After Young, 1962.)

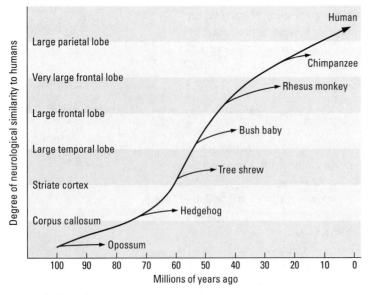

Figure 2.3 Phylogenetic relationships among the experimental subjects forming a quasi-evolutionary lineage. Hedgehogs, tree shrews, bush babies, monkeys, and apes are living animals taken to be close approximations of the ancestors of humans. Note the brain changes that occurred at the branches in this lineage. (After Masterton and Skeen, 1972.)

development of the human brain may be as important to understanding what humans are as the study of infants is to understanding what adults are. The research is done in two ways. First, experiments with rats, cats, dogs, and rhesus monkeys permit inferences about how the environments in which such a species lived shaped its evolution, brain, and behavior. All these species evolved independently from some primitive mammalian ancestor, as shown in Figure 2.2. Second, because these species are related, commonalities can tell us something about what we inherited in common with them and especially with the species in our own primate lineage.

The Use of a Quasi-Evolutionary Sequence

To do comparative work from a phylogenetic perspective, researchers choose species that constitute what Hodos and Campbell termed a **quasi-evolutionary** sequence. That is, they use a series of animals thought to represent consecutive stages in evolutionary history. In some cases, an animal is chosen because it is the living descendant of an ancestor that is no longer available to be studied. For example, the lineage to which humans belong includes ancestors of hedgehogs, tree shrews, bush babies, monkeys, and apes (to name just a few). Researchers generally assume that these present-day animals resemble the common ancestor closely enough to stand in for it. Notice in Figure 2.3 that, when a quasi-evolutionary sequence is constructed, a comparison of the brains and behaviors of the animals in the sequence reveals a correspondence between new structural developments and new behaviors. For example, striate cortex (cortex with a striped appearance) is visual cortex, and its presence in tree shrews confers an ability to see branches, heights, and insects. This ability is not important to (and not present in) the ground-dwelling hedgehog, which represents an earlier stage in the sequence. By the same token, the large temporal lobe in the bush baby is related to this animal's ability to select for itself a highly varied diet of insects, fruits, leaves, and more. The large frontal lobes of the rhesus monkey are related to its very complex group social life. The large parietal lobe of humans is probably a correlate of our abilities to perform the skilled movements required in toolmaking. Thus, tracking the evolution of new brain features and the evolution of new behavioral features can be a source of insight into what the different parts of the brain do.

Human Origins

The story of our knowledge about human origins begins in 1859 with Darwin's publication of *Origin of Species*. Darwin carefully avoided the then inflammatory subject of human ancestry, preferring to emphasize his studies of barnacles, extinct clams, and exotic animals from the faraway Galapagos Islands. His only reference to human evolution appears at the end of the book, where he states: "Light will be thrown on the origin of man and his history." Later, in 1871 Darwin concluded in his book *The Descent of Man* that humans descended from a "hairy, tailed quadruped, probably arboreal in its habits." Through the years, the public has largely grown accustomed to the idea of being descended from apes.

Scientists study the evolution of modern humans by examining the fossil remains of **hominids,** our humanlike ancestors and their near relatives, and artifacts such as tools that are found with those remains. These scientists carefully examine the structure of hominid bones, make a morphological reconstruction of a specimen, and compare it with other examples in extinct and living species. Figure 2.4 shows a morphological reconstruction of Neanderthal, who lived in Europe and is related to modern humans but disappeared about 40,000 years ago. Contrary to the original assumption that the Neanderthal people were brutish, stooped characters, reconstructions demonstrate how similar to us they really were. Using the ages of the sediments within which the bones of

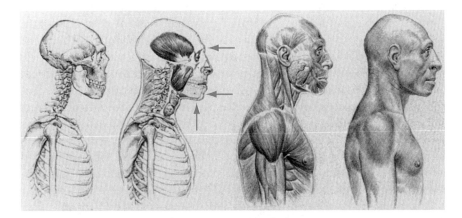

Figure 2.4 Reconstruction of the facial features of Neanderthal man. To the bare bones, temporal muscles and an outline of the skin are added. Arrows mark points where thickness is based on needle probes of humans or orangutans. Nose shape is based on projections from bony landmarks. The reconstruction contrasts markedly with previous depictions that represented Neanderthals as dull witted and stooped. (Reconstruction by Jay Matternes. From B. Rensberger. Facing the past. *Science* 41–81, October 1981. Copyright © 1981. Reprinted with permission.)

different hominids are found, researchers have created a lineage of hominid species that includes their approximate time of origin.

The Episodic Evolution of Humankind

According to Darwin, evolution is shaped largely by processes of natural selection and sexual selection. By *natural selection*, Darwin meant the accidental development of skills that allowed animals to exploit new habitats or niches and therefore survive when other animals didn't. By *sexual selection*, he meant the development of characteristics in one sex of a species that members of the other sex found appealing. Individual organisms with such characteristics would be more likely to mate, producing offspring with the same characteristics. Many of the differences in appearance of the two human sexes are the result of sexual selection. Darwin believed that the evolution of species was slow, occurring on time scales of tens of thousands of years.

Today, a hundred years after Darwin, the fossil record is well documented and has given rise to a new theory about the pace of evolution, the theory of **punctuated,** or episodic, evolution. This theory suggests that speciation occurs very rapidly, probably over a few hundred or a few thousand years. Instead of changing gradually throughout their existence, most species exhibit little significant change during their tenure on earth. They disappear in the fossil record looking much the same as when they appeared in it. Although modern humans do have ancestors, the appearance of modern humans was indeed sudden.

Although life may have existed on earth for some 650 million years, the fossil record shows that true mammals made their appearance only about 150 million years ago, and monkeylike mammals, or primates, first appeared only about 25 million years ago. Those first ancestors of ours lived during what was perhaps truly the age of primates. Almost the entire land mass of the planet was covered by jungles, a habitat in which primate species thrive.

Relatedness between humans and apes can be determined by comparing proteins, such as hemoglobin or albumin, two important constituents of blood. Proteins are chains of hundreds of amino acids, and in any protein many of the amino acids can vary without affecting the function of the protein. The amino acid sequence of a protein in one species can be compared with the amino acid sequence in the same protein in another species. A change in one amino acid may occur on average about once every million years; so the differences between proteins provide a molecular clock that can be used to compare the ages of different species. For example, geological evidence says Old- and New-World monkeys diverged from each other 30 million years ago. Their 24 differences in albumin amino acids suggest a rate of one amino acid change every 1.25 million years. If we apply this rate of change to apes, we can conclude that chimpanzees and humans diverged from each other about 5 million to 8 million years ago.

The relatedness of different species can also be determined by comparing their **deoxyribonucleic acid** (DNA), the genetic material in the nucleus of a cell. Genes are segments of DNA that specify what proteins a cell should make. Each gene is a long chain of four kinds of nucleotide bases. Through mutations, the sequence of bases can change to some extent and still leave a functional gene. Researchers use enzymes to cut DNA into short segments that they then place in a synthetic gel and subject to an electrical current. The current causes the segments to line up, longest to shortest, producing a signature of the gene's owner. Signatures of different species or even different individual members of the same species can be compared and calibrated by using known time relations (as described earlier) to establish relatedness. Signatures of modern humans and chimpanzees suggest that they have 99% of their genes in common and are each other's closest living relatives. So chimps and humans have a common ancestor. Obviously, the difference of 1% still produces a huge difference between the two species.

Behavioral studies also indicate that humans and chimps are closely related. Ethologist Jane Goodall's behavioral studies of chimpanzees paint a picture of a species so similar to humans that one has the impression of looking into a mirror. These animals occupy large territories that the males defend as a group. The males wage war and kill neighbors to expand their territories. The animals are great travelers, ambulating along the ground, at a rate that humans have difficulty matching, for distances of 8 km or more a day. They are omnivores, eating vegetation, fruit, and insects, but they can also hunt cooperatively to catch monkeys, pigs, and other mammals. They have complex social groups within which family relations are important both for the individual chimpanzee and for the group structure. Finally, they have rich manual, facial, and vocal communication capabilities, and they construct and use tools for defense and to obtain food and water.

Australopithecus: The East Side Story

The evolution of humans from an ape ancestor to *Homo sapiens* was not as linear as people tend to imagine. The human (hominid) family tree is really a bush: for much of hominid history, many family members were alive at the same time. Today, however, our species is the only surviving member, sitting alone on the last living branch (Figure 2.5). In this section, we will trace some of the major steps in the origins of modern humans, but we caution that there are many assumptions underlying this story. There is no certainty about the relationships between the different members of the human family. Each year new hominid fossils are discovered. Some of the discoveries add new species to our family tree, others trace our family further back in time.

The ancestor of all hominids was probably an animal somewhat like *Australopithecus* (*Australo*, meaning "southern" and *pithecus*, meaning "ape"). The name was coined by an Australian anthropologist, R. A. Dart, for a find he made in South Africa (he was probably feeling homesick). These animals lived in eastern Africa and possessed a distinctly human

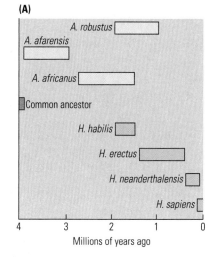

(A)

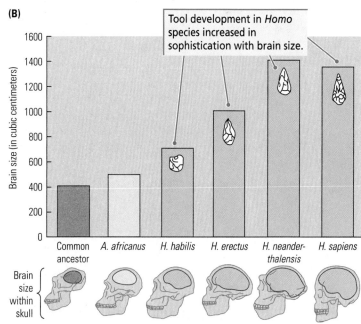

(B)

Tool development in *Homo* species increased in sophistication with brain size.

Figure 2.5 Summary of some of the recognized species of the human family. Notice the development of tools by *Homo.* (After Stanley, 1981, and Johanson and Edey, 1981.)

characteristic: they walked upright. The conclusion that they walked upright is based on the description of numerous bones and on the discovery of fossilized footprints dated from 3.6 million to 3.8 million years ago. The footprints feature a well-developed arch and big toe and point straight ahead, a pattern much more like that of humans than that of apes. Fossilized remains show that there were a number of distinct species of *Australopithecus* living in East Africa and Ethiopia. (For an enjoyable account of the discovery of the Ethiopian fossils, we recommend D. Johanson and M. Edey's book, *Lucy: The Beginnings of Humankind.*) According to Pickford, the first hominids may have appeared much earlier, as long ago as 6 million years, making *Australopithecus* a long-lived family group consisting of many species, one of which gave rise to the ancestors of modern humans.

Why did the hominid lineage diverge from its ape ancestor? Coppens advanced what he calls the "east side theory." Geological deposits on the east side of the Great Rift Valley, which runs from north to south dividing Africa in two, have yielded many fossils of hominids deposited through millions of years, but no fossils of apes at all. On the west side of the rift valley, the fossil record indicates that chimpanzees and gorillas currently live pretty much unchanged from what they were more than 15 million years ago. Coppens proposed that about 8 million years ago a tectonic crisis (a deformation of the earth's crust) produced the Great Rift Valley, leaving a wet jungle climate to the west and a much drier climate to the east. To the west the apes continued unchanged, whereas to the east the apes had to evolve rapidly to survive in the mixture of trees and grass that formed their new brushwood habitat. According to Teaford and Ungar, a distinctive feature of the new hominids was a change in dentition that included a reduction in the size of the incisors and a flattening of the molars. These animals were able to consume a much more varied diet than that consumed by ancestral apes. Their legs were longer, too, and thus better suited to over-ground locomotion.

There are two versions of how the evolution of hominids took place. The *down-from-trees hypothesis* proposes that the trees' being farther apart required apes to adopt bipedal locomotion. The accompanying change in posture reduced the area of the body exposed to the sun and permitted the loss of body hair. The *water-baby hypothesis*, proposed by Hardy, suggests a different order of events, beginning with a hypothetical naked ape swimming and foraging on the beaches of the ocean and later forced to abandon its semiaquatic habitat when the ocean receded. In this scenario the animal is described as finding bipedalism and lack of body hair advantageous in swimming; it then retains these features when it adapts to the land. Whichever story is correct, the ape continued to climb trees but changed to an upright posture and adopted a much more varied diet. Brain size did not change much, an indication that changes in brain size could not have been due simply to adopting an upright posture and thus having the hands free.

Homo Habilis: The Omo Story

The oldest fossils to be designated as *Homo* (the genus to which modern humans belong) were found by English anthropologist Louis Leakey in the Olduvai Gorge in Tanzania in 1964, dated at about 1.75 million years old. The specimens bear a strong resemblance to *Australopithecus*, but Leakey argued that the dental pattern is more similar to that of modern humans. The animal apparently made simple stone tools, which were also found in the Olduvai Gorge, and so Leakey named the species *Homo habilis* (that is, "handyman"). There were a number of species of *Homo* alive at this time, which raises the question whether *Homo habilis* or some other, similar species is the ancestor of modern humans. *Homo habilis* was not necessarily the first toolmaker. Semaw suggested that stone tools were made as early as 2.6 million years ago by *Australopithecus*.

Coppens argued that the appearance of *Homo habilis* was related to climatic change. He studied a site on the Omo River that contained a continuous stratigraphic record starting 4 million years ago and ending 1 million years ago. The record indicates that 4 million years ago the climate was more humid and the vegetation was brushwood, whereas 1 million years ago the area was less humid and the vegetation was savanna or grassland with only occasional trees. It was during the latter period that *Homo habilis* appeared, having a distinctively larger brain and using tools.

In early descriptions, *Homo habilis* was characterized as a hunter-gatherer, with the males specializing in hunting and the females specializing in collecting nuts and digging for roots. One consequence of the hunter-gatherer theory was the idea that men's superiority in spatial skills (compared with those of women) can be explained by the *Homo habilis* males' having to navigate long distances in search of prey, which they then killed by throwing spears. A corollary to this idea was that females, confined to the home base, developed social, language, and clothes-making skills that were important for instructing children and maintaining the social structure of the group.

This theory has some improbable features. Early hominids were not large: males were less than 5 feet tall and weighed about 100 pounds; females were smaller still. The animals on the savannas were much like the animals that live there today, and it is difficult to see how these early hominids could have been successful in hunting them. The animals are much too fast and dangerous, and, furthermore, the hominids would have been relatively defenseless and subject to predation from large cats and packs of dogs.

A more recent theory, suggested by Blumenschine and Cavallo, is that the most likely ecological niche for a savanna hominid to occupy was that of a scavenger. Many animals would die as a result of age, hunger during droughts, or predation. Carcasses could be found on the open savanna, around water holes, or in trees where they had been placed by leopards. The meat would be fresh for a day or two after death. A scavenger that could locate and butcher them quickly by daylight could compete with nocturnal scavengers such as jackals and large cats and so would have an ample supply of food. Such a scavenger would have to learn to read the environment and watch the activities of vultures, predators, and animal herds. Lacking the sharp teeth (for tearing skin) and strong jaws (for crushing bones to get the marrow) that other scavengers possessed, the new scavenger would need to be adept with sharp flakes of rock and hammers. It would also have to be a good carrier to retreat quickly to the safety of trees or rocks without abandoning the meat and bones. Importantly, scavenging, toolmaking, and butchering would have been a family affair. Children, with their keen eyesight, would have made an important contribution by locating carcasses, and the entire community would have participated in toolmaking, butchering, and carrying.

There was a big difference in brain size between *Australopithecus* and *Homo habilis*, which may have been related to scavenging. Such a life-style would have depended heavily on sensory, motor, and social skills. The fact that *Homo habilis* artifacts include the tools required for scavenging—stone flakes and hammers—but not the tools used for hunting provides additional support for the scavenging hypothesis.

Homo Erectus: The Traveler

Homo habilis is thought to have given rise to another species, *Homo erectus* ("upright human"), so named because of a mistaken notion that its predecessors were stooped. It first shows up in the fossil record about 1.9 million years ago and lasts until at least 400,000 years ago. *Homo erectus* has a pivotal position in this history. Its brain was significantly larger than that of any preceding animal and, unlike *Australopithecus* and *Homo habilis*, this creature was a globetrotter; its remains are found in East Africa as well as in Java (Java man) and China (Peking man). It first left Africa about 1.9 million years ago, making a number of new invasions into Europe and Asia in the next million years.

Homo Sapiens: The Eve Story

There are two explanations of the origins of modern humans. Until about 30,000 years ago, Africa, Europe, and Asia were occupied by a variety of human groups. The Neanderthal group occupied Europe. Neanderthal looked very much like us, having as large a brain but a stockier and stronger body, built more for strength than for swiftness. Neanderthals apparently buried their dead with flowers, arguably the first evidence of religious belief. Thorne and Wolpoff point out that modern humans living in Asia have physical features that resemble those of ancient hominids who lived there as long ago as 500,000 years. Modern humans living in Europe have the physical features of ancient hominids who lived in Europe. Thus, argue Thorne and Wolpoff, modern humans evolved in many places, from many hominid groups, at about the same rate. New adaptive genes, such as those that might have increased brain size, were disseminated throughout these diverse populations by migration, trade, and other social interactions.

The other explanation is based on biochemical evidence. A mitochondrial analysis of modern people by Cann and her coworkers suggests that all modern people descended from an ancestral "Eve" who lived in Africa about 200,000 years ago. Mitochondria are tiny, DNA-containing structures found in every cell and help produce energy for the cell's use. They are passed from females to their offspring in the cytoplasm (inner fluid) of the ovum. In other words, whereas humans receive nuclear DNA from both parents, they receive mitochondrial DNA from the mother only. The DNA of mitochondria is analyzed in the way described earlier for nuclear DNA.

Besides confirming a common ancestor for all modern humans within the past 200,000 years, Cann's analysis also suggests that there has been extensive intermingling between different modern human populations. These conclusions have since been supported by an analysis by Jin and Su of DNA from the Y chromosome (the male sex chromosome), which permits the tracking of relationships through substances passed only between males. Asiatic males have mutations on the Y chromosome that are similar to the mutations on the Y chromosome of African males. The logic of parsimony says it is unlikely that these mutations occurred twice. Instead, the ancestors of Asiatic males probably originated in Africa. In sum, the evidence points to an ancestral stock that divided into two groups, one of which remained in Africa while the other migrated into Europe and elsewhere. The analysis further suggests that modern humans did not simply migrate, settle, and develop into different races. Rather, modern humans migrated continually, populating and repopulating all habitable parts of the world and intermingling several times, as they continue to do today. The kind of migration, intergroup contact, and intermingling that so typifies the past few centuries has apparently been the historical pattern for *Homo sapiens*.

There is considerable debate about what happened to the Neanderthals in Europe, as well as to similar populations elsewhere, with the arrival of modern humans. The biochemical measures give no evidence that the new arrivals mated with the local inhabitants, even though the archeological record indicates that the groups overlapped for a considerable period of time. Perhaps they intermingled but have no living descendants. A failure to mix and mate would be difficult to explain. Perhaps modern humans had such advanced language abilities that they were effectively separated from any lasting interaction with the Neanderthals and others.

If we consider the effects that Europeans have had on several of the human populations that they have encountered in more recent times, then we can imagine some of the ways in which the Neanderthals and other early populations were completely replaced. Within a few years of the Europeans' arriving in the Americas, the numbers of indigenous people were drastically reduced by alien diseases and war, and in some places whole populations disappeared. Much the same thing happened in Tasmania. It is possible that the early history of *Homo* included similar interactions.

The Origin of Brain Size

Brain size presents a fascinating problem. According to Jerison's "principle of proper mass," the size of a brain, or a given part of a brain, is related to the complexity of its owner's behavior. The human brain ranges in size (that is, mass) from 1000 to 2000 g, with an average size ranging between 1300 and 1400 g. This mass is larger than that of the brains of most other animals, but how can we know whether it is simply proportional to the mass of the human body? The elephant's body size would lead us to expect its brain to be larger than the human brain, and indeed it is roughly three times as large.

The Encephalization Quotient

Neuroanatomists long ago realized that to compare brain sizes across species, it is necessary to factor out body size. Jerison developed what he terms the **encephalization quotient** (EQ): the ratio of actual brain size to expected brain size. The expected brain size is based on an average for living mammals that takes body size into account. Thus, the average typical mammal (which incidentally is the cat) has an EQ of 1.0. As animals increase in body size, the size of the brain increases somewhat less, about two-thirds the extent of the increase in body size. With the use of Jerison's formula, an EQ can be calculated for an animal of any size by knowing only its body size and brain size. Figure 2.6 shows a graph of the body and brain sizes of some common mammals. Animals that deviate from 1.0, the diagonal line, have brains larger or smaller than would be expected for a mammal of that particular body size. Relatively larger brains are above the line and relatively smaller brains are below the line. Note that the modern human brain is the farthest above the diagonal line, indicating that it has the relatively largest size.

Table 2.1 summarizes the EQs for common laboratory animals and for humans. Notice that the rat's EQ is only 0.4, whereas the human's EQ is 7.3. The rat's brain, then, has about half the mass expected for a mammal of the rat's body size, and the brain of a human is 7.3 times as large as that expected for a mammal of our body size. Note that the chimpanzee brain is about 2.5 times as large as that predicted for a mammal of a chimpanzee's body size (EQ = 2.48), but its EQ is still only about one-third the EQ of humans. These measurements make it clear that the human brain really is larger than those of other primates. An EQ of this magnitude is not unique to humans, however; the EQ of the dolphin is comparable, having a value of about 6.0. The EQ of an elephant, 1.3, on the other hand, is only a little bigger than expected for an animal of its size.

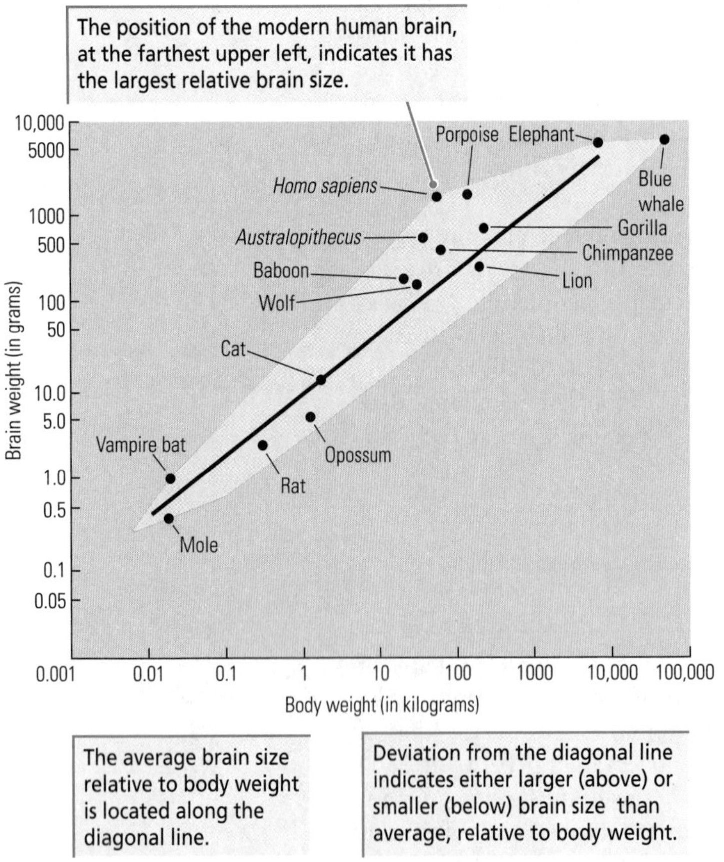

Changes in the Neocortex

Stephan and colleagues compared the brains of more than 60 species of mammals and found that, although nearly all structures of the brain increase in size as the EQ increases, the cortex shows the most dramatic increase. Thus, it seems reasonable to suppose that, if the human brain is different in some way, the difference is most likely to be found in the cortex. This idea has been explored by comparing the human brain with the brains of other primates, by using a variety of measures of cortical structure, in-

The position of the modern human brain, at the farthest upper left, indicates it has the largest relative brain size.

The average brain size relative to body weight is located along the diagonal line.

Deviation from the diagonal line indicates either larger (above) or smaller (below) brain size than average, relative to body weight.

Figure 2.6 Brain and body sizes of some common mammals. The measurements along the axes increase logarithmically to represent the wide range of body and brain sizes. The shaded polygon contains the brain and body sizes of all mammals. The line through the polygon illustrates the expected increase in brain size as body weight increases. Animals that lie above the diagonal line have brain sizes that are larger than would be expected for an animal of that size. Modern humans have the largest brain relative to body size of any animal and lie farthest away from the diagonal line. (After Jerison, 1973.)

cluding cell density and the volume and distribution of the cortex. Stephan and his coworkers calculated that the volume of the human neocortex is 3.2 times as great as the predicted volume for nonhuman primates in general and nearly 3 times as great as what would be predicted for a chimpanzee of the same body weight. In other words, the human cortex is very large.

The human cortex, as well as the cortexes of other animals with disproportionately big brains, is distinctive in another way. The typical mammalian cortex can be divided into areas that are specialized for movement, body senses, audition, and vision. In general, the frontal (movement), parietal (body senses), temporal (audition), and occipital (vision) lobes subserve these functions in humans (Figure 2.7). In very simple animals, each of these regions is relatively homogeneous but, in more complex animals, each lobe can be divided into a number of subregions. For example, although the visual cortex is in the occipital lobe of all animals, the squirrel has 4 separate visual areas, the cat appears to have at least 12, and the owl monkey has as many as 14 (the actual number in humans is not known but is probably about 30 or more). If each of these areas has a special function, as is supposed, then the growth of the human cortex is characterized not only by a larger size but by many more functional areas as well.

The processes that increase brain size can be illustrated by the following model. Figure 2.8A shows the brain of a primitive mammal, such as a hedgehog, and indicates the various regions that participate in movement and sensory processes. Iwaniuk and colleagues proposed that, if the forepaw area expands in size by means of mutation, then more-complex skilled forepaw movements for food handling become possible, allowing the animal to exploit a new habitat. Accordingly, the motor cortex in Figure 2.8B has acquired a new subregion, becoming comparatively larger and enabling the animal to use its forepaws more dexterously. Rodents, such as the laboratory rat, are representative of animals that have undergone such an increase in motor-cortex size: they have a large forepaw representation in the motor cortex and correspondingly good food-handling skills.

Table 2.1 Comparison of brain sizes of species most commonly studied in neuropsychology

Species	Brain volume (ml)	Encephalization quotient
Rat	2.3	0.40
Cat	25.3	1.01
Rhesus monkey	106.4	2.09
Chimpanzee	440.0	2.48
Human	1350.0	7.30

(A)

Frontal lobe
Central sulcus
Parietal lobe
Body senses
Motor
Vision
Hearing
Lateral fissure
Temporal lobe
Occipital lobe

(B)

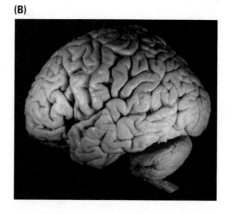

Figure 2.7 A lateral view of the human brain illustrating the lobes of the brain and their general functional correlates. The functional regions of the human brain consist of many subregions, each representing a subfunction within that modality. (Photo courtesy of Yakolev Collection/AFIP.)

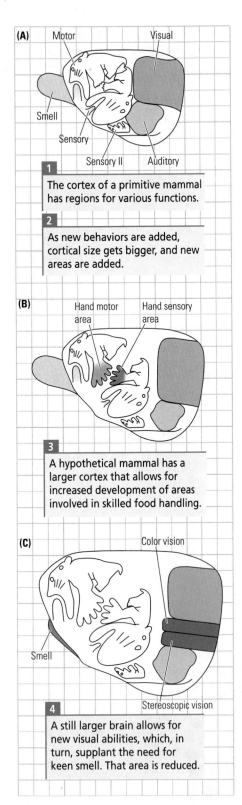

(A)
Motor
Visual
Smell
Sensory
Sensory II
Auditory

1 The cortex of a primitive mammal has regions for various functions.

2 As new behaviors are added, cortical size gets bigger, and new areas are added.

(B)
Hand motor area
Hand sensory area

3 A hypothetical mammal has a larger cortex that allows for increased development of areas involved in skilled food handling.

(C)
Color vision
Smell
Stereoscopic vision

4 A still larger brain allows for new visual abilities, which, in turn, supplant the need for keen smell. That area is reduced.

Figure 2.8 (A) The brain of a hedgehog, illustrating the extent and number of the sensory and motor areas of the cortex. (B) A hypothetical rodent that developed skilled forelimbs for food handling. The paw area of the sensory and motor cortex has increased in size to represent new receptors in the hands and the increased complexity of muscle arrangement. (C) A hypothetical primate that has developed color vision and vision for depth to improve further locomotion and feeding in the trees. There are two new visual areas in the cortex, one to represent each new ability. Note the increase in brain size associated with the expansion of areas and the addition of areas.

Primates are characterized by their ability to get around in an arboreal habitat. Good depth perception is useful to them in gauging their jumps from one small branch to another. They acquired depth perception because some cells in each eye became specialized for seeing the same object from different views, a development made possible by the association of these cells with a new region of the visual cortex. The new cortical area added mass to the primate brain, as is shown in Figure 2.8C.

Animals that are antecedent to primates have a very large olfactory system, and most of their motor behavior, such as locating food, is done by sniffing. Primates use vision to locate food. The switch from olfaction to vision in primates is associated with a sudden growth of the neocortex. The shift is not surprising, because the use of vision to control motor behavior would not only require new visual areas, but would also require the visual part of the cortex to connect to the motor cortex and control it. If other new abilities became adaptive, such as color vision for detecting ripe fruit, the brains of primates would acquire still more areas and grow still larger. Thus, both an increase in the size of existing areas and the development of new areas increase cortical size. Note that both the increase in the motor cortex allowing increased forepaw skill and the increase in the number of areas in the visual cortex increase cortical size.

Growth of the Hominid Brain

Unlike skulls and other bones, soft tissues such as brains do not leave fossil records. The size and organization of a fossil's brain must, therefore, be inferred from the shape, size, and other features of the inside of the skull. A measure commonly used for such inferences is cranial capacity, the volume of the cranial cavity. The cranial capacity of a skull can provide a reasonable estimate of the size of an animal's brain.

The brain of the early australopithecines was about the same size as that of a modern chimpanzee, about 400 g. None of the australopithecine species developed particularly large brains, despite the genus's lasting for about 5 million years. *Homo habilis* had a slightly larger brain. The great expansion in brain size occurred in *Homo erectus*, whose brain shows an increase in size equal to that of the entire australopithecine brain (Figure 2.9). The sudden appearance of large-brained *Homo erectus* implies that there probably was not a gradual selection of individuals with larger brains but rather that having a larger brain must have conferred a decisive and immediate advantage.

There are many theories for why the human brain changed in size, and they can be divided into two groups. **Prime mover theories** are theories that point to single causes. For example, it was once proposed that having free hands led to toolmaking and that toolmaking led to having a larger brain. We now know that chimpanzees and many other animals use tools and that the first upright apes did not have larger brains than other apes, which weakens this particular prime mover argument. **General mover theories** point to many simultaneously acting causes. Whatever the driving factors, any increase in brain size would have produced selective advantages in the form of increased abilities, and these increased abilities in turn would have rapidly reinforced the trend.

One prime mover theory is proposed by Dean Falk. Impressed by the observation that a car engine can get bigger only if its cooling system is improved, she investigated the way in which blood cools the brain. She suggested that a change in the brain's venous blood flow (blood that is returning to the heart) removed a constraint that had to that point placed an upper limit on the growth of the ape's brain. Although the brain comprises less than 2% of the body, it uses 25% of the body's oxygen and 70% of its glucose. As a result it generates a great deal of heat and is at risk of overheating under conditions of exercise or heat stress. Falk suggests that this risk of overheating places a limit on how big the brain can be and has kept the brain of the chimpanzee at its current size. When examining the holes in the skull through which blood vessels pass, Falk noted a difference in pattern between the skull holes of australopithecines and those of *Homo erectus*. In *Homo erectus* and their descendents, the holes suggest a much more widely dispersed outward flow of blood from the brain, which Falk speculates served as a radiator to help cool the brain. She suggests that it was selected in response to the upright posture of *Homo erectus* and helped to cool a body that was exposed to daytime savanna heat.

The blood-flow change had the fortuitous effect of allowing the brain to grow larger in response to other kinds of pressure. A condition that could fortuitously lead to further developments is called a **preadaption,** and improved blood cooling was a preadaption for the growth of the brain. When a behavior has been changed to exploit a new habitat, other new sources of influence may come into play to encourage further change. The sequence of effects in regard to brain size might have been as follows:

Bipedalism → development of a radiator → opportunity for brain expansion

General mover theories point to a number of mechanisms through which subsequent increases in brain size may have taken place. One is **neoteny,** a process in which an individual's rate of maturation slows down in such a way that some of the juvenile features of predecessors become the adult features of

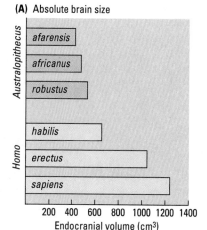

(A) Absolute brain size

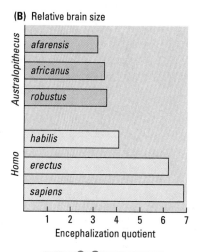

(B) Relative brain size

Figure 2.9 Endocranial volume (A) and encephalization quotients (B) for fossil hominids. Notice the sudden increase in brain size in *H. erectus*. (Data from McHenry, 1975.)

(A) Juvenile chimp

(B) Adult chimp

Figure 2.10 A juvenile (A) and adult (B) chimpanzee, showing the greater resemblance of the baby chimp to humans and illustrating the principle of neoteny in human evolution. (After Gould, 1981.)

descendants. Because an infant's head is large relative to body size, this process is postulated as having led to "adult babies" with large brains. Many features of the human anatomy resemble juvenile stages of other primates, including a small face; a vaulted cranium; a large brain-to-body size ratio; an unrotated big toe; an upright posture; and primary distribution of hair on the head, armpits, and pubic areas (Figure 2.10). Humans also retain behavioral features of their forebears' infants, including exploration, play, and flexible behavior. An important part of the answer to the Sphinx's riddle about the nature of humans is that the adult who walks on two legs is sort of an infant chimpanzee.

Other influences that could have led to brain growth include social development and changes in food-gathering practices. Humans are social, and as their groups increased in size and complexity, individuals with larger brains may have had an advantage. Hominids also changed diet, which changed the face and head structure; this change in turn may also have contributed to increased brain size. From the beginning, hominids were tool users, and changes in hand structure and increasing dexterity may have contributed to an increase in brain size. Even sexual selection could have contributed to increased brain size. There is evidence that males favor females who have more infantile facial features, and one such infantile facial feature is a greater head size relative to body size.

Variations in Modern Human Brain Size

Given species differences in brain size and the general association between the brain size and the behavioral complexity of different species, it is logical to ask whether variations in the size of the modern human brain are similarly related to behavioral complexity. The answer is yes—but in ways that are perhaps surprising.

Nineteenth-century investigators attempted to correlate gross human brain size and behavior with three questions in mind. They asked whether brain size was related to individual intelligence, whether brain size was related to intelligence differences between sexes, and whether brain size was related to intelligence differences between nationalities and races. Gould reviews these investigations in his book *The Mismeasure of Man* and concludes that they were completely invalidated by inadequate procedures for measuring brain size and by the absence of any method for measuring intelligence. For example, the investigators made little attempt to control for body size, were insensitive to the fact that head size and brain size are not closely correlated, and were not aware that the brain loses mass with age (most of the brains that were measured came from people who had died in old age). In the end, French investigators concluded that the French had the largest brains and German investigators concluded that Germans had the largest brains.

This line of investigation was no more successful in the twentieth century, even though the investigators had by that time solved two of the previous problems. First, with magnetic resonance imaging (MRI, described in Chapter 7), they were able to create a virtual representation of the brain of a young healthy adult. Figure 2.11 shows such an image juxtaposed with a photograph of a brain. Second, IQ tests allowed the investigators to estimate and compare intelligence by using a single number, the IQ. The IQ is the average of a subject's scores on a number of tests, including tests of information, arithmetic, memory, and so on. The twentieth-century investigators found wide variation in gross brain size among individuals, among members of the same national and racial groups, and among people of the same sex (as well as a statistical difference between the sexes), together with wide variation in intelligence, but little or no correlation between gross brain size and intelligence when individuals, nations, races, or sexes are compared.

(A)

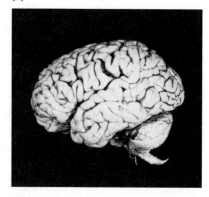

In addition to the absence of a strong relation between gross brain size and intelligence among humans, there are other good reasons to believe this line of inquiry is a superficial one. First, even though between-species differences in brain size may be correlated with between-species differences in behavior, to apply the correlation within a species is faulty, because within-species behavior is much more uniform. Second, intelligence is not well defined or understood, and IQ is a superficial measurement at best, one markedly influenced by culture. For example, when IQ tests that were given to young adults 50 years ago are given to young adults today, today's subjects score as much as 25 points higher (a phenomenon called the Flynn effect). Taken at face value (though it shouldn't be), the increase would suggest that intelligence has risen to such a degree in two generations that most young adults fall in the superior IQ category relative to their grandparents. (Obviously, the change has not been accompanied by a similar increase in brain size.)

(B)

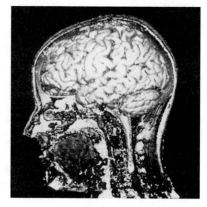

Attempts to correlate overall brain size and intelligence also overlook much more interesting issues. For one thing, the brain appears to be organized in functional units, each of which mediates a different kind of behavior. Variation in the size of specific functional units may be related to specific skills. For example, Nottebohm and colleagues showed that, in song birds, the size of the auditory and vocal regions of the brain are related to the complexity of song. Gardner and colleagues argued that there is not just one but many different kinds of human intelligence, each related to a different region of the brain. A second interesting observation is that brain size can be markedly affected by injury, especially if the injury occurs early in life. Kolb and colleagues reported that slight injury to the rat cortex within the first 10 days of life can result in disproportionate brain-size reductions of more than 25%. Rat pups at 10 days are equivalent in age to late-stage human embryos. Consequently, it is likely that a host of prenatal injuries can and do affect human brain size. A third observation is that, beginning with findings obtained by Rosensweig and colleagues more than 50 years ago, it is now well established that environmental experiences can affect cortical size. The Rosensweig team found that rats raised in a visually enriched environment undergo an increase in cortical size and a disproportionate increase in the size of visual regions of the cortex. Storfer suggested that similar enrichment of human experience, such as learning to read and write, also enlarges the size of the human cortex.

Figure 2.11 Comparison of an actual human brain (A) and a virtual brain produced by functional MRI (B). (Part A from Holser/Visuals Unlimited, Inc.; part B from Collection CNRI/Phototake)

The Acquisition of Culture

The evolution of humans, from the first "hominid" to the appearance of morphologically modern men and women, took less than 6 million years, an extremely short span of time in evolutionary terms. Thus, the evolution of the modern human brain was very rapid. Even so, most of the changes in behavior that differentiate us from our primate ancestors took place more rapidly still, long after the modern brain had evolved to its present condition. Only 25,000 years ago did modern humans leave the first human artistic relics: elaborate paintings on cave walls and carved ivory and stone figurines. The tempo of change has quickened further in the past 10,000 years. Agriculture and animal husbandry were established in the Middle East by 7000 B.C., followed by ideographic writing in the same region by 3000 B.C. Saint Ambrose, who lived in the fourth century A.D., is reported to have been the first person who could read silently. The modern technological age began in about A.D. 1500: it was after this time that most of what we see around us today was invented or discovered. How interesting that most of what we associate with modern humans is of such very recent origin, considering that the basic tools (a big brain, free hands, and bipedal locomotion) had been with us long before.

Summary

The divergence of the human brain from that of other living species has a history of at least 5 million years. In the past 2 million years, this history has been characterized by a major expansion of the brain that apparently took place in a number of quick steps, resulting in a number of different humanlike animals being alive at one time. Climatic changes seem to be closely correlated with the appearance of new hominid species. Today's humans have been around for only about 200,000 years, and they have replaced all of their predecessors.

The general structure of the human brain is quite similar to that of other animals, even to very simple animals such as rats. The human brain is proportionately larger in size, however, especially the size of the neocortex, and has more subregions. The enlargement and subregions probably allowed the development of many advantageous new skills (rather than a single decisive skill or ability). The increase in brain size in mammals generally and in the primate lineage in particular is also associated with the appearance of new cortical areas for mediating new behavior.

References

Beals, K. L., C. L. Smith, and S. M. Dodd. Brain size, cranial morphology, climate, and time machines. *Current Anthropology* 25:301–330, 1984.

Blinkov, S. M., and J. I. Glesner. *The Human Brain in Figures and Tables*. New York: Basic Books, 1968.

Blumenschine, R. J., and J. Q. Cavallo. Scavenging and human evolution. *Scientific American*, 90–96, October 1992.

Campbell, C. B. G., and W. Hodos. The concept of homology and the evolution of the nervous system. *Brain, Behavior and Evolution* 3:353–367, 1970.

Cann, R. L. Genetic clues to dispersal in human populations: Retracing the past from the present. *Science* 291:1742–1748, 2001.

Coppens, Y. The east side story: The origin of humankind. *Scientific American*, 88–95, May 1994.

Diamond, I. T., and K. L. Chow. Biological psychology. In S. Koch, Ed. *Psychology: A Study of a Science*, vol. 4. New York: McGraw-Hill, 1962.

Falk, D. A reanalysis of the South African australopithecine natural endocasts. *American Journal of Physical Anthropology* 53:525–539, 1980.

Falk, D. Brain evolution in *Homo*: The "radiator" theory. *Behavioral and Brain Sciences* 13:344–368, 1990.

Gardner, H. E., M. L. Kornhaber, and W. E. Wake. *Intelligence: Multiple Perspectives*. Fort Worth, TX, and Toronto: Harcourt Brace College, 1997.

Goodall, J. *The Chimpanzees of Gombe.* Cambridge, MA: The Belknap Press of Harvard University Press, 1986.

Gould, S. J. *The Mismeasure of Man.* New York: Norton, 1981.

Hardy, A. Was man more aquatic in the past? *New Scientist* 7:642–645, 1960.

Hetzer-Egger, C., M. Schorpp, and T. Boehm. Evolutionary conservation of gene structures of the Pax1/9 gene family. *Biochemistry and Biophysics Acta* 1492:517–521, 2000.

Hodos, W., and C. B. G. Campbell. Scale naturae: Why there is no theory in comparative psychology. *Psychological Review* 76:337–350, 1969.

Holloway, R. L. Revisiting the South African Tuang australopithecine endocast: The position of the lunate sulcus as determined by the stereoplotting technique. *American Journal of Physical Anthropology* 56:43–58, 1981.

Iwaniuk, A. N., and I. Q. Whishaw. On the origin of skilled forelimb movements. *Trends in Neurosciences* 23:372–376, 2000.

Jerison, H. J. *Evolution of the Brain and Intelligence.* New York: Academic Press, 1973.

Jin, L., and B. Su. Natives or immigrants: Modern human origin in east Asia. *National Review of Genetics* 1:126–133, 2000.

Johanson, D., and M. Edey. *Lucy: The Beginnings of Humankind.* New York: Warner Books, 1982.

Jorde, L. B. Human genetic distance studies: Present status and future prospects. *Annual Review of Anthropology* 14:343–373, 1987.

Kolb, B. *Brain Plasticity and Behavior.* Mahwah, NJ: Lawrence Erlbaum Associates, Inc., 1997.

Lockhart, R. B. The albino rat: A defensible choice or bad habit. *American Psychologist* 23:734–742, 1968.

Masterton, B., and L. C. Skeen. Origins of anthropoid intelligence: Prefrontal system and delayed alternation in hedgehog, tree shrew and baby. *Journal of Comparative and Physiological Psychology* 81:423–433, 1972.

McHenry, H. M. Fossils and the mosaic nature of human evolution. *Science* 190:425–431, 1975.

Nottebohm F. The King Solomon Lectures in Neuroethology: A white canary on Mount Acropolis. *Journal of Comparative Physiology* 179:149–156, 1996.

Passingham, R. E. *The Human Primate.* San Francisco: W. H. Freeman and Company, 1982.

Pickford, M. Discovery of earliest hominid remains. *Science* 291:986, 2001.

Rosensweig, M. R., D. Krech, E. L. Bennett, and M. C. Diamond. Effects of environmental complexity and training on brain chemistry and anatomy: A replication and extension. *Journal of Comparative and Physiological Psychology* 55:427–429, 1962.

Sarnat, H. B., and M. G. Netsky. *Evolution of the Nervous System.* New York: Oxford University Press, 1974.

Semaw, S. The world's oldest stone artifacts from Gona, Ethiopia: Their implications for understanding stone technology and patterns of human evolution between 2.6–1.5 million years ago. *Journal of Archaeological Science* 27:1197–1214, 2000.

Stanley, S. M. *The New Evolutionary Timetable.* New York: Basic Books, 1981.

Stephen, H., R. Bauchot, and O. J. Andy. Data on the size of the brain and of various parts in insectivores and primates. In C. R. Noback and W. Montagna, Eds. *The Primate Brain.* New York: Appleton, 1970, pp. 289–297.

Storfer, M. Myopia, intelligence, and the expanding human neocortex: Behavioral influences and evolutionary implications. *International Journal of Neuroscience* 98:153–276, 1999.

Teaford, M. F., and P. S. Ungar. Diet and the evolution of the earliest human ancestors. *Proceedings of the National Academy of Sciences of the United States of America* 97:13506–13511, 2000.

Thorne, A., and M. H. Wolpoff. The multiregional evolution of humans. *Scientific American,* 76–83, April 1992.

White, T. H. *The Once and Future King.* London: Collins, 1958.

Young, J. Z. *The Life of Vertebrates.* New York: Oxford University Press, 1962.

Organization of the Nervous System

To say that the human cerebral cortex is the organ of civilization is to lay a very heavy burden on so small a mass of matter. One is reminded of Darwin's amazement that the wonderfully efficient and diversified behavior of an ant can be carried on with so small a brain, which is "not so large as the quarter of a small pin's head." The complexity of the human brain is as far beyond that of an ant as human conduct is higher than ant's behavior. (C. Juston Herrick, 1926)

The complexity of the human brain and the complexity of human behavior present a major challenge to anyone trying to explain how the one produces the other. The human brain is composed of more than 180 billion cells, more than 80 billion of which are directly engaged in information processing. Each cell receives as many as 15,000 connections from other cells. If there were no order in this complexity, we would have to give up hope of ever understanding how the brain functions. Fortunately, we can obtain some tentative answers about how this machinery works, because it is possible to see a great deal of organization in the way that things are arranged. For example, cells that are close together make most of their connections with one another. Thus, they are like human communities, whose inhabitants share most of their work and engage in social interactions with others who live nearby. Each community of cells also makes connections with more-distant communities through quite large pathways made by their axons. These connections are analogous to the thoroughfares linking human communities.

Although the sizes and shapes of the brains of different people vary, just as their facial features do, the component structures—the communities and main roads of the brain—are common to all human beings. In fact, most of these structures seem to be common to all mammals. About a hundred years ago, anatomist Lorente de Nó examined a mouse brain through a microscope and discovered to his surprise that its fine structure is similar to that of the human brain. Because brain cells are similar in all animals with nervous systems, it is possible to show through experiments that these cells are responsible for behavior. Because the brains of different kinds of animals show structural differences as well as similarities, it is possible to learn about the function of specific brain structures by comparing the behavior of creatures that have those structures with the behavior of creatures that do not. This chapter begins with an overview of the anatomy of the brain and then describes some of its major structures and their function in more detail.

An Overview of the Nervous System

The nervous system is composed of many parts. Individually and in interactions with one another, they are responsible for different aspects of behavior. This section describes the cells of the nervous system and some of the ways in which they are organized to form the different anatomical structures of the brain.

Neurons and Glia

The brain of the embryo has its origin in a single undifferentiated cell called a **stem cell** (also called a germinal cell). Not only do this stem cell and its progeny produce the various specialized kinds of cells that make up the adult brain, but they also produce additional stem cells that persist into adulthood in a brain region called the **ventricular zone,** a region adjacent to the ventricles of the brain, as well as in the retina and spinal cord. A stem cell has an extensive capacity for self-renewal. To initially form a brain, it divides and produces two stem cells, both of which can divide again (Figure 3.1). In the adult, one stem cell dies after each division; so the brain contains a constant number of dividing stem cells. These stem cells serve as a source of new cells for certain parts of the adult brain and so may play a role in brain repair after brain injury.

In the developing embryo, stem cells give rise to precursor cells, which in turn give rise to primitive types of nervous system cells called **blasts.** Some blasts differentiate into the neurons of the nervous system, whereas others differentiate into the glia. These two basic brain-cell types—neurons and glia—take many forms and make up the entire adult brain. Neuroscientists once thought that the newborn child had all the neurons it would ever possess. Among

Figure 3.1 Cells in the brain begin as multipotential stem cells, which become precursor cells, which become blasts, which finally develop into specialized neurons and glia.

Cell type	Process
Stem	Self-renewal
Precursor	Precursor produced
Blast	Neuroblasts and glioblasts produced
Specialized	Neurons and glia differentiate

Neural   Glial

Interneuron   Projecting neuron   Oligodendrocyte   Astrocyte

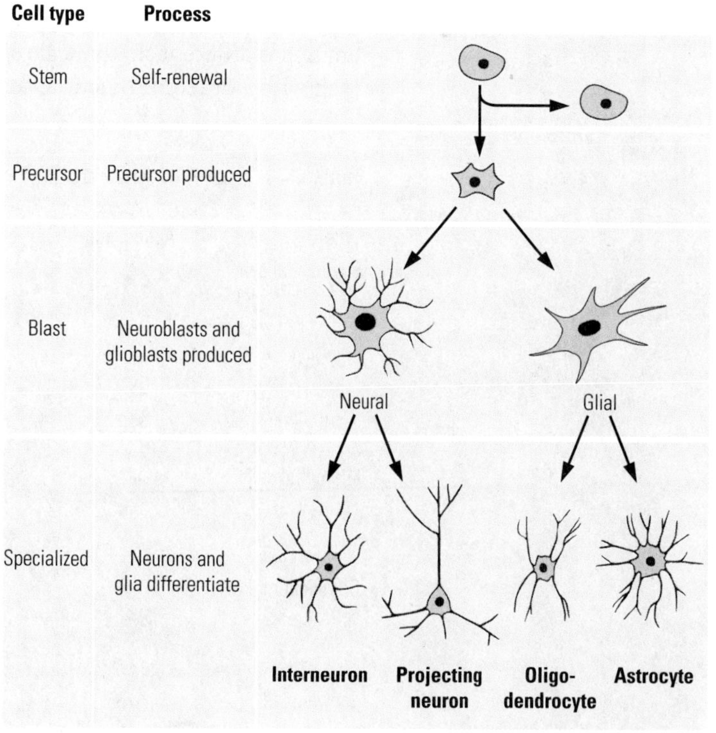

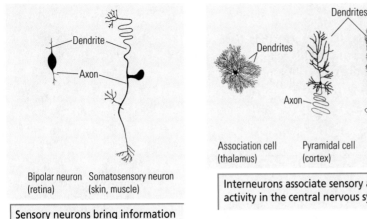

(A)

Dendrite

Axon

Bipolar neuron (retina)   Somatosensory neuron (skin, muscle)

Sensory neurons bring information to the central nervous system.

(B)

Dendrites

Dendrites

Axon

Axon

Association cell (thalamus)   Pyramidal cell (cortex)   Purkinje cell (cerebellum)

Interneurons associate sensory and motor activity in the central nervous system.

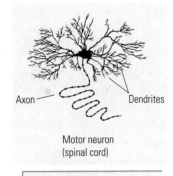

(C)

Axon   Dendrites

Motor neuron (spinal cord)

Motor neurons send signals from the brain and spinal cord to muscles.

Figure 3.2 The nervous system is composed of neurons, or nerve cells, each of which is specialized in regard to function. Schematic representations showing the relative sizes and configurations of (A) sensory neurons, (B) neurons in the brain, and (C) motor neurons in the spinal cord.

the most remarkable discoveries of the past few years is that, in fact, new neurons are produced after birth and, in some regions of the brain, continue to be produced into adulthood.

Neurons differ chiefly in overall size and in the complexity of their dendritic processes. Figure 3.2 shows examples of the differences in size and shape that characterize neurons from different parts of the nervous system. Note that the simplest neuron, called a bipolar neuron, consists of a cell body with a dendrite on one side and an axon on the other. Sensory neurons that project from the body's sensory receptors into the spinal cord are modified so that the dendrite and axon are connected, which speeds information conduction because messages do not have to pass through the cell body. Neurons within the brain and spinal cord have many dendrites that branch extensively but, like all neurons, a brain or spinal-cord neuron has only one axon. The architecture of cells differs from region to region in the brain. These differences provide the basis for dividing the brain into different anatomical regions. There are also various types of glial cells, each with a different function; some of them are described in Table 3.1.

Table 3.1 Types of glial cells

Type	Appearance	Features and function
Ependymal cell		Small, ovoid; secretes cerebrospinal fluid (CSF)
Astrocyte		Star shaped, symmetrical; nutritive and support function
Microglial cell		Small, mesodermally derived; defensive function
Oligodendroglial cell		Asymmetrical; forms myelin around axons in brain and spinal cord
Schwann cell		Asymmetrical; wraps around peripheral nerves to form myelin

Gray, White, and Reticular Matter

When a human brain is cut open to reveal its internal structures, some parts appear gray, some white, and some mottled. In general, these visually contrasting parts are described as gray matter, white matter, and reticular matter (Figure 3.3). With respect to our analogy equating brain regions with communities and roads, communities are gray and roads are white.

Gray matter acquires its characteristic gray brown color from the capillary blood vessels and neuronal cell bodies that predominate there. **White matter** consists largely of axons that extend from these cell bodies to form connections with neurons in other brain areas. These axons are covered with an insulating layer of glial cells, which are composed of the same fatty substance (lipid) that gives milk its white appearance. As a result, an area of the nervous system rich in axons covered with glial cells looks white. **Reticular matter** (from the Latin *rete*, meaning "net") contains a mixture of cell bodies and axons, from which it acquires its mottled gray and white, or netlike, appearance.

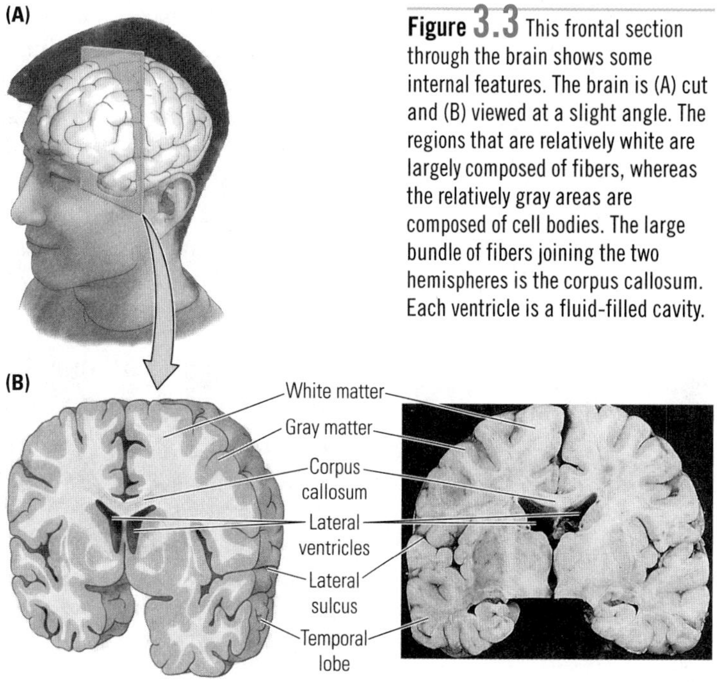

(A)

(B)

White matter
Gray matter
Corpus callosum
Lateral ventricles
Lateral sulcus
Temporal lobe

Figure 3.3 This frontal section through the brain shows some internal features. The brain is (A) cut and (B) viewed at a slight angle. The regions that are relatively white are largely composed of fibers, whereas the relatively gray areas are composed of cell bodies. The large bundle of fibers joining the two hemispheres is the corpus callosum. Each ventricle is a fluid-filled cavity.

Nuclei Nerves and Tracts

A large, well-defined group of cell bodies is called a **nucleus** (from the Latin *nux*, meaning "nut") because of its appearance. Some groups of cells are organized linearly, in a row, and are called layers. The ease with which we can visually distinguish these groupings suggests that each nucleus or layer has a particular function, and such is indeed the case. A large collection of axons projecting to or away from a nucleus or layer is called a **tract** (from Old French, meaning "path") or, sometimes, a fiber pathway. Tracts carry information from one place to another within the central nervous system; for example, the corticospinal (pyramidal) tract carries information from the cortex to the spinal cord. The optic tract carries information from the retina of the eye (the retina, strictly speaking, is actually part of the brain) to other visual centers in the brain. Fibers and fiber pathways that enter and leave the central nervous system are called **nerves,** such as the auditory nerve or the vagus nerve, but once they enter the central nervous system they, too, are called tracts. Because cell bodies are gray, nuclei are a distinctive gray; because glial cells make axons appear white, tracts and nerves are a distinctive white. Thus, the nuclei and layers of the brain are its communities, and the tracts are their connecting roadways.

Staining

Because of their respective gray and white coloring, the larger nuclei and tracts of the brain are easy to see in fresh brain tissue or in brain tissue cut into thin sections. The differences in the appearance of smaller nuclei and tracts must be enhanced to make them visible. The technique of staining to differentiate brain tissue consists of placing brain tissue into dyes or certain biochemical agents. Variations in the chemical composition of cells cause them to respond differently to particular coloring agents.

Staining techniques have an important role in neuroscience and are continually being refined. Stains now exist for coloring different parts of a cell, different kinds of cells, cells that contain distinctive proteins or other chemicals, immature or mature cells, sick cells, dead cells, and even cells that have recently played a part in learning some new behavior.

A Wonderland of Nomenclature

To the beginning student, the nomenclature for nuclei and tracts of the nervous system might seem chaotic. It is. Many structures have several names, often used interchangeably. For example, the **precentral gyrus,** which we introduce later in this chapter as the primary motor cortex, is variously referred to as "the primary motor cortex," "area 4," "the motor strip," "the motor homunculus," "Jackson's strip," "area pyramidalis," "the somatomotor strip," "gyrus precentralis," and "M1" (it can be seen in Figure 3.13 under the name "precentral"). This proliferation of terminology corresponds to the long, complex history of the neurosciences. Greek, Latin, and French terminology alternate with English: *mesencephalon* is Greek for "midbrain," *fasciculus opticus* is Latin for "optic tract," and *bouton termineau* is French for "synaptic knob."

The neuroanatomist's imagination has compared brain structures to body anatomy (mammillary bodies), flora (amygdala, or "almond"), fauna (hippocampus, or "sea horse"), and mythology (Ammon's horn). Some terminology is a tribute to early pioneers: the fields of Forel, Rolando's fissure, and Deiters's nucleus. Other terms make use of color: substantia nigra ("black substance"), locus coeruleus ("blue area"), and red nucleus. The longest name for a brain structure is nucleus reticularis tegmenti pontis Bechterewi, affectionately known as NRPT because, as you will observe, scientists have a special fondness for abbreviations. Some labels describe consistency: substantia gelatinosa ("gelatinous substance"); some a lack of knowledge: substantia innominata ("unnamable substance"), zone incerta ("uncertain area"), nucleus ambiguus ("ambiguous nucleus"). Some are based entirely on expediency: cell groups A-1 to A-15 or B1 to B9 (which, incidentally, were named only recently).

We attempt to use consistent and simple terms in this book, but in many cases alternative terms are widely used, and so we have included them where necessary.

Describing Locations in the Brain

Many structures of the brain are labeled according to their locations relative to other structures and landmarks. One convention makes use of seven terms that indicate anatomical direction: *superior* or *dorsal* (above), *lateral* (to the side), *medial* (to the inside), *ventral* (below), *anterior* (in front of), and *posterior* (behind). Thus one structure can be said to lie superior, lateral, medial, ventral, anterior, or posterior to another.

The nervous system is arranged symmetrically, with a left side and a right side. If two structures lie on the same side, they are said to be **ipsilateral;** if they lie on opposite sides, they are said to be **contralateral** to each other; if one lies on each side, they are said to be **bilateral;** that is, there is one in each hemisphere. Moreover, structures that are close to one another are said to be **proximal;** those far from one another are said to be **distal.** Finally, a projection that carries messages toward a given structure is said to be **afferent;** one that carries messages away from the structure is said to be **efferent.**

Approaches to the Study of Anatomy

Neuroanatomists study the structure of the brain by using any of four main conceptual approaches: (1) comparative, (2) developmental, (3) cytoarchitectonic, and (4) functional.

The Comparative Approach

The **comparative approach** examines the brain's evolution from the primitive cord in simple wormlike animals to the large, complex "ravelled knot" in the human head. In addition, it looks for correlations between the increasing complexity of the nervous system and the emergence of new and more complex behaviors in the animals under study. For example, comparing the nervous systems of animals that do not move with those of animals able to swim, crawl, walk, climb, or fly enabled scientists to piece together the story of how neurons and muscles evolved together to produce various movements and behaviors. Such analysis is not necessarily simple. The limbic system, a middle layer in the mammalian brain, first became prominent in the brains of amphibians and reptiles. Is its function to control the new modes of locomotion those animals employ, to orient their travels through a terrestrial rather than an aquatic world, to negotiate the more complex social groups in which they live, or to confer more advanced learning abilities on them than fish seem to enjoy? The answer is uncertain.

The comparative approach has yielded a key piece of information in neuropsychology: a mammal can be distinguished from other animals by its large cortex, and this structure is particularly large in humans. This observation first suggested to neuroscientists that the cortex must have an important function in conferring abilities unique to mammals, especially humans. As a result, the cortex receives proportionately more attention in human neuropsychology than do other structures.

The Developmental Approach

The **developmental approach** (also called the ontogenetic approach) examines the changes in brain structure and size that take place as an individual mammal develops from an egg to an adult.

As each individual organism matures, it passes through the same general phylogenetic stages as its ancestral species did in the course of evolution. This principle has been stated as "ontogeny recapitulates phylogeny" (*ontogeny* is the development of an individual organism, and *phylogeny* is the evolutionary history of a species). Thus, human babies are at first able to make only gross body movements; later they crawl, then walk, and eventually perform highly skilled motions with their hands and mouths. What changes take place in their nervous systems to make each new behavior possible? Like the comparative approach, the developmental approach allows the development and maturation of structures to be correlated with emerging behaviors.

In addition, the developmental approach acquires general information about brain function by studying immature brains as if they were simplified models of the adult brain. Neuropsychologists widely assume, for example, that the neocortex is particularly immature in newborn infants. Thus they believe that, by correlating the development of the neocortex with emerging complex and conscious behavior, they may discover the relations between neocortical structure and function.

Cytoarchitectonic Analysis

Cytoarchitectonic analysis examines the architecture of cells: their differences in structure, size, shape, and connections, as well as their distribution in different parts of the brain. The cytoarchitectonic approach has been used to particular advantage by neuroanatomists to produce various kinds of maps of the brain.

The newest cytoarchitectonic technique analyzes the brain's organization by looking at differences in the cells' biochemical activity. Cellular activity and growth are governed by a cell's nucleus, which releases biochemical "messages" into the cell that initiate the production of whatever new proteins the cell requires. These message molecules can be stained, allowing cells that are undergoing change to be located, mapped, and observed. It is a useful way of identifying cells that may be active in specific processes, such as learning or mediating recovery from brain damage.

Functional Approaches

Functional analysis seeks to discover the roles of the various brain areas, largely by observing changes in behavior that occur after injury or changes in metabolic activity that occur in the course of ongoing behavior. For example, an active brain area will increase its use of oxygen; so, if oxygen use can be detected, active areas of the brain can be distinguished from less-active areas. Various imaging techniques—based on methods for detecting the activity of cells, measuring their uptake of oxygen, recognizing their biochemical changes, and so on—allow the activity of different brain regions to be compared under varying circumstances. These methods have been used to study changes in brain function in the course of development, during movement, in responses to stimuli, and even during thinking. For example, injury to certain brain regions leads to language difficulties. Those same regions are observed to use more oxygen during thinking and speech in normal subjects.

The Origin and Development of the Brain

The developing brain is less complex than the adult brain and provides a clearer picture of the brain's basic three-part structural plan (Figure 3.4). Later, two of the three regions, the front and back components, expand greatly in mammals and become further subdivided, giving five regions in all. Embryologists use rather cumbersome names for the regions of the three-part and five-part brain plans; because some of these names are also used to describe parts of the adult brain, they are given in Figure 3.4.

The three regions of the primitive developing brain are recognizable as a series of three enlargements at the end of the embryonic spinal cord. The adult brain of a fish, amphibian, or reptile is roughly equivalent to this three-part brain: the **prosencephalon** ("front brain") is responsible for olfaction, the **mesencephalon** ("middle brain") is the seat of vision and hearing, and the **rhombencephalon** (hindbrain) controls movement and balance (Figure 3.4A). The spinal cord is considered part of the hindbrain. In mammals (Figure 3.4B), the prosencephalon develops further to form the cerebral hemispheres (the cortex and related structures), which are known collectively as the **telencephalon** ("endbrain"). The remaining part of the old prosencephalon is referred to as the **diencephalon** ("between brain") and includes the hypothalamus. The back part of the brain also develops further. It is subdivided into the **metencephalon** ("across brain," which includes the enlarged cerebellum) and the **myelencephalon** ("spinal brain").

Figure 3.4 Steps in the ontogenic development of the brain. (A) A three-chambered brain. (B) A five-chambered brain. (C) Side view through the center of the human brain.

(A) Fish, amphibian, reptile, human embryo at 25 days	(B) Mammals such as rat, human embryo at 50 days	(C) Fully developed human brain	
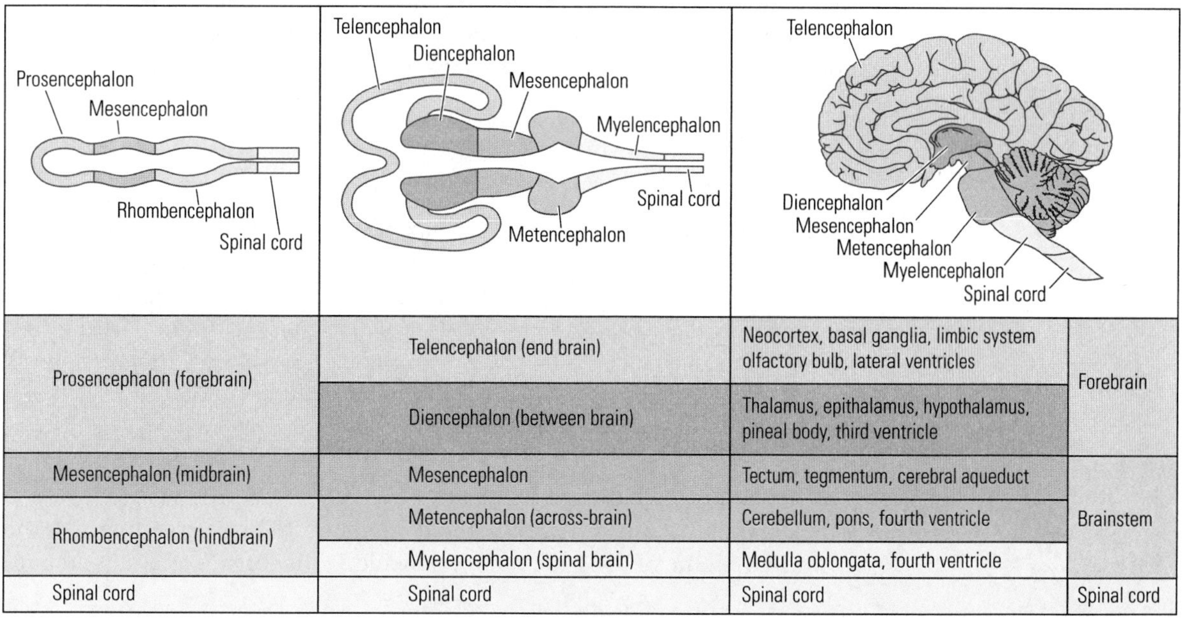 Prosencephalon (forebrain)	Telencephalon (end brain)	Neocortex, basal ganglia, limbic system olfactory bulb, lateral ventricles	Forebrain
	Diencephalon (between brain)	Thalamus, epithalamus, hypothalamus, pineal body, third ventricle	
Mesencephalon (midbrain)	Mesencephalon	Tectum, tegmentum, cerebral aqueduct	Brainstem
Rhombencephalon (hindbrain)	Metencephalon (across-brain)	Cerebellum, pons, fourth ventricle	
	Myelencephalon (spinal brain)	Medulla oblongata, fourth ventricle	
Spinal cord	Spinal cord	Spinal cord	Spinal cord

Figure 3.5 There are two lateral cerebral ventricles, one in each hemisphere, and a third and fourth ventricle, each of which lies in the midline of the brain.

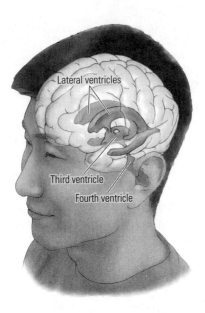

Figure 3.5 There are two lateral cerebral ventricles, one in each hemisphere, and a third and fourth ventricle, each of which lies in the midline of the brain.

The human brain is a more complex mammalian brain, retaining most of the features of other mammalian brains and possessing especially large cerebral hemispheres (Figure 3.4C).

The brain begins as a tube and, even after it folds and matures, its interior remains "hollow." The four prominent pockets created by the folding of this hollow interior are called **ventricles** ("bladders") and are numbered 1 through 4 (see Figure 3.4B). The "lateral ventricles" (first and second) form C-shaped lakes underlying the cerebral cortex, whereas the third and fourth ventricles extend into the brainstem (Figure 3.5). All are filled with a fluid—**cerebrospinal fluid,** or CSF—which is produced by ependymal glial cells located adjacent to the ventricles. The CSF flows from the lateral ventricles out through the fourth ventricle and eventually into the circulatory system.

The Spinal Cord

In a very simple animal, such as the earthworm, the body is a tube divided into segments. Within the body is a tube of nerve cells that also is divided into segments. Each segment receives fibers from sensory receptors of the part of the body adjacent to it and sends fibers to the muscles of that part of the body. Each segment functions relatively independently, although fibers interconnect the segments and coordinate their activity. This basic plan also holds for the human body. Let us take a look at our "tube of nerves."

Spinal-Cord Structure

Figure 3.6 shows the segmental organization of the human body. The segments, called **dermatomes** (meaning "skin cuts"), encircle the spinal column as a stack of rings. Originally, mammalian limbs developed perpendicularly to the spinal cord, but early humans developed an upright posture; so the ring formation in our bodies is distorted into the pattern shown in Figure 3.6. As many as six segments (C4 through T2) can be represented on the arm. If you imagine the person in the drawing standing on all fours, you can see how this pattern makes sense.

There are 30 spinal-cord segments: 8 cervical (C), 12 thoracic (T), 5 lumbar (L), and 5 sacral (S). Each segment is connected by nerve fibers to the body dermatome of the same number, including the organs and musculature

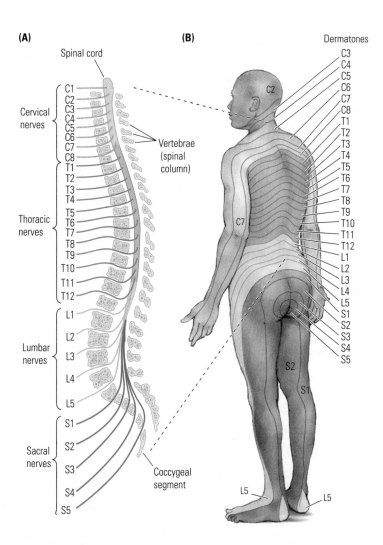

(A)

Spinal cord

Cervical nerves { C1 C2 C3 C4 C5 C6 C7 C8

T1 T2 T3 T4

Thoracic nerves { T5 T6 T7 T8 T9 T10 T11 T12

Lumbar nerves { L1 L2 L3 L4 L5

Sacral nerves { S1 S2 S3 S4 S5

(B)

Vertebrae (spinal column)

C2

C7

C7

S2

S1

L5   L5

Coccygeal segment

Dermatones

C3 C4 C5 C6 C7 C8 T1 T2 T3 T4 T5 T6 T7 T8 T9 T10 T11 T12 L1 L2 L3 L4 L5 S1 S2 S3 S4 S5

Figure 3.6 (A) The five groups of spinal-cord segments making up the spinal column (cervical, C; thoracic, T; lumbar, L; sacral, S; and coccygeal vertebrae) are shown in this side view. (B) Each spinal segment corresponds to a region of body surface (a dermatome) that is identified by the segment number.

that lie within the dermatome. In the main, the cervical segments control the forelimbs, the thoracic segments control the trunk, and the lumbar segments control the hind limbs.

Figure 3.7 shows a cross section of the spinal cord. Fibers entering the dorsal part of the spinal cord bring information from the sensory receptors of the body. These fibers converge as they enter the spinal cord, forming a strand of fibers referred to as a **dorsal root.** Fibers leaving the ventral part of the spinal cord, carrying information from the spinal cord to the muscles, form a similar strand known as a **ventral root.**

In the spinal cord itself, the outer part consists of white matter or tracts, arranged so that with a few exceptions the dorsally located tracts are motor and the ventrally located tracts are sensory. The tracts carry information to the brain and from the brain. The inner part of the cord consists of gray matter; that is, it is composed largely of cell bodies, which in this case organize movements and give rise to the ventral roots. In cross section, this gray region has the shape of a butterfly.

Figure 3.7 A cross section of the spinal cord illustrating a sensory neuron in the dorsal root and a motor neuron in the ventral root. Collateral branches of the sensory fiber cross to the other side of the spinal cord to influence motor neurons on that side and extend to adjacent segments to influence adjacent body parts. The inner regions of the spinal cord consist of cell bodies (gray matter) and the outer regions consist of tracts traveling to and from the brain (white matter).

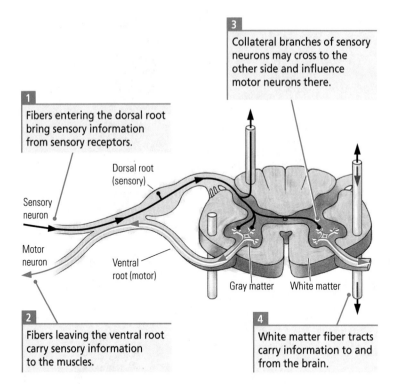

1 Fibers entering the dorsal root bring sensory information from sensory receptors.

3 Collateral branches of sensory neurons may cross to the other side and influence motor neurons there.

Sensory neuron

Dorsal root (sensory)

Motor neuron

Ventral root (motor)

Gray matter   White matter

2 Fibers leaving the ventral root carry sensory information to the muscles.

4 White matter fiber tracts carry information to and from the brain.

Spinal-Cord Function

Francois Magendie, a French experimental physiologist, reported in a three-page paper in 1822 that he had succeeded in cutting the dorsal roots of one group of puppies and the ventral roots of another group (the youth of the dogs allowed the different surgeries; in adult dogs, the roots are fused). He found that cutting the dorsal roots caused loss of sensation and cutting the ventral roots caused loss of movement. Eleven years earlier, in 1811, Charles Bell, a Scot, had suggested the opposite functions for each of the roots, basing his conclusions on anatomical information and the results from somewhat inconclusive experiments on rabbits. When Magendie's paper appeared, Bell hotly disputed priority for the discovery, with some success. Today the principle that the dorsal part of the spinal cord is sensory and the ventral part is motor is called the **Bell-Magendie law.** Magendie's experiment has been called the most important ever conducted on the nervous system. It enabled neurologists for the first time to distinguish sensory from motor impairments, as well as to draw general conclusions about the location of neural damage, on the basis of the symptoms displayed by patients. Because of the segmental structure of the spinal cord and the body, rather good inferences can also be made about the location of spinal-cord damage or disease on the basis of changes in sensation or movement in particular body parts. The internal organs, however, although also arranged segmentally, appear not to have their own sensory representation within the spinal cord. Pain in these organs is perceived as coming from the outer parts of the dermatome and so is called **referred pain.** For example, pains in the heart are felt in the shoulder and arm, and kidney pain is felt in the back. Physicians use what is known about the location of referred pains to diagnose problems within the body.

Other major advances in the understanding of spinal-cord function came from the work of Sir Charles Sherrington and his students, who showed that the spinal cord retains many functions even after it has been separated from the brain. Sherrington, a British physiologist, published a summary of this research in 1906, and it had an important influence in the treatment of humans with spinal-cord injury. Persons whose spinal cords are cut so that they no longer have control over their legs are called **paraplegic;** if the cut is higher on the cord so that they cannot use their arms either, they are called **quadriplegic.** Although it was once thought that there was no way to treat such injuries, an understanding of spinal-cord function has led to such huge improvements in treatment that spinal-cord patients today can lead long and active lives.

Sensory information plays a central role in eliciting different kinds of movements organized by the spinal cord. Movements dependent only on spinal-cord function are referred to as reflexes and are specific movements elicited by specific forms of sensory stimulation. There are many kinds of sensory receptors in the body, including receptors for pain, temperature, touch and pressure, and the sensations of muscle and joint movement. The size of fiber coming from each kind of receptor is distinctive; generally, pain and temperature fibers are smaller, and those for touch and muscle sense are larger. The stimulation of pain and temperature receptors in a limb usually produces **flexion** movements—movements that bring the limb inward, toward the body. If the stimulus is mild, only the distal part of the limb flexes in response to it but, with successively stronger stimuli, the size of the movement increases until the whole limb is drawn back. The stimulation of fine touch and muscle receptors in a limb usually produces **extension** movements, which extend the limb outward, away from the body. The **extensor reflex** causes the touched part of the limb to maintain contact with the stimulus; for example, the foot or hand touching a surface will maintain contact with the surface through this reflex. Thus, both withdrawal reflexes and following reflexes, as these reflexes are called, are activated by sensory stimulation. Because each of the senses has its own receptors, fibers, connections, and reflex movements, each can be thought of as an independent sensory system. Furthermore, because the movement produced by each sense is distinct and independent, the senses are thought of as each operating independently of the rest.

In addition to the local connections that they make within the segment of the spinal cord corresponding to their dermatome, pain and tactile receptors communicate with fibers in many other segments of the spinal cord and thus can produce appropriate adjustments in many body parts. For example, when one leg is withdrawn in response to a painful stimulus, the other leg must simultaneously extend to support the body's weight. The spinal cord is capable of producing actions that are more complex than just adjustments of a limb. If the body of an animal that has had its spinal cord sectioned from the brain is held in a sling with its feet touching a conveyor belt, the animal is even capable of walking. Thus, the spinal cord contains all of the connections required for allowing an animal to walk.

Despite the fact that the spinal cord controls both simple and complex behavior, it does depend on the brain, as evidenced by the severe behavioral impairments that follow spinal-cord injury. Because the main effect of spinal-cord injury is to sever connections between the cord and the brain, scientists believe that simply reestablishing these connections can restore function to spinal-cord-injured people. Unfortunately, although the fibers in the spinal tracts do regrow in some vertebrates, such as fish, and in the early stages of development in other animals, they do not regrow in adult mammals. Researchers are experimenting with various approaches to induce regrowth. One approach is based on the idea that new growth is prevented by the presence of certain inhibitory molecules on the tracts of the cord below the cut. The idea under investigation is that, if these inhibitory molecules can in turn be inhibited, fibers will begin to grow across the injured zone. Another line of research is focused on the scarring that accompanies most spinal-cord damage and the possibility that scarring inhibits new growth. Some scientists are conducting experiments in which they attempt to remove the scar, whereas other scientists are attempting to build bridges across the scar over which fibers can grow. All of these approaches have been partly successful in nonhuman animal studies, but they have not been attempted on humans with spinal-cord injury.

The Brainstem

The section of human brain portrayed in Figure 3.8 shows several of the main structures of the brainstem. In general, the brainstem produces more-complex movements than does the spinal cord. In addition to responding to most sensory stimuli in the environment and regulating eating and drinking, body

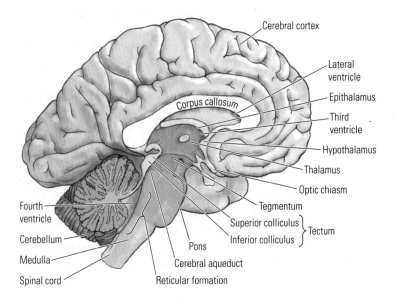

Figure 3.8 Medial view through the center of the brain showing structures of the brainstem.

temperature, sleep and waking, the brain stem can produce the movements of walking and running, grooming, and sexual behavior (all of which are more complex than the reflexive movements produced by the spinal cord). The brains of fish, amphibians, and reptiles are basically equivalent to a mammalian brainstem; in consequence, the behavior of these animals is a good indication of the functions of the brainstem. The brainstem can be subdivided into three parts: the diencephalon, the midbrain, and the hindbrain. Their main structures and functions are summarized next.

The Diencephalon

The diencephalon consists of the three thalamic structures: the thalamus ("inner room, or chamber"); the epithalamus ("upper room"); and the hypothalamus ("lower room").

The **thalamus** is composed of a number of nuclei, each of which projects to a specific area of the neocortex, as shown in Figure 3.9. These nuclei route information from three sources to the cortex.

1. One group of nuclei relays information from sensory systems to their appropriate targets. For example, the lateral geniculate body (LGB) receives visual projections; the medial geniculate body (MGB) receives auditory projections; and the ventral-posterior lateral nuclei (VPL) receive touch, pressure, pain, and temperature projections from the body. In turn, these areas project to the visual, auditory, and somatosensory regions of the cortex (see page 64 for more details on the organization of the cortex).

2. Some nuclei relay information between cortical areas. For example, a large area of the posterior cortex sends projections to and receives projections back from the pulvinar nucleus (P).

3. Some of the thalamic nuclei relay information from other forebrain and brainstem regions.

In short, almost all the information that the cortex receives is first relayed through the thalamus.

The function of the **epithalamus** is not well understood, but one of its structures, the **pineal body,** seems to regulate seasonal body rhythms. Recall

Figure 3.9 Relation between thalamic nuclei and various areas of the cortex to which they project. The arrows indicate the sources of input and output from the thalamus: anterior nucleus, A; dorsal medial nucleus, DM; ventral anterior nucleus, VA; ventral lateral nucleus, VL; lateral posterior nucleus, LP; ventral lateral posterior nucleus, VLP; pulvinar, P; lateral geniculate body, LGB; and medial geniculate body, MGB.

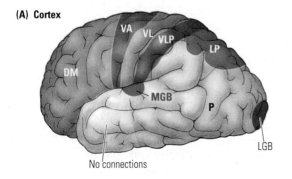

(A) Cortex

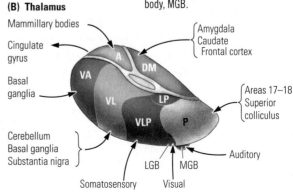

(B) Thalamus

that Descartes, impressed by the unitary character of the pineal body in comparison with other brain structures, suggested that it is the rendezvous for mind and matter and the source of the cerebral spinal fluid that he believed powers movements.

The **hypothalamus** is composed of about 22 small nuclei, fiber systems that pass through it, and the **pituitary gland.** Although comprising only about 0.3% of the brain's weight, the hypothalamus takes part in nearly all aspects of motivated behavior, including feeding, sexual behavior, sleeping, temperature regulation, emotional behavior, endocrine function, and movement.

The Midbrain

The **midbrain** has two main subdivisions: the **tectum,** or "roof," which is the roof of the third ventricle, and the **tegmentum,** or "floor," which is its floor. The tectum consists primarily of two sets of bilaterally symmetrical nuclei. The **superior colliculi** ("upper hills") are the anterior pair. They receive projections from the retina of the eye, and they mediate many visually related behaviors. The **inferior colliculi** ("lower hills") are the posterior pair. They receive projections from the ear, and they mediate many auditory-related behaviors. A class of behaviors mediated by the colliculi are orienting behaviors. For example, when an owl hears the sound of a moving mouse or a cat sees a moving mouse, each quickly orients its head toward the stimuli. In each case, the movement is enabled by the respective colliculi for vision and audition. The tegmentum contains nuclei for some of the cranial nerves, including a number of motor nuclei. Thus, in the midbrain as in the spinal cord, the dorsal part is sensory and the ventral part is motor.

The Hindbrain

The **hindbrain** is organized in much the same way as the midbrain: the part above the fourth ventricle is sensory and the part below the ventricle is motor. Sensory nuclei of the **vestibular system,** the sensory system governing balance and orientation, lie above the fourth ventricle; beneath this ventricle are more motor nuclei of the cranial nerves.

Perhaps the most distinctive part of the hindbrain is the **cerebellum.** It protrudes above the core of the brainstem, and its surface is gathered into narrow folds, or **folia,** which are like the gyri of the cortex but smaller (Figure 3.10). At the base of the cerebellum are several nuclei, which send connections to other parts of the brain.

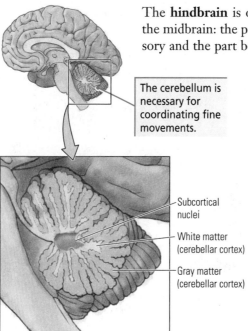

Figure 3.10 The cerebellum is necessary for fine coordinated movements. Like the cerebrum, the cerebellum (shown in the detailed cross section) has a cortex, containing gray and white matter and subcortical nuclei.

The cerebellum is necessary for coordinating fine movements.

Subcortical nuclei

White matter (cerebellar cortex)

Gray matter (cerebellar cortex)

The cerebellum plays a role in the coordination and learning of skilled movement. Thus, damage to the cerebellum results in equilibrium problems, postural defects, and impairments of skilled motor activity. The parts that receive most of their impulses from the vestibular system (the receptors for balance and movement, located in the middle ear) help to maintain the body's equilibrium, whereas parts receiving impulses mainly from the receptors in the trunk and limbs control postural reflexes and coordinate functionally related groups of muscles.

The core of the brainstem consists of nuclei, including those of the cranial nerves, as well as many bundles of fibers. Fibers from the spinal cord pass through the brainstem on their way to the forebrain; conversely, fibers from the forebrain connect with the brainstem or pass through it on their way to the spinal cord. The brainstem's mixture of nuclei and fibers creates a network referred to as the **reticular formation.**

The reticular formation is more commonly known as the **reticular activating system.** It obtained this designation in 1949 when Moruzzi and Magoun stimulated it electrically in anesthetized cats and found that the stimulation produced a waking pattern of electrical activity in the cats' cortexes. Moruzzi and Magoun concluded that the function of the reticular formation was to control sleeping and waking—that is, to maintain "general arousal" or "consciousness." As a result, the reticular formation came to be known as the reticular *activating* system. Neuroscientists now recognize that the various nuclei within the brainstem serve many functions and that only a few take part in waking and sleeping.

Cranial Nerves

Also leaving or entering the brainstem are the 12 sets of **cranial nerves.** The cranial nerves convey sensory information from the specialized sensory systems of the head, and many have nuclei in the brainstem and send axons to the muscles of the head. For example, movements of the eyes and tongue are produced by cranial nerves. In addition, one of the cranial nerves, the vagus, makes connections with many body organs, including the heart. A knowledge of the organization and function of the cranial nerves is important for making neurological diagnoses. Figure 3.11 illustrates the location of the cranial nerves, and Table 3.2 describes their functions and some of the more common symptoms that arise when they are damaged.

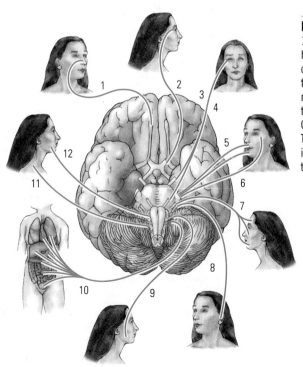

Figure 3.11 Each of the 12 pairs of cranial nerves has a different function. A common device for learning the order of the cranial nerves is, "On old Olympus's towering top, a Finn and German view some hops." The first letter of each word is, in order, the first letter of the name of each nerve.

Table **3.2** The cranial nerves

Number	Name	Functions	Method of examination	Typical symptoms of dysfunction
1	Olfactory	(s) Smell*	Various odors applied to each nostril	Loss of sense of smell (anosmia)
2	Optic	(s) Vision	Visual acuity, map field of vision	Loss of vision (anopsia)
3	Oculomotor	(m) Eye movement*	Reaction to light, lateral movements of eyes, eyelid movement	Double vision (Diplopia), large pupil, uneven dilation of pupils, drooping eyelid (ptosis), deviation of eye outward
4	Trochlear	(m) Eye movement	Upward and downward eye movements	Double vision, defect of downward gaze
5	Trigeminal	(s, m) Masticatory movements	Light touch by cotton baton; pain by pinprick; thermal by hot and cold tubes, corneal reflex by touching cornea; jaw reflex by tapping chin, jaw movements	Decreased sensitivity or numbness of face, brief attacks of severe pain (trigeminal neuralgia); weakness and wasting of facial muscles, asymmetrical chewing
6	Abducens	(m) Eye movement	Lateral movements	Double vision, inward deviation of the eye
7	Facial	(s, m) Facial movement	Facial movements, facial expression, test for taste	Facial paralysis, loss of taste over anterior two-thirds of tongue
8	Auditory vestibular	(s) Hearing	Audiogram for testing hearing; stimulate by rotating patient or by irrigating the ear with hot or cold water (caloric test)	Deafness, sensation of noise in ear (tinnitus); disequilibrium, feeling of disorientation in space
9	Glossopharyngeal	(s, m) Tongue and pharynx	Test for sweet, salt, bitter, and sour tastes on tongue; touch walls of pharynx for pharyngeal or gag reflex	Partial dry mouth, loss of taste (ageusia) over posterior third of tongue, anesthesia and paralysis of upper pharynx
10	Vagus	(s, m) Heart, blood vessels, viscera, movement of larynx and pharynx	Observe palate in phonation, touching palate for palatal reflex	Hoarseness, lower pharyngeal anesthesia and paralysis, indefinite visceral disturbance
11	Spinal accessory	(m) Neck muscles and viscera	Movement, strength, and bulk of neck and shoulder muscles	Wasting of neck with weakened rotation, inability to shrug
12	Hypoglossal	(m) Tongue muscles	Tongue movements, tremor, wasting or wrinkling of tongue	Wasting of tongue with deviation to side of lesion on protrusion

*The letters *s* and *m* refer to sensory and motor function, respectively, of the nerve.

The Cortex

Anatomists use the term *cortex* (from the Latin for "bark," as in a tree's bark) to refer to any outer layer of cells. In neuroscience, the terms *cortex* and *neocortex* (new cortex) are often used interchangeably to refer to the outer part of the forebrain, and so by convention "cortex" refers to "neocortex" unless otherwise indicated. The cortex is the part of the brain that has expanded the most in the course of evolution; it comprises 80% by volume of the human brain.

The human neocortex has an area as large as 2500 cm² but a thickness of only 1.5 to 3.0 mm. It consists of four to six layers of cells (gray matter) and is heavily wrinkled. This wrinkling is nature's solution to the problem of confining the huge neocortical surface area within a skull that is still small enough to pass through the birth canal. Just as crumpling a sheet of paper enables it to fit into a smaller box than it could when flat, the folding of the neocortex permits the human brain to fit comfortably within the relatively fixed volume of the skull.

Hemispheres and Lobes

As Figure 3.12 (dorsal view) shows, the cortex consists of two nearly symmetrical **hemispheres,** the left and the right, separated by the **longitudinal fissure.** Each hemisphere is subdivided into four lobes: frontal, parietal, temporal, and occipital. The **frontal lobes** have fixed boundaries: they are bounded posteriorly by the central sulcus, inferiorly by the lateral fissure, and medially by the **cingulate sulcus.** The anterior boundary of the **parietal lobes** is the central sulcus, and their inferior boundary is the lateral fissure. The **temporal lobes** are bounded dorsally by the lateral fissure. On the lateral surface of the brain, there are no definite boundaries between the occipital lobes and the parietal and temporal lobes.

Figure 3.12 In these views of the human brain (from top, dorsal; bottom, ventral; side, lateral; and middle, medial), the locations of the frontal, parietal, occipital, and temporal lobes of the cerebral hemispheres are shown, as are the cerebellum and the three major sulci (the central sulcus, lateral fissure, and longitudinal fissure) of the cerebral hemispheres.

Dorsal view

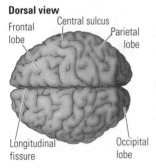
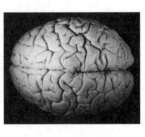

Lateral view

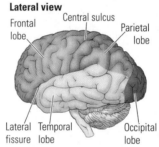
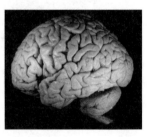

Ventral view

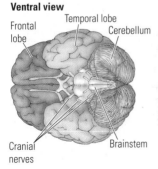
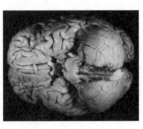

Medial view

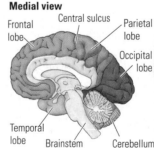
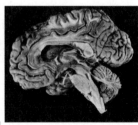

Fissures, Sulci, and Gyri

To review some of the main features of the cortex that were introduced in Chapter 1, the wrinkled surface of the neocortex consists of clefts and ridges. A cleft is called a **fissure** if it extends deeply enough into the brain to indent the ventricles, whereas it is a **sulcus** (plural sulci) if it is shallower. A ridge is called a **gyrus** (plural gyri).

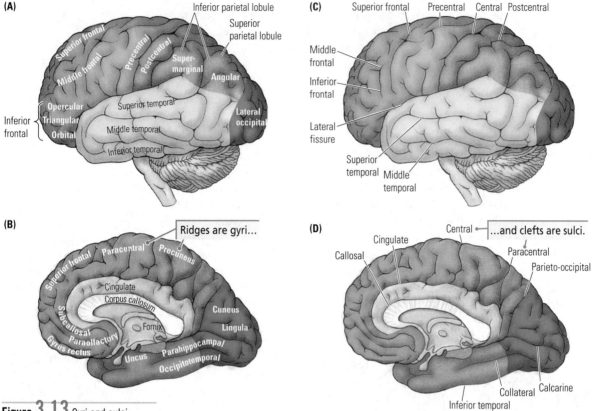

Figure 3.13 Gyri and sulci: lateral (A) and medial (B) views of the gyri; lateral (C) and medial (D) views of the sulci.

Figure 3.13 shows the location of some of the more important fissures, sulci, and gyri of the brain. There is *some* variation in the location of these features on the two sides of a single individual's brain, and *substantial* variation in the location, size, and shape of the gyri and sulci in the brains of different individuals. Adjacent gyri differ in the way that cells are organized within them; the shift from one kind of arrangement to another is usually at the sulcus. There is some evidence that gyri can be associated with specific functions.

As shown in Figure 3.13A, there are four major gyri in the frontal lobe: the superior frontal, middle frontal, inferior frontal, and precentral (which lies in front of the central sulcus). There are five major gyri in the parietal lobe: the superior and inferior lobule (small lobe), the postcentral (lying behind the central sulcus), and the supermarginal and angular (on either side of the lateral fissure). There are three gyri in the temporal lobe: the superior, middle, and inferior. Only the lateral gyrus is evident in the occipital cortex in this lateral view.

The Organization of the Cortex in Relation to Its Inputs and Outputs

Different regions of the neocortex have different functions. Some regions receive information from sensory systems, other regions command movements, and still other regions are the sites of connections between the sensory and the motor areas, enabling them to work in concert. Recall that the inputs are relayed through the thalamic nuclei. The locations of these various inputs and outputs can be represented by a map called a **projection map.** Such a map is constructed by tracing axons from the sensory systems into the brain and tracing axons from the neocortex to the motor systems of the brainstem and spinal cord.

The projection map in Figure 3.14 was constructed in part by following the axons projected by sensory receptors to see where they end in the neocortex and in part by locating the sources in the neocortex of motor axons projected from there to the spinal cord. As Figure 3.14 shows, the projections from the eye can be traced to the occipital lobe, the projections from the ear to the temporal lobe, and the projections from the somatosensory system to the parietal lobe. The olfactory system sends projections to the ventral frontal lobe. The major motor projection to the spinal cord originates in the frontal lobe. These areas that receive projections from structures outside the neocortex or send projections to it are called **primary projection areas.** Note that the lateral view of the brain presented in Figure 3.14 does not represent the entire extent of these primary projection areas, because they also extend down into the gyri and fissures. Much of the auditory zone, for example, is located within the lateral fissure. Nevertheless, the primary projection areas of the neocortex are small relative to the total size of the cortex.

The primary sensory areas send projections into the areas adjacent to them, and the motor areas receive fibers from areas adjacent to them. These adjacent areas, less directly connected with the sensory receptors and motor neurons, are referred to as **secondary areas.** The secondary areas are thought to be more engaged in interpreting perceptions or organizing movements than are the primary areas. The areas that lie between the various secondary areas are referred to as **tertiary areas.** Often referred to as association areas, tertiary areas serve to connect and coordinate the functions of the secondary areas. Tertiary areas mediate complex activities such as language, planning, memory, and attention.

Overall, the neocortex can be conceptualized as consisting of a number of fields: visual, auditory, body senses, and motor. Because vision, audition, and body senses are functions of the posterior cortex, this region of the brain (parietal, temporal, and occipital lobes) is considered to be largely sensory; and, because the motor cortex is located in the frontal neocortex, that lobe is considered to be largely motor. Finally, because each lobe contains one of the primary projection areas, it can roughly be associated with a general function:

Frontal lobes: motor

Parietal lobes: body senses

Temporal lobes: auditory function

Occipital lobes: visual functions

Figure 3.14 A projection map. The darkest shading indicates primary projection areas, which receive input from the sensory systems or project to spinal motor systems. The lighter shading represents secondary areas. The unshaded regions are higher-order association, or tertiary, areas. Arrows indicate that information flows from primary to secondary sensory areas and from secondary motor areas to primary motor areas. Information also flows from secondary to association areas and between association areas of the lobes.

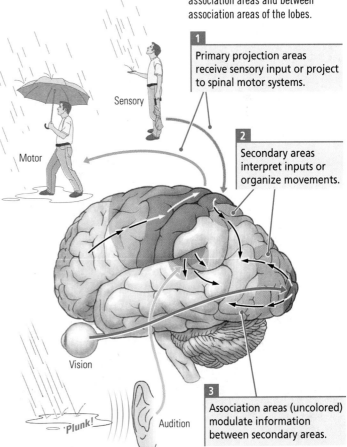

1 Primary projection areas receive sensory input or project to spinal motor systems.

Sensory

2 Secondary areas interpret inputs or organize movements.

Motor

Vision

Plunk!

Audition

3 Association areas (uncolored) modulate information between secondary areas.

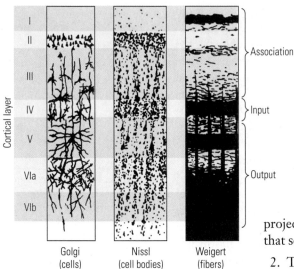

Figure 3.15 The cells of the cortex revealed through the use of three different stains. The Golgi stain penetrates only a few neurons but reveals all of their processes, the Nissl stain highlights only cell bodies, and the Weigert myelin stain reveals the location of axons. Note that these staining procedures highlight the different cell types of the cortex and show that they are organized into a number of layers, each of which contains typical cell types. (After Brodmann, 1909.)

The Organization of the Cells of the Cortex

Examination of the cells of the cortex shows that the cortex can be divided into different areas on the basis of cell organization. Maps of the cortex that are based on cell structure are called cytoarchitectonic maps. The neurons of the neocortex are arranged in about six layers, as shown in Figure 3.15. These six layers can be separated into three groups by function.

1. The **output cell layers,** layers V and VI, send axons to other brain areas. Both of these layers and the cells of which they are composed are particularly large and distinctive in the motor cortex, which sends projections to the spinal cord. (Large size is typical of cells that send information long distances.)

2. The **input cell layer,** layer IV, receives axons from sensory systems and other cortical areas. This layer features large numbers of small, densely packed cells in the primary areas of vision, somatosensation, audition, and taste-olfaction, which receive large projections from their respective sensory organs.

3. The **association cell layers,** layers I, II, and III, receive input mainly from layer IV and are quite well developed in the secondary and tertiary areas of the cortex.

In short, sensory areas have many layer IV cells, motor areas have many layer V and VI cells, and association areas have many layer I, II, and III cells.

One widely used map of the cortex, known as **Brodmann's map,** is presented in Figure 3.16A. This map represents differences in the density of different kinds of neocortical neurons. In Brodmann's map, the different areas are numbered, but the numbers themselves have no special meaning. To do his

Figure 3.16 (A) Brodmann's areas of the cortex. A few numbers are missing from the original sources of this drawing, including 12 through 16 and 48 through 51. Some areas have histologically distinctive boundaries and are outlined with heavy solid lines; others, such as 6, 18, and 19, have less-distinctive boundaries and are outlined with light solid lines; the remaining areas have no distinct boundaries but gradually merge into one another and are outlined with dotted lines. (B) Functional areas and Broadmann cytoarchitectonic areas. (Part A after Elliott, 1969.)

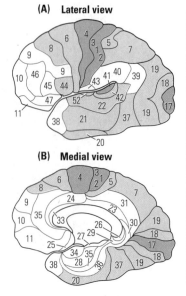

Function	Map code	Brodmann area
Vision		
primary		17
secondary		18, 19, 20, 21, 37
Auditory		
primary		41
secondary		22, 42
Body senses		
primary		1, 2, 3
secondary		5, 7
Sensory, tertiary		7, 22, 37, 39, 40
Motor		
primary		4
secondary		6
eye movement		8
speech		44
Motor, tertiary		9, 10, 11, 45, 46, 47

analysis, Brodmann divided the brain at the central sulcus and then examined the front and back halves of the brain separately, numbering new conformations of cells as he found them but without following a methodical path over the surface or through the layers. Thus, he found areas 1 and 2 in the posterior section, then switched to the anterior section and found areas 3 and 4, and then switched back again, and then looked somewhere else.

As it turns out, Brodmann's map is very useful because the regions depicted in it correspond quite closely with regions discovered with the use of noncytoarchitectonic techniques. Figure 3.16B summarizes some of the relations between areas on Brodmann's map and areas that have been mapped according to their known functions. For example, area 17 corresponds to the primary visual projection area, whereas areas 18 and 19 correspond to the secondary visual projection areas. Area 4 is the primary motor cortex. Broca's area, an area related to the articulation of words, is area 44. Similar relations exist for other areas and functions.

One of the problems with Brodmann's map is that new, more powerful analytical techniques have shown that many Brodmann areas actually consist of two architectonically distinct areas or more. For this reason, the map is continually being updated and now consists of an unwieldy mixture of numbers, letters, and names.

Connections Between Cortical Areas

The various regions of the neocortex are interconnected by three types of axon projections: (1) relatively short connections between one part of a lobe and another, (2) longer connections between one lobe and another, and (3) interhemispheric connections, or **commissures,** between one hemisphere and another. Figure 3.17 shows the locations and names of some of these connections.

Most of the interhemispheric connections link **homotopic** points in the two hemispheres—that is, contralateral points that correspond to one another in the brain's mirror-image structure. Thus, the commissures act as a zipper to link the two sides of the neocortical representation of the world and of the body together. The two main interhemispheric commissures are the corpus callosum and the anterior commissure.

Figure 3.17 Connections between various regions of the cortex.

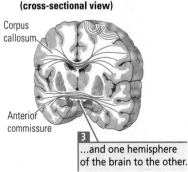

(A) Lateral view

1 | Axon fibers connect one lobe of the brain to another,...

Inferior occipital frontal tract
Superior occipital frontal tract
Superior longitudinal tract
Uncinate tract
Inferior longitudinal tract

(B) Medial view

2 | ...one part of a lobe to another part,...

Cingulum
Arcuate fibers
Corpus callosum
Inferior longitudinal tract

(C) Connections between hemispheres (cross-sectional view)

Corpus callosum
Anterior commissure
3 | ...and one hemisphere of the brain to the other.

The cortex also makes other types of connections with itself. Cells in any area, for example, may send axons to cells in a subcortical area such as the thalamus, and the cells there may then send their axons to some other cortical area. These types of relations are more difficult to establish anatomically than are those based on direct connections.

The various connections between regions of the cortex are of considerable functional interest, because damage to a pathway can have consequences as severe as damage to the functional areas connected by the pathway. A glance at Figure 3.17 shows that it is difficult indeed to damage any area of the cortex without damaging one or more of its interconnecting pathways.

The Limbic Lobe and Basal Ganglia

In addition to the neocortex, there are two other main forebrain structures: the limbic system and the basal ganglia. A brief description of the anatomy and function of these regions follows.

The Limbic Lobe

In the course of the evolution of the amphibians and reptiles, a number of three-layer cortical structures that sheath the periphery of the brainstem developed. With the subsequent growth of the neocortex, they became sandwiched between the new brain and the old. Because of the evolutionary origin of these structures, some anatomists have referred to them as the reptilian brain, but the term **limbic lobe** (from the Latin *limbus*, meaning "border" or "hem"), coined by Broca in 1878, is more widely recognized today.

The limbic lobe is also referred to as the **limbic system** (although that may very well be a misnomer, as we soon explain). The limbic lobe consists of a number of interrelated structures, including the **hippocampus** ("sea horse"), **septum** ("partition"), and cingulate ("girdle") gyrus (Figure 3.18). The history of how the limbic "lobe" became the limbic "system" is one of the most interesting chapters in neuroscience.

Figure 3.18 (A) This medial view of the right hemisphere illustrates the principal structures of the limbic system, including the cingulate cortex, the hippocampus, and the amygdala. (B) A model of the human limbic system and its major structures. Note: As proposed by Papez, the limbic system forms a circuit in which the hypothalamus (mammillary bodies) connect to the hippocampus through the cingulate gyrus, and the hippocampus connects to the hypothalamus through the fornix. (After Hamilton, 1976.)

(A) The limbic lobe, medial view

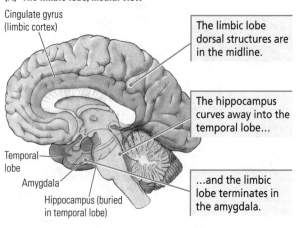

Cingulate gyrus (limbic cortex)

The limbic lobe dorsal structures are in the midline.

The hippocampus curves away into the temporal lobe...

Temporal lobe

Amygdala

Hippocampus (buried in temporal lobe)

...and the limbic lobe terminates in the amygdala.

(B) The limbic lobe (dissected out)

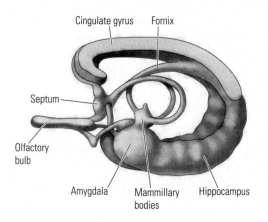

Cingulate gyrus   Fornix

Septum

Olfactory bulb

Amygdala   Mammillary bodies   Hippocampus

The first theory of limbic function stemmed from the observation that there are connections between the olfactory system and the limbic lobe. On this evidence, anatomists hypothesized that the limbic structures processed olfactory information, and so collectively the structures became known as the **rhinencephalon,** or "smell-brain." Subsequently, a number of experiments demonstrated that some limbic structures had little olfactory function. Then, in 1937, Papez, in what at the time amounted to a scientific tour de force, asked, "Is emotion a magic product, or is it a physiologic process which depends on an anatomic mechanism?" He suggested that emotion, which had no known anatomic substrate, is a product of the limbic lobe, which had no recognized function. He proposed that the emotional brain consists of a circuit in which information flows from the mammillary bodies in the hypothalamus to the anterior thalamic nucleus to the cingulate cortex to the hippocampus and back to the mammillary bodies. Input could enter this circuit from other structures to be elaborated as emotion. For example, an idea ("It is dangerous to walk in the dark") from the neocortex could enter the circuit to be elaborated as fear ("I feel frightened in the dark") and ultimately to influence the hypothalamus to release a hormone that would create the appropriate physical response to the idea and its emotional corollary.

In 1957, Scoville and Milner described the now-famous patient H. M., who had had his medial temporal lobe, including his hippocampus, removed bilaterally as a treatment for epilepsy. His primary deficits were not emotional. He displayed little ability to learn new information, although his presurgery memories were largely intact. Thereafter it was proposed that the limbic system is the memory system of the brain; but, in the years since H. M. was first described, many other regions of the brain also have become recognized as playing a part in memory, diminishing the apparent role of the limbic system in that function. Today, along with evidence that the limbic lobe has some involvement in olfaction, emotion, and memory, most major lines of research also suggest that the limbic system plays a special role in spatial behavior.

The Basal Ganglia

The **basal ganglia** ("lower knots," referring to "knots below the cortex") are a collection of nuclei lying mainly beneath the anterior regions of the neocortex (Figure 3.19). They include the **putamen** ("shell"), the **globus pallidus** ("pale globe"), the **caudate nucleus** ("tailed nucleus"), and the **amygdala** ("almond"). These structures form a circuit with the cortex. The caudate nucleus receives projections from all areas of the neocortex and sends its own projections through the putamen and globus pallidus to the thalamus and from there to the motor areas of the cortex. The basal ganglia also have reciprocal connections with the midbrain, especially with a nucleus called the **substantia nigra** ("black area").

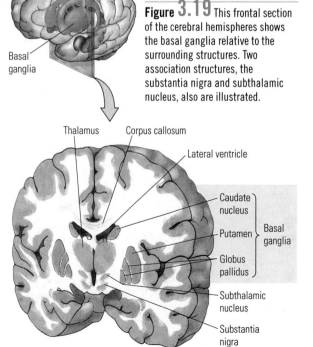

Figure 3.19 This frontal section of the cerebral hemispheres shows the basal ganglia relative to the surrounding structures. Two association structures, the substantia nigra and subthalamic nucleus, also are illustrated.

Basal ganglia

Thalamus   Corpus callosum

Lateral ventricle

Caudate nucleus

Putamen

Globus pallidus

Basal ganglia

Subthalamic nucleus

Substantia nigra

The basal ganglia historically have been described as having two functions. First, damage to different parts of the basal ganglia can produce changes in posture, increases or decreases in muscle tone, and abnormal movements such as twitches, jerks, and tremors; so the ganglia are thought to take part in such motor functions as the sequencing of movements into a smoothly executed response, as occurs during talking. Second, the basal ganglia are also thought to support stimulus-response, or habit, learning. For example, a bird that learns after a number of experiences that brightly colored butterflies have a bitter taste would use its basal ganglia to learn the association between taste and color and refrain from eating the insects.

The Crossed Brain

One of the most peculiar features of the organization of the brain is that each of its symmetrical halves responds to sensory stimulation from the contralateral side of the body or sensory world and controls the musculature on the contralateral side of the body (Figure 3.20). The visual system achieves this end by crossing half the fibers of the optic tract and by reversing the image through the lens of the eye. Nearly all the fibers of the motor and somatosensory systems cross. Projections from each ear go to both hemispheres, but there is substantial evidence that auditory excitation from one ear sends a stronger signal to the opposite hemisphere. As a result of this arrangement, numerous crossings, or **decussations,** of sensory and motor fibers are found along the center of the nervous system. Later chapters contain detailed descriptions of some of these crossings, when they are relevant to the discussion of how a given system works. It is sufficient to say here that, because of this arrangement, damage to one side of the brain generally causes sensory and motor impairments not to the same side of the body but to the opposite side.

Figure 3.20 (Left) This schematic representation of a rat's brain from a dorsal view shows the projection of visual and somatosensory input to contralateral (opposite-side) areas of the cortex and the projection of the motor cortex to the contralateral side of the body. The eyes of the rat are laterally placed such that most of the input from each eye travels to the opposite hemisphere. (Right) In the human head, the two eyes are frontally placed. As a result, the visual input is split in two, and so input from the right side of the world as seen by both eyes goes to the left hemisphere and input from the left side of the world as seen by both eyes goes to the right hemisphere. The somatosensory input of both rats and humans is completely crossed, and so information coming from the right paw or hand goes to the left hemisphere. Note that, although single arrows are used in the diagrams to depict the flow of information going to and from the brain, there are actually connectors along each route.

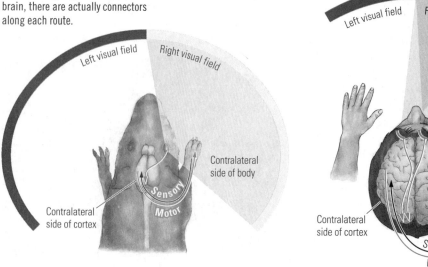

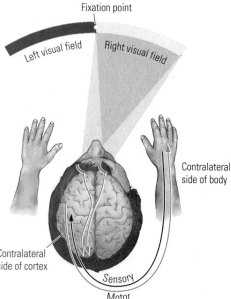

Blood Supply

The brain receives its blood supply from two **internal carotid arteries** and two **vertebral arteries;** one of each courses up each side of the neck. The internal carotid arteries enter the skull at the base of the brain, branching off into a number of smaller arteries and two major arteries, the **anterior cerebral artery** and the **middle cerebral artery,** that irrigate the anterior and middle parts of the cortex. The vertebral arteries also enter at the base of the brain but then join together to form the basilar artery. After branching off into several smaller arteries that irrigate the cerebellum, the basilar artery gives rise to the **posterior cerebral artery,** which irrigates the medial temporal lobe and the posterior occipital lobe.

The distribution zones of the anterior, middle, and posterior cerebral arteries are shown in Figure 3.21. Note that, if the hand is placed so that the wrist is on the artery trunk, the extended digits will give an approximate representation of the area of the cortex that is irrigated. These arteries irrigate not only the cortex but also subcortical structures. Thus, a disruption of blood flow to one of these arteries has serious consequences for subcortical as well as cortical structures.

Such a disruption occurs in a condition called **stroke:** an artery becomes blocked by the formation of a blood clot, depriving part of the brain of its blood supply. Within a few minutes of this deprivation, the cells in the region begin to die. Sometimes immediate treatment with an anticoagulant can restore the flow of blood within a couple of hours, rescuing significant numbers of cells. The symptoms of stroke vary according to the location of the loss of blood supply. Note in Figure 3.21 that blockade of the anterior cerebral artery results in loss of functions of the medial cortex, which include limbic functions; stroke of the middle cerebral artery results in impairments in motor function; and blockade of the posterior cerebral artery results in loss of visual functions.

The veins of the brain, through which spent blood returns to the lungs, are classified as external and internal cerebral and cerebellar veins. The venous flow does not follow the course of the major arteries but instead follows a pattern of its own, eventually entering a system of venous sinuses, or cavities, that drain the dura mater (one of the membranes that protect the brain from injury, as described next).

Figure 3.21 Distribution of the major cerebral arteries in the hemispheres: (left) lateral view; (right) medial view. If you align your hand so that your wrist represents the base of the artery, the extended digits will spread over the area of cortex to which blood is distributed by that artery.

Anterior cerebral artery

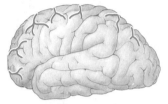

Middle cerebral artery

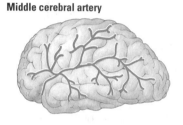

Posterior cerebral artery

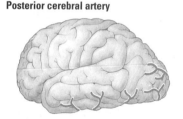

Lateral view **Medial view**

Figure 3.22 The brain is protected by the skull and a number of thick membranes—the dura, arachnoid, and pia. The subarachnoid space between the arachnoid layer and the pia layer contains cerebral spinal fluid (CSF).

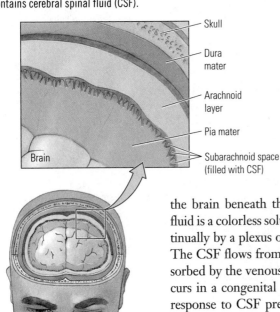

Figure 3.22 The brain is protected by the skull and a number of thick membranes—the dura, arachnoid, and pia. The subarachnoid space between the arachnoid layer and the pia layer contains cerebral spinal fluid (CSF).

Skull
Dura mater
Arachnoid layer
Pia mater
Subarachnoid space (filled with CSF)
Brain

Protection

The brain and spinal cord are supported and protected from injury and infection in four ways (Figure 3.22). First, the brain is enclosed in a thick bone, the **skull,** and the spinal cord is encased in a series of interlocking bony vertebrae. Second, within these bony cases are three membranes: the outer *dura mater* (from the Latin, meaning "hard mother"), a tough double layer of tissue enclosing the brain in a kind of loose sack; the middle *arachnoid membrane* (from the Greek, meaning "resembling a spider's web"), a very thin sheet of delicate tissue that follows the contours of the brain; and the inner *pia mater* (from the Latin, meaning "soft mother"), which is a moderately tough tissue that clings to the surface of the brain.

Third, the brain is cushioned from shock and sudden changes of pressure by the cerebrospinal fluid, which fills the ventricles inside the brain and circulates around the brain beneath the arachnoid membrane, in the subarachnoid space. This fluid is a colorless solution of sodium chloride and other salts and is secreted continually by a plexus of glial (ependymal) cells that protrudes into each ventricle. The CSF flows from the ventricles, circulates around the brain, and is then absorbed by the venous sinuses of the dura mater. If the outflow is blocked, as occurs in a congenital condition called **hydrocephalus,** the ventricles enlarge in response to CSF pressure and, in turn, dilate the skull. The condition can be ameliorated by draining the ventricles through a tube. Although CSF is not thought to nourish the brain, it may play a role in removing metabolic wastes from the brain.

Fourth, the brain is protected from many chemical substances circulating in the rest of the body by the **blood–brain barrier.** To form this barrier, the cells of the capillaries, the very small blood vessels, form tight junctions with one another, thus preventing many substances from crossing into or out of the capillaries.

Summary

The brain is composed of neurons and glial cells, each of which are present in many forms. The brain is organized into nuclei and tracts, with the nuclei appearing gray and the tracts appearing white to visual inspection. Visualization of brain anatomy in greater detail requires that tissue be stained to highlight differences in the biochemical structures of different groups of nuclei and tracts.

The developing brain first consists of three divisions surrounding a canal filled with cerebrospinal fluid. In adult mammals, increases in the size and complexity of the first and third division produce a brain consisting of five separate divisions. The spinal cord communicates with the body through dorsal roots, which are sensory, and ventral roots, which are motor. The spinal cord is also divided into segments, each representing a dermatome, or segment, of the body. This segmentation and the dorsal-is-sensory and ventral-is-motor organization continue into the brainstem, which functions to orchestrate more-complex behaviors pertaining to balance, vision, audition, and olfaction.

The neocortex, or cortex, comprising about 80% of the adult human brain, consists of a large sheet of neurons organized into six layers. In the adult brain, the sheet is crinkled to form gyri and sulci. The cortex can be divided into function regions, with motor functions in the front and sensory functions in the rear.

Individual lobes also can be associated with general functions: vision in the occipital lobe, audition in the temporal lobe, somatosensation in the parietal lobe, and movement in the frontal lobe. The lobes can be further subdivided into primary, secondary, and tertiary regions, each of which deals with more-complex and associative functions.

The cortex does not function in isolation but receives sensory information through the thalamus and works through the basal ganglia to produce movement and through the limbic system to organize spatial and emotional behavior.

The brain is protected by the skull and three membranes, the dura, arachnoid, and pia mater. The brain receives its blood supply from the internal carotid arteries and the vertebral arteries.

References

Brodmann, K. *Vergleichende Lokalisationlehr der Grosshirnrinde in ihren Prinzipien dargestellt auf Grund des Zellenbaues.* Leipzig: J. A. Barth, 1909.

Curtis, B. A., S. Jacobson, and E. M. Marcus. *An Introduction to the Neurosciences.* Philadelphia: Saunders, 1972.

Elliott, H. *Textbook of Neuroanatomy.* Philadelphia: Lippincott, 1969.

Everett, N. B. *Functional Neuroanatomy.* Philadelphia: Lea & Febiger, 1965.

Hamilton, L. W. *Basic Limbic System Anatomy of the Rat.* New York and London: Plenum, 1976.

Herrick, C. J. *Brains of Rats and Men.* Chicago: University of Chicago Press, 1926.

MacLean, P. D. Psychosomatic disease and the "visceral brain": Recent developments bearing on the Papez theory of emotion. *Psychosomatic Medicine* 11:338–353, 1949.

Moruzzi, G., and Magoun, W. H. Brain stem reticular formation and activation of the EEG. *Electroencephalography and Clinical Neurophysiology* 1:455–473, 1949.

Papez, J. W. A proposed mechanism of emotion. *Archives of Neurology and Psychiatry* 38:724–744, 1937.

Passingham, R. E. Brain size and intelligence in man. *Brain Behavior and Evolution* 16:253–270, 1979.

Penfield, W., and E. Boldrey. Somatic motor and sensory representation in the cerebral cortex as studied by electrical stimulation. *Brain* 60:389–443, 1958.

Penfield, W., and H. H. Jasper. *Epilepsy and the Functional Anatomy of the Human Brain.* Boston: Little, Brown, 1954.

Ranson, S. W., and S. L. Clark. *The Anatomy of the Nervous System.* Philadelphia: Saunders, 1959.

Sarnat, H. B., and M. G. Netsky. *Evolution of the Nervous System.* New York: Oxford University Press, 1974.

Scoville, W. G., and B. Milner. Loss of recent memory after bilateral hippocampal lesions. *Journal of Neurology, Neurosurgery, and Psychiatry* 20:11–21, 1957.

Truex, R. C., and M. B. Carpenter. *Human Neuroanatomy.* Baltimore: Williams & Wilkins, 1969.

The Structure and Electrical Activity of Neurons

When male grayling butterflies are ready to mate, they begin to notice and pursue female graylings passing overhead. The male's recognition of grayling females is not unerringly accurate, however; sometimes he pursues other passing objects instead. Observing this behavior, ethologist Nikolaas Tinbergen, working in the first half of the twentieth century, devised a series of controlled experiments to discover what stimulus or group of stimuli was eliciting the male's approach response. Tinbergen made various model female butterflies, attached one at a time to the line of a fishing rod, and "flew" them past males to determine which exerted the greatest attraction. Although the female graylings are brightly colored and the males can see color, Tinbergen found that color itself was not an important stimulus. The males were most strongly attracted by dark, large, darting stimuli. Furthermore, two or more of these stimulus properties produced a larger response than did one presented alone, which suggested to Tinbergen that the nervous system of male butterflies sums the different features of the stimulating object and then produces a proportional response.

The results of Tinbergen's experiments, done with no knowledge or study of the butterfly's nervous system, nevertheless yield important clues to how that system must work; thus, his experiments are a classic example of well-designed behavioral research. But to progress to the next level of understanding—to discover *how* the male butterfly produces a response—requires discovering how information from various stimuli affects neurons, how the information is conducted into the brain, and how it is added to produce an appropriate response. This story is applicable to neuropsychology. Much can be learned about people's behavior through careful observations and controlled experiments; but, to discover the details of how the nervous system controls behavior, we need to know the structure of its cells and how they work. This chapter gives a brief description of (1) the physical features of neurons, (2) the techniques used to study them, (3) the electrical activity of neurons, and (4) and the way that neurons send messages.

The Neuron's Structure

Neurons are cells that act as the information-conducting units of the nervous system, and, although they have many characteristics in common with other cells in the body, they also have special characteristics that help them perform their information-conducting functions. The word "information" is used loosely here to mean that we believe the activity of the neuron is meaningful with respect to the behavior of the animal.

An Overview of a Neuron

Figure 4.1 displays the external and internal features of a neuron. Perhaps the most prominent distinguishing features are the dendrites, whose presence greatly increases the cell's surface area. The dendrites' surface area is further increased by many subbranches and by many small protrusions called **dendritic spines** that cover each branch. A neuron may have from 1 to 20 dendrites, each of which may have one or many branches, and the spines on the branches may number in the many thousands. Because dendrites collect information from other cells, their surface areas determine how much information a neuron can gather. Because the dendritic spines are the points of communication between neurons, the many thousands of spines provide some indication of how much information a neuron may receive.

Each neuron has a single axon, extending out of an expansion of the cell body known as the **axon hillock** (hillock means "little hill"). The axon may have branches called **axon collaterals,** which usually emerge from it at right angles. Toward its end, the axon may divide into

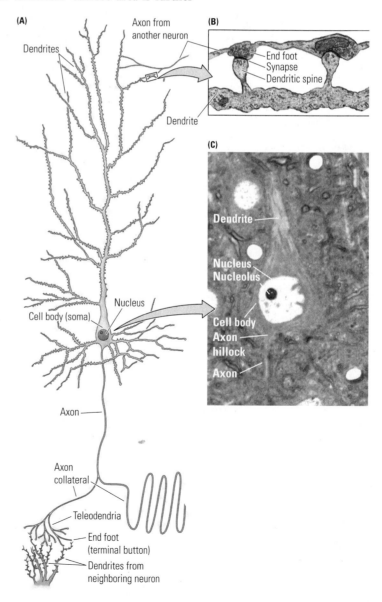

Figure 4.1 The major parts of a neuron. (A) A typical neuron that has been stained by using the Golgi technique to reveal some of its major physical features, including the dendrites and cell body. (B) A drawing of the neuron highlights its dendrites, cell body, and axon. (C) An electron micrograph image illustrating the synapse formed where the end foot of the axon of one neuron connects with the dendritic spine of a dendrite of another neuron. (D) A high-power light microscopic view of the cell body revealing the nucleus and the nucleolus.

a number of smaller branches called **teleodendria** ("end branches"). At the end of each teleodendrion is a knob called an **end foot** or terminal button. The end foot sits very close to a dendritic spine of another neuron, although it does not touch it (see inset in Figure 4.1). This "almost connection," consisting of the surface of the end foot, the corresponding surface of the neighboring dendritic spine, and the space between the two, is called a **synapse.** In contrast with the extensive information-gathering capacity of the dendrites and spines, the single axon limits the neuron to having only one output channel for communication.

Later, we will describe the neuron's activities in some detail. Here we'll simply generalize about its function by examining its shape, by using the analogy of a river system in which the flow of water represents the flow of information. A neuron has a cell wall enclosing its contents, much as the banks of a river enclose the water. The dendrites and the axon are simply fluid-filled extensions of the cell body. Information flows from the dendrites to the cell body and axon, just as tributaries feed a river. The axon's dividing into teleodendria is analogous to the main river channel's breaking up into a number of smaller channels at the river delta before discharging its contents into the sea. At each end foot, the information, in the form of a chemical message, is released onto a target. This flow of information from the dendritic tree to the end feet is illustrated in Figure 4.2.

Although information does flow from the dendrites to the cell body and then along the axon, a neuron does not function simply like an unregulated river system, carrying all the input that it receives to the delta that disgorges it into the sea. Rather, a neuron is both an information-collecting and an information-processing device. It receives a great deal of information on its hundreds to thousands of dendritic spines, but it has only one axon; so the message that it sends must be an averaged or summarized version of all the incoming signals. Therefore it could also be compared to a river system regulated by a dam located at the axon hillock. A dam can be opened or closed to allow more water flow at some times and less at others.

Here the river analogy ends. The information that travels along a neuron does not consist of a flow of liquid. Instead, it consists of a flow of electrical current that begins on the dendrites and then travels along the axon to the terminals. In the axon, the electrical flow consists of discrete impulses. When each impulse reaches an end foot, the end foot releases a chemical into its synapse, and the chemical influences the electrical activity of the receiving cell, thus passing the message along. The chemical is known as a **neuro-**

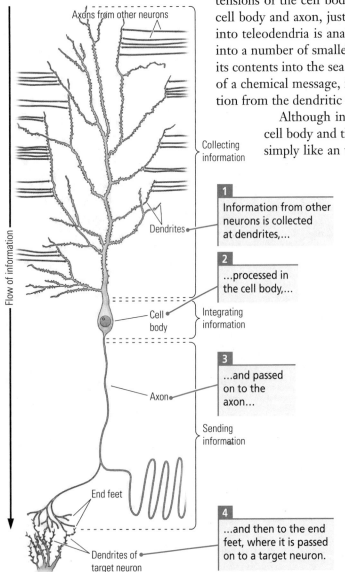

Figure 4.2 A schematic representation of information flow in a neuron.

Axons from other neurons

Flow of information

Collecting information

Dendrites

1 Information from other neurons is collected at dendrites,...

2 ...processed in the cell body,...

Cell body

Integrating information

Axon

3 ...and passed on to the axon...

Sending information

End feet

4 ...and then to the end feet, where it is passed on to a target neuron.

Dendrites of target neuron

transmitter substance or a neurotransmitter, for short, because it transmits the message across the synapse.

The next sections of this chapter will describe how neurons become electrically charged and how changes in electrical charge are able to transmit information.

The Cell as a Factory

We can picture the cell as a miniature factory, with departments that cooperate to make and ship the cell's products, which are proteins. Figure 4.3 illustrates many of the parts of a cell. As we describe these parts and their functions, you will see that the factory analogy is apt indeed.

Just as a factory has outer walls that separate it from the rest of the world and discourage unwanted intruders from entering, a cell has an outer cell membrane that separates it from its surroundings and allows it to regulate the materials that enter and leave its domain. The cell membrane envelops the cell body, the dendrites and their spines, and the axon and its terminals and so forms a boundary around a continuous intracellular compartment. Unassisted, very few substances can enter or leave a cell, because the cell membrane presents an almost impenetrable barrier. Proteins embedded in the cell membrane serve as the factory's gates, allowing some substances to leave or enter and denying passage to the rest. Because the role of proteins is important, we will be describing what

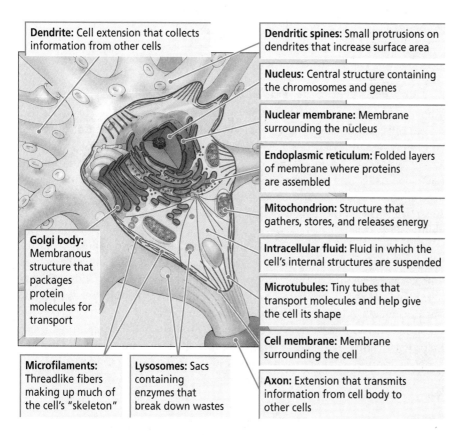

Dendrite: Cell extension that collects information from other cells

Dendritic spines: Small protrusions on dendrites that increase surface area

Nucleus: Central structure containing the chromosomes and genes

Nuclear membrane: Membrane surrounding the nucleus

Endoplasmic reticulum: Folded layers of membrane where proteins are assembled

Mitochondrion: Structure that gathers, stores, and releases energy

Golgi body: Membranous structure that packages protein molecules for transport

Intracellular fluid: Fluid in which the cell's internal structures are suspended

Microtubules: Tiny tubes that transport molecules and help give the cell its shape

Cell membrane: Membrane surrounding the cell

Microfilaments: Threadlike fibers making up much of the cell's "skeleton"

Lysosomes: Sacs containing enzymes that break down wastes

Axon: Extension that transmits information from cell body to other cells

Figure 4.3 The internal structure of a typical cell. The cell contains a nucleus and a number of other organelles (including lysosomes and the endoplasmic reticulum) enclosed within their own membranes. It also contains Golgi bodies to package and ship the cell products, as well as an internal tubule system to provide motility, support, and material transport. Mitochondria are organelles that provide the cell with energy. Many of these structures and organelles are found in the dendrites and axon, as well as in the body of the neuron.

proteins are in some detail. Within the cell are other membranes that divide its interior into compartments, similar to the work areas created by a factory's inner partitions. This compartmentalization allows the cell to concentrate chemicals where they are needed and otherwise keep them out of the way. Prominent among the cell's internal membranes is the **nuclear membrane,** which surrounds the cell's nucleus.

The **nucleus,** like the executive office of a factory, is where the blueprints—genes and chromosomes—for the cell's proteins are stored and copied. When needed, the copies are sent to the factory floor, the part of the cell called the **endoplasmic reticulum** (ER). The ER, actually an extension of the nuclear membrane, is where the cell's protein products are assembled in accordance with the nucleus's blueprint instructions. The finished products are packed and addressed in the **Golgi bodies,** which then pass them along to the cell's transportation network, a system of **tubules** that carries the packaged proteins to their final destinations (much like the factory's interior system of trucks and forklifts). Other kinds of tubules constitute the cell's structural framework; still others are contractile and aid in the cell's movements.

Two other important components of the cell factory are the mitochondria and lysosomes. The **mitochondria** are the cell's power plants that supply its energy needs, whereas the **lysosomes** are sacklike vesicles that not only transport incoming supplies, but also move and store wastes. Interestingly, more lysosomes are found in old cells than in young ones. Cells apparently have trouble disposing of their garbage just as we do.

With this overview of the cell's internal structure in mind, let's look at some of the components in more detail, beginning with the cell membrane.

The Cell Membrane: Barrier and Gatekeeper

The neurons and glia of the brain may appear to be tightly packed together but, like all cells, they are separated and cushioned by **extracellular fluid.** This fluid is composed mainly of water in which salts and many other chemical substances are dissolved. Fluid is found inside a cell as well. The **intracellular fluid** is also made up mainly of water with dissolved salts and other chemicals, but the concentrations of dissolved substances inside and outside the cell are very different. Later, we will see how this difference helps explain the information-conducting ability of neurons.

The cell membrane that encases a cell separates the intracellular from the extracellular fluid and so allows the cell to function as an independent unit. The special structure of the membrane makes this separation possible (Figure 4.4). The cell membrane also regulates the movement of substances into and out of the cell. For example, if too much water entered a cell, the cell could burst and, if too much water left, the cell could shrivel. The cell membrane helps ensure that neither will happen. The cell membrane also regulates the concentration of salts and other chemicals on either side. This regulation is important because precise concentrations of chemicals within a cell are essential to its normal function.

What properties of a cell membrane allow it to regulate water and salt concentrations within the cell? To answer this question, we have to look not only at the cell membrane but also at the composition of the intra- and extracellular fluids. The fluid is composed mainly of water molecules, which are slightly polar. That is, one part of each water molecule is slightly negatively charged and another part of the water molecule is slightly positively charged. Salts are molecules that separate into two parts when dissolved in water, with one part carrying a positive charge and the other part carrying a negative charge. These charged particles are collectively called ions. Some salts are relatively simple, such as common table salt, sodium chloride (NaCl). In water, NaCl dissolves into sodium ions (Na^+) and chloride ions (Cl^-), both of which are quite small. Other salts are much more complicated. For example, protein molecules can ionize in water, but proteins consist of hundreds of atoms, and so protein ions are hundreds of times as large as the ions of table salt. The cell membrane can regulate the movement of a substance because it is sensitive to the electrical charge on the substance; it can also regulate the movement of ions that differ in size.

The cell membrane is composed of a special kind of molecule called a phospholipid. This name comes from the molecule's structure, which features a "head" that contains the element phosphorus (P) and two "tails" that are lipids, or fats. The head is polar, which means that it has a slight positive charge in one location and a slight negative charge in another. The tails consist of hydrogen and carbon atoms that are tightly bound to each other in such a way that there are no polar regions. Figure 4.4 shows a model of this molecule and a symbol used to represent it.

The polar head and the nonpolar tails of a phospholipid molecule are the underlying reasons why it can form membranes. The head, being polar, is hydrophilic (from the Greek *hydro*, meaning "water," and *philic* meaning "love": literally, "water loving"), which means that it is attracted to water molecules because they, too, are polar. The nonpolar tails have no such attraction for water. They are hydrophobic, or "water hating" (the suffix phobic comes from the Greek word *phobia*, meaning "fear"). Quite literally, then, the head of a phospholipid loves water and the tails hate it. These phospholipid molecules form a two-layered membrane—a bilayer. That is, the phospholipid molecules form a double layer arranged so that the heads of one layer are in contact with the intracellular fluid and the heads of the other layer are in contact with the extracellular fluid. The tails of both layers point toward the inside of the bilayer, where they are hidden from the

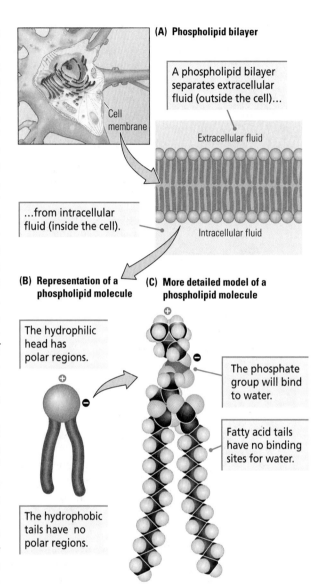

(A) Phospholipid bilayer

A phospholipid bilayer separates extracellular fluid (outside the cell)...

Extracellular fluid

...from intracellular fluid (inside the cell).

Intracellular fluid

(B) Representation of a phospholipid molecule

The hydrophilic head has polar regions.

The hydrophobic tails have no polar regions.

(C) More detailed model of a phospholipid molecule

The phosphate group will bind to water.

Fatty acid tails have no binding sites for water.

Figure 4.4 The basic structure of a cell membrane, which separates the fluid outside a cell from the fluid within the cell. (A) The membrane is composed of a bilayer (double layer) of phospholipid cells, with the tail side of one of the two layers facing the tail side of the other. (B) A conventional symbol for a phospholipid molecule, distinguishing its head and tail regions. (C) A space-filling model of a phospholipid molecule. The head has polar regions and so is hydrophilic; the tail has no polar regions and is hydrophobic.

water. The cell membrane is pliant and yet impermeable to a wide variety of substances. It is impenetrable to intracellular and extracellular water because polar water molecules can't pass through the hydrophobic tails of the membrane. Other polar molecules in the extracellular and intracellular fluid are prevented from crossing the membrane because they carry charges that are repelled by the phospholipid heads. In fact, only a few, small, nonpolar molecules, such as oxygen (O_2), can pass freely through a phospholipid bilayer.

If cell membranes are such effective barriers, the cell must also have mechanisms that enable substances necessary to the function of the cell to pass in and out. In other words, the cell factory must have doors of some kind to facilitate the delivery of supplies, disposal of wastes, and shipment of products. Proteins that are embedded in the cell membrane provide one way for substances to cross the membrane. Proteins can act as gates and transportation systems that allow selected substances to pass through the membrane.

We will describe these mechanisms for crossing the cell membrane a little later. First, however, we will describe how these proteins are manufactured by the cell and transported within it to the cell membrane.

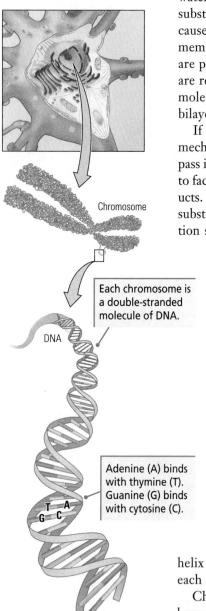

Chromosome

Each chromosome is a double-stranded molecule of DNA.

DNA

Adenine (A) binds with thymine (T). Guanine (G) binds with cytosine (C).

Figure 4.5 The cell nucleus contains chromosomes, each of which contains many genes. A chromosome is made up of two strands of DNA twisted in a helix and bound to each other by their nucleotide bases. The nucleotide base adenine (A) binds with thiamine (T), and the nucleotide base guanine (G) binds with cytosine (C).

The Nucleus: The Blueprints for Proteins

The nucleus, as we said, is the cell's executive office. Here the blueprints for making proteins are stored and copied; the copies are then sent out to the factory floor. These blueprints are called **genes,** which are embedded in the chemical structure of special giant molecular complexes in the nucleus called **chromosomes.** (The name chromosome means "colored body," referring to the fact that chromosomes can be readily stained with certain dyes.) Collectively, the chromosomes are like a set of books containing all the blueprints necessary for making a complex building, whereas a gene is like a page containing a single blueprint—the plan for a door, for example, or for a corridor between rooms. Each chromosome has a double-helix structure in which its two strands of molecules are wrapped around each other, and each chromosome contains hundreds of genes (Figure 4.5).

Chromosomes consist chiefly of a substance called DNA (for deoxyribonucleic acid), which in turn consists of long chains of four nucleotide bases. A gene is a segment of a DNA strand that encodes the synthesis of a particular type of protein molecule. The code is contained in the sequence of the nucleotide bases, much as a sequence of letters spells out a word. The sequence of bases "spells out" the particular order in which **amino acids,** the building blocks of **proteins,** should be assembled to construct a certain kind of protein.

To initiate the production of a protein, the appropriate gene segment of the DNA double helix first unwinds. The exposed sequence of nucleotide bases on one of the DNA strands then serves as a template on which a complementary strand of ribonucleic acid (RNA) is constructed from free-floating nucleotides.

This process is called **transcription** (Figure 4.6). (Transcribe means to copy, as one would copy in writing a piece of printed text. The sequence of nucleotide bases in the DNA is reproduced as a similar set of nucleotide bases composing RNA.) The strand of RNA is called **messenger RNA** (mRNA) because it carries the genetic code out of the nucleus to the part of the cellular factory where proteins are manufactured. This protein-manufacturing center is the endoplasmic reticulum.

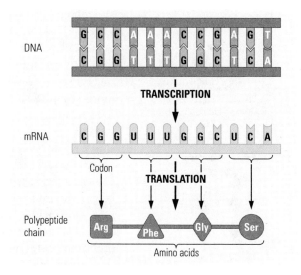

Figure 4.6 In preparation for the synthesis of a protein, a strand of DNA is transcribed into mRNA. Each sequence of three bases in the mRNA adds one amino acid to a chain. The chain of amino acids twists and folds to form a protein. The amino acids in this illustration are arganine (Arg), phenylalanine (Phe), glycine (Gly), and serine (Ser).

The Endoplasmic Reticulum: Site of Protein Synthesis

The endoplasmic reticulum consists of membranous sheets folded to form numerous channels. A distinguishing feature of the ER is that it is studded with **ribosomes,** structures that play a vital role in the building of proteins. When an mRNA molecule reaches the ER, it passes through a ribosome, where its genetic code is "read." Each group of three consecutive nucleotide bases along an mRNA molecule selects one amino acid from the surrounding fluid. These three-base sequences are called codons. For example, the nucleotide sequence uracil, guanine, guanine (abbreviated CGG) encodes the amino acid tryptophan (Trp), whereas the nucleotide sequence uracil, uracil, uracil (UUU) encodes the amino acid phenylalanine (Phe). Essentially, each of the different nucleotide codons encodes 1 of the 20 different amino acids found in protein molecules.

As each codon passes through a ribosome, the appropriate amino acid is added to the amino acid encoded by the preceding codon. In this way, a chain of amino acids is formed. The amino acids are linked to one another by a special bond called a peptide bond. A chain of amino acids is often called a **polypeptide chain** (meaning "many peptides"). Just as a remarkable number of words can be made from the 26 letters of our alphabet, a remarkable number of different peptide chains can be made from the 20 different kinds of amino acids that form proteins. These amino acids can form 400 (20 × 20) different dipeptides (two-peptide combinations), 8000 (20 × 20 × 20) different tripeptides (three-peptide combinations), and an almost endless number of polypeptides. The process of forming an amino acid chain is called **translation** because, in effect, it translates the particular sequence of nucleotide bases in the mRNA into a particular sequence of amino acids. ("Translation" means the conversion of one language into another and is distinguished from transcription, in which one chain of nucleotide bases produces another chain of nucleotide bases.)

A polypeptide chain and a protein are related, but they are not the same thing. The relation is somewhat analogous to that between a ribbon

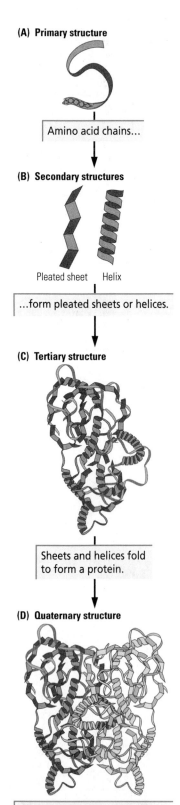

(A) Primary structure

Amino acid chains...

(B) Secondary structures

Pleated sheet   Helix

...form pleated sheets or helices.

(C) Tertiary structure

Sheets and helices fold to form a protein.

(D) Quaternary structure

A number of proteins combine to form a more complex protein.

and a bow of a particular size and shape that can be made from the ribbon. Figure 4.7 shows how a protein is formed when polypeptide chains assume a particular, functional shape. Long polypeptide chains have a strong tendency to curl into helixes (spirals) or to form pleated sheets, and these secondary structures, in turn, have a strong tendency to fold together to form more-complex shapes. The folded-up polypeptide chains constitute a protein. In addition, two or more polypeptide chains may combine, and the result also is a protein. Many proteins are globular in shape (roundish), whereas others are fibrous (threadlike), but within these broad categories countless variations are possible. Humans have about 30,000 active genes and can therefore make about 30,000 polypeptide chains. These chains can be cleaved into pieces or combined with others, leading to recombinations that, in principle, could result in millions of proteins. What make a protein functional are its shape and its ability to change shape in the presence of other molecules, as we will soon describe. Thus, in principle, the nature of the genetic code is quite simple:

$$DNA \rightarrow mRNA \rightarrow protein$$

Golgi Bodies and Microtubules: Protein Packaging and Shipment

Within any one neuron, there may be as many as 10,000 protein molecules, all of which the cell has manufactured. Some of these proteins are destined to be incorporated into the structure of the cell, becoming part of the cell membrane, the nucleus, the ER, and so forth. Other proteins remain in the intracellular fluid where they act as enzymes, facilitating many of the cell's chemical reactions. Still other proteins are excreted out of the cell as hormones or neurotransmitters. To deliver all these different proteins to the right destinations, the cell contains a set of components that operate much like a postal service, dedicated to packaging, labeling, and shipping.

Organelles called Golgi bodies wrap newly formed protein molecules in membranes and give them labels that indicate where they are to go (Figure 4.8). The packaged proteins are then loaded onto motor molecules that "walk" along the tubules radiating throughout the cell and carry each protein to its destination.

If a protein is destined to remain within the cell, it is unloaded into the intracellular fluid. If it is intended to be incorporated into the cell membrane, it is carried to the membrane and inserts itself there. When a protein is destined to be excreted at the cell membrane, a process called **exocytosis**,

Figure 4.7 Levels of protein structure. (A) The primary structure consists of the chain of amino acids—that is, the polypeptide chain. (B) Secondary structures are helixes (coils) or pleated sheets formed by the primary chain. (C) The tertiary structure emerges when the helixes, sheets, and other parts of the chain fold to form a three-dimensional structure. (D) A quaternary structure is an association between two or more folded polypeptides. The folding and ultimate shape assumed by a polypeptide chain are determined by the sequence of its amino acids.

the membrane in which the protein is wrapped will fuse with the membrane of the cell, allowing the protein to be expelled into the extracellular fluid.

What Do Proteins Do?

Proteins embedded in the cell membrane play a number of important roles, one of which is transporting substances across the membrane. Knowing something about how membrane proteins work is useful for understanding many of the functions of neurons. We will describe three categories of membrane proteins that assist in the transport of substances across the membrane. In each case, the protein's function is an emergent property of its shape.

1. *Channels.* Some of these membrane proteins are shaped in such a way that they create **channels,** or holes, through which substances can pass. Different proteins with different-sized holes allow different substances to enter or leave the cell. Figure 4.9A illustrates a protein whose shape forms a channel large enough for potassium ions (K^+) to travel through. Other protein molecules serve as channels for other ions.

2. *Gates.* An important feature of some protein molecules is that they can change shape. Figure 4.9B illustrates a channel, called a **gated channel,** that opens and closes to allow Na^+ ions to enter at some times but not at others. Some gates work by changing shape when another chemical binds to them. In these cases, the embedded protein molecule acts as a door lock. When a key of the

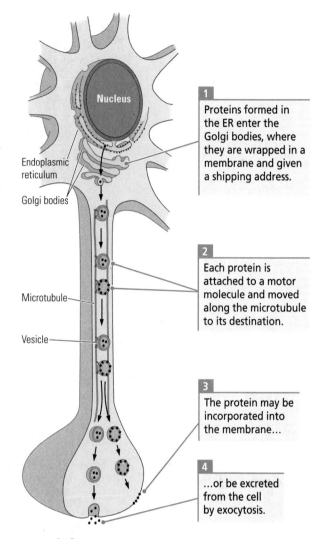

1 — Proteins formed in the ER enter the Golgi bodies, where they are wrapped in a membrane and given a shipping address.

2 — Each protein is attached to a motor molecule and moved along the microtubule to its destination.

3 — The protein may be incorporated into the membrane...

4 — ...or be excreted from the cell by exocytosis.

Endoplasmic reticulum
Golgi bodies
Microtubule
Vesicle

Figure 4.8 The steps in handling a protein consist of packaging, transport, and in some cases exocytosis.

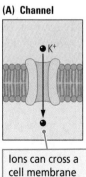

(A) Channel

Ions can cross a cell membrane through an appropriately shaped channel.

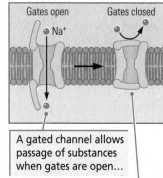

(B) Gated channel

Gates open   Gates closed

A gated channel allows passage of substances when gates are open...

...and prevents the passage when gates are closed.

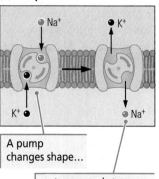

(C) Pump

A pump changes shape...

...to carry substances across a cell membrane.

Figure 4.9 Transmembrane proteins form channels that allow substances to enter and exit the cell.

appropriate size and shape is inserted into it and turned, the locking device changes shape and becomes activated. Other gates change shape when certain conditions in their environment, such as electrical charge or temperature, change.

3. *Pumps.* In some cases, a membrane protein acts as a **pump** or **transporter** to move substances across the membrane. The protein shown in Figure 4.9C changes its shape to pump sodium ions (Na^+) in one direction and chlorine (Cl^-) ions in the other direction. These pumps require energy to function. Many substances are transported across cell membranes by such mechanisms.

Channels, gates, and pumps play an important role in a neuron's ability to convey information, a process whose underlying mechanism we describe in the next sections.

The Neuron's Electrical Activity

The neurons of most animals, including humans, are very tiny, on the order of 1 to 20 micrometers (μm) in diameter (1 μm = one-thousandth of a millimeter). This size makes the neuron too small to be seen by the eye and too small to facilitate experimentation. To measure a neuron's electrical charge requires a much larger neuron.

British zoologist J. Z. Young, dissecting the North Atlantic squid *Loligo*, noticed that it has truly giant axons, as much as a millimeter (1000 μm) in diameter. These axons lead to the squid's body wall, or mantle, which contracts to propel the squid through the water. The squid itself, portrayed in Figure 4.10, is not giant. It is only about a foot long. But these particular axons are giant as axons go. Each is formed by the fusion of many smaller axons into a single large one. Because larger axons send messages faster than smaller axons, these giant axons allow the squid to jet propel away from predators.

In 1936, Young suggested to Alan Hodgkin and Andrew Huxley, two neuroscientists at Cambridge University in England, that these axons were large enough to be used for electrical recording studies. A giant axon could be removed from a live squid and kept functional in a bath of liquid designed to approximate the squid's body fluids. In this way, Hodgkin and Huxley could easily study the neuron's electrical activity and so lay the foundation for what we now know about the electrical activity of neurons.

Recording from an Axon

Hodgkin and Huxley's experiments with the giant squid axon were made possible by the invention of the **oscilloscope,** an instrument that turns electrical fluctuations into visible signals. You are familiar with one form of oscilloscope, a television set. An oscilloscope can also be used as a sensitive voltmeter to measure the very small and rapid changes in electrical currents that come from an axon, as shown in Figure 4.11. Sensitivity is important because the durations and size of electrical charges are very small, on the order of **milliseconds** (ms;

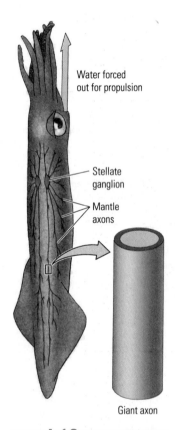

Water forced out for propulsion

Stellate ganglion

Mantle axons

Giant axon

Figure 4.10 The giant axons, projecting from the stellate ganglion to the mantle, form by the fusion of many smaller axons. Their size allows them to convey messages with extreme rapidity, instructing the mantle to contract.

1 ms = one-thousandth of a second) and **millivolts** (mV; 1 mV = one-thousandth of a volt). Oscilloscopes are still used today for recording the activities of neurons, although the job also can be—and frequently is—performed with the use of computers.

Recordings from the axon are made with microelectrodes, which are insulated wires with very tiny, uninsulated tips. Placing the tip of a microelectrode on an axon provides an extracellular measure of the electrical current from a very small part of the axon. If a second microelectrode is used as a reference, one tip can be placed on the surface of the axon and the other inserted into the axon. This technique provides a measure of voltage or electrical charge across the cell membrane. The voltage is a measure of the current that will flow from one electrode, through a wire to the voltmeter, and from there through another wire to the tip of the other electrode, when there is a difference in charge at the tips of the two electrodes. Using the giant axon of the squid, an oscilloscope, and two microelectrodes, Hodgkin and Huxley recorded the electrical voltage across the axon's membrane and proposed a model for explaining a nerve impulse. The basis of this electrical activity is the movement of intracellular and extracellular ions, which carry positive and negative charges. Therefore, before exploring the neuron's electrical activity, we will briefly summarize the principles underlying the movement of ions.

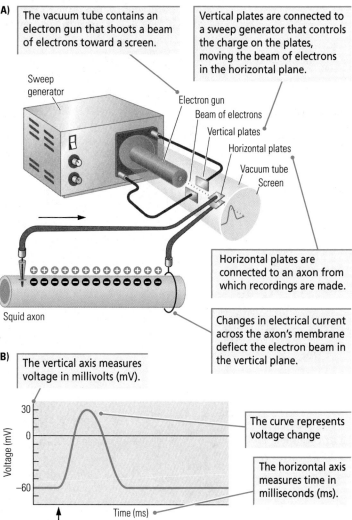

(A) The vacuum tube contains an electron gun that shoots a beam of electrons toward a screen.

Sweep generator

Electron gun
Beam of electrons
Vertical plates
Horizontal plates
Vacuum tube
Screen

Vertical plates are connected to a sweep generator that controls the charge on the plates, moving the beam of electrons in the horizontal plane.

Horizontal plates are connected to an axon from which recordings are made.

Squid axon

Changes in electrical current across the axon's membrane deflect the electron beam in the vertical plane.

(B) The vertical axis measures voltage in millivolts (mV).

Voltage (mV)
30
0
−60

The curve represents voltage change

The horizontal axis measures time in milliseconds (ms).

Time (ms)

Stimulation

Figure 4.11 (A) The principal parts of an oscilloscope. The vacuum tube contains an electron gun that shoots a beam of electrons toward a screen. Vertical plates are connected to a sweep generator that controls charge on the plates, moving the beam of electrons in the horizontal plane. Horizontal plates are connected to an axon from which recordings are made. Changes in electrical current across the axon's membrane deflect the electron beam in the vertical plane. (B) A recording of voltage change. The horizontal axis measures time in milliseconds (ms), whereas the vertical axis measures voltage in millivolts (mV). The graph illustrates a change in voltage (from −60 to +30) recorded from the axon.

How the Movement of Ions Creates Electrical Charges

The intracellular and extracellular fluids of a neuron are filled with various kinds of ions, including positively charged Na^+ (sodium) and K^+ (potassium) ions, and negatively charged Cl^- (chloride) ions. These fluids also contain numerous negatively charged protein molecules. Negatively charged ions are called **anions** (A^-), a term that we will use for negatively charged protein molecules, too. Three factors influence the movement of ions into and out of cells: (1) concentration gradient, (2) voltage gradient, and (3) the structure of the membrane.

All molecules have an intrinsic kinetic energy called thermal motion or heat: they move constantly. Because of this motion, they spontaneously spread out from where they are more concentrated to where they are less concentrated. This spreading out is called **diffusion.** Requiring no work, diffusion results from the random motion of molecules as they jostle and bounce about, gradually dispersing through the solution. Ink poured into water diffuses from its initial point of contact to every part of the liquid. When salts are placed in water, they dissolve into ions surrounded by water molecules. Carried by the random motion of the water molecules, the ions diffuse throughout the solution until every part of it has very nearly the same concentration. When diffusion is complete, the system is in equilibrium, with each kind of component molecule distributed evenly throughout.

Concentration gradient describes the relative difference in the concentration of a substance at different locations in space when the substance is not evenly dispersed. As illustrated in Figure 4.12A, a little ink placed in water will start out concentrated at the site of first contact; but, even in the absence of mechanical stirring, the ink will quickly spread away from that site. The ink spontaneously diffuses down a gradient from a place of high concentration to places of low concentration until it is equally distributed throughout the water. At that point, all of the water in the container will be equally dark. The process is similar when a salt solution is poured into water. The solution's concentration is initially high in the location where the solution enters the water, but it then diffuses from that location to other regions of the water until the concentrations of ions are uniform throughout.

The second factor that influences the movement of ions is their **voltage gradient,** a measure of relative concentrations of electrical charge. Because ions carry an electrical charge, their movement can be described not only by a concentration gradient but also by a voltage gradient. Ions will move down a voltage gradient from an area of high charge to an area of lower charge, just as they move down a concentration gradient from an area of high concentration to an area of lower concentration. Figure 4.12B illustrates this process. It shows that, when salt is dissolved in water, its diffusion can be described either as movement down a concentration gradient (for sodium and chloride) or as movement down a voltage gradient (for the positive and negative charges).

The third factor that influences the movement of ions in the nervous system is the cell membrane. The container in Figure 4.12B allows unimpeded movement of ions throughout the mixture. Fully dispersed, the ions and their positive and negative charges balance one another, and so there is no concentration gradient or voltage gradient. Such is not the case with intracellular and extracellular fluid, because the cell membrane acts as a partial barrier to the movement of ions between the cell's interior and its exterior. As stated earlier, a cell membrane is composed of a phospholipid bilayer with its hydrophobic tails pointing inward, toward one another, and its hydrophobic heads pointing outward. This membrane is impermeable to salty solutions because the salt ions,

(A) A concentration gradient

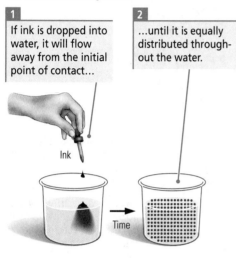

1	2
If ink is dropped into water, it will flow away from the initial point of contact...	...until it is equally distributed throughout the water.

Ink

Time

(B) An electrostatic gradient

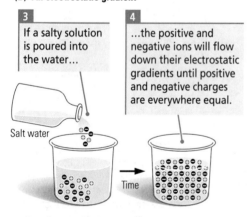

3	4
If a salty solution is poured into the water...	...the positive and negative ions will flow down their electrostatic gradients until positive and negative charges are everywhere equal.

Salt water

Time

Figure 4.12 (A) A concentration gradient. If a small amount of ink is dropped into a beaker of water, the ink will flow away from the point of initial contact, where it has a high concentration, into areas of lower concentration until it is equally distributed throughout the water. (B) An electrostatic gradient. If a salty solution is poured into a beaker of water, the positive and negative ions will flow down their electrostatic gradients until positive and negative charges are everywhere equal.

which are encased in water molecules, will not pass through the membrane's hydrophobic tails.

An imaginary experiment will help illustrate how a cell membrane influences the movement of ions. Figure 4.13A shows a container of water that is divided in half by a membrane. If we place a few grains of salt (NaCl) in one half of the container, the salt dissolves and the ions diffuse down their concentration gradients until the water in that side of the container is in equilibrium. At this point, *within* that side of the container, there is no longer a concentration gradient for either sodium or chloride ions, because the water everywhere in that side is equally salty. There are no concentration gradients for these ions *within* the other side of the container either, because there are no sodium and chloride ions there. But notice how there *are* concentration gradients for both sodium and chloride ions *across* the membrane—that is, from one side of it to the other.

You learned earlier that various protein molecules are embedded in the cell membrane and that some of these protein molecules form channels that act as pores to allow certain kinds of ions to pass through the membrane. Returning to our mental experiment, we'll place a chloride channel in the membrane and imagine how the channel will affect the activity of the dissolved particles. Chloride ions are now permitted to cross the membrane and will move down their concentration gradient from the side of the container where they are abundant to the side of the container from which they were previously excluded. The sodium ions, in contrast, will still be unable to cross the membrane. Although chloride ions are larger than sodium ions, sodium ions have a greater tendency to hold on to water molecules; as a result, the sodium ions are bulkier and unable to enter the chloride channels.

If the only factor influencing the movement of chloride ions were the chloride concentration gradient, the efflux (outward flow) of chloride from the salty to the unsalty side of the container would continue until chloride ions were in equilibrium on both sides. But this result is not what actually happens. Because the chloride ions carry a negative charge, they are attracted back toward the positively charged sodium ions (opposite charges attract). Consequently, the concentration of chloride ions remains higher in the first half of the container

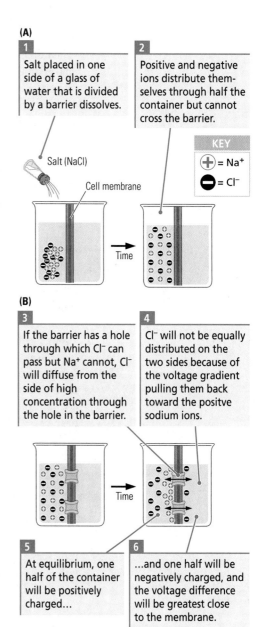

(A)

1 Salt placed in one side of a glass of water that is divided by a barrier dissolves.

2 Positive and negative ions distribute themselves through half the container but cannot cross the barrier.

Salt (NaCl)

Cell membrane

KEY

$\oplus$ = Na$^+$

$\ominus$ = Cl$^-$

Time

(B)

3 If the barrier has a hole through which Cl$^-$ can pass but Na$^+$ cannot, Cl$^-$ will diffuse from the side of high concentration through the hole in the barrier.

4 Cl$^-$ will not be equally distributed on the two sides because of the voltage gradient pulling them back toward the positve sodium ions.

Time

5 At equilibrium, one half of the container will be positively charged...

6 ...and one half will be negatively charged, and the voltage difference will be greatest close to the membrane.

Figure 4.13 (A) When salt is placed in one side of a glass of water that is divided by a barrier, the salt dissolves. Positive and negative ions distribute themselves throughout half of the container but cannot cross the barrier. (B) If the barrier has a hole through which Cl$^-$ can pass but Na$^+$ cannot pass, Cl$^-$ will diffuse from the side of high concentration through the hole in the barrier. The Cl$^-$ ions will not be equally distributed on the two sides of the container, because of the voltage gradient pulling the negative chloride ions back toward the positive sodium ions. At equilibrium, one side of the container will be positively charged, the other side will be negatively charged, and the voltage difference will be greatest close to the membrane.

than in the second half, as illustrated in Figure 4.13B. In short, with reference to Figure 4.13B, the movement of chloride ions from the left side of the container to the right side, down the chloride concentration gradient, is counteracted by the movement of chloride ions from right to left down the chloride voltage gradient. At some point, an equilibrium is reached in which the concentration gradient of chloride ions is balanced by the voltage gradient of negative charge. At that point,

Concentration gradient = volgate gradient

At this equilibrium, there are different ratios of positive and negative ions on each side of the membrane, and so a voltage gradient exists across the membrane. The first side of the container is positively charged because some chloride ions have crossed to the other side, leaving a preponderance of positive (Na^+) charges behind them. The second side of the container is negatively charged because some chloride ions (Cl^-) have crossed into it, and no ions (of any charge) were there before. The charges are highest on the surfaces of the membrane, where positive and negative ions accumulate in an attempt to balance each other.

This example is similar to what happens in a real cell, as we are about to see. Keep it in mind as we describe and explain five aspects of the cell membrane's electrical activity—(1) the resting potential, (2) graded potentials, (3) the action potential, (4) the nerve impulse, and (5) saltatory conduction—and the role that ion channels, gates, and pumps play in these processes.

The Resting Potential

An undisturbed axon has a difference in electrical charge across its membrane, much like the charge difference across the membrane in our thought experiment. This difference is called the **resting potential.** Figure 4.14A graphs the voltage difference recorded in the laboratory when one microelectrode is placed on the outer surface of an axon's membrane and another microelectrode is placed on its inner surface. The difference is about 70 mV. Although the charge on the outside of the membrane is actually positive, scientists follow the convention of assigning it a charge of 0 mV. Therefore, the inside of the membrane is −70 mV *relative* to the outside.

If we were to continue recording for a long period of time, the charge across the membrane would remain much the same. This charge has the potential to change, however, given certain changes in the membrane. In other words, the charge is currently stable but is a store of *potential* energy (thus the expression "resting potential"). The word "potential" here is used in the same way as we might use it in talking about the financial potential of someone who has money in the bank. Just as the money can be spent at some future time, the resting potential is a store of energy that can be used at a later time. The resting potential is not identical on every axon. It can vary from −40 mV to −90 mV on axons of different animal species.

Four kinds of charged particles interact to produce the resting potential: sodium ions (Na^+), chloride ions (Cl^-), potassium ions (K^+), and large protein anions (A⁻). As Figure 4.14B shows, these charged particles are distributed unequally across the axon's membrane, with more protein anions and K⁺ ions in the intracellular fluid, and more Cl⁻ and Na⁺ ions in the extracellular fluid. Let's consider how each contributes to the membrane's resting potential.

Large protein anions are manufactured inside cells. Because there are no membrane channels through which they can leave the cell, they remain in the intracellular fluid, and their charge contributes to the negative charge on the inside of the cell membrane. The negative charge of protein anions alone is sufficient to produce a transmembrane voltage gradient. Because most cells in the body manufacture these large, negatively charged protein molecules, most cells have a charge across their membranes.

To balance the negative charge of the large protein anions in the intracellular fluid, cells accumulate positively charged potassium ions (K⁺) inside their membranes. Potassium ions pass through the cell membrane through open potassium channels—to the extent that about 20 times as much potassium is inside the cell as outside it. With this very high concentration of potassium inside the cell, however, an efflux of K⁺ ions also is produced, owing to the potassium concentration gradient across the membrane. In other words, some potassium leaves the cell because the internal concentration of K⁺ ions is much higher than the external K⁺ concentration. The efflux of even a very small number of K⁺ ions is enough to contribute to the charge across the membrane, with the inside of the membrane being negatively charged relative to the outside.

You may be wondering whether you read that last sentence correctly. If there are 20 times as many positively charged potassium ions on the inside of the cell as on the outside, why should the inside of the membrane have a *negative* charge? Shouldn't all of those K⁺ ions in the intracellular fluid give the inside of the cell a positive charge instead? No, because of the negatively charged protein anions. Think of it this way. If there were no restriction on the number of potassium ions that could accumulate on the inside of the membrane, the positive charges on the intracellular potassium ions would exactly match the negative charges on the intracellular protein anions, and there would be no charge across the membrane at all. But there *is* a limit on the number of K⁺ ions that accumulate inside the

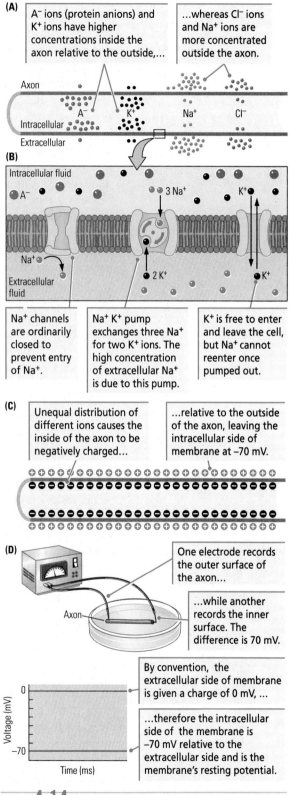

Figure 4.14 The basis and method of recording a resting potential. Protein ions are represented by A⁻.

cell because, when the intracellular potassium concentration becomes higher than the extracellular concentration, potassium starts moving out of the cell down its concentration gradient. The equilibrium of the potassium voltage gradient and the potassium concentration gradient results in some potassium ions remaining outside the membrane. Only a few potassium ions are needed outside the membrane to produce a relative negative charge on the inside of the membrane. As a result, potassium contributes to the charge across the membrane.

But what about the other two ions that contribute to the production of the resting potential—sodium (Na^+) and chloride (Cl^-)? If positively charged sodium ions were free to move across the membrane, they could diffuse into the cell and reduce the transmembrane charge produced by the unequal distribution of potassium ions. In fact, a cell membrane does have sodium channels, but they are ordinarily closed, blocking the entry of most sodium ions. Still, given enough time, sufficient sodium could leak into the cell to reduce its membrane potential to zero. What prevents this from occurring?

The high concentration of sodium outside relative to inside the cell membrane is caused by the action of a **sodium–potassium pump.** This pump is a protein molecule embedded in the membrane. A nerve membrane's many thousands of sodium–potassium pumps work continuously, each one exchanging three intracellular Na^+ ions for two K^+ ions with each pumping action. The K^+ ions are free to leave the cell through open potassium channels, but closed sodium channels prevent reentry of the Na^+. Consequently, there are about 10 times as many sodium ions on the outside of the axon membrane as there are on the membrane's inside.

Unlike sodium ions, Cl^- ions move in and out of the cell through open chloride channels in the membrane. The equilibrium at which the chloride concentration gradient equals the chloride voltage gradient is approximately the membrane's resting potential; so ordinarily chloride ions contribute little to the resting potential of the membrane. At this equilibrium point, there are about 12 times as many Cl^- ions outside the cell as inside it.

As summarized in Figure 4.14C, this unequal distribution of ions leaves a neuron's intracellular fluid negatively charged relative to the outside of the cell. We have seen that the membrane's bilayer structure, as well as the presence of channels and pumps, contributes to this resting potential. First, it keeps in large negatively charged protein molecules, keeps out positively charged Na^+ ions, and allows K^+ and Cl^- ions to pass relatively freely. Second, the membrane has a Na^+–K^+ pump that extrudes Na^+. The summed charges of the unequally distributed ions give the inside of the membrane a charge of -70 mV relative to the outside. This charge is the membrane's resting potential.

Graded Potentials

The resting potential provides an energy store that can be expended if the membrane's barrier to ion movement is suddenly removed. This energy store can also be restored by other modifications to the flow of ions. More specifically, if the barrier to the flow of ions is changed, the voltage across the membrane will change. Slight, sudden changes in the voltage of an axon's membrane are called **graded potentials,** which are highly localized, being restricted to the vicinity of the spot on the axon where they are produced. Just as a small wave produced in the middle of a large, smooth pond disappears before traveling much of a distance, graded potentials produced on a membrane decay before traveling very far.

Note that there is no reason for an isolated axon to experience a spontaneous change in charge. In order for a graded potential to occur, an axon must receive some kind of stimulation that changes the flow of ions. Stimulating the axon electrically through a microelectrode is one way to alter its membrane's voltage and produce a graded potential. If the current applied to the membrane is negative, the membrane potential becomes more negative by a few millivolts (increasing its charge). As illustrated in Figure 4.15A, it may suddenly change from the resting potential of -70 mV to a new, slightly higher potential of, say, -73 mV. This type of change is called **hyperpolarization,** to indicate that the polarity of the membrane becomes larger. Conversely, if the current applied to the membrane is positive, the membrane potential becomes more positive by a few millivolts (decreasing its charge). As illustrated in Figure 4.15B, it may suddenly change from a resting potential of -70 mV to a new, slightly lower potential of, say, -65 mV. This type of change is called **depolarization,** because the polarity of the membrane becomes smaller. Such changes are brief, lasting no more than milliseconds.

What are the specific causes of these changes in the membrane's polarity? The answer is that electrical stimulation influences the opening and closing of protein gates on membrane channels, and the opening and closing of various gates causes the membrane potential to change. For the membrane to become hyperpolarized, the outside must become more positive, which can be accomplished with an efflux of K^+ ions (or an influx of Cl^- ions). When gates that allow the passage of K^+ ions or Cl^- ions open, K^+ or Cl^- efflux can take place.

One piece of evidence that gated potassium channels have a role in hyperpolarization is that the chemical *tetraethylammonium* (TEA), which blocks potassium channels, also blocks hyperpolarization. But, if potassium channels are ordinarily open, how can a greater-than-normal efflux of K^+ ions take place? Apparently, even though potassium channels are open, they still present some resistance to the outward flow of potassium ions. The reduction of this resistance enables hyperpolarization.

Depolarization, on the other hand, is due to the influx of sodium ions and is produced by the opening of gated sodium

Figure 4.15 (A) Stimulation (S) that increases membrane voltage produces a hyperpolarizing graded potential. (B) Stimulation that decreases the membrane voltage produces a depolarizing graded potential.

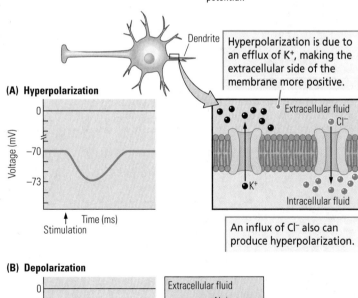

(A) Hyperpolarization

Hyperpolarization is due to an efflux of K^+, making the extracellular side of the membrane more positive.

An influx of Cl^- also can produce hyperpolarization.

(B) Depolarization

Depolarization is due to an influx of Na^+ through normally closed Na^+ channels.

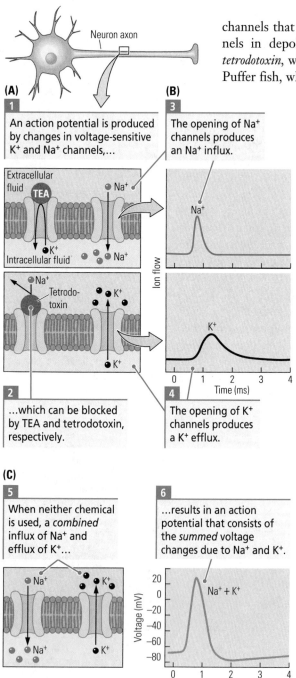

(A)

1 An action potential is produced by changes in voltage-sensitive K⁺ and Na⁺ channels,...

Extracellular fluid

TEA

Na⁺

K⁺

Intracellular fluid

Na⁺

Na⁺

Tetrodo-toxin

K⁺

Na⁺

K⁺

2 ...which can be blocked by TEA and tetrodotoxin, respectively.

(B)

3 The opening of Na⁺ channels produces an Na⁺ influx.

Na⁺

Ion flow

K⁺

4 The opening of K⁺ channels produces a K⁺ efflux.

Time (ms) 0 1 2 3 4

(C)

5 When neither chemical is used, a *combined* influx of Na⁺ and efflux of K⁺...

Na⁺

K⁺

Na⁺

K⁺

6 ...results in an action potential that consists of the *summed* voltage changes due to Na⁺ and K⁺.

Voltage (mV) 20 0 −20 −40 −60 −80

Na⁺ + K⁺

Time (ms) 0 1 2 3 4

Figure 4.16 Experiment demonstrating that the action potential on an axon is due to an inward flow of sodium ions and an outward flow of potassium ions. (A) The separate contributions of sodium and potassium channels can be demonstrated by blocking potassium channels with tetraethylammonium (TEA) and sodium channels with tetrodotoxin. (B) Sodium channels open first, allowing an influx of Na⁺ ions, and potassium channels open slightly later, allowing an efflux of K⁺ ions. (C) The combined influx of sodium and efflux of potassium is responsible for the action potential.

channels that are normally closed. The involvement of sodium channels in depolarization is indicated by the fact that the chemical *tetrodotoxin*, which blocks sodium channels, also blocks depolarization. Puffer fish, which are considered a delicacy in certain countries, especially Japan, secrete this potentially deadly poison; so skill is required to prepare this fish for dinner. The fish is lethal to the guests of careless cooks because its toxin impedes the electrical activity of neurons.

The Action Potential

An **action potential** is a brief but extremely large change in the polarity of an axon's membrane, lasting about 1 millisecond (Figure 4.16). In an action potential, the voltage across the membrane suddenly reverses, making the inside positive relative to the outside, and then abruptly reverses again, after which the resting potential is restored. Because the duration of the action potential is so brief, many action potentials can occur within a second.

This rapid change in the polarity of the membrane takes place when electrical stimulation produces a large graded potential that causes the membrane's potential to drop to about −50 mV. At this voltage level, called the **threshold potential,** the membrane undergoes a remarkable change without any further contribution from the stimulation. When the threshold potential has been reached, the voltage of the membrane suddenly drops to 0 mV and then continues to become more positive until the charge on the inside of the membrane is as great as +30 mV. This is a total voltage change of 100 mV. Then, almost as quickly, the membrane potential reverses again, returning to its resting potential and then bypassing it and becoming slightly hyperpolarized. This change is a reversal of a little more than 100 mV. After this second reversal, the membrane gradually returns to its resting potential.

The changes in voltage that produce an action potential are caused by a brief, large influx of sodium ions and a brief, large efflux of potassium ions. If an axon's membrane is stimulated to produce an action potential while immersed in a solution containing TEA (to block potassium channels), a somewhat smaller-than-normal action potential occurs that is due entirely to sodium influx. Similarly, if an axon's membrane is stimulated to produce an action potential while the axon is immersed in a solution containing tetrodotoxin (to block sodium channels), a slightly different action potential occurs that is due entirely to the efflux of potassium. These results show that the action potential on an axon normally consists of the summed voltage changes caused by the flow of both sodium and potassium ions through their respective gated channels.

The Role of Voltage-Sensitive Channels

There are many different kinds of sodium and potassium channels in the membrane of a neuron. The channels responsible for initiating the action potential belong to a class of gated ion channels that are sensitive to the membrane's voltage. These channels are called **voltage-sensitive sodium channels** and **voltage-sensitive potassium channels.** Voltage-sensitive channels are closed when an axon's membrane is at its resting potential, and so ions cannot pass through them. But, when the membrane reaches the threshold voltage, the configuration of the voltage-sensitive channels alters, enabling them to open and let ions pass through (Figure 4.17). In other words, the voltage to which these channels are sensitive is the threshold voltage of -50 mV. At this point, sodium and potassium ions are free to cross the membrane. The voltage-sensitive sodium channels are more sensitive than the potassium ones, and so the voltage change due to sodium influx occurs slightly before the voltage change due to potassium efflux.

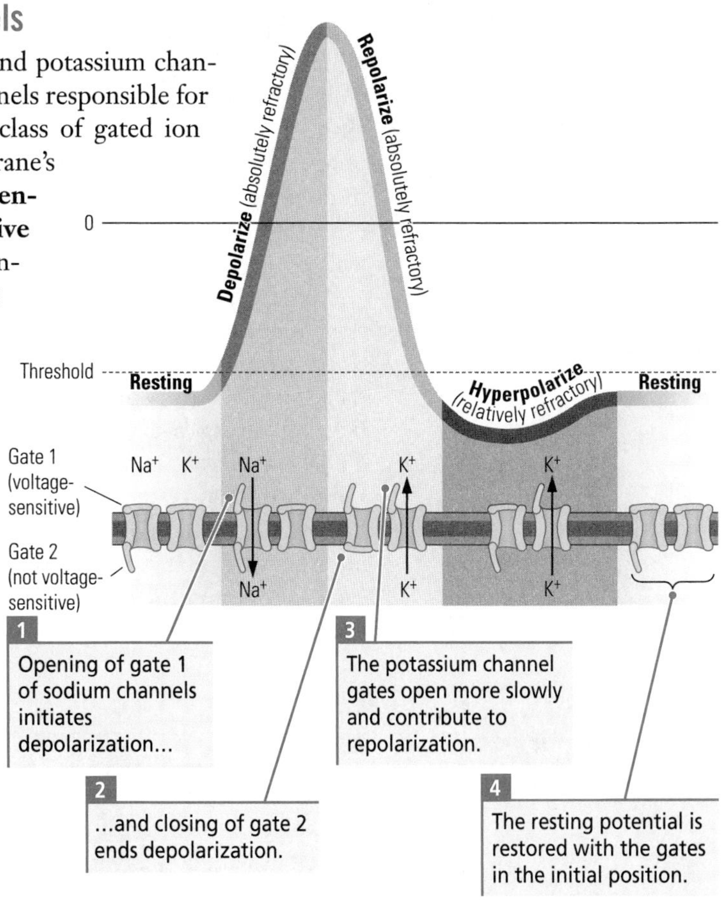

1 Opening of gate 1 of sodium channels initiates depolarization...

2 ...and closing of gate 2 ends depolarization.

3 The potassium channel gates open more slowly and contribute to repolarization.

4 The resting potential is restored with the gates in the initial position.

Refractory Periods

Although a nerve can exhibit hundreds of action potentials in a second, their frequency has an upper limit. If the axon membrane is stimulated during the depolarizing or repolarizing phases of the action potential, it does not respond with a new action potential. The axon in this phase is described as **absolutely refractory.** If, on the other hand, the axon membrane is stimulated during the hyperpolarization phase, a new action potential can be induced, but only if the intensity of stimulation is higher than that which initiated the first action potential. During this phase, the membrane is described as **relatively refractory.** The refractory periods place a limit on how frequently action potentials can occur. An axon can produce action potentials at a maximum rate of about 200 per second, but neurons typically fire at a much lower rate of about 30 action potentials per second.

Refractory periods are caused by the way in which the gates of the voltage-sensitive sodium and potassium channels open and close. The sodium channels have two gates and the potassium channels have one gate. Figure 4.17 illustrates

Figure 4.17 Changes in voltage-sensitive sodium and potassium channels are responsible for the phases of the action potential. The opening of gate 1 of the sodium channel initiates depolarization, and the closing of gate 2 ends depolarization. The potassium channel gates open more slowly and contribute to repolarization and hyperpolarization. Restoration of the initial condition of the gates is associated with restoration of the resting potential. The membrane is absolutely refractory when gate 2 of the sodium channels closes and relatively refractory until the resting membrane potential is restored.

the position of these gates before, during, and after the various phases of the action potential. During the resting potential, gate 1 of the sodium channel is closed and only gate 2 is open. At the threshold level of stimulation, gate 1 also opens. Gate 2, however, closes very quickly after gate 1 opens. This sequence produces a brief period during which both gates are open followed by a brief period when gate 2 is closed. When gate 2 is closed, the membrane cannot be changed by further stimulation, at which time the axon membrane is absolutely refractory. Both of the sodium gates are eventually restored to their resting potential positions, with gate 1 closed and gate 2 open. But, because the potassium channels close more slowly than the sodium channels, the hyperpolarization produced by a continuing efflux of potassium ions makes the membrane relatively refractory for a period of time after the action potential has occurred. The refractory periods have very practical uses in conducting information, as you will see when we consider the nerve impulse.

A lever-activated toilet provides an analogy for some of the stages of an action potential. Pushing the lever slightly produces a slight flow of water, which stops when the lever is released. This is analogous to a graded potential. A harder press of the lever brings the toilet to threshold and initiates flushing, a response that is out of all proportion to the pressure on the lever. This is analogous to the action potential. During the flush, the toilet is absolutely refractory, meaning that another flush cannot be induced at that time. During the refilling of the bowl, in contrast, the toilet is relatively refractory, meaning that reflushing is possible, but harder to bring about. Only after the cycle is over and the toilet is once again "resting" can the usual flush be produced again.

Sending a Message Along an Axon

The ability of the membrane of an axon to produce an action potential does not of itself explain how a neuron sends messages. A message has to travel along the length of the axon. In some cases, the trip is a long one, as it is along the axons of corticospinal tract neurons, which extend from the cortex to the spinal cord, and in squid, where the message must travel from the ganglia to the mantle muscles. In this section, we will describe how the action potential travels and serves to carry information.

The Nerve Impulse

Suppose you place two recording electrodes at a distance from each other on an axon's membrane and then electrically stimulate an area adjacent to one of these electrodes with a current sufficient to bring the membrane to threshold (Figure 4.18). That electrode would immediately record an action potential, which would very quickly be followed by a similar recording by the second electrode. Apparently, an action potential has arisen near the second electrode also, even though the electrode is some distance from the original point of stimulation. Is this second action potential simply an echo of the first, being felt along the axon?

No, that cannot be the case, because the size and shape of the action potential is exactly the same at the two electrodes. The second is not just a faint, degraded version of the first but instead is equal to the first in magnitude. Somehow the full action potential has moved along the axon. This movement of an action potential along an axon is called a **nerve impulse.**

Why does an action potential move? Remember that the voltage change during an action potential is 100 mV, which is far beyond the 20-mV change needed to bring the membrane to the threshold level of −50 mV. A 100-mV voltage change at the point of the original action potential is large enough to bring adjacent parts of the membrane to a threshold of −50 mV. When the membrane of an adjacent part of the axon reaches −50 mV, the voltage-sensitive channels at that location pop open to produce an action potential there as well. This action potential, in turn, induces a change in the voltage of the membrane still farther along the axon, and so on, and so on, down the axon's length. Figure 4.18 illustrates this process by which a nerve impulse travels along an axon. The nerve impulse is produced because each action potential propagates another action potential on an adjacent part of the axon membrane. The word *propagate* means to give birth, which is exactly what happens. Each successive action potential gives birth to another down the length of the axon. Because a membrane is refractory for a brief period of time during an action potential, the action potential cannot reverse direction and move back to where it came from. Thus the creation of a single, discrete impulse that travels in one direction is ensured.

To summarize the action of a nerve impulse, another analogy may help. Think of the voltage-sensitive ion channels along an axon as a series of dominoes. When one domino falls, it knocks over its neighbor, and so on down the line. The wave cannot return to its starting position until the dominoes are set back up again. There is also no decrement in the size of the propagated event: the last domino falls exactly the same distance and just as heavily as did the first one. Essentially the same can be said about voltage-sensitive ion channels: the opening of one channel triggers the opening of the next, just as one domino knocks over its neighbor. When gate 2 on a voltage-sensitive sodium channel closes, that channel is inactivated, much as a domino is temporarily

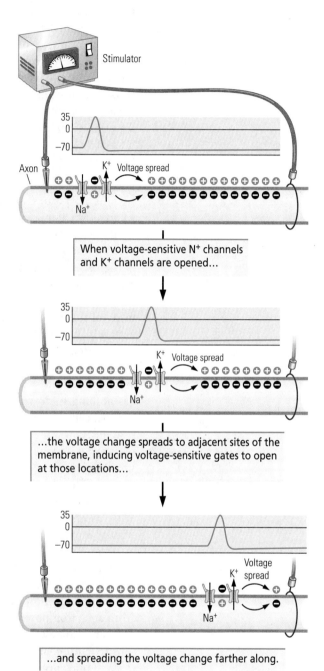

When voltage-sensitive N⁺ channels and K⁺ channels are opened...

...the voltage change spreads to adjacent sites of the membrane, inducing voltage-sensitive gates to open at those locations...

...and spreading the voltage change farther along.

Figure 4.18 A nerve impulse is a series of action potentials along an axon. When voltage-sensitive N⁺ channels and K⁺ channels are opened, the voltage change spreads to adjacent sites of the membrane, inducing voltage-sensitive gates to open at those locations and spreading the voltage change farther along. Because the gates are briefly inactivated after closing, the impulse cannot travel back in the direction from which it has come. Here, the voltage changes are shown in one direction and on one side of the membrane only.

inactivated after it has fallen over. Both channel and domino must be restored to their original condition before they can work again, and this restoration requires the same expenditure of energy for each domino. Furthermore, the channel-opening response does not grow any weaker as it moves along the axon. The last channel opens exactly like the first, just as the domino action stays constant until the end of the line. Because of this behavior of voltage-sensitive ion channels, a single nerve impulse of constant size moves in one direction along an axon.

Saltatory Conduction and Myelin Sheaths

Various properties of axons allow large axons to convey impulses quickly, whereas smaller axons convey impulses slowly. Because the giant axons of squids are so large, they can send nerve impulses very quickly. But large axons take up a substantial amount of space; so a squid cannot accommodate many of them, because its body would become too bulky. For us mammals, with our repertoires of complex behaviors, giant axons are out of the question. Our axons must be extremely slender because our complex behaviors require a great many of them. Our largest axons are only about 30 μm wide, and so the speed with which they convey information should not be especially fast. And yet most mammals are far from sluggish creatures. We process information and generate responses with impressive speed. How do we manage to do so if our axons are so thin? The mammalian nervous system has evolved a solution that has nothing to do with axon size.

Glial cells play a role in speeding nerve impulses in the mammalian nervous system. Schwann cells in the peripheral nervous system and oligodendroglia in the central nervous system wrap around each axon, insulating it except for the small region between each glial cell. This insulation is referred to as myelin or a myelin sheath, and insulated axons are said to be myelinated. The uninsulated regions between the myelinated segments of the axon are called nodes of Ranvier. Larger mammalian axons tend to be more heavily myelinated than smaller axons, and on larger axons the nodes are farther apart.

Action potentials cannot be produced where myelin surrounds an axon. For one thing, the myelin creates a barrier to the flow of ionic currents. For another, regions of an axon that lie under myelin have few channels through which ions can flow and, as you know, such channels are essential to generating an action potential. But, as we have just seen, the axons are not totally encased in myelin. The nodes of Ranvier are richly endowed with voltage-sensitive ion channels. These tiny gaps in the myelin sheath are sufficiently close to one another that an action potential at one of them can trigger voltage-sensitive gates to open at an adjacent one. In this way, an action potential jumps from node to node, as shown in Figure 4.19. This mode of conduction is called **saltatory conduction** (from the Latin verb *saltare*, meaning "to leap").

Jumping from node to node greatly speeds the rate at which an action potential can travel along an axon. On the largest myelinated mammalian axons, the nerve impulse can travel at a rate as high as 120 meters per second, compared with only about 30 meters per second on smaller, less-myelinated axons.

Think of how a wave made by spectators consecutively rising to their feet travels around a football stadium. As one person rises, the person's immediate neighbor begins to rise also, producing the wave effect. This wave is like conduction along an uninsulated axon. Now think of how much faster the wave would complete its circuit around the field if only spectators in the corners rose to produce it. This is analogous to a nerve impulse that travels by jumping from one node of Ranvier to another. That humans and other mammals are capable of quick reactions is due in part to this saltatory conduction in their nervous systems.

The Next Neuron

When an action potential reaches the terminal of an axon, it triggers the release of a chemical neurotransmitter from the terminal. This chemical crosses the space between the sending axon's terminal and the terminal of an adjacent neuron and there attaches to protein molecules that act as receptors. The neurotransmitter causes changes in the receptors, which in turn cause changes in the channels of the receiving membrane. Remember from Figure 3.1 that many neurons have many dendrites covered with dendritic spines. Input from some neurons onto these spines causes inhibitory graded potentials while input from some other neurons onto other spines causes inhibitory graded potentials. If the summed influence of these inputs is sufficient to depolarize the axon hillock to the neuron's threshold for firing, an action potential is propagated at the axon hillock. This action potential then travels down that neuron's axon. Thus the nerve impulse is passed along from one neuron to the next. We will take up this aspect of transmission in the next chapter, but let's return to Tinbergen's butterfly for a moment. The explanation of how information is conducted into the nervous system of the butterfly is that it is sent in the form of action potentials. When two different sensory stimuli are presented to a butterfly, separate neurons carry information about each stimulus. These action-potential messages can converge because the separate neurons can release their neurotransmitters onto a common neuron. Thus, a larger message than that conveyed by each alone can be sent to the wings of the butterfly to produce a proportional response.

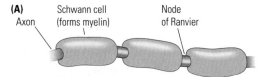

Long, myelin-sheathed stretches of axons are interrupted by short nodes of Ranvier, rich in voltage-sensitive channels.

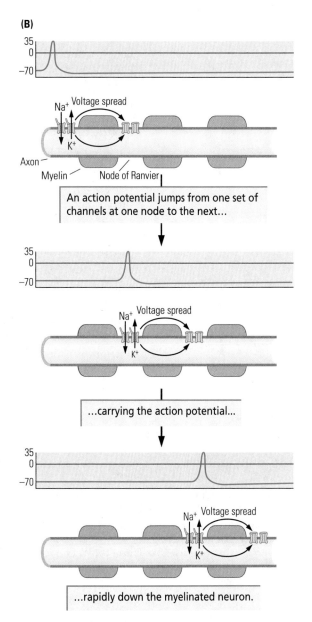

An action potential jumps from one set of channels at one node to the next...

...carrying the action potential...

...rapidly down the myelinated neuron.

Figure 4.19 Saltatory conduction. (A) The nodes of Ranvier have no myelin and are rich in voltage-sensitive channels. (B) The action potential jumps from node to node.

Summary

This chapter has described the various parts of a neuron and illustrated how an understanding of the parts leads to an understanding of various aspects of neuron function.

Neurons act as factories for making protein molecules. The chromosomes of the nucleus contain genes, and each gene contains the code for one polypeptide chain. The DNA of a gene is transcribed into mRNA, which then carries the code for the polypeptide to a ribosome. The code contained in the mRNA is translated on the ribosome into a series of amino acids connected by peptide bonds. The resulting long chains of amino acids fold in different ways and combine to form proteins. The proteins are packaged and shipped by Golgi bodies and travel on microtubules to various destinations within the cell. Some of these proteins are embedded in the neuron's membrane, forming channels, gates, and pumps that regulate the flow of ions across the cell membrane.

Neurons carry an electrical charge, called the resting potential, across their membranes. This charge is produced by unequal concentrations of ions across the membrane, an inequity that is maintained and regulated by membrane ion channels, gates, and pumps. If the gates on the membrane open briefly, ion efflux or influx can occur briefly, changing the membrane's charge. Such a change is called a graded potential. If a graded potential is sufficient to change the membrane's charge to the threshold at which voltage-sensitive sodium and potassium channels open, an action potential is produced. The voltage change of an action potential on one part of the membrane is sufficiently large to open adjacent voltage-sensitive channels, thus propagating the action potential along the membrane. The propagated action potential is called a nerve impulse. On myelinated axons, the action potential can be propagated only at the nodes between glial cells, and this form of propagation, called saltatory conduction, is especially rapid. These functions underlie the way in which cells communicate with one another and how they contribute to behavior.

References

Eccles, J. The synapse. *Scientific American* 212:56–66, January 1965.

Hodgkin, A. L., and A. F. Huxley. Action potentials recorded from inside nerve fiber. *Nature* 144:710–711, 1939.

Kandel, E. R., J. H. Schwartz, and T. M. Jessell. *Principles of Neural Science*. New York: McGraw-Hill, 2000.

Katz, B. How cells communicate. In J. L. McGaugh, N. M. Weinberger, and R. H. Whalen, Eds. *Psychobiology: Readings from Scientific American*. San Francisco: W. H. Freeman and Company, 1972.

Penfield, W., and H. H. Jasper. *Epilepsy and the Functional Anatomy of the Human Brain*. Boston: Little, Brown, 1954.

Posner, M. I., and M. E. Raichle. *Images of Mind*. New York: W. H. Freeman and Company, 1994.

Shepherd, G. M. *Neurobiology*. New York: Oxford University Press, 1997.

Tinbergen, N. *The Animal in Its World*. London: Allen & Unwin, 1972.

Communication Between Neurons

In 1921, Otto Loewi conducted a now well known experiment on the control of heart rate, the design of which came to him in a dream. One night, having fallen asleep while reading a short novel, he awoke suddenly and completely, with the idea fully formed. He scribbled the plan of the experiment on a scrap of paper and went back to sleep. The next morning, he could not decipher what he had written, yet he felt it was important. All day he went about distracted, looking occasionally at his notes but wholly mystified about their meaning. That night he again awoke, vividly recalling the ideas in his previous night's dream. Fortunately, he still remembered them the next morning. Loewi immediately set up and successfully performed the experiment.

Loewi's experiment consisted of electrically stimulating a frog's vagus nerve, which leads from the brain to the heart, while the heart was immersed in a fluid-filled container. Meanwhile, the fluid in the container was channeled to a second container holding a second heart that Loewi did not stimulate electrically. As illustrated in Figure 5.1, the fluid simply flowed

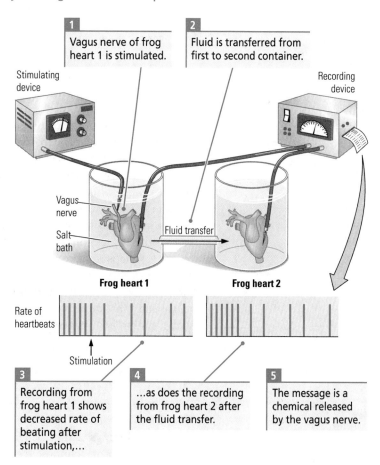

1 Vagus nerve of frog heart 1 is stimulated.

2 Fluid is transferred from first to second container.

Stimulating device

Recording device

Vagus nerve

Salt bath

Fluid transfer

Frog heart 1

Frog heart 2

Rate of heartbeats

Stimulation

3 Recording from frog heart 1 shows decreased rate of beating after stimulation,...

4 ...as does the recording from frog heart 2 after the fluid transfer.

5 The message is a chemical released by the vagus nerve.

Figure 5.1 Otto Loewi's 1921 experiment demonstrating neurotransmission. The vagus nerve leading to a frog heart maintained in a salt bath is electrically stimulated, decreasing the heart rate. Fluid from the bath is transferred to a second bath containing a second heart. The electrical recording from the second heart shows that its rate of beating also decreases. The experiment demonstrates that a chemical released from the vagus of the first heart can reduce the beating rate of the second heart.

from one container to the other through a tube. Loewi recorded the rate of beating of both hearts. The electrical stimulation decreased the rate of beating of the first heart, but what was much more important was that the fluid transferred from the first to the second container slowed the rate of beating of the second heart, too. Clearly, the fluid was somehow carrying a message about the speed at which to beat.

But where did the message originally come from? The only way that it could have gotten into the fluid was by a chemical released from the vagus nerve. This chemical must have dissolved into the fluid in sufficient quantity to influence the second heart. The experiment therefore demonstrated that the vagus nerve contains a chemical that tells the heart to slow its rate of beating. Loewi subsequently identified that chemical as acetylcholine (ACh).

In further experiments, Loewi stimulated another nerve, called the accelerator nerve, and obtained a speeding-up of heart rate. Moreover, the fluid that bathed the accelerated heart increased the rate of beating of a second heart that was not electrically stimulated. Loewi identified the chemical that carried the message to speed up heart rate as *epinephrine* (EP). Together, these complementary experiments showed that chemicals from the vagus nerve and the accelerator nerve modulate heart rate, with one inhibiting the heart and the other exciting it.

Chemicals that are released by a neuron onto a target are now referred to as **chemical neurotransmitters** or, simply, neurotransmitters. Neurons that release a chemical neurotransmitter of a certain type are named after that neurotransmitter. For example, neurons with terminals that release ACh are called acetylcholine neurons, and neurons that release EP are called epinephrine neurons. This naming of neurons by their chemical neurotransmitters helps to tell us something about the behavior in which the neuron takes part.

The synapse is the site where chemical communication by means of a neurotransmitter takes place. In this chapter, we examine, first, the general structure of synapses; second, the mechanisms that allow the release of a neurotransmitter into a synapse; and, third, the types of synapses that exist in the brain. We see how a group of neurons that all use the same neurotransmitter can constitute a system that mediates a certain aspect of behavior. When such a system is damaged, neurological disorders result.

The Structure of Synapses

Otto Loewi's discovery about the regulation of heart rate was the first of two important findings that provided the foundation for our current understanding of how neurons communicate. The second had to wait for the invention

(A)

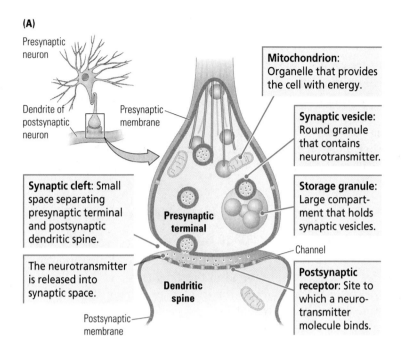

Presynaptic neuron

Dendrite of postsynaptic neuron

Presynaptic membrane

Mitochondrion: Organelle that provides the cell with energy.

Synaptic vesicle: Round granule that contains neurotransmitter.

Synaptic cleft: Small space separating presynaptic terminal and postsynaptic dendritic spine.

Presynaptic terminal

Storage granule: Large compartment that holds synaptic vesicles.

The neurotransmitter is released into synaptic space.

Dendritic spine

Channel

Postsynaptic receptor: Site to which a neurotransmitter molecule binds.

Postsynaptic membrane

(B)

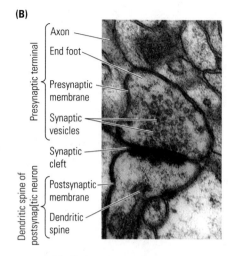

Presynaptic terminal

Dendritic spine of postsynaptic neuron

Axon

End foot

Presynaptic membrane

Synaptic vesicles

Synaptic cleft

Postsynaptic membrane

Dendritic spine

Figure 5.2 The major parts of a synapse. (A) The parts of this synapse are characteristic of most synapses. Note that vesicles in the terminal release the neurotransmitter into the synaptic cleft through exocytosis, and then the neurotransmitter binds to receptors on the postsynaptic membrane. (B) An electron photomicrograph of a synapse in which an axon terminal connects with a dendritic spine. Surrounding the centrally located synapse are other synapses, glial cells, axons, and dendrites. Round vesicles containing neurotransmitter substance are visible within the terminal. The dark material on the postsynaptic side of the synapse contains receptors and substances related to receptor function. (Photomicrograph courtesy of Jeffrey Kleim.)

of the electron microscope, which enabled scientists to see the structure of a synapse.

The first usable electron micrographs, made in the 1950s, revealed many of the structures of a synapse, such as the typical synapse seen in the center of the micrograph in Figure 5.2. The axon and its terminal are visible in the upper part of this photomicrograph; the dendrite is seen in the lower part. The round granular substances in the terminal are vesicles filled with neurotransmitter. The dark band of material just inside the dendrite contains the receptors for the neurotransmitter. The terminal and the dendrite do not touch but are separated by a small space.

The three main parts of a synapse, as illustrated in Figure 5.2, are an axon terminal, the membrane encasing the tip of an adjacent dendritic spine, and the very small space separating these two structures. That tiny space is called the **synaptic cleft.** The membrane on the tip of the dendritic spine is known as the **postsynaptic membrane.** The patch of dark material in the postsynaptic membrane consists largely of protein molecules specialized for receiving chemical messages. There are some dark patches in the **presynaptic membrane**— the membrane of the axon terminal—as well, but these patches are harder to see. They, too, consist largely of protein molecules, most of them serving as channels and pumps, although some are receptor sites. Within the axon terminal are many other specialized structures, including mitochondria (the organelles that supply the cell's energy needs) and round granules, called synaptic **vesicles,** that contain the chemical neurotransmitter. Some axon terminals have larger granules, called **storage granules,** which hold a number of synaptic vesicles. In the micrograph, you can also see that the synapse (located at the center) is closely surrounded by many other structures, including glial cells, other axons and dendritic processes, and other synapses.

Stages in Neurotransmission

Information is transmitted across a synapse in four basic steps: (1) the transmitter molecules are synthesized and stored in the axon terminal, (2) the transmitter is transported to the presynaptic membrane and released in response to an action potential, (3) the transmitter interacts with the receptors on the membrane of the target cell located on the other side of the synapse, and (4) the transmitter is inactivated (or it will continue to work indefinitely). These steps are illustrated in Figure 5.3.

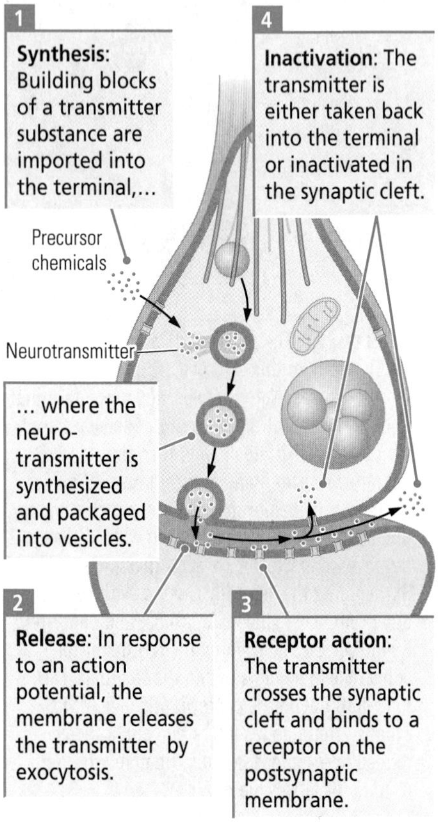

1

Synthesis: Building blocks of a transmitter substance are imported into the terminal,...

Precursor chemicals

Neurotransmitter

... where the neurotransmitter is synthesized and packaged into vesicles.

4

Inactivation: The transmitter is either taken back into the terminal or inactivated in the synaptic cleft.

2

Release: In response to an action potential, the membrane releases the transmitter by exocytosis.

3

Receptor action: The transmitter crosses the synaptic cleft and binds to a receptor on the postsynaptic membrane.

Figure 5.3 Steps in synaptic transmission in a generalized synapse.

Transmitter Synthesis and Storage

There are two basic paths for the manufacture of neurotransmitters. Some are manufactured in the axon terminal from building blocks derived from food. Transporter proteins in the cell membrane absorb the required precursor chemicals from the blood supply. (Sometimes these transporter proteins absorb entire, readymade neurotransmitters from the blood.) Mitochondria in the axon terminal provide the energy for the synthesis of these neurotransmitters from their precursor chemicals. Other neurotransmitters are manufactured in the cell body according to instructions contained in the neuron's DNA. These neurotransmitters are then packaged in membranes on the Golgi bodies and transported on microtubules to the axon terminal. There is also evidence that mRNA is transported to the synapse, where it serves as the message for the manufacture of a transmitter within the synapse, rather than in the ribosomes surrounding the nucleus. These two basic modes of synthesis, one in which the transmitter is synthesized or obtained from nutrient building blocks and one in which it is a protein derived from DNA, divide neurotransmitter substances into two large classes, as will be described in a later section of this chapter.

In the axon terminal, neurotransmitters manufactured in either of these ways are gathered in membranes that form synaptic vesicles. Synaptic vesicles are stored in three ways: (1) some are collected in storage granules, as mentioned earlier; (2) others are attached to the filaments in the terminal; and (3) still others are attached to the presynaptic membrane, ready for release into the synaptic cleft. When a vesicle is released from the presynaptic membrane, other vesicles move to take its place, so that they, too, are ready for release when needed.

Release of the Neurotransmitter

What, exactly, triggers the release of a synaptic vesicle and the spewing of its neurotransmitter into the synaptic cleft? The answer is an action potential. When an action potential is propagated on the presynaptic membrane, the voltage changes on the membrane set the release process in motion. Calcium

(Ca^{2+}) ions play an important role in these events. The presynaptic membrane is rich in voltage-sensitive calcium channels, and the surrounding extracellular fluid is rich in Ca^{2+}. As illustrated in Figure 5.4, the arrival of the action potential opens these voltage-sensitive calcium channels, allowing an influx of calcium into the axon terminal.

The incoming calcium ions bind to a chemical called **calmodulin,** forming a complex that participates in two chemical actions: one reaction releases vesicles bound to the presynaptic membrane, and the other releases vesicles bound to filaments in the axon terminal. The vesicles released from the presynaptic membrane empty their contents into the synaptic cleft through the process called **exocytosis,** in which the membrane surrounding the transmitter substances fuses with the membrane of the synapse. The vesicles that were formerly bound to the filaments are then transported to the membrane to replace the vesicles that were just released there.

Activation of Receptor Sites

When the neurotransmitter has been released from vesicles on the presynaptic membrane, it diffuses across the synaptic cleft and binds to specialized protein molecules imbedded in the postsynaptic membrane. These protein molecules are called **transmitter-activated receptors** or just receptors, because they receive the transmitter substance. The postsynaptic cell may be affected in one of three general ways, depending on the type of neurotransmitter and the kind of receptors on the postsynaptic membrane. First, the transmitter may depolarize the postsynaptic membrane and so have an excitatory action on the postsynaptic cell; second, the transmitter may hyperpolarize the postsynaptic membrane and so have an inhibitory action on the postsynaptic cell; or, third, the transmitter may initiate one of a wide variety of chemical reaction sequences that can cause morphological changes in the synapse, create new synapses, or bring about other changes in the cell. Later we describe the types of receptors that mediate these different effects.

In addition to acting on the postsynaptic membrane's receptors, a neurotransmitter may interact with receptors on the presynaptic membrane. That is, it may have an influence on the cell that just released it. The presynaptic receptors that a neurotransmitter may activate are called **autoreceptors** to indicate that they receive messages from their own axon terminal.

How much neurotransmitter is needed to send a message? In the 1950s, Bernard Katz and his colleagues provided an answer. Recording electrical activity from postsynaptic membranes in muscles, they detected small spontaneous depolarizations. They called these depolarizations **miniature postsynaptic potentials** (MPPs). The MPPs varied in size, but their size always appeared to be a multiple of the smallest potential. The researchers concluded that the smallest potential is produced by releasing the contents of just one synaptic vesicle. They called this amount of neurotransmitter a **quantum.** To

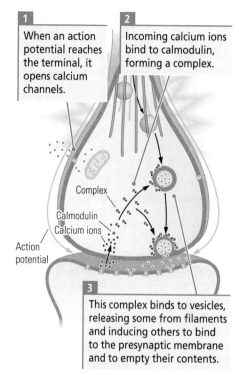

1 When an action potential reaches the terminal, it opens calcium channels.

2 Incoming calcium ions bind to calmodulin, forming a complex.

Complex

Calmodulin
Calcium ions

Action potential

3 This complex binds to vesicles, releasing some from filaments and inducing others to bind to the presynaptic membrane and to empty their contents.

Figure 5.4 Release of a transmitter. When an action potential reaches the terminal, it opens voltage-sensitive calcium (Ca^{2+}) channels. The extracellular fluid adjacent to the synapse has a high concentration of calcium ions that then flow into the axon terminal. The calcium binds to synaptic vesicles in the free vesicle pool to induce them to bind to the presynaptic membrane and expel their contents into the synaptic cleft. Calcium also binds to vesicles attached to filaments, freeing the vesicles so that they can move to the presynaptic membrane, where they are available for release.

produce a postsynaptic potential that has a major influence on the postsynaptic membrane, such as propagating an action potential, a presynaptic neuron must release many quanta simultaneously.

The results of subsequent experiments showed that the number of quanta released from the presynaptic membrane in response to a single action potential depends on two things. One is the amount of Ca^{2+} that enters the axon terminal in response to the action potential, and the other is the number of vesicles that are docked at the membrane, waiting to be released. Synapses that are put to frequent use, such as those that contract an exercised muscle, develop more Ca^{2+} and synaptic vesicles than do synapses that receive little use.

Deactivation of the Neurotransmitter

Chemical transmission would not be a very effective messenger system if the neurotransmitter molecules lingered within the synaptic cleft, continuing to occupy and stimulate receptors. If they did so, the postsynaptic cell could not respond to subsequent messages that the presynaptic cell might send. Therefore, after a neurotransmitter has done its work, it is removed quickly from receptor sites and from the synaptic cleft.

This removal of a neurotransmitter takes place in at least four ways. First, some of the neurotransmitter simply diffuses away from the synapse and is no longer available to bind to receptors. Second, the transmitter is inactivated or degraded by enzymes that are present in the synaptic cleft. Third, the transmitter may be taken back up into the axon terminal for subsequent reuse or the by-products of degradation by enzymes may be taken up into the terminal to be used again in the cell. The protein molecule responsible for this reuptake is a membrane pump or transporter. Fourth, some neurotransmitters are taken up by neighboring glial cells that also have appropriate transporters. The glial cells may contain enzymes that further degrade the transmitter to its constituent parts. The glial cells may export the transmitter or its parts back to neurons for reuse.

As already mentioned, an axon terminal has chemical mechanisms that enable the axon to regulate the amount of neurotransmitter in its terminal. If the terminal is not put to frequent use, enzymes located within it may break down excess transmitter. The by-products of this breakdown are then put to other uses or excreted from the cell. On the other hand, if the terminal is very active, the amount of neurotransmitter made and stored there increases. For example, intense physical exercise that creates a high demand for ACh at nerve–muscle junctions leads to an increase in the amount of ACh being produced in the terminals, thus preparing the terminals to respond to future high demands.

Types of Synapses

So far we have described a generic synapse, with features that most synapses possess. But actually there are many different kinds of synapses, specialized in regard to location, structure, and function.

Variations in Synaptic Connections

Figure 5.5 shows several kinds of synapses. In one kind, the axon terminal of a neuron meets a dendrite or dendritic spine of another neuron. Called an **axodendritic synapse,** it is the kind shown in Figure 5.2. Another kind of synapse with which you are already familiar is an **axomuscular synapse,** in which an axon synapses with a muscle, such as that studied by Otto Loewi.

The many other types of synapses include **axosomatic synapses,** in which an axon terminal ends on a cell body; **axoaxonic synapses,** in which an axon terminal ends on another axon; and **axosynaptic synapses,** in which an axon terminal ends at another synapse. Axon terminals that have no specific target but instead secrete their transmitter chemicals nonspecifically into the extracellular fluid are called **axoextracellular synapses.** In addition, there are **axosecretory synapses,** in which an axon terminal synapses with a tiny blood vessel called a capillary and secretes its transmitter directly into the blood. Finally, synapses need not include even a single axon terminal. Instead, dendrites may send messages to other dendrites through **dendrodendritic synapses.**

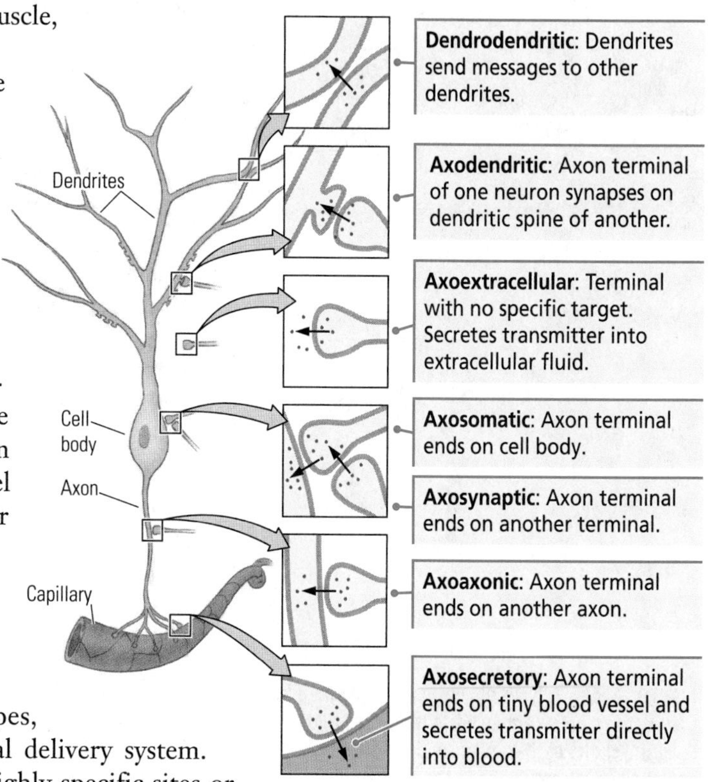

With this wide range of synaptic types, synapses are an extremely versatile chemical delivery system. They can deliver chemical transmitters to highly specific sites or distribute their messages more diffusely. For example, they can exercise direct control over the actions of a neuron by sending chemical transmitters to the dendrites, cell body, or axon. Through axosynaptic connections, they can also exert exquisite control over another neuron's input onto a cell. And, by excreting transmitters into extracellular fluid or into the blood, they can modulate the function of large areas of tissue or even of the entire body. In fact, many of the hormones that circulate in your blood and have widespread influences on your body are actually transmitters secreted by neurons.

Dendrodendritic: Dendrites send messages to other dendrites.

Axodendritic: Axon terminal of one neuron synapses on dendritic spine of another.

Axoextracellular: Terminal with no specific target. Secretes transmitter into extracellular fluid.

Axosomatic: Axon terminal ends on cell body.

Axosynaptic: Axon terminal ends on another terminal.

Axoaxonic: Axon terminal ends on another axon.

Axosecretory: Axon terminal ends on tiny blood vessel and secretes transmitter directly into blood.

Figure 5.5 Types of synapses in the central nervous system. An axon terminal can end on a dendrite, on another axon terminal, on a cell body, or on an axon. It may also end on a blood capillary or on muscles or end freely in the extracellular space. Additionally, dendrites may make synaptic connections with each other.

Excitatory and Inhibitory Messages

Despite the great variety of synapses and the many levels of control that the versatility of synapses implies, in the end they convey only two types of messages: excitatory or inhibitory. That is to say, a neurotransmitter either increases or decreases the probability that the cell with which it comes in contact will produce an action potential. In keeping with this dual message

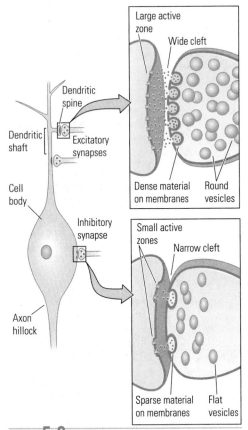

Figure 5.6 Two types of nervous system synapses. Excitatory synapses are found on the spines and dendritic shafts of the neuron, and inhibitory synapses are found on the neuron body. The structural features of excitatory and inhibitory synapses differ in the vesicles' shapes, the density of material on the presynaptic membrane, the cleft size, and the size of the postsynaptic active zone.

system, synapses can be divided into excitatory and inhibitory synapses. These two types of synapses vary both in location and in appearance. As shown in Figure 5.6, excitatory synapses are typically located on the shafts or the spines of dendrites, whereas inhibitory synapses are typically located on a cell body. Additionally, excitatory synapses have round synaptic vesicles, whereas the vesicles of inhibitory synapses are flattened. Furthermore, the material making up the presynaptic and postsynaptic membranes is denser at an excitatory synapse than it is at an inhibitory synapse, and the excitatory cleft is wider. Finally, the active zone on an excitatory synapse is larger than that on an inhibitory synapse.

The different locations of excitatory and inhibitory synapses divide a neuron into two zones: an excitatory dendritic tree and an inhibitory cell body. This arrangement suggests two alternate ways for excitatory and inhibitory messages to interact. One model pictures excitation coming in over the dendrites and spreading to the axon hillock, where it may trigger an action potential that travels down the length of the axon. If the message is to be stopped, the most efficient place to inhibit it is close to the axon hillock, the origin of the action potential. This model is one of excitatory–inhibitory interaction viewed from an inhibitory perspective, in which inhibition is defined as the blocking of excitation—essentially a "cut 'em off at the pass" strategy.

Another model of how these two kinds of messages might interact pictures excitatory stimulation as overcoming an otherwise constant state of inhibition. If the cell body is normally in an inhibited state, the only way for an action potential to be generated at the axon hillock is for the cell body's ongoing inhibition to be reduced. In this "open the gates" strategy, the excitatory message is like a racehorse ready to run down the track, but first the inhibition of the starting gate must be removed. Both types of mechanism probably exist in the nervous system, depending on the neural circuit and the behavior in question.

English neurologist John Hughlings-Jackson recognized an apparent pathological absence of inhibition in certain human neurological disorders, many of which are characterized by symptoms that seem to be "released" owing to the loss of a normal inhibitory influence. Hughlings-Jackson termed this process "release of function." In this situation, a given behavior is always ready to be produced but normally takes place only when inhibition is released. When the inhibitory mechanism is damaged, the behavior takes place continuously and is unwanted. An example is an involuntary movement, such as a tremor, called a **dyskinesia** (from the Greek *dys*, meaning "disordered," and *kinesia*, meaning "movement"). In a dyskinesia, something appears to be missing that would otherwise prevent the unwanted movement. Later on in this chapter, we will describe some other examples of released behavior.

Kinds of Neurotransmitters

In the 1920s, after Otto Loewi's discovery that excitatory and inhibitory chemicals control the heart's rate of beating, many researchers thought that the brain must work in much the same way. They assumed there must be excitatory and inhibitory brain cells and that epinephrine and acetylcholine were the transmitters through which these neurons worked. At that time, they could never have imagined what we know today: the human brain employs as many as 100 neurotransmitters to control our highly complex and adaptable behaviors. Although we are now certain of only about 50 substances that act as transmitters, we are in the midst of a research revolution in this field. Few scientists are willing to put an upper limit on the eventual number of transmitters that will be found. In this section, we describe how these neurotransmitters are identified and examine the categories of those currently known.

Identifying Neurotransmitters

Figure 5.7 shows four criteria for identifying neurotransmitters: (1) the chemical must be synthesized in the neuron or otherwise be present in it; (2) when the neuron is active, the chemical must be released and produce a response in some target cell; (3) the same response must be obtained when the chemical is experimentally placed on the target; and (4) there must be a mechanism for removing the chemical from its site of action after its work is done. By systematically applying these criteria, researchers can determine which of the many thousands of chemical molecules that exist in every neuron are neurotransmitters.

The criteria for identifying a neurotransmitter are relatively easy to apply to the peripheral nervous system, especially to the study of accessible nerve–muscle junctions, where there is only one main neurotransmitter, acetylcholine. But identifying chemical transmitters in the central nervous system is not so easy. In the brain and spinal cord, thousands of synapses are packed around every neuron, preventing easy access to a single synapse and its activities. Consequently, for many of the substances thought to be central nervous system neurotransmitters, the four criteria needed as proof have been only partly met. A chemical that is suspected of being a neurotransmitter but has not yet met all the proofs for one is called a *putative* (supposed) *transmitter.*

Acetylcholine was the first substance identified as a neurotransmitter in the central nervous system. This identification was greatly facilitated by a logical argument predicting its presence there even before experimental proof had been obtained. All of the motor neuron axons leaving the spinal cord contain acetylcholine, and each of these axons has an axon collateral within the spinal cord that synapses on a nearby interneuron that is part of the central nervous system. Because the main axon to the muscle

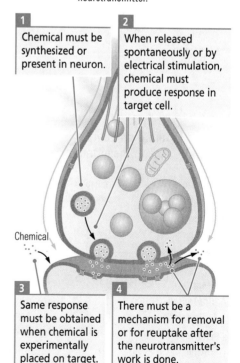

Figure 5.7 Four criteria for determining whether a chemical is a neurotransmitter.

1 Chemical must be synthesized or present in neuron.

2 When released spontaneously or by electrical stimulation, chemical must produce response in target cell.

Chemical

3 Same response must be obtained when chemical is experimentally placed on target.

4 There must be a mechanism for removal or for reuptake after the neurotransmitter's work is done.

releases acetylcholine, investigators suspected that its axon collateral also might release acetylcholine. It seemed unlikely that two terminals of the same axon would use different transmitters. Knowing what chemical to look for greatly simplified the task of finding it and then proving that it was in fact a neurotransmitter in this location, too. Incidentally, the loop formed by the axon collateral and the interneuron in the spinal cord acts as a feedback circuit that enables the motor neuron to inhibit itself and not become overexcited if it receives a great many excitatory inputs from other parts of the central nervous system.

Today the term neurotransmitter is used more broadly than when researchers first started trying to identify these chemicals. No longer limited to substances that carry a message from one neuron to another by influencing the voltage on the postsynaptic membrane, it also includes chemicals that have little effect on membrane voltage but instead induce effects such as changing the structure of a synapse. Furthermore, researchers have discovered that neurotransmitters communicate not only in the orthodox fashion, by delivering a message from the presynaptic side of a synapse to the postsynaptic side, but also, in some cases, in the opposite direction. To make matters even more complex, different kinds of neurotransmitters can coexist within the same synapse, raising the question of what exactly each contributes in relaying a message. To find out, researchers have to apply various transmitter cocktails to the postsynaptic membrane. Yet another complication is that some transmitters are gases and act so differently from a classic neurotransmitter such as acetylcholine that it is hard to compare the two. Because neurotransmitters are so diverse and work in such a variety of ways, the definition of what a transmitter is and the criteria used to identify one have become increasingly flexible in recent years.

Some order can be imposed on this confusing situation by classifying neurotransmitters into three groups on the basis of their composition: (1) small-molecule transmitters, (2) peptide transmitters (also called neuropeptides), and (3) transmitter gases. Here we briefly describe the major characteristics of each group and list some of the representative members.

Small-Molecule Transmitters

The first transmitters to be identified were **small-molecule transmitters,** one of which is acetylcholine. As the name of this category suggests, all these transmitters are small molecules. In most cases, they are synthesized and packaged for use in the axon terminals. When a small-molecule transmitter is released from an axon terminal, it can be quickly replaced at the presynaptic membrane. These transmitters also act relatively quickly compared with others.

Small-molecule transmitters or their main components are derived from the foods that we eat. Therefore, their levels and activities in the body can be influenced by diet. This fact is important in the design of drugs that affect the nervous system. Many of the neuroactive drugs are designed to reach the brain in the same way that small-molecule transmitters or their precursor chemicals do.

Table 5.1 lists some of the best known and most extensively studied small-molecule transmitters. In addition to acetylcholine, this list includes four amines,

Table 5.1 **Small-molecule neurotransmitters**

Transmitter	Abbreviation
Acetylcholine	ACh
Amines	
Dopamine	DA
Norepinephrine	NE
Epinephrine	EP
Serotonin	5-HT
Amino acids	
Glutamate	Glu
γ-Aminobutyric acid	GABA
Glycine	Gly
Histamine	H

which are chemicals that contain an amine group (—NH) in their chemical structure, and four amino acids that contain a carboxyl group (COO) in addition to an amine. A few other substances are sometimes classified as small-molecule transmitters. In the future, researchers are likely to find additional ones as well.

Some of the amines included in Table 5.1 are synthesized by the same biochemical pathway and so are related to one another. They are grouped together in the table. One such grouping consists of the amines **dopamine, norepinephrine,** and epinephrine (which, as you already know, is the excitatory transmitter in the heart). Figure 5.8 shows that epinephrine is the third transmitter produced by a single biochemical sequence. The precursor chemical is tyrosine, an amino acid that is abundant in food. The enzyme tyrosine hydroxylase changes tyrosine into L-dopa, which is sequentially converted by other enzymes into dopamine, norepinephrine, and finally epinephrine.

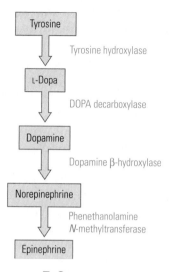

Figure 5.8 A single biochemical sequence produces three neurotransmitters: dopamine, noradrenaline, and epinephrine. A different enzyme is responsible for each synthetic step.

An interesting fact about this biochemical sequence is that the amount of the enzyme tyrosine hydroxylase in the body is limited and, consequently, so is the rate at which dopamine, norepinephrine, and epinephrine can be produced, regardless of how much tyrosine is present or ingested. This **rate-limiting factor** can be bypassed by orally ingesting L-dopa, which is why L-dopa is a medication used in the treatment of Parkinson's disease, a disease produced by an insufficiency of dopamine.

Two of the amino acid transmitters, **glutamate** and **gamma-aminobutyric acid** (GABA), also are closely related: GABA is formed by a simple modification of glutamate (Figure 5.9). These two transmitters are called "the work-horses of the nervous system" because so many synapses use them. In the forebrain and cerebellum, glutamate is the main excitatory transmitter and GABA is the main inhibitory transmitter. (The amino acid glycine is a much more common inhibitory transmitter in the brainstem and spinal cord.) Interestingly, glutamate is widely distributed in neurons, but it becomes a neurotransmitter only if it is appropriately packaged in vesicles in the axon terminal.

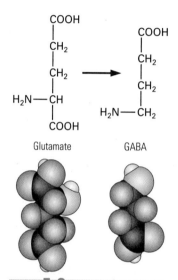

Figure 5.9 Glutamate, the major excitatory neurotransmitter in the brain, and γ-aminobutyric acid (GABA), the major inhibitory neurotransmitter in the brain, are related. The removal of the carboxyl (COOH) group from glutamate produces GABA. The space-filling models of the two neurotransmitters show that their shapes are different, thus allowing them to bind to different receptors.

Peptide Transmitters

The more than 50 known peptide transmitters—short chains of amino acids—have been grouped into the families listed in Table 5.2. As you learned in Chapter 3, amino acids link together by peptide bonds to form chains, which accounts for the name of this class of neurotransmitters. Peptide transmitters are made directly

Table 5.2 Peptide neurotransmitters

Family	Example
Opioids	Enkephaline, dynorphin
Neurohypophyseals	Vasopressin, oxytocin
Secretins	Gastric inhibitory peptide, growth-hormone-releasing peptide
Insulins	Insulin, insulin growth factors
Gastrins	Gastrin, cholecystokinin
Somatostatins	Pancreatic polypeptides

from instructions contained in the cell's DNA. Although in some neurons these transmitters are produced in the axon terminal, most are assembled on the cell's ribosomes, packaged inside a membrane by Golgi bodies, and transported on the microtubule highway to the axon terminals. The entire process of synthesis and transport is relatively slow compared with small-molecule transmitters. Consequently, once used, these transmitters are not replaced quickly.

Peptides have an enormous range of functions in the nervous system, as might be expected from the large number that are found there. They serve as hormones, are active in responses to stress, encourage a mother to bond to her infant, probably facilitate learning, help to regulate eating and drinking, and help to regulate pleasure and pain. For example, opium, obtained from seeds of the poppy flower, has long been known to both produce euphoria and reduce pain. Opium and a group of related synthetic chemicals, such as morphine, appear to mimic the actions of not one but three peptides: **Met-enkephalin, Leu-enkephalin,** and **β-endorphin.** (The term enkephalin derives from the phrase "in the cephalon," meaning "in the brain or head," whereas the term endorphin is a shortened form of "endogenous morphine.") A part of the amino acid chain is structurally similar in all three of these peptide transmitters. Presumably, opium mimics this part of the chain. The discovery of these naturally occurring opium-like peptides suggested that one or more of them might have a role in the management of pain. Opioid peptides, however, appear to have a number of functions in the brain and so may not just be pain-specific transmitters.

Unlike small-molecule transmitters, peptide transmitters do not bind to ion channels and so have no direct effects on the voltage of the postsynaptic membrane. Instead, peptide transmitters activate receptors that indirectly influence cell structure and function. Because peptides are amino acid chains that are degraded by digestive processes, they generally cannot be taken orally as drugs, unlike the small-molecule transmitters.

Transmitter Gases

The soluble gases **nitric oxide** (NO) and **carbon monoxide** (CO) are the most unusual neurotransmitters yet to have been identified. They are neither stored in synaptic vesicles nor released from them; instead, they are synthesized as needed. On synthesis, each gas diffuses away from the site where it was made, easily crossing the cell membrane and immediately becoming active.

Nitric oxide is a particularly important neurotransmitter because it serves as a messenger in many parts of the body. It controls the muscles in intestinal walls, and it dilates blood vessels in brain regions that are in active use (allowing these regions to receive more blood). It also dilates blood vessels in the genital organs and is therefore active in producing penile erections in males. Unlike classical neurotransmitters, nitric oxide is produced in many regions of a neuron, including the dendrites. The drug sildenafil citrate (trade name Viagra) is a widely used treatment for male erectile dysfunction and acts by enhancing the action of NO.

Types of Receptors for Neurotransmitters

When a neurotransmitter is released from a synapse, it crosses the synaptic cleft and binds to a receptor. What happens next depends on the kind of receptor. There are two general classes of receptors: ionotropic receptors and metabotropic receptors. Each produces a different effect on the postsynaptic membrane.

Ionotropic Receptors

Ionotropic receptors allow the movement of ions across a membrane (the suffix *tropic* means "to move toward"). As Figure 5.10 illustrates, an ionotropic receptor has two parts: a binding site for a neurotransmitter and a pore or channel. When the neurotransmitter attaches to the binding site, the receptor changes its shape, either opening the pore and allowing ions to flow through it or closing the pore and blocking the flow of ions. Because the binding of the transmitter to the receptor is quickly followed by a one-step response (the opening or closing of the receptor pore) that directly affects the flow of ions, ionotropic receptors bring about very rapid changes in membrane voltage.

Structurally, ionotropic receptors are similar to voltage-sensitive channels, discussed in Chapter 4. They are composed of a number of membrane-spanning subunits that form petals around the pore, which lies in the center. Within the pore is a shape-changing segment that causes the pore to open or close, which regulates the flow of ions through the pore.

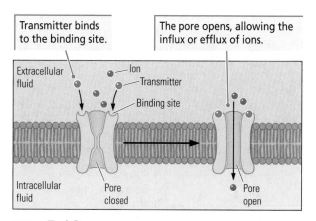

Figure 5.10 Ionotropic receptors are proteins that consist of two functional parts: a binding site and a pore. When a transmitter binds to the binding site, the shape of the receptor changes, opening or closing the pore. In the example shown here, when the transmitter binds to the binding site, the pore opens and ions are able to flow through it.

Metabotropic Receptors

In contrast with ionotropic receptors, a **metabotropic receptor** does not possess a pore of its own through which ions can flow, although it does have a binding site for a neurotransmitter. Through a series of steps, metabotropic receptors either produce changes in nearby ion channels or bring about changes in the cell's metabolic activity (that is, an activity that requires an expenditure of energy, which is what the term metabolic means).

Figure 5.11A shows the first of these two effects. The metabotropic receptor consists of a single protein, which spans the cell membrane. The outer part of the receptor is a site for transmitter binding, whereas the inner part translates the transmitter's message into biochemical activity within the cell. The internal part of a receptor is associated with one of a family of proteins called **guanyl nucleotide-binding proteins** (**G proteins** for short). A G protein consists of three subunits, one of which is the α subunit. When a neurotransmitter binds

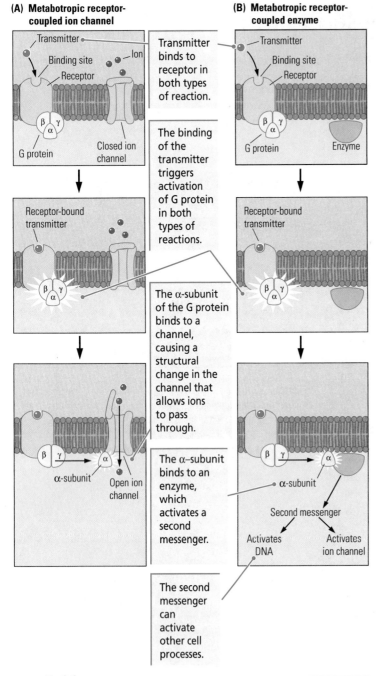

(A) Metabotropic receptor-coupled ion channel

Transmitter

Binding site

Receptor

Ion

G protein

Closed ion channel

Transmitter binds to receptor in both types of reaction.

Receptor-bound transmitter

The binding of the transmitter triggers activation of G protein in both types of reactions.

α-subunit

Open ion channel

The α-subunit of the G protein binds to a channel, causing a structural change in the channel that allows ions to pass through.

The α-subunit binds to an enzyme, which activates a second messenger.

The second messenger can activate other cell processes.

(B) Metabotropic receptor-coupled enzyme

Transmitter

Binding site

Receptor

G protein

Enzyme

Receptor-bound transmitter

α-subunit

Second messenger

Activates DNA

Activates ion channel

Figure 5.11 (A) A metabotropic receptor coupled to an ion channel has a binding site and is attached to a G protein. When a neurotransmitter binds to the binding site, the α subunit of the G protein detaches from the receptor and attaches to the ion channel, causing the channel to change its conformation so that—in this drawing—ions can flow through its pore. (B) A metabotropic receptor coupled to an enzyme also has a binding site and an attached G protein. When a neurotransmitter binds to the binding site, the α subunit of the G protein detaches and attaches to an enzyme. The enzyme then activates a compound called a second messenger, which initiates a series of biochemical steps that activate either ion channels or other cell processes (in some cases, the second messenger activates the cell's DNA).

to the G protein's associated metabotropic receptor, the α subunit detaches from the other two units and can then bind to other proteins within the cell membrane or within the cytoplasm of the cell. If the α subunit binds to a nearby ion channel in the membrane, the structure of the channel changes, modifying the flow of ions through it. If the channel is already open, the α subunit may close it or, if already closed, the α subunit may open it. This change in the channel and the flow of ions across the membrane influences the membrane's electrical potential.

The binding of a neurotransmitter to a metabotropic receptor can also trigger cellular reactions that are more complicated than the one shown in Figure 5.11A. These other reactions are summarized in Figure 5.11B. They all begin when the detached α subunit binds to an enzyme, which in turn activates another chemical called a **second messenger** (the neurotransmitter is the "first messenger"). A second messenger, as the name implies, carries a message to other structures within the cell. First, it can bind to a membrane channel, causing the channel to change its structure and thus alter ion flow through the membrane. Second, it can initiate a reaction that causes protein molecules within the cell to become incorporated into the cell membrane, as a result forming new ion channels. Third, it can send a message to the cell's DNA instructing it to initiate the production of a new protein.

No one neurotransmitter is associated with a single kind of receptor or a single kind of influence on the postsynaptic cell. At one location, a particular transmitter may bind to an ionotropic receptor and have an excitatory effect on the target cell. At another location, the same transmitter may bind to a metabotropic receptor and have an inhibitory influence. For example, acetylcholine has an excitatory effect on skeletal muscles, where it activates an ionotropic receptor; but it has an inhibitory effect on the heart, where it activates a metabotropic receptor. In addition, each transmitter may bind to a number of different kinds of ionotropic or metabotropic receptors. Elsewhere in the nervous system, acetylcholine, for example, may activate various versions of either type of receptor.

Neurotransmitter Functions

When Otto Loewi described acetylcholine as an inhibitory transmitter in the heart and epinephrine as an excitatory transmitter, the idea arose that these respective transmitters could be part of larger systems that were excitatory or inhibitory with respect to all behaviors. The notion that specific transmitters, wherever found, form systems with a common function has led to the notion that the nervous system could be divided into systems based on the neurotransmitter type. When researchers first began to study neurotransmitters, they also thought that any given neuron would contain only one transmitter at all of its axon terminals. This belief was called Dale's law, after its originator. New methods of staining neurochemicals, however, have revealed that Dale's law is an oversimplification. A single neuron may use one transmitter at one synapse and a different transmitter at another synapse, as David Sulzer and his coworkers have shown. Moreover, different transmitters may coexist in the same terminal or in the same synapse. For example, in some terminals, peptides have been found to coexist with small-molecule transmitters; and more than one small-molecule transmitter may be found in a single synapse. In some cases, more than one transmitter may even be packaged within a single vesicle.

All this complexity makes for a bewildering number of combinations of neurotransmitters and receptors for them. What are the functions of so many combinations? We do not have a complete answer. Very likely, however, this large number of combinations is critically related to the many different kinds of behavior of which humans are capable.

Fortunately, the study of neurotransmission can be simplified by concentrating on the dominant transmitter located within any given axon terminal. In most cases, the neuron and its dominant transmitter can then be linked to a certain kind of behavioral function. In this section, we describe some of the connections between neurotransmitters and behavior.

Some neurotransmitters in the central nervous system have very specific functions. For instance, a variety of chemical transmitters specifically prepare female white-tailed deer for the fall mating season. With the onset of winter, a different set of biochemicals takes on the new specific function of facilitating the development of the fetus. The mother gives birth in the spring and is subject to yet another set of biochemicals with highly specific functions, such as the chemical influence that enables her to recognize her own fawn and the one that enables her to nurse. The transmitters taking part in these very specific functions are usually neuropeptides.

In contrast, other neurotransmitters in the central nervous system have more general functions, helping an organism carry out routine daily tasks. These more general functions are mainly the work of small-molecule transmitters. For example, as already mentioned, the small-molecule transmitters

Cholinergic system (acetylcholine): Active in maintaining waking EEG patterns of the neocortex. Thought to play a role in memory by maintaining neuron excitability. Death of acetylcholine neurons and decrease in acetylcholine in the neocortex are thought to be related to Alzheimer's disease. (Receptor types: five types of muscarinic receptors, M1–M5; four subtypes of nicotinic receptors, N1–N4.)

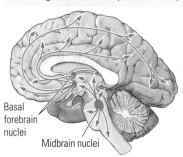

Basal forebrain nuclei

Midbrain nuclei

Adrenergic system (noradrenaline): Active in maintaining emotional tone. Decreases in noradrenalin activity thought to be related to depression, whereas increases in it are thought to be related to mania (excitable behavior). (Receptors: α1, α2, β1, β2).

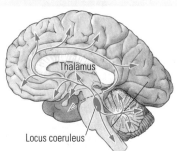

Thalamus

Locus coeruleus

Dopaminergic system (dopamine): Active in maintaining normal motor behavior. Loss of dopamine is related to Parkinson's disease, in which muscles are rigid and movement is difficult. Increases in dopamine activity may be related to schizophrenia. (Receptors: D1–D6.)

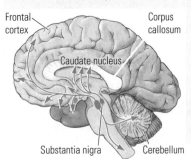

Frontal cortex

Corpus callosum

Caudate nucleus

Substantia nigra   Cerebellum

Serotonergic system (serotonin): Active in maintaining waking patterns of EEG activity. Increases in serotonin activity are related to obsessive compulsive disorders, tics, and schizophrenia. Decreases in serotonin activity are related to depression. (Receptors: 1A–1D, 2, 3, 1p.)

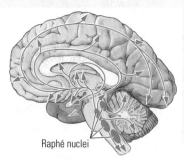

Raphé nuclei

GABA and glutamate are the most common neurotransmitters in the brain, with GABA having an inhibitory effect and glutamate an excitatory one.

Four other small-molecule transmitters—acetylcholine, dopamine, norepinephrine, and serotonin—seem to have the general function of ensuring that neurons in distant parts of the brain act in concert by being stimulated by the same neurotransmitter. The neurons containing these transmitters are commonly called **ascending activating systems.** They can be envisioned as something like the power supply to a house, in which a branch of the power line goes to each room of the house, but the electrical appliance powered in each room differs, depending on the room. We will describe this function in a little more detail.

The four ascending activating systems, classified by the dominant transmitter in their neurons, are the cholinergic, dopaminergic, noradrenergic, and serotonergic systems. Figure 5.12 shows the location of neurons in each of these four systems, with arrow shafts indicating the pathways of axons and arrow tips indicating axon terminals. The four ascending activating systems are similarly organized in that the cell bodies of their neurons are clustered together in only a few nuclei located in or near the brainstem, whereas the axons of the cells are widely distributed in the forebrain, brainstem, and spinal cord.

Figure 5.12 summarizes the behavioral functions as well as the brain disorders in which each of the four ascending activating systems has been implicated. The ascending cholinergic system contributes to the normal electrical activity of the cells of the cortex in an alert, mentally active person and so seems to play a role in normal wakeful behavior. People who suffer from Alzheimer's disease, which starts with minor forgetfulness and progresses to major memory dysfunction, show a loss of these cholinergic neurons at autopsy. One treatment strategy currently being pursued for Alzheimer's is to develop drugs that stimulate the cholinergic system to enhance behavioral alertness. The brain abnormalities associated with Alzheimer's disease are not limited to the cholinergic neurons, however. They also include

Figure 5.12 Four major nonspecific ascending systems. In all of these systems, the cell bodies are located in nuclei (ovals shown in color) in the brainstem. The axons of these neurons project diffusely to the forebrain, cerebellum, and spinal cord, where they synapse with most of the other neurons of the structure. Each system has been associated with one or more behaviors or nervous system diseases. Note: Numbers and letters are used in the names of many receptors.

extensive damage to the neocortex and other brain regions. As a result, the role played by the cholinergic neurons in the progress of the disorder is not yet clear. Perhaps their death causes degeneration in the cortex or perhaps the cause-and-effect relation is the other way around, with cortical degeneration being the cause of cholinergic cell death. Then, too, the loss of cholinergic neurons may be just one of many neural symptoms of Alzheimer's disease.

One function of the ascending dopaminergic system is an involvement in motor behavior. If dopamine neurons in the brain are lost, the result is a condition of extreme rigidity, in which opposing muscles are contracted, making it difficult for the person to move. Patients also show rhythmical tremors of the limbs. This condition is called Parkinson's disease. Although Parkinson's disease usually arises for no known cause, it can also be triggered by the ingestion of certain drugs, which suggests that those drugs act as selective poisons, or neurotoxins, to the dopamine neurons. The dopaminergic system also has an integral role in reward, in that many drugs that people abuse seem to act by stimulating it. In addition, this system is implicated in a condition called schizophrenia, one of the most common and debilitating psychiatric disorders. One explanation of schizophrenia is that the dopaminergic system is overactive.

Behaviors and disorders pertaining to the noradrenergic ascending system have been very difficult to identify. Some of the symptoms of depression may be related to decreases in the activity of norepinephrine neurons, whereas some of the symptoms of manic behavior (excessive excitability) may be related to increases in the activity of these same neurons.

Both the serotonergic ascending system and the cholinergic system work to produce a waking electroencephalogram (EEG) in the forebrain, but other behavioral functions of serotonin are not well understood. There is some evidence that certain symptoms of depression are related to decreases in the activity of serotonin neurons. Consequently, there may be two forms of depression, one related to norepinephrine and one related to serotonin. The results of other research suggest that some of the symptoms of schizophrenia may be related to serotonin. Again, the implication is that there may be different forms of schizophrenia.

Summary

Neurons communicate with one another by releasing chemicals at their terminals. A terminal forms a synapse, which consists of a presynaptic membrane, a space, and a postsynaptic membrane. A chemical is released by the terminal, crosses the synaptic space, and activates the postsynaptic membrane. On the postsynaptic membrane, the chemicals act on the receptors to activate or inhibit those neurons' electrical activity or to change their function in other ways. There are four general steps in transmitter action: synthesis, release, action, and reuptake of neurotransmitter substances. Drugs can influence each biochemical event. Thus, understanding how neurotransmitters work can be a source of insight not only into normal behavior but also into the mechanisms by which many drugs influence behavior. Likewise, a large number of diseases and other neurological conditions may have their bases in neurotransmitter malfunction. For example, acetylcholine, dopamine, norepinephrine, and serotonin nonspecific systems have each been associated with different brain diseases. Their treatment also is thus facilitated by an understanding of neurotransmitter function.

References

Cooper, J. R., F. E. Bloom, and R. H. Roth. *The Biochemical Basis of Neuropharmacology.* New York: Oxford University Press, 2002.

Hebb, D. O., *The Organization of Behavior.* New York: Wiley, 1949.

Kandel, E. *Cellular Basis of Behavior.* San Francisco: W. H. Freeman and Company, 1976.

Kandel, E. R., J. H. Schwartz, and T. M. Jessell. *Principles of Neural Science.* New York: Elsevier North Holland, 2000.

Sulzer, D., M. P. Joyce, L. Lin, D. Geldwert, S. N. Haber, T. Hatton, and S. Rayport. Dopamine neurons make glutamatergic synapses in vitro. *Journal of Neuroscience* 18:4588–4602, 1998.

The Influence of Drugs on Behavior

During the first 4 days of July 1982, a 42-year-old man used 4.4 grams of a new synthetic heroin. The substance was injected intravenously three or four times daily and caused a burning sensation at the site of injection. The immediate effects were different from heroin, producing an unusual "spacey" high as well as transient visual distortions and hallucination. Two days after the final injection, he awoke to find that he was "frozen" and could move only in "slow motion." He had to "think through each movement" to carry it out. He was described as stiff, slow, nearly mute, and catatonic during repeated emergency room visits from July 9 to July 11. He was admitted to a psychiatric service on July 15, 1982, with a diagnosis of "catatonic schizophrenia" and was transferred to our neurobehavioral unit the next day. (Ballard et al., 1985, p. 949)

This patient was one of seven young adults who were hospitalized at about the same time in California, all showing symptoms of Parkinson's disease, which is extremely unusual in people of their age. One of the paradoxes of drug use, researchers have discovered, is that subtle variations in the synthesis of well-known compounds can have entirely unexpected consequences. Heroin is a derivative of opium, which has been used as a therapeutic and recreational drug for centuries. Although highly addictive, heroin is a dependably effective treatment for severe pain and is not known to produce any kind of brain injury. Nevertheless, in the case just cited, a contaminant produced by a slight error in heroin synthesis produced a compound called MPTP that acts as a selective neurotoxin, attacking the cells of the substantia nigra and producing a relatively instantaneous condition of Parkinson's disease (a condition usually associated with aging) in the user.

Researchers began to use MPTP for producing experimental Parkinson's disease in animals in the search for cures and treatments for the disease. This research led to the finding that inserting dopamine-producing cells into rodents' brains could reverse some of the symptoms of the disorder. Then, in 1988, the patient just described was taken to Lund, Sweden, where fetal dopamine cells were inserted into his caudate and putamen region. Twenty-four months after the surgery, he was improved and could function more independently. He could dress and feed himself, visit the bathroom without help, and make trips outside his home.

In this chapter, we define the term "drug," describe how drugs enter the body and are eventually metabolized, and examine the effects of psychoactive drugs on the nervous system and behavior.

Routes of Drug Administration

A **drug** is a chemical compound that is administered to bring about some desired change in the body. Usually drugs are used to diagnose, treat, or prevent illness, to relieve pain and suffering, or to improve some adverse physiological condition. On the other hand, throughout human history, they have also been used as food substances and for recreation and even as poisons. Today they are also used as research tools.

The kinds of drugs that we mainly cover in this chapter are **psychoactive drugs**—substances that act to alter mood, thought, or behavior and are used to manage neuropsychological illness. Many psychoactive drugs are also *abused substances*. That is, people take them for nonmedical reasons to the point at which their functioning becomes impaired. Many psychoactive drugs produce addiction. Some can also act as toxins, producing sickness, brain damage, or death.

To be effective, a psychoactive drug has to reach its target in the nervous system. The way in which a drug enters and passes through the body to reach that target is called its *route of administration*. Many drugs are administered orally—the most natural and generally the safest way to consume a substance. Drugs can also be inhaled, administered through rectal suppositories, absorbed from patches applied to the skin, or injected into the bloodstream, into a muscle, or even into the brain.

These different routes pose different barriers through which a drug must pass to reach its target (Table 6.1). Taking a drug by mouth is easy and convenient, but not all drugs can withstand the acidity of the gastric secretions or are able to penetrate the digestive-tract walls. Generally, there are fewer barriers between a drug and its target if the drug is inhaled rather than swallowed, and fewer still if it is injected into the blood. The fewest obstacles are encountered if a drug is injected directly into the brain.

To reach the bloodstream, an ingested drug must first be absorbed through the lining of the stomach or small intestine. If the drug is liquid, it is absorbed more readily than if it is a solid. Drugs taken in solid form are not absorbed unless they can be dissolved by the stomach's gastric juices. Absorption is also affected by other physical and chemical properties of the drug, as well as by the presence of other stomach

Table 6.1 Characteristics that allow drugs to pass through barriers in the body

Barrier	Drug characteristic
Stomach	Drugs that are weak acids are absorbed from the stomach and enter the bloodstream.
Intestine	Drugs that are weak bases are absorbed by the intestine and enter the bloodstream.
Bloodstream	Drugs that are hydrophilic or are bound to proteins to make them hydrophilic can be carried in the blood; however, such proteins may be too large to pass through capillary pores.
Extracellular fluid	Drugs not bound to a protein may be small enough to pass through capillary pores and enter the extracellular fluid.
Blood–brain barrier	Drugs must be water soluble to pass through capillary pores and must be fat soluble to pass through the glial cell membrane encasing the capillaries.
Cell membrane	Drugs must be fat soluble or must be carried into the cell by a membrane transporter.

or intestinal contents. In general, if a drug is a weak acid, such as alcohol, it is readily absorbed across the stomach lining. If it is a weak base, it cannot be absorbed until it passes through the stomach and into the intestine—by which time the digestive juices may have destroyed it.

After absorption by the stomach or intestine, the drug must next enter the bloodstream. This part of the journey presents a different set of barriers. Blood has a high water concentration, and so a drug must be hydrophilic to mix with it. A hydrophobic substance will be blocked from entering the bloodstream. If a drug does make its way into the circulatory system, it becomes diluted by the blood's 6-liter volume.

To reach a neurological target, a drug must also travel from the blood into the extracellular fluid. This part of the journey requires that molecules of the drug be small enough to pass through the pores of capillaries, the tiny vessels that carry blood to the body's cells. Even if the drug makes this passage, it encounters other obstacles to effectiveness. For one thing, the extracellular fluid's roughly 35 liters of water dilute the drug even further. For another, the drug is at risk of being modified or destroyed by various metabolic processes taking place in the cells.

The Blood–Brain Barrier

In the brain, the passage of drugs across capillaries is much more difficult than elsewhere in the body because of the **blood–brain barrier.** The problem (for the drug) is not that the brain is deficient in capillaries. The brain has a rich capillary network. In fact, none of its neurons is farther than about 50 µm (1 micrometer is one-millionth of a meter) away from a capillary. But capillaries in the brain are impermeable to many substances, and this impermeability creates the blood–brain barrier.

Figure 6.1 shows the structure of brain capillaries, whose walls, as in all capillaries, are composed of a single layer of **endothelial cells.** In most parts of the body, substances can enter and exit the capillaries by passing through the clefts between these cells. In the brain, however, at least in most parts of it, the endothelial cells are fused together to form **tight junctions;** so molecules of most substances cannot squeeze between them.

Figure 6.1 also shows that the endothelial cells of a brain capillary are surrounded by end feet of astrocyte glial cells, covering about 80% of the capillary's outer surface. The glial end feet play only minor roles in the blood–brain barrier. The glial cells' main function is to provide a route for the exchange of food and waste between the capillaries and the brain's extracellular fluid and from there to other cells; but they may also play a role in maintaining the tight junctions

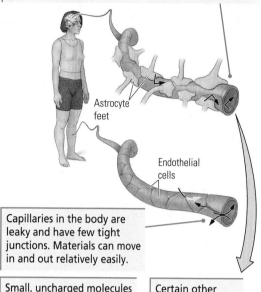

Capillaries in the brain are not leaky, have tight junctions, and are covered with astrocyte feet. These properties prevent materials from moving in and out easily, and are the basis of the blood–brain barrier.

Astrocyte feet

Endothelial cells

Capillaries in the body are leaky and have few tight junctions. Materials can move in and out relatively easily.

Small, uncharged molecules are able to pass through the endothelial membrane and reach the brain.

Certain other molecules are carried across the the membrane by active transport.

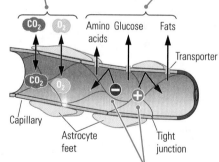

Large and electrically charged molecules are unable to pass out of the capillary.

Figure 6.1 The blood–brain barrier. Capillaries in the periphery of the body allow substances to pass between the capillary cell walls, but capillaries in the brain are made of cells with tight junctions and are blanketed by astrocytes. Some substances, such as oxygen and carbon dioxide, can travel freely across this blood–brain barrier. Some other substances, such as amino acids, glucose, and fats, must be transported through it. Most other substances, especially large charged molecules, are unable to cross at all.

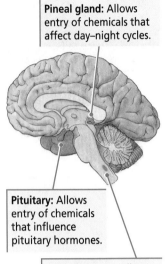

Pineal gland: Allows entry of chemicals that affect day–night cycles.

Pituitary: Allows entry of chemicals that influence pituitary hormones.

Area postrema: Allows entry of toxic substances that induce vomiting.

Figure 6.2 Three sites in the brain that have no blood–brain barrier. The median eminence of the pituitary is a target of many blood-borne hormones; the pineal gland is a target for hormones that affect behavioral rhythms; and the area postrema initiates vomiting of noxious substances.

between endothelial cells and in making capillaries dilate to increase blood flow to areas of the brain in which neurons are very active.

Many substances—for instance, oxygen, glucose, and amino acids (the building blocks of proteins)—must routinely travel from the blood to brain cells, just as carbon dioxide and other waste products must routinely be excreted from brain cells into the blood. There are two ways that molecules of these substances cross the blood–brain barrier. First, small molecules such as oxygen and carbon dioxide, which are not ionized and so are fat soluble, can pass right through the capillary wall. Second, molecules of glucose, amino acids, and other nutrients can be carried across the capillary by **active-transport systems.** These systems are pumps, such as the sodium–potassium pump described in Chapter 4, that are specialized for the transport of a particular substance.

There are a few brain regions that lack tight junctions between the cells of capillary walls and so lack a blood–brain barrier. These regions are shown in Figure 6.2. One is the **median eminence** of the hypothalamus, constructed to allow the passage of hormones into the pituitary gland. Another is the **area postrema** of the lower brainstem. The absence of a blood–brain barrier there allows toxic substances in the blood to trigger a vomiting response. The **pineal body** also lacks a blood–brain barrier and is therefore open to the hormones that modulate the day–night cycles controlled by this structure.

To summarize, drugs that can make the entire trip from the mouth to the brain have certain chemical properties. The most effective consist of molecules that are small in size, weakly acidic, water and fat soluble, potent in small amounts, and not easily degraded.

Given the many obstacles that psychoactive drugs encounter on their journey from the mouth to the brain, it is clear why inhaling a drug or injecting it into the bloodstream has advantages. These alternative routes of administration bypass the obstacle of the stomach. In fact, with each obstacle eliminated on the route to the brain, the dosage of a drug can be reduced by a factor of 10 and the drug will still have the same effects. For example, 1 milligram (1000 µg) of amphetamine, a psychomotor stimulant, produces a noticeable behavioral change when ingested orally. If inhaled into the lungs or injected into the blood, thereby circumventing the stomach, 100 µg of the drug (1000 µg ÷ 10) produces the same results. Similarly, if amphetamine is injected into the cerebrospinal fluid, thereby bypassing both the stomach *and* the blood, 10 µg is enough to produce an identical outcome, as is 1 µg if dilution in the cerebrospinal fluid also is skirted and the drug is injected directly onto target neurons. These numbers are well known to users of illicit drugs. Drugs that can be inhaled or injected intravenously are much cheaper to use because the doses required are smaller than those needed for drugs taken by mouth.

Metabolism

Soon after a drug is administered, the body begins to remove it. Drugs are metabolized throughout the body, but particularly in the kidneys, liver, and bile. They are excreted in urine, feces, sweat, breast milk, and exhaled air.

Drugs manufactured for therapeutic purposes are usually designed so as to optimize their chances of reaching their targets and to prolong their survival in the body.

There are some other substances, however, that the body has trouble removing. Such substances are potentially dangerous because, if large doses of them are taken, they can build up in the body and become poisonous. For instance, certain metals, such as mercury, are not easily eliminated from the body and, when they accumulate there, they can cause severe neurological problems.

Drug Actions in Synapses

Most psychoactive drugs work by influencing the chemical reactions at synapses. To understand their psychoactive effects, we must therefore explore the ways in which they modify synaptic activity.

Steps in Synaptic Transmission

Figure 6.3 summarizes the seven major events that contribute to synaptic neurotransmission. The first, synthesis of the neurotransmitter, can take place in the cell body, the axon, or the terminal. The neurotransmitter is then stored (event number 2) in storage granules or in vesicles until it is released (number 3) from the terminal's presynaptic membrane. The amount of transmitter released into the synapse is regulated by the effects of previous experience. When released, the transmitter acts on a receptor (number 4) embedded in the postsynaptic membrane. It is then either destroyed (number 5) or taken back into the terminal from which it came for reuse (number 6). The synapse also has mechanisms for degrading excess neurotransmitter (number 7) and removing unneeded by-products from the synapse.

Each of these components of neurotransmission entails one or more chemical reactions that drugs can potentially influence in one of two ways: either increasing the effectiveness of neurotransmission or diminishing it. Drugs that increase the effectiveness of neurotransmission are called **agonists,** whereas those that decrease its effectiveness are called **antagonists.** Agonists and antagonists can work in a variety of ways, but their end results are always the same. For example, all drugs that stimulate the release of the neurotransmitter dopamine, or block the reuptake of dopamine, or block dopamine's inactivation are considered dopamine agonists because they all increase the amount of dopamine available in the synapse. Conversely, all drugs that block the synthesis of dopamine or its release from the presynaptic membrane or that block dopamine receptors or speed up dopamine's inactivation are considered dopamine antagonists because they all decrease the biochemical effect of this transmitter in the synapse.

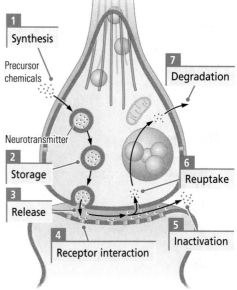

Figure 6.3 Seven points at which a drug can influence synaptic transmission. In principle, drugs could enhance or block a chemical process at any of these stages, reducing or enhancing synaptic transmission.

1 Synthesis

Precursor chemicals

7 Degradation

Neurotransmitter

2 Storage

6 Reuptake

3 Release

4 Receptor interaction

5 Inactivation

Examples of Drug Action: An Acetylcholine Synapse

Figure 6.4 uses the acetylcholine synapse between motor neurons and muscles to show how several representative drugs and toxins affect neurotransmission. Some of these drugs will be new to you, but you have probably heard of others. Knowing their effects at the synapse will enable you to understand the behavioral effects that they produce.

Two of the substances named in Figure 6.4 are toxins—black widow spider venom and botulinum toxin—that influence the release of acetylcholine from the axon terminal. **Black widow spider venom** is an agonist because it promotes the release of acetylcholine. In the insects on which black widow spiders prey, the excitation caused by excess acetylcholine at neuromuscular synapses is sufficient to cause paralysis and death. Fortunately, a black widow spider bite does not contain enough toxins to similarly affect a human. **Botulinum toxin** is a poisonous agent produced by a bacterium that sometimes grows in improperly processed canned foods. The toxin acts as an antagonist because it blocks the release of acetylcholine. The effects of botulinum poisoning can last from weeks to months. A severe case can result in paralysis of movement and breathing, leading to death. It might surprise you to know that this poison has medical uses. If injected into a muscle, it paralyzes that muscle, blocking unwanted muscular twitches or contractions in conditions such as cerebral palsy, and it is used in cosmetic surgery to reduce wrinkles.

Figure 6.4 also includes two drugs that act on receptors for acetylcholine: nicotine and curare. **Nicotine,** one of the chemicals in cigarette smoke, acts as an agonist to stimulate cholinergic receptors. Its molecular structure is enough like that of acetylcholine to fit into the receptors' binding sites. **Curare,** on the other hand, acts as an antagonist. It, too, occupies cholinergic receptors but, rather than activating them, curare simply blocks them, preventing acetylcholine from acting on them. When introduced into the body, curare acts quickly and is then cleared from the body in minutes. Large doses of it, however, arrest movement and breathing long enough to result in death. Early explorers of South America encountered Indians along the Amazon River who killed small animals by using arrows coated with curare prepared from the seeds of a plant. The hunters themselves did not become poisoned when eating the animals, because ingested curare cannot pass from the gut into the body. Many curare-like drugs have been synthesized. Some are used to briefly paralyze large animals so that they can be tagged for identification or examined. Skeletal muscles are more sensitive to curare-like drugs than respiratory muscles are; so an appropriate dose will paralyze an animal's movement but still allow it to breathe.

A fifth drug action shown in Figure 6.4 is that of physostigmine, which inhibits cholinesterase, the enzyme that breaks down acetylcholine. Physostigmine therefore acts as an agonist to increase the amount of acetylcholine available in the synapse. Physostigmine, obtained from a species of African bean, was used as a poison by tribes in Africa. Large

Figure 6.4 Examples of drugs that affect the cholinergic synapse. Agonists increase the effect of acetylcholine on the postsynaptic receptor, whereas antagonists decrease its effect. Note the many different ways that drugs can accomplish these results by acting on synthesis, affecting release, affecting binding to the postsynaptic receptor, or affecting inactivation.

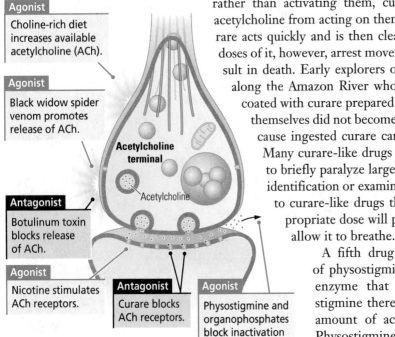

Agonist
Choline-rich diet increases available acetylcholine (ACh).

Agonist
Black widow spider venom promotes release of ACh.

Acetylcholine terminal

Acetylcholine

Antagonist
Botulinum toxin blocks release of ACh.

Agonist
Nicotine stimulates ACh receptors.

Antagonist
Curare blocks ACh receptors.

Agonist
Physostigmine and organophosphates block inactivation of ACh.

doses can be toxic because they produce excessive excitation of the neuro-muscular synapse and so disrupt movement and breathing. In small doses, however, physostigmine is used to treat a condition called myasthenia gravis (the name means "muscular weakness") in which muscle receptors are less than normally responsive to acetylcholine. The action of physostigmine is short-lived, lasting from only a few minutes to at most half an hour, but another class of compounds, called **organophosphates,** bind irreversibly to acetylcholinesterase and consequently are extremely toxic. Many insecticides are organophosphates. Organophosphates are also used in chemical warfare.

If a drug or toxin that is ingested affects neuromuscular synapses, will it also affect acetylcholine synapses in the brain? That depends on whether the substance can cross the blood–brain barrier, which depends in turn on the size and structure of the substance's molecules. Some of the drugs that act on acetylcholine synapses at the muscles—physostigmine and nicotine, for example—do cross the blood–brain barrier and act on acetylcholine synapses in the brain. Curare, on the other hand, cannot and therefore has no psychoactive effects.

Classification of Psychoactive Drugs

It has been difficult to devise a classification system for the many thousands of psychoactive drugs. Classification based on a drug's chemical structure has not been very successful, because drugs with similar structures can have quite different effects, whereas drugs with different structures can have effects that are very similar. Classification schemes based on receptors in the brain also have been problematic, because a single drug can act on many different receptors. The same problem exists with classification systems based on the neurotransmitter that a drug affects, because many drugs act on more than one transmitter. The classification system used in this book, summarized in Table 6.2, divides drugs into seven classes, according to the most pronounced psychoactive effect that a drug produces. The classes are further divided into subcategories containing from a few to many thousand different chemicals.

Drugs that are used to treat neuropsychological illness are listed in Table 6.3, along with the dates of their discovery and the names of their discoverers. The therapeutic action of every drug in Table 6.3 was originally discovered by accident and is still not fully understood. Nevertheless, scientists and pharmaceutical companies have developed many forms of each drug in attempts to increase effectiveness and reduce side effects. At the same time, experimental researchers have been working to explain each drug's action on the nervous system. Those efforts are examined here.

Table 6.2 Classification of psychoactive drugs

I.   Sedative hypnotics and antianxiety agents
     Barbiturates (anesthetic agents), alcohol
     Benzodiazepines: diazepam (Valium)

II. Antipsychotic agents
     Phenothiazines: chlorpromazine
     Butyrophenones: haloperidol

III. Antidepressants
     Monoamine oxidase (MAO) inhibitors
     Tricyclic antidepressants: imipramine (Tofranil)
     Atypical antidepressants: fluoxetine (Prozac)

IV. Mood stabilizers
     Lithium

V.   Narcotic analgesics
     Morphine, codeine, heroin

VI. Psychomotor stimulants
     Cocaine, amphetamine, caffeine, nicotine

VII. Psychedelics and hallucinogens
     Anticholinergics: atropine
     Noradrenergics: mescaline
     Serotonergics: LSD (lysergic acid diethylamide), psilocybin
     Tetrahydrocannabinol: marijuana

Table 6.3 Drugs used for the treatment of mental illness

Illness	Drug class	Representative drug	Common trade name	Discoverer
Schizophrenia	Phenothiazines	Chlorpromazine	Largactile, Thorazine	Jean Delay and Pierre Deniker (France), 1952
	Butyrophenone	Haloperidol	Haldol	Paul Janssen (Belgium), 1957
Depression	Monoamine oxidase (MAO) inhibitors	Iproniazid	Marsilid	Nathan S. Kline and J. C. Saunders (United States), 1956
	Tricyclic antidepressants	Imipramine	Tofranil	Roland Kuhn (Switzerland), 1957
	Selective serotonin reuptake inhibitors	Fluoxetine	Prozac	Eli Lilly Company, 1986
Bipolar disorder		Lithium (metallic element)		John Cade (Australia), 1949
Anxiety disorders	Benzodiazepines	Chlordiazepoxide	Valium, Miltown	Leo Sternbach (Poland), 1940
		Meprobamate	Equanil	Frank Berger and William Bradley (Czechoslovakia), 1946

Sedative-Hypnotics and Antianxiety Agents

The effects of sedative-hypnotics ("sedate," to make sleepy, and "hypnotic," to put to sleep) and antianxiety agents differ, depending on dose, as shown in Figure 6.5. At low doses, they reduce anxiety; at medium doses, they sedate (that is, they have a tranquilizing effect); and, at high doses, they produce anesthesia or coma. At very high doses, they can kill.

The most common members of this diverse group of drugs are **alcohol, barbiturates,** and **benzodiazepines.** Alcohol is well known to most people because it is so widely consumed, both as a beverage and an intoxicant. Its potentially devastating effects on fetuses produce a syndrome of retardation called fetal alcohol syndrome (FAS). Barbiturates are sometimes prescribed as a sleeping medication, but they are mainly used to induce anesthesia before surgery. Benzodiazepines, also known as **minor tranquilizers** or **antianxiety agents,** are often given to people who are having trouble coping with some major life stress, such as a traumatic accident or a death in the family. An example is the widely prescribed drug called Valium. Whereas both alcohol and barbiturates can produce sleep, anesthesia, and coma at doses only slightly higher than those that produce sedation, the dose of benzodiazepines that produces sleep and anesthesia is substantially higher than that which is needed to relieve anxiety.

A characteristic feature of sedative-hypnotics is that they cause weaker and weaker responses in the user who takes repeated doses. A larger dose is then required to produce the drug's initial effect. This lessening of response to a drug over time is called **tolerance. Cross-tolerance** results when the tolerance that develops for one drug carries over to a different drug. Cross-tolerance suggests that the two drugs are similar in their actions on the nervous system. That alcohol, barbiturates, and benzodiazepines show cross-tolerance alerted researchers to the likelihood that they affect a common nervous system tar-

Figure 6.5 This continuum of behavioral sedation shows how increasing doses of sedative-hypnotic drugs affect behavior, with low doses reducing anxiety and very high doses resulting in death.

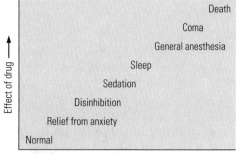

Death
Coma
General anesthesia
Sleep
Sedation
Disinhibition
Relief from anxiety
Normal

Effect of drug →

Increasing dose of sedative-hypnotic drug ⟶

get. This common target is now known to be the molecule containing a receptor site for the major inhibitory neurotransmitter γ-aminobutyric acid (GABA). Neurons that contain GABA are widely distributed in the nervous system and function to inhibit the activity of other neurons.

One of the receptors affected by GABA is the **GABA$_A$ receptor.** As illustrated in Figure 6.6, this receptor controls a chloride channel, and excitation of the receptor produces an influx of Cl$^-$ ions. Remember that an influx of Cl$^-$ ions increases the concentration of negative charges on the inside of the cell membrane, hyperpolarizing the membrane and thus making it less likely to propagate an action potential. GABA, therefore, produces its inhibitory effect by decreasing a neuron's rate of firing.

The GABA$_A$ receptor is a complex molecule that not only possesses a binding site for GABA but has two other important binding sites as well. One of the two binding sites accepts alcohol and barbiturates (the sedative-hypnotic site), whereas the other site accepts benzodiazepines (the antianxiety site). Drugs binding to the sedative-hypnotic site directly increase the influx of chloride ions and so produce the same effect as that of GABA. Consequently, the higher the dose of these drugs, the greater their inhibitory effect on neurons. The effect of antianxiety drugs is different. Excitation of the antianxiety site enhances the binding of GABA to its receptors, which means that the availability of GABA determines the potency of an antianxiety drug. Because GABA is very quickly reabsorbed by the neurons that secrete it and by surrounding glial cells, GABA concentrations are never excessive; as a result, people are generally unlikely to overdose on antianxiety drugs.

Scientists do not know what natural substances other than GABA bind to the GABA$_A$ receptor binding sites. Morrow and her coworkers suggest that a natural brain steroid called allopregnanolone may bind to the sedative-hypnotic site. Allopregnanolone is produced by activation of the pituitary. Thus, an additional mechanism by which alcohol may produce its effects is by facilitating the production of allopregnanolone, which in turn activates the sedative-hypnotic site of the GABA$_A$ receptor, producing sedation. One explanation of why alcohol has a less potent effect on human males than on females is that females have higher levels of allopregnanolone, thus making them more sensitive to the effects of alcohol and causing them to drink less and to be less likely to become alcoholic.

Because of their different actions on the GABA$_A$ receptor, sedative-hypnotic and antianxiety drugs should never be taken together. A sedative-hypnotic acts like GABA but, unlike GABA, is not quickly absorbed by surrounding cells. Instead, it remains on the site, allowing its effects to be enhanced by an antianxiety drug. The cumulative action of the two drugs will therefore exceed the individual action of either one. Even small combined doses of antianxiety and sedative-hypnotic drugs can produce coma or death.

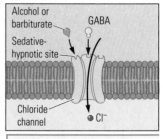

Binding of sedative-hypnotic drugs (such as alcohol or barbiturates) act like GABA, causing increased chloride conductance.

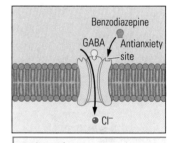

Binding of antianxiety drugs (benzodiazepines) enhances binding effects of GABA, increasing Cl$^-$ conductance.

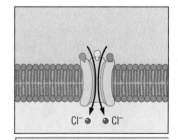

Because of their different actions, these drugs should never be taken together. Combined doses can cause coma or death, because they allow too much Cl$^-$ to enter the cell.

Figure 6.6 Sedative hypnotics bind to the GABA$_A$ receptor. Barbiturates and alcohol bind to one receptor site, the sedative-hypnotic site, and thus mimic the effects of GABA. Benzodiazepines bind to a different receptor site, the antianxiety site, and potentiate the action of GABA. Note that sedative-hypnotics bind at one site on the receptor, antianxiety agents at another, and GABA at yet another.

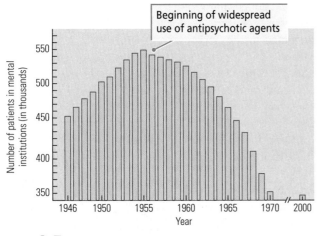

Figure 6.7 Numbers of resident patients in state and local government mental hospitals in the United States from 1946 to 2000. Note the dramatic decrease in the total patient population that began after 1955, when the therapeutic use of psychoactive drugs was introduced. (After Efron, 1968.)

Antipsychotic Agents

The term **psychosis** refers to various neuropsychological conditions, such as schizophrenia, that are characterized by hallucinations or delusions. Drugs used to treat psychosis are known as antipsychotic agents (also **major tranquilizers** and neuroleptics). The use of these agents has greatly reduced the number of patients held in mental institutions, as Figure 6.7 shows. Improving the functioning of schizophrenics has been a particularly important achievement because the incidence of schizophrenia is high—about 1 in every 100 people.

Although major tranquilizers have been widely used for nearly 50 years, their therapeutic actions are still not understood. One effect that all have in common is an immediate reduction of motor activity, which helps to alleviate the excessive agitation of some schizophrenic patients. Unfortunately, one of their negative side effects can be to produce symptoms reminiscent of Parkinson's disease, in which control over movement is impaired. With prolonged use, they can cause **dyskinesia** (involuntary movements). This condition includes rhythmical movements of the mouth, hands, and other body parts. The effects are usually reversible if the person stops taking the drug.

At least part of the action of antipsychotic drugs is to block one kind of dopamine receptor, called the **D_2 receptor.** This action of antipsychotic drugs led to the **dopamine hypothesis of schizophrenia.** It holds that some forms of schizophrenia may be related to excessive dopamine activity, which antipsychotic drugs control. Other support for the dopamine hypothesis comes from the schizophrenia-like symptoms of chronic users of amphetamine, a stimulant drug. As Figure 6.8 shows, amphetamine is a dopamine agonist that fosters the release of dopamine from the presynaptic membrane of dopamine synapses and blocks the reuptake of dopamine from the synaptic cleft. If amphetamine causes schizophrenia-like symptoms by increasing dopamine activity, perhaps naturally occurring schizophrenia is related to excessive dopamine action, too.

Even though such drug effects suggest that the dopamine hypothesis may have merit, consistent dopamine-related differences between normal people and schizophrenics have not been found in experimental

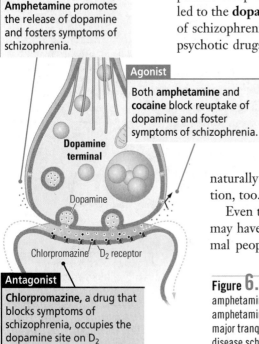

Agonist

Amphetamine promotes the release of dopamine and fosters symptoms of schizophrenia.

Agonist

Both **amphetamine** and **cocaine** block reuptake of dopamine and foster symptoms of schizophrenia.

Dopamine terminal

Dopamine

Chlorpromazine D_2 receptor

Antagonist

Chlorpromazine, a drug that blocks symptoms of schizophrenia, occupies the dopamine site on D_2 receptor, preventing receptor activation by dopamine.

Figure 6.8 Chlorpromazine blocks D_2 dopamine receptors, whereas the stimulant drug amphetamine causes the release of dopamine from the axon terminal. Both cocaine and amphetamine block the transporter that takes dopamine back into the terminal. Evidence that major tranquilizers, such as chlorpromazine, are helpful in treating the neuropsychiatric disease schizophrenia and that abuse of the stimulant drugs amphetamine and cocaine can produce schizophrenia-like behavior suggests that excessive activity at the dopamine receptor is related to schizophrenia.

studies. Compared with the brains of normal subjects, Kestler and colleagues found that the brains of patients with schizophrenia do not contain a greater number of dopamine synapses, do not release more dopamine from presynaptic membranes, and do not necessarily possess more D_2 receptors for dopamine. Consequently, the cause of schizophrenia and the mechanism by which antipsychotic agents work currently remain unclear.

Antidepressants

Depression is a common psychological disorder. At any given time, about 5% of the adult population worldwide suffer from it, and as many as 30% of all people may experience at least one episode of depression in their lives. Most people recover from depression within a year of its onset; but, if the condition is left untreated, the incidence of suicide is high. Two different types of drugs have antidepressant effects: the **monoamine oxidase inhibitors** (MAO inhibitors) and the **tricyclic antidepressants.** The so-called **second-generation antidepressants,** which include fluoxetine (Prozac), are similar to the tricyclic antidepressants.

Antidepressants are thought to act by improving chemical transmission in serotonin, noradrenaline, histamine, and acetylcholine synapses, and perhaps in dopamine synapses, too. Figure 6.9 shows their action at a serotonin synapse, the synapse on which most antidepressant research is focused. As you can see, MAO inhibitors and the tricyclic and second-generation antidepressants have different mechanisms for increasing the availability of serotonin. Monoamine oxidase is an enzyme that breaks down serotonin within the axon terminal. The inhibition of MAO by an MAO inhibitor therefore provides more serotonin for release with each action potential. The tricyclic antidepressants and the second-generation antidepressants block the transporter that takes serotonin back into the axon terminal. The second-generation antidepressants are thought to be especially selective in blocking serotonin uptake, and consequently some are also called **selective serotonin uptake blockers.** Because the transporter is blocked, serotonin remains in the synaptic cleft for a longer period, thus prolonging its action on postsynaptic receptors.

These discoveries notwithstanding, there are significant questions concerning how antidepressants work. For example, the drugs begin to affect synapses very quickly, and yet their antidepressant effects take weeks to develop. No one is sure why. In addition, about 20% of patients with depression fail to respond to antidepressant drugs.

Antidepressant side effects constitute another type of problem. These side effects include increased anxiety, sexual dysfunction, sedation, dry mouth, blurred vision, and memory impairments. Many people hoped that

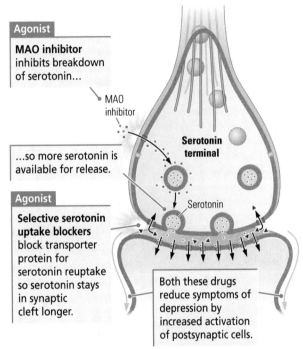

Agonist

MAO inhibitor inhibits breakdown of serotonin...

MAO inhibitor

Serotonin terminal

...so more serotonin is available for release.

Agonist

Selective serotonin uptake blockers block transporter protein for serotonin reuptake so serotonin stays in synaptic cleft longer.

Serotonin

Both these drugs reduce symptoms of depression by increased activation of postsynaptic cells.

Figure 6.9 Postulated mechanisms of action of antidepressant drugs on the serotonin synapse. MAO inhibitors block MAO from breaking down serotonin within the terminal. Reuptake blockers block the transporter protein that takes serotonin back up into the terminal after use. Thus, both types of drugs result in increased levels of serotonin available to act on serotonin receptors.

the second-generation antidepressants would produce fewer side effects than the tricyclic antidepressants, but that hope has not been fully realized. In fact, most antidepressants do not appear to be particularly selective in their action on the brain. Even Prozac, one of the more selective antidepressant compounds, is advertised as a treatment not only for depression but for obsessive-compulsive disorder, too. The major symptoms of obsessive-compulsive disorder are obsessive thoughts and behaviors, such as ideas that people cannot get out of their heads and ritual-like actions that they perform endlessly. Although obsessive-compulsive disorder, like depression, is associated with guilt and anxiety, most experts consider it to be a separate disorder.

Narcotic Analgesics

The **narcotic analgesics** are drugs with sleep-inducing (narcotic) and pain-relieving (analgesic) properties. Many of these drugs are derived from **opium,** an extract of the seeds of the opium poppy, *Papaver somniferum.* Opium has been used for thousands of years to produce euphoria, analgesia, sleep, and relief from diarrhea and coughing.

In 1805, German chemist Friedrich Sertürner synthesized two pure substances from the poppy plant—**codeine** and **morphine**—both of which demonstrated narcotic properties. Codeine is often included in cough medicine and in pain relievers such as aspirin (although not in the United States). Morphine, which was named after Morpheus, the Greek god of dreams, is a very powerful pain reliever. Despite decades of research, no other drug has been found that exceeds morphine's effectiveness as an analgesic. Opium antagonists such as **nalorphine** and **naloxone** block the actions of morphine and so are useful in treating overdoses of it. **Heroin,** another opiate drug, can be synthesized from morphine. It is more fat soluble than morphine is and penetrates the blood–brain barrier more quickly, allowing it to produce very rapid relief from pain. Although heroin is legal in some countries, it is illegal in others, including the United States.

What are the mechanisms through which opiates act on the central nervous system? In the 1970s, Pert and her colleagues provided an important part of the answer to this question by injecting radioactive opiates into the brain and identifying special receptors to which the opiates bound. But what were these receptors doing in the brain? Opiates, such as morphine, after all, are not naturally occurring brain chemicals. This question was answered at about the same time by Hughes and his coworkers, who identified two short peptides that had opioid properties and that appeared to be neurotransmitters. They called these opiate-like transmitters **endorphins,** an abridgement of the phrase *end*ogenous *morphin*elike substances.

We now know that there are endorphin-containing neurons in many brain regions and that morphine is similar enough to endorphins to mimic their action in the brain. Researchers have extensively studied whether endorphins can be used to relieve pain. The answer, so far, is mixed. Although endorphins do alleviate pain, they are not easily delivered to the brain. Consequently, morphine remains a preferred pain treatment.

Stimulants

Stimulants are a diverse class of drugs that increase the activity of neurons in a number of ways. They are subdivided into four groups: behavioral stimulants, convulsants, general stimulants, and psychedelic drugs.

Behavioral stimulants are drugs that cause an increase in motor behavior, as well as elevating a person's mood and level of alertness. Two examples are **cocaine** and **amphetamine.** Cocaine is extracted from the Peruvian coca shrub. The indigenous people of Peru originally discovered it in coca leaves, which they chewed. Purified cocaine can be taken either by sniffing (snorting) or by injection. Many cocaine users do not like to inject cocaine intravenously, and so they sniff a highly concentrated form of it called "crack." Crack is chemically altered so that it vaporizes at low temperatures, and the vapors are inhaled. Amphetamine is a synthetic compound that was discovered in attempts to synthesize the neurotransmitter epinephrine. Both amphetamine and cocaine are dopamine agonists that act by blocking dopamine transport back into the terminal, leaving more dopamine available in the synaptic cleft. Amphetamine also stimulates the release of dopamine from presynaptic membranes. Both these mechanisms increase the amount of dopamine available in synapses to stimulate dopamine receptors.

Cocaine was originally popularized as an antidepressant by Viennese psychoanalyst Sigmund Freud. In an 1884 paper titled "In Praise of Coca," Freud concluded that "The main use of coca will undoubtedly remain that which the Indians have made of it for centuries: it is of value in all cases where the primary aim is to increase the physical capacity of the body for a given short period of time and to hold strength in reserve to meet further demands—especially when outward circumstances exclude the possibility of obtaining the rest and nourishment normally necessary for great exertion." Freud also recommended that cocaine be used as a local anesthetic.

Cocaine was once widely used in soft drinks and wine mixtures, which were promoted as invigorating tonics. It is responsible for the origin of the trade name Coca-Cola, because this soft drink once contained cocaine, as suggested by the ad in Figure 6.10. The addictive properties of cocaine soon became apparent, however. There is also evidence that cocaine can produce circulatory disturbances, some of which can result in sudden death. Nevertheless, cocaine did prove to be valuable as a local anesthetic, and many derivatives, such as Novocaine, are used for this purpose today.

Amphetamine was first used as a treatment for asthma. A form of amphetamine, Benzedrine, was sold in inhalers as a nonprescription drug through the

Figure 6.10 Cocaine was once used as an ingredient in drinks such as Coca-Cola and Vin Mariani that promised to boost the user's energy. (The Granger Collection.)

1940s. Soon people discovered that they could open the container and swallow its contents to obtain a sudden energizing effect. In 1937, an article in the *Journal of the American Medical Association* reported that Benzedrine tablets improved performance on mental-efficiency tests. This information was quickly disseminated among students, who began to use the drug when studying for exams. Amphetamine was widely used in World War II to help keep troops and pilots alert and to improve the productivity of wartime workers. It was also used as a diet aid. In the 1960s, drug users discovered that they could obtain an immediate pleasurable "rush," often described as a whole-body orgasm, by intravenous injection of amphetamine. People who took amphetamine in this way, called "speed freaks," would inject the drug every few hours for days, remaining in a wide-awake, excited state without eating. They would then crash in exhaustion and hunger and, after a few days of recovery, would begin the cycle again. One explanation for repeated injections was to prevent the depressive crash that occurred when the drug wore off.

General stimulants are drugs that cause a general increase in the metabolic activity of cells. A widely used stimulant of this type is caffeine. **Caffeine** inhibits an enzyme that ordinarily breaks down the important regulatory biochemical cyclic adenosine monophosphate (cyclic AMP). The resulting increase in cyclic AMP leads to an increase in glucose production within cells, thus making available more energy and allowing higher rates of cellular activity.

The final class of stimulants, **psychedelic drugs,** alter sensory perception and cognitive processes. There are four major groups of psychedelics. One group consists of acetylcholine psychedelics, which either block or facilitate transmission at acetylcholine synapses in the brain. A second is made up of norepinephrine psychedelics. These drugs include **mescaline,** obtained from the peyote cactus, which is legal for use by Native Americans for religious practices.

A third type of psychedelic drug is tetrahydrocannabinol, or THC. Tetrahydrocannabinol is the active ingredient in marijuana, which is obtained from the hemp plant *Cannabis sativa.* There is growing evidence that *Cannabis* acts on two receptors, called the CB1 and CB2 receptors, thought by scientists to be the receptors for an endogeneous neurotransmitter called anandamide. Surprisingly, the results of numerous studies suggest that anandamide plays a role in forgetting, a mechanism that prevents memory systems of the brain from being overwhelmed by the information to which the brain is exposed each day. Thus, THC may have a detrimental effect on memory.

The fourth and last subtype in this drug category consists of the serotonin psychedelics. They include both LSD **(lysergic acid diethylamide)** and **psilocybin** (obtained from a certain mushroom). These drugs are thought to affect the activity of the serotonin synapses of serotonin neurons. In addition, these drugs may affect other transmitter systems, including norepinephrine.

The Effects of Experience, Context, and Genes

Many behaviors trigger consistently predictable results. When you strike the same key of a piano repeatedly, you hear the same note each time. When you flick a light switch over and over again, the same bulb goes on exactly as before. This kind of cause-and-effect consistency, to which we are exposed every-day, leads some people to assume that a drug will produce the same results every time it is taken. That assumption is incorrect, however, for several reasons. For one thing, the effect of a drug may change from one administration to another because the drug is taken in different contexts, with different accompanying behaviors that cause the brain to respond to it differently. In addition, the actions of a drug on one person may be quite different from its actions on someone else. The reason is that previous experience and the influence of genes also determine drug reactions. Finally, with repeated use, the effect of a drug can be dramatically different from the effect obtained with the first use. The reason for this difference is that many drugs produce an enduring change in the brain that over time can be quite substantial and that can alter what subsequent doses do. In the following sections, we describe a number of ways that repeated use of drugs changes the brain and behavior.

Tolerance

Isbell and coworkers described a dramatic example of tolerance—the decline in response to the repeated administration of a drug—in a group of prisoners who had volunteered for the study. These researchers gave subjects enough alcohol daily in a 13-week period to keep them in a constant state of intoxication. Yet they found that the subjects did not stay drunk for 3 months straight. In the first days of the experiment, all of the subjects showed rapidly rising levels of blood alcohol and behavioral signs of intoxication after consuming alcohol, as shown in Figure 6.11. Between the 12th and 20th days, however, blood-alcohol concentrations and the signs of intoxication fell to very low levels, even though the subjects maintained a constant alcohol intake. Interestingly, too, although blood-alcohol levels and signs of intoxication fluctuated in subsequent days of the study, the one did not always correlate with the other. A relatively high blood-alcohol level was sometimes associated with a low outward appearance of being drunk. Why?

These results were likely the products of three different kinds of tolerance—metabolic tolerance, cellular tolerance, and learned tolerance. **Metabolic tolerance** consists of an increase in the enzymes needed to break down alcohol in the liver, blood, and brain. As a result, the body metabolizes alcohol more quickly, and so blood alcohol levels are reduced. **Cellular tolerance** consists of adjustments in the activities of brain cells so as to minimize the effects of alcohol in the blood. This kind of tolerance helps explain why the behavioral signs of intoxication may be very low despite a relatively high blood-alcohol level. **Learned tolerance** also contributes to the drop in outward signs of intoxication. As people learn to cope with the daily demands of

Figure 6.11 Relative change in intoxication, blood-alcohol level, and alcohol intake in subjects over 20 days of steady drinking. Note that, as alcohol intake increases initially, so do blood-alcohol level and the degree of intoxication. With continued consumption, blood-alcohol level and behavioral intoxication decrease, owing to tolerance. (After H. Isbell, H. F. Fraser, A. Winkler, R. E. Belleville, and A. J. Eisenman. 1955. An experimental study of the etiology of "rum fits" and delirium tremens. *Quarterly Journal of Studies on Alcohol* 16, p. 16.)

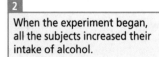

1 Subjects were given alcohol every day for 13 weeks—enough to keep them intoxicated.

2 When the experiment began, all the subjects increased their intake of alcohol.

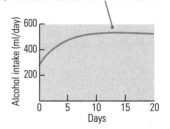

3 After 15–20 days of alcohol consumption, blood-alcohol levels began to fall,...

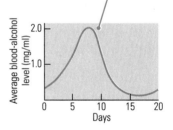

4 ...and the signs of intoxication fell, too.

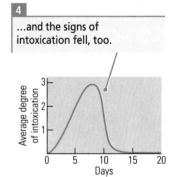

5 Because of tolerance, much more alcohol was required by the end of the study to obtain the same level of intoxication that was produced at the beginning.

living while under the influence of alcohol, they may no longer appear to be drunk.

The results of many studies confirm that learning plays a role in tolerance to alcohol. For instance, Wenger and his coworkers trained rats to walk on a narrow conveyor belt to prevent electric shock to their feet from a grid over which the belt was traveling. One group of rats received alcohol after having been trained to walk on the belt, whereas another group received alcohol just before their training sessions. A third group received training only, and a fourth group alcohol only. After several days of exposure to their respective conditions, all groups were given alcohol before a walking test. The rats that had previously received alcohol before training performed well, whereas those that had received training and alcohol separately performed just as poorly as those that had never had alcohol before or those that had never been trained. Apparently, animals can acquire the motor skills needed to balance on a narrow belt even when intoxicated with alcohol. Over time, in other words, they can learn to compensate for being drunk.

Tolerance can develop to many other drugs besides alcohol, such as barbiturates, amphetamines, and narcotics. In humans, for instance, a dose of 100 mg of morphine is sufficient to cause profound sedation and even death in some first-time users, but those who have developed tolerance to this drug have been known to take 4000 mg without adverse effects. Similarly, long-time users of amphetamine may need to take doses 100 or more times as great as the doses that they initially took to produce the same behavioral effect. In other words, with repeated administration of a drug, the effect produced by the drug may progressively diminish owing to tolerance.

Sensitization

Exposure to the same drug more than once doesn't always result in tolerance. Sometimes people show the opposite reaction, *increasing* their response with subsequent doses taken. This increased responsiveness to successive equal doses of a drug is called **sensitization.** Whereas tolerance generally develops with constantly repeated use of a given drug, sensitization is much more likely to develop with occasional use.

To demonstrate sensitization, Robinson and Becker isolated rats in observation boxes and recorded their reactions to an injection of amphetamine, paying particular attention to increases in sniffing, rearing, and walking, which are typical rat responses to this drug. Every 3 or 4 days, the investigators repeated the procedure. The results are given in Figure 6.12A. They show that the rats' level of activity increased to a new high level with each periodic trial. This increased response on successive tests was not due to the animals becoming "comfortable" with the test situation. Control animals that received no drug did not display a similar escalation in sniffing, rearing, and walking. Moreover, the sensitization to amphetamine was enduring. Even when two injections of amphetamine were separated by months, the animals still showed an increased response to the drug.

Sensitization also develops with depressant drugs, such as the major tranquilizer Flupentixol, which is a dopamine antagonist that blocks dopamine receptors. Figure 6.12B shows the changing effects of Flupentixol on the swimming behavior of rats in a study conducted by Whishaw and his colleagues. The researchers trained the rats to swim a short distance to a platform in a swimming pool. When the rats were reaching the platform within 1 to 2 seconds of immersion, they were given an injection of Flupentixol. On the first few swims after the injections, the rats swam normally; but, in subsequent trials, they began to slow down. After about 12 trials separated by a few minutes, they simply sank when placed in the water and had to be removed to prevent them from drowning. This effect was not simply the result of administering 12 successive trials on the same day. If the rats were injected and placed in water only once each day for 12 days, the same pattern of results was obtained. On the first few days, the rats swam normally, but thereafter they began to slow down, until by the 12th day they simply sank after being injected and placed in the water. Sensitization to the drug was dependent on the number of trials regardless of the time that elapsed between them or the number of times that the drug was given. Presumably, Flupentixol changes dopamine neurons that mediate the behavior in which the rat is engaging.

Sensitization is difficult to demonstrate in an animal that is tested in its home cage. Animals are accustomed to performing a certain repertoire of behaviors in their home environments and are unlikely to change that behavior even under the influence of a drug. When animals are placed in a novel environment, however, and given widely spaced injections of a drug, their responses to the drug can

(A) Procedure #1

In the Robinson and Becker study, animals were given periodic injections of the same dose of amphetamine. Then the researchers measured the number of times the rat reared in its cage.

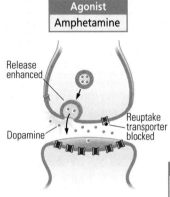

Agonist
Amphetamine

Release enhanced

Dopamine

Reuptake transporter blocked

Results #1

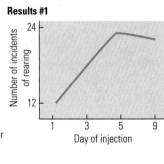

Number of incidents of rearing

Day of injection

Conclusion #1

Sensitization, as indicated by increased rearing, develops with periodic repeated injections.

(B) Procedure #2

In the Whishaw study, animals were given different numbers of swims after being injected with Flupentixol. Then the researchers measured their speed to escape to a platform in a swimming pool.

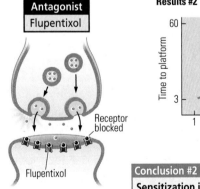

Antagonist
Flupentixol

Receptor blocked

Flupentixol

Results #2

Time to platform

Number of trials

Conclusion #2

Sensitization is also dependent on the occurrence of the behavior. The number of swims, not the spacing of swims or the treatment, causes an increase in the time it takes for the rat to reach the platform.

Figure 6.12 Two examples of sensitization. (A) Amphetamine stimulates dopamine release and blocks reuptake. Each injection of the same dose of the drug in rats produces a greater effect as measured by an increase in locomotion. (B) Flupentixol blocks dopamine receptors. After each injection, a swimming trial is slower until the rat can no longer escape from the swimming pool. (After Robinson and Becker, 1986, and Whishaw et al., 1989.)

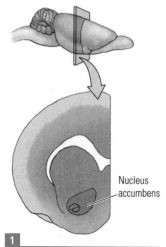

Nucleus accumbens

1

Animals received multiple doses of amphetamine. Neurons were drawn from the nucleus accumbens.

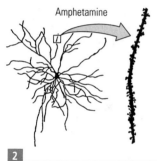

Amphetamine

2

Rats that show sensitization to amphetamine have increased dendritic growth and spine density...

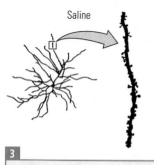

Saline

3

...relative to saline-treated rats.

4

The sensitization induced by repeated exposure to amphetamine changes the structure of neurons in certain brain areas.

Figure 6.13 Neurons in the nucleus accumbens of saline- and amphetamine-treated rats. Rats that show sensitization to amphetamine (or cocaine) undergo increased dendritic growth and increased spine density in comparison with saline-treated rats. Repeated exposure to psychoactive stimulant drugs thus alters the structure of cells in the brain. (After T. E. Robinson and B. Kolb. 1997. Persistent structural adaptations in nucleus accumbens and prefrontal cortex neurons produced by prior experience with amphetamine. *Journal of Neuroscience* 17, p. 8495.)

be seen to increase. Presumably, humans, too, will show sensitization to a drug when they take it periodically and in novel circumstances.

Because sensitization is long lasting, it is reasonable to ask whether it is accompanied by structural changes in the brain. Robinson and his colleagues found a dramatic increase in dendritic growth and spine density in rats that were sensitized to amphetamine or cocaine relative to rats that received injections of a saline solution. Figure 6.13 compares the effects of amphetamine and saline treatments on cells in the nucleus accumbens. Neurons in the amphetamine-treated brains can be seen to have more dendritic branches and an increased number of spines. These plastic changes were not found throughout the brain, however. Rather they were limited to regions of the brain that receive a large dopamine projection, as the nucleus accumbens and frontal cortex do (see Figure 3.14, bottom).

Addiction and Dependence

Substance abuse is a pattern of drug use in which people rely on a drug chronically and excessively, allowing it to occupy a central place in their lives. A more advanced state of drug abuse is **substance dependence,** also popularly known as **addiction.** People who are substance dependent have developed a **physical dependence** on a drug in addition to abusing it. They need to take the drug to feel normal. This physical dependence is usually accompanied by tolerance to the drug, and so the user requires increased doses to obtain the desired effect. The person may also experience unpleasant, sometimes dangerous **withdrawal symptoms** if he or she suddenly stops taking the drug. These symptoms can include muscle aches and cramps, anxiety attacks, sweating, nausea, and, for some drugs, even convulsions and death. Withdrawal symptoms can begin within hours of the last dose of a drug and tend to intensify for several days before they subside.

Many different kinds of drugs are abused or cause addiction, including sedative-hypnotics, antianxiety agents, narcotics, and stimulants. Drugs that are abused have a property in common: they produce psychomotor activation over some part of their dose range. That is, at certain levels of consumption, these drugs make the user feel energetic and in control. This common effect has led to the hypothesis that abused drugs may all act on the same target in the brain. One proposed target is the dopamine system, because stimulation of dopamine neurons is associated with psychomotor activity. Brain imaging of subjects who have taken nicotine shows that many brain regions display increased activity under the drug, including the nucleus accumbens, amygdala, the thalamus, and the prefrontal cortex (see this Snapshot on page 135). All of these structures receive projections from dopamine neurons.

Imaging the Effects of Nicotine

Cigarette smoking is the most common substance-abuse disorder and the leading preventable cause of death. Approximately 26% of North Americans are regular smokers. People who smoke two packs a day are 22 times as likely as nonsmokers to die from lung cancer. Nonsmokers who inhale cigarette smoke from the environment also have an elevated risk of lung cancer and other diseases. Smokers display compulsive use, difficulty in quitting, and withdrawal symptoms on cessation of chronic use. Only about 3% of smokers who quit remain abstinent for 1 year.

Although there are thousands of compounds in cigarette smoke, nicotine has been shown to produce tolerance, dependence, and a distinct withdrawal syndrome in both animals and humans. Thus, it is generally considered to be the addictive and reinforcing agent responsible for continued smoking behavior. Although the mechanisms underlying the reinforcing properties of nicotine are not well understood, nicotine is thought to interact with the mesolimbic dopamine system in a manner similar to that of other abused drugs.

Functional magnetic resonance imaging (fMRI) allows for the noninvasive study of human brain activity by measuring localized signal changes that are related to neuronal activity. One study used MRI to identify active regions in the brains of 16 cigarette smokers soon after having been injected with nicotine. Specifically, a dose of saline solution was followed by three doses of nicotine (0.75, 1.50, and 2.25 mg/70 kg of weight); each dose was administered intravenously in a 1-minute period in an ascending, cumulative-dosing paradigm while whole-brain images were acquired.

The nicotine induced a dose-dependent increase in several behavioral parameters, including feelings of "rush" and "high" and drug liking. It also induced a dose-dependent increase in neuronal activity in many brain regions, includ-

(A) Cingulate–orbital frontal

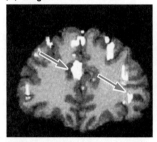

(C) Amygdala

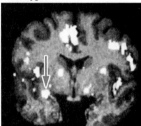

(B) Nucleus accumbens

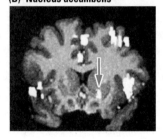

Functional magnetic resonance imaging of brain regions activated by nicotine: (A) cingulate orbital frontal cortex, (B) nucleus accumbens, and (C) amygdala. Arrows indicate areas of the brain that became activated.

ing the nucleus accumbens, amygdala, cingulate gyrus, and frontal lobes, which are the targets of dopamine projections. Activation in these structures is consistent with the idea that the activation of dopamine systems is related to addiction. The analysis of data did not distinguish between areas that are activated because they have nicotine receptors and areas of the brain in which nicotine-activated neurons activate other neurons, including dopamine neurons.

(F. A. Stein, J. Pankiewicz, H. H. Harsch, J. K. Cho, S. A. Fuller, R. G. Hoffmann, M. Hawkins, S. M. Rao, P. A. Bandettini, and A. S. Bloom. Nicotine-induced limbic cortical activation in the human brain: A functional MRI study. *The American Journal of Psychiatry* 155:1009–1015, 1998.)

Three lines of evidence support a central role for dopamine in drug abuse. First, animals are easily trained to press a bar to receive electrical stimulation of the dopamine system in the brain, but they quickly discontinue that behavior if the dopamine system is subsequently blocked or damaged. This evidence suggests that the release of dopamine is somehow rewarding. Second, abused drugs seem to cause the release of dopamine or to prolong its availability in synaptic clefts. Even drugs that have no primary action on do-pamine synapses have been found to increase dopamine's effects. Apparently, when activated, many brain regions that contain no dopamine neurons them-selves may stimulate dopamine neurons elsewhere in the brain. Finally, drugs that block dopamine receptors or decrease the availability of dopamine at dopamine receptors are not substances that people abuse. For example, the major tranquilizers that are widely available for treating psychosis are not abused drugs.

Explaining Drug Abuse

Why do people become addicted to drugs? One of the first explanations to gain widespread acceptance was the **dependence hypothesis.** According to this hypothesis, habitual users of a drug experience psychological or physio-logical withdrawal symptoms when the effects of the drug wear off. They feel anxious, insecure, or just plain sick in the absence of the drug, and so they take the drug again to alleviate those symptoms. In other words, they are "hooked" on the drug. Although this hypothesis may account for part of drug-taking be-havior, it has shortcomings as a general explanation. For example, an addict may abstain from a drug for months, long after any withdrawal symptoms have abated, and yet still be drawn back to using the drug. Moreover, the depen-dence hypothesis fails to explain why certain drugs that produce withdrawal symptoms when discontinued, such as the tricyclic antidepressants, are not abused. The **hedonic hypothesis,** that people take drugs because they pro-duce pleasure, was proposed to explain such observations. It in turn is sub-stantially weakened by reports from addicted people who say that the drugs that they take give them little pleasure.

To account for all the observations about drug abuse and addiction, Robinson and Berridge proposed the **incentive-sensitization theory.** They see addiction as developing in a series of stages. The first stage is the activa-tion of pleasure as a consequence of drug taking. Using the drug produces a positive subjective sensation in the person. In other words, the user *likes* the experience. In the second stage, pleasure becomes linked through **associa-tive learning** to mental representations of objects, acts, places, and events connected to taking the drug. This associative learning may occur through **classical** (also called **Pavlovian**) **conditioning.** That is, the sight of the drug and the drug-taking context and equipment are repeatedly paired with the use of the drug, which produces a pleasurable reaction. The third stage is at-tributing **incentive salience** to the cues associated with drug use. In other words, those cues become highly desired and sought-after incentives in themselves. Stimuli that signal availability of these incentives also become attractive. For instance, acts that have led to the drug-taking situation be-come attractive, as do new acts that the drug taker predicts will lead again to the drug. In this sequence of events, then, a number of repetitions of the drug-taking behavior lead from that act being liked to its being sought out or wanted regardless of its current consequences. This perspective is also called the *wanting-and-liking theory* because, in it, wanting and liking for a drug are affected differently, as is illustrated in Figure 6.14. *Wanting* is equivalent

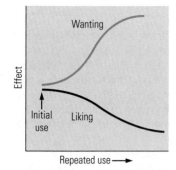

Figure 6.14 The incentive-sensitization theory of drug addiction. When first used, a drug produces a moderate amount of wanting and liking. With repeated use, tolerance for liking develops and consequently the expression of liking decreases. At the same time, the system that mediates wanting becomes sensitized so that wanting the drug increases. Wanting becomes associated with cues encountered in typical situations in which the drug is used.

to craving a drug, whereas *liking* is defined as the pleasure produced by drug taking.

The neural bases for liking and wanting are not completely understood. The important point is that each may be mediated by a separate neural system. Liking may be due to the activity of opioid neurons, whereas wanting may be due to activity in a part of the dopamine system called the **mesolimbic dopamine system.** This dopamine pathway consists of dopamine neurons in the midbrain that have axons projecting to the nucleus accumbens, the frontal cortex, and the limbic system, as shown in Figure 6.15. Cues that have been previously associated with drug taking may cause the dopamine system to become active, producing the subjective experience of wanting. The process that awakens the desire for the drug would not be one of which the user is conscious. Rather, the wanting would derive from unconsciously acquired associations between drug taking and various cues related to it.

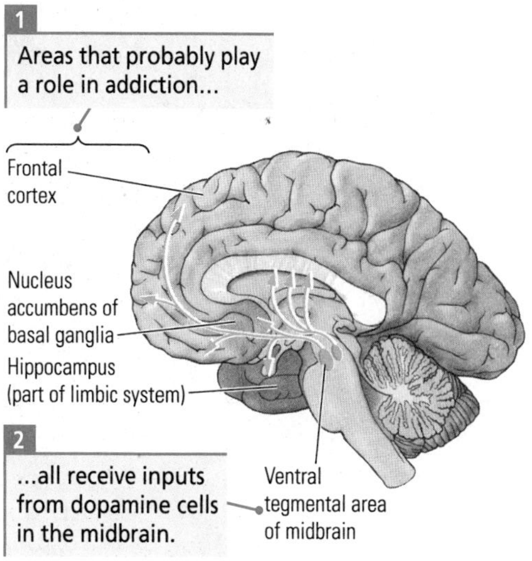

1
Areas that probably play a role in addiction...

Frontal cortex

Nucleus accumbens of basal ganglia

Hippocampus (part of limbic system)

2
...all receive inputs from dopamine cells in the midbrain.

Ventral tegmental area of midbrain

Figure 6.15 The dopamine hypothesis of addiction proposes that the mesolimbic dopamine system plays a role in drug craving. The dopamine cells in the ventral tegmental area of the midbrain project to the nucleus accumbens of the basal ganglia, to the limbic system, including the hippocampus, and to the frontal cortex, suggesting that these areas of the brain may play a role in addiction.

Drug-Induced Behavior

Drugs can cause behavior and mood changes that are as unpredictable as they are extreme. People who have taken alcohol, for example, may feel happy at one moment, sad the next, and perhaps belligerent or reckless the next. What accounts for such wide variability? An early and still popular explanation of the effects of alcohol is the **disinhibition theory.** It holds that alcohol has a selective depressant effect on the cortex, which is the region of the brain dealing with judgment, while sparing subcortical structures, which are the sites of more-primitive instincts. Stated differently, alcohol presumably depresses learned inhibitions based on reasoning and judgment, thus releasing the "beast" within. This theory is the basis for such often-heard excuses for alcohol-related behavior as, "She was too drunk to know better" or "The boys had a few too many and got carried away."

Craig MacAndrew and Robert Edgerton challenged the disinhibition theory in their book titled *Drunken Comportment.* They cite many instances in which behavior under the influence of alcohol changes from one context to another in ways that contradict the idea that alcohol lowers inhibitions. They also cite examples of cultures in which people are disinhibited when sober only to become inhibited after consuming alcohol and cultures in which people are inhibited when sober and become *more* inhibited when drinking. How can all these differences in alcohol's effects be explained? MacAndrew and Edgerton conclude that behavior under the effects of alcohol is learned behavior that is specific to the drug, culture, group, and setting. Often it simply represents *time out* from the rules of daily life that would normally apply.

MacDonald and her coworkers suggest that alcohol-related behavior can be explained by what they call **alcohol myopia** (myopia means "nearsightedness"). They coined this term to describe what they see as a tendency for people under the influence of alcohol to respond to a restricted set of very salient cues while ignoring more remote cues and potential consequences. By "salient cues" MacDonald means very strong and obvious ones that are close at hand. For example, if there is a fight, the person with alcohol myopia will be quicker than normal to swing a punch because the cue of the fight is so highly salient. Similarly, if there is a raucous party, the myopic drinker will be more eager than usual to join it because the salient cue of boisterous fun dominates the person's senses. This explanation can be applied to many other lapses in judgment that lead to risky behavior while on drugs, including aggression, date rape, and reckless driving (or driving at all).

Why Doesn't Everyone Abuse Drugs?

There are vast individual differences in people's responses to drugs, as well as differences that correlate with age, sex, body size, and other factors that affect sensitivity to a given substance. Large people are generally less sensitive to a given dose of a drug than smaller people are because the drug is more diluted in a large person's body fluids. Females are about twice as sensitive to drugs as males are. This difference is due in part to a female's relatively smaller body size, but it is also due to hormonal differences between females and males. Old people also may be twice as sensitive to drugs as young people are. The elderly often have less-effective barriers to drug absorption, as well as less-effective processes for metabolizing and eliminating drugs from their bodies. Similarly, there are differences in the susceptibility of individual people and of different groups to become addicted to drugs.

Observing that some people are more prone to drug abuse and dependence than other people are, scientists have wondered if this difference might be genetically based. Three lines of evidence suggest a genetic contribution. First, the results of studies show that if one of a pair of twins abuses alcohol, there is a greater likelihood for the other twin to abuse it, too, if the twins are identical (have the same genetic makeup) rather than fraternal (have only some of their genes in common). Second, the results of studies of people adopted shortly after birth reveal that they are more likely to abuse alcohol if their biological parents were alcoholic, even though they have had almost no contact with those parents. And, third, although most animals do not care for alcohol, selective breeding of mice, rats, and monkeys can produce strains that consume large quantities of it.

There are problems with all these lines of evidence, however. Perhaps identical twins show greater concordance for alcohol abuse because they are exposed to more-similar environments than fraternal twins are. And perhaps the link between alcoholism in adoptees and their biological parents has to do with nervous system changes due to prebirth exposure to the drug. Finally, just because animals can be selectively bred for alcohol consumption does not mean that human alcoholics have a similar genetic makeup. The evidence for a genetic basis of alcohol abuse will become compelling only when a gene or set of genes related to alcoholism is found in humans.

Although researchers continue to study the characteristics that appear to influence drug use, there is no unequivocal evidence as yet to suggest that a specific gene determines substance abuse. Nor is there unequivocal evidence that differences in the dopamine system make some individuals more prone to drug abuse than others. And, even if a particular substance-abuse gene or genes could be found, that genetic factor would not provide a full explanation of drug addiction. Identical twins have all their genes in common, and yet, when one twin becomes a drug abuser, the other doesn't necessarily become one, too. Clearly, learning also plays an important role in developing drug abuse and addiction.

Can Psychoactive Drugs Cause Brain Damage?

Table 6.4 shows that many substances can act as neurotoxins, causing damage to neurons. Given the widespread use of psychoactive drugs in our society, it is important to ask whether any of them can do the same. In this section, we both examine the evidence that commonly used psychoactive drugs can act as neurotoxins and investigate the processes by which they might have toxic effects.

In the late 1960s, there were many reports that monosodium glutamate (commonly known as MSG), a salty-tasting, flavor-enhancing food additive, produced headaches in some people. In the process of investigating why this happened, scientists placed large doses of monosodium glutamate on cultured neurons and noticed that the neurons died. Subsequently, they injected monosodium glutamate into the brains of experimental animals, where it also produced neuron death. These findings raised the question whether large doses of the neurotransmitter glutamate, which monosodium glutamate resembles structurally, also might be toxic to neurons. It turns out that they are. This finding suggests that a large dose of *any* substance that acts like glutamate might be toxic.

In 1987, in Canada, there was an outbreak of food poisoning that occurred after people had eaten mussels. In all, nine people died and a number suffered confusion and memory loss that proved to be permanent. Autopsies revealed extensive cell loss in the hippocampus, amygdala, and surrounding cortex and

Table 6.4 Some neurotoxins, their sources, and their actions

Substance	Origin	Action
Tetrodotoxin	Puffer fish	Blocks membrane permeability to Na^+ ions
Magnesium	Natural element	Blocks Ca^{2+} channels
Reserpine	*Rauwulfia* shrubs	Destroys storage granules
Colchicine	Crocus plant	Blocks microtubules
Caffeine	Coffee bean	Blocks adenosine receptors and Ca^{2+} channels
Spider venom	Black widow spider	Stimulates ACh release
Botulinum toxin	Food poisoning (*Clostridium botulinum* bacteria)	Blocks ACh release
Curare	Berry of *Strychnos* vine	Blocks ACh receptors
Rabies virus	Animal bite	Blocks ACh receptors
Ibotenic acid	*Amanita muscaria* and *Amanita pantherina* mushrooms	Similar to that of domoic acid
Strychnine	Plants of genus *Strychnos*	Blocks glycine
Apamin	Bees and wasps	Blocks Ca^{2+} channels

in the thalamus. An examination of the mussels showed that they contained a chemical called domoic acid, a substance that, like glutamate, acts on glutamate receptors. Domoic acid in large quantities excessively stimulates the glutamate receptors of certain brain cells and kills them.

This finding not only demonstrated that certain substances can cause brain damage, but further suggested that excessive stimulation of glutamate receptors by glutamate itself could potentially cause brain damage. Researchers have since discovered that many brain insults—including traumatic blows to the head, strokes in which blood supply is temporarily stopped, and epilepsy, or abnormal electrical discharges—can result in excessive glutamate release and subsequent brain injury from glutamate's action. Glutamate is thought to kill cells in two ways. First, it causes an increase in intracellular calcium that poisons the cell. Second, the increase in intracellular calcium can activate genes in the cell's DNA to produce proteins that kill the cell. This cell suicide is called **apoptosis** and can take place weeks or months after the initial injury.

These discoveries do not mean that people should totally avoid glutamate. In fact, our bodies need glutamate to function properly. Recent findings show that we even have taste-bud receptors for glutamate in the mouth, in addition to our receptors for sweet, salty, bitter, and sour. The taste-bud receptor for glutamate is called the umani receptor or **mGluR4,** and its probable function is to encourage us to eat glutamate or protein, inasmuch as glutamate is commonly found in meat. Clearly, the amounts of glutamate typically found in food are required by the body and are not toxic. Only excessive doses of glutamate cause harm.

The Potential Harmfulness of Recreational Drugs

What about the many recreational drugs that affect the nervous system? Are any of them potentially harmful to the nervous system? The answer is not always easy to determine, as McCann and her coworkers found in their recent review of studies. For one thing, there is the problem of sorting out the effects of the drug itself from the effects of other factors related to taking the drug. For instance, although chronic alcohol use can be associated with damage to the thalamus and limbic system, producing severe memory disorders, related complications of alcohol abuse (including vitamin deficiencies resulting from poor diet), rather than the alcohol itself, seem to cause this damage. Alcoholics typically consume insufficient amounts of thiamine (vitamin B_1), and the alcohol in their systems compounds that problem by interfering with the absorption of thiamine by the liver. Thiamine plays a vital role in maintaining cell-membrane structure. Similarly, though there are many reports of people who suffer some severe psychiatric disorder subsequent to the abuse of other recreational drugs, it is difficult in most of these cases to determine whether the drug initiated the condition or just aggravated a previously existing problem. It is also hard to determine whether the drug itself or some contaminant in it might be producing a harmful outcome. For example, in the case of Parkinson's disease described at the beginning of this chapter, the onset of the disease followed the use of synthetic heroin, but the disease was actually caused by a contaminant (MPTP) and not by the heroin itself. There have also been a number of cases of chronic use of marijuana (*Cannabis sativa*) being associated with psychotic attacks. But the marijuana plant contains at least 400 chemicals, 60 or more of which are structurally related to its active ingredient tetrahydrocannabinol (THC). Clearly, it is almost impossible to determine whether the psychotic attacks are related to THC or to some other ingredient in marijuana.

Perhaps the best evidence that a recreational drug can cause brain damage comes from the study of MDMA, also called "ecstasy," a widely used synthetic amphetamine. Although MDMA is structurally related to amphetamine, it produces hallucinogenic effects that have earned it the name "hallucinogenic amphetamine." The results of animal studies show that doses of MDMA approximating those taken by human users result in the degeneration of very fine serotonergic nerve terminals. In rodents, these terminals regrow within a few months after drug use is stopped; but, in monkeys, the terminal loss may be permanent, as shown in Figure 6.16. Morgan reports that there are cognitive declines in MDMA users, but researchers still want to know if human use of MDMA is associated with the same loss of serotonergic terminals as that in rodents and monkeys. Answering this question is complicated by the fact that many MDMA users have also used other drugs. Another obstacle is that the types of anatomical analysis used with laboratory animals cannot be used with humans.

The finding that MDMA can be toxic to neurons has led to investigations of whether amphetamine also is toxic. The results of studies with rodents have shown that high doses of amphetamine can result in the loss of dopamine terminals, but again no behavioral deficits have been associated with this loss. Whether humans using amphetamine show similar neuron damage is not known. The drug doses used in the rodent studies are typically higher than those taken by human amphetamine users; so the implications of the rodent studies are open to question.

The psychoactive actions of cocaine are similar to those of amphetamine, and its possible deleterious effects have been subjected to intense investigation. The results of many studies have shown that cocaine use is related to blockage of cerebral blood flow and other changes in blood circulation. It is not clear, however, whether cocaine causes these abnormalities or aggravates preexisting conditions.

Phencyclidine (PCP), or "angel dust," originally developed as an anesthetic, blocks one of the glutamate receptors called the NMDA receptor. Its use as an anesthetic was discontinued after studies found that about half of treated patients displayed psychotic symptoms for as long as a week after coming out of anesthesia. Users of PCP report perceptual changes and the slurring of speech after small doses, with high doses producing perceptual disorders and hallucinations. Some of the symptoms can last for weeks. The mechanisms by which PCP produces enduring behavioral changes are unknown, but Olney and his colleagues observed abnormal changes in neurons, as well as loss of neurons, in rats that had been given a

Figure 6.16 Change in the density of serotonin axons in the neocortex of a squirrel monkey that had been treated with MDMA 18 months previously: (left) normal monkey and (right) treated monkey. (After McCann et al., 1997.)

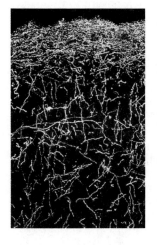

related drug (MK-801). This finding suggests that the altered behavior of PCP users may be related to neuron damage.

Some drugs that produce altered perceptual experiences and changes in mood, however, do not appear to cause brain damage. For instance, the psychedelic drug LSD, believed to act on serotonergic neurons, produces hallucinations but does not seem to cause enduring brain changes in rats. Similarly, although opiates produce mood changes, long-term studies of opiate users have not revealed persistent cognitive impairments or brain damage.

Summary

Synapses play a central role in the way that drugs produce their effects on behavior. Any of the biochemical events pertaining to neurotransmission—the synthesis of a transmitter, its release from the terminal so that it can excite another neuron, its degradation, or its reabsorption—can be influenced by drugs. Any modification of synaptic communication will result in increased or decreased action by the transmitter. In this way, drugs can act as agonists to increase synaptic transmission or as antagonists to decrease synaptic transmission.

Although there are an extraordinary number of drugs, they can be classified according to the behavioral effects that they produce. Thus, drugs can act as sedative-hypnotics, antianxiety agents, antipsychotic agents, antidepressants, narcotic analgesics, and stimulants. Drugs are also extremely variable in producing their effects, both with respect to different individuals and with respect to the same individual on different occasions. A decrease in the response to a drug with use is called tolerance, whereas an increase in response is called sensitization. Responses to drugs may be affected by an individual's genetic makeup and by other factors.

In addition to their therapeutic effects, drugs can cause addiction. The incentive-sensitization theory suggests that a liking for the effects that the drug produces develops in the initial stage of drug use, but, with repeated use, the user becomes conditioned to the cues associated with drug use; subsequent exposure to these cues then elicits a craving for the drug. Drugs can also act as neurotoxins, and some drugs that are used for recreational purposes have been implicated in producing brain injury.

References

Ballard, P. A., J. W. Tetrud, and J. W. Langston. Permanent human Parkinsonism due to 1-methyl-4-phenyl-1,2,3,6-tetrahydropyridine (MPTP). *Neurology* 35:949–956, 1985.

Comings, D. E., R. J. Rosenthal, H. R. Lesieur, L. J. Rugle, D. Muhleman, C. Chiu, G. Dietz, and R. Gade. A study of the dopamine D2 receptor gene in pathological gambling. *Pharmacogenetics* 6:223–234, 1996.

Cooper, J. R., F. E. Bloom, and R. H. Roth. *The Biochemical Basis of Neuropharmacology*. New York: Oxford University Press, 2002.

Efron, D. H., Ed. *Psychopharmacology: A Review of Progress*. Washington, DC: U.S. Department of Health, Education, and Welfare, 1988.

Feldman, R. S., J. S. Meyer, and L. F. Quenzer. *Principles of Neuropsychopharmacology*. Sunderland, MA: Sinauer, 1997.

Fraioli, S., H. S. Crombag, A. Badiani, and T. E. Robinson. Susceptibility to amphetamine-induced locomotor sensitization is modulated by environmental stimuli. *Neuropsychopharmacology* 20:533–541, 1999.

Hughes, J., and H. W. Kosterlitz. Opioid peptides: Introduction. *British Medical Bulletin* 39:1–3, 1983.

Hynie, I., and E. C. D. Todd. Domoic acid toxicity. *Canada Diseases Weekly Report* 16:1–77, 1990.

Isbell, H., H. F. Fraser, R. E. Wikler, R. E. Belleville, and A. J. Eisenman. An experimental study of the etiology of "rum fits" and delirium tremens. *Quarterly Journal for Studies of Alcohol* 16:1–35, 1955.

Julien, R. M. *A Primer of Drug Action*. New York: W. H. Freeman and Company, 2001.

Kestler, L. P., E. Walker, and E. M. Vega. Dopamine receptors in the brains of schizophrenia patients: a meta-analysis of the findings. *Behavioural Pharmacology* 12;355–371, 2001.

MacAndrew, C., and R. B. Edgerton. *Drunken Comportment: A Social Explanation*. Chicago: Aldine, 1969.

MacDonald, T. K., M. P. Zanna, and G. T. Fong. Alcohol and intentions to engage in risky health-related behaviours: Experimental evidence for a casual relationship. In J. Adair and F. Craik, Eds. *Advances in Psychological Science*, vol. 2, *Developmental, Personal, and Social Aspects*. East Sussex, UK: Psychology Press, 1998.

McCann, U. D., K. A. Lowe, and G. A. Ricaurte. Long-lasting effects of recreational drugs of abuse on the central nervous system. *The Neurologist* 3:399–411, 1997.

Morgan, M. S. Memory deficits associated with recreational use of "ecstasy" (MDMA). *Psychopharmacology* 141:30–36, 1999.

Morrow, A. L., G. C. Janis, M. J. VanDoren, D. B. Matthews, H. H. Samson, P. H. Janak, and K. A. Grant. Neurosteroids mediate pharmacological effects of ethanol: A new mechanism of ethanol action? *Alcohol and Clinical and Experimental Research* 23:1933–1940, 1999.

Olney, J. W., O. L. Ho, and V. Rhee. Cytotoxic effects of acidic and sulphur-containing amino acids on the infant mouse central nervous system. *Experimental Brain Research* 14:61–67, 1971.

Pert, C. B., M. J. Kuhar, and S. H. Snyder. Opiate receptor: Autoradiographic localization in rat brain. *Proceedings of the National Academy of Sciences of the United States of America* 73:3729–3733, 1976.

Robinson, T. E., and J. B. Becker. Enduring changes in brain and behavior produced by chronic amphetamine administration: A review and evaluation of animal models of amphetamine psychosis. *Brain Research Reviews* 11:157–198, 1986.

Robinson, T. E., and K. C. Berridge. The neural basis of drug craving: An incentive-sensitization theory of addiction. *Brain Research Reviews* 18:247–291, 1993.

Robinson, T. E., and B. Kolb. Persistent structural adaptations in nucleus accumbens and prefrontal cortex neurons produced by prior experience with amphetamine. *Journal of Neuroscience* 17:8491–8498, 1997.

Teitelbaum, J. S., R. J. Zatorre, S. Carpenter, D. Gendron, A. C. Evans, A. Gjedde, and N. R. Cashman. Neurologic sequelae of domoic acid intoxication due to the ingestion of contaminated mussels. *The New England Journal of Medicine* 322:1781–1787, 1990.

Wenger, J. R., T. M. Tiffany, C. Bombardier, K. Nicholls, and S. C. Woods. Ethanol tolerance in the rat is learned. *Science* 213:575–577, 1981.

Whishaw, I. Q., G. Mittleman, and J. L. Evenden. Training-dependent decay in performance produced by the neuroleptic *cis*(Z)-Flupentixol on spatial navigation by rats in a swimming pool. *Pharmacology, Biochemistry, and Behavior* 32:211–220, 1989.

Imaging the Brain's Activity

In the late nineteenth century, Italian physiologist Angelo Mosso (1846–1910) became the first to experiment with the idea that changes in the flow of blood in the brain might provide a way of assessing brain function during mental activity. Mosso knew that the fontanelles in newborn children—the soft areas on a baby's head where the bones of the skull are not yet fused—can be seen to pulsate with the rhythm of the heartbeat. He noticed similar pulsations in two adults who had suffered head injuries that left them with defects of the skull and observed, in particular, a sudden increase in the magnitude of those pulsations when the subjects engaged in mental activities (Figure 7.1). For example, when one of the subjects, a farmer named Signore Bertino, heard church bells ring and was asked whether the bells signified the time for prayer, the pulsations increased. While recording the pressure of the pulsations on Bertino's head, Mosso simultaneously recorded the blood pressure in Bertino's arm. He discovered that, when Bertino solved mathematical problems, the pressure in the farmer's skull increased but not the pressure in his arm. In other words, Signore Bertino's mental activity was accompanied by a selective increase in blood flow in the brain.

Recordings were taken from the forearm (black) and the brain (blue).

Forearm

Brain

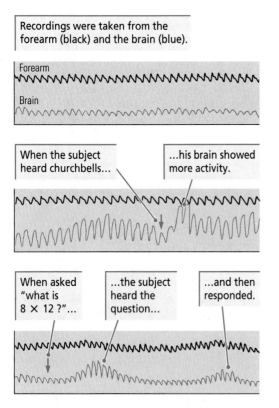

When the subject heard churchbells...

...his brain showed more activity.

When asked "what is 8 × 12 ?"...

...the subject heard the question...

...and then responded.

In each case, brain pulsations increased in amplitude, but those in the arm did not.

Figure 7.1 Mosso's recordings taken from Bertino's forearm and brain. When the subject heard church bells or when he was given a multiplication problem, Mosso found an increase in amplitude in the subject's brain pulsations but none in the subject's arm. (After Posner and Raichle, 1994.)

Mosso's results suggest that activity in the brain changes as it engages in problem solving. The increased pulsations suggest increased blood flow, which in turn suggests that the active region of the brain requires more oxygen to perform ongoing functions. This need for more oxygen in turn suggests that active areas of the brain have a way of signaling the circulatory system to increase the flow of blood to those areas. The signaling mechanism may be quite simple. When neurons are active, there is an increased outward flow of potassium through the cell membrane. Potassium could signal local capillaries to dilate and so import more blood. Alternatively, nitric oxide, a gaseous neurotransmitter, might be released by active neurons to stimulate the dilation of blood vessels. Or the signal could be heat. Metabolically active areas of the brain give off more heat. (The results of some early experiments suggested that a thermometer placed on the skull could detect changes in activity of the underlying brain.)

Modern computerized methods of measuring brain changes have led to the invention of numerous new "imaging" methods with which the normal brain and its activity can be observed. These imaging methods are of two general types: static and dynamic. Static imaging methods provide snapshots of the brain that are useful for studying its anatomy and for localizing injury. Dynamic imaging methods record ongoing changes in brain activity, including the electrical activity of cells, biochemical events, differences in glucose consumption, and, yes, the flow of blood to various regions. These methods, too, are helpful for locating brain injury, but, as Mosso proposed, they are also useful for studying cognitive function.

Historically, brain researchers studied brain function by examining the effects of brain injuries on behavior. Imaging methods have provided a new and complementary approach. The strength of brain-injury studies is that they allow behavior to be reduced to its component parts. For example, as we saw in the examples of language impairments after brain injury that were described in Chapter 1, patients suffering from Broca's aphasia are unable to articulate words and yet are able to understand them. Those who have Wernicke's aphasia are impaired in comprehension and yet are able to articulate words. Thus, language must have at least two components—articulation and comprehension—that are governed by at least two different areas in the brain. Now, with the new imaging techniques, researchers can literally "watch" these two areas in action, as well as identify other brain regions that control language.

We begin our survey by examining imaging techniques that make use of the brain's electrical activity. All such techniques produce dynamic images. In later sections, we examine techniques that make use of differences in the physical and chemical properties of brain substances or of differences in brain metabolic activity. Some of these techniques produce static images and others produce dynamic ones.

The Brain's Electrical Activity

Because the activity of nerve cells has an electrochemical basis, it can be recorded with instruments sensitive to small changes in electrical activity. Researchers then attempt to correlate these recordings with observed differences in behavior; such correlations serve as sources of insight into how the brain processes information. The techniques for recording the brain's electrical activity include (1) single-cell recording; (2) electroencephalographic (EEG) recording; and (3) event-related potential (ERP) recording. The main advantage of single-cell recording is that it provides the highest resolution of all of the functional imaging techniques. In other words, it provides a lot of information about what a few neurons are doing. Its weakness is that it has the lowest generalizability. Electroencephalographic recording provides information about the function of the brain as a whole but has little to say about the activity of single neurons. Event-related potential recording has lower resolution than single-unit recordings but greater resolution than EEGs. Single-cell recordings are mainly performed by using nonhuman animals because surgery is required. In contrast, the EEG and ERP imaging techniques—uncomplicated, inexpensive, and noninvasive—are easy to use with any kind of experimental subject.

After exploring the techniques for recording electrical activity, we will look at transcranial magnetic stimulation, a related technique for noninvasively stimulating the brain through the skull. In this method, researchers, turning the table, do not record *from* neurons but apply stimulation *to* them to discover functional relations between brain anatomy and observed behavior.

Single-Cell Recording

What is each of the brain's 10 billion neurons doing at any given moment? If you are watching television, are your visual and auditory neurons active while the neurons responsible for olfaction, taste, and movement remain at rest? When you are watching an actor jump from the roof of one building to the roof of another, do the motor regions of *your* brain become active, even though your arms and legs remain still? Why does the actor's distance above the ground give you a feeling of vertigo, even though you feel no sensation of contact or pain as he lands on the roof of the second building?

Such questions can be addressed with single-cell recording techniques, refinements of the historical experiments that detected the electrical activity of individual squid axons (Chapter 4). An electrode is inserted directly into an animal's brain, adjacent to a single neuron, and the neuron's electrical activity is recorded on a computer, thus supplying information about the activity of that neuron.

Various behaviors in mammals and other animals can be sources of remarkable insight into what single neurons are up to during these behaviors. Most experiments must be done with nonhuman animals, however, because single-cell recording calls for placing the electrodes directly on the brain tissue, and there are only a few occasions (such as brain surgery) during which researchers can have such access to a living human brain. Some animal species are preferable for studying given behaviors to other species. For example, nonhuman primates and cats are favored for recording the single-cell activity of visual functions because these species have excellent vision. The barn owl is frequently used for studying auditory function because of its excellent hearing and because it automatically orients its head to locate the sound of its prey. Rats are used for recording single-cell activity associated with spatial behavior because they are small enough to be physically active in a limited space. For studies of reaching, in which recordings are made as the animal uses a single hand to grasp objects, nonhuman primates are again preferred. Their reaching movements are under visual control and therefore resemble human reaching movements.

In early studies, only a single recording electrode was used, thus recording only one cell at a time. Today, however, multiunit techniques allow researchers to insert arrays of as many as 50 thin wires into a brain region to record from many individual neurons simultaneously. Furthermore, techniques have been developed to identify specific neurons so that their activity can be followed over long periods of time. For example, an electrode that is quite close to a neuron will provide a large-amplitude signal of that neuron's activity, whereas an electrode a little farther away will provide a smaller-amplitude signal produced by the same activity. The ratio of the amplitude of the two signals will provide a unique "signature," allowing researchers to monitor the ongoing activity of that specific neuron.

The visual recordings produced in single-cell studies differ somewhat from the graphs of action potentials that we have looked at in earlier chapters. Graphs of single action potentials, such as those examined in Chapter 2, are usually drawn with the *x*-axis (indicating the passage of time) scaled in milliseconds. In contrast, graphs for single-cell studies are usually drawn with the *x*-axis scaled on the order of seconds. This practice allows researchers to correlate the serial action potentials produced by a given neuron with the ongoing behavior (measured in seconds) of the animal under observation. Figure 7.2 illustrates the different graphical representations that can be obtained by changing the time base. In graph A, which represents the passage of two milliseconds, only a single action potential can be graphed. In graph B, which represents a period of a number of milliseconds, a couple of action potentials can be graphed. Graph C represents a longer period, during which many action potentials are graphed, but, because they must be packed together so tightly, each is seen as only a single vertical stroke.

Action potentials are the currency with which the brain operates. The sensation of a mosquito landing on one's arm is conveyed from one neuron to the next in the form of action potentials: somatosensory neurons convey action potentials to the spinal cord, and spinal neurons convey them to the cortex. In the cortex, action potentials record the perception that it is a mosquito that is on one's arm. When the cortex instructs the hand to swat at the mosquito, it sends the message in the form of action potentials. Action potentials in the brain represent sights, sounds, smells, tastes, sensations of pain and temperature, and even one's desires and emotions. A longstanding puzzle in the study of perception is the question of how an action potential in one neuron represents a visual signal, whereas a similar action potential in another, similar neuron represents an auditory signal, and an action potential in still another neuron records the face of a relative. This puzzle has not been satisfactorily solved.

Neurons exhibit many patterns of firing. Some of them discharge at a steady rate that appears unrelated to behavior. Other neurons fire in bursts in association with an observable behavior. Others hardly ever discharge at all. Some neurons discharge in the morning and in the evening, in rhythm with the cycle of days. Other neurons discharge once a year, in association with some important annual event. Many neurons exhibit a rhythmical dis-

(A)

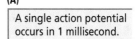

A single action potential occurs in 1 millisecond.

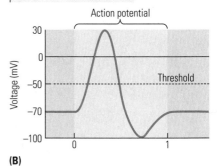

(B)

Two action potentials occur in 3 milliseconds.

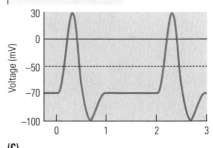

(C)

A changing pattern of activity can be seen with the occurence of many action potentials in a 40-millisecond period.

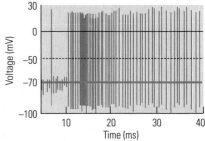

Figure 7.2 In these representations of an action potential, the scale of the horizontal (*x*) axis is changed (A) to illustrate the phases of a single action potential; (B) to illustrate that each action potential is a discrete event; and (C) to illustrate that a membrane can produce many action potentials with varying patterns of occurrence during a short period of time.

charge that is in some way related to breathing or heart rate. Some neurons behave differently in different circumstances. Certain neurons in a jellyfish, for example, discharge rhythmically to move the mantel and keep the jellyfish swimming slowly. When the animal is threatened, however, these same neurons change their discharge pattern to fire at a high, steady rate, allowing the animal to speed up and escape. In more complicated organisms, such as humans, the activity patterns of neurons not only produce behavior but also form the representations and perceptions that we associate with being conscious.

More than a hundred years ago, theorists speculated that neurons in the visual system might provide a representation of our visual world in very much the way that bits of silver produce an image in a photograph. In a photograph, bits of silver or spots of dye are packed close together to produce the picture. Likewise it seemed reasonable that, in the visual areas of the brain, action potentials in different neurons might be the units of the perceived image. Bright areas of the visual image might be represented by neurons firing more rapidly, whereas dark areas might be represented by reduced or absent firing. The pattern of brightness and darkness across the visual cortex would create a picture of the scene being picked up by the eyes. It is now clear, however, that this theory is incorrect. Single-cell recording techniques have been an important source of insight into this and other aspects of the neural code.

Neurons encode information in several ways. A simple way of representing sensory events is with a time code, in which the presence of an event is signaled by neural firing. For example, as long as a light is present, a neuron discharges; the discharging stops when the light is turned off. Alternatively, this same information could be represented as an event code: a neuron might discharge when the light comes on and then discharge again when the light goes off. In this case, a given neuron's firing might signal the onset of light, whereas another neuron's firing would signal its disappearance. The intensity of an event might be represented by a frequency code. For example, the brightness of a light or the intensity of a pain stimulus could be represented by the rapidity of a cell's firing. The frequency with which a neuron fires could also represent much more complicated information. For example, when a neuron in the visual system is very active, it could represent the color red; when it is less active, it could represent the color green. Neurons that encode bimodal information in this way might have a "resting" state characterized by moderate activity; then, an increase in activity could serve as one signal, and a decrease in activity could serve as the other signal.

Both the anatomy of the brain and the results of single-cell recording studies suggested to researchers that the brain does use such codes to represent information. One anatomical clue lies in the different numbers of cells at various levels of the visual system, from the receptors in the retina of the eye to cortical areas that presumably take part in perception, as diagrammatically represented in Figure 7.3A and B. Note that, relative to the large number of rods and cones, which are the receptor cells for light in the retina, the numbers of ganglion cells and lateral geniculate body (LGB) cells carrying visual information to area 17, the first visual area of the neocortex, are very low. In higher visual cortical areas, the numbers of cells are again larger. From single-cell recordings at these different levels (Figure 7.3C), researchers learned that ganglion cells and lateral geniculate cells respond only to dots of light, whereas the cells in the visual cortex respond to bars of light of specific orientation. Cells in higher visual areas respond to more-complex stimuli, including the sight and movement of objects, and perhaps even to the specific features of the face known as "Grandmother." In some way, the visual cortex takes information encoded in dots and bars and translates it into the complex ongoing visual experience that tells us the "look" of our world. It is unlikely, however, that only one brain cell would be assigned the job of recognizing one of our grandmothers. It is more likely that from hundreds to thousands of cells would be required.

The single-cell recordings made from human neocortex (usually made during neurosurgery) illustrate a number of interesting features of single-cell activity in the human brain. Generally, cortical neurons fire at a relatively low level of fewer than 3 discharges per minute, which may increase to about 10 discharges per minute when the neurons become more active. Furthermore, most neurons have a narrow behavioral repertory, responding to only one kind of sensory event or behavior. Neurons that are nearby may have very different behavioral repertories, which suggests that, in association areas of the brain, the networks subserving different behaviors interact closely. For example, in Broca's area, one neuron may be active during word perception and its neighbor during word production. At the same time, specific stimuli or events may be associated with neuronal activity in a surprisingly large number of areas in both hemispheres. In addition, the recordings show that the inhibition of activity also is an extremely common response. Lastly, in single-cell recordings, well-learned behaviors seem to be encoded by relatively sparse cortical activity, whereas behaviors that are being newly learned are accompanied by much more widespread

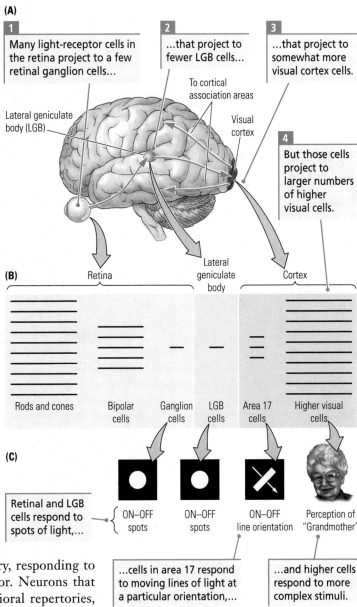

Figure 7.3 (A) A schematic representation of the brain illustrating the eye and projections from the eye to the visual cortex. (B) A schematic illustration of the relative numbers of cells at each level of the visual projection. These relative numbers are indicated both by the number of lines and the length of the lines. Note that there are very few neurons carrying information from the retina to the visual cortex, but cell numbers increase again in the visual cortex. (C) Coding of information in the visual pathways. Ganglion and lateral geniculate (LGB) cells in the visual pathway respond to spots of light, cells in area 17 respond to lines of light of particular orientation, and higher visual areas respond to more-complex stimuli.

excitability in the cortex. These general findings suggest that not only is the type of behavior or stimulus event important for determining whether a neuron changes its rate of firing, but so is context and experience.

With the assumption that single cells are the units of brain function, would it be possible to understand brain function and consciousness after recording a large enough sample of cells individually? Perhaps, if one were also able to discover the relation of each neuron to all the rest. At present, however, it does not seem likely that researchers will ever be able to record from each and every neuron and fully chart the relations between them. Thus, other imaging techniques that allow the activity of large areas of the brain to be viewed concurrently provide important alternative approaches to understanding brain function.

Electroencephalographic Recording

A simple technique for recording the electrical activity of large regions of the human brain was developed in the early 1930s by German physiologist Hans Berger. He found that it was possible to record "brain waves" by placing the leads from a voltmeter on the skull. These recordings, called **electroencephalograms** or **EEGs,** have proved to be a valuable tool for (1) studying sleep, (2) monitoring the depth of anesthesia, (3) diagnosing epilepsy and brain damage, and (4) studying normal brain function.

In a typical EEG recording arrangement (Figure 7.4), one electrode (a small metal disc called the "active electrode") is attached to the scalp to detect the electrical activity of neurons in the underlying brain area, and a second electrode (called the "indifferent electrode") is attached to the ear lobe, where there is no electrical activity to detect. At least two electrodes are needed because the EEG is a recording of the difference in the electrical potentials detected by the electrodes. The electrodes are fixed in place with a paste that is a good electrical conductor. The electrical fluctuations in the brain are rather small, usually much less than a millivolt, but when amplified they can be displayed on an oscilloscope and transferred to paper on a chart recorder. They can also be stored on a tape recorder for later replay on a paper chart recorder or for analysis requiring the use of a computer.

When electrodes on the skull are recording the electrical activity of the underlying brain, they are actually summing the graded potentials of many thousands of underlying neurons. The neurons of the neocortex are arranged in horizontal layers, and a substantial part of the EEG signal comes from the large pyramidal neurons of layers 5 and 6. In response to synaptic events, the dendrites of these neurons become more positively or more negatively charged than the axon hillock. If the synaptic inputs are rhythmical, then the graded potentials on the pyramidal cells fluctuate rhythmically.

The rhythms of the pyramidal cells are produced in a number of ways. Cells in the thalamus or brainstem can act as pacemaker cells, driving the graded potentials rhythmically. Interneurons within the cortex that are connected to many dozens of pyramidal cells also can discharge rhythmically, thus driving the rhythm of the pyramidal cells. Additionally, the pyramidal

1
Electrodes attached to the skull and corresponding to specific areas of the brain...

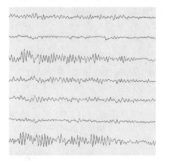

2
...are connected to magnets, which are connected to pens...

Electrodes

Pen

Polygraph pen recorder

3
...that produce a paper record of electrical activity in the brain. The record shown here indicates a relaxed person.

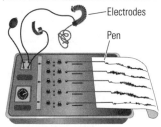

Figure 7.4 A typical electroencephalographic recording arrangement. (Photograph from Michael Rosenfeld/Stone Images; chart from SIU/Photo Researchers.)

cells can have intrinsic rhythms, and the connections between adjacent neurons can serve to synchronize those patterns. Finally, the rhythm of the cells can fluctuate with heart rate or respiration, events that provide oxygen and glucose to the cells and thus influence their activity. No matter how a given signal is produced, the neurons that produce it are referred to as the signal's **generator.**

That the electrical activity detected through the skull actually comes from generators in the brain has been demonstrated in a number of ways. During surgery, neurologists have taken EEG recordings both from the skull and directly from the underlying brain and have found that the rhythms from the two locations are similar, although the waves are larger in amplitude when recorded from the brain tissue. In research with animals, microelectrodes placed across the dendritic field of the pyramidal neurons (with one electrode on the dendrites and the other at the axon hillock, to obtain the maximum amplitude rhythms), have demonstrated that these neurons do generate the waves.

The waves recorded from the skull are **volume conducted** through the brain and through the skull—that is, conducted in the way that waves travel through water. As the electrodes are moved farther away from the source, the amplitude of the waves from a given generator becomes smaller. Thus, if a number of electrodes are placed on the skull, amplitude differences can be used to estimate the approximate location of the generator that is producing a given set of waves.

Subsequent to Berger's discovery, EEG recordings were soon found to be useful in a number of ways. Figure 7.5 shows, for example, that certain patterns of waves are associated with particular behavioral states. When a person is aroused, excited, or even just alert, the EEG pattern has a low amplitude (the height of the brain waves) and a high frequency (the number of brain waves per second), as seen in Figure 7.5A. This pattern, called the *beta* (β) **rhythm,** is typical of an EEG taken from anywhere on the skull of an alert subject—not only a human subject, but other animals, too. In contrast, when a person is calm and resting quietly, especially with eyes closed, the rhythmical brain waves shown in Figure 7.5B often emerge. These so-called alpha (α) waves are extremely rhythmical but with waxing and waning amplitude and a frequency of approximately 11 cycles per second. In humans, alpha rhythms are detected coming from the region of the visual cortex, which lies at the back of the head. If a relaxed person is disturbed or opens his or her eyes, the alpha rhythm abruptly stops.

Not everyone displays alpha rhythms, and some people display them much more consistently than others. You can buy a small voltmeter for monitoring your own alpha rhythms if you're interested. The voltmeter transforms EEG waves into

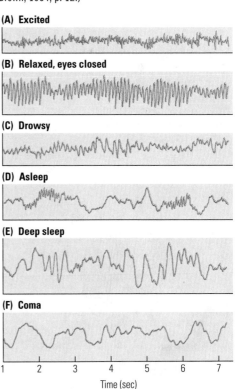

Figure 7.5 These characteristic EEGs recorded during various behavioral states in humans show (A) the beta brain-wave pattern in an awake, alert person; (B) the alpha rhythm associated with relaxing with the eyes closed; (C) the slowing in frequency and increase in amplitude of theta waves associated with a drowsy condition; (D) the slow, high-amplitude delta waves associated with sleep; (E) the larger, slow waves associated with deep sleep; and (F) the further slowing of electroencephalographic waves associated with coma. (After *Epilepsy and the Functional Anatomy of the Human Brain* by W. Penfield and H. H. Jasper. Boston: Little, Brown, 1954, p. 12.)

(A) Excited

(B) Relaxed, eyes closed

(C) Drowsy

(D) Asleep

(E) Deep sleep

(F) Coma

1   2   3   4   5   6   7

Time (sec)

"beeps" so that the brain-wave rhythm can be heard. After attaching a lead from one pole of the voltmeter to your skull and attaching the reference wire to your ear lobe (by using a paste that conducts an electrical current), you relax with eyes closed and try to make the voltmeter "beep" in an alpha rhythm. Many people quickly learn to turn alpha waves on and off in this way. Beeping voltmeters were once promoted as a tool for learning transcendental meditation.

An EEG is a sensitive indicator of states other than arousal and relaxation. Figure 7.5C through E illustrates the electroencephalographic changes that take place as a person goes from drowsiness to sleep and finally enters deep sleep. As the electroencephalographic rhythms become slower in frequency and larger in amplitude, 4- to 7-cycle-per-second theta (θ) waves and finally 1- to 3- cycle-per-second **delta** (δ) **waves** are produced. If the brain ceases to function (the condition called brain death), the EEG becomes a flat line. These distinctive brain-wave patterns make the EEG a reliable tool for monitoring waking and consciousness, estimating the depth of anesthesia, evaluating the severity of head injury, and searching for other brain abnormalities.

A **polygraph** (*poly*, meaning "many") is a machine that graphs many biological events simultaneously (Figure 7.6). In a typical polygraph arrangement, electrodes are pasted to standard locations on the skull's surface to obtain an EEG (see Figure 7.6A); onto muscles of the neck to obtain an electromyogram (EMG), a record of muscle activity (see Figure 7.6B); and over the eyes to obtain an **electrooculogram** (EOG), a record of eye movements (see Figure 7.6C). A thermometer is often added to keep a record of body temperature. Together, these recordings provide a comprehensive and reliable description of sleep–waking states. On the bases of polygraph data, researchers have divided sleep into four stages.

Observers of sleep have long known that sleepers exhibit periods of relative inactivity and periods characterized by twitching movements of the mouth, fingers, and toes. These two different aspects of sleep are readily observable in household pets and partners. In 1955, Eugene Aserinsky and Nathaniel Kleitman, working at the University of Chicago, discovered that the twitching periods were associated with rapid eye movements, or REMs. More remarkably, they discovered that, during the REMs, the neocortical EEG record displayed a

Figure 7.6 Typical electrode placements for polygraph recordings. (A) Electroencephalogram made from a point on the skull relative to a neutral point on the ear. (B) Electromyogram made from a comparison of two muscles, such as those on the chin and throat. (C) Electrooculogram based on signals from the eye and a neutral point on the ear.

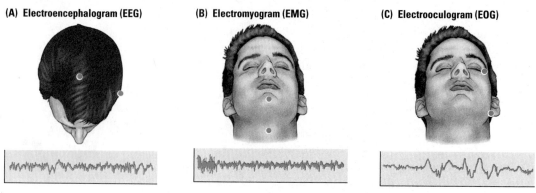

(A) Electroencephalogram (EEG)   **(B) Electromyogram (EMG)**   **(C) Electrooculogram (EOG)**

(A) EEG

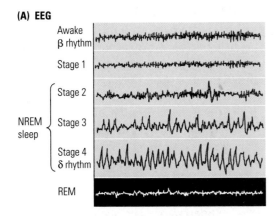

(B) Sleep

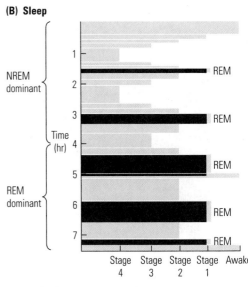

Figure 7.7 (A) Electroencephalographic patterns associated with waking and the four stages of sleep. Stage 1 is also called REM sleep, and stages 2 through 4 are called slow-wave sleep. (B) In a typical night's sleep, a subject undergoes a number of sleep-state changes. Stage 4 sleep dominates the early sleep hours, and stage 1 sleep dominates the later sleep hours. (After D. D. Kelley, 1991.)

fast-wave pattern. That is, the EEG record suggested that the subjects were awake. After further investigation, Aserinsky and Kleitman were able to confirm that, in spite of their brain-wave patterns, the subjects really were asleep.

The sleep stage in which fast-wave (beta) activity is associated with REMs is referred to as **REM sleep.** The other phase of sleep, associated with slowing of the EEG, is called **non-REM** or **NREM sleep** (or sometimes **slow-wave sleep**). With these distinctions in mind, we can describe the electroencephalographic patterns associated with a typical night's sleep.

A summary of the brain activity recorded from one subject during a typical night's sleep is illustrated in Figure 7.7. Part A of the figure displays the EEG patterns associated with waking and with the four stages of sleep. Notice that the main change characterizing a sleeper's progression from stage 1 sleep through stage 4 sleep is that the EEG waves become larger and slower. The numbering of these stages assumes that the sleeper moves from relatively shallow sleep in stage 1 to deeper sleep in stage 4.

Figure 7.7B shows the subject moving from one stage of sleep to another as the night progresses. Notice that the depth of sleep is shown by steps indicating when the subject descends and ascends through the four sleep stages and how long each stage lasts. Notice also that the depth of sleep changes several times in the course of the night. The subject shows a gradual descent from waking to stage 4 sleep that takes about one-half hour, stays in stage 4 sleep for about one-half hour, and then ascends to stage 1 sleep. This descent and ascent is then repeated four times, except that, as the night progresses, the stages of sleep associated with the slowest EEG patterns are less frequent. The EEG of stage 1 sleep is similar in appearance to the EEG of waking, but the subject is asleep. The electrooculograph records that the subject's eyes are moving during this stage of sleep, indicating that this stage is REM sleep. The time spent in REM sleep is indicated by the bars above the periods of stage 4 sleep.

The EEG finds its most useful clinical application in the diagnosis of epilepsy, a condition characterized by changes in consciousness or by

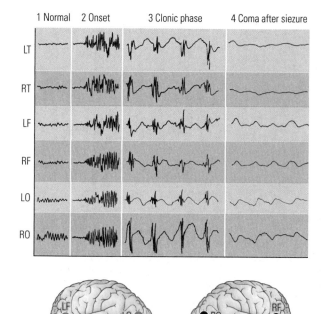

Figure 7.8 Examples of electroencephalographic patterns recorded during a grand mal seizure. Abbreviations: LT and RT, left and right temporal; LF and RF, left and right frontal; LO and RO, left and right occipital. Dots on the hemispheres indicate the approximate recording sites. Numbers refer to the stages of the seizure: (1) normal record before the attack; (2) onset of the attack; (3) clonic phase, in which the person makes rhythmic movements in time with the large abnormal discharges; and (4) period of coma after the seizure ends.

convulsions of the body. The cause of epileptic seizures was unknown until the results of electroencephalographic experiments demonstrated that different varieties of epilepsy are associated with different abnormal electrical rhythms in the brain (Figure 7.8). Some forms of epilepsy, called **petit mal** (from the French meaning "little bad" or "little evil") **epilepsy** are generally associated with brief losses of consciousness, perhaps lasting only a few seconds. Other forms of epilepsy may be associated with a loss of memory lasting for many minutes. Still other forms, called **grand mal** (meaning "big bad" or "big evil") **epilepsy,** are characterized by convulsions of the body, falling down, and loss of consciousness.

Electroencephalographic recordings can provide information both about the cause of epilepsy and about the location of the problem. First, the duration of an epileptic attack correlates closely with the duration of abnormalities in the EEG, which may consist of a loss of EEG recording, a slowing of EEG recording, or large distinctive spikes. This correspondence indicates that epilepsy is associated with the abnormal activity of neurons. Second, the EEG can identify the region of the brain in which the abnormal rhythm is produced. The focus of the abnormality is usually located in the brain region that first generates the abnormal electrical activity. For example, although abnormal waves might be recorded from a number of regions of the brain, all of them may be produced in one location and volume conducted across the brain to be detected by electrodes at other locations. Alternatively, the waves may originate in a particular location, then recruit adjacent regions, and in that way spread across the brain. Note that the largest abnormal spikes in Figure 7.8 appear to be coming from the right occipital (RO) cortex recording site, suggesting that the abnormality producing the epileptic attack is located in this region of the brain. Computerized techniques can be used to make comparisons of the onset times and amplitude of EEG waves and thus indicate the region of the brain in which the abnormal waves originate.

Electroencephalographic imaging can also be used to study cognitive functions. With modern computing techniques, it is possible to record many channels of EEG information simultaneously and to compare the amplitudes and frequencies of the EEGs from the different channels as they change from one moment to the next. The miniaturization of the equipment allows recordings to be taken from many more sites on the skull, sometimes from as many as 125 locations. The computer then makes a two-dimensional map of the brain surface, with different colors indicating the relative activity of different brain regions. This technique produces an ongoing "on line" representation of brain activity.

Event-Related Potentials

Event-related potentials, or ERPs, are brief changes in an EEG signal in response to a discrete sensory stimulus. An ERP is not as easy to detect in an EEG as one might think. The problem is that an ERP of interest is mixed in with so many other electrical signals in the brain that it is impossible to spot just by visually inspecting an EEG. One way to detect an ERP is to produce the stimulus repeatedly and average the recorded responses. Averaging tends to cancel out any irregular and unrelated electrical activity, leaving only the potentials generated by the stimulus event.

An analogy will help to clarify this procedure. Imagine throwing a small stone into a lake of choppy water. Although the stone produces a splash, that splash is hard to see among all of the water's ripples and waves. The splash made by the stone is analogous to an event-related potential caused by a sensory stimulus. Like the splash surrounded by choppy water, the ERP is hard to detect because of all the other electrical activity taking place at the same time. A solution is to throw a number of stones exactly the same size, always hitting the same spot in the water and producing the same splash over and over. If a computer is then used to calculate an average of the water's activity, random wave movements will tend to cancel each other out, and the splashes produced by the stones will stand out as clearly as if a single stone had been thrown into a pool of calm water.

Figure 7.9 shows how averaging reveals an ERP in response to an auditory stimulus—in this case, a tone. Notice that the EEG made when the tone is first presented is very irregular. But when the recordings of more than 100 stimulus presentations are averaged, a distinctive wave pattern appears. This ERP consists of a number of negative (N) and positive (P) waves produced in a period of a few hundred milliseconds after the stimulus is presented. By convention, the waves depicted as going downward on the ERP graph are called positive, and the waves depicted as going upward are called negative. Positive and negative waves are numbered according to the time at which they are produced. For instance, P_1 in Figure 7.9 is a positive wave produced about 100 ms after the presentation of the stimulus. Not all of the waves in the ERP are unique to this particular stimulus. Some are common to any auditory stimulus perceived by the brain. The waves produced from 100 to 300 ms after a stimulus is presented are likely to be related to the meaning of a stimulus. For example, the ERPs produced in response to the spoken words "cat"

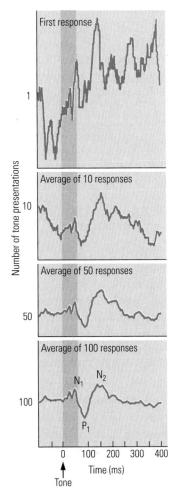

Figure 7.9 An illustration of the averaging process for obtaining an ERP. A stimulus is presented at time 0, as indicated by the vertical shaded bar, and the electroencephalographic activity that occurs in response to the tone is recorded (First response). The second, third, and fourth graphs then show the results of averaging the electroencephalographic responses after 10, 50, and 100 presentations, respectively. The averaged wave sequence develops a more and more distinctive shape until, after 100 presentations, the ERP pattern is sharp and clear. Positive (P) and negative (N) waves produced at every repetition of the stimulus are used for analysis.

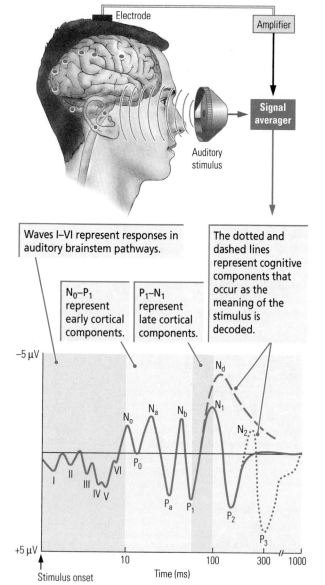

Electrode

Amplifier

Auditory
stimulus

Signal
averager

Waves I–VI represent responses in
auditory brainstem pathways.

N_0–P_1
represent
early cortical
components.

P_1–N_1
represent
late cortical
components.

The dotted and
dashed lines
represent cognitive
components that
occur as the
meaning of the
stimulus is
decoded.

−5 µV

+5 µV

N_d

N_a N_b N_1

N_0 N_2

P_0

I II VI

III
IV V

P_a P_1

P_2

P_3

10 100 300 1000

Stimulus onset

Time (ms)

Figure 7.10 Event-related
potential (ERP) from the parietal
cortex of a subject in response to the
presentation of an auditory stimulus.
(After Neville, 1980.)

and "rat" contain distinctive peaks and patterns that allow researchers to differentiate one response from the other.

Many interesting questions can be investigated with the use of ERPs. Figure 7.10 shows an ERP produced by the parietal cortex in response to the presentation of an auditory stimulus. Note that the ERP is made up of many positive and negative waves. Each wave is produced by a different generator; that is, by a different group of neurons responding to the signal with a change in their electrical activity. To understand how such a series of waves is produced, imagine the brain as a bowl of jelly in which a number of vibrators have been buried, all connected in a series. If a stimulus sets off the vibrators one after another, a recording electrode would record a jiggle moving through the jelly as each vibrator became activated in succession. The signals shown in Figure 7.10 correspond to the successive activation of many regions of the brain by an auditory stimulus. The signals identified as I though VI are from brainstem generators, those designated N_0 through P_1 are from primary auditory cortex regions, and those designated N_1 though P_3 are from secondary and tertiary regions of the cortex. The dotted lines indicate waves that are believed to be associated with thought processes in response to the signal. For example, P_3, produced 300 milliseconds after stimulus presentation, is thought to represent the process of decoding the meaning of the sounds.

Figure 7.11 shows a multiple-recording method that uses 64 electrodes simultaneously to detect ERPs at many cortical sites. Computerized averaging techniques reduce the masses of information obtained to simpler comparisons between electrode sites. For example, if the focus of interest is P_3, a computer record can display an image of the skull in which only the amplitude of P_3 is shown. A computer can also convert the averages at different sites into a color code, creating a graphical representation showing which brain regions are most responsive. The left-hand part of Figure 7.11 shows a subject being monitored while viewing a picture of a rat that flashes repeatedly in the same place on a computer screen. The P_3 wave recorded on the posterior right side of the subject's head is larger than the same P_3 wave recorded anywhere else, showing that this region is a "hot spot" for processing the visual stimulus. Presumably, for this particular subject, the right posterior part of the brain performs an important operation in the decoding of the picture of the rat 200 ms after it is presented. In this way, ERPs can be used not only to detect which areas of the brain process particular stimuli, but also to study the order in which different regions play a role. This second use of

ERPs is important because it shows us the route taken by the information as it travels through the brain.

Because an ERP produced in response to a stimulus represents the activity of the entire pathway and all of the nuclei engaged in processing the signal evoked by that stimulus, the ERP has many experimental uses. It can be used to study the normal function of the pathway through which the signal passes, the normal function of the nuclei taking part in processing the signal, and the cognitive processes in the neocortex that are employed in discriminating or learning about the signal. Because measures are taken from both hemispheres, studies of ERPs recorded during cognitive tasks compare the responses of the different hemispheres with the stimulus signal. Finally, ERPs can also reveal electrical changes associated with the planning and execution of movements. For example, researchers have identified certain potentials produced in the motor cortex later than 300 ms after the presentation of a given stimulus. They call it a **readiness potential** because they have discovered that it signals an impending movement.

Magnetoencephalography

When a magnetic field passes across a wire, it induces a current in the wire. When a current flows along a wire, it induces a magnetic field around the wire. This reciprocal relation between electricity and magnetism is also seen in neurons. Neural activity, by generating an electrical field, also produces a magnetic field. Although the magnetic field produced by a single neuron is extremely small, the field produced by many neurons is sufficiently strong to be recorded on the surface of the skull. Such a record is called a **magnetoencephalogram** (MEG), and it is the magnetic counterpart of the EEG or ERP.

Calculations based on MEG measurements not only provide a description of the electrical activity of neurons but also permit a three-dimensional localization of the cell groups generating the measured field. Magnetic waves being conducted through tissue undergo less distortion than electrical signals do, and so a MEG can have a higher resolution than an ERP. Thus, a major advantage of the MEG over the EEG and ERP is its ability to more precisely identify the source of the activity being recorded. For example, the MEG has proved useful in locating the source of epileptic discharges. The disadvantage of the MEG is its cost. The equipment for producing it is expensive in comparison with the apparatus used to produce EEGs and ERPs.

The heart of a magnetoencephalographic probe is a sensing device containing the special superconducting coils needed to detect the brain's very weak magnetic fields. This so-called SQUID (**superconducting quantum interference device**) is immersed in liquid helium to keep it at the low temperature necessary for superconductivity. One or more probes are moved across the surface of the skull, sending signals to the SQUID. Each probe produces an "iso-contour map," a chart with concentric circles representing different intensities of the magnetic field. Such gradient maps allow the calculation of the three-dimensional location of the neurons generating the field. They are also converted into a graph of electrical events very similar to the electrical potentials recorded by electroencephalographic instruments.

Figure 7.11 Imaging brain activity by using ERPs.

64 electrodes attached to a research subject's scalp are connected to...

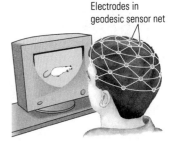

Electrodes in geodesic sensor net

...a computer display of electrical activity, showing a large positive (P₃) wave at the posterior right side of the head.

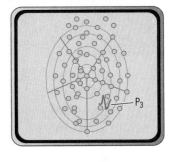

This electrical activity can be converted into a color representation showing the hot spot for the visual stimulus.

Resting   300 ms after viewing

Transcranial Magnetic Stimulation

Neuroscientists discovered long ago that they could learn about the functions of different brain areas by electrically stimulating the tissue. The results of the earliest studies of brain stimulation indicated that movements could be elicited by stimulating the motor cortex, sensations could be elicited by stimulating the sensory cortex, and complex cognitive functions such as speech could be disrupted by stimulating speech areas of the cortex. These techniques, however, can be used only during brain surgery (which on humans is done only for the purpose of repairing a problem in or near the brain); in most surgeries, the surgical procedures must take precedence over any detailed electrical mapping studies. A newer method has been developed that allows the brain to be stimulated through the skull.

When a magnetic stimulus is placed near the skull, brain function is disrupted in the region immediately adjacent to the magnet. In the new, nonsurgical mapping technique called **transcranial magnetic stimulation** (TMS), a small coil placed on the skull stimulates neurons in the brain regions directly under the coil. Figure 7.12 shows a typical experimental setup, including a possible placement of the coil on the skull (Figure 7.12A) and the area of the brain that the coil, so placed, would stimulate (Figure 7.12B, dotted line). Transcranial magnetic stimulation can be applied without danger to the normal brain.

One of the interesting findings obtained with the use of TMS is that individual brains differ substantially in the sizes of neocortex areas dedicated to different functions. For example, the area of the motor cortex from which movements of the body can be produced varies in size from one person to another. Furthermore, motor-cortex size varies as a function of experience (that is, a person who has learned complex motor skills tends to have a larger motor cortex). Likewise, language areas of the brain differ in size among individuals and as a function of how many languages a person speaks. Through the use of TMS, both individual differences in the organization of the cortex and differences due to a person's experiences can be analyzed.

In his early studies of electrical stimulation of the brain, Wilder Penfield was able to evoke memories in his patients by electrically stimulating their brains. It was unclear, however, whether the stimulation itself evoked the memories or whether the stimulation initiated an epileptic event that evoked an apparent memory. Similar mnemonic events have not been induced in normal subjects during TMS, suggesting that perhaps it was an epileptic event that evoked the memory-like experiences.

Figure 7.12 Transcranial magnetic stimulation. (Composite scan from Tomas Paul, Montreal Neurological Institute.)

A transcranial magnetic stimulator (TMS) is placed over a region of the cortex.

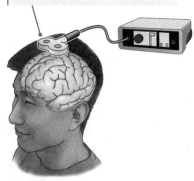

The TMS coil, shown here in composite MRI/PET scan photograph, interferes with brain function in the adjacent area, indicated by the dotted line.

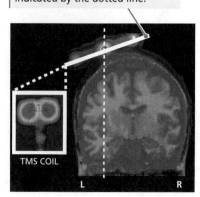

TMS COIL

L   R

Static Brain-Imaging Techniques

Aside from surgery, the first methods for peering into the living brain to see what was "in there" required taking X-rays of the brain. These methods were and continue to be important for medical diagnosis, especially to the neurologist looking for evidence of a brain tumor, stroke, or abnormality in brain vasculature. The most obvious limitation of these techniques, however, is that they produce a static two-dimensional image of what, in contrast, is a dynamic three-dimensional structure. Today, with the assistance of powerful computing techniques, it is possible to produce dynamic three-dimensional images of the living brain, not only to locate abnormalities more precisely, but also to detect changes in normal brain activity that are associated with ongoing behavior. These new methods allow brain structure and function to be imaged together.

We will first consider some of the early static techniques and then look at new, dynamic methods of imaging the changing brain.

Conventional Radiography

The first widely used method for producing a visual image of the brain, **conventional radiography** consists of passing X-rays through the skull onto an X-ray-sensitive film. As the X-rays travel through the head, they are absorbed to different degrees by different tissues: to a great degree by dense tissue such as bone, to a lesser degree by neural tissue, and less still by fluid such as that in the blood vessels and ventricles. Thus some parts of the film receive a greater dose of X-rays emerging from the far side of the skull than do others. When the film is developed, a shadowy negative image is revealed, showing the locations of different kinds of tissue. Radiography is still used for examining the skull for fractures and the brain for gross abnormalities.

Pneumoencephalography

Pneumoencephalography (literally *air-brain-graph*) is a method for enhancing conventional X-ray radiography by taking advantage of the fact that X-rays are not absorbed by air. First, a small amount of cerebrospinal fluid is removed from the subarachnoid space in the subject's spinal cord and replaced by air; then, with the subject sitting upright, X-rays are taken as the air moves up the spinal cord and enters the ventricular system. Because of the air inside them, the ventricles stand out clearly in the resulting image. Although it has diagnostic value (because expanded ventricles can mean loss of brain tissue and because constricted ventricles can indicate the presence of tumors), pneumoencephalography is painful and has been supplanted by newer imaging methods.

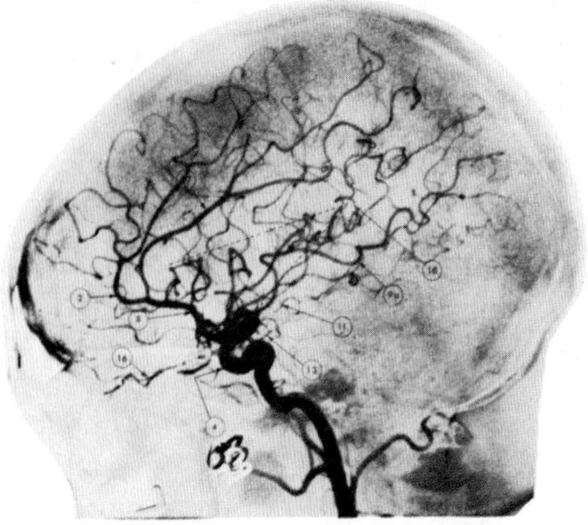

Figure 7.13 A normal carotid angiogram showing the large blood vessels. The face is pointing down toward the left. (From S. J. DeArmond et al., 1976. Copyright 1976 by Oxford University Press, Inc. Reprinted with permission.)

Angiography

Angiography is similar to pneumoencephalography except that a substance that absorbs X-rays is injected into the bloodstream (Figure 7.13). The presence of this "radioopaque" material in the blood produces an excellent image of the blood vessels, thus revealing circulatory abnormalities that might affect blood flow. Injecting a substance into the bloodstream is dangerous, however, and can be painful, and newer imaging methods are supplanting angiography.

(A) CT scan

Lesion

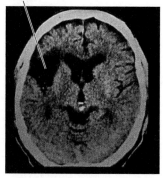

(B) Horizontal section

Anterior

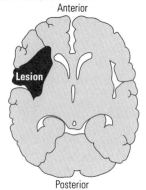

Lesion

Posterior

(C) Reconstruction, lateral view

Lesion

Plane of section in (A) and (B)

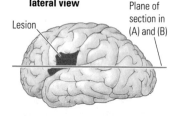

Figure 7.14 (A) A horizontal computerized tomography (CT) scan of a subject who presented with Broca's aphasia. The dark region at the left anterior is the location of the lesion. (B) A schematic representation of the horizontal section, with the area of the lesion shown in black. (C) A reconstruction of the brain, showing a lateral view of the left hemisphere with the lesion shown in black. (After H. Damasio and A. R. Damasio, *Lesion Analysis in Neuropsychology.* New York: Oxford University Press, 1989, p. 56.)

Computerized Tomography

The modern era of brain imaging began in the early 1970s, when Allan Cormack and Godfrey Hounsfield independently developed an approach now called X-ray **computerized tomography** (*tomo* meaning "cut," thus a picture through one section) or the **CT scan.** Cormack and Hounsfield both recognized that one could pass a narrow X-ray beam through the same object at many different angles, creating many different images of it, and then combine the images with the use of computing and mathematical techniques to create a three-dimensional image of the brain. The method has some resemblance to the way in which our two eyes (and our brains) work in concert to perceive depth and distance so as to locate an object in space. The CT scan, however, coordinates many more than two images, analogous perhaps to our walking to a new vantage point to obtain another view.

As we saw earlier, the absorption of X-ray radiation varies with tissue density. High-density tissue, such as bone, will absorb a lot of radiation. Low-density material, such as ventricular fluid or blood, will absorb little radiation. Neural-tissue absorption lies between these two extremes. The software of CT scanning translates these differences in absorption into a contrast-reversed image of the brain. In other words, light colors indicate low-density regions, and dark colors indicate high-density regions.

Figure 7.14A shows a typical example. The skull is seen as a white circle. The density of gray matter does not differ sufficiently from that of white matter for a CT scan to clearly distinguish between the two, and so the cortex and its underlying white matter show up as a more or less homogeneous gray. Ventricles can be visualized, however, because the fluid in them is far less dense; they, as well as some of the major fissures, are rendered darker in the CT scan. Each point on this image represents about a 1-mm-diameter circle of tissue, a resolution that is sufficient to distinguish two objects about 5 mm apart and is appropriate for localizing brain tumors and lesions. The lesion revealed in Figure 7.14A is a damaged region where the presence of fewer neurons and more fluid produces a contrast that appears as a darker area in the CT scan. The subject presented with symptoms of Broca's aphasia, a diagnosis confirmed by the location of the lesion in the left frontal cortex (adjacent to the butterfly-shaped lateral ventricles). Figure 7.14B, a drawing of the same horizontal section, uses shading to portray the lesion. Figure 7.14C is a lateral drawing of the left hemisphere showing the extent of the lesion, reconstructed from a series of horizontal CT scans.

Dynamic Brain Imaging

The development of the CT scan was momentous in two respects. First, it changed the practice of neurology by providing a way to look inside the head without using unpleasant or dangerous procedures. Second, it inspired other scientists to use clever mathematics and computer strategies to develop even more kinds of image reconstruction, such as positron-emission tomography

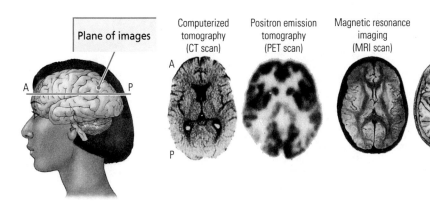

Figure **7.15** The CT, PET, and MRI scans shown here were created by three different techniques for imaging a slice of the brain. The fourth image is a photograph of a brain removed from a cadaver. (After Posner and Raichle, 1994.)

(PET), magnetic resonance imaging (MRI), and functional magnetic resonance imaging (fMRI). Figure 7.15 displays images obtained by each of these methods, along with a photograph of a dissected brain. The clarity of the photograph, in which the gray matter of the cortical surface and the white matter of the underlying fibers are easily distinguishable, provides a useful frame of reference for evaluating the resolution of the other techniques.

Positron-Emission Tomography

Positron-emission tomography was the first post-CT development in imaging. A PET camera, like the one shown in Figure 7.16, is a doughnut-shaped array of radiation detectors positioned to encircle a subject's head. Either a small amount of water, containing radioactive molecules to label it, is injected into the bloodstream or a gas containing the radioactive molecule is inhaled. The radioactive molecules pose little danger to the subject because they are very unstable and break down in just a few minutes. In the process, they release particles that are detected by the PET camera. A computer reconstructs variations in the density of the flow of particles from different locations to produce an image of a section of the brain. Because the radioactive molecules are carried in the bloodstream, the variations in the image represent areas of higher and lower blood flow. These differences are usually portrayed by a color gradient proceeding from white through reds, greens, and then blues. Color images made during different kinds of mental activity indicate which areas of the brain are active during the execution of particular cognitive functions.

Figure **7.16** A subject lying in a PET scanner, the design of which is illustrated in the drawing. In the scan, the bright areas are regions of high blood flow. (PET scan from Alan Carruthers/Photo Researchers.)

A small amount of radioactively labeled water is injected into a subject. Active areas of the brain use more blood and thus have more radioactive labels.

Positrons from the radioactivity are released; they collide with electrons in the brain, and photons (a form of energy) are produced, exit the head, and are detected.

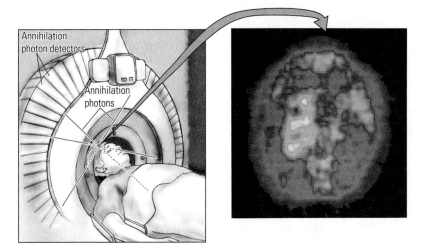

(A)

A positron released by an unstable nucleus of ^{15}O meets an electron and their mass is converted to two annihilation photons traveling at 180 degrees from each other.

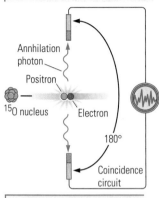

Opposing radiation detectors record the event when struck simultaneously by annihilation photons.

(B) Annihilation photon detectors

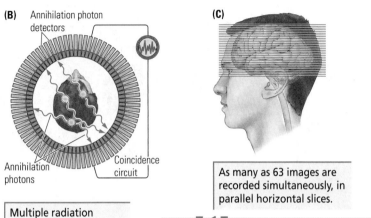

Annihilation photons

Coincidence circuit

Multiple radiation detectors are arranged about the subject's head.

(C)

As many as 63 images are recorded simultaneously, in parallel horizontal slices.

Figure 7.17 The technique of PET imaging. (After M. I. Posner and M. E. Raichle, *Images of Mind.* New York: Scientific American Library, 1996, p. 19.)

The particles detected by the PET camera are produced as illustrated in Figure 7.17. Briefly, positron-emission tomography is based on the unique behavior of positrons. When a radioactive substance is injected into the blood or enters the bloodstream through the lungs, it is carried by the blood to the brain and, as it travels, it decays by releasing positrons. These tiny, positively charged radioactive particles emerge from the nucleus of a radioactive atom because the nucleus has a deficiency of neutrons and so is unstable (Figure 7.17A). The nucleus of a radioactive form of oxygen, ^{15}O, for example, has eight protons and seven neutrons, whereas the stable, nonradioactive form of oxygen that we breath, ^{16}O, has eight of each. In the unstable nucleus, the extra proton breaks down into a positron and a neutron. The positron is expelled from the nucleus and the neutron stays. Positrons released from the nucleus lose their kinetic energy after traveling just a few millimeters in brain tissue and, when they come to rest, are attracted to the negative charge of electrons. A positron and an electron are annihilated when they come together, and the resulting energy creates two very powerful annihilation gamma rays (a gamma ray is a photon of a certain frequency) that leave the area of the annihilation event in exactly opposite directions. Because of their energy (511 kiloelectron volts), the annihilation photons exit the head at the speed of light. In PET, pairs of radiation detectors, each member of a pair opposing the other, are placed around the head to record these events. The paired detectors are programmed so that they record an event only when both are struck by annihilation photons simultaneously. The simultaneous collisions are counted, and the counts are converted into an image of the blood flow in the brain during the first minute after injection. Because the radioactive substance has been injected into the blood, areas of the brain with more blood flow will emit more photons.

A PET camera, as we have seen, is composed of many radiation detectors arranged in a ring about the subject's head (Figure 7.17B). Each detector in the ring is coupled to a detector directly opposite so that annihilation events in any region through the horizontal plane of the ring can be detected. Through the use of multiple rings of detectors, each of which can sample a slice of brain, annihilation events in many brain slices can be recorded. Modern PET cameras can obtain multiple parallel slices simultaneously, as shown in Figure 7.17C. Each image consists of **voxels,** or three-dimensional imaging regions, that are 2 mm³ in size. The shades indicate the density of annihilation events, as shown in Figure 7.18 (white = maximum density). Note that PET does not measure local neural activity directly; rather, it provides an inferential indication of neural activity on the assumption that blood flow increases in areas where neuron activity increases.

We can conclude from Figure 7.18 that the distribution of blood flow in the brain is not uniform. To arrive at conclusions about the link between blood flow and mental activity, however, PET researchers must resort to a statistical trick. They take the pattern of blood flow recorded when a subject is engaged in an experimental task and subtract from it the blood-flow pattern seen when the brain is in a selected control state (such as when the subject is lying quietly with eyes closed). As illustrated in Figure 7.19, this subtraction provides an image of the *change* in blood flow from state to state. The change can be averaged across subjects to yield an average image difference, revealing which areas of the brain are selectively active under different circumstances.

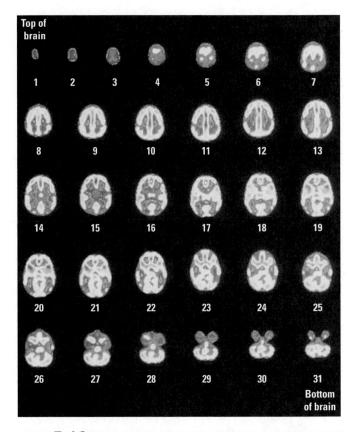

Figure 7.18 The PET images of blood flow obtained from a single subject resting quietly with eyes closed. Each scan represents a horizontal plane, or section, from the top (1) to the bottom (31) of the brain. (From M. E. Raichle, Mallinckrodt Institute of Radiology, Washington University School of Medicine.)

The radioactive materials used in PET have a half-life ranging from minutes to hours—for example, from 2.2 minutes for radioactive oxygen to a little more than an hour for radioactive fluorine. Consequently, the radioactive

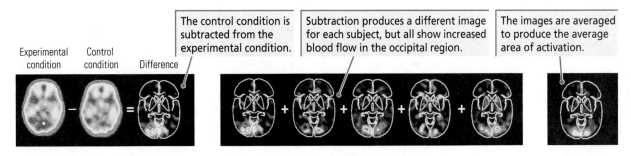

Figure 7.19 The procedure of subtraction. In the scans on the left, the control condition (in this case, resting while looking at a static fixation point) is subtracted from the experimental condition of looking at a flickering checkerboard. The subtraction produces a somewhat different image for each of the five subjects shown in the middle row, but all show increased blood flow in the occipital region. The images are averaged to produce the image on the right. (From M. E. Raichle, Mallinckrodt Institute of Radiology, Washington University School of Medicine.)

materials must be prepared close to the PET apparatus just before use, requiring the presence of a cyclotron in the vicinity of the experimental room. In spite of the expense incurred by this requirement, PET has important advantages over other imaging methods. One advantage is that it can be used to detect the decay of a wide range of radiochemicals. Literally hundreds of radiochemicals are used with PET to map a wide range of brain changes and conditions, including changes in pH, glucose, oxygen, amino acids, and proteins. PET can also be used to detect relative amounts of a given neural transmitter, the density of neurotransmitter receptors, or metabolic activities associated with learning, brain poisoning, or degenerative processes that might be related to aging.

Positron-emission tomography is widely used for the study of cognitive function, and here it has also had great success. For example, PET confirms that various regions of the brain have different functions. An early study of PET relating blood flow to language use not only confirmed that areas such as Broca's area and Wernicke's area are centers of language, but also indicated that a number of other areas, such as the dorsolateral frontal cortex, take part as well, in both the left and the right hemispheres (Figure 7.20). This finding resolved a longstanding debate in neuroscience. When Broca proposed that language was highly localized and lateralized in the brain, Hughlings-Jackson dissented on theoretical grounds, claiming that all areas of the brain contribute to language but in different ways. PET reveals that both positions are correct: language is localized, but many areas of the brain contribute to it.

In spite of their value, PET studies of cognitive function also have certain limitations. One has already been mentioned: PET imaging is indirect; it is measuring regional blood flow rather than neuronal activity. A second limitation is that PET imaging requires a subtraction process. A neutral condition of cognitive function is used as a baseline and is subtracted from an active condition of cognitive function. This process provides researchers not with a specific list of what areas of the brain are taking part in a task but with an indication of what areas become relatively more or less active as a task is performed. In some experiments, a number of subtractions are made. For example, a state in which a subject is reading a book may be subtracted from a resting state, and this resultant may be subtracted from a state in which a subject is reading only nouns. Each subtraction provides a more refined view of brain function but one that is more artificial. A third weakness of PET is that, in interpreting the data, researchers are making certain assumptions that might not be equally valid in every circumstance. For example, when a subject is given a visual task, researchers might be assuming that lower visual areas are active during all forms of visual activity, whereas higher visual areas are much more specific in function. Even if this assumption turns out to be correct when applied to vision, it may be incorrect when applied elsewhere.

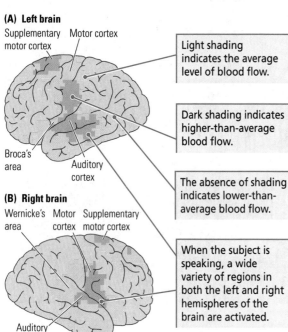

(A) Left brain

Supplementary motor cortex

Motor cortex

Broca's area

Auditory cortex

(B) Right brain

Wernicke's area

Motor cortex

Supplementary motor cortex

Auditory cortex

Light shading indicates the average level of blood flow.

Dark shading indicates higher-than-average blood flow.

The absence of shading indicates lower-than-average blood flow.

When the subject is speaking, a wide variety of regions in both the left and right hemispheres of the brain are activated.

Figure 7.20 Relating brain function to regional blood flow. Because the pattern of blood flow varies with the behavioral task, the relative importance of different areas in different functions can be inferred from PET scans showing blood flow under different experimental conditions.

Magnetic Resonance Imaging

Magnetic resonance imaging, or MRI, is a technology for noninvasively creating pictures of the soft tissues of the human body. It is named for its use of a large magnet (M) and a radiofrequency pulse of a certain resonance (R) to generate a signal from the brain in order to produce an image (I). Magnetic resonance imaging can be used to study both brain anatomy and neural function; and, because it does not make use of ionizing radiation, it is safe enough to use repeatedly on volunteers and patients, adult and child alike. A standard clinical MRI scanner typically has a three-dimensional resolution or voxel size better than 1 mm³, meaning that it can discriminate the activity in a piece of tissue of that size. Our description of MRI will be simplified in several ways, because the phenomenon would have to be described by using quantum mechanics to be completely accurate.

Magnetic resonance imaging is based on the principle that a hydrogen atom's nucleus, which consists of a single proton, behaves like a spinning bar magnet. In other words, each proton has a dipole, and so, as the proton spins, one end of its axis acts like the north pole of a bar magnet and the other end acts like the south pole. Ordinarily, protons are oriented at random, and so a given piece of tissue (all soft tissue contains water, which contains hydrogen) has no net dipole (Figure 7.21). When placed in a magnetic field, however, the spinning protons orient themselves with respect to the field's lines of force and thus all line up in parallel. In other words, the protons behave like the needle of a compass that aligns itself with the earth's magnetic field. Because of their spin, protons

(A)

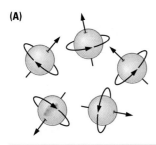

Each proton of a hydrogen atom rotates about its axis, acting as a small magnet with its own dipole. Normally the protons of hydrogen atoms are randomly positioned so that the tissue has no net charge.

(B)

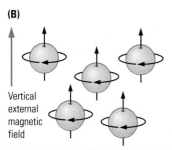

Vertical external magnetic field

When placed in a magnetic field the protons become aligned in parallel.

(C)

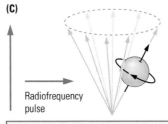

Radiofrequency pulse

A radiofrequency pulse applied to the tissue pushes the protons to their sides, causing them to wobble about their axes.

(D)

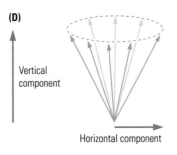

Vertical component

Horizontal component

This wobbling, called precession, produces two components of the magnetic field, a vertical component and a horizontal component.

Figure 7.21 The physics of MRI. The movements of hydrogen protons (A) under normal conditions, (B) under the influence of a magnetic field, and (C) under the additional influence of a horizontal radiofrequency pulse provide the basis for magnetic resonance imaging. (D) The wobbling (called precession) of the protons in the third condition produces two measurable magnetic-field components.

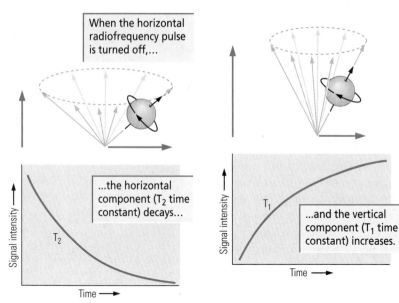

When the horizontal radiofrequency pulse is turned off,...

...the horizontal component (T_2 time constant) decays...

Signal intensity →

T_2

Time →

...and the vertical component (T_1 time constant) increases.

T_1

Signal intensity →

Time →

Figure 7.22 Magnetic resonance imaging time constants. When the horizontal radiofrequency pulse is turned off, relaxation in the vertical and horizontal components of the magnetic field provides two time constants that measure the recovery of the vertical component of the magnetic field (T_1) and the decay of the horizontal component (synchronous spinning) of the magnetic field (T_2).

generate an electrical current, and, because proton density varies in different brain tissue (cerebral spinal fluid, myelin, neurons), a recorder sensitive to such a current can be used to produce proton-density images of the brain when the photons are all aligned. Most such imaging is done with a magnetic field measuring 1.5 teslas in strength. Considering that 1 tesla is 10,000 gauss and the earth's magnetic field is only about 0.5 gauss, it is a big magnet.

Another way to make an image is to perturb the protons when they are aligned and record the changes in the electrical field that take place as a result of the perturbation. A brief radio pulse of a frequency that resonates with the target molecule is applied to a brain in which the atoms have been aligned in a magnetic field, and the radio pulses form a second magnetic field; the pulses generated by the second magnetic field can push the protons over onto their sides. Such "tipped" protons will now have two motions: their spin around their own axes and a spin around their longitudinal orientation. This second spin is like the wobble in a spinning top and is called **precession.** Imagine a dancer doing a never-ending pirouette while falling onto the floor to do a break-dance spin, all the time continuing to pirouette. This behavior in protons forms the basis for two other ways of making a magnetic resonance image.

When the second magnetic field is turned off, the protons that are spinning around their horizontal axis in synchrony begin to relax; that is, they begin to stand up again and to fall out of synchrony with one another. These relaxation processes are usually described by two time constants, T_1 and T_2 (Figure 7.22). For T_1, a current detector having an orientation horizontal to the vertical axis of the protons' initial alignment measures the time that it takes them to "right" from their tipped position and realign with the original magnetic field. For T_2, a second detector, having an orientation perpendicular to that of the first detector, measures the rate at which the protons lose synchrony around the horizontal axis after the magnetic pulse is turned off.

Protons have different relaxation rates and corresponding T_1 and T_2 time constants, depending on whether they are in fat, cerebrospinal fluid, neurons, bone, or other tissue (Figure 7.23). Therefore, if a measure is made of electrical current at a set time—for example, at the midpoint of relaxation—differences related to the composition of surrounding tissue can be measured. For example, the relaxation rates for cerebrospinal fluid are slower than those for white matter. These differences in time constants can be translated into images of the brain made up of gradients that correspond to its different tissues. Either T_1 or T_2 constants can be used, though one may be more suitable than the other in a given situation. For example, T_2 imaging is more sensitive to differences between damaged tissue and intact tissue and so is useful for detecting lesions.

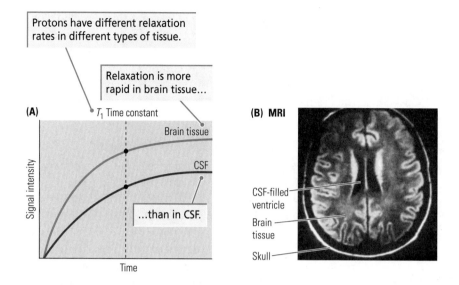

(A)

Protons have different relaxation rates in different types of tissue.

Relaxation is more rapid in brain tissue...

T_1 Time constant

Brain tissue

CSF

...than in CSF.

Signal intensity

Time

(B) MRI

CSF-filled ventricle

Brain tissue

Skull

Figure 7.23 Translating relaxation rates into brain images. (A) Protons have different relaxation rates in different tissue. (B) The differences can be translated into an image of the brain. (Magnetic resonance image from Gregory G. Dimijian/Photo Researchers.)

The MRI procedure is illustrated in Figure 7.24. The subject, lying prone on a bed with his or her head inserted into the center of the magnetic coils, must remain as still as possible. (Corrections are made for the slight head and brain movement produced by pulsations of the blood flow through the brain.) Density differences in the slice through the head are portrayed as colors (seen in the insert), producing a cross-sectional image of the head and of the brain. Two- or three-dimensional readings are obtained by the placement of three

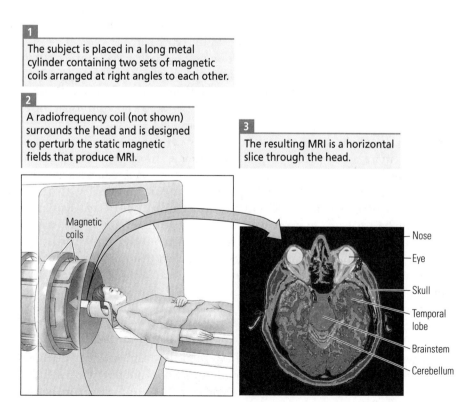

1
The subject is placed in a long metal cylinder containing two sets of magnetic coils arranged at right angles to each other.

2
A radiofrequency coil (not shown) surrounds the head and is designed to perturb the static magnetic fields that produce MRI.

3
The resulting MRI is a horizontal slice through the head.

Magnetic coils

Nose

Eye

Skull

Temporal lobe

Brainstem

Cerebellum

Figure 7.24 The machine used to obtain magnetic resonance images. (Magnetic resonance image from Gregory G. Dimijian/Photo Researchers.)

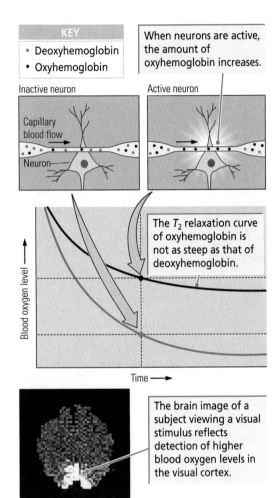

KEY
- Deoxyhemoglobin
- Oxyhemoglobin

When neurons are active, the amount of oxyhemoglobin increases.

Inactive neuron

Active neuron

Capillary blood flow

Neuron

Blood oxygen level

The T_2 relaxation curve of oxyhemoglobin is not as steep as that of deoxyhemoglobin.

Time

The brain image of a subject viewing a visual stimulus reflects detection of higher blood oxygen levels in the visual cortex.

Figure 7.25 The different relaxation curves of protons in unoxygenated (blue) and oxygenated (black) blood provide a measure of brain activity.

magnetic fields around the head, each of them graded along an axis. These gradients effectively divide the tissue into slices. The intersection of the slices provides 1-mm voxels, each having a unique signal. A computer performs a mathematical transformation on the voxels to produce an image of the brain (see the Snapshot on page 170).

Functional Magnetic Resonance Imaging

A discovery by Fox and colleagues revealed that, during increases in functional activity within the human brain, the increase in oxygen produced by increased blood flow actually exceeds the tissue's need for oxygen. As a result, the amount of oxygen in an area of activated brain increases. More specifically, as neurons become active, they increase their use of oxygen, resulting in a temporary dip in the amount of oxygen in the blood. At the same time, they signal the blood vessels to dilate to increase blood flow. The resulting increase in blood flow brings more oxygen to the area than the neurons can actually use, thus producing a relative increase in local oxygen. Before neuronal activation, the amounts of deoxyhemoglobin (hemoglobin without oxygen) and oxyhemoglobin (hemoglobin with oxygen) are about equal, but, after neuronal activation, the amount of oxyhemoglobin is higher. Changes in the oxygen content of the blood alter the magnetic properties of the blood's water, affecting the MRI signal (Figure 7.25). The T_2 signal is steeper in the unoxygenated state than it is in the oxygenated state.

Ogawa and his colleagues showed that MRI can accurately match these changes in magnetic properties to specific locations in the brain. The resulting images are known as **functional MRIs** (fMRIs). Figure 7.26 illustrates changes in the fMRI signal in the visual cortex of a person who is being stimulated visually with light. These changes indicate that, when the light is turned on, the visual cortex (bottom of the brain image) becomes more active than it was during baseline. In other words, from increases and decreases in the MRI signal produced by changes in oxygen levels, functional changes in the brain can be inferred.

When superimposed on MRI-produced brain images, fMRI changes in activity can be attributed to particular structures. The dense blood-vessel supply to the cerebral cortex allows for a spatial resolution of fMRI on the order of 1 mm. Thus, fMRI has better spatial resolution than that of PET. (Moreover, because fMRI can be used to accurately estimate metabolic changes in the brain of a single subject, no averaging across subjects is required.) On the other hand, because changes in blood flow take as long as a third of a second, the temporal resolution of fMRI is not as precise as that obtained with EEG recordings and ERPs.

There are other drawbacks to fMRI. Magnetic resonance imaging machines are expensive. The standard hospital MRI usually does not have the resolution required for brain research; so neuroscientists need to buy even more expen-

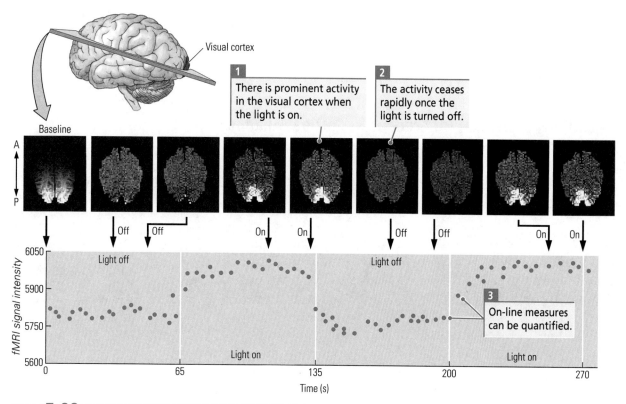

Figure 7.26 Functional MRI (fMRI) of a normal human brain during visual stimulation. The occipital cortex is at the bottom of each image. A baseline acquired in darkness (far left) was subtracted from the subsequent images. The subject wore tightly fitting goggles containing light-emitting diodes that were turned on and off as a rapid sequence of scans was obtained in a period of 270 seconds. (After Dynamic magnetic resonance imaging of human brain activity during primary sensory stimulation, by K. K. Kwong et al., *Proceedings of the National Academy of Sciences of the United States of America* 89, 1992, p. 5678.)

sive equipment to do their specialized research. In addition, fMRI can be difficult for subjects to endure. They must lie motionless in a long, noisy tube, an experience that can be quite claustrophobic. The confined space also restricts the types of behavioral experiments that can be performed. A typical solution to the lack of space and mobility is to have subjects look at images presented on mirrors and signal their responses with finger movements. Despite these drawbacks, MRI and fMRI provide wonderful information concerning brain structure and function.

Magnetic Resonance Spectroscopy

The images produced by MRI are actually depictions of differences in water density in the various tissues of the brain. The hydrogen nuclei affected by MRI's magnetic fields belong to water molecules, and water makes up 80% of the brain's soft-tissue composition. Thus, MRI does not image the remaining 20% of brain material, including all macromolecules (DNA, RNA, most proteins, and phospholipids), cell membranes, organelles (such as mitochondria),

S N A P S H O T

Describing Individual Differences in Cortical Anatomy

Individual A

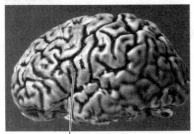

Pars opecularis with
one gyrus

Individual B

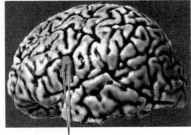

Pars opecularis with
two gyri

Individual C

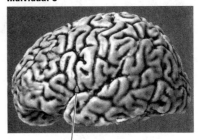

Pars opecularis hidden
in sulcus between gyri

A major advantage of magnetic resonance imaging is the clarity with
which it can distinguish between different regions of the brain and even
different regions of the cortex.
Consequently, fissures and gyri can
be visualized, and individual differences in brain anatomy
can be examined. The illustration in this box shows some
of the variations found by Tomaiuolo and colleagues with
the use of T_1 imaging of a part of the frontal cortex called
the **pars opercularis,** a region that constitutes part of
Broca's area. Electrical stimulation of this area in human
surgical patients reliably interferes with speech production, confirming that the area has a role in speech. The
MRI analysis showed individual differences there, with
some people having two small convolutions, some having

Magnetic resonance imaging of the human brain can be used for anatomical studies. A study
of Broca's area shows that one part of it, the pars opercularis, can consist of one gyrus (left),
two gyri (middle), or a gyrus that is hidden beneath adjacent gyri (right). (After Tomaiuolo
et al., 1999.)

one convolution, and others having convolutions hidden
within the surrounding gyri. The researchers also looked
for hemispheric differences and sex differences (by comparing the left and right hemispheres in male and female subjects) and found the size of the pars opercularis
to be similar in the two hemispheres and uncorrelated with
the subject's sex. These results suggest that, if there are
sex and hemispheric differences in this part of Broca's
area, they must reside in the function of the region rather
than in its gross structure.

and glial cells. This remaining 20% of the brain is imaged by using a magnetic
technique called **magnetic resonance spectroscopy** (MRS). In MRS, the frequency of the radio waves determine what tissue can be imaged. Varying the
frequency of the radio waves allows different components of the remaining
20% of brain tissue to be imaged.

One example of MRS's utility is provided by *N*-acetylaspartate, a substance
that is found in both neurons and glial cells and thus serves as a marker for
brain cells. Magnetic resonance spectroscopic imaging of this substance distinguishes brain cells from other substances. Analyses of *N*-acetylaspartate can
be used to detect the loss of brain cells in degenerative disease or the loss of

myelin in demyelinating disease (such as multiple sclerosis). Creatin is used in a further refinement of MRS analysis. It is present in much higher concentrations in neurons than in glia and so can be used as a neuronal marker (for example, to detect the loss of brain neurons in certain degenerative diseases). Magnetic resonance spectroscopy can also image some of the molecules involved in the transmission of information between neurons, including choline, the precursor molecule for acetylcholine, and glutamate, the major excitatory neurotransmitter molecule in the brain. In the future, MRS will likely be able to image many other brain molecules and so provide new avenues for investigating brain development, brain function, and brain disease.

Summary

In this chapter, a number of brain-imaging methods have been described: those that provide a static image of the structure of the brain and those that provide a functional image of the brain as it changes. What have researchers learned about brain function by using these techniques?

Electroencephalographic recordings tell us that, when a person is awake and engaged in some behavior, the whole brain is in an active state: the entire neocortex is displaying the beta electroencephalographic pattern. Similarly, when a person is resting or sleeping, the entire brain rests or sleeps, as indicated by the slower electroencephalographic alpha and delta patterns. Electroencephalograms also tells us that, during REM sleep, the brain displays a waking beta pattern. On the other hand, event-related potentials tell us that, even though the entire brain is active during waking, certain parts of it are momentarily much more active than others. The location of increased activity changes as information moves from one brain area to another. For example, ERPs produced by visual stimuli are first seen in primary visual cortex and later are seen in higher visual areas (which presumably function in perceptual or thought processes). From single-cell recordings, we know that the neurons employ a code and that cortical neurons are organized into functional groups.

The results of brain-lesion studies suggest that functions are highly localized, but metabolic imaging studies suggest that any behavior requires the collaboration of widespread circuits within the brain. For example, findings from the first PET studies indicated that language functions are performed not only by Broca's and Wernicke's areas of the left hemisphere but by similar areas in the right hemisphere as well, along with other brain areas, such as the dorsolateral cortex. The PET and fMRI methods record blood flow and other metabolic changes over periods of time measured in minutes and require complex subtraction procedures and the averaging of responses across a number of subjects.

Magnetic resonance imaging provides an exceptionally clear image of the brain and indicates that different people's brains can be structurally quite different. Records of blood flow obtained by using fMRI can be combined with MRI to identify the location of changes in the individual brain. In subsequent chapters, we will describe how these methods have revealed that more of the brain is active when a person performs novel tasks and less of the brain is active when a person performs familiar tasks. We will also describe how functional imaging shows that, when certain parts of the brain become active in response to a sensory stimulus, these same areas are frequently also active when the person remembers the stimulus.

Not only are all these techniques useful for understanding how the brain produces normal behavior, but they are also useful in diagnosing disease. In the past, the neurologist and neuropsychologist depended on laborious and imprecise behavioral testing to localize a tumor or diagnose a disease. Today, with the use of static and dynamic imaging procedures, tumors and lesions can be quickly localized. For example, because MRS can distinguish gray and white matter, it can be used to detect the degeneration of myelin that occurs in multiple sclerosis or the degeneration of neurons that occurs in Alzheimer's disease. Because all these imaging methods are central to many ongoing lines of research into brain function and dysfunction, further examples of their use will be presented in subsequent chapters.

References

Cormack, A. M. Reconstructions of densities from their projections, with applications in radiological physics. *Physics, Medicine, and Biology* 18:195–207, 1973.

Damasio, H., and A. R. Damasio. *Lesion Analysis in Neuropsychology*. New York: Oxford University Press, 1989.

Fox, P. T., and M. E. Raichle. Focal physiological uncoupling of cerebral blood flow and oxidative metabolism during somatosensory stimulation in human subjects. *Proceedings of the National Academy of Sciences of the United States of America* 83:1140–1144, 1986.

Housfield, G. N. Computerized transverse axial scanning (tomography) I: Description of system. *British Journal of Radiology* 46:1016–1022, 1973.

Kelley, D. D. Sleeping and dreaming. In E. R. Kandel, J. H. Schwartz, and T. M. Jessell, Eds. Principles of Neuroscience, 3d ed. New York: Elsevier, 1991, pp. 792–803.

Kleitman, N. *Sleep and Wakefulness*. Chicago: University of Chicago Press, 1965.

Neville, H. Event-related potentials in neuropsychological studies of language. *Brain and Language* 11:300–318, 1980.

Ogawa, S. L., L. M. Lee, A. R. Kay, and D. W. Tank. Brain magnetic resonance imaging with contrast dependent on blood oxygenation. *Proceedings of the National Academy of Sciences of the United States of America* 87:9868–9872, 1990.

Ojemann, G. A., S. G. Ojemann, and I. Fried. Lessons from human brain: Neuronal activity related to cognition. *The Neuroscientist* 4:285–300, 1998.

Posner, M. I., and M. E. Raichle. *Images of Mind*. New York: Scientific American Library, 1994.

Toga, A. W., and J. C. Mazziotta. *Brain Mapping: The Methods*. New York: Academic Press, 1996.

Tomaiuolo, F., J. D. MacDonald, S. Caramanos, G. Posner, M. Chivaras, A. C. Evans, and M. Petrides. Morphology, morphometry and probability mapping of the pars opercularis of the inferior frontal gyrus: An in vivo MRI analysis. *European Journal of Neuroscience* 11:3033–3064, 1999.

Windhorst, U., and H. Johansson. *Modern Techniques in Neuroscience Research*. New York: Springer, 1999.

chapter **8**

Organization of the Sensory Systems

One day in May 1971, when he was 19, Ian Waterman cut his finger. Because he was a butcher, the event was hardly unusual. The cut became infected, however, and over the next day or so the redness and inflammation spread a little way up his arm. Nevertheless, Ian ignored it, and eventually the problem seemed to disappear. Shortly after this occurrence, Ian began to suffer alternating hot and cold spells and was very tired, to such an extent that he was forced to take time off work. One day, although tired, he attempted to mow the lawn but lost control of the motorized lawn mower and stood helplessly as it careened away. About a week later, after falling as he tried to get out of bed, Ian was taken to the hospital. By this time, he could not move, had no sense of touch or pressure in his hands and feet (although he felt a tingling sensation in those areas), and was having trouble talking. The physicians in the hospital, who had never seen a case like Ian's, diagnosed him as having a neuropathy (a disorder of the peripheral nerves) and suggested that he would soon recover. Seven months later, he still had difficulty moving, and he still could not feel touch or pressure, although he was sensitive to temperature and pain. His mother tried to look after him at home, but he could do little for himself, and any attempt at activity exhausted him. He eventually was sent to a rehabilitation hospital where he began to learn some alternative ways of accomplishing everyday tasks.

His physicians finally concluded that Ian had lost all of the fine touch and pressure fibers and all of the sensory fibers that provided his nervous system with information about the position of his limbs and their movements. He had lost the vital sense, called proprioception, by which the body is aware of itself. Without proprioception, what some have called our "sixth sense," we are largely unable to engage in the "melody of movement."

Ian Waterman never did recover from his sensory loss, although with enormous effort he did learn to walk, to care for himself, and to drive a car. He did so by learning to replace proprioception with vision: by watching his hands as he made them perform and by watching his feet as he made them step. He was able to drive by using vision to estimate his movement speed and direction. But, if the lights went out or if his eyes were covered, he lost all ability to control the voluntary movements of his body. Ian was eventually able to hold a job, to marry, and to enjoy life, but movement always required an enormous conscious effort of him. He describes the effects of his loss of proprioception in this way.

> I am trying not to sound melodramatic and I'm sorry if it does, but sometimes I wake up in the morning and the knowledge of how much mental effort I'll have to put in to get by makes me feel down. It is like having to do a marathon everyday, a daily marathon. (Cole, 1991)

We may believe that we see, hear, touch, and taste real things in a real world. In fact, the only input that our brains receive from the "real" world is a series of action potentials passed along the neurons of our various sensory pathways. Although we experience sensations such as vision and olfaction as being fundamentally different from one another, the nerve impulses in the neurons of these two sensory systems are very similar, as are the neurons themselves. Neuroscientists understand a lot about how nerves can turn energy, such as light waves, into nerve impulses. They also know the pathways taken by those nerve impulses to reach the brain. But they do not yet know how we end up perceiving that one set of nerve impulses is what the world looks like and another set is what it tastes like.

Some scientists propose that everything that we know comes to us through our senses. Taken at face value, this statement seems reasonable. At the same time, we realize that our senses can deceive us, that two people can look at the same optical illusion and see very different images, and that a person dreaming does not normally think that the dream images are real. Therefore, other scientists have proposed the presence of some innate organization in the brain that helps create perceptions and helps us to distinguish between those that are real and those that are imaginary. Again, taken at face value, this proposal, too, seems reasonable.

This chapter presents an overview of how sensory information reaches the cortex, placing special emphasis on two features of sensory organization: (1) the presence of many submodalities in each of the sensory systems and (2) the fact that each submodality is designed for a specific function.

General Principles of Sensory System Function

We are accustomed to thinking of ourselves as having five sensory systems (touch, taste, smell, vision, and hearing), but a more accurate statement would be that there are five modalities, or groups of senses, through which we receive information. Each of these modalities consists of submodalities that may differ from one another with respect to the receptors that respond to sensory events, the size of the fibers that travel from the receptors to the brain, the connections that are made within the brain, and any actions that the submodalities produce.

Sensory Receptors

Sensory receptors are specialized parts of cells that transduce or convert sensory energy (for example, light photons) into neural activity. Each sensory system has a different type of receptor, specialized to be sensitive to a different form of energy. For vision, light energy is converted into chemical energy in the receptors of the retina, and this chemical energy is in turn converted into neural activity. In the auditory system, air pressure waves are converted into a number of forms of mechanical energy, the last of which eventually activates the receptors, which then produce a neural discharge. In the somatosensory system, mechanical energy activates mechanoreceptors, which in turn generate neural activity. For taste and olfaction, various molecules carried by the air or contained in food fit themselves into receptors of various shapes to activate neural activity. For pain sensation, tissue damage releases a chemical that acts like a neurotransmitter to activate pain fibers and thus produce a nerve impulse.

All sensory receptors also act as filters. If we put flour into a sieve and shake it, the more finely ground particles will go through the holes, whereas the coarser particles and lumps will not. Similarly, receptors of each sensory modality are designed to respond to only a narrow band of energy—analogous to particles of certain sizes—within the given modality's energy spectrum. Figure 8.1 illustrates the entire electromagnetic spectrum, for example, and indicates the very small part of it that our visual system can detect. Were our visual receptors somewhat different, we would be able to see in the ultraviolet or infrared parts of the electromagnetic spectrum, as some other animals are able to do. There are even some people who do not have receptors for parts of the usual visual spectrum, and we refer to those people as color-blind.

There are many other slight differences in the visual receptors of individual people that affect the color that they can see. Joris Winderickx and his colleagues report that about 60% of men have one form of the red receptor and 40% have another form. Many females may have both forms. Hence different people may see different "reds." For audition, the receptors of the human ear respond to sound waves between 20 and 20,000 Hz (cycles per second), but elephants can hear and produce sounds that are less than 20 Hz, and bats can hear and produce sounds that are as high as 120,000 Hz. In fact, in comparison with those of other animals, human sensory abilities are rather average. Even our pet dogs have "superhuman" powers: they can detect odors that we cannot detect, they can hear the ultrasounds emitted by rodents and bats, they can hear the low-range sounds of elephants, and they can see in the dark. (We can hold up only our superior color vision.) Different species have different sets of sensory system filters; each set produces an idiosyncratic representation of reality.

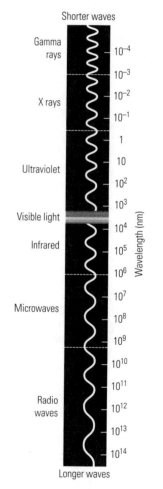

Figure 8.1 The part of the electromagnetic spectrum that is visible to the human eye lies within a narrow range.

Energy Transduction

Each type of sensory receptor performs some kind of transduction, the changing of energy received by the receptor into action potentials. In the visual system, the chemical reactions induced by photons of light striking the receptor

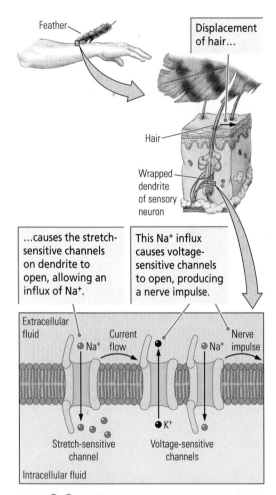

Feather

Displacement of hair...

Hair

Wrapped dendrite of sensory neuron

...causes the stretch-sensitive channels on dendrite to open, allowing an influx of Na⁺.

This Na⁺ influx causes voltage-sensitive channels to open, producing a nerve impulse.

Extracellular fluid

Na⁺

Current flow

Na⁺

Nerve impulse

K⁺

Stretch-sensitive channel

Voltage-sensitive channels

Intracellular fluid

Figure 8.2 A hair's touch receptor is activated by a feather. The dendrite of a sensory neuron is wrapped around the hair so that, when the hair is displaced, the dendrite stretches. Stretch-sensitive sodium channels on the dendrite open up, depolarizing the dendrite membrane to threshold, which causes voltage-sensitive channels to open. The opening of the voltage-sensitive channels produces an action potential that is conducted along the dendrite as a nerve impulse.

must be turned into action potentials. In the taste system, the receptors that respond to molecules of food must turn that chemical energy into action potentials. For touch, the receptors on our skin must convert the mechanical energy of an object touching the skin into action potentials. Figure 8.2 illustrates how the displacement of a single hair on the arm results in an action potential that we interpret as touch. The dendrite of a sensory neuron is wrapped around the base of the hair. When the hair is displaced, the dendrite is stretched by the displacement. The dendrite has Na^+ channels that are "stretch sensitive" and open in response to the stretching of the dendrite's membrane. If the influx of sodium in the stretch-sensitive sodium channels is sufficient to depolarize the dendrite to its threshold for an action potential, the voltage-sensitive Ka^+ and Na^+ channels will open to produce an action potential.

The receptors for hearing and balance also have hairs that, when displaced, activate stretch-sensitive channels. In contrast, in the visual system, light particles striking chemicals in the receptors in the eye cause a chemical reaction that activates ion channels in the membranes of relay neurons. An odorous molecule in the air lands on an olfactory receptor in the nose and fits itself into a specially shaped compartment, thereby opening ion channels on the nerve membrane. When tissue is damaged, injured cells release a chemical that activates ion channels on a pain nerve.

Receptive Fields

Every receptor organ and cell has a **receptive field,** a specific part of the world to which it responds. For example, if you fix your eyes on a point directly in front of you, the part of the world that you see is your eyes' receptive field. If you close one eye, what the remaining eye sees is the receptive field for that eye. Within the eye is a cup-shaped retina that contains thousands of receptor cells called rods and cones. The little part of the world from which each receptor cell receives light at a given moment is the receptive field of that rod or cone.

Cells in the central nervous system that receive input from receptors also have receptive fields. For example, the neurons in the visual cortex that receive information from a given rod or cone have the same receptive field as that rod or cone does. Movements of the head or eyes can change the rod's or cone's or visual system's receptive field. Other receptive fields are more permanent. The part of the skin on which a skin receptor is located forms that receptor's receptive field and generally consists of a few square millimeters of tissue, whereas the receptive field for all tactile sensation consists of the entire body surface. Receptive fields not only sample sensory information but also, in contrast with what neighboring receptors detect, locate sensory events in space.

Researchers discover the receptive fields for various parts of the brain by monitoring the activity of a cell or part of the brain while moving an appropriate stimulus around until the cell or brain region responds. The location of the stimulus when it elicits the response is the location of the receptive field. With this technique, brain researchers have produced a map of the cortex's various sensory fields.

Rapidly and Slowly Adapting Receptors

By means of dedicated receptors that differ in their sensitivity, each sensory system is able to answer questions such as, Is something there? And is it still there? The receptors that detect whether something is there are of a type that is easy to activate but then stops responding after a very short time. They are called **rapidly adapting receptors.** If you touch your arm very lightly with a finger, for example, you will immediately detect the touch, but, if you then keep your finger still, the sensation will fade as the receptors adapt. That is because the rapidly adapting hair receptors on the skin are designed to detect the movement of objects on the skin. If you push a little harder when you first touch your arm, you will be able to feel the touch for much longer because many of the body's pressure-sensitive receptors are **slowly adapting receptors,** receptors that adapt more slowly to stimulation. In the visual system, the rod-shaped receptors are responsive to light of any wavelength, have lower response thresholds, and adapt more rapidly than do the cone-shaped receptors, which are sensitive to color but adapt more slowly. A dog, with mainly black–white vision, is thus very sensitive to moving objects but has more difficulty detecting objects when they are still.

Self and Other Receptors

Our sensory systems are organized in such a way that they tell us both what is happening in the world around us and what we ourselves are doing. Receptors that respond to external stimuli are called **exteroceptive;** receptors that respond to our own activity are called **interoceptive.** For example, objects in the world that we see, that touch us, or are touched by us and objects that we smell or taste act on exteroceptive receptors, and we know that they are produced by an external agent.

When we move, however, we ourselves change the perceived properties of objects in the world, and we experience sensations that have little to do with the external world. When we walk, visual stimuli appear to stream by us, a stimulus configuration called **optic flow.** When we move past a sound source, we hear **auditory flow,** changes in the intensity of the sound that occur because of our changing location. Some of the information about these changes comes to us through our exteroceptive receptors, but we also learn about them from our interoceptive receptors; that is, receptors in our muscles and joints and in the vestibular organs of the middle ear that tell us about the position and movement of the body itself.

Not only do interoceptive receptors play an important role in helping to distinguish what we ourselves do from what is done to us, but they also help us to interpret the meaning of external stimuli. For example, their interpretation of optic or auditory flow is useful in telling us how fast we are going and whether we are going in a straight line or up or down and whether it is we who are moving or whether it is an object in the world that is moving. Try this experiment. Slowly move your hand back and forth before your eyes and gradually increase the speed of the movement. Your hand will eventually get a little blurry because your eye movements are not quick enough to follow its movement. Now keep your hand still and move your head back and forth. The image of the hand remains clear. When the interoceptive receptors in the vestibular system inform your visual system that your head is moving, the visual system responds by compensating for the head movements so that the hand is observed as a stationary image.

Localization and Identification

Sensory systems are able to locate stimuli because the receptive fields of individual receptors overlap. If one receptor is more activated by a stimulus than its neighbor is, then more of that stimulus must be located in the receptive field of the first receptor than in its neighbor's.

Overlap in combination with receptor density helps sensory systems to identify stimuli as well. Receptor density is particularly important in touch, demonstrated by the fact that tactile receptors on the fingers are numerous compared with those on the back. This difference explains why the fingers can discriminate remarkably well and the back not so well. You can prove it by moving the tips of two pencils apart to different degrees as you touch different parts of your body. The ability to recognize the presence of two pencil points close together, a measure called **two-point discrimination,** is highest on the parts of the body with the most receptors.

The visual system uses two quite different organizational strategies to facilitate detection. In the fovea (a small area of the retina that provides color vision), the receptors—all cone cells—are small and densely packed to make fine discriminations in bright light. In the periphery of the retina, the rod cells that are the receptors for black–white vision are larger and more scattered, but they are connected to the rest of the visual system in such a way that large numbers of rods give their input to only a few neurons. The discrimination ability of rods is not good but, because of their converging connections, their ability to detect light (say, a lighted match at a distance of 2 miles on a dark night) is quite remarkable.

Neural Relays

In each sensory system, the receptor connects to the cortex through a sequence of three or four intervening neurons (for example, the visual and somatosensory systems have three, and the auditory system has four). There is no straight-through, point-to-point correspondence between one relay and the next but rather a recoding of activity in each successive relay. Moreover, different stages in the relay allow the sensory system to mediate different responses.

Three important kinds of events can take place at the neuronal synapses between one relay and the next.

- First, a motor response can be produced. For example, axons from pain receptors synapse first in the spinal cord, where they can produce a withdrawal reflex of the hand or foot. They next synapse in the brainstem, where they can produce whole-limb or whole-body movements, presumably away from the painful stimulus. Finally, they synapse in the thalamus, where, in conjunction with their connections in the cortex, they can produce awareness and hence avoidance of the noxious stimulus.
- Second, the messages carried by these systems can be modified. For example, descending impulses from the cortex can block or amplify pain signals. When we are excited by an activity, as occurs when we are playing a sport, we may not notice an injury, because a descending message from the brain inhibits the transfer of a pain stimulus from the spinal cord to the brain. Later, when we think about the injury, it begins to be much more painful because a descending signal from the brain now amplifies the pain signal from the spinal cord.
- Third, systems can interact with one another. For example, we often rub the area around an injury to reduce the pain. This activation of fine touch and pressure receptors can block the transmission of information along the pain pathways.

Information Coding

After having been transduced, all sensory information from all sensory systems is encoded by action potentials. They travel into the brain along bundles of axons—called **nerves** until they enter the brain or spinal cord and called **tracts** thereafter—and every bundle carries the same kind of signal. How do action potentials encode the different kinds of sensations (how does vision differ from touch), and how do they encode the features of particular sensations (how does purple differ from blue)?

Parts of these questions seem easy to answer and other parts are very difficult. The presence of a stimulus can be encoded by an increase or decrease in the discharge rate of a neuron, and the amount of increase or decrease can encode the stimulus intensity. Qualitative visual changes, such as a change from red to green, can be encoded by activity in different neurons or even by different levels of discharge in the same neuron (for example, more activity might signify redder and less activity greener).

What is less clear, however, is how we perceive such sensations as touch, sound, and smell as being different from one another. Part of the explanation is that these different sensations are processed in distinct regions of the cortex. Another part is that we learn through experience to distinguish them. A third part is that each sensory system has a preferential link with certain kinds of reflex movements, constituting a distinct wiring that helps keep each system distinct at all levels of neural organization. For example, pain stimuli produce withdrawal responses, and fine touch and pressure stimuli produce approach responses. The distinctions between the sensory systems, however, are not *always* clear: there are people who can hear in color or identify smells by how the smells sound to them. This mixing of the senses is called

synesthesia. Anyone who has shivered when hearing certain notes of a piece of music (or at the noise that chalk or fingernails can make on a blackboard) has "felt" sound.

Sensory Subsystems

We are used to thinking of vision as the product of a single sensory system, but, if we refer to Figure 8.3, we can see that it is really the work of a number of submodalities. We are aware of the operation of some of these submodalities, but we will not know of the operation of others until they are discovered through further study of the brain. These visual submodalities each consist of a discrete visual center in the brain (numbered 1 through 7 in Figure 8.3) and the pathway that connects it to the retina. There is a pathway to the suprachiasmatic nucleus (number 1) of the hypothalamus, which controls the daily rhythms of such behaviors as feeding and sleeping in response to light changes. There is a pathway to the pretectum (2) in the midbrain, which controls pupillary responses to light. There is a pathway to the superior colliculus (3) in the midbrain, which controls head orientation to objects. There is a pathway to the pineal body (4), which controls long-term circadian rhythms. There is a pathway to the accessory optic nucleus (5), which moves the eyes to compensate for head movements. There is a pathway to the visual cortex (6), which controls pattern perception, depth perception, color vision, and the tracking of moving objects. Finally, there is a pathway to the frontal cortex (7), which controls voluntary eye movements. Many of these pathways are less direct than the illustration indicates, and they may connect with other brain centers as well.

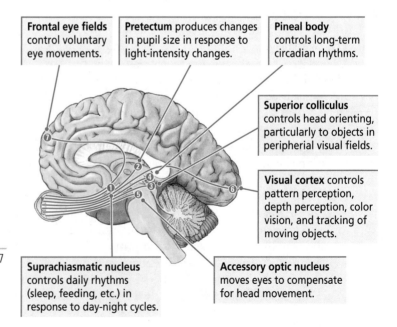

Frontal eye fields control voluntary eye movements.

Pretectum produces changes in pupil size in response to light-intensity changes.

Pineal body controls long-term circadian rhythms.

Superior colliculus controls head orienting, particularly to objects in peripherial visual fields.

Visual cortex controls pattern perception, depth perception, color vision, and tracking of moving objects.

Suprachiasmatic nucleus controls daily rhythms (sleep, feeding, etc.) in response to day-night cycles.

Accessory optic nucleus moves eyes to compensate for head movement.

Figure 8.3 The visual subsystems. The numbers 1–7 represent visual centers in the brain; the lines are a simplification of the individual pathways leading to them. Each pathway and its number represents a particular subsystem.

Many of the visual subsystems projecting into different brain regions have multiple submodalities of their own. In the projection to the visual cortex, for example, the systems for pattern perception, color vision, depth perception, and visual tracking are as independent from one another as the systems that encode hearing are independent from those that encode taste. The fact that they are in close anatomical proximity cannot be taken to mean that they are functionally identical or interchangeable. And, like vision, all of the other sensory modalities contain subsystems that perform distinct and specific roles. One indication that taste, for example, consists of more than one submodality is that the taste receptors of the first two-thirds of the tongue send information to the brain through the facial nerve (VII), whereas the taste receptors of the posterior third of the tongue send information to the brain through the glossopharyngial (IX) nerve.

Multiple Representations

In most mammals, the neocortex represents the sensory field of each modality (that is, of vision, hearing, touch, smell, or taste) not once but a number of times (Figure 8.4). How many times a representation occurs depends on the species of animal. Note that the squirrel in Figure 8.4 has 3 visual areas, whereas the owl monkey has 14. If each of these visual areas responds to one feature of the environment—assuming that the visual areas of these species have been mapped adequately—then owl monkeys can see 11 kinds of things that squirrels cannot see. Considering that both species live in trees, have color vision, have good depth perception, and so on, what those 11 things might be is not immediately obvious. Monkeys, however, make better use of their fingers, make use of facial expressions, and have a more varied diet than squirrels do, and these differences might account for some of the monkey's additional visual areas. We humans, in turn, have many more representations than do rhesus monkeys, and so we presumably perceive the visual world in ways that rhesus monkeys cannot. (Perhaps some of the additional visual areas are necessary for reading.)

All mammals have at least one primary cortical area for each sensory system. Additional areas are usually referred to as secondary areas because most of the information that reaches them is relayed through the primary area. Each additional representation is probably dedicated to encoding one specific aspect of the sensory modality. Thus, for vision, different areas may be take part in the perception of color, of movement, and of form.

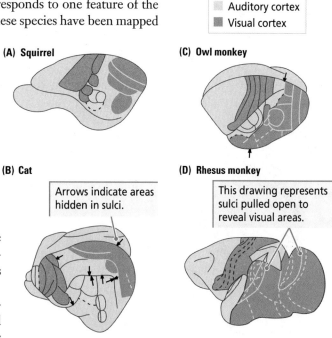

KEY
- ■ Somatic cortex
- ■ Auditory cortex
- ■ Visual cortex

(A) Squirrel

(C) Owl monkey

(B) Cat

Arrows indicate areas hidden in sulci.

(D) Rhesus monkey

This drawing represents sulci pulled open to reveal visual areas.

Figure 8.4 Subdivisions of the sensory cortex in several well-studied mammals. (A) Researchers have identified 5 somatic regions, 2 or 3 auditory regions, and from 2 to 4 visual regions in the squirrel. (B) Twelve visual areas, 4 somatic areas, and 5 auditory areas have been defined in the cat. (C) Fourteen visual areas, 4 auditory areas, and 5 somatic areas have been demonstrated in the owl monkey. (D) Twelve visual areas, 4 auditory areas, and 8 somatic areas have been defined in the rhesus monkey. (After Kaas, 1987.)

(A)

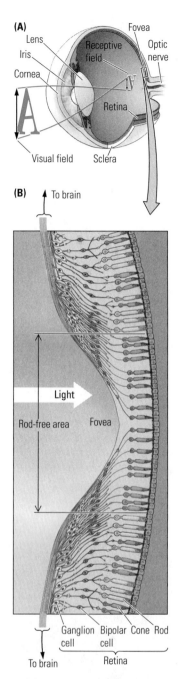

(B)

Light

Rod-free area Fovea

Ganglion Bipolar Cone Rod
cell   cell

Retina

To brain

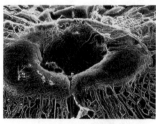

SEM of fovea

Vision

Visual Receptors

A schematic illustration of the eye and its visual receptor surface, the retina, is presented in Figure 8.5. Rays of light enter the eye through the cornea, which bends them slightly, and then through the lens, which bends them to a much greater degree so that the visual image is focused on the receptors at the back of the eye. The light then passes through the photoreceptors to the **sclera,** which reflects the light back into the photoreceptors. The light's having to pass through the layer of retinal cells (to be bounced back at them by the sclera) poses little obstacle to our visual acuity for two reasons. First, the cells are relatively transparent and the photoreceptors are extremely sensitive; they can be excited by the absorption of a single photon of light. Second, many of the fibers forming the optic nerve bend away from the retina's central part, or **fovea,** so as not to interfere with the passage of light through the retina. Because of this bending, the fovea is seen as a depression on the retinal surface.

The retina contains two types of photoreceptive cells—rods and cones—both of which function to transduce light energy into action potentials. **Rods,** which are sensitive to dim light, are used mainly for night vision. **Cones** are better able to transduce bright light and are used for daytime vision. There are three types of cones, each type maximally responsive to a different set of wavelengths—either red, blue, or yellow—and thus they mediate color vision. Rods and cones differ in their distribution across the retina: cones are packed together densely in the foveal region, whereas rods are absent from the fovea entirely and more sparsely distributed in the rest of the retina. Thus, to see in bright light, it is best to look directly at things and, to see in dim light, it is best to look slightly away.

The photoreceptive cells synapse with, and induce graded potentials in, a very simple type of neuron called a **bipolar cell.** Bipolar cells, in turn, induce action potentials in ganglion cells. The **ganglion cells** send axons into the brain proper (remember that the retina is considered to be part of the brain). In addition to the photoreceptive cells that relay information to the cortex, other cells in the retina—including horizontal and amacrine cells—play a role in the retina's encoding of information. The retina contains at least one other receptor, a specialized ganglion cell that forms the retinohypothalamic tract to the suprachiasmatic nucleus; this specialized receptor-ganglion cell plays a role in regulating circadian rhythms.

Visual Pathways

The axons of ganglion cells leave the retina to form the optic nerve. Just before entering the brain, the two optic nerves (one from each eye) meet and form the **optic chiasm** (from the Greek letter X, or chi). At this point, about half the

Figure 8.5 (A) The anatomy of the eye. (B) The anatomy of the retina. (Photomicrograph from Professor P. Motta, Dept. of Anatomy, University La Sapienza, Rome/Science Photo Library/Photo Researchers.)

fibers from each eye cross as illustrated in Figure 8.6; so the right half of each eye's visual field is represented in the left hemisphere of the brain and the left half of each eye's visual field is represented in the right hemisphere of the brain. In an animal with eyes on the side of its head (the rat, for example), as many as 95% of its optic fibers cross to ensure this crossed representation.

Having entered the brain proper, the optic tract, still consisting of the axons of ganglion cells, diverges to form a number of separate pathways. The largest of them is the **geniculostriate pathway,** the projection that goes to the lateral geniculate nucleus or body (LGB) of the thalamus and then to layer IV of the visual cortex, a layer called the **striate cortex** (it is very large in primates and has the appearance of a stripe across the visual cortex; hence the name striate, or "striped," cortex). The ganglion cells of the geniculostriate system synapse in the LGB.

The LGB has six well-defined layers: layers 2, 3, and 5 receive fibers from the ipsilateral eye, and layers 1, 4, and 6 receive fibers from the contralateral eye. The topography of the visual field is reproduced in the LGB: the central parts of each layer represent the central visual field, and the peripheral parts represent the peripheral visual field.

The LGB cells project mainly to area 17 of the visual cortex (there are smaller projections to other areas), where they are distributed in such a way that the visual field is again topographically represented, although, as illustrated in Figure 8.7, the representation is upside down, inverted, and reversed. The central part of the visual field is represented at the back of the visual cortex, and the peripheral part is represented toward the front of the visual cortex. The upper part of the visual field is represented below the calcarine fissure, and the lower

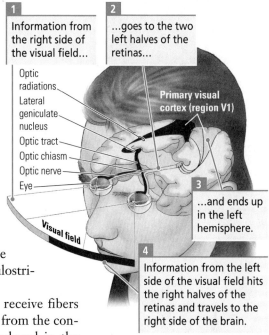

1 Information from the right side of the visual field...

2 ...goes to the two left halves of the retinas...

Optic radiations
Lateral geniculate nucleus
Optic tract
Optic chiasm
Optic nerve
Eye

Primary visual cortex (region V1)

Visual field

3 ...and ends up in the left hemisphere.

4 Information from the left side of the visual field hits the right halves of the retinas and travels to the right side of the brain.

Figure 8.6 This horizontal slice through the brain shows the visual pathways from each eye to region V1 of each hemisphere.

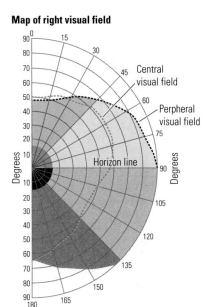

Map of right visual field

Central visual field
Peripheral visual field
Horizon line
Degrees

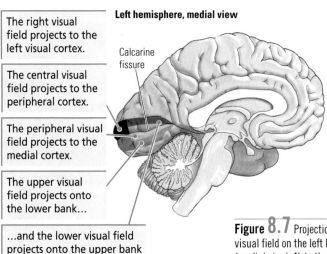

The right visual field projects to the left visual cortex.

The central visual field projects to the peripheral cortex.

The peripheral visual field projects to the medial cortex.

The upper visual field projects onto the lower bank...

...and the lower visual field projects onto the upper bank of the calcarine fissure.

Left hemisphere, medial view

Calcarine fissure

Figure 8.7 Projection of the right visual field on the left hemisphere (medial view). Note the relation between the topography of the visual field and the topography of the cortex. (After Poggio, 1968.)

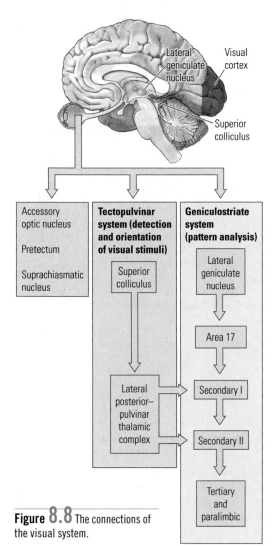

part of the visual world is represented above the calcarine fissure. Figure 8.7 also shows that the visual input striking the left side of each retina, and therefore originating from the right side of the world, eventually travels to the left hemisphere.

Other visual pathways go to the superior colliculus, accessory optic nucleus, pretectum, and suprachiasmatic nucleus, as summarized in Figure 8.8. Note also that the projections to the superior colliculus can reach the cortex through relays in the lateral posterior-pulvinar complex of the thalamus. Because this so-called **tectopulvinar pathway** constitutes the visual system in fish, amphibians, and reptiles, we can expect it to be capable of reasonably sophisticated vision. Because there are two visual pathways to the neocortex, complete destruction of the main pathway, the geniculostrate pathway, does not render a subject completely blind.

Figure 8.8 The connections of the visual system.

Hearing

Auditory Receptors

Sound consists of changes in air pressure. The frequency, size, and complexity of these changes determine what we hear. We hear the frequency of pressure changes as changes in pitch; we hear the size of pressure changes as loudness; and we hear the complexity of pressure changes as timbre, the perceived uniqueness of a sound (Figure 8.9). These differences in pressure are detected by receptors in the inner

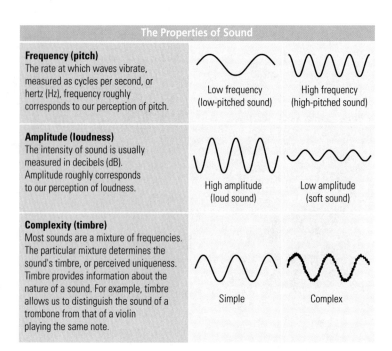

The Properties of Sound

Frequency (pitch)
The rate at which waves vibrate, measured as cycles per second, or hertz (Hz), frequency roughly corresponds to our perception of pitch.

Low frequency (low-pitched sound)   High frequency (high-pitched sound)

Amplitude (loudness)
The intensity of sound is usually measured in decibels (dB). Amplitude roughly corresponds to our perception of loudness.

High amplitude (loud sound)   Low amplitude (soft sound)

Complexity (timbre)
Most sounds are a mixture of frequencies. The particular mixture determines the sound's timbre, or perceived uniqueness. Timbre provides information about the nature of a sound. For example, timbre allows us to distinguish the sound of a trombone from that of a violin playing the same note.

Simple   Complex

Figure 8.9 Sound has three physical dimensions: frequency, amplitude, and complexity. These dimensions correspond to the perceptual dimensions of pitch, loudness, and timbre.

ear, and from there they are conveyed to the brain as action potentials. Areas of the cortex in the temporal lobe interpret the action potentials as sounds, language, and music.

The ear is described has having three major divisions: the outer ear, middle ear, and inner ear (Figure 8.10). The outer ear consists of the **pinna** and the external ear canal. The pinna catches the waves of pressure and directs them into the external ear canal, which amplifies the waves somewhat and directs them to the eardrum. The middle ear consists of the eardrum and a series of three little bones (ossicles) connected to it called the **hammer, anvil,** and **stirrup.** The bones in turn connect to the **oval window** of the inner ear. When sound waves strike the eardrum, it vibrates. The vibrations are transferred to the bones, producing an action like that of a piston that not only conveys the vibrations to the round window but also amplifies them, much as a drumstick amplifies the movement of the drummer striking a drum. In short, pressure waves in the air are amplified and transformed

Figure 8.10 The ear has three major anatomical divisions: the outer ear, middle ear, and inner ear.

1 The pinna catches sound waves and deflects them into the external ear canal.

2 Waves are amplified and directed to the eardrum, causing it to vibrate,...

3 ...which in turn vibrates ossicles.

4 Ossicles amplify and convey vibrations to the oval window.

7 ...which in turn cause cilia of outer hair cells, embedded in the tectorial membrane, to bend. This bending generates neural activity in hair cells.

6 ...causing the basilar and tectorial membranes to bend,...

5 Vibration of oval window sends waves through cochlear fluid,...

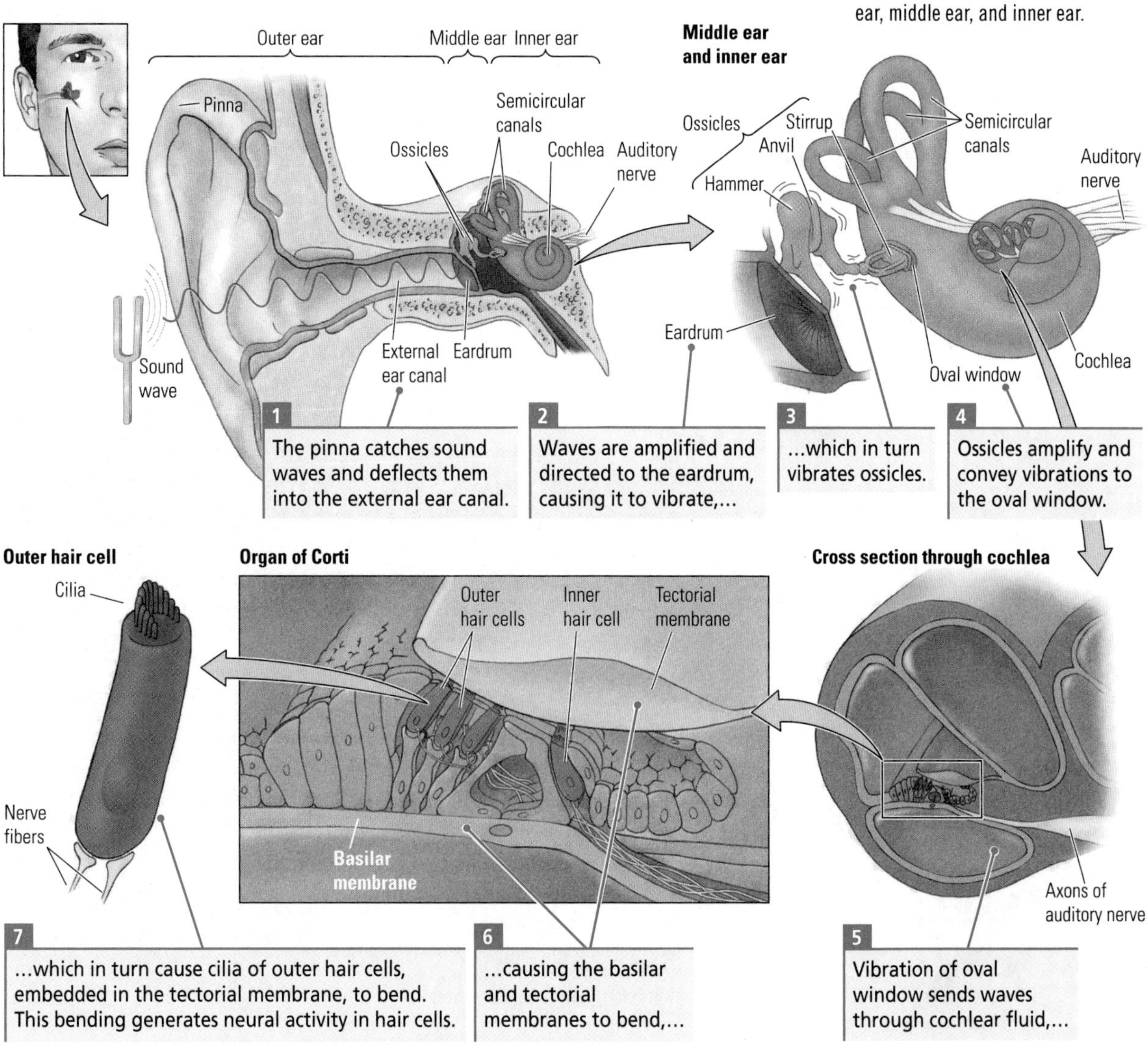

a number of times in the ear: by deflection in the pinna, by oscillation as they travel through the external ear canal, and by the movement of the bones of the middle ear.

In the inner ear is the **cochlea,** which is the part of the ear that contains the sensory receptors. The cochlea is rolled up into the shape of a snail (see Figure 8.10). It is filled with fluid, and floating in the middle of this fluid is a membrane called the **basilar membrane.** The ear's sensory receptors are hair cells embedded in a part of the basilar membrane called the **organ of Corti.** When the round window vibrates, it sends waves through the fluid, causing the basilar membrane to bend and thus stimulating the hair cells to produce an action potential. The larger the air pressure changes are, the more the basilar membrane bends, causing larger numbers of hair cells to generate action potentials.

The frequency of a sound is transduced by the longitudinal structure of the basilar membrane, which proves to be a sheet of tissue when the cochlea is unrolled (Figure 8.11A). The basilar membrane is not uniform from end to end; rather, it is narrow and thick near the round window and thinner and wider at its other end. In 1960, George von Békésy found a way of observing the actual movement of a wave along the membrane. He placed particles of silver on the membrane and filmed them jumping to different heights in different places, depending on the sound frequency. Higher sound frequencies caused maximum peaks near the base of the basilar membrane (that is, near the oval window), and lower sound frequencies caused maximum peaks near the apex (farthest from the

Figure 8.11 (A) The cochlea has been unwound to show the progression of a sound wave along the basilar membrane. (B) The tonotopic representation of sound on the basilar membrane and on the primary auditory cortex. A retractor has been used to open the Sylvian fissure and reveal the auditory cortex which is buried within it.

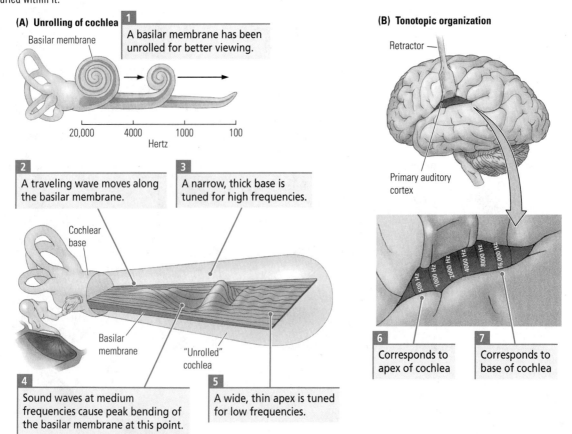

(A) Unrolling of cochlea

Basilar membrane

1 A basilar membrane has been unrolled for better viewing.

20,000   4000   1000   100
Hertz

2 A traveling wave moves along the basilar membrane.

3 A narrow, thick base is tuned for high frequencies.

Cochlear base

Basilar membrane

"Unrolled" cochlea

4 Sound waves at medium frequencies cause peak bending of the basilar membrane at this point.

5 A wide, thin apex is tuned for low frequencies.

(B) Tonotopic organization

Retractor

Primary auditory cortex

500 Hz   1000 Hz   2000 Hz   4000 Hz   8000 Hz   16,000 Hz

6 Corresponds to apex of cochlea

7 Corresponds to base of cochlea

oval window). These patterns are roughly analogous to what happens when you shake a towel. If you shake it very quickly, the waves are very small and remain close to the part of the towel that you are holding. But if you shake the towel slowly with a large movement of your arms, the waves reach their peak farther away from you. The hair cells in the organ of Corti are maximally disturbed at the point where the wave peaks, producing their maximal neural discharge at that place. A signal composed of many frequencies will cause several different points along the basilar membrane to vibrate and will excite hair cells at all those points.

Single-cell recordings from the primary auditory cortex in the temporal lobes show that different points in the cortex respond maximally to different frequencies, just as occurs in the basilar membrane (Figure 8.11B). Thus, the **tonotopic theory,** which states that different points on the basilar membrane represent different sound frequencies, also applies to the auditory cortex: there, too, different locations represent different sound frequencies. Presumably, projections from hair cells of the organ of Corti create a representation of the basilar membrane in the neocortex.

As in the visual system, each receptor cell in the auditory system has a receptive field, and so does each cell in the higher auditory centers. The receptive field of a hair cell is not a point in space, as it is in the visual system, but rather a particular frequency of sound. Thus, in contrast with the retinotopic maps in the visual system, the auditory system is composed of tonotopic maps. Because the auditory system locates sound in space by comparing the time of the sound's arrival at each ear, it must also possess some representation of the space around the body, a map on which it locates the sources of sound.

Auditory Pathways

The axons of the hair cells leave the cochlea to form the major part of the auditory nerve, the eighth cranial nerve (Figure 8.12). This nerve first projects to the level of the medulla in the lower brainstem, synapsing either in the dorsal or ventral cochlear nuclei or in the superior olivary nucleus. The axons of cells in these areas form the lateral lemniscus, which terminates in discrete zones of the inferior colliculus. (Note that the superior colliculus functions to orient the head toward the direction of sounds.) Two distinct pathways emerge from the colliculus, coursing to the ventral and the dorsal medial geniculate bodies. The ventral region projects to the core auditory cortex (AI or Brodmann's area 41), and the dorsal region projects to the secondary regions, thus adhering to the sensory systems' general pattern of having multiple, independent ascending pathways to the cortex. In contrast with the visual-system pathways, the projections of the auditory system provide both ipsilateral and contralateral inputs to the cortex; so there is bilateral representation of each cochlear nucleus in both hemispheres.

Balance

The inner ear also contains the receptor system that allows us to stand upright without losing our balance. This system is made up of two parts: (1) the **semicircular canals** and (2) the **otolith organs** consisting of the **utricle** and **saccule.** All these structures contain hair cells that are bent when the head changes position. The three semicircular canals lie in different

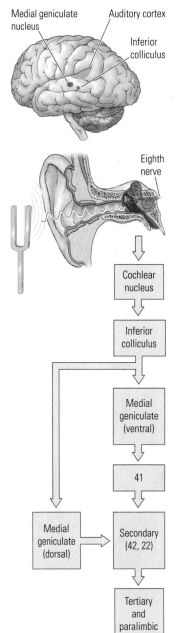

Figure 8.12 The major connections of the auditory system.

planes perpendicular to one another and so can respond to any movement of the head. The otolith organs detect linear acceleration of the head and are also responsive to changes in the position of the head with respect to gravity. In addition, the otoliths are sensitive to the static position of the head in space, in contrast with the semicircular canals' sensitivity to head movement. Fibers from the balance receptors project over the eighth nerve to a number of nuclei in the brainstem. These nuclei help keep us balanced while we move and also aid in controlling eye movements.

Body Senses

Figure 8.13 The perceptions derived from the body senses depend on different receptors located variously in skin, muscles, joints, and tendons.

The visual and auditory systems are known as exteroceptive systems because they are sensitive to stimuli from the external environment. The somatosensory system—literally, the "body sense" system—also has an exteroceptive function: it feels the world around us. In addition, however, it is interoceptive, meaning that it provides information about the position of body segments relative to one another and the position of the body in space; it also records internal bodily events. Thus, the somatosensory system, like the others, is not a single sensory system but a multiple one composed of several submodalities. Three major submodalities are pain and temperature (the perception of unpleasant stimuli, touch, and pressure), also called nocioception; the perception of objects using fine touch and pressure receptors, or hapsis; and the perception of body awareness, called **proprioception.** The various receptors that mediate perception in each of these three submodalities are listed in Figure 8.13.

Meissner's corpuscle

Free nerve endings for pain

Free nerve endings for temperature

Pancinian corpuscle

Ruffini corpuscle

Merkel's receptor

Hair receptor

Nocioception (pain and temperature)	Adaptation
Free nerve endings for pain (sharp pain and dull pain)	Slow
Free nerve endings for temperature (heat or cold)	Slow

Damage to the dendrite or to surrounding cells releases chemicals that stimulate the dendrite to produce action potentials.

Hapsis (fine touch and pressure)	Adaptation
Meissner's corpuscle (touch)	Rapid
Pacinian corpuscle (flutter)	Rapid
Ruffini corpuscle (vibration)	Slow
Merkel's receptor (steady skin indentation)	Slow
Hair receptors (flutter or steady skin indentation)	Slow

Pressure on the various types of tissue capsules mechanically stimulates the dendrites within them to produce action potentials.

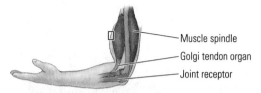

Muscle spindle

Golgi tendon organ

Joint receptor

Proprioception (body awareness)	Adaptation
Muscle spindles (muscle stretch)	Rapid
Golgi tendon organs (tendon stretch)	Rapid
Joint receptors (joint movement)	Rapid

Movements stretch the receptors to mechanically stimulate the dendrites to produce action potentials.

Somatosensory Pathways

Two major somatosensory pathways extend from the spinal cord to the brain: one for touch and proprioception, the other for pain and temperature (Figure 8.14). The fibers of the sensory neurons that make up the first system are relatively large and heavily myelinated. Their cell bodies are located in the dorsal-root ganglia, their dendrites project to the sensory receptors in the body, and their axons project into the spinal cord. The dendrite and axon of each cell are joined into one continuous nerve fiber. In the spinal cord, the axons of this system ascend through the dorsal columns to synapse in the dorsal-column nuclei in the base of the brainstem. The cell bodies of these nuclei send their axons across the spinal cord to form the medial lemniscus that ascends to synapse in the ventrobasal thalamus. This thalamic nucleus then projects primarily to Brodmann's area 3-1-2, as well as to area 4.

Initially, the fibers of the second pathway, for pain and temperature sensation, are somewhat smaller and less myelinated than those of touch and proprioception. They follow the same course as that of the touch and proprioception fibers to enter the spinal cord but, once there, they project to neurons in the more central region of the spinal cord, the **substantia gelatinosa.** The second-relay cells then send their axons across to the other side of the cord, where they form the ventral spinothalamic tract. These fibers eventually join the touch and proprioception fibers in the medial lemniscus. They, too, terminate primarily in the ventrobasal thalamus, as well as in the posterior thalamus; and these messages, too, are relayed in turn to area 3-1-2 of the cortex. Thus we see that there are two somatosensory pathways, each taking a somewhat different route to the cortex, as in other sensory systems.

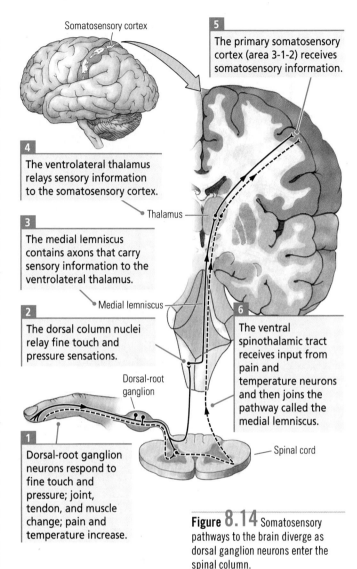

Somatosensory cortex

5 The primary somatosensory cortex (area 3-1-2) receives somatosensory information.

4 The ventrolateral thalamus relays sensory information to the somatosensory cortex.

Thalamus

3 The medial lemniscus contains axons that carry sensory information to the ventrolateral thalamus.

Medial lemniscus

2 The dorsal column nuclei relay fine touch and pressure sensations.

Dorsal-root ganglion

1 Dorsal-root ganglion neurons respond to fine touch and pressure; joint, tendon, and muscle change; pain and temperature increase.

6 The ventral spinothalamic tract receives input from pain and temperature neurons and then joins the pathway called the medial lemniscus.

Spinal cord

Figure 8.14 Somatosensory pathways to the brain diverge as dorsal ganglion neurons enter the spinal column.

Somatosensory Cortex

Like other sensory systems in the cortex, the somatosensory cortex is composed of a primary area and a number of secondary areas. As illustrated in Figure 8.15, SI (somatosensory area I, or Brodmann's area 3-1-2) is the primary area, and it sends projections into SII and areas 5 and 7. Area SI also sends projections into the adjacent motor cortex, area 4.

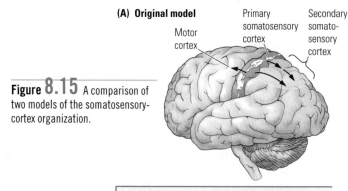

Figure 8.15 A comparison of two models of the somatosensory-cortex organization.

(A) Original model

Motor cortex

Primary somatosensory cortex

Secondary somatosensory cortex

In this model, the primary somatosensory cortex is organized as a single homunculus with large areas representing body parts that are very sensitive to sensory stimulation.

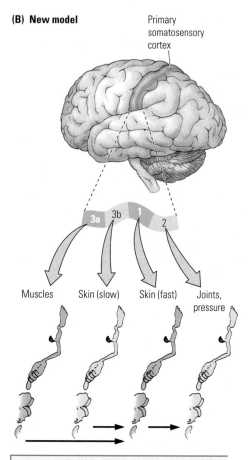

(B) New model

Primary somatosensory cortex

3a   3b   1   2

Muscles   Skin (slow)   Skin (fast)   Joints, pressure

In this model, the primary somatosensory cortex is organized into four separate homunculi consisting of areas 3a, 3b, 1, and 2. Information is passed from other areas into area 2, which is responsive to combined somatosensory information.

When Wilder Penfield first stimulated the sensory cortex in conscious epilepsy patients and had them report the sensations that they felt, he created a map that topographically represented the body surface on the primary somatosensory cortex. The regions representing feeling in the mouth and eyes were in the ventral part of SI, the regions representing hand and finger sensation were in the middle, and the regions corresponding to feet were in the dorsal area (Figure 8.15A). The map is called a homunculus, meaning "little man," because it can be drawn as a distorted human figure.

The results of subsequent studies, mainly using monkeys and making use of smaller recording electrodes, suggest that the primary somatosensory cortex contains a number of homunculi, one for each of its four known subregions, 3a, 3b, 1, and 2, as shown in the lower part of Figure 8.15B. The results of recording experiments show that each of these areas is dominated by responses to one type of body receptor, although there is overlap. Area 3a represents muscle sense (position and movement of muscles), area 3b represents both slowly and rapidly adapting skin receptors, area 1 represents rapidly adapting skin receptors, and area 2 represents deep pressure and joint sense. Thus, the body is represented at least four times in SI. Additionally, a number of other receptor types are represented in each area; so it is possible that there are still more body-representation areas.

Although Penfield underestimated the number of homunculi, he was correct about the disproportion in the sizes of some parts of the homunculi relative to other parts (Figure 8.16). The density of somatosensory receptors varies greatly from one place to another on the body surface (and varies from species to species), and somatotopic maps manifest this variability. Thus in humans, the areas representing the hands and tongue are extremely large, whereas the areas representing the trunk and legs are small. The area representing the face of the rat, including input from the tactile hairs known as vibrissae on its face, is very large relative to that representing any other body part. The face and vibrissae of the rat are extremely sensitive, enabling rats to make tactile discriminations with only a single vibrissa. In contrast, an anteater, which uses its tongue to explore for ants, should have a truly impressive tongue representation on its sensory cortex.

Taste and Smell

In humans, the senses of taste and smell (or olfaction) do not have the extensive cortical representation that vision, audition, and touch do, and thus they do not appear as attractive (perhaps we should say glamorous!) to neuroscientists for study. As a result, less is known about these senses than about the other ones. Our discussion of them therefore will be limited, especially with respect to cortical contributions to taste and olfaction.

Receptors

In contrast with the other senses, in which the stimuli are various physical forms of energy, the stimuli for taste and smell are chemical. Specialized receptors have evolved for each of these systems, as for all the rest. For taste, the receptors are the taste buds, which most people mistakenly believe to be the bumps on the tongue. In fact, the bumps, called papillae, are probably there to help the tongue grasp food; the taste buds lie buried around them. Chemicals in food dissolve in the saliva that coats the tongue and disperse through the saliva to reach the taste receptors. Thus, if the tongue is dry, the taste buds receive few chemical signals, and food is difficult to taste.

There are five different taste-receptor types, each responding to a different chemical component of food. The four most familiar are sweet, sour, salty, and bitter. The fifth type of receptor—sometimes called the *umami* receptor—is specifically responsive to glutamate, and perhaps to protein. The specificity of any given taste receptor is not absolute, however; single fibers can respond to a variety of chemical stimuli. It therefore appears likely that the perceived taste of any stimulus results from a pattern of firing of the entire population of taste receptors.

Curiously, there are significant differences in taste preferences both within and between species. For example, humans and rats like sucrose and saccharin solutions, but dogs reject saccharin and cats are indifferent to both. Similarly, within the human species, there are clear differences in taste thresholds. Older people generally have higher thresholds, largely because there is a dramatic reduction in the number of taste buds as we age. Children tolerate spices poorly because their sense of taste is stronger. In addition, as Bartoshuk has shown, there are absolute differences among adults: some people perceive certain tastes as being strong and offensive, whereas other people are indifferent to them.

The receptor surface for olfaction is the olfactory epithelium, which is located in the nasal cavity. It is composed of three cell types: receptor cells and supporting cells on an underlying layer of basal cells. The axons projecting

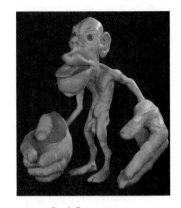

Figure 8.16 The misshapen appearance of this homunculus represents the disproportion among the areas of the somatic sensory cortex dedicated to different parts of the body. (After Bloom and Lazereson, 1988.)

from the receptor cells form the olfactory tract. The epithelium's outer surface is covered by a layer of mucus in which the receptor cell's cilia are embedded. Thus, odors must pass through the mucus to reach the receptors, which means that changes in the properties of the mucus (such as occur when we have a cold) may influence how easily an odor can be detected. It is interesting to note the extent to which the area of the olfactory epithelium varies across species. In humans, the area is estimated to range from 2 to 4 cm²; in dogs, the area is about 18 cm²; and, in cats, it is about 21 cm². Such differences support the observation that some species are more sensitive to odors than others. How different odors produce different activity in the olfactory receptors is not clear. Individual receptors are not specific to single odors, and so that each receptor is likely to contain various proteins that respond differently to different molecules. Perhaps different receptors have different distributions of receptor proteins. Again, it is the summed action of many receptors, leading to a particular pattern of neural activity, that the olfactory system identifies as a particular odor.

Pathways

Three cranial nerves carry information from the tongue: the glossopharyngeal nerve (IX), the vagus nerve (X), and the chorda tympani branch of the facial nerve (VII). All three nerves enter the solitary tract, which forms the main gustatory nerve. At that point, as illustrated in Figure 8.17, the pathway divides in two. One route goes to the ventroposterior medial nucleus of the thalamus, which in turn sends out two pathways, one going to SI and the other to a region just rostral to SII, in the insular cortex. The latter region is probably dedicated

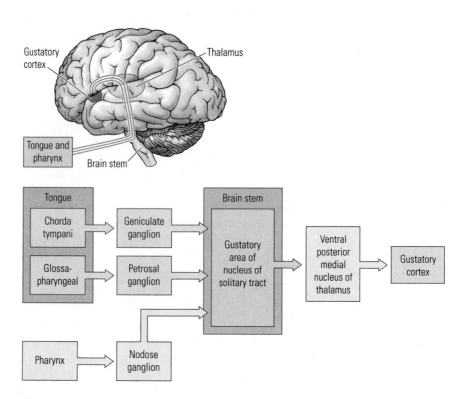

Figure 8.17 The major connections of the taste system.

entirely to taste, because it is not responsive to tactile stimulation. In contrast, the SI projection is sensitive to tactile stimuli and is probably responsible for the localization of tastes on the tongue. (Those who enjoy wine are familiar with this distinction because wines are described not only by their gustatory qualities but also by the way that they taste on different parts of the tongue.) These areas project in turn to the orbital frontal cortex, which may be the secondary taste area. The second pathway from the solitary tract leads to the pontine taste area, which in turn projects to the lateral hypothalamus and amygdala. Both of these areas have roles in feeding, although the precise contribution to this behavior of the gustatory input is uncertain.

The axons of the olfactory-receptor cells synapse in the olfactory bulb, which is made up of several layers and may be conceptualized as an analogue to the retina. The major output of the bulb is the lateral olfactory tract, which passes ipsilaterally to the pyriform cortex, the amygdala, and the entorhinal cortex (Figure 8.18). The primary projection of the pyriform cortex goes to the central part of the dorsal medial nucleus of the thalamus, which in turn projects to the orbitofrontal cortex. Thus, the orbitofrontal cortex can be considered the primary olfactory neocortex.

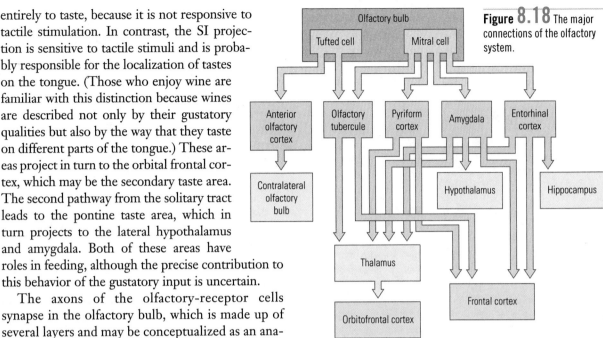

Figure 8.18 The major connections of the olfactory system.

Perception

We have reviewed the basic organization of the sensory systems, traced their neural pathways from the receptors to the cortex, and identified some of the principles governing their operation. But there is far more to sensation than the simple transduction of physical energy into nervous activity. When compared with the richness of actual sensory experience, this chapter's description of sensory anatomy and physiology is bound to seem rather sterile. Part of the reason for this disparity is that our sensory impressions are affected by the contexts in which they take place, by our emotional states, and by our past experiences. All these factors contribute to **perception,** the subjective experience of the transduction events outlined in this chapter, and perception, rather than sensory transduction, is of most interest to the neuropsychologists (see the Snapshot on page 194).

As clear proof that perception is more than sensation, consider that different people may transform the same sensory stimulation into totally different perceptions and that perceptions are affected by the context of the sensory input. The classic demonstration of the former phenomenon is an ambiguous image such as the well-known Rubin's vase shown in Figure 8.19A. This image may be seen either as a vase or as two faces. If you fix your eyes on the center of the picture, the two perceptions will alternate even though the sensory

(A) Ambiguous reversible figure

(B) Müller-Lyer illusion

Figure 8.19 Demonstration of the distinction between sensation and perception. (A) This ambiguous or reversible image first described by Rubin can be seen as a vase or as two faces. (B) In this Müller-Lyer illusion, the top line appears longer than the bottom line because of the contextual cues provided by the arrowheads.

SNAPSHOT

Watching the Brain Taste

After falling from a horse while riding in the mountains of Iran, J. H. required surgery to remove a blood clot from her right frontal cortex. She recovered quickly from her accident and the surgery but experienced a lingering disability from the accident in the form of an inability to enjoy food. Although she had always enjoyed cooking and took pride in her expertise in preparing food from many regions of the world, hardly a meal now went by when she did not complain that she wished she could taste what she was eating. Flavor, our sense of the taste of food, is a marriage of stimuli from the tongue and the nose. Where in the brain does this union of senses take place? Imaging methods are helping researchers to answer this question.

To image the effects of odors and tastes, researchers must first eliminate the effects of the movement of air through the nostrils and the effects of moving the tongue and mouth from the imaging record. This separation of "sniffing" from "smelling" can be accomplished in part by having subjects sample air on control trials or by anesthetizing the nostrils so that the movement of air is not perceived. The usual "sip and spit" method employed in laboratory taste tests cannot be used, because the movements of the mouth produce movement artifacts that interfere with recording the brain image; but special delivery techniques that use droppers or even the electrical stimulation of taste buds can partly circumvent the problem.

A review of various imaging studies suggests that the orbital frontal cortex, especially the right orbital frontal cortex, plays a special role in the perception of odors and taste (Zatorre and Jones-Gotman, 2000). The adjoining illustration, for example, presents the results of a number of independent studies (including studies on odor recognition, odor intensity, and the connection between odor and affect, or mood) in which PET or MRI was used to record responses to olfactory stimuli. The locations of the brain activity recorded in each study, represented by crosses, are clustered in the midlateral part of the orbital frontal cortex of both the left and the right hemispheres, although in most cases the right-hemisphere response was both stronger and more localized. A similar review of studies of taste shows that a similar region of the orbital frontal cortex is activated by taste stimuli. These summaries of olfactory and taste research suggest that the union of olfac-

stimulation remains constant. Similarly, the Müller-Lyer illusion in Figure 8.19B demonstrates the influence of context. The top line is perceived as longer than the bottom line, although both lines are exactly the same length. The contextual cues (the arrowheads) alter the perception of each line's length. Such ambiguous images and illusions demonstrate the workings of complex perceptual phenomena that are mediated by the neocortex. They are an enlightening source of insight into cognitive processes.

Summary

This chapter has provided an overview of the sensory systems. Historically, five sensory abilities have been recognized, but the results of research have revealed that each consists of many submodalities, each with different receptors, different pathways, and different brain targets. Some sensory systems also have both exteroceptive and interoceptive receptors, which respond to stimuli outside

(A) Olfactory stimuli **(B) Taste stimuli**

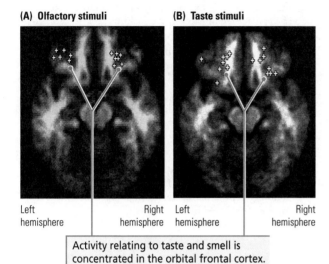

Left hemisphere   Right hemisphere   Left hemisphere   Right hemisphere

Activity relating to taste and smell is concentrated in the orbital frontal cortex.

(A) A horizontal section of the brain illustrating the locations of responses to olfactory stimuli in six different studies. (B) A horizontal section of the brain illustrating the locations of responses to taste stimuli in four different studies. (From Zatorre and Jones-Gottman, 2000).

(E. T. Rolls. The orbitofrontal cortex. In A. C. Roberts, T. W. Robbins, and L. Weiskrantz, Eds. *The Prefrontal Cortex*. Oxford: Oxford University Press, 1998, pp. 67–86.
R. J. Zatorre and M. Jones-Gotman. Function imaging in the chemical senses. In A. W. Toga and J. C. Mazziota, Eds. *Brain Mapping: The Applications*. San Diego: Academic Press, 2000, pp. 403–424.)

tion and taste to produce flavor is likely to take place in the orbital frontal cortex.

Although there have been no PET or MRI studies specifically directed at the perception of flavor, the results of single-cell recording studies have been helpful in answering the question of where flavor perception takes place. Rolls (1998), recording the activity of neurons in the orbital frontal cortex of rhesus monkeys, found that some neurons respond to taste stimuli, others to olfactory stimuli, and still others to both olfaction and taste. He suggested that this third group of neurons are flavor neurons that participate in the learning of flavor discriminations, the association of flavor with the visual images of foods that might have a flavor, and the learning that some flavors are pleasant and reinforcing, whereas others are not.

and within the body, respectively. This division no doubt helps us to distinguish between "self" and "other," as well as to interpret the stimuli themselves.

All the sensory systems use a common code, sending information to the brain in the currency of action potentials. At the same time, the primary brain targets for different modalities and submodalities are discrete. Any sensory information that converges does so in higher cortical areas. Our motor responses to different submodalities also are quite specific. We are conscious of the operation of some submodalities but unconscious of others, such as visual submodalities that control eye movements or circadian rhythms. The anatomical organization is similar for each of the different senses in that each sensory system has many receptors, each has more than one pathway to the brain, and each sends information to the cortex through a sequence of three or four neuron relays. In addition, although each of the sensory modalities has a primary cortical target, such as area 17, or V1, for vision, each modality also has a number of other brain targets. For all of the sensory systems, the primary cortical area projects to a number of secondary areas, and in these areas sensory information is recoded in more-complex ways.

References

Bartoshuk, L. M. Gustatory system. In R. B. Masterton, Ed. *Handbook of Behavioral Neurobiology*, vol. 1. New York: Plenum, 1978.

Bloom, F. E., and A. Lazerson. *Brain, Mind, and Behavior.* New York: W. H. Freeman and Company, 1988.

Cole, J. *Pride and a Daily Marathon.* London: MIT Press, 1991.

Galaburda, A., and F. Sanides. Cytoarchitectonic organization of the human auditory cortex. *Journal of Comparative Neurology* 190:597–610, 1980.

Imig, T. J., M. A. Ruggero, L. M. Kitzes, E. Javel, and J. F. Brugge. Organization of auditory cortex in the owl monkey (*Aotus trivirgatus*). *Journal of Comparative Neurology* 171:111–128, 1977.

Kaas, J. H. The organization and evolution of neocortex. In S. P. Wise, Ed. *Higher Brain Functions.* New York: Wiley, 1987.

Kandel, E. R., J. H. Schwartz, and T. M. Jessell. *Principles of Neural Science.* New York: Elsevier, 2000.

Lashley, K. S. The mechanisms of vision XVI: The functioning of small remnants of the visual cortex. *Journal of Comparative Neurology* 70:45–67, 1939.

Livingston, M., and D. Hubel. Segregation of form, color, movement and depth: Anatomy, physiology, and perception. *Science* 240:740–749, 1988.

Masterton, R. B., Ed. *Handbook of Behavioral Neurobiology*, vol. 1. New York: Plenum, 1978.

Merzenich, M. M., and J. F. Brugge. Representation of the cochlear partition on the superior temporal plane of the macaque monkey. *Brain Research* 50:276–296, 1973.

Poggio, G. F. Central neural mechanisms in vision. In V. B. Mountcastle, Ed. *Medical Physiology.* St Louis: Mosby, 1968.

Rothwell, J. C., M. M. Traub, B. L. Day, J. A. Obeso, P. K. Thomas, and C. D. Marsden. Manual motor performance in a deafferented man. *Brain* 105:515–542, 1982.

von Békésy, G. *Experiments in Hearing.* Toronto: McGraw-Hill, 1960.

Winderickx, J., D. T. Lindsey, E. Sanocki, D. Y. Teller, B. G. Motulsky, and S. S. Deeb Polymorphism in red photopigment underlies variation in color matching. *Nature* 356:431–433, 1992.

Organization of the Motor System

In 1995, Christopher Reeve, a well-known actor who portrayed Superman in film, was thrown from his horse at the third jump of a riding competition. Reeve's spinal cord was severed at the C1–C2 level, near the upper end of the vertebral column. The injury left his brain and the remainder of his spinal cord intact and functioning—but his brain and spinal cord were no longer connected. Reeve's body below the neck was completely paralyzed.

A few decades ago, such a severe injury would have been fatal. Modern and timely medical treatment allowed Christopher Reeve to survive. Today, Reeve campaigns energetically on behalf of the disabled, fighting to prevent the imposition of lifetime caps on compensation for spinal-cord injuries and raising money for spinal-cord research. He is optimistic about the possibilities of such research, knowing that, if even just a few fibers between the brain and the spinal cord can be reestablished after the spinal cord has been severed, the result will be enormously beneficial. As he documents in his recent book, *Nothing Is Impossible*, Reeve continues to make remarkable recovery, facilitated by an intense exercise program and some remaining fibers, confirmed by MRI, that bypass the injury. He can wiggle his toes on both feet, move the fingers of his left hand, raise his right hand, and distinguish between hot and cold, and sharp and dull sensations over his body. With the assistance of aquatherapy he has the ability to kick his legs and make his way across the pool. His experience with physical therapy, has made Reeve an advocate of activity-dependent training for people with nervous system injury.

Reeve's injury left the major structures of his motor system—the neocortical motor regions of the frontal cortex, the basal ganglia (the collection of nuclei and tracts that lie beneath the frontal cortex), the brainstem, and the cerebellum—intact and functioning but cut them off from most of their connections to the neural circuits of the spinal cord that would normally allow them to produce movement. The central motor regions also had most of their connections cut off from sensory information that normally flows from the skin, muscle, and joint receptors of the body to the motor regions of the brain. In this chapter, we will look at how these various components of the brain and spinal cord work together to produce movement. We begin by exploring the contribution of the neocortex to the control of movement and then consider the functions of the brainstem, basal ganglia, and cerebellum.

The Three Principles of Motor-System Function

To illustrate the large number of brain regions that may be brought into play in the execution of a movement, Figure 9.1 shows the steps by which the human nervous system directs a hand to pick up a coffee mug. The visual system must first inspect the cup to determine what part of it should be grasped. This information is then relayed from the visual cortex to cortical motor regions, which plan and initiate the movement, sending instructions to the part of the spinal cord that controls the muscles of the arm and hand. As the handle of the cup is grasped, information from sensory receptors in the fingers travels to the spinal cord, and from there messages are sent to sensory regions of the cortex that interpret touch. The sensory cortex informs the motor cortex that the cup is now being held. Meanwhile, other regions of the brain have been modulating and adjusting the movement: the basal ganglia help to produce the appropriate amount of force, and the cerebellum helps to regulate timing and corrects any errors as the movement takes place.

A relatively small part of the neocortex consists of the primary motor cortex, the area that sends motor instructions from the cortex to the spinal cord. Nevertheless, many regions of the neocortex send instructions to the primary motor cortex, making them also part of the brain's motor system.

Three principles govern the motor system's production of movement: the principle of motor sequences, the principle of hierarchy, and the principle of parallel processing. In the 1930s, a widely accepted explanation of movement

Figure 9.1 (A) The brain tells the hand to reach, and the hand tells the brain that it has succeeded. Movements such as reaching for a cup require the participation of many nervous system components in various parts of the body. Other regions of the brain also play a role: the basal ganglia participate in the movement by estimating the force required to make the grasp, and the cerebellum participates by correcting errors in the movement as it is made. (B) Hierarchical control of movement such as reaching for a cup.

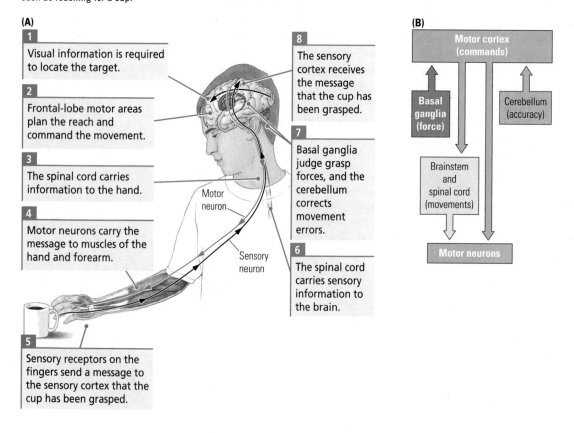

(A)

1 Visual information is required to locate the target.

2 Frontal-lobe motor areas plan the reach and command the movement.

3 The spinal cord carries information to the hand.

4 Motor neurons carry the message to muscles of the hand and forearm.

5 Sensory receptors on the fingers send a message to the sensory cortex that the cup has been grasped.

Motor neuron

Sensory neuron

8 The sensory cortex receives the message that the cup has been grasped.

7 Basal ganglia judge grasp forces, and the cerebellum corrects movement errors.

6 The spinal cord carries sensory information to the brain.

(B)

Motor cortex (commands)

Basal ganglia (force)

Cerebellum (accuracy)

Brainstem and spinal cord (movements)

Motor neurons

control was developed around the concept of feedback. The explanation proposed that, after we perform an action, we wait for feedback about how well the action has succeeded, and then we make the next movement accordingly. But, in a paper titled "The Problem of Serial Order in Behavior," Karl Lashley argued that complex movements are performed too quickly for feedback about one movement-recent to have shaped the next. The time required to receive feedback about the first movement combined with the time needed to develop a plan for the subsequent movement and send a message to the muscles was simply too long. Lashley suggested that movements must instead be performed as sets of motor sequences, with one sequence being held in readiness while an ongoing sequence is being completed. Lashley's view seems to be borne out in how we execute speech. When we speak, we produce sequences of words interspersed with pauses. The more complex the idea that we wish to express, the more likely we are to pause and make "umm" and "ahh" sounds, suggesting that it is taking us more time than usual to organize our word sequences.

The idea of hierarchy in movement production dates to John Hughlings-Jackson in the 1800s. Hughlings-Jackson thought of the nervous system as being organized in levels, with successively higher levels controlling movements by acting through the lower levels. The three major levels in Hughlings-Jackson's model were the forebrain, the brainstem, and the spinal cord. Hughlings-Jackson also proposed that, within these divisions, further levels of organization could be found. Hughlings-Jackson adopted the concept of hierarchical organization from evolutionary theory. He knew that the chordate nervous system had evolved in a series of steps: the spinal cord had developed in worms; the brainstem in fish, amphibians, and reptiles; and the forebrain in birds and mammals. With each addition, movement became a bit more complex. Because each level of the nervous system had developed at a different time, Hughlings-Jackson assumed that each must have some functional independence. Consequently, if higher levels were damaged, the result would be regression to the simpler behaviors of a "lower" animal, a phenomenon that Hughlings-Jackson called **dissolution.** The damaged nervous system would still possess a repertoire of behaviors, but it would be more typical of an animal that had not yet evolved the damaged brain structure. We recognize today that many reflex actions, including the neural basis of walking, are encoded by the spinal cord. Many more actions, such as eating, drinking, certain sexual or maternal behaviors, and grooming routines, are produced by circuitry in the brainstem. Movements that require a certain amount of acquired skill and include the manipulation of objects or communication are encoded in the circuitry of the forebrain.

More-recent study of how movements are controlled has introduced the notion of parallel systems. According to this idea, a number of controlling systems function partly in parallel. For example, movements that have become automatic, such as opening a door or catching a ball before it hits you, may be produced by one movement system, and movements that require attention, skill, and ongoing adjustments, such as lifting a full glass of water, performing surgery, or speaking, will be produced by other systems. This parallel operation of various systems may explain how we are able to perform certain combinations of less-demanding actions and more-demanding actions simultaneously.

Neocortical Contributions to Movement Control

A good place to begin our exploration of how the brain controls movement is by considering the complexity of the movements required to play basketball. At every moment of the game, decisions must be made and actions must be performed. Dribble, pass, and shoot are very different actions, and each can be carried out in numerous ways. Good players make their choices effortlessly and execute them seemingly without thought. Players who excel in quick and accurate execution are sometimes described as being "unconscious" or "in the zone." There are also movements that require a certain level of thought, care, and communication with others, and players who excel in this kind of decision making are sometimes described as "court generals." In this section, after first presenting a theory of how the neocortex produces movement and how different regions of the neocortex contribute to movement, we describe how the more automatic and the more reflective kinds of movement are produced.

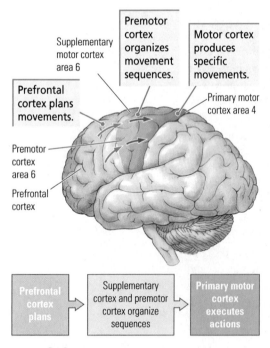

Figure 9.2 Subdivisions of the frontal lobe that collaborate to produce movement. The prefrontal cortex of the frontal lobe plans movements. The premotor cortex and the supplementary motor cortex control the organization of sequences of movements. The primary motor cortex executes specific movements. Information flows from the prefrontal cortex to the supplementary and the premotor cortex and then to the primary motor cortex. Posterior sensory regions of the cortex can directly instruct the primary motor cortex or the prefrontal cortex. Numbered areas refer to areas of the cortex as mapped by Brodmann's system.

A Theory of Neocortical Control of Movement

Four general regions of the neocortex, as shown in Figure 9.2, are thought to produce most voluntary movements—that is, movements that we choose to make. If we start at the front and move backward, these regions are the prefrontal cortex, the premotor cortex (Brodmann's area 6), the supplementary motor cortex (Brodmann's area 6), the primary motor cortex (Brodmann's area 4), and the posterior sensory regions of the cortex.

According to current theory, the primary motor cortex and the premotor cortex can be thought of as containing a dictionary of movements—a lexicon—from which appropriate selections are made. These regions receive instructions from the prefrontal cortex, which produces plans for movements. (The instructions travel from the prefrontal cortex to the premotor cortex to the primary motor cortex.) The lexicon of the primary motor cortex consists of movements that are somewhat more elementary than those of the premotor cortex. The posterior sensory regions of the cortex send information to the primary motor cortex for the execution of relatively automatic movements and send information to the prefrontal cortex for the planning of more-complex movements. Thus, in general, the planning of movement takes place in the prefrontal cortex, the sequencing of movement is arranged by the premotor cortex, and the individual elements of movement are produced by the primary motor cortex. The sensory information used for producing movements comes from the posterior neocortex.

Support for this general theory of how the neocortex produces movement comes from the results of Roland's studies of cerebral blood flow (which, as we have seen, serves as an indi-

(A)

Blood flow increased in the hand area of the primary somatosensory and primary motor cortex when subjects were tapping a finger.

Motor cortex   Sensory cortex

(B)

Blood flow increased in the premotor cortex when subjects performed a sequence of movements.

Dorsal premotor cortex

(C)

Blood flow increased in the prefrontal and posterior sensory cortex when subjects used a finger to find a route through a maze.

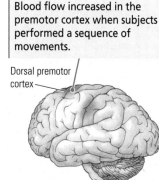
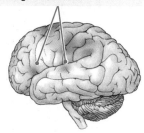

Figure 9.3 Blood flow in the cerebral cortex in subjects performing three different tasks. Blood flow increases in the cerebral cortex depend on the motor task being performed by the subject. The pattern of activation supports the idea that simple motor movements are mainly controlled by the motor cortex, movements requiring sequencing are additionally controlled by the premotor cortex, and movements requiring planning are controlled by other cortical areas, including the prefrontal cortex and regions of the parietal and temporal cortex. (After P. E. Roland, 1993. *Brain Activation.* New York: Wiley-Liss, p. 63.)

cator of neural activity). Figure 9.3 shows the regions of the brain that were active when subjects in one such study were performing particular tasks. When a subject was tapping a finger, increases in blood flow were limited to the primary motor cortex. When the subject was executing a sequence of finger movements, the blood flow increased in the premotor motor cortex as well. And, when the subject was using a finger to navigate a drawing of a maze—a task that requires the coordination of movements in pursuit of a goal as well as specific movements corresponding to the shape of the maze—blood flow increased in the prefrontal cortex and posterior sensory cortex, too. Notice that blood flow did not increase throughout the entire neocortex as the subjects were performing these tasks. Blood flow increased only in the regions contributing to the particular movements.

The following sections describe the anatomies and functions of the motor cortex and premotor cortex and then the contributions of the prefrontal and frontal cortex.

Identification of the Motor Cortex by Using Electrical Stimulation

The specialization of body parts for the performance of skilled movements is widespread among animals. Elephants use their trunks to manipulate objects; dolphins and seals deftly do the same with their noses; and many other animals, including domestic dogs, accomplish the same ends by using their mouths. Different bird species have beaks designed for obtaining particular foods, for building nests, and sometimes even for making and using tools. Tails can be handy, too. Some marsupials and some New-World primates can grasp and carry objects with them. Among horses, the lips are dexterous enough to manipulate small items. Humans tend to rely primarily on their hands for manipulating objects, but they can do manual tasks with other body parts, such as the mouth or a foot, if they have to. (Some people without arms have become extremely proficient at writing with a foot, for example.) What are the properties of the motor system that explain these differences in carrying out skilled movements?

In 1870, Prussian physicians Gustav Fritsch and Eduard Hitzig electrically stimulated the neocortex of an anesthetized dog, producing movements of the mouth, limbs, and paws on the opposite side of the dog's body. This finding

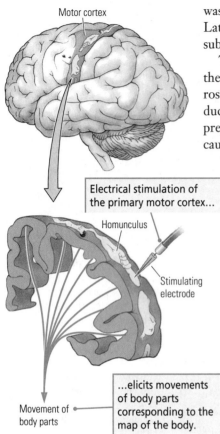

Motor cortex

Electrical stimulation of the primary motor cortex...

Homunculus

Stimulating electrode

Movement of body parts

...elicits movements of body parts corresponding to the map of the body.

Figure 9.4 Penfield's homunculus. Electrical stimulation of the primary motor cortex in conscious human patients elicits movement of the body parts corresponding to this map of the body. Movements are organized topographically such that stimulation of the dorsal medial regions of the cortex produces movements or sensations in the lower limbs, and stimulation in the ventral regions of the cortex produces movements or sensations in the upper body, hands, and face.

was the first direct evidence that the neocortex could control movement. Later researchers confirmed the finding by using a variety of animals as subjects, including primates such as monkeys.

Then, in the 1950s, Wilder Penfield used electrical stimulation to map the cortex of conscious human patients who were about to undergo neurosurgery. He and his colleagues found that most of the movements induced by their experiments were triggered by stimulation of the precentral gyrus, also known as *Brodmann's area 4*, the region that, because of its role in movement, is now called the primary motor cortex.

Penfield also obtained evidence that movement can be produced by stimulating the dorsal part of premotor cortex. Penfield summarized his results by drawing cartoons of body parts to represent the areas of the primary motor cortex and premotor cortex where stimulation caused those parts to move. The result was a **homunculus** ("little person") spread out across the motor cortex, as illustrated for the primary motor cortex in Figure 9.4. (It is similar to the somatosensory homunculi described in Chapter 8.) Because the body is symmetrical, each hemisphere contains a more-or-less mirror-image representation of this homunculus.

The most striking feature of the motor homunculus is the disproportion in the relative sizes of its body parts compared with their relative sizes in the body itself. The homunculus has very large hands with an especially large thumb. It also has very large lips and a large tongue. In contrast, the trunk, arms, and legs, which constitute most of the area of a real body, occupy much less space, relatively speaking, in the motor cortex. These size distortions are due to the fact that large parts of the motor cortex regulate the hands, fingers, lips, and tongue, giving us precise motor control over those body parts. Parts of the body over which we have much less motor control have a much smaller representation in the motor cortex.

Another distinctive feature of the homunculus when it is sketched according to its representation in the motor cortex is that the arrangement of body parts is somewhat different from that of the body itself. For instance, the area of the cortex that produces eye movements is located in front of the area that produces movement in the head, as is the area that produces movement of the lips. In addition, the head of the homunculus is oriented with the chin up and the forehead down, rather than the other way around as Penfield originally drew it. But these details do not prevent the homunculus from being a useful concept for understanding the **topographic organization,** or functional layout, of the primary motor cortex. It shows at a glance that relatively larger areas of the brain control the parts of the body that are able to make the most-complex and finely tuned movements.

The Pathways from the Motor Cortex to the Spinal Cord

Franz Gall and Johann Spurzheim discovered the main pathway out of the motor cortex in the early 1800s. They dissected a pathway that went from the motor cortex all the way to the spinal cord. We now know that this pathway projects both to the lower brainstem, as the **cortico-bulbar tracts,** and to the spinal cord, as the **corticospinal tracts.** (The term *cortico* indicates that these tracts begin in the neocortex, and the terms *bulbar* and *spinal* indicate where the tracts end.) The corticobulbar tracts terminate in nuclei that control facial muscles and thus take part in controlling facial movements. The corticospinal tracts terminate in the vicinity of the motor neurons in the spinal cord and control movements of the limbs and body.

The axons that form the corticobulbar and corticospinal tracts do not come *only* from the primary motor cortex. Some parts of the tracts come from the somatosensory cortex (area 3-1-2), others come from the primary motor cortex (area 4), and still others come from the premotor cortex (area 6). The part of the corticospinal tract that comes from the somatosensory cortex terminates in nuclei of the ascending sensory tracts and modulates sensory signals that are sent to the neocortex. The parts of the tract that originate in the primary motor cortex and premotor cortex descend to the interneurons and motor neurons of the brainstem and spinal cord and more directly control movement.

The axons of the corticobulbar and corticospinal tracts originate in layer-5 pyramidal cells of the neocortex. These neurons have especially large cell bodies, in keeping with the fact that they support axons that travel a long way. The axons of the corticospinal tract descend into the brainstem, sending collaterals to a few brainstem nuclei and eventually emerging on the brainstem's ventral surface, where they form a large bump on each side of that surface. These bumps, known as **pyramids,** give the corticospinal tracts their alternate name, the **pyramidal tracts.** From this location, some of the axons descending from the left hemisphere cross over to the right side of the brainstem, whereas some of the axons descending from the right hemisphere cross over to the left side of the brainstem. The rest of the axons stay on their original sides. The division produces two corticospinal tracts entering each side of the spinal cord. (Figure 9.5 illustrates the division of axons for the tract originating in the left-hemisphere cortex.) The dual tracts on each side of the brainstem then descend into the spinal cord. The corticospinal tract fibers that cross to the other side of the brainstem originate mainly in the hand-and-arm and leg-and-foot regions of the cortical homunculi. The fibers that do not cross originate in the trunk region of the homunculi. Therefore, each motor cortex controls the limbs of the opposite side of the body but the trunk on the same side of the body.

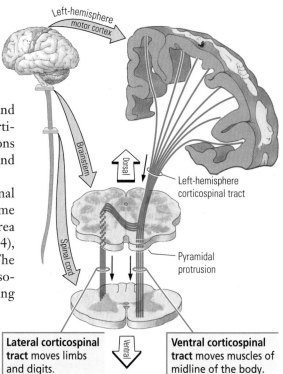

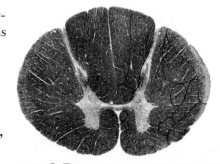

Lateral corticospinal tract moves limbs and digits.

Ventral corticospinal tract moves muscles of midline of the body.

Figure 9.5 The corticospinal (from cortex to spinal cord) tracts descend from the motor cortex to the brainstem. Their location in the lower brainstem produces protrusions called pyramids on the ventral surfaces of the brain. ("Pyramid" is the origin of the corticospinal tracts' other name, the pyramidal tracts.) Each tract divides into a lateral spinothalamic tract, which crosses the midline to the other side of the spinal cord, and a ventral spinothalamic tract, which remains on the same side. Fibers in the lateral spinothalamic tracts represent the limbs and digits of the cortical homunculus and are destined to move muscles of the limbs and digits. Fibers of the ventral spinothalamic tracts represent the midline of the body of the homunculus and are destined to move muscles of the midline of the body. (Photograph of spinal cord reproduced from *The Human Brain: Dissections of the Real Brain,* by T. H. Williams, N. Gluhbegovic, and J. Jew, on CD-ROM. Published by Brain University, brain-university.com, 2000.)

Figure 9.6 The relation between interneurons, motor neurons, and muscles. (A) The ventral horns of the spinal cord contain the interneurons and motor neurons. Interneurons project to motor neurons, and motor neurons project to muscles. (B) The lateral motor neurons innervate arm and hand muscles, whereas the medial motor neurons innervate trunk and shoulder muscles. Thus, the interneurons and motor neurons of the spinal cord can be envisioned as a homunculus representing the muscles that they will innervate.

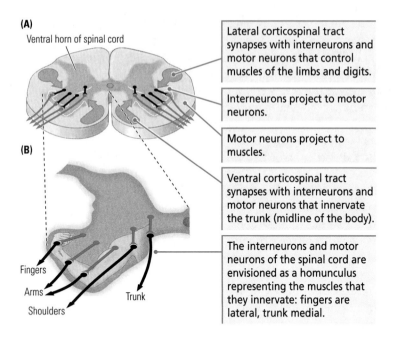

(A)
Ventral horn of spinal cord

Lateral corticospinal tract synapses with interneurons and motor neurons that control muscles of the limbs and digits.

Interneurons project to motor neurons.

Motor neurons project to muscles.

(B)

Ventral corticospinal tract synapses with interneurons and motor neurons that innervate the trunk (midline of the body).

The interneurons and motor neurons of the spinal cord are envisioned as a homunculus representing the muscles that they innervate: fingers are lateral, trunk medial.

Fingers
Arms
Shoulders
Trunk

Looking at the cross section of the spinal cord in Figure 9.6, you can see the location of the two tracts—the one that crosses and the one that remains uncrossed—on each side. Those fibers that cross to the opposite side of the brainstem descend the spinal cord in a lateral location, giving them the name **lateral corticospinal tract.** Those fibers that remain on their original side of the brainstem continue down the spinal cord in a ventral location, giving them the name **ventral corticospinal tract.** The lateral corticospinal tract sends messages to the limbs, whereas the ventral corticospinal tract sends messages to the trunk.

The Motor Neurons

The spinal-cord motor neurons that connect to muscles are located in the spinal cord's ventral horns. Interneurons lie just medially to the motor neurons and project onto them. The fibers of the corticospinal tracts make synaptic connections with both the interneurons and the motor neurons, but all nervous system commands to the muscles are carried by the motor neurons. Figure 9.6 shows that the more laterally located motor neurons project to muscles that control the fingers and hands; intermediately located motor neurons project to muscles that control the arms and shoulders; and the most medially located motor neurons project to muscles that control the trunk. The lateral corticospinal tract axons connect mainly with the lateral motor neurons, whereas the ventral corticospinal tract axons connect mainly to the medial motor neurons.

The muscles with which spinal-cord motor neurons synapse contract to produce the movements of the body. Some muscles cause a part of the body to extend outward, away from the body midline, and these muscles are called **extensor** muscles. Other muscles draw a body part inward, toward the body midline, and these are called **flexor** muscles. For example, the arm muscles are arranged in pairs as shown in Figure 9.7. The extensor member of the pair in Figure 9.7 causes the lower arm to move out, and the flexor member of the pair pulls the lower arm in. Connections between the interneurons and motor neurons of the spinal cord cause the muscles to work in concert: when one muscle of the pair contracts, the other relaxes.

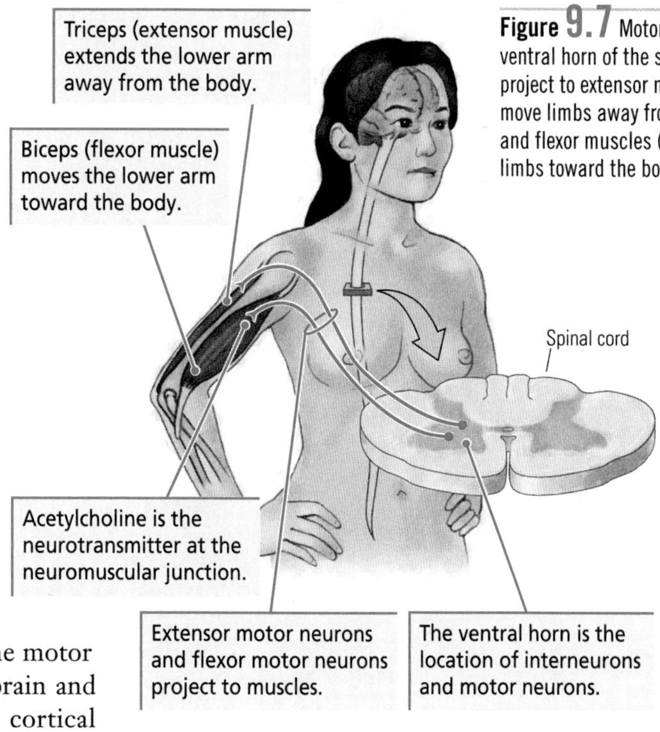

Overview of the Motor System

To picture how the motor homunculus in the cortex is related to motor neurons in the spinal cord, imagine placing your right index finger on the index finger of the motor homunculus on the left side of the brain and then following the axons of the cortical neurons downward. Your route takes you through the brainstem, across its midline, and down the lateral corticospinal tract, ending on interneurons and motor neurons in the most lateral region of the spinal cord's right ventral horn—the horn on the side opposite the side of the nervous system on which you began. If you next follow the axons of these motor neurons, you will find that they synapse with muscles that move the index finger on that same, right-hand side of the body. (By the way, the neurons that your brain is using to carry out this task are the same neurons whose pathway you are tracing.) If you repeat the procedure, but this time trace the pathway from the trunk of the motor homunculus on the left side of the brain, you will follow the same route through the upper part of the brainstem. There, however, instead of crossing over to the brainstem's opposite side, you will descend into the spinal cord on the side of the nervous system on which you began (the left side), eventually ending up in the most medially located interneurons and motor neurons of that side's ventral horn. Finally, if you follow the axons of these motor neurons, you will end up at their synapses with muscles that move the trunk on the left side of the body.

This imaginary exercise should help you to remember the routes taken by axons of the motor system. The limb regions of the motor homunculus contribute most of their fibers to the lateral corticospinal tract. Because these fibers have crossed over to the opposite side of the brainstem, they activate motor neurons that move the arm, hand, leg, and foot on *the opposite side of the body.* In contrast, the trunk regions of the motor homunculus contribute their fibers to the ventral corticospinal tract, and, because these fibers do not cross over at the brainstem, they activate motor neurons that move the trunk on *the same side of the body.* In short, the neurons of the motor homunculus in the left-hemisphere cortex control the trunk on the left side of the body but the limbs

Figure 9.7 Motor neurons of the ventral horn of the spinal cord project to extensor muscles (which move limbs away from the body) and flexor muscles (which move limbs toward the body).

Triceps (extensor muscle) extends the lower arm away from the body.

Biceps (flexor muscle) moves the lower arm toward the body.

Acetylcholine is the neurotransmitter at the neuromuscular junction.

Extensor motor neurons and flexor motor neurons project to muscles.

The ventral horn is the location of interneurons and motor neurons.

Spinal cord

on the body's right side. Similarly, neurons of the motor homunculus in the right-hemisphere cortex control the trunk on the right side of the body but the limbs on the body's left side.

Movement Coding by Cells in the Neocortex

The debate over how the motor cortex contributes to movement is of long standing. The results of certain single-cell studies of the motor regions of the neocortex suggest that the cells play a direct role in instructing particular muscles to contract, whereas findings from other studies suggest that the cells specify the target of the movement. We can also *imagine* movements; so other cells must take part in producing movement images (see the Snapshot on page 208). In the following sections, we will review evidence in favor of a third view—that the cells of the neocortex specify movements.

The Motor Cortex Contains a Lexicon of Movements

The discovery of the topographical representation of the motor cortex (the homunculus) suggested to some neuroscientists that movements might be produced as follows. Information from elsewhere in the neocortex could be sent to the motor homunculus, and neurons in the appropriate part of the homunculus could then execute the requisite movements by sending messages to appropriate muscles. If a finger movement were needed, for example, a message could be sent to the appropriate finger neurons of the motor homunculus, and these neurons would send a message to the appropriate muscles to move the finger. If this model of how the motor system works is correct, damage to a part of the homunculus would result in a loss of movement in the corresponding part of the body.

As summarized by Schieber, more-detailed mapping of the motor cortex (by using smaller electrodes than those used by Penfield) and the results of more-detailed studies of the effects of damage to it indicate that the picture is a bit more complex. First, detailed mapping of the premotor and motor cortex reveals that there are many motor homunculi, perhaps as many as ten. Second, loci from which electrical stimulation can elicit the movement of a finger are not located in a discrete area representing that finger, adjacent to areas representing the other fingers, as the original Penfield homunculus suggests. Finger movements can be obtained from many points, and many of the locations from which finger movements are obtained also elicit movements of other body parts. In addition, anatomical evidence suggests that a cell in a particular region of the motor cortex that might represent a finger not only connects to spinal motor neurons that activate the finger but also connects to motor neurons representing muscles of other fingers and even connects to motor neurons representing muscles of other parts of the limb and body. Each cell in the motor cortex sends horizontal connections to many groups of surrounding cells, many of which represent other body parts. Further evidence against the discrete homunculus concept comes from the results of single-unit recording studies in which motor-cortex cells that were active during the movement of one finger were also active during the movements of other fingers. All of this evidence argues against the idea of a point-to-point relation between topographic areas of the motor cortex and muscles of the body.

To explain these more complex findings, researchers now propose that the motor cortex is organized not for the control of individual muscles but for the control of movements, any of which might require the coordinated action of many muscles. In other words, we have a lexicon, or vocabulary, of movements in the motor cortex. An observation that supports this idea is the remarkable similarity in the ways in which different people perform skilled movements. Most people who reach for a small object use a pincer grip—that is, the thumb and index finger are used to grasp the object (Figure 9.8A). This movement entails moving the thumb, the second digit, and the arm. The pincer grasp could be learned by watching other people use it, but there is no evidence that any of us needed to do that as children. In fact, at about 12 months of age, most healthy babies begin spontaneously to use the pincer grip to pick up tiny objects such as breadcrumbs. Other evidence includes the fact that most primate species use this same grip pattern and the fact that people who have incurred small lesions of the motor cortex in the area of the thumb region of the homunculus have a weakness not only in the thumb but in the other fingers of the hand and in the arm as well. The latter finding suggests to Schieber that neurons controlling a number of arm and finger muscles have been affected. After incurring such a lesion, a person is likely to begin using a whole-hand grip in place of the pincer grasp (Figure 9.8B). Apparently, then, the pincer grip and other skilled movements are not learned but are part of an integral movement lexicon in the motor cortex. They are encoded in the neural connections there as basic patterns of movement that are common to the particular species, to be called on as situations demand.

Findings from lesion studies suggest that the premotor cortex and the primary motor cortex each have a movement lexicon and that the lexicon of the premotor cortex is more complex than that of the motor cortex. Brinkman showed that damage to the premotor cortex does not produce muscle weakness, but it does disrupt more-complex movements. For example, the monkey depicted in Figure 9.9, with a lesion in the dorsal part of its premotor cortex, has

(A) Pincer grasp

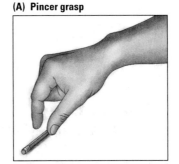

A control subject picks up a small object using the forefinger and thumb, the pincer grasp.

(B) Whole-hand grasp

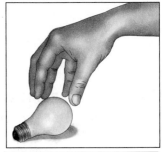

A subject with motor cortex damage has difficulty executing the pincer grasp but can grasp an object using the entire hand.

Figure 9.8 A comparison of (A) pincer and (B) whole-hand grasps. (After Jeannerod, 1988.)

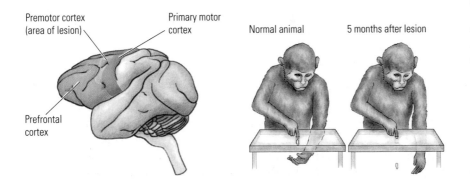

Premotor cortex (area of lesion)

Primary motor cortex

Prefrontal cortex

Normal animal

5 months after lesion

Figure 9.9 A unilateral lesion in the premotor cortex impairs a monkey's performance on a task in which both hands are required. The normal monkey can push the peanut out of a hole with one hand and catch it in the other, but the experimental monkey is unable to do so. (After C. Brinkman. 1984. Supplementary motor area of the monkey's cerebral cortex: Short- and long-term effects after unilateral ablation and the effects of subsequent callosal section. *Journal of Neuroscience* 4, p. 925.)

The Motor Regions of the Neocortex: Observing, Remembering, and Imagining Movements

Before ascending the diving tower, a diver mentally rehearses the movements of the perfect dive that she hopes to make. Once on the tower, she may again imagine and rehearse the sequence of movements that she is about to execute. Does this mental preparation help? Is she activating the circuits of the motor system that she is about to use in performing the dive? These questions are important. We can be reasonably certain that, if we practiced diving in our imagination only, we would never be able to actually perform a polished dive. Similarly, if we paid close attention to the movements of seasoned basketball players but had never actually dribbled, passed, or thrown a basketball, we would not be able to go onto a basketball court and play the game with any competence.

Scientists have used various imaging techniques to study the role of the motor regions of the neocortex in observing, remembering, and imagining movements. Martin and colleagues, for example, used positron emission tomography (PET) to identify regions of the brain that were active when subjects silently rehearsed various words. The scans revealed increases in blood flow in the hand regions of the motor cortex when subjects named tools. This finding suggests a connection of some kind between the hand region of the motor cortex and knowledge about the tool and its use.

Haueisen and Knosche, intrigued by reports that pianists involuntarily move their fingers as if playing when in fact they are only listening to a piece of music they have often practiced, used magnetoencephalography (MEG) to compare the motor activation in pianists and nonpianists while the subjects listened to piano pieces. Only the pianists exhibited an increase of activity above the region of the motor cortex. Furthermore, when the piece that they were listening to required more thumb than little-finger activity, the pianists' brain scans showed more activity in the thumb region of the motor cortex than in the digit region, and vice versa. Thus, for piano players, the motor cortex is active during listening, suggesting that it plays a role in music appreciation.

Nyberg and colleagues made a more direct comparison of the brain activity evoked by performing a movement and the activity evoked by imagining a movement. They made PET scans of subjects who were performing certain movements with the right hand (such as rolling a ball with the hand) and compared these scans with PET scans of subjects who were verbally encoding the same movement by silently describing the movement to themselves in their minds. The results are presented in the accompanying illustration. The areas of the brain that were most active during the overt performance of the task included the sensory and motor cortex, the premotor cortex of the left hemisphere, and the cerebellum of the right hemisphere (there are preferential connections between the right neocortex and the left cerebellum). The areas that were most active during covert rehearsal of the task also included the somatosensory and motor cortex (though not to the same extent as in the overt condition) but did not include the cerebellum. Thus, there is some overlap of brain activity in the overt performance of a movement and its verbal rehearsal, but there are also large differences.

been given the task of extracting a piece of food wedged in a hole in a table. If the monkey merely pushes the food through with a finger, the food will drop to the floor and be lost. The monkey has to catch the food by holding one palm beneath the hole while using the other hand to push the food out. Unlike a normal monkey, this one is unable to make the two complementary movements together. It can push the food with a finger and it can extend an open palm, but

The results of these studies are consistent with the notion that practice, rather than dreaming, makes perfect but that dreaming may help. They also indicate that, after we have become proficient at a skill that requires movement, such as playing the piano, the brain's representations of the imagined performance and the real performance of those movements may become more alike.

(J. Haueisen and T. R. Knosche. Involuntary motor activity in pianists evoked by music perception. *Journal of Cognitive Neuroscience* 13:786–792, 2001.
A. Martin, C. L. Wiggs, L. G. Ungerleider, and J. V. Haxby. Neural correlates of category-specific knowledge. *Nature* 379:649–652, 1996.
L. Nybert, K. M. Petersson, L.-G. Nmilsson, J. Sandblom, C. Aberg, and M. Ingvar. Reactivation of motor brain areas during explicit memory for actions. *NeuroImage* 14:521–528, 2001.)

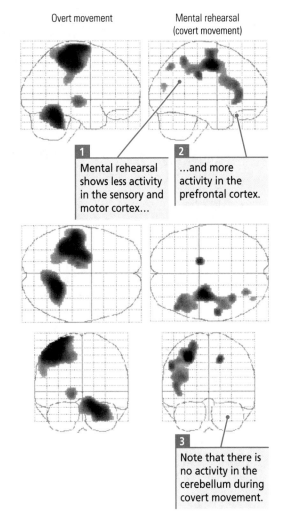

Overt movement   Mental rehearsal (covert movement)

1 Mental rehearsal shows less activity in the sensory and motor cortex...

2 ...and more activity in the prefrontal cortex.

3 Note that there is no activity in the cerebellum during covert movement.

Comparisons of brain activation measured with PET for movements that are overtly performed (top) and movements that are covertly performed (bottom). Note that there are some similarities in neocortical activation, but there are also some differences, especially with respect to the absence of cerebellar activation during covert movement. (After Nyberg et al., 2001.)

it cannot coordinate these actions of its two hands. The supplementary motor cortex may have a greater role in organizing whole-body movements, whereas the prefrontal cortex may have a greater role in organizing movements of the limbs and the mouth.

Movements encoded by the neocortex are not limited to movements of the hand and arm but include movements in which many parts of the body are used.

Figure 9.10 Baseball pitcher winding up. Movement patterns used in sports are similar to the movements used in everyday activities. Apparently, the nervous system has a set of basic plans for movement.

Figure 9.11 The motor cortical neurons are active in planning and executing movements. (A) The setup for recording requires the monkey to flex its wrist to rotate a lever. Different weights are attached to the lever to vary the force that the monkey must exert to move the lever. (B) This recording from a corticospinal neuron shows that the neuron's activity increases before the movement, which suggests that the neuron has a role in planning the movement. Its activity continues throughout the movement, suggesting that it also takes part in making the movement. The activity in the neuron increases when additional force is exerted (after a heavier weight has been attached to the lever), suggesting that the rate of discharge is related to the force of the movement (After E. V. Evarts, 1968. Relation of pyramidal tract activity to force exerted during voluntary movement. *Journal of Neurophysiology* 31, p. 15.)

For example, a person throwing a ball, as illustrated in Figure 9.10, must coordinate the entire body to deliver the ball to the target. The action requires stepping movements of the leg, constant adjustments of the trunk to maintain balance, and the throwing movement of the arm. Note, by the way, that some of these movements are also used in walking, particularly the coordinated movements of the diagonal limb couplets: the pitcher has the left arm forward and the right leg back, just as you would if you were stepping forward with your left leg. In an extensive analysis of body reflexes, Fukuda suggests that a large part of training in skilled sports consists of learning how to use preorganized patterns of movement to improve both skill and strength.

Motor-Cortex Cells Specify Movements, Their Force, and Their Direction

To investigate how the cells of the motor cortex produce movement, Evarts used the simple procedure illustrated in Figure 9.11. He trained a monkey to flex its wrist in order to move a bar to which weights of different heaviness could be attached. An electrode implanted in the wrist region of the motor cortex recorded the activity of neurons there. Evarts discovered that these neurons began to discharge even before the monkey flexed its wrist. Apparently, they participated in planning the movement as well as initiating it. The neurons then continued to discharge during the wrist movement, confirming that they also played a role in the execution of the movement. The neurons also discharged at a higher rate when the bar was loaded with a weight, an indication that motor-cortex neurons

(A) Procedure

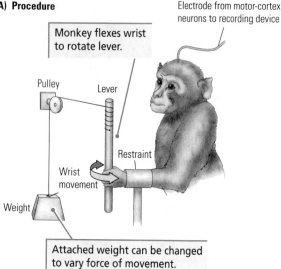

Monkey flexes wrist to rotate lever.

Pulley

Lever

Wrist movement

Restraint

Weight

Attached weight can be changed to vary force of movement.

Electrode from motor-cortex neurons to recording device

(B) Results

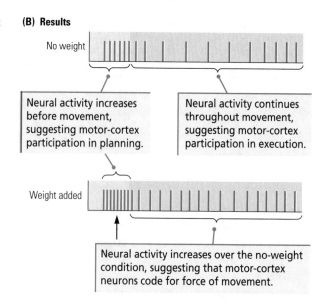

No weight

Neural activity increases before movement, suggesting motor-cortex participation in planning.

Neural activity continues throughout movement, suggesting motor-cortex participation in execution.

Weight added

Neural activity increases over the no-weight condition, suggesting that motor-cortex neurons code for force of movement.

increase the force of a movement by increasing their rate of firing.

The results of Evarts's experiment also revealed that the motor cortex specifies the direction of a movement. The neurons of the motor-cortex wrist area discharged when the monkey flexed its wrist to bring the hand inward but not when the monkey extended its wrist to move the hand back to its starting position. These on–off responses of the neurons, depending on whether the flexor or extensor muscle is being used, are a simple way of encoding the direction in which the wrist is moving.

Georgopoulos and his coworkers used a method similar to that of Evarts to further examine the encoding of movement direction. They trained monkeys to move a lever in different directions across the surface of a table. Recording from single cells in the arm region of the motor cortex, they found that each cell was maximally active when the monkey moved its arm in a particular direction. Figure 9.12 summarizes these results. As the monkey's arm moved in directions other than the one to which a particular cell maximally responded, the cell would decrease its activity in proportion to the displacement from the "preferred" direction. For example, if a neuron discharged maximally as the arm moved directly forward, its discharge would be halved if the arm moved to one side and would cease altogether if the arm moved backward. According to Georgopoulos and his coworkers, the motor cortex seems to calculate both the direction and the distance of movements. Each neuron in a large population of motor-cortex neurons could participate in producing a particular movement, but the discharge rate of a particular neuron would depend on that movement's direction.

To compare how the premotor cortex and the primary motor cortex contribute to movement, Kakei and his colleagues made a slight modification to Georgopoulos's task. The monkey still moved its arm in different directions, but it did so with the palm facing downward, sideways, or upward. They found that about half of the neurons from which they recorded in the primary motor cortex were active in relation to the orientation of the hand, suggesting that these neurons activated muscles to produce the appropriate hand orientation. The remaining neurons were sensitive to the direction of the hand's movement, suggesting they encoded the target of the movement. When Kakei and his colleagues recorded premotor cortex cells, they found that the neurons responded exclusively to a target. Thus, it would appear that the primary motor cortex specifies the movement to be made by the hand as well as the target to which the hand is directed, whereas premotor-cortex neurons make a more abstract contribution and are especially concerned with the objective of the movement.

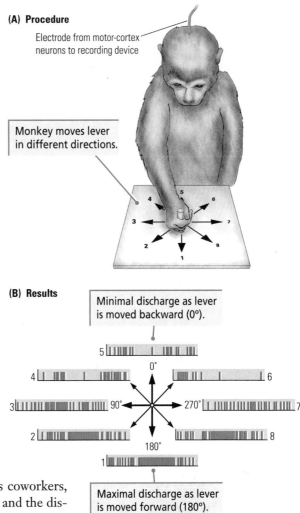

(A) Procedure

Electrode from motor-cortex neurons to recording device

Monkey moves lever in different directions.

(B) Results

Minimal discharge as lever is moved backward (0°).

Maximal discharge as lever is moved forward (180°).

Figure 9.12 Individual cortical neurons are tuned to the direction of a movement. (A)The monkey moves a lever in different directions on a table. (B) The activity of a single motor-cortex neuron as a function of movement direction suggests that motor-cortex neurons encode movement direction. (After A. P. Georgopoulos et al., 1982. On the relations between the direction of two-dimensional arm movements and cell discharge in primate motor cortex. *Journal of Neuroscience* 2, p. 1530.)

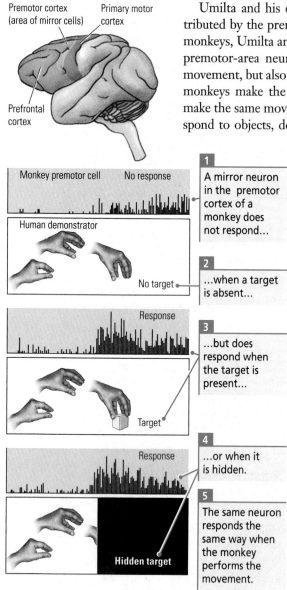

Figure 9.13 The activity of a mirror neuron in the premotor cortex of a monkey in response to hand movements made by a human demonstrator. The same neuron would perform in the same way were the monkey to perform the movement. (After Umilta et al., 2001.)

Umilta and his colleagues further clarified the more complex control contributed by the premotor cortex to movement. In the course of their studies in monkeys, Umilta and coworkers made the remarkable finding that many ventral premotor-area neurons not only discharge when the monkey itself makes a movement, but also discharge, and in the same way, when the monkey sees other monkeys make the same movement and even when the monkey sees people make the same movement. These neurons, now called *mirror neurons*, do not respond to objects, do not respond to isolated hand movements, and do not respond very well to pictures or movies of movements. They are interested in a completed action. Some of the neurons have very exacting requirements, responding only to a particular hand movement and only if it is used to pick up a small object rather than a large object, for example. Other neurons are more broadly tuned and continue to respond when the grip pattern changes or the size of the target varies somewhat. The researchers proposed that all these neurons represent actions, whether one's own or others', and that the representations could be used both for imitating others' actions and for understanding the meaning of those actions, thus permitting the selection of appropriate responses. These neurons therefore provide a link between the sender and the receiver of communication. Humans also have mirror neurons, but a major difference between humans and monkeys is that in humans the mirror neurons are found largely in the left hemisphere.

Umilta and colleagues also report that mirror neurons can recognize a given movement made by a demonstrator even when the monkey is unable to see part of the movement. Figure 9.13 shows an instance in which such a neuron responded when the human demonstrator reached for a block but not when the demonstrator reached for an object that was not there; however, the neuron did respond when the demonstrator reached for an object that was hidden behind a screen. That premotor mirror cells can reason in this way means that the motor representation of an action performed by others can be internally generated, even when the visual description of the action is incomplete. Such a result suggests that mirror-neuron activation could be at the root of action recognition.

The Roles of the Prefrontal and Posterior Cortex

Movements are usually made in response to sensory stimuli—information from touch, vision, audition, and so forth—although they can also be made in the absence of such information. Sensory information may instruct movements in two ways. First, direct connections from the parietal cortex to the primary motor cortex suggest that movements can be made in direct response to sensory stimulation. Such movements are likely to be simple and reflexive. Second, the various sensory systems also send information to the prefrontal cortex, which can use the information to formulate plans for more-complex movements that can then be sent to the premotor cortex for execution.

The importance of sensory information for movement is illustrated by the severe motor disabilities that arise after **deafferentation,** the loss of somatosensory input that results from damage to the fibers that would otherwise convey sensory information from the body to the brain. The importance of sensory information for normal walking in humans is demonstrated by people who suffer from a genetic disorder called *Friedreich's ataxia,* a degeneration of the dorsal columns of the spinal cord, through which fine touch and pressure information is conveyed from the body to the cortex. These people have little or no position sense and a poor sense of passive movement and vibration. When they walk, they support the body on a broad base, legs apart, and tend to shuffle, reel, and stagger. (*Ataxia* comes from the Greek for "disorderly.") For humans, walking is a balancing act: we shift our weight forward from one leg to the other while balancing on one leg at a time. This balancing obviously requires ongoing afferent input, because ataxia does not lessen with time or practice. Locomotion is more severely impaired in people with ataxia than in monkeys with the same condition because of our more complex mode of locomotion (monkeys walk with four feet on the ground).

Rothwell and coworkers described the motor abilities of G. O., who was deafferented by a severe peripheral-nervous-system sensory disease. His motor power was unaffected, and he could produce a range of finger movements with accuracy, including simple, isolated finger movements; outlining figures in the air with his eyes closed; and moving his thumb accurately through different distances and at different speeds. He could judge weights and match forces with his thumb. (He could also drive his old car but was unable to learn to drive a new car.) Yet, in spite of all that he could still do, G. O.'s hands were relatively useless to him in daily life. He was unable to write, to fasten shirt buttons, or to hold a cup. His difficulties lay in *maintaining* force for any length of time. He could begin movements quite normally, but the patterns would gradually fall apart and become unrecognizable. When he tried to carry a suitcase, for example, he would soon drop it unless he continually looked down at it to confirm that it was there. G. O.'s symptoms support the findings with monkeys by suggesting that sensory feedback is not required to generate a movement. Instead, his symptoms suggest that sensory feedback is necessary to sustain a single movement or series of movements.

The Brainstem

In addition to the corticospinal pathways that carry messages to the spinal cord, about 26 pathways to the spinal cord originate in various locations in the brainstem. These pathways are important for carrying information pertaining to posture and balance from the brainstem and for controlling the autonomic nervous system. For all motor functions, the motor neurons are the final common path, but movements produced by the brainstem differ from those produced by the neocortex in that brainstem movements tend to be whole-body movements, unlike the skilled movements of the limbs organized by the neocortex.

The general idea that the brainstem is responsible for many movements performed by animals was most dramatically revealed by a series of studies done by Swiss neuroscientist Walter R. Hess. Hess developed the technique of implanting and cementing electrodes into the brains of cats and other animals. These electrodes could subsequently be attached to stimulating leads, causing little discomfort to the animal and allowing it to move freely.

When Hess stimulated the brainstem of a freely moving animal, he was able to elicit almost every innate movement that an animal of that species might be expected to make. For example, a resting cat could be induced to suddenly leap up with an arched back and erect hair, as though frightened by an approaching dog. The movements would begin abruptly when the stimulating current was turned on and end equally abruptly when the stimulating current was turned off. The behaviors were performed without vigor when the stimulating current was low but increased in vigor as the stimulating current was turned up. Some stimulation sites produced turning of the head, others produced walking or running, others produced aggressive or fear movements, and so forth. The emotional behavior of the animal also could be modulated. When shown a stuffed toy, a cat might respond to electrical stimulation of some sites by stalking the toy, whereas it would respond to stimulation of other sites with fear and withdrawal.

Other functions of the brainstem pertain to the control of the movements used in eating and drinking and in sexual behavior. The brainstem is also important for posture, for the ability to stand upright and make coordinated movements of the limbs, for swimming and walking, and for movements used in grooming and making nests. Grooming is in fact a particularly complex example of a movement pattern coordinated mainly by the brainstem. When grooming, a rat sits back on its haunches, licks its paws, wipes its nose with its paws, wipes its paws across its face, and finally turns to lick the fur on its body. These movements are always performed in the same order. The next time you dry off after a shower or swimming, note the "grooming sequence" that you use. Your grooming sequence is very similar to the sequence used by the rat.

The Basal Ganglia and Cerebellum

The main evidence that the basal ganglia and the cerebellum have motor functions is that damage to either structure impairs movement. Both structures also have extensive connections to the motor cortex, further suggesting their participation in movement. In this section, we review the anatomy of the basal ganglia and cerebellum and look at some of the symptoms that appear after they are damaged. We also consider some experiments illustrating the roles that the basal ganglia and cerebellum might play in controlling movement.

The Basal Ganglia and Movement Force

The basal ganglia are a collection of nuclei in the forebrain that make connections with the motor cortex and with the midbrain. As shown in Figure 9.14, one of the most prominent of these structures is the **caudate putamen,** itself a large cluster of nuclei located beneath the frontal cortex. Part of the caudate extends as a "tail" (*caudate* means "tailed") into the temporal lobe, ending in the amygdala.

The basal ganglia receive inputs from two main sources. First, all areas of the neocortex and limbic cortex, including the motor cortex, project to the basal ganglia. Second, there is a dopaminergic projection to the basal ganglia from the **substantia nigra,** a cluster of darkly pigmented cells of the midbrain. Conversely, the basal ganglia send projections back to both the motor cortex and the substantia nigra.

Two different, and in many ways opposite, kinds of movement disorders result from basal ganglia damage. If cells of the caudate putamen are damaged, unwanted choreiform (writhing and twitching) movements result. For example, Huntington's chorea destroys caudate putamen cells and is characterized by involuntary and exaggerated movements. Another example of involuntary movements related to caudate putamen damage consists of the unwanted tics and vocalizations peculiar to Tourette's syndrome. People with Tourette's syndrome make involuntary movements such as head twists or sudden movements of a hand or arm or will often utter a cry. But, in addition to causing involuntary movements, called **hyperkinetic symptoms,** damage to the basal ganglia can also result in difficulty in making movements—that is, in hypokinetic symptoms. Parkinson's disease, for example, caused by the loss of dopamine cells in the substantia nigra, is characterized by muscular rigidity, impairments in posture and balance, and rhythmic tremors of the hands, legs, and body. These two very different kinds of symptoms—hyperkinetic and hypokinetic—after basal ganglia damage suggest that a major function of the basal ganglia is to *modulate* movement.

Keele and Ivry tried to connect the two different kinds of basal ganglia symptoms by hypothesizing that the underlying function of the basal ganglia is to generate the force required for each particular movement. According to this idea, some types of basal ganglia damage cause errors of too much force and so result in excessive movement, whereas other types of damage cause errors of too little force and so result in insufficient movement. Keele and Ivry tested their hypothesis by giving healthy subjects as well as patients with various kinds of basal ganglia disorders a task that tested their ability to exert appropriate amounts of force. While looking at a line projected on a television screen, the experimental and control subjects attempted to produce a second line of the same length by pressing a button with the appropriate amount of force. After a number of practice trials, the subjects were then asked to press the button with appropriate force even when the first line was no longer visible as a guide. Patients with basal ganglia disorders were unable to do this task reliably. The force that they exerted was usually too little or too much, resulting in a line too short or too long.

What neural pathways enable the basal ganglia to modulate the force of movements? Basal ganglia circuits are quite complex, but Alexander and Crutcher proposed that there are two pathways through which they affect

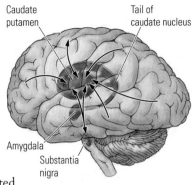

Caudate putamen · Tail of caudate nucleus · Amygdala · Substantia nigra

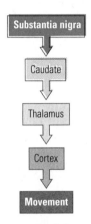

Substantia nigra → Caudate → Thalamus → Cortex → Movement

Figure 9.14 The basal ganglia consist of the caudate putamen, the tail of the caudate nucleus, and the amygdala. The caudate putamen makes reciprocal connections with the neocortex and with the substantia nigra.

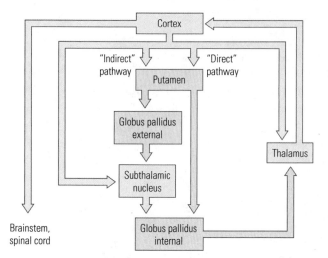

Figure 9.15 Two pathways in the basal ganglia modulate cortically produced movements. Blue indicates parts of the pathways that are excitatory; gray indicates parts of the pathways that are inhibitory. The indirect pathway has an excitatory effect on the internal part of the globus pallidus (GPi), whereas the direct pathway has an inhibitory influence on the GPi. If inhibition dominates, the thalamus is shut down and the cortex is unable to produce movement. If excitation predominates, the thalamus can become overactive, thus amplifying movement. (After Alexander and Crutcher, 1990.)

the activity of the motor cortex: an inhibitory pathway and an excitatory pathway. Both these pathways converge on an area of the basal ganglia called the internal part of the **globus pallidus** (GPi), as shown in Figure 9.15. The GPi in turn projects to the thalamus (more specifically, to the anterior thalamic nucleus), and the thalamus projects to the motor cortex. The thalamic projection modulates the size or force of a movement that the cortex produces, but the GPi influences the thalamic projection. The GPi is thought of as acting like the volume dial on a radio, because its output determines whether a movement will be weak or strong.

Figure 9.15 portrays the inputs to the GPi in color to illustrate how they affect movement. If activity in the inhibitory pathway is high relative to that in the excitatory pathway, inhibition of the GPi will predominate and the thalamus will be free to excite the cortex, thus amplifying movement. If, on the other hand, activity in the excitatory pathway is high relative to that in the inhibitory pathway, excitation of the GPi will predominate and the thalamus will be inhibited, thus reducing input to the cortex and decreasing the force of movements.

The idea that the GPi acts like a volume control over movement is currently receiving a great deal of attention. If the GPi is surgically destroyed in Parkinson patients, muscular rigidity has been found to be reduced and the ability to make normal movements is improved. Also consistent with this "volume theory," recordings made from cells of the globus pallidus show excessive activity in people with Parkinson's disease. Thus, destroying these inhibitory cells reduces rigidity and improves movement.

The Cerebellum and Motor Learning

Concerning the amount of practice required to play a musical instrument, musicians have a saying: "Miss a day of practice and you're OK; miss two days and you notice; miss three days and the world notices." Apparently, changes take place in the brain when practice of a motor skill is neglected. Evidence of the enormous amount of practice required to maintain motor skills is summarized in Table 9.1. The cerebellum seems to be the part of the motor system that participates in acquiring and maintaining motor skills, from playing a musical instrument to pitching a baseball to typing on a computer keyboard.

Large and conspicuous, the cerebellum sits on top of the brainstem and is clearly visible just behind the cerebral cortex. Like the cerebral cortex, it is divided into two hemispheres. A small lobe called the **flocculus** projects from its ventral surface. Despite the cerebellum's small size, it contains about half of all the neurons of the nervous system.

Table 9.1 Repetitions required to master skilled movements

Activity	Subjects	Repetitions
Cigar making	Women	3 million cigars
Knitting	Women	1.5 million stitches
Rug making	Women	1.5 million knots
Violin playing	Children	2.5 million notes
Basketball	Professional athletes	1.0 million shots
Baseball pitching	Professional athletes	1.6 million pitches

As Figure 9.16 shows, the cerebellum can be divided into several regions, each specializing in a different aspect of motor control. The flocculus receives projections from the vestibular system (the sensory receptors in the middle ear that tell us when we are off-balance) and takes part in the control of balance and eye movements. Many of the flocculus's projections go to the spinal cord and to the motor nuclei that control eye movements. The hemispheres of the cerebellum can be subdivided, as shown by the white lines in the drawing. The most medial parts control the face and the midline of the body. The more lateral parts are connected to areas of the motor cortex and are associated with movements of the limbs, hands, feet, and digits. The pathways from the hemispheres project to nuclei of the cerebellum, which in turn project to other brain regions, including the motor cortex.

To summarize the cerebellum's topographic organization, the midline of the homunculus is represented in the central part of the cerebellum, whereas the limbs and digits are represented in the cerebellum's lateral parts. Tumors in midline areas of the cerebellum or damage to them disrupt balance, eye movements, upright posture, and walking but do not substantially disrupt other movements, such as reaching, grasping, and using the fingers. When lying down, a person with medial damage to the cerebellum may show few symptoms. In contrast, damage to lateral parts of the cerebellum disrupts arm, hand, and finger movements much more than movements of the body's trunk.

Attempts to understand how the cerebellum controls movements have centered on two major ideas: (1) that the cerebellum has a role in the timing of movements and (2) that the cerebellum helps maintain movement accuracy. Keele and Ivry support the first of these two hypotheses. According to them, the cerebellum acts like a clock or pacemaker to ensure that both movements and perceptions are appropriately timed. In a motor test of timing, subjects were asked to tap a finger in rhythm with a metronome. After a number of taps, the metronome was turned off, and the subjects attempted to go on tapping with the same beat. Those with damage to the cerebellum, especially to the lateral cerebellum, performed poorly. In a perceptual test of timing, subjects were presented with two pairs of tones. The silent period between the first two tones was always the same length, whereas the silent period between the second two tones changed from trial to trial. The subjects had to tell whether the second silent period was longer or shorter than the first. Those with damage to the cerebellum performed poorly on this task, too. Apparently, the underlying impairment in disorders of the cerebellum is a loss of timing, both in movement and in perception.

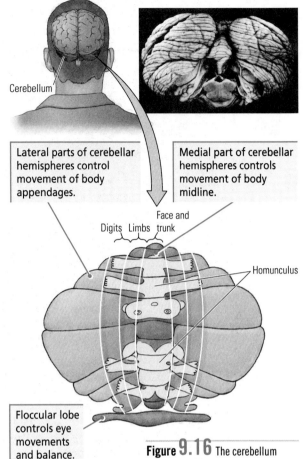

Cerebellum

Lateral parts of cerebellar hemispheres control movement of body appendages.

Medial part of cerebellar hemispheres controls movement of body midline.

Digits Limbs Face and trunk

Homunculus

Floccular lobe controls eye movements and balance.

Figure 9.16 The cerebellum consists of the cerebellar hemispheres and the flocculus. The hemispheres encode body movements, and the flocculus encodes balance. The cerebellum is organized topographically, with more-medial parts representing the midline of the body and more-lateral parts representing the limbs and digits. (Photograph of cerebellum reproduced from *The Human Brain: Dissections of the Real Brain,* by T. H. Williams, N. Gluhbegovic, and J. Jew, on CD-ROM. Published by Brain University, brain-university.com, 2000.)

(A) Procedure

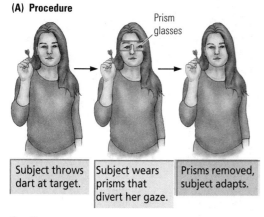

Prism glasses

| Subject throws dart at target. | Subject wears prisms that divert her gaze. | Prisms removed, subject adapts. |

Results

(B) Normal subject

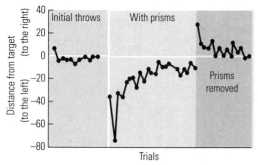

(C) Patient with damage to cerebellum

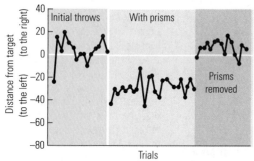

Figure 9.17 A task demonstrating that the cerebellum is making fine adjustment to movements. (A) A subject throws darts at a target. After some practice, the subject dons prisms that divert her gaze to the left. After practicing with the prisms, the subject takes them off, resumes the task, and adapts to the absence of the prisms. (B) A graph of the performance of a normal subject in the three throwing conditions. The normal subject throws the dart accurately without prisms; initially throws to the left and then corrects the throws when wearing prisms; and finally throws to the right and then corrects the throws when the prisms are removed. (C) A patient with damage to the cerebellum fails to correct throws when wearing prisms and shows no aftereffect when the prisms are removed. (After W. T. Thatch, H. P. Goodkin, and J. G. Keating, 1992. The cerebellum and the adaptive coordination of movement. *Annual Review of Neuroscience* 15, p. 429.)

Not all researchers believe that the cerebellum's major contribution to controlling movements is only one of timing. Thatch and coworkers argue that the primary role of the cerebellum is to help make the adjustments needed to keep movements accurate. They gathered evidence in support of this view by having subjects throw darts at a target, as shown in Figure 9.17. After a number of throws, the subjects put on glasses containing wedge-shaped prisms that displaced the apparent location of the target to the left. Then when a subject threw a dart, it landed to the left of the intended target. All subjects showed this initial distortion in aim. But then came an important difference. When normal subjects saw the dart miss the mark, they adjusted each successive throw until reasonable accuracy was restored. In contrast, subjects with damage to the cerebellum could not correct for this error. They kept missing the target far to the left time after time. Next the subjects removed the prism glasses and threw a few more darts. Again, another significant difference emerged. Normal subjects threw their first darts much too far to the right (corresponding to the previous adjustment they had learned to make), but soon they adjusted once again until they regained their former accuracy. In contrast, subjects with damage to the cerebellum showed no aftereffects from having worn the prisms, seeming to confirm the impression that they had never compensated for the glasses to begin with. This experiment suggests that many movements that we make—throwing a dart, hitting a ball with a bat, writing neatly, painting a work of art—depend on moment-to-moment learning and adjustments that are made by the cerebellum.

To better understand how the cerebellum improves motor skills by making required adjustments to movements, imagine throwing a dart yourself. Suppose you aim at the bull's eye, throw the dart, and find that it misses the board completely. On your next throw, you aim in such a way as to correct for the original error. Notice that there are actually two versions of each throw: (1) the movement that you intended to make and (2) the actual movement as recorded by sensory receptors in your arm and shoulder. If the throw is successful, you need make no correction on your next try. But, if you miss, an adjustment is called for. One way in which the adjustment might be accomplished is through the circuit shown in Figure 9.18. The cortex sends instructions to the spinal cord to throw a dart at the target. A copy of the same instructions is sent to the cerebellum through the inferior olivary nucleus. When you first throw the dart, the sensory receptors in your arm and shoulder encode the actual movement that you make and send a message about it to the cerebellum. The cerebellum now has information about both versions of the movement: what you intended to do and what you actually did. The cerebellum can now calculate the error and tell the cortex how it should correct the movement. When you next throw the dart, you incorporate that correction into your throw.

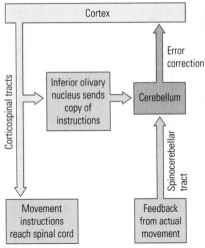

Figure 9.18 A feedback circuit allows the cerebellum to correct movements. The cerebellum receives information about the *instructions* sent to motor neurons by the inferior olivary nucleus. It receives information about the *actual* movement through the spinocerebellar tract (a sensory pathway carrying information from the spinal cord to the cerebellum that provides information about movements that have been made). By comparing the message for the intended movement with the movement that was actually performed, the cerebellum can send an error message to the cortex to improve the accuracy of a subsequent movement.

Summary

Movement of the body's muscles is represented in the motor regions of the brain. Skilled movements of the mouth and limbs are controlled by the motor cortex; whole-body movements requiring a certain level of coordination are controlled by the brainstem; and many reflex and walking movements are controlled by the spinal cord. Within the neocortex, elementary movements are controlled by the primary motor cortex, whereas coordinated movements are controlled by the premotor cortex. The prefrontal cortex organizes movement plans and instructs the premotor cortex in regard to how the plans should be executed. The sensory regions of the posterior cortex can initiate rapid responses to sensory events through projections made to the primary motor cortex and can influence plans for movements through projections to the prefrontal cortex.

Single-cell recordings in the neocortex suggest that cells in the primary motor cortex specify the movement that is to be made, as well as its force and its direction. Cells in the premotor cortex are active during more-complex movements in which not only the movement itself but also the movement's target must be considered. One class of cells, mirror neurons, studied in monkeys, is active when a monkey makes a particular goal-oriented movement, when it observes another monkey make the same movement, and even when it observes a human make the movement.

The basal ganglia contribute to motor control by adjusting the force associated with each movement. Consequently, damage to the basal ganglia results either in unwanted involuntary movements (too much force being exerted) or in such rigidity that movements are difficult to perform (too little force being exerted). The cerebellum contributes to the control of movement by improving movement skill. One way in which it seems to do so is by keeping track of the timing of movements. Another way is by making adjustments in movements to maintain their accuracy. In this case, the cerebellum compares an intended movement with an actual movement and calculates any necessary corrections.

References

Alexander, R. E., and M. D. Crutcher. Functional architecture of basal ganglia circuits: Neural substrates of parallel processing. *Trends in Neuroscience* 13:266–271, 1990.

Asanuma, H. *The Motor Cortex.* New York: Raven Press, 1989.

Bauman, M. L., and T. L. Kemper, *The Neurobiology of Autism.* Baltimore: Johns Hopkins University Press, 1994.

Berridge, K. C. Progressive degradation of serial grooming chains by descending decerebration. *Behavioural Brain Research* 33:24–253, 1989.

Brinkman, C. Supplementary motor area of the monkey's cerebral cortex: Short-and-long-term deficits after unilateral ablation and the effects of subsequent callosal section. *Journal of Neuroscience* 4:918–992, 1984.

Evarts, E. V. Relation of pyramidal tract activity to force exerted during voluntary movement. *Journal of Neurophysiology* 31:14–27, 1968.

Friedhoff, A. J., and T. N. Chase, Eds. *Advances in Neurology,* vol. 35, *Gilles de la Tourette Syndrome.* New York: Raven Press, 1982.

Fukuda, T. *Statokinetic Reflexes in Equilibrium and Movement.* Tokyo: University of Tokyo Press, 1981.

Galea, M. P., and I. Darian-Smith. Multiple corticospinal neuron populations in the Macaque monkey are specified by their unique cortical origins, spinal terminations, and connections. *Cerebral Cortex* 4:166–194, 1994.

Georgopoulos, A. P., J. F. Kalaska, R. Caminiti, and J. T. Massey. On the relations between the direction of two-dimensional arm movements and cell discharge in primate motor cortex. *Journal of Neuroscience* 2:1527–1537, 1982.

Georgopoulos, A. P., G. Pellizzer, A. V. Poliakov, and M. H. Schieber. Neural coding of finger and wrist movements. *Journal of Computational Neuroscience* 6:279–288, 1999.

Georgopoulos, A. P., M. Taira, and A. Lukashin. Cognitive neurophysiology of the motor cortex, *Science* 260:47–52, 1993.

Hughlings-Jackson, J. *Selected Writings of John Hughlings-Jackson,* J. Taylor, Ed. London: Hodder, 1931.

Hess, W. R. *The Functional Organization of the Diencephalon.* London: Grune and Stratton, 1957.

Jeannerod, M. *The Neural and Behavioural Organization of Goal-Directed Movements.* Oxford: Clarendon Press, 1988.

Kaas, J. H. The organization and evolution of neocortex. In S. P. Wise, Ed. *Higher Brain Functions.* New York: Wiley, 1987, pp. 237–298.

Kakei, S., D. Hoffman, and P. L. Strick. Direction of action is represented in the ventral premotor cortex. *Nature Neuroscience* 4:1020–1025, 2001.

Kakei, S., D. Hoffman, and P. L. Strick. Muscle and movement representations in the primary motor cortex. *Science* 285:2136–2139, 1999.

Kandel, E. R., J. H. Schwartz, and T. M. Jessell. *Principles of Neural Science,* vol. 4. New York, Elsevier, 2000.

Keele, S. W., and R. Ivry. Does the cerebellum provide a common computation for diverse tasks? A timing hypothesis. In A. Diamond, Ed., The Development and Neural Bases of Higher Cognitive Functions. *Annals of the New York Academy of Sciences* 608:197–211, 1991.

Kuypers, H. G. J. M. Anatomy of descending pathways. In V. B. Brooks, Ed. *The Nervous System,* vol. 7, *Handbook of Physiology.* Bethesda, MD: American Physiological Society, 1981.

Lashley, K. S. The problem of serial order in behavior. In L. A. Jeffress, Ed. *Cerebral Mechanisms and Behavior.* New York: Wiley, 1951, pp. 112–136.

Leonard, C. M., D. S. Glendinning, T. Wilfong, B. Y. Cooper, and C. J. Vierck, Jr. Alterations of natural hand movements after interruption of fasciculus cuneatus in the macaque. *Somatosensory and Motor Research* 9:61–75, 1991.

Melzack, R., and P. D. Wall. Pain mechanisms: A new theory. *Science* 150:971–979, 1965.

Mountcastle, V. B. An organizing principle for cerebral function: The unit module and the distributed system. In G. M. Edelman and V. B. Mountcastle, Eds. *The Mindful Brain.* Cambridge, MA: MIT Press, 1978, pp. 7–50.

Napier, J. *Hands.* Princeton NJ: Princeton University Press, 1980.

Nudo, R. J., B. M. Wise, F. SiFuentes, and G. W. Milliken. Neural substrates for the effects of rehabilitative training on motor recovery after ischemic infarct, *Science* 272:1791–1794, 1996.

Penfield, W., and E. Boldrey. Somatic motor and sensory representation in the cerebral cortex as studied by electrical stimulation. *Brain* 60:389–443, 1958.

Pons, T. P., P. E. Garraghty, A. K. Ommaya, J. H. Kaas, E. Taum, and M. Mishkin. Massive cortical reorganization after sensory deafferentation in adult macaques. *Science* 252:1857–1860, 1991.

Reeve, C. *Nothing Is Impossible.* New York: Random House, 2002.

Roland, P. E. *Brain Activation.* New York: Wiley-Liss, 1993.

Rothwell, J. C., M. M. Taube, B. L. Day, J. A. Obeso, P. K. Thomas, and C. D. Marsden. Manual motor performance in a deafferented man. *Brain* 105:515–542, 1982.

Sacks, O. W. *The Man Who Mistook His Wife for a Hat.* New York: Touchstone Books, 1998.

Schieber, M. H. Constraints on somatotopic organization in the primary motor cortex. *Journal of Neurophysiology* 86:2125–2143, 2001.

Schieber, M. H. Somatotopic gradients in the distributed organization of the human primary motor cortex hand area: Evidence from small infarcts. *Experimental Brain Research* 128:139–148, 1999.

Thatch, W. T., H. P. Goodkin, and J. G. Keating. The cerebellum and the adaptive coordination of movement. *Annual Review of Neuroscience* 15:403–442, 1992.

Umilta, M. A., K. Kohler, V. Gallese, L. Fogassi, L. Fadiga, C. Keysers, and G. Rizzolatti. I know what you are doing: A neurophysiological study *Neuron* 31:155–165, 2001.

Principles of Neocortical Function

A. R. was a strictly average boy until the age of 11, when he developed seizures, but only on the right side of his body. In time, he developed a persistent right-side weakness and increasing difficulty in talking (dysphasia).

In the next six years and multiple hospital admissions, the cause of the seizures and A. R.'s language and motor problems remained undetermined. Although he was initially right-handed, he was unable to use his right hand and began to write and draw with his left. (Recall from Chapter 3 that the motor and sensory nerves cross over, for example, from the right side of the body to the left cerebral hemisphere.)

By age 15, A. R.'s IQ score had dropped 30 points and, by age 17, his language and emotional problems made psychological testing impossible. At 17, his condition was diagnosed as Rasmussen's encephalitis, a chronic brain infection that slowly leads to a virtual loss of function in one cerebral hemisphere. Because the only successful treatment is hemispherectomy, removal of the diseased tissue, most of A. R.'s left cerebral hemisphere was surgically removed.

When A. R. was reassessed 10 years later, at age 27, he showed remarkable improvement. His oral language skills appeared to be average. He communicated freely and could both initiate and respond to conversation. He was, however, functionally illiterate and unable to read or write except at a very simple level.

His motor skills also had improved: he could move about on his own, although he still had a significant limp; he could lift his right arm to shoulder level; and he could open and close his hands to grasp objects with his right hand. (Taylor, 1991)

A surprising lesson from A. R.'s case is that people can lose an enormous amount of cerebral tissue and still show remarkable cognitive and motor abilities. The achievements of patients such as A. R., even those with severe neuron loss in both cerebral hemispheres, prompts the question, What roles do the cerebral hemispheres and the subcortical regions play in the control of behavior? To search for answers, in this chapter we focus on the brain's hierarchical organization from spinal cord to cortex, on the structure of the cortex, and on theories of functional organization.

A Hierarchy of Function from Spinal Cord to Cortex

The brain is organized in a *functional* hierarchy, the higher levels providing an animal with more precision and flexibility in behavior. A. R.'s intelligence test score was borderline retarded with an IQ of 70 after his surgery, which is much below his earlier IQ score of about 100. Nonetheless, although severely impaired, A. R. functioned rather well with so much of his brain gone. He did so for two reasons:

1. Subcortical structures are capable of mediating complex behavioral processes. The relation of the cortex to subcortical structures is analogous to that of a piano player to a piano. The cortex is the piano player, producing behavior by playing on subcortical keys. This idea dates to Herbert Spencer's mid-nineteenth-century speculation that each step in evolution added a new level of brain and of behavioral complexity. Hughlings-Jackson adopted Spencer's idea, and it became a central focus of neurological theories of the twentieth century (see Chapter 1).

2. The brain has considerable capacity to compensate for loss, a property known as **plasticity.** At the time of his surgery, A. R. had no language ability at all, but that was partly because the dysfunctioning left hemisphere, where language functions are concentrated in most of us, was interfering with the right hemisphere's ability to engage in language functions. Shortly after the left hemisphere was removed, at least some language functions reemerged, as though the left hemisphere had been surpressing functioning in the right.

Indeed, the focus on functional levels of nervous system organization can be traced in part to early findings that the brain has remarkable plasticity. The brain's resiliency to damage gained popular exposure in 1700 by Joseph Du Verney. In a public demonstration, he showed that, when a nerve and muscle were dissected away from a frog, the nerve continued to function, because it produced muscle contractions when touched.

In the 300 years since then, it has become clear that both laboratory animals and humans can function surprisingly well with rather large amounts of the brain removed. We hasten to point out that the mere fact that people can live fairly normally with large amounts of brain tissue missing does not imply that those parts of the brain are not needed. People can compensate for lost brain tissue just as they can compensate for lost limbs. But this ability to compensate does not mean that such people would not be better off with all their limbs intact.

Throughout the twentieth century, the capacities of animals with extensive regions of the nervous system removed were recorded in many neurologic studies. One study was conducted by Kent Berridge on grooming in the rat. Rats (as well as other animals, including ourselves) begin by grooming the head and then work their way down the body. As illustrated in Figure 10.1, rats begin to groom using their paws, rubbing the nose with symmetrical circular movements. Then, they sweep their paws across the face and behind the ears before turning to lick the body. This series of actions can be divided into as many as 50 linked movements.

Rats have a fixed grooming sequence, which starts with ellipical strokes to the head,...

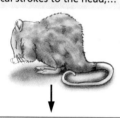

...followed by grooming of each side of the face.

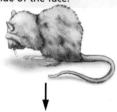

They move to the ears, using bilateral strokes,...

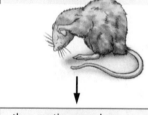

...then continue moving toward the rear of the body.

Figure 10.1 Grooming sequences in the rat. Rats have a stereotyped grooming sequence in which they begin by washing the face with bilateral eliptical movements, followed first by a slight turning of the head with a unilateral paw stroke over one ear, eye, and the face and then by a turning of the head to the body. The rat then proceeds down the body, ending at the rump. (After Berridge and Whishaw, 1992.)

In examining this movement complex, Berridge found that many levels of the nervous system take part in producing the elements and the syntax (the organization) of the behavior. That is, grooming behavior is produced not by one locus in the brain but rather by many brain areas and levels, including the spinal cord, hindbrain, midbrain, diencephalon, basal ganglia, and cortex. These different nervous system layers do not simply replicate function; rather, each region adds a different dimension to the behavior.

This hierarchical organization is true not only of grooming but also of virtually every behavior in which we (as well as rats) engage. Understanding this general principle is critical to understanding what role the cortex plays in controlling behavior. The following sections summarize some of the functions mediated by different anatomical levels of the nervous system (Figure 10.2). We note parallel functions that may exist in humans as appropriate. We begin with the "lowest" level of the nervous system, the spinal cord, and add structures to see how the corresponding behaviors increase in complexity.

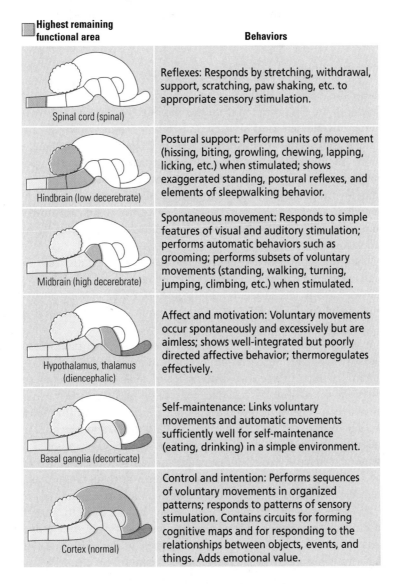

Highest remaining functional area

Behaviors

Spinal cord (spinal)
Reflexes: Responds by stretching, withdrawal, support, scratching, paw shaking, etc. to appropriate sensory stimulation.

Hindbrain (low decerebrate)
Postural support: Performs units of movement (hissing, biting, growling, chewing, lapping, licking, etc.) when stimulated; shows exaggerated standing, postural reflexes, and elements of sleepwalking behavior.

Midbrain (high decerebrate)
Spontaneous movement: Responds to simple features of visual and auditory stimulation; performs automatic behaviors such as grooming; performs subsets of voluntary movements (standing, walking, turning, jumping, climbing, etc.) when stimulated.

Hypothalamus, thalamus (diencephalic)
Affect and motivation: Voluntary movements occur spontaneously and excessively but are aimless; shows well-integrated but poorly directed affective behavior; thermoregulates effectively.

Basal ganglia (decorticate)
Self-maintenance: Links voluntary movements and automatic movements sufficiently well for self-maintenance (eating, drinking) in a simple environment.

Cortex (normal)
Control and intention: Performs sequences of voluntary movements in organized patterns; responds to patterns of sensory stimulation. Contains circuits for forming cognitive maps and for responding to the relationships between objects, events, and things. Adds emotional value.

Figure 10.2 The anatomical and behavioral levels of the nervous system. Shading indicates the highest remaining functional area, in a hierarchy from spinal cord to cortex.

Figure 10.3 Spinal animal walking on treadmill.

The Spinal Cord and Reflexes

In Chapter 9, we met the actor Christopher Reeve, whose spinal cord was severed just below the brain in a tragic equestrian accident. This spinal-cord injury left the Superman of the movies unable to move or even to breathe without the aid of a respirator. The question we wish to ask is, What behaviors can his spinal cord initiate without any descending influence from the brain?

Like Christopher Reeve, an animal whose spinal cord is disconnected from the brain is unable to move voluntarily, because the brain has no way to communicate with the spinal neurons. Nonetheless, the spinal cord is intact and can mediate many reflexes, such as limb approach to a tactile stimulus and limb withdrawal from a noxious stimulus. The spinal cord also contains the circuitry to produce stepping responses and walking, provided that body weight is supported. For example, if animals are suspended in a hammock and placed such that their limbs are in light contact with a moving treadmill, their legs will begin to make stepping movements automatically, as illustrated in Figure 10.3. This behavior tells us that circuitry in the spinal cord, not the brain, produces the stepping movements. The role of the brain is control—to make those movements at the right time and place.

The Hindbrain and Postural Support

If the brain is injured such that the hindbrain and spinal cord are still connected but both are disconnected from the rest of the brain, the subject is called a **low decerebrate** (see Figure 10.2). This type of injury produces a very different type of syndrome from that produced in an animal with a spinal-cord transection. An animal that has undergone the transection is alert; a person who has sustained such an injury can still talk, express emotion, and so on. However, the low-decerebrate animal no longer shows any alertness, because many essential inputs to the brain regions above the injury are now disconnected, presumably leaving the forebrain "in the dark," with difficulty in maintaining consciousness.

Sensory input into the hindbrain comes predominantly from the head and is carried over cranial nerves IV to XII (see Figure 3.11). Most of these nerves also have motor nuclei in the hindbrain, whose efferent (outgoing) fibers control muscles in the head and neck. Sensory input to the hindbrain is not limited to the cranial nerves: the spinal somatosensory system has access to hindbrain motor systems, just as the hindbrain has access to spinal motor systems. But the sensory input into the hindbrain can no longer reach the upper parts of the brain, resulting in a serious disturbance of consciousness in low decerebrates.

A classic example of the effects of low-decerebrate injury can be seen in the results of extensive studies on cats done in the early part of the twentieth century by researchers such as Bazett, Penfield, Bard, and Macht. The researchers kept low-decerebrate cats alive for periods of weeks or months. The cats were generally inactive when undisturbed and showed no effective thermoregulatory ability, but they swallowed food placed on their tongues and so could be fed. If the animals were stimulated lightly in any of a variety of sensory modalities (such as touch, pain, or sounds), they moved from their normal reclining position into a crouch. If the stimulation was stronger, they walked, somewhat unsteadily. These stimuli also elicited such normal affective (emotional) behaviors as biting, hissing, growling, and lashing of the tail.

A characteristic aspect of behavior accorded by the hindbrain is a peculiar kind of stiffness called **decerebrate rigidity.** This stiffness is due to excessive muscle tone, particularly in the antigravity muscles (those that hold the body up), which are the body's strongest. When a low-decerebrate animal is placed in an upright position, its limbs extend and its head flexes upward in a posture that is often referred to as "exaggerated standing."

Against the background of decerebrate rigidity, a number of *postural reflexes* can be elicited by changes in head position. If the head of a standing animal is pushed down toward the floor, the front limbs flex and the hind limbs extend; if the head is pushed upward, the hind legs flex and the front legs extend. The first posture would be used by a normal cat looking under a couch, the second by a normal cat looking upward onto a shelf. Turning the head to the side elicits extension of the limbs on the same side and flexion of the limbs on the opposite side of the body. This response occurs in a normal cat that has turned its head to look at some object and is prepared to pursue it.

Normal animals exhibit two types of sleep: *quiet sleep*, characterized by muscle tone and commonly referred to as slow-wave sleep, and *active sleep*, characterized by an absence of muscle tone and commonly referred to as dream, or REM, sleep (Figure 10.4). Low-decerebrate animals display both types of sleep at different times. Animals left undisturbed gradually lose their rigidity and subside or droop into a prone posture. Any mild stimulus such as a noise or a touch reinstates rigidity. This behavioral change seems analogous to quiet sleep. The animals also show a sudden collapse, accompanied by the loss of all body tone, which lasts from 15 seconds to 12 minutes, analogous to active, or dream, sleep. People with an illness called **narcolepsy** similarly collapse uncontrollably into active sleep. The results of research with low-decerebrate animals thus demonstrate that the neural centers that produce sleep are located in the hindbrain.

The behavioral changes seen in low-decerebrate animals are paralleled in people who are rendered comatose by brainstem damage of the type that essentially separates the lower brainstem from the rest of the brain. Barrett and his colleagues documented numerous cases. These people may alternate between states of consciousness resembling sleeping and waking, make eye movements to follow moving stimuli, cough, smile, swallow food, and display decerebrate rigidity and postural adjustments when moved. When cared for, people with such brain damage may live for months or years with little change in their condition.

Awake

Quiet sleep
(slow wave sleep)

Active sleep
(REM, or dream sleep)

Figure 10.4 Postures of a cat when awake, and in quiet and active sleep.

The Midbrain and Spontaneous Movement

The next level of brain organization can be seen in an animal that has an intact midbrain but lacks higher-center functioning. Damage that separates the diencephalon from the midbrain regions containing, in the tectum, the coordinating centers for vision (superior colliculus) and hearing (inferior colliculus) and, in the tegmentum, a number of motor nuclei produces this condition, called **high decerebration** (see Figure 10.2). Visual and auditory inputs allow the animal to perceive events at a distance, and so the high-decerebrate animal can respond to distant objects by moving toward them.

Bard and Macht reported that high-decerebrate cats can walk, stand, resume upright posture when turned on their backs, and even run and climb when stimulated. Bignall and Schramm found that kittens decerebrated in infancy could orient themselves toward visual and auditory stimuli. The animals could even execute an attack response and pounce on objects at the source of a sound. In fact, Bignall and Schramm fed the cats by exploiting this behavior: they placed food near the source of the sound. Attacking the sound source, the cats then consumed the food. Although the cats attacked moving objects, they gave no evidence of being able to see, because they bumped into things when they walked.

These experiments demonstrate that all the components (or subsets) of **voluntary movements**—movements that take an animal from one place to another, such as turning, walking, climbing, and swimming—are present at the subcortical level of the midbrain. Normal animals use voluntary movements to satisfy a variety of needs; for example, to find food, water, or a new home territory or to escape a predator. Voluntary movements have also been variously called appetitive, instrumental, purposive, or operant.

Because they are executed through lower-level postural support and reflex systems, voluntary movements can also be elicited by lower-level sensory input; that is, a pinch or postural displacement can elicit turning, walking, or climbing. Thus, this new functional level is integrated with lower levels by both ascending and descending connections, exactly as the hindbrain and spinal levels are interconnected.

High-decerebrate animals can also effectively perform **automatic movements:** units of stereotyped behavior linked in a sequence. Grooming, chewing food, lapping water, and rejecting food are representative automatic behaviors of the rat. Generally, automatic behaviors (also variously called reflexive, consummatory, or respondent behaviors) are directed toward completing some act and are not specifically directed toward moving an animal from one place to another.

Grooming is an excellent example of an automatic behavior, because it consists of a large number of movements executed sequentially in an organized and stereotyped fashion (see Figure 10.1). Food rejection comprises a similarly complex series of behaviors. If decerebrate rats are given food when they are not hungry, they perform a series of movements consisting of tongue flicks, chin rubbing, and paw shaking to reject the food. These behaviors are similar to the rejection behaviors of normal rats (as well as people, as illustrated in Figure 10.5) in response to food that they find noxious. If the animals are not sated, they will lap water and chew food brought to their mouths.

Among the accounts of infants born with large parts of the forebrain missing, one child studied by Gamper had no brain present above the diencephalon and

Figure 10.5 Human reactions to taste. Positive reactions (such as licking the fingers or lips) are elicited by sweet and other palatable tastes. Negative (aversive) reactions, elicited by bitter tastes (such as quinine) and by other unpalatable flavors, include spitting, making a face of distaste, and wiping the mouth with the back of the hand. (After K. C. Berridge. 1996. Food reward: Brain substrates of wanting and liking. *Neuroscience and Biobehavioral Reviews* 20, p. 6.)

Positive actions

Negative actions

only a few traces of the diencephalon intact (Figure 10.6). This child was, therefore, anatomically and behaviorally equivalent to a high-decerebrate animal. The child could sit up and showed many behaviors of newborn infants, periodically asleep and wakeful, sucking, yawning, stretching, crying, and following visual stimuli with the eyes. However, the child showed little spontaneous activity and, if left alone, remained mostly in a drowsy state.

Brackbill studied a similar child and found that, in response to moderately loud sounds (60–90 decibels), this infant oriented to stimuli in much the same way as normal infants do. Unlike normal babies, however this child's responses did not change in magnitude and did not habituate (gradually decrease in intensity) to repeated presentation. Brackbill concluded that the forebrain is not important in producing movements but is important in attenuating and inhibiting them. Generally, babies born with such extensive brain abnormalities do not live long, and, among those who live for a number of months, there is no development of the complex behaviors seen in normal infants.

The Diencephalon and Affect and Motivation

The **diencephalic** animal, although lacking the basal ganglia and cerebral hemispheres (see Figure 10.2), has an intact olfactory system, enabling it to smell odors at a distance. The hypothalamus and pituitary also are intact, and their control over hormonal systems no doubt integrates the body's physiology with the brain's activity. The hypothalamus is thought to be implicated in **homeostasis**—that is, in maintaining body temperature, chemical balance, energy reserves, and so forth. Diencephalic animals maintain normal body temperature, but they do not eat or drink well enough to sustain themselves.

The diencephalon adds a dimension of affect and motivation to behavior in the sense that behavior becomes "energized" and sustained. As already mentioned, high-decerebrate animals show many of the component behaviors of rage, but the behaviors are not energetic, well integrated, or sustained. Cannon and Britton studied diencephalic cats and described what they called "quasi-emotional phenomena," or sham rage, such as that usually seen in an infuriated animal. This affective behavior is inappropriately displayed and is thus called sham rage to distinguish it from the directed rage of the normal cat. Sham rage consists of lashing the tail, arching the trunk, making limb movements, displaying claws, snarling, and biting. The animal displays sympathetic signs of rage, including erection of the tail hair, sweating of the toe pads, dilation of the pupils, urination, high blood pressure, high heart rate, and increases in epinephrine and blood sugar. These emotional attacks sometimes last for hours.

Bard removed varying amounts of forebrain and brainstem and found that, for sham rage to occur, it was necessary to leave at least the posterior part of the hypothalamus intact. Clinical reports indicate that similar sham emotional attacks can occur in people who have suffered hypothalamic lesions. These people show unchecked rage or literally laugh until they die.

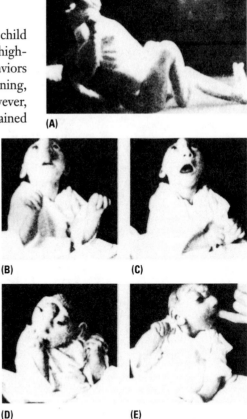

(A)

(B) (C)

(D) (E)

Figure 10.6 Instinctive behavior and oral automatisms in a mesencephalic human infant studied by Gamper: yawning, spreading arms (A); sucking after lips are touched, with deviation of eyes (B); coordinated gaze and mouth snapping after finger is removed from view (C); spontaneous sucking of own hand (D); and turning left to suck, with deviation of head and eyes and tonic neck reflexes in arms (E). (From E. Gamper. 1926. *Z. ges. Neurol. Psychiat.* 104, p. 49.)

In addition to sham rage, another pronounced feature of the diencephalic animal's behavior is its constant activity. For example, when placed in an open field, it wanders aimlessly. These two behaviors suggest that the diencephalon energizes the animal's behavior, which may have led some researchers to label the behavior affective or motivated. Perhaps the hyperactivity of the diencephalic animal should be called *sham motivation* to distinguish it from the normal animal's goal-oriented behavior.

In this sense the sham affect and sham motivation of the diencephalic animal are akin to the exaggerated standing observed in low-decerebrate animals. Under appropriate forebrain control the behavior can be released for functional purposes, but in the absence of that control the behavior of the diencephalic animal is excessive and seems inappropriate.

The Basal Ganglia and Self-Maintenance

Decortication is the removal of the neocortex, leaving the basal ganglia and brainstem intact (see Figure 10.2). Decorticate animals have been studied more closely than any other neurologically impaired class because they are able to maintain themselves without special care in laboratory conditions.

The first careful experiments were done by Goltz with decorticate dogs (see Chapter 1), but the most thorough studies have used rats as subjects. Within a day after surgery, rats eat and maintain body weight on a wet mash diet and eat dry food and drink water brought in contact with the mouth. With a little training in drinking (holding the water spout to the mouth), they find water and become able to maintain themselves on water and laboratory chow. They have normal sleeping–waking cycles; run, climb, and swim; and even negotiate simple mazes.

They can also sequence series of movements. For example, copulation consists of a number of movements that take place sequentially and last for hours, yet decorticate animals can perform these acts almost normally. As described early in this chapter, grooming also requires the sequential use of about 50 discrete movements, and decorticated rats also perform it normally.

In sum, to a casual observer, the decorticated rat appears indistinguishable from normal animals. In fact, in laboratory exercises for students in which their job is to distinguish between normal and decorticated animals, students not only find this task difficult, but often fail. The decorticate rat does indeed have a lot of behavioral difficulties, but seeing these problems requires a trained eye. All the elementary movements that animals might make seem to be part of their behavioral repertoire after decortication. They can walk, eat, drink, mate, and raise litters of pups in a seemingly adequate fashion.

What is observed in the decorticate rat, and what is presumably conferred by functions in the basal ganglia, is the ability to link automatic movements to voluntary movements so that the behaviors are biologically adaptive. A major part of this linking probably includes the inhibition or facilitation of voluntary movements. For example, the animal walks until it finds food or water and then inhibits walking to consume the food or water. Thus, the basal ganglia probably provide the circuitry required for the stimulus to inhibit movement so that ingestion can occur.

The Cortex and Intention

What the cortex *does* can also be ascertained by studying what decorticate animals (with the neocortex alone removed or with the limbic system also removed) do *not* do. They do not build nests, although they engage in some nest-building behaviors. They do not hoard food, although they might carry food around. They also have difficulty making skilled movements with the tongue and limbs, because they are unable to reach for food by protruding the tongue or by reaching with one forelimb.

They can do pattern discriminations in different sensory modalities but only if these tasks are relatively simple. For example, a decorticate could discriminate two pure tones but would be unable to distinguish complex sounds such as the noises from a lawnmower and an automobile. The results of a series of experiments by David Oakley show that the animals can perform well in tests of classical conditioning, operant conditioning, approach learning, cue learning, and pattern discrimination. These experiments confirm that the cortex is not essential for learning itself. However, decorticate animals fail at learning, for example, complex pattern discriminations and how to find their way around in space.

The results of studies of decortication tell us that the cortex does not add much in the way of new movements to an animal's behavioral repertory. Rather, the cortex appears to extend the usefulness of all behaviors or to make them adaptive in new situations. An animal without a cortex can see and hear and can use its limbs for many purposes, but an animal with a cortex can make plans and combine movement sequences together to generate more-complex behavioral patterns.

The Structure of the Cortex

As our summary of the behaviors of animals with only subcortical brain function makes clear, the cortex adds new dimensions to the analysis of sensory events and new levels of control to movements. What structural features of the cortex permit these enhancements?

As already noted, the cortex can be divided by topographic maps, which are based on various anatomical and functional criteria (see Chapter 3). The first complete cortical map of the human brain was published in 1905 by Alfred Campbell, and it was based on both cell structure and myelin distribution. Soon after several alternative versions emerged, the most notable by Korbinian Brodmann (Figure 10.7). The various maps do not correspond exactly, and they use different criteria and nomenclature. Furthermore, as new staining techniques are devised, it is possible to subdivide and to redefine cortical areas in a truly bewildering manner, with estimates of the number of cortical areas in the human brain ranging from the approximately 50 of Brodmann to more than 200. Indeed, one neuroanatomical wag was quoted as concluding that "in cortical anatomy the gain is in the stain!" Most recently, it has been possible to map the human brain using MRI technology, as illustrated in the Snapshot on page 230.

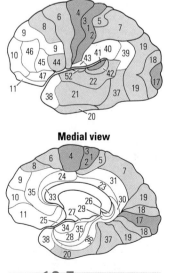

Lateral view

Medial view

Figure 10.7 Brodmann's map.

Mapping the Human Cortex

About 70% of the human cerebral cortex is buried in sulci, which complicates our ability to visualize its extent from a surface view or topographic map. Surface views of the brain thus hide the source of the majority of activation recorded in imaging studies. One display format that solves this problem is the flat map, which allows imagers to visualize the entire surface area of a hemisphere in a single view. (For a flat map of the cortical areas in the macaque monkey, see Figure 10.17.)

van Essen and Drury used the MRI analysis of the Visible Man, a digital atlas of the human body, to generate flat maps of the human cortex. Figure A shows a surface view of the Visible Man's two hemispheres, with the lobes identified by different shadings. Flat maps display the sulci and gyri in an alternative format (Figure B), in which buried cortex (not visible from the exterior of the hemisphere) is shown in darker shades. The table summarizes the surface areas of the cortical lobes and the paralimbic cortex.

The location of brain areas in a whole brain can be calculated by using a three-dimensional atlas. Sections are taken at regular intervals (typically 4 mm in the human brain), much as if an atlas of the earth were made by taking sequential cuts through the globe at regular intervals and then displaying the map obtained of each cut on a single page. As you flip through the pages, it thus becomes possible to visualize how

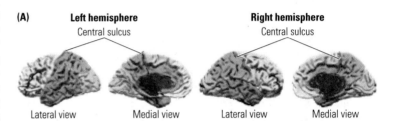

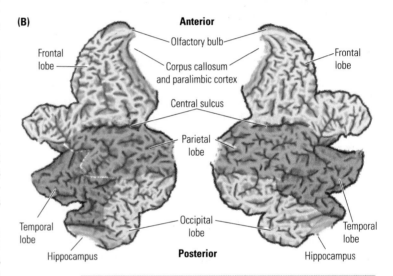

Cortical maps. (A) A digital surface map. (B) The cortex has been "flattened" so that all tissues hidden in sulci are visible. Flat maps provide a perspective on the relative size of various cortical regions and on the amount of tissue dedicated to different functions, as detailed in the table.

the earth appears going from one side to the other in space. By linking the data from the Visible Man to so-called Talairach space, van Essen and Drury were able to identify the coordinates for the regions in their flat map. Their coordinate system makes it possible to identify the location of activations in imaging studies with respect to cortical surface.

(D. C. van Essen and H. A. Drury. Structural and functional analyses of human cerebral cortex using a surface-based atlas. *Journal of Neuroscience* 17:7082–7102, 1997.)

Cortical surface-area measurements

Region	Left hemisphere cm² (%)	Right hemisphere cm² (%)
Frontal	278 (36)	297 (37)
Temporal	161 (21)	161 (21)
Parietal	139 (18)	161 (20)
Occipital	144 (19)	145 (18)
Paralimbic	46 (6)	40 (5)
Total	766 (100)	803 (100)

A consistent theme in neuroanatomy throughout the past century is that cortical regions can be categorized as **primary sensory cortex, primary motor cortex,** and **association cortex.** The last of these categories, association cortex, is usually also categorized as **secondary cortex,** which elaborates information coming from primary areas, and as **higher-order areas,** which may combine information from more than one system. This idea can be traced to Paul Flechsig and his studies of the development of myelin in the cortex.

Flechsig divided cortical regions into (1) an early-myelinating primordial zone including the motor cortex and a region of visual, auditory, and somatosensory cortex; (2) a field bordering the primordial zone that myelinates next; and (3) a late-myelinating zone, which he called "association." Flechsig hypothesized psychological functions for his hierarchy, with the general idea being that the primary zones perform simple sensorimotor functions, whereas the association areas conduct the highest mental analyses. Flechsig's ideas greatly influenced neurological thinking throughout the twentieth century.

Cortical Cells

Nerve cells can be easily distinguished in the cortex as **spiny neurons** or **aspiny neurons** by the presence or absence, respectively, of dendritic spines. Much as rose thorns extend the surface area of rose-bush branches, dendritic spines (see Figure 4.1) are essentially an extension of the surface area of dendrites. Dendritic spines serve as functional compartments for chemicals as well as a location for synaptic connections with other cells. About 95% of all excitatory synapses on spiny neurons occur on the spines. (For an extensive series of books on the structure of the cortex, see Peters and Jones, 1984–1999).

Spiny neurons include **pyramidal cells,** which have pyramid-shaped cell bodies and generally send information from one region of the cortex to some other brain area, and spiny **stellate cells,** which are smaller, star-shaped interneurons whose processes remain within the region of the brain in which the cell body is located. Spiny neurons are excitatory and are likely to use glutamate or aspartate as transmitters. Pyramidal cells, which constitute the largest population of cortical neurons (70%–85%), are the efferent projection neurons of the cortex. They are found in layers II, III, V, and VI. In general, the largest cells send their axons the farthest. The pyramidal cells of layer V are the largest, projecting to the brainstem and spinal cord. Those in layers II and III are smaller and project to other cortical regions (Figure 10.8).

Aspiny neurons are interneurons with short axons and no dendritic spines. They are diverse in appearance, with different types named largely on the basis of the configurations of their axons and dendrites. One type of aspiny stellate cell is called a basket cell because its axon projects horizontally, forming synapses that envelop the postsynaptic cell like a basket. Another, the double-bouquet type, has a proliferation of dendrites on either side of the cell body, much as if two bouquets of flowers were aligned stem to stem. Despite differences in shape, all aspiny neurons are inhibitory and are likely to use GABA as a transmitter. Aspiny neurons also use many other transmitters; virtually every classical transmitter and neuropeptide has been colocalized with GABA in aspiny cells. Thus, not only are aspiny cells morphologically diverse, but they show a remarkable chemical diversity.

Figure 10.8 Neocortical cell types. The most important neuron types, pyramidal cells and stellate cells, are elaborated here. The direction of the arrows indicates afferents (up) or efferents (down). (After Szentagothai, 1969.)

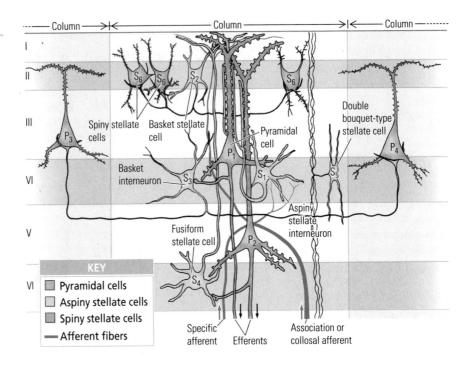

Cortical Layers, Efferents, and Afferents

Each of the four to six layers of the cortex has different functions, different afferents (inputs), and different efferents (outputs). The cells of the middle layers of the cortex (especially in and around layer IV) constitute a zone of sensory analysis in that they receive projections from other areas of the cortex and other areas of the brain. The cells of layers V and VI constitute a zone of output in that they send axons to other cortical areas or other brain areas. Therefore, it is hardly surprising that the somatosensory cortex has a relatively large layer IV and a small layer V, whereas the motor cortex has a relatively large layer V and a small layer IV. Figure 10.9 illustrates this difference and shows that the different cortical layers can be distinguished by the neuronal elements that each contains and that the thickness of the layers also corresponds to their function.

Figure 10.9 illustrates another feature of cortical organization: afferents to the cortex are of two general types, specific and nonspecific:

1. *Specific afferents* bring information (sensory information, for example) to an area of the cortex and terminate in relatively discrete cortical regions, usually in only one or two layers. Specific afferents include projections from the thalamus as well as from the amygdala. Most of these projections terminate in layer IV, although projections from the amygdala and certain thalamic nuclei may terminate in the more superficial layers.

2. *Nonspecific afferents* presumably serve general functions, such as maintaining a level of tone or arousal, so that the cortex can process information. They terminate diffusely over large regions of the cortex—in some cases, over all of it. Nonspecific afferents even release their transmitter substances into the extracellular space. The norepinephrinergic projections from the brainstem, the cholinergic projections from the basal forebrain, and the projections from certain thalamic nuclei are examples of nonspecific afferents.

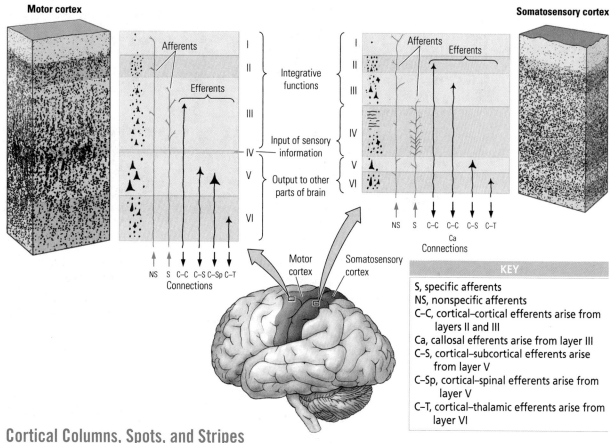

Motor cortex

Somatosensory cortex

Afferents

Efferents

I

II

III

IV

V

VI

Integrative functions

Input of sensory information

Output to other parts of brain

NS S C–C C–S C–Sp C–T
Connections

Afferents

Efferents

I

II

III

IV

V

VI

NS S C–C C–C C–S C–T
Ca
Connections

Motor cortex

Somatosensory cortex

KEY
S, specific afferents
NS, nonspecific afferents
C–C, cortical–cortical efferents arise from layers II and III
Ca, callosal efferents arise from layer III
C–S, cortical–subcortical efferents arise from layer V
C–Sp, cortical–spinal efferents arise from layer V
C–T, cortical–thalamic efferents arise from layer VI

Cortical Columns, Spots, and Stripes

Most interactions between the layers of the cortex take place within the cells directly above or below adjacent layers. Less interaction takes place with cells more than a couple of millimeters on either side (see Figure 10.9). This vertical bias in cortical organization forms the basis for a second type of neocortical organization.

There have been many terms for the vertical organization of the cortex, two of the most common being **column** and **module.** Although these terms are not always interchangeable, the underlying idea is that groups of 150 to 300 neurons form little circuits ranging from about 0.5 to 2.0 mm wide, depending on the cortical region. Evidence for some kind of modular unit comes from two principal sources: staining and probing.

When the brain is cut horizontally and stained in special ways, patterns of spots or stripes in the cortex are visible. Some examples will illustrate:

- If a radioactive amino acid is injected into one eye of a monkey, the radioactivity is transported across synapses to the primary visual cortex. The radioactivity is not evenly distributed across the cortex, however, in that it travels only to places that connect with the affected eye (Figure 10.10A). Thus, the pattern of radioactivity seen in the primary visual cortex (area 17) is a series of stripes, much like those on a zebra.

- A different pattern is seen in the same visual cortex when a different technique is used, however. If the cortex is stained with cytochrome oxidase, which shows areas of high metabolic activity by staining mitochondria, the visual cortex appears spotted. These spots, known as "blobs," have a role in color perception (Figure 10.10B).

Figure 10.9 Cortical layers. A comparison of cortical layers in the somatosensory and motor cortexes shows that layer IV is thicker in the somatosensory cortex than in the motor cortex. Diagrams of the neuronal elements of the somatosensory and motor cortexes show that the somatosensory cortex is much thinner than the motor cortex and that the size of each layer is markedly different in the two. The specific and nonspecific inputs to the cortex illustrate the distribution of these afferents to the different layers. The outputs (efferents) from the cortex arise from different layers, depending on the destination. (After Shepherd, 1979.)

Figure 10.10 Spots and stripes in the cortex, obtained by staining. (After Purves et al., 1992.)

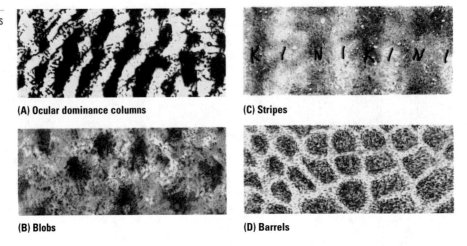

(A) Ocular dominance columns

(C) Stripes

(B) Blobs

(D) Barrels

- Curiously, if the same stain is applied to area 18, which is an adjacent visual region, the pattern of staining is more like stripes (Figure 10.10C) than like spots.

- Finally, if the primary somatosensory cortex of a rat is stained with succinic dehydrogenase, the cortex shows a pattern of spots that are known as "barrels" (Figure 10.10D). Each barrel corresponds to one of the vibrissae on the face of the rat.

As these examples illustrate, there appear to be many types of modules, and even the same stain shows a different modular organization in different regions.

A second way to demonstrate modular organization is shown physiologically in the sensory cortex. If a microelectrode is moved vertically through the sensory cortex from layer I to layer VI, all the neurons encountered appear to be functionally similar. For example, if an electrode is placed in the somatosensory cortex and lowered vertically from layer I to layer VI, neurons in each layer are excited by a particular tactile stimulus (for example, a light touch) in a particular part of the body (for example, the left thumb). The cells of layer IV are activated earliest by an afferent input, as would be expected from the direct afferent connections to this layer. Cells of the other layers must have longer latencies: they would have at least one more synapse on an interneuron in layer IV before receiving the sensory input. The pyramidal neurons of layer V are the last to be activated, again as would be expected because the efferents are there (see Figure 10.8).

The functional similarity of cells across all six layers at any point in the cortex suggests that the simplest functional unit of the cortex is a vertically oriented column of cells that composes a minicircuit. Groups of these columns may be organized in somewhat larger units as well. If an electrode samples the cells of area 17 (visual cortex), all the cells in a column will respond to a line of a given orientation (for example, 45°). If the electrode is moved laterally across the cortex, adjacent columns will respond to successively different orientations (for example, 60°, 90°, and so on) until all orientations over 360° are sampled. The pattern will then repeat itself. Thus, in the visual cortex, columns are arranged in larger modules.

As interesting as cortical spots, stripes, and columns are, there is considerable controversy over what the definition of a module is and what the presence of a module means functionally. One problem is that, although modules are apparent in primary sensory regions, they are less apparent in the association or motor areas of the cortex. Another problem is that, if we are looking for a common definition of the dimensions of a module, then the stripes and spots are a problem because they differ greatly in size. Furthermore, closely related species often have very different patterns of spots and stripes, which seems strange if they are fundamental units of cortical function. For example, although Old-World monkeys have beautiful ocular dominance columns, these columns are not found in New-World monkeys, even though the visual abilities of the two species are similar.

Semir Zeki suggested that the search for the basic module of cortical organization is akin to the physicist's search for the basic unit of all matter. The underlying assumption is that the cortical module might be performing the same basic function throughout the cortex. In this view, the evolutionary expansion of the cortex corresponds to an increase in the number of basic units, much as one would add chips to a computer to expand its memory or processing speed. This notion has some appeal, but we are left wondering what the basic function and operation of the cortical module might be.

Dale Purves and his colleagues have offered a provocative answer. They noted that the spots and stripes on the cortex resemble markings on the fur of many animals. They suggested that, though these patterns may provide camouflage or broadcast sexual signals, these functions are secondary to the fur's fundamental purpose of maintaining body temperature. Pursuing this analogy, the researchers proposed that some modular patterns in the cortex may well correspond to secondary functions of cortical organization. One suggested possibility is that cortical modules may be an incidental consequence of the nature of synaptic processing in the cortex. In other words, as the cortex forms its intrinsic connections to process information, one efficient pattern of connectivity is the vertical module.

The module certainly *conforms* to an important aspect of cortical connectivity, but it does not *cause* cortical connectivity. There must be an alternative way (or ways) of organizing complex neural activity that does not require a constant module. In fact, the bird brain provides an example. Birds clearly exhibit complex behavior, and some birds, such as crows, are extremely intelligent, likely more intelligent than many mammals (such as mice). In spite of their complex behavior, birds do not have a cortex but rather a neural organization in which different nuclei function rather like cortical layers. We can see therefore that, although a cortical organization with columns is a useful arrangement, it is not the only way to organize a brain.

The conclusion to be drawn from this discussion is that there is clearly a vertical component to cortical organization, but the structure and function of a basic module is difficult to define at present. Further, it seems unlikely that there is a single way of organizing cortical connectivity across all mammalian species and cortical regions.

Multiple Representations: Mapping Reality

Early ideas about visual, auditory, and somatic function held that one or two representations of the external environment in the cortex are responsible for our basic sensations. When Wilder Penfield and his colleagues stimulated the motor and somatosensory strips of their patients at the Montreal Neurological Hospital, they identified two regions of the parietal cortex that appeared to represent localized body parts such as the leg, hand, and face (see Figure 3.3). These regions, called *homunculi*, were seen as the areas of the cortex responsible for basic tactile sensations such as touch, pressure, and temperature. Subsequent investigations of nonhuman subjects led to the identification of analogous maps of the visual and auditory worlds as well. Thus the vast majority of the human cortex was generally believed to be occupied by complex mental analyses that we might loosely call cognition.

Doubt about this simple view of cortical organization arose in the late 1970s and the 1980s, however, as more refined physiological and anatomical research techniques began to reveal literally dozens of maps in each sensory modality, rather than just one or two. For example, between 25 and 32 regions in the monkey cortex have roles in visual functioning, depending on the definition used.

Although the somatosensory and auditory maps are less numerous, from about 10 to 15 cortical maps in each of these modalities do not duplicate the original maps but rather process different aspects of sensory experience. For example, visual areas are specialized for analyzing basic features such as form, color, and movement. Furthermore, many psychological processes, such as visual object memory and visually guided movements, require visual information.

In addition to the demonstration of multiple maps, areas were identified that function in more than one modality (for example, vision and touch). These areas, known as **multimodal** or **polymodal cortex,** presumably function to combine characteristics of stimuli across different modalities. For example, we can visually identify objects that we have only touched, which implies some common perceptual system linking the visual and somatic systems.

There are three distinct regions of multimodal cortex, one in each of the parietal, temporal, and frontal lobes. The existence of these three areas implies that more than one process requires polymodal information, although exactly what these processes might be is not known. We can speculate, however, that different regions could take part in different memory processes, object perception, emotion, movement control, and so on.

An interesting implication of the discovery of so many cortical maps is that little cortex is left over for the more-complex cognitive functions in Flechsig's hierarchy. In fact, it is now clear that virtually the entire cortex behind the central fissure has some kind of sensory function. And the frontal lobe receives connections from many maps, suggesting some type of sensory function there as well.

Multimodal cortex appears to be of two general types, one type related to the recognition and related processing of information and the other type controlling movement related to the information in some manner. This important concept suggests that we have parallel cortical systems: one system functions to understand the world, whereas the other system functions to move us around in the world and allows us to manipulate our world. This distinction is counterintuitive because our impression is that our sensory and motor worlds are the same. We shall see that they are not.

The emerging view is that the cortex is fundamentally an organ of sensory perception and related motor processes. This idea has an interesting implication: animals with more cortex must engage in more sensory processing than do animals with less or no cortex and must experience a different perception of the world as well. Harry Jerison pursued this idea by suggesting that our knowledge of reality is related directly to the structure and number of our cortical maps. As the number of maps possessed by an animal brain increases, more of the external world is known to the animal and more behavioral options are available to it. For instance, animals such as rats and dogs, whose brains do not have a cortical region analyzing color, perceive the world in black and white. This lack must limit their behavioral options, at least with respect to color. Similarly, although it is difficult for us to imagine, species, such as dogs that are not "smell blind" as we are, may know their world through object-specific olfactory images that are as useful to them as our visual images are to us.

Jerison suggested that cortical maps determine reality for a given species. Furthermore, he noted that, the more maps that a species has, the more complex the internal representation of the external world must be. Thus, if humans have more maps than dogs, then our representation of reality must be more complex than that of a dog. Similarly, if dogs have more maps than mice, then a dog's understanding of the world is more complex than that of a mouse. This viewpoint suggests an interesting implication: the relative intelligence of different mammalian species may be related to the number of maps that the cortex uses to represent the world. Dogs would have more olfactory maps than people and would thus be more intelligent about smells, but the total number of maps in all sensory regions taken together is far greater in humans than in dogs.

Cortical Systems: The Frontal Lobe, Paralimbic Cortex, and Subcortical Loops

The connections among cortical areas in a sensory system constitute only a part of all cortical connections. The four other principal connections in the cortical hierarchy are with the frontal lobe, paralimbic cortex, multimodal cortex, and subcortical connections and loops (Figure 10.11).

The frontal lobe can be subdivided into (1) the **motor cortex,** forming the motor homunculus; (2) the **premotor cortex** lying just in front of the motor cortex; and (3) the **prefrontal cortex,** which occupies the remainder of the frontal lobe. Sensory regions do not connect directly with the motor cortex but may project to either the premotor or the prefrontal cortex. Connections to the premotor cortex participate in ordering movements in time and controlling hand, limb, or eye movements with respect to specific sensory stimuli. Projections to the prefrontal cortex take part in the control of movements in time and short-term memories of sensory information (see Chapter 18).

The **paralimbic cortex**—phylogenetically the older cortex— is adjacent and directly connected to the limbic structures and it

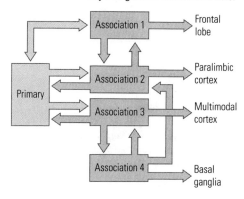

Figure 10.11 Levels of organization in the cortex. The primary sensory cortex projects to sensory association regions that are interconnected. These regions project to several cortical targets— including the frontal lobe, paralimbic cortex, and multimodal cortex—and a subcortical target, the basal ganglia. There are several levels of association cortex, but for simplicity only a single level is illustrated here.

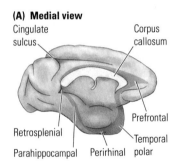

(A) Medial view

Cingulate
sulcus

Corpus
callosum

Prefrontal

Retrosplenial

Temporal
polar

Parahippocampal   Perirhinal

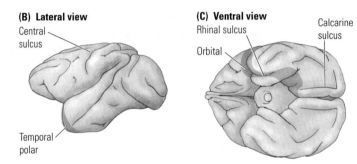

(B) Lateral view

Central
sulcus

Temporal
polar

(C) Ventral view

Rhinal sulcus

Calcarine
sulcus

Orbital

Figure 10.12 The paralimbic cortex. Medial (A), lateral (B), and ventral (C) surfaces of the cerebral cortex of the rhesus monkey. Blue indicates the paralimbic areas in the frontal and temporal lobes, and in the cingulate gyrus. Note that the medial view in part A is upside down so that the top of the brain in the medial and lateral views are adjacent. Similarly, in the ventral view in part C, the hemisphere has been tipped on its side so that the tip of the temporal lobe is adjacent in the medial and ventral views.

comprises roughly three layers (Figure 10.12). It can be seen in two places: (1) on the medial surface of the temporal lobe, where it is known as *pyriform cortex, entorhinal cortex,* and *parahippocampal cortex;* and (2) just above the corpus callosum, where it is referred to as *cingulate cortex.* The paralimbic cortex plays a role in the formation of long-term memories.

The cortex receives all its sensory input from subcortical structures, either directly from the thalamus or indirectly through midbrain structures, such as the tectum. These cortical–subcortical connections are reciprocal feedback loops, or **subcortical loops** (Figure 10.13). Each level interacts and is integrated with higher and lower levels by ascending and descending connections. Subcortical loops connect the cortex, thalamus, amygdala, and hippocampus; an indirect loop with the striatum connects with the thalamus.

Subcortical loops are presumed to play some role in amplifying or modulating cortical activity. Consider, for example, how the amygdala adds affective tone to visual input. A ferocious dog may generate a strong affective response in us as it charges, in part because the amygdala adds affective tone to the visual threat of the dog. Indeed, in the absence of the amygdala, laboratory ani-

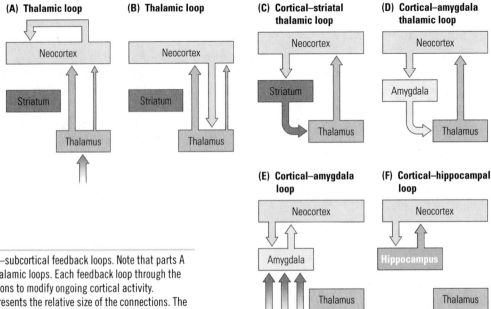

Figure 10.13 Cortical–subcortical feedback loops. Note that parts A and B show two different thalamic loops. Each feedback loop through the midbrain presumably functions to modify ongoing cortical activity. Thickness of the arrows represents the relative size of the connections. The dashed lines indicate various subcortical inputs to the amygdala.

mals display absolutely no fear of threatening objects. Cats whose amygdalas have been removed take leisurely strolls through rooms housing large monkeys, whereas no normal cat would even contemplate doing such a thing.

Cortical Connections, Reentry, and the Binding Problem

We have seen that the cortex has multiple anatomically segregated and functionally specialized areas. How does brain organization translate into our perception of the world as a **gestalt**—a unified and coherent whole? When you look at the face of a person, for example, why do shape, color, and size combine into a coherent, unchanging image? This question identifies the **binding problem,** which asks how sensations in specific channels (touch, vision, hearing, and so forth) combine into perceptions that translate as a unified experience that we call reality.

There seem to be three possible solutions to the binding problem. One is a high-order cortical center that receives input from all the different cortical areas and integrates (binds) them into a single perception. Although this hierarchical idea makes sense, there is unfortunately no such area. A second solution is to interconnect all the different cortical areas so that information is somehow shared. The problem is that not all cortical areas are connected with one another, not even within a sensory modality. Various researchers have tried to determine the rules of connectivity, but they are not simple and are beyond the scope of our discussion here (for details, see Felleman and van Essen, 1991; Pandya and Yeterian, 1985; and Zeki, 1993).

Suffice it to say that only about 40% of the possible intercortical connections within a sensory modality are actually found, which leads us to the third solution: intracortical networks of connections among subsets of cortical regions. This idea has considerable appeal.

First, all cortical areas have internal connections among units with similar properties. These connections link neurons that are neighbors and synchronize their activity. Second, through a mechanism called **reentry,** any cortical area can influence the area from which it receives input. This remarkable, interactive aspect of cortical connectivity means that, when area A sends information to area B, area B reciprocates and sends a return message to area A (Figure 10.14). Zeki suggested that an area could actually modify its inputs from another area before it even received them. An important point is that the connections from areas A and B do not originate from the same layers, suggesting that they play different roles in influencing each other's activity.

How can the flow of information through intraareal and interareal connections and interaction through reentry solve the binding problem? Computer modeling suggests that the primary function of the neural connections is to coordinate activity within and between areas to produce a globally coherent pattern, known as *integration*, over all areas of the perceptual system.

Figure 10.14 Inter- and intraareal connections. (A) The flow of information to and from the cortex. Information from the thalamus goes to the primary cortex, which then projects to the association cortex. Note the reciprocal connections at each level, representing feedback loops. (B) The principle of reentry. When one cortical area sends information to another the projection arises from layers II and III and terminates in layer IV. The receiver returns a connection (reentry) from layers V and VI to layers I and VI of the first area. In this way, a receiving cortical area can modify the inputs that it is getting. This reentry principle holds for all levels of cortical–cortical connectivity.

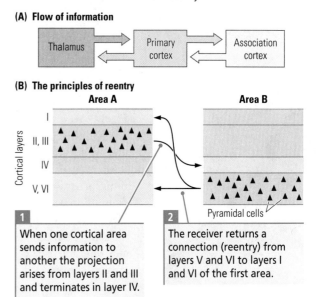

(A) Flow of information

(B) The principles of reentry

Cortical layers — I, II, III, IV, V, VI

Area A — Area B

Pyramidal cells

1 When one cortical area sends information to another the projection arises from layers II and III and terminates in layer IV.

2 The receiver returns a connection (reentry) from layers V and VI to layers I and VI of the first area.

Integration requires a way of binding the areas together briefly to form a unified percept. The computer models show that perceptual integration can be almost immediate, on a time scale of 50 to 500 ms. (This concept of cortical organization is likely to be foreign to many readers. We recommend Zeki's readable book for a longer discussion.)

Jerison related the binding problem to his analogy of multiple cortical maps. The evolutionary expansion of the cortex in area has implications for a brain with multiple neurosensory channels that are trying to integrate information into a single reality. Because so many different kinds of sensory information reach the cortex, it is necessary somehow to discriminate equivalent features in the external world. It would be useful to the brain to label these equivalencies and organize them.

Suppose that the brain creates labels to designate objects and a coordinate system to locate objects in the external world—that is, in space and time. Suppose also that some sensory information must be tagged to persist through time and must be categorized to be retrieved (remembered) when needed.

Labels, coordinates, and categories are products of **cognition** (knowledge and thought). Viewed in this way, Jerison's analogy of multiple cortical maps provides a basis for thinking about how the information that is arriving to the cortex is integrated into perception and organized as knowledge and thought. It should not be a surprise that injuries to discrete cortical areas alter the way that people perceive the world and the way that they think about it. In Chapter 13, we shall see that one form of sensory deficit, **agnosia** (literally, not knowing), renders a partial or complete inability to recognize sensory stimuli. Agnosias are unexplainable by subcortical deficits in elementary sensation or alertness.

Functional Organization of the Cortex

Knowledge of the world is constructed by the brain. To Jerison, this knowledge is *mind*. As cortical maps develop, the brain must also develop the mind to organize the maps in such a way as to produce knowledge of the external world. It is a small jump to the idea that the next step in mental development is language. After all, language is a way of representing knowledge.

A Hierarchical Model of Cortical Function

Flechsig was the first to suggest that anatomical criteria could be used to delineate a hierarchy of cortical areas, but Alexander Luria fully developed the idea in the 1960s. Luria divided the cortex into two functional units. The posterior part of the cortex is the *sensory unit* (Figure 10.15A). It receives sensations, processes them, and stores them as information. The anterior cortex (the frontal lobe) is the *motor unit* (Figure 10.15B). It formulates intentions, organizes them into programs of action, and executes the programs. Both cortical units have a hierarchical structure with three cortical zones arranged functionally one above the other. The first zone corresponds to Flechsig's primary cortex; the second corresponds to the slower-developing cortex bordering the primary cortex, which Luria labeled *secondary cortex;* and the third is the slowest-developing cortex, which Luria labeled *tertiary cortex.*

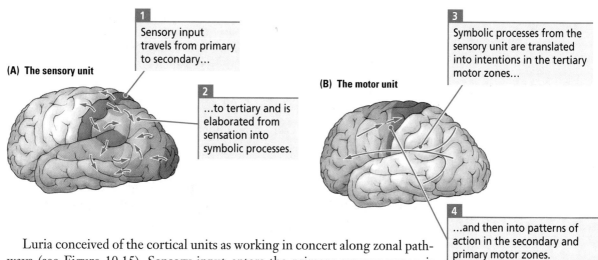

(A) The sensory unit

1 Sensory input travels from primary to secondary...

2 ...to tertiary and is elaborated from sensation into symbolic processes.

(B) The motor unit

3 Symbolic processes from the sensory unit are translated into intentions in the tertiary motor zones...

4 ...and then into patterns of action in the secondary and primary motor zones.

Figure 10.15 Functional units of the cortex. (A) The first functional unit of the cortex—the sensory unit. Dark-shaded areas are primary zones; medium-shaded areas secondary zones; light-shaded areas tertiary zones. Sensory input travels from primary to secondary to tertiary and is thereby elaborated from sensation into symbolic processes. (B) The second functional unit of the cortex—the motor unit. Symbolic processes from the sensory unit are translated into intentions in the tertiary motor zones and then into patterns of action in the secondary and primary motor zones. (After A. R. Luria. © 1973. The Copyright Agency of the USSR. Reprinted with permission.)

Luria conceived of the cortical units as working in concert along zonal pathways (see Figure 10.15). Sensory input enters the primary sensory zones, is elaborated in the secondary zones, and is integrated in the tertiary zones of the posterior unit. To execute an action, activation is sent from the posterior tertiary sensory zones to the tertiary frontal motor zone for formulation, to the secondary motor zone for elaboration, and then to the primary frontal zone for execution.

Consider a simplified example of Luria's model. Say you were walking along and came upon a soccer game. The actual perception of the movements of players and the ball would be in the primary visual area. The secondary visual sensory zone would recognize that those activities constituted a soccer game. In the tertiary zone, the sounds and movements of the game would be synthesized into the realization that one team had scored and was ahead and that the game had a certain significance for league standings. By the time the information is integrated in the tertiary zone, there is considerably more to it than what we would think of as "sensory." Rather, there is knowledge.

Information in the tertiary sensory zone activates the paralimbic cortex for memory processing and the amygdala for emotional assessment. These cortical events could then activate, in the tertiary zone of the frontal (motor) cortex, the intention to find a viewing spot and root for your team. The execution of this plan would be formulated in the secondary frontal zones. The actual movements required to join the crowd would be initiated in the primary zone of the frontal cortex.

Using the example of a soccer game, we can also describe the effects of brain lesions on levels of processing. A lesion in the primary visual zone would produce a blind spot in some part of the visual field, requiring the spectator to move his or her head backward and forward to see the entire game. A lesion in the secondary visual zone might produce a perceptual deficit, making the person unable to recognize the activity as a soccer game. A lesion in the tertiary sensory zone might make it impossible to recognize the significance of the game in its abstract form—that is, that one team wins.

Damage to the paralimbic cortex would leave no memory of the event, and damage to the amygdala would render the person unresponsive to the event's emotional significance. A lesion in the tertiary motor area might prevent the formation of the intention to become a soccer player and join a club, buy a uniform, or get to practice on time. A lesion in the secondary motor zone might make it difficult to execute the sequences of movements required in play. A lesion in the primary zone might make it difficult to execute a discrete movement required in the game—for example, kicking the ball.

Evaluating the Hierarchical Model

Luria based his theory on three assumptions:

1. The brain processes information serially—that is, one step at a time. Thus, information from sensory receptors goes to the thalamus, then to the primary cortex, then to the secondary cortex, and finally to the tertiary sensory cortex. Similarly, the output goes from tertiary sensory to tertiary motor, then to secondary motor, and finally to primary motor.

2. Serial processing is hierarchical; that is, each level of processing adds complexity that is qualitatively different from the processing in the preceding levels. The tertiary cortex could be considered a "terminal station" insofar as it receives input from the sensorimotor and perceptual areas and performs higher cognitive processes on that input.

3. Our perceptions of the world are unified and coherent entities. Luria's formulation was in accord with the commonsense view that some active process creates each percept, and naturally the simplest way to do so is to form it in the tertiary cortex.

The beauty of Luria's theory is that it used the then-known anatomical organization of the cortex to provide a simple explanation for observations that Luria made daily in his clinic and published in 1973. The difficulty is that its basic assumptions have been questioned by newer anatomical and physiological findings. Consider the following problems.

First, a strictly hierarchical processing model requires that all cortical areas be linked serially, but this serial linkage is not the case. We have seen that all cortical areas have reciprocal (reentrant) connections with the regions to which they connect, which means that there is no simple "feed forward" system. Furthermore, as noted earlier, only about 40% of the possible connections among different areas in a sensory modality are actually found. Thus no single area receives input from all other areas, which presents a difficulty in actively forming a single percept in one area.

Second, Zeki made the interesting point that, because a zone of cortex has connections with many cortical areas, it follows that each cortical zone is probably undertaking more than one operation, which is subsequently relayed to different cortical areas. In addition, the results of the same operation are likely to be of interest to more than one cortical area, which would account for multiple connections.

These principles can be seen in the primary visual cortex, which appears to make calculations related to color, motion, and form. These calculations are relayed to specific cortical regions for these processes. And the same calculation may be sent to cortical as well as to subcortical regions.

The fact that cortical operations are relayed directly to subcortical areas is important because it implies that cortical processing can bypass Luria's motor hierarchy and go directly to subcortical motor structures. Further, the fact that given cortical areas can do multiple calculations that are sent to multiple areas raises a question about what is hierarchical in the processing. Can we assume that areas that are serially connected are actually undertaking more complicated operations? It would seem that an area such as the primary visual cortex, which is processing color, form, and movement, might be considered more complex than an area that processes only color.

Finally, Luria assumed that his introspection about perception being a unitary phenomenon was correct. It appears, however, that it is not. Thus, we can experience a single percept despite the fact that there is no single terminal area producing it. Indeed, this ability is the essence of the binding problem discussed earlier.

How can we put this knowledge together in a meaningful way to see organization in the cortex? There are two logical possibilities. One possibility is that there is no hierarchical organization but rather some sort of nonordered neural network. As individual organisms gain experiences, this network becomes ordered in some way and so produces perceptions, cognitions, and memories. Many neural network models of brain function propose that this possibility is exactly what happens. However, the results of a wealth of perceptual research suggest that the brain filters and orders sensory information in a species-typical fashion.

The other possibility, suggested by Daniel Felleman and David van Essen, is that cortical areas are hierarchically organized in some well-defined sense, with each area occupying a specific position relative to other areas, but with more than one area allowed to occupy a given hierarchical level. Felleman and van Essen proposed that the pattern of forward and backward connections could be used to determine hierarchical position. Thus, ascending (or forward) connections terminate in layer IV whereas descending (or feedback) connections do not enter layer IV, usually terminating in the superficial and deep layers (see Figure 10.14B). They also recognize a third type of connection, which is columnar in its distribution, terminating in all layers. This type of connection is uncommon but provides a basis for placing areas in the same location in the hierarchy.

By analyzing the patterns of connectivity among the visual, auditory, and somatosensory areas, Felleman and van Essen found evidence of what they call a distributed hierarchical system. Figure 10.16 contrasts Luria's model and this model. Notice in Figure 10.16 the several levels of processing and, across the levels, interconnected processing streams that presumably represent different elements of the sensory experience. Note, too, that some connections skip levels and the number of areas expands as the hierarchy unfolds.

Figure 10.16 Hierarchical models. (A) Luria's simple serial hierarchical model of cortical processing. (B) Felleman and van Essen's distributed hierarchical model, which features several levels of association areas. Areas at each level are interconnected with one another.

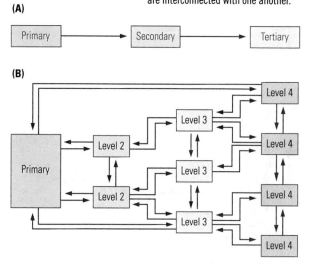

A New Model of Cortical Function

The Felleman and van Essen distributed hierarchical model proposes a relatively simple organization for sensory processing in the cortex. With the addition of the idea that the backward or lateral connections provide a basis for

Figure 10.17 Flat map of cortical areas in the macaque (see the Snapshot on page 230). The locations of 32 visual areas are indicated by blue shading. The abbreviations are summarized in Table 10.1. (After Felleman and van Essen, 1991.)

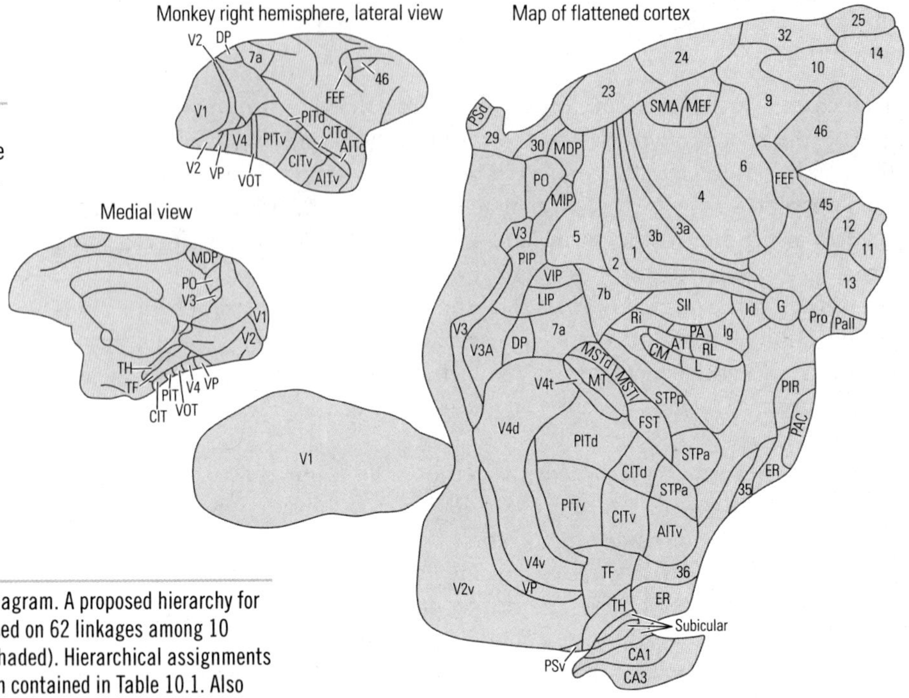

Figure 10.18 Cortical wiring diagram. A proposed hierarchy for somatosensory and motor areas, based on 62 linkages among 10 somatosensory and 3 motor areas (shaded). Hierarchical assignments are based on the laminar information contained in Table 10.1. Also included in the hierarchy are connections with visual area 7a and with higher associational areas 35 and 36. With the highest level included, there are 10 levels in the hierarchy, and possibly an 11th, depending on uncertainties with regard to interconnections among motor areas. (After Felleman and van Essen, 1991.)

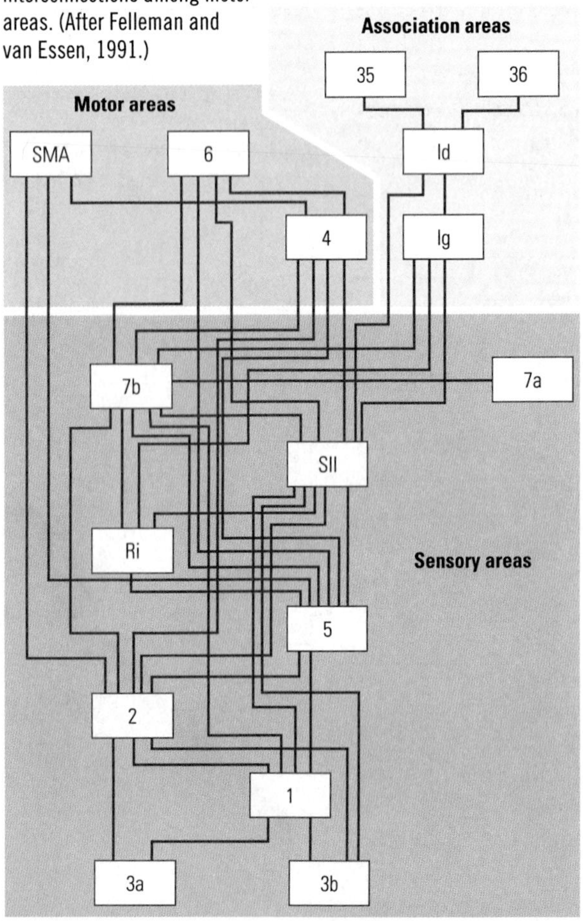

solving the binding problem, the model offers an explanation of our experience of a single, coherent perception of the world.

To illustrate the distributed hierarchy model, we will not use the soccer example used to illustrate Luria's model, but we certainly invite the reader to attempt the exercise. Rather, we begin with some simpler examples, and, because this information was obtained from studies of rhesus monkeys, we use some examples relevant to monkeys.

Let us imagine that we set a monkey the task of reaching into a box in which, among other things, there are some jellybeans. If the monkey finds a jellybean, it is allowed to keep it; if it takes something else, it loses that object and, as punishment, has to wait before getting another trial. Thus, the monkey has to feel the objects until it finds a jellybean, and then it has to grasp the jellybean by using a pincer grasp.

Using the model to speculate about how information flows through and gets organized by the monkey's cortex, we follow Felleman and van Essen's cortical map (Figure 10.17) and their wiring diagrams of how to get from one area of the somatosensory system to the next (Figure 10.18) and from one area of the visual system to the next (Figures 10.18 and 10.19). Table 10.1 charts the functions of each mapped area.

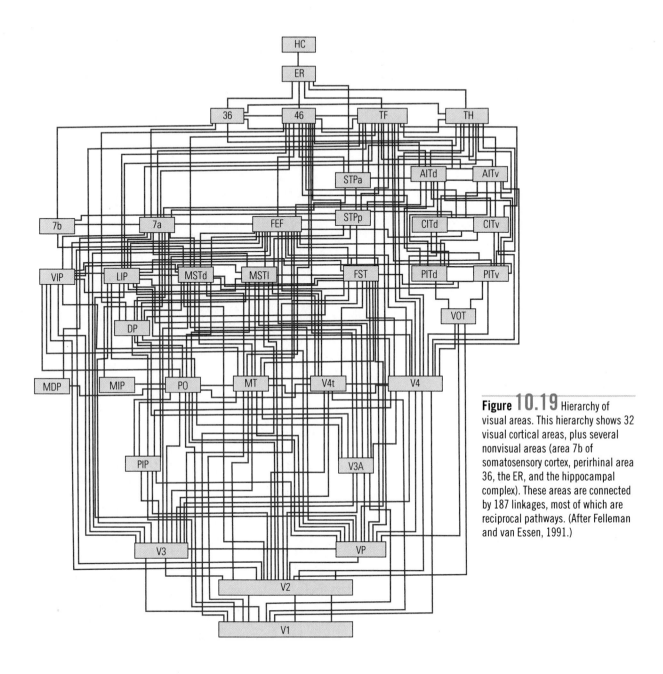

Figure 10.19 Hierarchy of visual areas. This hierarchy shows 32 visual cortical areas, plus several nonvisual areas (area 7b of somatosensory cortex, perirhinal area 36, the ER, and the hippocampal complex). These areas are connected by 187 linkages, most of which are reciprocal pathways. (After Felleman and van Essen, 1991.)

From Table 10.1, we see that tactile information is first analyzed in area 3b of the somatosensory cortex and that the motor output to grasp comes from area 4 of the motor cortex. Although areas 3b and 4 are side by side on the cortical map in Figure 10.17, the wiring diagram in Figure 10.18 shows that these somatosensory areas are not connected. Figure 10.18 also shows that three visual streams go to area 4. One goes through areas 1, 5, and SII (SII is important for pattern discriminations); one goes through areas 2 and 7b (possibly important for shape discrimination); and the third goes through areas 2 and SMA (supplementary motor cortex, which may be important for producing a series of movements). It is possible that the monkey's problem

Table 10.1 Summary of cortical areas in the monkey

Lobe	Structure	Name	Putative function
Occipital	V1	Visual area 1 (17)	Visual sorting
	V2	Visual area 2 (18)	Visual sorting
	V3	Visual area 3	Vision-dynamic form
	V3A	Visual area 3A	Vision-?
	V4	Visual area 4	Vision-color
	V4t	V4 transitional	Vision-?
	MT (V5)	Visual area 5	Motion
	VP	Ventral posterior visual	Vision-?
	VOT	Ventral occipital-temporal	Vision-?
Temporal	FST	Floor of superior temporal	Vision
	PITd	Posterior inferotemporal, dorsal	Vision
	PITv	Posterior inferotemporal, ventral	Vision
	CITd	Central inferotemporal, dorsal	Vision
	CITv	Central inferotemporal, ventral	Vision
	AITd	Anterior inferotemporal, dorsal	Vision
	AITv	Anterior inferotemporal, ventral	Vision
	STPp	Superior temporal polysensory, posterior	Polymodal
	STPa	Superior temporal polysensory, anterior	Polymodal
	FT	FT (hippocampal formation)	Memory
	TH	TH (hippocampal formation)	Memory
	AI	Primary auditory	Audition
	RL	Rostrolateral auditory	Audition
	CM	Caudomedial auditory	Audition
	L	Lateral auditory	Audition
	PA	Postauditory	Somato or auditory?
Hippocampus	ER	Entorhinal cortex	Memory or space or both
	35	Brodmann's 35	Memory or space or both
	36	Brodmann's 36	Memory or space or both
	Subicular	(Pre, post, sub)	Memory or space or both
	CAI	Ammon's horn, area 1	Memory or space or both
	CA3	Ammon's horn, area 3	Memory or space or both
Parietal	3a	Primary somatosensory	Cutaneous?
	3b	Primary somatosensory	Tactile; muscle, joint
	1	Somatosensory	Tactile-?
	2	Somatosensory	Vestibular
	SII	Secondary somatosensory map	Tactile patterns
	5	Secondary somatosensory (area PE)	Tactile patterns
	7a	Secondary visual (area PG)	Visuomotor guidance
	7b	Secondary somatosensory (area PF)	Visuomotor guidance
	MSTd	Medial superior temporal, dorsal	Visuomotor guidance
	MSTl	Medial superior temporal, lateral	Visuomotor guidance
	PO	Parietal-occipital	Visuomotor guidance
	PIP	Posterior intraparietal	Visuomotor guidance
	LIP	Lateral intraparietal	Visuomotor
	VIP	Ventral intraparietal	Visuomotor
	MIP	Medial intraparietal	Visuomotor
	MDP	Medial dorsal parietal	Visuomotor
	DP	Dorsal prelunate	Visuomotor
Frontal	4	Primary motor	Fine movements
	6	Secondary motor	Sequences
	SMA	Supplementary motor cortex	Bimanual movements
	MEF	Supplementary eye fields	Eye movements
	FEF	Frontal eye fields	Eye movements

Table 10.1 Summary of cortical areas in the monkey (*continued*)

Lobe	Structure	Name	Putative function
Frontal (*continued*)			
	46	Dorsolateral prefrontal	Memory, movement, planning
	9, 10, 14	Dorsal prefrontal	Memory, movement, planning
	11, 12, 13	Orbital prefrontal	Emotion, memory
	25–32	Medial prefrontal	Memory, movement, planning
	G	Gustatory	Taste
	PRO	Prosiocortex	?
	PAL	Periallocortex	?
	PIR	Olfactory	Olfaction
	PAC	Olfactory	Olfaction
	ER	Olfactory	Olfaction
Cingulate	23, 24, 29, 30		Motivation, emotion, space, memory

could be solved by only one of the three streams, but it could also be solved by all of them working together.

Here is a second problem for the monkey, who is presented with a television screen that displays some jellybeans of various colors. If the monkey touches a red jellybean on the screen, it receives a reward, but there is no reward for touching other jellybeans. Using the list of functions in Table 10.1, we can hypothesize that the monkey uses the color vision system, beginning in V1 (area 17), to identify the correct jellybean, and uses area 4 of the motor system to point. Turning to the wiring diagram in Figure 10.19, we can imagine that the monkey must use the parvocellular system for color vision, which passes into V1 and then V2, and from there information must go to V4 (the color module of the visual system). We already know that area 7b will reach area 4; it is logical that this route is at least one of the possible routes.

The second jellybean problem is still very simple. Consider what would happen if the correct jellybean not only were red but also had to be large and moving. The monkey would now have to use area V4 (color), area V3 (dynamic form), and MT, or area V5 (motion) and have all this information converge on area 7b. But even this trial is a simple problem for a monkey (although the wiring diagram may be becoming a little complex for some of us).

Let us give the monkey a problem that poses a challenge: if, on the last trial, a large moving red jellybean was correct, then, on the present trial, a small green stationary jellybean is correct. Now the monkey has to remember what it did on the last trial, and Table 10.1 tells us that the temporal cortex and perhaps even the hippocampus (HC) is required for memory. It is no longer sufficient to take a route to area 7a; the temporal cortical areas also must take part. Now the solution to the problem requires activity in the occipital, parietal, temporal, and motor cortex almost simultaneously. It is a simple matter to select a set of connections that could do the job, but now the question is whether that is how the monkey is doing it.

When we think of all the areas and connections that are required, the question is not so easily answered. As experimenters, we can always simplify the problem a little by creating a computer program that is regularly updated with areas, functions, and connections and that generates solutions to problems such as the ones that we have posed here. When we have done so, we can begin to work on different problems, such as why monkeys are inordinately fond of red jellybeans.

Summary

The primary interest in neuropsychology is the function of the human neocortex. This chapter has described the levels of function in the brain hierarchically and then focused on the structure and functional organization of the cortex. The levels of function begin in the spinal cord and end in the cortex. The functional hierarchy can be demonstrated by studying animals with surgical removals of successively more brain tissue.

The cortex comprises two basic types of neurons—spiny and aspiny—organized into about six layers. The cortical layers can be considered sensory, motor, and associational. The cortex has a vertical organization, referred to as columns or modules. Cortical modules can be seen in the spots and stripes visible in specific histological preparations and with the use of neuroimaging technologies.

Multiple representations of sensory and motor functions exist in the cortex. One evolutionary change in mammals has been an increase in the number of representations. A characteristic of cortical connectivity is reentry: each cortical area is reciprocally connected with many, but not all, other regions in a given sensory modality. The cortex processes information about the world in multiple representations, and these representations are not formally connected; yet we perceive the world as a unified whole. This conundrum is the "binding problem."

Cortical activity is influenced by feedback loops not only from other cortical regions but also from subcortical forebrain regions such as the amygdala and hippocampus. The cortex is functionally organized as a distributed hierarchical network.

References

Bard, P., and M. B. Macht. The behavior of chronically decerebrate cats. In G. E. W. Wolstenholm, and C. M. O'Connor, Eds. *Ciba Foundation Symposium on Neurological Basis of Behavior.* London: Churchill, 1958.

Barrett, R., H. H. Merritt, and A. Wolf. Depression of consciousness as a result of cerebral lesions. *Research Publications of the Association for Research in Nervous and Mental Disease* 45:241–276, 1967.

Bazett, H. C., and W. G. Penfield. A study of the Sherrington decerebrate animal in the chronic as well as the acute condition. *Brain* 45:185–265, 1922.

Berridge, K. C. Measuring hedonic impact in animals and infants: Microstructure of affective taste reactivity patterns. *Neuroscience and Biobehavioral Reviews* 24:173–98, 2000.

Berridge, K. C., and I. Q. Whishaw. Cortex, striatum, and cerebellum: Control of serial order in a grooming sequence. *Experimental Brain Research* 90:275–290, 1992.

Bignall, K. E., and L. Schramm. Behavior of chronically decerebrate kittens. *Experimental Neurology* 42:519–531, 1974.

Brackbill, Y. The role of the cortex in orienting: Orienting reflex in an encephalic human infant. *Developmental Psychology* 5:195–201, 1971.

Cannon, W. B., and S. W. Britton. Pseudoaffective medulliadrenal secretion. *American Journal of Physiology* 72:283–294, 1924.

Felleman, D. J., and D. C. van Essen. Distributed hierarchical processing in the primate cerebral cortex. *Cerebral Cortex* 1:1–47, 1991.

Flechsig, P. *Anatomie des menschlichen Gehirns und Rückenmarks*. Leipzig: Georg Thieme, 1920.

Gamper, E. As cited in Jung, R., and R. Hassler. The extrapyramidal system. In J. Field, H. W. Magoun, and V. E. Hall, Eds. *Handbook of Physiology*, vol. 2. Washington, DC: American Physiological Society, 1960, pp. 863–927.

Goltz, F. On the functions of the hemispheres. In G. von Bonin, Ed. *The Cerebral Cortex*. Springfield, IL.: Charles C. Thomas, 1960.

Grill, H. J., and R. Norgren. Neurological tests and behavioral deficits in chronic thalamic and chronic decerebrate rats. *Brain Research* 143:299–312, 1978.

Grillner, S. Locomotion in the spinal cat. In R. B. Stein, Ed. *Control of Posture and Locomotion*. New York: Plenum, 1973.

Jerison, H. J. *Brain Size and the Evolution of Mind*. New York: American Museum of Natural History, 1991.

Kuhn, R. A. Functional capacity of the isolated human spinal cord. *Brain* 73:1–51, 1950.

Luria, A. R. *The Working Brain*. Harmondsworth, England: Penguin, 1973.

Oakley, D. A. Cerebral cortex and adaptive behavior. In D. A. Oakley and H. C. Plotkin, Eds. *Brain, Evolution and Behavior*. London: Methuen, 1979.

Pandya, D. N., and E. H. Yeterian. Architecture and connections of cortical association areas. In A. Peters and E. G. Jones, Eds. *Cerebral Cortex*, vol. 4. New York: Plenum Press, 1985.

Penfield, W., and E. Boldrey. Somatic and motor sensory representation in the cerebral cortex of man as studied by electrical stimulation. *Brain* 60:389–443, 1937.

Peters, A., and E. G. Jones. *Cerebral Cortex*, vols. 1–14. New York: Plenum, 1984–1999.

Purves, D., D. R. Riddle, and A.-S. LaMantia. Iterated patterns of brain circuitry (or how the brain gets its spots). *Trends in Neuroscience* 15:362–368, 1992.

Shepherd, G. M. *The Synaptic Organization of the Brain*, 2d ed. New York: Oxford University Press, 1979.

Sherrington, C. S. *The Integrative Action of the Nervous System*. New Haven: Yale University Press, 1906.

Szentagothai, J. Architecture of the cerebral cortex. In H. H. Jasper, A. A. Ward, and A. Pope, Eds. *Basic Mechanisms of the Epilepsies*. Boston: Little, Brown, 1969.

Tailairach, J., and P. Tournoux. *Coplanar Stereotaxic Atlas of the Human Brain*. New York: Thieme, 1988.

Tononi, G., O. Sporns, and G. M. Edelman. Reentry and the problem of integrating multiple cortical areas: Simulation of dynamic integration in the visual system. *Cerebral Cortex* 2:336–352, 1991.

van Essen, D. C., and H. A. Drury. Structural and functional analyses of human cerebral cortex using a surface-based atlas. *Journal of Neuroscience* 17:7092–7102, 1997.

Whishaw, I. Q. The decorticate rat. In B. Kolb and R. Tees, Eds. *The Neocortex of the Rat*. Cambridge, MA: MIT Press, 1989.

Woods, J. W. Behavior of chronic decerebrate rats. *Journal of Neurophysiology* 27:634–644, 1964.

Zeki, S. *A Vision of the Brain*. London: Blackwell Scientific, 1993.

chapter **11**

Cerebral Asymmetry

M. S., a 25-year-old mother of two, had a lifetime history of epilepsy. Her seizures were well controlled by medication until after her second child was born. From that time, she endured about one uncontrolled seizure a month on average. Neurological examination revealed that the source of her seizures was a long-standing cyst in her left temporal lobe. M. S. agreed to neurosurgery to remove the cyst and the surrounding abnormal brain tissue.

Her immediate postoperative course was initially uneventful, and her seizures appeared to have been cured. Unexpectedly, she developed an infection that proved resistant to antibiotics. Within a few days, M. S. suffered extensive damage to her left hemisphere. The illness left her unable either to produce or to understand language, a condition known as global aphasia. For weeks, the only words that she was able to say were "I love you," and she said them to everyone she knew well.

In spite of her severe language problems, her ability to enjoy music was unimpaired. M. S. could sing versions of songs that she had known before her surgery. Thus, although she could not use or understand words to talk or read, she could use words in music and could tell immediately if the words in songs were wrong. Learning the words to new songs proved to be very difficult, however, though she was able to learn new tunes and hum along.

The case of M. S. illustrates the single most curious feature of human brain organization: the left and right cerebral hemispheres have partly separate functions. For M. S., this cerebral asymmetry was especially apparent in her loss of language skills but her maintenance of musical skills.

This chapter reviews research on cerebral asymmetry in humans. To set the stage, we address the basic anatomical principles. Next, we review and contrast neurological and behavioral research on damaged brains and on intact persons. In the concluding sections, we compare experimental results with brain scans, contrast sets of theories about cerebral asymmetry, and evaluate the quest to measure behavior. In Chapter 12, we will examine the biological and environmental factors that produce variations in cerebral asymmetry.

Anatomical Asymmetry in the Human Brain

Perhaps no idea about human brain organization has so fascinated neuroscientists as **laterality,** the idea that the two cerebral hemispheres have separate functions. In Chapter 10, we focused on how an anatomical and functional hierarchy in the cortex leads to unity of experience and the idea of a mind. Laterality leads to the notion that *two* different minds control our behavior.

After more than 100 years of studying cerebral asymmetry, psychologists now know that the hemispheres do perform separate functions. The left hemisphere plays a special role in producing and understanding language and in controlling movement on the right side of the body, whereas the right hemisphere specializes in perceiving and synthesizing nonverbal information, including music and facial expression. The right hemisphere controls movement on the left side of the body.

Four variables complicate the research on laterality:

1. *Laterality is relative, not absolute.* Both hemispheres play a role in nearly every behavior; thus, although the left hemisphere is especially important for the production of language, the right hemisphere also has some language capabilities.

2. *Cerebral site is at least as important in understanding brain function as cerebral side.* The frontal lobes are asymmetrical, but their functions are more similar to each other than they are to those of the posterior cortex on the same side. In fact, it is often very difficult to localize lesions in neurological patients to one hemisphere in the absence of neurological data, even though the site (frontal rather than temporal or parietal) may be immediately obvious. Perhaps it is best to think of the functions of the cerebral cortex as being localized and of hemispheric side as being only one step in localizing them.

3. *Laterality is affected by environmental and genetic factors.* For example, the cerebral organization of some left-handers and females appears to be more integrated than that of right-handers and males.

4. *Laterality is exhibited by a range of animals.* A functionally asymmetrical brain was once believed to be a uniquely human characteristic and related to language, but certain songbirds, rats, cats, monkeys, and apes have functionally and anatomically asymmetrical brains as well.

Cerebral Asymmetry

According to John Hughlings-Jackson, Pierre Gratiolet first observed in the 1860s that the cortical convolutions (clefts and ridges) on the left hemisphere mature more rapidly than those on the right. Anatomical asymmetry was described again later in the nineteenth century by a number of researchers, but these observations were largely ignored until the 1960s, when Norman Geschwind and Walter Levitsky described a significant anatomical asymmetry of the planum temporale in the temporal lobes.

Also called Wernicke's area, the planum temporale lies just posterior to the primary auditory cortex (Heschl's gyrus) within the Sylvian, or lateral, fissure (Figure 11.1, left). On the average, in 65 of the 100 brains studied by Geschwind and Levitsky, the planum temporale in the left hemisphere was nearly 1 cm longer than that in the right (Figure 11.1, right).

Geschwind and Levitsky's finding has been replicated by numerous investigators, with the percentage of cases having a larger planum temporale on the left varying from 65% to 90% in different samples. In contrast, the neighboring primary auditory cortex of Heschl's gyrus is larger on the right because there are usually two Heschl's gyri on the right and only one on the left (see Figure 11.1).

MRI scans of living brains confirm eight major anatomical differences between the two hemispheres:

1. The right hemisphere is slightly larger and heavier than the left, but the left contains more gray matter.

2. The temporal lobes display a marked structural asymmetry that may provide an anatomical basis for the observed specialization of the left and right temporal lobes in language and in music functions, respectively. (See Geschwind and Levitsky).

3. The asymmetry in the cortex of the temporal lobes is correlated with a corresponding midbrain asymmetry in the thalamus. This anatomical asymmetry complements an apparent functional asymmetry in the thalamus, the left thalamus being dominant for language functions. (See Eidelberg and Galaburda.)

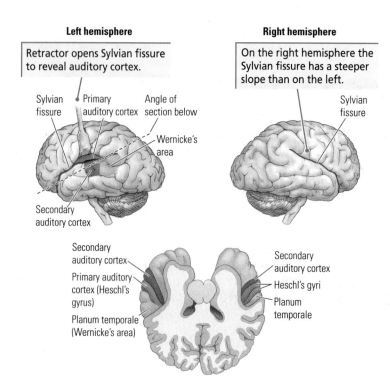

Figure 11.1 Anatomical differences between the two hemispheres. (Top) The Sylvian fissure has a different slope in the two hemispheres. (Bottom) A knife has been moved along the Sylvian fissure of each hemisphere and through the brain, cutting away the top part. The auditory areas and planum temporale are now visible. The planum temporale is larger on the left than on the right, whereas there are two Heschl's gyri on the right but only one on the left.

Left hemisphere

Retractor opens Sylvian fissure to reveal auditory cortex.

Sylvian fissure
Primary auditory cortex
Angle of section below
Wernicke's area
Secondary auditory cortex

Right hemisphere

On the right hemisphere the Sylvian fissure has a steeper slope than on the left.

Sylvian fissure

Secondary auditory cortex
Primary auditory cortex (Heschl's gyrus)
Planum temporale (Wernicke's area)

Secondary auditory cortex
Heschl's gyri
Planum temporale

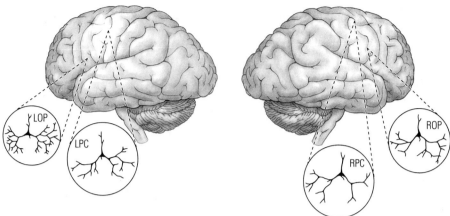

Figure 11.2 Differences in the dendritic morphology in neurons in four locations in the frontal lobe. Left and right frontal operculum (LOP, ROP); left and right precentral cortex (LPC, RPC). (After Scheibel et al., 1985.)

4. The slope of the lateral fissure is gentler on the left hemisphere than on the right (Figure 11.2). The region of the temporoparietal cortex lying ventral to the lateral fissure therefore appears larger on the right.

5. The frontal operculum (Broca's area) is organized differently on the left and right. The area visible on the surface of the brain is about one-third larger on the right than on the left, whereas the area of cortex buried in the sulci (ridges) of the region is greater on the left than on the right. This anatomical asymmetry probably corresponds to the functional dissociation—that is, the lateralization—of the regions, the left side affecting the production of grammar in language and the right side possibly influencing tone of voice.

6. The distribution of various neurotransmitters is asymmetrical, in both the cortical and the subcortical regions. The particular asymmetries in the distribution of acetylcholine, GABA, norepinephrine, and dopamine depend on the structure under consideration. (See Falzi et al., Glick et al., and Oke et al.)

7. The right hemisphere extends farther anteriorly than does the left, the left hemisphere extends farther posteriorly than does the right, and the occipital horns of the lateral ventricles are five times as likely to be longer on the right as on the left. These asymmetries presumably correspond to some gross difference in cerebral organization that has yet to be identified.

8. The details of anatomical asymmetry are affected by both sex and handedness, as we shall see in the next chapter.

Many more anatomical asymmetries between the two cerebral hemispheres have been reported (Table 11.1). Overall, anatomical asymmetries center on the language areas, and it is tempting to speculate that they evolved to subserve language. Moreover, these asymmetries are present in preterm infants, which seems to support the proposition that language is innate in humans.

In fact, the brains of australopithecines had many anatomical asymmetries in common with modern humans, but the hominids had no vocal apparatus that allowed language as we conceive of it. And some asymmetries, such as a heavier and larger right hemisphere and a longer lateral fissure, can also be seen in many nonhuman species.

Table 11.1 Summary of studies demonstrating anatomical asymmetry

Measure	Basic reference
Asymmetries Favoring the Left Hemisphere	
Greater specific gravity	von Bonin, 1962
Longer Sylvian fissure	Eberstaller, 1884; LeMay and Culebras, 1972; Heschl, 1878
Larger insula	Kodama, 1934
Doubling of cingulate gyrus	Eberstaller, 1884
Relatively more gray matter	von Bonin, 1962; Gur et al., 1980
Larger planum temporale	Geschwind and Levitsky, 1968; Galaburda et al., 1978; Teszner et al., 1972; Witelson and Pallie, 1973; Wada et al., 1975; Rubens et al., 1976; Kopp et al., 1977
Larger lateral posterior nucleus	Eidelberg and Galaburda, 1982
Larger inferior parietal lobule	Lemay and Culebras, 1972
Larger area Tpt of temporoparietal cortex	Galaburda and Sanides, 1980
Wider occipital lobe	LeMay, 1977
Longer occipital horn of lateral ventricles	McRae et al., 1968; Strauss and Fitz, 1980
Larger total area of frontal operculum	Falzi et al., 1982
Asymmetries Favoring the Right Hemisphere	
Heavier	Broca, 1865; Crichton-Browne, 1880
Longer internal skull size	Hoadley and Pearson, 1929
Doubling of Heschl's gyrus	von Economo and Horn, 1930; Chi et al., 1977
Larger medial geniculate nucleus	Eidelberg and Galaburda, 1982
Larger area of convexity of frontal operculum	Wada et al., 1975
Wider frontal lobe	LeMay, 1977

With all the emphasis on finding anatomical asymmetries that can be associated with language, research on right-hemisphere function has lagged. If the left hemisphere has asymmetries related to language, then the right hemisphere must have specialized for some other function. After all, the two hemispheres are quite similar in size and other symmetries: it is not as though language areas evolved on the left and nothing happened on the right.

Neuronal Asymmetry

The emphasis on the demonstration of gross morphological asymmetries in the human brain is a natural starting point in comparing the two hemispheres structurally. But remember that the activities of the brain are carried out by neurons. Do the structures of neurons differ on the two sides of the brain?

The identification of structural differences in the neurons in any two areas of the brain is a formidable task in view of the sheer number of neurons. Nonetheless, Arnold Scheibel and his colleagues compared the dendritic fields of pyramidal cells in Broca's area, the left frontal operculum, with those in the facial area of the motor cortex in the left precentral hemisphere and with homologous regions in the right hemisphere (see Figure 11.2).

Their results show that the neurons in each of these regions have a distinct pattern of branching. The degree or pattern of branching is important because each branch is a potential location for the enhancement or suppression of the graded potentials in the dendritic tree. Thus, more branch points allow more degrees of freedom with respect to the final activity of the cell. Note the abundant branches in neurons in Broca's area, far more than in the other areas.

We must approach Scheibel's data on neural asymmetry with caution, because the sample of brains was small ($n = 6$). Curiously, however, five of the six brains were similar to the pattern shown in Figure 11.2. These five brains came from right-handers; the atypical brain came from a left-handed person.

Asymmetry in Neurological Patients

Cerebral asymmetry was first established by studying patients with neurological disease, such as epilepsy, that is lateralized to one hemisphere. Improved neurosurgical treatment for such disorders has provided researchers with a large source of subsequently healthy subjects who are usually very willing to participate in neuropsychological studies. Current knowledge about both the lateralization and the localization of functions in the cerebral cortex owes a great debt to these patients.

In this section, we consider the evidence demonstrating the lateralization of function, emphasizing the study of patients with lateralized lesions and those undergoing commissurotomy, as well as of those who had one hemisphere anesthetized.

Patients with Lateralized Lesions

The oldest research on hemispheric specialization infers function from behavioral deficits that arise as a result of strokes or surgery. Such circumscribed unilateral lesions in the left hemisphere of right-handed patients can produce aphasias that do not develop from lesions of the right hemisphere. Recall, for example, the case history of M. S. presented at the beginning of this chapter. The study of such patients demonstrates that functions of the two hemispheres are lateralized, or dissociated.

To conclude that the cortical area has a special or lateralized function, however, it is also necessary to show that lesions in other areas of the brain do not produce a similar deficit. In the strongest experimental method for demonstrating lateralization of function, called **double dissociation** by Hans-Leukas Teuber, two areas of the neocortex are functionally dissociated by two behavioral tests, each test being affected by a lesion in one zone and not in the other. Lesions in the left hemisphere of right-handed patients have been consistently demonstrated to produce deficits in language functions (speech, writing, and reading) that are not produced by lesions of the right hemisphere. Thus, the functions of the two hemispheres are dissociated. However, performing spatial tasks, singing, playing musical instruments, and discriminating tonal patterns are more disrupted by right-hemisphere than by left-hemisphere lesions. Because right-hemisphere lesions disturb tasks not disrupted by left-hemisphere lesions and vice versa, the two hemispheres are doubly dissociated.

Table 11.2 Hypothetical example of a double-dissociation behavioral test

Neocortical lesion site	Reading	Writing
102	Impaired	Normal
107	Normal	Impaired

A similar logic is used to localize functions within a hemisphere. Behavioral tests that are especially sensitive to damage to a specific locus and not to others can be used to localize functions within a hemisphere. As illustrated in Table 11.2, two hypothetical cortical regions, 102 and 107, are doubly dissociated on tests of reading and writing: damage to area 102 disturbs reading, whereas damage to area 107 impairs writing. In principle, this logic can be extended to dissociate the functions of additional areas concurrently by triple dissociation, quadruple dissociation, and so on.

To illustrate the nature of lateralized functions in neurological cases, we contrast two patients from the Montreal Neurological Hospital, neither of whom was aphasic at the time of assessment. The first patient, P. G., was a 31-year-old man who had developed seizures in the 6 years preceding his surgery. At the time of his admission to the hospital, his seizures were poorly controlled by medication, and subsequent neurological investigations revealed a large tumor in the anterior part of the left temporal lobe. Preoperative psychological tests showed this man to be of superior intelligence, with the only significant deficits being on tests of verbal memory. Two weeks after surgery, psychological testing showed a general decrease in intelligence ratings and a further decrease in the verbal memory scores. Performance on other tests, including tests of recall of complex drawings, was normal. The second patient, S. K., had a tumor removed from the right temporal lobe. In contrast with P. G.'s test results, preoperative testing of S. K. showed a low score on the recall of complex drawings. Two weeks after surgery, repeat testing showed a marked decrease in the performance IQ rating and a decline in the nonverbal memory score, both on simple and on complex designs.

The comparison of these two patients in Figure 11.3 provides a clear example of double dissociation: the patient with removal of the left temporal lobe

Figure 11.3 A comparison of psychological test results for patient P. G. after a left temporal lobectomy (A) and patient S. K. after a right temporal lobectomy (B). The respective regions removed, represented by the shaded zones, are as estimated by the surgeon at the time of operation. (After Taylor, 1969.)

(A)

Left temporal lobectomy

Test	Preoperative	Postoperative
Full scale IQ	123	109
Verbal IQ	122	103
Performance IQ	121	114
Memory quotient	96[a]	73[a]
Verbal recall	7.0[a]	2.0[a]
Nonverbal recall	10.5	10.5
Card sorting	6 categories	6 categories
Drawings: Copy	34/36	34/36
Recall	22.5/36	23.5/36

[a] Significantly low score

(B)

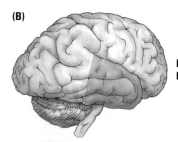

Right temporal lobectomy

Test	Preoperative	Postoperative
Full scale IQ	114	103
Verbal IQ	115	115
Performance IQ	110	89[a]
Memory quotient	121	101
Verbal recall	16.0	12
Nonverbal recall	7.5	5.5[a]
Card sorting	3 categories	3 categories
Drawings: Copy	31/36	28/36[a]
Recall	11/36[a]	13/36[a]

[a] Significantly low score

was impaired only on verbal tests, whereas the patient with removal of the right temporal lobe was impaired only on nonverbal tests. Furthermore, both patients performed normally on many tests, providing evidence for localization, as well as lateralization, of function.

Patients with Commissurotomy

Epileptic seizures may begin in a restricted region of one hemisphere and then spread through the fibers of the corpus callosum (the commissure) to the homologous location in the opposite hemisphere. To prevent the spread of a seizure when medication has failed to impose control, commissurotomy, the procedure of cutting the 200 million nerve fibers of the corpus callosum, was performed in the early 1940s by William Van Wagnen, an American neurosurgeon. The procedure initially appeared to be too variable in its therapeutic outcome and was subsequently abandoned until the 1960s, when research with monkeys and cats by Ron Myers and by Roger Sperry led neurologists to reconsider it.

Two California surgeons, Joseph Bogen and Philip Vogel, performed complete sections of the corpus callosum and of the smaller anterior commissure in a new series of about two dozen patients suffering from intractable epilepsy. The procedure was medically beneficial, leaving some patients virtually seizure free afterward, with minimal effects on their everyday behavior. More extensive psychological testing by Sperry and his colleagues soon demonstrated, however, a unique behavioral syndrome that has been a source of new insights into the nature of cerebral asymmetry.

Figure 11.4 illustrates the effect of commissurotomy on the normal function of the brain. After sectioning, the two hemispheres are independent; each receives sensory input from all sensory systems, and each can control the muscles of the body, but the two hemispheres can no longer communicate with each other. Because the functions in these separate cortexes, or "split brains," are thus isolated, sensory information can be presented to one hemisphere and its function can be studied without the other hemisphere having access to the information.

Figure 11.5 illustrates how the information seen in a particular part of the visual world by both eyes is sent to only one hemisphere: input from the left side of the world (the left visual field) goes to the right hemisphere, whereas input from the

Figure 11.4 The effect of commissurotomy on connections between the hemispheres.

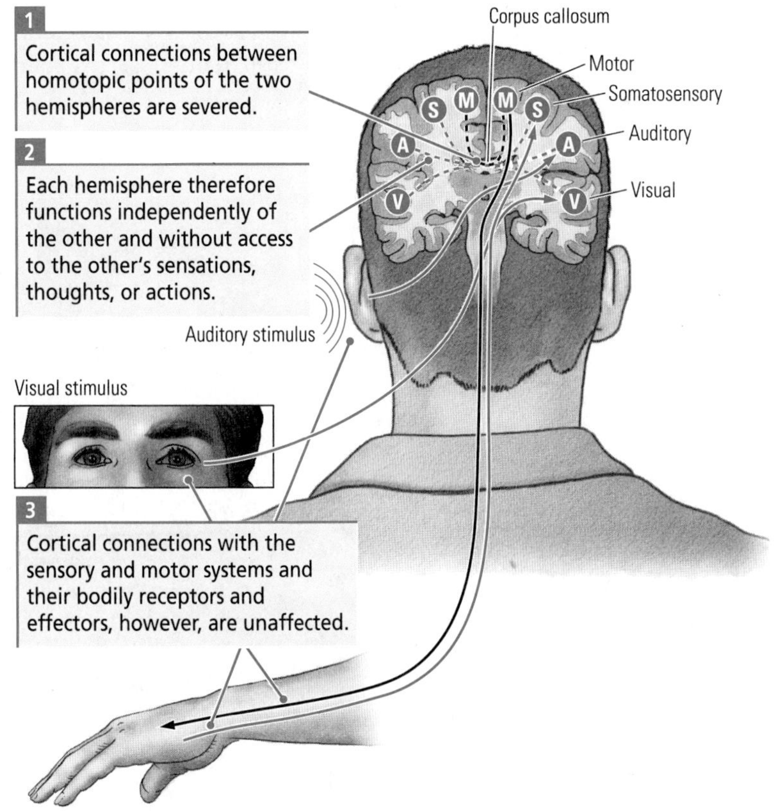

1. Cortical connections between homotopic points of the two hemispheres are severed.

2. Each hemisphere therefore functions independently of the other and without access to the other's sensations, thoughts, or actions.

3. Cortical connections with the sensory and motor systems and their bodily receptors and effectors, however, are unaffected.

Corpus callosum
Motor
Somatosensory
Auditory
Visual
Auditory stimulus
Visual stimulus

Figure 11.5 Visual pathways are crossed, and thus both visual fields (not eyes) are represented in each hemisphere. The entire field left of the fixation point (gray region) is represented in the right visual cortex, and the entire field right of the fixation point (blue region) is represented in the left visual cortex.

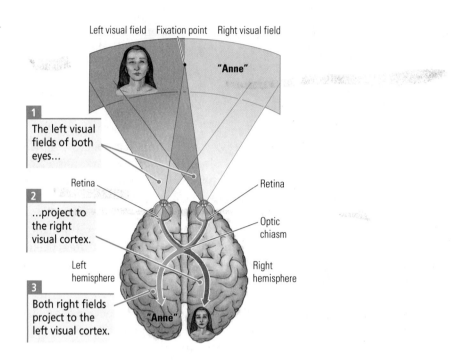

right side of the world (the right visual field) goes to the left hemisphere. The two sides of the world are joined by a connection through the corpus callosum, as illustrated in Figure 11.6. With the corpus callosum severed, the brain cannot relate the different views of the left and right hemispheres.

When the left hemisphere of a split-brain patient has access to information, it can initiate speech and hence communicate about the information. The right hemisphere apparently has reasonably good recognition abilities but is unable

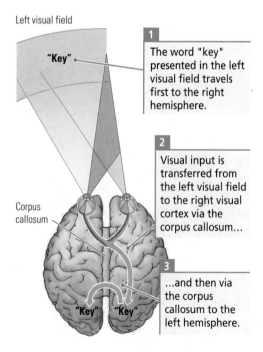

Figure 11.6 Connection between two sides of the world. The word "key" presented in the left visual field travels first to the right hemisphere and then through the corpus callosum to the left hemisphere. Cutting the callosum prevents the transfer.

to initiate speech, because it lacks access to the speech mechanisms of the left hemisphere. The following example illustrates the split-brain phenomenon:

> Patient N. G., a California housewife, sits in front of a screen with a small black dot in the center [illustrated in another patient in Figure 11.7]. She is asked to look directly at the dot. When the experimenter is sure she is doing so, a picture of a cup is flashed briefly to the right of the dot. N. G. reports that she has seen a cup. Again she is asked to fix her gaze on the dot. This time, a picture of a spoon is flashed to the left of the dot. She is asked what she saw. She replies, "No, nothing." She is then asked to reach under the screen with her left hand and to select, by touch only, from among several items the one object that is the same as she has just seen. Her left hand manipulates each object and then holds up the spoon. When asked what she is holding, she says "pencil." (Springer and Deutsch, 1981, pp. 29–30)

Figure 11.7 Basic testing arrangement used to lateralize visual and tactile information and allow tactile responses. (Adapted with permission from S. P. Springer and G. Deutsch. *Left Brain, Right Brain: Perspectives from Cognitive Neuroscience*. New York: W. H. Freeman and Company, 1998, p. 37.)

1

The split-brain subject fixates on the dot in the center of the screen while an image is projected to the left or right visual field. The subject is asked to identify verbally what he sees.

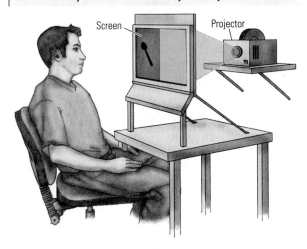

Screen Projector

2

If the picture is presented to the right visual field, the subject answers, "Spoon."

3

If the picture is presented to the left visual field, the subject says, "I see nothing."

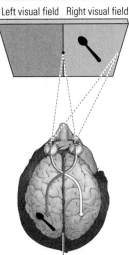

Left visual field Right visual field   Left visual field Right visual field

Severed corpus callosum

4

When the left hemisphere, which can speak, sees the spoon in the right visual field, the subject responds correctly. When the right hemisphere, which cannot speak, sees the spoon in the left visual field, the subject does not respond.

The behavior of patient N. G. clearly demonstrates the behavior of the two hemispheres when they are not interacting. The picture of the cup was presented to the speaking left hemisphere, which could respond. The picture of the spoon was presented to the right hemisphere and, because the right hemisphere does not speak and the speaking left hemisphere was not connected to the right, N. G. failed to identify the picture correctly (see Figures 11.6 and 11.7). The abilities of the right hemisphere were demonstrated when the left hand, which is controlled by the right hemisphere, picked up the spoon. Finally, when asked what the still-out-of-sight left hand was holding, the left hemisphere did not know and incorrectly guessed "pencil."

The special capacities of the right hemisphere in facial recognition can also be demonstrated in the split-brain patient. Jere Levy devised the chimeric-figures test, which consists of pictures of faces and other patterns that have been

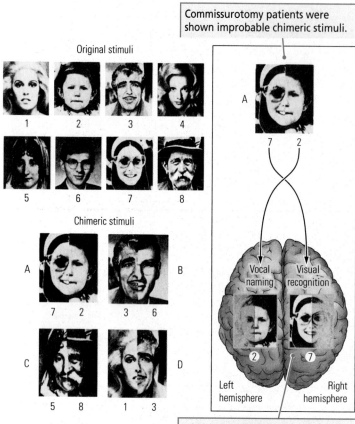

Commissurotomy patients were shown improbable chimeric stimuli.

Original stimuli

1 2 3 4

5 6 7 8

Chimeric stimuli

A 7 2 3 6 B

C 5 8 1 3 D

A

7 2

Vocal naming   Visual recognition

2   7

Left hemisphere   Right hemisphere

When asked to choose the face they had seen from the array of original pictures, the patients chose the face that was presented to the left visual field.

Figure 11.8 Chimeric figures used to demonstrate the special role of the right hemisphere in facial recognition. (Left) Levy and coworkers used photographs 1 through 8 to create composite pictures A through D to produce chimeric stimuli. (Right) When asked to choose the face that they had seen from the array of original pictures 1 through 8, the patients chose the face that was presented to the left visual field. (From J. Levy et al., 1972. Reprinted with the permission of Oxford University Press, Oxford.)

split down the center and recombined in improbable ways (Figure 11.8). When the recombined faces were presented selectively to each hemisphere, the patients appeared to be unaware of the gross discordance between the two sides of the pictures. When asked to pick out the picture that they had seen, they chose the face seen in the left visual field (that is, by their right hemisphere), demonstrating that the right hemisphere has a special role in the recognition of faces.

In summary, the results of careful and sometimes ingenious studies of patients with commissurotomies provide clear evidence of the complementary specialization of the two cerebral hemispheres. It must be recognized, however, that, as interesting as these patients are, they represent only a very small population and their two hemispheres are by no means normal. Most of these patients had focal lesions, which caused the initial seizure disorder, and some may have had brain damage early in life, leading to a significant reorganization of cerebral function. Thus, generalizations and inferences must be made cautiously from these fascinating patients. We shall return to them in Chapter 17.

Brain Stimulation

In the early 1930s, Wilder Penfield and his associates at the Montreal Neurological Institute pioneered the use of surgical treatment for epilepsy in patients whose seizures were poorly controlled by drug therapy. The logic of this procedure is to remove the region of cortex where the abnormal neural discharge originates. Because this therapeutic surgery is elective, it can be planned for, and considerable care can be taken to ensure that areas of the cortex critical for the control of speech and movement are not damaged.

To identify speech and movement areas and to localize the extent of the epileptogenic tissue, the surgeon stimulates the exposed cortex and records the responses of the conscious patient, as illustrated in Figure 11.9. The careful study of hundreds of patients in Montreal by Penfield and his students and more recently by George Ojemann and his colleagues at the University of Washington, provides clear evidence of cerebral asymmetry. Stimulation of the left hemisphere can block the ability to speak, whereas stimulation of the right hemisphere seldom does so.

Application of an electrical current to the cortex of a conscious patient has four general effects—three excitatory and one inhibitory:

1. Stimulation can produce localized movements, localized dysthesias (numbness or tingling in the skin), light flashes, or buzzing sensations. These effects are normally evoked from primary motor, somatosensory, visual, and auditory areas and pathways, respectively, and are produced by the stimulation of either hemisphere with about the same frequency, a result that illustrates the often overlooked fact that the brain has symmetrical as well as asymmetrical functions.

2. Stimulation can produce what Penfield called "interpretive" and "experiential" responses. These uncommon but often highly reliable phenomena include alterations in the interpretation of the patient's surroundings, such as deja vu, fear, and dreaming states, and the reproduction of visual or auditory aspects of specific earlier experiences. That is, patients report specific "memories" in response to specific stimulation. These phenomena usually arise from tissue showing epileptogenic discharge, but there is an asymmetry in their occurrence: stimulation of the right temporal lobe produces these phenomena more frequently than does stimulation of the left temporal lobe, which suggests that the right hemisphere has perceptual functions not shared by the left.

3. Stimulation of the left frontal or temporal regions may accelerate the production of speech. Ojemann suggested that this acceleration may result from a type of "alerting response" and may occur in other cognitive processes, especially memory, although this possibility is difficult to demonstrate unequivocally.

4. Stimulation blocks function. This inhibitory effect is most evident in complex functions such as language and memory and is apparent only when current is applied while a patient is actively engaged in these behaviors. Stimulation of the same site in a quiet patient has no discernible effect. Disruption of speech is a well-documented effect of stimulation of the left hemisphere, but only recently has stimulation of the right hemisphere been shown to disrupt behavior. Ojemann and his colleagues reported that stimulation of the right hemisphere disrupts judgments of line orientation, labeling of facial expressions, and short-term memory for faces. These effects come almost exclusively from the right temporoparietal cortex, a result consistent with the presumed role of this cortical area in visuospatial behavior.

In summary, stimulation of the cortex has proved a useful tool in demonstrating both localization and lateralization of function. The effect of disrupting stimulation can be quite localized, often changing as the site of stimulation is moved as little as a few millimeters, and it is often very reliable for individual patients. An additional intriguing aspect of data from cortical

(A)

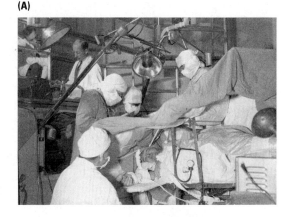

(B)

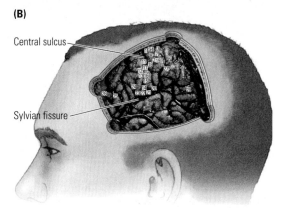

Central sulcus

Sylvian fissure

Figure 11.9 Identifying speech and movement areas of the brain. (A) Localizing an eleptogenic focus in the brain. The patient is fully conscious, lying on his right side, with the left hemisphere of his brain exposed. He is kept comfortable with local anesthesia. In the background, the neurologist studies the electro-encephalogram recording from the patient's cortex. The EEG will help to identify the source of seizures. (B) Identifying critical cortical areas. A drawing of the entire skull overlies a photograph of the patient's exposed brain at surgery. The numbered tickets identify the points that the surgeon stimulated. The application of a stimulating electrode at points 26, 27, and 28, for example, interfered with speech. (Montreal Neurological Institute.)

stimulation is the great variation from patient to patient in the exact location and extent of sites with particular effects on behavior. One can speculate that this variation forms a basis for individual differences in skills, because people presumably have different amounts of cortex for particular functions.

Carotid Sodium Amobarbital Injection

Although language is usually located in the left hemisphere, in a small percentage of people, most of them left-handed, language is represented in the right hemisphere. In the event of elective surgery, preventing inadvertent damage to the speech zones requires that the surgeon be certain of their location. To achieve certainty in doubtful cases, Jun Wada pioneered the technique of injecting sodium amobarbital into the carotid artery to produce a brief period of anesthesia of the ipsilateral hemisphere, as shown in Figure 11.10. (Injections are now normally made through a catheter inserted into the femoral artery.)

This procedure results in an unequivocal localization of speech, because injection into the speech hemisphere results in an arrest of speech lasting up to several minutes; as speech returns, it is characterized by aphasic errors. Injection into the nonspeaking hemisphere may produce no speech arrest or only brief arrest. The amobarbital procedure has the advantage that each hemisphere can be studied separately in the functional absence of the other, anesthetized one. Because the period of anesthesia lasts several minutes, it is possible to study a variety of functions, including memory and movement, to determine the capabilities of one hemisphere in the absence of the anesthetized one.

In a typical Wada test, a patient is given a "dry run" to become familiar with the tests that will be done during and after the drug injection. This dry run establishes a baseline performance level against which to compare the postinjection performance. The patient is then given a series of simple tasks, entailing immediate and delayed memory for both verbal (sentences or words) and nonverbal (photographs of faces or objects) material, for the same purpose.

Moments before the drug is injected, the supine patient raises both arms and wiggles the fingers and toes. The patient is asked to start counting from 1, and, without warning, the neurosurgeon injects the drug through the catheter for 2 to 3 seconds. Within seconds, dramatic changes in behavior are apparent.

The contralateral arm falls to the bed with a flaccid paralysis, and there is no response whatsoever to a firm pinch of the skin of the affected limbs. If the injected hemisphere is nondominant for speech, the patient may continue to count and carry out the verbal tasks while the temporary hemiparesis is present, although often the patient appears confused and is silent for as long as 20 to 30 seconds but can typically resume speech with urging. When the injected hemisphere is dominant for speech, the patient typically stops talking and remains completely aphasic until recovery from the hemiparesis is well along, usually in 4 to 10 minutes.

Speech is tested by asking the patient to name a number of common objects presented in quick succession, to count and recite the days of the week forward and backward, and to perform simple object naming and spelling. In addition

Figure 11.10 The Wada test. To prevent damage to the speech zones of patients about to undergo brain surgery, surgeons inject sodium amobarbital into the carotid artery. The sodium amobarbital anesthetizes the hemisphere where it is injected (in this case, the left hemisphere), allowing the surgeon to determine whether that hemisphere is dominant for speech.

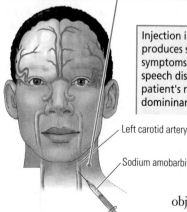

When the left carotid artery is injected, the left hemisphere is briefly anesthetized, so the person cannot speak, move the right arm, or see on the right visual field. Although the right hemisphere is awake, for most people it is nondominant for speech, and the patient can neither speak nor later report on the experience.

Injection into the right side produces sensory and motor symptoms on the left but no speech disturbance, unless the patient's right hemisphere is domininant for speech.

Left carotid artery

Sodium amobarbital

to aphasia and paresis, patients with anesthesia of either hemisphere are totally nonresponsive to visual stimulation in the contralateral visual field. For example, there is no reflexive blinking or orientation toward suddenly looming objects.

The sodium amobarbital test, like direct brain stimulation, has been very useful in determining which hemisphere controls speech. In a series of studies, Brenda Milner and her colleagues demonstrated that about 98% of right-handers and 70% of left-handers show speech disturbance after sodium amobarbital injection into the left hemisphere and not after injection into the right. Curiously, roughly 2% of right-handers have their speech functions lateralized to the right cerebral hemisphere, which is roughly the proportion of right-handed people who show aphasia from right-hemisphere lesions. This finding reminds us that speech is sometimes found in the right hemisphere of right-handed people. The results for left-handed patients support the view that the pattern of speech representation is less predictable in left-handed and ambidextrous subjects than in right-handers but that the majority of left-handers do have speech represented in the left hemisphere.

Whereas none of the right-handers showed evidence of bilateral speech organization, however, 15% of the non-right-handers displayed some significant speech disturbance subsequent to the injection of either side. These patients probably did not have a symmetrical duplication of language functions in the two hemispheres; the injection of one hemisphere tended to disrupt naming (for example, names of the days of the week), whereas the injection of the other hemisphere disrupted serial ordering (for example, ordering the days of the week). Hence, although people may have bilateral representation of speech, this representation is probably asymmetrical and need not imply that the person has "two left hemispheres." Further study of these patients probably would have revealed that visuospatial functions were bilaterally and asymmetrically represented as well, although this is mere conjecture on our part.

Behavioral Asymmetry in the Intact Brain

The study of neurological patients demonstrates a clear difference between the effects of lesions in the two hemispheres, particularly in the control of language. The reason for this difference is not so clear, however, because there are many problems in trying to make inferences about the functioning of the normal brain from the results of clinical studies of the dysfunctioning brain. Just because a specific behavioral symptom is associated with damage to a particular brain area does not necessarily mean that the region once controlled the disrupted function. For example, the fact that 98% of right-handers have a disruption of language function with a left hemisphere stroke in the "language areas" does not mean that the function of the left hemisphere is language. Rather, it means that the left hemisphere executes instructions that are required for normal language functions.

What are these functions? One experimental approach is to study the normal brain noninvasively and to make inferences about the functions of its components from the behavior produced by each component. The most common behavioral approach is the laterality experiment, which takes advantage of the anatomical organization of the sensory and motor systems to "trick" the brain into revealing its mode of operation. Laterality studies, then, are designed to determine which side of the brain controls various functions. Laterality studies are not without problems of their own, however, as we shall see.

Asymmetry in the Visual System

The organization of the visual system provides an opportunity to present each hemisphere selectively with specific visual information. As seen in Figure 11.5, stimuli in the right visual field travel to the left visual cortex, whereas stimuli in the left visual field project to the right visual cortex. With the use of a special instrument called a *tachistoscope*, visual information can be presented to each visual field independently. Normal subjects fixate on a center point marked by a dot or cross (see Figure 11.7). An image is then flashed in one visual field for about 50 ms—a time short enough to allow the image to be processed before the eyes can shift from the fixation point. By comparing the accuracy with which information from the two visual fields is processed, one can infer which hemisphere is best suited to processing different types of information.

The simple conclusion to be drawn from the results of 50 years of tachistoscopic studies is that information presented to only one visual field is processed most efficiently by the hemisphere that is specialized to receive it. Words presented to the verbal left hemisphere, therefore, are processed more efficiently than are words presented to the nonverbal right hemisphere. Similarly, a left-visual-field advantage is found for faces and other visuospatial stimuli thought to be processed by the right hemisphere. These results with normal subjects are consistent with those demonstrated anatomically with neurological patients and reinforce the evidence for a fundamental difference in the perceptual processes of the two hemispheres.

Asymmetry in the Auditory System

The auditory system is not as completely crossed as the visual, because both hemispheres receive projections from each ear. The crossed auditory connections are more numerous, however, and faster conducting than the ipsilateral projections.

In the early 1960s, Doreen Kimura studied neurological patients while they performed dichotic listening tasks, such as the one illustrated in Figure 11.11. Pairs of spoken digits (say, "two" and "six") were presented simultaneously through headphones, but one digit only was heard in each ear. The subjects heard three pairs of digits and then were asked to recall as many of the six digits as possible, in any order. Kimura noticed that subjects recalled more digits that had been presented to the right ear than had been presented to the left.

This result led Kimura to propose that, when different stimuli are presented simultaneously to each ear, the pathway from the right ear to the speaking hemisphere has preferred access and the ipsilateral pathway from the left ear is relatively suppressed. Thus, during a dichotic task, the stimulus to the left ear must travel to the right hemisphere and then across the cerebral commissures to the left hemisphere. This longer route puts the left ear at a disadvantage, and words played to the right ear are recalled more accurately.

Having found a right-ear advantage for the perception of dichotically presented speech stimuli, an obvious next step was to search for tasks that gave a left-ear superiority. In 1964, Kimura reported just such an effect in the perception of melodies. Two excerpts of instrumental chamber music were played simultaneously through headphones, one to each ear. After each pair, four excerpts (in-

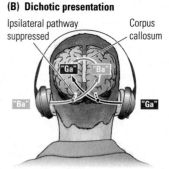

(A) Monaural presentation

Ipsilateral pathway

Contralateral pathway

(B) Dichotic presentation

Ipsilateral pathway suppressed

Corpus callosum

Figure 11.11 Kimura's model of dichotic listening. (A) If information is played to either ear, it reaches both hemispheres by both ipsilateral and contralateral pathways. (B) In dichotic presentation, the contralateral pathways have preferred access to the hemisphere, possibly because the ipsilateral pathways are suppressed. Thus, the syllable "ba" presented to the left ear can gain access to the left hemisphere only through the corpus callosum. If the callosum is cut, the patient can only report hearing "ga." (Adapted with permission from S. P. Springer and G. Deutsch. *Left Brain, Right Brain: Perspectives from Cognitive Neuroscience.* New York: W. H. Freeman and Company, 1998, p. 99.)

cluding the two that had been played dichotically) were presented binaurally (to both ears), and the subject's task was to identify the two that had been heard previously. Amazingly, Kimura found a left-ear advantage on this task.

Not all normal subjects show the expected ear advantages in dichotic studies, the effects are not large when they occur (seldom exceeding a twofold difference in accuracy in the two ears), and dichotic results are apparently affected by various contextual and practice effects. Nonetheless, the Kimura studies are seminal in laterality research, because Kimura's behavioral methods complement results from the neurological literature (Table 11.3). As a result, her research opened up an entire field of experimentation to anyone with imagination and a stereo tape recorder.

Table 11.3 Examples of ear advantages for various dichotic signals

Test	Basic reference
Tests Showing a Right-Ear Advantage	
Digits	Kimura, 1961
Words	Kimura, 1967
Nonsense syllables	Kimura, 1967
Formant transitions	Lauter, 1982
Backward speech	Kimura and Folb, 1968
Morse code	Papcun et al., 1974
Difficult rhythms	Natale, 1977
Tone used in linguistic decisions	Zurif, 1974
Tonal sequences with frequency transitions	Halperin et al., 1973
Ordering temporal information	Divenyi and Efron, 1979
Movement-related tonal signals	Sussman, 1979
Tests Showing a Left-Ear Advantage	
Melodies	Kimura, 1964
Musical chords	Gelfand et al., 1980
Environmental sounds	Curry, 1967
Emotional sounds and hummed melodies	King and Kimura, 1972
Tones processed independently of linguistic content	Zurif, 1974
Complex pitch perception	Sidtis, 1982
Tests Showing No Ear Advantage	
Vowels	Blumstein et al., 1977
Isolated fricatives	Darwin, 1974
Rhythms	Gordon, 1970
Nonmelodic hums	van Lancker and Fromkin, 1973

Source: After Noffsinger, 1985.

More importantly, Kimura's experiments provide a noninvasive technique for identifying the hemisphere dominant for language—a question of special clinical importance, particularly in left-handed patients. And the dichotic test has other clinical uses. It turns out that patients with left-temporal-lobe damage are very poor at this task. Patients with damage to the corpus callosum exhibit an almost complete inhibition of words presented to the left ear, even though they can recall words presented to this ear if there is no competing stimulus to the right ear.

The Kimura experiments imply that the left hemisphere is specialized for processing language-related sounds, whereas the right hemisphere processes music-related sounds. There is, however, another interpretation. It is possible that the asymmetry is related to the temporal or spectral structure of the sounds—their rhythm and frequency—rather than to language and music themselves. Consider, for example, the finding by Papcun and colleagues. They showed that Morse-code operators have a right-ear superiority for the perception of the code, even though the sounds are distinguished only by their *temporal* structure. Thus, the results of this study might be taken as evidence that the left hemisphere is not specialized for language so much as for "something else." One possibility is the analysis of signals with a complex temporal microstructure. We will return to this idea later.

Asymmetry in the Somatosensory System

Experiments on laterality in somatosensation are not as numerous as those on vision and audition. The primary somatosensory system is almost completely crossed, as illustrated in Figure 11.12, which allows an easy behavioral comparison of the two sides by testing right and left limbs separately. By blindfolding subjects and requiring them to perform various tasks separately with each hand, for example, one can identify differences in each hand's efficiency—differences that can be taken to imply functional asymmetry in cerebral organization.

One line of somatosensory research compares the performance of the left and right hands in the recognition of shapes, angles, and patterns. The left hand of right-handed subjects is superior at nearly all tasks of this type. Rudel and coworkers found that both blind and sighted subjects read Braille more rapidly with the left hand. Some children are actually fluent readers with the left hand but are totally unable to read with the right. Because Braille patterns are spatial configurations of dots, this observation is congruent with the proposal that the right hemisphere has a role in processing spatial information that is not shared by the left.

A second type of somatosensory test employs an analogue of the dichotic listening procedure, the *dichaptic test*. Subjects feel objects and then look at an array of objects and select those that they had previously touched. Using this task, Candace Gibson and Phil Bryden presented subjects with cutouts of irregular shapes or letters made of sandpaper, which were moved slowly across the fingertips. Their subjects showed a right-hand advantage for identifying letters and a left-hand advantage for identifying other shapes.

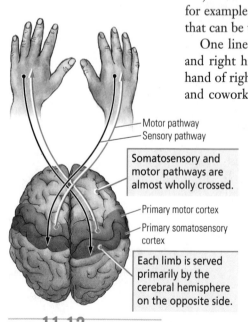

Motor pathway
Sensory pathway

Somatosensory and motor pathways are almost wholly crossed.

Primary motor cortex
Primary somatosensory cortex

Each limb is served primarily by the cerebral hemisphere on the opposite side.

Figure 11.12 Primary sensorimotor cortex.

Asymmetry in the Motor System

Neuroscientists have long known that left hemisphere lesions can produce severe deficits in copying sequences of movements, a condition known as **apraxia.** The logic of studying asymmetry in intact sensory systems makes it seem reasonable to look for asymmetries in motor control. A difficulty that immediately confronts researchers, however, is that, because an asymmetry exists in the processing of sensory input, the study of motor asymmetries is potentially confounded by the fact that the two sides do not start off equally. For example, if we found that the right hand reacts to verbal stimuli faster than the left, we would be unable to conclude that this difference is due to motor asymmetry itself; it could be entirely due to perceptual asymmetry. Therefore, two different types of experiments have been devised to assess motor asymmetries: (1) direct observation of motor asymmetry and (2) interference tasks.

Direct Observation

If asymmetry in the control of movement is inherent, this asymmetry might be observable when people are engaged in other behaviors. For example, perhaps the right hand is more active during the performance of verbal tasks, which do not require a manual response, and the left hand is more active during the performance of nonverbal tasks, such as listening to music, which also do not require a manual response. To examine this possibility, Kimura and her colleagues videotaped subjects talking or humming. They found that right-handed people tend to gesture with their right hands when talking but are equally likely to scratch, rub their noses, or touch their bodies with either hand. Kimura interpreted the observed gesturing with the limb contralateral to the speaking hemisphere to indicate a relation between speech and certain manual activities.

Differences in gesturing, which favor the right hand in right-handed subjects, could simply be due to a difference in preferred hand rather than to functional asymmetry in motor control. Thus, another series of observational studies compared hand-movement asymmetries during analogous verbal and nonverbal tasks. The procedure consisted of videotaping right-handed subjects while they assembled blocks in three different tests. The first, a "neutral task," required subjects to combine white blocks to form a five-by-five matrix. The second test, a "verbal task," required subjects to combine blocks with letters on them in a series of crossword-puzzle tasks. In the third test, a "nonverbal task," subjects did jigsaw puzzles with the same size blocks as those used in the preceding two types of tasks.

Analysis of the movements showed that, in the neutral task, subjects manipulated blocks with the right hand while supporting them with the left. Other movements seldom occurred. In the verbal test, most task-directed movements showed a right-hand preference. In the nonverbal test, in contrast, task-directed movements showed a leftward shift from the neutral condition, subjects now making far more movements with the left hand. These results suggest that the two hemispheres may have complementary roles in the control of movement—an asymmetry that is moderated by a native hand preference.

A second observed motor asymmetry was reported in the performance of complex movements of the mouth. Wolf and Goodale did single-frame analyses

(A) Start of speaking "ma"

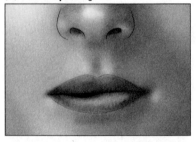

(B) 67 ms later

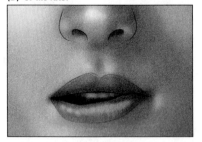

Figure 11.13 Motor asymmetry. Successive video frames illustrate that the right side of the mouth opens more quickly and wider during the production of the syllable "ma" in the sequence "mabopi." (Adapted with permission from *Neuropsychologia* 25, Wolf and Goodale, Oral asymmetries during oral and nonoral movements of the mouth, copyright © 1987.)

of videotaped mouth movements produced when people make verbal or nonverbal sounds. Figure 11.13 illustrates their principal finding: the right side of the mouth opens wider and more quickly than the left for both verbal and nonverbal tasks. Goodale's observations support the idea that the left hemisphere has a special role in the selection, programming, and production of verbal and nonverbal oral movements.

Is there an analogous role for the right hemisphere? Indeed there is. Considerable evidence shows that the left side of the face displays emotions more strongly than the right side, and Goodale showed that the onset of facial expressions occurs sooner on the left side of the face. Thus, it is not the control of movement itself that is asymmetrical but rather movement for a particular purpose.

Interference Tasks

A variety of interference tasks examine a well-known phenomenon that most people manifest: the difficulty of doing two complex tasks at the same time. Perhaps the most interesting interference study known to us is an unpublished experiment by Robert Hicks and Marcel Kinsbourne. They persuaded several unemployed musicians to come to their laboratory daily to play the piano. The task was to learn a different piece of music with each hand so that the two pieces could be played simultaneously. When the musicians had mastered this very difficult task, the experimenters then asked them to speak or to hum while playing. Speaking disrupted playing with the right hand, and humming disrupted playing with the left.

Interference studies provide a useful way to study the roles of the two hemispheres in controlling movement, but much more work is needed before researchers can identify the complementary roles of the two hemispheres (see reviews by Murphy and Peters and by Caroselli et al.). It will be necessary to identify which types of movements each hemisphere is especially good at controlling, because these movements will probably be resilient to interference effects. Further, there should be studies of the capacities of the hemispheres to produce simultaneous finger-versus-limb movements. Perhaps finger movements are more sensitive to interference effects when performed by the right hemisphere than by the left.

Studies of interference effects are intriguing because they may be sources of fresh insights into the cortical organization of the motor systems, but interference effects are poorly understood and appear to be capricious. In addition, as we become proficient at motor tasks, we are less prone to interference effects. Consider the difficulty of talking while learning to play tennis, an interference paradigm of little challenge to a tennis professional.

What Do Laterality Studies Tell Us about Brain Function?

Laterality studies provide a behavioral complement to the anatomical study of neurological patients. Much current theorizing about the nature of cerebral asymmetry is based on laterality research. However, these noninvasive studies are indirect measures of brain function and are far less precise than anatomical measures. Consider the following problems.

Behavioral measures of laterality do not correlate perfectly with invasive measures of cerebral asymmetry. For example, the results of dichotic-listening studies show a right-ear bias for words in about 80% of right-handed subjects, but sodium amobarbital testing and brain stimulation show language to be represented in the left hemisphere in more than 98% of right-handers. What causes this discrepancy? One possibility is that the behavioral test is measuring several things, only one of which is relative cerebral dominance.

A curious paradox is that the behavioral tests may correlate with anatomical asymmetries more closely than data from the invasive tests do. Thus, it is known from anatomical studies that only about 75% to 80% of brains show a left-sided advantage in the posterior lateral area of right-handers, yet 98% of these brains show language in the left hemisphere in a sodium amobarbital test. Strauss and colleagues proposed that the results of laterality studies may provide correlations between anatomy and behavior. One way to test this proposal would be to perform a battery of laterality tests with subjects for whom MRIs also are available. Yet the question remains, Why do the results of both the amobarbital test and brain-stimulation studies show a larger percentage of people with left-hemisphere speech?

Nor do measures of laterality correlate very highly with one another. We might expect tachistoscopic and dichotic measures in the same subjects to be highly concordant, but they are not. Perhaps these tests are not really measuring the same things. Further, the behavioral strategies that subjects adopt in laterality tasks can alter performance significantly. If subjects are instructed to pay particular attention to words entering the left ear in dichotic tasks, they can do so, abolishing the right-ear effect. Subjects can also enter tests with preconceived biases that may affect test performance. Finally, laterality effects may simply be a result of experiential, rather than biological, factors. Suspicion about laterality effects is reinforced by the observation that repeated testing of the same subjects does not always produce the same results.

Skepticism regarding the usefulness of laterality research reaches its peak in an insightful and provocative book by Robert Efron. His thesis is that the apparent right–left difference in laterality studies can be explained entirely by the way in which the brain "scans" sensory input. Imagine the following experiment. Six numbers are presented for 100 ms in a line going from left to right. Three appear in each visual field such that 1, 2, and 3 fall in the left visual field and 4, 5, and 6 fall in the right visual field. Subjects are asked to repeat the numbers that they saw in sequence. As it turns out, they tend to respond with the sequence 4, 5, 6, 1, 2, 3. It appears that the subjects are scanning, from left to right, the contents of the right visual field followed by the contents of the left visual field.

Note that the apparent scanning has nothing to do with actually moving the eyes to read the numbers, because the numbers are present for only 100 ms, which is not enough time for one eye movement. Thus, the sequencing scan is taking place after the presentation of the stimuli has ended. One would predict that, the longer it took to scan, the poorer the performance would be at the end of the scan because the information is decaying. Subsequent experiments confirm this expectation. Efron's numerous scanning experiments led him to conclude that the brain has a tendency to scan information serially. If this is so, then the brain must necessarily examine some stimuli before others. If there is a tendency to examine stimuli in one visual half-field earlier than those in the other half-field, the result would be a left–right performance asymmetry without entailing any hemispheric differences in processing capacity.

There is still a bias in what is scanned first, but that is a different question. Efron does not argue that the two hemispheres are functionally and anatomically identical. He does argue that the evidence of laterality does not constitute an explanation and that we should be very skeptical when we read about descriptions of hemispheric "specialization." What, indeed, is actually lateralized?

Neuroimaging and Asymmetry

Neuroimaging studies, described in Chapter 7, allow researchers to map cerebral activity as it takes place in normal subjects. The primary interest in most imaging studies is the localization, rather than lateralization, of functions. Because both hemispheres are scanned, however, it is possible to assess left–right differences in cerebral activation during a large range of behavioral measures. Virtually all imaging measures, including those by PET, fMRI, ERP, and MEG, reveal the expected asymmetry in cerebral activation in tasks similar to those used in laterality studies.

For example, as expected, asymmetrical cerebral activity takes place when subjects either listen to conversation or engage in it (Figure 11.14). Thus, when a subject is listening to speech, both hemispheres show regional changes in cerebral activity, especially within the auditory cortex, but the left

(A) Left hemisphere, speaking

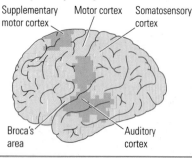

Supplementary motor cortex   Motor cortex   Somatosensory cortex

Broca's area   Auditory cortex

1 Speaking activates the mouth, tongue, and larynx representations in the motor and somatosensory cortex, the supplementary motor area, the auditory cortex, and the language zones in the left hemisphere.

(B) Right hemisphere, speaking

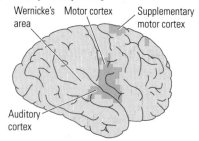

Wernicke's area   Motor cortex   Supplementary motor cortex

Auditory cortex

2 In the right hemisphere, the mouth area and auditory cortex are active but less active than in the left hemisphere.

(C) Left hemisphere, listening

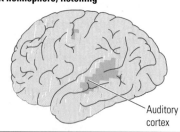

Auditory cortex

3 Sensation changes the pattern of blood flow in the cortex, revealing the localization of areas that mediate perception. Here the subject listened to spoken words, resulting in increased activity localized to the auditory cortex.

Figure 11.14 Relating brain function to regional blood flow. These images, averaged from nine different subjects, show differences in the activity of the left and right hemispheres as the pattern of blood flow varies with the behavioral task. Light shading indicates the average level of blood flow; dark shading indicates higher-than-average blood flow; the absence of shading indicates lower-than-average blood flow. Note that the position of the Sylvian and central fissures is approximate; the actual position could be determined only by opening the skull. The squared shapes are an artifact of the recording and averaging procedure and thus do not accurately indicate the shapes of areas in the brain. (After Lassen et al., 1978.)

hemisphere also shows increased activity in Broca's and Wernicke's areas. When speaking, subjects also show activity in the motor areas that represent the face and mouth, as well as activity of the supplementary motor cortex. Curiously, repetition of what has been called "automatic" speech, such as naming the days of the week over and over again, fails to produce increased activity in Broca's area. This result would not be predicted from the idea that this area takes part in producing movement or from the results of the sodium amobarbital or stimulation studies discussed earlier. In contrast with the increased activity on the left side during speech perception, right-side activity in the temporal lobe increases when subjects hear music.

The mere demonstration of asymmetry is not going to be the principal advantage of imaging studies in the future. Rather, that advantage will be in examples in which predicted asymmetries are *not* found, such as the example of absent activity in Broca's area during automatic speech noted earlier.

The changes in cerebral perfusion during cognitive tasks that underlie fMRI result in alterations of blood flow velocities in the feeding basal arteries. The changes in blood flow in these arteries can be measured using a procedure known as functional transcranial doppler ultrasonography (fTCD). Knecht and colleagues have shown that the changes in blood flow velocity in the basal arteries can be used to identify the language-dominant hemisphere. The authors tested each patient with both fTCD and the Wada procedure to determine the speaking hemisphere. In every case both tests found the same hemisphere to be dominant for speech. The advantage of fTCD is that it is noninvasive and thus may be preferable to the Wada procedure. The unknown question at this point is how the blood flow of people with bilateral speech representation would change with fTCD.

Theoretical Arguments: What Is Lateralized?

It is tempting to conclude that the functional asymmetries described thus far indicate a fundamental difference in the basic cognitive processes of the left and right cerebral hemispheres. However, before turning to this matter, we will consider a summary of the data, because any theoretical statements are best considered in light of available information.

Table 11.4 summarizes the major data on cerebral lateralization and illustrates the range of functions lateralized principally in the left and right hemispheres. In right-handed people, the left hemisphere has a greater role in language and in the control of complex voluntary movements than does the right hemisphere, and the right hemisphere has a greater role in the control of certain visuospatial and nonverbal abilities.

Table 11.4 Summary of data on cerebral lateralization

Function	Left hemisphere	Right hemisphere
Visual system	Letters, words	Complex geometric patterns Faces
Auditory system	Language-related sound	Nonlanguage environmental sounds Music
Somatosensory system	?	Tactile recognition of complex patterns Braille
Movement	Complex voluntary movement	Movements in spatial patterns
Memory	Verbal memory	Nonverbal memory
Language	Speech Reading Writing Arithmetic	Prosody?
Spatial processes		Geometry Sense of direction Mental rotation of shapes

Note: Functions of the respective hemispheres that are predominantly mediated by one hemisphere in right-handed people.

A truly enormous number of proposals have been made on what is lateralized in the brain (see Allen for a readable summary). At the broadest level, these theories fall into two groups: specialization theories propose unique functions for each hemisphere, and interaction theories propose cooperation between the two hemispheres.

Specialization Models

At the extreme, a unilateral specialization model states that only one hemisphere facilitates a given psychological process. For example, it has been argued since Broca that the left hemisphere alone performs language functions. Perhaps the most thorough modern version of the "left for language" theory is Eric Lenneberg's modification of the language theory proposed by Hugo Liepmann at the turn of the century. Liepmann proposed that the left hemisphere is specialized for some form of motor control, which would account for both aphasia and apraxia as the major symptoms of left-hemisphere damage.

Kimura extended this idea by proposing that, although the left hemisphere mediates verbal function, it is specialized not for verbal function itself but rather for certain kinds of motor function, both verbal and nonverbal. Kimura's argument is based on two premises. First, lesions of the left hemisphere disturb the production of voluntary movement—an impairment correlated with disturbance in speech. Second, Kimura proposed that verbal communication among humans evolved from a stage that was primarily gestural, though with vocal concomitants, to one that is primarily vocal but that retains the capacity for manual communication. Because the neurological control of speech and language thus evolved out of a system of motor control of gesture, the left hemisphere is specialized not for language itself but rather for motor control.

Several authors (for example, Efron) have suggested that it is not motor control itself that is located in the left hemisphere but rather the capacity for the fine resolution of stimuli in time. In other words, because the analysis and production of speech require fine discrimination over very short intervals, the left hemisphere might be specialized for temporal sequencing (organizing behavior or information or both over time). Elaborations of this idea have stressed the capacity of the left hemisphere to make fine discriminations in time, whether or not the stimuli are verbal (see, for example, Sergent). Recall the study of Morse-code operators discussed earlier: there is a left-hemisphere advantage even though the code is not verbal—it is a temporal sequence.

Zatorre and his colleagues expanded the Efron timing idea by emphasizing that speech and musical sounds exploit different acoustical cues: speech is highly dependent on rapidly changing broadband sounds, whereas tonal patterns of music tend to be slower, although small and precise changes in frequency are important. Zatorre proposed that the auditory cortices in the two hemispheres are therefore specialized such that temporal resolution is better in the left and spectral resolution is better in the right auditory areas. Zatorre made the point that, because an acoustical system cannot simultaneously analyze both temporal and spectral aspects of sound, the cortical asymmetries related to acoustical processing may have developed as a solution to the need to optimize the processing of acoustical stimuli.

Rather than specifying different processing of specified psychological processes, other specialization models focus on the idea that the two hemispheres might process information in distinctly different ways. The first clear proposal of this sort was made by Josephine Semmes in 1968. On the basis of the results of her previous studies of World War II veterans suffering from penetrating brain injuries, Semmes concluded that the left hemisphere functions as a collection of focalized regions, whereas the right hemisphere functions more diffusely. Her logic was as follows. She had noticed that small lesions in the left hemisphere produced a wide variety of specific deficits (for example, impaired spelling and reading), the precise deficit depending on the locus of the lesion; similar-sized lesions within the right hemisphere were often without obvious effect. In contrast, large lesions of *either* hemisphere produced a large number of deficits.

To account for these differences, Semmes argued that a person with a small lesion in the right hemisphere exhibits no deficits, because specific functions are not localized in discrete regions in the right hemisphere, the functions being diffusely represented. A large lesion of the right hemisphere produces many more deficits than would be predicted from the total of smaller lesions because an entire functional field is removed. A large lesion of the left hemisphere produces many deficits simply because many small focal regions have been destroyed; that is, in the left hemisphere, the total is equal to the sum of the parts.

Semmes proposed that this differential organization of the two hemispheres is advantageous for efficient control of their respective functions. The diffuse organization of the right hemisphere is seen as advantageous for spatial abilities, because spatial analysis requires that different sensations (visual, auditory, tactile) be integrated into a single percept. Language functions, in contrast, remain discrete individual units in the left hemisphere.

From these basic ideas about distinct functions of the two hemispheres has arisen the idea that the hemispheres represent two distinct modes of cognitive processing (see Springer and Deutch). The left hemisphere operates in a more logical, analytical, computer-like fashion, analyzing stimuli input sequentially and abstracting the relevant details to which it attaches verbal labels. The right hemisphere is primarily a synthesizer, more concerned with the overall stimulus configuration, and organizes and processes information as gestalts, or wholes.

Although specialization models have stimulated interest among philosophers and the general public, it is important to remember that they are based entirely on inference and have jumped a long way from the data (such as those summarized in Table 11.4).

Interaction Models

All interaction models have in common the idea that both hemispheres have the capacity to perform all functions but they do not. The specific reasons "why not" have spawned debates, experiments, and models. Three versions of the interaction model are:

1. The two hemispheres function simultaneously but work on different aspects of processing. This version is a direct analogue of the multiple-channel idea of sensory processing. It is merely taken one step further so that the two hemispheres represent a class of sensory channel. Although

simultaneous processing is generally appealing as a model, this theory has yet to offer a satisfactory explanation of how information is combined into a single percept or behavior.

2. An entire group of interaction models proposes that, although the two hemispheres have the capacity to perform a given function, they inhibit or suppress each other's activity (see Kinsbourne, for example, and Moscovitch). Thus, the left hemisphere inhibits language processing in the right hemisphere, and the right hemisphere inhibits music processing in the left. Developmentally, this inhibition model has appeal because it appears that functions such as language can develop in the "wrong" hemisphere if the normally dominant hemisphere is damaged, as illustrated in the Snapshot on page 275. Thus, if the language zones are damaged in infancy, language can develop in the right hemisphere. A difficulty with these models is that the physiological mechanisms of inhibition have not been clearly specified.

3. Interaction models based on information processing suggest either that the two hemispheres receive information preferentially and thus perform different analyses simultaneously or that some mechanism enables each hemisphere to "pay attention" to specific types of information, thus leading to different hemispheric analyses (see, for example, Moscovitch). Information-processing models are complex, detailed, and based heavily on theories of cognitive psychology. An interesting proposal of the simultaneous-processing models is analogous to networked, or distributed, processing by computer. That is, if one hemisphere is busy, it ought to be able to allocate functions to the other hemisphere. A problem with attention-based information-processing models is that they are necessarily vague on what physiological mechanisms might be responsible for selective attention.

In summary, the question of what is lateralized does not have a simple or a generally accepted answer. There is no shortage of theory. What is needed is more information about the nature of asymmetry and its origins, both developmentally and phylogenetically.

Preferred Cognitive Mode

From the preceding theoretical arguments, it is possible to speculate that individual differences in the behavior of normal subjects result, at least in part, from individual differences in how the cerebral hemispheres are organized and how functions are lateralized. **Preferred cognitive mode** refers to the use of one thought process in preference to another. At one extreme, people who are logical, analytical, and verbal are assumed to rely more on their left hemispheres to solve problems in everyday life, whereas people who are visual, intuitive, and tend to look at the big picture are assumed to rely more on their right hemispheres. Consider an example, albeit a tongue-in-cheek one.

Two professors, Alpha and Beta, are both excellent scholars, but they work and think in totally different ways.

Alpha is meticulous and leaves no detail to chance; when learning new material, he masters every detail and has total command of the topic. Alpha is verbal and easily wins debates with his quick thinking and elegant arguments. His

S N A P S H O T

Imaging the Brain's Plasticity

Recall from Chapter 10 that hemispherectomy is sometimes performed to treat children with severe seizures. These disorders can arise from progressive viral infections such as Rasmussen's encephalitis or as congenital or acquired dysfunction of one cerebral hemisphere. Although such children may have severe behavioral difficulties after the surgery, they often compensate remarkably, communicating freely and, in some cases, showing considerable motor control over the limbs opposite the excised hemisphere.

Using both functional magnetic resonance imaging (fMRI) and somatosensory evoked potentials (SEPs), Holloway and colleagues investigated the sensorimotor functions of 17 hemispherectomy patients. Ten patients showed SEPs in the normal hemisphere when the nerves of the limb opposite the excised hemisphere were stimulated. Similarly, as illustrated in the adjoining micrographs, fMRI shows that, for at least some of the patients, passive movement of the same limb produced activation in a region of somatosensory cortex that normally responds to the opposite hand. The Holloway team concluded that the responses to the hand ipsilateral to the normal hemisphere must occur because direct ipsilateral pathways run from the normal hemisphere to the affected limb.

Curiously, the novel ipsilateral responses were found in patients with both congenital and acquired disease, suggesting that, although age at injury may be important, other factors must be influencing the cerebral reorganization. The injury-induced reorganization is characteristic of

Damage to right hemisphere

Passive movement of right hand is seen in the left sensorimotor cortex.

Passive movement of the left (hemiplegic) hand shows an abnormal ipsilateral pathway.

the brain's plasticity—the ability of the nervous system to alter its organization to compensate for injury. We will return to plasticity in the context of brain development in Chapter 23.

(V. Holloway, D. G. Gadian, F. Vargha-Khadem, D. A. Porter, S. G. Boyd, and A. Connelly. The reorganization of sensorimotor function in children after hemispherectomy. *Brain* 123:2432–2444, 2000.)

writing is clear and concise, with flawless grammar and spelling. Alpha is athletic and is a nationally ranked tennis player. Curiously, he is only mediocre at other sports, but with prolonged practice he is able to master them. Alpha's office is neat and tidy, with every item carefully placed in its correct location. On his desk is the project on which he is currently working and nothing else.

Beta appears to be messy and disorganized compared with Alpha and has poor recall for details. He grasps the heart of an idea quickly, however, and can tie diverse concepts into a meaningful picture. Communicating his thinking poses Beta a challenge, however, for he has difficulty expressing his ideas in words. Like Alpha, Beta is athletic, but Beta acquires the general motor skills of new sports rapidly, although he has never been able to become a top participant in any event. In contrast with Alpha, who works on only one project at a time, Beta works on several projects concurrently, leading to piles of papers and books in his work space, unlike Alpha's meticulous desk.

In both the cognitive and the motor skills of Alpha and Beta is a basic difference that is assumed to correspond to a fundamental difference either in brain organization or in the "dominance" of one hemisphere over the other. Alpha and Beta represent extreme left-hemisphere and right-hemisphere people, respectively. The fundamental difference between them is their preferred cognitive mode. Alpha is analytical, logical, verbal, and meticulous, whereas Beta is a synthesizer more concerned with organizing concepts and visualizing meaningful wholes.

As intriguing as the Alpha and Beta analysis might be, we caution that it is pure speculation, without empirical basis. Factors other than brain organization probably contribute to preferred cognitive mode. For example, the results of a study by William Webster and Ann Thurber demonstrate that **cognitive set,** the tendency to approach a problem with a particular bias in thought, can affect some tests of lateralization. They repeated Witelson and Pallie's dichaptic test (described earlier) but added an additional variable. One group (the gestalt bias) was encouraged to learn the shapes by imagining their overall appearance; a second group (the analytic bias) was encouraged to identify distinctive features of each shape and list them to themselves.

This manipulation of cognitive set demonstrably influenced the degree of left-hand superiority, because the gestalt group had a significantly larger performance difference between the hands than did the analytic group. Although the basis for this effect is uncertain, it implies that strategies used by subjects can significantly influence tests of lateralization. Thus it seems reasonable to assume that differences in preferred cognitive mode may be due to biases in socialization or environmental factors in addition to neuronal, genetic, or constitutional biases. Nevertheless, the idea that individual differences in behavior result in part from individual differences in brain organization is a provocative assumption worthy of serious study.

Measuring Behavior in Neuropsychology

It is appropriate at this point to briefly consider the problem of measuring behavior. It might be thought that, of all the procedures used in neuropsychology, the measurement of things or events may be the easiest to perform and replicate. This is not true. Many measurements are made to obtain inferences about some other processes. For example, in dichotic listening, if more words are recalled from the right ear than from the left, the inference is made that speech is lateralized to the left hemisphere. The assumptions underlying this inference are relatively simple, yet so many variables affect the result that Phil Bryden has written an entire book on the problem. Perhaps, one may ask, If a more objective measure of something like brain size were used, would the results be clearer? This outcome, however, seems unlikely. There appear to be so many different ways to measure objects that almost any result can be obtained. Consider the following example.

Probably everyone has had the feeling that his or her feet are not exactly the same size. Often the difference manifests itself as greater discomfort in one foot when breaking in a new pair of shoes (we have never heard anyone suggest that the shoes might be different sizes). Foot size may be related to differences in brain organization. For example, people in medicine have known for a long time that damage to one hemisphere at an early age leads to smaller limbs on the contralateral side of the body (Figure 11.15).

Jere and Jerome Levy attempted to measure differences in foot size in normal people in order to make inferences about cerebral organization. They measured foot size in 150 persons and found that significantly more right-handed females had larger left than right feet, whereas significantly more right-handed males had larger right than left feet. Just the opposite result was obtained with left-handed females and males.

The Levys' measures were made by converting foot size into shoe size and then converting differences into a seven-point rating scale. A number of studies attempted to repeat the Levys' work. Mascie-Taylor and his coworkers measured foot size by using a "standard anthropometric technique" (described elsewhere as heel to longest toe with the subject seated and with the toenails cut). They found that the left foot was longer than the right in both sexes, confirming the results of seven earlier studies. There were no handedness effects. Michael Peters and his coworkers measured the actual foot length from the heel to the longest toe in 365 seated subjects. They found no significant differences between the left and the right foot for any sex or handedness group, and they claimed partial support for their results from three other studies. Yanowitz and his colleagues traced the outline of 105 subjects' feet on a large sheet of paper. They found no differences in foot size with regard to sex or handedness.

The final score on this series of studies is as follows: one study for sex and handedness effects, eight studies for a left-foot effect, and two studies for no differences, with the results of three additional studies in partial support of no differences. This story—like all good stories—has a sequel, and we refer the interested reader to Peters's review.

Measuring foot size might seem relatively easy. This series of studies shows that it is not. The results obtained depend on the measuring device, the points across which length is measured, whether subjects are seated or standing, the time of day, and perhaps even shoe type worn before measurement. In many of the studies, the importance of these variables was not recognized; in others, the procedure was not described in sufficient detail to permit exact replication. It is interesting that the most objective measure, photography, was not used in any of the studies (see Figure 11.15). A photographic record of the feet would have permitted a reevaluation of the results at any time by investigators interested in the question of appropriate measurement.

Perhaps three lessons should be derived from this example (one of them is not that it is impossible to make measurements). The first is that, if measuring something like feet is difficult, then inferring something about the brain from such measurements should be done with caution. The second is that there is nothing wrong with making multiple measurements. If they correlate, then each is measuring the same thing; if they do not, then either multiple factors are at work or some of the measures are not reliable. The third is that, if a measurement is to be made, it should be the most meaningful one that can be made.

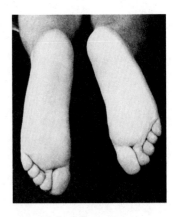

Figure 11.15 Growth and the brain. Destruction of the left frontoparietal region at the time of birth produced this growth asymmetry in the right foot. Such cases demonstrate that growth affecting limb size has a cortical component, quite aside from the effect of disuse of the limb. (From W. Penfield and H. Jasper, Copyright © 1954. Reprinted with permission.)

Summary

A striking feature of the organization of the human brain is that the two hemispheres of the human brain are anatomically and functionally asymmetrical. The asymmetries in structure are visible not only in an overall view but also at the level of the morphology of the individual neuron, and the asymmetries in function exist not only in neurological patients but also in the normal brain. Although there is little disagreement about the facts of asymmetry in the human brain, there is considerable disagreement about why the two hemispheres are asymmetrical and about what the asymmetry means in regard to how we humans process information.

The observed asymmetries can be assumed to represent functional specializations of the hemispheres. Thus, the increased size of the language areas in certain auditory regions of the temporal lobe presumably corresponds to the special role of this tissue in processing acoustical stimuli related to language. But, given that the total area of the auditory cortex is similar in the two hemispheres, the tissue of the right hemisphere must be specialized for the analysis of some other characteristic of language, which is likely the characteristic of sound related to music.

The analysis of patients undergoing specialized neurological and surgical procedures provides an opportunity to study functional aspects of the anatomical asymmetries. Converging evidence from patients with lateralized lesions or split brains, as well as those undergoing brain stimulation and sodium amobarbital injection, confirm the left hemisphere's special role in language and motor functions and the right hemisphere's complementary role in musical and spatial functions. Asymmetry in the intact brain can also be studied by using imaging procedures as well as by behavioral experiments that trick the brain into revealing that sensory information from the left or right side of space is processed differently by the brain.

Four cautions must be reiterated before we consider variations in the "textbook pattern" of cerebral asymmetry in the next chapter. The first is that many functions of the cerebral hemispheres are symmetrical rather than asymmetrical. In an examination in our undergraduate course in human neuropsychology, we asked, In what ways is the human brain symmetrical? Thinking it to be a trick question, a majority of the students answered, "It isn't symmetrical, it's asymmetrical." This answer is wrong, because many functions—especially of the primary sensory and motor areas—appear to be identical on the two sides of the brain.

Second, the functional differences between the two hemispheres are not absolute, but relative. Just because sodium amobarbital renders one hemisphere aphasic does not mean that language functions are carried out only in the aphasic hemisphere.

Third, cerebral *site* is at least as important in understanding brain function as cerebral *side*. Thus the functions of the two frontal lobes, though asymmetrical, are more similar to each other than they are to those of the posterior cortex on the same side. We can think of the functions of the cerebral cortex as being localized and of hemispheric side as being only one step in localizing them.

Fourth, it is a long inferential leap from the data available to explanations of what those data mean. Although it is tempting to conclude, for example, that the function of the left hemisphere is "language," the appropriate conclusion is that the left hemisphere takes part in processes that are necessary for certain aspects of language. Similarly, the right hemisphere appears to take part in processing required for visuospatial functions. Indeed, at present, it is safe to conclude that we do not know what processes the two hemispheres are specialized to perform.

References

Allen, M. Models of hemispheric specialization. *Psychological Bulletin* 93:73–104, 1983.

Amaducci, L., S. Sorbi, A. Albanese, and G. Gainotti. Choline acetyltransferase (ChAT) activity differs in right and left human temporal lobes. *Neurology* 31:799–805, 1981.

Blumstein, S., V. Tartter, D. Michel, B. Hirsch, and E. Leiter. The role of distinctive features in the dichotic perception of words. *Brain and Language* 4:508–520, 1977.

Brandeis, D., and D. Lehmann. Event-related potentials of the brain and cognitive processes: Approaches and applications. *Neuropsychologia* 24:151–168, 1986.

Broca, P. Sur la faculté du langage articule. *Bulletins et Memoires de la Societé D'Anthropologie de Paris* 6:377–393, 1865.

Bryden, M. P. *Laterality: Functional Asymmetry in the Intact Brain.* New York: Academic Press, 1982.

Carmon, A., Y. Harishanu, E. Lowinger, and L. Lavy. Asymmetries in hemispheric blood volume and cerebral dominance. *Behavioral Biology* 7:853–859, 1972.

Caroselli, J. S., M. Hiscock, and T. Roebuck. Asymmetric interference between concurrent tasks: An evaluation of competing explanatory models. *Neuropsychologia* 35:457–469, 1997.

Chi, J. G., E. C. Dooling, and F. H. Gilles. Left-right asymmetries of the temporal speech areas of the human fetus. *Archives of Neurology* 34:346–348, 1977.

Crichton-Browne, J. On the weight of the brain: Its component parts in the insane. *Brain* 2:42–67, 1880.

Cunningham, D. F. *Contribution to the Surface Anatomy of the Cerebral Hemispheres.* Dublin: Royal Irish Academy, 1892.

Curry, F. A comparison of left-handed subjects on verbal and nonverbal dichotic listening tasks. *Cortex* 3:343–352, 1967.

Dabbs, J. M. Left-right differences in cerebral blood flow and cognition. *Psychophysiology* 17:548–551, 1980.

Darwin, C. Ear differences and hemispheric specialization. In F. O. Schmitt and F. G. Worden, Eds. *The Neurosciences: Third Study Program.* Cambridge, MA: MIT Press, 1974.

Divenyi, P., and R. Efron. Spectral versus temporal features in dichotic listening. *Brain and Language* 7:375–386, 1979.

Eberstaller, O. Zur Oberflächenanatomie der Grosshirnhemispharen. *Wien. Med. Blätter* 7:479–482, 542–582, 644–646, 1884.

Efron, R. *The Decline and Fall of Hemispheric Specialization.* Hillsdale, NJ: Lawrence Erlbaum, 1990.

Eidelberg, D., and A. M. Galaburda. Symmetry and asymmetry in the human posterior thalamus. *Archives of Neurology* 39:325–332, 1982.

Falzi, G., P. Perrone, and L. A. Vignolo. Right-left asymmetry in anterior speech region. *Archives of Neurology* 39:239–240, 1982.

Galaburda, A. M., M. LeMay, T. L. Kemper, and N. Geschwind. Right-left asymmetries in the brain. *Science* 199:852–856, 1978.

Galaburda, A. M., and F. Sanides. Cytoarchitectonic organization of the human auditory cortex. *Journal of Comparative Neurology* 190:597–610, 1980.

Gelfand, S., S. Hoffmand, S. Waltzman, and N. Piper. Dichotic CV recognition at various interaural temporal onset asynchronies: Effect of age. *Journal of the Acoustical Society of America* 68:1258–1261, 1980.

Geschwind, N., and W. Levitsky. Left-right asymmetries in temporal speech region. *Science* 161:186–187, 1968.

Gibson, C., and M. P. Bryden. Dichaptic recognition of shapes and letters in children. *Canadian Journal of Psychology* 37:132–143, 1983.

Glick, S. D., D. A. Ross, and L. B. Hough. Lateral asymmetry of neurotransmitters in human brain. *Brain Research* 234:53–63, 1982.

Gordon, H. Hemispheric asymmetries in the perception of musical chords. *Cortex* 6:387–398, 1970.

Graves, R., H. Goodglass, and T. Landis. Mouth asymmetry during spontaneous speech. *Neuropsychologia* 20:371–381, 1982.

Gur, R. C., I. K. Packer, J. P. Hungerbuhler, M. Reivich, W. D. Obrist, W. S. Amarnek, and H. Sackheim. Differences in distribution of gray and white matter in human cerebral hemispheres. *Science* 207:1226–1228, 1980.

Halperin, Y., I. Nachson, and A. Carmon. Shift of ear superiority in dichotic listening to temporally patterned nonverbal stimuli. *Journal of the Acoutistical Society of America* 53:46–50, 1973.

Hampson, E., and D. Kimura. Hand movement asymmetries during verbal and nonverbal tasks. *Canadian Journal of Psychology* 38:102–125, 1984.

Heschl, R. L. *Über die vordere quere Schlafentwindung des Meschlichen Grosshirns.* Wien: Braumüller, 1878.

Hoadley, M. D., and K. Pearson. Measurement of internal diameter of skull in relation to "pre-eminence" of left hemisphere. *Biometrika* 21:94–123, 1929.

Kimura, D. Some effects of temporal-lobe damage on auditory perception. *Canadian Journal of Psychology* 15:156–165, 1961.

Kimura, D. Left-right differences in the perception of melodies. *Quarterly Journal of Experimental Psychology* 16:355–358, 1964.

Kimura, D. Functional asymmetry of the brain in dichotic listening. *Cortex* 3:163–178, 1967.

Kimura D. The asymmetry of the human brain. *Scientific American* 228:70–78, 1973.

Kimura D., and S. Folb. Neural processing of background sounds. *Science* 161:395–396, 1968.

King, F., and D. Kimura. Left-ear superiority in dichotic perception of vocal, non-verbal sounds. *Canadian Journal of Psychology* 26:111–116, 1972.

Kinsbourne, M. Eye and head turning indicates cerebral lateralization. *Science* 176:539–541, 1971.

Kinsbourne, M., and J. Cook. Generalized and lateralized effects of concurrent verbalization on a unimanual skill. *Quarterly Journal of Experimental Psychology* 23:341–345, 1971.

Kinsbourne, M., and R. E. Hicks. Functional cerebral space: A model for overflow, transfer and interference effects in human performance. In J. Requin, Ed. *Attention and Performance*, vol. 7. New York: Academic Press, 1978.

Kodama, L. Beitrage zur Anatomie des Zentralnervensystems der Japaner. VIII. Insula Reil ii. *Folia Anatomica Japan* 12:423–444, 1934.

Kopp, N., F. Michel, H. Carrier, A. Biron, and P. Duvillard. Hemispheric asymmetries of the human brain. *Journal of Neurological Sciences* 34:349–363, 1977.

Lassen, N. A., D. H. Ingvar, and E. Skinhøj. Brain function and blood flow. *Scientific American* 239:62–71, 1978.

Lauter, J. Dichotic identification of complex sounds: Absolute and relative ear advantages. *Journal of the Acoustical Society of America* 71:701–707, 1982.

LeMay, M. Asymmetries of the skull and handedness. *Journal of the Neurological Sciences* 32:243–253, 1977.

LeMay, M. Morphological aspects of human brain asymmetry. *Trends in Neurosciences* 5:273–275, 1982.

LeMay, M., and A. Culebras. Human brain-morphologic differences in the hemispheres demonstrable by carotid arteriography. *New England Journal of Medicine* 287:168–170, 1972.

Levy, J., and J. M. Levy. Human lateralization from head to foot: Sex-related factors. *Science* 200:1291–1292, 1978.

Levy, J., and J. M. Levy. Foot-length asymmetry, sex, and handedness. *Science* 212:1418–1419, 1981.

Levy, J., C. Trevarthen, and R. W. Sperry. Perception of bilateral chimeric figures following hemispheric deconnection. *Brain* 95:61–78, 1972.

Mascie-Taylor, C. G. N., A. M. MacLarnon, P. M. Lanigan, and I. C. McManus. Foot-length asymmetry, sex, and handedness. *Science* 212:1416–1417, 1981.

McRae, D. L., C. L. Branch, and B. Milner. The occipital horns and cerebral dominance. *Neurology* 18:95–98, 1968.

Moscovitch, M. Information processing and the cerebral hemispheres. In M. Gazzaniga, Ed. *Handbook of Behavioral Neurobiology*, vol. 2. New York: Plenum, 1979.

Murphy, K., and M. Peters. Right-handers and left-handers show differences and important similarities in task integration when performing manual and vocal tasks concurrently. *Neuropsychologia* 32:663–674, 1994.

Nachson, I., and A. Carmon. Hand preference in sequential and spatial discrimination tasks. *Cortex* 11:123–131, 1975.

Natale, M. Perception of nonlinguistic auditory rhythms by the speech hemisphere. *Brain and Language* 4:32–44, 1977.

Noffsinger, D. Dichotic-listening techniques in the study of hemispheric asymmetries. In D. F. Benson and E. Zaidel, Eds. *The Dual Brain.* New York: Guilford Press, 1985.

Ojemann, G. A. Brain organization for language from the perspective of electrical stimulation mapping. *Behavioral and Brain Sciences* 6:189–230, 1983.

Oke, A., R. Keller, I. Mefford, and R. N. Adams. Lateralization of norepinephrine in human thalamus. *Science* 200:1411–1413, 1978.

Papcun, G., S. Krashen, D. Terbeek, R. Remington, and R. Harshman. Is the left hemisphere organized for speech, language and/or something else? *Journal of the Acoustical Society of America* 55:319–327, 1974.

Penfield, W., and H. Jasper. *Epilepsy and the Functional Anatomy of the Human Brain.* Boston: Little, Brown, 1954.

Peters, M. Footedness: Asymmetries in foot preference and skill and neuropsychological assessment of foot movement. *Psychological Bulletin* 103:179–192, 1988.

Peters, M. B., B. Petries, and D. Oddie. Foot-length asymmetry, sex, and handedness. *Science* 212:1417–1418, 1981.

Posner, M. I., and M. E. Raichle. *Images of Mind.* New York: Scientific American Library, 1994.

Rasmussen, T., and B. Milner. The role of early left brain injury in determining lateralization of cerebral speech functions. *Annals of the New York Academy of Sciences* 299:355–369, 1977.

Rubens, A. B. Anatomical asymmetries of human cerebral cortex. In S. Harnad, R. W. Doty, L. Goldstein, J. Jaynes, and G. Krauthamer, Eds. *Lateralization in the Nervous System.* New York: Academic Press, 1977.

Rubens, A. M., M. W. Mahowald, and J. T. Hutton. Asymmetry of the lateral (Sylvian) fissures in man. *Neurology* 26:620–624, 1976.

Rudel, R. G., M. B. Denckla, and E. Spalten. The functional asymmetry of Braille letter learning in normal sighted children. *Neurology* 24:733–738, 1974.

Scheibel, A. B., I. Fried, L. Paul, A. Forsythe, U. Tomiyasu, A. Wechsler, A. Kao, and J. Slotnick. Differentiating characteristics of the human speech cortex: A quantitative Golgi study. In D. F. Benson and E. Zaidel, Eds. *The Dual Brain*. New York: Guilford Press, 1985.

Semmes, J. Hemispheric specialization: A possible clue to mechanism. *Neuropsychologia* 6:11–26, 1968.

Sergent, J. Role of the input in visual hemispheric asymmetries. *Psychological Bulletin* 93:481–512, 1983.

Sidtis, J. Predicting brain organization from dichotic listening performance: Cortical and subcortical functional asymmetries contribute to perceptual asymmetries. *Brain and Language* 17:287–300, 1982.

Springer, S. P., and G. Deutsch. *Left Brain, Right Brain*, 5th ed. New York: W. H. Freeman and Company, 1998.

Squires, N. K., and C. Ollo. Human evoked potential techniques: Possible applications to neuropsychology. In H. J. Hannay, Ed. *Experimental Techniques in Human Neuropsychology*. New York: Oxford University Press, 1986.

Steinmetz, H., J. Volkman, L. Jancke, and H. Freund. Anatomical left-right asymmetry of language-related temporal cortex is different in left and right-handers. *Annals of Neurology* 29:315–319, 1991.

Strauss, E., and C. Fitz. Occipital horn asymmetry in children. *Annals of Neurology* 18:437–439, 1980.

Strauss, E., B. Kosaka, and J. Wada. The neurological basis of lateralized cerebral function: A review. *Human Neurobiology* 2:115–127, 1983.

Strauss, E., B. Kosaka, and J. Wada. Visual laterality effects and cerebral speech dominance determined by the carotid Amytal test. *Neuropsychologia* 23:567–570, 1985.

Sussman, H. M. Evidence for left hemisphere superiority in processing movement-related tonal signals. *Journal of Speech and Hearing Research* 22:224–235, 1979.

Taylor, L. B. Localisation of cerebral lesions by psychological testing. *Clinical Neurology* 16:269–287, 1969.

Teszner, D., A. Tzavaras, and H. Hécaen. L'asymetries droite-gauche du planum temporale: A-propos de l'étude de 100 cerveaux. *Revue Neurologique* 126:444–452, 1972.

Teuber, H.-L. Physiological psychology. *Annual Review of Psychology* 6:267–296, 1955.

Van Lancker, D., and V. Fromkin. Hemispheric specialization for pitch and "tone": Evidence from Thai. *Journal of Phonetics* 1:101–109, 1973.

von Bonin, B. Anatomical asymmetries of the cerebral hemispheres. In V. B. Mountcastle, Ed. *Interhemispheric Relations and Cerebral Dominance*. Baltimore: Johns Hopkins Press, 1962.

von Economo, C. V., and L. Horn. über Windungsrelief, Masse and Rindenarchitektonik der Supratemporalfläche, ihre individuellen und ihre Seitenunterschiede. *Zeitschrift für Neurologie and Psychiatrie* 130:678–757, 1930.

Wada, J. A., R. Clarke, and A. Hamm. Cerebral hemispheric asymmetry in humans: Cortical speech zones in 100 adult and 100 infant brains. *Archives of Neurology* 32:239–246, 1975.

Wada, J., and T. Rasmussen. Intracarotid injection of sodium amytal for the lateralization of cerebral speech dominance. *Journal of Neurosurgery* 17:266–282, 1960.

Webster, W. G., and A. D. Thurber. Problem solving strategies and manifest brain asymmetry. *Cortex* 14:474–484, 1978.

Witelson, S. F., and W. Pallie. Left hemisphere specialization for language in the newborn: Neuroanatomical evidence of asymmetry. *Brain* 96:641–646, 1973.

Wolf, M. E., and M. A. Goodale. Oral asymmetries during verbal and non-verbal movements of the mouth. *Neuropsychologia* 25:375–396, 1987.

Wyke, M. The effect of brain lesions on an arm-hand precision task. *Neuropsychologia* 6:125–134, 1968.

Zangwill, O. L. *Cerebral Dominance and Its Relation to Psychological Function*. Springfield, IL: Charles C. Thomas, 1960.

Zatorre, R. J., P. Belin, and V. B. Penhume. Structure and function of auditory cortex: Music and speech. *Trends in Cognitive Sciences* 6:37–46, 2002.

Zurif, E. Auditory lateralization: Prosodic and syntactic factors. *Brain and Language* 1:391–401, 1974.

Variations in Cerebral Asymmetry

No two brains are alike; indeed, no two hemispheres are even grossly alike, as Figure 12.1 illustrates. Brains (and hemispheres) differ in size, gyral patterns, distribution of gray and white matter, cytoarchitectonics, vascular patterns, and neurochemistry, among other things. Do variations in the brain's anatomical asymmetry correlate with functional asymmetries?

Consider the case of A. B. and L. P., two middle-aged college graduates who suffered similar brain injuries but responded very differently. After an injury to the posterior part of the left temporal lobe, A. B. had verbal difficulties, in reading, speaking, and remembering words. In contrast, L. P., whose injury was similar, had no language difficulties. But L. P. had trouble recognizing faces and drawing pictures, symptoms that A. B. did not exhibit.

Given their similar injuries and education (both were psychology majors in college and presumably above average in intelligence before their injuries), we would expect their symptoms to be quite similar, but they were, in a sense, opposite.

Two significant differences between these people help explain the difference in symptoms: A. B. was a right-handed man, and L. P. was a left-handed woman. We shall see that these two factors—sex and handedness—influence the organization of the cerebral hemispheres and ultimately the effects of cerebral injury. In this case, L. P. was found to have language in the right hemisphere, which explains why she had no language impairments.

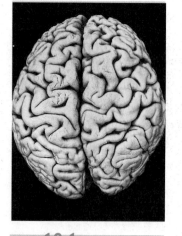

Figure 12.1 Photograph of a human brain taken from above. In this photograph, the two hemispheres appear very different.

Handedness and sex are easily identified factors influencing cerebral asymmetry, but they are not the only factors leading to individual differences in brain organization and behavior. This chapter examines a range of biological and environmental factors that produce individual variations in cerebral asymmetry. We review the effects of the relations between brain organization and hand preference, sex differences, and genes and environment on individual patterns of asymmetry. In the final section, we consider the incidence of asymmetry in nonhuman animals.

Handedness and Functional Asymmetry

People use the word *sinister* as a synonym for wicked or evil. Originally a Latin word meaning "left-hand side," our contemporary English meaning implies that left-handedness has been historically viewed at best as strange or unusual. Today, terms such as southpaw in baseball suggest an evolution of tolerance toward left-handers and, in professional sports, even admiration.

The most commonly cited statistic for left-handedness in the general population is 10%, referring to the percentage of people who write with the left hand. But, when broader criteria are used, estimates range from 10% to 30%. The problem is that handedness is not absolute; some people are nearly totally left- or right-handed, whereas others are ambidextrous (that is, they use either hand with equal facility).

A useful distribution of handedness was constructed by Marion Annett (Table 12.1), who asked more than 2000 adults to indicate the hand that they use to perform each of 12 different tasks. The evidence of left-handedness on Annett's tasks varies from a low of about 6% when cutting with scissors to a high of about 17% when dealing cards.

Table 12.1   Summary of handedness in performing various tasks

Task	Left (%)	Either (%)	Right (%)
Dealing cards	17.02	3.32	79.66
Unscrewing jar	6.50	17.49	66.01
Shoveling	13.53	11.89	74.58
Sweeping	13.49	16.89	69.62
Threading needle	13.10	9.74	77.16
Writing	10.60	0.34	89.06
Striking match	9.95	8.74	81.31
Throwing ball	9.44	1.29	89.47
Hammering	9.22	2.54	88.24
Using toothbrush	9.18	8.49	82.33
Using racket	8.10	2.59	89.31
Using scissors	6.20	6.81	86.99

Note: Percentages are based on 2321 respondents.
Source: Annett, 1970.

Anatomical Studies

Hand preference is correlated with differential patterns of right–left asymmetry in the parietal operculum, frontal cortex, occipital region, vascular patterns, and cerebral blood flow, as summarized in Table 12.2. Thus, in comparison with right-handers, a higher proportion of left-handers show no asymmetry or, like L. P. at the beginning of this chapter, a reversal of left and right anatomical asymmetries.

Are variations in anatomical organization related in any meaningful way to handedness? To answer this question, Graham Ratcliffe and his colleagues correlated the asymmetry in the course of the Sylvian (lateral) fissure, as revealed by carotid angiogram, with the results of carotid sodium amobarbital speech testing (see Chapter 11). They found that left- and right-handers with speech in the left hemisphere had a mean right–left difference of 27° in the angle formed by the vessels leaving the posterior end of the Sylvian fissure. In left- and right-handers with speech in the right hemisphere or with bilaterally represented speech, the mean difference shrank to 0°.

Table 12.2   Variations in anatomical asymmetry related to handedness

Measure	Handedness	ANATOMICAL DIFFERENCES Left larger (%)	Right larger (%)	No difference (%)
Blood volume	Right	25	62	13
	Left	64	28	8
Parietal operculum	Right	67	8	25
	Left	22	7	71
Frontal width	Right	19	61	20
	Left	27	40	33
Occipital width	Right	66	9	25
	Left	38	27	35
Occipital horns	Right	60	10	30
	Left	38	31	31

Sources: Hochberg and LeMay (1975), LeMay (1977), and Carmon et al. (1972).

Thus, the anatomical asymmetry in their population was related to speech representation and not necessarily to handedness. The location of speech proved a better predictor of individual variation in cerebral organization than handedness.

Handedness may appear to be more closely related to anatomical anomalies because left-handers display more variation in lateralization of speech. A series of studies by Yakovlev and Rakic are germane. In a study of more than 300 cases, they found that, in 80%, the pyramidal tract descending to the right hand contains more fibers than does the same tract going to the left hand. Apparently, more fibers descend to the right hand both from the contralateral left hemisphere and from the ipsilateral right hemisphere than to the left hand. In addition, the contralateral tract from the left hemisphere crosses at a higher level in the medulla than does the contralateral tract from the right hemisphere.

Even though their sample was small—only 11 left-handers—the pattern was remarkably similar to that observed in the population at large: 9 of 11 (82%) had the typical right-side bias. Statistically, we expect that two-thirds of these left-handers have speech localized on the left; so there appears to be a closer relation between locus of language and pyramidal tract organization than between handedness and pyramidal tract organization.

A difficulty in accounting for variations in anatomical asymmetries is that some left- and right-handers show a marked dissociation between morphological (structural) and functional asymmetry. Thus, carotid sodium amobarbital testing may show speech to reside in the left hemisphere, but the enlarged temporoparietal speech zone is inferred from other neurological studies to be in the right hemisphere. Consider also that a large percentage of the right-handed cases summarized in Table 12.2 do not show the expected asymmetries but have reversed asymmetries or no differences at all. These cases do pose a significant interpretation problem, and they suggest that other variables, still unknown, may also account for individual differences in both left- and right-handers.

One possible variable is that the connections between the two hemispheres may differ. To test this idea Sandra Witelson studied the hand preference of terminally ill subjects on a variety of unimanual tasks. She later did postmortem studies of their brains, paying particular attention to the size of the corpus callosum. She found that the cross-sectional area was 11% greater in left-handed and ambidextrous people than in right-handed people.

Whether the larger callosum of non-right-handers contains a greater total number of fibers, thicker axons, or more myelin remains to be determined. If the larger callosum is due to the number of fibers, the difference would consist of some 25 million fibers. Confirmation of Witelson's result by others will imply greater interaction between the hemispheres of left-handers and will suggest that the pattern of cerebral organization may be fundamentally different in left- and right-handers.

Functional Cerebral Organization in Left-Handers

Although the belief that cognitive functions are more bilaterally organized in left-handers than in right-handers is widespread in the neurological literature, little evidence exists for this generalization. In Chapter 11, we considered the sodium amobarbital procedure and referred to the data of Rasmussen and Milner. They found that, in left-handers, language is represented in the left hemisphere in 70%, in the right hemisphere in 15%, and bilaterally in 15%.

Similarly, Kimura reported the incidence of aphasia and apraxia in a consecutive series of 520 patients selected for unilateral brain damage only. The frequency of left-handedness in her population was within the expected range, and these patients did not have a higher incidence of either aphasia or apraxia than right-handers did. In fact, the incidence of aphasia in left-handed patients was approximately 70% of the incidence in right-handers, exactly what would be predicted from the sodium amobarbital studies. Thus, although a small proportion of left-handers have bilateral speech or right-hemisphere speech, the majority of left-handers do not.

It has been suggested that left-handers can be subdivided into two genetic populations differing in cerebral organization: familial left-handers, who have a family history of left-handedness, and nonfamilial left-handers, who have no such family history. According to Hécaen and Sauguet, the performance of nonfamilial left-handed patients with unilateral lesions is like that of right-handed patients on neuropsychological tests. In contrast, familial left-handers perform much differently, suggesting to Hécaen and Sauguet that they have a different pattern of cerebral organization.

In summary, we can find little evidence that the cerebral organization of speech or nonspeech functions in the 70% of left-handers with speech represented in the left hemisphere differs from the cerebral organization of these functions in right-handers. One caveat must be stated, however: there is a larger incidence of left-handedness among mentally defective children and children with various neurological disorders than is found in the general population. This finding is not surprising, because, if the dominant hemisphere is injured at an early age, handedness and dominance can move under the control of what would normally be the nondominant hemisphere. Because there are so many more right-handed children, it can be expected by probability alone that more right-handed children with left-hemisphere damage would switch to right-hemisphere dominance than would switch in the reverse direction. That such switching can take place, however, cannot be used as grounds for predicting cognitive deficits or differences in cerebral organization in the general population of left-handers.

An additional question concerns the organization of the cerebral hemispheres in left-handers who have right-hemisphere speech. Is there simply a straight reversal of functions from one hemisphere to the other? Unfortunately, little is known about cerebral organization in people who have right-hemisphere speech and otherwise typical asymmetries.

Theories of Hand Preference

The many theories put forward to account for hand preference can be categorized broadly according to their environmental, anatomical, hormonal, or genetic emphases. Each category shelters widely varied points of view.

Environmental Theories

Three variations on an environmental theory of handedness stress either the utility of the behavior or reinforcement for hand use or a cerebral deficit caused by accident.

Behavioral utility. Sometimes called the theory of the Peloponnesian Wars, or the sword-and-shield hypothesis, the behavioral theory proposes that a soldier who held his shield in his left hand better protected his heart and improved his chances of survival. Because the left hand was holding the shield, the right hand became more skilled at various offensive and defensive movements, and eventually was used for most tasks. A female-oriented variant hypothesizes that it is adaptive for a mother to hold an infant in her left hand, to be soothed by the rhythm of her heart. The mother, like the soldier, uses the free right hand for executing skilled movements. Utility-of-behavior theories have difficulties, the most obvious being their failure to consider the probability that right-handedness preceded and is thus responsible for the behavior.

Environmental reinforcement. This variation states that handedness is established by a bias in the environment. The child's world is right-handed in many ways, which reinforces the use of that hand. In addition, children in many countries, including the United States, have been forced to write with their right hands. Although reinforcement theory emphasizes the potential importance of environmental factors, it does not account for biological factors such as differences between patterns of familial and nonfamilial handedness or the relation of handedness to cerebral dominance. Reinforcement theory also seems to be contradicted by what happened when children were given their choice of hand in learning to write: the incidence of left-handed writing rose to only 10%, which is the norm in most societies that have been studied.

Environmental accident. The third variation on environmental theory, postulates a genetically determined bias toward being right-handed. Left-handedness develops through a cerebral deficit caused by accident. This idea comes from correlating statistics on the incidence of left-handedness and neurological disorders in twins. About 18% of twins are left-handed, close to twice the occurrence in the population at large. Twins also show a high incidence of neurological disorders, which are suspected to result overwhelmingly from intrauterine crowding during fetal development and stress during delivery.

It is logical to conclude that stressful gestation and birth result in an elevated incidence of brain damage. Is left-handedness a form of brain damage? Bakan and his colleagues extended this logic to nontwins. They argued for a high probability of stressful births among left-handers, which increases the risk of brain damage to the infant and so maintains the statistical incidence of left-handedness. This theory was tested directly by Murray Schwartz, who tracked children beginning at age 2 and examined hospital records and maternal reports of birth stress. He did not find compelling support for the environmental accident theory.

Anatomical Theories

Among the several anatomical theories of handedness, two explain hand preference on the basis of anatomical asymmetry.

The first theory attributes right-handedness to enhanced maturation and ultimately greater development of the left hemisphere. Generalizing from this assumption, the theory predicts that nonfamilial left-handers will show an asymmetry mirroring that of right-handers, whereas familial left-handers will show no anatomical asymmetry. These predictions are difficult to assess, because no studies have specifically considered anatomical asymmetry with respect to handedness or to familial history and handedness. A major problem with this theory is that it simply pushes the question one step backward, asking not, "Why handedness?" but instead, "Why anatomical asymmetry?"

The second theory addresses this question in part. Many animals have a left-sided developmental advantage that is not genetically coded. For example, there is a left-sided bias for the location of the heart, the size of the ovaries in birds, the control of birdsong, the size of the left temporal cortex in humans, the size of the left side of the skull in the great apes, and so on. This predominance of left-favoring asymmetries puts the more celebrated left-hemisphere speech dominance in the more general, structural perspective of all anatomical asymmetries.

Because neither genetic evidence nor genetic theory accurately predicts these human asymmetries, Michael Morgan assumes that they all result from some fundamental asymmetries in human body chemistry. The problem with Morgan's theory as applied to handedness is that it fails to explain left-handedness in the presence of other "normal" asymmetries such as the location of the heart.

Hormonal Theories

Norman Geschwind and Albert Galaburda proposed that brain plasticity can modify cerebral asymmetry significantly during early life, leading to anomalous patterns of hemispheric organization. A central factor in their theory is the action of the sex-linked male hormone testosterone in altering cerebral organization during development. Testosterone does affect cerebral organization (discussed in detail later); so it is reasonable to suggest that differences in testosterone level might influence cerebral asymmetry, particularly if the testosterone receptors were asymmetrically distributed.

Geschwind and Galaburda suggested that testosterone's effect is largely inhibitory, meaning that higher-than-normal levels of testosterone will slow development, possibly acting directly on the brain or indirectly through an action on genes. Central to the Geschwind-Galaburda theory is the idea that testosterone's inhibitory action is largely in the left hemisphere, thus allowing the right hemisphere to grow more rapidly, which leads to altered cerebral organization and, in some people, to left-handedness. A further feature of the theory is that testosterone also affects the immune system, leading to more diseases related to a malfunctioning immune system. (A parallel theory of the relation between the immune system and male afflictions has been proposed by Gualtieri and Hicks.)

The Geschwind-Galaburda theory is elaborate and has generated considerable research. Unfortunately, the bulk of available evidence does not support the model (for a thorough review, see Bryden et al.). For example, in one study, Grimshaw and colleagues studied handedness in children whose mothers had undergone amniocentesis and therefore fetal levels of testosterone could be assessed. Increased testosterone levels did not result in increased left-handedness. Nonetheless, the data in the literature do show that left-handers are at greater risk for allergies and asthma, whereas autoimmune disorders such as arthritis are more prevalent in right-handers. These differences still require explanation.

Genetic Theories

Most genetic models for handedness postulate a dominant gene or genes for right-handedness and a recessive gene or genes for left-handedness (see Hardyck and Petrinovich for a review of these models). But the model that best predicts the actual number of left-handers in the population, by Annett, rejects this idea in favor of a dominant gene (rs^+) responsible for the development of speech in the left hemisphere.

Annett hypothesizes further that the processes necessary for left-hemisphere speech also confer an advantage on motor control in the right hand. The recessive form of the gene (rs^-) results in no systematic bias either for speech or for handedness. If both alleles occurred equally often statistically, then 50% of the population would be (rs^{+-}) and the rest would be equally divided, 25% (rs^{++}) and 25% (rs^{--}). People in the rs^{+-} and rs^{++} groups, constituting 75% of the population, would show a left-for-speech and right-handedness shift. The remaining 25%, people in the rs^{--} group, would show no bias; so half would, by chance, be left-handed.

Thus, Arnett's model predicts about 12.5% left-handers, which is pretty close to what we see in the population. Unfortunately, her theory neither predicts the number of left-handers with right-hemisphere speech nor attempts to differentiate between familial and nonfamilial left-handers.

From this review of theories of handedness, it is clear that we do not know why handedness occurs, and we may never know. From the various theories just presented, it does seem likely, however, that there is no single cause. There is undoubtedly some genetic basis for the development of left-handedness in some people, but how it relates to cerebral organization remains a mystery. For more on genetic relationship and brain structure, see the Snapshot on page 291.

Sex Differences in Cerebral Organization

One obvious source of individual variation in human behavior is sex: men and women behave differently. The question is whether any differences in cognitive behavior between men and women can be attributed to biological differences between the brains of the two sexes. Substantial anecdotal and experimental evidence reveals cognitive differences, and several researchers have attempted to relate them to differences in brain organization.

If one neurological principle can be abstracted to distinguish the sexes, it is that, on average, women tend to be more fluent than men in using language, and men tend to perform better than women in spatial analysis. But sex, like handedness, is not absolute. All men and women exhibit both male and female traits to greater and lesser degrees. As always, before considering the theories on differences in the pattern of cerebral organization between the sexes, we shall review the data.

Sex Differences in Behavior

In her book *Sex and Cognition*, Kimura examines five cognitive behaviors and finds compelling sex differences in all—namely, motor skills, spatial analysis, mathematical aptitude, perception, and verbal abilities. Table 12.3 summarizes her major conclusions and shows that the verbal–spatial dichotomy noted earlier is a gross oversimplification. We will briefly consider each class of behavior, as well as sex differences in aggression.

Table **12.3** Summary of sex differences in cognitive behavior

Behavior	Sex difference	Basic reference
Motor Skills		
Target throwing and catching	M > F	Hall and Kimura, 1995
Fine motor skills	F > M	Nicholson and Kimura, 1996
Spatial Analysis		
Mental rotation	M > F	Collins and Kimura, 1997
Spatial navigation	M > F	Astur et al., 2002
Geographical knowledge	M > F	Beatty and Troster, 1987
Spatial memory	F > M	McBurney et al., 1997
Mathematical Aptitude		
Computation	F > M	Hyde et al., 1990
Mathematical reasoning	M > F	Benbow, 1988
Perception		
Sensitivity to sensory stimuli	F > M	Velle, 1987
Perceptual speed	F > M	Majeres, 1983
Sensitivity to facial and body expression	F > M	Hall, 1984
Visual recognition memory	F > M	McGivern et al., 1998
Verbal Abilities		
Fluency	F > M	Hyde and Linn, 1988
Verbal memory	F > M	McGuinness et al., 1990

Motor Skills

One obvious difference in motor skills is that, on average, men are superior in throwing objects, such as balls or darts at targets, and are superior at intercepting objects thrown toward them. Although it could be concluded that the difference is related to practice, this conclusion is unlikely, because these differences are present in children as young as 3 years of age. Chimpanzees show a similar sexual dimorphism, although their motor control is far less accurate than that of humans. In contrast, women have superior fine motor control and surpass men in executing sequential and intricate hand movements. This difference is also unlikely to be related to experience, because young girls are superior to young boys at each of these skills.

Spatial Analysis

Although men are generally believed to be superior to women at spatial analysis, this belief applies to only some types of spatial behaviors. Men are superior at tasks requiring the mental rotation of objects, such as those illustrated in Figure 12.2, and they are superior at spatial navigation tasks. An example of the latter difference can be seen in a task illustrated in Figure 12.3. Subjects are given a tabletop map on which they must learn a designated route. On average, men learn such tasks faster and with fewer errors than women do. Although this map test is not a real-world test of spatial navigation, the findings are consistent with those of studies showing that men have better overall map knowledge than women.

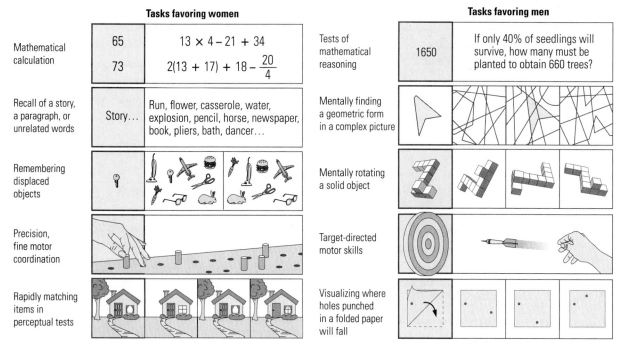

	Tasks favoring women			Tasks favoring men	
Mathematical calculation	65 73	$13 \times 4 - 21 + 34$ $2(13 + 17) + 18 - \dfrac{20}{4}$	Tests of mathematical reasoning	1650	If only 40% of seedlings will survive, how many must be planted to obtain 660 trees?
Recall of a story, a paragraph, or unrelated words	Story...	Run, flower, casserole, water, explosion, pencil, horse, newspaper, book, pliers, bath, dancer...	Mentally finding a geometric form in a complex picture		
Remembering displaced objects			Mentally rotating a solid object		
Precision, fine motor coordination			Target-directed motor skills		
Rapidly matching items in perceptual tests			Visualizing where holes punched in a folded paper will fall		

Figure 12.2 Tasks that illustrate sex differences in behavior. On average, women perform tests of calculation, verbal memory, object memory, fine motor skills, and perception better than men do. In contrast, on average, men perform tests of mathematical reasoning, geometric form perception, mental rotation, target-directed motor skills, and visual imaging better than women do.

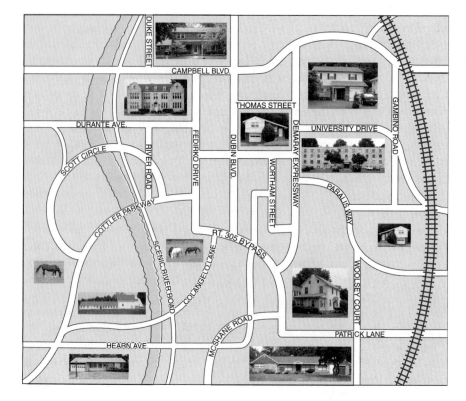

Figure 12.3 A representation of a tabletop map for route learning. Men learn routes in fewer trials than women do, but women recall more landmarks along the way. (After Kimura, 1999.)

Genetic Influences on Brain Structure

One way to investigate the contributions of genes and experience to cerebral organization is to analyze MRIs from normal brains and to vary the genetic relationships among the subjects. Thompson and colleagues varied genetic relatedness by comparing the MRIs of unrelated people, dizygotic twins, and monozygotic twins. They took advantage of recent advances in MRI mapping technology that allows detailed mapping of gray-matter distribution across the cerebral hemispheres.

The results were striking, as you can see in the adjoining illustration. The quantity of gray matter, especially in frontal, sensorimotor, and posterior language cortexes was dissimilar in unrelated people but almost identical in monozygotic twins. Because monozygotic twins are genetically identical, we can presume that any differences must be attributable to environmental effects. Curiously, there was an asymmetry in the degree of similarity, the left-hemisphere language zones being significantly more similar than the right in the monozygotic twins.

The high similarities among monozygotic twins likely accounts for their highly similar cognitive abilities. Similarly, given that various diseases, such as schizophrenia and some dementias, affect the integrity of the cortex, the high correlation between the brain structures of identical twins could account for the strong genetic component to these diseases.

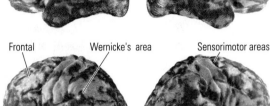

Unrelated subjects
Average differences in quantity of gray matter are shown as an even texture.

Fraternal twins
Lighter shading shows about a 30% reduction in differences especially in Wernicke's area.

Identical twins
The differences are even less (10–30%) and include frontal and sensorimotor areas.

Left hemisphere — Right hemisphere

Wernicke's area

Frontal — Wernicke's area — Sensorimotor areas

Average differences in quantity of gray matter in each cortical region for identical and fraternal twins, compared with average differences between pairs of randomly selected, unrelated persons. (After Thompson et al., 2001, p. 1254.)

(P. M. Thompson, T. D. Cannon, K. L. Narr, T. van Erp, V. P. Poutanen, M. Huttunen, J. Lonnqvist, C. G. Standertskjold-Nordenstam, J. Kaprio, M. Khaledy, R. Dail, C. I. Zoumalan, and A. W. Toga. Genetic influences on brain structure. *Nature Neuroscience* 4:1253–1258, 2001.)

Male superiority in spatial-navigation tasks contrasts with female superiority on tests of spatial memory, such as the one illustrated in Figure 12.2. Women are better than men at identifying which objects have been moved. In the map test (Figure 12.3), women have better recall for landmarks along the route. Thus, the spatial information itself is not the critical factor in this sex difference; rather, the critical factor is the required behavior—that is, the way in which the spatial information is to be used.

Mathematical Aptitude

The difference in mathematical ability is perhaps the oldest-established sex difference and it is undoubtedly the most controversial. On average, men get better scores on tests of mathematical reasoning, whereas women do better at tests of computation.

Perhaps the most interesting studies to date on mathematical aptitude were done by Camille Benbow and Julian Stanley. In 1971, Stanley founded the Study of Mathematically Precocious Youth. Within a 15-year period, thousands of 12-year-old children were given the Scholastic Aptitude Test Mathematics exam. Stanley was particularly interested in the children with the highest scores because they might be assumed to be least affected by extraneous environmental factors such as social pressures.

The curious thing discovered in the Stanley study is that the sex difference increased as the scores increased. That is, although the average score was only marginally higher for boys than for girls, when the researchers looked only at the children with the highest scores, they found an enormous sex difference: 12 times as many "gifted" boys as girls at the top. Furthermore, this ratio was found worldwide across different cultures, although the absolute scores varied with educational system. Benbow and Stanley have searched for support for a primarily environmental explanation of their data but have not found it.

Perception

Perception refers to the recognition and interpretation of the sensory information that we take in from the external world. There would appear to be no a priori reason to expect a sex difference, but the evidence suggests that women are more sensitive to all forms of sensory stimulation, except for vision. That is not to say that there is no difference in the perception of some types of visual material, however, because women are more sensitive than men to facial expressions and body postures. Not only do women have lower thresholds for detection, they also detect sensory stimuli faster. Males may have one perceptual advantage, however, in that their drawings of mechanical things such as bicycles are superior (Figure 12.4A). This particular advantage does not mean that they have a general advantage in drawing, as illustrated in Figure 12.4C.

Figure 12.4 Performance of boys and girls of different ages on three neuropsychological tests. (Whishaw and Kolb, unpublished.)

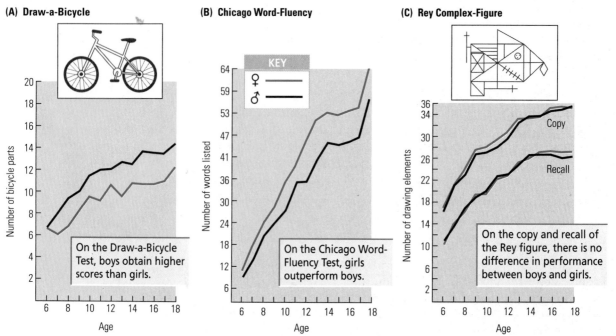

(A) Draw-a-Bicycle

Number of bicycle parts

On the Draw-a-Bicycle Test, boys obtain higher scores than girls.

Age

(B) Chicago Word-Fluency

KEY
♀
♂

Number of words listed

On the Chicago Word-Fluency Test, girls outperform boys.

Age

(C) Rey Complex-Figure

Number of drawing elements

Copy

Recall

On the copy and recall of the Rey figure, there is no difference in performance between boys and girls.

Age

Verbal Ability

Women are superior to men on tests of verbal fluency, on average, and they have superior verbal memory. The sex difference in verbal ability has long been known, in part because girls begin talking before boys and appear to be more fluent throughout life. For example, the Chicago Word-Fluency Test asks subjects to write as many words beginning with "s" as possible in 5 minutes and as many four-letter words beginning with "c" as possible in 4 minutes. As Figure 12.4B illustrates, girls performed better—at some ages by as many as 10 words—in a broad study that we did with children.

Aggression

Although not a cognitive behavior in the sense of verbal or spatial abilities, men are physically more aggressive than women. A sex difference is present as early as social play begins, at age 2 to 3 years, and remains through the college years. The results of studies on nonhuman primates and rodents show that the increased aggression in males is probably a result of the male hormone testosterone both pre- and postnatally. Castrating infant male rats or monkeys decreases aggression, and treating females with testosterone increases aggression.

Genes or Experience?

It is often argued that sex-related differences are related to life experience, but Kimura argues compellingly that this relation is unlikely for the cognitive behaviors summarized in Table 12.3. In particular, most if not all these differences, as well as differences in aggression, are found in both children and adults, and the differences are largely unaffected by training. There are certainly training effects on most tests, but the effects tend to be of similar magnitude in both sexes.

Furthermore, some sex differences seem unrelated to life experience. Consider the test illustrated in Figure 12.5. The task is to draw in the water line in a series of half-filled, tilted glass jars. Women consistently underperform on this task relative to men, and this difference is seen in both young and old subjects and in university students whether science or nonscience majors. The difference in performance is due not to the inability of women to understand the concept that the water line will always be horizontal but rather to the fact that women are more affected by the tilt of the jar than are men. The difference remains even if women are given training on the test.

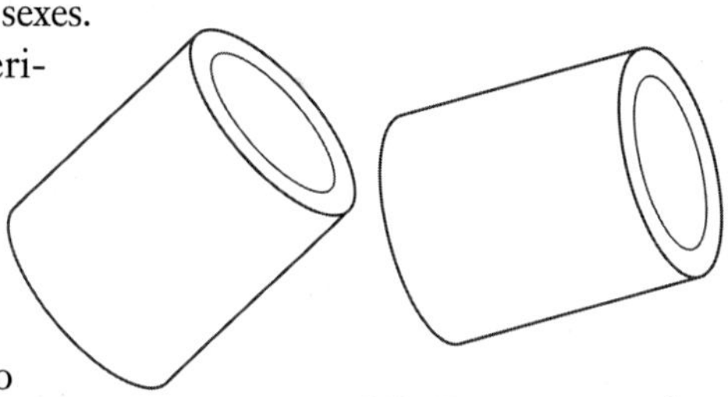

Figure 12.5 A water-level task. In each jar, the water line must be drawn.

Sex Differences in Brain Structure

A complicating factor in analyzing sex differences in cerebral organization is that the male brain is larger than the female brain, and differences in body size cannot account for this difference. In one study, Ankney compared the brains of men and women of the same body size and found that men's brains are about 100 g heavier than women's throughout the range of body sizes. In another study, Pakkenberg and Gundersen found that the male brains in their sample had about 4 billion more neurons than the female brains, and body size did not account for this difference.

What such a difference might mean is not immediately apparent, in part because the connections of the neurons give clues to how they might function. Nonetheless, some researchers (Alexopoulis, for example, and Lynn) have

Table 12.4 **Summary of sex differences in gross brain anatomy**

Sex difference	Basic reference
Differences Favoring Female Brains	
Larger language areas	Harasty et al., 1997
Larger medial paralimbic areas	Filipek et al., 1994
Larger lateral frontal areas	Schlaepfer et al., 1995
Greater relative amount of gray matter	Gur et al., 1999
More densely packed neurons in temporal lobe	Witelson et al., 1995
Differences Favoring Male Brains	
Larger medial frontal areas	Goldstein et al., 2001
Larger cingulate areas	Paus et al., 1996
Larger amygdala and hypothalamus	Swaab et al., 1985
Larger overall white matter volume	Gur et al., 1999
Larger cerebral ventricles	Murphy et al., 1996
Larger right planum parietale	Janke et al., 1994
More neurons overall	Pakkenberg and Gunderson, 1997

concluded that men have a small (4 points) advantage in IQ scores, on average. Needless to say, this idea has proved to be controversial (as indicated by other articles published in the same issue of the journal containing the Lynn article).

Is the sex difference in brain size related to a sex difference in cerebral asymmetry? When different cerebral regions are examined separately, with the results being corrected for relative size of the cerebrum of different brains, the findings of many studies show areal-dependent sex differences, as summarized in Table 12.4. Sex-related differences in brain volume are not diffusely spread across the cerebral hemispheres. In general, female brains appear to have larger volumes in regions associated with language functions, in medial paralimbic regions, and in some frontal lobe regions. In addition, women have a greater relative amount of gray matter and, at least in the planum temporale, they have more densely packed neurons. Conversely, men have a larger medial frontal and cingulate region, a larger amygdala, and a larger hypothalamus. They also have a larger overall white matter volume and larger cerebral ventricles.

A proposed contrasting organizational difference is that male brains tend to have more neurons and female brains more neuropil (that is, dendrites and axons) per neuron. This conclusion is likely an overgeneralization and may depend on the particular brain region or cortical layer under investigation.

Figure 12.6 Sex differences in brain volume relative to cerebral size. Women have significantly higher volumes in the major frontal and medial paralimbic regions (blue) than those of men, whereas men have larger relative volumes in the medial frontal cortex and the angular gyrus (dark gray). The blue areas correspond to regions in which there are high levels of estrogen receptors during development; the dark gray to regions high in androgen receptors during development. (After Goldstein et al., 2001.)

The Influence of Sex Hormones

The presence of sex differences in brain structure has been related to differences in the distribution of estrogen and androgen receptors during development. Goldstein and her colleagues did a large MRI study of sexual dimorphism in the male and female brain (Figure 12.6). Sex differences were largest in regions of the human brain in which the results of studies of nonhumans have shown that there are sex differences in the developmental expression of estrogen or androgen receptors. Thus, the Goldstein team proposed that a large part of the observed sex differences in cerebral organization is related to differences in the distribution of receptors for gonadal hormones during development.

The investigators noted that their conclusions have limitations because they do not consider differences in cerebral organization that might be related to circulating hormones in adulthood. Furthermore, the findings in many studies suggest that the rate of cell death during aging may be higher in men than in women, especially in the frontal lobe; so we must consider the possibility that some of the sex differences observed in adults may not be present in childhood.

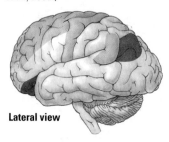

Lateral view   **Medial view**

Established Asymmetries

The presence of sex differences in overall size and in relative size of different regions does not speak directly to the question of whether there are sex differences in the degree of cerebral asymmetry. Although the cerebral hemispheres of women are often said to be more symmetrical than those of men, this conclusion is based largely on nonsignificant trends or impressions. There are, however, several reliable sex differences in anatomical asymmetry:

1. Asymmetry (left larger than right) in the planum temporale is seen more often in men than in women. In fact, an MRI study by Kulynych and colleagues found a large asymmetry in males (left 38% larger) but no asymmetry in females. This result is not found universally, however (Aboitiz et al. obtained different results); so we must interpret it with caution.

2. Witelson and Kigar quantified the slope of the Sylvian fissure with reference to various cortical landmarks (Figure 12.7A). This quantification led to a separate measure of the horizontal and vertical components of the Sylvian fissure. They found that, although the horizontal component was longer in the left hemisphere of both sexes, men had a larger horizontal component in the left hemisphere than did women. There was no difference in the right hemisphere. Thus, male brains have a larger asymmetry in the Sylvian fissure than do female brains. Taken together, the results of the studies of the planum temporale and the Sylvian fissure reinforce evidence of a sex difference in the organization of language-related functions.

3. Jancke and colleagues found that the asymmetry in the planum parietale, which favors the right hemisphere, is about twice as large in men as in women.

4. Numerous studies claim that women have more interhemispheric connections, in both the corpus callosum and the anterior commissure, than do men. The callosal studies have proved controversial, but the consensus appears to be that the posterior part of the callosum (the **splenium**) is significantly larger in women than in men (Figure 12.7B and Table 12.5). The sex difference found in the anterior commissure, a structure that connects the temporal lobes, appears to be less controversial (see Chapter 17). Allen and Gorski found that women have a larger anterior commissure than do men, even without correcting for brain size. This difference is likely due to a difference in the number of neural fibers in the two sexes, a difference presumably due to some difference in the way in which the two hemispheres interact.

5. The ridges in our fingerprints, which are established early in fetal life, are asymmetrical, with the fingers on the right hand having more ridges

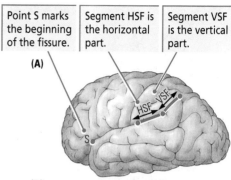

| Point S marks the beginning of the fissure. | Segment HSF is the horizontal part. | Segment VSF is the vertical part. |

(A)

(B)

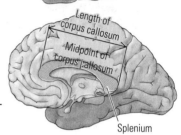

Length of corpus callosum

Midpoint of corpus callosum

Splenium

Figure 12.7 Measuring the brain. (A) Side view of the human brain illustrating the measuring points on the Sylvian fissure. (B) The human corpus callosum shown in midsagittal section. The subdivisions that are typically measured are indicated: the entire length and cross-sectional area; the anterior and posterior halves; and the splenium.

Table 12.5 Summary of brain measures in four groups classified by handedness and sex

Group	Number in group	Age (years)	Brain weight (g)	Callosal area (mm²)
Males				
RH	7	48	1442	672
MH	5	49	1511	801[a]
Females				
RH	20	51	1269	655
MH	10	49	1237	697[a]

Note: RH, consistently right-handed; MH, left-handed or ambidextrous.
[a]Differs significantly from other same-sex group.
Source: Simplified from Witelson, 1985.

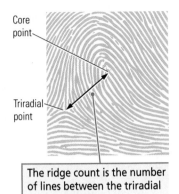

Core point

Triradial point

The ridge count is the number of lines between the triradial and core points.

Figure 12.8 A fingerprint pattern. A line is drawn from the triradial point at the left to the core point at the right.

than fingers on the left (see Figure 12.8). Given that this pattern is visible in utero, it could not be influenced by environmental factors such as differences in limb use. Kimura found that most people have the asymmetry, but women are far more likely to show an atypical pattern, much as we saw for brain asymmetries. The critical part of the Kimura studies (and later studies by others) is that the pattern of ridges is correlated with performance on certain cognitive tests, a finding we shall return to shortly.

Kimura also followed up on the studies of others looking at asymmetries in sexually dimorphic body parts—namely, the size of the testes in men and of the ovaries and breasts in women. She found that, whereas the right testicle tends to be larger than the left testicle, the ovaries and breasts tend to be larger on the left than on the right. Importantly, the sex difference in gonad size is found in fetuses. Once again, we must ask what such a finding might mean. At this time, the meaning is not obvious, but one conclusion is inescapable. If there is an asymmetry in gonad size that is sexually dimorphic, then there is every reason to also expect sex differences in other body regions, especially in those, such as the brain, that are influenced by gonadal hormones.

Sex Differences Revealed in Imaging Studies

The results of virtually all types of neuroimaging studies show sex-related differences, as summarized in Table 12.6. In general, EEG, MEG, and fMRI studies show more asymmetrical activity in men than in women, particularly in language-related activities. Measures of blood flow, including those obtained with the use of PET, show that women have more rapid overall blood exchange than do men, possibly due to the difference in the density of neurons or the distribution of gray matter and white matter.

The main point to take from these results is that not only are there differences in the anatomical organization of the male and female brain, but there are differences in the functional activity of the brains as well, a result that is hardly surprising. Presumably, the anatomical differences correspond to the functional differences that researchers have found.

Table 12.6 Sex differences in imaging studies

Measure	Result	Representative reference
EEG	Males more asymmetrical	Corsi-Cabrera et al., 1997
MEG	Males more asymmetrical	Reite et al., 1995
Blood flow	Females > males	Gur et al., 1982
	Females > males in frontal lobe tests	Esposito et al., 1996
PET	Males > females in anterior blood flow	Haverkort et al., 1999
	Females > males in posterior blood flow	
fMRI	More left-hemisphere activity in language-related tasks (but see Frost et al., 1999) in males	Pugh et al., 1996

Research with Neurological Patients

If the brains of females and males differ in anatomical organization as well as in metabolic activity as indicated by the results of blood-flow and fMRI studies, then the effects of injury also might differ. Two types of lesion-related differences are possible:

1. *Degree of asymmetry in the lesion effects.* Such a difference might exist if the two hemispheres were more similar functionally in one sex than in the

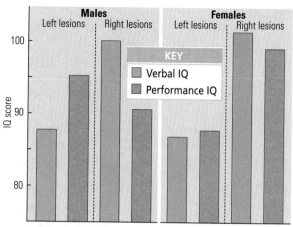

other sex. Indeed, the greater asymmetry observed in EEG, MEG, and fMRI studies in men suggests that men might show more asymmetrical effects of unilateral lesions than women.

2. *Intrahemispheric organization.* Injury to the frontal lobe might have greater effects in one sex than in the other, a difference that would be consistent with greater relative volume of much of the frontal lobes of women.

In fact, there is evidence of both effects.

One way to assess the asymmetry of left- or right-hemisphere lesions is to look at the effects of the lesions on general tests of verbal and nonverbal abilities. A way of measuring this difference is to examine the pattern of results in the effects of lateralized lesions on the performance and verbal achievement subscales of the Wechsler Adult Intelligence Scale (WAIS; see Chapter 28 for details on this IQ test). By using various statistical procedures with these data, Inglis and Lawson showed that, although left- and right-hemisphere lesions in men affected the verbal and performance subscales differently, left-hemisphere lesions in women depressed both IQ scores equally, and right-hemisphere lesions in women failed to depress either score (Figure 12.9).

Thus, Inglis and Lawson found an equivalent effect of left-hemisphere lesions on verbal IQ in both sexes, but men with right-hemisphere lesions were more disrupted than women were. This finding could imply that right-hemisphere organization differed in men and women. This conclusion seems unlikely, however, because there is no evidence of a sex difference in a variety of symptoms commonly associated with right-hemisphere damage. On the other hand, women could be more likely than men to use verbal strategies (that is, a verbal cognitive mode) to solve the tests in the WAIS.

Work by Kimura shows that the pattern of cerebral organization *within* each hemisphere also differs between the sexes. Men and women are almost equally likely to be aphasic subsequent to left-hemisphere lesions. But men are likely to be aphasic and apraxic after damage to the left posterior cortex, whereas women are far more likely to experience speech disorders and apraxia after anterior lesions (Figure 12.10). Kimura also obtained data from a small sample of patients that suggest an analogous sex-related difference subsequent to right-hemisphere lesions. Anterior, but not posterior, lesions in women impaired their performance of the block-design and object-assembly subtests of the WAIS, whereas men were equally affected on these tests by either anterior or posterior lesions.

Figure 12.9 Summary of Inglis and Lawson's tabulation of studies reporting verbal and performance IQ scores in neurological patients. A clear sex difference emerged in which males with left-hemisphere lesions exhibited a depression in verbal IQ, whereas males with right-hemisphere lesions exhibited a complementary deficit in performance IQ. In contrast, females with right-hemisphere lesions showed no significant depression in either IQ scale.

Figure 12.10 Evidence for intrahemispheric differences in cortical organization of males and females. Apraxia is associated with frontal damage to the left hemisphere in women and with posterior damage in men. Aphasia develops most often when damage is to the front of the brain in women but to the rear of the brain in men. (After Kimura, 1999.)

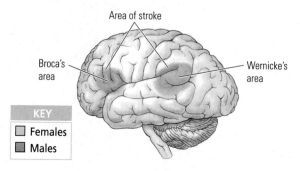

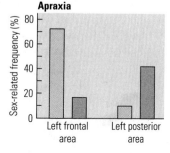

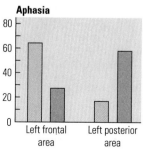

We have found parallel results in our studies of rats with prefrontal lesions: male rats with these lesions have much smaller deficits in various tests of spatial navigation than do female rats with similar lesions. This finding may suggest a fundamental difference between the sexes in the intracerebral organization in mammals. In fact, in an anatomical study, we were able to show a large difference between male and female rats in the dendritic organization of neurons in the prefrontal cortex. This sex difference was affected by treatments that either increased or decreased testosterone levels during prenatal development.

Finally, Esther Strauss and her colleagues obtained a surprising result. They gave sodium amobarbital to 94 epileptic patients who were being considered for elective surgery after infant brain damage. It is well known that left-hemisphere injury in infancy leads to the shifting of language to the right hemisphere; so Strauss expected this shift to happen in those patients with left-hemisphere injury. The unexpected result was a sex difference in the likelihood of cerebral reorganization subsequent to left-hemisphere injury after 1 year of age: girls were unlikely to show reorganization, whereas boys appeared likely to shift language, perhaps as late as puberty. This unexpected result suggests that the male brain may be more plastic after cortical injury, a conclusion that has important implications if it proves reliable. Curiously, this greater plasticity is exactly what was found (in a study by Kolb and Stewart) for rats with neonatal prefrontal lesions: males showed better recovery and more synaptic changes than did females.

Taken together, the data from neurological patients support the idea that unilateral cortical lesions have different effects on male and female brains. The precise nature of the differences is still under debate, however.

Explanations of Sex Differences

We have considered sex differences in cerebral organization as inferred from studies of behavior, anatomy, imaging, and neurological patients. Why are these differences present? We can identify five explanations commonly advanced to account for sex differences: (1) hormonal effects on cerebral function, (2) genetic sex linkage, (3) maturation rate, (4) environment, and (5) preferred cognitive mode.

Hormonal Effects

Clear sex differences are apparent in the neural control of a wide variety of reproductive and nonreproductive behavioral patterns in most vertebrate species. In birds and mammals, the presence of testosterone at critical times in the course of development has unequivocal effects on the organization of both hypothalamic and forebrain structures, and the observed morphological effects are believed to be responsible for the behavioral dimorphism. The influence of gonadal hormones on brain and behavioral development is often referred to as an *inductive* or *organizing* effect and, in the brain, this organizing effect is said to lead to *sexual differentiation*.

The actions of gonadal hormones (largely androgens) during development are permanent, but the mechanisms of action are still not well understood. Androgens (typically "male" hormones) appear to be converted into estradiol (normally "female" hormones) in the brain, and the binding of this estradiol to receptors leads to masculinization of the brain. Estradiol receptors have been found in the cortexes of developing rodents and nonhuman primates, but they are not found in the adults. This finding suggests that the hormones may have an organizing effect on the brains of mammals only during development, although they can still influence neuronal function later in life. As mentioned earlier, regions of the human brain that have clear sex-related differences in adulthood are the same ones that have a high density of estrogen receptors during development (see Figure 12.6).

Although the principal organizing action of sex hormones is assumed to occur during development, there might be longer significant functional effects of hormones in adulthood. One way to test this hypothesis would be to see if there is a relation between behavior and the level of hormones observed at different times in adults of each sex. The collection of data relating hormone levels to cognitive functions has been made much easier in recent years by the advent of testing hormone levels in saliva. For example, Hampson and Kimura showed that the performance of women on certain tasks changes throughout the menstrual cycle as estrogen levels rise and fall. High estrogen levels are associated with relatively depressed spatial ability as well as enhanced articulatory and motor capability.

The effect of estrogen fluctuations during the menstrual cycle may be direct or indirect. Catecholamine (for example, epinephrine and dopamine) levels are affected by estrogen, and catecholamine levels fluctuate during the estrous cycle in rats. In view of the importance of catecholamines in movement and other behaviors, estrogen could obviously alter behavior through its stimulation of dopamine receptors in particular. There are dopamine receptors in the prefrontal cortex and medial temporal region; so the possibility that estrogen alters functioning in these regions is reasonable.

Estrogen also directly affects the structure of neurons. Woolley and her colleagues showed that, during the female rat's estrous cycle, there are large changes in the number of dendritic spines on hippocampal neurons (Figure 12.11). Thus the number of synapses in the female rat's hippocampus goes up and down *in 4-day cycles*. There is little reason to believe that similar changes are not also taking place in the human brain, albeit at a slower pace. Similarly, female rats that have their ovaries removed in middle age show a dramatic increase in dendrites and spines of cortical neurons (see Stewart and Kolb). Although in the latter study such changes were not correlated with cyclic fluctuations in the estrogen levels, the results are consistent with the general idea that estrogen has direct effects on cerebral neurons in the adult animal.

There is also reason to believe that testosterone affects cognition in men. The level of testosterone in men fluctuates both seasonally and daily. Testosterone levels in men are higher in the fall than in the spring, and they are higher in the morning than in the evening. Kimura showed that men's spatial scores fluctuate with testosterone levels: men with *lower* testosterone levels get the highest scores. So there appears to be an optimal level of testosterone, and increasing the level is actually detrimental to cognitive performance.

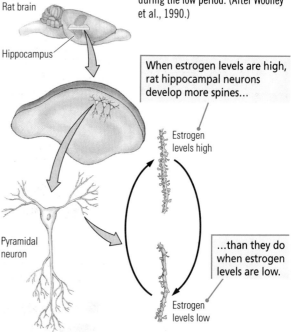

Figure 12.11 Dendrites of hippocampal pyramidal neurons at high and low levels of estrogen in the rat's (4-day) estrous cycle. There are many fewer dendritic spines during the low period. (After Woolley et al., 1990.)

Rat brain

Hippocampus

When estrogen levels are high, rat hippocampal neurons develop more spines...

Estrogen levels high

Pyramidal neuron

...than they do when estrogen levels are low.

Estrogen levels low

Thus, men do better at the spatial tests in the spring and in the evening. Furthermore, men with lower average levels of testosterone do better on both spatial tests and on mathematical reasoning tests than do those with higher levels. A reasonable question is whether there is also a relation between testosterone level and spatial ability in women. There is. Women with higher levels do better, again suggesting that some optimal hormone level benefits at least some cognitive activities.

Finally, we might ask whether administering testosterone to men with very low levels might improve spatial ability. In the early part of the twentieth century, testosterone was believed to be able to reverse senescence, but there is little evidence that the hundreds of men given testicular implants actually benefited from this treatment (an interesting book about this treatment is *The Monkey Gland Affair* by Hamilton). Nonetheless, recent evidence suggests that testosterone treatments may influence spatial cognition in older men. Jery Janowsky and her colleagues gave retired men testosterone (or placebo) in scrotal patches and found a significant improvement in the performance of spatial tasks but not in verbal or other cognitive measures.

Interestingly, when the researchers measured blood-hormone levels, they found a decrease in estradiol as well as an increase in testosterone. The low estradiol levels correlated with the improved spatial performance, which would be predicted from the results of Hampson's study of monthly fluctuations in women. In other words, it may be that the suppression of estrogen is more beneficial than the presence of testosterone.

The results from studies of men lead to the question of the role of hormone replacement therapy in menopausal women. The data are controversial, but one consistent finding is that estrogen treatment in postmenopausal women improves verbal memory.

In summary, gonadal hormones unquestionably have significant effects on brain development and function. Although little direct evidence points to how these effects might relate to the sex differences in cognitive function, there is good reason to suppose that at least some sex differences are related to gonadal hormones.

Perhaps the most interesting possibility is that gonadal hormones alter the brain and make male and female brains more or less responsive in different environments. One way that they have such an influence is by altering the susceptibility of cortical neurons to the effects of environmental stimuli. For example, Janice Juraska found that exposure to gonadal hormones perinatally (that is, near birth) determines the later ability of environmental stimulation to alter the synaptic organization of the cerebrum. Furthermore, she showed that environmentally induced changes in the hippocampus and neocortex are affected differently by gonadal hormones. For instance, the female hippocampus is far more plastic in new environments than the male hippocampus, and this plasticity depends on estrogen.

This type of hormonally mediated selective effect of experience on the brain is important because it provides a route whereby experiential factors (including social factors) could influence the male and female brain differently, leading to sex-related variations in brain and behavior. The fact that sex hormones are important to cerebral function in adults leads to an interesting possibility: the cognitive functions of the two sexes may diverge functionally at puberty and begin to converge again after menopause. We are unaware of any direct test of this hypothesis.

Genetic Sex Linkage

A number of investigators have proposed that the major factor in determining variation in spatial ability is genetic. A recessive gene on the X (female) chromosome is postulated to be responsible. Every normal person has 46 chromosomes arranged in 23 pairs, one set from the father and one from the mother. The 23rd pair is composed of the sex chromosomes; if both sex chromosomes are X, the child is female (XX) but, if one sex chromosome is X and the other is Y, the child is male (XY).

If a gene for a particular trait, such as spatial analysis, is recessive, the trait will not be expressed in a girl unless the recessive gene is present on both X chromosomes. However, the recessive gene need be present only on one chromosome if the child is a boy. Thus, if a mother carries the gene on both X chromosomes, all her sons will have the trait, but her daughters will possess it only if their father also carries the recessive gene on his X chromosome. This hypothesis has generated a lot of interest and research, but a thorough review by Boles concludes that it has yet to be proved.

Maturation Rate

The results of developmental studies indicate that a fundamental difference in male and female cerebral maturation may help to account for the sex differences observed in adulthood. It has long been known that girls begin to speak sooner than boys, develop larger vocabularies in childhood, and, as children, use more complex linguistic constructions than boys do. Further, the speech of young girls may be better enunciated than boys' speech, and girls are generally better readers.

Although developmental studies of laterality in children yield conflicting results, findings from dichotic and tachistoscopic studies often indicate an earlier evolution of cerebral asymmetry in girls than in boys. Because girls attain physical maturity at an earlier age than boys do, it is reasonable to propose that the male brain matures more slowly than the female brain and that maturation rate is a critical determinant of brain asymmetry. That is, the more slowly a child matures, the greater the observed cerebral asymmetry.

A study by Waber demonstrates just this finding. She found that, regardless of sex, early-maturing adolescents performed better on tests of verbal abilities than on tests of spatial ones, whereas late-maturing adolescents did the opposite. Her findings, then, imply that maturation rate may affect the organization of cortical function. Because, on average, girls mature faster than boys, superior spatial abilities in boys may be directly related to their relatively slow development.

Environment

Probably the most influential psychological view of sex-related differences is that environmental factors shape the behaviors. For example, in regard to spatial ability, boys are expected to exhibit greater independence than girls and thus to engage in activities such as exploring and manipulating the environment—activities that improve spatial skills.

Harris considered all the research support for this argument and concluded that, although a few studies can be found to support the environmental view, the bulk of the evidence fails to do so. For example, in the study by Hoben Thomas and colleagues on the horizontality of a liquid (see Figure 12.5), women who failed the task were repeatedly shown a bottle half-filled with red water that was tilted at various angles. They were asked to adjust the "pretend waterline" by moving a disk, half red, half white, in a second bottle. Even when the subjects simply had to adjust the pretend waterline to match the visible real waterline, these women failed to show much improvement and were likely to state that "water is level when the bottle is upright but is inclined when the bottle is tilted."

Men and women who perform correctly state that "water is always level." A priori, one would expect that women have as much experience as men with tilting vessels and, even if they do not, that special instruction would be helpful. This, however, does not seem to be the case. In conclusion, although environmental theories may be appealing, there is no evidence that environmental or social factors can solely account for the observed sex differences in verbal and spatial behaviors.

Preferred Cognitive Mode

As already mentioned, the difference in strategies used by men and women to solve problems may be at least partly responsible for the observed sex differences in behavior. Genetic, maturational, and environmental factors may predispose men and women to prefer different modes of cognitive analysis. Women solve problems primarily by using a verbal mode, for example. Because this cognitive mode is less efficient in solving spatial problems, women exhibit an apparent deficit, on average. By the same logic, women should do better than men at primarily verbal tasks, on average. This proposition has yet to be thoroughly investigated.

Conclusions

At least six significant behavioral differences are sex related: verbal ability, visuospatial analysis, mathematical ability, perception, motor skills, and aggression. Although the precise causes of cognitive sex-related differences are unknown, biology likely plays a part. Consider the following data: Richard Harshman and his associates, in a very ambitious study of the interaction of sex and handedness in cognitive abilities, found a significant interaction between sex and handedness; that is, sex-related differences in verbal and visuospatial behavior vary as a function of handedness. (Recall that Witelson found that callosal size also varies by sex and handedness.) It is difficult to imagine how biological or environmental factors alone could account for this result. It is thus very plausible to account for sex-related differences partly by neurological factors that may be modulated by the environment.

Environmental Effects on Asymmetry

The environment produces significant effects on brain growth in laboratory animals, and so it is reasonable to hypothesize that different environments affect the human brain differently and produce variation in the pattern of cerebral asymmetry. Two broad environmental variables are especially good candidates: culture, especially language, and a range of environmental deficits.

Culture and Language

Most studies of cultural differences center on language. Asian languages such as Japanese and Chinese might promote more right-hemisphere involvement than European languages, because the Asian languages appear to have more prosody (or song). Those who speak two or more languages may develop a different pattern of language organization from that of those who speak only one.

The results of laterality studies lend some support to the idea that Asian and Native American languages may be represented more bilaterally in the brain than, for example, Spanish. However, as we have seen, laterality studies can be influenced by many factors, such as strategy and task requirements. Thus inferring cultural differences in brain organization from the results of these studies should be done with caution. (Good discussions of the difficulties can be found in Uyehara and Cooper, as well as in Obler et al.)

The results of studies of neurological patients provide no evidence for culturally or linguistically based differences in cerebral organization. A good example is a study by Rapport and coworkers. They evaluated the language functions of seven Chinese-English polyglots whose mother tongues were Malay, Cantonese, or Hokkien. Their methods included the use of carotid sodium amobarbital, cortical stimulation, and clinical examination. They found that all these patients were left-hemisphere dominant for both the Chinese and the English languages; there was no consistent evidence of increased participation by the right hemisphere for language functions.

All language is probably located in the left hemisphere of bilingual people, but the possibility that their left-hemisphere language zones are enlarged or slightly different in microorganization from those who speak only a single language cannot be ruled out. Experience is known to alter somatosensory organization; so an analogous effect of experience on the language zones is a reasonable expectation. However, the major effects of language and environment on the brain are likely on the development of particular styles of problem solving (that is, preferred cognitive mode) that heavily depend on culture rather than on changes in cerebral asymmetry.

Exposure to multiple languages could be expected to change the normal pattern of brain organization, but, again, this change does not appear to happen. The results of PET studies by Klein and her colleagues showed, for example, that no difference appears in the cerebral activation for various language tasks performed in English and French or English and Chinese by bilingual subjects. In particular, no activation of the right hemisphere was recorded for any task in either language. There may, however, be subtle differences in the cerebral representation of different languages within the left hemisphere. Using fMRI, Kim and coworkers showed that languages acquired later in life may activate different, although adjacent, frontal regions from those activated by first languages or second languages acquired early in life.

The Japanese writing system provides an unusual opportunity for studying cerebral organization because, unlike Indo-European writing, it consists of two types of symbols: phonograms (kana) and ideograms (kanji). Phonograms are analogous to English letters; each phonogram represents a spoken sound. In contrast, the ideogram represents a unit of meaning, which may correspond to a word or words. In reading, the brain may process these two types of characters differently; furthermore, the right hemisphere might process kanji while the left hemisphere processes kana. There is little support for either idea. For example, in a large series of patients, Sugishita and his colleagues found no clear relation between deficits in reading either script and locus of left-hemisphere injury. In fact, most of their cases were impaired equally in both forms of reading.

Sensory or Environmental Deficits

Both education and congenital deafness are alleged to alter hemispheric specialization. The evidence that schooling changes cerebral organization is scanty and inconclusive. However, this evidence is based largely on the results of laterality studies, which are difficult to interpret. Furthermore, illiterate aphasics do not appear to differ from those who are educated. On the other hand, there is some evidence that congenital deafness may alter cerebral processing.

Brain Organization in Nonhearing People

As for hearing people, left-hemisphere damage produces aphasia in people who converse by using American Sign Language (Ameslan), possibly because of the praxic requirements. But there is evidence that the congenitally deaf may have atypical patterns of cerebral organization.

First, several laboratories report independently that congenitally deaf persons fail to show the usual right-visual-field superiority in tasks of linguistic processing. This failure could be interpreted as evidence that, if experience with auditory language is absent, lateralization of some aspect or aspects of nonauditory language function is abolished. Or these data could result from strategy differences (cognitive mode again) due to the absence of auditory experience.

Second, Helen Neville reported that, during the perception of line drawings, visual evoked potentials were significantly larger on the right in children with normal hearing and significantly larger on the left in deaf children who used Ameslan to communicate. Curiously, there was no asymmetry at all in deaf children who could not sign but merely used pantomime to communicate. From the signers' left-hemisphere effect for line drawings, Neville inferred that the deaf signers acquire their visual signing symbols much as hearing children acquire auditory verbal symbols: with the left hemisphere.

Thus, visuospatial functions may have developed in the left hemisphere of people who sign, producing an unexpected left-hemisphere effect. The lack of asymmetry in nonsigners could mean that the absence of language experience somehow abolished certain aspects of cerebral asymmetry or, alternatively, that the expression of cerebral asymmetry depends on language experience. If the nonsigners learn Ameslan and do so before puberty, they might develop an asymmetrical evoked-potential pattern similar to that of their contemporaries who already sign.

Although congenital deafness may be suspected to affect the development of certain aspects of cerebral lateralization, the results of studies of brain-injured patients show little difference between hearing and nonhearing subjects. Hickock and coworkers studied 34 congenitally deaf patients who had unilateral brain injury. Left-hemisphere patients performed poorly on all measures of language use, whereas right-hemisphere patients performed poorly on visuospatial tasks—exactly what would be expected in hearing people. Exposure to spoken language obviously was not necessary for hemispheric specialization.

Environmental Deprivation

Evidence pointing to early environment as a factor in asymmetry is based on a study of Genie, an adolescent girl who endured nearly 12 years of extreme social and experiential deprivation and malnutrition. She was discovered at the age of 13½, after having spent most of her life isolated in a small closed room, during which time she was punished for making any noise. After her rescue, Genie's cognitive development was rapid, although her language lagged behind other abilities.

Results of her dichotic listening tests proved provocative for a right-handed person: although both ears showed normal hearing, there was a strong left-ear (hence right-hemisphere) effect for both verbal and nonverbal (environmental) sounds. In fact, the right ear was nearly totally suppressed, a phenomenon characteristic of people with severe left-hemisphere injury. Genie's right hemisphere appeared to be processing both verbal and nonverbal acoustical stimuli, as would be the case in people with a left hemispherectomy in childhood.

At least three explanations for Genie's abnormal lateralization are plausible. The first is that disuse of the left hemisphere may simply have resulted in degeneration, which seems unlikely. The second is that, in the absence of appropriate auditory stimulation, the left hemisphere lost the ability to process linguistic stimuli. This explanation is possible because, without early exposure to foreign languages, adults have difficulty in learning many phoneme discriminations, even though they were able to make these discriminations as infants (see Werker and Tees). The third explanation is that Genie's left hemisphere was either being inhibited by the right hemisphere or by some other structure or it was performing other functions.

Effects of Hemispherectomy

If life-threatening seizures result from severe infantile cerebral injury, the neocortex of an entire hemisphere may be surgically removed to control the seizures (see the vignette about A. R. at the beginning of Chapter 10). Although most hemispherectomies are performed in the patient's early adolescence, the surgery is sometimes done in the first year of life, before speech has developed. The latter case is particularly germane to the question of how cerebral lateralization develops. If the hemispheres vary functionally at birth, then the left and right hemispherectomies would be expected to produce different effects on cognitive abilities. If they do not vary at birth, then no cognitive differences would result from left or right hemispherectomies.

The general results of studies of linguistic and visuospatial abilities in patients with unilateral hemidecortications support the conclusion that both

Table 12.7 Summary of effects of hemidecortication on verbal and visuospatial abilities

	Left hemidecorticate	Right hemidecorticate
Intelligence	Low normal	Low normal
Language Tests		
Simple	Normal	Normal
Complex	Poor	Normal
Visuospatial Tests		
Simple	Normal	Normal
Complex	Normal	Poor

hemispheres are functionally specialized at birth, although both hemispheres appear capable of assuming some functions usually performed by the missing hemisphere. Table 12.7 summarizes these data. Note that the left hemidecortication produces no severe deficits in visuospatial abilities. Yet the left hemisphere cannot completely compensate for the right hemisphere, as evidenced by the patients' difficulty in performing complex visuospatial tasks.

In an analysis of language abilities, Maureen Dennis and Harry Whitaker found that, unlike right-hemisphere removals, left hemispherectomies produce deficits in understanding spoken language when the meaning is conveyed by complex syntactic structure, particularly if the sentence contains an error (for example, "The tall guard wasn't shot by the armed robber"). Likewise, removing the left hemisphere leads to difficulty in determining sentence implication, in integrating semantic and syntactic information to replace missing pronouns, and in forming judgments of word interrelations in sentences.

In an analysis of word comprehension, Dennis found that both hemispheres understand the meaning of words and both can spontaneously produce lists of names of things. In a search for words by using different cues, however, the left hemisphere has an advantage over the right. Both hemispheres can name an object from its picture or from its description, but the left hemisphere can identify the object on the basis of "rhymes with," whereas the right hemisphere is oblivious to this type of cue.

In an analysis of reading skills, Dennis and her coworkers found that both hemispheres had almost equal ability in higher-order reading comprehension; however, the left hemisphere is superior to the right in reading and spelling unfamiliar words and in using sentence structure to achieve fluent reading. The left hemisphere also reads prose passages with greater decoding accuracy, more fluency, and fewer errors that violate the semantic and syntactic structure of the sentence. The superiority of the left hemisphere seems to be its ability to manipulate and exploit language rules. Yet the right hemisphere is not without its strengths in language. Performance is better with the right hemisphere in a task that requires learning an association between nonsense words and symbols.

In summarizing the results of studies on language, Dennis suggests that, if written language structure is thought of as a combination of meaning cues (morphology), sound cues (phonology), and picture cues (logography), then the isolated left hemisphere will show superior performance with morphology and phonology and inferior performance with logographic cues. The isolated right hemisphere will show superior performance with logographic cues and inferior performance with morphological and phonological cues.

Kohn and Dennis found an almost analogous pattern of results on tests of visuospatial function. They observed that, although patients with right hemispherectomies performed normally on simple tests of visuospatial functions such as drawing, they were significantly impaired on complex tests such as negotiating a maze and reading a map.

To summarize, each hemisphere can assume some of its opposite's functions if the opposite hemisphere is removed in the course of development, but neither hemisphere is totally capable of mediating all of the missing hemisphere's functions. Thus, although the developing brain gives evidence of considerable plasticity, there is convincing evidence against **equipotentiality:** both hemispheres appear to have a processing capacity that probably has an innate structural basis. Furthermore, there seems to be a price for assuming new responsibilities. With few exceptions, patients undergoing hemispherectomy are of below-average or, at best, average intelligence, and their proficiency at tests of the intact hemisphere's function is often less than normal.

Ontogeny of Asymmetry

The results of anatomical studies generally show that adultlike cerebral asymmetries are present before birth, a result that supports an innate predisposition for cerebral asymmetry in humans. Findings in a recent MRI study in which Sowell and colleagues examined asymmetries in the sulcal patterns in a large sample of children, adolescents, and young adults confirm this general impression. In addition, the findings show that the extent of asymmetries in the sulcal patterns increases even past adolescence and well into adulthood.

Thus a basic template for cortical development appears to lay down an asymmetrical organization prenatally, and the pattern progresses after birth. Presumably this pattern can be influenced by the environment, especially by injury. The results of ERP studies by Dennis and Victoria Molfese confirm a functional asymmetry in which the left hemisphere shows a greater response to speech stimuli as early as 1 week of age. There is apparently little change in this difference during development.

Recall from Chapter 11 that two polar theoretical positions postulate the ontogeny (development in the individual) of cerebral specialization. Unilateral specialization culminates in a left-for-language hypothesis: the left hemisphere is genetically organized to develop language skills; the right hemisphere is dumb. At the opposite pole of cerebral interaction, the parallel-development hypothesis posits that both hemispheres, by virtue of their construction, play special roles, one destined to specialize in language and the other in nonlanguage functions.

Research points to a parallel-development theory that initially permits some flexibility or equipotentiality to most usefully explain most of the available data. The cognitive functions of each hemisphere can be conceived as hierarchical. Simple, lower-level functions are represented at the base of the hierarchy, corresponding to functions in the primary sensory, motor, language, or visuospatial areas. More complex, higher-level functions ascend the hierarchy, the most complex being at the top. These advanced functions are the most lateralized.

At birth, the two hemispheres overlap functionally because each is processing low-level behaviors. By age 5, the newly developing higher-order cognitive

Figure 12.12 Development of cognitive function in the left and right hemispheres. At birth (the base of the hierarchy) cognitive functioning is simple, and the functions of the two hemispheres overlap considerably. At the top of the hierarchy are the most complex cognitive abilities, and the functions of the two hemispheres do not overlap at all. The hemispheres are not themselves becoming more lateralized with respect to a given function; rather, they are developing more highly specialized functions.

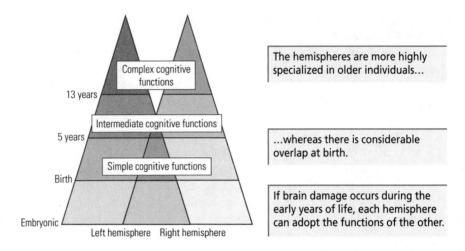

The hemispheres are more highly specialized in older individuals...

...whereas there is considerable overlap at birth.

If brain damage occurs during the early years of life, each hemisphere can adopt the functions of the other.

processes have very little overlap, and each hemisphere thus becomes increasingly specialized. By puberty, each hemisphere has developed its own unique functions (Figure 12.12). Note that the cerebral hemispheres are not becoming more lateralized in development; rather, the developing cognitive functions are built on the lower functions, which are innately located in one hemisphere or the other.

All models of cerebral development must answer the question of how functions become restricted to one hemisphere rather than becoming bilateral. The interactive parallel-development hypothesis answers that question. In a series of papers, Morris Moscovitch emphasized the possibility that one hemisphere actively inhibits the other, thus preventing the contralateral hemisphere from developing similar functions. This active inhibition presumably develops at about age 5, as the corpus callosum becomes functional.

Moscovitch proposed that this inhibitory process not only prevents the subsequent development of language processes in the right hemisphere but also inhibits the expression of the language processes already in the right hemisphere. Support for this idea comes from the observation that the right hemispheres of commissurotomy patients appear to have greater language abilities than expected from the study of normal patients, presumably because the right hemisphere is no longer subject to inhibition by the left. Furthermore, Netley reports that people born with no corpus callosum demonstrate little or no functional asymmetry as inferred from dichotic listening, suggesting that the absence of interhemispheric connection results in attenuated hemispheric asymmetry. This phenomenon follows directly from the Moscovitch proposal.

Asymmetry in Nonhumans

Many participants in discussions on the nature of cerebral asymmetry and its role in behavioral diversity in humans implicitly assume that asymmetry is linked with especially human intellectual characteristics such as language. Asymmetry is not a uniquely human characteristic, however. Elements of communicative vocalizations in frogs and salamanders are lateralized to the left side of the brain. Thus, understanding the origins and evolution of lateral asymmetries in the nonhuman brain is germane to any understanding of the nature of asymmetry in the human brain. Here we present the most stimulating and robust data so far gathered on birds, rodents, and nonhuman primates. For a complete discussion, we recommend the book by Bradshaw and Rogers listed in the References.

Asymmetry in Birds

Fernando Nottebohm made a startling discovery in 1971. He severed the hypoglossal nerve in canaries and found a severe disruption in the birds' song after left lesions but not after right ones. Subsequent work in his laboratory, as well as in many others, showed anatomical differences in the structures controlling birdsong in the two avian hemispheres and identified many song-related regions as sexually dimorphic.

Curiously, although a left-hemisphere dominance for song has been shown in many species of songbirds (and even chickens), it is not characteristic of all songbirds. Apparently, the zebra finch has little anatomical or functional asymmetry, even though it sings. It may be that the lateralization is not for singing itself but for some other still-unrecognized feature of bird vocalizations.

Nottebohm's discovery led to interest in the possibility of asymmetry in the visual system of birds because the optic nerves of most birds cross over almost completely at the optic chiasm. Thus, each hemisphere receives most input from a single eye. The beauty of this arrangement is that lateralization of visual function can be investigated by testing birds monocularly. Furthermore, birds have no corpus callosum and, although other small commissures connect the hemispheres, there is less interhemispheric transfer in birds than in mammals.

Lateralization has now been shown for a range of visually guided functions in birds. According to Bradshaw and Rogers, the right-eye system is specialized for categorizing objects, such as food versus nonfood items, whereas the left-eye system is specialized for responding to the unique properties of each stimulus (color, size, shape, and so forth), including topographical information. Thus, the left hemisphere of birds appears to be specialized for categorizing objects and the right for processing topographical information. The results of research by Gabriel Horn and his colleagues showed an asymmetry for memory formation in the chicken brain. Different synaptic and neurochemical changes take place in each hemisphere when the animals learn, which is presumably due to some difference in information processing by the two hemispheres.

One curious asymmetry is in sleep. Birds spend much of their sleep time with only one hemisphere asleep, which presumably allows them to monitor the environment. On the other hand, it also means that there is a transient asymmetry in sensory processing, which might have significant implications for the animals. We note parenthetically that unilateral sleep is also characteristic of cetaceans (whales, dolphins) and seals, a sensible adaptation in mammals that can drown.

In summary, the results of studies of birds reveal that lateralization takes many forms in the brain and is not a unique property of mammals. Indeed,

Bradshaw and Rogers suggested that, in view of the growing list of functional and structural asymmetries in birds, one begins to wonder whether it is not cerebral *symmetry* that needs to be explained.

Asymmetry in Rodents

Studies in rats and mice focus on two rather different types of asymmetry. The first emphasizes postural and motor asymmetries such as paw preference and direction of movement. This form of lateralization is present in individual animals and correlates with individual differences in the distribution of neurotransmitters, especially dopamine. Unlike handedness in humans, most postural asymmetries in rodents are random across the population. Thus, although the neural bases of individual preferences may be relevant for understanding motor or postural asymmetries in humans, the directions of the asymmetries do not relate directly to human brain-behavior relations.

The second type of lateralization in rodents is more interesting in the current context because it is seen in the population, much as we saw in birds. As in humans, there is an asymmetry in the anatomy of the two cerebral hemispheres, with the right hemisphere being larger. In addition, the cortex of the right hemisphere is thicker, especially in the visual and posterior parietal regions, and this difference is modulated by hormones. For example, several groups of researchers have seen a sex difference in the asymmetry: male rodents have a greater difference than females. Furthermore, both prenatal stress and postnatal castration were shown to abolish the anatomical asymmetry in males, presumably owing to alterations in the normal hormonal environment (Stewart and Kolb).

Studies of functional correlates of the anatomical asymmetries have proved controversial. Nonetheless, evidence is accumulating to support the conclusion that the left hemisphere is specialized for the processing of species-specific calls. The auditory asymmetry may represent a left-hemisphere advantage in the processing of rapidly changing acoustical stimuli, a conclusion that has also been made for the human left temporal lobe (see Chapter 15). Claims that the right hemisphere is specialized for controlling emotional and spatial behavior remain speculative.

An intriguing asymmetry in rodents is an apparent lateralization of the modulation of immune responses. For example, lesions in the left hemisphere of mice, but not in the right, suppress T-cell functions. (T-cells are specialized cells that respond to immune challenges, such as infections.) The T-cell suppression may be due to lateralized control of the secretion of specific hormones, such as prolactin. Whether similar asymmetries exist in the control of immune functions in humans is not yet known, although such asymmetry has been hypothesized by Kang and colleagues.

As noted earlier, stress may alter anatomical asymmetries in the rat cortex, and many research groups have suggested that stress may also alter functional asymmetries. For example, Denneberg and his coworkers hypothesized that specific experiences might alter the two hemispheres differentially during development. One could imagine that, if different experiences differ in stress levels, then Denneberg's results could be explained by the lateralized responses to various stress-related hormones, such as glucocorticoids.

Asymmetry in Nonhuman Primates

A trend in primate brain evolution is the shift of the Sylvian fissure from an almost vertical orientation to a more horizontal orientation. This shift implies an expansion of the parietal lobe, which pushes the Sylvian fissure down, especially in the left hemisphere. Thus, as with human brains, there is a greater upward slope in the Sylvian fissure in the right hemisphere in apes and Old-World monkeys. In addition, the right frontal lobe and left occipital lobe extend farther in the same species, again as in humans. Data for New-World monkeys are more variable, but even here there is likely to be an asymmetry in the Sylvian fissure.

The existence of asymmetries in the nonhuman primates is not to be interpreted as being identical with that in humans. Bradshaw and Rogers concluded that the asymmetries in the language-related parietal and temporal lobe structures were not fully developed until the arrival of hominids (that is, they are seen in fossil hominids and human brains). Thus the increased development of language-related structures in the posterior part of the brain is suggested to have occurred after the advent of hominids.

The results of studies of hand preference in nonhuman primates are controversial. Studies in the 1960s by Warren unequivocally failed to find any systematic hand preference in rhesus monkeys, and he concluded that observed preferences are task dependent and are strongly affected by learning.

More recently, MacNeilage and his colleagues argued that, because earlier studies concentrated on particular types of movements, a hand preference in monkeys has been overlooked. Their basic premise is that primates evolved a preference for reaching with one limb (the left) while supporting the body with the other (the right). As the prehensile hand developed and primates began to adopt a more upright posture, the need for a hand used primarily for postural support diminished and, because this hand was free, it became specialized for manipulating objects. They later proposed that the hand specializations were accompanied by hemispheric specializations: a right-hemisphere (left-hand) perceptuomotor specialization for unimanual predation (grasping fast-moving insects or small animals) and a left-hemisphere specialization for whole-body movements.

This hypothesis has been hotly debated. A significant difficulty is that studies of limb use in primates are hampered by poor control of myriad confounding factors including species, age, sex, task difficulty, learning, and sample size. Nonetheless, evidence is accumulating in support of at least some components of the theory. For example, Ward's group showed left-hand preferences for prey catching and food retrieval in prosimians and some Old-World monkeys.

One objection to the theory is that cerebral asymmetry must precede handedness, and whether this asymmetry did indeed precede handedness and why it might have done so are not clear. If anything akin to cerebral asymmetry in humans is to be demonstrated in nonhuman primates, tests of tactile, visual, and auditory perception would be a good place to start looking. Consider the following examples.

Horster and Ettlinger trained 155 rhesus monkeys to make a tactile response in a task in which the subjects had to discriminate a cylinder from a sphere. The results showed that the 78 monkeys spontaneously using the left hand outperformed the 77 using the right hand. Thus, as in humans, the right hemisphere outperformed the left one, suggesting an asymmetry.

Hamilton and Vermeire took a different approach. They taught 25 split-brain monkeys to discriminate two types of visual stimuli that have shown lateralization in humans. In one task, the animals had to discriminate between pairs of lines differing in slope by 15° (15° versus 30°, for example, or 105° versus 120°). For each pair, the more vertical line was designated as positive, and the monkey received a food reward for choosing it.

Each hemisphere was tested separately, and the results showed that most monkeys learned the line-orientation discriminations faster with the left hemisphere. The second task required the animals to discriminate different monkey faces. The right hemispheres of most animals showed better discrimination and memory of the faces. There was no hemispheric difference in making a simple discrimination of black-and-white patterns.

The curious thing about these results is that, a priori, the line-orientation task appears to be one in which humans would show a *right*-hemisphere bias, rather than the left-hemisphere bias shown by the monkeys. At any rate, it is safe to conclude that there appears to be evidence in nonhuman primates of hemispheric specialization for the processing of different types of visual information.

There is also evidence from primates that the two hemispheres may differ in their production of facial expressions. Split-brain monkeys viewed videotapes of people, monkeys, other animals, and scenery, and the amount of time spent watching the recordings and the number of species-typical facial expressions made were recorded. The number of facial expressions elicited from the right hemisphere was greater than the number made when using the left hemisphere, which is what one would predict from studies of humans. In another study, Hauser found that the left side of the monkey's face began to display facial expression before the right, and it was more expressive. Recall from Chapter 11 that a similar result was reported for humans.

Finally, many studies look for asymmetries in auditory perception. In an early study, Dewson removed the superior temporal gyrus (roughly equivalent to Wernicke's area in humans) in four rhesus monkeys, producing a lasting deficit on an auditory–visual task if the lesion was in the left hemisphere but not if it was in the right. The monkeys were required to press a panel that activated one of two acoustical stimuli, either a 1-kilohertz (kHz) tone or white noise. They were then presented with two panels, one green and one red. If the tone was heard, the monkeys pressed the red panel; if the white noise was heard, they pressed the green panel to receive the reward. Lesions on the left impaired performance of this task, but lesions on the analogous area on the right did not.

The possibility of asymmetry in the auditory system was confirmed, however, by the work of Petersen and colleagues. They compared the ability of Japanese macaques to discriminate between communicatively relevant sounds and irrelevant sounds. The animals could discriminate relevant sounds presented to the right ear better than those presented to the left. The researchers suggested that the Japanese macaques engage in left-hemisphere processing in a way that is analogous to that in humans.

The results of a further study by Heffner and Heffner support this conclusion. They trained monkeys to discriminate between two forms of their "coo" vocalization. Then they removed the left or right superior temporal gyrus or the left or right parietal cortex. Removal of the left, but not the right, temporal cortex produced impairment in the performance of this task. Parietal lesions were without effect. Curiously, with training, the animals with left temporal lesions were able to relearn the task. When the remaining side was later removed, the animals had a permanent deficit in the task and were unable to relearn it.

Summary

Considerable individual variation exists in the pattern of left–right hemisphere asymmetry. Neuropsychologists study anatomical and functional variations in individual persons—the ontogeny of asymmetry—to separate the processes that are lateralized, which can be a source of insight into the nature of cerebral asymmetry in our species (phylogeny).

Systematic relations exist between normal variations in cerebral organization and individual differences in cognitive abilities. Each of us has unique behavioral capacities as well as shortcomings that are related to cerebral organization. Demonstrations related to handedness and sex imply that some asymmetric variation is biologically based, although environmental variables certainly modify cerebral organization as well. The basis for handedness in humans has been the focus of much debate and theorizing, yet there is still no adequate explanation for why people are either right- or left-handed. More progress has been made in understanding the nature of sex differences. The most likely explanation is that gonadal hormones alter brain organization during development and continue to influence brain activity during adulthood. This altered brain organization and activity interacts with experience to enhance or diminish the sex-related differences. Although it seems likely that experience and environment certainly alter cerebral organization, the nature of experience-dependent variations in brain organization is not yet understood.

The results of studies of nonhuman species show that lateral asymmetry is a property not unique to humans. The demonstration of asymmetry in nonhuman brains implies that asymmetry in the human brain is directly related neither to handedness nor to language but rather to analysis of sensory information and control of movement.

References

Aboitiz, F., A. B. Scheibel, and E. Zaidel. Morphometry of the Sylvian fissure and the corpus callosum, with emphasis on sex differences. *Brain* 115:1521–1541, 1992.

Allen L. S., and R. A. Gorski. Sexual orientation and the size of the anterior commissure in the human brain. *Journal of Comparative Neurology* 312:97–104, 1991.

Alexopoulos, D. S. Sex differences and IQ. *Personality and Individual Differences* 20:445–450, 1996.

Ankney, C. D. Sex differences in relative brain size: The mismeasure of woman too? *Intelligence* 16:329–336, 1992.

Annett, M. A classification of hand preference by association analysis. *British Journal of Psychology* 61:303–321, 1970.

Astur, R. S., M. L. Ortiz, and R. J. Sutherland. A characterization of performance by men and women in a virtual Morris water task: A large and reliable sex difference. *Behavioural Brain Research* 93:185–190, 1998.

Bakan, P., G. Dibb, and P. Reed. Handedness and birth stress. *Neuropsychologia* 11:363–366, 1973.

Barrera, A., L. Jimenez, G. M. Gonzalez, J. Montiel, and F. Aboitiz. Dendritic structure of single hippocampal neurons according to sex and hemisphere of origin in middle-aged and elderly human subjects. *Brain Research* 906:31–37, 2001.

Beatty, W. W., and A. I. Troster. Gender differences in geographic knowledge. *Sex Roles* 16:202–229, 1987.

Benbow, C. P. Sex differences in mathematical reasoning ability in intellectually talented preadolescents: Their nature, effects, and possible causes. *Behavioral and Brain Sciences* 11:169–232, 1988.

Benbow, C. P., and J. C. Stanley. Sex differences in mathematical ability: Fact or artifact? *Science* 210:1262–1264, 1980.

Bishop, K. M., and D. Wahlsten. Sex differences in the human corpus callosum: myth or reality? *Neuroscience and Biobehavioral Review* 21:581–601, 1997.

Boles, D. B. X-linkage of spatial ability: A critical review. *Child Development* 51:625–635, 1980.

Bradshaw, J., and L. Rogers. *The Evolution of Lateral Asymmetries, Language, Tool Use, and Intellect.* New York: Academic Press, 1993.

Bryden, M. P., I. C. McManus, and M. B. Bulman-Fleming. Evaluating the empirical support for the Geschwind-Behan-Galaburda model of cerebral lateralization. *Brain and Cognition* 26:103–167, 1994.

Carmon, A., Y. Harishanu, E. Lowinger, and S. Lavy. Asymmetries in hemispheric blood volume and cerebral dominance. *Behavioral Biology* 7:853–859, 1972.

Collins, R. L. Toward an admissible genetic model for the inheritance of the degree and direction of asymmetry. In S. Harnad, R. W. Doty, L. Goldstein, J. Jaynes, and G. Krauthamer, Eds. *Lateralization of the Nervous System.* New York: Academic Press, 1977.

Collins, D. W., and D. Kimura. A large sex difference on a two-dimensional mental rotation task. *Behavioral Neuroscience* 111:845–849, 1997.

Corballis, M. C. The genetics and evolution of handedness. *Psychological Review* 104:714–727, 1997.

Corballis, M. C. Is the handedness gene on the X chromosome? *Psychological Review* 108(4):805–810, 2001.

Corsi-Cabrera, M., C. Arce, J. Ramos, and M. A. Guevara. Effect of spatial ability and sex on inter- and intrahemispheric correlation of EEG activity. *Neurophysiology* 102:5–11, 1997.

Curtiss, S. *Genie: A Psycholinguistic Study of a Modern-Day "Wild Child."* New York: Academic Press, 1978.

de Lacaste-Utamsing, C., and R. L. Holloway. Sexual dimorphism in the human corpus callosum. *Science* 216:1431–1432, 1982.

Dennenberg, V. H. Hemispheric laterality in animals and the effects of early experience. *Behavioral and Brain Sciences* 4:1–50, 1981.

Dennis, M. Capacity and strategy for syntactic comprehension after left or right hemidecortication. *Brain and Language* 10:287–317, 1980.

Dennis, M. Language acquisition in a single hemisphere: Semantic organization. In D. Caplan, Ed. *Biological Studies of Mental Processes.* Cambridge, MA: MIT Press, 1980.

Dennis, M., M. Lovett, and C. A. Wiegel-Crump. Written language acquisition after left or right hemidecortication in infancy. *Brain and Language* 12:54–91, 1981.

Dennis, M., and H. A. Whitaker. Language acquisition following hemidecortication: Linguistic superiority of the left over the right hemisphere. *Brain and Language* 3:404–433, 1976.

Dewson, J. H. Preliminary evidence of hemispheric asymmetry of auditory function in monkeys. In S. Harnad, R. W. Doty, L. Goldstein, J. Jaynes, and G. Krauthamer, Eds. *Lateralization in the Nervous System.* New York: Academic Press, 1977.

Esposito G., J. D. van Horn, D. R. Weinberger, and K. F. Berman. Gender differences in cerebral blood flow as a function of cognitive state with PET. *Journal of Nuclear Medicine* 37:559–564, 1996.

Filipek, P. A, C. Richelme, D. N. Kennedy, and V. S. Caviness, Jr. The young adult human brain: An MRI-based morphometric analysis. *Cerebral Cortex* 4:344–360, 1994.

Frost, J. A., J. R. Binder, J. A. Springer, T. A. Hammeke, P. S. F. Bellgowan, S. M. Rao, and R. W. Cox. Language processing is strongly left literalized in both sexes: Evidence from functional MRI. *Brain* 122:199–208, 1999.

Geschwind, N., and A. M. Galaburda. *Cerebral Lateralization: Biological Mechanisms, Associations, and Pathology.* Cambridge, MA: MIT Press, 1987.

Goldstein, J. M., L. J. Seidman, N. J. Horton, N. Makris, D. N. Kennedy, V. S. Caviness, Jr., S. V. Faraone, and M. T. Tsuang. Normal sexual dimorphism of the adult human brain assessed by in vivo magnetic resonance imaging. *Cerebral Cortex* 11:490–497, 2001.

Grimshaw, G. M., M. P. Bryden, and J. K. Finegan. Relations between prenatal testosterone and cerebral lateralization at age 10. *Journal of Clinical and Experimental Neuropsychology* 15:39–40, 1993.

Gualtieri, T., and R. E. Hicks. An immunoreactive theory of selective male affliction. *Behavioral and Brain Sciences* 8:427–477, 1985.

Gur, R. C., R. E. Gur, W. D. Obrist, J. P. Hungerbuhler, D. Younkin, A. D. Rosen, B. E. Skolnick, and M. Reivich. Sex and handedness differences in cerebral blood flow during test and cognitive activity. *Science* 217:659–660, 1982.

Gur, R. C., B. I. Turetsky, M. Yan, W. Bilker, P. Hughett, and R. E. Gur. Sex differences in brain gray and white matter in healthy young adults: Correlations with cognitive performance. *Journal of Neuroscience* 19:4065–4072, 1999.

Hall, J. A. Y., and D. Kimura. Sexual orientation and performance on sexually dimorphic motor tasks. *Archives of Sexual Behavior* 24:395–407, 1995.

Hall, J. *Nonverbal Sex Differences.* Baltimore: Johns Hopkins University Press, 1984.

Hamilton, C. R., and B. A. Vermeire. Complementary hemispheric superiorities in monkeys. *Science* 242:1691–1694, 1988.

Hamilton, D. *The Monkey Gland Affair.* London: Chatto & Windus, 1986.

Hampson, E. Variations in sex-related cognitive abilities across the menstrual cycle. *Brain and Cognition* 14:26–43, 1990.

Hampson, E., and D. Kimura. Sex differences and hormonal influences on cognitive function in humans. In J. B. Becker, S. M. Breedlove, and D. Crews, Eds. *Behavioral Endocrinology.* Cambridge, MA: MIT Press, 1992.

Harasty, J., K. L. Double, G. M. Halliday, J. J. Kril, and A. McRitchie. Language-associated cortical regions are proportionally larger in the female brain. *Archives of Neurology* 54:171–175, 1997.

Hardyck, C., and L. F. Petrinovich. Left-handedness. *Psychological Bulletin* 84:384–404, 1977.

Harris, L. J. Sex differences in spatial ability: Possible environmental, genetic, and neurological factors. In M. Kinsbourne, Ed. *Asymmetrical Function of the Brain.* Cambridge, UK: Cambridge University Press, 1978.

Harshman, R. A., E. Hampson, and S. A. Berenbaum. Individual differences in cognitive abilities and brain organization I: Sex and handedness—Differences in ability. *Canadian Journal of Psychology* 37:144–192. 1983.

Haverkort, M., L. Stowe, B. Wijers, and A. Paans. Familial handedness and sex in language comprehension. *Neuroimage* 9:12–18, 1999.

Hauser, M. D. Right hemisphere dominance for the production of facial expression in monkeys. *Science* 261:475–477, 1993.

Hécaen, H., M. DeAgostini, and A. Monzon-Montes. Cerebral organization in left-handers. *Brain and Language* 12:261–284, 1981.

Hécaen, H., and J. Sauguet. Cerebral dominance in left-handed subjects. *Cortex* 7:19–48, 1971.

Heffner, H. E., and R. S. Heffner. Temporal lobe lesions and perception of species-specific vocalizations by macaques. *Science* 226:75–76, 1984.

Hickok, G., U. Bellugi, and E. S. Klima. Sign language in the brain. *Scientific American* 284(6):58–65, 2001.

Hochberg, F. H., and M. LeMay. Arteriographic correlates of handedness. *Neurology* 25:218–222, 1975.

Horn, G. Neural basis of recognition memory investigated through an analysis of imprinting. *Philosophical Transactions of the Royal Society London B* 329:133–142, 1990.

Horster, W., and G. Ettlinger. An association between hand preferences and tactile discrimination performance in the rhesus monkey. *Neuropsychologica* 21:411–413, 1985.

Hyde, J. S., E. Fennema, and S. J. Lamon. Gender differences in mathematics performance: A meta-analysis. *Psychological Bulletin* 107:139–155, 1990.

Hyde, J. S., and M. C. Linn. Gender differences in verbal ability: A meta-analysis. *Psychological Bulletin* 104:53–69, 1988.

Ide, A., and F. Aboitiz. A sex difference in the postcentral sulcus of the human brain. *Brain Research* 890:330–332, 2001.

Ifune, C. K., B. A. Vermeire, and C. R. Hamilton. Hemispheric differences in split-brain monkeys viewing and responding to videotape recordings. *Behavioral and Neural Biology* 41:231–235, 1984.

Inglis, J., and J. S. Lawson. A meta-analysis of sex differences in the effects of unilateral brain damage on intelligence test results. *Canadian Journal of Psychology* 36:670–683, 1982.

Inglis, J., M. Rickman, J. S. Lawson, A. W. MacLean, and T. N. Monga. Sex differences in the cognitive effects of unilateral brain damage. *Cortex* 18:257–276, 1982.

Janke, L., G. Schlaug, Y. Huang, and H. Steinmetz. Asymmetry of the planum parietale. *Neuroreport* 5:1161–1163, 1994.

Janowsky, J. S., S. K. Oviatt, and E. S. Orwoll. Testosterone influences spatial cognition in older men. *Behavioral Neuroscience* 108:325–332, 1994.

Juraska, J. Sex differences in developmental plasticity of behavior and the brain. In W. T. Greenough and J. M. Juraska, Eds. *Developmental Neuropsychology.* New York: Academic Press, 1986.

Kang, D.-H., R. J. Davidson, C. L. Coe, R. E. Wheeler, A. J. Tomarken, and W. B. Ershler. Frontal brain asymmetry and immune function. *Behavior Neuroscience* 105:860–869, 1991.

Kertesz, A., and N. Geschwind. Patterns of pyramidal decussation and their relationship to handedness. *Archives of Neurology* 24:326–332, 1971.

Kim, K., N. R. Relkin, K. Lee, and J. Hirsch. Distinct cortical areas associated with native and second languages. *Nature* 388:171–174, 1997.

Kimura, D. *Sex and Cognition.* Cambridge, MA: MIT Press, 1999.

Kimura, D. Sex differences in cerebral organization for speech and praxic functions. *Canadian Journal of Psychology* 37:9–35, 1983.

Klein, D., B. Milner, R. J. Zatorre, E. Meyer, and A. C. Evans. The neural substrates underlying word generation: A bilingual functional-imaging study. *Proceedings of the National Academy of Sciences of the United States of America* 92:2899–2903, 1995.

Klein, D., B. Milner, R. J. Zatorre, V. Zhao, and J. Nikelski. Cerebral organization in bilinguals: A PET study of Chinese-English verb generation. *Neuroreport* 10:2841–2846, 1999.

Kohn, B., and M. Dennis. Selective impairments of visuo-spatial abilities in infantile hemiplegics after right cerebral hemidecortication. *Neuropsychologia* 12:505–512, 1974.

Kolb, B., and J. Stewart. Sex-related differences in dendritic branching of cells in the prefrontal cortex of rats. *Journal of Neuroendocrinology* 3:95–99, 1991.

Kolb, B., R. J. Sutherland, A. J. Nonneman, and I. Q. Whishaw. Asymmetry in the cerebral hemispheres of the rat, mouse, rabbit, and cat: The right hemisphere is larger. *Experimental Neurology* 78:348–359, 1982.

Kulynych, J. J., K. Vladar, D. W. Jones, and D. R. Weinberger. Gender differences in the normal lateralization of the supratemporal cortex: MRI surface-rendering morphometry of Heschl's gyrus and the planum temporale. *Cerebral Cortex* 4:107–118, 1994.

Lansdell, H. A sex difference in effect of temporal-lobe neurosurgery on design preference. *Nature* 194:852–854, 1962.

LeMay, M. Asymmetries of the skull and handedness: Phrenology revisited. *Journal of Neurological Science* 32:243–253, 1977.

Levy, J. Possible basis for the evolution of lateral specialization of the human brain. *Nature* 224:614–615, 1969.

Levy, J., and T. Nagylaki. A model for the genetics of handedness. *Genetics* 72:117–128, 1972.

Lynn, R. Sex differences in intelligence and brain size: A paradox resolved. *Personality and Individual Differences* 17:257–271, 1993.

MacCoby, E., and C. Jacklin. *The Psychology of Sex Differences.* Stanford, CA: Stanford University Press, 1974.

MacNeilage, P. F., M. G. Studdert-Kennedy, and B. Lindblom. Primate handedness reconsidered. *Behavioral and Brain Sciences* 10:247–303, 1987.

MacNeilage, P. F., M. G. Studdert-Kennedy, and B. Lindblom. Primate handedness: A foot in the door. *Behavioral and Brain Sciences* 11:737–746, 1988.

Majeres, R. L. Sex differences in symbol-digit substitution and speeded matching. *Intelligence* 7:313–327, 1983.

Manning, A. A., W. Gobel, R. Markman, and T. LaBrech. Lateral cerebral differences in the deaf in response to linguistic and nonlinguistic stimuli. *Brain and Language* 4:309–321, 1977.

McBurney, D. H., S. J. C. Gaulin, T. Devineni, and C. Adams. Superior spatial memory of women: Stronger evidence for the gathering hypothesis. *Evolution and Human Behavior* 19:73–87, 1997.

McGivern, R. F., K. L. Mutter, J. Anderson, G. Wideman, M. Bodnar, and P. J. Huston. Gender differences in incidental learning and visual recognition memory: Support for a sex difference in unconscious environmental awareness. *Personality and Individual Differences* 25:223–232, 1998.

McGlone, J. Sex differences in the cerebral organization of verbal function to patients with unilateral brain lesions. *Brain* 100:775–793, 1977.

McGlone, J. Sex differences in human brain asymmetry: A critical survey. *Behavioral and Brain Sciences* 3:215–263, 1980.

McGuinness, D., A. Olson, and J. Chapman. Sex differences in incidental recall for words and pictures. *Learning and Individual Differences* 2:263–285, 1990.

McKeever, W. F., H. W. Hoemann, V. A. Florina, and A. D. Van Deventer. Evidence of minimal cerebral asymmetries in the congenitally deaf. *Neuropsychologia* 14:413–423, 1976.

Molfese, D. L., and V. J. Molfese. Right-hemisphere responses from preschool children to temporal cues to speech and nonspeech materials: Electrophysiological correlates. *Brain and Language* 33:245–259, 1988.

Morgan, M. Embryology and inheritance of asymmetry. In S. Harnad, R. W. Doty, L. Goldstein, J. Jaynes, and G.

Krauthamer, Eds. *Lateralization in the Nervous System.* New York: Academic Press, 1977.

Moscovitch, M. The development of lateralization of language functions and its relation to cognitive and linguistic development: A review and some theoretical speculations. In S. J. Segalowitz and F. A. Gruber, Eds. *Language Development and Neurological Theory.* New York: Academic Press, 1977.

Murphy, D. G. M., C. DeCarli, A. R., McIntosh, E. Daly, M. J. Mentis, P. Peitrini, J. Szczepanik, M. B. Schapiro, C. L. O. Grady, B. Horwitz, and S. I. Rapaport. Sex differences in human brain morphometry and metabolism: An in vivo quantitative magnetic resonance imaging and positron emission tomography study on the effect of aging. *Archives of General Psychiatry* 53:585–594, 1996.

Netley, C. Dichotic listening of callosal agenesis and Turner's syndrome patients. In S. J. Segalowitz and F. A. Gruber, Eds. *Language Development and Neurological Theory.* New York: Academic Press, 1977.

Neville, H. Electroencephalographic testing of cerebral specialization in normal and congenitally deaf children: A preliminary report. In S. J. Segalowitz and F. A. Gruber, Eds. *Language Development and Neurological Theory.* New York: Academic Press, 1977.

Nicholson, K. G., and D. Kimura. Sex differences for speech and manual skill. *Perceptual and Motor Skills* 82:3–13, 1996.

Nottebohm, F. Brain pathways for vocal learning in birds: A review of the first 10 years. *Progress in Psychobiology and Physiological Psychology* 9:85–124, 1980.

Obler, L. K., R. J. Zatoree, L. Galloway, Jr., and J. Vaid. Cerebral lateralization in bilinguals: Methodological issues. *Brain and Language* 15:40–54, 1982.

Pakkenberg, B., and H. J. Gundersen. Neocortical neuron number in humans: Effect of sex and age. *Journal of Comparative Neurology* 384:312–320, 1997.

Paus, T., N. Otaky, Z. Caramanos, D. MacDonald, A. Zijdenbos, D. D'Avirro, D. Gutmans, C. Holmes, F. Tomaiuolo, and A. C. Evans. In vivo morphometry of the intrasulcal gray matter in the human cingulate, paracingulate, and superior-rostral sulci: Hemispheric asymmetries, gender differences, and probability maps. *Journal of Comparative Neurology* 376:664–673, 1996.

Peters, M. Corpus callosum. *Canadian Journal of Psychology* 42:313–324, 1988.

Peters, M. Description and validation of a flexible and broadly usable handedness questionnaire. *Laterality* 3:77–96, 1998.

Petersen, M. R., M. D. Beecher, S. R. Zoloth, D. B. Moody, and W. C. Stebbins. Neural lateralization: Evidence from studies of the perception of species-specific vocalizations by Japanese macaques (*Macada puscata*). *Science* 202:324–326, 1978.

Pugh, K. R., B. A. Shaywitz, S. E. Shaywitz, R. T. Constable, P. Skudlarski, R. K. Fulbright, R. A. Bronen, J. M. Fletcher, D. P. Shankweiler, L. Katz, J. M. Fletcher, and J. C. Gore. Cerebral organization of component process in reading. *Brain* 119:1221–1238, 1996.

Rapport, R. L., C. T. Tan, and H. A. Whitaker. Language function and dysfunction among Chinese- and English-speaking polyglots: Cortical stimulation, Wada testing, and clinical studies. *Brain and Language* 18:342–366, 1983.

Ratcliffe, G., C. Dila, L. Taylor, and B. Milner. The morphological asymmetry of the hemispheres and cerebral dominance for speech: A possible relationship. *Brain and Language* 11:87–98, 1980.

Reite, M., J. Sheeder, P. Teale, D. Richardson, M. Adams, and J. Simon. MEG based brain laterality: Sex differences in normal adults. *Neuropsychologia* 33:1607–1616, 1995.

Schlaepfer, T. E., G. J. Harris, A. Y. Tien, L. Peng, S. Lee, and G. D. Pearlson. Structural differences in the cerebral cortex of healthy female and male subjects: A magnetic resonance imaging study. *Psychiatry Research* 61:129–135, 1995.

Sowell, E. R., D. A. Trauner, A. Gamst, and T. L. Jernigan. Development of cortical and subcortical brain structures in childhood and adolescence: A structural MRI study. *Developmental Medicine and Child Neurology* 44:4–16, 2002.

Sowell, E. R., P. M. Thompson, D. Rex, D. Kornsand, K. D. Tessner, T. L. Jernigan, and A. W. Toga. Mapping sulcal pattern asymmetry and local cortical surface gray matter distribution in vivo: Maturation in perisylvian cortices. *Cerebral Cortex* 12:17–26, 2002.

Springer, S. P., and G. Deutsch. *Left Brain, Right Brain,* 5th ed. New York: W. H. Freeman and Company, 1998.

Stark, R. E., K. Bleile, J. Brandt, J. Freeman, and E. P. G. Vining. Speech-language outcomes of hemispherectomy in children and young adults. *Brain and Language* 51:406–421.

Stewart, J., and B. Kolb. The effects of neonatal gonadectomy and prenatal stress on cortical thickness and asymmetry in rats. *Behavioral and Neural Biology* 49:344–360, 1988.

Stewart, J., and B. Kolb. Dendritic branching in cortical pyramidal cells in response to ovariectomy in adult female rats: Suppression by neonatal exposure to testosterone. *Brain Research* 654:149–154, 1994.

Strauss, E., J. Wada, and M. Hunter. Sex-related differences in the cognitive consequences of early left-hemisphere lesions. *Journal of Clinical and Experimental Neuropsychology* 14:738–748, 1992.

Sugishita, M., K. Otomo, S. Kabe, and K. Yunoki. A critical appraisal of neuropsychological correlates of Japanese ideogram (kanji) and phonogram (kana) reading. *Brain* 115:1563–1585, 1992.

Swaab, D. F., and E. Fliers. A sexually dimorphic nucleus in the human brain. *Science* 228:1112–1115, 1985.

Thomas, H., W. Jamison, and D. D. Hummel. Observation is insufficient for discovering that the surface of still water is invariantly horizontal. *Science* 191:173–174, 1973.

Tzavaras, A., G. Kaprinis, and A. Gatzoyas. Literacy and hemispheric specialization for language: Dichotic listening in illiterates. *Neuropsychologia* 19:565–570, 1981.

Uyehara, J. M., and W. C. Cooper, Jr. Hemispheric differences for verbal and nonverbal stimuli in Japanese- and English-speaking subjects assessed by Tsunoda's method. *Brain and Language* 10:405–417, 1980.

Velle, W. Sex differences in sensory functions. *Perspectives in Biology and Medicine* 30:490–522, 1987.

Waber, D. P. Sex differences in cognition: A function of maturation rate. *Science* 192:572–573, 1976.

Wada, J. A., R. Clarke, and A. Hamm. Cerebral asymmetry in humans: Cortical speech zones in 100 adult and 100 infant brains. *Archives of Neurology* 32:239–246, 1975.

Warren, J. M. Functional lateralization in the brain. *Annals of the New York Academy of Sciences* 299:273–280, 1977.

Wechsler, A. F. Crossed aphasia in an illiterate dextral. *Brain and Language* 3:164–172, 1976.

Werker, J. F., and R. C. Tees. The organization and reorganization of human speech perception. *Annual Review of Neuroscience* 15:377–402, 1992.

Witelson, S. F. Early hemisphere specialization and interhemispheric plasticity: An empirical and theoretical review. In S. J. Segalowitz and F. A. Gruber, Eds. *Language Development and Neurological Theory.* New York: Academic Press, 1977.

Witelson, S. F. The brain connection: The corpus callosum is larger in left-handers. *Science* 229:665–668, 1985.

Witelson, S. F. Hand and sex differences in the isthmus and genu of the human corpus callosum. *Brain* 112:799–835, 1989.

Witelson, S. F., and C. H. Goldsmith. The relationship of hand preference to anatomy of the corpus callosum in men. *Brain Research* 545:175–182, 1991.

Witelson, S. F., and D. L. Kigar. Sylvian fissure morphology and asymmetry in men and women: Bilateral differences in relation to handedness in men. *Journal of Comparative Neurology* 323:326–340, 1992.

Witelson, S. F., I. I. Lezner, and D. L. Kigar. Women have greater density of neurons in posterior temporal cortex. *Journal of Neuroscience* 15:3418–3428, 1995.

Wittig, M. A., and A. C. Petersen. *Sex-Related Differences in Cognitive Functioning.* New York: Academic Press, 1979.

Woolley, C. S., E. Gould, M. Frankfurt, and B. S. McEwen. Naturally occurring fluctuation in dendritic spine density on adult hippocampal pyramidal neurons. *Journal of Neuroscience* 10:4035–4039, 1990.

Yakovlev, P. I., and P. Rakic. Patterns of decussation of bulbar pyramids and distribution of pyramidal tracts on two sides of the spinal cord. *Transactions of the American Neurological Association* 91:366–367, 1966.

The Occipital Lobes

P. M., a colonel in the British army who fought in North Africa during the Second World War, was struck by a bullet that went through the back of his brain. Miraculously, P. M. survived, but his vision was severely affected. He completely lost sight in the right visual field but the central part of his left visual field survived. He reported that he could see "normally" in a region of the left visual world that was about the diameter of your fist held at arm's length directly in front of your face.

P. M.'s symptoms reveal a topographical map of the visual world in the occipital cortex and the possibility of seeing through only a small part of it. But what did P. M. experience in the rest of the visual world? Shortly after his injury, he reported that the lost world appeared black, as though the lights were out. Occasionally, however, he was aware that the lost regions were different, "almost gray," although he could never express specifically what exactly was different other than the grayness.

P. M. also experienced a phenomenon that many patients with extensive visual-field defects experience: if asked to guess whether a spot of light had blinked in his blind field, he could "guess" at above-chance levels. He was not consciously aware that the light had appeared and seemed bemused that he could guess, sometimes quite accurately, about the presence or absence of the light.

In spite of his residual central vision, P. M. had two particular (and, for him, aggravating) problems: he found it very difficult to read and he had difficulty recognizing faces. Curiously, however, P. M. could recognize other objects more easily, even though he could not see any more of them than he could the faces.

Cases such as P. M.'s are especially interesting because our brains are organized around vision. Our perception of the world is predominantly visual, our movements are guided by visual information, our social and sexual behavior is highly visual, our entertainment is largely visual, and our nights are enriched by visual dreams. In this chapter, we first consider the anatomical organization of the occipital lobes and then examine the extent of the visual system within the brain. Next, we examine disorders of the visual pathways and of the visual system. We shall see why faces present a special problem for the visual system and why the ability to visualize presents humans a unique opportunity.

Anatomy of the Occipital Lobes

The occipital lobes form the posterior pole of the cerebral hemispheres, lying under the occipital bone at the back of the skull. On the medial surface of the hemisphere, the occipital lobe is distinguished from the parietal lobe by the parieto-occipital sulcus, as illustrated in Figure 13.1. No clear landmarks separate the occipital cortex from the temporal or parietal cortex on the lateral surface of the hemisphere, however, because the occipital tissue merges with the other regions. The lack of clear landmarks makes it difficult to define the extent of the occipital areas precisely and has led to much confusion about the exact boundaries.

Within the visual cortex, however, are three clear landmarks. The most prominent is the calcarine sulcus, which contains much of the primary cortex (see Figure 13.1). The calcarine fissure divides the upper and lower halves of the visual world. On the ventral surface of the hemisphere are two gyri (lingual and fusiform). The lingual gyrus includes part of visual cortical regions V2 and VP, whereas V4 is in the fusiform gyrus.

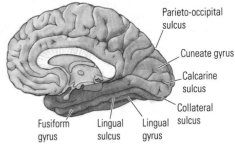

Figure 13.1 Medial view of the occipital lobe, illustrating the major landmarks.

Subdivisions of the Occipital Cortex

The monkey cortex was first divided by Brodmann into three regions (areas 17, 18, and 19, see Figure 10.7), but studies using imaging, physiological, and newer anatomical techniques have produced much finer subdivisions. Although the map is still not complete, the consensus is that the occipital cortex contains at least nine different visual areas, as illustrated in Figure 13.2: V1, V2, V3, VP, V3a, V4d, V4v, DP, and MT (also known as V5).

Figure 13.2 shows the locations of some of these areas on the lateral surface of the monkey brain as well as their locations on a two-dimensional flattened map that includes both the lateral areas and those

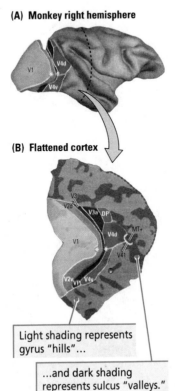

Figure 13.2 Topography of the visual cortex of the macaque monkey. (A) A nearly normal rendition of the lateral surface of the brain in which the sulci are opened slightly. (B) A flattened cortical surface showing both the lateral and the medial regions. The shaded areas represent regions that are normally curved up (gyri) or down (sulci). The asterisks refer to the foveal representation in areas B1 and V4. (After Tootell and Hadjikhani, 2001, with permission.)

Figure 13.3 Topography of the human visual cortex. (A) A nearly normal rendition of the lateral surface of the brain in which the sulci are opened slightly. (B) The medial surface in which the sulci are opened slightly. (C) A flattened cortical surface showing both the lateral and medial regions. The shaded areas represent regions that are normally curved up (gyri) or down (sulci). The asterisks refer to the foveal representation in areas V1 and V4. (After Tootell and Hadjikhani, 2001, with permission.)

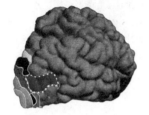

(A) Human right hemisphere (lateral, viewed slightly from behind)

(B) Right hemisphere (medial, viewed slightly from below)

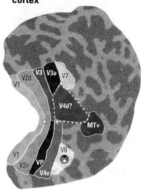

(C) Flattened view of occipital cortex

located on the medial surface of the hemisphere. The precise locations of the human homologues are still not settled, but Figure 13.3 presents a recent map constructed by Tootell and Hadjikhani that includes all of the monkey areas as well as an additional color-sensitive area (V8).

Some of the areas contain a complete visual field, whereas others have only an upper or lower visual field. This distinction is curious, and Previc has suggested that the upper and lower fields may have different functions, with the upper more specialized for visual search and recognition and the lower more specialized for visuomotor guidance.

A remarkable feature of area V1 is its complex laminar organization, which, as illustrated in Figure 13.4, is probably the most distinct of all cortical areas. Although we usually say that the cortex has six layers, it is possible to see many more in area V1, partly because layer IV alone features four distinct layers. Another surprising feature of area V1 is that, although it appears to be anatomically homogenous, it can be shown to actually be heterogeneous by staining it for the enzyme cytochrome oxidase, which is crucial in making energy available to cells. Regions of cytochrome-rich areas, known as blobs, are separated by interblob regions of little cytochrome activity (see Figure 10.10). It turns out that cells in the blobs take part in color perception and the interblobs have a role in form and motion perception.

The discovery that area V1 is functionally heterogeneous—that a given cortical area may have more than one distinct function—was unexpected. It

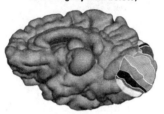

Parietal lobe

Striate cortex

Occipital lobe

Temporal lobe

Cell-body stain

Myelin stain

Because of the distinct stripes the visual cortex is sometimes called the striate cortex.

Figure 13.4 The visual cortex is highly laminated, as can be seen in a cell body stain (left) or a myelin stain (right) in these sections from a monkey brain. Because of the distinct stripes, the visual cortex is sometimes called the striate cortex.

turns out that area V2 also is heterogeneous when stained with cytochrome oxidase, but, instead of blobs, stripes are revealed (see Figure 10.10). One type, the "thin stripe," takes part in color perception. Two other types, known as thick stripes and pale stripes, have roles in form and motion perception, respectively. Thus, we see that the heterogeneity of function observed in area V1—representing color, form, and motion—is preserved in area V2, although it is organized in a different way.

The distribution of color function across much of the occipital cortex and beyond (i.e., areas V1, V2, V4, V8) is important because, until recently, the perception of form or movement was believed to be colorblind. It has now become clear that color vision is integral to the analysis of position, depth, motion, and structure of objects (see a review by Tanaka et al., 2001).

A key point here is that, although the relative amount of color processing certainly varies across occipital regions, with area V4 having color processing as its major function, the processing of color-related information does more than simply allow us to tell red from green. The appreciation of color also enriches our capacity to detect motion, depth, and position. In the absence of significant color analysis, dogs and cats thus not only see an essentially black-and-white world, but have reduced visual capacities more generally as well.

An example of the advantage of color vision can be seen in the type of photoreceptors in primates. Sumner and Mollon found that the color system of primates is optimized for differentiating edible fruits from a background of leaves. This ability to differentiate is an important advantage when having to select edible fruits from a complex scene and is especially important when the fruits are partly occluded by leaves, which is fairly common. In fact, color provides important information for object recognition in such cases. A partly occluded yellow banana is quickly seen, whereas a gray banana would be difficult to detect in a black-and-white scene.

Connections of the Visual Cortex

By the late 1960s, the consensus was that the visual cortex is hierarchically organized, with visual information proceeding from area 17 to area 18 to area 19. Each visual area was thought to provide some sort of elaboration on the processing of the preceding area. This strictly hierarchical view is now considered too simple, and has been replaced by the notion of a distributed hierarchical process with multiple parallel and interconnecting pathways at each level, much as illustrated in Figure 10.16.

There is still a hierarchy for vision, but with separate functions. As indicated in Chapter 10, the details of all the connections between the occipital areas and from them to the parietal, temporal, and frontal regions are bewildering, but it is possible to extract a few simple principles (Figure 13.5):

1. **V1** (the striate cortex) is the primary vision area: it receives the largest input from the lateral geniculate nucleus of the thalamus and it projects to all other occipital regions. V1 is the first processing level in the hierarchy.

Figure 13.5 Streams of visual processing. The occipitoparietal (dorsal) stream takes part in visual action and flows from area V1 to the posterior parietal visual areas. The occipitotemporal (ventral) stream takes part in object recognition and flows from area V1 to the temporal visual areas. The superior temporal sulcus (STS) stream, where information to and from the dorsal and ventral streams converges, flows from area V1 into the superior temporal sulcus.

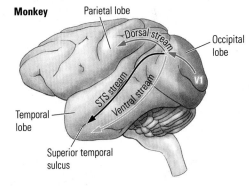

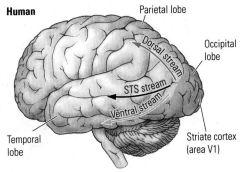

2. V2 also projects to all other occipital regions. V2 is the second level.

3. After V2, three distinct parallel pathways emerge en route to the parietal cortex, superior temporal sulcus, and inferior temporal cortex, for further processing.

As we shall see in more detail shortly, the parietal pathway, or **dorsal stream,** has a role in the visual guidance of movement, and the inferior temporal pathway, or **ventral stream,** is concerned with object perception (including color). The middle pathway along the superior temporal sulcus is probably important in visuospatial functions.

A Theory of Occipital-Lobe Function

We have seen that areas V1 and V2 are functionally heterogeneous and that both segregate processing for color, form, and motion. The heterogeneous functions of areas V1 and V2 contrast with the functions of the areas that follow in the hierarchy. In a sense, areas V1 and V2 appear to serve as little mailboxes into which different types of information are assembled before being sent on to the more specialized visual areas.

From areas V1 and V2 flow three parallel pathways that convey different attributes of vision. The information derived from the blob areas of area V1 goes to area V4, considered to be a color area. Cells in area V4 are not solely responsive to color, however; some cells respond to both form and color.

Other information from area V1 (the magnocellular input discussed in Chapter 8) also goes to area V2 and then to area V5, which is specialized to detect motion. Finally, an input from areas V1 and V2 to area V3 is concerned with what Zeki calls "dynamic form"—that is, the shape of objects in motion. Thus, we see that vision begins in the primary cortex (V1), which has multiple functions, and then continues in more specialized zones.

It is not surprising to discover that selective lesions up the hierarchy in areas V3, V4, and V5 produce specific deficits in visual processing. People who suffer damage to area V4 are able to see only in shades of gray. Curiously, patients not only fail to perceive colors but also fail to recall colors from before their injuries or even to imagine colors. In a real sense, the loss of area V4 results in the loss of color cognition, or the ability to think about color. Similarly, a lesion in area V5 produces an inability to perceive objects in motion. Objects at rest are perceived but, when the objects begin to move, they vanish. In principle, a lesion in area V3 will affect form perception but, because area V4 also processes form, a rather large lesion of both V3 and V4 would be required to eliminate form perception.

An important constraint on the functions of areas V3, V4, and V5 is that all these areas receive major input from area V1. People like Colonel P. M., with lesions in area V1, act as though they are blind, but visual input can still get through to higher levels—partly through small projections of the lateral geniculate nucleus to area V2 and partly through projections from the colliculus to the thalamus (the pulvinar) to the cortex. (This system is the tectopulvinar pathway described in Chapter 8.)

People with V1 lesions seem not to be aware of visual input and can be shown to have some aspects of vision only by special testing. Thus, when asked what they see, patients with V1 damage often reply that they see nothing. Nonetheless, they can act on visual information, indicating that they do indeed "see."

Area V1 thus appears to be primary for vision in yet another sense: V1 must function for the brain to make sense out of what the more specialized visual areas are processing. We must note, however, reports of people with significant V1 damage who are capable of some awareness of visual information, such as motion. Barbur and colleagues suggested that the integrity of area V3 may allow this conscious awareness, but this suggestion remains a hypothesis.

Visual Functions Beyond the Occipital Lobe

Neuroscientists have known since the early 1900s that the occipital lobes house vision, but only in the past two decades have they begun to understand the extent of visual processing that takes place beyond the occipital lobes. In fact, it is now clear that more cortex is concerned with vision than with any other function in the primate brain.

Felleman and van Essen's flattened cortical map in Figure 10.17 illustrates that, of the 32 cortical areas (of a total of about 70 in their scheme) that have visual functions in the monkey brain, only 9 are actually in the occipital lobe. The total surface area of the vision-related regions is about 55% of the whole cortical surface, which compares with 11% and 3% for the somatosensory and auditory regions, respectively. (It is interesting that so little of the monkey cortex represents audition, which is certainly evidence of a major difference between the brains of humans and those of monkeys; we humans have a much larger auditory representation, which is no doubt responsible for our preoccupation with both language and music.)

Visual processing in humans therefore does not culminate in secondary visual areas such as areas V3, V4, and V5 but continues within multiple visual regions in the parietal, temporal, and frontal lobes (see Figure 10.17). Functions have not been assigned to all these additional visual regions, but it is possible to speculate on what their functions must be. To do so, we can divide visual phenomena into five general categories: vision for action, action for vision, visual recognition, visual space, and visual attention.

Vision for Action

This category is visual processing required to direct specific movements. For example, when reaching for a particular object such as a cup, the fingers form a specific pattern that allows grasping of the cup. This movement is obviously guided by vision, because people do not need to shape their hands consciously as they reach.

In addition to that for grasping, there must be visual areas that guide all kinds of specific movements, including those of the eyes, head, and whole body. A single system could not easily guide all movements, because the requirements are so different. Reaching to pick up a jellybean requires a very different kind of motor control than that required to duck from a snowball, but both are visually guided.

(A) Normal subject

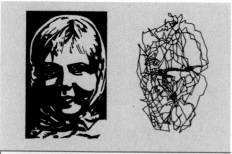

Eye movements of a normal subject concentrate on facial features and are directed more to the left side of the photograph.

(B) Normal subject

Sphere Bust

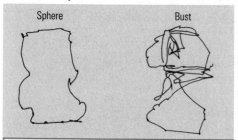

Eye movements of a normal subject concentrate on the shapes of the objects examined,...

(C) Agnosic subject

Sphere Bust

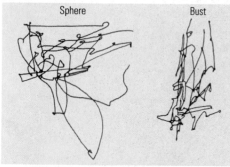

...but those of an agnosic subject are random.

Figure 13.6 Eye movements during the examination of a visual stimulus. (A) The concentration of eye movements (by a normal subject) to distinctive features of the face (eyes, nose, mouth); these movements are directed more to the left side of the photograph. (B) The eye movements of a normal subject examining a sphere (left) and a bust (right). (C) The eye movements of an agnosic subject examining the same shapes. Note the random movements of the agnosic subject. (From A. R. Luria, *The Working Brain*, © 1973, The Copyright Agency of the USSR. Reprinted with permission.)

Finally, vision for action must be sensitive to movement of the target. Catching a moving ball requires specific information about the location, trajectory, speed, and shape of the object. Vision for action is thought to be a function of the parietal visual areas.

Action for Vision

In a more "top down" process, the viewer actively searches for only part of the target object and attends selectively it (Figure 13.6). When we look at a visual stimulus, we do not simply stare at it; rather, we scan the stimulus with numerous eye movements. These movements are not random but tend to focus on important or distinct features of the stimulus.

When we scan a face, we make a lot of eye movements directed toward the eyes and mouth. Curiously, we also make more eye scans directed to the left visual field (the right side of the person's face) than to the right visual field. This scanning bias may be important in the way that we process faces, because it is not found in the scanning of other stimuli. People with deficits in action for vision are likely to have significant deficits in visual perception, although such deficits have not been studied systematically.

An interesting aspect of action for vision consists of the eye movements that we often make when we visualize information. For example, when people are asked to rotate objects mentally in order to answer simple questions about the objects' appearance, they usually make many eye movements, especially to the left. When people are doing things in the dark, such as winding photographic film onto spools for processing, they also make many eye movements. Curiously, if the eyes are closed, these movements stop. Indeed, it appears that it is easier to do many tasks in the dark if the eyes are closed. Because things are done by touch in the dark, the visual system may interfere until the eyes are closed.

Visual Recognition

We enjoy the ability both to recognize objects and to respond to visual information. For example, we can both recognize specific faces and discriminate and interpret different expressions in those faces. Similarly, we can recognize letters or symbols and assign meaning to them.

We can recognize different foods, tools, or body parts, but it is not reasonable to expect that we have different visual regions for each category or object. We may have at least some specialized areas for biologically significant information, such as faces, however. Cells in the temporal cortex appear to be highly specific in their preference for particular faces or hands. These visual areas in the temporal lobe are specialized for visual recognition.

Visual Space

Visual information comes from specific locations in space. This information allows us to direct our movements to objects in space and to assign meaning to objects. But spatial location is not a unitary characteristic. Objects have location both relative to an individual (**egocentric space**) and relative to one another (**allocentric space**).

Egocentric visual space is central to the control of your actions toward objects. It therefore seems likely that visual space is coded in neural systems related to vision for action. In contrast, allocentric properties of objects are necessary for you to construct a memory of spatial location.

A key feature of allocentric spatial coding is that it depends on the identity of particular features of the world. Thus, it is likely to be associated with the regions of visual recognition. In summary, different aspects of spatial processing probably take place in both the parietal and the temporal visual regions, and respective functions are integrated in areas that interact and exchange information.

Visual Attention

We cannot possibly process all the visual information available. This page has shape, color, texture, location, and so on, but the only really important characteristic is that it has words. Thus, when we read the page, we select a specific aspect of visual input and attend to it selectively.

In fact, neurons in the cortex show various attentional mechanisms. For example, neurons may respond selectively to stimuli in particular places or at particular times or if a particular movement is to be executed. Independent mechanisms of attention are probably required both for the guidance of movements (in the parietal lobe) and for object recognition (in the temporal lobe).

Visual Pathways Beyond the Occipital Lobe

Vision evolved first for motion, not for recognition. Simple organisms can detect light and move to or from the light. For example, the single-cell organism *Euglena* alters its swimming pattern as a function of the ambient light levels in different parts of the pond in which it lives. Because sunlight helps manufacture food in this aquatic environment, it is an advantage for *Euglena* to move toward the light.

Notice that *Euglena* need not "perceive" the light or make an internal map of the outside world. Rather, it is only necessary that some type of link exist between the amount of ambient light and locomotion. For *Euglena*, "vision" acts to guide movement—the most primitive form of vision for action.

However, our vision is far more complicated than that of *Euglena*. But even much of human vision can be understood without reference to recognition. Consider, for example, a major-league baseball batter who swings at a ball before it is possible for him to perceive what the object actually is. The visual guidance of his movement is independent of his recognition of the ball.

Nonetheless, as primitive animals interacted with their environment, they are adapted to learn more about their environment. Thus distinct visual systems evolved to recognize objects in the environment. The system of knowing what an object is includes the flow of visual information from area V1 to the temporal lobe, called the ventral stream (see Figure 13.5). The system controlling the visual guidance of movements includes the flow of information from area V1 to the parietal lobe, known as the dorsal stream.

The distinction between the ventral and the dorsal streams can be seen clearly in a series of patients studied by Milner and Goodale. They first described D. F., a patient who was blind but who nevertheless shaped her hand appropriately when asked to reach for objects. Her dorsal stream was intact, as revealed by the fact that she could "unconsciously" see location, size, and shape. On the other hand, Milner and Goodale noted that patients with dorsal-stream damage consciously reported seeing objects but could not reach accurately or shape the hand appropriately when reaching.

Milner and Goodale proposed that the dorsal stream should be thought of as a set of systems for the on-line visual control of action. Their argument is based on three main lines of evidence:

1. The predominant characteristic of the neurons in posterior parietal regions is that they are active during a combination of visual stimulation and associated behavior. For example, cells may be active only when a monkey reaches out to a particular object. Looking at an object in the absence of movement does not activate the neurons. Thus, these "visual" neurons are unique in that they are active only when the brain acts on visual information.

2. These posterior parietal neurons can therefore be characterized as an interface between analysis of the visual world and motor action taken on it. The demands of action have important implications for what type of information must be sent to the parietal cortex—information such as object shape, movement, and location. Each of these visual features is likely to be coded separately, and at least three distinct pathways within the dorsal stream run from area V1 to the parietal cortex. As illustrated on the right in Figure 13.7, one pathway goes from area V1 directly to area V5 to parietal cortex, a second goes from area V1 to areas V5 and V3a and then to parietal regions, and a third goes from area V1 to area V2 to the parietal cortex. These three pathways must certainly be functionally dissociable.

3. Most of the visual impairments associated with lesions to the parietal cortex can be characterized as visuomotor or orientational. (We return to this subject in Chapter 14.)

The Milner-Goodale model is an important theoretical advance in understanding how our visual brain is organized. As detailed in Figure 13.7, two distinct visual streams have evolved to use visual information in two fundamentally different ways: the dorsal stream for guiding movements and the ventral for identifying objects. This model can likely be applied to the organization of the auditory and somatosensory systems as well—both systems also function to guide movements and identify stimuli. An important point here is that we are conscious of only a small amount of what the brain actually does; even with effort, we cannot gain awareness of much of our sensory processing.

One wrinkle must be added to the Milner-Goodale model—the third stream of visual processing, which originates from

Figure 13.7 A summary of the visual processing hierarchy. The dorsal stream, which takes part in visual action, guides movements such as the hand postures for grasping a mug or pen, as illustrated. The ventral stream, which takes part in object recognition, identifies objects such as mugs and pens in our visual world. The dorsal and ventral streams exchange information through polysensory neurons in the superior temporal sulcus stream, as shown by double-headed arrows. (After Goodale, 1993.)

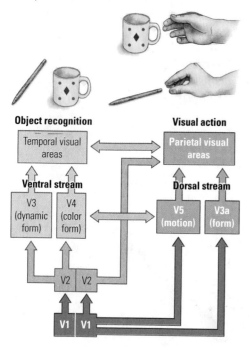

structures associated with both the parietal and the temporal pathways and flows to a region of the temporal lobe that is buried in the superior temporal sulcus (see Figure 13.5). The superior temporal sulcus is characterized by **polysensory neurons**—neurons that are responsive to both visual and auditory or both visual and somatosensory input. The interaction of the parietal and temporal streams in the superior temporal sulcus is probably due to interaction between the dorsal and the ventral—the "action" and "recognition"—streams.

Imaging Studies of Dorsal and Ventral Streams

Brain regions associated with specific visual pathways can be identified by measuring regional blood flow as people perform visual tasks. Ungerleider and Haxby reviewed such PET studies, as summarized in Figure 13.8.

In studies by Haxby and colleagues, subjects were given two tasks. In the first, the subjects indicated which of two faces was identical with a sample face. In the second, the subjects were asked to identify which of two stimuli had a dot (or square) in the same location as in a sample. The results showed activation of the temporal regions for the facial stimuli and activation of the posterior parietal region for the location task (see Figure 13.8A). Note, in addition, the activation of frontal areas for the spatial task, supporting the idea that the frontal lobe plays a role in certain aspects of visual processing.

One difficulty with interpretation of the spatial-task PET images is that subjects have to make eye movements, which activate regions in the dorsal stream; so whether the spatial or the movement components activate the parietal region is not clear. The important point, however, is that different regions take part in the two tasks.

A similar dissociation was identified among the processes that detect motion, color, and shape (see Figure 13.8B). Detection of motion activates regions in the

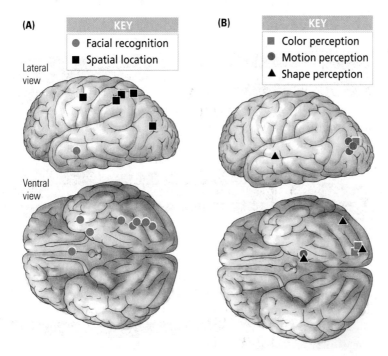

Figure 13.8 Summary of results of PET studies illustrating selective activation of (A) cortical regions by tasks of facial recognition (circles) versus spatial location (squares) and (B) areas associated with perception of color (squares), motion (circles), and shape (triangles). (After Ungerleider and Haxby, 1994.)

vicinity of area V5, whereas detection of shape activates regions along the superior temporal sulcus and the ventral region of the temporal lobe. The perception of color is associated with activation of the region of the lingual gyrus, which is the location of area V4. One study also found activation of a lateral occipital region, which is difficult to interpret in the light of lesion studies. This study made special visual attention demands of its participants, potentially an important factor in interpreting the observed activation.

In summary, studies of regional blood flow in normal subjects show results consistent with the general notion of two separate visual streams, one to the parietal lobe and the other to the temporal lobe. In addition, it is clear that separate visual functions reside in different temporo-occipital regions.

Figure 13.9 Visual defects subsequent to damage at different levels of the visual system, keyed by number. A darkened region in the visual field denotes a blind area. (After Curtis, 1972.)

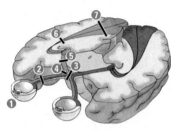

Patient's actual visual field

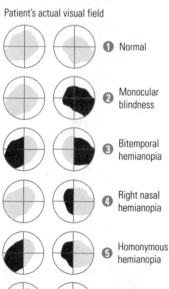

1. Normal

2. Monocular blindness

3. Bitemporal hemianopia

4. Right nasal hemianopia

5. Homonymous hemianopia

6. Quadrant-anopia

7. Macular sparing

Disorders of Visual Pathways

Before we consider the deficits associated with damage to the visual pathways, we must revisit two key elements in the way in which the brain organizes the visual fields:

1. The left half of each retina sends its projections to the right side of the brain, whereas the right half of each retina sends its projections to the left side of the brain (see Figure 11.5). Thus, the representation of each side of the visual world seen by each eye is sent to the same place in area V1. As a result, damage to area V1 affects vision in both eyes. Conversely, if a visual disturbance is restricted to just one eye, then the damage must be outside the brain, either in the retina or in the optic nerve.

2. Different parts of the visual field are topographically represented in different parts of area V1 (Figure 13.9). Thus, injury to a specific region of area V1 produces a loss of vision in a specific part of the visual world.

Now let us consider what happens when there is damage to different places in the visual pathways, as keyed on Figure 13.9.

Destruction of the retina or optic nerve of one eye produces monocular blindness—the loss of sight in that eye. A lesion of the medial region of the optic chiasm severs the crossing fibers, producing **bitemporal hemianopia**—loss of vision of both temporal fields. This symptom can arise when a tumor develops in the pituitary gland, which sits medially, next to the chiasm. As the tumor grows, it can put pressure on the medial part of the chiasm and produce the loss, or disturbance, of lateral vision.

A lesion of the lateral chiasm results in a loss of vision of one nasal field, or *nasal hemianopia*. Complete cuts of the optic tract, lateral geniculate body, or area V1 result in **homonymous hemianopia**—blindness of one entire visual field (see Figures 13.9 and 13.10A). Note that, because the disturbance affects information coming from both eyes, the visual defect is present in both eyes.

Indeed, the effects of such injuries enable investigators to determine whether a lesion is in the eye or optic tract versus the optic nerve or brain. The former injuries produce visual disturbance in one eye, whereas the latter injuries produce visual disturbance in the visual field and thus in both eyes. Should this lesion be partial, as is often the case, only a part (quadrant) of the visual field is destroyed (see Figures 13.9 and 13.10).

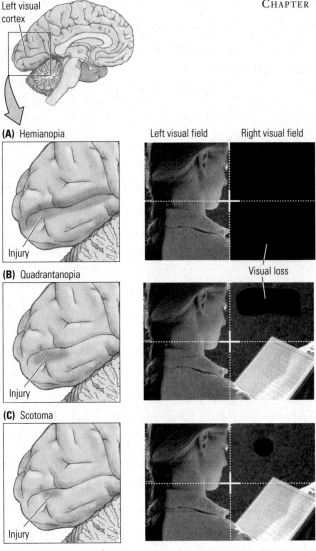

Left visual cortex

(A) Hemianopia

Injury

(B) Quadrantanopia

Injury

(C) Scotoma

Injury

Left visual field Right visual field

Visual loss

Figure 13.10 Consequences of lesions in area V1. The bluedark areas indicate the regions of visual loss. (A) The effect of a complete lesion of area V1 in the left hemisphere is hemianopia affecting the right visual field. (B) A large lesion of the lower lip of the calcarine fissure produces a quadrantanopia that affects most of the upper-right visual quadrant. (C) A smaller lesion of the lower lip of the calcarine fissure results in a smaller injury, a scotoma. (Jim Pickerell/Stock Connection/PictureQuest.)

Lesions of the occipital lobe often spare the central, or macular, region of the visual field, although the reason is uncertain. The most reasonable explanations are that (1) the macular region receives a double vascular supply, from both the middle and the posterior cerebral arteries, making it more resilient to large hemispheric lesions, or (2) the foveal region of the retina projects to both hemispheres, and so, even if one occipital lobe is destroyed, the other receives projections from the fovea. The first explanation is more likely.

Macular sparing of the central visual field helps to differentiate lesions of the optic tract or thalamus from cortical lesions, because macular sparing occurs only after lesions (usually large) to the visual cortex. Macular sparing does not always occur, however, and many people with visual-cortex lesions have a complete loss of vision in one-quarter (quadrantanopia) or one-half (hemianopia) of the fovea (see Figures 13.9 and 13.10B). A curious aspect of both hemianopia and quadrantanopia is that the border between the impaired visual area and the adjacent, intact visual field, or quadrant, is sharp, much as if a pair of scissors were used to cut away part of the visual field (see Figure 13.9). This sharp demarcation of intact and impaired visual regions is due to the anatomical segregation between the left and the right and the upper and the lower visual fields.

Small lesions of the occipital lobe often produce **scotomas,** small blind spots in the visual field (Figure 13.10C). A curious aspect of scotomas is that people are often totally unaware of them because of *nystagmus* (constant, tiny, involuntary eye movements) and "spontaneous filling in" by the visual system. The eyes are usually in constant motion; so the scotoma moves about the visual field, allowing the brain to perceive all the information in the field. If the eyes are held still, the visual system actually completes objects, faces, and so on, resulting in a normal percept of the stimulus.

The visual system may cover up the scotoma so successfully that its presence can be demonstrated to the patient only by "tricking" the visual system. Such tricking can be achieved by placing objects entirely within the scotoma region of the patient's visual field and, without allowing the patient to shift gaze, asking what the object is. If no object is reported, the examiner moves the object out of the scotoma so that it suddenly "appears" in the intact region of the patient's visual field, thus demonstrating the existence of a blind region.

A similar phenomenon can be demonstrated in your own "blind spot." Stand beside a table, close or cover one eye, stare at a spot on the table, and move a pencil along the table laterally, from directly below your nose to between 20 and 30 cm toward the periphery. Part of the pencil will vanish when you reach the blind spot. You can move the pencil through the blind spot slowly, and it will suddenly reappear on the other side. Notice that, like a scotoma, the normal blind spot is not noticeable, even when you look around the world with just one eye. Even the normal brain "fills in" missing bits of the visual world.

Disorders of Cortical Function

Research into selective disturbances of human visual functions is limited mainly to case studies, such as case P. M., whom you met at the beginning of this chapter, and these natural lesions seldom respect the boundaries of specific visual areas. Several case histories, each with distinctly different symptoms and pathology, will give you a feeling for the specific symptoms of injury to the visual cortex. We begin with damage to area V1 and proceed along the hierarchy to higher areas and more-complicated visual disturbances.

Case B. K.: V1 Damage and a Scotoma

One morning B. K. awoke to discover that he was hemianopic in the left visual field. Given a history of classic migraine, in which the aura was nearly always in the left visual field, it is likely that he had a migraine stroke. Within a few hours, the left lower field began to return, but the left upper quadrant was slow to show any change.

A CT scan (Figure 13.11A) showed a clear infarct (dead tissue) in the right occipital area. The size of a visual-field defect is routinely measured with perimetry, a standardized method in which the subject fixates on a black dot in the center of a large white hemisphere. A small light is moved around the field, and the task is to indicate when it can be seen. The brightness and size of the light can be varied, thus manipulating the difficulty of the task.

(A) Three planes of section through B.K.'s brain

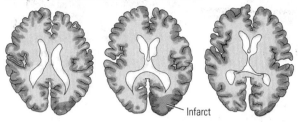

Infarct

(B) The visual fields of the left and right eyes

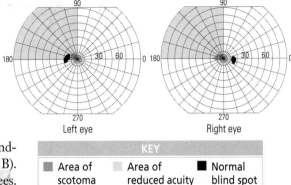

Left eye   Right eye

KEY		
■ Area of scotoma	Area of reduced acuity	■ Normal blind spot

Performance is mapped by indicating the area of "blindness" on a schematic map of the visual fields (Figure 13.11B). Size in the visual field is measured by visual angle, in degrees. (A degree is roughly the size of your thumb viewed at arm's length.) Thus, for B. K., the area of complete inability to perceive even a very large bright light is measured from the center, 6° upward along the vertical midline and about 15° laterally along the horizontal midline. The area beyond this zone in the left upper quadrant does not have normal vision, however, because B. K. is still unable to perceive less-bright lights in this area.

The nature of B. K.'s visual defects can be illustrated best in the context of their poststroke evolution. For the first 2 to 3 days, his visual field appeared dark, much as though a piece of smoked glass were blocking his view of the world beyond. On the fourth day, this darkness had disappeared and was replaced by "visual noise" (a scintillating scotoma) throughout much of the field, especially in the area of the scotoma. Visual noise is best described as being like colored "snow" on a television screen. At about the same time, B. K. first perceived movement in the field as a traveling "wave," much like ripples on a pond. There was no perception of form or pattern.

A curious phenomenon was first observed during perimetry testing 4 days after the stroke. If the stimulus light was moved into the blind field, it was not perceived until it moved into another quadrant. Curiously, however, B. K. immediately became aware (in hindsight) that the light had been present in the blind field and could accurately state where it entered the blind field. In other words, B. K. perceived location without being able to perceive content. Recall that Colonel P. M also experienced this phenomenon, known as **blindsight**.

In the ensuing 4 to 6 months, the area of blindness decreased somewhat and acuity in the periphery improved significantly for B. K. Nonetheless, roughly 15 years later, form vision remains poor in the left upper quadrant, outside the scotoma. The scintillating colored snow is still present, showing little change from the first few days after the stroke.

The visual phenomena observed by B. K. indicate that area V1 (and perhaps area V2) probably has an area of total cell death (the dense scotoma). The presence of poor form vision in the rest of the quadrant may be due to a loss of some but not all neurons in area V1, possibly only those neurons that are especially sensitive to a period of reduced blood flow, known as ischemia. The poor form vision might also be attributed to the fact that other visual areas, especially area V2, remain intact.

B. K.'s symptoms show that other occipital areas are functional, because he perceives color and motion even though there is no form perception. Thus, B. K. can accurately perceive the color or motion of objects that he cannot

Figure 13.11 Scan and map of B. K.'s brain. (A) Schematic representation of B. K.'s CT scan, showing the infarct in the right occipital area in different views. (B) Map of B. K.'s visual fields 6 months after the stroke. Subnormal vision persists in the upper-left quadrant.

identify. Those who are myopic (nearsighted) experience a similar phenomenon: the colors of objects or lights can be perceived, whereas the form is not recognizable. B. K.'s stroke thus indicates the presence of at least four independent visual functions: form (which is absent), as well as color, movement, and location (which are spared).

The loss of one-quarter of the fovea leads B. K. to make a variety of visual errors. Immediately after the stroke, he was able to read only with great difficulty. When we look at a word, the fixation point is in the center of the word; so, for B. K., half of the word is absent. Indeed, he had difficulty finding the edge of the page because it was in the blind field. Normal reading returned as B. K. learned to direct his gaze slightly to the left and upward (probably about 2° in each direction), which allowed words to fall in the normal visual field.

This "recovery" took about 6 weeks. Returning to playing squash and tennis was equally challenging because, when a ball entered the scotoma, it was lost. Similarly, facial recognition was slower than it had been before the stroke, because the information in the left visual field appears to be particularly important for face recognition.

Case D. B.: V1 Damage and Blindsight

D. B. is one of the most extensively studied people with visual disturbance from an occipital lesion (see the detailed monograph by Weiskrantz). D. B.'s right calcarine fissure was removed surgically to excise an angioma, which is a collection of abnormal blood vessels. D. B. therefore has a hemianopia based on standard perimetry but nevertheless has surprising visual capacities.

When questioned about his vision in the left field, D. B. usually reports that he sees nothing, as did P. M. and B. K. Occasionally, D. B. indicates that he had a "feeling" that a stimulus was "approaching" or was "smooth" or "jagged." But, according to Weiskrantz, D. B. always stresses that he "saw" nothing, that typically he is guessing, and that he is at a loss for words to describe any conscious perception.

In contrast, when D. B. was asked to point to locations in the impaired field in which spots of light were turned on briefly, he was surprisingly accurate. His blindsight contrasts with his subjective impression that he saw nothing at all. Furthermore, he appears to be able to discriminate the orientation of lines, which he could not report "seeing." Thus, he can discriminate a 10° difference in orientation between two successively presented gratings in his impaired field.

Finally, D. B. can detect some forms of movement. When a vigorously moving stimulus was used, he reported "seeing" something. In this case, he did not report actually seeing a visual stimulus but rather spoke of complex patterns of lines and grids. These patterns may have been something like B. K.'s moving lines. In summary, D. B. has "cortical blindness," or blindsight, in which he reports no conscious awareness of "seeing" but still is able to report the movement and location of objects that he cannot recognize.

Case J. I.: V4 Damage and Color

Oliver Sacks and Robert Wasserman report the touching story of J. I., an artist who suddenly became color-blind. In 1986, the man was in a car accident in which he sustained a concussion. His principal symptoms after the injury were an inability to distinguish any colors whatsoever, but his visual acuity had actually improved. "Within days . . . my vision was that of an eagle—I can see a worm wiggling a block away. The sharpness of focus is incredible."

The effect of the loss of color vision was far greater than one would have expected. J. I. could barely stand the pain of living in a world that appeared in shades of gray. He found the changed appearance of people unbearable, because their flesh was an abhorrent gray ("rat-colored") to him. He found foods disgusting in their grayish, dead appearance, and he had to close his eyes to eat. He could not even imagine colors any longer. The mental image of a tomato looked as black as its actual appearance. Even his dreams, which had once been in vivid colors, were now in black and gray.

Detailed visual testing by Sacks and Wasserman, and later by Zeki, revealed that J. I. was color-blind by the usual definitions, but this color blindness was attributed to specific damage to the occipital cortex. In addition, it did appear that his acuity had improved, especially at twilight or at night. Two years after his injury, J. I.'s despair had declined, and he appeared to no longer be able to remember color well. This failure to remember color is curious, because people who become blind through injury to the eyes or optic nerves do not lose their imagery or memory of color. There is little doubt from J. I.'s case that imagery and memory rely on the operation of at least some cortical structures necessary for the original perception.

Case P. B.: Conscious Color Perception in a Blind Patient

Zeki and his colleagues described the case of a man who was electrocuted, resulting in cardiac and respiratory arrest. P. B. was resuscitated but had suffered brain ischemia that produced a large area of posterior cortical damage. P. B. was left virtually blind, although he can detect the presence or absence of light. The remarkable visual feature, however, is that P. B.'s capacity to identify and name colors remains intact, as does his ability to name the typical color of imagined objects.

P. B.'s vision is in many ways opposite that of J. I.; the results of fMRI studies show that P. B. has activation in areas V1 and V2 in response to colored stimuli. As we reflect on the visual capacity of P. B., it is hard to imagine a world that is filled with color but no form, almost like an out-of-focus kaleidoscope that changes as we gaze around the world.

Case L. M.: V5 Damage and the Perception of Movement

Zihl and his colleagues reported the case of a 43-year-old woman who had a bilateral posterior injury resulting from a vascular abnormality. Her primary chronic complaint was a loss of movement vision. For example, she had difficulty pouring tea into a cup because the fluid appeared to be frozen. And she could not stop pouring, because she could not see the fluid level rise.

L. M. found being in a room with other people disturbing because she could not see them moving; they suddenly appeared "here or there," but she did not see them move in between. The results of other tests of visual function appeared essentially normal. She could discriminate colors, recognize objects, and read and write.

Her condition is especially intriguing because we would not believe intuitively that such a syndrome is likely. Loss of color or form vision fits with our everyday experience that people can be color-blind or myopic; loss of the ability to see moving objects is counterintuitive indeed. Case L. M. is important because she shows that the brain must analyze movement of form separately from the form itself.

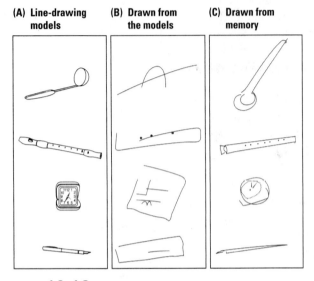

(A) Line-drawing models   **(B) Drawn from the models**   **(C) Drawn from memory**

Figure 13.12 Samples of D. F.'s drawings. (A) Examples of the original line drawings presented to D. F. (B) Examples of D. F.'s drawings of the models. (C) D. F.'s drawings based on memory of the models. Note that the drawings from memory are superior to the copies of the line drawings of the models.

Case D. F.: Occipital Damage and Visual Agnosia

Visual agnosia is the term coined by Sigmund Freud for an inability to combine individual visual impressions into complete patterns—thus, the inability to recognize objects or their pictorial representations or the inability to draw or copy them. Goodale and Milner and their colleagues have extensively studied a 35-year-old visual agnosic who suffered carbon monoxide poisoning that resulted in bilateral damage to the lateral occipital region (mainly areas 18 and 19) and in the tissue at the junction of the parietal and occipital cortex.

D. F., whom we met earlier in the chapter in considering Goodale and Milner's distinction between the dorsal and the ventral streams, has essentially normal color vision and can see well enough to get around in the world. Her principal deficit is *visual-form agnosia*, a severe inability to recognize line drawings of objects. Thus, although D. F. can recognize many actual objects, she is unable to recognize drawings of them. Furthermore, as illustrated in Figure 13.12, although she can draw objects from memory, she has real difficulty in drawing objects from life and even more difficulty in copying line drawings. Thus, D. F. appears to have a serious defect in form perception.

Recall that the remarkable thing about D. F. is her apparently nearly intact ability to guide hand and finger movements toward objects that she cannot recognize. For example, although D. F. had a gross deficit in judging lines as horizontal or vertical, she could reach out and "post" a hand-held card into a slot rotated to different orientations, as illustrated in Figure 13.13. Indeed, analysis of video records of D. F.'s reaching revealed that, like normal control subjects, she began to orient the card correctly even as her hand was being raised

Figure 13.13 Testing visuomotor guidance. (A) The apparatus that was used to test sensitivity to orientation in patient D. F. The slot could be placed in any orientation around the clock. The task is to "post" the card into the slot as shown. (B) Plots of the orientation of the card in a perceptual matching task and in the visuomotor posting task. For illustration, the correct orientation has been rotated to vertical. D. F. was unable to match the orientation of the card to that of the slot unless she made a movement to post it. (Adapted with permission from Goodale, 2000.)

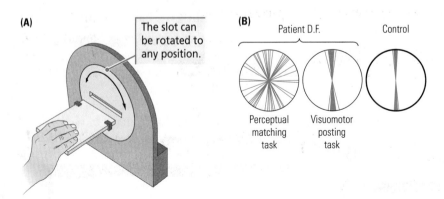

(A) The slot can be rotated to any position.

(B) Patient D.F.   Control

Perceptual matching task   Visuomotor posting task

from the start position of the task. In other words, D. F. could use visual form information to guide movements to objects (the dorsal stream), but she could not use visual information to recognize the same objects (the ventral stream).

Case V. K.: Parietal Damage and Visuomotor Guidance

Damage to the posterior parietal lobe produces a disorder known as **optic ataxia**, a deficit in visually guided hand movements, such as reaching, that cannot be ascribed to motor, somatosensory, or visual-field or -acuity deficits. V. K. is a woman with bilateral hemorrhages in the occipitoparietal regions, as described by Jakobson and colleagues. Although V. K. initially appeared virtually blind, her symptoms dissipated in a month, and she was left with disordered control of her gaze, impairment in visual attention, and optic ataxia. (Collectively, these symptoms are known as Balint's syndrome; see Chapter 14.)

V. K. had good form and color vision and could recognize and name objects; however, her ability to reach for objects was grossly impaired. Thus, in contrast with D. F., who was able to reach and orient her hand posture toward different objects that she could not perceive, V. K. was unable to coordinate reaching and grasping for objects that she could perceive.

This difficulty was not merely one of being unable to direct movements in space, because V. K. could point to objects. What she could not do was to form the appropriate hand postures needed to grasp objects of different shapes, as illustrated in Figure 13.14. Taken together, cases D. F. and V. K. suggest that the mechanisms underlying the conscious perception of object form are dissociable from the mechanisms controlling visually guided movements to the same objects.

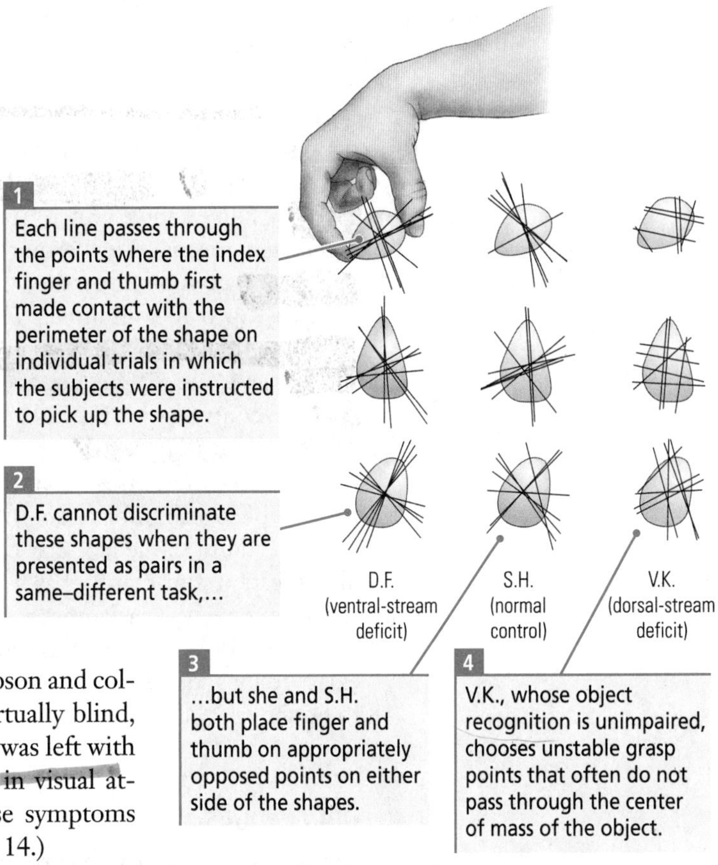

Cases D. and T.: Higher-Level Visual Processes

Two cases described by Campbell and colleagues illustrate an intriguing dissociation of visual functions. Case D. has a right occipitotemporal lesion associated with a left upper quadrantanopia that extends into the lower quadrant. As would be expected from B. K.'s case, D. had some initial difficulties in reading, but her language abilities were intact. Curiously, she was completely unable to recognize people by their faces and had difficulty identifying handwriting, including her own.

Recall from the case presented at the beginning of this chapter that P. M. also had difficulty in recognizing faces. His view on his difficulty was that, although he could see the different bits of the face quite clearly, he had trouble putting it all together because, unless a person was a long way off, the entire face was not in the visual field all at once. You can imagine what it would be like to try to recognize people by looking at snapshots of different parts of their faces.

1 Each line passes through the points where the index finger and thumb first made contact with the perimeter of the shape on individual trials in which the subjects were instructed to pick up the shape.

2 D.F. cannot discriminate these shapes when they are presented as pairs in a same–different task,...

D.F. (ventral-stream deficit) S.H. (normal control) V.K. (dorsal-stream deficit)

3 ...but she and S.H. both place finger and thumb on appropriately opposed points on either side of the shapes.

4 V.K., whose object recognition is unimpaired, chooses unstable grasp points that often do not pass through the center of mass of the object.

Figure 13.14 The brain has different systems for visual object recognition and visual guidance of movement. Representative "grasping" axes for three different shapes by patient D. F. with visual form agnosia (ventral-stream deficit), by control subject S. H. with no brain damage and by V. K., a patient with bilateral occipitoparietal damage resulting in optic ataxia (dorsal-stream deficit). Even though D. F. does not recognize the object, she perceives enough information about shape to control her grasp as she picks it up. In contrast, V. K. recognizes objects but cannot control her movements in relation to them. (Adapted from Milner and Goodale, 1995.)

The facial-recognition deficit, **prosopagnosia,** is particularly interesting because many prosopagnosics cannot recognize even their own faces in a mirror. Although D. could not recognize faces, she could make use of information in faces. For example, when given various tests of lip reading, she appeared completely normal. Furthermore, she could imitate the facial movements and expressions of another person.

Case T. provides an interesting contrast to case D. Case T. has a left occipitotemporal lesion with a right hemianopia. She had great difficulty reading (**alexia**) and was unable to name colors, even though she could discriminate them. In contrast with D., T. had no difficulty in recognizing familiar faces but was impaired in lip reading.

Taken together, cases D. and T. indicate that face identification and the extraction of speech information from faces do not call on the same cortical systems. In addition, the fact that D. has a lesion on the right and a deficit in face identification and that T. has a lesion on the left and a deficit in lip reading suggests a relative asymmetry in some aspects of occipital-lobe functions. Exactly what visual processes are impaired in the two cases and what the necessary lesions for deficits in facial recognition and lip reading might be remain to be shown.

Conclusions from Case Studies

Several conclusions can be extracted from the behavior and pathology of these cases:

- There are clearly distinct syndromes of visual disturbance.

- Some symptoms can be taken as evidence of a fundamental dissociation between vision for guiding movements (the dorsal stream) and visual recognition (the ventral stream).

- The dissociability of the symptoms in the various patients implies that our introspective view of a unified visual experience is false. The fact that objects can be seen when they are still but not when they are moving is particularly disturbing, because it seems to defy the commonsense view that an object is the same object whether it is moving or still. Clearly the brain does not treat objects in the same way in the two conditions.

- Neuroscientists have at least suggestive evidence of an asymmetry in occipital-lobe functions.

Visual Agnosia

A difficulty in describing the symptomatology and pathology of agnosia is the bewildering variety of patients and symptoms discussed in the neurological literature. Another, as Farah has pointed out, is that there is no agreement on a taxonomy of agnosia, which makes classifying different patterns of symptoms very difficult. We shall separate visual agnosias into object agnosias and other agnosias.

Object Agnosias

The traditional way to classify visual-object agnosia is to distinguish two broad forms: apperceptive agnosia and associative agnosia.

Apperceptive Agnosia

Any failure of object recognition in which relatively basic visual functions (acuity, color, motion) are preserved is apperceptive. This agnosia category has been applied to an extremely heterogeneous set of patients, but the fundamental deficit is an inability to develop a percept of the structure of an object or objects. In the simplest case, patients are simply unable to recognize, copy, or match simple shapes, much like case D. F.

Many patients have another unusual symptom, too—often referred to as **simultagnosia.** In this case, patients can perceive the basic shape of an object, but they are unable to perceive more than one object at a time. Thus, if two objects are presented together, only one is perceived. Such patients often act as though they were blind, possibly because they are simply overwhelmed by the task at hand. Imagine trying to see the world one object at a time.

Apperceptive agnosia does not result from a restricted lesion but usually follows gross bilateral damage to the lateral parts of the occipital lobes, including regions sending outputs to the ventral stream. Such injuries are probably most commonly associated with carbon monoxide poisoning, which appears to produce neuronal death in "watershed" regions—that is, regions lying in the border areas between territories of different arterial systems.

Associative Agnosia

The inability to recognize an object despite an apparent perception of the object is associative agnosia. Thus, the associative agnosic can copy a drawing rather accurately, indicating a coherent percept, but cannot identify it. Associative agnosia is therefore conceived as being at a "higher cognitive" level of processing that is associated with stored information about objects—that is, with memory.

In effect, failure of object recognition is a defect in memory that affects not only past knowledge about the object but also the acquisition of new knowledge. Associative agnosias are more likely with damage to regions in the ventral stream that are farther up the processing hierarchy, such as the anterior temporal lobe.

Other Agnosias

A critical point in understanding the nature of visual agnosia is that the most commonly affected region is the tissue at the occipitotemporal border, which is part of the ventral visual pathway. Visual agnosias do not appear to result from damage to the dorsal stream. Note, however, that agnosias are at least partly dissociable, which means that there must be different streams of visual information processing within the ventral pathway. We now briefly consider three other visual agnosias.

Prosopagnosia

Patients with facial agnosia (recall cases D. and P. M.) cannot recognize any previously known faces, including their own as seen in a mirror or photograph. They can recognize people by face information, however, such as a birthmark, mustache, or characteristic hairdo.

Prosopagnosics may not accept the fact that they cannot recognize their own faces, probably because they know who must be in the mirror and thus see themselves. We saw one young woman who was convinced of the severity of her problem only when she was presented with her identical twin sister. When asked who her twin was, she indicated that she had never seen the woman before. Imagine her amazement to discover that the person was her twin sister.

According to Damasio and colleagues, most facial agnosics can tell human from nonhuman faces and can recognize facial expressions normally. All postmortem studies on facial agnosics have found bilateral damage, and the results of imaging studies in living patients confirm the bilateral nature of the injury in most patients, with the damage centered in the region below the calcarine fissure at the temporal junction. These results imply that the process of facial recognition is probably bilateral, but asymmetrical.

Alexia

An inability to read has often been seen as the complementary symptom to facial-recognition deficits. Alexia is most likely to result from damage to the left fusiform and lingual areas. Either hemisphere can read letters, but only the left hemisphere appears able to combine the letters to form lexical representations (that is, words). Alexia can be conceived to be a form of object agnosia in which there is an inability to construct perceptual wholes from parts or to be a form of associative agnosia, in which case word memory (the lexical store) is either damaged or inaccessible.

Visuospatial Agnosia

Among this variety of disorders of spatial perception and orientation, one disruptive form is *topographical disorientation*—the inability to find one's way around familiar environments such as one's neighborhood. People with this deficit seem unable to recognize landmarks that would indicate the appropriate direction in which to travel. Most people with topographical disorientation have other visual deficits, especially defects in facial recognition. Thus, it is not surprising to find that the critical area for this disorder lies in the right medial occipitotemporal region, including the fusiform and lingual gyri.

Why Are Faces Special?

Most of us probably spend more time looking at faces than at any other single stimulus. Infants prefer to look at faces almost from birth, and adults are excellent at identifying familiar faces despite large variations in expression and viewing angles, even when the faces are disguised with beards, spectacles, or hats. Faces also convey a wealth of social information, and we humans are unique among primates in spending a good deal of time looking directly at the faces of other members of our species.

Figure 13.15 The "Thatcher illusion." Look at the face of former British Prime Minister Margaret Thatcher as presented (upside down) and then invert the page and look again. There is a compelling illusion of normalcy in the inverted face but, in the upright view, the reconfigured face appears hideous. Lady Thatcher was the original subject of the illusion that now bears her name.

The importance of faces as visual stimuli has led to the idea that a special pathway exists in the visual system for the analysis of faces (see Farah, 1998, for a review). Several lines of evidence support this view. In the first place, the results of studies of monkeys show neurons in the temporal lobe that are specifically tuned to different faces, with some cells attuned to facial identity and others to facial expression. (We return to these cells in Chapter 15.) In the second place, inverting a photograph of any object that has a usual right side up makes it harder to recognize, but the effect on faces is disproportionate (see a review by Valentine).

Similarly, we are particularly sensitive to the configuration of upright faces. Consider the illusion shown in Figure 13.15, which illustrates this effect. The importance of an upright orientation to facial perception is also seen in imaging studies. For example, Haxby and his colleagues showed that inverted faces are processed by the same cortical regions as are other visual stimuli, whereas upright faces are processed in a separate face-perception system. This face-perception system is surprisingly extensive and includes regions not only in the occipital lobe but also in several different regions of the temporal lobe.

Figure 13.16 summarizes a model by Haxby and colleagues in which different aspects of facial perception (such as facial expression versus identity) are analyzed in core visual areas in the temporal part of the ventral stream. The model also includes other cortical regions as an "extended system" that includes the analysis of other facial characteristics such as emotion and lip reading. The key point here is that the analysis of faces is unlike that of other visual stimuli.

Figure 13.16 A model of the distributed human neural system for face perception. The model is divided into a core system, consisting of occipital and temporal regions, and an extended system, including regions that are part of neural systems for other cognitive functions. The fusiform gyrus is an occipital region lying on the ventral surface of the temporal lobe. (After Haxby, Hoffman, and Gobbini, 2000.)

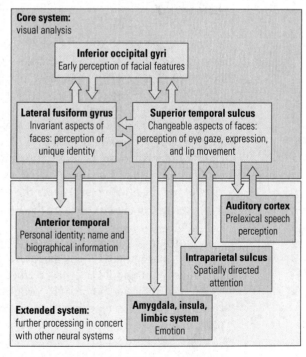

Core system:
visual analysis

Inferior occipital gyri
Early perception of facial features

Lateral fusiform gyrus
Invariant aspects of faces: perception of unique identity

Superior temporal sulcus
Changeable aspects of faces: perception of eye gaze, expression, and lip movement

Auditory cortex
Prelexical speech perception

Anterior temporal
Personal identity: name and biographical information

Intraparietal sulcus
Spatially directed attention

Extended system:
further processing in concert with other neural systems

Amygdala, insula, limbic system
Emotion

(A) Original face

(B) Composite of right sides

(C) Composite of the left sides

Figure 13.17 The split-faces test. Subjects were asked which of the two pictures, B or C, most closely resembles picture A. Control subjects chose picture C significantly more often than picture B. Picture C corresponds to that part of picture A falling in a subject's left visual field. The woman pictured chose B, the view that she is accustomed to seeing in the mirror. (After Kolb, Milner, and Taylor, 1983.)

Finally, a clear asymmetry exists in the role of the temporal lobes in the analysis of faces. Right temporal lesions have a greater effect on facial processing than do similar left temporal lesions. Even in control subjects, researchers can see an asymmetry in face perception.

We presented subjects with photographs of faces, as illustrated in Figure 13.17. Photographs B and C are composites of the right or the left sides, respectively, of the original face shown in photograph A. Asked to identify which composite most resembled the original, normal subjects consistently matched the left side of photograph A to its composite in photograph C, whether the photographs were presented upright or inverted. Furthermore, patients with either right temporal or right parietal removals failed to consistently match either side of the face in either the upright or the inverted presentation.

The results of this split-faces test not only show an asymmetry in facial processing but also speak to the nature of our perceptions of our own faces. Self-perception provides a unique example of visual perception, because your own image of your face comes largely from looking in a mirror, where the image is reversed, whereas the image that others have of your face comes from direct view. Inspection of Figure 13.17 illustrates the implications of this difference. Photograph A is the image that other people see of this woman and, because there is a left-visual-field bias in our perception, most right-handers choose photograph C as the picture most resembling the original. Consider the choice of the woman herself, however. Her common view of her face (in the mirror) is the reverse of ours, and hence she is more likely to choose (and in fact did choose) composite photograph B as most resembling her own face.

An intriguing consequence of our biased self-facial image is our opinion of personal photographs. Many people complain about not being photogenic, that their photographs are never taken at the correct angle, that their hair wasn't just right, and so on. The problem may be rather different: we are accustomed to seeing ourselves in a mirror image and hence, when we view a photograph, we are biased to look at the side of the face that we do not normally perceive selectively in the mirror. Indeed, we appear not to see ourselves as others see us. The more asymmetrical the face, the less flattering the person will see his or her image to be.

Visual Imagery

Our ability to conjure up mental images of things that cannot be perceived is central to human thought. Visualization is crucial in problem-solving tasks such as mental arithmetic, map reading, and mechanical reasoning. How crucial can be seen in a patient such as D. F., who was unable to copy drawings or to recognize actual objects but who could nonetheless produce drawings of the same objects from memory (see Figure 13.12).

Behrmann and colleagues described another such patient, C. K. The curious thing about C. K. is that, although he cannot recognize objects, he can imagine them and can draw them in considerable detail from memory. This ability implies some dissociation between the neural system dealing with object perception and that dealing with the generation of images. We can conclude that neural structures mediating the perception and visualization of objects are unlikely to be completely independent, but it is clear that a deficit in object perception cannot be due simply to a loss of mental representations (that is, memory) of objects.

There has been considerable controversy over whether mental rotation of objects might be localized to some region of the right hemisphere. In her review of this literature, Farah concludes that the studies have been "distressingly inconsistent." She proposes that mental rotation probably entails both hemispheres, with some degree of right-hemisphere superiority. (For more detail, see both Farah and Kosslyn.)

Nonetheless, it does seem likely that mental rotation implicates structures related to the dorsal stream. We can imagine that, before a brain could visualize rotating an object, it would first have to have actually rotated it manually. It is a small step to presume that visualizing an object rotating requires the activation of at least part of the motor cortex—the regions needed to actually do it.

In the past two decades, cognitive neuroscientists have conducted a flurry of imaging studies designed to identify the neural events underlying the generation of a mental image. Farah concludes that, although the data are noisy, a reasonably consistent answer is emerging from the results of imaging studies such as the one described in the Snapshot on page 342. Mental imagery appears to be a top-down activation of a subset of the brain's visual areas. In other words, at least some cortical areas are used both for perception and for visualization.

These common areas carry the same representational functions for both purposes, carrying information specifically about color, shape, spatial location, and so on. There is evidence for a distinct mechanism for image generation as well, one separate from the processes needed for perception. Farah notes that the evidence, although mixed, points to a region in the left temporo-occipital region as the key location for this mechanism.

Generating Mental Images

What is the neural basis for visual imagery? It may result from activity in the same visual areas that are active when an image is actually viewed. Another possibility is that some other region of the brain is selectively active when we imagine.

D'Esposito and colleagues addressed this question in an fMRI study by asking subjects to generate mental images from memory, cued by an aurally presented word such as "tree." These cues were common objects rather than abstract representations ("tree" rather than "love," for example). The subjects kept their eyes closed throughout the experiment so that any neural activation could be attributed to imagery rather than to direct activation of the visual pathways. In the baseline condition, the subjects heard abstract words that would not easily allow any image formation, and they were asked simply to listen to the words.

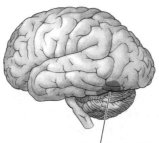

Left temporo-occipital region
(fusiform gyrus, area 37)

The results (illustrated here) show that visualizing concrete words increases activation in the left posterior temporo-occipital region, corresponding to the fusiform gyrus (area 37). There was no activation in area V1. The fMRI data are consistent with those of other imaging studies, as well as with a case history of a patient with a left-occipital lobectomy (including area 37) who had a hemianopia in both real and imagined stimuli. The pronounced asymmetry is consistent with Farah's hypothesis that, in most people, the left hemisphere is specialized for image generation.

(M. D'Esposito, J. A. Detre, G. K. Aguirre, M. Stallcup, D. C. Alsop, L. J. Tippet, and M. J. Farah. A functional MRI study of mental image generation. *Neuropsychologia* 35:725–730, 1997.)

Summary

The function of the occipital lobe is vision, but visual functions extend beyond the occipital lobe. Separate anatomical regions within the occipital lobe take part in the perception of form, movement, and color. Occipital structures are merely the beginning of visual processing because multiple visual systems can be divided into at least three major routes, one going ventrally into the temporal lobe, another going dorsally into the parietal lobe, and a middle route going to the superior temporal sulcus. The ventral stream is most certainly implicated in various aspects of stimulus recognition. The dorsal stream is for the guidance of movement in space. The representation of spatial information relies on the recognition of cues within the environment, which would therefore make visuospatial recognition dependent on processing in the ventral stream. An important aspect of the dorsal–ventral distinction in visual processing is that neither route is a single system. Rather, clearly dissociable subsystems take part in various functions. Finally, some occipital regions, especially those adjoining the temporal cortex, may be functionally asymmetrical. In particular, there appears to be some specialization for word recognition on the left and facial recognition and mental rotation on the right.

References

Barbur, J. L., J. D. G. Watson, R. S. J. Frackowiak, and S. Zeki. Conscious visual perception without V1. *Brain* 116:1293–1302, 1993.

Behrmann, M., G. Winocur, and M. Moscovitch. Dissociation between mental imagery and object recognition in a brain-damaged patient. *Nature* 359:636–637, 1992.

Boussaud, D., L. G. Ungerleider, and R. Desimone. Pathways for motion analysis: Cortical connections of the medial superior temporal and fundus of the superior temporal visual areas in the macaque. *Journal of Comparative Neurology* 296:462–495, 1990.

Campbell, R., T. Landis, and M. Regard. Face recognition and lip reading: A neurological dissociation. *Brain* 109:509–521, 1986.

Clarke, S., and J. Miklossy. Occipital cortex in man: Organization of callosal connections, related myelo- and cytoarchitecture, and putative boundaries of functional visual areas. *Journal of Comparative Neurology* 298:188–214, 1990.

Curtis, B. Visual system. In B. A. Curtis, S. Jacobson, and E. M. Marcus, Eds. *An Introduction to the Neurosciences*. Philadelphia and Toronto: Saunders, 1972.

Damasio, A. R., H. Damasio, and G. W. Van Hoesen. Prosopagnosia: Anatomical basis and behavioral mechanisms. *Neurology* 32:331–341, 1982.

Damasio, A. R., D. Tranel, and H. Damasio. Disorders of visual recognition. In F. Boller and J. Grafman, Eds. *Handbook of Neuropsychology*, vol. 2. Amsterdam: Elsevier, 1989.

Diamond, R., and S. Carey. Why faces are and are not special: An effect of expertise. *Journal of Experimental Psychology: General* 15:107–117, 1986.

Farah, M. J. The neurological basis of mental imagery: A componential analysis. *Cognition* 18:245–272, 1984.

Farah, M. J. The neuropsychology of mental imagery. In F. Boller and J. Grafman, Eds. *Handbook of Neuropsychology*, vol. 2. Amsterdam: Elsevier, 1990.

Farah, M. J. *Visual Agnosia*. Cambridge, MA: MIT Press, 1990.

Farah, M. J. What is "special" about face perception? *Psychological Review* 105:482–498, 1998.

Farah, M. J. The neural basis of mental imagery. In M. S. Gazzaniga, Ed. *The New Cognitive Neurosciences*, 2d ed. Cambridge, MA: MIT Press, 2000, pp. 965–974.

Felleman, D. J., and D. C. van Essen. Distributed hierarchical processing in primate cerebral cortex. *Cerebral Cortex* 1:1–47, 1991.

Goodale, M. A. Visual pathways supporting perception and action in the primate cerebral cortex. *Current Opinion in Neurobiology* 3:578–585, 1993.

Goodale, M. A. Perception and action in the human visual system. In M. Gazzaniga, Ed. *The New Cognitive Neurosciences*. Cambridge, MA: MIT Press, 2000, pp. 365–377.

Goodale, M. A., D. A. Milner, L. S. Jakobson, and J. D. P. Carey. A neurological dissociation between perceiving objects and grasping them. *Nature* 349:154–156, 1991.

Hancock, P. J. B., V. Bruce, and A. M. Burton. Recognition of unfamiliar faces. *Trends in Cognitive Sciences* 4:330–337, 2000.

Haxby, J. V., E. A. Hoffman, and M. I. Gobbini. The distributed human neural system for face perception. *Trends in Cognitive Science* 4:223–233, 2000.

Haxby, J. V., L. G. Ungerleider, V. P. Clark, J. L. Schouten, E. A. Hoffman, and A. Martin. The effect of face inversion on activity in human neural systems for face and object perception. *Neuron* 22:189–199, 1999.

Jakobson, L. S., Y. M. Archibald, D. P. Carey, and M. A. Goodale. A kinematic analysis of reaching and grasping movements in a patient recovering from optic ataxia. *Neuropsychologia* 29:803–809, 1991.

Kingdom, F., H.-C. O. Li, and E. J. MacAulay. The role of chromatic contrast and luminance polarity in stereoscopic segmentation. *Vision Research* 41:375–383, 2001.

Kolb, B., B. Milner, and L. Taylor. Perception of faces by patients with localized cortical excisions. *Canadian Journal of Psychology* 37:8–18, 1983.

Kosslyn, S. M., and W. L. Thompson. Shared mechanisms in visual imagery and visual perception: Insights from cognitive neuroscience. In M. Gazzaniga, Ed. *The New Cognitive Neurosciences*. Cambridge, MA: MIT Press, 2000, pp. 975–986.

Luria, A. R. *The Working Brain*. New York: Penguin, 1973.

Meadows, J. C. Disturbed perception of colors associated with localized cerebral lesions. *Brain* 97:615–632, 1974.

Milner, A. D., and M. A. Goodale. *The Visual Brain in Action*. Oxford: Oxford University Press, 1995.

Previc, F. H. Functional specialization in the lower and upper visual fields in humans: Its ecological origins and neurophysiological implications. *Behavioral and Brain Sciences* 13:519–575, 1990.

Sacks, O., and R. Wasserman. The case of the colorblind painter. *New York Review of Books* 34:25–33, 1987.

Servos, P., M. A. Goodale, and G. K. Humphrey. The drawing of objects by a visual form agnosic: Contribution of surface properties and memorial representations. *Neuropsychologia* 31:251–259, 1993.

Sumner, P., and J. D. Mollon. Catarrhine photopigments are optimized for detecting targets against a foliage background. *Journal of Experimental Biology* 203:1963–1986, 2000.

Tanaka, J., D. Weiskopf, and P. Williams. The role of color in high-level vision. *Trends in Cognitive Sciences* 5:211–215, 2001.

Tootell, R. B. H., and N. Hadjikhani. Where is "dorsal V4" in human visual cortex? Retinotopic, topographic and functional evidence. *Cerebral Cortex* 11:298–311, 2001.

Ungerleider, L. G., and J. V. Haxby. "What" and "where" in the human brain. *Current Opinion in Neurobiology* 4:15–165, 1994.

Valentine, T. Upside-down faces: A review of the effect of inversion upon face recognition. *British Journal of Psychology* 79:471–491, 1988.

Weiskrantz, L. *Blindsight: A Case History and Implications.* Oxford: Oxford University Press, 1986.

Zeki, S. *A Vision of the Brain.* Oxford: Blackwell, 1993.

Zeki, S., S. Aglioti, D. McKeefry, and G. Berlucchi. The neurological basis of conscious color perception in a blind patient. *Proceedings of the National Academy of Sciences of the United States of America* 96:14124–14129, 1999.

Zihl, J., D. von Cramon, and N. Mai. Selective disturbance of movement vision after bilateral brain damage. *Brain* 106:313–340, 1983.

The Parietal Lobes

H. P. was a 28-year-old accountant who was planning his wedding with his fiancée when she noticed that he was making addition errors as he calculated the budget for their reception. At first, they joked about it, especially given his occupation, but in the following weeks H. P.'s problem with numbers became serious. In fact, he was no longer able to do a simple subtraction such as 30 − 19 in which the solution requires "borrowing" 10 when subtracting 9 from 0.

At first, H. P. simply put it down to working too hard, but soon he began to have trouble reaching for objects. He was constantly knocking over his water glass, because his reach was clumsy and misdirected. He began confusing left and right and having difficulties reading. Some of the words appeared to be backward or upside down, and he could not make sense of them.

Finally, when H. P. visited a neurologist for testing, it was obvious that something was seriously wrong. Indeed something was: he had a fast-growing tumor in his left parietal lobe. Unfortunately, the tumor was extremely virulent and, within a couple of months, he died.

The parietal cortex processes and integrates somatosensory and visual information, especially with regard to the control of movement. In this chapter, we first describe the anatomy of the parietal lobes and then present a theoretical model of parietal-lobe organization. Next, we consider the major somatosensory symptoms of parietal injury, survey the most commonly observed disorders of the posterior parietal region, and conclude the chapter with a survey of behavioral tests that reliably predict brain injury.

Anatomy of the Parietal Lobes

H. P.'s symptoms are typical of left parietal injury and illustrative of the curious pattern of symptoms that have proved a challenge for neuropsychologists to understand. Part of the challenge is that these symptoms are difficult to demonstrate in animals. Common laboratory animals such as rats and cats have very modest parietal "lobes," and, although monkeys with parietal damage show many symptoms similar to those seen in human patients, symptoms related to language or cognition are difficult to study in monkeys. Furthermore, the parietal lobes in the human brain have evolved to a much larger size, which might imply that humans will show some symptoms not seen in monkeys.

Subdivisions of the Parietal Cortex

The parietal lobe is the region of cerebral cortex between the frontal and occipital lobes, underlying the parietal bone at the roof of the skull. This area is roughly demarcated anteriorly by the central fissure, ventrally by the Sylvian fissure, dorsally by the cingulate gyrus, and posteriorly by the parieto-occipital sulcus (Figure 14.1A). The principal regions of the parietal lobe include the postcentral gyrus (Brodmann's areas 1, 2, and 3), the superior parietal lobule (areas 5 and 7), the parietal operculum (area 43), the supramarginal gyrus (area 40), and the angular gyrus (area 39) (Figure 14.1A and B).

Together, the supramarginal gyrus and angular gyrus are often referred to as the inferior parietal lobe. The parietal lobe can be divided into two functional zones: an anterior zone including areas 1, 2, 3, and 43; and a posterior zone, which includes the remaining areas. The anterior zone is the somatosensory cortex; the posterior zone is referred to as the **posterior parietal cortex.**

The parietal lobes have undergone a major expansion in the course of human evolution, largely in the inferior parietal region. This increase in size has made comparisons of various areas in the human brain with those in the monkey brain confusing, especially because Brodmann did not identify areas 39 and 40 in the monkey. Whether monkeys actually have regions homologous to areas 39 and 40 is debatable. One solution to this problem is to consult another anatomist, Constantin von Economo.

On von Economo's maps, in which parietal areas are called PA (parietal area A), PB, and so forth, are three posterior parietal areas (PE, PF, PG) that von Economo described in both humans and monkeys (Figure 14.1C). If we use this system, area PF is equivalent to area 7b and PE to area 5 in Felleman and van Essen's flat map of cortical areas in the macaque (see Figure10.17). Similarly, area PG in the monkey includes areas 7a, VIP, LIP, IPG, PP, MSTc, and MSTp. These PG areas are primarily visual (see Chapter 15).

An area of significant expansion in the human brain appears to consist of the polymodal parts of area PG and the adjoining polymodal cortex in the superior temporal sulcus. (Polymodal cells are those that receive inputs from more than one sensory modality.) Those in PG respond to both somatosensory and visual inputs, whereas those in the superior temporal sulcus (the third visual pathway discussed in Chapter 13) respond to various combinations of auditory, visual, and somatosensory inputs.

The increase in size of area PG and the superior temporal sulcus is especially interesting because this region is anatomically asymmetrical in the human brain (see Figure 11.1). This asymmetry may be due to a much larger area PG (and possibly superior temporal sulcus) on the right than on the left. If PG has a visual function and is larger in humans, especially in the right hemisphere, then we might expect unique visual symptoms after right parietal le-

(A) Major parietal lobe gyri and sulci

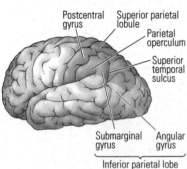

Postcentral gyrus
Superior parietal lobule
Parietal operculum
Superior temporal sulcus
Submarginal gyrus
Angular gyrus
Inferior parietal lobe

(B) Brodmann's cytoarchetectonic regions

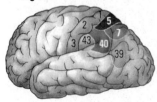

(C) von Economo's cytoarchetectonic regions

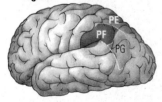

Figure 14.1 Gross anatomy of the parietal lobe.

sions, which is indeed the case. Note, however, that PG is also larger on the left in the human than in the monkey, which would lead us to expect humans to have unique deficits after left hemisphere lesions. This, too, is the case.

Connections of the Parietal Cortex

The anterior parietal cortex has rather straightforward connections, which are illustrated in Felleman and van Essen's hierarchy (see Figure 10.19). There are projections from the primary somatosensory cortex to area PE, which has a tactile recognition function, as well as to motor areas, including the primary motor cortex (area 4) and the supplementary motor and premotor regions. The motor connections must be important for providing sensory information about limb position in the control of movement (see Chapter 9).

Although more than 100 inputs and outputs of areas 5 and 7 in the monkey (PE, PF, and PG) have been described (see Figure 10.19), a few basic principles will summarize the connections diagrammed in Figure 14.2:

1. Area PE (Brodmann's area 5) is basically a somatosensory area, receiving most of its connections from the primary somatosensory cortex (areas 1, 2, and 3). Its cortical outputs are to the primary motor cortex (area 4) and to the supplementary motor (SMA) and premotor (6 and 8) regions, as well as to PF. Area PE therefore plays some role in guiding movement by providing information about limb position.

2. Area PF (area 7b) has a heavy somatosensory input from the primary cortex (areas 1, 2, and 3) through area PE. It also receives inputs from the motor and premotor cortex and a small visual input through area PG. Its efferent connections are similar to those of area PE, and these connections presumably provide some elaboration of similar information for the motor systems.

3. Area PG (area 7b and visual areas) receives more-complex connections including visual, somesthetic, proprioceptive (internal stimuli), auditory, vestibular (balance), oculomotor (eye movement), and cingulate (motivational?). This region was described by MacDonald Critchley as the "parieto-temporo-occipital crossroads," which is apparent from the connectivity. It seems likely that its function corresponds to this intermodal mixing. Area PG is part of the dorsal stream discussed in Chapter 13. It is assumed to have a role in controlling spatially guided behavior with respect to visual and tactile information.

4. There is a close relation between the posterior parietal connections and the prefrontal cortex (especially area 46). Thus, there are connections between the posterior parietal cortex (PG and PF) and the dorsolateral prefrontal region. Additionally, both the prefrontal and the posterior parietal regions project to the same areas of the paralimbic cortex and the temporal cortex as well as to the hippocampus and various subcortical regions. These connections emphasize a close functional relation between the prefrontal cortex and the parietal cortex. This relation probably has an important role in the control of spatially guided behavior.

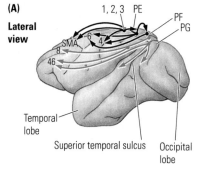

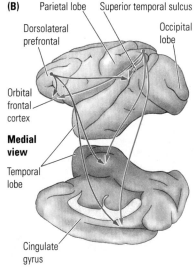

Figure 14.2 Connections of the parietal lobe. (A) The major cortical–cortical projections of the parietal lobe. (B) The posterior parietal and dorsolateral prefrontal projections to cingulate, orbital frontal, and temporal regions.

A Theory of Parietal-Lobe Function

If we consider the anterior (somatosensory) and posterior parietal zones as functionally distinct regions, we can identify two independent contributions of the parietal lobes. The anterior zone processes somatic sensations and perceptions; the posterior zone is specialized primarily for integrating sensory input from the somatic and visual regions and, to a lesser extent, from other sensory regions, mostly for the control of movement. We are concerned here mostly with the function of the posterior parietal zone; the anterior zone's somatosensory functions were discussed in Chapter 8.

Imagine that you are having dinner with a friend in a restaurant. You are confronted with a set of cutlery, some dishes, a basket of bread, a glass of water, perhaps a glass of wine or a cup of coffee, a napkin, and of course your companion. Seemingly without effort you select various utensils and foods as you chat with your friend.

If we analyze what is required to do all these things, however, we see that your brain is faced with several complex tasks. For example, you must reach and correctly grasp a glass or cup or fork or piece of bread. Each of those movements is directed toward a different place and requires a different hand posture and or limb movement or both. Your eyes and head must be directed toward various places in space, and you must coordinate the movements of your limbs and your head to get food to your mouth.

Furthermore, you must attend to certain objects and ignore others. (You do not take your companion's fork or drink.) You also must attend to the conversation with your friend and ignore other conversations around you. When you eat items from your plate, you must choose which one you want and select the correct utensil. It would be inappropriate to try to eat your peas with a knife. You must also make movements in the correct order. For example, you must cut your food before picking it up. Similarly, when you choose a bit of bread you must pick up a knife, get some butter, place the butter on the bread, and then eat the bread.

As we think about how the brain can manage these tasks, it seems obvious that there must be some sort of internal representation of the location of different objects around us, a sort of map in the brain of where things are. Furthermore, we assume that the map must be common to all our senses because we can move without apparent effort from visual to auditory to tactile information. On the basis of clinical observations of patients with parietal injury, it has been widely believed for nearly 60 years that the parietal lobe plays a central role in the creation of this brain map. But what is the map?

The commonly held introspective view is that real space must be mapped topographically because that is how it appears to us. That is, we take it for granted that the world around us is as we perceive it, and thus that the brain must employ some sort of unified spatial map. (This view is a form of the binding problem discussed in Chapter 10.) Unfortunately, there is very little evidence for the existence of such a map in the brain. Rather, it seems likely that there is no single map, but a series of representations of space, which vary in two ways. First, different representations are used for different behavioral needs. Second, representations of space vary from simple ones, which are applicable to the control of simple movements, to abstract ones, which may represent information such as topographical knowledge. We consider each of these aspects of brain maps in turn.

Uses of Spatial Information

Goodale and Milner emphasize that spatial information about the location of objects in the world is needed both to direct actions at those objects and to assign meaning and significance to them. In this sense, spatial information is simply another property of visual information, much like form, motion, and color. However, just as form is coded in more than one way in visual processing, so is spatial information. The critical factor for both form and space is how the information is to be used.

Recall that form recognition is of two basic types: one is for object recognition and the other is for the guidance of movement. Spatial information can be thought of in the same way.

Object Recognition

The spatial information needed to determine the relations between objects, independent of what the subject's behavior might be, is very different from the spatial information needed to guide eye, head, or limb movements to objects. In the latter case, the visuomotor control must be viewer centered—that is, the location of an object and its local orientation and motion must be determined relative to the viewer. Furthermore, because the eyes, head, limbs, and body are constantly moving, computations about orientation, motion, and location must take place every time we wish to undertake an action. Details of object characteristics, such as color, are irrelevant to visuomotor guidance of the viewer-centered movements. That is, a detailed visual representation is not needed to guide hand action.

Milner suggests that the brain operates on a "need to know" basis. Having too much information may be counterproductive for any given system. In contrast with the viewer-centered system, the object-centered system must be concerned with such properties of objects as size, shape, color, and relative location so that the objects can be recognized when they are encountered in different visual contexts or from different vantage points. In this case, the details of the objects themselves (color, shape) are important. Knowing where the red cup is relative to the green one requires identifying each of them.

The temporal lobe codes relational properties of objects. Part of this control is probably in the polymodal region of the superior temporal sulcus, and another part is in the hippocampal formation. We return to the role of the temporal cortex in Chapter 15.

Guidance of Movement

The posterior parietal cortex has a role in the viewer-centered system. To accommodate the many different types of viewer-centered movements (eyes, head, limbs, body, and combinations of them) requires separate control systems. Consider, for example, that the control of the eyes is based on the optical axis of the eye, whereas the control of the limbs is probably based on the positions of the shoulders and hips. These movements are of very different types.

We have seen many visual areas in the posterior parietal region and multiple projections from the posterior parietal regions to the motor structures for the eyes (frontal eye fields, area 8) and limbs (premotor and supplementary motor). There also are connections to the prefrontal region (area 46) that have a role in short-term memory of the location of events in space.

The role of the posterior parietal region in visuomotor guidance is confirmed by the results of studies of neurons in the posterior parietal lobe of monkeys. The activity of these neurons depends on the concurrent behavior of the animal with respect to visual stimulation. In fact, most neurons in the posterior parietal region are active both during sensory input *and* during movement. For example, some cells show only weak responses to stationary visual stimuli but, if the animal makes an active eye or arm movement toward the stimulus *or even if it just shifts its attention to the object*, the discharge of these cells is strongly enhanced.

Some cells are active when a monkey manipulates an object and also respond to the structural features of the object, such as size and orientation. That is, the neurons are sensitive to the features of an object that determine the posture of the hand during manipulation.

A characteristic common to all the posterior parietal neurons is their responsiveness to movements of the eyes and to the location of the eye in its socket. When cells are stimulated at the optimum spot in their receptive fields, they discharge at the highest rate when the eyes are in a particular position. This discharge appears to signal the size of the eye movement, or **saccade**, necessary to move the visual target to the fovea of the retina.

In other words, these cells detect visual information and then move the eye to get the fine vision of the fovea to examine it. A curious aspect of many posterior parietal eye-movement cells is that they are particularly responsive to visual stimuli that are behaviorally relevant, such as a cue signaling the availability of a reward. This responsiveness has been interpreted as suggesting that these cells are affected by the "motivational" characteristics of information.

Stein summarized the responses of posterior parietal neurons by emphasizing that they all have two important characteristics in common. First, they receive combinations of sensory, motivational, and related motor inputs. Second, their discharge is enhanced when the animal attends to a target or makes a movement toward it. These neurons therefore are well suited to transforming the necessary sensory information into commands for directing attention and guiding motor output.

It is not possible to study the activity of single cells in the human posterior parietal region, but event-related potentials (ERPs) in response to visual stimuli can be recorded. Thus, when a stimulus is presented in one visual field, activation would be expected in the opposite hemisphere, which receives information from the contralateral visual field. Stephen Hillyard showed that, when a visual stimulus is presented, there is a large negative wave from about 100 to 200 ms later in the posterior parietal region. The wave is larger than that seen in the occipital cortex and is largest in the hemisphere contralateral to the stimulus.

Two interesting characteristics of these waves are reminiscent of neurons in monkeys. First, if a subject is asked to pay attention to a particular spot in one visual field, the ERP is largest when the stimulus is presented there rather than elsewhere. Second, there is a large parietal response between 100 and 200 ms before eye movements. Pere Roland also showed that, when subjects direct their attention to visual targets, blood flow increases preferentially in the posterior parietal region.

Taken together, the results of electrophysiological and blood-flow studies in monkeys and humans support the general idea that the posterior parietal region plays a significant role in directing movements in space and in detecting stimuli in space. We can predict, therefore, that posterior parietal lesions impair the guidance of movements and perhaps the detection of sensory events.

The role of the superior parietal cortex in the control of eye movements has important implications for PET studies of visual processing. Recall from Chapter 13 that Haxby and colleagues showed an increase in blood flow in the posterior parietal cortex when subjects identified different spatial locations. This finding was taken as evidence that the dorsal stream of processing deals with "spatial processing."

One difficulty with this interpretation, however, is that, when people solve spatial tasks, they move their eyes. The increased PET activation, therefore, could be due to the movement of the eyes, rather than to the processing of *where* the target actually is in space. Indeed, it has been demonstrated that, when people solve problems in which they must rotate objects mentally, they move their eyes back and forth. These saccades may indicate the ongoing activity of parietal circuits, but they also present a problem for PET studies. Thus there is a practical difficulty in constructing watertight experimental designs in brain-imaging studies.

The Complexity of Spatial Information

The second aspect of spatial representation is complexity. The control of limb or eye movements is concrete and relatively simple, but other types of viewer-centered representations are far more complex. For example, the concept of "left" and "right" is viewer centered but need not require movement. Patients, such as H. P., with posterior parietal lesions are impaired at distinguishing left from right. But there are spatial relations that are even more complex. For example, you can visualize objects and manipulate these mental images spatially as was done in the experiments described in the Snapshot on page 352. Patients with posterior parietal lesions are impaired at mental manipulations, such as those illustrated in Figure B in the Snapshot.

It seems likely that the ability to manipulate objects mentally is an extension of the ability to manipulate objects with the hands. Thus, mental manipulation is really just an elaboration of the neural control of actual manipulation, much as visual imagery is an elaboration of the neural record of actual visual input. The actual location of the cells taking part in mental manipulation is not known, but one guess is that it includes the temporoparietal polysensory regions that show such significant expansion in the human brain. (These regions constitute the third stream of processing illustrated in Figure 13.5.) This idea is speculative but based on the knowledge that this region is larger in the right hemisphere and that larger deficits in mental "spatial tasks" follow right-hemisphere lesions.

S N A P S H O T

Measuring Parietal-Lobe Activation During Mental Rotation

To determine whether the posterior parietal cortex shows functional activation during a mental-rotation task, Alivisatos and Petrides used PET to measure regional blood flow during two different test conditions. Subjects were first presented with letters or numbers and asked merely to press one key in response to a number and a different key in response to a letter. Their responses established a baseline level of activation, or control condition, for the experiment.

In the mirror-image test condition, subjects were presented letters or numbers either in the "normal" or backward, "mirror-image" orientation, as shown in Figure A. Their task was to press a different key to indicate each ori-

(B) Mental-rotation test condition

(B) An example of the rotation of the stimuli in the mental-rotation task.

entation. In the mental-rotation test, subjects were presented with the same stimuli, but in different orientations, as shown in Figure B. The subjects were required to make the same normal-versus-backward discrimination as in the mirror-image condition.

To determine whether the mirror-image or mental-rotation tasks activated the parietal lobe, the baseline discrimination was subtracted from each test. Both tasks increased activation in the parietal cortex on the left and in a slightly more posterior temporal region on the left (Figure C). In addition, bilateral activation of the posterior temporal cortex was recorded. When the activation in the mirror-image condition was subtracted from that in the mental-rotation condition, the right hemisphere activation in the parietal and temporal lobes was no longer significant. Evidently both

(A) Mirror-image test condition

(A) The alphanumeric stimuli used in their "normal" form (left) and in their "backward" form (right).

Other Aspects of Parietal Function

Three parietal-lobe symptoms do not fit obviously into a simple view of the parietal lobe as a visuomotor control center. These symptoms include difficulties with arithmetic, certain aspects of language, and movement sequences—deficits encountered in H. P.'s case.

Luria proposed that mathematics and arithmetic have a quasi-spatial nature analogous to the mental manipulation of concrete shapes but entailing abstract symbols. For example, addition and subtraction have spatial properties that are important to calculating a correct solution. Consider the problem of subtracting 25 from 52. The "2" and "5" occupy different positions and have different meanings in the two numbers. There must be a "borrowing" from the 10's column in 52 in order to subtract, and so on.

From this perspective, the reason that parietal-lobe patients such as H. P. experience **acalculia** (an inability to do arithmetic) stems from the spatial na-

(C) Average brain scan

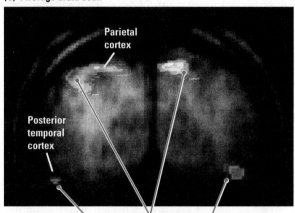

Parietal cortex

Posterior temporal cortex

After subtracting baseline discrimination from each test, both tasks increased activation in the parietal cortex and posterior temporal cortex.

(C) PET reactivity in the parietal cortex during mental rotation.

tasks require the same right parietal and temporal activation, whereas there was something different about the left parietal involvement in the two tasks.

The left difference is likely related to the increased difficulty in identifying alpha–numeric stimuli when they are rotated, which makes sense given that the left hemisphere is dominant for verbal processing. One puzzle, however, is that, in a parallel study, these researchers found that making similar manipulations with abstract stimuli produced a similar pattern of activation, even though the stimuli were not verbal. This finding suggests that the left parietal cortex has a role in active mental transformations of stimuli, regardless of the content of the stimulus material.

Notably, parietal activation in the two hemispheres is not in the same location, as you can see in the MRI in Figure C. The activation on the left is more rostral and inferior (area 40) than the activation on the right, which is more posterior and superior (area 7). This difference suggests that each hemisphere contributes a different type of processing to mental manipulation.

(B. Alivisatos and M. Petrides. Functional activation of the human brain during mental rotation. *Neuropsychologia* 35:111–118, 1997.)

ture of the task. Indeed, if parietal-lobe patients are given simple problems such as 6 − 4, they usually solve them because the spatial demands are few. Even when the problems are somewhat more difficult, such as 984 − 23, the patients have little problem. When more-complex manipulations, such as borrowing, must be made, however, the patients' abilities to do arithmetic break down, as in 983 − 24. Thus, arithmetic operations may depend on the polysensory tissue at the left temporoparietal junction.

Language has many of the same demands as arithmetic. The words "tap" and "pat" have the same letters, but the spatial organization is different. Similarly, the phrases "my son's wife" and "my wife's son" have identical words but very different meanings. These observations have led Luria and others to suggest that language can be seen as quasispatial. Patients such as H. P. may have a clear understanding of individual elements, but they are unable to understand the whole when the syntax becomes important. This ability, too, may depend on the polysensory region at the temporoparietal junction.

The deficit in organizing individual elements of behavior can be seen not only in language but in movement as well. People with parietal-lobe injuries have difficulty in copying sequences of movements, a problem that we shall return to shortly.

In summary, the posterior parietal lobe controls the visuomotor guidance of movements in egocentric (that is, viewer-centered) space. This control is most obvious in regard to reaching and to eye movements needed to grasp or manipulate objects. The eye movements are important, because they allow the visual system to attend to particular sensory cues in the environment. The polymodal region of the posterior parietal cortex is also important in various aspects of "mental space," ranging from arithmetic and reading to the mental rotation and manipulation of visual images to sequencing movements.

Somatosensory Symptoms of Parietal-Lobe Lesions

In this section, we consider the somatosensory symptoms associated with damage to the postcentral gyrus (see Figure 14.1A and areas 1, 2, and 3 in Figure 14.1B) and the adjacent cortex (areas PE and PF in Figure 14.1C).

Somatosensory Thresholds

Damage to the postcentral gyrus is typically associated with marked changes in somatosensory thresholds. The most thorough studies of these changes were done by Josephine Semmes and her colleagues on World War II veterans with missile wounds to the brain and by Suzanne Corkin and her coworkers on patients who had undergone cortical surgery for the relief of epilepsy.

Both research groups found that lesions of the postcentral gyrus produced abnormally high sensory thresholds, impaired position sense, and deficits in stereognosis (tactile perception). For example, in the Corkin study, patients performed poorly at detecting a light touch to the skin (pressure sensitivity), at determining if they were touched by one or two sharp points (two-point threshold), and at localizing points of touch on the skin on the side of the body contralateral to the lesion. If blindfolded, the patients also had difficulty in reporting whether the fingers of the contralateral hand were passively moved.

Lesions of the postcentral gyrus may also produce a symptom that Luria called **afferent paresis.** Movements of the fingers are clumsy because the person has lost the necessary feedback about their exact position.

Somatoperceptual Disorders

The presence of normal somatosensory thresholds does not preclude the possibility of other types of somatosensory abnormalities. First, there is **astereognosis** (from the Greek *stereo*, meaning "solid"), which is the inability to

(A)

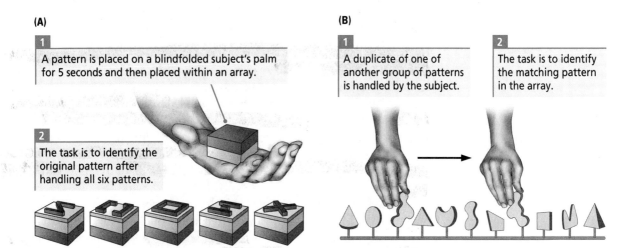

> **1** A pattern is placed on a blindfolded subject's palm for 5 seconds and then placed within an array.

> **2** The task is to identify the original pattern after handling all six patterns.

(B)

> **1** A duplicate of one of another group of patterns is handled by the subject.

> **2** The task is to identify the matching pattern in the array.

Figure 14.3 Tests for tactile appreciation of objects. (A) A pattern is placed on the blindfolded subject's palm for 5 seconds and then placed within the array. The task is to handle all six patterns and identify which of them is the original pattern. (B) The subject handles a duplicate of one of the patterns. The task is to identify, again by handling, the matching pattern in the array. (After Teuber, 1978.)

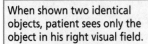recognize the nature of an object by touch. This disturbance can be demonstrated in tests of tactile appreciation of object qualities, illustrated in Figure 14.3. In these tests, objects are placed on the palms of blindfolded subjects or the subjects are told to handle shapes. The task is to match the original shape or object to one of several alternatives solely on the basis of tactile information.

A second somatoperceptual disorder, **simultaneous extinction,** can be demonstrated only by special testing procedures. The logic of this test is that a person is ordinarily confronted by an environment in which many sensory stimuli impinge simultaneously, yet the person is able to distinguish and perceive each of these individual sensory impressions. Thus, a task that presents stimuli one at a time represents an unnatural situation that may underestimate sensory disturbances or miss them altogether.

To offer more-complicated sensory stimulation, two tactile stimuli are presented simultaneously to the same or different body parts. The objective of such double simultaneous stimulation is to uncover those situations in which both stimuli would be reported if applied singly, but only one would be reported if both were applied together, as illustrated in Figure 14.4. A failure to report one stimulus is usually called **extinction** and is most commonly associated with damage to the somatic secondary cortex (areas PE and PF), especially in the right parietal lobe.

> When shown two identical objects, patient sees only the object in his right visual field.

> When shown two different objects, patient sees the object in both visual fields.

> When shown two kinds of an object, patient sees only the object in his right visual field.

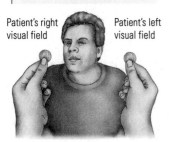

Patient's right visual field

Patient's left visual field

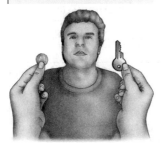

Figure 14.4 Testing for extinction in a stroke patient. The patient responds differently, depending on whether objects in the left and right visual fields are similar or different.

Blind Touch

Evidence that patients can identify the location of a visual stimulus even though they deny "seeing" it was presented in Chapter 13. Jacques Paillard and his colleagues reported the case of a woman who appears to have a tactile analogue of blindsight. This woman had a large lesion of areas PE, PF, and some of PG, resulting in a complete anesthesia of the right side of the body so severe that she was likely to cut or burn herself without being aware of it. Nevertheless, she was able to point with her left hand to locations on her right hand where she had been touched, even though she failed to report feeling the touch.

Although reported in a single case, the phenomenon is clearly reminiscent of blindsight. The presence of a tactile analogue of blindsight is important because it suggests the existence of two tactile systems—one specialized for detection and the other for localization. Such specialization may be a general feature of sensory system organization.

Somatosensory Agnosias

There are two major types of somatosensory agnosias: astereognosis (see the preceding discussion of somatoperceptual disorders) and **asomatognosia**—the loss of knowledge or sense of one's own body and bodily condition. Although astereognosis is essentially a disorder of tactile appreciation (see Figure 14.3), it is included here because it is often described clinically simply as an agnosia.

Asomatognosia is one of the most curious of all agnosias. It is an almost unbelievable syndrome—until you actually observe it. The varieties of asomatognosias include **anosognosia,** the unawareness or denial of illness; **anosodiaphoria,** indifference to illness; **autopagnosia,** an inability to localize and name body parts; and **asymbolia for pain,** the absence of normal reactions to pain, such as reflexive withdrawal from a painful stimulus.

Asomatognosias may affect one or both sides of the body, although most commonly the left side, as a result of lesions in the right hemisphere. An exception comprises the autopagnosias, which usually result from lesions of the left parietal cortex. The most common autopagnosia is **finger agnosia,** a condition in which a person is unable either to point to the various fingers of either hand or show them to an examiner. A curious relation exists between finger agnosia and dyscalculia (difficulty in performing arithmetic operations). When children learn arithmetic, they normally use their fingers to count. We might predict that children who are unable to use their fingers to count, such as those with finger agnosia, would have difficulty learning arithmetic. In fact, children with a condition known as spina bifida have finger agnosia and have been found to be terrible at arithmetic.

Symptoms of Posterior Parietal Damage

The clinical literature describes a bewildering array of symptoms of posterior parietal injury. We will restrict our consideration here to the most commonly observed disorders.

Balint's Syndrome

In 1909, R. Balint described a patient whose bilateral parietal lesion was associated with rather peculiar visual symptoms. The patient had full visual fields and could recognize, use, and name objects, pictures, and colors normally. Nevertheless, he had three unusual symptoms:

1. Although he spontaneously looked straight ahead, when an array of stimuli was placed in front of him, he directed his gaze 35° to 40° to the right and perceived only what was lying in that direction. Thus, he could move his eyes but could not fixate on specific visual stimuli.

2. When his attention was directed toward an object, he did not notice other stimuli. With urging, he could identify other stimuli placed before him, but he quickly relapsed into his former neglect. Balint concluded that the patient's field of attention was limited to one object at a time, a disorder that made reading very difficult because each letter was perceived separately. (This disorder is often referred to as *simultagnosia*.)

3. The patient had a severe deficit in reaching under visual guidance. Balint described this symptom as *optic ataxia*. He noted that the patient could still make accurate movements directed toward the body, presumably by using tactile or proprioceptive information, but could not make visually guided movements.

Although Balint's syndrome is quite rare, optic ataxia is a common symptom of posterior parietal lesions and can develop after unilateral lesions. Consider the following description of a patient of Damasio and Benton:

> She consistently misreached for targets located in the nearby space, such as pencils, cigarettes, matches, ashtrays and cutlery. Usually she underreached by 2 to 5 inches, and then explored, by tact [touch], the surface path leading to the target. This exploration, performed in one or two groping attempts, was often successful and led straight to the object. Occasionally, however, the hand would again misreach, this time on the side of the target and beyond it. Another quick tactually guided correction would then place the hand in contact with the object. . . . In striking contrast to the above difficulties was the performance of movements which did not require visual guidance, such as buttoning and unbuttoning of garments, bringing a cigarette to the mouth, or pointing to some part of her body. These movements were smooth, quick and on target. (Damasio and Benton, 1979, p. 171)

The deficits in eye gaze and visually guided reaching are most likely to result from lesions in the superior parietal region (area PE). Optic ataxia does not accompany lesions in the inferior parietal region, suggesting a clear functional dissociation of the two posterior parietal regions.

Contralateral Neglect and Other Symptoms of Right Parietal Lesions

Critchley remarked in his 1953 textbook on the parietal lobes that the symptoms of parietal lesions differ widely—one patient showing only a few abnormal signs that are mild in nature but another showing an intricate clinical picture with elaborate symptoms. What causes this diversity is still not known. We must keep this uncertainty in mind as we consider the symptoms of right parietal lesions because the range and severity of symptoms varies widely among individual patients.

Contralateral Neglect

A perceptual disorder subsequent to right parietal lesions was described by John Hughlings-Jackson in 1874. Not until the 1940s, however, was the effect of right parietal lesions clearly defined by Alan Paterson and Oliver Zangwill. A classic paper by John McFie and Zangwill, published in 1960, reviewed much of the previous work and described several symptoms of right parietal lesions, which are illustrated in the following patient.

Mr. P., a 67-year-old man, had suffered a right parietal stroke. At the time of our first seeing him (24 hours after admission), he had no visual-field defect or paresis. He did, however, have a variety of other symptoms:

- Mr. P. neglected the left side of his body and of the world. When asked to lift up his arms, he failed to lift his left arm but could do so if one took his arm and asked him to lift it. When asked to draw a clock face, he crowded all the numbers onto the right side of the clock. When asked to read compound words such as "ice cream" and "football," he read "cream" and "ball." When he dressed, he did not attempt to put on the left side of his clothing (a form of dressing apraxia), and when he shaved, he shaved only the right side of his face. He ignored tactile sensation on the left side of his body. Finally, he appeared unaware that anything was wrong with him and was uncertain about what all the fuss was about (anosagnosia). Collectively, these symptoms are referred to as **contralateral neglect.**

- He was impaired at combining blocks to form designs (constructional apraxia) and was generally impaired at drawing freehand with either hand, copying drawings, or cutting out paper figures. When drawing, he often added extra strokes in an effort to make the pictures correct, but the drawings generally lacked accurate spatial relations. In fact, it is common for patients showing neglect to fail to complete the left side of the drawing, as illustrated in Figure 14.5.

- Mr. P. had a topographical disability, being unable to draw maps of well-known regions from memory. He attempted to draw a map of his neighborhood, but it was badly distorted with respect to directions, the spatial arrangement of landmarks, and distances. Despite all these disturbances, Mr. P. knew where he was and what day it was, and he could recognize his family's faces. He also had good language functions: he could talk, read, and write normally.

Contralateral neglect as observed in Mr. P. is one of the most fascinating symptoms of brain dysfunction. Neglect occurs in visual, auditory, and somesthetic (somatosensory) stimulation on the side of the body or space or both opposite the lesion, Neglect may be accompanied by denial of the deficit.

Recovery passes through two stages. **Allesthesia** is characterized by the person's beginning to respond to stimuli on the neglected side as if the stimuli were on the unlesioned side. The person responds and orients to visual, tactile, or auditory stimuli on the left side of the body as if they were on the right.

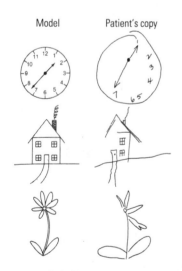

Model   Patient's copy

Figure 14.5 Drawings copied by a patient with contralateral neglect. (From F. E. Bloom and A. Lazerson. *Brain, Mind, and Behavior,* 2d ed. New York: W. H. Freeman and Company, p. 300. Copyright © 1988.)

The second stage of recovery, noted earlier, is simultaneous extinction (see Figure 14.4). The person responds to stimuli on the hitherto neglected side unless both sides are stimulated simultaneously, in which case he or she notices only the stimulation on the side ipsilateral to the lesion.

Neglect presents obstacles to understanding. What is the location of the lesion that produces this effect? Figure 14.6A is a composite drawing of the region damaged (as inferred from brain scans) in 13 patients with neglect as described by Ken Heilman and Robert Watson. The area of most overlap (Figure 14.6B) among the lesions was the right inferior parietal lobule.

Note, however, that contralateral neglect is occasionally observed subsequent to lesions to the frontal lobe and cingulate cortex, as well as to subcortical structures including the superior colliculus and lateral hypothalamus. What is not clear is whether the same phenomenon results from lesions in these various locations.

Why does neglect occur? The two main theories argue that neglect is caused by either (1) defective sensation or perception or (2) defective attention or orientation. The strongest argument favoring the theory of defective sensation or perception is that a lesion to the parietal lobes, which receive input from all the sensory regions, can disturb the integration of sensation into perception. Derek Denny-Brown and Robert Chambers termed this function *morphosynthesis* and its disruption *amorphosynthesis*.

A current elaboration of this theory proposes that neglect follows a right parietal lesion because the integration of the spatial properties of stimuli becomes disturbed. As a result, although stimuli are perceived, their location is uncertain to the nervous system and they are consequently ignored. The neglect is thought to be unilateral because, in the absence of right-hemisphere function, the left hemisphere is assumed to be capable of some rudimentary spatial synthesis that prevents neglect of the right side of the world. This rudimentary spatial ability cannot compensate, however, for the many other behavioral deficits resulting from right parietal lesions.

Critchley and, later, others suggested that neglect results from defective attention or orientation; that is, an inability to attend to input that has in fact been registered. This suggestion was elaborated most recently by Heilman and Watson. They propose that neglect is manifested by a defect in orienting to stimuli; the defect results from the disruption of a system whose function is to "arouse" the person when new sensory stimulation is present.

Object Recognition

Elizabeth Warrington and her colleagues described another common symptom of right-parietal-lobe lesion: although able to recognize objects shown in familiar views, patients having these lesions are badly impaired at recognizing objects shown in unfamiliar views (Figure 14.7). Warrington concluded that the deficit is not in forming a gestalt, or concept—in this case, of "bucket"—but rather in perceptual classification—the mechanism for categorizing information as being part of the idea "bucket." Such allocation can be seen as a type of a spatial matching in which the common view of an object must be rotated spatially to match the novel view. Warrington and Taylor suggested that the focus for this deficit is roughly the right inferior parietal lobule, the same region proposed as the locus of contralateral neglect (see Figure 14.6B).

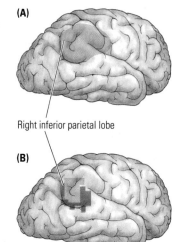

Right inferior parietal lobe

Figure 14.6 The locus of right parietal symptoms. (A) Composite map of the region damaged (inferred from brain scans) in 13 patients with contralateral neglect as described by Heilman and Watson. The area of greatest overlap is the right inferior parietal lobule. (B) Composite outline of the region of overlap among lesions producing deficits in Warrington and Taylor's test of recognition of objects seen in unfamiliar views. The lightly shaded region is the area of maximal overlap. Note the locational similarity between parts A and B.

Figure 14.7 Drawing of a bucket in (A) familiar and (B) unfamiliar views. Patients with right parietal lesions have difficulty in recognizing objects in unfamiliar views, such as that shown in part B.

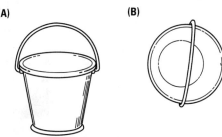

The Gerstmann Syndrome and Other Left Parietal Symptoms

In 1924, Josef Gerstmann described a patient with an unusual disorder subsequent to a left parietal stroke: finger agnosia, an asomatognosia described earlier in the chapter. Gerstmann's patient was unable to name or indicate recognition of the fingers on either hand. This symptom aroused considerable interest, and, in the ensuing years, three other symptoms were reported to accompany finger agnosia: right–left confusion, **agraphia** (inability to write), and acalculia. These four symptoms collectively became known as the Gerstmann syndrome.

Gerstmann and others argued that these symptoms accompany a circumscribed lesion in the left parietal lobe, roughly corresponding to the angular gyrus (area PG). If these four symptoms arose as a group, the patient was said to demonstrate the Gerstmann syndrome, and the lesions could be localized in the angular gyrus (see Figure 14.1A). The Gerstmann syndrome is a doubtful diagnostic tool in routine investigations, but all the symptoms can be associated with left parietal lesions.

Various other symptoms of left parietal lesions are illustrated in the following case history. On 24 August 1975, S. S., an 11-year-old boy, suddenly had a seizure, which was characterized by twitching on the right side of the body, particularly the arm and face. He was given anticonvulsant medication and was free of symptoms until 16 September 1975, when he began to write upside down and backward. S. S. was immediately referred to a neurologist, who diagnosed a left parietal malignant astrocytoma. Careful neuropsychological assessment revealed a number of symptoms characteristic of left parietal lesions:

- *Disturbed language function*. S. S. was unable to write even his name (agraphia), had serious difficulties in reading (dyslexia), and spoke slowly and deliberately, making many errors in grammar (dysphasia).
- *Apraxia*. S. S. was unable to combine blocks to form designs and had difficulty learning a sequence of novel movements of the limbs (see the next subsection).
- *Dyscalculia*. He was very poor at mental arithmetic and could not solve even simple additions and subtractions.
- *Recall*. He had an especially low digit span, being able to master the immediate recall of only three digits, whether they were presented orally or visually.
- *Right–left discrimination*. He was totally unable to distinguish left from right, responding at random on all tests of this ability.
- *Right hemianopia*. Probably because his tumor had damaged the geniculostriate connections, as S. S.'s tumor progressed, movement of the right side of his body became disturbed as the tumor placed pressure on the frontal lobe.

By the end of October 1975 S. S. died; neither surgery nor drug therapy could stop the growth of the tumor. The symptoms that S. S. exhibited resemble those of other patients whom we have seen with left parietal lesions, including H. P., whose story begins this chapter. Curiously, S. S. did not have finger agnosia, one of the Gerstmann symptoms, illustrating the point that even very large lesions do not produce the same effects in every patient.

Apraxia and the Parietal Lobe

Apraxia is a disorder of movement in which loss of skilled movement is not caused by weakness, an inability to move, abnormal muscle tone or posture, intellectual deterioration, poor comprehension, or other disorders of movement such as tremor. Among the many types of apraxia, we shall focus on two: ideomotor apraxia and constructional apraxia.

In ideomotor apraxia, patients are unable to copy movements or to make gestures (for example, to wave "hello"). Patients with left posterior parietal lesions often present ideomotor apraxia. Kimura showed that the deficits in such patients can be quantified by asking them to copy a series of arm movements such as those illustrated in Figure 14.8A. Patients with left-parietal-lobe lesions are grossly impaired at this task, whereas people with right-parietal-lobe lesions perform the task normally. We return to ideomotor apraxia in Chapter 22.

(A) Serial arm-movement copying test

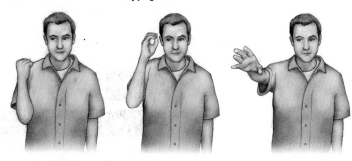

(B) Serial facial-movement copying test

Figure 14.8 Testing for apraxia. (A) Sample items from a serial arm-movement copying test. To assess ideomotor apraxia, subjects are asked to copy each movement in the series as accurately as they can. (B) Sample items from a serial facial-movement copying test used to assess constructional apraxia.

In constructional apraxia, a visuomotor disorder, spatial organization is disordered. Patients with constructional apraxia cannot assemble a puzzle, build a tree house, draw a picture, or copy a series of facial movements (Figure 14.8B). Constructional apraxia can develop after injury to either parietal lobe, although debate over whether the symptoms are the same after left- and right-side lesions is considerable (see the review by Benton). Nonetheless, constructional apraxia often accompanies posterior parietal lesions.

You can view both ideomotor and constructional apraxia as disturbances of movement that result from a disruption of the parietofrontal connections that control movement. Mountcastle proposed that the posterior parietal cortex receives afferent signals not only of the tactile and visual representation of the world but also of the position and movement of the body. He proposed that the region uses this information to function as "a command apparatus for operation of the limbs, hands, and eyes within immediate extrapersonal space."

Thus, the parietal lobe not only integrates sensory and spatial information to allow accurate movements in space but also functions to direct or guide movements in the immediate vicinity of the body. Both ideomotor and constructional apraxia can be seen as examples of a dysfunction in this guidance system.

Drawing

Although drawing deficits are known to arise subsequent to lesions in either hemisphere, the deficits in drawing are generally believed to be greater after damage to the right hemisphere than after damage to the left, and the right parietal damage is believed to have the greatest influence on drawing ability.

This conclusion is consistent with the general idea that the right hemisphere plays a dominant role in spatial abilities, but it may not be correct. Rather, it appears that disturbances in drawing differ, depending on whether the lesion is in the right or the left hemisphere. For example, Kimura and Faust asked a large sample of patients to draw a house and a man. Apraxic or aphasic left-hemisphere patients did very poorly, producing fewer recognizable drawings and fewer lines than did right-hemisphere patients. In contrast, right-hemisphere patients tended to omit details from the left side of their drawings and to rotate the drawings on the page.

In sum, drawing is a complex behavior that may require verbal as well as nonverbal (for example, spatial) processes. If asked to draw a bicycle, many people will make a mental checklist of items to include (fenders, spokes, chain, and so on). In the absence of language, we would expect such people to draw less-complete bicycles. Further, if patients are apraxic, there is likely to be a deficit in making the required movements. Similarly, the parts of a bicycle have a particular spatial organization. If spatial organization is poor, the drawing is likely to be distorted.

Spatial Attention

As we move about the world, we are confronted with a vast array of sensory information that cannot possibly all be treated equally by the nervous system. Thus, the brain must select certain information to process. Consider, for example, the sensory overload to which we are subjected when we stop to chat with an old friend in a department store. Several other people may be around, and there will certainly be displays of various items to purchase, competing sounds (others talking, music, cash registers), novel odors, and so on. Nonetheless, we can orient to a small sample of the incoming information and ignore most of the other input. In fact, we may focus to the exclusion of other, potentially more important information. Cognitive psychologists refer to this orienting of the sensory systems as *selective attention.* Thus, we are said to attend to particular stimuli.

Posner proposed that one function of the parietal cortex is to allow attention to shift from one stimulus to another, a process that he calls **disengagement.** Consider our earlier example of dining with a friend. As we eat, we shift from peas to bread to wine. We are disengaging each time that we shift from one food to another. One aspect of this disengagement is that we must reset our visuomotor guidance system to form the appropriate movements for the next target. We can extend this idea to mental manipulation of objects and spatial information, too: we must reset the system for the next operation. We return to the problem of selective attention in Chapter 22.

Disorders of Spatial Cognition

We use the term "spatial cognition" to refer to a broad category of abilities that require mentally using or manipulating spatial properties of stimuli, including the ability to mentally manipulate images of objects and maps. The mental-rotation tasks illustrated in Figures 12.2 and 21.11 provide good examples. Another is the ability to follow an upside-down map.

There is little doubt that posterior lesions, most likely including the region of PG and the polymodal cortex of the superior temporal sulcus, produce deficits in mental-rotation and map-reading tasks. Although it is widely assumed in the neuropsychological literature that the right hemisphere is "spatial" and that deficits in spatial cognition should thus result from right posterior lesions, the clinical evidence is far from convincing. Indeed, there is little doubt that both left- and right-hemisphere lesions produce deficits in spatial-cognition tasks.

The emerging view, however, is that left- and right-hemisphere lesions have different effects on the performance of spatial cognition. For example, Corballis suggested that mental rotation requires two different operations: (1) the mental imaging of the stimulus and (2) the manipulation of the image. Newcombe and Ratcliff suggested that the left-hemisphere deficit may result from an inability to generate an appropriate mental image. In Chapter 13, we saw that visual-imaging deficits result from left occipital lesions. In contrast, the right-hemisphere deficit may be due to an inability to perform operations on this mental image.

Deficits in the ability to use topographical information are more likely to be associated with damage to the right hemisphere than to the left. Such disorders include the loss of memory of familiar surroundings, the inability to locate items such as countries or cities on a map, and the inability to find one's way about the environment. Not surprisingly, such deficits are likely to be associated with other visual deficits (such as contralateral neglect or visual agnosia), but patients have been described with relatively specific disorders of topographical orientation.

Emillio de Renzi concluded that injury to the right posterior hemisphere is a prerequisite for such disorders. Newcombe and Ratcliff noted that such disorders are often associated with injury to the right posterior cerebral artery and thus are likely to include right occipitotemporal and right hippocampal regions. When the parietal cortex is affected, it is most likely to be the inferior part, probably including area PG and the superior temporal sulcus.

Left and Right Parietal Lobes Compared

In their classic paper, McFie and Zangwill compared the symptoms of patients with left or right parietal lesions. Although they found some overlapping symptoms, the asymmetry was clear (Table 14.1). In addition, as noted earlier, ideomotor apraxia is more likely to be associated with left parietal lesions.

A puzzling feature of the McFie and Zangwill study noted in Table 14.1 is that lesions to the two hemispheres produce some overlapping symptoms, despite the clear asymmetry. The results of neuropsychological studies tend to emphasize the asymmetry of lesion effects, but the overlapping symptoms are important theoretically. Indeed, as noted earlier, both constructional apraxia and disorders of spatial cognition are poorly lateralized. Many theories of hemispheric asymmetry discussed in Chapter 11 do not predict such ambiguity

Table 14.1 Effects of left- and right-parietal-lobe lesions compared

	PERCENTAGE OF SUBJECTS WITH DEFICIT*	
	Left (%)	Right(%)
Unilateral neglect	13	67
Dressing disability	13	67
Cube counting	0	86
Paper cutting	0	90
Topographical loss	13	50
Right–left discrimination	63	0
Weigl's sorting test	83	6

*Note the small but significant overlap in symptoms of left and right lesions.
Source: Based on data presented by McFie and Zangwill, 1960.

in symptom localization and tend to assume far greater dissociation of lesion effects than is actually observed.

One explanation for the overlapping symptoms relates to the concept of preferred cognitive mode, introduced in Chapter 11. There it was noted that many problems can be solved by using either a verbal cognitive mode or a spatial nonverbal cognitive mode. Genetic, maturational, and environmental factors may predispose people to use different cognitive modes. For example, a complex spatial problem, such as reading an upside-down map, can be solved either directly, by "spatial cognition" (the directions to travel are intuited spatially) or indirectly, by "verbal cognition" (the spatial information is encoded into words and the problem is solved by being "talked" through step by step).

People who are highly verbal prefer the verbal mode even when it is less efficient; we expect lesions of the left parietal lobe in these people to disturb functions that ordinarily are disrupted preferentially by right parietal lesions. Little direct evidence favors this explanation of functional overlap, but it is a provocative idea that accounts in part for individual differences as well as for the apparent functional overlap revealed by the results of lesion studies.

Major Symptoms and Their Assessment

Table 14.2 summarizes the major symptoms of parietal-lobe lesions. Damage to the anterior parietal cortex, including area PE, produces deficits in various somatosensory functions. Damage to the posterior parietal regions produces most of the other disorders.

Table 14.2 Summary of major symptoms of parietal-lobe damage

Symptom	Most probable lesion site	Basic reference
Disorders of tactile function	Areas 1, 2, 3	Semmes et al., 1960 Corkin et al., 1970
Tactile agnosia	Area PE	Hecaen and Albert, 1978 Brown, 1972
Defects in eye movement	Areas PE, PF	Tyler, 1968
Misreaching	Areas 5, 7	Damasio and Benton, 1979
Manipulation of objects	Areas PF, PG	Pause et al., 1989
Apraxia	Areas PF, PG, left	Heilman and Rothi, 1993 Kimura, 1980
Constructional apraxia	Area PG	Benton, 1990
Acalculia	Areas PG, STS*	Levin et al., 1993
Impaired cross-modal matching	Areas PG, STS	Butters and Brody, 1968
Contralateral neglect	Area PG right	Heilman et al., 1993
Impaired object recognition	Area PG right	Warrington and Taylor, 1973
Disorders of body image	Area PE?	Benton and Sivan, 1993
Right–left confusion	Areas PF, PG	Semmes et al., 1960
Disorders of spatial ability	Areas PE, PG	Newcombe and Ratcliff, 1990
Disorders of drawing	Area PG	Warrington et al., 1966 Kimura and Faust, 1987

*STS, superior temporal sulcus.

Table 14.2 also lists the regions most likely to be associated with the deficits, but few studies clearly demonstrate anatomical dissociations of such deficits. A major difficulty in dissociating the regions is that natural lesions rarely respect anatomical boundaries and affect only the neocortex. And, in contrast with the frontal and temporal lobes, which are often implicated in epilepsy and thus may be removed surgically, the parietal lobe is rarely epileptogenic, and so surgical removal is rare, as is the opportunity for follow-up research.

Clinical Neuropsychological Assessment

As we have seen, restricted lesions of the parietal cortex produce a wide variety of behavioral changes. Behavioral tests used to evaluate brain damage in neurologically verified cases could be logically employed to predict the locus and extent of damage or dysfunction in new cases. (See Chapter 28 for more detail on the rationale of neuropsychological assessment.) This section briefly summarizes the behavioral tests that have proved sensitive and valid predictors of brain injury (Table 14.3). Although these tests do not assess all the symptoms of parietal injury, they do evaluate a broad range of parietal-lobe functions. It would be highly unusual for a person to perform normally on all these tests yet show other symptoms of parietal-lobe damage. In addition to these tests, Howard Goodglass and Edith Kaplan describe a good series of tests in their "parietal lobe battery."

Table 14.3 Standardized clinical neuropsychological tests for parietal-lobe damage

Function	Test	Basic reference
Somatosensory threshold	Two-point discrimination	Corkin et al., 1970
Tactile form recognition	Seguin-Goddard Form Board	Teuber and Weinstein, 1954
	Tactile patterns	Benton et al., 1983
Contralateral neglect	Line bisection	Schenkenberg et al., 1980
Visual perception	Gollin Incomplete Figures	Warrington and Rabin, 1970
	Mooney Closure	Milner, 1980
Spatial relations	Right–left differentiation	Benton et al., 1983
Language		
Speech comprehension	Token	de Renzi and Faglioni, 1978
Reading comprehension	Token	
Apraxia	Kimura Box	Kimura, 1977

Note: These standardized tests have been validated on large samples of patients with known localized brain damage.

Somatosensory Threshold

Recall that subsequent to lesions of the postcentral gyrus, the somatosensory threshold increases on the contralateral side of the body. The two-point discrimination test requires the blindfolded subject to report whether he or she felt one or two points touch the skin (usually on the face or on the palm of the hand). The distance between the points is at first very large (say, 3 cm) and is gradually reduced until the subject can no longer perceive two points. In extreme cases, the process is reversed: the distance must be increased to find when the subject first perceives two points.

Tactile Form Recognition

In the Seguin-Goddard Form Board test, the blindfolded subject manipulates 10 blocks of different shapes (star, triangle, and so forth) and attempts to place them in similarly shaped holes on a form board. When the test is completed, the form board and blocks are removed and the subject is asked to draw the board from memory. The precise locus of the lesion producing deficits on this test is controversial, and no claims have been proved. Nevertheless, the results of research on tactile performance in monkeys with parietal lesions indicate that blindfolded tactile recognition is probably sensitive to lesions of areas PE and PF, whereas, in humans, the drawing part—a test of both memory and cross-modal matching—is probably sensitive to lesions in area PG.

Contralateral Neglect

A variety of tests have been devised, but we favor the line-bisection test by Schenkenberg and colleagues because it is particularly sensitive. In this test, the subject is asked to mark the middle of each of a set of 20 lines. Each line is a different length and is located at a different position on the page—some left of center, some in the middle, and some right of center. Patients showing contralateral neglect typically fail to mark the lines on the left side of the page.

Visual Perception

Visual perceptual capacity is easily assessed by either the Mooney Closure Test or the Gollin Incomplete-Figures Test. In both tasks, a series of incomplete representations of faces or objects is presented, and the subject must combine the elements to form a gestalt and identify the picture. These tests are especially sensitive to damage at the right parietotemporal junction, presumably in regions of the ventral visual stream.

Spatial Relations

In the right–left differentiation test, a series of drawings of hands, feet, ears, and so on, are presented in different orientations (upside down, rear view, and so forth), and the subject's task is to indicate whether the drawing is of the left or the right body part. In a verbal variant of this test, subjects are read a series of commands (for example, "Touch your right ear with your left hand") that are to be carried out. Both tests are very sensitive to left-parietal-lobe damage, but caution is advised, because subjects with left-frontal-lobe damage also are often impaired at these tasks.

Language

The Token Test is an easily administered test of language comprehension. Twenty tokens—four shapes (large and small circles, large and small squares) in each of five colors (white, black, yellow, green, red)—are placed in front of the subject. The test begins with simple tasks (for example, touching the white circle) and becomes progressively more difficult (for example, touching the large yellow circle and the large green square).

A Token Test of reading comprehension can also be given by having the subject read the instructions out loud and then carry them out. We have not considered language a function of the parietal lobe, but the posterior speech zone borders on area PG. Thus, injuries affecting PG often include temporal speech-related cortex, and aphasia is observed.

Apraxia

It is unfortunate that there are no standard-ized tests of apraxia analogous to the token test for aphasia. However, the Kimura box test (Figure 14.9) is probably the best test cur-rently available. The subject is required to make consecutive movements of pushing a button with the index finger, pulling a handle with four fingers, and pressing a bar with the thumb. This test is done very poorly by apraxics, and many of them appear unable to perform this very simple series of movements even with extensive practice.

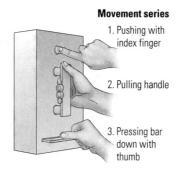

Movement series

1. Pushing with index finger

2. Pulling handle

3. Pressing bar down with thumb

Figure 14.9 Kimura box test. Subjects are required to learn the movement series that consists of pushing the top button with the index finger, pulling the handle with four fingers, and pressing a bar with the thumb. Apraxic subjects are impaired at this task, and they may be unable to learn it at all.

Summary

The parietal lobe can be divided into three functional zones for somatosensory processes, movement, and spatial cognition. The most anterior zones primar-ily take part in somatosensory functions. The superior parietal region primar-ily controls the visual guidance of movements of the hands and fingers, limbs, head, and eyes. This region has expanded in humans to include regions con-trolling not only the actual manipulation of objects but also the mental ma-nipulation of objects. Movements around the body, or in the imagination, necessarily include the space around the body and the object. Thus, the poste-rior parietal region can be conceived of as having a "spatial" function, although the precise nature of this spatial function is far from clear.

The inferior parietal region has a role in processes related to spatial cogni-tion and in what have been described as quasi-spatial processes, such as are used in arithmetic and reading.

Damage to the somatosensory regions of the parietal lobe produces deficits in tactile functions, ranging from simple somatosensation to the recognition of objects by touch.

Posterior parietal-lobe injury interferes with the visual guidance of hand and limb movements. Thus, for left parietal injury, there may be limb aprax-ias; whereas, for right parietal injury, constructional apraxias may result. Left parietal injury also produces a range of cognitive symptoms including deficits in arithmetic and writing; right parietal injury produces a complementary range of symptoms including contralateral neglect and various deficits in spa-tial cognition.

Neuropsychological analyses of parietal-lobe functions utilize tests that are sensitive to discrete parietal-lobe injuries. Such tests include the assessment of tactile functioning, visual guidance of movement, and cognitive functions such as spatial orientation, including both the copying of complex geometric figures and mental rotation.

References

Andersen, R. A. Inferior parietal lobule function in spatial perception and visuomotor integration. *Handbook of Physiology* 5:483–518, 1987.

Balint, R. Seelenlahmung des "Schauens," optische Ataxie, raumliche Störung der Aufmerksamkeit. *Monatsschrift fuer Psychiatrie und Neurologie* 25:51–81, 1909.

Benton, A. L. Constructional apraxia. In F. Boller and J. Grafman, Eds. *Handbook of Neuropsychology*, vol. 2. Amsterdam: Elsevier, 1990.

Benton, A. L., K. de S. Hamsher, N. R. Varney, and O. Spreen. *Contributions to Neuropsychological Assessment.* New York: Oxford University Press, 1983.

Benton, A. L., and A. B. Sivan. Disturbances of body schema. In K. M. Heilman and E. Valenstein, Eds. *Clinical Neuropsychology*, 3d ed. New York: Oxford University Press, 1993.

Blum, B. The functional relationship of monkey infra parietal cortex (IPL) to behavior in extrapersonal space. *Metabolic, Pediatric and Systemic Ophthalmology* 19:13–19, 1998.

Brown, J. *Aphasia, Apraxia, and Agnosia: Clinical and Theoretical Aspects.* Springfield, IL: Charles C. Thomas, 1972.

Butters, N., and B. A. Brody. The role of the left parietal lobe in the mediation of intra- and cross-modal associations. *Cortex* 4:328–343, 1968.

Corballis, M. C. Mental rotation: Anatomy of a paradigm. In M. Potegal, Ed. *Spatial Abilities: Development and Physiological Foundations.* New York: Academic Press, 1900.

Corkin, S., B. Milner, and T. Rasmussen. Somatosensory thresholds. *Archives of Neurology* 23:41–58, 1970.

Critchley, M. *The Parietal Lobes.* London: Arnold, 1953.

Damasio, A. R., and A. L. Benton. Impairment of hand movements under visual guidance. *Neurology* 29:170–178, 1979.

Denny-Brown, D., and R. A. Chambers. The parietal lobe and behavior. *Research Publications, Association for Research in Nervous and Mental Disease* 36:35–117, 1958.

de Renzi, E., and P. Faglioni. Normative data and screening power of a shortened version of the token test. *Cortex* 14:41–49, 1978.

Eidelberg, D., and A. M. Galaburda. Inferior parietal lobule: Divergent architectonic asymmetries in the human brain. *Archives of Neurology* 41:843–852, 1984.

Gerstmann, J. Some notes on the Gerstmann syndrome. *Neurology* 7:866–869, 1957.

Geschwind, N. The apraxias: Neural mechanisms of disorders of learned movement. *American Scientist* 63:188–195, 1975.

Goodale, M. A. Visual pathways supporting perception and action in the primate cerebral cortex. *Current Opinion in Neurobiology* 3:578–585, 1993.

Goodglass, H., and E. Kaplan. *The Assessment of Aphasia.* Philadelphia: Lea & Febiger, 1972.

Hécaen, H. Aphasic, apraxic, and agnosic syndromes in right and left hemisphere lesions. In P. Vincken and G. Bruyn, Eds. *Handbook of Clinical Neurology*, vol. 4. Amsterdam: North-Holland, 1969.

Hécaen, H., and M. L. Albert. *Human Neuropsychology.* New York: Wiley, 1978.

Heilman, K. M., and L. J. Gonzalez Rothi. Apraxia. In K. M. Heilman and E. Valenstein, Eds. *Clinical Neuropsychology*, 3d ed. New York: Oxford University Press, 1993.

Heilman, K. M., R. T. Watson, and E. Valenstein. Neglect and related disorders. In K. M. Heilman and E. Valenstein, Eds. *Clinical Neuropsychology*, 3d ed. New York: Oxford University Press, 1993.

Hillyard, S. A., and L. Anllo-Vento. Event-related brain potentials in the study of visual selective attention. *Proceedings of the National Academy of Sciences of the United States of America* 95:781–787, 1998.

Hyvarinen, J. *The Parietal Cortex of Monkey and Man.* Berlin: Springer Verlag, 1982.

Kimura, D. Acquisition of a motor skill after left hemisphere damage. *Brain* 100:527–542, 1977.

Kimura, D. Neuromotor mechanisms in the evolution of human communication. In H. D. Steklis and M. J. Raleigh, Eds. *Neurobiology of Social Communication in Primates: An Evolutionary Perspective.* New York: Academic Press, 1980.

Kimura, D., and R. Faust. Spontaneous drawing in an unselected sample of patients with unilateral cerebral damage. In D. Ottoson, Ed. *Duality and Unity of the Brain.* Wenner-Gren Center International Symposium Series (vol. 47). New York: MacMillan, 1987.

Levin, H. S., F. C. Goldstein, and P. A. Spiers. Acalculia. In K. M. Heilman and E. Valenstein, Eds. *Clinical Neuropsychology*, 3d ed. New York: Oxford University Press, 1993.

Luria, A. R. *The Working Brain.* Harmondsworth, England: Penguin, 1973.

McFie, J., and O. L. Zangwill. Visual-constructive disabilities associated with lesions of the left cerebral hemisphere. *Brain* 83:243–260, 1960.

Milner, B. Complementary functional specializations of the human cerebral hemispheres. In R. Levy-Montalcini, Ed. *Neurons, Transmitters, and Behavior.* Vatican City: Pontificiae Academiae Scientiarum Scripta Varia, 1980.

Milner, D. A., D. P. Carey, and M. Harvey. Visually guided action and the "need to know." *Behavioral and Brain Sciences* 17:213–214, 1994.

Mountcastle, V. B., J. C. Lynch, A. Georgopoulos, H. Sakata, and C. Acuna. Posterior parietal association cortex of the monkey: Command functions for operation within extra-personal space. *Journal of Neurophysiology* 38:871–908, 1975.

Newcombe, F., and G. Ratcliff. Disorders of visuospatial analysis. In F. Boller and J. Grafman, Eds. *Handbook of Neuropsychology*, vol. 2. Amsterdam: Elsevier, 1990.

Paillard, J., F. Michel, and G. Stelmach. Localization without content: A tactile analogue of "blindsight." *Archives of Neurology* 40:548–551, 1983.

Paterson, A., and O. L. Zangwill. Disorders of space perception association with lesions of the right cerebral hemisphere. *Brain* 67:331–358, 1944.

Pause, M., E. Kunesch, F. Binkofski, and H.-J. Freund. Sensorimotor disturbances in patients with lesions of the parietal cortex. *Brain* 112:1599–1625, 1989.

Posner, M. I., A. W. Inhoff, F. J. Friedrich, and A. Cohen. Isolating attentional systems: A cognitive-anatomical analysis. *Psychobiology* 15:107–121, 1987.

Posner, M. I., J. A. Walker, J. J. Friedrich, and R. D. Rafal. Effects of parietal lobe injury on covert orienting of visual attention. *Journal of Neuroscience* 4:1863–1874, 1984.

Roland, P. E. *Brain Activation.* New York: Wiley, 1993.

Schenkenberg, T., D. C. Bradford, and E. T. Ajax. Line bisection and unilateral visual neglect in patients with neurologic impairment. *Neurology* 30:509–517, 1980.

Semmes, J., and B. Turner. Effects of cortical lesions on somatosensory task. *Journal of Investigations in Dermatology* 69:181–189, 1977.

Semmes, J., S. Weinstein, L. Ghent, and H.-L. Teuber. *Somatosensory Changes after Penetrating Brain Wounds in Man.* Cambridge, MA: Harvard University Press, 1960.

Semmes, J., S. Weinstein, L. Ghent, and H.-L. Teuber. Correlates of impaired orientation in personal and extrapersonal space. *Brain* 86:747–772, 1963.

Stein, J. F. The representation of egocentric space in the posterior parietal cortex. *Behavioral and Brain Sciences* 15:691–700, 1992.

Teuber, H.-L. The brain and human behavior. In R. Held, W. Leibowitz, and H.-L. Teuber, Eds. *Handbook of Sensory Physiology*, vol. 7, *Perception.* Berlin: Springer, 1978.

Teuber, H.-L., and S. Weinstein. Performance on a formboard task after penetrating brain injury. *Journal of Psychology* 38:177–190, 1954.

Traverse, J., and R. Latto. Impairments in route negotiation through a maze after dorsolateral frontal, inferior parietal or premotor lesions in cynomolgus monkeys. *Behavioural Brain Research* 20:203–215, 1986.

Tyler, H. R. Abnormalities of perception with defective eye movements (Balint's syndrome). *Cortex* 4:154–171, 1968.

Warrington, E. K., M. James, and M. Kinsbourne. Drawing disability in relation to laterality of cerebral lesion. *Brain* 89:53–82, 1966.

Warrington, E. K., and P. Rabin. Perceptual matching in patients with cerebral lesions. *Neuropsychologia* 8:475–487, 1970.

Warrington, E. K., and A. M. Taylor. The contribution of the right parietal lobe to object recognition. *Cortex* 9:152–164, 1973.

Warrington, E. K., and L. Weiskrantz. An analysis of short-term and long-term memory defects in man. In J. A. Deutsch, Ed. *The Physiological Basis of Memory.* New York: Academic Press, 1993.

15

The Temporal Lobes

When he was 40 years old, H. H., a successful corporate lawyer with a wife and two school-age children, was finding his job increasingly stressful. His wife was taken off guard when he suddenly announced that he was quitting his law firm. He complained of being so stressed that he simply could not remember cases on which he was working and felt that he could not continue as a lawyer. He had no plan about how he would support his family but, curiously, he seemed unconcerned about it.

A couple weeks later, H. H. shaved his hair off, donned a flowing robe, and left his family to join a fringe religious group. His wife of 15 years was stunned by this sudden change in behavior: up to this point, H. H. had been an atheist. She was notified a couple of weeks later that he had collapsed with a seizure while handing out flowers and peace pamphlets in a large U.S. airport. He was taken to a hospital in a confused state, and a neurological examination revealed a left-temporal-lobe tumor. Fortunately, it was operable and was removed.

H. H. was aphasic after his surgery, but this condition cleared in a matter of weeks. He was left with enduring word-finding difficulties, problematic only when he was tired. He continued to complain of verbal memory problems, however. And his wife said that his personality remained different from what it had been, largely because he remained religious. Eventually, H. H. successfully returned to his law firm, although with a reduced caseload from that of his pretumor days.

H. H. showed typical symptoms of temporal-lobe disorder, including radical changes in affect and personality, memory disturbance, and at least a transient disturbance of language. In this chapter, we survey the anatomy of the temporal lobe, present a theoretical model of its function, describe the basic symptoms of damage to it, and briefly describe clinical tests of temporal-lobe function.

Anatomy of the Temporal Lobe

The temporal lobe comprises all the tissue that lies below the Sylvian sulcus and anterior to the occipital cortex (Figure 15.1). Subcortical temporal-lobe structures include the limbic cortex, the amygdala, and the hippocampal formation (Figure 15.2). Connections to and from the temporal lobe extend throughout the brain.

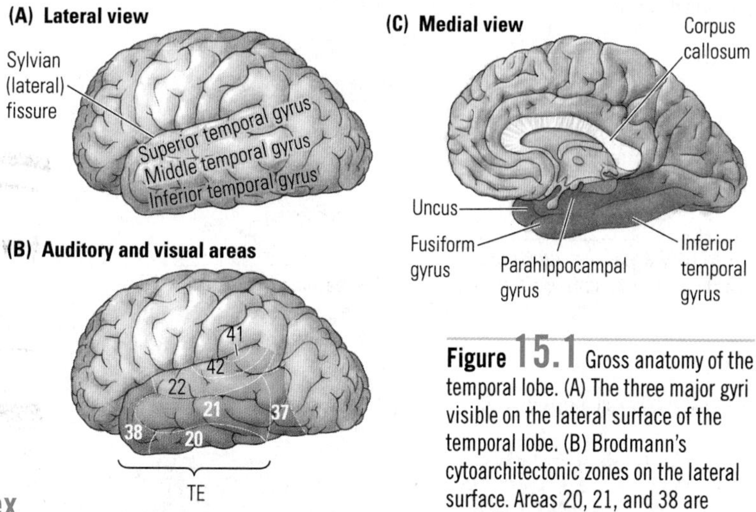

Subdivisions of the Temporal Cortex

Brodmann identified 10 temporal areas, but many more areas in the monkey were identified in more-recent studies (see Felleman and van Essen's map, Figure 10.19). Likely there are more areas in the human as well. We can divide the temporal regions on the lateral surface into those that are auditory (Brodmann's areas 41, 42, and 22 in Figure 15.1B) and those that form the ventral visual stream on the lateral temporal lobe (areas 20, 21, 37, and 38 in Figure 15.1B). The visual regions are often referred to as inferotemporal cortex or by von Economo's designation, TE.

(A) Lateral view

(B) Auditory and visual areas

(C) Medial view

Figure 15.1 Gross anatomy of the temporal lobe. (A) The three major gyri visible on the lateral surface of the temporal lobe. (B) Brodmann's cytoarchitectonic zones on the lateral surface. Areas 20, 21, and 38 are often referred to by von Bonin and Bailey's designation TE. (C) The gyri visible on a medial view of the temporal lobe. The uncus refers to the anterior extension of the hippocampal formation. The parahippocampal gyrus includes areas TF and TH.

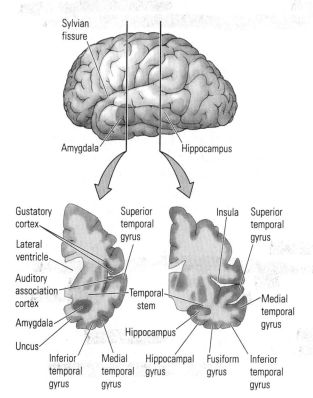

Figure 15.2 Internal structure of the temporal lobe. (Top) Lateral view of the left hemisphere illustrating the relative positions of the amygdala and hippocampus buried deep in the temporal lobe. The vertical lines indicate the approximate location of the sections in the bottom illustration. (Bottom) Frontal sections through the left hemisphere illustrating the cortical and subcortical regions of the temporal lobe.

(A) Brodmann's areas

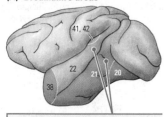

Auditory areas are light blue and visual areas are dark blue.

(B) Von Bonin and Bailey's areas

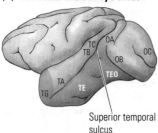

Superior temporal sulcus

Figure 15.3 Cytoarchitectonic regions of the temporal cortex of the rhesus monkey. (A) Brodmann's areas. (B) Von Bonin and Bailey's areas. (C and D) Lateral and ventral views of Seltzer and Pandya's parcellation showing the multimodal areas in the superior temporal sulcus. The sulcus has been opened up to reveal many subareas on its banks. These subareas are normally not visible from the surface.

(C) Lateral view

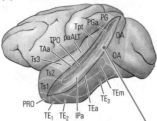

The banks of the sulcus have been spread to show many subareas on the bank.

(D) Ventral view

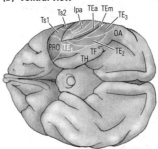

The sulci of the temporal lobe contain a lot of cortex, as can be seen in Figure 15.2. In particular, the Sylvian fissure contains tissue forming the *insula*, which includes the gustatory cortex as well as the auditory association cortex. The superior temporal sulcus, which separates the superior and middle temporal gyri, also contains a significant amount of neocortex, which can be divided into many subregions (Figure 15.3). The cortex of the superior temporal sulcus is multimodal, receiving input from auditory, visual, and somatic regions, as well as from the other two polymodal regions (frontal and parietal) and the paralimbic cortex.

The medial temporal region (limbic cortex) includes the amygdala and adjacent cortex (uncus), the hippocampus and surrounding cortex (subiculum, entorhinal cortex, perirhinal cortex), and the fusiform gyrus. The entorhinal cortex is Brodmann's area 28, and the perirhinal cortex comprises Brodmann's areas 35 and 36. Cortical areas TH and TF at the posterior end of the temporal lobe are often referred to as the *parahippocampal cortex* (see Figure 15.3). The fusiform gyrus and inferior temporal gyrus are functionally part of the lateral temporal cortex (see Figure 15.2).

Connections of the Temporal Cortex

The temporal lobes are rich in internal connections, afferent projections from the sensory systems, and efferent projections to the parietal and frontal association regions, limbic system, and basal ganglia. The neocortex of the left and right temporal lobes is connected by the corpus callosum, whereas the medial temporal cortex and amygdala are connected by the anterior commissure.

The results of studies on the temporal–cortical connections of the monkey reveal five distinct types of cortical–cortical connections, which are illustrated in Figure 15.4:

1. *A hierarchical sensory pathway*. The hierarchical progression of connections emanate from the primary and secondary auditory and visual areas, ending in the temporal pole. The visual projections form the ventral stream of visual processing, whereas the auditory projections form a parallel ventral stream of auditory processing (see Figure 15.4A).

2. *A dorsal auditory pathway*. Traveling from the auditory areas to the posterior parietal cortex, this pathway is analogous to the dorsal visual pathway and thus concerned with directing movements with respect to auditory information (see Figure 15.4A).

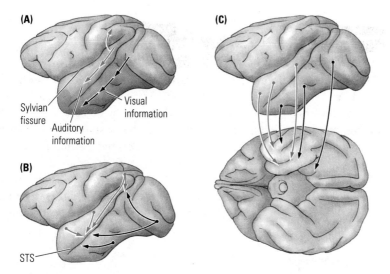

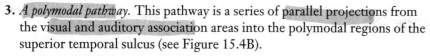

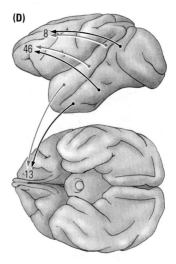

3. *A polymodal pathway.* This pathway is a series of parallel projections from the visual and auditory association areas into the polymodal regions of the superior temporal sulcus (see Figure 15.4B).

4. *A medial temporal projection.* The projection from the auditory and visual association areas into the medial temporal, or limbic, regions goes first to the perirhinal cortex, then to the entorhinal cortex, and finally into the hippocampal formation or the amygdala or both (see Figure 15.4C). The hippocampal projection is a major one, forming the **perforant pathway.** A disturbance of this projection results in a major dysfunction in hippocampal activity.

5. *A frontal-lobe projection.* This series of parallel projections reaches from the association areas to the frontal lobe (see Figure 15.4D).

These five projection pathways presumably subserve different functions, which will become apparent in the next section. Briefly, the hierarchical sensory pathway probably subserves stimulus recognition; the dorsal auditory pathway may play some role in detecting the spatial location of auditory inputs; the polymodal pathway probably underlies stimulus categorization; the medial temporal projection is crucial to long-term memory; and the frontal-lobe projection is necessary for various aspects of movement control, short-term memory, and affect.

Figure 15.4 Major intracortical connections of the temporal lobe. (A) Auditory and visual information progress ventrally from the primary regions toward the temporal pole, en route to the medial temporal regions. Auditory information also forms a dorsal pathway to the posterior parietal cortex. (B) Auditory, visual, and somatic outputs go to the multimodal regions of the superior temporal sulcus. (C) Auditory and visual information goes to the medial temporal region, including the amygdala and the hippocampal formation. (D) Auditory and visual information goes to two prefrontal regions, one on the dorsolateral surface and the other in the orbital region (area 13).

A Theory of Temporal-Lobe Function

The temporal lobe does not have a unitary function, in that it houses the primary auditory cortex, the secondary auditory and visual cortex, the limbic cortex, and the amygdala and hippocampus. On the basis of the cortical anatomy, we can identify three basic sensory functions of the temporal cortex: one concerned primarily with the processing of auditory input, another specialized for visual object recognition, and still another associated with long-term storage of sensory input (that is, memory). The hippocampus works in concert with the object-recognition and memory functions of the neocortex and plays a special role in organizing the memory of objects in space. The remaining temporal-lobe region, the amygdala, adds affective tone (that is, emotion) to sensory input and memories.

Temporal-lobe functions are best understood by considering how the brain analyzes sensory stimuli as they enter the nervous system. Imagine that you are hiking in the woods. On your journey, you notice many different birds, and you decide to keep a mental list of the species that you encounter so that you can tell your sister, who is an avid birder. As you walk along, you suddenly stop and back up—you have encountered a rattlesnake in the middle of the path. You decide to change routes and look for birds elsewhere! What temporal-lobe functions took part in your experience?

Sensory Processes

As you searched for different birds, you needed to be aware of specific colors, shapes, and sizes of birds that you might encounter. This process is object recognition and is the function of the ventral visual pathway in the temporal lobe.

You also needed to be able to categorize the birds quickly, because they were often flying away, and you had to do so by using information that varied in perspective from sighting to sighting (for example, lateral view versus rear view). This process of categorization is crucial to both perception and memory and probably depends on the cortex in the superior temporal sulcus. Categorization may require a form of directed attention because certain characteristics of stimuli are likely to play a more important role in classification than others. For example, classifying two different yellow birds requires that attention be directed away from color and focused on shape, size, and other characteristics. Thus, damage to the temporal cortex leads to deficits in identifying and categorizing stimuli. There is no difficulty in locating the stimulus or in recognizing that a stimulus is present, however, because these activities are functions of the posterior parietal and primary sensory areas, respectively.

As you walked along, you also may have heard birdsong, and you needed to match songs with the visual input. This process of matching visual and auditory information is called **cross-modal matching.** It, too, is likely to depend on the cortex of the superior temporal sulcus. As you saw more and more birds, you had to form memories that you could later access. Furthermore, as you saw different birds, you needed to access their names from your memory. These processes of long-term memory depend on the entire ventral visual stream as well as the paralimbic cortex of the medial temporal region.

Affective Responses

When you encountered the snake, you first heard the rattle, which alerted you, and you stopped. As you scanned the ground, you saw and identified the snake, and your heart rate and blood pressure rose. The affective response that you exhibited is a function of the amygdala. The association of sensory input and emotion is crucial for learning because stimuli become associated with their positive, negative, or neutral consequences, and behavior is modified accordingly.

In the absence of this system, all stimuli would be treated as equivalent. Consider the consequences of failing to associate the rattlesnake, which is poisonous, with the consequences of being bitten. Or consider being unable to associate good feelings (such as love) with a specific person. Laboratory animals with amygdala lesions become very placid and do not react emotionally to threatening stimuli. For example, monkeys that were previously terrified of snakes become indifferent to them.

Spatial Navigation

When you changed routes and went elsewhere, you used the hippocampus. The hippocampus contains cells that code places in space; together, these cells allow us to navigate space and to remember where we are.

As we consider these general functions of the temporal lobes, you can see that their loss would have devastating consequences for behavior. There would be an inability to perceive or to remember events, including language. There would be a loss of affect. Note, however, that a person would be able to use the dorsal visual system to make visually guided movements and, under many circumstances, would appear rather normal.

The Superior Temporal Sulcus and Biological Motion

An additional temporal-lobe function was not included in our hiking example. Animals engage in what we can call *biological motion*, or movements that have particular relevance to a species. For example, our eyes, faces, mouths, hands, and bodies make movements that can have social meanings. We shall see that the superior temporal sulcus analyzes these types of movements.

As already mentioned, the superior temporal sulcus receives multimodal inputs, and these inputs play a role in categorizing stimuli. A major category of stimuli is social perception, which includes the analysis of actual or implied bodily movements that provide socially relevant information. This information plays an important role in allowing us to develop hypotheses about the intentions of other people, an ability that is sometimes referred to as *theory of mind* or *social cognition*. For example, the direction in which a person's eyes are looking provides us with considerable information about what that person is attending (or not attending) to.

In a nice review, Allison and colleagues propose that cells in the superior temporal sulcus play a key role in social cognition. For example, cells in the monkey superior temporal sulcus respond to various forms of biological motion including the direction of eye gaze, head movement, mouth movement, facial expression, and hand movement. For social animals such as primates, knowledge about biological motion is critical information needed to guess the intentions of others. As illustrated in Figure 15.5, imaging studies show activation along the superior temporal sulcus during the perception of various forms of biological motion.

An important correlate of mouth movements is vocalization, and so we might predict that regions of the superior temporal sulcus are also implicated in the perception of species-typical sounds. In monkeys, cells in the superior temporal gyrus, which is adjacent to the superior temporal sulcus and sends connections

Figure 15.5 A summary of the activation (shaded areas) of the superior temporal sulcus (STS) region in the left (A) and right (B) hemispheres during the perception of biological motion. (After Allison, Puce, and McCarthy, 2000.)

(A) Left hemisphere

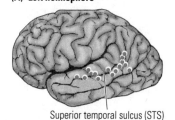

Superior temporal sulcus (STS)

(B) Right hemisphere

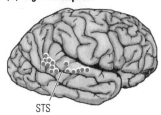

STS

to it, show a preference for "monkey calls," and imaging studies in humans have shown that the superior temporal gyrus is activated both by human vocalizations and by melodic sequences.

We could predict activation in the some part of the superior temporal sulcus in response to the combination of the visual stimulus (mouth movements) and talking or singing. Presumably talking and singing can be perceived as complex forms of biological motion. We could predict that, if people have temporal-lobe injuries that lead to impairments in analyzing biological motion, there is likely to be a correlated deficit in social awareness. Indeed, there is.

Asymmetry of Temporal-Lobe Function

The temporal lobes are sensitive to epileptiform abnormalities, and surgical removal of the abnormal temporal lobe is often of benefit in treating epilepsy. These circumstances also allow neuropsychologists to study the complementary specialization of the temporal lobes.

A comparison of the effects of left and right temporal lobectomy by Brenda Milner and her colleagues revealed that specific memory defects vary according to which side the lesion is on. Damage to the left temporal lobe is associated with deficits in verbal memory; damage to the right with deficits in nonverbal memory (for example, of faces). Similarly, left temporal lesions are associated with deficits in processing speech sounds, whereas right temporal lesions are associated with deficits in processing certain aspects of music.

Little is known, however, about the relative roles of the left and right temporal lobes in social and affective behavior. Right, but not left, temporal-lobe lesions lead to impairments in the recognition of faces and facial expression; so it seems likely that the two sides play different roles in social cognition. In fact, clinical experience dictates that left and right temporal-lobe lesions have different effects on personality.

Although the left and right temporal lobes are relatively specialized in their functions, do not be overly impressed by the apparent functional asymmetry. Substantial functional overlap is revealed in the relatively minor effects of *unilateral* temporal lobectomy, a striking result considering that such a large zone of the cerebral hemispheres is removed. Recall, for example, the striking recovery of function in H. H., whom we met at the beginning of the chapter. It is incorrect to assume, however, that removing both temporal lobes merely doubles the symptoms of damage seen in unilateral temporal lobectomy. Bilateral temporal-lobe removal produces dramatic effects on both memory and affect that are orders of magnitude greater than those observed subsequent to unilateral lesions.

Symptoms of Temporal-Lobe Lesions

Nine principal symptoms are associated with disease of the temporal lobes: (1) disturbance of auditory sensation and perception, (2) disorders of music perception, (3) disorders of visual perception, (4) disturbance in the selection of visual and auditory input, (5) impaired organization and categorization of sensory

Table 15.1 Summary of major symptoms of temporal-lobe damage

Symptoms	Most probable lesion site	Basic reference
Disturbance of auditory sensation	Areas 41, 42, 22	Vignolo, 1969 Hécaen and Albert, 1978
Disturbance of selection of visual and auditory input	Areas TE, superior temporal sulcus	Sparks et al., 1970 Dorff et al., 1965
Disorders of visual perception	Areas TE, superior temporal sulcus, amygdala	Milner, 1968 Meier and French, 1968
Disorders of auditory perception	Areas 41, 42, 22	Samson and Zatorre, 1988 Swisher and Hirsch, 1972
Disorders of music perception	Superior temporal gyrus	Zatorre et al., 2002
Impaired organization and categorization of material	Areas TE, superior temporal sulcus	Wilkins and Moscovitch, 1978 Read, 1981
Poor contextual use	Area TE	Milner, 1958
Disturbance of language comprehension	Area 22 left	Hécaen and Albert, 1978
Poor long-term memory	Areas TE, TF, TH, 28	Milner, 1970
Changes in personality and affect	Areas TE, plus amygdala	Blumer and Benson, 1975 Pincus and Tucker, 1974
Changes in sexual activity	Amygdala, plus?	Blumer and Walker, 1975

input, (6), inability to use contextual information, (7) impaired long-term memory, (8) altered personality and affective behavior, and (9) altered sexual behavior. Table 15.1 summarizes the major symptoms of temporal-lobe damage, lists the most probable lesion sites, and cites basic references. The sections that follow sample the range of temporal-lobe disorders and their clinical assessment.

Disorders of Auditory Perception

Damage to the primary visual or somatic cortex leads to a loss of conscious sensation; so it is reasonable to predict that bilateral damage to the auditory cortex will produce *cortical deafness*, an absence of neural activity in the auditory regions. The results of neither clinical nor animal laboratory studies support this prediction, however. As the Snapshot on page 378 illustrates, auditory hallucinations, which result from spontaneous activity in the auditory regions, are essentially the opposite of cortical deafness. Auditory hallucination is the perception of sounds (hearing voices) that are not actually present. The auditory cortex does play an actual role in discriminating two forms of auditory processing—namely, rapidly presented stimuli and complex patterns of stimuli. Language is fast and must be analyzed quickly, whereas music generally contains relatively slower changes in frequency, but the ear must be sensitive to the small differences in frequency important in music.

Speech Perception

Impaired auditory processing can be seen in the difficulty that temporal-lobe patients have in discriminating speech sounds. Although related to the common complaint among patients with left-temporal-lobe damage that people

S N A P S H O T

Imaging Auditory Hallucinations

Auditory hallucinations are the most common symptom of schizophrenia, being reported by about 65% of people diagnosed with the disease. Auditory hallucinations are not simply sounds; a patient hears fully formed verbal passages that appear to be coming from an external source. The patient's thoughts are usually hostile or paranoid, as in the following example:

> Days later while in the Metropolis again, I was once more startled by those same pursuers, who had threatened me several days before. It was night-time. As before, I could catch part of their talk, but, in the theatre crowds, I could see them nowhere. I heard one them a woman, say: "You can't get away from us; we'll lay for you and get you after a while!" To add to the mystery, one of these "pursuers" repeated my thoughts aloud verbatim. I tried to elude those pursuers as before, but this time I tried to escape from them by means of subway trains, darting up and down subway exits and entrances, jumping on and off trains, until after midnight. But, at every station where I got off a train, I heard the voices of these pursuers as close as ever (L. Percy King, from a letter written in the 1940s protesting the writer's imprisonment in a mental hospital and published in Firth, 1999, p. 414)

Dierks and colleagues described an experiment with paranoid schizophrenia patients whose hallucinations could be monitored within one fMRI session. In this study, the verbal hallucinations activated the primary auditory

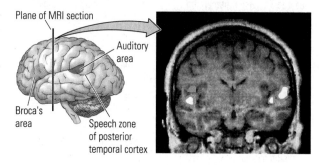

fMRI activation of auditory cortex during hallucinations in a schizophrenic subject. (After T. Dierks et al., 1999.)

cortex, Broca's area, and the speech zone in the posterior temporal cortex in the left hemisphere. In addition, there was some activation of the limbic areas (see the illustration above).

These results suggest that the hallucinations have their origin in the patients' own inner language systems. The researchers propose that activation in the auditory cortex leads to the perception that the voices are coming from an external source. The limbic activity presumably results from the anxiety generated by hearing voices, especially hostile voices.

(T. Dierks, D. E. J. Kinden, M. Jandl, E. Formisano, R. Goebel, H. Lanfermann, and W. Singer. Activation of Heschl's gyrus during auditory hallucinations. *Neuron* 22:615–621, 1999.)

are talking too quickly, the problem is not so much the quickness of the speech but rather the patient's inability to discriminate sounds presented quickly. This difficulty is commonly encountered by normal people trying to learn a new language.

The problem is not just in discriminating the speech sounds, however, but also in judging the temporal order in sounds heard. If a normal subject is presented with two sounds, a temporal separation of only 50 to 60 ms is sufficient to identify which sound was presented first. Subjects with temporal-lobe lesions may require as much as 500 ms between two sounds (a 10-fold increase) to perform at the same level. Each of these audioperceptual impairments appears more severe after left-temporal-lobe lesions than after right-temporal-lobe lesions—a result suggesting that these auditory skills are especially important in the discrimination of speech sounds.

Speech differs from other auditory input in three fundamental ways:

1. Speech sounds come largely from three restricted ranges of frequencies, which are known as *formants*. Figure 15.6A illustrates sound spectrograms of different two-formant syllables. The dark bars indicate the frequency bands seen in more detail in Figure 15.6B, which shows that the syllables differ both in the onset frequency of the second (higher) formant and in the onset time of the consonant. Notice that vowel sounds are in a constant frequency band, but consonants show rapid changes in frequency.

2. The same speech sounds vary from one context in which they are heard to another, yet they are all perceived as being the same. Thus, the sound spectrogram of the letter "d" in English is different in the words "deep," "deck," and "duke," yet a listener perceives all of them as "d." The auditory system must have a mechanism for categorizing varying sounds as equivalent, and this mechanism must be affected by experience, because a major obstacle to learning foreign languages in adulthood is the difficulty of learning equivalent sound categories. Thus, a word's spectrogram depends on context—the words that precede and follow it. (There may be a parallel mechanism for musical categorization as well.)

3. Speech sounds change very rapidly in relation to one another, and the sequential order of the sounds is critical to understanding. According to Liberman, we can perceive speech at rates of up to 30 segments per second, although normal speech is on the order of 8 to 10 segments per second. Speech perception at the higher rates is truly amazing, because it far exceeds the auditory system's ability to transmit all the speech as separate pieces of auditory information. For example, nonspeech noise is perceived as a buzz at a rate of only about 5 segments per second. Clearly, language sounds must be recognized and analyzed in a special way by the brain, much as the echolocation system of the bat is specialized in the bat brain. It is likely that the special mechanism for speech perception is in the left temporal lobe. This function may not be unique to humans, because the results of studies in both monkeys and rats have shown specific deficits in the perception of species-typical vocalizations after temporal lesions.

The fact that left-temporal-lobe lesions alter the perception of speech sounds ought not to be surprising: since the time of Wernicke, lesions of the left temporal association cortex (primarily area 22) have been known to produce aphasia (see Chapter 1). The classical view of Wernicke's aphasia is that it is associated with disturbed recognition of words, the extreme form being "word deafness"—an inability to recognize words as such despite intact hearing of pure tones.

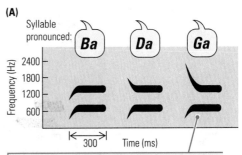

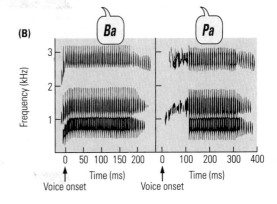

These shapes represent simplified renderings of spectrograms like those shown below.

Figure 15.6 Speech sounds. (A) Schematic spectrograms of three different syllables, each made up of two formants. (B) Spectrograms of syllables differing in voice onset time. (After Springer, 1979.)

Music Perception

The second category of auditory deficit is in processing sounds related to music. Musical sounds may differ from one another in three aspects: loudness, timbre, and pitch.

- *Loudness* refers to the magnitude of a sensation as judged by a given person. Loudness, although related to the intensity of a sound as measured in decibels, is in fact a subjective evaluation described by such terms as "very loud," "soft," "very soft," and so forth.

- *Timbre* refers to the distinctive character of a sound, the quality by which it can be distinguished from all other sounds of similar pitch and loudness. For example, we can distinguish the sound of a violin from that of a trombone even though they may play the same note at the same loudness.

- *Pitch* refers to the position of a sound in a musical scale, as judged by the listener. Pitch is clearly related to frequency. Consider the note middle C, described as a pattern of sound frequencies as depicted in Figure 15.7. The amplitude of acoustic energy is conveyed by the darkness of the tracing in the figure. The lowest component of this note is the *fundamental frequency* of the sound pattern, which is 264 Hz, or middle C. The sound frequencies above the fundamental frequency are known as *overtones* or *partials*. The overtones are generally simple multiples of the fundamental (for example, 2 × 264, or 528 Hz; 4 × 264, or 1056 Hz), as can be seen in Figure 15.7. Those overtones that are multiples of the fundamental are known as *harmonics*.

The classic view, dating to Hermann Helmholtz in the late 1800s, held that pitch perception depends on the fundamental frequency, and the overtones provide timbre. This view now appears to be incorrect. If the fundamental frequency is removed from a note by means of electronic filters, the overtones are sufficient to determine the pitch of the fundamental frequency—a phenomenon known as *periodicity pitch*. The ability to determine pitch from the overtones alone is probably due to the fact that the difference between the frequencies of the various harmonics is equal to the fundamental frequency (for example, 792 Hz − 528 Hz = 264 Hz = the fundamental). The auditory system can determine this difference, and we perceive the fundamental frequency.

The primary auditory cortex of the right temporal lobe appears to make this periodicity pitch discrimination. For example, Zatorre found that patients with right temporal lobectomies that include the primary auditory cortex are impaired at making pitch discriminations when the fundamental is absent but normal at making such discriminations when the fundamental is present. Right temporal lesions that spare the primary auditory cortex or left temporal lobectomies do not impair performance. Zatorre suggested that the right temporal lobe has a

Figure 15.7 Spectrographic display of the steady-state part of middle C (264 Hz) played on a piano. Bands of acoustical energy are present at the fundamental frequency, as well as at integer multiples of the fundamental (harmonics). (After Ritsma, 1967.)

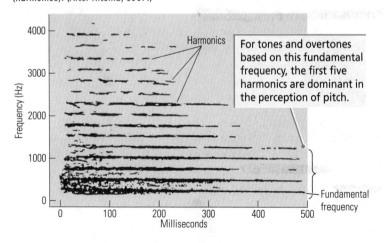

For tones and overtones based on this fundamental frequency, the first five harmonics are dominant in the perception of pitch.

Harmonics

Fundamental frequency

special function in extracting pitch from sound, regardless of whether the sound is speech or music. In regard to speech, the pitch will contribute to "tone" of voice, which is known as **prosody.**

Other aspects of music are also specially processed in the right temporal lobe. The simplest is the perception of timbre, which is impaired by right temporal lesions. In addition, more-complex aspects of music, such as scales, chords, and progressions, are all constructed from single musical notes. Although speculative, it seems likely that we humans develop a "musical store" much as we develop a "syntactic store" of words. Thus, when we encounter a musical scale or progression, we recognize it as such. The mechanism of such a hypothetical store is unknown, but it may be a function of the right auditory association cortex.

Finally, Liegeois-Chauval and colleagues point out that distinct musical processes may depend on specific cortical sites in the superior temporal gyrus (see Figure 15.2). Thus, in their study of patients with temporal lobectomies, these investigators found that rhythm discrimination was most affected by right posterior superior temporal gyrus damage, whereas distinguishing meter (for example, distinguishing a waltz and a march) was more affected by anterior damage to either temporal lobe.

Although it is tempting to compartmentalize music and language on opposite sides of the brain, it seems unlikely that the brain is specifically designed to treat them differently; rather, certain characteristics of musical and language input are probably analyzed selectively by the two hemispheres. Zatorre emphasized the key difference: the left hemisphere is concerned more with speed and the right hemisphere with distinguishing frequency differences, a process called *spectral sensitivity*.

Disorders of Music Perception

The fact that the brain appears to have neural networks dedicated to the processing of language and music leads to the conclusion that both language and music have biological roots. Although this conclusion seems obvious for language, it is less obvious for music, which has often been perceived as an artifact of culture. But considerable evidence suggests that humans are born with a predisposition for processing music.

Infants show learning preferences for musical scales and are biased toward perceiving the regularity (such as harmonics) on which music is built. Peretz argued that one of the strongest bits of evidence favoring the biological basis of music is that a surprising number of people have a condition known as *congenital amusia*. They are tone deaf. Apparently, amusic people have an abnormality in their neural networks for music, and no amount of training makes much difference. In fact, we have a colleague whose parents were both music teachers and, to the chagrin of her parents, she is amusic. She likes to note that she knows that the national anthem is being played because people stand up!

Liegeois-Chauvel and colleagues studied musical processing in a large group of patients with temporal lobectomies and found that injury to the right superior temporal gyrus impairs various aspects of processing necessary for discriminating melodies. In addition, a dissociation between the roles of the posterior and anterior regions of the superior temporal gyrus on different aspects of musical processing suggests their relative localization within the superior temporal gyrus.

(A)

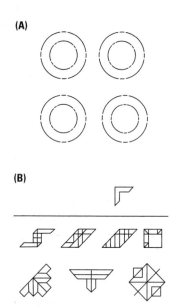

(B)

(C)

(D)

Figure 15.8 Tests for visual disorders. (A) Meier and French's test, in which the subject must identify the drawing that is different. (B) Sample of the Gottschaldt Hidden-Figures Test, in which the task is to detect and trace the sample (upper drawing) in each of the figures below it. (C) Rey Complex-Figure Test, in which the subject is asked to copy the drawing as exactly as possible. (D) Sample of the Mooney Closure Test, in which the task is to identify the face within the ambiguous shadows.

Disorders of Visual Perception

Although persons with temporal lobectomies do not normally have large defects in their visual fields, they do have deficits in visual perception. Such deficits were first demonstrated by Milner, who found that her patients with right temporal lobectomies were impaired in the interpretation of cartoon drawings in the McGill Picture-Anomalies Test. For example, one item illustrating a monkey in a cage features an oil painting on the wall of the cage—an obvious oddity or anomaly. But, although patients with right temporal lesions can describe the contents of the cartoon accurately, they are impaired at recognizing the anomalous aspects of this picture and others. Similarly, on a test such as the Mooney Closure Test or tests requiring the discrimination of complex patterns (Figure 15.8), patients with temporal-lobe damage perform very poorly.

Facial Recognition and Biological Motion

One of the most interesting visual perceptual deficits is in facial perception and recognition. When one of us (B. K.) and his associates presented patients with the split-faces test (see Figure 13.17), they found that those with right temporal-lobe resections fail to show a bias for that part of the face falling in the left visual field, suggesting that these patients perceive faces abnormally. This conclusion is consistent with reports that patients with right temporal-lobe damage are impaired at the recognition and recall of faces or photographs of faces.

Furthermore, these patients do not appear able to perceive subtle social signals such as discreet but obvious glances at one's watch, a gesture often intended as a cue to break off a conversation. Presumably the patients fail to perceive the significance of the visual signal. Facial signals are a form of biological motion, the analysis of which we have seen to be a function of the temporal lobe.

The description of deficits in visual perception in people with temporal-lobe injury is consistent with the hypothetical role of the inferior temporal cortex in the ventral visual stream (see Chapter 13). An extensive literature shows that monkeys with inferior temporal lesions have severe and selective deficits in learning tasks that require the visual recognition of objects. Furthermore, inferior temporal cortex neurons in monkeys have long been known to have selective characteristics, such as a preference for faces or hands.

These preferences may be quite specific. For example, Perrett and colleagues showed that neurons in the superior temporal sulcus may be responsive to particular faces seen head-on, faces viewed in profile, posture of the head, or even particular facial expressions. More recently, Perrett also showed that some superior temporal sulcus cells are maximally sensitive to primate bodies that are moving in a particular direction, another characteristic biological motion (Figure 15.9). This finding is quite remarkable because the basic configuration of the stimulus is identical as the body moves in different directions; it is only the direction that changes.

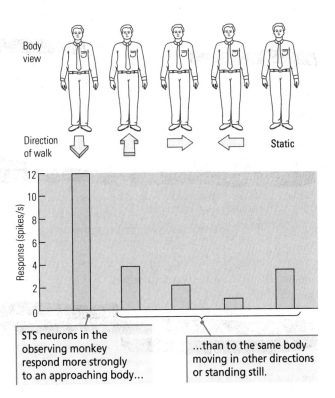

Body view

Direction of walk

Static

Response (spikes/s)

12
10
8
6
4
2
0

STS neurons in the observing monkey respond more strongly to an approaching body...

...than to the same body moving in other directions or standing still.

Figure 15.9 Neuronal sensitivity to direction of body movements. (Top) Schematic representation of the front view of a body. (Bottom) The histogram illustrates a greater neuronal response of superior temporal sulcus (STS) neurons to the front view of a body that approaches the observing monkey compared with the same body views when the body is moving away to the right and to the left or is static. (After Perrett et al., 1990.)

Activation of Inferior Temporal Neurons

One problem with the identification of specialized temporal visual neurons is that the dedication of specific temporal cortex cells for every possible object feature in the world is impractical. Tanaka approached this problem by attempting to determine the features that are critical for activating neurons in the monkey inferior temporal cortex. He and his colleagues presented many three-dimensional animal and plant representations to find the effective stimuli for given cells. Then they tried to determine the necessary and sufficient properties of these cells.

Tanaka found that most cells in area TE require rather complex features for activation. These features contain a combination of characteristics such as orientation, size, color, and texture. Furthermore, as illustrated in Figure 15.10, he found that cells with similar, although slightly different, selectivity tend to cluster vertically in columns.

Organizationally, the cortex has an important vertical component (see Chapter 10), but the neurons organized in columns in the temporal cortex are not identical in their stimulus selectivity. Thus it seems likely that an object is not represented by the activity of a single cell but rather by the activity of many cells within a columnar module. This important finding provides an explanation for the phenomenon of stimulus equivalence—that is, the common observation that an object viewed at different orientations remains the same object. Tanaka speculates that the representation of objects by multiple cells in a columnar module in which the selectivity varies from cell to cell and effective stimuli largely overlap can provide a way for the brain to minimize the effect of small changes in input images.

Figure 15.10 Schematic representation of the columnar organization in area TE. Cells with similar but slightly different selectivity cluster in elongated vertical columns, perpendicular to the cortical surface.

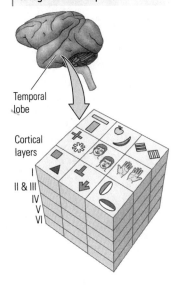

Neurons in the temporal lobe form columns that respond to categories of shapes.

Temporal lobe

Cortical layers

I
II & III
IV
V
VI

Tanaka and others have described two other remarkable features of inferior temporal neurons in monkeys. First, the stimulus specificity of these neurons is altered by experience. In a period of 1 year, monkeys were trained to discriminate 28 complex shapes. The stimulus preferences of inferior temporal neurons were then determined from a larger set of animal and plant models. In the trained monkeys, 39% of the inferior temporal neurons gave a maximum response to some of the stimuli used in training. This percentage compared with only 9% of the neurons in naive monkeys.

This result is exciting, because it shows that the temporal lobe's role in visual processing is not determined genetically but is subject to experience even in the adult. We can speculate that this experience-dependent characteristic allows the visual system to adapt to different demands in a changing visual environment. This feature is important for human visual recognition abilities that have very different demands in forests from those on open plains or in urban environments. In addition, experience-dependent visual neurons ensure that we can identify visual stimuli that were never encountered in the evolution of the human brain.

The second interesting feature of inferior temporal neurons is that they may not only process visual input but also provide a mechanism for the internal representation of the images of objects. Fuster and Jervey first demonstrated that, if monkeys are shown specific objects that are to be remembered, neurons in the monkey cortex continue to discharge during the "memory" period. These selective discharges of neurons may provide the basis of working memory for the stimuli. Furthermore, the discharges of these neurons may provide the basis for imagery. That is, the discharge of groups of neurons that are selective for characteristics of particular objects may provide a mental image of the object in its absence.

Disturbance of Selection of Visual and Auditory Input

We must select which inputs to process from the wealth of information in our environment. This selectivity is generally not conscious, because the nervous system automatically scans input and selectively perceives the environment. (Conscious control can be exerted, of course, as when you search for a mailbox to post a letter.)

Selectivity in auditory perception is best illustrated by the problem of listening to two conversations simultaneously. Because it is impossible to process the two competing inputs concurrently, the auditory system adopts one of two strategies: either one conversation is ignored or attention shifts back and forth from one conversation to the other. In either case, there is a selection of input. Selective perception in the visual system operates similarly. For example, because it is not possible to watch all floor events at a gymnastics meet simultaneously, either we focus our attention entirely on one event or shift it from one event to another.

Let us now consider the person with temporal-lobe damage. Selection of both auditory and visual input is impaired, which is ordinarily demonstrated only by special testing procedures. Selective attention to auditory input can be tested by dichotic listening (see Chapter 11). Recall that, when subjects are presented with two words simultaneously, one to each ear, normal subjects report more of the words presented to the right ear; if tonal sequences are presented dichotically, there will be a left-ear advantage.

This left-ear advantage is maintained in patients with temporal-lobe lesions, but left-temporal-lobe lesions result in an overall drop in the number of words recalled. One explanation for this effect is that the nervous system has difficulty focusing selectively on the input into one ear and attempts to process all the input concurrently; as a result, performance drops significantly.

Analogous findings are reported for visual input. If two different visual stimuli are presented simultaneously, one to each visual field, damage to the left temporal lobe impairs recall of content of the right visual field, but damage to the right temporal lobe impairs recall of content in *both* visual fields. Again, it may be that the nervous system is now unable to focus on distinctive features of the stimuli to allow efficient perception and storage of the input. In regard to visual input, however, it is noteworthy that right temporal lesions produce bilateral deficits, whereas left temporal lesions produce unilateral ones. This difference implies that the right temporal lobe may have a greater role than the left in selective attention to visual input.

Organization and Categorization

Asked to learn a list of words such as "dog, car, bus, apple, rat, lemon, cat, truck, orange," most of us will organize the words into three different categories—animals, vehicles, and fruit. If the list is later recalled, the items are likely to be recalled by category, and recall of the categories is likely to be used as an aid in recall of the items.

The ability to organize material is especially important for language and memory. For example, categorizing makes it possible to comprehend complex, extended sentences, including both the meaning of individual clauses and the information inferred from them. Organization of sensory input appears to be a function of the temporal lobes. Patients with left temporal lobectomies are impaired in their ability to categorize even single words or pictures of familiar objects.

Thus, patients have difficulty placing words or pictures into discrete categories, even when they are requested to, and they also have difficulty in using categories that most of us use automatically. For example, Milner has found that, when these patients are given a category name (such as animal) and are asked to recall exemplars of the category (such as dog, cat, rat), they have difficulty, even though they are fluent in other types of tests. Given that these patients have difficulty in simple types of categorization tasks studied in the laboratory, you can imagine that their difficulty in spontaneous organization may represent a significant deficit in cognition, especially in memory for complex material.

Neurolinguists propose that another type of categorization may take place in the left temporal lobe. Semantic categories are hierarchies of meaning in which a single word might belong to several categories simultaneously. For example, a duck belongs to the categories animal, bird, and waterfowl. Each of these categories is a refinement of the preceding one. Patients with posterior temporal lesions may show dysphasic symptoms in which they can recognize the broader categorization but have difficulty with the more specific ones.

Using Contextual Information

The meaning of identical stimuli can vary, depending on the context. For example, a word such as "fall" can refer to a season or to a tumble, depending on the context. Similarly, context may be a major cue for facial recognition. Most of us have encountered someone completely out of context (for example, while in Paris you encounter a clerk from your neighborhood store at home) and have been unable to recall who the person is until information about the context is provided.

A more complex example of extracting meaning from context is found in social situations. The interpretation of events, and indeed our role in events, depends on the social context. Thus, stimuli may be interpreted in one way when we are with our parents and in a different way when we are with our peers, an ability that is referred to as social cognition. (We return to social cognition in Chapter 22.) A simple example of the use of contextual information can be found in the McGill Picture-Anomalies Test described in the section on visual perceptual deficits. The only clue to the correct choice in the McGill anomalies is the context.

Memory

Interest in the temporal lobes' function in memory was stimulated in the early 1950s by the discovery that bilateral removal of the medial temporal lobes, including the hippocampus and amygdala, results in amnesia for all events after the surgery (**anterograde amnesia**). It is now clear that both the medial temporal regions and the temporal neocortex are important for memory functions (see Chapter 18).

Damage to the inferior temporal cortex specifically interferes with conscious recall of information, the extent of the memory disturbance increasing in direct proportion to the amount of temporal-lobe damaged. Lesions of the left temporal lobe result in impaired recall of verbal material, such as short stories and word lists, whether presented visually or aurally; lesions of the right temporal lobe result in impaired recall of nonverbal material, such as geometric drawings, faces, and tunes. Two case histories demonstrate the roles of the left and right temporal lobes in memory.

Mr. B., age 38, was suffering from an astrocytoma in the left temporal lobe. Before onset, he had been a successful executive in an oil company and was noted for his efficiency. As his tumor developed, he became forgetful, and at the time of hospital admission his efficiency had dropped drastically; he had begun to forget appointments and other important events. Forgetfulness had become such a problem that he had begun to write notes to himself to cover his memory problem, but he often mislaid the notes, leading to even greater embarrassment.

On formal tests of memory Mr. B. had special difficulty in recalling short stories read to him a few minutes earlier. In one test, he was read the following story from the Wechsler Memory Scale and was asked to repeat it as exactly as possible. "Anna Thompson of South Boston, employed as a scrub woman in an office building, was held up on State Street the night before and robbed of $15. She had four little children, the rent was due and they had not eaten for two days. The officers, touched by the woman's story, made up a purse for her."

Mr. B. recalled: "A woman was robbed and went to the police station where they made her a new purse. She had some children too." This performance is very poor for a person of Mr. B.'s intelligence and education. On the other hand, his immediate recall of digits was good; he could repeat strings of seven digits accurately. Similarly, his recall of geometric designs was within normal limits, illustrating the asymmetry of memory functions, because his right temporal lobe was intact.

Ms. C. illustrates the complement of Mr. B.'s syndrome. She was a bright 22-year-old college student who had an indolent tumor of the right temporal lobe. When we first saw her, after surgery, she complained of memory loss. She was within normal limits on formal tests of verbal memory, such as the story of Anna Thompson, but was seriously impaired on formal tests of visual memory, especially geometric drawings. For example, in one test she was shown geometric designs for 10 seconds and then asked to draw them from memory. Ten minutes later, she was asked to draw them again. She had difficulty with immediate recall (Figure 15.11) and, after 10 minutes, was unable to recall any of the drawings.

Affect and Personality

Although temporal-lobe disorder has been associated with disturbance of affect in humans for nearly 100 years, knowledge about the details of this role is still surprisingly fragmentary. Wilder Penfield and others reported that stimulation of the anterior and medial temporal cortex produces feelings of fear, an effect also occasionally obtained from stimulating the amygdala. Recall, too, that H. H.'s wife complained that H. H.'s personality was different after his tumor and surgery from what it had been before.

Temporal-lobe epilepsy has traditionally been associated with personality characteristics that overemphasize trivia and the petty details of daily life. Pincus and Tucker described several symptoms of this personality, including pedantic speech, egocentricity, perseveration in discussions of personal problems (sometimes referred to as "stickiness," because one is stuck talking to the person), paranoia, preoccupation with religion, and proneness to aggressive outbursts. This constellation of behaviors produces what is described as *temporal-lobe personality*, although very few people combine all these traits.

Similar personality traits arise after temporal lobectomy. There appears to be a relative asymmetry in the symptoms, with right temporal lobectomy more likely to be associated with these personality traits than left temporal lobectomy. This observation has not been quantified, however, and warrants further study.

Stimulus drawing   Ms. C.'s sketch

Figure 15.11 Impaired recall of geometric figures by Ms. C. In each set shown, the drawing at the left is the original stimulus and the drawing at the right is Ms. C.'s sketch made immediately after viewing each figure for 10 seconds. Note that Ms. C.'s impairment is worse with the more complex figures. Ms. C. was unable to recall even the simplest figure 10 minutes after viewing it.

Clinical Neuropsychological Assessment of Temporal-Lobe Damage

A number of standardized assessment tools have proved sensitive and valid predictors of temporal-lobe injury (Table 15.2). Like the clinical neuropsychological tests of parietal-lobe function reviewed in Chapter 14, these tests do not assess all possible temporal-lobe symptoms, but it would be highly unusual for a person to perform normally on all these tests if there were damage to either temporal lobe.

- Auditory and visual processing capacity can be assessed by using dichotic listening and the McGill Picture-Anomalies Test. The picture-anomalies task is not as sensitive an indicator today as it was when first used in the 1950s, perhaps because video-based home entertainment has made the

Table 15.2 **Standardized clinical neuropsychological tests for temporal-lobe damage**

Function	Test	Basic reference
Auditory processing capacity	Dichotic words and melodies	Sparks et al., 1970
Visual processing capacity	McGill Picture Anomalies	Milner, 1958
Verbal memory	Revised Wechsler Memory Scale; logical stories and paired associates	Milner, 1975
Nonverbal memory	Rey Complex Figure	Taylor, 1969
Language	Token	de Renzi and Faglioni, 1978

average person more sophisticated visually. Nevertheless, a poor score on this test almost invariably denotes right temporal abnormality.

- The best test of general verbal memory ability is the revised Wechsler Memory Scale. However, because the Wechsler memory quotient is affected by nonspecific disorders of attention, two subtests—paired associates and logical stories—are often used as a purer measure of verbal memory capacity. The paired-associates subtest requires a subject to learn a series of word pairs (for example, north–south, cabbage–pen) such that, when one word is read (north, cabbage), its paired-associate word (south, pen) can be recalled. An example of the logical memory test was presented in reference to Mr. B.'s verbal memory defect.

- The Rey Complex-Figure Test has proved to be one of the best for evaluating nonverbal memory function of the right temporal lobe (see Figure 15.8C). A printed copy of a complex geometric pattern is placed before the subject with the instructions, "Copy the drawing as accurately as you can." Forty-five minutes later, the subject is asked to reproduce as much of the figure as he or she can remember. Although the scoring criteria provide an objective measure of nonverbal memory, the test has the drawback that depressed or poorly motivated subjects may perform poorly, not because of right temporal-lobe damage but because they refuse to try to recall the figure. There is no easy solution to this problem, because all tests of nonverbal memory are subject to this complication.

- A deficit in language comprehension could be the result of a lesion in any of the language zones of the left hemisphere (that is, in the parietal, temporal, or frontal lobes). No current neuropsychological assessment tool can localize the area of damage within the left hemisphere. For this reason, we once again recommend the token test as the test of choice for language comprehension.

Summary

The temporal lobe can be divided into four functional zones for auditory processes (superior temporal gyrus), visual processes (inferior temporal cortex), and the integration of these processes for emotion (amygdala) and spatial navigation and spatial and object memory (hippocampus and associated cortex).

The processing of auditory information is specialized for two characteristics: speed and frequency. Language processing requires analysis of rapid changes in sounds but, because people talk at different pitches (that is, high squeaky voices versus deep resonant voices), the understanding of language sounds can tolerate differences in frequencies. In contrast, music is relatively slower than language, but differences in frequency are critical. The left temporal lobe is more concerned with speed, whereas the right is more concerned with complex frequency patterns. Damage to the auditory regions of the temporal lobe produces deficits in the recognition of language (primarily left) and music (primarily right), as well as in sound localization.

The temporal lobe adds two features to both auditory and visual information—namely, tone (affect) and categorization. These aspects are important for understanding sensory input as well as for using it in biologically relevant ways, such as in biological motion. Whereas the parietal lobe processes spatial location with respect to movement, the temporal lobe uses spatial location as a feature of object recognition and in the development of memories for object location. Damage to the visual regions of the temporal lobe disrupt the recognition of complex visual stimuli, such as faces. Damage to medial temporal regions produces deficits in affect, personality, spatial navigation, and object memory.

Neuropsychological analyses of temporal-lobe functions utilize tests that are sensitive to discrete temporal-lobe injuries. Such tests include those of auditory processing (dichotic listening), visual processing (object recognition), memory (both verbal and nonverbal), and language.

References

Allison, T., A. Puce, and G. McCarthy. Social perception from visual cues: Role of the STS region. *Trends in Cognitive Sciences* 4:267–278, 2000.

Belin, P., R. J. Zatorre, P. Lafaille, P. Ahad, and B. Pike. Voice-selective areas in human auditory cortex. *Nature* 403:309–312, 2000.

Blumer, D., and D. F. Benson. Personality changes with frontal and temporal lesions. In D. F. Benson and F. Blumer, Eds. *Psychiatric Aspects of Neurologic Disease.* New York: Grune & Stratton, 1975.

Blumer, D., and D. E. Walker. The neural basis of sexual behavior. In D. F. Benson and D. Blumer, Eds. *Psychiatric Aspects of Neurologic Disease.* New York: Grune & Stratton, 1975.

Chedru, F., V. Bastard, and R. Efron. Auditory micropattern discrimination in brain damaged patients. *Neuropsychologia* 16:141–149, 1978.

Dierks, T., D. E. J. Kinden, M. Jandl, E. Formisano, R. Goebel, H. Lanfermann, and W. Singer. Activation of Heschl's gyrus during auditory hallucinations. *Neuron* 22:615–621, 1999.

de Renzi, E., and P. Faglioni. Normative data and screening power of a shortened version of the token test. *Cortex* 14:41–49, 1978.

Dorff, J. E., A. F. Mirsky, and M. Mishkin. Effects of unilateral temporal lobe removals on tachistoscopic recognition in the left and right visual fields. *Neuropsychologia* 3:39–51, 1965.

Frith, C. How hallucinations make themselves heard. *Neuron* 22:414–415, 1999.

Fuster, J. M., and J. P. Jervey. Neuronal firing in the inferotemporal cortex of the monkey in a visual memory task. *Journal of Neuroscience* 2:361–375, 1982.

Geschwind, N. Disconnexion syndromes in animals and man. *Brain* 88:237–294, 585–644, 1965.

Hécaen, H., and M. L. Albert. *Human Neuropsychology.* New York: Wiley, 1978.

Kolb, B., B. Milner, and L. Taylor. Perception of faces by patients with localized cortical excisions. *Canadian Journal of Psychology* 37:8–18, 1983.

Kolb, B., and L. Taylor. Facial expression and the neocortex. *Society for Neuroscience Abstracts* 14:219, 1988.

Lackner, J. R., and H.-L. Teuber. Alterations in auditory fusion thresholds after cerebral injury in man. *Neuropsychologia* 11:409–415, 1973.

Liberman, A. On finding that speech is special. *American Psychologist* 37:148–167, 1982.

Liegeois-Chauvel, C., I. Peretz, M. Babai, V. Laguitton, and P. Chauvel. Contribution of different cortical areas in the temporal lobes to music processing. *Brain* 121:1853–1867, 1998.

Meier, M. S., and L. A. French. Lateralized deficits in complex visual discrimination and bilateral transfer of reminiscence following unilateral temporal lobectomy. *Neuropsychologia* 3:261–272, 1968.

Milner, B. Psychological defects produced by temporal lobe excision. *Research Publications of the Association for Research in Nervous and Mental Disease* 38:244–257, 1958.

Milner, B. Visual recognition and recall after right temporal lobe excision in man. *Neuropsychologia* 6:191–209, 1968.

Milner, B. Memory and the medial temporal regions of the brain. In K. H. Pribram and D. E. Broadbent, Eds. *Biological Bases of Memory.* New York: Academic Press, 1970.

Milner, B. Psychological aspects of focal epilepsy and its neurosurgical management. *Advances in Neurology* 8:299–321, 1975.

Penfield, W., and H. H. Jasper. *Epilepsy and the Functional Anatomy of the Human Brain.* Boston: Little, Brown, 1959.

Peretz, I. Brain specialization for music: New evidence from congenital amusia. *Annals of the New York Academy of Sciences* 930:153–165, 2001.

Perrett, D. I., M. H. Harries, P. J. Benson, A. J. Chitty, and A. J. Mistlin. Retrieval of structure from rigid and biological motion: An analysis of the visual responses of neurones in the macaque temporal cortex. In A. Blake and T. Troscianko, Eds. *AI and the Eye.* New York: Wiley, 1990.

Perrett, D. I., P. Smith, D. D. Potter, A. J. Mistlin, A. S. Head, A. D. Milner, and M. A. Jeeves. Neurones responsive to faces in the temporal cortex: Studies of functional organization, sensitivity to identity and relation to perception. *Human Neurobiology* 3:197–208, 1984.

Pincus, J. H., and G. J. Tucker. *Behavioral Neurology.* New York: Oxford University Press, 1974.

Rauschecker, J. P., and B. Tian. Mechanisms and streams for processing of "what" and "where" in auditory cortex. *Proceedings of the National Academy of Sciences of the United States of America* 97:11800–11806, 2000.

Read, D. E. Solving deductive-reasoning problems after unilateral temporal lobectomy. *Brain and Language* 12:116–127, 1981.

Ritsma, R. Frequencies dominant in the perception of pitch of complex sounds. *Journal of the Acoustical Society of America* 42:191–198, 1967.

Samson, S., and R. J. Zatorre. Discrimination of melodic and harmonic stimuli after unilateral cerebral excisions. *Brain and Cognition* 7:348–360, 1988.

Schulhoff, C., and H. Goodglass. Dichotic listening: Side of brain injury and cerebral dominance. *Neuropsychologia* 7:149–160, 1969.

Sidtis, J. J. Music, pitch perception, and the mechanisms of cortical hearing. In M. S. Gazzaniga, Ed. *Handbook of Cognitive Neuroscience.* New York: Plenum, 1984.

Sparks, R., H. Goodglass, and B. Nickel. Ipsilateral versus contralateral extinction in dichotic listening from hemispheric lesions. *Cortex* 6:249–260, 1970.

Springer, S. P. Speech perception and the biology of language. In M. S. Gazzaniga, Ed. *Handbook of Behavioral Neurology: Neuropsychology.* New York: Plenum, 1979.

Swisher, L., and I. J. Hirsch. Brain damage and the ordering of two temporally successive stimuli. *Neuropsychologia* 10:137–152, 1972.

Tanaka, K. Neuronal mechanisms of object recognition. *Science* 262:685–688, 1993.

Taylor, L. B. Localization of cerebral lesions by psychological testing. *Clinical Neurosurgery* 16:269–287, 1969.

Trehub, S., E. G. Schellenberg, and S. B. Kamenetsky. Infants' and adults' perception of scale structure. *Journal of Experimental Psychology: Human Perception and Performance* 25:383–396, 1999.

Ungerleider, L. G., and M. Mishkin. Two cortical visual systems. In D. J. Ingle, M. H. Goodale, and R. J. W. Mansfield, Eds. *The Analysis of Visual Behavior.* Cambridge, MA: MIT Press, 1982.

Vignolo, L. A. Auditory agnosia: A review and report of recent evidence. In A. L. Benton, Ed. *Contributions to Clinical Neuropsychology.* Chicago: Aldine, 1969.

Wilkins, A., and M. Moscovitch. Selective impairment of semantic memory after temporal lobectomy. *Neuropsychologia* 16:73–79, 1978.

Wolberg, Z., and J. D. Newman. Auditory cortex of squirrel monkey: Response patterns of single cells to species-specific vocalizations. *Science* 175:212–214, 1972.

Zatorre, R. J. Musical perception and cerebral function: A critical review. *Music Perception* 2:196–221, 1984.

Zatorre, R. J. Neural specializations for tonal processing. *Annals of the New York Academy of Sciences* 930:193–210, 2001.

Zatorre, R. J., and P. Belin. Spectral and temporal processing in human auditory cortex. *Cerebral Cortex* 11:946–953, 2001.

Zatorre, R. J., P. Belin, and V. Penhume. Structure and function of the auditory cortex: Music and speech. *Trends in Cognitive Science* 6:37–46, 2002.

Zatorre, R. J., and A. R. Halpern. Effect of unilateral temporal-lobe excision on perception and imagery of songs. *Neuropsychologia* 31:221–232, 1993.

chapter 16

The Frontal Lobes

E. L. was a professor of botany at a college in upstate New York. Known for his organizational skills, E. L. had developed a large herbarium at the college and truly enjoyed having students working with him on various research projects. Late in the spring semester when he was 60 years old, E. L. began to have headaches and felt as if he had the flu; after a few days bed rest, however, he was not getting any better. He eventually visited his physician, who determined that E. L. had an infection, although the source was difficult to identify.

Meanwhile, E. L. began to develop cognitive symptoms that his wife found very worrisome. He seemed disorganized, showed little emotion, and, although a chapter of his unpublished book was due and he was never late in doing such things, he said that he just could not think of anything to write.

The most striking thing about E. L. when he arrived for his neuropsychological assessment was his flat affect and the virtual absence of facial expression—symptoms typical of left-frontal-lobe patients. This lack of affect was not associated with a lack of effort on the tests, however, because the assessment ranked his intelligence and general memory scores in the superior range. He did, nevertheless, register significant impairments on tests sensitive to frontal-lobe functions.

Talking with E. L. and his wife of more than 30 years made it clear that E. L. was having difficulty not only with his academic work but also with his social interactions with colleagues, friends, and his family. He found it difficult to interact even with close friends, and his wife was concerned that her husband was "not the man I married."

In a real sense, all neural roads eventually lead to the frontal lobes. As is apparent in E. L.'s case, when some of the roads lead nowhere, people can have major problems in generating appropriate behavior. In this chapter, we consider the anatomical organization of the frontal lobes, including the neural roads for information flow to and from them, before looking at a general theory of frontal-lobe function, the various symptoms associated with frontal-lobe injury, and diseases that affect the frontal lobes.

Anatomy of the Frontal Lobes

Children are notorious for their social faux pas because they do not recognize that the rules of behavior change with the social and environmental circumstances. Indeed, controlling our behavior in response to the social or environmental situation that we are in requires considerable skill, and we can all relate examples in which we goofed and behaved inappropriately. Fortunately, most of us do not err often, because our frontal lobes control our behavior with respect to time and place. Yet the frontal lobe can perform such a function only if it is provided with all the relevant sensory and mnemonic (that is, memory) information available.

Subdivisions of the Frontal Cortex

In the human brain, the frontal lobes comprise all the tissue in front of the central sulcus. This vast area, constituting 20% of the neocortex, is made up of several functionally distinct regions that we shall group into three general categories—motor, premotor, and prefrontal (Figures 16.1 and 16.2).

The motor cortex is area 4. The premotor cortex includes areas 6 and 8, which can be divided into four regions:

lateral area 6: premotor cortex
medial area 6: supplementary motor cortex
area 8: frontal eye field
area 8A: supplementary eye field

In humans, the lateral premotor area expanded as Broca's area (area 44) developed.

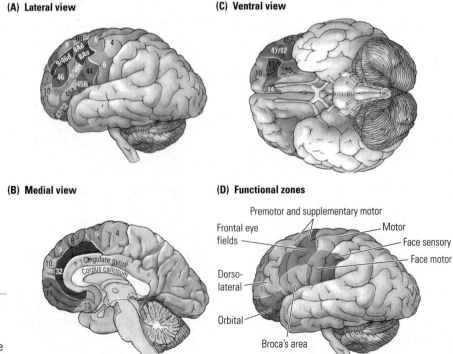

(A) Lateral view

(C) Ventral view

(B) Medial view

(D) Functional zones

Premotor and supplementary motor
Frontal eye fields
Motor
Face sensory
Face motor
Dorso-lateral
Orbital
Broca's area

Figure 16.1 Petrides and Pandya's cytoarchitectonic map of the frontal lobe. Approximate boundaries of functional zones of the frontal lobe are shown in part D.

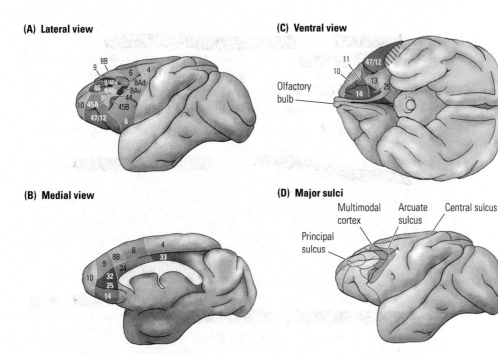

(A) Lateral view

(B) Medial view

(C) Ventral view

Olfactory bulb

(D) Major sulci

Multimodal cortex   Arcuate sulcus   Central sulcus

Principal sulcus

Figure 16.2
Petrides and Pandya's cytoarchitectonic map of the frontal lobe of the rhesus monkey. The two major sulci in the monkey frontal lobe are the principal sulcus and the arcuate sulcus, as shown in part D.

Prefrontal cortex is a peculiar name that derives from Jersey Rose and Clinton Woolsey's observation that the frontal lobes of all the mammalian species that they examined have a region that receives projections from the dorsomedial nucleus of the thalamus. They saw this thalamic projection as being parallel to the projections of the lateral and medial geniculate nuclei to the visual and the auditory cortex, respectively, and concluded that the dorsomedial projection could be used to define a similar region in different animal species. They termed this region the prefrontal cortex.

In primates, the prefrontal cortex can be divided into three regions (refer to Figures 16.1 and 16.2): (1) dorsolateral prefrontal cortex (areas 9 and 46); (2) inferior (ventral) prefrontal cortex (areas 11, 12, 13, and 14); and (3) medial frontal cortex (areas 25 and 32). The inferior frontal cortex is sometimes referred to as the **orbital frontal cortex** because of its relation to the orbit (eye socket). The medial frontal area is sometimes considered part of the anterior cingulate region rather than part of the prefrontal cortex, even though it may receive dorsomedial projections.

As in the temporal lobe, many areas in the frontal lobe are multimodal. Cells responsive to combinations of visual, auditory, and somatic stimuli are found in the lateral premotor cortex (area 6) and in area 46. In contrast, cells responsive to taste and olfaction are found in area 13. The latter cells likely produce our perception of flavor in foods.

Connections of the Motor and Premotor Areas

The motor and premotor areas are part of a functional system to control movements directly. Several groups of connections bind up this system:

- The motor cortex projects to the spinal motor neurons to control limb, hand, foot, and digit movements and to the appropriate cranial nerve motor neurons to control facial movements. It also projects to other motor structures such as the basal ganglia and the red nucleus.

- The premotor areas can influence movement directly through corticospinal projections or indirectly through projections to the motor cortex. The premotor regions also receive projections from the posterior parietal areas PE and PF. Thus, the premotor regions are connected to areas concerned with the execution of limb movements.

- The frontal eye fields (areas 8 and 8A) receive projections from regions controlling eye movements and send projections to these regions. Thus, these regions receive visual input from posterior parietal region PG and the superior colliculus.

- All premotor areas receive projections from the dorsolateral prefrontal cortex, which implies that this prefrontal area has some role in the control of limb and eye movements.

Connections of the Prefrontal Areas

The prefrontal areas can be viewed as the end points of the dorsal (object recognition) and ventral (spatial behavior) visual streams. In fact, Felleman and van Essen included prefrontal regions as part of the visual cortex (see Figure 10.19).

The dorsolateral prefrontal cortex (areas 9 and 46) receives its main inputs from the posterior parietal areas and the superior temporal sulcus. These connections are reciprocal. In addition, the dorsolateral cortex has extensive connections to regions to which the posterior parietal cortex also projects, including the cingulate cortex, basal ganglia, and superior colliculus (see Figure 14.2). The key to understanding the functions of the dorsolateral cortex lies in its relation to the posterior parietal cortex (Figure 16.3A).

The orbital frontal cortex (areas 11 through 14) receives its main afferents from the temporal lobe, including the auditory regions of the superior temporal gyrus, the visual regions of TE and the superior temporal sulcus, and the amygdala (Figure 16.3B). In addition, there are connections from the somatosensory cortex (area 43), gustatory cortex (in the insula), and olfactory regions of the pyriform cortex, as illustrated in Figure 16.4. The orbital cortex therefore gains input from all sensory modalities. The orbital frontal area projects subcortically to the amygdala and hypothalamus, providing a route for influencing the autonomic system, which controls changes in blood pressure, respiration, and so on. These physiological changes are important in emotional responses.

Figure 16.3 The corticocortical connections to the frontal lobe of the rhesus monkey (see Figure 16.2). (A) The connections to the dorsolateral surface include projections from posterior parietal as well as temporal regions. (B) The connections to the inferior frontal region are from the temporal lobe. Connections from the insula and olfactory cortex are not shown.

(A) Spatial behavior

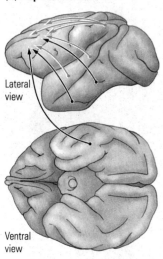

Lateral view

Ventral view

(B) Object recognition

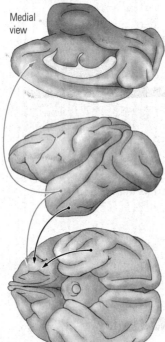

Medial view

The prefrontal regions receive significant input from dopaminergic cells in the tegmentum. This modulatory input plays an important role in regulating how prefrontal neurons react to stimuli, including stressful stimuli, and probably plays some role in our different emotional states. Abnormalities in this projection play a central role in schizophrenia.

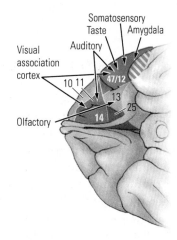

Figure 16.4 Inputs to the orbitofrontal cortex. Schematic illustration of the ventral surface of the monkey orbitofrontal cortex, including inputs from all sensory regions. (After Rolls, 1998.)

A Theory of Frontal-Lobe Function

Imagine the following scenario. At the last moment, you have invited friends for dinner. Because you have nothing to serve, you must go shopping after you leave work at 5:00 P.M. Before leaving, you prepare a list of items to buy. You are working under a time constraint because you must return home before your guests arrive and you need time to prepare. Because the items you need are not all at the same store, you must make an efficient plan of travel. You also must not be distracted by stores selling items (such as shoes) that you do not need or by extended chats with store clerks or friends whom you might encounter.

The task that you have set yourself is a bit rushed, but for most people it offers little challenge. People with frontal-lobe injury, however, cannot manage it. The fundamental requirements of the task that challenge frontal-lobe patients are as follows:

- Planning in advance and selecting from many options
- Ignoring extraneous stimuli and persisting in the task at hand
- Keeping track of the stores to which they have gone and the items that they have already purchased

The behavioral requirements of this task can be described as the temporal organization of behavior, and this organization is the general function of the frontal lobe. Thus, the frontal lobe contains control systems that implement different behavioral strategies in response to both internal and external cues. In recent years, it has become fashionable to refer to these temporal systems as *executive functions,* although we do not want to read too much into this label. The premotor and prefrontal regions contribute in different ways to this control function, and so we will consider them separately.

Functions of the Premotor Cortex

Whereas the motor cortex provides a mechanism for the execution of individual movements, the premotor cortex selects the movements to be executed. Consider the behavior of a resting dog. It may get up and respond to its owner's call or it may get up for no apparent reason and wander about the yard.

The former movements are made in response to a specific environmental cue, whereas the latter behavior can be regarded as a response to an internal event. Passingham suggested that the premotor region functions primarily to choose behavior in response to external cues and the supplementary motor region makes a greater internal contribution when no such cues are available.

Just as we choose limb movements, we must select eye movements. This selection is the function of the frontal eye fields. Like limb movements, eye movements can be made to specific targets that are visible or they can be made on the basis of internal cues. Thus, we can make eye movements to look at specific objects or we can gaze around, seemingly without purpose. Passingham suggested that area 8 is specialized for stimulus-directed movements, whereas area 8A is responsible for internally driven movements.

The role of the premotor cortex in response selection was first shown in normal subjects by Roland and his colleagues. They compared the cerebral blood flow in subjects making either a repetitive movement of one finger or a complex sequence of 16 movements of the fingers of one hand. The increase in blood flow in the supplementary motor cortexes *in both hemispheres* was larger in the sequence task than in the repetitive task. There was, however, no increase in blood flow in the premotor region.

Roland concluded that the supplementary motor region plays a special role in the selection and direction of motor sequences. An important aspect of Roland's experiment is that there was no external cue for the movements. That is, the production of the movement sequence was self-paced, or internally driven.

Deiber and colleagues showed that the premotor cortex is activated when movement sequences are paced externally by a cue. In their experiment, the subjects performed one of two tasks. In the first task, whenever a tone sounded, they made a fixed movement, which was to move a joystick forward. In this case, there was no response selection; the same response was made each time. In the second task, when the subjects heard the tone, they randomly made one of four movements of the joystick (forward, backward, left, or right). This task required a choice of movement. The results showed a significant effect of response selection: there was an increase in blood flow to both premotor areas in the choice condition relative to the fixed condition.

It is curious that both premotor regions were activated in the Deiber task, but an experiment by Jenkins and colleagues may provide an explanation. These researchers compared the performance of a prelearned sequence of finger movements with the learning of a sequence in which a tone indicated whether the sequence was correct or incorrect. The medial region was relatively more activated during the prelearned sequence, and the lateral region was more activated during the learning sequence. It seems likely that, during the prelearned movement, the cues were internal, whereas, on the learning task, the subjects had to attend to external cues.

Functions of the Prefrontal Cortex

The motor cortex is responsible for making movements. The premotor cortex selects movements. The prefrontal cortex controls cognitive processes so that appropriate movements are selected at the correct time and place. This selection may be controlled by internalized information or external cues or it may be made in response to context or self-knowledge. We consider these aspects separately.

Internal Cues

The internalized record of what has just taken place is independent of the existing sensory information and can be called *temporal memory*, *working memory*, or *short-term memory*. We use **temporal memory** here to refer to a neural record of recent events and their order. These events may be related to things or to movements and thus derive their information from the object-recognition or motor streams of sensory processing.

Recall that both streams project to the prefrontal cortex, although to different places (see Figure 16.3), which suggests temporal memory for both motor and object information, although the memory will be localized in different places in the frontal cortex. The dorsolateral areas are especially engaged in the selection of behavior based on temporal memory.

External Cues

People whose temporal memory is defective become dependent on environmental cues to determine their behavior. That is, behavior is not under the control of internalized knowledge but is controlled directly by external cues. One effect of this condition is that people with frontal-lobe injuries have difficulty in inhibiting behavior directed to external stimuli. In our dinner-party example, frontal-lobe patients would enter a shoe store or chat with friends as they responded to environmental cues that they encountered. (We have probably all experienced occasions when the temporal organization of our behavior failed and we were controlled by external cues rather than internalized information. How many times have you started to do something, been distracted by a question or event, and then been unable to recall what you were going to do? Sadly, this phenomenon increases with age, which is not reassuring information about the state of one's prefrontal cortex.)

One type of environmental cue is feedback about the rewarding properties of stimuli. For example, if you imagine that a certain stimulus, such as a photograph of your grandmother, is always associated with a reward, such as wonderful food, then you learn the association between the visual stimulus (the photograph of grandma) and the reinforcement (food). The learning of such associations is central to much of what we do as we learn about the world, and the orbital cortex is central to learning by associations.

Context Cues

We humans live complex lives. We live in social groups in which we have multiple simultaneous roles as children, parents, friends, siblings, lovers, workers, and so on. Each of these roles is governed by rules of behavior that we are expected to follow: our behavior around our grandparents is certainly different from our behavior with our high-school friends. Similarly, our behavior varies with the environment: we are quiet at a movie theater or in a library, but we may be noisy at a football game or at a picnic.

Behavior, then, is context dependent. Hence, behavior that is appropriate at one moment may not be appropriate if there are subtle changes in the context. This point is beautifully illustrated in Jane Goodall's graphic descriptions of the different behavioral patterns exhibited by chimpanzees. The makeup of the social group at any given time dictates the behavior of each chimpanzee. Given the presence and position of certain animals, a particular chimp may be bold and relaxed, whereas, with a different group of animals, the chimp is quiet and nervous. Further, an error in evaluating the context can have grievous consequences.

It may be no accident that the frontal lobe has grown so large in primates that are highly social. We can easily see the importance of social context when we reflect on our behavior with our grandparents versus that with our closest friends. It is common experience that our tone of voice, the use of slang or swear words, and the content of conversations are quite different in the two contexts.

The choice of behaviors in context requires detailed sensory information, which is conveyed to the inferior frontal cortex from the temporal lobe. Context also means affective context, and this contribution comes from the amygdala. People with orbital frontal lesions, which are common in closed-head injuries (damage that results from a blow to the head), have difficulty with context, especially in social situations, and are notorious for making social gaffes. Closed-head injuries are considered in detail in Chapter 26.

Autonoetic Awareness

Not only is our behavior under the control of ongoing sensory input, temporal memory, and context, but it is also affected by a lifetime of experiences and goals. Tulving called this autobiographical knowledge **autonoetic awareness** (that is, self-knowing). Tulving's idea is that autonoetic awareness makes it possible to bind together the awareness of oneself as a continuous entity through time.

Impairment in autonoetic awareness results in a deficit in the self-regulation of behavior. Thus, our behavior is under the influence of our personal past experiences and life goals for the future such that we interpret the world in our daily life within our own frames of reference. Patients with orbital frontal injury often lose this self-knowledge and have real difficulty in daily living. Levine and colleagues described M. L., a salesman whose orbital frontal injury resulted from a closed-head injury. M. L. noted that maintaining a close relation with his wife of 10 years was very difficult. "I have a hard time relating to my wife. I don't know why I married this person. . . . I told myself I must have been happy, and they said I was." This type of symptom surely would be very disruptive to daily living, but it is not easy to capture with a neuropsychological test, in part because the symptoms are so individual.

Asymmetry of Frontal-Lobe Function

In keeping with the general complementary organization of the left and right hemispheres, as a rule the left frontal lobe has a preferential role in language-related movements, including speech, whereas the right frontal lobe plays a greater role in nonverbal movements such as facial expression. Like the asymmetry of the parietal and temporal lobes, the asymmetry of frontal-lobe function is relative rather than absolute; the results of studies of patients with frontal lesions indicate that both frontal lobes play a role in nearly all behavior. Thus, the laterality of function disturbed by frontal-

Table 16.1 Relative frequency of defective performance on neuropsychological tests

| Test | PERCENTAGE OF GROUP SHOWING A DEFICIT | | |
	Left hemisphere (%)	Right hemisphere (%)	Bilateral (%)
Verbal fluency	70	38	71
Verbal learning	30	13	86
Block construction	10	50	43
Design copying	10	38	43
Time orientation	0	0	57
Proverbs	20	25	71

Source: After Benton, 1968.

lobe lesions is far less striking than that observed from lesions in the more-posterior lobes.

Nonetheless, as with the temporal lobe, there is reason to believe that some effects of bifrontal lesions cannot be duplicated by lesions of either hemisphere alone. Table 16.1 summarizes a study comparing the behavioral effects of unilateral and bilateral frontal lesions. People with bifrontal lesions are severely impaired in reporting the time of day and in decoding proverbs, effects seldom seen subsequent to unilateral frontal lesions.

Recently, Tulving and his colleagues proposed that the left and right frontal lobes may play different roles in memory processing: the left prefrontal cortex is proposed to be have a greater role in encoding information into memory, whereas the right prefrontal cortex is more engaged than the left in retrieval. This hypothesis remains controversial, in part because it is difficult to fit such a finding with our notions of what cerebral asymmetry represents. We shall return to the Tulving proposal in Chapter 18 (for a review, see Lepage et al., 2000, and Tulving, 2002).

Heterogeneity of Frontal-Lobe Function

Shallice and Burgess noted that correlations among performance on tasks sensitive to frontal-lobe injury are relatively low. Among the many explanations offered for low interest correlations, one is that the tests require different cognitive operations for their successful solution. These different functions require different bits of the frontal lobe, and, given that the exact site of injury will vary among patients, the different tests are impaired to different degrees.

Thus, as we consider the different symptoms of frontal-lobe injury, we must remember that any individual patient is unlikely to show all the symptoms, and the severity of symptoms will vary with lesion location. Few imaging studies have addressed the matter of heterogeneity and, as we shall see, the trend has been for evidence favoring homogeneity of function. The Snapshot on page 401 shows, however, that, at least in the orbital frontal cortex, there is evidence of discrete localization of functions.

Symptoms of Frontal-Lobe Lesions

Of primary concern here are the effects of unilateral lesions to the frontal cortex. In an effort to organize the symptoms conceptually, we have grouped them into eight major categories (Table 16.2). We do not mean to imply that the brain respects these categories but rather that the categories provide a conceptual framework within which to consider the symptoms.

Disturbances of Motor Function

Frontal lesions can impair a person's ability to make a wide variety of movements, to order movement sequences, and even to speak.

Fine Movements, Speed, and Strength

Damage to the primary motor cortex is typically associated with a chronic loss of the ability to make fine, independent finger movements, presumably owing to a loss of direct corticospinal projections onto motor neurons. In addition, there is a loss of speed and strength in both hand and limb movements in the contralateral limbs. The loss of strength is not merely a symptom of damage to area 4, because lesions restricted to the prefrontal cortex also lead to a reduction in hand strength.

Movement Programming

In a classic paper in 1950, Karl Lashley asked how movements are put together in a particular order. How is it, he asked, that a violinist can play an arpeggio so quickly and flawlessly? Clearly, each note is not "thought of" separately. And how is it that, in a tennis game, a player can make very rapid movements, seemingly much too fast to have considered each movement by itself?

Lashley presumed that this function—serially ordering complex chains of behavior in relation to varying stimuli—must somehow be a function of the neocortex. Although he believed it to be a function of the entire neocortex, it appears more likely to be a function of the frontal lobes. Removal of the supplementary motor cortex results in a transient disruption of nearly all voluntary movements (including speech, if the removal is on the left). There is rapid recovery, however, and the only permanent disability appears to be in the performance of rapidly alternating movements with the hands or fingers.

The likely reason that relatively minor symptoms result from rather large supplementary motor lesions is that both the left and the right premotor cortexes participate in the control of movement. This idea is supported by observations that both left and right premotor areas show an increase in blood flow during unimanual tasks in humans; in monkeys, cells in both the left and the right areas show increased activity regardless of which hand is moving. There is also a bilateral projection from each supplementary motor cortex to the basal ganglia.

Further evidence favoring a role for the frontal cortex in movement programming comes from the results of a study by Kolb and Milner, in which patients with localized unilateral frontal lobectomies (most of which did not include the premotor cortex) were asked to copy a series of arm or facial movements (see Figure 14.8). Although the patients showed mild impairment in copying the arm

S N A P S H O T

Heterogeneity of Function in the Orbital Frontal Cortex

The orbital frontal cortex is a large region of the frontal lobe that includes at least five subregions—namely, Brodmann's areas 10 through 14. Different regions have different patterns of connectivity. Area 13, for example, has extensive connections with the amygdala and hypothalamus, whereas area 11 has connections with medial temporal cortical areas taking part in recognition memory.

The orbital frontal cortex is a challenge to study functionally in the laboratory because its location makes discrete lesions difficult to produce. Furthermore, although the orbital frontal cortex is often affected in closed-head injuries, these injuries are not focal but tend to be diffuse across the orbital region.

Frey and Petrides examined functional heterogeneity in the orbital region in two parallel PET studies. In one study, subjects heard either the sounds of violent car crashes, which they suspected would be perceived as unpleasant, or familiar abstract sounds generated from an electronic keyboard. In the other study, the subjects were presented with novel abstract visual designs that they had to either commit to memory or just view. Abstract designs were used to prevent subjects from verbalizing the images and thus provoking semantic associations.

As shown in the adjoining figure, area 13 showed increased activation in response to the unpleasant auditory stimuli, whereas area 11 showed increased activation when subjects had to learn new visual information. These results show a clear functional dissociation of the two orbital regions: area 13 (richly connected to the amygdala and hypothalamus) processes unpleasant auditory information; area

Area 11 showed increased activation when subjects had to learn new visual information...

...whereas area 13 showed increased activation in response to unpleasant auditory stimuli.

Activation of the orbital frontal cortex by sensory stimulation. (After Frey and Petrides, 2000, and Frey, Kostopoulous, and Petrides, 2000.)

11 (medial temporal cortical connections) processes the encoding of new visual information.

Area 13 can be seen as a region that can alert an organism to attend to stimuli that have affective qualities. We might predict that people with damage to area 13 would be less responsive to threatening stimuli, and they are. It would be interesting to determine whether both areas would be implicated if unpleasant stimuli were to be encoded.

(After S. Frey and M. Petrides. Orbitofrontal cortex: A key prefrontal region for encoding information. *Proceedings of the National Academy of Sciences of the United States of America* 97:8723–8727, 2000; S. Frey, P. Kostopoulous, and M. Petrides. Orbitofrontal involvement in the processing of unpleasant auditory information. *European Journal of Neuroscience* 12:3709–3712, 2000.)

movements, it was small compared with the performance of patients with left-parietal-lobe lesions. In contrast, patients with both left- and right-frontal-lobe damage were very poor at copying a series of facial movements.

An analysis of the facial-movement task showed that the groups with frontal-lobe lesions made more errors of sequence than did normal controls or other groups of patients. In other words, patients with frontal-lobe lesions had

Table 16.2 Summary of major symptoms of frontal-lobe damage

Most probable symptom	Lesion site	Basic reference
Disturbances of Motor Function		
Loss of fine movements	Area 4	Kuypers, 1981
Loss of strength	Areas 4 and 6; dorsolateral	Leonard et al., 1988
Poor movement programming	Premotor	Roland et al., 1980
	Dorsolateral	Kolb and Milner, 1981
Poor voluntary eye gaze	Frontal eye fields	Guitton et al., 1982
Poor corollary discharge	Dorsolateral, premotor	Teuber, 1964
Broca's aphasia	Area 44	Brown, 1972
Loss of Divergent Thinking		
Reduced spontaneity	Orbital	Jones-Gotman and Milner, 1977
Poor strategy formation	Dorsolateral?	Shallice, 1988
Poor frequency estimate	Dorsolateral	Smith and Milner, 1984
Environmental Control of Behavior		
Poor response inhibition	Prefrontal	Milner, 1964
Impaired associative learning	Dorsolateral	Petrides, 1997
Risk taking and rule breaking	Prefrontal	Miller, 1985
Gambling	Orbital	Bechara et al., 2000
Self-regulatory disorder	Orbital	Levine et al., 1998
Poor Temporal Memory		
Poor working memory	Dorsolateral	Petrides, 2000
Poor delayed response	Dorsolateral	Freedman and Oscar-Berman, 1986a
Other Symptoms		
Impaired social behavior	Orbital; dorsolateral	Blumer and Benson, 1975
Altered sexual behavior	Orbital	Walker and Blumer, 1975
Impaired olfactory discrimination	Orbital	Jones-Gotman and Zatorre, 1993
Disorders associated with damage to the facial area	Face	Taylor, 1979

difficulty ordering the various components of the sequence into a chain of movements. The components were recalled correctly but in the wrong order. To be sure, these patients made other sorts of errors as well, especially errors of memory in which items were not recalled. The reproduction of movement sequences requires temporal memory, and our impression is that the largest deficits come from dorsolateral lesions.

The observation that frontal injury severely disrupts the copying of facial but not arm movements implies that the frontal lobe may play a special role in the control of the face, perhaps even including the tongue. We shall see in the next section that patients with frontal-lobe damage exhibit relatively little spontaneous facial expression—a result in accordance with the possible special role of the frontal lobe in the control of the face.

Voluntary Gaze

A number of studies using quite different procedures have been reported in which frontal-lobe lesions produce alterations in voluntary eye gaze. For example, Teuber presented patients with an array of 48 patterns on a screen. The patterns could be distinguished by shape or color or both (Figure 16.5). At a warning signal, a duplicate of one of the 48 patterns appeared in the center of the array, and the subject's task was to identify the matching pattern by pointing to it. Patients with frontal-lobe lesions were impaired at finding the duplicate pattern.

Luria recorded patients' eye movements as they examined a picture of a complex scene. The eye-movement patterns of the patients with large frontal-lobe lesions were quite different from those of normal control subjects or those of patients with more-posterior lesions. For example, if a normal control was asked about the age of the people in a picture, his or her eyes fixed on the heads; if asked how they are dressed, the eyes fixed on the clothing. Patients with large frontal-lobe lesions tended to glance over the picture more or less at random, and a change in the question about the picture failed to alter the direction or the pattern of eye movements. Visual search in Luria's task would require internalized knowledge to direct the eyes.

Guitton and his colleagues examined a different type of oculomotor defect in frontal-lobe patients. They studied the ability of patients to make voluntary eye movements toward or away from briefly appearing targets presented at random to the right or the left of a fixation point. Normally, if a stimulus cue is presented briefly in either visual field, a person will make a quick eye movement (a saccade) toward the stimulus.

Patients with frontal-lobe lesions had no difficulty doing so, and so Guitton and his coworkers added a second feature to the task. Rather than making eye movements toward a target, the patients had to move their eyes to the same place in the opposite visual field. The task therefore required inhibition of the normal saccade and a voluntary saccade toward a similar point in the opposite direction.

Patients with frontal lesions had two deficits on this variation of the task. First, although normal subjects failed to inhibit a short-latency response toward the cue in about 20% of the trials, patients with frontal lesions had much more difficulty. Second, after the initial saccade in the incorrect direction, normal subjects had no difficulty in making a large corrective saccade toward the opposite field. In contrast, patients with frontal lesions, which included the frontal eye fields, had difficulty in executing the corrective response when the response had to be generated by the damaged hemisphere. In other words, they had difficulty in moving the eyes to the field contralateral to the frontal lesion. Corrective movements could be made normally in the field on the same side as the lesion.

The difficulty that patients with frontal lesions encounter in the visual-search task and in the saccade task indicates the importance of the frontal cortex for certain aspects of oculomotor control. Only the study by Guitton and associates localized the effect in the frontal eye fields, but it is likely that the most severe deficits in performing such tasks are associated with damage to those fields.

Corollary Discharge

If you push on your eyeball, the world appears to move. If you move your eyes, the world remains stable. Why? Teuber proposed that, for a movement to take place, a neural signal must produce the movement as well as a signal that the movement is going to take place. If the eyes are moved mechanically, there is

Figure 16.5 Visual search task used by Teuber. The subject must locate a duplicate of the shape inside the central box by pointing to it. (After Teuber, 1964.)

no such signal and the world moves. However, when you move your eyes, there is a neural signal that movement will happen and the world stays still. This signal has been termed **corollary discharge** or **reafference.**

Teuber argued that voluntary movements require two sets of signals rather than one. A movement command, through the motor system, effects the movements, and a signal (corollary discharge) from the frontal lobe to the parietal and temporal association cortex presets the sensory system to anticipate the motor act. Thus, a person's sensory system can interpret changes in the external world in light of information about his or her movement. For example, when you are running, the external world remains stable even though your sense organs are in motion, because the corollary discharge from the frontal lobe to the parietotemporal cortex signals that the movements are taking place. A frontal lesion therefore can not only disturb the production of a movement but also interfere with the message to the rest of the brain that a movement is taking place. By this indirect means, perception of the world by the posterior association cortex is altered.

One source of evidence that the frontal lobe plays a role in corollary discharge comes from the results of studies of cells in the frontal eye fields. Bizzi and Schiller, among others, found that some cells in the frontal eye fields fire simultaneously with movements of the eyes. These cells cannot be causing the eyes to move, because to do so they would have to fire before the eye movements (just as to accelerate an automobile, you must first depress the gas pedal). Rather, these cells must be monitoring the ongoing movement—a process suspiciously similar to what would be expected from a region controlling corollary discharge.

Speech

Speech is an example of movement selection. Passingham suggested that words are responses generated in the context of both internal and external stimuli. If the frontal lobe has a mechanism for selecting responses, then it must select words, too. The frontal lobe contains two speech zones: Broca's area, which can be regarded as an extension of the lateral premotor area, and the supplementary speech area, which may be an extension of the supplementary motor area (see Figure 16.1D).

Viewed in this way, Broca's area has a critical role when a word must be retrieved on the basis of an object, word, letter, or meaning. That is, like the premotor area's role in other behaviors, Broca's area selects words on the basis of cues. In contrast, the supplementary speech area is required to retrieve words without external cues, which also is consistent with the general function of the supplementary motor area.

People with strokes in Broca's area are impaired in their ability to use verbs and to produce appropriate grammar, a symptom known as agrammatism. People with strokes that include the supplementary speech area and extend into the left medial frontal region are often mute. The ability to speak usually returns after a few weeks in people with unilateral lesions but not in those with bilateral lesions. This outcome again supports the bilateral participation of the supplementary motor areas in movement selection. The role of the supplementary motor region is corroborated by the results of blood-flow studies done by Roland, who showed activation of the medial premotor area when subjects recall the months of the year, which is done without external cues.

Loss of Divergent Thinking

One of the clearest differences between the effects of parietal- and temporal-lobe lesions and the effects of frontal-lobe lesions is in performance on standard intelligence tests. Posterior lesions produce reliable, and often large, decreases in IQ scores, but frontal lesions do not. The puzzle is why patients with frontal-lobe damage appear to do such "stupid" things.

Guilford noted that traditional intelligence tests appear to measure what can be called **convergent thinking,** in the sense that there is just one correct answer to each question. Thus, definitions of words, questions of fact, arithmetic problems, puzzles, and block designs all require correct answers that are easily scored. Another type of intelligence test, in which the number and variety of responses to a single question rather than a single correct answer are emphasized, can measure **divergent thinking.** An example is a question asking for a list of the possible uses of a coat hanger. Frontal-lobe injury interferes with the intelligence required by divergent thinking, rather than the convergent type measured by standard IQ tests. Several lines of evidence support Guilford's idea.

Behavioral Spontaneity

Patients with frontal-lobe lesions have long been recognized to exhibit a loss of spontaneous speech. Various investigators have been able to quantify this loss by using tests such as the Thurstone Word-Fluency Test (also referred to as the Chicago Word-Fluency Test). Patients are asked to write or to say, first, as many words starting with a given letter as they can think of in 5 minutes and, then, as many four-letter words starting with a given letter in 4 minutes.

Patients with frontal-lobe lesions have a low output of words in this test. For example, when asked to generate as many words as he could think of beginning with a specific letter, E. L., introduced at the beginning of this chapter, sat for about 2 minutes before asking if he could use the Latin names of plants. He was assured that he could do so but, after another couple of minutes, he remarked, "I can't think of any!" He abandoned the plant names but, even with an additional 5 minutes, he could think of only six words.

Although the principal locus of this defect appears to be in the left orbital frontal region, lesions in the right orbital frontal region also may produce a marked reduction in verbal fluency. Again we see less asymmetry in the frontal lobes than we might expect. The following case is an example of low spontaneous verbal fluency resulting from a lesion of the right frontal lobe.

Mrs. P., a 63-year-old woman with a college degree, was suffering from a large astrocytoma of the right frontal lobe. Her word fluency is reproduced in Figure 16.6A. Four features of frontal-lobe damage are illustrated in her test performance:

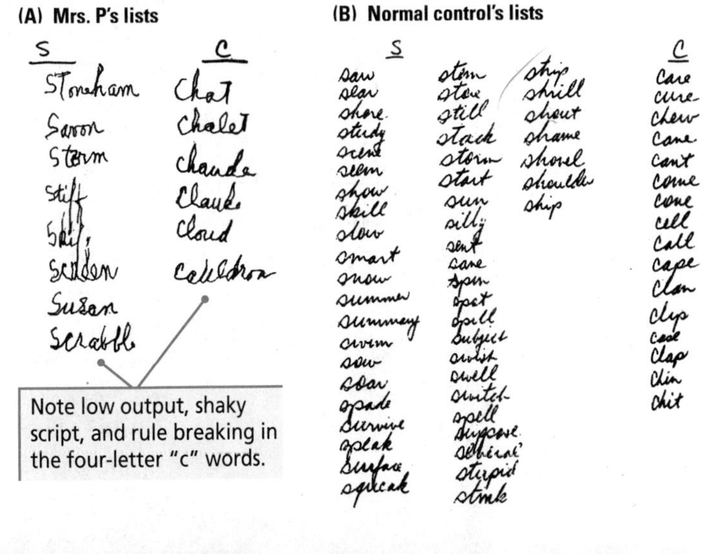

1. Her total output of words is remarkably low: only 8 words beginning with the letter "s" and 6 words beginning with the letter "c." (Control subjects of

Figure 16.6 Word fluency. Subjects were given 5 minutes to write as many English words as possible starting with the letter "s" and 4 minutes to write as many four-letter words as possible starting with the letter "c."

(A) Mrs. P's lists

Note low output, shaky script, and rule breaking in the four-letter "c" words.

(B) Normal control's lists

similar age and education produce a total of about 60 words in the same time period, as shown in Figure 16.6B.)

2. Rule breaking is a common characteristic of patients on this test. We told Mrs. P. several times that the words starting with "c" could have only four letters. She replied. "Yes, yes, I know, I keep using more each time." Even though she understood the instructions, she could not organize her behavior to follow them successfully.

3. Her writing was not fluid but rather jerky, much like that seen in a child learning to write, implying that her tumor had invaded the motor or premotor cortex.

4. Mrs. P. insisted on talking throughout the test—complaining that she simply could not think of any more words—and kept looking around the room for objects starting with the required letter.

A study by Jones-Gotman and Milner raises the question of whether this verbal-fluency deficit might have a nonverbal analogue. The researchers devised an ingenious experiment in which they asked patients to draw as many different designs as they could in 5 minutes. The drawings were not supposed to be representational of anything, but rather much like the doodles that students are prone to put in the margins of their notes or textbooks. The patients were then asked to draw as many different designs as they could, but this time using only four lines (a circle was counted as a single line).

The results show a beautiful analogue to the verbal-fluency results. As can be seen in Figure 16.7, lesions in the right frontal lobe produced a large decrease in the number of different drawings produced. Normal controls drew about 35 drawings, left-frontal-lobe patients drew about 24 drawings, and right-frontal-lobe patients drew about 15 drawings. This deficit appears to be related to an impoverished output, high perseveration, and, in some cases, the drawing of nameable things (that is, representational drawings). As with verbal fluency, lesions in the orbital cortex or central facial area in the frontal lobe appeared to produce a larger deficit than did the more-dorsal lesions.

It seems likely that frontal-lobe patients show reduced spontaneity not only in speech or doodling but in their behaviors in general. For example, Kolb and Taylor recorded the spontaneous behavior of frontal-lobe patients taking a battery of neuropsychological tests. Patients with frontal-lobe removals displayed fewer spontaneous facial movements and expressions than did normal controls or patients with more-posterior lesions. In addition, there were dramatic differences in the number of words spoken by the patients in a neuropsychological interview: patients with left frontal removals rarely spoke, whereas patients with right frontal lesions were excessively talkative.

Although the range of behaviors studied to date is small, there is reason to believe that frontal-lobe patients have a general loss of spontaneous behavior. Frontal-lobe patients characteristically appear lethargic or lazy: they often have difficulty getting out of bed in the morning, getting dressed, or initiat-

Figure 16.7 Design fluency. In an analog to the word-fluency test, subjects were allowed 5 minutes to draw as many nonrepresentational doodles as they could.

(A) Normal subject

(B) Frontal lobe patient showing perseveration

(C) Frontal lobe patient showing lack of spontaneity

ing other daily activities such as going to work. One patient is a particularly dramatic example. He was a prominent lawyer who suffered a midline meningioma in the frontal lobe. The tumor was removed surgically, but he was left with bilateral damage to the superior aspect of both frontal lobes.

His IQ score was still superior (higher than 140), and his memory for legal matters was unimpaired. Nonetheless he was unable to function in his profession, because he could not get up in the morning to go to work, preferring to stay in bed and watch television. When his wife forced him to get up and go to work, he was disruptive at the office because he could not concentrate on any law-related work. Rather, he was distracted by anything else going on in the office. Curiously, he remained an excellent resource for his colleagues, who nonetheless found his behavior intolerable and consequently preferred to consult him by telephone.

Strategy Formation

Patients with frontal-lobe lesions are especially impaired at developing novel cognitive plans or strategies for solving problems. For example, when Shallice and Evans asked subjects questions that required reasoning based on general knowledge for which no immediate obvious strategy was available, they found that frontal-lobe patients did very poorly and often gave bizarre responses. In a later study, Shallice and Burgess gave patients a task very much like our dinner-party problem. The subjects were given a list of six errands (for example, "Buy a loaf of brown bread") and an instruction to be at a particular place 15 minutes after starting. They were also to get answers to four questions (for instance, the price of a pound of tomatoes). They were not to enter shops except to buy something and were to complete the tasks as quickly as possible, without rushing.

The frontal-lobe patients found this simple task very difficult. They were inefficient, they broke rules (for example, entered unnecessary shops), and two of the three patients failed at least four of the tasks. Yet, when quizzed, all the patients understood the task and attempted to comply. Similar difficulty with everyday problems is seen in a study by Smith and Milner. They asked subjects to estimate the average price of a particular object, such as a sewing machine. They suggested that to perform such a task one must develop a strategy that might include deciding what a typical sewing machine is, judging the range of possible prices, and selecting a representative price for a machine of average quality. They found that patients with frontal-lobe lesions—especially right frontal lesions—were very poor at this task. In contrast, patients with temporal-lobe damage who showed memory deficits on other tasks performed like controls on this task. Thus, it seems unlikely that a simple explanation of impaired memory will account for the poor performance of the frontal-lobe patients.

Shallice and Burgess argued that, although the frontal lobe may have a general role in planning behavior, it has a critical role in coping with novel situations in contrast with routine ones. They suggested that coping with a novel situation, by which they mean a novel set of external and internal states, entails the activation of a wide variety of processes to solve the problem. In contrast, the solution of a familiar task can rely on strategies that have been well practiced and therefore are more easily accessed.

The extreme case of novel situations is during development, when most situations are novel. Hebb noted in the 1940s that, relative to frontal-lobe injuries acquired in adulthood, people whose frontal-lobe injuries were acquired in childhood often show surprisingly severe deficits in behavioral control. He believed that these people were not able to properly develop the behavioral schematas necessary to solve problems. That is, they would find few situations routine.

Environmental Control of Behavior: Impaired Response Inhibition and Inflexible Behavior

Perhaps the most commonly observed trait of frontal-lobe patients is their difficulty in using information from environmental cues (feedback) to regulate or change their behavior. This difficulty manifests itself in a number of ways.

Response Inhibition

Patients with frontal-lobe lesions consistently perseverate on responses in a variety of test situations, particularly those in which there are changing demands. The best example of this phenomenon is observed in the Wisconsin Card-Sorting Test, which has become one of the standard clinical tests of frontal-lobe injury. As Figure 16.8 shows, a subject is presented with four stimulus cards, bearing designs that differ in color, form, and number of elements. The subject's task is to sort the cards into piles in front of one or another of the stimulus cards. The only help given the subject is to be told whether the choice is correct or incorrect.

The test works on the following principle: the correct solution is, first, color; when the subject has figured out this solution, the correct solution then becomes, without warning, form. Thus, the subject must now inhibit classifying the cards on the basis of color and shift to form. When the subject has succeeded at selecting by form, the correct solution again changes unexpectedly, this time to the number of elements. It will later become color again, and so on.

Shifting response strategies is particularly difficult for people with frontal lesions. They may continue responding to the original stimulus (color) for as many as 100 cards until testing is terminated. Throughout this period, they may comment that they know that color is no longer correct. They nevertheless continue to sort on the basis of color. For example, one person stated (correctly): "Form is probably the correct solution now so this [sorting to color] will be wrong, and this will be wrong, and wrong again."

Such perseveration is common on any task in which a frontal-lobe patient is required to shift response strategies, demonstrating that the frontal lobe is necessary for flexibility in behavior. It is important to note that, on card-sorting tasks, the subjects must not be given any hint that they are to expect a change in the correct solution, because many frontal-lobe patients improve dramatically when given this warning. The cue apparently allows enough flexibility in behavior to solve the problem.

From the results of Milner's work, the principal locus of this card-sorting effect appears to be roughly around Brodmann's area 9 in the left hemisphere. Lesions elsewhere in the left frontal lobe, and often in the right, will also produce a deficit on this task, although an attenuated one.

Figure 16.8 The Wisconsin Card-Sorting Test, showing test material as presented to the subject. The task is to place each card from the bottom pile with the appropriate card in the top row, sorting by one of three possible categories: color, number of elements, or shape. Subjects are never told the correct sorting category but only whether their responses are correct or incorrect. When the subject selects the correct category, the correct solution changes unexpectedly. (After Milner, 1964.)

Performance of the Stroop Test (Figure 16.9) further demonstrates loss of response inhibition subsequent to frontal-lobe damage. Subjects are presented with a list of color words (blue, green, red, and so forth), each word being printed in colored ink but never in the color denoted by the word (for example, the word "yellow" is printed in blue, green, or red ink). The subject's task is to name the color in which each word is printed as quickly as possible. Correct response requires the inhibition of reading the color name, an inhibition that is difficult for many control subjects. Perret found that patients with left frontal lesions were unable to inhibit reading the words and thus were impaired in this task.

Risk Taking and Rule Breaking

Frontal-lobe patients are distinguished from other patients in their common failure to comply with task instructions. Milner found this failure to comply to be especially common on tests of stylus-maze learning in which a buzzer indicates that the patient has made an error and is to stop and start at the beginning of the maze again. Subjects with frontal-lobe lesions tended to disregard the signal, thereby continuing the incorrect path and making more errors. This behavior is reminiscent of their inability to modify their responses in the card-sorting task.

Miller gave subjects a task in which words had to be guessed on the basis of partial information. With each additional clue, a subject was assigned a successively lower point value for a correct answer, but points could be collected only if the answer was correct. An incorrect answer forfeited all the points for an item. Frontal-lobe patients took more risks (and made more mistakes) than did other patients, and the risk taking was greatest in those frontal-lobe patients who also had temporal-lobe damage.

The role of the orbital frontal cortex in risk taking has been studied extensively by Antoine Bechera, Antonio Damasio and their colleagues, who designed a gambling task in which subjects gradually learn how to play a unique card game. They are presented with four decks of cards and are asked to turn over the first card in any deck. Some cards are associated with a payoff ($50 or $100), whereas other cards result in a $50 or $100 penalty being assessed. Each subject is given $2000 in play money to play the game, and the goal is to make as much money in the game as possible.

The trick in the game is that the reward and penalty contingencies of each deck differ. For example, one deck may have high payoffs but also has high penalties, whereas another may have a lower payoff but also a low penalty. The game is set so that playing two of the four decks results in a net loss, whereas playing the other two yields a net gain.

The results from the Bechera studies are clear: normal subjects and patients without frontal damage sample from all the decks for a while but quickly learn which decks have the best payoff. In contrast, patients with orbital frontal injuries do not learn this strategy and play predominantly from the bad decks, thus losing all their money. An important aspect of the task is that subjects are not allowed to keep a running tally of how they are doing; rather they must "sense" which decks are risky and which are profitable. This ability is clearly a function of the prefrontal cortex and its loss makes it difficult for orbital frontal patients to make wise decisions, especially in social or personal matters—that is, situations in which an exact calculation of future outcomes is not possible.

BLUE	WHITE
BLACK	GRAY
GRAY	WHITE
BLUE	**BLACK**

Figure 16.9 The Stroop test. The task is to give the color of the ink for each word as quickly as possible. When the ink color and the color name are the same, the task is simple. When they are different, there is a tendency to read the word rather than give the ink color.

Self-regulation

We noted earlier that people with ventral frontal injuries, such as M. L., have deficits in the self-regulation of behavior in unstructured situations, in part because of a loss of autonoetic awareness. M. L. had been a salesman, and he knew what his job had been and that he had traveled a great deal. When pressed, however, he was unable to provide a single personal example of this job. For example, when asked if he traveled to conferences, he said that, yes, he traveled to conferences often; it was a major part of his job. Yet he could not name a single instance of an experience at a conference. His autobiographical knowledge was lost.

You can imagine what this impairment would be like if you think about your high-school experience. We are all aware of having gone to high school and can describe what high school was like, and presumably so could patients such as M. L. The difference, however, is that we can describe personal events that happened in high school, whereas M. L. would not be able to do so. We can immediately see why M. L. had difficulty in relating to his wife—he simply could not recall instances that would explain why they were married.

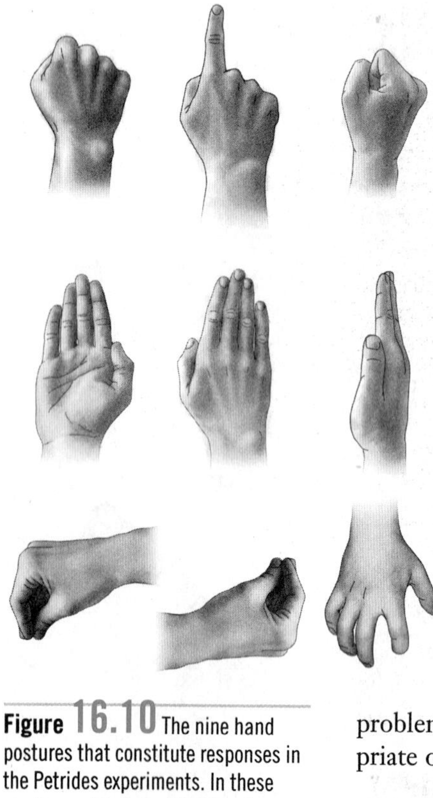

Associative Learning

Patients with large frontal-lobe lesions have often been claimed to be unable to regulate their behavior in response to external stimuli—that is, to learn from experience. Luria and Homskaya described patients with massive frontal-lobe tumors who could not be trained to respond consistently with the right hand to a red light and with the left hand to a green light, even though the patients could indicate which hand was which and could repeat the instructions.

In an extensive series of studies, Petrides examined the ability of both human patients and monkeys with frontal lesions to make arbitrary stimulus-response associations. In one study, Petrides asked frontal-lobe patients to learn arbitrary associations between colors and hand postures, as illustrated in Figure 16.10. For example, patients were presented with nine colored stimuli, and the their task was to learn which posture was associated with which colored stimulus. Damage to either the left or the right hemisphere resulted in poor performance on this task. Again, the behavioral impairments in the frontal-lobe patients could not be attributed to a deficit in memory, because temporal-lobe patients who performed poorly on other tests of memory performed normally at these tasks. Rather, the problem is in learning to select, from a set of competing responses, the appropriate ones for the various stimuli.

Figure 16.10 The nine hand postures that constitute responses in the Petrides experiments. In these studies, subjects had to learn to associate each hand posture with one of nine different colors and to perform the movement in response to the presentation of the appropriate color.

Poor Temporal Memory

Perhaps the single most important experimental discovery for understanding the functions of the frontal lobe was Carlyle Jacobsen's finding that chimpanzees with frontal-lobe lesions were impaired in the delayed-response test. In this task, an animal observes a reward being placed under a plaque, in a well. The chimp's view is blocked for a few seconds, and then it is allowed to retrieve the reward. Animals with prefrontal lesions perform at chance, even with extended practice. Although the behavioral impairment is unlikely to be due to a single deficit, the deficit is difficult to interpret without recourse to some sort of memory difficulty. Four additional experiments are especially germane here.

In the first experiment, Passingham presented monkeys with a task in which the animals were required to open each of 25 doors to obtain a food reward. Food was placed behind each door only once per day; so the animals had to learn not to return to locations where the reward had been obtained already. Passingham found that lesions in area 46 produced marked impairments in this task. Thus, whereas the normal monkeys developed a door-opening strategy that led to few repetitions, the lesioned animals were inefficient, often returning to previously accessed doors (Figure 16.11A).

In the second experiment, Funahashi, Bruce, and Goldman-Rakic trained monkeys to fixate on a central spot of light while target lights were flashed in different parts of the visual field. The monkeys had to wait for the fixation spot to disappear before moving their eyes to the spot where the target light had been flashed. The researchers found that unilateral lesions in the principal sulcus (part of area 46) impaired the monkeys' ability to remember the location of the target in a restricted region of the contralateral visual field, as illustrated in Figure 6.11B. They interpret this result as showing that the principal sulcus contains a mechanism for guiding responses on the basis of stored information, which in this case is spatial.

The third experiment was conducted by Mishkin and Manning. They trained monkeys in a task known as delayed nonmatching to sample. In this test, a monkey is confronted with an unfamiliar object, which it displaces to

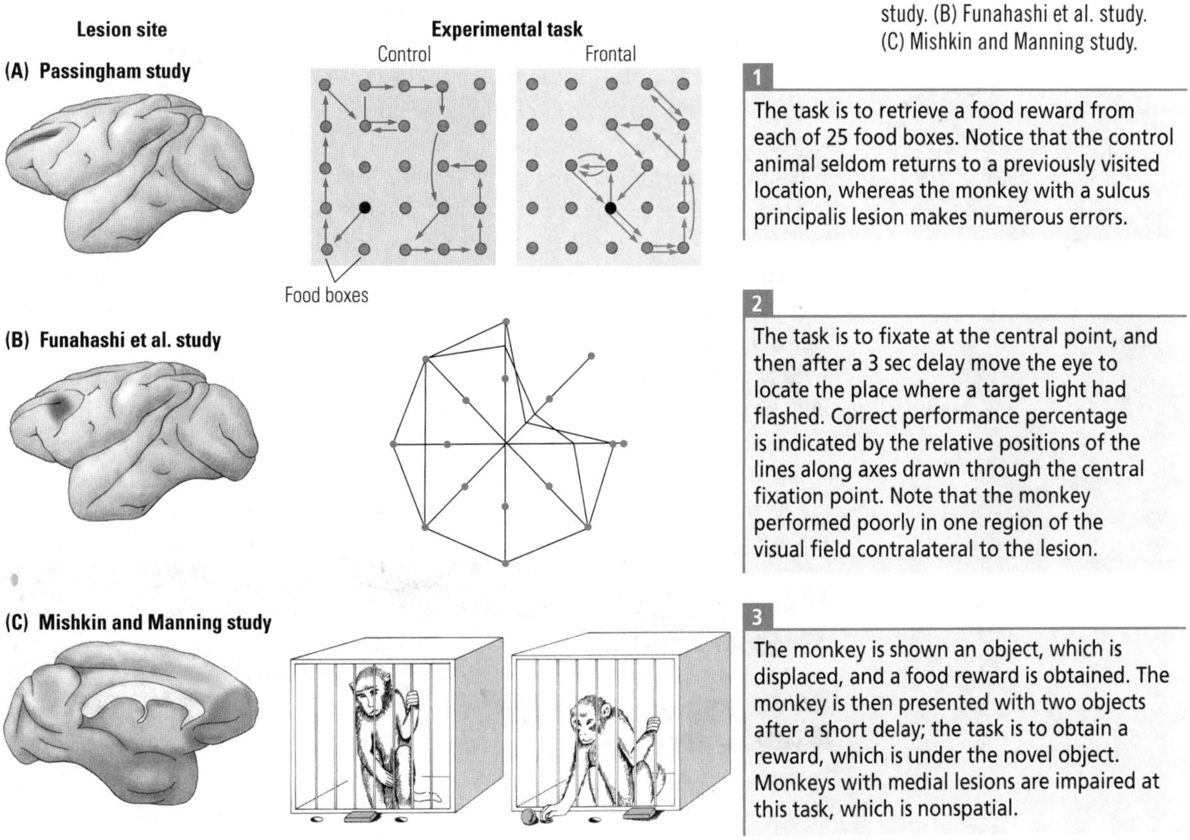

Figure 16.11 Testing for temporal memory. Schematic illustrations of frontal lesions in monkeys are shown at the left. The shaded areas represent lesion sites in three experiments, illustrated on the right, that reveal a temporal memory deficit. (A) Passingham study. (B) Funahashi et al. study. (C) Mishkin and Manning study.

Lesion site

(A) Passingham study

Experimental task

Control   Frontal

Food boxes

(B) Funahashi et al. study

(C) Mishkin and Manning study

1 — The task is to retrieve a food reward from each of 25 food boxes. Notice that the control animal seldom returns to a previously visited location, whereas the monkey with a sulcus principalis lesion makes numerous errors.

2 — The task is to fixate at the central point, and then after a 3 sec delay move the eye to locate the place where a target light had flashed. Correct performance percentage is indicated by the relative positions of the lines along axes drawn through the central fixation point. Note that the monkey performed poorly in one region of the visual field contralateral to the lesion.

3 — The monkey is shown an object, which is displaced, and a food reward is obtained. The monkey is then presented with two objects after a short delay; the task is to obtain a reward, which is under the novel object. Monkeys with medial lesions are impaired at this task, which is nonspatial.

find a reward. After a delay the animal sees the same object paired with a new one. The monkey must recognize the object that it saw earlier and move the new one instead to get a reward (Figure 6.11C). Monkeys with lesions of areas 10 and 32 are impaired in this task. Mishkin and Manning interpret this result as showing that this area of the frontal cortex participates in the short-term storage of object information.

The fourth experiment was a 1991 study by Petrides in which monkeys were given two different tasks. In the first task, the animals were presented with three objects and allowed to choose one for reward. The animals were then given an option between the chosen object and one of the other objects, with the correct choice being the one that was not previously selected. In the second task, the animals were again presented with three objects and allowed one choice. On this task, however, they were then presented with the previously selected object and a novel object.

In the first task, a monkey must recall what it did with the objects. In the second task, the monkey must recall only which object was seen before. Monkeys with dorsolateral lesions performed at chance on the first task but performed as well as controls on the second. This result suggests that the dorsolateral cortex plays a role in monitoring self-generated responses.

Taken together, these five experiments point to an unequivocal role for the frontal cortex in short-term memory process and to the fact that different regions of the prefrontal cortex control the storage of different types of information. In view of the anatomical connections, it seems likely that area 46 plays a role in providing an internal representation of spatial information and that the medial regions play a similar role with object information.

The results of electrophysiological studies lend further support for the role of area 46: cells in this area are active during the intervals in delayed-response tests and their activity ends abruptly when the animal responds. Some neurons respond selectively to the spatial position of the cues, and we might expect to find similar neurons coding some features of objects as well.

Studies of temporal memory have taken a slightly different slant with human subjects. On the basis of earlier works by others, Milner, Corsi, and Leonard designed an ingenious test of memory for the order in which things have happened, which is often called recency memory. Subjects were shown a long series of cards, each card bearing two stimulus items, which were either words or pictures. On some cards a question mark appeared between the items, and the subjects' task was to indicate which of the two items had been seen more recently. Successful performance required the subjects to recall the order of presentation of the stimuli.

On most test trials, both the items had appeared previously, but, on some, one item was new. In this case, the task became one of simple recognition memory. Patients with frontal-lobe lesions performed normally on the recognition trials, but they were impaired in judging the relative recency of two previously seen items. Further, there is relative asymmetry in the frontal lobes in this regard: the right frontal lobe appears to be more important for memory for nonverbal or pictorial recency; the left frontal lobe appears to be more important for verbal recency. In contrast, patients with temporal-lobe lesions were impaired in the recognition test but not in the recency test. (This latter finding is curious, because it seems to be analogous to blindsight in that people who fail to recognize items can identify which was observed most recently.

Might this suggest a memory location system that is separate from a memory recognition system?)

Petrides and Milner designed an experiment that is conceptually similar to Passingham's self-ordering task for monkeys. Subjects were presented with stacks of cards on which were displayed an array of 12 stimuli, including words or drawings in parallel versions of the task. The stimuli in the array remained constant, but the position of each stimulus varied randomly from card to card. The subjects' task appeared rather simple: go through the stack and point to only one item on each card, taking care not to point to the same item twice. Thus, the subjects themselves initiated the plan to follow and determined the order of responding. Although the task appears easy to us, frontal-lobe patients did not find it so: left-frontal-lobe lesions were associated with impaired performance of both verbal and nonverbal versions of the task, whereas right-frontal-lobe lesions were associated with poor performance only on the nonverbal test.

Petrides and Milner suggested that, in contrast with the recency tests, the self-ordered tasks require subjects to organize and carry out a sequence of responses. From the moment the subjects begin to respond, they must constantly compare the responses that they have made with those that still remain to be carried out. Hence, the self-ordered task demands an accurate memory as well as an organized strategy.

When questioned about their approach to the task at the end of testing, patients with frontal lesions were less likely than other subjects to report that they had used a particular strategy, and, when they had, the strategy often appeared to be ill defined and to have been used inconsistently. The deficit is unlikely to have been one of simple memory, because temporal-lobe patients, who would have been expected to have defects of memory, performed normally at this task.

The temporal memory deficits in both laboratory animals and in human patients have caught the imagination of researchers for more than 60 years. Recently, both imaging studies and single-unit studies in monkeys have confirmed what the lesion studies had suggested—namely, that the prefrontal cortex plays a critical role in temporal memory. A study by Fuster and colleagues serves as a nice illustration. In this experiment, monkeys were trained to associate two different tones each with one of two different colors, as illustrated in Figure 16.12. The trick was that a monkey heard the tone and then had to remember which tone it had heard for 10 seconds before making a response to obtain reward. A large contingent of cells in dorsolateral prefrontal area (areas 8, 9, and 46) responded selectively to one tone or the other and, later, to its associated color. These cells appear to integrate sound and color across time. Curiously, in trials on which the animals made errors, the cells failed to respond, indicating no temporal correlation of the sound and color.

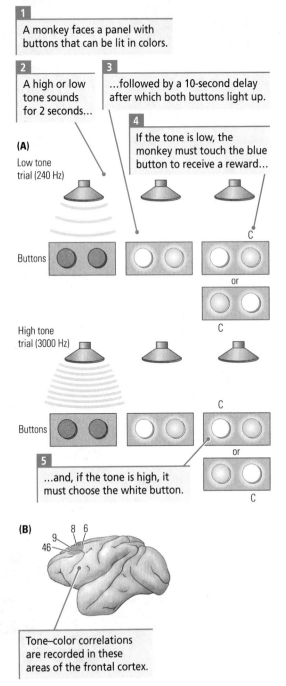

Figure 16.12 Prefrontal cells that code sensory associations.

1 A monkey faces a panel with buttons that can be lit in colors.

2 A high or low tone sounds for 2 seconds...

3 ...followed by a 10-second delay after which both buttons light up.

4 If the tone is low, the monkey must touch the blue button to receive a reward...

(A)
Low tone trial (240 Hz)

Buttons

High tone trial (3000 Hz)

Buttons

5 ...and, if the tone is high, it must choose the white button.

(B)

Tone–color correlations are recorded in these areas of the frontal cortex.

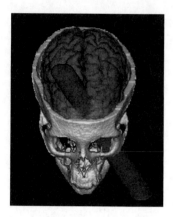

Figure 16.13 When Phineas Gage died in 1861, no autopsy was performed, but his skull was later recovered. Measurements from Gage's skull were combined with imaging techniques to reconstruct the accident and determine the probable location of the lesioning. The image makes it obvious that the frontal cortex of both hemispheres was damaged. (Department of Neurology and Image Analysis Facility, University of Iowa.)

Impaired Social and Sexual Behavior

Social and sexual behaviors require flexible responses that are highly dependent on contextual cues. It is hardly surprising, therefore, that frontal-lobe lesions interfere with both. Perhaps the most obvious and striking effect of frontal-lobe damage in humans is a marked change in social behavior and personality. The most publicized example of personality change subsequent to frontal-lobe lesions is that of Phineas Gage, first reported by John Harlow in 1868. Gage was a dynamite worker who survived an explosion that blasted an iron tamping bar (about a meter long and 3 centimeters wide at its widest point) through the front of his head (Figure 16.13). After the accident, his behavior changed completely. Gage had been of average intelligence and was "energetic and persistent in executing all of his plans of operation." His personality after the injury was described by Harlow as follows:

> The equilibrium or balance, so to speak, between his intellectual faculties and animal propensities seems to have been destroyed. He is fitful, irreverent, indulging at times in the grossest profanity, manifesting but little deference to his fellows, impatient of restraint or advice when it conflicts with his desires, at times pertinaciously obstinate, yet capricious and vacillating, devising many plans of operation, which are no sooner arranged than they are abandoned in turn for others appearing more feasible. A child in his intellectual capacity and manifestations, he has the animal passions of a strong man. (Blumer and Benson, 1975, p. 153)

Gage's injury affected primarily the left frontal lobe from the medial orbital region upward to the precentral region. Although Gage's skull has been examined carefully, the first person with extensive frontal damage to undergo close scrutiny at autopsy was a furrier who fell 30 meters from a window. He suffered a compound fracture of the frontal bones and severe injury to the right frontal lobe but, remarkably, was never unconscious and was confused only briefly. Before the fall, the man had been good natured and sociable, but, afterward, he became nasty and cantankerous. Autopsy, about a year after the accident, revealed deep scarring of the orbital part of both frontal lobes, although it was more extensive on the right.

From 1900 until about 1950, there were many excellent psychiatric studies of the effect of brain lesions on personality. A consistent finding of this work (especially Kleist's, cited in Zangwill) was that damage to the orbital regions of the frontal lobe is associated with more-dramatic changes in personality than are dorsolateral lesions, although the latter also have significant effects. Clinical descriptions of the effects of frontal-lobe lesions on personality abound, but there are few systematic studies.

At least two types of personality change have been clinically observed in such patients: Blumer and Benson have termed them **pseudodepression** and **pseudopsychopathy.** Patients classified as being pseudodepressed exhibit such symptoms as outward apathy and indifference, loss of initiative, reduced sexual interest, little overt emotion, and little or no verbal output. Patients classified as pseudopsychopathic exhibit immature behavior, lack of tact and restraint, coarse language, promiscuous sexual behavior, increased motor activity, and a general lack of social graces. Two case histories illustrate these personalities.

Pseudodepression

At the age of 46, a successful salesman sustained a compound depressed fracture of the left frontal bone in a traffic accident. Treatment included debridement [surgical removal] and amputation of the left frontal pole. Recovery was slow, and 9 months after the injury he was referred for long-term custodial management. By this time, he had recovered motor function with only a minimal limp and slight hyperreflexia on the right side, had normal sensation, no evidence of aphasia, and normal memory and cognitive ability (IQ 118). Nonetheless, he remained under hospital care because of marked changes in personal habits.

Prior to the accident, the patient had been garrulous, enjoyed people, had many friends and talked freely. He was active in community affairs, including Little League, church activities, men's clubs, and so forth. It was stated by one acquaintance that the patient had a true charisma, "whenever he entered a room there was a change in the atmosphere, everything became more animated, happy and friendly."

Following the head injury, he was quiet and remote. He would speak when spoken to and made sensible replies but would then lapse into silence. He made no friends on the ward, spent most of his time sitting alone smoking. He was frequently incontinent of urine, occasionally of stool. He remained unconcerned about either and was frequently found soaking wet, calmly sitting and smoking. If asked, he would matter-of-factly state that he had not been able to get to the bathroom in time but that this didn't bother him. Because of objectionable eating habits he always ate alone on the ward. His sleep pattern was reversed; he stayed up much of the night and slept during the day. He did not resent being awakened or questioned. He could discuss many subjects intelligently, but was never known to initiate either a conversation or a request. He could give detailed accounts of his life prior to the accident, of the hospitals he had been in, the doctors and treatment he had had, but there was an unreality to his conversation. When asked, he would deny illness, state emphatically that he could return to work at any time, and that the only reason he was not working was that he was being held in the hospital by the doctors. At no time did he request a discharge or weekend pass. He was totally unconcerned about his wife and children. Formerly a warm and loving father, he did not seem to care about his family. Eventually, the family ceased visiting because of his indifference and unconcern. (Blumer and Benson, 1975, pp. 156–157)

Pseudopsychopathy

A 32-year-old white male was admitted for behavioral evaluation. History revealed that he had sustained a gunshot wound in Vietnam 5 years previously. A high-velocity missile had entered the left temple and emerged through the right orbit. Infection necessitated surgical removal of most of the orbital surface of the right frontal lobe. On recovery, he was neither paralyzed nor aphasic but suffered a remarkable change in personality.

Prior to injury he had been quiet, intelligent, proper, and compulsive. He was a West Point graduate and spent the ensuing years as a military officer attaining the rank of captain. Both as a cadet and later as an officer, he was known to be quiet, strict, and rigid. He was considered a good commander, trusted by his men, but never shared camaraderie with his troops or with his peers.

Subsequent to injury, he was outspoken, facetious, brash, and disrespectful. There was no evidence of self-pity, although he frequently made rather morbid jokes about his condition (for example, "dummy's head"). On admission to the hospital, he had just failed at an extremely simple job.

He was not aphasic but misused words in a manner that suggested inability to maintain specific meanings. For instance, when asked whether the injury had affected his thinking his response was, "Yeah—it's affected the way I think—it's affected my senses—the only things I can taste are sugar and salt—I can't detect a pungent odor—ha ha—to tell you the truth it's a blessing this way." When the examiner persisted, "How had it affected the way you think?" his response was "Yes—I'm not as spry on my feet as I was before." He was never incontinent, but did show a messiness in attire. His remarks to the nurses and other female personnel were open and frank but were never blatantly sexual. His premorbid IQ was reported at about 130. Present examination showed a full-scale IQ of 113. (Blumer and Benson, 1974, pp. 155–156)

Blumer and Benson are probably correct in their assertion that all elements of these syndromes are observable only after bilateral frontal-lobe damage. Nevertheless, some elements of these two rather different syndromes can be observed in most, if not all, persons with unilateral frontal-lobe lesions. Pseudodepression appears most likely to follow lesions of the left frontal lobe, pseudopsychopathic behavior to follow lesions of the right frontal lobe.

Changes in sexual behavior are among the most difficult symptoms of frontal-lobe damage to document properly, largely because of social taboos against investigating people's sexual lives. To date, there are no such empirical studies, but there is anecdotal evidence that frontal lesions do alter libido and related behavior. Orbital frontal lesions may introduce abnormal sexual behavior (such as public masturbation) by reducing inhibitions, although the frequency of sexual behavior is not affected. On the other hand, dorsolateral lesions appear to reduce interest in sexual behavior, although patients are still capable of the necessary motor acts and can perform sexually if led through the activity "step by step."

The results of several studies show that frontal-lobe lesions in monkeys significantly alter social behavior. In one interesting study, Butter and Snyder removed the dominant (so-called alpha) male from each of several groups of monkeys. They removed the frontal lobes from half of these alpha monkeys. When the animals were later returned to their groups, they all resumed the position of dominant male, but within a couple of days all the monkeys without frontal lobes were deposed and fell to the bottom of the group hierarchy.

Analogous studies of wild monkeys have shown similar results: monkeys with frontal-lobe lesions fall to the bottom of the group hierarchy and eventually die, because they are helpless alone. Exactly how the social behavior of these animals changed is not known, but there is little doubt that the changes are as dramatic as those in the social behavior of humans. The social interactions of monkeys are complex and include a significant amount of context-dependent behavior; the behavior of a monkey will change in accord with the configuration of the proximal social group, and monkeys may lose this ability after frontal-lobe lesions. There are likely to be additional components of this behavioral change, however, that relate to the interpretation of species-typical sensory cues, whether they be odors, facial expressions, or sounds.

The deficit in the perception of facial expression by frontal-lobe patients may be related to the loss of cells that code for facial expression. Certain cells in the temporal lobe are especially responsive to facial expression (see Chapter 15), and Rolls and his colleagues showed that a population of cells in the orbital frontal cortex also codes for faces. Some of these face-selective neurons are responsive to facial expression or movement. It is thus not surprising that patients with orbital frontal lesions might have difficulty in understanding facial expression. We could speculate that there are also likely to be cells in the prefrontal cortex that are responsive to tone of voice, which would be a verbal analogue of facial expression.

Is There a Spatial Deficit?

We have indicated that a key to understanding the functions of the dorsolateral cortex is to be found in its relation to the posterior parietal cortex. The posterior parietal cortex plays a central role in visuomotor guidance of movements in space, and region PG and the superior temporal sulcus play some role in more-complex spatial behavior such as mental rotation (see Chapter 14). These parietotemporal regions provide a major input into the dorsolateral region, which implies some role of this frontal area in spatially guided behavior.

The precise role has been difficult to determine, however. It is clear that dorsolateral lesions impair short-term memory for the location of events, and this deficit presumably could interfere with the selection of behaviors with respect to places in space. Indeed, the delayed-response deficit, as well as the deficit in Passingham's and Goldman-Rakic's tasks (see Figure 16.11), have spatial components.

The role of the dorsolateral cortex in "spatial thinking" can also be seen in a blood-flow study by Roland and Frieberg. They asked subjects to imagine walking along a familiar route and taking first a left turn, then a right, and so on, alternating turns along the path. A major increase in blood flow in the dorsolateral region suggests a role for the dorsolateral cortex in the selection of spatially guided behaviors.

Taken together, results of the blood-flow and lesion studies suggest that the frontal lobe has a role in selecting between different visual locations. This role may be related to some aspect of attention, an idea that we return to in Chapter 22. Note, however, that little evidence favors the role of the prefrontal cortex in parietal-lobe functions such as topographic orientation or in the ability to mentally manipulate or organize spatial information (see Chapter 14).

Symptoms Associated with Damage to the Facial Area

Through the years, Taylor and his colleagues have accumulated some remarkable data from a small group of patients with localized surgical removals of the precentral and postcentral gyri, containing, respectively, the motor and sensory representations of the face (see Figure 16.1D). Unlike the removal of cortical areas for the hand, the removal of areas for the face is seldom associated with long-lasting somatosensory deficits on the face, even if both the sensory and the motor representations are removed completely. This finding is in keeping with the evidence that the face is represented bilaterally in the cortex.

There has been no systematic study of the facial motor abilities of patients who have undergone the removal of both precentral and postcentral gyri, but Kolb and Milner found such patients able to perform facial-movement sequences normally. Furthermore, although these patients had difficulty in making individual facial movements in the initial postoperative period, especially on the side of the face contralateral to the lesion, they appeared to have regained normal voluntary facial control a month after surgery, although closer examination might have revealed subtle defects. In addition, their faces were expressive, and they displayed normal spontaneous facial expressions at frequencies well within normal limits.

In the immediate postoperative period, patients with left-hemisphere facial-area lesions are aphasic, being impaired at both language comprehension and language production, as well as being alexic. However, these symptoms subside rapidly, probably having resulted from swelling and trauma associated with the surgical procedure. Within about 6 months to a year after surgery, only a slight residual expressive dysphasia remains. Yet these same patients are severely impaired at certain other language tests. In particular, they perform very poorly on tests of word fluency and are unable to make effective use of the phonetic elements of language.

In addition, these same patients are very poor spellers, occasionally writing words that are unrecognizable. Their low verbal fluency is complemented by a very low design fluency (see Figure 16.7). Patients with right facial-area lesions are worse at design fluency than are patients with very large anterior frontal lesions. This lack of spontaneity in verbal and design fluency is remarkable, considering the normal spontaneity of facial expressions.

In summary, unilateral removal of the cortical area representing the face results in no significant chronic loss in sensory or motor control of the face, presumably because of the face's bilateral representation in the cortex. But it does result surprisingly in chronic deficits in phonetic discrimination, spelling, verbal fluency, and design fluency. Taylor has preliminary data suggesting that these deficits may result primarily from damage to the precentral motor representation of the face, rather than from damage to the postcentral sensory representation. The origin of these deficits, however, is unexplained to date.

Clinical Neuropsychological Assessment of Frontal-Lobe Damage

Considering the number and variety of symptoms associated with frontal-lobe damage, surprisingly few standardized neuropsychological tests are useful for assessing frontal-lobe function. Furthermore, some of the symptoms of frontal-lobe injury, such as the loss of self-regulation of behavior, are not easily assessed by a neuropsychological test. Nonetheless, there are a number of very good clinical tests, which are summarized in Table 16.3. As with the parietal- and temporal-lobe tests discussed in Chapters 14 and 15, for a person to perform normally on all these tests if there were damage to either frontal lobe would be highly unusual.

The Wisconsin Card-Sorting Test (see Figure 16.8) is the best available test of dorsolateral frontal cortex function. As described earlier, a subject is told to sort the cards into piles in front of one or another of the stimulus cards bearing designs that differ in color, form, and number of elements. The correct so-

Table **16.3** Standardized clinical neuropsychological tests for frontal-lobe damage

Function	Test	Basic reference
Response inhibition	Wisconsin Card Sorting	Milner, 1964
	Stroop	Perret, 1974
Verbal fluency	Thurstone Word Fluency	Milner, 1964
		Ramier and Hecaen, 1970
Nonverbal fluency	Design Fluency	Jones-Gotman and Milner, 1977
Motor	Hand dynamometry	Taylor, 1979
	Finger tapping	Reitan and Davison, 1974
	Sequencing	Kolb and Milner, 1981
Language comprehension	Token	de Renzi and Faglioni, 1978
	Spelling	Taylor, 1979
	Phonetic discrimination	Taylor, 1979
Working memory	Self-ordering	Owen et al., 1990
		Pouchon et al., 2001
Planning	Tower of London	Owen et al., 1995

lution shifts without the subject's knowledge when he or she has figured out each solution.

Recall that the Thurstone Word-Fluency Test requires subjects to say or write as many words beginning with a given letter as possible in 5 minutes, and then as many four-letter words beginning with a given letter in 4 minutes (see Figure 16.6). Although subjects with lesions anywhere in the prefrontal cortex are apt to do poorly on this test, subjects with facial-area lesions perform the worst, and those with orbital lesions perform only slightly better. Performance is poorest when the lesion is in the left hemisphere.

The Gotman-Milner Design-Fluency Test (see Figure 16.7) also is very useful, although somewhat difficult to score. Subjects are asked to draw as many unnameable, abstract drawings as they can in 5 minutes. Frontal-lobe patients will draw very few items, draw nameable objects, or draw the same figure repeatedly. Like the verbal-fluency tests, the design-fluency task appears most sensitive to orbital injury.

Two tests, the Tower of Hanoi and the Tower of London, have proved sensitive to frontal injury, although the Tower of London appears to be a purer test of planning functions. In both tests, a person is presented with several pegs and several discs of varying size. The discs must be moved from the presented location to another configuration and location according to different rules. For example, only one disc can be moved at a time, and a large disc may never be placed on a smaller one. Damage to either the left or the right prefrontal cortex produces impairments on these tasks.

Tests of motor function include tests of strength (hand dynamometry), finger-tapping speed, and movement sequencing. Strength and finger-tapping speed are significantly reduced contralaterally to a lesion that is in the vicinity of the precentral or postcentral gyri. Motor sequencing can be assessed by using Kolb and Milner's facial-sequence test, although this test requires considerable practice to administer and scoring should be from videotaped records. Simpler tests of movement programming such as the Kimura Box Test (see Chapter 14) are not suitable, because frontal-lobe patients are unlikely to perform very poorly unless the lesion extends into the basal ganglia.

As in preceding chapters, we recommend the token test as a quick screening test for aphasia, to be followed if necessary by more-extensive aphasia testing (see Chapter 19). Although damage to Broca's area is widely believed to result in deficits only in language production and not in comprehension, this outcome is not strictly true. Left frontal lesions in the vicinity of Broca's area produce deficits in comprehension as well as in production.

Spelling is seriously impaired by facial-area lesions and can be assessed by any standardized spelling test. Phonetic differentiation, a test described by Stitt and Huntington and used for neurological patients by Taylor, is another means of assessing facial-area function. A series of nonsense words, such as "agma," is presented and a subject's task is to identify the first consonant sound. This test proves difficult even for controls, but it is performed most poorly by subjects with facial-area damage, especially damage on the left side. However, frontal-lobe lesions outside the facial area also may impair performance on this test significantly.

In the absence of language deficits, localizing frontal-lobe damage in either the left or the right hemisphere with neuropsychological tests may prove to be difficult, presumably because the functions of the two frontal lobes overlap significantly. Clinical evaluation of personality as pseudodepressed or pseudopsychopathic (as discussed earlier) may prove useful in localizing the dysfunction to the left or the right hemisphere, respectively, but caution is advised. Unfortunately, no standardized quantitative measures of these symptoms are available.

Imaging Frontal-Lobe Function

In general, the results of imaging studies have shown specific activation for prefrontal functions that were identified historically in lesion studies, as illustrated in Table 16.4. Thus, for example, the results of many studies have shown dorsolateral prefrontal participation in tasks tapping verbal and nonverbal working temporal memory. An especially intriguing finding, however, comes

Table 16.4 Examples of functional imaging studies of frontal-lobe function

Presumed function	Locus of activation	Basic reference
Self-ordering	Dorsolateral	Petrides, 2000
Conditioned learning	Dorsolateral	
Spatial working memory	Dorsolateral; Ventrolateral	Owen et al., 1996
Visuomotor skill learning	Dorsolateral	Doyon et al., 1996
Verbal memory retrieval	Dorsolateral	Buckner et al., 1995 Tulving et al., 1994
	Ventrolateral	Petrides et al., 1995
Encoding visual information	Orbital frontal	Frey and Petrides, 2000
Encoding unpleasant auditory information	Orbital frontal	Frey et al., 2000
Facial expression or recognition or both	Inferior prefrontal	Idaka et al., 2001

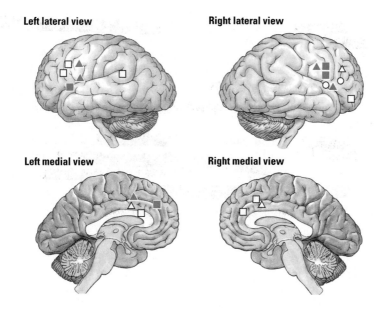

KEY

○ Auditory discrimination
● Visual divided attention
△ Self-paced response production
▲ Task switching
□ Spatial problem solving
■ Semantic processing of words

Figure 16.14 Prefrontal activations produced by widely different cognitive demands. Shown are lateral and medial views of each hemisphere. Despite the diversity of cognitive demands in these experiments, frontal activations show apparent clustering, with most points within middorsolateral, midventrolateral, and dorsal anterior cingulate regions.

from a review by Duncan and Owen. They reviewed the patterns of frontal-lobe activation associated with a broad range of different cognitive demands, including aspects of perception, response selection, executive functions, working memory, long-term memory, and problem solving.

Given such a diverse set of presumed cognitive functions, one can reasonably imagine that different regions of the frontal lobe are active during the performance of cognitive tasks that require different cognitive functions. The surprising finding, however, is that a striking regularity in activation emerged: for most cognitive demands, there was a similar recruitment of the dorsolateral, ventrolateral, and anterior cingulate regions, as summarized in Figure 16.14. The reviewers concluded that, although regional specialization exists within the frontal lobe, a frontal lobe network is consistently recruited for the solution of a diverse set of cognitive problems. How these three regions work in concert to produce behavior is not immediately obvious, but the overlap of activation in such diverse cognitive processes makes it easy to see how the frontal lobe is central to the control of such a diversity of behavior.

Diseases Affecting the Frontal Lobe

Many symptoms of frontal-lobe injury are characteristic of people with psychiatric or neurological disorders, including especially schizophrenia (see Chapter 20), Parkinson's disease (see Chapter 22), and Korsakoff's disease (see Chapter 18). In each case, a disturbance of frontal-lobe function likely contributes significantly to the behavioral symptoms of the disease.

In schizophrenia, there are believed to be an abnormality in the mesocortical dopamine projection, which terminates largely in the frontal lobe, a decrease in blood flow to the frontal lobe, and possible frontal-lobe atrophy. Schizophrenic patients perform poorly on all tests of frontal-lobe function and exhibit abnormalities in the control of eye movements, but they perform normally on tests of parietal-lobe function.

Parkinson's disease results from a loss of the dopamine cells of the substantia nigra. Although the primary projection of these cells is to the caudate nucleus, they project directly to the prefrontal cortex, too, and indirectly through the dorsomedial nucleus of the thalamus. Parkinson patients are characterized by a lack of facial expression similar to that seen in frontal-lobe patients, and they are impaired in the Wisconsin Card-Sorting Test and at delayed-response tasks.

Korsakoff patients suffer from alcohol-induced damage to the dorsomedial thalamus and may have a deficiency in catecholamines in the frontal cortex. They perform poorly on the Wisconsin Card-Sorting Test, as well as on tests of spatial memory such as delayed response.

Summary

The frontal lobe can be conceived as the end point for the visuomotor and object-recognition functions that are initiated in the occipital lobe. The frontal lobe's function in these processes is to select behaviors with respect to context and internalized knowledge.

It is possible to subdivide the frontal lobe into three distinct functional zones: motor cortex, premotor cortex, and prefrontal cortex. The motor cortex is responsible for making movements. The premotor cortex selects movements. The prefrontal cortex controls the cognitive processes so that appropriate movements are selected at the correct time and place. The premotor cortex can be divided into two regions: the lateral area responsible for selecting behaviors in response to environmental cues and the supplementary area responsible for selecting behaviors on the basis of internalized knowledge. The prefrontal cortex can be divided into two general zones: a dorsolateral zone responsible for selecting behavior with respect to temporal memory and the inferior prefrontal region responsible for selecting behavior with respect to context. Context may be current or based on previous knowledge, including self-knowledge.

The wide range of symptoms of frontal-lobe lesions can be grouped, conceptually, into several categories: (1) disturbances of motor functions; (2) loss of divergent thinking; (3) impaired response inhibition and inflexible behavior; (4) poor temporal memory; and (5) impaired social and sexual behavior imaging.

There is a complementary effect of left and right frontal lesions, in that left frontal lesions are more likely to affect language or movement-related behaviors, and right frontal lesions are more likely to alter nonlanguage functions, such as emotion.

The results of imaging studies show frontal participation in tasks with widely different cognitive demands including attentional tasks, sensory discrimination tasks, motor tasks, spatial problem solving; and semantic processing of words. Dysfunction of the frontal lobe is implicated in many behavioral disorders, including particularly schizophrenia, Parkinson's disease, and Korsakoff's disease.

References

Bechara, A., D. Tranel, and H. Damasio. Characterization of the decision-making deficit of patients with ventromedial prefrontal cortex lesions. *Brain* 123:2189–2202, 2000.

Benton, A. L. Differential effects of frontal lobe disease. *Neuropsychologia* 6:53–60, 1968.

Bizzi, E., and P. H. Schiller. Single unit activity in the frontal eye fields of unanesthetized monkeys during head and eye movement. *Experimental Brain Research* 10:151–158, 1970.

Blumer, D., and D. F. Benson. Personality changes with frontal and temporal lobe lesions. In D. F. Benson and D. Blumer, Eds. *Psychiatric Aspects of Neurologic Disease.* New York: Grune & Stratton, 1975.

Brown, J. W. *Aphasia, Apraxia, and Agnosia: Clinical and Theoretical Aspects.* Springfield, IL: Charles C. Thomas, 1972.

Buckner, R. L., M. E. Raichle, and S. E. Petersen. Dissociation of human prefrontal cortical areas across different speech production tasks and gender groups. *Journal of Neurophysiology* 74:2163–2173, 1995.

Butter, C. M., and D. R. Snyder. Alterations in aversive and aggressive behaviors following orbital frontal lesions in rhesus monkeys. *Acta Neurobiologiae Experimentalis* 32:525–565, 1972.

Deiber, M.-P., R. E. Passingham, J. G. Colebatch, K. J. Friston, P. D. Nixon, and R. S. J. Frackowiak. Cortical areas and the selection of movement: A study with positron emission tomography. *Experimental Brain Research* 84:393–402, 1991.

de Renzi, E., and P. Faglioni. Normative data and screening power of a shortened version of the token test. *Cortex* 14:41–49, 1978.

Doyon J., R. Laforce, G. Bouchard, D. Gaudreau, J. Roy, M. Poirier, P. J. Bedard, F. Bedard, and J. P. Bouchard. Role of the striatum, cerebellum and frontal lobes in the automatization of a repeated visuomotor sequence of movements. *Neuropsychologia* 36:625–641, 1998.

Doyon, J., A. M. Owen, M. Petrides, V. Sziklas, and A. C. Evans. Functional anatomy of visuomotor skill learning in human subjects examined with positron emission tomography. *European Journal of Neuroscience* 8:637–648, 1996.

Drewe, E. A. Go–no-go learning after frontal lobe lesions in humans. *Cortex* 11:8–16, 1975.

Duncan, J., and A. M. Owen. Common origins of the human frontal lobe recruited by diverse cognitive demands. *Trends in Neuroscience* 23:475–483, 2000.

Freedman, M., and M. Oscar-Berman. Bilateral frontal lobe disease and selective delayed response deficits in humans. *Behavioral Neuroscience* 100:337–342, 1986a.

Freedman, M., and M. Oscar-Berman. Comparative neuropsychology of cortical and subcortical dementia. *Canadian Journal of Neurological Science* 13(4 Suppl):410–414, 1986b.

Frey, S., and M. Petrides. Orbitofrontal cortex: A key prefrontal region for encoding information. *Proceedings of the National Academy of Sciences of the United States of America* 97:8723–8727, 2000.

Frey, S., P. Kostopoulous, and M. Petrides. Orbitofrontal involvement in the processing of unpleasant auditory information. *European Journal of Neuroscience* 12:3709–3712, 2000.

Funahashi, S., C. J. Bruce, and P. S. Goldman-Rakic. Perimetry of spatial memory representation in primate prefrontal cortex. *Society for Neuroscience Abstracts* 12:554, 1986.

Fuster, J. M. The prefrontal cortex—an update: Time is of the essence. *Neuron* 30:319–333, 2001.

Fuster, J. M., M. Bodner, and J. K. Kroger. Cross-modal and cross-temporal association in neurons of frontal cortex. *Nature* 405:347–351, 2000.

Goel, V., and J. Grafman. Are the frontal lobes implicated in "planning" functions? Interpreting data from the Tower of Hanoi. *Neuropsychologia* 5:623–642, 1995.

Goldman-Rakic, P. S. Circuitry of the primate prefrontal cortex and regulation of behavior by representational memory. In F. Plum, Ed. *Handbook of Physiology; The Nervous System*, vol. 5, *Higher Functions of the Brain*, Part 1. Bethesda, MD: American Physiological Society, 1987.

Guilford, J. P. *The Nature of Human Intelligence.* New York: McGraw-Hill, 1967.

Guitton, D., H. A. Buchtel, and R. M. Douglas. Disturbances of voluntary saccadic eye-movement mechanisms following discrete unilateral frontal-lobe removals. In G. Lennerstrand, D. S. Lee, and E. L. Keller, Eds. *Functional Basis of Ocular Motility Disorders.* Oxford: Pergamon, 1982.

Iidaka, T., M. Omori, T. Murata, H. Kosaka, Y. Yonekura, T. Okada, and N. Sadato. Neural interaction of the amygdala with the prefrontal and temporal cortices in the processing of facial expressions as revealed by fMRI. *Journal of Cognitive Neuroscience* 15:1035–1047, 2001.

Jacobsen, C. F. Studies of cerebral function in primates. *Comparative Psychology Monographs* 13:1–68, 1936.

Jenkins, I. H., R. E. Passingham, P. D. Nixon, R. S. J. Frackowiak, and D. J. Brooks. The learning of motor sequences: A PET study. *European Journal of Neuroscience* (Suppl. 5):3215, 1992.

Jones-Gotman, M., and B. Milner. Design fluency: The invention of nonsense drawings after focal cortical lesions. *Neuropsychologia* 15:653–674, 1977.

Jones-Gotman, M., and R. J. Zatorre. Odor recognition memory in humans: Role of right temporal and orbitofrontal regions. *Brain and Cognition* 22:182–198, 1993.

Kolb, B., and B. Milner. Performance of complex arm and facial movements after focal brain lesions. *Neuropsychologia* 19:505–514, 1981.

Kolb, B., and B. Milner. Observations on spontaneous facial expression after focal cerebral excisions and after intracarotid injection of sodium amytal. *Neuropsychologia* 19:514–515, 1981.

Kolb, B., and L. Taylor. Affective behavior in patients with localized cortical excisions: An analysis of lesion site and side. *Science* 214:89–91, 1981.

Kuypers, H. G. J. M. Anatomy of the descending pathways. In V. B. Brooks, Ed. *Handbook of Physiology; The Nervous System*, vol. 2, *The Motor Systems*. Baltimore: Williams & Wilkins, 1981.

Lashley, K. S. The problem of serial order in behavior. In F. A. Beach, D. O. Hebb, C. T. Morgan, and H. W. Nissen, Eds. *The Neuropsychology of Lashley*. New York: McGraw-Hill, 1960.

Lepage, M., Ghaffar, O., Nyberg, L., and E. Tulving. Prefrontal cortex and episodic memory retrieval mode. *Proceedings of the National Academy of Sciences of the United States of America* 97:506–511, 2000.

Leonard, G., L. Jones, and B. Milner. Residual impairment in handgrip strength after unilateral frontal-lobe lesions. *Neuropsychologia* 26:555–564, 1988.

Levine, B., S. E. Black, R. Cabeza, M. Sinden, A. R. Mcintosh, J. P. Toth, E. Tulving, and D. T. Stuss. Episodic memory and the self in a case of isolated retrograde amnesia. *Brain* 121:1951–1973, 1998.

Luria, A. R. *The Working Brain*. New York: Penguin, 1973.

Luria, A. R., and E. D. Homskaya. Disturbance in the regulative role of speech with frontal lobe lesions. In J. M. Warren and K. Akert, Eds. *The Frontal Granular Cortex and Behavior*. New York: McGraw-Hill, 1964.

Miller, L. Cognitive risk taking after frontal or temporal lobectomy I: The synthesis of fragmented visual information. *Neuropsychologia* 23:359–369, 1985.

Miller, L., and B. Milner. Cognitive risk taking after frontal or temporal lobectomy II: The synthesis of phonemic and semantic information. *Neuropsychologia* 23:371–379, 1985.

Milner, B. Some effects of frontal lobectomy in man. In J. M. Warren and K. Akert, Eds. *The Frontal Granular Cortex and Behavior*. New York: McGraw-Hill, 1964.

Milner, B., P. Corsi, and G. Leonard. Frontal cortex contribution to recency judgements. *Neuropsychologia* 29:601–618, 1991.

Milner, B., and M. Petrides. Behavioural effects of frontal-lobe lesions in man. *Trends in Neurosciences* 7:403–407, 1984.

Mishkin, M., and F. J. Manning. Non-spatial memory after selective prefrontal lesions in monkeys. *Brain Research* 143:313–323, 1978.

Owen, A. M., J. J. Downes, B. J. Sahakian, C. E. Polkey, and T. W. Robbins. Planning and spatial working memory following frontal lobe lesions in man. *Neuropsychologia* 28:1021–1034, 1990.

Owen, A. M., B. Milner, M. Petrides, and A. C. Evans. Memory for object features versus memory for object location: A positron-emission tomography study of encoding and retrieval processes. *Proceedings of the National Academy of Sciences of the United States of America* 93:9212–9217, 1996.

Owen, A. M., B. J. Sahakian, J. R. Hodges, R. A. Summers, C. E. Polkey, and T. W. Robbins. Dopamine-dependent fronto-striatal planning deficits in early Parkinson's disease. *Neuropsychology* 9:126–140, 1995.

Passingham, R. E. Memory of monkeys (*Macaca mulatta*) with lesions in prefrontal cortex. *Behavioral Neuroscience* 99:3–21, 1985.

Passingham, R. E. *The Frontal Lobes and Voluntary Action*. Oxford: Oxford University Press, 1993.

Perret, E. The left frontal lobe of man and the suppression of habitual responses in verbal categorical behavior. *Neuropsychologia* 12:323–330, 1974.

Petrides, M. Motor conditional associative learning after selective prefrontal lesions in the monkey. *Behavioural Brain Research* 5:407–413, 1982.

Petrides, M. Functional specialization within the dorsolateral frontal cortex for serial order memory. *Proceedings of the Royal Society, London* B246:299–306, 1991.

Petrides, M. Visuo-motor conditional associative learning after frontal and temporal lesions in the human brain. *Neuropsychologia* 35:989–997, 1997.

Petrides, M. Mapping prefrontal cortical systems for the control of cognition. In A. W. Toga and J. C. Mazziotta, Eds. *Brain Mapping: The Systems*. San Diego: Academic Press, 2000, pp. 159–176.

Petrides, M., B. Alivisatos, and A. C. Evans. Functional activation of the human ventrolateral frontal cortex during mnemonic retrieval of verbal information. *Proceedings of the National Academy of Sciences of the United States of America* 92:5803–5807, 1995.

Petrides, M., and B. Milner. Deficit on subject ordered tasks after frontal- and temporal-lobe lesions in man. *Neuropsychologia* 20:249–262, 1982.

Potter, H., and N. Butters. An assessment of olfactory deficits in patients with damage to prefrontal cortex. *Neuropsychologia* 18:621–628, 1980.

Pouchon, J.-B., R. Levy, J.-B Poline, S. Crozier, S. Lehericy, B. Pillon, B. Deweer, D. Le Bihan, and B. Dubois. The role of dorsolateral prefrontal cortex in the preparation of forthcoming actions: An fMRI study. *Cerebral Cortex* 11:260–266, 2001.

Ramier, A.-M., and H. Hecaen. Role respectif des atteintes frontales et de la lateralisation lesionnelle dans les deficits de la "fluence verbale." *Revue de Neurologie* 123:17–22, 1970.

Reitan, R. M., and L. A. Davison. *Clinical Neuropsychology: Current Status and Application*. New York: Wiley, 1974.

Roberts, A. C., T. W. Robbins, and L. Weizkrantz, Eds. *The Prefrontal Cortex: Executive and Cognitive Functions*. Oxford: Oxford University Press, 1998.

Roland, P. E. Metabolic measurements of the working frontal cortex in man. *Trends in Neuroscience* 7:430–435, 1984.

Roland, P. E., and L. Friberg. Localization of cortical areas activated by thinking. *Journal of Neurophysiology* 3:1219–1243, 1985.

Roland, P. E., B. Larsen, N. A. Lassen, and E. Skinhoj. Supplementary motor area and other cortical areas in organization of voluntary movements in man. *Journal of Neurophysiology* 43:118–136, 1980.

Rolls, E. T. The orbitofrontal cortex. In A. C. Roberts, T. W. Robbins, and L. Weizkrantz, Eds. *The Prefrontal Cortex: Executive and Cognitive Functions.* Oxford: Oxford University Press, 1998, pp. 67–86.

Rolls, E. T. *The Brain and Emotion.* Oxford: Oxford University Press, 2000.

Rose, J. E., and C. N. Woolsey. The orbitofrontal cortex and its connections with the mediodorsal nucleus in rabbit, sheep and cat. *Research Publications of the Association of Nervous and Mental Disease* 27:210–232, 1948.

Semmes, J., S. Weinstein, L. Ghent, and H.-L. Teuber. Impaired orientation in personal and extrapersonal space. *Brain* 6:747–772, 1963.

Shallice, T. *From Neuropsychology to Mental Structure.* Cambridge, UK: Cambridge University Press, 1988.

Shallice, T., and P. Burgess. Deficits in strategy application following frontal lobe damage in man. *Brain* 114:727–741, 1991.

Shallice, T., and M. E. Evans. The involvement of the frontal lobes in cognitive estimation. *Cortex* 14:294–303, 1978.

Smith, M. L., and B. Milner. Differential effects of frontal-lobe lesions on cognitive estimation and spatial memory. *Neuropsychologia* 22:697–705, 1984.

Stitt, C., and D. Huntington. Some relationships among articulation, auditory abilities, and certain other variables. *Journal of Speech and Learning Research* 12:576–593, 1969.

Taylor, L. Psychological assessment of neurosurgical patients. In T. Rasmussen and R. Marino, Eds. *Functional Neurosurgery.* New York: Raven, 1979.

Teuber, H.-L. The riddle of frontal lobe function in man. In J. M. Warren and K. Akert, Eds. *The Frontal Granular Cortex and Behavior.* New York: McGraw-Hill, 1964.

Teuber, H.-L. Unity and diversity of frontal lobe function. *Acta Neurobiologiae Experimentalis* 32:615–656, 1972.

Tulving, E. Episodic memory: From mind to brain. *Annual Review of Psychology* 53:1–25, 2002.

Tulving E., S. Kapur, F. I. Craik, M. Moscovitch, and S. Houle. Hemispheric encoding/retrieval asymmetry in episodic memory: Positron emission tomography findings. *Proceedings of the National Academy of Sciences of the United States of America* 91:2016–2020, 1994.

Tyler, H. R. Disorders of visual scanning with frontal lobe lesions. In S. Locke, Ed. *Modern Neurology.* London: Churchill, 1969.

Walker, E. A., and D. Blumer. The localization of sex in the brain. In K. J. Zulch, O. Creutzfeldt, and G. C. Galbraith, Eds. *Cerebral Localization.* Berlin and New York: Springer-Verlag, 1975.

Zangwill, O. L. Psychological deficits associated with frontal lobe lesions. *International Journal of Neurology* 5:395–402, 1966.

chapter 17

Disconnection Syndromes

D. M. was the director of a large psychiatric hospital. He began to complain of headaches and memory problems, and a neurological examination found a cyst in the third ventricle. The only available treatment was to drain the cyst and relieve the pressure that was causing D. M.'s symptoms. The surgical procedure was simple and required that the neurosurgeon insert a cannula from the top of the brain through the corpus callosum and a bit of brainstem to get to the ventricle.

The cyst was drained successfully and D. M. showed good recovery: his headaches disappeared, his memory improved, and he returned to work. A year later, D. M. still had some residual memory difficulties but, on the whole, he considered himself a lucky man. One new symptom that bothered D. M., however, was that he had difficulty assembling jigsaw puzzles such as large landscapes. Throughout his life, he had found large-project jigsaw puzzles relaxing, but he was now having difficulty and was finding the whole experience frustrating.

On further examination, his neurologist discovered that, for certain types of tasks, such as puzzles, D. M.'s two hands did not seem to be working together. For example, the left hand would pick up one piece and the right hand another, and, seemingly without realizing it, D. M. would try to put both pieces into the same place, one with each hand. No wonder D. M. was getting frustrated! His surgeon had cut a part of the corpus callosum, and the connections linking the hands in the two hemispheres were severed. The right hand literally did not know what the left hand was doing.

In the preceding chapters, we considered the connections among different cortical regions, the most obvious being the dorsal and ventral pathways of visual processing. But we have not yet considered what happens when the pathways are disturbed. This chapter deals with the effects of cutting cerebral connections, beginning with a summary of cortical connectivity and the anatomy of cerebral connections. In the remainder of the chapter, we revisit

Sperry's research on the "split brain" patient as a model of disconnection syndromes. We then reconsider Geschwind's reinterpretation of three classic symptoms of cortical damage (aphasia, apraxia, and agnosia) as disconnection syndromes and briefly study Mishkin's animal model of disconnection in the visual system before considering some unresolved questions on disconnection at the chapter's end.

Disconnecting Cognitive Functions

To understand D. M.'s symptoms, we need to look back on the effects of cortical injuries on behavior. In Chapters 13 through 16, we associated particular behavioral deficits with different brain lesions and from these deficits have tried to infer the function of the missing region. Similarly, we considered the results of imaging studies showing localized activity in the performance of different behavioral tasks. Two inescapable conclusions emerge from these discussions:

1. The different anatomically defined cortical lobes are each engaged in a wide range of cognitive activities. Thus, for example, the temporal lobe appears to play a significant role not in only vision and audition but also in more-complex cognitive functions such as memory, language, and emotion.

2. Although the various lobes are engaged in different cognitive activities, they overlap remarkably in function. Recall, for example, that the frontal lobe has cells that are responsive to visual, auditory, somatosensory, olfactory, and taste inputs. Furthermore, we identified a frontal role in functions such as memory, language, and emotion. Clearly, if we presume that the functions of the different anatomical regions differ in some manner, then the simplest explanation of how the cerebral regions function together is that they form some sort of neural network that combines their different contributions to virtually every function that we can describe.

By its very nature, a network implies connections. The cutting of cerebral connections is called **disconnection,** and the ensuing behavioral effects are called **disconnection syndromes.** Thus, we can see that D. M.'s disconnection syndrome was an accidental result of his surgical procedure to drain the third ventricle cyst.

The behavioral changes that result from disconnecting cerebral regions can be rather odd and are different from what could be expected if either area were damaged but remained connected. Figure 17.1 presents an example in which Downer performed two different forms of disconnection on a monkey. In Downer's study, all commissures connecting the two halves of the brain were cut and the amygdala on the left side was removed.

Downer then covered one of the animal's eyes with an occluder and presented objects to the other eye. If the objects were presented to the eye ipsilateral to the hemisphere with the ablated amygdala, the animal appeared "tame,"

(A) Normal monkey

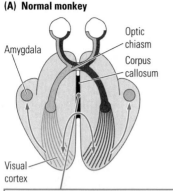

(B) "Tame" monkey

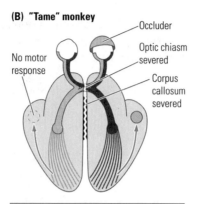

(C) "Wild" monkey

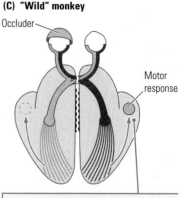

In the anatomically normal monkey, the hemispheres are connected by commissures, including the optic chiasm and the corpus callosum.

With the commissures disconnected, the right eye covered, and the left amygdala removed, visual information is unavailable to the motor system.

With the commissures disconnected, the right amygdala intact, and the left eye covered, the circuit in the right hemisphere for activating species-typical behavior is intact.

Figure 17.1 Downer's experiment. (A) Normal anatomy of the monkey brain. (B) The commissures between the two hemispheres are severed, the amygdala on the left is removed, and an occluder covers the right eye. The monkey displays no species-typical responses to visual stimuli and is described as "tame." (C) The left eye is occluded; the monkey displays species-typical behavior in response to visual stimuli and is classified as "wild."

even if the objects were typically frightening to monkeys (Figure 17.1B). If the objects were presented to the eye ipsilateral to the intact amygdala, the animal made its usual species-typical responses to threats and appeared "wild" (Figure 17.1C). The results can be explained as follows.

For an animal to display species-typical responses to a visual stimulus, the information must be projected from the eye to the visual cortex, through the temporal lobes to the amygdala, and from the amygdala to the brainstem and frontal cortex, where autonomic responses, movements, and facial expressions, respectively, are activated. When the commissures between the two halves of the brain are disconnected, visual information from one eye can project only to the ipsilateral hemisphere. If that hemisphere contains an intact amygdala, the circuit for activating species-typical behavior is complete and behavior will be normal. If the hemisphere does not have an intact amygdala, visual information will be disconnected from motor systems and cannot elicit species-typical behavior.

Had the commissures not been cut, the experiment would not have worked, because information from one hemisphere could have crossed to the other, and each eye would thus have had access to the intact amygdala. As the experiment was performed, however, the right hemisphere had access to an amygdala whereas the left hemisphere did not.

Anatomy of Cerebral Connections

Three major types of neural fibers connect the neocortex—association, projection, and commissural fibers:

- Association fibers can be distinguished as (1) long fiber bundles that connect distant neocortical areas, and (2) short subcortical U-shaped fibers that connect adjacent neocortical areas. The long fiber bundles include the uncinate fasciculus, the superior longitudinal fasciculus, the cingulum, the inferior longitudinal fasciculus, and the inferior frontal occipital fasciculus.

- Projection fibers include ascending fibers from lower centers to the neocortex, such as projections from the thalamus, and descending fibers from the neocortex to the brainstem and spinal cord.

- Commissural fibers function primarily to connect the two hemispheres and include principally the corpus callosum, the anterior commissure, and the hippocampal commissures. The corpus callosum (from the Latin *callus*, meaning "hard body") provides the major connection of neocortical areas. In humans, it is made up of 200 million to 800 million fibers, about half of which are unmyelinated and quite small. Most, but not all, areas of the two hemispheres are connected.

Figure 17.2 illustrates the patterns of connections between the hemispheres in a rhesus monkey. Most of the primary visual cortex (area V1) is devoid of interhemispheric connections, except for that part representing the midline of the visual world, the *visual meridian*. The lack of such connections has been explained in functional terms: this cortex represents the visual world topographically, and there is no need for one half of the representation to be connected to the other. The motor and sensory areas for distal parts of the limbs (mainly the hands and feet) also lack connections. It could be argued that, because their essential function is to work independently of one another, connections are not necessary.

Among the areas that do receive interhemispheric connections, the density of projections is not homogeneous (Figure 17.2A). Areas of the cortex that represent the midline of the body—such as the central meridian of the visual fields, auditory fields, and trunk of the body on the somatosensory and motor cortex—have the densest connections. The functional utility of this arrangement is that movements of the body or actions in central space require

Figure 17.2 Patterns of commissural connections. (A) The areas shaded blue show regions of the cortex of a rhesus monkey that receive projections from the contralateral hemisphere through the corpus callosum. (B) Regions of the corpus callosum showing zones through which a radioactive label was transported after injections into specific locations in the cortex. (After Pandya and Seltzer, 1986.)

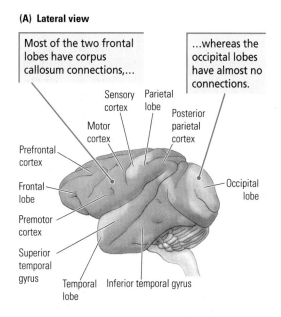

(A) Lateral view

Most of the two frontal lobes have corpus callosum connections,...

...whereas the occipital lobes have almost no connections.

Prefrontal cortex
Frontal lobe
Premotor cortex
Superior temporal gyrus
Motor cortex
Sensory cortex
Parietal lobe
Posterior parietal cortex
Temporal lobe
Inferior temporal gyrus
Occipital lobe

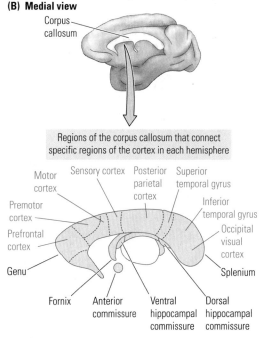

(B) Medial view

Corpus callosum

Regions of the corpus callosum that connect specific regions of the cortex in each hemisphere

Motor cortex
Sensory cortex
Posterior parietal cortex
Superior temporal gyrus
Premotor cortex
Prefrontal cortex
Genu
Fornix
Anterior commissure
Ventral hippocampal commissure
Dorsal hippocampal commissure
Inferior temporal gyrus
Occipital visual cortex
Splenium

interhemispheric cooperation. A prominent working hypothesis concerning callosal function is the *zipper hypothesis*, which suggests that the corpus callosum knits together the representations of the midpoints of the body and space that are divided by the longitudinal fissure.

The connections of the corpus callosum appear to fall into three general classes:

1. Most of the projections are topographical. That is, they connect to identical points in the contralateral hemisphere. Presumably, these projections knit the two areas together functionally.

2. One group of projections goes to areas to which the homotopic area on the contralateral side projects. Thus, projection zones within a hemisphere also maintain close relations with parallel zones in the contralateral hemisphere. For example, recall that area V1 is connected to area V2. Not only are these areas connected within a hemisphere, but they are also connected across hemispheres; so area V1 in one hemisphere also sends connections to area V2 in the opposite hemisphere.

3. Another group of projections has a diffuse terminal distribution. Possibly these projections alert the appropriate zones of one hemisphere that the other is active.

The location of fiber projections within the corpus callosum is precise. The pattern in the rhesus monkey is illustrated in Figure 17.2B. The anterior part of the corpus callosum is called the genu (the knee), and it contains the fibers from the prefrontal cortex. Fibers through the body of the corpus callosum are, proceeding from front to back, from the premotor, motor, somatosensory, and posterior parietal cortex. Fibers in the posterior part, or splenium, are from the superior temporal, inferior temporal, and visual cortex.

The anterior commissure is much smaller than the corpus callosum and connects parts of the anterior temporal lobe, the amygdala, and the paleocortex of the temporal lobe surrounding the amygdala (see Figure 17.2B). In humans born with no corpus callosum (agenesis of the corpus callosum), the anterior commissure is greatly enlarged to connect far greater regions of the neocortex.

A variety of individual differences in callosal size and patterns are suggested to exist. For example, Witelson reported that the corpus callosum is larger in left-handers than in right-handers and in women than in men (see Chapter 12).

The Behavioral Effects of Disconnection

Colonnier recounted the conclusions of Monsieur de la Peyronie, who in 1741 reviewed all the literature concerning areas claimed to be the seat of the soul and dismissed each claim in turn. Peyronie then recounted some of his own patients' cases, from which he claimed that, "whereby it appears that the corpus callosum cannot be either compressed, sphacelated [affected with gangrene] or otherwise injured, but for both reason and all sensations are abolished" (Colonnier, p. 35), the corpus callosum must necessarily be the immediate seat of the soul. Colonnier then noted that, by 1941, McCulloch and Garol had reviewed the literature and concluded that few impairments could be found after callosum damage except perhaps in complicated symbolic activity.

The clinical effects of disconnection, however, were first seriously considered by Carl Wernicke in 1874 and were very much a part of early neurology. He predicted the existence of an aphasic syndrome (conduction aphasia) that would result from severing fiber connections between the anterior and posterior speech zones. Later, in 1892, Joseph Dejerine was the first to demonstrate a distinctive behavioral deficit resulting from pathology of the corpus callosum. In a series of papers published in about 1900, Hugo Liepmann most clearly demonstrated the importance of severed connections as an underlying factor in the effects of cerebral damage.

Having carefully analyzed the behavior of a particular patient, Liepmann predicted a series of disconnections of the neocortex that could account for the behavior. In 1906, after a patient died, Liepmann published the postmortem findings, which supported his hypothesis. He wrote extensively on the principle of disconnection, particularly about the idea that some apraxias might result from disconnection.

Liepmann reasoned that, if a patient were given a verbal command to use the left hand in a particular way, only the verbal left hemisphere would understand the command. To move the left hand, a signal would then have to travel from the left hemisphere through the corpus callosum to the right hemispheric region that controls movements of the left hand, as illustrated in Figure 17.3A. Interrupting the part of the corpus callosum that carries the command from the left hemisphere to the right would disconnect the right hemisphere's motor region from the command. Thus, although the subject would comprehend the command, the left hand would be unable to obey it (Figure 17.3B). This apraxia would occur in the absence of the weakness or incoordination of the left hand that would develop if there were a lesion in the motor cortex of the right hemisphere, which controls the actual movement of the left hand.

Liepmann's deduction, although brilliant, was ignored for a number of reasons. For one, it was published in German and so was not widely read by English-speaking neurologists (Liepmann's papers have been translated into English only recently by Doreen Kimura.) Additionally, except in the extremely unusual case of a patient with a natural lesion of only the corpus callosum, any observed behavioral deficits should be attributed to damage of gray matter itself without reference to connections. Finally, the results of a large number of animal studies consistently purported to demonstrate that no significant behavioral

(A) Normal response

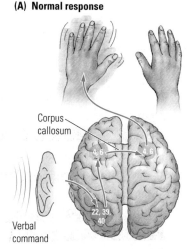

Corpus callosum

Verbal command

(B) Apraxic response

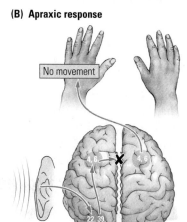

No movement

Verbal command

Figure 17.3 Liepmann's theory of apraxia resulting from lesions of the corpus callosum. (A) Normal response to a verbal command to move the left hand. The command is processed through the posterior speech zone (areas 22, 39, and 40) from the motor cortex of the left hemisphere through the corpus callosum to the motor cortex (area 4) of the right hemisphere to move the left hand. (B) Apraxic response. The jagged line through the callosal area indicates sectioning of the callosum. The verbal command has no way of informing the right-hemisphere motor cortex to move the left hand. Geschwind proposed that bilateral apraxia could result from a lesion disconnecting the posterior speech zone from the motor cortex of the left hemisphere because the verbal command cannot gain access to either the left or the right motor cortex.

effects followed the cutting of the corpus callosum. Not until the late 1950s and 1960s did it become clear that the results from the animal studies could be attributed largely to crude behavioral testing.

An important series of papers by Ronald Myers and by Roger Sperry in the early 1950s revived interest in the effects of disconnecting neocortical regions. They examined the behavioral effects of severing the cat corpus callosum. Their work confirmed others' earlier observations that the animals were virtually indistinguishable from their surgically intact counterparts and indeed appeared normal under most testing and training conditions.

Unlike those of earlier studies, however, the results of their studies revealed that, under special training procedures, the animals could be shown to have severe deficits. Thus, if the sensory information were allowed separate access to each hemisphere, each could be shown to have its own independent perceptual, learning, and memory processes. The corpus callosum does indeed serve an important function. This conclusion has been confirmed in subsequent studies by Sperry and his colleagues on the effects of surgical disconnection of the cerebral hemispheres of humans for the treatment of intractable epilepsy (see Chapter 11).

The success of the Myers and Sperry experiments stimulated interest in other connections of the brain. Geschwind began to reassess the clinical effects of naturally occurring neocortical lesions as possibly indicating disconnection of various regions of the cerebral hemispheres. In parallel work, Mishkin began to construct animal models of human disconnection syndromes by disconnecting related neocortical regions from one another. These researchers have demonstrated the critical interdependence of these normally connected regions.

In fact, the anatomical organization of the neocortex allows for fairly easy disconnection:

- The primary sensory areas have no direct connections among one another and so can be disconnected quite easily.

- Even in higher-order sensory zones, there are few if any direct connections among sensory systems, and so they can be disconnected easily.

- Because the hemispheres are in large part duplicate and are connected by only a few projection systems, they are easy to separate and, as noted earlier, are sometimes found separated congenitally.

Hemispheric Disconnection

The results of studies on surgical disconnection of the hemispheres indicate that many symptoms, including aphasia, alexia, agnosia, agraphia, acopia, and apraxia, can be demonstrated in the *absence of any direct damage* to particular cytoarchitectonic or functional neocortical regions. They can also be present for one side of the body and not the other.

There are three conditions in which the hemispheres become completely separated. First, in humans, the interhemispheric fibers are sometimes cut as a therapy for epilepsy. Second, people are born with congenitally reduced or completely missing interhemispheric connections. Third, in animals, disconnections are performed to trace functional systems, to model human conditions, and to answer basic questions about interhemispheric development.

Epileptic seizures may begin in a restricted region of one hemisphere (most often the temporal lobes) and then spread through the fibers of the corpus callosum or anterior commissure to the homologous location in the opposite hemisphere. These seizures can usually be controlled by anticonvulsant medication, but in some cases the medication is of little value, and the seizures may actually become life threatening because they recur often, sometimes several times in an hour.

To relieve this seizure condition, the corpus callosum and anterior commissure can be surgically sectioned to prevent the spread of abnormal electrical activity from one hemisphere to the other. Patients who have received this treatment obtain substantial relief from their epilepsy and often show marked improvements in personal well being, competence, and intelligence.

The reason for a congenital lack of interhemispheric connections is not known. Interestingly, albinos of nearly all species and Siamese cats have peculiarities in fiber crossings, mostly a reduced number of uncrossed fibers in the visual system. A number of summaries of research on interhemispheric connections have been published, including one by Steele-Russell and colleagues in 1979 and another by Lepore and associates in 1986.

Commissurotomy

Commissurotomy is the surgical cutting of the cerebral commissures as an elective treatment for epilepsy. Surgeons Philip Vogel and Joseph Bogen at the White Memorial Medical Center in Los Angeles reintroduced this technique, and the results obtained by Sperry and his coworkers with their "split brain" patients are now well known (see Chapter 11). As a result of the surgery, each hemisphere retains fibers that allow it to see only the opposite side of the visual world. Likewise, each hemisphere predominantly receives information from the opposite side of the body and controls movements on the opposite side of the body.

The surgery also isolates speech in those persons with lateralized speech. Consequently, the dominant hemisphere (usually the left) is able to speak, and the nondominant hemisphere is not. About a year or so is required for recovery from the surgical trauma. Within 2 years, the typical patient is able to return to school or work. A standard medical examination would not reveal anything unusual in the behavior of these patients, and their scores on standardized tests are normal. The patients' everyday behavior appears similar to that of normal, "unified" people.

Specific tests, however, can show differences between the functioning of split-brain patients and that of people with normal cerebral connections. In the split brain, each hemisphere can be shown to have its own sensations, percepts, thoughts, and memories that are not accessible to the other hemisphere. The usual test procedures include the presentation of stimuli to one hemisphere and then the testing of each hemisphere for what transpired. For example, a person who is asked to touch an out-of-view object with one hand and then find a similar object with the other hand is unable to match the objects correctly (see Figure 11.7).

Odors presented to one nostril cannot be identified by the other, objects seen in one visual field cannot be recognized in the other, and so on. Although the hemispheres function independently, they both do so at a high level. High levels of function apply even to language skills. The nondominant hemisphere, although unable to speak, can understand instructions, read written words, match pictures to words, and match written to spoken words. Nondominant language ability is best for nouns and poorest for verbs.

The nondominant hemisphere performs in a superior fashion on a variety of spatial tasks, including copying designs, reading facial expressions, and fitting forms into molds. The nondominant hemisphere also has a concept of self and can recognize and identify social relations, pictures of the person in a social relation, pictures of family members, acquaintances, pets and belongings, and historical and social figures. Each hemisphere also has a general awareness of body states such as hunger and fatigue.

Callosal Agenesis and Early Transections

Exceptions to the pattern of results obtained with adult commissurotomy patients are found in persons who are born without a corpus callosum. These patients can perform interhemispheric comparisons of visual and tactile information. The interpretation of these results is that the patients have enhanced conduction in the remaining commissures (for example, for vision) and that they develop enhanced abilities to use their few uncrossed projections (for example, for tactile information).

These patients do have deficits in some features of the tasks, however. There are a number of reports of poor transfer of information if stimuli are complex. Furthermore, nonspecific deficits in task performance have been reported in these patients. Lassonde presented pairs of stimuli to six patients with agenesis of the corpus callosum, asking them if the pairs were the same or different. Letters, numbers, colors, or forms were used. Either the pairs were presented one on top of the other in one visual field (intrahemispheric task) or one stimulus was presented in one visual field and the other stimulus in the other visual field (interhemispheric task).

The acallosal group was equally accurate in identifying same–different pairs under both conditions. Their reactions, however, were very slow for both forms of presentation. Lassonde suggested that the callosum participates in hemispheric activation as well as in the transfer of information. Thus, the acallosal group has alternative ways of obtaining the interhemispheric transfer of information but not of activation.

A particularly interesting question concerning the development of language laterality and other asymmetries discussed by Jeeves, in regard to agenesis patients. One explanation of why language is lateralized to one hemisphere is that it gets a start there and then that hemisphere actively inhibits its development in the other hemisphere. In people with callosal agenesis, the opportunity for such an inhibitory process to work is much reduced. Yet the lateralization of language and other functions in most of these people is similar to that in the general population. They also tend to be right-handed, as is the general population. Thus the corpus callosum and other commissures are not necessary for the development of asymmetries.

There are similarities in the effects of callosal agenesis and the effects of transections made early in life. Lassonde and coworkers compared the performance of five children aged 6 to 16 years on the interhemispheric transfer of tactile information and motor learning. The younger children were less affected by the callosal transections than the older children. The researchers suggest that the younger children come to rely on ipsilateral pathways to obtain information and execute movements. That older children are more impaired suggests that, if transections occur early, ipsilateral pathways may make new connections, become functionally validated, or simply become more sensitive.

Disconnecting Sensorimotor Systems

Sperry, Gazzaniga, and others have extensively studied the effects of hemispheric disconnection on behaviors related to both sensory and motor systems. Their findings are summarized here, followed by a consideration of the effects of partial disconnection.

Olfaction

Unlike all the other senses, the olfactory system is not crossed. Input from the left nostril goes straight back to the left hemisphere, and input from the right nostril goes to the right hemisphere. Fibers traveling through the anterior commissure join the olfactory regions in each hemisphere, just as fibers traveling through the corpus callosum join the motor cortex of each hemisphere (see Figure 17.2).

A patient whose anterior commissure is severed cannot name odors presented to the right nostril, because the speaking left hemisphere is disconnected from the information. The right hemisphere has the information but has no control of speech. The olfactory function is still intact, however, because the patient can use the left hand to pick out an object, such as an orange, that corresponds to the odor smelled.

In this case, no connection with speech is necessary, because the right hemisphere both contains the olfactory information and controls the left hand. If requested to use the right hand, the patient would be unable to pick out the object, because the left hemisphere, which controls the right hand, is disconnected from the sensory information. Thus, the patient appears normal with one hand and anosmic (lacking the sense of smell) with the other (Figure 17.4).

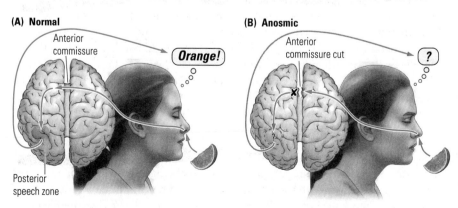

(A) Normal

Anterior commissure

Orange!

Posterior speech zone

(B) Anosmic

Anterior commissure cut

?

Figure 17.4 Anosmia. (A) In the normal condition, olfactory input to the right nostril travels directly back into the right hemisphere and crosses the anterior commissure, thus gaining access to the left (speech) hemisphere. (B) Anosmia results from section of the anterior commissure. (The jagged line indicates the lesion.) When the pathway is severed, the information is blocked, and the left hemisphere has no way of knowing what odor the right hemisphere perceived.

Vision

The visual system is crossed, so information flashed to one visual field travels selectively to the contralateral hemisphere. Recall that, by using this fact, researchers have demonstrated left- and right-visual-field superiority for different types of input. For example, verbal material (such as words) is perceived more accurately when presented to the right visual field, presumably because the input travels to the left, speaking, hemisphere. On the other hand, visuospatial input (such as a map) produces a left-visual-field superiority, because the right hemisphere appears to have a more important role in analyzing spatial information.

Note, however, that the visual-field superiority observed in normal subjects is *relative.* That is, words presented to the left visual field, and hence right hemisphere, are sometimes perceived, although not as accurately or consistently as when they are presented to the right visual field. The relative effects occur because either hemisphere potentially has access to input to the opposite hemisphere through the corpus callosum, which connects the visual areas.

A commissurotomy patient no longer has such access, because the connection is severed. Given that speech is usually housed in the left hemisphere of right-handed patients, visual information presented to the left visual field will be disconnected from verbal associations because the input goes to the right, nonlinguistic, hemisphere. Similarly, complex visual material presented to the right visual field will be inadequately processed, because it will not have access to the visuospatial abilities of the right hemisphere. It follows that, if material is appropriately presented, it will be possible to demonstrate aphasia, agnosia, alexia, and acopia (the inability to copy a geometric design) in a patient who ordinarily exhibits none of these symptoms, as we now demonstrate.

If verbal material is presented to the left visual field, the commissurotomy patient will be unable to read it or to answer questions about it verbally, because the input is disconnected from the speech zones of the left hemisphere. Presentation of the same verbal material to the right visual field presents no difficulties, because the visual input projects to the verbal left hemisphere.

Similarly, if an object is presented to the left visual field, the patient will be unable to name it and thus will appear agnosic and aphasic. If presented to the right visual field, this same object will be correctly named, because the left visual cortex perceives the object and has access to the speech zones. Thus, we can see that the split-brain patient is aphasic, alexic, and agnosic if verbal material or an object requiring a verbal response is presented visually to the right hemisphere, but this person appears normal if material is presented to the left hemisphere.

A further deficit can be seen if the patient is asked to copy a complex visual figure. Because the right hemisphere controls the left hand, we might predict that the left hand will be able to copy the figure but the right hand, deprived of the expertise of the right hemisphere, will be severely impaired. This result is indeed the case: the left hand draws the figure well, whereas the right hand cannot and is thus acopic.

Somesthesis

Like the visual system, the somatosensory system is completely crossed. Sensations of touch in the left hand travel to the right hemisphere, and those in the right hand travel to the left hemisphere. An object placed in the left hand can be named because the tactile information projects to the right hemisphere, crosses to the left, and subsequently has access to the speech zones. Similarly, if a subject is blindfolded and the right hand is molded to form a particular shape, the left hand is able to copy the shape. The tactile information goes from the right hand to the left hemisphere and then across the corpus callosum to the right hemisphere, and the left hand forms the same shape.

If, however, the two hemispheres are disconnected, the somatosensory functions of the left and right parts of the body become independent. For example, if some object is placed in the left hand of a blindfolded callosal patient, who is then asked to choose the presented object from an array of objects, the left hand can pick out the object, but the right hand cannot. If an object is placed in a blindfolded patient's right hand, the patient can name it but cannot do so if the object is placed in the left hand, because the sensory input is disconnected from the left (speech) hemisphere.

Disconnection effects can also be demonstrated without the use of objects. For example, if the callosal patient is blindfolded and one hand is shaped in a particular way, the opposite hand is unable to mimic the posture. One hand has no way of "knowing" what the other hand is doing in the absence of input coming from the opposite hemisphere through the corpus callosum. If the patient is not blindfolded, however, he or she can find out what the opposite hand is doing simply by looking at it.

Audition

The auditory system is more complex than the other sensory systems because it has both crossed and uncrossed connections. Although the left hemisphere appears to receive most of its input from the right ear, it also receives input from the left ear. Therefore, words played into the left ear can travel directly to the left hemisphere or can go to the right hemisphere and then to the left through the corpus callosum.

In normal subjects, dichotic-listening tasks clearly show that the contralateral input is preferred: words presented to the right ear are selectively perceived over words presented to the left ear. Remember, however, that this difference is relative, because some words presented to the left ear also are reported.

The bilateral anatomical arrangement just described appears to reduce the effects of disconnection, but nevertheless one effect has been demonstrated. In the dichotic-listening task, input from the left ear is totally suppressed; the patient reports only those words played to the right ear. That is, digits or words played to the right ear are reported, but no input to the left ear is reported. This effect is a little surprising, because words played to the left ear, even under these conditions, would be expected to attain some direct access to the left hemisphere. This direct access does not appear to exist when the hemispheres are disconnected.

Movement

Because the motor system is largely crossed, we might predict that disconnection of the hemispheres will induce motor difficulties. Here we consider responses to verbal commands and tasks requiring the cooperation of both hands.

On any task in which the left hand must either respond to a verbal command or write in response to verbal material, a form of apraxia and agraphia could be expected, because the left hand would not receive instructions from the left hemisphere. That is, the left hand would be unable to obey the command (apraxia) or to write (agraphia). These disabilities would not be seen in the right hand, because it has access to the speech hemisphere.

Similarly, if a patient were asked to use the right hand to copy a geometric design, it might be impaired (acopia) because it is disconnected from the right hemisphere, which ordinarily has a preferred role in rendering. These symptoms of disconnection are in fact observed in commissurotomy patients, although the severity of the deficit declines significantly with the passage of time after surgery, possibly because the left hemisphere's ipsilateral control of movement is being used.

A second situation that might produce severe motor deficits in commissurotomy patients is one in which the two arms must be used in cooperation. Ordinarily, one hand is informed of what the other is doing through the corpus callosum. Preilowski and, later, Zaidel and Sperry examined the effect of the disconnection of this type of bimanual cooperative movement.

Patients were severely impaired at alternating tapping movements of the index fingers. Likewise, in a task similar to using an Etch-a-Sketch, one requiring that a line inclined at an angle be traced, callosal patients did very poorly. This task requires the use of two cranks, one operated by each hand; one crank moves the tracing pen vertically, and the other moves it horizontally.

A high degree of manual cooperation is required to trace a diagonal line smoothly. If the hemispheres have been disconnected, this cooperation is severely retarded, because the left and right motor systems cannot gain information about what the opposite side is doing, except indirectly by the patient's watching them. Recall D. M.'s frustration with his jigsaw puzzles.

Dramatic illustrations of conflict between hands abound. In one case, a patient repeatedly picked up a newspaper with his right hand and laid it down with his left hand. He performed this sequence several times until, finally, the left hand threw the newspaper on the floor. Another patient was described by a physiotherapist: "He was buttoning his shirt with his right hand and the left hand was coming along just behind it undoing the buttons just as quickly as he could fasten them."

However, as in the praxic impairments described earlier, instances of intermanual conflict are generally confined to the first postoperative months and again seem related to the age of the patient and extent of extra-callosal damage. It is of interest to note that the same patients while inhibiting these episodes of intermanual conflict were able to use their left hands in a purposeful and cooperative manner when "not thinking of what they were doing" (Preilowski, 1975, p. 119). For example, they could pour coffee from a pot held in the right hand into a cup held by its handle with the left hand. The aforementioned peculiarities in motor functions were observed only in complete-split-brain patients and not in patients with partial disconnections.

The Effects of Partial Disconnection

Would a partial section of the corpus callosum have effects as severe as those of a complete disconnection? Surgeons have experimented with partial surgical disconnection of the hemispheres, hoping to attain the same clinical relief

An fMRI Study of Disconnection

Various imaging studies have revealed that, if one hand is subjected to tactile stimulation, areas SI and SII in both the contralateral and the ipsilateral hemispheres become activated. To relieve drug-resistant epilepsy, M. C., age 41, underwent a partial callosotomy, which severed the anterior corpus callosum. Because his seizures were unaffected by the surgery, M. C. later had the posterior callosum severed as well.

M. C. was placed in an MRI scanner a week before the second surgery, and his fMRI was recorded in response to the brushing of his palm and fingers of the right or left hand with a sponge at the rate of about 1 Hz (Figure A). He was retested in the same manner 6 months after the second surgery. Figure B shows that, whereas M. C. retained bilateral activation in response to tactile stimulation of either hand after the first surgery, he showed activation only in the contralateral hemisphere after the second surgery.

This result is due to the absence of callosal transfer of the tactile information after the posterior callosum was severed. This loss of activation was correlated with a functional loss as well: before the second surgery, M. C. was able to name objects placed into either hand, whereas, after the second surgery, he could no longer name objects placed into his left hand.

(A) Before surgery

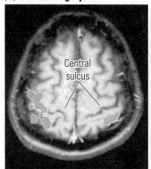

(B) After surgery

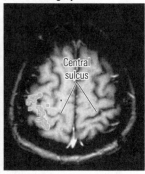

Activation in response to tactile stimulation. Before the second disconnection surgery (A), M. C. showed bilateral activation of somatosensory cortex, whereas, after surgery (B), he showed only unilateral activation. The second surgery prevented the transfer of information from one hemisphere to the other.

(M. Fabri, G. Polonara, M. Del Pesce, A. Quatrinni, U. Salvolini, and T. Manzoni. Posterior corpus callosum and interhemispheric transfer of somatosensory information: An fMRI and neuropsychological study of a partially callosotomized patient. *Journal of Cognitive Neuroscience* 13: 1071–1079, 2001.)

from seizures but with fewer neuropsychological side effects. Although the results are still preliminary, partial disconnection, in which the posterior part of the corpus callosum is left intact, appears to combine markedly milder effects than those of complete commissurotomy with the same therapeutic benefits. For example, Sperry and colleagues have found that patients with partial disconnection are significantly better at motor tasks such as those needed to use the Etch-a-Sketch.

The results of research on monkeys with partial commissurotomies suggest that the posterior part of the corpus callosum (splenium) subserves visual transfer (as does the anterior commissure), whereas the region just in front of the splenium affects somatosensory transfer (see Figure 17.2B). The functions of the more anterior parts of the corpus callosum are largely unknown, but the transfer of motor information is presumed to be one such function. The effect of the transection of the anterior versus the posterior part of the callosum is illustrated nicely in the Snapshot on this page.

Lesion Effects Reinterpreted As Disconnection Syndromes

In 1965, Norman Geschwind wrote a theoretically significant paper titled "Disconnexion Syndromes in Animals and Man" that tied together a vast amount of literature and anticipated many of the effects of callosal surgery. Geschwind's thesis was that certain types of behavioral deficits result from disconnections between the hemispheres, within a hemisphere, or a combination of both. That is, symptoms such as aphasia and agnosia can be thought of as resulting from the *disconnection* of cortical regions rather than necessarily from *damage to* cortical regions.

The value of this monograph is not its review of the data but rather its reintroduction of the concept first proposed by Dejerine and Liepmann nearly 70 years earlier: disconnecting neocortical regions can cause a variety of neurological symptoms. To demonstrate the utility of the model, we will consider only the three classic symptoms of left hemisphere damage: apraxia, agnosia, and alexia.

Apraxia

As noted early in this chapter, if a lesion of the corpus callosum disconnects the left hand from the left hemisphere, that hand is unable to respond to verbal commands and is considered apraxic. Suppose, however, that the right hand is unable to respond to verbal commands. Geschwind speculated that this deficit results from a lesion in the left hemisphere that disconnects its motor cortex (which controls the right hand) from the speech zone (see Figure 17.3B). Thus the right hand cannot respond to verbal commands and is considered apraxic.

Although Geschwind's model can explain bilateral apraxia in some patients, it must be emphasized that disconnection is not the only cause of apraxia. Because the posterior cortex has direct access to the subcortical neural mechanisms of arm and body movements (see Chapter 9), parietal input need not go through the motor cortex except for the control of finger movements. Further, as noted earlier, patients with sections of the corpus callosum are initially apraxic but show substantial recovery despite a disconnection of the motor cortex of the left and right hemispheres.

Agnosia and Alexia

Geschwind theorized that agnosia and alexia can disconnect the posterior speech area from the visual association cortex. Both symptoms can be produced by a lesion that disconnects the visual association region on the left from the speech zone or by a lesion that disconnects the right visual association cortex from the speech zone by damaging the corpus callosum, as illustrated in Figure 17.5. Thus the patient, although able to talk, is unable to identify words or objects, because the visual information is disconnected from the posterior speech zone in the left hemisphere.

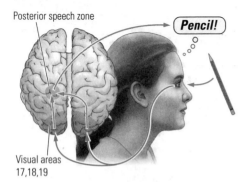

(A) Normal

Posterior speech zone

Pencil!

Visual areas 17,18,19

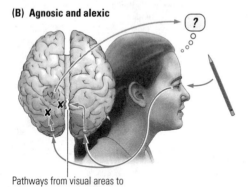

(B) Agnosic and alexic

?

Pathways from visual areas to posterior speech zone cut

Figure 17.5 Geschwind's model of agnosia and alexia resulting from disconnection of the visual cortex from the posterior speech zone. (A) Normally, the visual input of both hemispheres travels to the posterior speech zone and association cortex, where it is processed to allow speech describing the written word or the object. (B) In the absence of the connection, processing of the visual input is no longer possible, and agnosia and alexia result. The jagged lines indicate the lesion of the pathways.

Experimental Verification of Disconnection Effect

Disconnection can be used experimentally to demonstrate the function of various brain regions. This chapter began with a discussion of Downer's ingenious experiment to demonstrate the effects of disconnection. Mishkin and others have disconnected different brain areas in animals to demonstrate the functional connections in the hierarchical organization of the visual system and the somatosensory system. The results of this research clearly demonstrate the usefulness of the disconnection approach and have led to significant progress in understanding the sensory systems.

Disconnecting the Visual System

In the visual system, connections in each hemisphere run from area V1 to area V2 and to areas V3, V4, and V5 in the same hemisphere (Figure 17.6A). Connections from V3, V4, and V5 cross the corpus callosum to the analogous

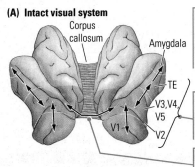

(A) Intact visual system

Corpus callosum

Amygdala

TE

V3, V4, V5

V1

V2

This view of the monkey brain shows both hemispheres in lateral view, with an exaggerated corpus callosum connecting them.

In each hemisphere, connections run from V1 to V2 and to V3, V4, V5, TE, and the amygdala.

Connections from V3, V4, and V5 cross the corpus callosum.

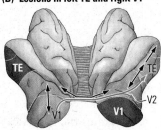

(B) Lesions in left TE and right V1

TE

TE

V1

V1

V2

A lesion in V1 on the right and TE on the left does not disturb performance, because an intact triad of V1 on the left, V2, and TE on the right remains.

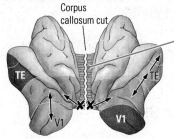

(C) Lesioned and disconnected

Corpus callosum cut

TE

TE

V1

V1

Sectioning the corpus callosum disconnects the remaining pathway, severely impairing vision.

Figure 17.6 Disconnection effects in the visual system of monkeys. (A) The visual system is intact. (B) After lesioning (dark gray areas), the left visual cortex still has access to the visual association cortex of the right hemisphere, and so vision is still possible. (C) The intact components of the visual system are disconnected (jagged line) after lesioning, producing major visual deficits. (After Mishkin, 1979.)

areas on the opposite side, as well as connecting with area TE on the same side. Area TE connects to the anterior temporal cortex and the amygdala on the same side and connects, through the anterior commissure, to these structures on the opposite side. What would happen to vision if the connections were cut? This question has been addressed in experiments with the use of monkeys.

Such experiments require that the monkeys first be tested to determine their visual capabilities. The easiest method is to teach the animals a visual discrimination, such as between a "+" and a "0." Food reinforcement is associated with one stimulus and not with the other.

A monkey's task is to identify the correct stimulus and respond to it. Control monkeys learn this problem in 100 to 150 trials or fewer. If a monkey that has been lesioned fails to learn this problem in 1000 trials, the assumption is that it will not learn the task at all. The lesion can be inferred to have some important effect on the monkey's ability to discriminate between visual stimuli.

By using tasks of this sort, Mishkin and others have demonstrated that bilateral lesions in areas V1, V2, or TE result in an impaired or abolished ability to solve visual-discrimination problems. Because unilateral lesions do not have such an effect, what seems to be necessary is one intact trio of areas V1, V2, and TE. There is, however, one constraint: the remaining cortical regions must be connected.

Thus, as illustrated in Figure 17.6B, a lesion in area V1 on the right and in area TE on the left does not disturb performance, because an intact system still functions. If the connection between the hemispheres is now severed, the neocortical areas are still intact but are not connected, and the result is failure on the visual-discrimination problem (Figure 17.6C). Clearly, the neocortical regions do not function properly if they are not connected to one another.

Disconnecting Nonvisual Regions from the Visual System

Mishkin first studied area TE, thinking it the final step in the neocortical visual system. He later studied the problem of how visual stimuli might gain what he calls "motivational" or "emotional" significance. Monkeys with bilateral temporal lobectomies including the amygdalae attach no significance to visual stimuli. That is, they will repeatedly eat nasty-tasting objects or place inedible objects in their mouths.

In his 1965 paper, Geschwind proposed that this symptom represents a disconnection of the amygdala from the visual system. That is, although an animal's visuosensory system might be intact, the animal would behave as if it were not, because it is disconnected from another system that attaches meaning to visual information. Figure 17.7A illustrates the additional connections when the amygdala is included in an extended visual system. Area TE connects with the amygdala on the same side and connects with the amygdala on the opposite side through the anterior commissure.

To test Geschwind's proposal, Mishkin devised an experiment. The amygdala was lesioned on the left and the inferior temporal cortex (area TE) on the right (Figure 17.7C). This arrangement left one complete system of areas V1, V2, TE, and the amygdala; using it, the monkey's performance on visual problems was normal, as would be expected.

The anterior commissure was then cut, leaving all the necessary pieces of the system intact but disconnecting the intact amygdala from the neocortical

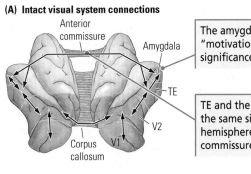

(A) Intact visual system connections

Anterior commissure

Amygdala

TE

V2

Corpus callosum

V1

The amygdala attaches "motivational" or "emotional" significance to visual stimuli.

TE and the amygdala connect on the same side, and on opposite hemispheres via the anterior commissure.

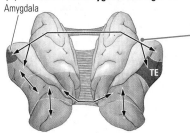

(B) Lesions to left amygdala and right TE

Amygdala

TE

Even when the amygdala on the left and TE on the right are lesioned, one intact visual system remains and behavior is normal.

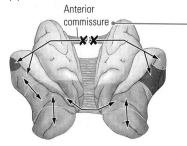

(C) Lesioned and disconnected

Anterior commissure

Severing the anterior commissure cuts the connections between contralateral TE and amygdala, resulting in visual performance deficits.

Figure 17.7 Disconnection of affect from visual input. (A) The connections of the intact visual system, including the callosal and anterior commissural connections. (B) Even if parts of the system are damaged (dark gray areas), it can still function. (C) If the anterior commissure is severed after lesioning, visual input is separated from affect, resulting in visual deficits. (After Mishkin, 1979.)

part of the system. Performance on visual problems instantly deteriorated, indicating some interruption of the normal processing of visual material, as would be predicted from Geschwind's model.

In another application of the disconnection model to the study of the visual system, Nakamura and Mishkin showed blindness in monkeys after disconnection of the intact visual system from nonvisual regions. Monkeys underwent unilateral decortications in which the visual areas (in addition to the motor and limbic cortex) were spared. Then the cerebral commissures and contralateral optic tract were severed. Unexpectedly, the animals acted as though they were blind! None showed any detectable reaction to visually presented stimuli, whether food, fearful objects, threats, or sudden movements. When placed in an unfamiliar environment, they bumped into obstacles and found food objects only by touching them accidentally on tactile exploration.

Although some of the monkeys showed some recovery with the passage of time, others did not, remaining functionally blind even 2 years after surgery. Further experiments revealed that the visual cortex was still functioning electrophysiologically, yet the animals behaved as though it no longer functioned at all. The results point to an important role of the nonvisual cortex in visual perception and demonstrate the importance of studying the connections to a functional system as well as its areas. In the present case, if an animal cannot move in response to visual information, it appears to be essentially blind, even though the visual system may be processing the sensory input.

We can speculate at this point about what a person whose brain is placed in a bottle and kept alive might experience, which, in a real sense, is an extreme example of a disconnection syndrome because the brain is disconnected from both its inputs and its outputs. It seems likely that, although the brain could still function, it would be unconscious in the absence of inputs or outputs.

Unresolved Questions

Here we touch on questions related to cerebral disconnection, ranging from species differences to philosophical arguments.

Species Differences

Significant species differences exist in the anatomy and functions of interconnecting hemispheric commissures. Some primitive marsupials do not have a corpus callosum. Some birds, although having interhemispheric commissures, behave as might humans who have no corpus callosum. Sherry reported that, if an occluder is placed over the eye of a food-caching bird, the information stored by the bird in its contralateral hemisphere about where its food is located is not accessible to the other eye. The animals apparently have separate memory stores for each eye.

Development

Disconnection hypotheses could be applicable to interpretations of various developmental stages of infants. It is well known that myelination of fibers is one of the last events in the maturation of neural systems. Therefore, if certain connections have not matured while others have, features of behavior may parallel symptoms observed in disconnection cases.

For example, young infants will extend their arms to reach for objects in the visual field of the limb. If an object moves across the visual midline, the hand will not follow it, but the other hand will be extended to grasp for it. A little later in development, the infant will follow the object with a hand even if the object crosses the midline. This behavior could be a result of hemispheric disconnection, attributable to immaturity or a lack of myelination of the interhemispheric pathways.

Other behaviors displayed by infants could be interpreted in the same way. Mitchel found that human infants younger than about 1 year are like split-brain patients in that they are unable to transfer information about objects obtained by touch. In the experiments, infants were conditioned to expect that someone would play "peek-a-boo" on one or the other side of their bodies, shortly after they were allowed to feel an object of a certain texture in one hand. Then they were allowed to feel the object in the other hand. If information was transferred from one hand to the other in the infant's brain, the infants were expected to display the conditioned response, which they did not.

Rudy and Stadler-Morris found that rats trained on a spatial-navigation task learned the task with one hemisphere at 22 days of age but could not learn it with the other. By the time they were 25 days old, they did display interocular equivalence. The researchers suggest that the 22-day-old rat behaves like a split-brain animal.

Head Trauma

Disconnection may be especially relevant to one other line of inquiry. People working with patients who have suffered head trauma (see Chapter 26) are often puzzled by the severe chronic impairments that these patients may display even with minimal direct brain injury. Gennarelli and his coworkers suggested that the impairments may be due to diffuse axonal injury. Head trauma often causes twisting and shearing of the two hemispheres, which could result in a traumatic form of disconnection.

In contrast, head-trauma patients can also show surprisingly small and selective deficits. Fantie studied a group of university graduate students with relatively mild closed-head injuries and no apparent deficits and found impairments in callosal transfer of tactile information. That these people were able to obtain graduate degrees in a variety of fields speaks to the specific nature of their brain pathology, which was likely largely restricted to the corpus callosum.

Philosophical Arguments

Many people have written about the implications of the split-brain cases to support theories of mind and concepts of individuality. Certainly for dualists, who hold that the brain has a separate corresponding mental representation (the mind), there are compelling reasons to consider that a split-brain person possesses two brains and two minds. For materialists, who hold that behavior is explained as a function of the nervous system, without recourse to mind, the philosophical implications are not so weighty. But, for everyone, there is a challenge to understand how persons with separated hemispheres function in a seemingly integrated way.

Summary

Historically enigmatic, the functions of the corpus callosum and associated forebrain commissures are now well understood. In general, the commissures function to allow the two hemispheres to engage in complementary functions and to do so in concert. But there is more to connectivity than the interhemispheric connections; there are also intrahemispheric connections. These connections function to allow each hemisphere to work as a coordinated unit. The major interhemispheric connection is the corpus callosum, which joins most neocortical regions. The medial temporal regions, especially the amygdalae, are connected by the anterior commissure. The intrahemispheric connections include long fiber bundles that connect distant cortical areas, as well as short fibers that connect adjacent neocortical areas. Disconnection of either inter- or intrahemispheric connections can produce a variety of neurological syndromes including apraxia, aphasia, agnosia, and acopia. Thus, such classic symptoms may result from damage to specific cortical regions or from damage to the connections between the cortical regions.

Researchers have taken advantage of disconnection syndromes to study the function of discrete cortical regions. This approach has proved especially useful in studies examining the hierarchical organization of the sensory systems. Disconnection principles can be extended to understanding other observations, too, including interspecies differences in cognitive processing, developmental stages in infants, and various behavioral disorders resulting from conditions such as head trauma.

References

Colonnier, M. Notes on the early history of the corpus callosum with an introduction to the morphological papers published in this festschrift. In F. Lepore, M. Ptito, and H. H. Jasper, Eds. *Two Hemispheres—One Brain*. New York: Liss, 1986.

Downer, J. L. de C. Changes in visual gnostic functions and emotional behavior following unilateral temporal pole damage in the "split-brain" monkey. *Nature* 191:50–51, 1961.

Fabri, M., G. Polonara, M. Del Pesce, A. Quatrinni, U. Salvolini, and T. Manzoni. Posterior corpus callosum and interhemispheric transfer of somatosensory information: An fMRI and neuropsychological study of a partially callosotomized patient. *Journal of Cognitive Neuroscience* 13:1071–1079, 2001.

Fantie, B., and B. Kolb. Tasks traditionally used to assess callosal function reveal performance deficits associated with mild head injury. *Neuroscience Abstracts* 15:132, 1989.

Gazzaniga, M. S. *The Bisected Brain*. New York: Appleton-Century-Crofts, 1970.

Gennarelli, T. A., J. H. Adams, and D. I. Graham. Diffuse axonal injury: A new conceptual approach to an old problem. In A. Baethmann, K. G. Go, and A. Unterberg, Eds. *Mechanisms of Secondary Brain Damage*. New York: Plenum, 1986.

Geschwind, N. Disconnexion syndromes in animals and man. *Brain* 88:237–294, 585–644, 1965.

Jeeves, M. A. Callosal agenesis: Neuronal and developmental adaptions. In F. Lepore, M. Ptito, and H. H. Jasper, Eds. *Two Hemispheres—One Brain*. New York: Liss, 1986.

Lassonde, M. The facilitatory influence of the corpus callosum on intrahemispheric processing. In F. Lepore, M. Ptito, and H. H. Jasper, Eds. *Two Hemispheres—One Brain*. New York: Liss, 1986.

Lassonde, M., H. Sauerwein, G. Geoffroy, and M. Decarie. Effects of early and late transection of the corpus callosum in children. *Brain* 109:953–967, 1986.

Lepore, F., M. Ptito, and H. H. Jasper, Eds. *Two Hemispheres—One Brain*. New York: Liss, 1986.

Mishkin, M. Analogous neural models for tactile and visual learning. *Neuropsychologia* 17:139–152, 1979.

Mitchel, G. F. Self-generated experience and the development of lateralized neurobehavioral organization in infants. *Advances in the Study of Behavior* 17:61–83, 1987.

Myers, R. E. Functions of the corpus callosum in interocular transfer. *Brain* 57:358–363, 1956.

Nakamura, R. K., and M. Mishkin. Blindness in monkeys following non-visual cortical lesions. *Brain Research* 188:572–577, 1980.

Pandya, D. N., and B. Seltzer. The topography of commissural fibers. In F. Lepore, M. Ptito, and H. H. Jasper, Eds. *Two Hemispheres—One Brain*. New York: Liss, 1986.

Preilowski, B. Bilateral motor interaction: Perceptual-motor performance of partial and complete "split-brain" patients. In K. J. Zulch, O. Creutzfeldt, and G. C. Galbraith, Eds. *Cerebral Localization*. Berlin and New York: Springer, 1975.

Rudy, J. W., and S. Stadler-Morris. Development of interocular equivalence in rats trained on a distal-cue navigation task. *Behavioral Neuroscience* 101:141–143, 1987.

Schrift, M. J., H. Bandla, P. Shah, and M. A. Taylor. Interhemispheric transfer in major psychoses. *Journal of Nervous and Mental Disease* 174:203–207, 1986.

Sherry, D. F. Food storage by birds and mammals. *Advances in the Study of Behavior* 15:153–183, 1985.

Sperry, R. W. Lateral specialization in the surgically separated hemispheres. In F. O. Schmitt and F. G. Worden, Eds. *Neurosciences: Third Study Program*. Cambridge, MA: MIT Press, 1974.

Spiegler, B. J., and M. Mishkin. Evidence for the sequential participation of inferior temporal cortex and amygdala in the acquisition of stimulus-reward associations. *Behavioral Brain Research* 3:303–317, 1981.

Steele-Russell, I., M. W. Van Hof, and G. Berlucchi, Eds. *Structure and Function of Cerebral Commissures*. London: Macmillan, 1979.

Witelson, S. F. Wires of the mind: Anatomical variation in the corpus callosum in relation to hemispheric specialization and integration. In F. Lepore, M. Ptito, and H. H. Jasper, Eds. *Two Hemispheres—One Brain*. New York: Liss, 1986.

Zaidel, D., and R. W. Sperry. Some long term motor effects of cerebral commissurotomy in man. *Neuropsychologia* 15:193–204, 1977.

chapter 18

Memory

H. M. had experienced generalized epileptic seizures that had grown progressively worse in frequency and severity despite very high doses of medication. On 23 August 1953, William Scoville performed a bilateral medial-temporal-lobe resection in an attempt to stop the seizures. Afterward H. M. experienced a severe anterograde amnesia that has persisted with little improvement to this day: H. M.'s IQ is above average (118 on the Wechsler Adult Intelligence Scale), and he performed normally on perceptual tests. H. M.'s memory of events that took place before the surgery is good, as is his capacity to recall remote events such as incidents from his school days or jobs that he held in his late teens or early twenties. Socially, H. M. is quiet and well mannered. He dresses neatly but has to be reminded when to shave. He speaks in a monotone but articulates his words well and has a vocabulary in keeping with his above-average intelligence. His language comprehension is normal; he understands complex verbal material, including jokes; and he can engage in sophisticated conversations.

In December 1967, H. M.'s father died suddenly, and H. M. is said to have become temporarily quite irritable and intractable, rushing out of the house in anger one evening. The cause of the anger was finding that some of his guns were missing. They had been prize possessions of which he often spoke and which he had kept in his room for many years, but an uncle had claimed them as his legacy after the father's death. The patient was upset by what to him was an inexplicable loss, but became calm when they were re-placed in his room. Since then, he has been his usual even-tempered self. When ques-tioned about his parents 2 months later, he seemed to be dimly aware of his father's death. In these and similar respects, he demonstrates some capacity to set up traces of constant features of his immediate environment.

After his father's death, H. M. was given protected employment in a state rehabilita-tion center, where he spends weekdays participating in rather monotonous work, pro-grammed for severely retarded patients. A typical task is the mounting of cigarette lighters on cardboard frames for display. He characteristically cannot give us any description of his place of work, the nature of his job, or the route along which he is driven each day, to and from the center.

In contrast with his inability to describe his job after 6 months of daily exposure (except for weekends), H. M. is able to draw an accurate floor plan of the bungalow in which he has lived for the past 8 years. He also seems to be familiar with the topography of the immediate neighborhood, at least within two or three blocks of his home, but is lost beyond that. His limitations in this respect are illustrated by the manner in which he attempted to guide us to his house, in June 1966. After leaving the main highway, we asked him for help in locating his house. He promptly and courteously indicated to us several turns, until we arrived at a street that he said was quite familiar to him. At the same time, he admitted that we were not at the right address. A phone call to his mother revealed that we were on the street where he lived before his operation. With her directions, we made our way to the residential area where H. M. now lives. He did not get his bearings until we were within two short blocks of the house, which he could just glimpse through the trees. (Milner et al., 1968, pp. 216–217)

A great deal of our knowledge about memory comes from case histories such as that of H. M., whose amnesia as a result of brain injury has been the subject of more than 100 scientific studies. Recently, growing numbers of studies have employed brain-imaging techniques to discover the neural bases of memory. The information obtained by studying H. M. and other people with memory problems has been enhanced through studies using nonhuman animals, which can be tested more systematically after undergoing deliberate, carefully controlled procedures that create lesions of specific dimensions in specific parts of the brain. In the following sections, we will examine what the results of these various lines of research have revealed about (1) amnesia, (2) types of memory, (3) the role of the hippocampus in memory, (4) the role of other brain regions in memory, and (5) the fascinating case of a person who could not forget.

Amnesia

When William Scoville operated on H. M. to bring the latter's epilepsy under control, he inadvertently produced one of the most widely studied cases of memory impairment in neuropsychological history. H. M.'s disorder has generated this intense interest not only because H. M. is severely **amnesic**—has lost the ability to acquire and retain memories—but also because his injury is confined to a relatively small region of the brain. The discovery that amnesia could be produced by a localized brain lesion was surprising to everyone, given what had been learned about memory before H. M.'s arrival on the scene.

Although an 1885 monograph by Hermann Ebbinghaus stands as the first psychological study of memory, the formal neuropsychological study of memory is considered to have begun about 1915, when Lashley embarked on a lifetime project to identify the neural locations of learned habits. In most of his experiments, performed on rats and monkeys, Lashley either removed parts of the animals' neocortex or severed different fiber pathways there, hoping to prevent communication between regions of the cortex. He then studied the effects of these lesions on the animals' abilities to find their way in mazes, manipulate puzzles to open doors, perform visual discriminations, and so on.

Even after hundreds of experiments, Lashley was unable to locate a center for memory. At the same time, he found that, as he damaged more and more tissue, the impairments in memory became greater and greater. In 1950, 35 years after beginning this research, Lashley concluded that "it is not possible to demonstrate the isolated localization of a memory trace anywhere in the nervous system. Limited regions may be essential for learning or retention of a particular activity, but the engram [the memory] is represented throughout the region" (Lashley, 1950).

No one could have predicted from Lashley's work that removal of any structure—let alone the small amount of tissue removed by Scoville—would result in a person's being capable of remembering things from the past but incapable of acquiring new memories. H. M.'s case seemed to demonstrate that a single structure in the temporal lobes is responsible for memory. As our story unfolds, however, we will see that H. M. and results of the studies inspired by his condition have shown that Lashley was correct after all. Many regions of the brain take part in memory.

The Medial Temporal Lobe and Amnesia

The idea that the temporal lobes have some role in memory is not based solely on H. M.'s case. The first evidence that the temporal lobes might play a role in human memory was provided by Vladimir Bekhterev in 1900. When he autopsied the brain of a patient who had shown a severe memory impairment, he discovered a bilateral softening in the region of the medial temporal cortex. Then, in the 1950s, several patients with bilateral temporal cortex damage, including H. M., were described as having severe memory defects. Milner subsequently described other such patients who are believed to have bilateral medial-temporal-lobe damage. One case, P. B., was a civil engineer whose left temporal lobe had been removed surgically for relief of seizures. Afterward, he had severe amnesia, which persisted and worsened until his death, from unrelated causes, 15 years later. At autopsy, P. B. was found to have atrophy in the right temporal lobe opposite the surgically excised left temporal lobe. Amnesia can be produced in ways other than selectively damaging the medial temporal lobe, as the following section describes.

Causes of Amnesia

We have all experienced amnesia to some degree. The most dramatic example of forgetting common to all of us is **infantile amnesia.** Although the early years of life are generally regarded as being critical in a child's development, they are not consciously remembered in adulthood. For example, we acquire many skills and much knowledge in those years but for the most part do not remember the experiences through which we acquired them. It is possible that the details of the experiences are still there but cannot be retrieved, because one memory system is used by infants and another one develops for adults. Perhaps memories seem to be lost because they are not stored in the new adult system.

Adults also forget, as witnessed by occasional reports of people who turn up far from home with no knowledge of their previous life but with skills and language intact. This form of memory loss is referred to as a **fugue state.** The word *fugue* means "flight," and one interpretation of the condition is that the person has in effect fled a previous life to form a new one. **Transient global amnesia** is another acute form of amnesia (that is, one with a sudden onset and, usually, a short course). Fisher and Adams described it as a loss of old memories and an inability to form new memories. The condition has been linked to a number of possible causes, including concussion, migraine, hypoglycemia, and epilepsy, as well as to interruption of blood flow in the posterior cerebral artery from either a transient ischemic attack or an embolism. Transient global amnesia can be a one-time event, but Markowitsch suggests that, even so, some of the memory loss can be permanent. Indeed, Mazzucchi and colleagues showed that a significant chronic memory loss is typical in transient global amnesia but is usually overlooked because of the dramatic recovery and because careful memory testing (after recovery) is seldom done.

Electroconvulsive shock therapy (ECT), used to treat depression, produces a similar memory loss. It was developed by Ladislas von Meduna in 1933 because he thought that people with epilepsy could not be schizophrenic and, therefore, that seizures could cure insanity. At first, the therapeutic seizures were induced with a drug called Metrazol, but, in 1937, Ugo Cerletti and Lucio Bini replaced Metrazol with electricity. In ECT, from 70 to 120 V of alternating current is passed briefly from one part of the brain to another through electrodes placed on the skull. Electroconvulsive shock therapy does not in fact cure schizophrenia, but it can be effective for depression. Taylor and his associates reach several conclusions about the nature of the memory loss that it often causes as a side effect: (1) even the standard number of bilateral ECT treatments (eight or nine) often induces memory changes; (2) the effects of ECT on memory appear to be cumulative, increasing with successive treatments; (3) the majority of ECT-induced cognitive and memory defects appear to be entirely reversible, with a return to pretreatment levels of function or better within 6 to 7 months; and (4) although some subtle but persistent defects may be found some months after ECT, especially in the recollection of personal or autobiographical material, (5) the persistent defects tend to be irritating rather than seriously incapacitating. Similar memory loss often follows the use of minor tranquilizers or alcohol.

Damage to restricted parts of the brain can cause amnesia that takes very curious forms. For example, there are clinical reports of people who become amnesic for the meaning of nouns but not verbs, and vice versa. There are other reports of people who become amnesic for recognizing animals but not people or who become amnesic for human faces but not for other objects.

There are also little everyday amnesias: we forget people's names or faces, where we put our keys, and so on. We also rapidly forget things that we do not need to know, such as telephone numbers that we won't need more than once. This kind of forgetting can increase with advanced age, in which case it is popularly known as "old timer's disease." Its onset is typically characterized by amnesias for the names of people we do not often meet and for items of information that we encounter in newspapers and in conversation. For some people, memory disorders of aging can become incapacitating, as happens in Alzheimer's disease, which is characterized by the extensive loss of past memories and is accompanied by the loss of neurons and by other pathologies in the cortex.

What can these examples tell us about memory? Why should infants suffer amnesia for some things and not others? Why should some people have selective loss of memories for one class of objects, whereas memories for other objects are preserved? Why should we have a greater tendency to forget people's names than to forget certain other things as we age? Is amnesia of all types due to damage to a common neural substrate? Read on for the answers to these and other questions about learning and memory.

Anterograde and Retrograde Amnesia

A careful study of H. M. and other amnesiac patients shows that his amnesia consists of two parts—anterograde amnesia and retrograde amnesia. H. M. is unable to acquire new memories, and he has also lost memories that must have been accessible to him before his surgery. H. M.'s inability to acquire new memories is called anterograde amnesia. The term *anterograde* refers to the future with respect to the time at which the patient incurred the damage to his or her brain (Figure 18.1). H. M.'s anterograde amnesia is frequently referred to as *global anterograde amnesia* because so many aspects of his ability to create new memories appear to be affected. He is impaired in spatial and topographical learning and in learning about all of the events that take place around him, including the death of his loved ones. He does not learn new words and does not learn about events and people who have made the news since his injury. As H. M. himself has said, "Every day is alone in itself, whatever enjoyment I've had, and whatever sorrow I've had."

In H. M. and many other amnesic patients, memories that were formed before the lesion or surgery are lost. This form of amnesia is called **retrograde amnesia,** to signify that it extends back in time relative to the time of brain injury. H. M.'s retrograde amnesia is obviously not as complete as his anterograde amnesia, because he remembers many things that he learned before his surgery. For example, he knows who he is; he can read, write, and speak; and he retains most of the skills that he acquired before his surgery. Typically, presurgical memory is much better for events that have taken place earlier in life than for events that have taken place more recently. H. M. was able to return to the house where he had lived before his surgery, and he remembered that he had possession of his father's guns.

When the severity of retrograde amnesia varies, depending on how old memories are, it is said to be time dependent. Head injuries commonly produce **time-dependent amnesia,** with the severity of the injury determining how far back in time the amnesia extends. For example, after a head injury, there is typically a transient loss of consciousness followed by a short period of

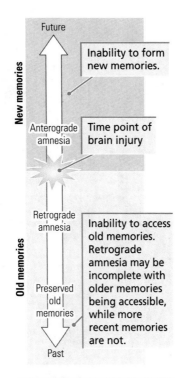

Figure 18.1 Possible consequences of brain injury on old and new memories. Note that retrograde amnesia may be incomplete, with older memories being more preserved than newer memories.

confusion and retrograde amnesia. The retrograde extent of the amnesia (the period of personal history that it covers, extending from the present to the farther past) generally shrinks with the passage of time, often leaving a residual amnesia of only a few seconds to a minute for events immediately preceding the injury. The duration of such posttraumatic amnesias can vary, however. In one series of patients with severe head injuries, Whitty and Zangwill found that 10% had durations of less than 1 week, 30% had durations of 2 to 3 weeks, and the remaining 60% had durations of more than 3 weeks. Sometimes certain isolated events, such as the visit of a relative or some unusual occurrence, are retained as "islands of memory" during this amnesic period.

Two Kinds of Memory

Schacter described the 1980s as the beginning of the modern memory revolution because of the realization during that decade that memory comes in different forms. Again, studies of H. M. contributed to this discovery, as did the development of new approaches to the investigation of the neural basis of memory. These approaches include new theoretical models, an increasing interest in brain function on the part of cognitive psychologists (those who study how we "think"), and the use of brain-imaging techniques to do research into all these areas. We begin our discussion of the different forms of memory with a description of the two broadest categories to which they may be assigned: explicit and implicit memory.

Explicit memory is the conscious, intentional recollection of previous experiences. You can probably describe what you had for breakfast this morning, how you traveled to school, and to whom you have spoken since you woke up, all explicit memories. You can also describe events that have taken place in the past, and you know the identity of many local or world leaders, as well as many famous personalities. These memories, too, are explicit. **Implicit memory** is an unconscious, nonintentional form of memory. Your ability to use language and to perform motor skills such as riding a bicycle or playing a sport are examples of implicit memory. Studies of H. M., whose explicit memory is extremely impaired while his implicit memory is largely intact, played an important role in the discovery that these two forms of memory are separate. This dissociation between explicit and implicit memory implies that implicit memory is stored independently of the temporal lobe, the brain region that in H. M. had been surgically removed. In the following description of implicit and explicit memory, we will demonstrate that the implicit memory systems of H. M. and other amnesiacs are remarkably intact.

Implicit and Explicit Memory

Although H. M. exhibits severe memory defects on many kinds of tests, he is found to be surprisingly competent at some kinds of learning. Remember that he was put to work making cigarette-lighter displays, and he was able to learn to do it. In one experiment, Milner trained H. M. on a mirror-drawing task that required drawing a third outline between the double outline of a star while looking only at the reflection of the star and his pencil in a mirror (Figure 18.2). This task is difficult at first even for normal subjects, but they improve with practice. H. M., too, had a normal learning curve on this task. Although he did not remember having performed the task previously, his skill improved each time he performed it in a series of days. Subsequently, Corkin trained H. M. on a variety of manual tracking and coordination tasks. Although his initial performances tended to be inferior to those of control subjects, he showed nearly normal improvement from session to session.

For a time, motor learning was considered a curious exception to the deficits that result from temporal-lobe damage but, in the 1980s, several lines of investigation indicated that other kinds of memory also survive in H. M. and other patients with amnesia. A phenomenon known as priming reveals the sparing of many kinds of implicit memory in amnesic subjects, and so we will describe priming and give examples of how it can be demonstrated.

Imagine a task in which a person is first given a list of words to read and is then given a list containing the beginnings of words and is asked to complete each of them with the first word that comes to mind. If one of the incomplete words is TAB, the person might complete it as "table," "tablet," "tabby," "tabulation," or something similar. If one of the words on the first list is "table," however, a control subject is more likely to complete TAB as "table" than as any other possibility, showing that he or she remembers the word from the previous list. Researchers would say that the first list "primed" the subject to give a certain response later on, which is why such tasks are referred to as priming tasks and the phenomenon is referred to as **priming**.

A property of priming is that the remembered item is remembered best in the form in which it was originally encountered. If a test list is printed in capital letters, then a priming list printed in capital letters produces better performance than does a priming list printed in lowercase letters. If a priming list is given in an auditory mode, then an auditory cue produces better performance than does a visual cue. Marsolek and coworkers further elaborated this finding by demonstrating evidence for simultaneous but different encoding in each hemisphere. In their experiment, a subject was given a priming list and later asked to complete three-letter stems with the first word that came to mind. On the completion test, the stems were presented to either the left or the right hemisphere by brief exposure of the three-letter stem to one visual hemifield or the other. Performance was lower when the case of the stem was changed in presentations to the right hemisphere (for example, when TAB was changed to tab), but changing the case of the stem in presentations to the left hemisphere did not reduce performance. Thus, the encoding in each hemisphere clearly was simultaneous but different. The authors of this study suggested that the left hemisphere encodes abstract word-form representations that do not

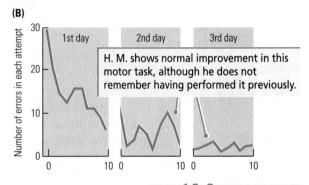

(A)

H. M.'s task is to trace between the two outlines of the star while looking only at his hand in a mirror.

Crossing a line constitutes an error.

(B)

H. M. shows normal improvement in this motor task, although he does not remember having performed it previously.

Figure 18.2 A test of motor memory. (A) The mirror drawing task. (B) The performance of the patient H. M. over three training sessions.

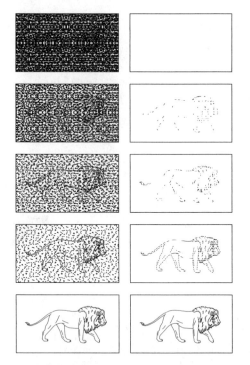

Figure 18.3 The Gollin test. Subjects are shown a series of drawings in sequence, from least to most clear, and asked to identify the object depicted. It is impossible to identify the object from the first sketch, and most people must see several of the panels before they can identify it correctly. On a retention test some time later, however, subjects identify the image sooner than they did on the first test, indicating some form of memory for the image. Amnesic subjects also show improvement on this test, even though they do not recall having done the test before.

preserve specific features of the letters, whereas the right hemisphere encodes perceptually specific letterforms. This division of labor can be thought of as representing phoneme (language) in contrast with grapheme (spatial) functions of the hemispheres.

Priming can also be demonstrated in the following way. Subjects are shown an incomplete sketch and asked what it is. If they fail to identify the sketch, they are shown another sketch that is slightly more complete. This process continues until they eventually recognize the picture. When control subjects and amnesiacs are shown the same sketch at a later date, both groups will identify the sketch at an earlier stage than was possible for them the first time. Thus, control and amnesic subjects will indicate through their performance that they remember the previous experience of seeing the lion in Figure 18.3 completed, even though the amnesic subjects cannot consciously recall ever having been shown the sketches before.

An important feature of a priming task is that amnesic subjects perform as well on it as control subjects do, indicating through their performance that they, too, remember what was on the previous study list even though they report no conscious recollection of ever having seen the list. That H. M., like many other amnesic patients, demonstrates the effects of priming in such tasks but has no conscious recall of having encountered the tasks before is taken as one kind of evidence that implicit and explicit memory are different.

The independence of implicit and explicit memory can also be demonstrated in other ways, especially in normal control subjects. If such subjects are asked to think about the meaning of a word or the shape of the word, their explicit recall of the word is greatly improved. Their scores on word completion, however, which taps implicit memory, are not affected by this manipulation. This phenomenon is known as the **depth-of-processing effect.** On the other hand, if subjects are shown a word in one modality (for example, if they hear the word) and are tested for recall in another modality (say, they must write the word or identify it by reading), their score on a word-completion test is greatly reduced, but their explicit recall is little affected. This phenomenon is called a **study-test modality shift.**

The Neural Basis of Explicit Memory

An important difference between explicit and implicit memory is that they are housed in different neural structures, which may in turn explain some of the differences in the way in which the information is processed. Implicit information is encoded in very much the same way as it is received. This type of processing is data-driven, or "bottom-up," processing. It is dependent simply on receiving the sensory information and does not require any manipulation of the information content by higher-level cortical processes. Explicit memory, on the other hand, depends on conceptually driven, or "top-down," processing, in which a subject reorganizes the data to store it. The later recall of information is thus greatly influenced by the way in which the information was originally processed. Because a person has a relatively passive role in encoding implicit

(A)

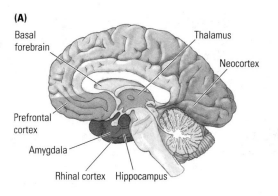

(B)

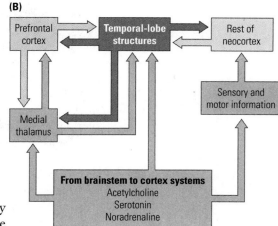

memory, he or she may have difficulty recalling the memory voluntarily but will recall it easily when primed by one of the features of the original stimulus. In contrast, because a person plays an active role in processing explicit information, the internal cues that he or she used in processing it can also be used to initiate spontaneous recall.

On the basis of animal and human studies, Petri and Mishkin proposed different neural circuits for explicit and implicit memory. Figure 18.4 illustrates the neural structures that they assign to explicit memory. Most are in the temporal lobe or closely related to it, such as the amygdala, the hippocampus, the rhinal cortexes in the temporal lobe, and the prefrontal cortex. Nuclei in the thalamus also are included, inasmuch as many connections between the prefrontal cortex and temporal cortex are made through the thalamus. The regions that make up the explicit memory circuit receive input from the neocortex and from brainstem systems, including acetylcholine, serotonin, and noradrenaline systems.

Figure 18.4 A neural circuit proposed for explicit memory. (A) The general anatomical areas of explicit memory. (B) A circuit diagram showing the flow of information through the circuits. Information flow begins with inputs from the sensory and motor systems, which themselves are not considered part of the circuit.

The Neural Basis of Implicit Memory

It seems reasonable to expect that, if the temporal-lobe circuitry has a role in explicit memory, other brain structures must take part in implicit memory. Petri and Mishkin suggested a brain circuit for implicit memory as well (Figure 18.5). The key structures in this proposed circuit are the neocortex and basal ganglia (the caudate nucleus and putamen). The basal ganglia receive projections from all regions of the neocortex and send projections through the globus pallidus and ventral thalamus to the premotor cortex. The basal ganglia also receive projections from cells in the substantia nigra.

Figure 18.5 A neural circuit proposed for implicit memory. (A) The general anatomical areas of implicit memory. (B) A circuit diagram showing the flow of information through the circuits. Information flow begins with inputs from the sensory and motor systems, which themselves are not considered part of the circuit.

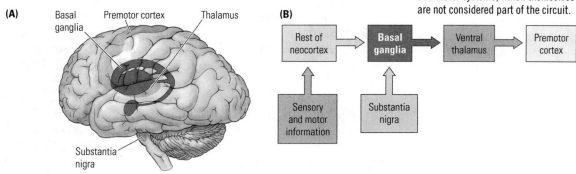

The projections to the basal ganglia from the substantia nigra contain the neurotransmitter dopamine. The fact that dopamine appears to be necessary for circuits in the basal ganglia to function suggests that it may have an indirect role in memory formation, and this role has been confirmed by Hay and coworkers. The case of J. K. is illustrative.

J. K. was born on 28 June 1914. He was above average in intelligence and worked as a petroleum engineer for 45 years. In his mid-70s, he began to show symptoms of Parkinson's disease (in which the projections from the dopaminergic cells of the brainstem to the basal ganglia die), and, at about age 78, he started to have memory difficulties. Curiously, J. K.'s memory disturbance seemed primarily to affect tasks that he had done all his life. On one occasion, he stood at the door of his bedroom frustrated by his inability to recall how to turn on the lights. He remarked, "I must be crazy. I've done this all my life, and now I can't remember how to do it!" On another occasion, he was seen trying to turn the radio off with the remote control for the television set. This time he explained, "I don't recall how to turn off the radio; so I thought I would try this thing!" J. K. clearly had a deficit in implicit memory. In contrast, he was aware of current events and new experiences and could recall explicit details about them as well as most men his age are able to. Once when we visited him, which is something that we seldom did together, one of us entered the room first and J. K. immediately asked where the other was, even though 2 weeks had elapsed since he had been told that both of us would be coming to visit.

Evidence from other clinical and experimental studies supports a formative role for the basal ganglia circuitry in implicit memory. In a study of patients with **Huntington's chorea,** a disorder characterized by the degeneration of cells in the basal ganglia, Martone and her colleagues demonstrated impairments in the mirror-drawing task, on which patients with temporal-lobe lesions are unimpaired. Conversely, the patients with Huntington's chorea were unimpaired on a verbal-recognition task. Grafton and coworkers made PET scans of regional cerebral blood flow in normal subjects as the subjects learned to perform a pursuit motor task. In this task, a subject attempts to keep a stylus in a particular location on a turning disc that is about the size of a longplaying phonograph record. The task draws on skills that are very much like the skills needed in mirror drawing. The researchers found that performance of this motor task was associated with increases in regional cerebral blood flow in the motor cortex, basal ganglia, and cerebellum and that acquisition of the skill was associated with a subset of these structures, including the primary motor cortex, the supplementary motor cortex, and the pulvinar nucleus of the thalamus.

A more dramatic demonstration of the role of the motor cortex in implicit learning comes from a study by Pascual-Leone and colleagues. In this study, subjects were required to press one of four numbered buttons by using a correspondingly numbered finger in response to numbered cues provided on a television monitor; for example, when number 1 appears on the screen, push button 1 with finger 1. The measure of learning was the decrease in reaction time between the appearance of the cue and the pushing of the button. The subjects were tested with sequences of 12 cues. For the control group, there was no order to the sequences, but the sequence presented to the brain-damaged group was repeated so that, after they learned the pattern, they could anticipate the cue provided by the monitor and so respond very quickly. The implicit-memory component of this task was the improvement in reaction time that occurred with practice, whereas the explicit-memory component was the subjects' recognition of the sequence so that they could generate responses without needing the cues. Transcranial magnetic stimulation was used to map the motor-cortex area representing the limb making the responses. In this technique, the motor cortex is stimulated through coils placed on the skull while muscle activity in the limb is recorded simultaneously. Thus, the researchers can discover which parts of the cortical area are sending commands to the muscles at various times in the course of learning. They found that the cortical maps of the muscles participating in the task became progressively larger as the task was mastered. That is, it appeared as if the area of the cortex controlling the limb increased in size as learning took place. When the subjects knew the sequence of the stimuli and thus had explicit knowledge of the task, however, the area of the motor cortex active during performance of the task returned to its baseline dimensions. In summary, the process of acquiring implicit knowledge required a reorganization of the motor cortex that was not required for explicit-memory performance.

The motor regions of the cortex also receive projections through the thalamus from the cerebellum. Thompson reviews many lines of evidence that the cerebellum occupies an important position in the brain circuits taking part in motor learning. He and his coworkers suggested, for example, that the cerebellum plays an important role in a form of learning called classical conditioning. In their model, a puff of air is administered to the eyelid of a rabbit, paired with a stimulus such as a tone. Eventually, the rabbit becomes "conditioned" to blink in expectation of the air puff whenever the tone is sounded. Lesions to pathways from the cerebellum abolish this response, known as a "conditioned response," but do not stop the rabbit from blinking in response to an actual air puff, the "unconditioned response." The researchers further demonstrated the importance of the cerebellum in learning by showing that the neocortex is not necessary for the development of a conditioned response. On the basis of such experiments, Thompson suggested that the cerebellum takes part in learning discrete, adaptive, behavioral responses to noxious events.

In conclusion, whereas it was initially thought that H. M. and other amnesiacs displayed a loss of all memory, research now shows that implicit memory is usually spared. Research also shows that there are likely many different kinds of implicit memory, such as motor memory, priming, and classical conditioning, all of which are spared. It is noteworthy that H. M.'s ability to demonstrate priming in tasks with words depends on his knowing the meaning of the words. If words are employed that came into use after his surgery, he is impaired. Thus, priming depends on the activation of existing memory.

Two Kinds of Explicit Memory

In the preceding section, we defined two subdivisions of memory, explicit and implicit. We also described a number of different kinds of implicit memory. The results of studies by Tulving suggest that explicit memory can itself be subdivided into two forms: episodic and semantic. We will describe each of them in turn.

Episodic Memory

Episodic memory consists of singular events that a person recalls. This form of memory is also referred to as *autobiographical memory*. Tulving proposes that episodic memory is a neurocognitive (that is, a thinking) system uniquely different from other memory systems that enable human beings to remember past personal experiences. It is memory of life experiences centered on the person himself or herself. The following excerpt illustrates a simple test for the presence of autobiographical memory. In reading through the example, note that the neuropsychologist is persistent in trying to determine whether the subject, G. O., can recall a single event or experience. Had he not been so persistent, G. O.'s impairment in episodic memory might well have been missed.

Do you have a memory of when you had to speak in public?

Well yes, I'm a call centre trainer with Modern Phone Systems; so I did a lot of speaking because I did a lot, a lot of training all across Canada. I also went to parts of the States.

Do you remember one time that you were speaking? Can you tell us about one incident?

Oh yes! Well I trained thousands and thousands of clients on a wide variety of topics including customer service, inbound and outbound telemarketing. Handling difficult customers.

Do you remember one training session that you gave? Something that may have happened, a specific incident?

Well for example I always recommended that people take customer-service first. And I always had people come up with four things about themselves, three that were true and one that was false. Not necessarily in that order.

But this was something ongoing, so every training session you would tell people this, right?

Yes.

So what we're looking for is one incident or one time that you gave a training session or any other speeches that you want to tell us about. A specific incident.

Oh well I customized a lot of material for many, many companies. And I also did lots of training at the home office.

OK, so what we're asking is do you remember one time that you gave a talk?

Oh! yes I do.

One specific time not over a series of times, one time, can you tell us about that?

Oh sure yes, it was at the home office and yes, many many people were there.

One occasion. When did that take place?

When? Well I left Modern voluntarily in 1990.

But this one occasion when did it take place?

Ummm, well I started in the Modern home office.

I'm getting the impression that you have a really good memory for all the training that you've done but you don't seem to be able to come up with a specific talk that maybe stands out in your mind for any reason? Would you agree with that?

Oh yes well I always trained customer service.

So there was no talk that maybe something went wrong or something strange happened?

No, No I was a very good trainer. (Levine, 2000)

According to Tulving, episodic memory requires three elements: (1) a sense of subjective time; (2) autonoetic awareness, the ability to be aware of subjective time; and (3) a "self" that can travel in subjective time. To illustrate his idea, Tulving uses the metaphor of time travel, stating that everything in nature travels forward in time, but humans can also travel backward in time, because of their episodic memory, which he views as uniquely human. Tulving says that nonhuman animals are as capable as humans at producing their own kind, that they have minds and are conscious of their world, and that they rely on learning and memory to acquire life skills, but he believes they do *not* have the ability to travel back in time in their own minds and revisit their past experiences in the way that humans can. He also believes that episodic memory also depends on maturation in humans and so will not be found in babies and young children. Tulving's patient K. C. further illustrates the effects of the loss of episodic memory.

K. C. was born in 1951. At the age of 30 he suffered a serious closed-head injury in a motorcycle accident, with extensive brain lesions in multiple cortical and subcortical brain regions, including medial temporal lobes, and consequent severe amnesia. Nevertheless, most of K. C.'s cognitive capabilities are intact and indistinguishable from those of many healthy adults. His intelligence and language are normal; he has no problems with reading or writing; his ability to concentrate and to maintain focused attention are normal; his thought processes are clear; he can play the organ, chess, and various card games; his ability to visualize things mentally is intact; and his performance on short-term-memory tasks is normal. He knows many objective facts concerning his own life, such as his date of birth, the address of his home for the first 9 years of his life, the names of some of the schools he attended, the make and color of the car he once owned, and the fact that his parents owned and still own a summer cottage. He knows the location of the cottage and can easily find it on a map. He knows the distance from his home to the cottage and how long it takes to drive there in weekend traffic. He also knows that he has spent a lot of time there. His knowledge of mathematics, history, geography, and other "school subjects," as well as his general knowledge of the world, is not greatly different from that of others at his educational level.

Along with all these normal abilities, K. C. has dense amnesia for personal experiences. Thus, he cannot recollect any personally experienced events, whether one-time happenings or repeating occurrences. This inability to remember any episodes or situations in which he was present covers his whole life, from birth to the present, although he does retain immediate experiences for a minute or two. K. C. has no particular difficulty understanding and discussing either himself or physical time. He knows many facts about himself, and he knows what most other people know about physical time, its units, its structure, and its measurement by clocks and calendars. Nevertheless, he cannot "time travel," either to the past or future. He cannot say what he is going to be doing later today, tomorrow, or at any time in the rest of his life. In short, he cannot imagine his future any more than he can remember his past.

Semantic Memory

Knowledge about the world—all knowledge that is not autobiographical—is referred to by Tulving as **semantic memory** and includes knowledge of historical events and of historical and literary figures. It includes the ability to recognize family, friends, and acquaintances. It also includes information learned in school, such as specialized vocabularies and reading, writing, and mathematics. Tulving's patient K. C. has retained his semantic memory. He recalls the information that he learned in school; he remembers that his parents had a cabin; and he knows where it is. He also remembers the games that he learned before his injury, and he can still play them well.

Because K. C. has diffuse damage, it is difficult to say which constellation of injuries accounts for his asymmetric retrograde amnesia, in which episodic memory is lost and semantic memory retained. Levine and his coworkers describe similar symptoms for M. L., whose lesion has been located through MRI, however. Densely amnesic for episodic experiences predating his injury, M. L shows damage to the right ventral frontal cortex and underlying white matter, including the uncinate fasciculus, a band of fibers that connects the temporal lobe and ventral frontal cortex (Figure 18.6). His impairment in episodic memory is therefore thought to be due to a disconnection between the right frontal lobe and the temporal lobe. Levine and Tulving also suggest that semantic memory may depend on the left hemisphere and thus on undisrupted uncinate connections between the left ventral frontal cortex and the right temporal lobe.

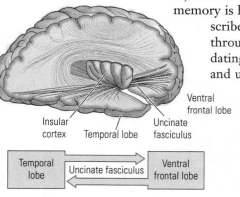

Figure 18.6 Brain regions of episodic memory. The ventral frontal lobe and the temporal lobe are reciprocally connected by the uncinate fasciculus.

Insular cortex   Temporal lobe   Uncinate fasciculus

Ventral frontal lobe

Temporal lobe → Uncinate fasciculus → Ventral frontal lobe

The Role of the Hippocampus in Memory

Even though H. M.'s surgery consisted of removal of the medial temporal lobe, Scoville and Milner, in their original paper, "Loss of recent memory after bilateral hippocampal lesions," implied that the loss of the hippocampus, specifically, was responsible for his memory deficits. Through the years, however, a number of lines of evidence indicate that it is incorrect to envision a one-to-one relation between the hippocampus and memory. First, H. M.'s surgery was not a selective lesion of the hippocampus but a removal of most of the medial temporal lobe. The hippocampus is but one of a number of structures in the medial temporal lobe; the amygdala and perirhinal cortex are others, and they, too, were damaged to some extent in H. M. and may be implicated in his memory impairment. Researchers have attempted to model H. M.'s memory impairment in rats and monkeys and have demonstrated that damage to the perirhinal cortex and amygdala, for example, can result in memory impairment (see section on multiple memory systems). Furthermore, Corkin and colleagues used MRI to reexamine H. M.'s lesion and found that his hippocampal lesion was not complete. In fact, about 40% of his hippocampus was spared (see the Snapshot on page 462). Taken together, these lines of evidence argue against the conclusion that H. M.'s memory impairment stems solely or primarily from damage to his hippocampus. Nevertheless, clinical and experimental research continues to implicate the hippocampus in some kind of memory. We will describe some of the evidence after first providing a description of hippocampus anatomy.

Anatomy of the Hippocampus

In the 1960s, anatomist H. Chandler Elliott described the hippocampus as "quite archaic and vestigial, possibly concerned with primitive feeding reflexes no longer emergent in man." Nevertheless, this structure, small in comparison with the rest of the human forebrain, now plays a dominant role in the discussion of memory.

The hippocampus has a tubelike appearance. It extends in a curve from the lateral neocortex of the medial temporal lobe toward the midline of the brain (Figure 18.7). *Hippocampus* means "seahorse," and the hippocampus derives its name from its curved seahorselike shape. It consists of two gyri, **Ammon's horn** (after a name for the horn of plenty, the mythological goat's horn from which fruits and vegetables flow endlessly) and the **dentate gyrus** (from the

Figure 18.7 The hippocampal formation. (A) The hippocampus lies within the temporal lobe. It is connected to temporal cortical structures by the perforant path and to the brainstem mammillary bodies, nucleus accumbens, and anterior thalamus by the fimbria/fornix. (B) A cross section through the hippocampus showing the location of Ammon's horn, with its pyramidal cells (CA1 through CA4), and the dentate gyrus. (C) A circuit diagram showing that that neocortical structures project to the hippocampus through the entorhinal cortex, which receives feedback from the subiculum.

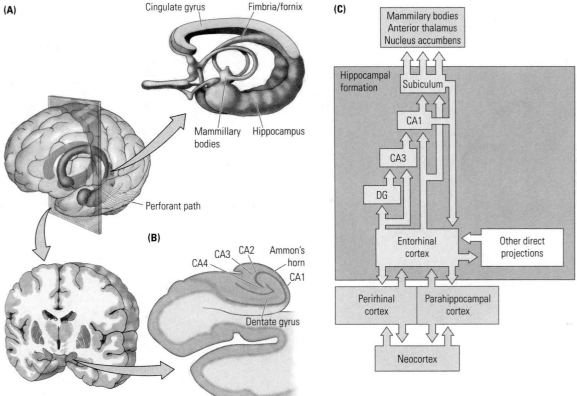

S N A P S H O T

Imaging H. M.'s Brain

Patient H. M. received elective surgery for the relief of epilepsy in 1953, when he was 27 years old. His neurosurgeon, William Scoville, estimated that the temporal-lobe resection removed 8 cm of medial-temporal-lobe tissue, including the temporal pole, amygdaloid complex, and approximately two-thirds of the rostral caudal extent of the intraventricular part of the hippocampal formation. Since then, H. M. has been studied by nearly 100 investigators and has contributed to many major lines of investigation into the neural basis of memory.

When H. M. was 66 and 67 years old, Corkin and her colleagues reexamined the extent of his temporal-lobe removal by using magnetic resonance imaging (MRI). They found that the resection was actually smaller than reported by Scoville. Specifically, it spared a part of the posterior hippocampus. They also found that the resection removed most of the entorhinal cortex, a major route of communication between the temporal lobe and the hippocampus.

The MRI analysis of H. M.'s brain also disproved one of the theories that had been advanced to explain H. M.'s amnesia. In 1978, Horel proposed that the surgery had cut the temporal stem connecting H. M.'s temporal lobe to much of the rest of his brain and that this temporal-stem lesion accounted for H. M.'s symptoms. Indeed, Horel demonstrated in primates that damage to the temporal stem could result in memory impairment. But the MRI scan of H. M.'s brain indicates that H. M.'s temporal stem is intact, confirming that H. M.'s amnesia arises instead from damage to his entorhinal cortex and hippocampus.

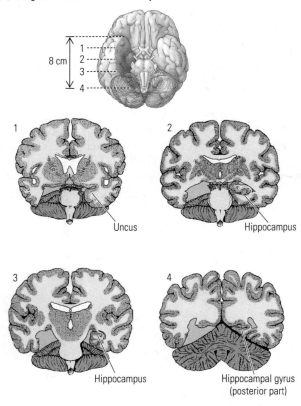

(A) Surgeon's 1953 estimate of temporal lobe ablation

(A) The surgeon's estimate of H. M.'s medial-temporal-lobe resection. The top drawing is a ventral view of a human brain showing the predicted rostrocaudal extent of the removal. Drawings 1 through 4 are of coronal sections, arranged from rostral (1) to caudal (4), showing the predicted extent of the surgery. Note that, although the lesion was made bilaterally, the right side is shown intact to illustrate structures that were removed. (After Scoville and Milner, 1957.)

(B) Amended 1997 version based on MRI images

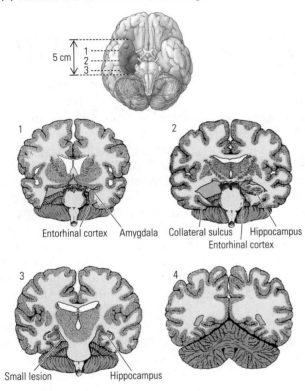

Corkin also studied H. M.'s residual memory abilities, reporting, for example, that, if H. M. is asked to examine novel pictures for 20 seconds, he subsequently shows normal recognition of the pictures as long as 6 months later. Functional MRI (fMRI) imaging of H. M.'s brain during novel picture viewing indicated activation in his caudal parahippocampal gyrus, suggesting that a remaining part of his medial temporal lobe can acquire memory of pictures. According to Corkin, this finding explains the answer to the most frequently asked question concerning H. M.'s amnesia: "What does he see when he looks in the mirror?" H. M.'s answer is, "Not a young man." Corkin explains that, because of the repeated exposure to his face year after year, H. M. is familiar with his face, and this familiarity may be supported through his intact parahippocampal gyrus.

(C. Corkin, D. G. Amaral, A. G. Gonzalez, K. A. Johnson, and B. T. Hyman. H. M.'s medial temporal lobe lesion: Findings from magnetic resonance imaging. *Journal of Neuroscience* 17:3964–3979, 1997.
Corkin, S. What's new with the amnesic patient H. M.? *Nature Reviews Neuroscience* 3:153–160, 2002.
J. A. Horel. The neuroanatomy of amnesia: A critique of the hippocampal memory hypothesis. *Brain* 101:403–445, 1978.)

(B) An amended version of the original diagram indicating the extent of the removal based on the MRI studies reported here. The rostrocaudal extent of the lesion is 5 cm rather than 8 cm, and the lesion does not extend as far laterally as was initially believed. (After Corkin et al., 1997.)

Latin *dentate*, meaning "tooth," because its main cell layer has a sharp bend like the edge of a tooth). If you imagine cutting a tube lengthwise and placing one half on top of the other so that their edges overlap (like two interlocking Cs), the upper half would represent Ammon's horn and the lower one the dentate gyrus (which can be pictured as flowing out of Ammon's horn). Each of these two gyri contains a distinctive type of cell. The cells of Ammon's horn are pyramidal cells, and the cells of the dentate gyrus are stellate (star-shaped) cells called **granule cells.** The pyramidal cells of Ammon's horn are divided into four groups: CA1, CA2, CA3, and CA4 (CA standing for *Cornu Ammonis*, the Latin name for Ammon's horn). For structural and functional reasons, the cells of Ammon's horn and the dentate gyrus are differentially sensitive to anoxia (lack of oxygen) and many toxins. For example, with mild anoxia, CA1 cells are the ones most likely to die; and, with more-severe anoxia, other CA cells and finally the dentate gyrus cells will die.

The hippocampus is reciprocally connected to the rest of the brain through two major pathways. One pathway, called the **perforant path** (because it perforates the hippocampus), connects the hippocampus to the posterior neocortex. The other, called the **fimbria-fornix** ("arch-fringe," because it arches along the edge of the hippocampus), connects the hippocampus to the thalamus and frontal cortex, the basal ganglia, and the hypothalamus. Through its connection to these two pathways, the hippocampus can be envisioned as a way station between the posterior neocortex on one end of the journey and the frontal cortex, basal ganglia, and brainstem on the other. Within the hippocampus, input from the neocortex goes to the dentate gyrus, and the dentate gyrus projects to Ammon's horn. Thus the granule cells are the "sensory" cells of the hippocampus, and the pyramidal cells are its "motor" cells. The CA1 cells project to another part of the temporal lobe called the subiculum, and the subicular cells project back to the temporal cortex and forward to the thalamus and brainstem.

Many forms of brain injury may damage not only Ammon's horn or the dentate gyrus but also the pathways that connect the hippocampus to the rest of the brain, thereby making it difficult for neuropsychologists to determine whether a behavioral impairment stems from damage to the hippocampus itself, damage to its pathways, or damage to its connecting structures. The connections between the dentate gyrus and Ammon's horn are extensive, such that almost every granule cell is connected to every pyramidal cell. This interconnectivity suggests that, after partial damage, the remaining parts may retain some of the functions of the intact structure.

Case Histories of Hippocampal Function

A number of research groups have described other amnesic patients whose symptoms are somewhat like those of H. M. Described here are the findings of three of these groups.

1. Squire and his colleagues report the results of various case studies that, taken together, suggest that the retrograde amnesia of such patients is time dependent and that larger lesions produce retrograde amnesia that goes back farther in time. They also suggest that memories formed early in

life—say, in the first 20 years or so—may be spared by hippocampal lesions but may be lost if the lesions extend into structures surrounding the hippocampus. Two of their patients, R. B. and D. G., whose lesions are limited to the CA1 region of the hippocampus, have a limited retrograde amnesia covering perhaps 1 or 2 years. Patients L. M. and W. H. have more extensive, but still incomplete, hippocampal damage, and their retrograde amnesia covers from 15 to 25 years. Patient E. P., with complete hippocampal damage plus some damage to surrounding structures, has retrograde amnesia covering from 40 to 50 years. All of these patients have access to memories from early life, as does H. M., who underwent surgery at age 27. Squire and colleagues concluded that the hippocampus itself is important for memory for a relatively short period of time after learning and that adjacent cortexes are responsible for memory that extends farther back in time. Additionally, they proposed that the earliest memories can be accessed directly in the neocortex and so survive temporal-lobe lesions.

2. Cipolottie and her colleagues report that a patient whom they have studied, V. C., whose hippocampus was entirely removed, though surrounding structures were undamaged, has retrograde amnesia that covers his entire life before the lesion was incurred. V. C. was born in 1926. Between 1992 and 1993, he suffered migraines and heart arrhythmia that left him by the age of 67 with profound amnesia. He had been a chief engineer on large ships, and before his amnesia had been described as being extremely intelligent with a good memory. In a test of memory for public events, the *"dead or alive test,"* V. C. was asked to indicate whether a famous person was dead or alive, whether that person had been killed or had died of natural causes, and when the person died by choosing from eight time periods between 1950 and 1989. V. C. was severely impaired relative to control subjects. His performance was equally impaired on a similar test of historic events, consisting of 15 questions for each of eight time periods between 1960 and 1998. On a test of well-known faces, consisting of 145 photographs divided into four 10-year periods between 1960 and 1998, V. C.'s score was extremely low. In all of these tests, his performance was slightly better when he was allowed to choose the answer from a number of alternatives, but it was still worse than that of control subjects. To assess whether V. C. had implicit memory, Cipolottie and her colleagues presented him with triplets of names, one of which was that of a famous person and two that were distractors, and asked him to choose or guess the famous name. His performance on this test was comparable to that of the control subjects. When given a vocabulary test for the period before his amnesia, he again performed at control levels. To assess V. C.'s autobiographical memory, the researchers asked him pointed questions about himself and events in his childhood, early adult life, and recent life. He was almost completely unable to respond to such autobiographical requests as "Describe an incident that occurred in the period when you were attending elementary school" for any time period. His performance was better on factual questions, such as "What was your address when you were attending high school?" But even that ability was impaired relative to

that of control subjects. In short, V. C.'s case suggests that the complete loss of the hippocampus results in complete retrograde and anterograde amnesia for explicit information for all age periods of life.

3. The symptoms seen in adult cases of hippocampal damage led some researchers to hypothesize that, if such damage occurred in infancy, the persons would be described not as amnesic but as severely retarded. That is, they would be unable to speak, being unable to learn new words; be unable to socialize, being unable to recognize other people; and be unable to develop problem-solving abilities, being unable to remember solutions to problems. Vargha-Khadem and her colleagues report on three cases in which hippocampal damage was incurred early in life: for one subject just after birth, for another at 4 years of age, and for the third at 9 years of age. None of these people can reliably find his or her way in familiar surroundings, remember where objects and belongings are usually located, or remember where the objects were last placed. None is well oriented in date and time, and all must frequently be reminded of regularly scheduled appointments and events, such as particular classes or extracurricular activities. None can provide a reliable account of the day's activities or reliably remember telephone conversations or messages, stories, television programs, visitors, holidays, and so on. According to all three sets of parents, these everyday memory losses are so disabling that none of the affected persons can be left alone, much less lead lives commensurate with their ages or social environments. They are not retarded, however. All have fared very well in mainstream educational settings. They are competent in speech and language, have learned to read, and can write and spell. When tested for factual knowledge, they score in the average range. When tested for their memory of faces and objects, they also score in the average range, although they are impaired on tasks requiring object–place associations and face–voice associations.

What Do We Learn about Explicit Memory from Hippocampal Patients?

The difficulty in understanding the contributions of the hippocampus to memory is due in part to the varying sizes of the lesions that have been studied, differences in the way that the lesions occurred, differences in the ages of the patients, and differences in testing methods. For example, H. M. was not originally described as having extensive retrograde amnesia, but reexamination of his autobiographical knowledge by Corkin revealed that he is unable to provide specific memories, even from as far back in his past as his childhood. In the three studies just described, the extent of amnesia was compared with the extent of damage to the hippocampus; but amnesia can also develop if pathways leading into the hippocampus are damaged, although the hippocampus remains intact. Gaffan and Gaffan described a series of patients who sustained damage to the fimbria-fornix. These patients apparently display retrograde and anterograde amnesia that is similar to that seen in patients with temporal-lobe damage, although perhaps not as extensive. Damage to the temporal stem, a pathway that connects the temporal lobe to the frontal lobe, also may contribute to amnesia. Finally, severing of the reciprocal connections between the posterior neocortex and the temporal lobe may produce amnesia. We might well ask whether there is anything that we *can* conclude with certainty from the results of studies on patients with amnesia. The answer is yes.

Even though the specific nature of the contribution of the hippocampus to memory is debatable, the studies of hippocampal patients allow important conclusions to be drawn. For one thing, the neural mechanisms underlying anterograde and retrograde amnesias do appear to be at least partly different in that anterograde deficits in memory are more severe than retrograde deficits. For another thing, memories for autobiographical material appear to be somewhat different from memories for other factual material (episodic memories versus semantic memories) in that some subjects are more impaired on episodic memory than on semantic memory. There is also some evidence that memories of early life may be different from those of later life in that many subjects with retrograde amnesia retain their early memories. Furthermore, semantic memory appears to have been spared in subjects who suffered early lesions relative to subjects who suffered lesions later in life. Lastly, with practice, even adult amnesic patients may learn. Recall that H. M. can draw the floor plan of a house into which he moved after incurring his lesion and in which he has lived for 8 years. Corkin postulates that he acquired this knowledge through the repetition of moving about the house. In addition, the results of studies of hippocampal function have led to a number of lines of inquiry into how memories are stored.

Memory Storage and the Hippocampus

There are at least four theories of the role of the hippocampus in memory. One theory describes the hippocampus as a storage site for memory. Most researchers doubt this theory, however, because it is difficult to reconcile the time-dependent effects of retrograde amnesia with a storage theory. If memories were stored there, presumably remote memories should be as likely to be lost as recent memories. A second theory says that the role of the hippocampus is to **consolidate** new memories, the process by which the memories are made permanent. When consolidation has been completed, the memories are stored somewhere else. According to this notion, memories are held in the hippocampus for a period of time, undergoing consolidation before transfer to the neocortex. The consolidation theory explains why older memories tend to be preserved in cases of hippocampal damage (they have been transferred elsewhere for storage), whereas more-recent memories are likely to be lost (they are still in the hippocampus). A difficulty with the consolidation theory is that retrograde amnesia sometimes extends back for decades, which, according to the theory, means that the hippocampus would have to hold the memories for storage for an exceedingly long time and the consolidation process would have to be exceedingly slow. A third theory suggests that the hippocampus plays the role of a librarian for memories. It knows how and where memories are stored elsewhere in the brain and can retrieve them when required. A problem with this theory is that it does not explain why explicit memories cannot be retrieved, whereas implicit memories can be retrieved. A fourth theory proposes that the hippocampus is responsible for tagging memories with respect to context—that is, with the location and time of their occurrence. According to this notion, the hippocampus is just one of many memory systems, but one with a special role in storing memories that are meaningful only if their context also is recalled. Episodic, or autobiographical, memory is especially context dependent.

Multiple Memory Systems

There is growing evidence that no single region of the brain is responsible for all memory and that each region makes a specific contribution. Even within the temporal lobes and frontal lobes, various subregions have memory functions that can be different from the functions of regions immediately adjacent to them. Memory functions of different brain regions are described in the following sections.

The Temporal Cortex

The temporal lobes are often the site of problems resulting in epilepsy. Because one treatment for epilepsy is removal of the affected temporal lobe, including both neocortical and limbic systems, a large number of patients have undergone such surgery and have subsequently undergone neuropsychological study. The results of these studies suggest that there are significant differences in the memory impairments stemming from damage to the left and right hemispheres. They also show that the temporal neocortex makes a significant contribution to these functional impairments.

After right-temporal-lobe removal, patients are impaired on face-recognition, spatial-position, and maze-learning tests (Figure 18.8). Impairments in memory for spatial position are apparent in the Corsi block-tapping test, in which a subject learns to tap out a sequence on a block board, illustrated in Figure 18.9. Just as there is a memory span for digits (which is about seven digits), there is a memory span for locations in space. Patients and normal (control) subjects are tested on sequences of block locations that contain one item more than their memory span. One sequence, however, is repeated every third trial. Normal subjects learn the repeating sequence in several trials, although they still have trouble with the novel sequences. Subjects with damage to the right temporal lobe either do not learn the repeating sequence or they learn it very slowly.

Left-temporal-lobe lesions are followed by functional impairments in the recall of word lists, recall of consonant trigrams, and nonspatial associations. They may also cause impairments on the Hebb recurring-digits test. This test is similar to the block-tapping test in that subjects are given lists of digits to repeat that exceed their digit span. Among the lists of digits is one digit sequence that repeats. Patients with left-temporal-lobe lesions do not display the typical learning-acquisition curve, illustrated in Figure 18.9C, but instead fail to learn the recurring digit sequence.

Much of our description of explicit-memory disorders has focused on patients with large medial-temporal-lobe lesions. The structures in the medial

Figure 18.8 A visually guided stylus maze. The black circles represent metal bolt heads on a wooden base. The task is to discover and remember the correct route by trial and error, indicated here by the line. Deficits on this task are correlated with the amount of right hippocampus damage.

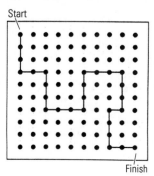

Start

Finish

(A) Hebb recurring-digits test

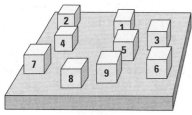

```
1 4 3 9 2 8 6 7 5
3 6 4 5 7 2 1 9 8
5 9 1 3 4 8 6 2 7  (R)
8 5 2 1 6 9 3 7 4
7 1 4 8 3 2 5 9 6
5 9 1 3 4 8 6 2 7  (R)
2 9 3 5 6 1 8 7 4
8 4 6 9 5 3 7 1 2
5 9 1 3 4 8 6 2 7  (R)
```

(B) Corsi block-tapping test

Examiner's view

(C) Learning-acquisition curve

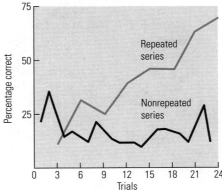

Repeated series

Nonrepeated series

Percentage correct

Trials

(D) Performance

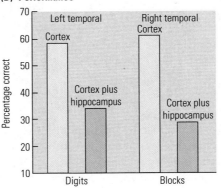

Left temporal Cortex

Right temporal Cortex

Cortex plus hippocampus

Cortex plus hippocampus

Percentage correct

Digits   Blocks

Figure 18.9 Assessment of the temporal lobes in memory. (A) Hebb recurring-digits test. The subjects are given multiple series of nine numbers, two digits longer than the usual digit-memory span. One series repeats (R) every third trial. (B) Corsi block-tapping test. The subject must copy a sequence that the examiner taps out on the blocks. The block's numbers are visible on the examiner's side but not on the subject's. Again, one numerical sequence repeats. (C) Performance on repeated-digit series improves as the number of trials increases, but there is no improvement on the nonrepeating series. (D) Patients with medial temporal lesions of the left hemisphere are impaired on the Hebb recurring-digits test; subjects with medial-temporal-lobe damage of the right hemisphere are impaired on the Corsi block-tapping test.

temporal lobe, however, receive their inputs from the adjacent cortex. We would therefore expect that neocortical lesions also could produce explicit explicit-memory deficits. Milner and her colleagues doubly dissociated the effects of damage to the neocortex of the temporal lobe of each hemisphere on several memory tasks. They conclude that lesions of the right temporal lobe result in impaired memory of nonverbal material. Lesions of the left temporal lobe, on the other hand, have little effect on the nonverbal tests but produce deficits on verbal tests such as the recall of previously presented stories and word pairs, as well as the recognition of words or numbers and recurring nonsense syllables. The results of these studies indicate not only that the medial temporal lobe is associated with severe deficits of memory but also that the adjacent temporal neocortex also is associated with memory disturbance.

Cortical injuries in the parietal, posterior temporal, and possibly occipital cortex sometimes produce specific long-term memory difficulties. Examples include color amnesia, "face amnesia" (prosopagnosia), object anomia (inability to recall the names of objects), and topographical amnesia (inability to recall the location of an object in the environment). Many of these deficits appear to develop in the presence of bilateral lesions only.

Other areas of the neocortex, including the frontal cortex, also participate in memory. An interesting pattern of hemispheric asymmetry is seen in comparisons of the encoding versus the retrieval of memory. The pattern is usually referred to as HERA, for hemispheric encoding and retrieval asymmetry. HERA makes three predictions: (1) the left prefrontal cortex is differentially more engaged in encoding semantic information than in retrieving it, (2) the left prefrontal cortex is differentially more engaged in encoding episodic

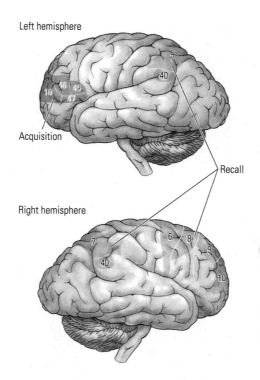

Left hemisphere

Acquisition

Recall

Right hemisphere

Figure 18.10 Areas of cortex that are active as revealed by PET during acquisition (dark blue) or recall (light blue) of verbal information. During acquisition, there is activation in the left ventrolateral prefrontal cortex (areas 10, 46, 45, and 47). During recall of the same material, there is activation in the right dorsolateral cortex (areas 6, 8, 9, and 10) and the parietal cortex bilaterally (areas 7 and 40). (After Tulving et al., 1994.)

information than in retrieving it, and (3) the right prefrontal cortex is differentially more engaged in episodic memory retrieval than is the left prefrontal cortex. For example, Tulving and coworkers show that the ventrolateral frontal cortex of the left hemisphere is preferentially active during memory encoding of words or series of words, but the same regions do not retrieve this information. The dorsolateral frontal cortex in the right hemisphere and the posterior parietal cortex in both hemispheres are active during memory retrieval (Figure 18.10). The asymmetry in encoding versus retrieving may be related to hemispheric asymmetry in the use of language and spatial processes. Most information storage may include the use of language in some way, whereas retrieval may additionally include the use of spatial processes to locate stored information. Thus, Cabeza and Nyberg in a review of 275 PET and fMRI studies note that brain activation during memory encoding and retrieval is likely due to general processes by which the brain handles information as well as local processes related to the storage and retrieval of specific kinds of information.

Memory impairments also result from diffuse damage, such as that in herpes simplex encephalitis and Alzheimer's disease. Damasio and coworkers described a number of herpes simplex encephalitis cases in which damage to the temporal lobes is accompanied by severe memory impairments. One herpes simplex encephalitis patient, Boswell, is described in considerable detail. Boswell resembles many temporal-lobe-injury patients in having extensive anterograde amnesia while demonstrating normal intelligence and language abilities and performing normally on implicit-memory tests. Boswell is different, however, in that he has retrograde amnesia much more severe than that displayed by most temporal-lobe-injury patients. He is described as being entirely unable to retrieve information from any part of his life history. The damage to the medial temporal cortex probably accounts for his anterograde amnesia, whereas additional damage in the lateral temporal cortex, the insula, and the medial frontal cortex is probably related to his retrograde amnesia. Damasio suggested that, in Boswell and other herpes simplex encephalitis patients, the insula may be especially implicated in retrograde amnesia. On the basis of the results of studies using a PET imaging approach, Posner and Raichle reported that the insula is active when subjects perform a well-practiced verbal task but is not active when they perform a novel verbal task. This finding seems consistent with Damasio's suggestion that the insula accesses previously acquired memories.

Alzheimer's disease is a progressive syndrome exhibiting loss of cells and the development of abnormalities in the association cortex. It is characterized at first by anterograde amnesia and later by retrograde amnesia as well. Among the first areas of the brain to show histological change is the medial temporal cortex but, as the disease progresses, other cortical areas are affected. Here, too, the pattern of brain change and the pattern of memory deficit suggest that damage to the medial temporal cortex is related to anterograde amnesia and that damage to other temporal association and frontal cortical areas is related to retrograde amnesia. As with the other amnesic patients described thus far, amnesia is displayed mainly on tests of explicit memory, but eventually implicit memory also may suffer.

The Amygdala

The amygdaloid complex is composed of a number of separate nuclei, each of which probably has specific functions, and so it is not entirely correct to consider them together, as we do here. These nuclei have been associated with emotional, olfactory, and visceral events. Sarter and Markowitsch, in reviewing the literature on studies of animals and humans, suggest that the amygdala has a role in memory processes associated with events that have emotional significance in a subject's life. Thus, if the amygdala makes any contribution to the amnesia of patients with medial-temporal-lobe lesions, it may be emotional in nature. The functions of the amygdala are described in more detail in Chapter 20.

The Perirhinal Cortex

The rhinal cortex—the cortex surrounding the rhinal fissure, including the entorhinal cortex and the perirhinal cortex (Figure 18.11)—is often damaged in patients with medial-temporal-lobe lesions. These regions project to the hippocampus, and so conventional surgeries and many forms of brain injury that affect the hippocampus may also damage the rhinal cortex or the pathways from the rhinal cortex to the hippocampus. In consequence, discriminating between deficits that stem from rhinal-cortex damage and deficits that result from

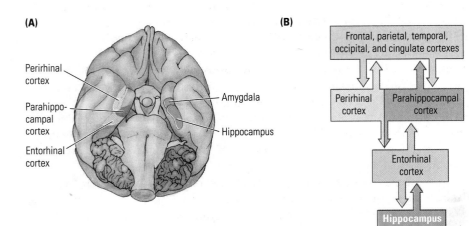

(A)

Perirhinal cortex

Parahippo-campal cortex

Entorhinal cortex

Amygdala

Hippocampus

(B)

Frontal, parietal, temporal, occipital, and cingulate cortexes

Perirhinal cortex

Parahippocampal cortex

Entorhinal cortex

Hippocampus

Figure 18.11 Structures in the medial temporal cortex that play a role in memory. (A) A rhesus monkey brain viewed from below, showing the medial temporal regions. On the left, three medial temporal cortical areas are shown: the perirhinal cortex, the parahippocampal cortex, and the entorhinal cortex. On the right, the amygdala and hippocampus are not directly visible because they lie beneath the medial temporal cortical regions illustrated on the left. (B) Connections among the medial temporal regions. Input from the sensory cortex flows to the parahippocampal and perirhinal regions, then to the entorhinal cortex, and finally to the hippocampus. There is feedback from the hippocampus to the medial temporal cortical regions.

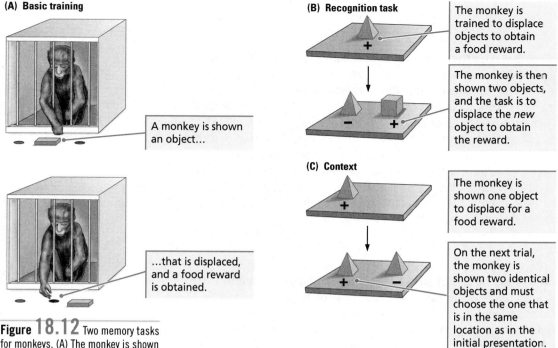

(A) Basic training

A monkey is shown an object...

...that is displaced, and a food reward is obtained.

(B) Recognition task

The monkey is trained to displace objects to obtain a food reward.

The monkey is then shown two objects, and the task is to displace the *new* object to obtain the reward.

(C) Context

The monkey is shown one object to displace for a food reward.

On the next trial, the monkey is shown two identical objects and must choose the one that is in the same location as in the initial presentation.

Figure 18.12 Two memory tasks for monkeys. (A) The monkey is shown an object that, when displaced, reveals a food reward. (B) A recognition task. (C) A context task.

disconnection of the hippocampus or damage to it can be difficult. Murray and her colleagues used neurotoxic lesion techniques to selectively damage the cells of either the hippocampus or the rhinal cortex in monkeys to examine the specific contributions of each structure to amnesia.

In Murray's studies, monkeys reach through the bars of their cage to displace objects under which a reward may be located. To find the reward, the animals must make use of their abilities to (1) recognize objects or (2) recognize a given object in a given context (Figure 18.12). The recognition tasks are of a number of different types. In a matching-to-sample task, a monkey sees a sample object that it displaces to retrieve a food reward hidden underneath. After a brief interval, the monkey is allowed to choose between the sample and some different object and is rewarded for choosing the familiar object. In an alternate, non-matching-to-sample version of the task, the monkey must choose the novel object. For both tasks, delays can be introduced between the sample part and the matching–nonmatching part of the test. There are many versions of this matching–nonmatching task; for example, a novel object can be paired with a familiar object on each trial. The same task can be modified so that it serves as an object-association task: if the sample is A, choose sample X when it is presented with any other object Y. Cross-modal versions of the recognition tasks include having an animal palpate an object in the dark and then choose it visually in the light.

A contextual version of the task requires a monkey to choose an object by using cues based on the object's spatial location—for example, choosing an object that remains in the same place or an object that appears in the same location in a visually presented scene in a picture.

In these studies of memory for objects and contexts, animals with selective hippocampal removal displayed no impairments on the object-recognition tests but were impaired when the test included context. In contrast, animals with rhinal-cortex lesions displayed severe anterograde and retrograde impairments on the object-recognition tests. Thus the conclusion from the results of these studies is that object recognition (factual, or semantic, knowledge) depends on the rhinal cortex, whereas contextual knowledge depends on the hippocampus.

The results of the primate studies are similar to those reported for human subjects. For example, the children with hippocampal damage described by Vargha-Khadem and colleagues were severely impaired in contextual learning but were able to acquire factual information.

The Diencephalon

Evidence of diencephalic amnesia comes from two sources: patients with focal lesions of the medial thalamus and patients with Korsakoff's syndrome. Focal lesions of the medial thalamic area most commonly result from vascular accidents and reliably produce memory problems, but few thorough behavioral and postmortem examinations have been done in such cases; so the critical lesion remains a mystery. More is known about alcohol-related diencephalic damage, although the anatomical location of that damage, too, remains in question.

Long-term alcoholism, especially when accompanied by malnutrition, has long been known to produce defects of memory. In the late 1800s, Russian physician Korsakoff called attention to a syndrome that he found to accompany chronic alcoholism, the most obvious symptom being a severe loss of memory. He wrote:

> The disorder of memory manifests itself in an extraordinarily peculiar amnesia, in which the memory of recent events, those that just happened, is chiefly disturbed, whereas the remote past is remembered fairly well. This reveals itself primarily in that the patient constantly asks the same questions and repeats the same stories. At first, during conversation with such a patient, it is difficult to note the presence of psychic disorder; the patient gives the impression of a person in complete possession of his faculties; he reasons about everything perfectly well, draws correct deductions from given premises, makes witty remarks, plays chess or a game of cards, in a word, comports himself as a mentally sound person. Only after a long conversation with the patient, one may note that at times he utterly confuses events and that he remembers absolutely nothing of what goes on around him: he does not remember whether he had his dinner, whether he was out of bed. On occasion the patient forgets what happened to him just an instant ago: you came in, conversed with him, and stepped out for one minute; then you come in again and the patient has absolutely no recollection that you had already been with him. . . . With all this, the remarkable fact is that, forgetting all events, which have just occurred, the patients usually remember quite accurately the past events, which occurred long before the illness. (Oscar-Berman, 1980, p. 410)

Korsakoff's syndrome has been studied intensively since a seminal article by Sanders and Warrington was published in 1971, because Korsakoff patients are far more readily available than are persons with other forms of global amnesia. There are six major symptoms of the syndrome: (1) anterograde amnesia; (2) retrograde amnesia; (3) **confabulation,** in which patients glibly produce plausible stories about past events rather than admit memory loss (the stories are plausible because they tend to be based on past experiences; for example, a man once told us that he had been at the Legion with his pals, which, though untrue, had been his practice in the past); (4) meager content in conversation; (5) lack of insight; and (6) apathy (the patients lose interest in things quickly and generally appear indifferent to change).

The symptoms of Korsakoff's syndrome may appear suddenly, within the space of a few days. The cause is a thiamine (vitamin B_1) deficiency resulting from prolonged intake of large quantities of alcohol. The syndrome, which is usually progressive, can be arrested by massive doses of vitamin B_1 but cannot be reversed. Prognosis is poor, with only about 20% of patients showing much recovery in a year on a B_1-enriched diet. Many patients demonstrate no recovery even after 10 to 20 years.

Although there has been some controversy over the exact effect of the vitamin deficiency on the brain, current thought is that there is damage in the medial thalamus and possibly in the mammillary bodies of the hypothalamus, as well as generalized cerebral atrophy.

Ascending Systems

The basal forebrain is an area just anterior to the hypothalamus. It is the source of a number of pathways to the forebrain, some of which are cholinergic fibers. The cholinergic cells project to all cortical areas and provide as much as 70% of the cholinergic synapses in these areas. The loss of these cholinergic cells has been proposed to be related to, even responsible for, the amnesia displayed by patients with Alzheimer's disease. In animal experiments, selective lesioning of the cholinergic cells, with the use of neurotoxins, does not result in amnesia. There are also serotonergic cells in the midbrain, projecting to the limbic system and cortex and helping to maintain activation in those areas. If only this cell group is removed in animals, no serious memory difficulty results. Profound amnesia can be produced, however, if the serotonergic cells in the midbrain and the cholinergic cells in the basal forebrain are damaged together. Vanderwolf demonstrates that animals receiving such treatment behave as if the entire neocortex had been removed, in that they no longer display any intelligent behavior. Additionally, cortical EEG recordings from such animals show a pattern typical of sleep.

Another example of the conjoint activity of the ascending systems is that between the acetylcholine and the noradrenaline systems. Decker and coworkers show that if either is pharmacologically blocked, there is very little effect on learning. If both systems are blocked together, experimental rats are extremely impaired on learning tasks. Because a number of diseases of aging are associated with loss of neurons of the ascending projections of the cholinergic, serotonergic, or noradrenergic systems, cell loss in more than one of these systems could be a cause of amnesia even when cortical or limbic structures are intact.

Short-Term Memory

In 1890, William James drew a distinction between memories that endure for a very brief time and longer-term memories. Not until 1958, however, were separate short-term and long-term memories specifically postulated by Broadbent. **Short-term memory,** sometimes also called **working memory,** is the type of memory that we use for holding digits, words, names, or other items in our minds for a brief period. Baddely described it aptly as "scratch-pad memory." Short-term and long-term memory are parallel memory systems in which material is processed separately and simultaneously.

There are probably a number of kinds of short-term memory, each with different neural correlates. Baddely suggested at least two kinds. One is a visual-spatial scratch pad on which object forms are located spatially. The second is a phonological scratch pad that holds verbal information. The function of both kinds of memory is to hold pieces of information "on line" until they can be dealt with physically or mentally. Both kinds of short-term memory can be subdivided further and can take different forms in the left and right hemispheres. Baddely's two scratch pads are synonymous with the dorsal spatial visual system and the ventral object-recognition visual system and entail both the posterior neocortex and the frontal neocortex.

Short-Term Memory and the Temporal Lobes

Warrington and her colleagues point out that short-term memory can be doubly dissociated from long-term memory with respect to the kinds of impairments seen in the different systems and with respect to the different kinds of structural damage from which those deficits arise. For example, one patient, K. F., received a left posterior temporal lesion that resulted in an almost total inability to repeat verbal stimuli such as digits, letters, words, and sentences. In contrast, his long-term recall of paired-associates words or short stories was nearly normal. On the other hand, patients who display anterograde amnesia for explicit information do not show impairments in short-term memory for words and digits. Warrington and colleagues also found that some patients apparently have defects in short-term recall of visually presented digits or letters but have normal short-term recall of the same stimuli presented aurally. Luria describes patients with just the opposite difficulty: specific deficits for aurally presented but not visually presented verbal items. Short-term-memory deficits can also result from damage to the polymodal sensory areas of the posterior parietal cortex and posterior temporal cortex. Warrington and Weiskrantz present several cases of specific short-term-memory deficits in patients with lesions at the junction of the parietal, temporal, and occipital cortexes.

Short-Term Memory in the Frontal Lobes

Historically, there have been extravagant claims that the frontal lobes are responsible for the highest intellectual functions, but until quite recently there was no evidence that the frontal lobes are implicated in memory. Now damage to the frontal cortex is recognized to be the cause of many impairments of short-term memory for tasks in which subjects must remember the temporary location of stimuli. The tasks themselves may be rather simple: given this cue, make that response after a delay. But as one trial follows another, both animals and people with frontal-lobe lesions start to mix up the previously presented stimuli.

Prisko devised a "compound stimulus" task in which two stimuli in the same sensory modality are presented in succession, separated by a short interval. The subject's task is to report whether the second stimulus of the pair is identical with the first. In half the trials, the stimuli were the same; in the other trials, they were different. Thus, the task required the subject to remember the first stimulus of a pair in order to compare it with the second, while suppressing the stimuli that had been presented in previous trials. Prisko used pairs of clicks, light flashes, tones, colors, and irregular visual nonsense patterns as the stimuli. In each task, a small set of stimuli was used repeatedly in different combinations. Patients with unilateral frontal-lobe removals showed a marked impairment in matching the first and second items of each pair.

Similarly, Corsi used two tasks, one verbal and one nonverbal. In this study, the subjects were required to decide which of two stimuli had been seen more recently. In the verbal task, they were asked to read pairs of words presented on a series of cards (for example, *cowboy–railroad*). From time to time, a card appeared bearing two words with a question mark between them. The subject had to indicate which of the words he or she had read most recently. Sometimes both words had been seen before, but at other times only one had been seen. In the latter case, the task became a simple test of recognition, whereas in the former case it was a test of recency memory. Patients with left temporal removals showed a mild deficit in recognition, in keeping with their difficulty with verbal memory; the frontal-lobe patients performed normally. On the recency test, however, both frontal-lobe groups (left and right) were impaired, although the left-side group was significantly worse.

The nonverbal task was identical with the verbal task except that the stimuli were photographs of paintings rather than words. Patients with right-temporal-lobe removals showed mild deficits in recognition, consistent with their visual memory deficit, whereas those with right-frontal-lobe lesions performed normally. On the recency test, the frontal-lobe groups were impaired, but now the right-side group was significantly worse.

Moscovitch devised a task in which patients were read five different lists of 12 words each and were instructed to recall as much as they could of each list immediately after presentation. In the first four lists, all the words were drawn from the same taxonomic category, such as sports; the words in the fifth list came from a different category, such as professions. Normal subjects show a decline from list 1 to list 4 in the number of words recalled correctly (that is, they exhibit *proactive interference*), but they also exhibit an additional phenomenon on list 5: they recall as many words as they did for list 1, thus demonstrating what is referred to as *release from proactive interference*. Frontal-lobe patients also showed strong proactive interference, as would be expected from the Prisko experiments, but they failed to show release from proactive interference on list 5.

Another memory deficit in patients with frontal-lobe lesions has been demonstrated in a test of movement copying. In a study in which patients with cortical lesions were asked to copy complex arm and facial movements, Kolb and Milner found that, in addition to making errors of sequence, frontal-lobe patients made many errors of intrusion and omission; that is, when asked to copy a series of three discrete facial movements, frontal-lobe patients left one movement out (error of omission) or added a movement seen in a previous sequence (error of intrusion).

The results of experiments with monkeys confirm that different areas of the prefrontal cortex take part in different types of short-term memory. Fuster demonstrated that, if monkeys are shown objects that they must remember for a short period before they are allowed to make a response, neurons in the

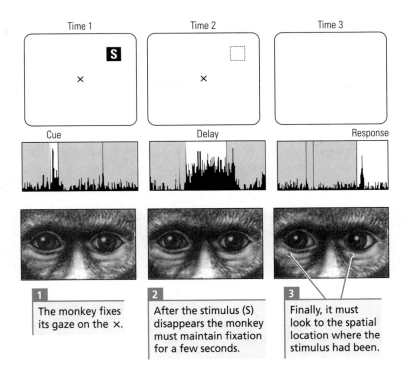

Time 1   Time 2   Time 3

Cue   Delay   Response

1 The monkey fixes its gaze on the ×.

2 After the stimulus (S) disappears the monkey must maintain fixation for a few seconds.

3 Finally, it must look to the spatial location where the stimulus had been.

Figure 18.13 Single cells can code the spatial location of objects. During the delay in step 2, single cells in area 8 code the memory for the location of the second stimulus. (After Goldman-Rakic, 1992.)

frontal cortex will fire during the delay. This finding suggests that these neurons are active in bridging the stimulus-response gap. Goldman-Rakic and her colleagues examined this phenomenon further in two tasks, one of memory for the location of objects and the other of memory for the identity of objects. For the first task, a monkey was required to fixate on a point in the center of a screen while a light was flashed in some part of its visual field. After a variable delay of a few seconds, the monkey was required to shift its eyes to look at the point where the light had been. In the second task, as the monkey fixated on the center of the screen, one of two objects appeared on the screen. The monkey was required to look to the left in response to one stimulus and to the right in response to the other (Figure 18.13). Cells that coded spatial vision were located in area 8 of the dorsolateral prefrontal cortex, whereas cells that coded object recognition were located in areas 9 and 46 of the middorsolateral frontal cortex (Figure 18.14A).

Figure 18.14 Two systems for short-term memory in frontal cortex. (A) Frontal cortex area 8 participates in short-term memory for the spatial location of objects. It receives projections from the parietal cortex. Frontal cortex areas 9 and 46 have roles in short-term memory for visual objects and receive information from the inferior temporal cortex. This conclusion is based on the results of single-cell recording experiments in monkeys. (B) Frontal cortex area 8 searches for an object when a stimulus is presented, and areas 9 and 46 remember objects that are identified sequentially. This conclusion is based on the results of PET recording experiments in human subjects. (Part A after Wilson et al., 1993; part B after Petrides et al., 1993.)

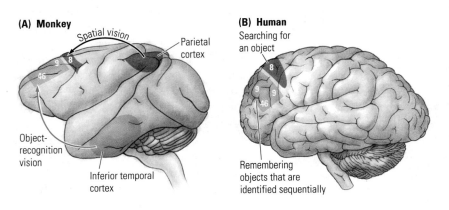

(A) Monkey

Spatial vision

Parietal cortex

Object-recognition vision

Inferior temporal cortex

(B) Human

Searching for an object

Remembering objects that are identified sequentially

Petrides and coworkers used PET along with MRI to demonstrate similar function–anatomy relations in humans (Figure 18.14B). A spatial vision test required subjects to point to one of eight patterns on each of eight cards in response to a colored bar at the top of the card. That is, in response to a cue, a subject had to search for a specific pattern. Performance of this task was accompanied by increases in activity in area 8 of the left hemisphere. In contrast, an object task required subjects to point to a different one of an array of eight patterns repeated on eight successive cards, which meant that they had to keep track of the patterns that they had indicated already. During this task, the researchers found increases in regional cerebral blood flow in the middorsolateral frontal cortex (areas 9 and 46, mainly on the right). Thus, findings from both sets of studies indicate that different areas of the prefrontal cortex are implicated in different kinds of short-term memory.

A Case of Total Recall

We end this chapter by noting that students may have had their own problems with different kinds of memory when studying for examinations and taking them. If a student underlines relevant passages in a textbook to study for a test, then that student will undoubtedly do well on an examination that calls for recognizing those relevant words and passages. Unfortunately, most examinations consist of the quite different activity of writing a summary of the text from memory. Students can prevent the unpleasant experience of "I knew the information but had a mental block when I had to produce it" by performing the same operations during the study phase that will be required of them during the test phase. These operations usually require top-down rather than bottom-up processing. It would be remiss of us not to explain how top-down processing can be done.

S. was a newspaper reporter with an extraordinary ability to form explicit memories that he could not forget. The fact that he never took notes at briefings as other reporters did brought him to the attention of his employer, who questioned him on the matter. S. responded by repeating verbatim the transcript of the briefing that they had just attended. S. did not consider himself unusual, although he wondered why other people relied so much on written notes. Nonetheless, at his employer's urging, he went to see a psychologist. In this way, S. met Luria, who began a study of this remarkable case of memory ability that continued for the following 30 years. Luria published an account of the investigation, and to this day *The Mind of a Mnemonist* is one of the most readable studies in the literature of memory.

For an example of S.'s abilities, consider Table 18.1. S. could look at this table for 2 or 3

Table 18.1 Example of tables memorized by S.

6	6	8	0
5	4	3	2
1	6	8	4
7	9	3	5
4	2	3	7
3	8	9	1
1	0	0	2
3	4	5	1
2	7	6	8
1	9	2	6
2	9	6	7
5	5	2	0
x	0	1	x

Note: With only 2 to 3 minutes' study of such a table, S. was able to reproduce it in reverse order, horizontally, or vertically and to reproduce the diagonals.

minutes and then repeat it from memory: by columns, by rows, by diagonals, in reverse, or in sums. Tested unexpectedly 16 or more years later, S. could still reproduce the table, reciting the columns in any order or combination, without error.

For a good part of his life, S. supported himself as an *mnemonist*—an entertainer who specializes in feats of memory. In the course of his career, he memorized hundreds of such lists or lists of names, letters, nonsense syllables, and so on; after memorizing any of them, he was able to recall it at any later date.

S.'s ability to commit things to memory hinged on three processes. He could visualize stimuli mentally, recalling them simply by reading them from this internal image. He also made multisensory impressions of things. This ability, called **synesthesia,** entails the processing of any sensory event in all sensory modalities simultaneously. Thus, a word was recorded as a sound, a splash of color, an odor, a taste, a texture, and a temperature. Finally, S. employed the pegboard technique used by many other mnemonists; that is, he kept a collection of standard images in his mind and associated them with new material that he wanted to remember. This trick and others employed by mnemonists serve as sources of insight into how explicit memories are usually formed and how such an understanding can be exploited to improve memory in normal people, as well as in people with memory impairments.

Here are some examples of how S. saw numbers:

> Even numbers remind me of images. Take the number 1. This is a proud, well-built man; 2 is a high-spirited woman; 3 a gloomy person (shy, I don't know); 6 a man with a swollen foot; 7 a man with a mustache; 8 a very stout woman—a sack within a sack. As for the number 87, what I see is a fat woman and a man twirling his mustache. (Luria, 1968)

From Luria's description of S., it seems safe to conclude that there was absolutely no limit to his ability to remember. At least Luria, in the many tests that he gave S., was never able to reach such a limit. Did S. forget? As already said, his long-term memory was amazing, but, from Luria's account, he also did not seem to forget in the same way as the rest of us do. When he missed an item, it was not because it was forgotten but because it was hidden from view or hard to see. He was always able to find it eventually.

Did S. pay a price for his memory abilities? Luria clearly has taken the position that he did. Luria characterizes S. as a person with little aim in life, seemingly dull and superficial. Luria suggests that S. was not able to reason, to categorize, and to see order in things, as ordinary people can. He also had little ability to use or understand metaphors (for example, the phrase "to weigh one's words"); he visualized and interpreted them literally and so was puzzled by what they meant. He often had difficulty understanding simple statements and had even more difficulty understanding the sense of poetry. Although we can see in the behavior of S. how top-down processing, or conscious manipulation, of information is an aid in forming long-term memories, we can also learn from him the value of short-term memory, which he appears to have lacked. Without it, he was unable to assess, compare, classify, change, and otherwise manipulate information in all the ways that allow us to create and understand.

Summary

Figure 18.15 provides an overview of different kinds of memory and their relation to different brain regions. The two major categories of memory are conscious, or explicit, memory and unconscious, or implicit, memory. Research findings suggest that explicit memory is associated with temporal-lobe structures and implicit memory with the basal ganglia and neocortical structures.

Explicit memory is further divided into episodic memory, or memory for personal experiences, and semantic memory, or memory for facts. Episodic memory seems to be closely associated with hippocampal function and semantic memory with temporal cortex function (including the rhinal cortex). Implicit memory can be divided into motor memory, priming, and classical conditioning, which are associated with the function of the neocortex and cerebellum, and emotional memory, which seems to be associated with the amygdala.

Research findings also suggest that there are differences in the processes of acquiring and storing memory. For example, anterograde amnesia, the inability to form new memories, is often more severe than retrograde amnesia, the inability to retrieve old memories.

Finally, there is evidence that short-term memory has a structural basis different from that of long-term memory. The parietal frontal spatial system (dorsal stream) appears to have a role in short-term memory for spatial locations, and the inferior temporal dorsolateral frontal system (ventral stream) appears to function in short-term memory for objects.

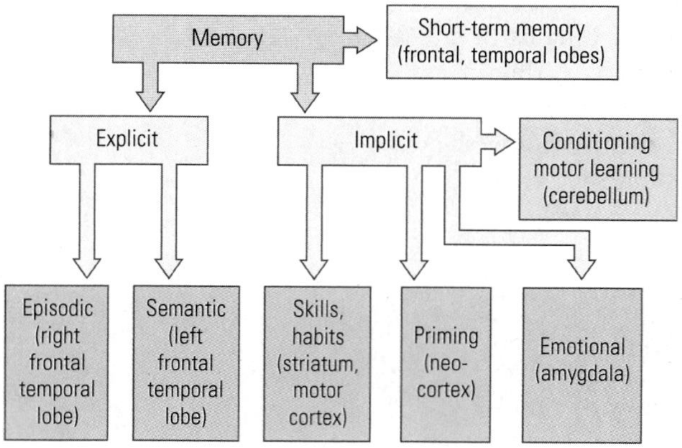

Figure 18.15 The types of memory and the neural structures most closely related to each one.

References

Amaral, D. G. Memory: Anatomical organization for candidate brain regions. In *Handbook of Physiology: The Nervous System*. Bethesda, MD: The American Physiological Society, 1987.

Baddely, A. *Working Memory*. London: Oxford University Press, 1986.

Bartlett, F. C. *Remembering*. Cambridge, UK: Cambridge University Press, 1932.

Bekhterev, V. M. Demonstration eines Gehirns mit Zerstörung der vorderen und inneren Theile der Hirnrinde beider Schlafenlappen. *Neurol. Zbl.* 19:990–991, 1900.

Broadbent, D. E. *Perception and Communication*. London: Pergamon, 1958.

Cabeza, R., and L. Nyberg. Imaging Cognition II: An empirical review of 275 PET and fMRI studies. *Journal of Cognitive Neuroscience* 12:1–47, 2000.

Cermak, L. S., Ed. *Human Memory and Amnesia*. Hillsdale, NJ: Lawrence Erlbaum Associates, 1982.

Cipolotti, L., T. Shallice, D. Chan, N. Fox, R. Scahill, G. Harrison, J. Stevens, and P. Rudge. Long term retrograde amnesia: The crucial role of the hippocampus. *Neuropsychologia* 39:151–172, 2001.

Corkin, S. Tactually-guided maze-learning in man: Effects on unilateral cortical excisions and bilateral hippocampal lesions. *Neuropsychologia* 3:339–351, 1965.

Corkin, S. Acquisition of motor skill after bilateral medial temporal-lobe excision. *Neuropsychologia* 6:255–265, 1968.

Corsi, P. M. Human Memory and the Medial Temporal Region of the Brain. Ph.D. dissertation. Montreal: McGill University, 1972.

Damasio, A. R., D. Tranel, and H. Damasio. Amnesia caused by herpes simplex encephalitis, infarctions in basal forebrain, Alzheimer's disease and anoxia/ischemia. In L. Squire and G. Gainotti, Eds. *Handbook of Neuropsychology*, vol 3. Amsterdam: Elsevier, 1991.

Decker, M. W., M. T. Gill, and J. L. McGaugh. Concurrent muscarenic and β-adrenergic blockade in rats impairs place learning in a water maze and retention of inhibitory avoidance. *Brain Research* 513:81–85, 1990.

Ebbinghaus, H. *Memory*. New York: Teachers College, 1913 (originally published in 1885). Reprinted by Dover, New York, 1964.

Elliott, H. C. *Textbook of Neuroanatomy*. Philadelphia: Lippincott, 1969.

Fisher, C. M., and R. O. Adams. Transient global amnesia. *Transactions of the American Neurological Association* 83:143, 1958.

Fuster, J. M. *The Prefrontal Cortex*. New York: Raven, 1989.

Gaffan, D. Monkey's recognition memory for complex pictures and the effect of fornix transection. *Quarterly Journal of Experimental Psychology* 29:505–514, 1977.

Gaffan, D., and E. Gaffan. Amnesia in man following transection of the fornix: A review. *Brain* 114:2611–2618, 1991.

Goldman-Rakic, P. S. Working memory and the mind. *Scientific American* 267(3):111–117, 1992.

Gollin, E. S. Developmental studies of visual recognition of incomplete objects. *Perceptual and Motor Skills* 11:289–298, 1960.

Grafton, S. T., J. C. Mazziotta, S. Presty, K. J. Friston, S. J. Frackowiak, and M. E. Phelps. Functional anatomy of human procedural learning determined with regional cerebral blood flow and PET. *Journal of Neuroscience* 12:2542–2548, 1992.

Hay, J. F., M. Moscovitch, and B. Levine. Dissociating habit and recollection: Evidence from Parkinson's disease, amnesia and focal lesion patients. *Neuropsychologia* 40:1324–1334. 2002.

James, W. *The Principles of Psychology*. New York: Holt, 1890.

Kolb, B., and B. Milner. Performance of complex arm and facial movements after focal brain lesions. *Neuropsychologia* 19:491–503, 1981.

Lashley, K. D. In search of the engram. *Symposia of the Society for Experimental Biology* 4:454–482, 1950.

Levine, B. Autonoetic consciousness and self-regulation in patients with brain injury. *International Journal of Psychology* 35:223, 2000.

Levine, B., S. E. Black, R. Cabeza, M. Sinden, A. R. Mcintosh, J. P. Toth, and E. Tulving. Episodic memory and the self in a case of isolated retrograde amnesia. *Brain* 121:1951–1973, 1998.

Luria, A. R. *The Mind of a Mnemonist*. New York: Basic Books, 1968.

Mair, W. G. P., E. K. Warrington, and L. Weiskrantz. Memory disorder in Korsakoff's psychosis. *Brain* 102:749–783, 1979.

Markowitsch, H. J. Transient global amnesia. *Neuroscience and Biobehavioral Reviews* 7:35–43, 1983.

Markowitsch, H. J., and M. Pritzel. The neuropathology of amnesia. *Progress in Neurobiology* 25:189–288, 1985.

Marsolek, C. J., S. M. Kosslyn, and L. R. Squire. Form-specific visual priming in the right cerebral hemisphere.

Journal of Experimental Psychology: Learning, Memory, and Cognition 18:492–508, 1992.

Martone, M., N. Butlers, M. Payne, J. T. Bker, and D. S. Sax. Dissociations between skill learning and verbal recognition in amnesia and dementia. *Archives of Neurology* 41:965–970, 1984.

Mazzucchi, A., G. Moretti, P. Caffara, and M. Parma. Neuropsychological functions in the follow-up of transient global amnesia. *Brain* 103:161–178, 1980.

Milner, B. Visually-guided maze learning in man: Effects of bilateral hippocampal, bilateral frontal, and unilateral cerebral lesions. *Neuropsychologia* 3:317–338, 1965.

Milner, B. Memory and the medial temporal regions of the brain. In K. H. Pribram and D. E. Broadbent, Eds. *Biology of Memory*. New York: Academic Press, 1970.

Milner, B., S. Corkin, and H.-L. Teuber. Further analysis of the hippocampal amnesic syndrome: 14-year follow up study of H. M. *Neuropsychologia* 6:215–234, 1968.

Moscovitch, M. Multiple dissociations of function in amnesia. In L. S. Cermak, Ed. *Human Memory and Amnesia*. Hillsdale, NJ: Lawrence Erlbaum Associates, 1982.

Murray, E. Memory for objects in nonhuman primates. In M. S. Gazzaniga, Ed. *The New Cognitive Neurosciences*, 2nd ed. London: MIT Press, 2000, pp. 753–763.

Oscar-Berman, M. Neuropsychological consequences of long-term chronic alcoholism. *American Scientist* 68:410–419, 1980.

Pascual-Leone, A., J. Grafman, and M. Hallett. Modulation of cortical motor output maps during development of implicit and explicit knowledge. *Science* 263:1287–1289, 1994.

Penfield, W., and B. Milner. Memory deficit produced by bilateral lesions in the hippocampal zone. *Archives of Neurology and Psychiatry* 79:475–497, 1958.

Petri, H. L., and M. Mishkin. Behaviorism, cognitivism, and the neuropsychology of memory. *American Scientist* 82:30–37, 1994.

Petrides, M. Deficits on conditional associative-learning tasks after frontal- and temporal-lobe lesions in man. *Neuropsychologia* 23:601–614, 1985.

Petrides, M., B. Alivisatos, A. C. Evans, and E. Meyer. Dissociation of human mid-dorsolateral from posterior dorsolateral frontal cortex in memory processing. *Proceedings of the National Academy of Sciences of the United States of America* 90:873–877, 1993.

Posner, M. I., and M. E. Raichle. *Images of Mind*. New York: Scientific American Library, 1994.

Prisko, L. Short-Term Memory in Focal Cerebral Damage. Ph.D. dissertation. Montreal: McGill University, 1963.

Sanders, H. I., and E. K. Warrington. Memory for remote events in amnesic patients. *Brain* 94:661–668, 1971.

Sarter, M., and H. J. Markowitsch. The amygdala's role in human mnemonic processing. *Cortex* 21:7–24, 1985.

Schacter, D. L. Memory, amnesia, and frontal lobe dysfunction. *Psychobiology* 15:21–36, 1987.

Schacter, D. L. Implicit knowledge: New perspectives on unconscious processes. *Proceedings of the National Academy of Sciences of the United States of America* 89:11113–11117, 1992.

Schacter, D. L., and H. F. Crovitz. Memory function after closed head injury: A review of the quantitative research. *Cortex* 13:150–176, 1977.

Scoville, W. B., and B. Milner. Loss of recent memory after bilateral hippocampal lesions. *Journal of Neurology, Neurosurgery and Psychiatry* 20:11–21, 1957.

Squire, L. R. The neuropsychology of human memory. *Neuroscience* 5:241–273, 1982.

Squire, L. R. *Memory and the Brain.* New York: Oxford University Press, 1987.

Squire, L. R., R. E. Clark, and B. J. Knowlton. Retrograde amnesia. *Hippocampus* 11:50–55, 2001.

Taylor, J. R., R. Tompkins, R. Demers, and D. Anderson. Electroconvulsive therapy and memory dysfunction: Is there evidence for prolonged defects? *Biological Psychiatry* 17:1169–1193, 1982.

Thompson, R. F. The neurobiology of learning and memory. *Science* 233:941–947, 1986.

Tulving, E. Episodic memory: From mind to brain. *Annual Review of Psychology* 53:1–25, 2002.

Tulving, E., S. Kapur, F. I. M. Craik, M. Moscovitch, and S. Houle. Hemispheric encoding/retrieval asymmetry in episodic memory: Positron emission tomography finding. *Proceedings of the National Academy of Sciences of the United States of America* 91:2016–2020, 1994.

Vanderwolf, C. H. Cerebral activity and behavior: Control by central cholinergic and serotonergic systems. *International Review of Neurobiology* 30:255–340, 1988.

Vargha-Khadem, F., D. G. Gadian, K. A. Watkins, W. Connelly, W. Van Paesschen, and M. Mishkin. Differential effects of early hippocampal pathology on episodic and semantic memory. *Science* 277:376–380, 1997.

von Cramen, D. Y., N. Hebel, and U. Schuri. A contribution of the anatomical basis of thalamic amnesia. *Brain* 108:993–1008, 1985.

Warrington, E., and M. James. An experimental investigation of facial recognition in patients with unilateral cerebral lesions. *Cortex* 3:317–326, 1967.

Warrington, E. K., and L. Weiskrantz. Further analysis of the prior learning effect in amnesic patients. *Neuropsychologia* 16:169–177, 1978.

Weiskrantz, L. Neuroanatomy of memory and amnesia: A case for multiple memory systems. *Human Neurobiology* 6:93–105, 1987.

Whitty, C. W. M., and O. L. Zangwill. Traumatic amnesia. In C. W. M. Whitty and O. L. Zangwill, Eds. *Amnesia.* London: Butterworth, 1966.

Wilson, F. A. W., S. P. O. Scalaidhe, and P. S. Goldman-Rakic. Dissociation of object and spatial processing domains in primate prefrontal cortex. *Science* 260:1955–1958, 1993.

chapter *19*

The Origins of Language

K. H. was a Swiss-born architect working as a professor of architecture at a major U.S. university. Although German was his first language and he was fluent in French and Italian, his primary language had become English. Because he had been an outstanding student, had excelled at writing, and was meticulous about his spelling and grammar, he was astonished when, several years ago, his mother complained that he was making spelling and grammatical errors in his letters to her, which of course were in German. He suspected that he must just be forgetting his German and resolved to prevent that from happening. A few weeks later, K. H. asked a colleague to review a manuscript that he had just completed. His colleague read the paper and commented that K. H. must be working too hard because the manuscript was filled with errors of a kind that K. H. would not have normally made. At about the same time, K. H. noticed that the right side of his face seemed to "feel funny." He went to a neurologist, who found a small tumor at the junction of the motor face area and Broca's area in K. H.'s left hemisphere. The tumor was benign and was successfully removed through surgery. In the first few days after surgery, K. H. was densely aphasic: he could not talk, and he could not understand either oral or written language. Although he had been warned that aphasia was likely and that it would be temporary, he was visibly upset about his language difficulties. By the end of the first week, he could understand oral language, but his speech was still unintelligible and he could not read. By the end of the second week, he could speak German fluently but had difficulty with English, although his English was certainly understandable. He was still unable to read in any language, but he believed that he could read German and could be convinced otherwise only when he was informed that the book that he was reading was upside down. His reading and English slowly improved, but even now, years later, he has difficulty spelling in any language, and his reading is slower than would be expected for a person of his intelligence and education.

anguage is one of our most precious abilities, yet most of us take it for granted, as K. H. did before his illness. We don't realize how much depends on our ability to talk, listen, and read. We even talk to ourselves. As children, we learn language long before we can catch a ball or ride a bicycle, using words to label and learn about the things in our environment. We use language to entertain ourselves in poetry, song, and humor. Indeed, much humor is based on nuances of language and on double entendres. Because the use of language is our most complex skill, there are many ways to approach the study of language. One place to start is to consider what language is.

What Is Language?

There is no universally accepted definition of language. Many species of animals use sound as a form of communication, and so do most humans. But animal sounds aren't really the equivalent of human language; and humans have found ways of communicating without sound. Nevertheless, sound is central to human language. In considering the components and origins of human language, we must consider the production of sound.

Components of Language

Although most of us probably think of words as the meaningful units of language, linguists break down language somewhat differently (Table 19.1). They view words as consisting of fundamental language sounds called **phonemes.** An analysis of how phonemes are processed is called a phonological analysis. Phonemes, in turn, are combined to form **morphemes,** the smallest meaningful units of words. A morpheme may be a base (*do* in un*do*), an affix (*un* in *un*do or *er* in do*er*), or an inflection (*ing* in do*ing* or *s* in girl*s*). Some morphemes are complete words by themselves; other morphemes must be combined to form words. A **lexicon** is the collection of all the words in a given language. Words are strung together in patterns and conform to rules of grammar, also known as **syntax.** A key aspect of syntax is the appropriate choice of verb tenses. It is

Table 19.1 Components of a sound-based language

Phonemes	The individual sound units whose concatenation, in particular order, produces morphemes
Morphemes	The smallest meaningful units of a word, whose combination creates a word
Syntax	The admissible combinations of words in phrases and sentences (called grammar in popular usage)
Lexicon	The collection of all words in a given language, each lexical entry includes all information with morphological or syntactic ramifications but does not include conceptual knowledge
Semantics	The meanings that correspond to all lexical items and all possible sentences
Prosody	The vocal intonation that can modify the literal meaning of words and sentences
Discourse	The linking of sentences such that they constitute a narrative

interesting that children develop syntactical skills independently of formal training, a characteristic that led Chomsky to suggest that humans possess an innate mechanism for developing language. The meaning connected to words and sentences is referred to, collectively, as **semantics.** Vocal intonations that can modify the literal meaning of words and sentences are collectively called prosody. Finally, the stringing together of sentences to form a meaningful narrative is called **discourse.** Although this discussion has emphasized the acoustical nature of these basic parts of language, there are analogues in visual language, such as American Sign Language (ASL, or Ameslan). A morpheme in ASL would be the smallest meaningful movement.

Although the presence of words and word components is the traditional criterion by which linguists recognize language, there are other ways to describe human language. MacNeilage noted that one unique characteristic of human language is its use of syllables that are made up of consonants and vowels. Nonhuman species do not produce syllables, primarily because they do not produce consonants. Thus, for MacNeilage, the unique thing about human language is that our mouths are capable of producing consonants and combining them with vowels to produce syllables.

The Production of Sound

Speech and language are different. Language is any system for representing and communicating ideas, whereas speech refers to a particular audible manner of communicating language. Most of us have heard talking birds such as parrots or mynahs, and we may have even heard talking seals or dolphins. We have not heard talking apes, however, and not for lack of trying. The Hayes family raised Vicki, a chimpanzee, and made a heroic effort to get her to produce words, but she accomplished little more than a feeble rendition of "cup." Whereas many researchers have demonstrated that chimpanzees can learn a rudimentary sign language, the ability of chimps to produce human speech sound remains negligible. Why do our nearest animal relatives lack vocal output capabilities comparable to ours?

The basic machinery that produces sound in apes and humans is similar (Figure 19.1). It consists of two sets of parts, one set acting as the sound source and the other set as filters. First, air exhaled from the lungs provides power to drive oscillations of the **vocal folds** (commonly known as the vocal cords), which are located in the **larynx,** or "voice box." The rate of vocal-fold oscillation (which varies from about 100 Hz in adult men to 500 Hz in small children) determines the pitch of the sound thus produced. The acoustical energy generated then passes through the vocal tract (the pharyngeal, oral, and nasal cavities) and finally out through the nostrils and lips. As this energy passes through the vocal tract, the structures there act as a series of "bandpass filters," which in the context of speech are called **formants.** The formants modify the sound that is emitted, allowing specific frequencies to pass unhindered but blocking the transmission of others. The filtering process plays a crucial role in speech. Formant characteristics are determined by the length and shape of the vocal tract and are modified rapidly during speech by the movements of the articulators (tongue, lips, soft palate, and so on).

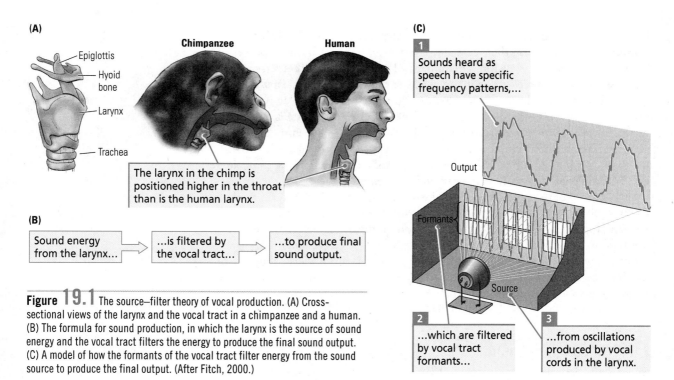

(A)

Epiglottis

Hyoid bone

Larynx

Trachea

Chimpanzee

Human

The larynx in the chimp is positioned higher in the throat than is the human larynx.

(B)

Sound energy from the larynx... → ...is filtered by the vocal tract... → ...to produce final sound output.

(C)

1 Sounds heard as speech have specific frequency patterns,...

Output

Formants

Source

2 ...which are filtered by vocal tract formants...

3 ...from oscillations produced by vocal cords in the larynx.

Figure 19.1 The source–filter theory of vocal production. (A) Cross-sectional views of the larynx and the vocal tract in a chimpanzee and a human. (B) The formula for sound production, in which the larynx is the source of sound energy and the vocal tract filters the energy to produce the final sound output. (C) A model of how the formants of the vocal tract filter energy from the sound source to produce the final output. (After Fitch, 2000.)

Part of the difference between apes and ourselves lies in the part of the vocal apparatus that produces formants. The human oral cavity is longer than that of the ape, and the human larynx is situated much lower. During development, starting at about 3 months of age, the human larynx begins a slow descent toward its adult position, which it reaches after 3 to 4 years. A second, shorter descent takes place in human males at puberty.

The descent of the larynx in humans was a key innovation in the evolution of speech, allowing humans to produce a much wider range of formant patterns than other mammals do. It allows the tongue to move both vertically and horizontally within the vocal tract, giving us the ability to vary the area of the oral and pharyngeal tubes independently, which adds to the variety of sounds that are easy for us to produce.

The Origins of Language

The emphasis on the uniqueness of human language poses certain obstacles to understanding how language evolved. Although no other species has language in the sense that linguists mean it, there can be little doubt that language did not appear all of a sudden—with no antecedents whatsoever—in *Homo sapiens*. There must be some evolutionary trace of the mechanisms necessary for producing human language. The search for such capacities is not a matter of idle curiosity. If we can determine which capacities were precursors of human language and why they were selected, we will have taken a giant step toward understanding how language is represented in our brains.

Predecessors of Language

One hypothetical explanation for language is that it evolved slowly from various kinds of animal vocalizations. Perhaps it is a tribute to the imagination with which speculators approached the question of *which* vocalizations, in 1866, that the Linguistic Society of Paris banned future discussion of it. We will not let that deter us, however.

Hewes reviewed many variants of the vocalization theory, including the "pooh-pooh" theory (language evolved from noises associated with strong emotion), the "bow-wow" theory (language evolved from noises first made to imitate natural sounds), the "yo-he-ho" theory (language evolved from sounds made to resonate with natural sounds), and the "sing-song" theory (language evolved from noises made while playing or dancing). These examples by no means exhaust the list of animal vocalization theories of language origin. A major drawback of these kinds of theories, however, is the difficulty of finding evidence to support them. Nevertheless, Steklis and Raleigh argue strongly for the theory that language evolved from vocalization. They claim that the theory has the advantage of parsimony, because it provides a direct rather than an indirect explanation: many nonhuman primates use nonemotional vocalizations in a rudimentary communicative style. The evolution of new types of skilled movements of the vocal system would have provided a neural basis for the further developments of those vocalizations into language. The results of Jane Goodall's studies on the chimpanzees of Gombe in Tanzania indicate that our closest relatives have as many as 32 separate vocalizations. Goodall notes that the chimps seem to understand these calls much better than humans do, although her field assistants, the people most familiar with the chimps, could distinguish them well enough to claim that the actual number was higher than 32. Figure 19.2 illustrates the wide range of vocalizations made by free-living chimpanzees.

Language As a Recently Evolved Ability

Let us consider the evidence that language (as modern humans use it) has a relatively recent origin. Swadish developed a list of 100 basic lexical concepts that he expected to be found in every language. These concepts included such words as "I," "two," "woman," "sun," and "green." He then calculated the rate at which these words would have changed as new dialects of language were formed. His estimates suggested a rate of change of 14% every 1000 years. When he compared the lists of words spoken in different parts of the world today, he estimated that between 10,000 and 100,000 years ago everyone spoke the same language. According to Swadish's logic, language would have had its origins at about this time (the time when everyone spoke the same language) because diversification would have begun almost as soon as language developed. Hominids have been around for 4 million years; so how can the possibility that they were speaking much earlier than 100,000 years ago be ruled out?

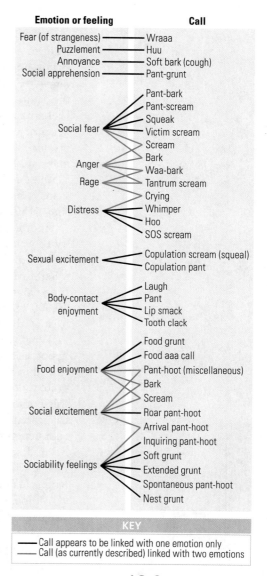

Figure 19.2 Chimpanzee calls and the emotion or feeling with which they are most closely associated. (After Goodall, 1986. Reprinted with permission.)

Lieberman studied the properties of the vocal tract that enable modern humans to make the sounds used for language. Modern humans have a low-placed larynx, and this feature makes them unique among primates. Modern apes and newborn humans have neither of these characteristics and cannot produce all the sounds used in human speech. On the basis of skull reconstructions, Lieberman suggests that Neanderthals also were unable to make the sounds necessary for modern speech. Specifically, they would not have been able to produce the vowels "a," "i," and "u." Because Neanderthals and modern humans are likely each other's closest relatives, having a common ancestor within the past 200,000 years, this inability is evidence that language in modern humans is recent. It is noteworthy, however, that X-rays of modern human skulls suggest no relation between skull morphology and larynx position.

Another argument for the recent development of language is that the ability to write and the ability to speak seem to have a lot in common. Most notably, both require very fine movements and many movement transitions. Therefore, it is possible that speech and writing appeared at about the same time. Marshack found that the first symbols made by humans date to about 30,000 years ago, which would be evidence that speech appeared before or at least at about this time.

What seems to link these three separate lines of evidence, making the recency hypothesis plausible, is that the first appearance of modern humans can be dated to within the past 200,000 years. Possibly the evolution of modern humans was quite sudden and one of their adaptive strategies was language. In opposition to this notion of recently acquired language, Holloway argues from paleontological evidence (for example, the size of Broca's area as revealed by endocasts) that rudimentary language was probably displayed by *Australopithecus* from roughly 2.5 million to 5.5 million years ago. An argument against the paleontological evidence will emerge later when we point out that many brain areas take part in language and that it is by no means clear that Broca's area is central.

Although the development of the vocal tract may have been crucial to human language, MacNeilage argues that the critical feature of language is articulation. This characteristic can be described, basically, as what the mouth does: the mouth is usually opened once for each vocal episode, and the shape of the cavity between the lips and the vocal tract modulates the sound. Articulation is unique to humans. Furthermore, it is employed in virtually every utterance of every one of the world's languages (with the exception of a few words consisting of a single vowel). In human speech, the mouth alternates more or less regularly between a relatively open and a relatively closed configuration, open for vowels and closed for consonants. To MacNeilage, the question raised by this observation is not how the vocal tract changed but how the brain changed to provide the motor control of the mouth necessary for making syllables. This perspective on language alerts us to its importance as a motor action as well as a perceptual capacity.

Speech As a Gestural Language

Some researchers suggest that primitive gestures and other body movements slowly evolved into modern language. This theory assumes that effective hunting and farming and the maintenance of social groups required some kind of communication system and provided the impetus for the evolution of language. Two lines of evidence support the **gestural theory.** First, gestural language and vocal language depend on similar neural systems. The cortical regions that produce mouth and hand movements are adjacent. Second, nonhuman primates can use gestures or symbols for at least rudimentary communication.

It has long been thought that an experiment showing that gestural language and vocal language depend on the same brain structure would support the idea that gestural language evolved into vocal language. As early as 1878, Hughlings-Jackson suggested that a natural experiment, the loss of certain sign-language abilities by people who had previously depended on sign language (specifically ASL), would provide the appropriate evidence, and he even observed a case that seemed to indicate that sign language was disrupted by a left-hemisphere lesion, as is vocal language. A definitive review of similar cases by Kimura confirms that lesions disrupting vocal speech also disrupt signing. Of 11 patients with signing disorders subsequent to brain lesions, 9 right-handers had disorders subsequent to a left-hemisphere lesion. One left-handed patient had a signing disorder subsequent to a left-hemisphere lesion, and another left-handed patient had a signing disorder subsequent to a right-hemisphere lesion. These proportions are identical with those found for vocal patients who become aphasic. Such results strongly support the idea that at least some of the language systems that control vocal speech also control signing.

The idea that verbal language and sign language depend on similar neural structures is supported by Newman and colleagues in fMRI imaging of areas of the brain active during speech and during signing by bilingual speakers. The Newman study also compared signers who acquired sign language early in life (native signers) with those who learned sign language later in life (late signers). As is illustrated in Figure 19.3, both native and late signers show activation in the frontal and temporal lobe of the left hemisphere. This finding confirms a left-hemisphere specialization for sign language implicating the same left-hemisphere brain regions that are active during the use of vocal and written language. There is also activation in the right hemisphere, however, and the area of this activation was larger in the native signers than in the late signers. Specifically, the region of the right angular gyrus was active in the native signers. Note that the corresponding region in the left hemisphere is important for spoken and written language.

If vocal language evolved from gestures used by the ancestors of modern humans, those gestures are likely to have been transmitted genetically rather than culturally. If so, the same gestures should still be transmitted genetically in humans and should still be found in all human groups. Our close relatives, the apes, should also use a subset of this group of gestures. The begging gesture, hand outstretched, of chimpanzees and humans is a likely example of these gestures.

A question that can be raised with respect to gestural theories is why there was a shift to vocalizing. There are at least two plausible explanations. First,

Figure 19.3 Functional MRI images comparing responses in native signers (top) and late signers (bottom) to American Sign Language sentences and to meaningless signlike gestures. Like spoken or written English, ASL activates extensive regions of the left hemisphere, as well as activating right-hemisphere superior temporal and inferior parietal regions. Right-hemisphere activation in native signers includes brain regions not active in later-learning signers. (From Newman et al., 2002.)

Native signers

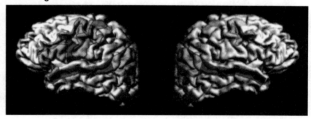

Late signers

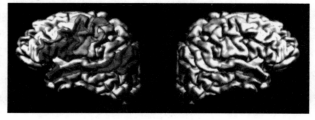

the increasing use of tools meant that our ancestors' hands were more frequently occupied and often could not be used for gesturing. Second, gesturing requires visual contact, but individuals picking fruit in trees or gathering food in tall grass needed to communicate about both food and predators without being able to see one another. A relevant observation in support of the gestural proposal is that hand gestures still accompany language. Indeed, in the absence of a common language, people use elaborate hand and facial gestures to communicate.

Evidence for Languagelike Processes in Apes

Although no nonhuman primates have a verbal language analogous to that of humans, there must be traces of phylogenetic development of the processes necessary for human language. Given that evolution is a matter of "descent with modification," it seems unlikely that language would have evolved de novo in humans. On the other hand, there are those who believe that what makes humans unique in having consciousness is language. A demonstration that other animals have language would deprive humans of this uniqueness. A large number of studies have attempted to explore these matters by examining language abilities in apes (Table 19.2).

One line of experimentation, begun by the Gardners, used versions of American Sign Language. The Gardners brought Washoe, a year-old chimp, into their home. They aimed to teach Washoe ASL hand movements, or signs, for various objects or actions (called exemplars). These signing gestures, analogous to words in spoken language, consist of specific movements that begin and end in a prescribed manner in relation to the signer's body (Figure 19.4). The Gardners molded Washoe's hands to form the desired shapes in the presence of the exemplars of the signs, reinforcing her for correct movements. In addition, rather than using verbal language, the Gardners used ASL to communicate with each other in Washoe's presence. Thus, Washoe was raised in an environment filled with signs. Washoe did learn to understand and to use not only nouns but also pronouns and action verbs. For example, she could sign statements such as "You go me," meaning "Come with me." Attempts to teach ASL to other species of great apes (gorilla, orangutan) have had similar results.

Table 19.2 Summary of language projects in apes

Project	Procedure	Basic reference
Washoe (chimp)	ASL	Gardner and Gardner, 1978
Sarah (chimp)	Plastic tokens to form simple "sentences" to communicate	Premack, 1983
Lana (chimp)	Keyboard communication using a language (Yerkish) based on lexigrams	Rumbaugh, 1977
Koko (gorilla)	ASL and spoken English	Patterson, 1987
Nim (chimp)	ASL	Terrace, 1979
Kanzi (pygmy chimp)	Keyboard communication with Yerkish and spoken English	Savage-Rumbaugh et al., 1986
Chantek (orang)	Pidgin Sign Language	Miles, 1983

Abbreviation: ASL, American Sign Language.

Cat: Draw out two wiskers with thumb and index finger

Fruit: Fingertip and thumbtip on cheek; twist

Me: Index finger points to and touches chest

Caterpillar: Pull hand along arm

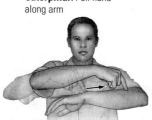

Orange: Squeeze fist in front of chin

Fond: Cross arms over heart

Figure 19.4 Examples from American Sign Language. The Gardners and others taught such symbols to the chimpanzees in their studies. (After Gustason et al., 1975.)

The sign-language studies have been criticized on a number of counts. One weakness is that the apes have not been unequivocally shown to use grammatical structure, an ability possessed even by very young human children. Another problem is that, even if there is some evidence of rudimentary grammar, apes have not been shown to understand that reordering words can give very different meanings. For example, Terrace and his colleagues analyzed more than 19,000 multisign utterances of an infant chimpanzee (Nim), as well as reanalyzing films of Washoe and other chimps. They claimed to have found no evidence of grammatical construction; most of the chimps' utterances were prompted by their teachers' prior utterances and thus could be explained by nonlinguistic processes. Instead, Terrace and his coworkers were struck by the absence of creativity in the apes' utterances and by their dependence on the prior utterances of their teachers. This finding is quite unlike the advanced multiword sequences produced by young children. In response, the Gardners have argued that Terrace used training methods with Nim that were inappropriate for a highly social animal such as a chimp.

Premack approached the study of the language abilities of chimpanzees in a different way. He taught his chimpanzee, Sarah, to read and write with variously shaped and colored pieces of plastic, each representing a word. Premack first taught Sarah that different symbols represented different nouns, just as Washoe had been taught in sign language. Thus, for example, Sarah learned that a pink square was the symbol for banana. Sarah was then taught verbs so that she could write and read such combinations as "give apple" or "wash apple." Her comprehension could be tested easily by "writing" messages to her (that is, by hanging up a series of symbols) and then observing her response. This procedure was followed by much more complicated tutoring in which Sarah mastered the interrogative ("Where is my banana?"), the negative, and finally the conditional (if, then). It is readily apparent that Sarah learned a fairly complicated communication system analogous in some ways to simple human language.

A more recent project has demonstrated even more complex language learning ability in the chimpanzee. After carefully studying the results of the Gardner and Premack projects, Rumbaugh and Gill launched Project Lana, which called for teaching their chimp, Lana, to communicate by means of a keyboard programmed by a computer. The keyboard was composed of nine stimulus elements and nine primary colors, which could be combined in nearly 1800 lexigrams (Figure 19.5) to form a language now known as Yerkish.

Lana had simply to type out her messages on the keyboard. First, she was trained to press keys for various single incentives. Then, the requirements became increasingly complex and she was taught to compose various types of statements, such as the indicative ("Tim move into room"), the interrogative ("Tim move into room?"), the imperative ("Please Tim move into room"), and the negative ("Don't Tim move into room"). Lana was eventually capable of composing strings of six lexigrams.

One of the weaknesses of Project Lana was its assumption that Lana was treating the lexigrams as symbols rather than as mere paired associates for certain stimuli. Indeed, some of the harshest criticisms have come from the Project Lana team itself, Rumbaugh and Gill. In their most recent project, Kanzi, they have altered the format.

Savage-Rumbaugh and coworkers began teaching Malatta, a pygmy chimpanzee caught in the wild, the Yerkish language used with Lana. Malatta was very slow at learning the language, probably because of her age and experience; so the workers tried using English words as well, but to no avail. Serendipitously, Malatta had a male offspring, Kanzi, that accompanied her during her language training. It turned out that, even though he was not specifically trained, Kanzi learned more Yerkish and English than his mother did. Remarkably, his knowledge of English words exceeded his knowledge of the lexigrams. To facilitate his learning, his keyboard was augmented with a speech synthesizer. In the fall of 1986, when he was 6 years old, Kanzi was tested on his comprehension of multisymbol utterances. He responded correctly to 298 of 310 spoken sentences of two or more utterances. In a critical review of the literature, Wallman concludes

Figure 19.5 Yerkish consists of nine basic design elements (A) that are combined to form lexigrams (B). (After von Glaserfeld, 1977. © 1977. Reprinted with permission.)

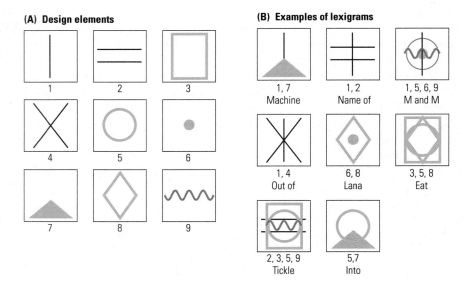

(A) Design elements

1 2 3
4 5 6
7 8 9

(B) Examples of lexigrams

1, 7 — Machine
1, 2 — Name of
1, 5, 6, 9 — M and M
1, 4 — Out of
6, 8 — Lana
3, 5, 8 — Eat
2, 3, 5, 9 — Tickle
5, 7 — Into

that Kanzi's use of lexigrams constitutes the best evidence available to date for the referential application of learned symbols by an ape.

In summary, it is clear that nonhuman primates can employ at least a rudimentary manual sign language and a referential graphic language when trained to do so. Additionally, they may have a much greater predisposition to understand language than to produce it. Anyone watching films of their performance cannot help but be impressed by their abilities. This body of research does suggest that the basic capacity for languagelike processes was there to be selected for in the common ancestor of humans and apes.

Language in Parrots

Although we are specifically interested in the antecedents of human language, it is important to note that, if the languagelike behavior of signing chimps is to be considered an antecedent form of language, then languagelike abilities may also be present in many different brains, even brains extremely different from our own. Irene Pepperberg's African gray parrot Alex deserves mention. Not only does Alex display elements of language, he uses speech. Pepperberg shows Alex a tray of four corks and asks, "How many?" Alex replies, "Four." He can correctly apply English labels to numerous colors, shapes, and materials and to various items made of metal, wood, plastic, or paper. He can use words to identify, request, and refuse items and to respond to questions about abstract ideas, such as the color, shape, material, relative size, and quantity of more than 100 different objects.

Birds do not possess a neocortex, and yet Alex is capable of forms of "thought," "speech," and "language." Perhaps if a brain reaches a certain level of complexity, it then has the ability to learn at least some form of language, even without the presence of a massive neocortex with dedicated neural structures. When a rudimentary language appears, it can be further selected for by evolutionary processes. Thus, we are back to the question with which we began: What has been selected? We consider a number of possibilities.

A Theory of Language

One theory defines language as a combination of four separate abilities: (1) the ability to categorize, (2) the ability to label categories, (3) the ability to sequence behaviors, and (4) the ability to mimic. We will describe these abilities and consider their role in language.

First, we have stressed the idea that sensory information is processed by multiple parallel hierarchical channels. Jerison suggested that, as the cortex expands and there are more channels processing parallel sensory information, it becomes increasingly difficult to integrate the information into a single reality. The brain must determine which of the many different kinds of sensory information reaching the cortex correspond to a given object in the external world. In other words, it becomes necessary to categorize information (for example, to designate some qualities as belonging to plants and others as belonging to animals). One could suppose that categorizing information makes it easier not only to perceive the information but also to retrieve it later when it is needed. It is likely that most animals are capable of categorizing objects to some extent.

Second, although words are the ultimate categorizers, the use of words to label categories must be based on a preexisting perception of categories. The development of human language may have entailed a selection for a novel means of categorization that not only allowed simple sensory stimuli to be combined and grouped but also provided a way of organizing events and relations. This system can take a concept (that is, a category) and stimulate the production of word forms about that concept; conversely, it can take words and cause the brain to evoke the concepts. Thus, a man who was once a painter but is now color-blind can know and use the words (labels) for colors even though he can no longer perceive or imagine what the labels mean. He has, in a sense, lost his concept of color, but words can still evoke it. In contrast, certain brain-lesion patients retain their perception of color, and thus the concept, but have lost the language with which to describe it. They experience colors but cannot attach labels to them.

Third, we have already considered the fact that a unique property of human language is the employment of transitional lip and mouth movements to form syllables. Kimura proposed that left-hemisphere structures associated with language are part of a system that has a fundamental role in the ordering of certain types of movements. Hence, she showed that patients with left-hemisphere lesions have deficits in the repetition of limb movements, oral movements, and syllables. This situation suggests to her that the left hemisphere has neural systems specialized for the selection and ordering of both speech and nonspeech movements.

Fourth, mimicking must play an important role in language development. Not only do babies begin to babble at an early age, but they also copy the sounds made by adults. By some estimates, in the formative period of development, children may add as many as 60 new words each day to their vocabularies. In our description of the organization of the motor system, we described "mirror neurons," neurons in a monkey's frontal cortex that discharge both when the monkey makes a hand movement and when it observes a demonstrator make a similar hand movement. Similar mirror neurons in the language regions of the frontal cortex may be responsible for the mimicking of sounds and words by human children.

This four-part organization both allows us to form concepts and prepares us to communicate them. Julien Jaynes and others have suggested that one of the fundamental functions of language is to allow us to talk to ourselves. Being able to use words to categorize objects and concepts *for ourselves* and then to organize them gives us a real advantage in understanding the world.

The Localization of Language

Current ideas about the localization of language processes come from four basic lines of inquiry: (1) anatomical studies of language, (2) studies of lesions in human patients, (3) studies of brain stimulation in awake human patients, and (4) brain-imaging studies. We consider each in turn.

Anatomical Areas Associated with Language

The anatomical landmarks used by researchers for describing brain regions associated with language vary considerably. Some researchers refer to sulci, others to Brodmann's areas, and still others to areas associated with

(A) Fissures and gyri

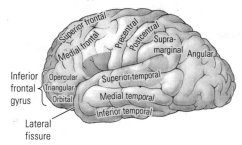

(C) Insula and medial superior temporal gyrus

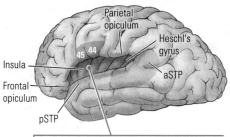

The temporal and frontal lobes have been pulled aside to reveal the insula.

Figure 19.6 Core regions of the brain associated with language functions. They are shown in relation to (A) fissures and gyri and (B) Brodmann's areas and (C) with the lateral fissure opened up to expose the insula and the medial bank of the superior temporal gyrus.

(B) Brodmann's areas

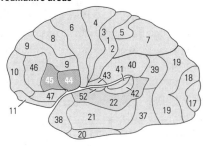

syndromes, such as Broca's area and Wernicke's area. Figure 19.6 illustrates various approaches to labeling the cortical regions that are most frequently described as playing a core role in language.

Figure 19.6A shows that these regions include the inferior frontal gyrus and the superior temporal gyrus, in which Broca's areas and Wernicke's areas, respectively, are located. Parts of surrounding gyri, including the ventral parts of the precentral and postcentral gyrus, the supramarginal gyrus, the angular gyrus, and the medial temporal gyrus, also are within the core language regions. Figure 19.6B depicts the language areas in accord with Brodmann's number system, in which Broca's area is equivalent to areas 45 and 44 and Wernicke's area is equivalent to area 22. Language regions also include parts of areas 9, 4, 3-1-2, 40, 39, and 21. Figure 19.6C shows that, if the lateral fissure is opened up, a number of language-related areas can be found within it, including the insula, Heschl's gyrus (primary auditory cortex), and parts of the superior temporal gyrus referred to as the anterior and posterior superior temporal planes (aSTP and pSTP). Together, Heschl's gyrus, aSTP, and pSTP are sometimes referred to as the **planum temporale.**

This survey by no means covers all language areas. Other regions taking part in language include the dorsal part of area 6 within the lateral fissure (also referred to as the supplementary motor area); parts of the thalamus, the dorsolateral parts of the caudate nucleus, and the cerebellum; visual areas (required for reading), sensory pathways, and motor pathways; and pathways connecting all of these various regions. Furthermore, many regions of the right hemisphere also have roles in language.

Lesion Studies in Humans

Most discussions of the neural basis of language have centered on Broca's area and Wernicke's area, whose historical backgrounds are described in Chapter 1. The early neurological model of language by Wernicke, as well as its later revival by Geschwind, now called the **Wernicke-Geschwind model,** was based

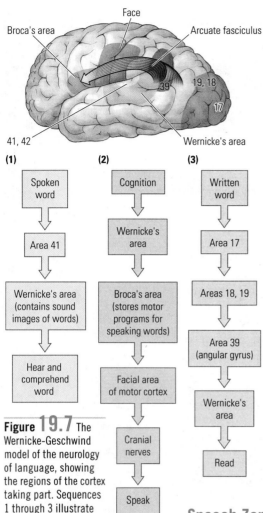

Figure 19.7 The Wernicke-Geschwind model of the neurology of language, showing the regions of the cortex taking part. Sequences 1 through 3 illustrate how the model explains different language functions.

entirely on lesion data (Figure 19.7). This model has played a formative role in directing research and organizing research results. It has three parts:

1. The meaning of words is represented in Wernicke's area. When a person listens to speech, word sounds are sent through the auditory pathways to the primary auditory cortex, Heschl's gyrus. From there, they are relayed to Wernicke's area, where the sense of the words is extracted.

2. To speak, it is necessary to send word meanings over the arcuate fasciculus to Broca's area, where morphemes are assembled. The model proposes that Broca's area holds a representation for articulating words. Instructions for speech are sent from Broca's area to the adjacent facial area of the motor cortex, and from there instructions are sent to facial motor neurons in the brainstem, which relay movement commands to facial muscles.

3. Reading requires that information concerning writing be sent from visual areas 17, 18, and 19 to the angular gyrus (area 39) and from there to Wernicke's area, which reads silently or, in conjunction with Broca's area, reads out loud.

Although useful conceptually, many aspects of this model have been modified by improved lesion analysis and by brain-imaging studies. In the sections that follow, we'll describe the ways in which newer findings are consistent or inconsistent with the Wernicke-Geschwind model.

Speech Zones Mapped by Electrical Stimulation

The language zones of the neocortex, particularly those pertaining to speech, were identified by Penfield and others by using cortical stimulation during surgery. Statistical analyses of results from hundreds of patients have made it possible to construct a map of these regions. The major findings are as follows:

1. Stimulation of a number of cortical areas (Figure 19.8) with a low-voltage electrical current interferes with speech. These areas include the classical areas of Broca and Wernicke in the left hemisphere, as well as the sensory and motor representations of the face and the supplementary speech area in both hemispheres. Recently, Duffau and colleagues reported that stimulation of the pathways that connect parietal areas of the brain with frontal areas also results in the alteration of speech.

2. Penfield and Roberts conclude that stimulation produces two effects on speech:

   a. Positive effects, meaning vocalization that is not speech but rather a sustained or interrupted vowel cry, such as "Oh." Vocalization can be elicited by stimulation of either the facial area or the supplementary motor region of either hemisphere.

b. Negative effects, meaning the inability to vocalize or to use words properly. These effects include a variety of aphasia-like errors:

   i. Total arrest of speech, or an inability to vocalize spontaneously; this error results from stimulation throughout the shaded zones in Figure 19.8.

   ii. Hesitation and slurring of speech; hesitation results from stimulation throughout the zones of Figure 19.8, whereas slurring results primarily from stimulation of the facial area in either hemisphere.

   iii. Distortion and repetition of words and syllables; distortion differs from slurring in that the distorted sound is an unintelligible noise rather than a word. These effects result primarily from stimulation of the classical speech zones, although occasionally from stimulation of the face area as well.

   iv. Confusion of numbers while counting; for example, a patient may jump from "6" to "19" to "4," and so on. Confusion in counting results from stimulation of Broca's or Wernicke's area.

   v. Inability to name despite retained ability to speak. An example is "That is a . . . I know. That is a. . . ." When the current was removed, the patient was able to name the object in the picture correctly. Another example is, "Oh, I know what it is. That is what you put in your shoes." After withdrawal of the stimulating electrodes, the patient immediately said "foot" (Penfield and Roberts, 1959, p. 123). Naming difficulties arise from stimulation throughout the anterior (Broca's) and posterior (Wernicke's) speech zones.

   vi. Misnaming may occur when the subject uses words related in sound, such as "camel" for "comb," uses synonyms, such as "cutters" for "scissors," or perseverates by using the same word twice. For example, the subject may name a picture of a bird correctly but may also call the next picture, a table, a bird. Misnaming, like other naming difficulties, occurs during stimulation of both the anterior and the posterior speech zones.

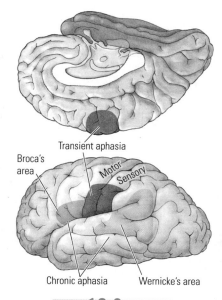

Figure 19.8 The regions where stimulation or surgical lesions have been shown to affect speech. Damage to the two blue areas produces chronic aphasia, damage to the gray areas produces transient aphasia, and damage outside these areas does not produce aphasia.

3. Ojemann and Mateer report that, during stimulation of Broca's area, patients are unable to make voluntary facial movements. Curiously, stimulation of these same points may also disrupt phonemic discrimination. These authors also describe defects in short-term memory resulting from stimulation in the posterior temporoparietal cortex.

4. Most reports agree that the extent of the cortical language zones as marked by stimulation varies considerably among subjects, although there is little indication of what this variation may signify. Ojemann has found that, on the whole, the language area is larger in males than in females. In view of the superior verbal skills of females, this result implies, paradoxically, that the size of the language area may be inversely related to ability. Such a hypothesis is supported by his observation that, in multilinguals, the weaker language is distributed over a larger area than the stronger one. The possibility that improved efficiency requires less neural activity is intriguing and warrants further study. A parallel result obtained by Haier is an inverse correlation between abstract reasoning and cerebral metabolic activity. One is tempted to conclude that "smart brains work better, not harder." A next step in pursuing these questions might be to correlate the size of the speech zones with performance on a variety of verbal tests.

5. Ojemann makes two additional observations. First, he notes that stimulation at particular points has very discrete effects. Stimulation of one cortical site will alter a language function, such as naming, on every trial, and it will alter only one of several language functions tested. Second, in view of the high variability among people in the extent of language representation, Ojemann suggests that the biological substrate for human language is capable of evolving rapidly. That is, it is a highly variable trait or set of traits that is almost certainly subject to selection by the environment.

Several important conclusions can be drawn from these results. First, the data do not support strict localizationist models of language, because the effects of stimulation of the anterior and posterior speech zones on speech functions are remarkably similar. Second, stimulation of the neocortex considerably beyond the classical areas of Broca and Wernicke disturbs speech functions. Third, stimulation of the speech zones affects more than just talking, because it produces deficits in voluntary motor control of facial musculature as well as in short-term memory and reading.

Speech Zones Mapped by Imaging

With the development of PET, fMRI, and event related potential procedures, cognitive psychologists have become more interested in the neural correlates of language processing. To interpret their imaging studies, we must first briefly consider some of the complexities of conducting such experiments.

Suppose the word "cake" is presented visually. Hypothetically, the brain could analyze this sensory input in several ways. It could analyze the surface visual characteristics of the word (for example, the shapes of the letters). It could analyze what are called the phonological aspects of the word. That is, it could consider the sound of the word and whether it rhymes with "bake." Finally, it could assess the meaning of the word, which is referred to as the word's semantic code. The semantic code and other perceptions of "cake" will likely vary considerably among listeners.

A question of particular interest in cognitive psychology is whether the brain does different types of analysis serially, with each depending on preceding levels of analysis, or whether the different types of analysis are done in parallel. This question is not trivial, because, if the analyses are done serially, perhaps, for example, words must be sounded mentally before they are understood. This would mean that nonwords that can be pronounced (such as the nonword "twips") would be analyzed differently from nonwords that cannot be pronounced (such as the nonword "tzpws"). It should be possible to show that the brain activity produced in each case is distinctive; furthermore, because there is no semantic code in these two cases, a third pattern of brain activity should be observed when real words are processed. This division of visual language inputs into visual patterns, phonological aspects, and semantic properties can be applied to the auditory system, too, in which case the words would be analyzed by their frequency, phonemes, and semantics.

The method of presentation (verbal versus written) as well as how and what instructions are given will influence which regions of the brain process words (or nonwords). In addition, the chosen method of image subtraction will also influence which area of the brain will be seen to respond to a word. For example if a word is presented aurally, areas of the brain that respond to any sound will be activated by the presentation. To control for this general response to sound, it is usual to present pseudomorphemes (sounds that could be words but are not) in one trial and true morphemes (real words) in a second trial. The differences between the regions that are active in the two trials will allow the researchers to differentiate between the brain's response to sounds that are not words and the brain's response to sounds that are words. There will, however, be considerable areas of overlap.

After having used fMRI to measure brain areas implicated in language, Binder and colleagues report that these areas make up a remarkably large part of the brain. These researchers presented either tones or meaningful words to 30 right-handed subjects, half of whom were male and half female. Tone stimuli consisted of a number of 500- and 750-Hz pure tones presented in sequence. The subjects pressed a button if they heard two 750-Hz tones in a sequence. Word stimuli were spoken English nouns designating animals (for example, "turtle"). Subjects pushed a button if an animal was native to the United States and used by humans. A rest condition consisted of no stimulus presentations. By subtracting the activation produced by tones from the activation seen during the rest condition, the researchers identified brain regions responding to tones. By subtracting the activation produced by words from the activation produced by tones, the researchers identified brain regions responding to words. Four general brain regions, mainly on the left side of the brain, were found to be activated by words (Figure 19.9): (1) most of the lateral and ventral temporal-lobe region that included the superior middle and inferior temporal gyri and parts of the fusiform and parahippocampal gyri; (2) a prefrontal region that included much of the inferior and superior frontal gyri, rostral and caudal aspects of the middle frontal gyrus, and a part of the anterior cingulate gyrus; (3) the angular gyrus; and (4) an extensive part of the cingulate cortex. Additional areas that were active included the caudate nucleus, the thalamus, and the cerebellum. The results confirm Hughlings-Jackson's prediction that much of the brain would be found to be engaged in language. They also confirm that Broca's and Wernicke's areas take part in language.

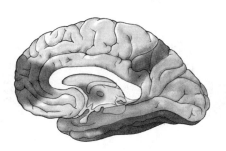

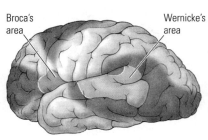

Broca's area

Wernicke's area

Figure 19.9 Left hemisphere brain regions activated while listening to speech, as measured by fMRI. Subjects listened to spoken English nouns designating animals and were required to decide, in each case, whether the word indicated an animal that was native to the United States and was used by humans. (After Binder et al., 1997.)

Using PET and a wider range of stimuli, a number of research groups have identified more-specific functions for some of these language areas (Figure 19.10). Peterson's group used a variety of different conditions to identify speech regions. In one task, they passively presented words (or in some cases pseudo-words or pseudosounds) either visually or aurally to passive subjects. In the next task, the subject was to repeat the word (an output task). In the final task (an association task), the subject was to suggest a use for the object named by the target word (for example, if "cake" was presented, the subject might say "eat"). The authors monitored blood flow by using PET and analyzed their data by using a subtraction technique. Thus, in the sensory (reading or listening) tasks, they identified changes from baseline blood flow by taking the difference between the activities in the two states. In the output task, they subtracted the sensory activity, and, in the association task, they subtracted the output activity.

Their results (Figure 19.10A) lead to several conclusions. First, in the word-viewing condition, blood flow increased bilaterally in the primary and secondary visual areas, whereas, for the word-hearing condition, blood flow increased in the secondary auditory areas. Hearing pronounceable words and nonwords appeared to activate Wernicke's area (area 22), whereas listening to simple tones and vowels did not. Second, there was absolutely no overlap in the visual and auditory activation during the passive task, implying that the processing of the word forms in the two modalities was completely independent. This finding would seem logical, except that it seems to contradict the view of language comprehension that claims that visual input is converted into a phonological code. Third, during the speaking tasks, there was bilateral activation of the motor and

(A) Word-processing areas

Broca's area Speaking words Hearing words Wernicke's area

Generating verbs Viewing words

Each of the tasks in the word-generation experiment activates a distinct set of areas in the brain.

(C) Tools

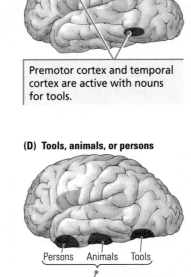

Premotor cortex and temporal cortex are active with nouns for tools.

(B) Selecting words

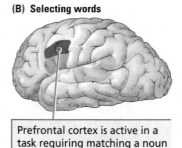

Prefrontal cortex is active in a task requiring matching a noun to one of four target words.

(D) Tools, animals, or persons

Persons Animals Tools

These locations are active for different kinds of nouns.

Figure 19.10 Brain areas activated by language tasks. (Part A after Posner and Raichle, 1994; part B after Wagner et al., 2001; part C after Martin et al., 1996; part D after Damasio et al., 1996.)

sensory facial areas, as well as bilateral activation of the supplementary speech area and activation of the right cerebellum. In addition, there was activation of the insular cortex. Surprisingly, neither Broca's area nor Wernicke's area was active during the repetition task. The activation of the cerebellum presumably corresponds to its role in motor behavior. Fourth, for the task that required generating verbs, there was activation of the frontal lobe, especially the left inferior region, including Broca's area. The verb-generation task also activated the posterior temporal cortex, the anterior cingulate cortex, and the cerebellum.

Other investigators have identified still other areas that are activated, depending on task demands. Wagner and colleagues presented subjects with a single cue word and four target words. A subject's task was to indicate which target word was most closely and globally related to the cue. Thus, the task measured the subject's ability to retrieve meaningful information. They found that an area in the left inferior frontal cortex just dorsal to Broca's area became active during this task (Figure 19.10B). Martin and colleagues asked subjects to name tools or animals and subtracted activation produced by the animal brain response from the tool brain response. They found that a region of premotor cortex was activated, a region that was also activated by imagined hand movements (Figure 19.10C). Finally, Damasio and colleagues report that naming persons, animals, and tools activates specific areas in the inferior temporal lobe (Figure 19.10D).

In summary, the results of studies of this sort are confirming the role of the classical anterior and posterior speech zones in language, but they also show that other regions are implicated. Furthermore, they suggest that the posterior speech zone may deal largely with the analysis of auditory input, inasmuch as there was no increase in blood flow in this region in response to visual stimuli. They also indicate that Broca's area is not simply a cortical representation of the movements of speech, as has been traditionally believed; and they provide evidence that "language" is mapped onto circuits that are ordinarily also engaged in more-primary functions, such that visual attributes of words are represented in visual areas, auditory attributes of words are mapped onto auditory regions of the brain, motor attributes are mapped onto motor regions of the brain, and so on.

It is unlikely that language is simply represented in the brain a number of times in a number of isolated regions. Language is probably organized in the brain in networks that connect both sensory and motor representations of words. Pulvermüller suggests that language is organized in word-related neural webs and that the webs are flexible and change as word use and meaning change. Some representative webs are illustrated in Figure 19.11. Note that, if a word contains visual content, the web includes visual areas of the brain, whereas, if it contains motor content, the web includes motor areas. Any given web will also include nodes within primary and secondary auditory areas as well as nodes within primary and secondary motor regions.

Figure 19.11 Neural webs for language tasks. Local neurons are symbolized by circles, and connecting axons are signified by lines. In this model, different word-related tasks are seen as using different webs. (After Pulvermüller, 2001.)

(A) Word sounds

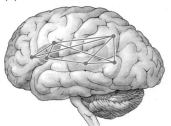

(C) Tool-related word

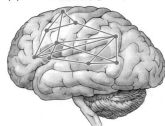

(B) Face-related word

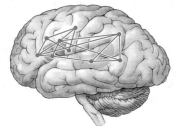

(D) Animal-related word

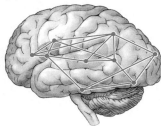

Disorders of Language

In this section, we will describe the classification of symptoms of language impairment. It is important to recognize that, whereas symptom classification was originally linked to brain regions (Broca's aphasia and Broca's area, for example), improved anatomical analysis suggests that such precise correlations do not exist.

Normal language depends on the complex interaction of sensory integration and symbolic association, motor skills, learned syntactical patterns, and verbal memory. Aphasia refers to a disorder of language apparent in speech, in writing (in this case also called **agraphia**), or in reading (also called **alexia**) produced by injury to brain areas specialized for these functions. Thus, disturbances of language due to severe intellectual impairment, to loss of sensory input (especially vision and hearing), or to paralysis or incoordination of the musculature of the mouth (called **anarthria**) or hand (for writing) are not considered to be aphasic disturbances. These disorders may accompany aphasia, and they complicate the study of it.

Table 19.3 Summary of symptoms of disorders of language

Disorders of Comprehension
Poor auditory comprehension
Poor visual comprehension
Disorders of Production
Poor articulation
Word-finding deficit (anomia)
Unintended words or phrases (paraphasia)
Loss of grammar and syntax
Inability to repeat aurally presented material
Low verbal fluency
Inability to write (agraphia)
Loss of tone in voice (aprosidia)

Goodglass and Kaplan have broken down language disturbances into 10 basic types, which we have subgrouped into disorders of comprehension and disorders of production in Table 19.3. Most of these language disorders were described earlier, in our discussions of parietal-, temporal-, and frontal-lobe functions. The one exception is **paraphasia,** which is the production of unintended syllables, words, or phrases in an effort to speak. Paraphasia differs from difficulties in articulation in that sounds are correctly articulated, but they are the wrong sounds; people with paraphasia either distort the intended word (for example, "pike" instead of "pipe") or produce a completely unintended word (for example, "my mother" instead of "my wife").

Despite disagreement among experts concerning the number of types of aphasias, certain classification systems are widely used. The system presented in Table 19.4 groups aphasias into three broadly defined categories: (1) **fluent aphasias,** in which there is fluent speech but difficulties either in auditory verbal comprehension or in the repetition of words, phrases, or sentences spoken by others; (2) **nonfluent aphasias,** in which there are difficulties in articulating but relatively good auditory verbal comprehension; and (3) **pure aphasias,** in which there are selective impairments in reading, writing, or the recognition of words. Within each of these broad categories, numerous subtypes are often distinguished, including Wernicke's aphasia, transcortical aphasia, conduction aphasia, anomic aphasia, and Broca's aphasia.

Table 19.4 Definition of aphasic syndromes

Syndrome	Type of speech production	Type of language errors
Fluent Aphasias		
Wernicke (sensory)	Fluent speech, without articulatory disorders	Neologism or anomias, or paraphasias, poor comprehension; poor repetition
Transcortical (isolation syndrome)	Fluent speech, without articulatory disorders; good repetition	Verbal paraphasias and anomias; poor comprehension
Conduction	Fluent, sometimes halting speech, but without articulatory disorders	Phonemic paraphasias and neologisms; phonemic groping; poor repetition; fairly good comprehension
Anomic	Fluent speech, without articulatory disorders	Anomia and occasional paraphasias
Nonfluent Aphasias		
Broca, severe	Laborious articulation	Speechlessness with recurring utterances or syndrome of phonetic disintegration; poor repetition
Broca, mild	Slight but obvious articulatory disorders	Phonemic paraphasias with anomia; agrammatism; dysprosody
Transcortical motor	Marked tendency to reduction and inertia; without articulatory disorders; good repetition	Uncompleted sentences and anomias; naming better than spontaneous speech
Global	Laborious articulation	Speechlessness with recurring utterances; poor comprehension; poor repetition
"Pure" Asphasias		
Alexia without agraphia	Normal	Poor reading
Agraphia	Normal	Poor writing
Word deafness	Normal	Poor comprehension; poor repetition

Source: After Mazzocchi and Vignolo, 1979.

Fluent Aphasias

Fluent aphasias are impairments related mostly to the input or reception of language. A listener who did not speak the language of a fluent aphasic would receive the impression that the subject was speaking easily and correctly.

Wernicke's aphasia, or **sensory aphasia,** is the inability to comprehend words or to arrange sounds into coherent speech. Luria proposed that this type of aphasia has three characteristics. First, to hear and make out the sounds of speech, one must be able to qualify sounds—that is, to recognize the different sounds in the system of phonemes that are the basic units of speech in a given language. For example, in the Japanese language, the sounds "l" and "r" are not distinguished; a Japanese-speaking person hearing English cannot distinguish these sounds, because the necessary template is not in the brain. Thus, although this distinction is perfectly clear to English-speaking persons, it is not clear to native Japanese. This problem is precisely what a person with Wernicke's aphasia has in his or her own language: the inability to isolate the significant phonemic characteristics and to classify sounds into known phonemic systems. Thus, we see in Wernicke's aphasia a deficit in the categorization of sounds. The second characteristic of Wernicke's aphasia is a defect in speech. The affected person can speak and may speak a great deal, but he or she confuses phonetic characteristics, producing what is often called **"word salad."** The third characteristic is impairment in writing. A person who cannot discern phonemic characteristics cannot be expected to write, because he or she does not know the graphemes (pictorial or written representations of a phoneme) that combine to form a word.

Transcortical aphasia, sometimes called **isolation syndrome,** is a curious type of aphasia in which people can repeat and understand words and name objects but cannot speak spontaneously or they cannot comprehend words, although they can repeat them. Comprehension could be poor because words fail to arouse associations. The production of meaningful speech could be poor because, even though the production of words is normal, words are not associated with other cognitive activities in the brain.

Conduction aphasia is a paradoxical deficit: people with this disorder can speak easily, name objects, and understand speech, but they cannot repeat words. The simplest explanation for this problem is that there is a disconnection between the "perceptual word image" and the motor systems producing the words.

People with anomic aphasia (sometimes called **amnesic aphasia**) comprehend speech, produce meaningful speech, and can repeat speech, but they have great difficulty in finding the names of objects. For example, we saw a patient who, when shown a picture of a ship anchor, simply could not think of the name and finally said, "I know what it does. . . . You use it to anchor a ship." Although he had actually used the word as a verb, he was unable to use it as a noun. Difficulties in finding nouns appear to result from damage throughout the temporal cortex. In contrast, verb-finding deficits are more likely to come from left frontal injuries. Although the extent to which the brain differentiates between nouns and verbs may seem surprising, we can see that they have very different functions. Nouns are categorizers. Verbs are action words that form the core of syntactical structure. It would make sense, therefore, to find that they are separated in such a way that nouns are a property of brain areas controlling recognition and classification, and verbs are a property of brain areas controlling movement.

Nonfluent Aphasias

In nonfluent aphasia (Broca's aphasia, or **expressive aphasia**), a person continues to understand speech but has to labor to produce it: the person speaks in short phrases interspersed with pauses, makes sound errors, makes repetitious errors in grammar, and frequently omits function words. Only the key words necessary for communication are used. Nevertheless, the deficit is not one of making sounds but rather of switching from one sound to another. Nonfluent aphasia can be mild or severe. In one form, transcortical motor aphasia, repetition is good but spontaneous production of speech is labored. In global aphasias, speech is labored and comprehension is poor.

Pure Aphasias

The pure aphasias include alexia, an inability to read; agraphia, an inability to write; and word deafness, in which a person cannot hear or repeat words. These disorders may be quite selective. For example, a person is able to read but not write or is able to write but not read.

The Localization of Lesions in Aphasia

Beginning students of language are intrigued by the simplicity of the Wernicke-Geschwind model of language. In this model, Wernicke's area is associated with speech comprehension, and Broca's area is associated with speech production, and the arcuate fibers that connect the two areas translate meaning into sound. Seasoned researchers, on the other hand, are equally excited to learn that the neural organization of language is more complex than the model suggests and that, in fact, the key deficits of Wernicke's aphasia do not come from damage to Wernicke's area and the key deficits of Broca's aphasia do not come from damage to Broca's area.

There are four reasons why the study of the neural basis of language is itself so complex.

1. As heretofore described, brain-imaging studies are now showing that most of the brain takes part in language in one way or another; and indeed it makes sense that a behavior as comprehensive and complex as language would not be the product of some small, circumscribed region of the brain.

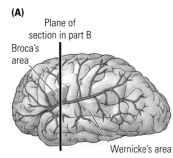

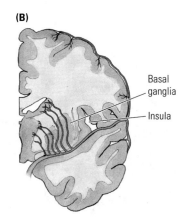

2. Most of the patients who contribute information to the study of language have suffered strokes, usually of the middle cerebral artery. Figure 19.12 illustrates the location of this artery and its tributaries. Because stroke results from a blockage or bleeding of the artery, it is clear that, depending on where a stroke occurs, all of the core language areas may be damaged or only smaller regions may be damaged. There are individual differences in the tributary pattern of the middle cerebral artery, which add to the variation seen in stroke symptoms and outcome. The artery supplies subcortical areas as well, including the basal ganglia, a region that is also thought to play a role in language.

Figure 19.12 The middle cerebral artery. Note that the amount of damage to the cortex by middle cerebral artery blockage can vary widely in the neocortex (A) and the basal ganglia (B), depending on the location of the blockage.

3. Immediately following a stroke, symptoms are generally severe, but as time progresses there is considerable improvement. Thus, the symptoms cannot be easily ascribed to damage in a particular brain region.

4. Aphasias described as nonfluent (Broca's) or fluent (Wernicke's) are syndromes consisting of a number of different symptoms, each of which may have a different neural basis. Keep these variables in mind as we consider some recently proposed ideas concerning the neural basis of language.

Cortical Components of Language

In studying a series of stroke patients with language disorders, Dronkers and coworkers attempted to correlate different symptoms of nonfluent and fluent aphasia with specific cortical regions. Their analysis suggests that nonfluent aphasia consists of at least five kinds of symptoms: apraxia of speech (difficulty in producing sequences of speech sounds), impairment in sentence compre-

Figure 19.13 Proposed relations between brain regions and symptoms of aphasia. Note these relations are different from those originally proposed by Broca and Wernicke.

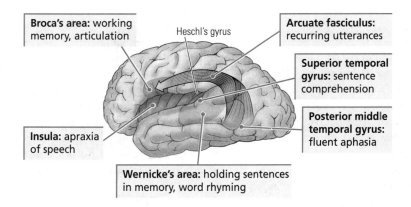

Broca's area: working memory, articulation

Heschl's gyrus

Arcuate fasciculus: recurring utterances

Superior temporal gyrus: sentence comprehension

Posterior middle temporal gyrus: fluent aphasia

Insula: apraxia of speech

Wernicke's area: holding sentences in memory, word rhyming

hension, recurring utterances, impairment in articulation of sounds, and impairment in working memory for sentences. After using overlaying maps of brain injury to identify areas of common damage, they concluded that each of these impairments has a somewhat different neural basis (Figure 19.13). Their analysis also suggests that the core deficit, apraxia, comes not from Broca's-area damage, but from damage to the insula, a large region of the neocortex lying within the dorsal bank of the lateral fissure. Impairments in sentence comprehension seemed to be associated with damage to the dorsal bank of the superior temporal gyrus, recurring utterances seemed to stem from damage to the arcuate fasciculus, and impairments in working memory and articulation seemed to be associated with damage to Broca's area.

Concerning fluent aphasia, Dronkers and colleagues propose that most of the core difficulties, especially the lack of comprehension in speech, comes from damage to the medial temporal lobe and underlying white matter. Damage in this area not only destroys local language regions but also cuts off most of the occipital, temporal, and parietal regions from the core language region. The researchers also propose that damage to Wernicke's area does not result in the core deficits of fluent aphasia but contributes to deficits in holding sentences in memory until they can be repeated and in word rhyming. Thus the patients appear to have impairment in the "iconic" memory for sounds but are not impaired in comprehension.

We must point out, however, that, as we continue with the analysis of the neural basis of language, the continuing localization of deficits only partly contributes to an understanding of language. Brain regions are interconnected, as the Wernicke-Geschwind model indicates. We will not have a complete understanding of language organization until we have a thorough understanding of neural "webs."

Subcortical Components of Language

At the same time that Broca was describing a cortical center for speech control, Hughlings-Jackson proposed that subcortical structures are critical to language. In 1866, he wrote: "I think it will be found that the nearer the disease is to the basal ganglia, the more likely is the defect of articulation to be the striking thing, and the farther off, the more likely it is to be one of mistakes of words."

There has been little study of the role of the basal ganglia in language, but the symptoms displayed by half of the members of the KE family, described in the Snapshot on page 508, suggest that this brain region may be important for the articulation of language.

Hughlings-Jackson's proposal that aphasias result from subcortical damage was not considered seriously until 1959, when Penfield and Roberts suggested that the thalamus, especially the pulvinar nucleus, functions to coordinate the activity of the cortical speech zones. In recent years, evidence from stimulation and lesion studies has supported Hughlings-Jackson's proposal, although the importance—and the precise role—of the thalamus is still being debated.

Some of this evidence was gathered in the course of surgical treatment of dyskinesia (the term for any disturbance of movement). In this kind of procedure, electrodes are used to stimulate different parts of the thalamus as a way of ascertaining the best site for the surgery. For example, if movements are evoked by the stimulation, then the electrode is probably positioned in the motor thalamus, whereas somatosensory changes, such as tingling sensations in the skin, would indicate that the electrode is positioned in the somatosensory thalamus. When the surgeons are satisfied that the electrode is in the desired location, a stronger current is applied, to produce a lesion that they hope will relieve the dyskinesia. Findings in the study of language functions during these procedures, especially by Ojemann's and Cooper's research teams, have indicated that the pulvinar nucleus and the lateral-posterior–lateral-central complex of the left thalamus have a role in language that is not common to other subcortical structures. Stimulation of the left ventrolateral and pulvinar nuclei of the thalamus produces speech arrest, difficulties in naming, preservation, and reduced speed of talking. Stimulation of the thalamus has also been reported to have a positive effect on memory, because it improves later retrieval of words heard during the stimulation. As a result, some researchers have proposed that the thalamus has a role in activating or arousing the cortex.

These lesion studies have documented a variety of disturbances of speech and language processes in association with lesions of the left ventrolateral thalamus or the pulvinar nucleus or both. Symptoms include postoperative dysphasia, which is usually transitory; increased verbal-response latency; decreases in voice volume; alterations in speaking rate and slurring or hesitation in speech; and impaired performance on tests of verbal IQ and memory.

Right-Hemisphere Contributions to Language

Although there is little doubt that the left hemisphere of right-handed people is the dominant hemisphere in language, there is growing evidence that the right hemisphere does have language abilities. The best evidence has come from studies of split-brain patients in whom the linguistic abilities of the right hemisphere have been studied systematically with the use of various techniques for lateralizing input to one hemisphere. The results of these studies have shown that the right hemisphere has little or no speech but surprisingly good auditory comprehension of language, including both nouns and verbs. There also appears to be some reading but little writing ability in the right hemisphere. In short, although the right hemisphere appears to be able to recognize words (semantic processing), it has virtually no understanding of grammatical rules and sentence structures (syntactical processing).

S N A P S H O T

Using MRI to Understand an Inherited Speech and Language Disorder

There is good evidence that language disorders can be inherited. To some scientists, this evidence has suggested that there may be genes for "grammar" or "language." Investigations in a large family, known as the KE family, however, point to the difficulty of relating genetic abnormalities to language abnormalities in any simple way.

Almost half the members of three generations of the KE family are affected by a severe disorder of speech and language that is inherited as an autosomal dominant trait. This language impairment, displayed by 15 of 37 family members, is best characterized as a deficit in the sequencing of articulation patterns, rendering speech sometimes agrammatical and often unintelligible. Genetic analysis of the family identified a locus, designated SPCH1, in chromosome 7q31 that seems to be the genetic basis for the abnormality.

Watkins and her colleagues have compared the performance of affected and unaffected KE family members on a thorough set of neuropsychological tests. A score on a test of repetition of nonwords with complex articulation patterns successfully discriminated between the two groups. Moreover, the affected family members were impaired on verbal and performance IQ tests, including such nonverbal subtests as picture completion and picture arrangement. They were also impaired on most tests of language function. The patients were impaired on tests of mouth movement (oral praxis), including simple movements of clicking the tongue and making sequences of movements (such as blowing up the cheeks, then licking the lips, and then smacking the lips).

Watkins and colleagues also investigated a subset of the affected and unaffected family members by using morphometric MRI analysis, which enabled the measurement of various brain regions. On the one hand, the affected family members were found to have significantly less gray matter in the caudate nuclei, sensorimotor cortex, inferior temporal cortex, cerebellum, and left inferior frontal cortex. On the other hand, the affected members were found to have *more* gray matter in the insula, inferior frontal cortex, and putamen. The reduction in the volume of the caudate nucleus was particularly noteworthy because difficulties in the use of expressive language subsequent to damage to the caudate nucleus have been reported in other studies. It is possible that the language impairments are also associated with regions in which there was an increase in gray matter, but there is no reason to suspect that having larger areas should be associated with language disorders.

The adjoining illustration shows a pedigree of the KE family (A) as well as the average volume of the caudate nucleus at different locations along its nostral-caudal extent in affected and nonaffected family members (B). Only the head, not the tail, of the caudate nucleus was measured. The photograph shows its location. These studies demon-

---

Complementary evidence of the right hemisphere's limited role in language comes from studies of people who have had the left hemisphere removed, a procedure known as **hemispherectomy.** If the left hemisphere is lost early in development, the right hemisphere can acquire considerable language abilities (see Chapter 10 for details), although people with left hemispherectomies are by no means normal. Left hemispherectomy in adulthood is far more debilitating, and in all such cases there are severe deficits in speech; but even these people have surprisingly good auditory comprehension. Their reading ability is limited, however, and writing is usually absent. In general, it appears that left

(A)

Generation
I

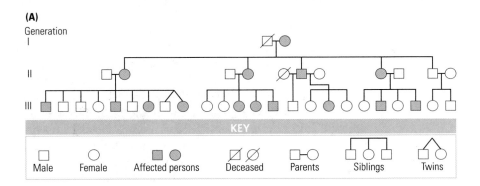

KEY

□ Male	○ Female	■ ● Affected persons	⊠ ⊘ Deceased	□—○ Parents	Siblings	Twins

(B)

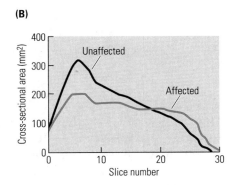

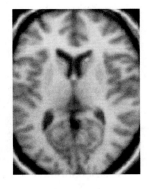

The KE family. (A) Pedigree. (B) The location of the caudate nucleus and its average volume. (After K. E. Watkins et al. *Brain* 125:453–464, 2002.)

strate the use of comprehensive testing procedures and brain-analysis procedures to show that a single genetic abnormality can result in a wide range of impairments that include language deficits as well as numerous associated brain abnormalities.

(K. E. Watkins, F. Vargha-Khadem, J. Ashburner, R. E. Passingham, A. Connelly, K. E. Friston, R. S. J. Frackowiak, M. Mishkin, and D. G. Gadian. MRI analysis of an inherited speech and language disorder: Structural brain abnormalities. *Brain* 125:465–478, 2001.)

hemispherectomy produces language abilities that are reminiscent of those achieved by the right hemisphere of commissurotomy patients.

The effects of right-hemisphere lesions on language functions provide further indication that the right hemisphere is capable of considerable language comprehension, especially of auditory material, even though it cannot control speech. For example, aphasia is rare after right-hemisphere lesions, even after right hemispherectomy, but more-subtle linguistic impairments have been noted, including changes in vocabulary selection, in responses to complex statements with unusual syntactical construction, and in the comprehension of metaphors. In addition,

Table 19.5 Language activities of the two hemispheres

Function	Left hemisphere	Right hemisphere
Gestural Language	+	+
Prosodic Language		
Rhythm	++	
Inflection	+	+
Timbre	+	++
Melody		++
Semantic Language		
Word recognition	+	+
Verbal meaning	++	+
Concepts	+	+
Visual meaning	+	++
Syntactical Language		
Sequencing	++	
Relations	++	
Grammar	++	

Source: After Benson, 1986.

right-orbital-frontal lesions reduce verbal fluency and lead to deficits in the comprehension of tone of voice and possibly in the production of similar emotional tone (prosody).

The differences between the functioning of the right and left hemispheres in language have been summarized in the following way. The wife of a patient with Broca's aphasia comments that her husband understands everything, even though he cannot match spoken words with their pictured representations and cannot follow two-step commands. The wife of a patient with an equivalent right-hemisphere lesion comments that her husband has difficulty following a conversation, makes irrelevant remarks, and generally seems to miss the point of what people are saying, even though he performs quite well on the same tests failed by the patient with a left-hemisphere lesion.

In reviewing the role of the right hemisphere in language, both Benson and Zaidel concluded that the only strictly left hemisphere function in language is syntax (Table 19.5). This function has many components, including production, timing, and sequencing of the movements required for speaking, as well as understanding the rules of grammar. The relative roles of the two hemispheres in other aspects of language comprehension remain to be ascertained.

The Assessment of Aphasia

Since World War II, there has been widespread interest in establishing a standard systematic procedure for assessing aphasia, both to provide standardized clinical descriptions of patients and to facilitate comparison of patient populations in neuropsychological research. In the past 25 years, a number of manuals on aphasia testing have appeared. Table 19.6 summarizes the most widely used tests. Those in the first group are in fact test batteries, in that they contain a large number of subtests so as to systematically explore the language capabilities of the subject. They typically include tests of (1) auditory and visual comprehension; (2) oral and written expression, including tests of repetition, reading, naming, and fluency; and (3) conversational speech. Because test batteries have the disadvantages of being lengthy and requiring special training to administer, some brief aphasia screening tests also have been devised. The two most popular, the Halstead-Wepman Aphasia Screening Test and the Token Test, are often used as part of standard neuropsychological test batteries (see Chapter 28) because they are short and easy to administer and score. These tests do not take the place of the detailed aphasia test batteries, but they provide

Table 19.6 Summary of the major tests of aphasia

Test	Basic reference
Aphasia Test Batteries	
Boston Diagnostic Aphasia Test	Goodglass and Kaplan, 1972
Functional communicative profile	Sarno, 1969
Neurosensory center comprehensive examination for aphasia	Spreen and Benton, 1969
Porch Index of Communicative Ability	Porch, 1967
Minnesota Test for Differential Diagnosis of Aphasia	Schuell, 1965
Wepman-Jones Language Modalities Test for Aphasia	Wepman and Jones, 1961
Aphasia Screening Tests	
Halstead-Wepman Aphasia Screening Test	Halstead and Wepman, 1959
Token Test	de Renzi and Vignolo, 1962

efficient means of discovering the presence of a language disorder. If a detailed description of the linguistic deficit is then desired, the more comprehensive aphasia batteries may be given.

Although theoretical models and test batteries may be useful for evaluating and classifying the status of a patient with aphasia, they are not a substitute for continued experimental analysis of language disorders. In an evaluation of current interpretations of aphasic language disorders, Marshall pointed out some of the inadequacies of the models and batteries and argued that the development of a psychobiology of language disorders is still needed. Whereas the test batteries attempt to classify patients into a number of groups, a psychobiological approach would concentrate on individual differences and peculiarities and from these differences would attempt to reconstruct the processes through which the brain produces language. On the practical side, Marshall notes that only about 60% of patients will fit into a classification scheme such as the one presented in Table 19.4. Similar inadequacies have been noted in the use of other classification methods. For example, most patients with a language impairment show a deficit in naming that can be elicited by having them look at pictures of objects and attempt to identify them. Scores on standard tests often tell little about this impairment. A number of patients might be able to name a violin, but one patient might know only that it is a musical instrument, another that it is a stringed instrument, and still another that it is similar to a cello and not a trumpet. Some patients have highly selective naming deficits, such as being unable to name buildings, or people, or colors, or objects found inside houses. Thus, it is inappropriate simply to classify all these different conditions as anomic and draw no further distinctions between them. The study of such differences can be a source of important insight into the neural organization of language.

The Assessment of Dyslexia

The assessment of reading disorders is becoming a special branch of the study of language for several reasons. First, it is possible to be more objective in the analysis of reading than in the analysis of writing and speaking. Additionally, there is a large pedagogical science of reading. Finally, in addition to the **acquired dyslexias**—impairments in reading subsequent to brain damage—cases of developmental **dyslexia,** or failure to learn to read during development, are common and require diagnosis and remediation.

Coltheart argued that model building is the most objective approach to the study of reading. A model is much like an algorithm, a set of steps to follow to answer a question. Reading models are used to test reading-disabled people, both as a way of defining the impairment and as a way of testing the utility of the model. The model-building approach differs from classical neurological approaches in two ways: (1) the latter define dyslexia according to whether it arises in conjunction with other disorders, such as dysgraphia or dysphasia, and (2) the primary intent is to correlate the impairment with the locus of brain damage. The model-building approach views reading as being composed of a number of independent skills or subsystems, one or another of which may not be functioning in an impaired reader.

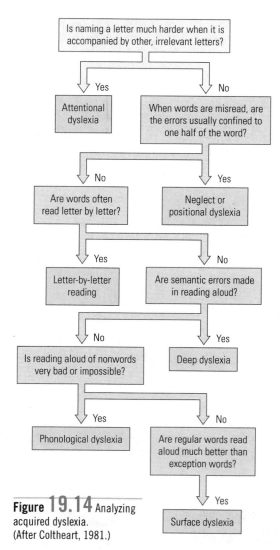

Figure 19.14 Analyzing acquired dyslexia. (After Coltheart, 1981.)

The model-building approach can be traced to an analysis by James Hinshelwood, first published in 1900, in which he identified different types of reading disorders: (1) the inability to name letters (letter blindness), (2) the inability to read words (word blindness), and (3) the inability to read sentences (sentence blindness). Hinshelwood's taxonomy and its subsequent elaboration led to the current hypothesis that reading is composed of a number of independent abilities that may each have an independent anatomical basis. Figure 19.14 shows a series of questions that an examiner might ask to identify the following impairments:

1. *Attentional dyslexia.* When one letter is present, letter naming is normal. When more than one letter is present, letter naming is difficult. Even if a letter is specially colored, underlined, has an arrow pointing to it, and is pointed to by the tester, it may be named incorrectly when it is not alone. The same phenomenon may occur for words when more than one is present.

2. *Neglect.* Persons displaying this impairment may misread the first half of a word (for example, reading "whether" as "smother") or they may misread the last part of a word (for example, reading "strong" as "stroke"). This syndrome has received little investigation.

3. *Letter-by-letter reading.* Affected persons read words only by spelling them out to themselves (aloud or silently). When the spelling is done silently, it can be detected by the additional time required for reading long words. Frequently, an affected person can write but then has difficulty reading what was written.

4. *Deep dyslexia.* The key symptoms of this disorder are semantic errors: persons with deep dyslexia read semantically related words in place of the word that they are trying to read (for instance, "tulip" as "crocus" and "merry" as "Christmas"). Nouns are easiest for them to read, followed by adjectives and then verbs. Function words present the greatest difficulty. Those who suffer from deep dyslexia also find it easier to read concrete words rather than abstract ones and are completely unable to read nonsense words. They are also generally impaired at writing and in their short-term verbal memory (digit span).

5. *Phonological dyslexia.* The one symptom of phonological dyslexia is an inability to read nonwords aloud; otherwise reading may be nearly flawless.

6. *Surface dyslexia.* The surface dyslexic cannot recognize words directly but can understand them by using letter-to-sound relations; that is, the word can be understood if it is sounded out. This reading procedure works well as long as the words are regular ones ("home," "dome"), but not if the words are irregular ("come" will be read as "comb"). Spelling is also

impaired but is phonetically correct. Surface dyslexia does not develop in languages that are totally phonetic (such as Italian). Surface dyslexia is a common symptom of children who have difficulty in learning to read.

Marshall cleverly demonstrates the model-building idea of reading with the following example of two lines of poetry that can be read either for sense or for sound:

> Kuh! Sie Kuh! Sie kann der . . .
> Wer Du ja Wanduhr?

This poetry can be read as two lines of German (which the reader may or may not understand) or it can be read phonetically as "Goosey, Goosey Gander / Where do you wander?" (By the way, the meaning in German is "Cow! You Cow! Who do you think you are / You and your clock on the wall?") The point of this example is that, in normal readers, sense and sound are computed in parallel, whereas, in the dyslexic, one process or the other may be absent. The deep dyslexic is unable to process for sound and so attempts to read for sense. This person, unless he or she spoke German, would not be able to read the lines at all. The surface dyslexic is able to process for sound but not for sense. This person might pronounce the English words correctly but still not realize what they were saying. A model of how parallel systems may be organized and interact in the normal reader is illustrated in Figure 19.15. Note that there are quite separate ways of obtaining speech from print and a still different way of producing letter names. The important features of the model-building approach are that it does not depend on function–anatomy relations, it can be applied to language disorders other than dyslexia, and it may eventually lead to an alternative perspective on the anatomical organization of language.

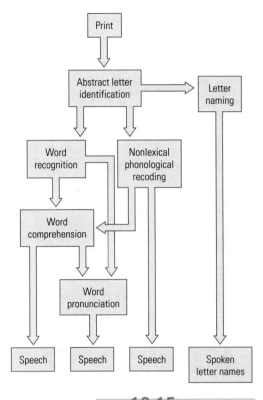

Figure 19.15 Subsystems used in reading. Note that speech from print can follow a number of different routes and can be independent of comprehension or pronunciation. (After Coltheart, 1981.)

Summary

Language is a unique human ability that extends the development of multiple sensory channels. It gives us a way to organize sensory inputs by assigning tags to information, which allows us to categorize objects and ultimately concepts. Language also includes the unique motor act of producing syllables, as well as the ability to impose grammatical rules, which dramatically increases the functional capacity of the system.

The various language functions take up a large part of the cortex. Some, such as the generation of verbs versus nouns or the understanding of visual versus auditory information, are found in precise locations. Like other cerebral functions, language seems to be organized in a series of parallel hierarchical channels. The evolution of language may not be the development of a single ability but rather the parallel development of several processes, such as the ability to categorize and the ability to use gestures for communication.

References

Benson, D. F. Aphasia and lateralization of language. *Cortex* 22:71–86, 1986.

Benson, D. F. Aphasia. In K. M. Heilman and E. Valenstein, Eds. *Clinical Neuropsychology*, 3d ed. New York: Oxford University Press, 1993.

Binder, J. R., J. A. Frost, T. A. Hammeke, R. W. Cox, S. M. Rao, and T. Prieto. Human brain language areas identified by functional magnetic resonance imaging. *Journal of Neuroscience* 17:353–362, 1997.

Caplan, D. *Language: Structure, Processing, and Disorders.* Cambridge, MA: MIT Press, 1992.

Caplan, D., and J. C. Marshall. Generative grammar and aphasic disorders: A theory of language representation in the human brain. *Foundations of Language* 12:583–596, 1976.

Chomsky, N. On the biological basis of language capabilities. In R. W. Rieber, Ed. *Neuropsychology of Language.* New York: Plenum, 1976.

Coltheart, M. Disorders of reading and their implications for models of normal reading. *Visible Language* 15:245–286, 1981.

Coltheart, M. Acquired dyslexias and normal reading. In R. N. Malatesha and H. A. Whitaker, Eds. *Dyslexia: A Global Issue.* The Hague: Martinus Nijhoff, 1984.

Cooper, I. S., I. Amin, R. Chandra, and J. M. Waltz. A surgical investigation of the clinical physiology of the LP-pulvinar complex in man. *Journal of Neurological Science* 18:89–100, 1973.

Damasio H., T. J. Grabowski, D. Tranel, R. D. Hichwa, and A. R. Damasio. A neural basis for lexical retrieval. *Nature* 380:499–505 1996.

Demonet, J. F., R. Wise, and R. S. J. Frackowiak. Language functions explored in normal subjects by positron emission tomography: A critical review. *Human Brain Mapping* 1:39–47, 1993.

de Renzi, E., and L. A. Vignolo. The Token Test: A sensitive test to detect disturbances in aphasics. *Brain* 85:665–678, 1962.

Dronkers, N. F., B. B. Redfern, and R. T. Knight. The neural architecture of language disorders. In M. S. Gazzaniga, Ed. *The New Cognitive Neurosciences.* Cambridge, MA: MIT Press, 1999, pp. 949–958.

Duffau, H., L. Capelle, N. Sichez, D. Denvil, M. Lopez, J.-P. Sichez, A. Bitar, and D. Fohanno. Intraoperative mapping of the subcortical language pathways using direct stimulations: An anatomo-functional study. *Brain* 125:199–214, 2002.

Fitch, W. T. The evolution of speech: A comparative review. *Trends in Cognitive Science* 4:258–267, 2000.

Gardner, R. A., and B. T. Gardner. Comparative psychology and language acquisition. *Annals of the New York Academy of Sciences* 309:37–76, 1978.

Geschwind, N. Language and the brain. *Scientific American* 226:76–83, 1972.

Goodall, J. *The Chimpanzees of Gombe.* Cambridge, MA: Harvard University Press, 1986.

Goodglass, H., and E. Kaplan. *The Assessment of Aphasia and Related Disorders.* Philadelphia: Lea & Febiger, 1972.

Green, E. Psycholinguistic approaches to aphasia. *Linguistics* 53:30–50, 1969.

Gustason, G., D. Pfetzing, and E. Zawoklow. *Signing Exact English.* Silver Spring, MD: Modern Signs Press, 1975.

Haier, R. J., B. V. Siegel, Jr., A. MacLachlan, E. Soderling, S. Lottenberg, and M. S. Baushbaum. Regional glucose metabolic changes after learning a complex visuospatial motor task: A positron emission tomographic study. *Brain Research* 570:134–143, 1992.

Halstead, W. C., and J. M. Wepman. The Halstead-Wepman aphasia screening test. *Journal of Speech and Hearing Disorders* 14:9–15, 1959.

Hewes, G. W. Language origin theories. In D. M. Rumbaugh, Ed. *Language Learning by a Chimpanzee.* New York: Academic Press, 1977.

Holloway, R. L. Human paleontological evidence relevant to language behavior. *Human Neurobiology* 2:105–114, 1983.

Jefferson, G. Localization of function in the cerebral cortex. *British Medical Bulletin* 5:333–340, 1949.

Jerison, H. J. *Brain Size and the Evolution of Mind.* New York: American Museum of Natural History, 1991.

Kellogg, W., and L. Kellogg. *The Ape and the Child.* New York: McGraw-Hill, 1933.

Kimura, D. Neural mechanisms in manual signing. *Sign Language Studies* 33:291–312, 1981.

Kimura, D. *Neuromotor Mechanisms in Human Communication.* Oxford: Oxford University Press, 1993.

Kimura, D., and N. Watson. The relation between oral movement control and speech. *Brain and Language* 37:565–590, 1989.

Levelt, W. J. M. *Speaking: From Intention to Articulation.* Cambridge, MA: MIT Press, 1989.

Lieberman, P. *On the Origins of Language: An Introduction to the Evolution of Human Speech.* New York: Macmillan, 1975.

Luria, A. R., and J. T. Hutton. A modern assessment of basic forms of aphasia. *Brain and Language* 4:129–151, 1977.

MacNeilage, P. F. The frame/context theory of evolution of speech production. *Behavioral Brain Sciences* 21:499–511, 1998.

Marshack, A. *The Roots of Civilization: The Cognitive Beginnings of Man's First Art, Symbol, and Notation.* New York: McGraw-Hill, 1971.

Marshall, J. C. Biological constraints on orthographic representation. *Philosophical Transactions of the Royal Society of London* 298:165–172, 1982.

Marshall, J. C. The description and interpretation of aphasic language disorder. *Neuropsychologia* 24:5–24, 1986.

Martin, A., C. L. Wigs, L. G. Ungerleider, and J. V. Haxby. Neural correlates of category-specific knowledge. *Nature* 379:649–652, 1966.

Mateer, C. Asymmetric effects of thalamic stimulation on rate of speech. *Neuropsychologia* 16:497–499, 1978.

Mazzocchi, R., and L. A. Vignolo. Localization of lesions in aphasia: Clinical-CT scan correlations in stroke patients. *Cortex* 15:627–654, 1979.

Miles, L. W. Apes and language: The search for communicative competence. In J. de Luce and H. T. Wilder, Eds. *Language in Primates: Perspectives and Implications.* New York: Springer, 1983.

Monrad-Krohn, H. The third element of speech: Prosody and its disorders. In L. Halpern, Ed. *Problems of Dynamic Neurology.* Jerusalem: Hebrew University Press, 1963.

Newcombe, F., and J. C. Marshall. On psycholinguistic classifications of the acquired dyslexias. *Bulletin of the Orton Society* 31:29–46, 1981.

Newman, A. J., D. Bavelier, D. Corina, P. Jezzard, and H. J. Neville. A critical period for right hemisphere recruitment in American Sign Language processing. *Nature Neuroscience* 5:76–80, 2002.

Ojemann, G. A. The thalamus and language. *Brain and Language* 2:1–120, 1975.

Ojemann, G. A. Models of the brain organization for higher integrative functions derived with electrical stimulation techniques. *Human Neurobiology* 1:243–250, 1982.

Ojemann, G. A., and O. D. Creutzfeldt. Language in humans and animals: Contribution of brain stimulation and recording. *Handbook of Physiology*, vol. 5, *The Nervous System.* Bethesda, MD: American Physiological Society, 1987.

Ojemann, G. A., and C. Mateer. Cortical and subcortical organization of human communication: Evidence from stimulation studies. In H. D. Steklis and M. J. Raleigh, Eds. *Neurobiology of Social Communication in Primates: An Evolutionary Perspective.* New York: Academic Press, 1979.

Patterson, F. G. *Koko's Story.* New York: Scholastic, 1987.

Penfield, W., and L. Roberts. *Speech and Brain Mechanisms.* Princeton, NJ: Princeton University Press, 1959.

Petersen, S. E., and J. A. Fiez. The processing of single words studied with positron emission tomography. *Annual Review of Neuroscience* 16:509–530, 1983.

Petersen, S. E., P. T. Fox, M. I. Posner, M. Mintun, and M. E. Raichle. Positron emission tomographic studies of the processing of single words. *Journal of Cognitive Neuroscience* 1:153–170, 1988.

Porch, B. E. *Index of Communicative Ability.* Palo Alto, CA: Consulting Psychologists Press, 1967.

Posner, M. I., and M. E. Raichle. *Images of Mind.* New York: Scientific American Library, 1994.

Premack, D. The codes of man and beasts. *Behavioral and Brain Sciences* 6:125–167, 1983.

Pulvermüller, F. Brain reflections of words and their meaning. *Trends in Cognitive Sciences* 5:517–524, 2001.

Raichle, M. E., J. A. Fiez, T. O. Videen, A. K. Macleod, J. V. Pardo, P. T. Fox, and S. E. Peterson. Practice-related changes in human brain functional anatomy during non-motor learning. *Cerebral Cortex* 4:8–26, 1994.

Ricklan, M., and I. S. Cooper. Psychometric studies of verbal functions following thalamic lesions in humans. *Brain and Language* 2:45–64, 1975.

Rumbaugh, D. M., and T. V. Gill. Lana's acquisition of language skills. In D. M. Rumbaugh, Ed. *Language Learning by a Chimpanzee.* New York: Academic Press, 1977.

Sarno, M. T. *The Functional Communication Profile: Manual of Directions.* New York: Institute of Rehabilitation Medicine, New York University Medical Center, 1969.

Savage-Rumbaugh, E. S., K. McDonald, R. A. Sevcik, W. D. Hopkins, and E. Rubert. Spontaneous symbol acquisition and communicative use by pygmy chimpanzees (*Pan paniscus*). *Journal of Experimental Psychology: General* 115:211–235, 1986.

Schuell, H. *Differential Diagnosis of Aphasia with the Minnesota Test.* Minneapolis: University of Minnesota Press, 1965.

Searleman, A. A review of right hemisphere linguistic capabilities. *Psychological Bulletin* 84:503–528, 1977.

Spreen, O., and A. L. Benton. *Neurosensory Center Comprehensive Examination for Aphasia.* Victoria, Canada: University of Victoria, 1969.

Steklis, H. D., and M. J. Raleigh. Requisites for language: Interspecific and evolutionary aspects. In H. D. Steklis and M. J. Raleigh, Eds. *Neurobiology of Social Communication in Primates: An Evolutionary Perspective.* New York: Academic Press, 1979.

Swadish, M. *The Origin and Diversification of Language.* J. Sherzer, Ed. Chicago: Aldine-Atherton, 1971.

Terrace, H. S. *Nim.* New York: Knopf, 1979.

von Glaserfeld, E. The Yerkish language and its automatic parser. In D. M. Rumbaugh, Ed. *Language Learning by a Chimpanzee.* New York: Academic Press, 1977.

Wagner, A. D., E. J. Paré-Blagoev, J. Clark, and R. A. Poldrack. Recovering meaning: Left prefrontal cortex guides controlled semantic retrieval. *Neuron* 31:329–338, 2001.

Wallman, J. *Aping Language.* Cambridge, UK: Cambridge University Press, 1992.

Wepman, J. M., and L. V. Jones. *Studies in Aphasia: An Approach to Testing.* Chicago: University of Chicago Education-Industry Service, 1961.

Whitaker, H. A. *On the Representation of Language in the Human Brain.* Edmonton, Canada: Linguistic Research, Inc., 1971.

Zaidel, E. Language in the right hemisphere. In D. F. Benson and E. Zaidel, Eds. *The Dual Brain.* New York: Guilford Press, 1985.

Zangwill, O. L. Excision of Broca's area without persistent aphasia. In K. J. Zulch, O. Creutzfeldt, and G. C. Galbraith, Eds. *Cerebral Localization.* Berlin and New York: Springer, 1975.

chapter 20

Emotion

The year was 1912. After a difficult labor of 22 hours, a baby boy was born. J. P. weighed 11.5 lb, but dropped to 5 lb after postpartum complications. Ackerly reports that J. P. appeared to recover from his early trauma and by age 1 was walking and talking with apparently normal intelligence. But he was a problem child. He was hyperactive and showed no emotion but anger, which he expressed in temper tantrums.

As J. P. grew to school age, he began to wander away. Police would find him miles from home, but evidently he never showed any fear of being lost. Even severe whippings did not deter him. School was a real problem. Although he was extremely well mannered most of the time, J. P. unexpectedly engaged in inappropriate behaviors such as exposing himself and masturbating in the classroom.

Growing up, he developed no close friendships and was generally disliked. The community blamed the parents for much of the boy's problems, but nothing the parents did was helpful. As an adolescent, J. P. pawned his mother's rings, stole his uncle's car, and drove to Chicago from Kentucky to spend the money. At 19, when his criminal record for theft began to mount, a psychiatrist began to investigate the nature of his behavioral problems, finding eventually that J. P.'s right frontal lobe was missing and his left was only 50% of normal size. It was the 1930s, and few treatment options existed.

As an adult, J. P. could not hold down a job for more than a few weeks, largely because of his erratic behavior. At one moment he was charming and at the next was reacting out of all proportion to some seemingly trivial matter. Even by age 50, J. P.'s behavior had not changed: he remained hyperactive and alone, largely detached from anything that gives meaning to life such as love or friendship. He had virtually no social feelings at all and evidently was unable to understand what such feelings would be like or to react to emotions in others. Absent frontal lobes, J. P. had no social skills and showed very little emotion, except in the form of temper tantrums.

Emotion entails cognitive processes that may either be conscious or lie outside our awareness. We begin this chapter by exploring the nature of emotion and how neuroscientists have studied emotion and developed theories over the past century. Then we consider contemporary neuropsychological theories of emotion and reported asymmetries in how the brain produces, interprets, and reacts to emotion.

The Nature of Emotion

J. P.'s behavior was extreme and certainly not common. More typical is the observation that seemingly minor brain injury can change a person's personality. To neuropsychologists, impairments of movement, perception, language, or memory affect how a person expresses and reacts to emotion and how that person's emotions are perceived by others. Not so evident to observers, however, is a subject's or patient's feeling of emotion. Indeed, some view emotion as an inconvenient remnant of our evolutionary past, a nonconscious time when humans literally were driven by "instincts" such as emotion.

Some believe that humans are fundamentally rational creatures, but emotion is older than thought. People such as J. P., with blunted or lost emotions, may behave in a completely rational manner most of the time, but, when making personal and social decisions, they act irrationally.

Damasio emphasizes that emotion is a cognitive process that actually contributes to logical thinking. He argues that the mechanisms of reasoning are influenced significantly by both unconscious and conscious signals that come from the neural machinery underlying emotion. Note the contrast in neuropsychologists' use of unconscious as a synonym for nonconscious brain activity with Freud's use as a hidden or repressed component of the mind. Neuropsychologists use unconscious as shorthand for von Helmholtz's notion of **unconscious inference,** processes outside of awareness and learned by experience, whereby observers use knowledge to perceive.

Feeling Emotion

What is the last strong emotion you felt? Perhaps you had a serious disagreement with a close friend or received some unexpected, wonderful news. An emotion cannot be described as a unitary event, because emotional processes differ in multiple ways from one another and from other cognitive processes.

An emotional experience may include all sorts of thoughts or plans about who said or did what or what will be done in the future. Your heart may pound, your throat tighten, you may sweat, tremble, or flush. Strong emotional feelings (rage or elation) are not always verbalized. Marked changes in facial expression, tone of voice, or body posture—even tears of sadness or joy—convey emotion to others.

These emotional signals are very powerful and little influenced by experience. It is well documented by Paul Ekman, for example, that basic emotional expressions of anger, fear, disgust, surprise, happiness, and sadness are universally recognized by people throughout the world (Figure 20.1). In this context, that J. P. did not recognize such expressions is all the more curious.

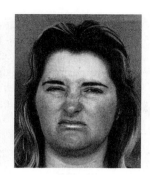
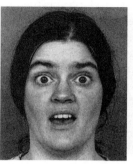

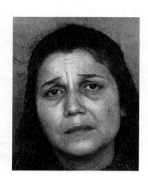

Figure 20.1 Paul Ekman and his colleagues showed these photographs to people in different types of societies throughout the world—societies ranging from hunting and gathering to postindustrial—and found that facial expressions of basic emotions are recognized by humans of all cultures regardless of experience. (Courtesy of Dr. Paul Ekman from P. Ekman, and W. V. Friesen, 1984.)

What Is Emotion?

Neuropsychologists view emotion not as a thing but rather as an inferred behavioral state called **affect**, a conscious, subjective feeling about a stimulus independent of where or what it is. Affective behavior is internal and subjective. As observers, we can infer emotion in others only from their behavior (what they say and do) and by measuring physiological changes associated with emotional processes.

Emotion has many components, and each, in principle, can be quantified as well as observed. A contemporary theory of emotion must include at least four principal behavioral components.

1. *Physiology*. Physiological components include central and autonomic nervous system activity and the resulting changes in neurohormonal and visceral activity. Hence, emotion produces changes in heart rate, blood pressure, the distribution of blood flow, perspiration, and the digestive system, among others, as well as the release of hormones that may affect the brain or the autonomic system. Although the idea is a topic of some debate, it seems likely that at least some emotional states (for example, happiness versus sadness) can be differentiated by their associated physiological changes.

2. *Distinctive motor behavior*. Facial expression, tone of voice, and posture express emotional states. These motor behaviors are especially important to observing emotions because they convey overt action that can differ from observed verbal behavior. Our perception of a person who says she is fine but is sobbing uncontrollably is different from our perception of the same person when smiling.

3. *Self-reported cognition*. Cognitive processes are inferred from self-reported rankings. Cognition operates in the realm of both subjective emotional feelings (feeling love or hate, feeling loved or hated) and other cognitive processes (plans, memories, or ideas).

4. *Unconscious behavior*. Cognitive processes influence behavior that is not conscious—behavior of which we are not aware. We may make decisions on the basis of "intuition" or a hunch or other apparently unfounded basis. Recall, for example, in Chapter 16 the gambling task in which normal subjects gradually changed their behavior to optimize the outcome but seemed unconscious of why they had chosen to play certain decks of cards over others to win the game. (In contrast, frontal-lobe patients behaved irrationally: they failed to choose these decks, lost all their play money, and had to "borrow" more to continue the experiment.)

The theoretical distinction among physiology, movement, self-reports, and unconscious action as component behaviors of emotional experience is significant because researchers detect little correlation among the physical states of emotion when all of them are measured in the same subjects. A brief review of a century's research on emotion will set the stage for exploring the anatomy of emotion and contemporary theories in depth.

Historical Views

Interest in the biology of emotion dates to Darwin's book titled *The Expression of the Emotions in Man and Animals*, published in 1872. Darwin believed that human emotional expression could be understood only in the context of expression in other animals because emotional behavior is determined by evolution. Although Darwin's book was a bestseller in its time, its influence was short lived and it was temporarily forgotten.

Investigating the Anatomy of Emotion

Psychologists began to speculate about emotions at the turn of the twentieth century, but they had little knowledge about the neural basis of emotional behavior. By the late 1920s, physiologists began to examine the relation between autonomic, endocrine, and neurohumoral factors and inferred emotional states, with particular emphasis on measuring indices such as heart rate, blood pressure, and skin temperature (see reviews by Dunbar and by Brady).

Philip Bard made one of the first major anatomical discoveries about emotion while working in Walter Cannon's laboratory in the late 1920s. Friedrich Goltz's studies in the 1890s had shown that decorticated dogs could show strong "rage" responses to seemingly trivial stimuli (recall J. P.'s behavior); the dogs behaved as though a seriously threatening stimulus confronted them. Working with cats, Bard showed that this response depended on the diencephalon, which includes the thalamus and hypothalamus. He found that, if the diencephalon was intact, animals showed strong "emotional" responses, but, if the animals were decerebrate (see Figure 10.2), leaving the diencephalon disconnected from the midbrain, they were unemotional.

The results of later studies by many investigators (especially Eckhard Hess in the 1940s and John Flynn in the 1960s) show that stimulating different regions of the hypothalamus elicits different "affective responses" in cats (see Chapter 15). Behaviors associated with attacking another cat (piloerection, hissing, baring of teeth) or attacking a prey animal (crouching, whiskers and ears forward, pouncing)—including eating the animal, among others—can result.

The lesion and stimulation studies on the diencephalon were important because they led to the idea that the thalamus and hypothalamus contain the neural circuits for the overt expression of emotion and for autonomic responses such as changes in blood pressure, heart rate, and respiration. The cortex was envisioned as inhibiting the thalamus and hypothalamus. Conversely, the thalamus was seen as activating the cortex during autonomic arousal, presumably to help direct the emotion to the appropriate stimulus.

The Emotional Brain

Papez proposed the first major theory in the neurology of emotions in 1937. The structure of the "limbic lobe" (see Figure 3.18) forms the anatomical basis of emotion, Papez reasoned, and the limbic structures act on the hypothalamus to produce emotional states. Although for Papez the neocortex played no part in producing emotional behavior, he did believe the cortex necessary for transforming events produced by limbic structures into our experience of emotion.

The Papez theory had appeal: it combined behavioral phenomena having no known neurological substrates with anatomical structures having no known function. The idea of an emotional brain gained instant broad approval because Freudian thinking predominated in the 1930s. That an ancient, deep part of the central nervous system controls emotions and instincts in Freud's unconscious, with the neocortex producing consciousness, was a concept with natural appeal for the psychology of the time.

The Cortical Connections of Emotion

Two contributions in the 1930s shed light on the nature of the cortical structures and connections implicated in emotion. In both cases, investigators were studying something other than emotion and made serendipitous findings that fundamentally changed our thinking about the emotional brain.

Klüver-Bucy Syndrome

A major finding came in 1939, when Heinrich Klüver and Paul Bucy announced the rediscovery of an extraordinary behavioral syndrome that had first been noted by Sanger Brown and Edward Schaefer in 1888. The *Klüver-Bucy syndrome* has been observed subsequently in people with a variety of neurological diseases. One obvious aspect of this extraordinary set of behaviors is lack of affect. For example, animals displaying Klüver-Bucy syndrome show no fear whatsoever to threatening stimuli such as snakes or to "threat" signals from humans or other animals, situations in which normal animals show strong aversion.

The behavioral syndrome, resulting experimentally from bilateral anterior temporal lobectomy in monkeys, includes

- tameness and a loss of fear;

- indiscriminate dietary behavior, the monkeys being willing to eat many types of previously rejected foods;

- greatly increased autoerotic, homosexual, and heterosexual activity, with inappropriate object choice (for example, sexual mounting of chairs);

- hypermetamorphosis, a tendency to attend and react to every visual stimulus;

- a tendency to examine all objects by mouth; and

- visual agnosia.

Marlowe and colleagues reported on a patient with Klüver-Bucy symptoms that resulted from meningoencephalitis (inflammation of the brain and the meninges):

> Behavioral patterns were distinctly abnormal. He exhibited a flat affect, and, although originally restless, ultimately became remarkably placid. He appeared indifferent to people or situations. He spent much time gazing at the television, but never learned to turn it on; when the set was off, he tended to watch reflections of others in the room on the glass screen. On occasion he became facetious, smiling inappropriately and mimicking the gestures and actions of others. Once initiating an imitative series, he would perseverate copying all movements made by another for extended periods of time. In addition, he commonly generated a series of idiosyncratic, stereotyped gestures employing primarily his two little fingers which he would raise and touch end-to-end in repetitive fashion.
>
> He engaged in oral exploration of all objects within his grasp, appearing unable to gain information via tactile or visual means alone. All objects that he could lift were placed in his mouth and sucked or chewed. He was commonly observed to place his fingers in his mouth and suck them. He did not attempt to pick up objects directly with his mouth, using his hands for that purpose, but was observed to engage in much olfactory behavior. When dining he would eat with his fingers until reprimanded and a fork placed in his hand; he was thereafter able to imitate use of a fork, but failed to remaster the task of eating with utensils spontaneously. He would eat one food item on his plate completely before turning to the next. Hyperbulimia [excessive, insatiable appetite] was prominent; he ingested virtually everything within reach, including the plastic wrapper from bread, cleaning pastes, ink, dog food, and feces. Although his tastes were clearly indiscriminate, he seemed to prefer liquids or soft solids.
>
> The patient's sexual behavior was a particular source of concern while in hospital. Although vigorously heterosexual prior to his illness, he was observed in hospital to make advances toward other male patients by stroking their legs and inviting fellatio by gesture; at times he attempted to kiss them. Although on a sexually mixed floor during a portion of his recovery, he never made advances toward women, and, in fact, his apparent reversal of sexual polarity prompted his fiancee to sever their relationship. (Marlowe et. al., 1975, pp. 55–56)

The appearance of the Klüver-Bucy syndrome in humans and monkeys apparently requires that the amygdala and inferior temporal cortex be removed bilaterally. H. M., the amnesic patient described in Chapter 18, does not exhibit the syndrome despite bilateral removal of the medial temporal structures. Furthermore, monkeys with bilateral amygdalectomies do not show the Klüver-Bucy syndrome unless the temporal cortex also is removed. Finally, there is a single case of a man with a bilateral temporal lobectomy identical with the Klüver-Bucy removal, and he showed all the Klüver-Bucy symptoms, with the exception of orality. Instead of placing novel objects in his mouth he repeatedly inspected them visually.

Psychosurgery

At about the time of Klüver and Bucy's discovery, a less dramatic, but in many ways more important, discovery was made. Carlyle Jacobsen studied the behavior of chimpanzees in a variety of learning tasks subsequent to frontal-lobe removals. In 1935, he reported his findings on the effects of the lesions at the Second International Neurology Congress in London. He casually noted that one particularly neurotic chimp appeared more relaxed after the surgery, leading a Portuguese neurologist, Egas Moniz, to propose that similar lesions in people might relieve various behavioral problems. Thus was born psychosurgery and the frontal lobotomy.

Unbelievably, not until the late 1960s was any systematic research done on the effects of frontal-lobe lesions on the affective behavior of nonhuman animals. Hence, frontal lobotomies were performed on humans without an empirical basis. Experimental findings by several laboratories clearly confirm the results of frontal lobotomies on humans: frontal-lobe lesions in rats, cats, and monkeys have severe effects on social and affective behavior across the board.

Studies in Normal Subjects

Laterality studies look not only at cognitive behaviors, as summarized in Chapter 11, but also at the lateralization of affective processes in normal subjects. The basic approach in these studies is to present stimuli to one hemisphere, by using dichotic (or tachistoscopic) techniques, to demonstrate a difference in the performance of the two hemispheres.

If one hemisphere were superior to the other at recognizing tone of voice or facial expression, for example, the superior hemisphere could be inferred to have a dominant role in emotion. We now survey these studies briefly, dividing them according to whether they investigate the production of affective behavior or its perception, and conclude by considering how personality differences might relate to brain structure.

The Production of Affective Behavior

The results of a series of studies by Campbell demonstrate that facial expressions are not always symmetrical but rather tend to be predominantly on the left side of the face. The asymmetries may range from the hardly noticeable—

such as the flicker of a smile on the left side of Mona Lisa's face (on the right in the painting)—to the pronounced—such as a raised eyebrow, wink, or lopsided smile on the left side of the face.

In one study, Moscovitch and Olds surreptitiously recorded the facial expressions of people in restaurants, finding a left-side preponderance of facial expression. They confirmed this observation by carefully analyzing video recordings of people recounting sad and humorous stories, again finding a left-side bias in facial expressions.

Asymmetrical facial expressions show right-hemisphere specialization in producing emotion consistent with its presumed specialization in perceiving facial expressions. It is tempting to speculate that right-hemisphere specialization in producing and interpreting nonverbal behavior is analogous to left-hemisphere specialization in producing and interpreting language, but it has yet to be proved. We caution that the apparent specialization of the right hemisphere in the perception of faces could easily be interpreted as a specialization for the perception of complex visual stimuli, of which faces are an example.

The Perception of Relevant Stimuli

To date, studies of perception of emotionally loaded stimuli by normal subjects have examined only vision and audition. For both modalities, the stimulus is usually presented to one hemisphere selectively, either alone or in competition with information presented simultaneously to the opposite hemisphere.

Vision

Two procedures are used for the visual presentation. In one procedure, faces with different expressions (for example, sad and happy) are presented tachistoscopically to the left or right visual field, and the subject is asked to identify the facial expression. The results show the left visual field to be superior at correct identification. This superiority can be interpreted as demonstrating a right-hemisphere specialization for the perception of facial expression, an important aspect of nonverbal communication.

The second procedure employs an ingenious technique devised by Dimond (see also a more recent study by Wittling and Roschmann). By using special contact lenses, Dimond and his colleagues were able to project several types of films selectively to the left or right hemisphere. Subjects rated each film on a scale of 1 to 9 on four emotional dimensions—humorous, pleasant, horrific, or unpleasant.

Films presented to the right hemisphere were judged more unpleasant and horrific and produced greater autonomic nervous system activation (as measured by heart rate) than did these same films presented to the left hemispheres of other subjects. Dimond and his colleagues concluded that the two hemispheres hold an essentially different emotional view of the world. Curiously, if the films were shown to both hemispheres simultaneously, the ratings closely resembled those of the right visual field (the left hemisphere), suggesting that left-hemisphere perception is dominant.

We could hypothesize that a left-hemisphere lesion would result in a more negative view of the films, although this possibility has not been studied. The idea that the left hemisphere has a more positive view of the world has proved controversial, although fMRI research by Canli and coworkers provides provocative support for the idea.

Audition

Studies of asymmetries in the auditory perception of emotions generally employ a dichotic-listening technique, which generally shows a left-ear superiority for emotion-laden sounds such as laughing or crying. A compelling experiment was conducted by Ley and Bryden, who employed as stimuli a number of short sentences spoken in happy, sad, angry, and neutral voices. These sentences were dichotically paired with neutral sentences of similar semantic content.

Subjects were instructed to attend to one ear and to report the emotional tone of the target sentence and indicate its content by checking off items on a multiple-choice recognition sheet. Virtually every subject showed a left-ear advantage for identifying the emotional tone of the voice and, at the same time, a right-ear advantage for identifying the content. This result is analogous to that obtained by Dimond and colleagues, who found that the two hemispheres deal with visual material in a similar manner: left eye for emotional tone and right eye for content.

Personality Differences and Brain Structure

Many personality traits or emotional behaviors characteristic of brain-damaged patients can be observed in people without known brain injury. This observation leads us to speculate that differences in cerebral organization, whether genetically or environmentally derived, form the basis of different human personalities. For example, one could hypothesize that people who are hypercritical may have relatively smaller or less-active temporal lobes than those of people who are not hypercritical. Or that people without much facial expression have smaller or less-active frontal lobes than normal.

Because people vary widely in their performance on neuropsychological tests of cognitive behavior, it would be interesting to explore the differences in performance on measures of cognitive and emotional behavior in the *same normal subjects*. An intriguing study by Canli and colleagues used fMRI to directly test whether individual differences in brain reactivity to emotional stimuli are correlated with extraversion and neuroticism in healthy women. Extraversion was correlated with brain reactivity to positive stimuli in localized brain regions, whereas neuroticism was correlated with brain reactivity to negative stimuli in localized brain regions. These findings suggest that personality traits are indeed associated with activity in distinct cerebral regions.

Candidate Structures in Emotional Behavior

A consistent principle of neural organization is that multiple systems control virtually every behavior. Sensory information enters the cortex through multiple, distinctly different sensory channels. When stimuli have been processed, information travels through multiple parallel systems subserving different functions.

Processing Emotional Stimuli

Recall that visual information follows a ventral route through the temporal lobe and a dorsal route through the parietal lobe. The former route appears to play a role in object recognition, and the latter in spatial location. In keeping with this general principle of brain organization, we can speculate that multiple systems, both cortical and subcortical, contribute to the experience of an emotion.

Neural systems must process sensory stimuli as being significant to social behavior. Presumably sensations are species specific for stimuli including olfactory (pheromones), tactile (especially to sensitive body zones), visual (facial expressions), and auditory (phonemes, crying, screaming, and so forth) stimuli. Arguably these socially significant stimuli are processed by the same systems that analyze other sensory inputs, but at least some sensory systems may be separate. Olfaction in cats provides a good example.

In many mammals, a receptor organ (Jacobson's organ) is specialized to analyze species-typical odors. When animals such as cats encounter certain odors (especially urine from other cats), they close their nostrils and appear to stare off into space with an odd look on their faces, a behavior known as *flehmen* (Figure 20.2). Actually, the cats are forcing the air through the roof of the mouth and into a special duct (which allows the air access to Jacobson's organ) that is connected to the accessory olfactory system. (The accessory olfactory system functions to analyze species-specific odors and has direct connections to the hypothalamus and amygdala.)

Virtually the only odors that produce flehmen in cats are from other cats, including urine and ear wax but not feces. (Curiously, we have found that human urine also is often effective.) This neural system is thus specialized for species-typical odors. An interesting property is that the system shows habituation (repeated exposure to the same urine reduces the likelihood of flehmen), and cats appear able to remember the odors of familiar cats. Thus, they do not show flehmen to their own urine or to that of cats with which they live. Urine from novel cats will produce prolonged episodes of flehmen, and urine from familiar, but not coresident, cats will produce shorter episodes.

Although little evidence points to such specialized systems for other senses, there is more evidence of specialized processing for emotionally relevant sensory information. Cells in the temporal lobes of monkeys are specially tuned for species-typical calls and are relatively insensitive to other sounds. Recall, too, the temporal cortical cells that are specialized for faces (see Chapter 15).

It is possible as well that higher-level systems process other aspects of sensory information, including the internal generation of feelings. In addition to

Figure 20.2 A cat sniffs a urine-soaked cotton ball (left), begins the gape response of the flehmen (middle), and follows with the full gape response (right). This behavior is mediated by the accessory olfactory system.

multiple systems that may encode specific species-typical information, a general cortical system may identify affective attributes of external stimuli. An interesting experiment by Gazzaniga and Le Doux illustrates such a system. They presented split-brain subjects with visual information to one or the other visual field. A subject's task was to describe the stimulus verbally and to give it a rating on a five-point scale from "dislike very much" to "like very much."

The results were striking. As expected, only the items in the right visual field (and therefore sent to the left, speaking, hemisphere) were described accurately. In contrast, the five-point rating was identical for stimuli in each visual field. Clearly, the pathways that process the affective significance of the stimuli are distinct from the pathways that process their objective properties.

This distinction is reminiscent of the difference between knowing what a stimulus is and knowing where it is, as illustrated by blindsight (see Chapter 13). There may be a third system that processes affect. We have all recognized an odor, sound, or other physical stimulus, even though we cannot identify what it is. We may say that we have a "feeling" or "intuition" about the stimulus. This effect is often true of sounds that may elicit a certain feeling because of the context in which they are normally heard. For example, music that is associated with being at some place or with some person may elicit emotional feelings when heard in another context, such as an elevator. We may not realize why we are suddenly melancholy or unusually happy.

Brain Circuits for Emotion

As noted earlier, in the early 1930s, when the psychiatrist was beginning to study J. P., the limbic lobe (including the amygdala) and prefrontal cortex were identified as brain regions implicated in emotion. Although the original limbic structures identified by Papez in the late 1930s focused on the hippocampus and its connections with the hypothalamus, modern views of the limbic system include the amygdala and prefrontal cortex. Figure 20.3 shows the amygdala lying adjacent to the hippocampus in the temporal lobe, with the prefrontal cortex lying just anteriorly.

Figure 20.4 schematically illustrates the limbic circuit. The hippocampus, amygdala, and prefrontal cortex all connect with the hypothalamus. The mammillary nucleus of the hypothalamus connects to the anterior thalamus, which in turn connects to the cingulate cortex. Connections from the cingulate complete the circuit by connecting to the hippocampus, amygdala, and prefrontal cortex.

Although the entire circuit is important for emotional behavior, the amygdala and prefrontal cortex hold the key to understanding the nature of emotional experience. We considered the anatomy of the prefrontal cortex in detail in Chapter 16, and so we will briefly examine only the amygdala here.

From the Greek, meaning "almond," the amygdala is formed by three principal subdivisions—the corticomedial, basolateral, and central areas.

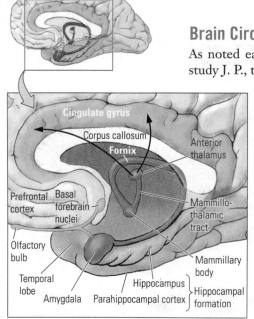

Figure 20.3 The limbic lobe, which encircles the brainstem, consists of the cingulate gyrus and hippocampal formation, the amygdala, the mammillothalamic tract, and the anterior thalamus.

(A)

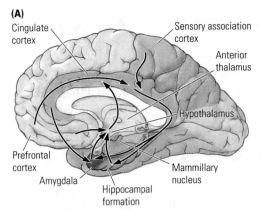

Cingulate cortex

Sensory association cortex

Anterior thalamus

Hypothalamus

Prefrontal cortex

Amygdala

Mammillary nucleus

Hippocampal formation

(B)

Prefrontal cortex | Sensory association cortex

Cingulate cortex

Amygdala

Hippocampal formation

Anterior thalamus

Mammillary nucleus

Hypothalamus

Behavior

Figure 20.4
Contemporary view of the limbic system. (A) An interconnected network of structures including the cortex, thalamus, hypothalamus, hippocampal formation, and amygdala forms the basis of emotional experience. (B) A schematic representation of the major connections in the limbic circuit. The prefrontal and sensory regions connect with the cingulate cortex, hippocampal formation, and amygdala. The last two structures connect with different regions in the hypothalamus, which in turn connects with the cingulate cortex through the thalamus.

Like the prefrontal cortex, the amygdala receives inputs from all sensory systems and, like the prefrontal cortex, the cells of the amygdala require complex stimuli (such as faces) to be excited. In addition, many cells in the amygdala are multi-modal. In fact, some neurons in the amygdala respond to visual, auditory, somatic, gustatory, *and* olfactory stimuli, just as prefrontal cells do. The amygdala can therefore create a complex image of the sensory world, and we shall see later that this image is especially sensitive to stimuli that might be threatening or dangerous.

Studies of Nonhuman Primates: Prefrontal and Paralimbic Lesions

Although spouses or relatives often complain of personality changes in brain-damaged patients, but the parameters of these changes have been poorly specified in human subjects. Even the behavioral changes in people such as Phineas Gage (see Chapter 16) are described in general, subjective terms and are seldom reported objectively. The results of research on animals, particularly nonhuman primates, has made it possible to identify brain regions that undoubtedly have a significant role in emotional processes.

In the past 30 years, studies have been conducted on several species of Old-World and New-World monkeys with lesions of the frontal cortex, paralimbic cortex, or amygdala—the forebrain areas that appear to be most important in emotional behavior. The results show six consistent changes in emotional behavior after frontal lesions.

1. *Reduced social interaction.* Especially after orbital frontal lesions, monkeys become socially withdrawn and fail even to reestablish close preoperative relations with family members. The animals sit alone; seldom if ever engage in social grooming or contact with other monkeys; and, in a free-ranging natural environment, become solitary, leaving the troop altogether. Anterior temporal lesions produce a milder version of this

interaction syndrome, reducing social grooming and social interaction with conspecific monkeys. Lesions elsewhere in the cortex have no obvious effect.

2. *Loss of social dominance.* As reported in Chapter 16, after orbital frontal lesions, monkeys that were formerly dominant in a group do not maintain their dominance, although the fall from power may take weeks to complete, depending on the aggressiveness of other monkeys in the group.

3. *Inappropriate social interaction.* Male monkeys are much larger than females. Yet female monkeys with orbital frontal lesions may challenge and threaten unfamiliar male monkeys. Normal females typically exhibit gestures of submission in response to dominance gestures displayed by unfamiliar males. Lesion monkeys may also approach any animal without hesitation, irrespective of that animal's social dominance. This behavior often results in retaliatory aggression from the dominant, intact animals. Similarly, when approached by dominant animals, monkeys with frontal lesions may simply ignore them or run away, rather than performing normal submissive gestures such as allowing mounting. Curiously, such monkeys show an increased aversion to threat by people, possibly owing to a decrease in aggressive behavior.

4. *Altered social preference.* When a normal monkey is released into a large enclosure that has conspecifics behind a glass barrier, it will generally sit against the glass next to an animal sitting on the opposite side. Although normal animals prefer to sit beside intact monkeys of the opposite sex, monkeys with large frontal lesions prefer to sit with other frontal monkeys of the same sex, presumably because they are less threatening.

5. *Reduced affect.* Monkeys with frontal lesions and those with anterior temporal lesions largely abandon facial expressions, posturings, and gesturings in social situations—the effects being larger after frontal than after temporal lesions. (Lesions of the cingulate or visual association cortex seem to have no effect.) Thus, monkeys with frontal lesions show a drastic drop in the frequency and variability of facial expressions and are described as "poker-faced." The one exception is in the frequency of submissive or agitated expressions such as the "grimace." This loss of facial expression is not a simple loss of muscle control of the face, because the animals do produce expressions, but not often.

6. *Reduced vocalization.* Lesions of the frontal or anterior limbic cortex reduce spontaneous social vocalizations. Indeed, after anterior cingulate lesions, rhesus monkeys effectively make no normal vocalizations at all. Curiously, the nonvocal social behavior of these animals is normal.

In general, lesions of the monkey orbital frontal cortex produce marked changes in social behavior. In particular, lesion monkeys become less socially responsive and fail to produce or respond to species-typical stimuli. Damage to the paralimbic cortex produces milder effects, the animals showing a reduction in social interaction. An important point is that, despite the significant changes in the sensory processing abilities of animals with visual association lesions, there appear to be very few obvious changes in their affective behavior.

The changes in emotional processes in monkeys with frontal lesions are especially intriguing because they suggest that similar changes might be found in humans with frontal-lobe injuries. In particular, because monkeys fail to make appropriate vocal and gestural behaviors and fail to respond normally to those made by conspecifics, we can predict that humans with frontal-lobe injuries or abnormalities, such as those endured by J. P., will show similar changes in social behavior. Furthermore, disorders such as schizophrenia, which are characterized by significant changes in social interactions, also might be due to frontal dysfunction.

Studies of Nonhuman Primates: Amygdalectomy

In their original studies, Klüver and Bucy observed grossly abnormal emotional behavior in monkeys after removal of the amygdala and the adjacent paralimbic cortex and temporal neocortex. Subsequent work showed that destruction of the amygdala alone produced much of the syndrome, inasmuch as monkeys whose amygdalas had been removed showed a reduced aversion to biologically relevant stimuli that normal monkeys found threatening. In general, there is a loss of fear of humans and a general taming in such monkeys.

Among the animals studied by Dicks and his colleagues, four of six with amygdalectomies failed to rejoin their original groups when freed, and all died within a short time. The two remaining animals were younger, and they did rejoin their group but rarely initiated social activity. The results of studies of single-unit activity in the amygdala have shown cells that respond to species-typical aversive visual stimuli, a result that is consistent with the loss of response to such stimuli after lesioning.

The close anatomical connections between the orbital prefrontal cortex and the amygdala and the emotional changes after lesions to either region suggest that these structures belong to a neural circuit regulating emotional behavior. Disconnecting the amygdala from its visual input through the temporal lobe also produces alterations in emotional behavior, which suggests that the amygdala may form part of a neural system for processing socially relevant visual information (see Chapter 17).

Recall that a region in the temporal lobe, the superior temporal sulcus, plays a central role in the analysis of biological motion (see Chapter 15). Certain aspects of biological motion, such as body posture, hand and facial movement, and eye gaze, are all components of social perception. The superior temporal sulcus has reciprocal connections with the amygdala and presumably is a major source of information allowing the amygdala to play a central role in the analysis of facial expression.

Premorbid Emotional Processes

The personality of a human brain-injured patient is at least partly dependent on his or her premorbid, or preinjury, state. A person who is depressive before the injury is likely to be depressive afterward; a person who is cheerful is likely to remain so. There has been no systematic study of this phenomenon, but in our experience there is far more intersubject variability in the emotional behavior of brain-damaged people than there is in most tests of cognitive function.

A study by Peters and Ploog on the social behavior of squirrel monkeys with frontal lesions is relevant here. Although these researchers found many of the changes in social behavior previously observed by others, they also noted that some monkeys seemed less changed by their lesions. Two dominant monkeys received similar orbital frontal lesions; but, whereas one of them completely lost his dominant position, the other remained dominant but did not exert the dominance strongly. In another social group, the second monkey might have been challenged and lost this position. Differences in the premorbid behavior of the lesioned monkeys, as well as in the group structure, appear to have contributed to the change in social behavior after lesioning.

In contrast, when monkeys with frontal lesions are given neuropsychological learning tests such as delayed-response tests, all animals typically show a much more similar behavioral change. This result is important because it is probably true of humans as well: the effects of brain damage on processes such as language and memory are more consistent than the effects on emotion. Or, stated differently, the premorbid personalities of human patients with cortical injuries are likely to influence the extent of postinjury changes in emotional processes. This possibility has been completely neglected in research to date and adds a major complication as we try to make generalizations about emotional processes.

The relation between premorbid behavior and the effects of cerebral injury leads to the logical idea that there must be some difference in the details of brain organization in response to social experience. One promising finding is that the density of serotonin receptors in the orbital frontal cortex of a monkey correlates with the animal's social status. In fact, Raleigh and colleagues have shown that pharmacologically increasing serotonin receptors alters social behavior and increases social status. This result may offer some explanation for how drugs that selectively block serotonin reuptake such as the SSRIs (for example, Prozac; see Figure 6.9) can alter social behavior in humans (see Panksepp's review for more on this idea).

General Theories of Emotion

One theme runs through all modern theories of emotion: emotion and cognition are intimately related and likely entail overlapping neural systems. It therefore follows that changes to cognitive abilities will be related to changes in emotion and vice versa. (For a thorough review of theories of emotion, see a recent review by Scherer.) Here, we outline three current theories that represent the major lines of thinking in cognitive neuroscience regarding emotion: Damasio's somatic marker hypothesis, Le Doux's cognitive–emotional interaction theory, and Gainotti's lateralization theory. The reader is directed to books and reviews by these authors in the References at the end of this chapter.

Somatic Marker Hypothesis

The core of Damasio's somatic marker hypothesis comes from William James's ideas, first formulated in the late nineteenth century. James argued that an emotion consists of a change in body and brain states in response to the evaluation of a particular event. For example, if you encounter a poisonous snake as you walk along a path, your heart rate, respiration, and sweating increase. We interpret these physiological changes as fear.

Thus, a person is confronted with a stimulus that has biological importance, and the brain and the body change as a result. One prediction that we could make here is that, if there is a reduction in the bodily reaction to a stimulus, then there should be a reduction in the intensity of emotions. Figure 20.5 illustrates that people with spinal-cord injuries do indeed experience reduced emotionality, the loss being proportional to the level of injury.

In contrast with James, who was really talking about intense emotions such as fear or anger, Damasio's theory is more encompassing and includes a much broader range of bodily changes. For example, there may be a change in motor behavior, facial expression, autonomic changes, or endocrine changes as well a change in how the brain processes this information and other information. Hence, for Damasio, emotions engage those neural structures that represent body states and those structures that somehow link the perception of external stimuli to body states.

The changes in the body (that is, the somatic markers) are thus linked to external events, and these two together influence cognitive processing. What is different in the Damasio theory is that he specifies that the neural control of emotions includes limbic structures and the prefrontal cortex, both of which are widely assumed to play a role in emotion, as well as structures that represent body states. These latter structures include the somatosensory cortex and components of the basal ganglia, all of which represent the state of the body. In addition, for cases in which an emotion produces a global change in neural processing, such as in depression or mania, the model includes neuromodulatory structures such as forebrain cholinergic systems and brainstem noradrenergic, dopaminergic, and serotinergic systems.

A key aspect of Damasio's somatic marker hypothesis is that emotion is fundamental to the survival of the individual within a particular environment. The environment for mammals, and certainly for humans, includes not only the physical environment but also the social environment. Emotions therefore affect the survival of members of a social group.

The social aspect is of great importance in humans and includes the study of social development, social communication, and even culture. These topics have barely been addressed by neuroscientists, and virtually nothing is known about the neural underpinnings of social emotions such as jealousy, pride, and embarrassment. Given that the frontal lobe has expanded so extensively in human evolution, these emotions probably require some form of frontal-lobe processing, but this is conjecture at this point.

Finally, Damasio's theory emphasizes that emotion is not only a fundamental experience for all higher animals but also a necessary experience for us to make rationale decisions. This is especially true in situations in which a person

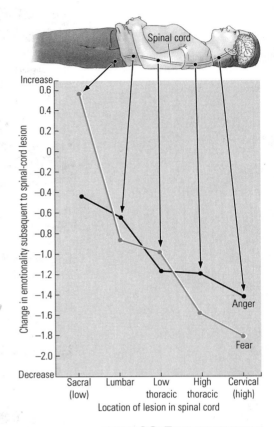

Figure 20.5 Spinal injury reduces the experience of emotion. The extent of emotional loss is greatest when the lesion is high on the spinal cord.

faces risk or conflict. People with reduced emotions, such as frontal-lobe patients, thus show impairments in personal or social matters, especially when they include the possibility of risk or conflict. The role of our emotions, especially subtle emotional states, is obviously not always conscious, and thus we may be unable to account for why we behave in certain ways.

Cognitive–Emotional Interactions

Le Doux's theory also is evolutionary. The general idea is that emotions evolved to enhance the survival of animals and, as the brain evolved, cognitive and emotional processes grew more and more interrelated. In contrast with Damasio, Le Doux has not tried to account for all emotions but rather has chosen one emotion—namely, fear—as an exemplar of how to study brain–behavior relations in emotion.

In Le Doux's view, all animals inherently detect and respond to danger, and the related neural activities eventually evolve to produce a feeling—in this case, fear. When a mouse detects a cat, fear is obviously related to predation, and in most situations animals such as mice have fear related either to predation or to danger from other mice who may take exception to their presence in a particular place. For humans, however, fear is a much broader emotion that today is only rarely of predation but routinely includes stress—situations in which we must "defend" ourselves on short notice.

Modern humans face wide-ranging physical and psychological dangers, from sports injuries to terrorism, as well as more subtle dangers such those posed by chronic stress. One important implication of the Le Doux theory is that our fear system includes both unconscious fear responses, such as the mouse would show to the cat, and conscious awareness of subjective feelings of fear. He presumes, however, that the neural system underlying fear is similar in both cases and that the neural basis of fear can be studied by using a model system, which is fear conditioning.

Most behavioral studies of fear employ classical conditioning, the pairing of some initially neutral stimulus, such as a tone, with some biologically significant event, such as pain from a shock (see Chapter 18). Rats (and people) rapidly learn when a neutral stimulus is paired with a negative event (such as a shock). In this case, the auditory information (the tone) passes through the auditory pathways to the thalamus, which in turn sends the information to the cortex and, in addition, to the amygdala, as illustrated in Figure 20.6.

The key brain structure in the development of conditioned fear is the amygdala, which sends outputs to stimulate hormone release and activate the autonomic nervous system and thus generates emotion, which we interpret in this case as fear. Physiological measures of fear conditioning can rank autonomic functioning (for example, heart rate or respiration), and quantitative measures can rank behavior (for example, standing motionless) after the tone is heard.

Figure 20.6 Processing an emotional stimulus. Information about an emotion-laden stimulus travels from the sensory thalamus to the amygdala and cortex. The cortex feeds back to the amygdala, where several projections initiate stress hormone release, activate the autonomic system, evoke emotion and suppress pain, and stimulate attention. The hippocampus provides information related to context. (After Le Doux, 2000.)

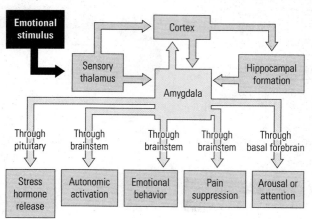

Damage to the amygdala interferes with fear conditioning, regardless of how it is measured. Humans with damage to the temporal lobe that includes the amygdala are impaired at fear conditioning, yet imaging studies show activation of the amygdala during fear conditioning (see, for example, LaBar et al., 1998). How does the amygdala "know" that a stimulus is dangerous? Le Doux proposes two possibilities. Both implicate neural networks, one genetically evolved and one shaped by learning.

Genetically based neural networks in the amygdala evolve with the animal (for example, the scent or appearance of a predator). Rats born in the laboratory, for example, show fear responses to the sound of owls or the scent of predators even though they have never encountered them. Most primates show intense fear of snakes on their first encounter, which suggests that a "snake detector" has evolved to sensitize us to stimuli associated with danger. Recall that Downer's split-brain monkey with one amygdala removed (Chapter 17) had no fear of a snake from the side of brain with no amygdala but showed intense fear from the intact side.

Similarly, neurons in the amygdalas of primates evolved a sensitivity to negative facial expressions in others. This evolution makes sense because presumably one cue to the presence of a threatening stimulus is the behavior of one's social group toward the stimulus.

Neural networks based in the amygdala likely also learn from experience about dangerous stimuli for which evolution could not prepare us. We may have learned, for instance, that a person wearing a certain type of insignia (such as one characteristic of a violent gang) is typically dangerous, whereas a person wearing another insignia (such as a police badge) is typically not dangerous.

Le Doux proposes that these circuits in the amygdala interact with cortical circuits to influence affective behavior. For example, if the amygdala functions to identify stimuli that signal danger, then the amygdala can act through the brainstem-activating systems to arouse the cortex and essentially to regulate cortical attention (awareness) on specific stimuli.

An important aspect of fear is context: a particular stimulus can be dangerous in one setting but not in another, and this distinction is clearly important to our behavior. A highly poisonous snake is extremely dangerous when suddenly encountered on a pathway but presents no danger behind a glass wall in a zoo. Furthermore, environmental contexts may acquire emotional properties through prior experiences (classical conditioning). If poisonous snakes are repeatedly encountered on a particular path in the woods, then the path itself becomes threatening.

Although the evidence is incomplete regarding exactly how context is associated with fear, the evidence is clear that hippocampal damage interferes with the development of contextual fear associations. How hippocampal activity normally acts to influence the association of context and fear remains to be understood.

How can the amygdala influence our thoughts about emotion-laden stimuli? People have all sorts of fears and worries that can interfere with everyday life, and for some people these fears become debilitating. People suffer from panic disorders, posttraumatic stress disorder, obsessive-compulsive disorders, anxiety disorders, and phobias. These examples illustrate the extreme power of fear-related events to affect cognition and suggest that evolution has crafted a powerful mechanism for forming such associations.

It is important in this context to recall that frontal-lobe patients show little anxiety or fear-related behavior. The orbital and medial prefrontal regions have significant reciprocal connections with the amygdala, suggesting that amygdaloprefrontal circuits play a significant role in the formation of thoughts about fearful stimuli. It is possible that the prefrontal cortex is somehow modified in people with pathological fears and anxieties, making it difficult for them to extinguish learned fears or to suppress fears of evolutionarily significant events.

Cognitive Asymmetry and Emotion

We have seen in both Damasio's and Le Doux's theories that emotion entails cognitive appraisals. Because there are significant asymmetries in a variety of cognitive functions, it follows that related emotional systems must also be lateralized. This idea is not new and can be traced to at least the 1930s, when clinicians reported detailed observations of patients with large unilateral lesions, noting an apparent asymmetry in the effects of left- and right-hemisphere lesions on emotional behavior. (Through the decades in neuropsychology, many versions of asymmetry theories of emotional control have been compiled, and the reader is directed to recent reviews by Gainotti and by Tucker et al. for details.)

The best-known early descriptions, contemporary with J. P.'s case presented at the beginning of the chapter, are those of Goldstein, who suggested that left-hemisphere lesions produce "catastrophic" reactions characterized by fearfulness and depression, whereas right-hemisphere lesions produce "indifference." The results of the first systematic study of these contrasting behavioral effects, by Gainotti in 1969, showed that catastrophic reactions were found in 62% of his left-hemisphere sample compared with only 10% of his right-hemisphere cases. In contrast, indifference was common in the right-hemisphere patients, found in 38% compared with only 11% of the left-hemisphere cases.

Significantly, however, Gainotti reported that catastrophic reactions were associated with aphasia and indifference reactions with contralateral neglect. A key point to remember in regard to Goldstein's and Gainotti's observations is that, if the left hemisphere is damaged extensively, then the behavior that we observe is in large part a function of what the right hemisphere can do. Thus, if we observe a catastrophic reaction after a left-hemisphere injury, one conclusion is that this behavior is coming from the right hemisphere. This conclusion leads directly to the idea that the right hemisphere normally plays a major role in the production of strong emotions, especially in emotions regarded as negative, such as fear and anger.

Gainotti concludes that the two sides of the brain play a complementary role in emotional behavior, the right hemisphere being more engaged in the automatic components of emotion and the left hemisphere in the overall cognitive control of emotion. The left hemisphere is presumed to have this general control because of language.

This idea is similar to one proposed by Gazzaniga, who suggests that a general control function of the speaking hemisphere characterizes the differences in thinking between humans and other animals. He labels the speaking hemisphere the "interpreter." What he means is illustrated in an experiment using split-brain patients as subjects. Each hemisphere is shown the same two pictures, such as a picture of a match followed by a picture of a piece of wood. A series of other pictures is then shown, and the task is to pick out a third picture that has an inferred relation with the other two. In our example, the third picture might be a bonfire.

The right hemisphere is incapable of making the inference that a match struck and held to a piece of wood could create a bonfire, whereas the left hemisphere can easily arrive at this interpretation. Evidently, the speaking left hemisphere can make logical inferences about sensory events that the nonspeaking right hemisphere cannot make. Gainotti applies this general idea to emotion and concludes that the right hemisphere generates emotional feelings, whereas the left hemisphere interprets these feelings, presumably through its language abilities, and produces a conceptual (cognitive) level of emotional processing (affective behavior).

Asymmetry in Emotional Processing

All three principal theories of the neuropsychology of emotional behavior overlap emotional and cognitive behaviors. We now turn our attention to studies that focused on the nature of this overlap. In the 1970s and 1980s, there was considerable interest in the possibility that the two cerebral hemispheres play complementary roles in controlling emotional behavior. Research on asymmetry has been less popular in the past 15 years, in part because of the shift in interest toward the Damasio and Le Doux theories, which do not focus on asymmetry as much as on the site within the cerebral hemispheres. We will briefly consider the asymmetry literature, providing examples of the type of research that has been done on the production and interpretation of emotional behavior as well as on changes in personality associated with temporal-lobe lesions.

The Production of Emotional Behavior

Mood is inferred largely from affect—facial expression, tone of voice, and frequency of talking—and so it is sensible to measure these behaviors first in an analysis of emotional behavior in brain-damaged people. Table 20.1 summarizes a range of measures of emotional behavior. The general picture is that left-hemisphere lesions, especially left-frontal-lobe lesions, produce a flattening of mood and in many people an appearance of depression, especially after strokes that produce language difficulties.

Facial expression is one of the most obvious cues to emotion in humans, and in recent years there has been a good deal of study of its production in normal people. Overall, studies of neurological patients find a reduction in the frequency and intensity of facial expressions in people with anterior lesions relative to those with more-posterior lesions. For example, in a series of studies,

Table 20.1 Summary of experiments on production of emotional behavior in neurological patients

Behavior	Characteristics	Basic reference
Clinical behavior of patients with natural lesions	Catastrophic reactions from left-hemisphere lesions; indifference from right-hemisphere lesions	Gainotti, 1969; Goldstein, 1939
Facial expression	Reduced by frontal lesions Reduced by right-hemisphere lesions Asymmetry altered	Kolb and Milner, 1981; Buck and Duffy, 1980; Borod et al., 1986 Bruyer, 1986
Spontaneous speech	Decreased by left-frontal-lobe lesions; increased by right-frontal-lobe lesions	Kolb and Taylor, 1981
Tone, or prosody, of speech	Right-hemisphere lesions impair mimicry of emotional states	Tucker et al., 1977; Kent and Rosenbek, 1982
Temporal-lobe traits	Temporal-lobe personality	Bear and Fedio, 1977; Waxman and Geshwind, 1974; Fedio and Martin, 1983
Sodium amytal	Catastrophic reactions to left injection; indifference reactions to right injection	Terzian, 1964; Rossi and Rosandini, 1974
	No evidence of asymmetric effects	Rovetta, 1960; Kolb and Milner, 1981

one of us (Kolb) and colleagues found that whether facial expressions are measured in terms of frequency, quantitative scoring of facial-movement elements, or subjective rating by judges, both left- and right-frontal-lobe patients show a reduction in facial expression relative to temporal lobe groups (Figure 20.7A). This result is obtained whether the expressions are spontaneous or posed.

Figure 20.7 Relative frequencies of facial expressions (A) and spontaneous talking (B) during routine neuropsychological testing. (After Kolb and Milner, 1981, and Kolb and Taylor, 1981.)

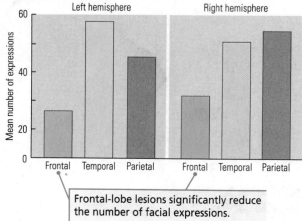

(A) Facial expressions

Frontal-lobe lesions significantly reduce the number of facial expressions.

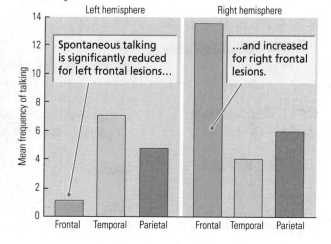

(B) Talking

Spontaneous talking is significantly reduced for left frontal lesions...

...and increased for right frontal lesions.

In contrast with the reduction in facial expression from both left- and right-frontal-lobe lesions, there is a difference in the effects of side of the lesion on spontaneous talking in frontal-lobe patients. Right-frontal-lobe lesions appear to increase talking markedly, whereas left-frontal-lobe lesions decrease it (Figure 20.7B). Without doubt, loss of facial expression and changes in talkativeness would be perceived by friends and relatives of frontal-lobe patients as marked changes in personality.

Spoken language carries two types of information: content and tone of voice. Typically, the former is a function of the left hemisphere, and there is reason to suspect that the latter is a function of the right. For example, when Tucker and colleagues asked patients to express particular affective states such as anger, happiness, and sadness as they read emotionally neutral sentences, patients with right-hemisphere lesions produced the sentences with relatively flat affect compared with patients with left-hemisphere lesions. This absence of tone in speech has been termed aprosodia, and it can be measured on a wide-band spectogram, as was done by Kent and Rosenbek.

Abnormalities in tone of voice in right-hemisphere patients led Ross to propose a set of aprosodias analogous to aphasias in left-hemisphere speech (Table 20.2). *Motor aprosodia,* an inability to produce affective components of language, is proposed to result from damage to Broca's area in the right hemisphere. *Sensory aprosodia,* a deficit in the interpretation of the emotional components of language, is presumed to result from damage to the region in the right hemisphere analogous to Wernicke's area. Ross's proposal may have merit and it deserves serious consideration, but at present it is without much scientific support. Furthermore, like aphasias, which are virtually never purely of one type, aprosodias may not be as pure as Ross has suggested.

Finally, although most brain-damaged people do not exhibit psychotic behaviors, symptoms such as hallucinations, mania, or delusions of persecution are occasionally reported. Curiously, such symptoms are virtually always associated with right-hemisphere lesions, although such symptoms are perhaps masked by aphasia after left-hemisphere lesions. In any event, the cause of psychotic symptoms in brain-damaged patients is obscure.

Table 20.2 Ross's proposed classification of aprosodias

Type	Spontaneous prosody and gesturing	Prosodic repetition	Prosodic comprehension	Comprehension of emotional gesturing
Motor	Poor	Poor	Good	Good
Sensory	Good	Poor	Poor	Poor
Global	Poor	Poor	Poor	Poor
Conduction	Good	Poor	Good	Good
Transcortical motor	Poor	Good	Good	Good
Transcortical sensory	Good	Good	Poor	Poor
Mixed transcortical	Poor	Good	Poor	Poor
Anomic (alexia with agraphia)	Good	Good	Good	Poor

The Interpretation of Emotional Behavior

Emotional behavior might appear abnormal not only because a person is unable to produce the appropriate behavior (expression, say) but also because he or she misinterprets the social or emotional signals coming from others. The importance of interpretation symptoms in understanding personality change after injury has led to the development of a variety of clinical tests of emotional perception, which are summarized by Borod and colleagues. As summarized in Table 20.3, right-hemisphere lesions produce deficits in a range of measures, especially including the comprehension of humor, as well as the judgment of mood, both in tone of voice and facial expression.

Table 20.3 Summary of experiments on interpretation of emotional behavior in neurological patients

Experiment	Characteristics	Basic reference
Judgment of mood in others	Right-hemisphere lesions impair comprehension	Heilman et al., 1993
	Right-temporal-lobe lesions impair perception of intonation	Tompkins and Mateer, 1985
Judgment of propositional affect	Left-hemisphere lesions impair comprehension	Kolb and Taylor, 1981
Comprehension of verbal humor	Right-hemisphere lesions alter humor appreciation	Gardner et al., 1975; Shammi and Stuss, 1999
Matching emotional expressions	Right-hemisphere lesions impair performance	DeKosky et al., 1980; Kolb and Taylor, 1981;
	Left-hemisphere lesions impair performance	Bowers et al., 1987; Young et al., 1993
Judgment of emotional expressions	Bilateral amygdala lesions impair perception of negative expressions	Adolphs et al., 1999

The ability to be humorous and to comprehend humor is one of humankind's most intriguing behaviors and certainly contributes to personality and is a basic ingredient in social life. Shammi and Stuss looked at humor in patients with focal injuries in various areas of the brain. Those patients with right-frontal injuries were the most affected in that they reacted less than other patients, with diminished laughter and smiling, and failed to get punch lines in jokes.

We should note here that not only do right-frontal-lobe patients fail to comprehend humor, in our experience they also have an almost perverse sense of humor. Figure 20.8 is the business card of a man who had a closed-head injury including injury to the right frontal lobe. This man was genuinely attempting to use humor to get business for his company.

Like humor, facial expression is a kind of social glue that bonds humans together: a lot of information is passed between and among us simply by changes in the nuances of facial expression. Recall that the superior temporal sulcus plays a central role in the analysis of biological motion, of which facial expression is an example. But, as the Snapshot on page 540 shows, much more of the brain than just the superior temporal sulcus is interested in facial expression.

Figure 20.8 Humor of a frontal-lobe subject. Depicted is the business card of a man who sold himself as an entrepreneur. Read carefully, the card says, "Holy cow, look at the ass on that tomato."

Situation 1 **Situation 2**

Figure 20.9 Examples of cartoon situations in which patients were asked either to produce the appropriate expression or to choose the appropriate expression from several choices for the blank face. See Figure 20.1 for a representative range of choices. (After Kolb and Taylor, 1988.)

In particular, patients with lesions of the right temporal or right frontal lobe or both have difficulty in recognizing facial expressions. Kolb and Taylor illustrate: subjects were asked to choose the appropriate facial expression for each of a set of cartoons in which one face was blank, as illustrated by situations 1 and 2 in Figure 20.9. As summarized in Figure 20.10A, both frontal- and temporal-lobe patients were impaired at this test but, curiously, there was no asymmetry: lesions of either hemisphere were equally effective in disrupting performance, regardless of the appropriate emotion.

One explanation is that, although the right hemisphere may be dominant for the processing of faces and facial expressions, the left hemisphere may play a role in understanding context. We noted earlier that Gazzaniga's studies of split-brain patients led him to conclude that the left hemisphere acts as an "interpreter" of behavior. This may also be true of social situations.

Are different facial expressions (for example, frightened, happy) analyzed by different cerebral regions? Recall, for example, that the amygdala is believed to selectively perceive fear, and the results of studies by Adolphs and colleagues showed that subjects with bilateral amygdala lesions are impaired at recognizing negative expressions (such as fear) but not at recognizing happy faces. In a similar study, Kolb and Taylor showed that patients with unilateral frontal-lobe lesions were severely impaired at matching negative but not positive faces to

Figure 20.10 Matching facial expressions. (A) Performance of control subjects and surgical-excision patients on a test of matching facial expressions to cartoon situations. (B) Performance of the same subjects on a test of matching photographs of negative emotions to the appropriate Ekman face. Lesions throughout the right hemisphere disturb this ability. (After Kolb and Taylor, 2000.)

(A) Cartoon matching

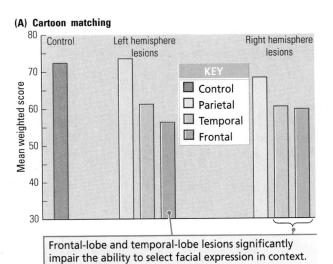

Frontal-lobe and temporal-lobe lesions significantly impair the ability to select facial expression in context.

(B) Matching photographs of negative emotions

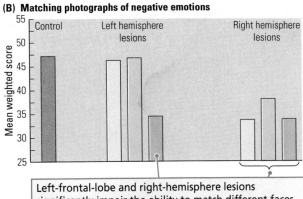

Left-frontal-lobe and right-hemisphere lesions significantly impair the ability to match different faces when the expression is fear or disgust.

Interpreting Facial Expressions Through Brain Activation

Faces are rich stimuli for humans. Expressions convey information about identity, mood, and intention. Such diverse information is presumably analyzed in an extensive neural network that includes the frontal and temporal cortex as well as the amygdala. Iidaka and colleagues used fMRI to investigate cerebral activation when normal subjects judged the sex of faces displaying negative (angry or disgusted), positive (happy), or neutral facial expressions.

The researchers found widespread activation in the occipital cortex, prefrontal cortex, medial temporal regions (including the amygdala), and the right parietal lobe, thus confirming that an extensive cerebral network processes facial expression.

To compare the activation in response to positive versus negative expressions Iidaka and colleagues used subtraction procedures across the conditions and showed that the left amygdala, right inferior frontal cortex, and temporal cortexes were predominantly engaged in the processing of negative expressions. Curiously, the right posterior temporoparietal region processed predominantly positive faces (see the adjoining illustration).

The researchers then correlated activity in different brain areas and found a positive correlation between activity in the prefrontal cortex and that in the left amygdala, especially for negative faces. This relation may suggest that the processing of negative facial expression is modulated by a neural circuit including both the left amygdala and the prefrontal cortex. This finding supports the findings that patients with left or right prefrontal lesions are impaired at the perception of negative facial expressions.

(A) Areas activated in processing facial emotion

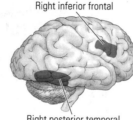

Right inferior frontal

Right posterior temporal

(B) Correlation of cortical and amygdala activity

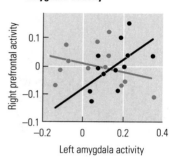

Facial expression and cerebral activity. (A) Emotional expressions activate posterior temporal, inferior frontal, and amygdala. (B) Plots and regression lines show a significant interaction between neural activity and the experimental condition. The x-axis represents activity in the left amygdala, and the y-axis represents activity in the right prefrontal cortex. Under the negative-expression condition (black), a positive correlation was observed between activities in these two regions; whereas, with positive expression (blue), there was a slight negative correlation. (After Iidaka et al., 2001.)

(T. Iidaka, M. Omori, T. Murata, H. Kosaka, Y. Yonekura, T. Okada, and N. Sadato. Neural interaction of the amygdala with the prefrontal and temporal cortices in the processing of facial expressions as revealed by fMRI. *Journal of Cognitive Neuroscience* 13:1035–1047, 2001.)

the appropriate Ekman face. Patients with right, but not left, temporal or parietal lesions showed a similar pattern of deficits, as illustrated in Figure 20.10B (see also the Snapshot above).

Thus, it appears that facial expressions are not a single stimulus category but rather that different expressions may be processed separately in the brain. An fMRI study by Phillips and colleagues addresses this idea by comparing the cerebral activation for fear and disgust. Given that expressions of disgust are normally related to bad-tasting food, these researchers predicted that the perception of expressions of disgust might include the gustatory cortex, which is located in the insula within the temporal lobe. Indeed, that is exactly what they found: fearful expressions activated the amygdala, whereas disgust expressions activated the insula.

Temporal-Lobe Personality

One way to quantify social or affective behavior is to have patients and their friends complete rating scales of behaviors related to traits such as "anger," "sadness," or "religiosity." In their study of the behavior of temporal-lobe patients, Bear and Fedio asked patients and their friends to do so, with the scales related to the traits summarized in Table 20.4. Each trait had previously been attributed to temporal-lobe epileptics, who presumably had temporal-lobe lesions that produced their epileptic condition.

Table 20.4 Summary of characteristics attributed to temporal-lobe epileptics

Emotionality	Deepening of all emotions; sustained intense manic-depressive disease
Elation, euphoria	Grandiosity, exhilarated mood; diagnosis of manic-depressive disease
Sadness	Discouragement, fearfulness, self-depreciation; diagnosis of depression; suicide attempt
Anger	Increased temper, irritability
Aggression	Overt hostility, rape attacks, violent crimes, murder
Altered sexual interest	Loss of libido, hyposexualism; fetishism, transvestism, exhibitionism, hypersexual episodes
Guilt	Tendency to self-scrutiny and self-recrimination
Hypermoralism	Attention to rules with inability to distinguish significant from minor infractions, desire to punish offenders
Obsessionalism	Ritualism; orderliness; compulsive attention to detail
Circumstantiality	Loquaciousness; pedantry; being overly detailed or peripheral
Viscosity	Stickiness; tendency to repetition
Sense of personal destiny	Events given highly charged, personalized significance; divine guidance ascribed to many features of patient's life
Hypergraphia	Keeping extensive diaries, detailed notes; writing autobiography or novel
Religiosity	Holding deep religious beliefs; often idiosyncratic multiple conversions, mystical states
Philosophical interest	Nascent metaphysical or moral speculations, cosmological theories
Dependence, passivity	Cosmic helplessness, "at hands of fate"; protestations of helplessness
Humorlessness, sobriety	Overgeneralized ponderous concern; humor lacking or idiosyncratic
Paranoia	Suspicious, overinterpretative of motives and events; diagnosis of paranoid schizophrenia

Source: After Bear and Fedio, 1977.

The epileptic patients self-reported a distinctive profile of humorless sobriety, dependence, and obsession. Raters differentiated the temporal-lobe patients on the basis of nearly every trait in Table 20.4 but rated them most strongly on the traits described as "circumstantiality," "philosophical interests," and "anger." Furthermore, right- and left-temporal-lobe patients could be distinguished: the right-temporal-lobe patients were described as more obsessional, and the left-temporal-lobe patients are more concerned with "personal destiny."

In a 1983 study, Fedio and Martin evaluated temporal-lobectomy patients on the same scale, finding that surgical removal of the epileptogenic tissue produced a decrease in the characteristic personality traits, presumably because the abnormal temporal-lobe tissue that produced the seizures also interfered with normal function. Nonetheless, these patients still differed from normal control subjects: the left-temporal-lobectomy cases rated themselves more harshly, reported hypergraphic tendencies, and professed a reflective style of thinking centered on themes of religiosity and personal destiny. Right-temporal-lobectomy patients rated themselves less adversely but claimed to have developed more feelings of anger, sadness, and aggression.

Summary

Emotions, or affective behaviors, are easily recognized but very difficult to quantify. Similarly, it is easy to identify structures in which injury can disrupt emotional behavior but difficult to determine what role different structures play in the control of emotional behavior. Like other cognitive processes, multiple neural systems control different aspects of emotional behavior. The key candidate structures in emotional behavior include the frontal lobes, primarily the inferior frontal cortex, the amygdala and associated paralimbic cortex, and the hypothalamus. To the extent that changes in perception, movement, memory, language, and so on, affect our emotional behavior, we can see that the vast cortical regions taking part in cognitive processing also take part in producing emotion.

One theme that runs through all major theories of emotion, especially Damasio's somatic marker hypothesis, Le Doux's cognitive–social interaction theory, and Gainotti's asymmetry theory, is that emotion and cognition are intimately related and are likely controlled by overlapping neural systems.

Studies of changes in emotional behavior after cerebral injury focus largely on changes in the production and perception of emotions. Overall, lesions of the left and right hemispheres have different effects on emotional behaviors, and damage to the right hemisphere appears to produce larger effects. Asymmetry in the effects of cerebral injury should not overshadow the importance of cortical site in understanding emotional behavior. Both the frontal lobes and the amygdala play special roles in emotional control, especially on behaviors related to the production and interpretation of facial expression. It appears that the left amygdala plays a special role in generating one particular emotion—namely, fear.

References

Ackerly, S. S. A case of paranatal bilateral frontal lobe defect observed for thirty years. In J. M. Warren and K. Akert, Eds. *The Frontal Granular Cortex and Behavior.* New York: McGraw-Hill, 1964, pp. 192–218.

Adolphs, R. Social cognition and the human brain. *Trends in Cognitive Science* 3:469–479, 1999.

Adolphs, R., D. Tranel, S. Hamann, A. W. Young, A. J. Calder, E. A. Phelps, A. Anderson, G. P. Lee, and A. R. Damasio. Recognition of emotional expression in nine individuals with bilateral amygdala damage. *Neuropsychologia* 37:1111–1117, 1999.

Bear, D. M., and P. Fedio. Quantitative analysis of interictal behavior in temporal lobe epilepsy. *Archives of Neurology* 34:454–467, 1977.

Bihrle, A. M., H. H. Brownell, J. A. Powelson, and H. Gardner. Comprehension of humorous and nonhumorous materials by left and right brain-damaged patients. *Brain and Cognition* 5:399–411, 1986.

Blonder, L. X., D. Bowers, and K. M. Heilman. The role of the right hemisphere on emotional communication. *Brain* 114:1115–1127, 1991.

Blumer, D. Temporal lobe epilepsy and its psychiatric significance. In D. F. Blumer and D. Benson, Eds. *Psychiatric Aspects of Neurological Disease.* New York: Grune & Stratton, 1975.

Borod, J. C., E. Koff, M. Perlman Lorch, and M. Nicholas. The expression and perception of facial emotion in brain-damaged patients. *Neuropsychologia* 24:169–180, 1986.

Borod, J. C., M. H. Tabert, C. Santschi, and E. H. Strauss. Neuropsychological assessment of emotional processing in brain-damaged patients. In J. C. Borod, Ed. *The Neuropsychology of Emotion.* New York: Oxford University Press, 2000, pp. 80–105.

Bowers, D., H. B. Coslett, R. M. Bauer, L. J. Speedie, and K. M. Heilman. Comprehension of emotional prosody following unilateral hemispheric lesions:Processing defect versus distraction defect. *Neuropsychologia* 25:317–328, 1987.

Brady, J. V. *Handbook of Physiology,* vol. 3, *Emotional Behavior.* Bethesda, MD: American Physiological Society, 1960.

Brown, S., and E. A. Schaefer. An investigation into the functions of the occipital and temporal lobe of the monkey's brain. *Philosophical Transactions of the Royal Society, Part B* 179:303–327, 1888.

Brownell, H. H., D. Michel, J. Powelson, and H. Gardner. Surprise but not coherence: Sensitivity to verbal humor in right-hemisphere patients. *Brain and Language* 18:20–27, 1983.

Bruyer, R., Ed. *The Neuropsychology of Face Perception and Facial Expression.* Hillsdale, NJ: Lawrence Erlbaum, 1986.

Buck, R., and R. J. Duffy. Nonverbal communication of affect in brain-damaged patients. *Cortex* 16:351–362, 1980.

Butter, C. M., and D. R. Snyder. Alterations in aversive and aggressive behaviors following orbital frontal lesions in rhesus monkeys. *Acta Neurobiologiae Experimentalis* 32:525–565, 1972.

Campbell, R. The lateralisation of emotion: A critical review. *International Journal of Psychology* 17:211–229, 1982.

Canli T., J. E. Desmond, Z. Zhao, G. Glover, and J. D. Gabrieli. Hemispheric asymmetry for emotional stimuli detected with fMRI. *Neuroreport* 9:3233–3239, 1998.

Canli T., Z. Zhao, J. E. Desmond, E. Kang, J. Gross, and J. D. Gabrieli. An fMRI study of personality influences on brain reactivity to emotional stimuli. *Behavioral Neuroscience* 115:33–42, 2001.

Damasio, A. R. *Descartes' Error: Emotion, Reason, and the Human Brain.* New York: Putnam, 1994.

Damasio, A. R. A second chance for emotion. In R. D. Lane and L. Nadel, Eds. *Cognitive Neuroscience of Emotion.* New York: Oxford University Press, 2000, pp. 12–23.

DeKosky, S. T., K. M. Heilman, D. Bowers, and E. Valenstein. Recognition and discrimination of emotional faces and pictures. *Brain and Language* 9:206–214, 1980.

Dicks, D., R. E. Myers, and A. Kling. Uncus and amygdala lesions: effects on social behavior in the free-ranging rhesus monkey. *Science* 165:69–71, 1968.

Dimond, S. J., and L. Farrington. Emotional response to films shown to the right or left hemisphere of the brain measured by heart rate. *Acta Psychologia* 41:255–260, 1977.

Dimond, S. J., L. Farrington, and P. Johnson. Differing emotional response from right and left hemispheres. *Nature* 261:690–692, 1976.

Dunbar, H. F. *Emotions and Bodily Changes,* 4th ed. New York: Columbia University Press, 1954.

Ekman, P., and W. V. Friesen. *Unmasking the Face.* Palo Alto, CA: Consulting Psychology Press, 1984.

Fedio, P., and A. Martin. Ideative-emotive behavioral characteristics of patients following left or right temporal lobectomy. *Epilepsia* 254:S117–S130, 1983.

Gainotti, G. Reactions "catastrophiques" et manifestations d'indifférence au cours des atteintes cerebrales. *Neuropsychologia* 7:195–204, 1969.

Gainotti, G. Emotional behavior and hemispheric side of the lesion. *Cortex* 8:41–55, 1972.

Gainotti, G. Neuropsychological theories of emotion. In J. C. Borod, Ed. *The Neuropsychology of Emotion.* New York: Oxford University Press, 2000, pp. 214–236.

Gardner, H., P. K. Ling, L. Flamm, and J. Silverman. Comprehension and appreciation of humorous material following brain damage. *Brain* 98:399–412, 1975.

Gazzaniga, M., and J. E. Le Doux. *The Integrated Mind.* New York: Plenum, 1978.

Goldstein, K. *The Organism: A Holistic Approach to Biology, Derived from Pathological Data in Man.* New York: American Book, 1939.

Haggard, M. P., and A. M. Parkinson. Stimulus and task factors as determinants of ear advantages. *Quarterly*

Journal of Experimental Psychology 23:168–177, 1971.

Heilman, K. M., D. Bowers, and E. Valenstein. Emotional disorders associated with neurological diseases. In K. M. Heilman and E. Valenstein, Eds. *Clinical Neuropsychology*, 3d ed. New York: Oxford University Press, 1993.

Iidaka, T., M. Omori, T. Murata, H. Kosaka, Y. Yonekura, T. Okada, and N. Sadato. Neural interaction of the amygdala with the prefrontal and temporal cortices in the processing of facial expressions as revealed by fMRI. *Journal of Cognitive Neuroscience* 13:1035–1047, 2001.

Kent, R. D., and J. C. Rosenbek. Prosodic disturbance and neurological lesion. *Brain and Language* 15:259–291, 1982.

Klüver, H., and P. C. Bucy. Preliminary analysis of the temporal lobes in monkeys. *Archives of Neurology and Psychiatry* 42:979–1000, 1939.

Kolb, B., and B. Milner. Observations on spontaneous facial expression after focal cerebral excisions and after intracarotid injection of sodium amytal. *Neuropsychologia* 19:505–514, 1981.

Kolb, B., and L. Taylor. Affective behavior in patients with localized cortical excisions: Role of lesion site and side. *Science* 214:89–91, 1981.

Kolb, B., and L. Taylor. Facial expression, emotion, and hemispheric organization. In R. D. Lane and L. Nadel, Eds. *Cognitive Neuroscience of Emotion*. New York: Oxford University Press, 2000, pp. 62–83.

LaBar, K. S., J. C. Gatenby, J. C. Gore, J. E. Le Doux, and E. A. Phelps. Human amygdala activation during conditioned fear acquisition and extinction: A mixed-trial fMRI study. *Neuron* 20:937–945, 1998.

Le Doux, J. E. Cognitive-emotional interactions. In R. D. Lane and L. Nadel, Eds. *Cognitive Neuroscience of Emotion*. New York: Oxford University Press, 2000, pp. 129–155.

Ley, R. G., and M. P. Bryden. Hemispheric differences in processing emotions and faces. *Brain and Language* 7:127–138, 1979.

Ley, R. G., and M. P. Bryden. A dissociation of right and left hemispheric effects for recognizing emotional tone and verbal content. *Brain and Cognition* 1:3–9, 1982.

Marlowe, W. B., E. L. Mancall, and J. J. Thomas. Complete Klüver-Bucy syndrome in man. *Cortex* 11:53–59, 1975.

Milner, B. Brain mechanisms suggested by studies of the temporal lobes. In C. H. Millikan and F. L. Darley, Eds. *Brain Mechanisms Underlying Speech and Language*. New York: Grune & Stratton, 1967.

Moscovitch, M., and J. Olds. Asymmetries in spontaneous facial expressions and their possible relation to hemispheric specialization. *Neuropsychologia* 20:71–82, 1982.

Myers, R. E. Role of the prefrontal and anterior temporal cortex in social behavior and affect in monkeys. *Acta Neurobiologiae Experimentalis* 32:567–579, 1972.

Myers, R. E., C. Swett, and M. Miller. Loss of social group affinities following prefrontal lesions in free-ranging macaques. *Brain Research* 64:257–269, 1973.

Panksepp, J., B. Knutson, and J. Burgdorf. The role of brain emotional systems in addictions: A neuro-evolutionary perspective and new "self-report" animal model. *Addiction* 97:459–69, 2002.

Papez, J. W. A proposed mechanism of emotion. *Archives of Neurology and Psychiatry* 38:725–744, 1937.

Peters, M., and D. Ploog. Frontal lobe lesions and social behavior in the squirrel monkey (*Saimiri*): A pilot study. *Acta Biologica Medica (Germany)* 35:1317–1326, 1976.

Phillips, M. L., A. W. Young, C. Senior, M. Brammer, C. Andrews, A. J. Calder, E. T. Bullmore, D. I. Perrett, D. Rowland, S. C. R. Williams, J. A. Gray, and A. S. David. A specific neural substrate for perceiving facial expressions of disgust. *Nature* 389:495–498, 1997.

Raleigh, M. J. Neural mechanisms supporting successful social decisions in simians. In Y. Christen, A. Damasio, and H. Damasio, Eds. *Neurobiology of Decision Making*. Berlin: Springer, 1996, pp. 63–82.

Raleigh, M. J., M. T. McGuire, G. L. Brammer, D. B. Pollack, and A. Yuwiler. Serotonergic mechanisms promote dominance acquisition in adult male vervet monkeys. *Brain Research* 559:181–190, 1991.

Raleigh, M. J., and H. D. Steklis. Effects of orbitofrontal and temporal neocortical lesions on the affiliative behavior of vervet monkeys (*Ceropithecus aethiops sabaeus*). *Experimental Neurology* 73:378–389, 1981.

Robinson, R. G., K. Kubos, L. B. Starr, K. Rao, and T. R. Price. Mood disorders in stroke patients. *Brain* 107:81–93, 1984.

Ross, E. D. The aprosodias: Functional-anatomical organization of the affective components of language in the right hemisphere. *Archives of Neurology* 38:561–569, 1981.

Ross, E. D., R. W. Homan, and R. Buck. Differential hemispheric lateralization of primary and social emotions. *Neuropsychiatry, Neuropsychology, and Behavioral Biology*. In press.

Ross, E. D., and A. J. Rush. Diagnosis and neuroanatomical correlates of depression in brain-damaged patients. *Archives of General Psychiatry* 38:1344–1354, 1981.

Rossi, G. F., and G. Rosadini. Experimental analysis of cerebral dominance in man. In C. J. Millikan and F. L. Darley, Eds. *Brain Mechanisms Underlying Speech and Language*. New York: Grune & Stratton, 1974, pp. 167–174.

Rovetta, P. Discussion of paper "Amytal intracaroitides per lo studio della dominanza emisferica." *Rivista di Neurologia* 30:460–470, 1960.

Sachdev, H. S., and S. G. Waxman. Frequency of hypergraphia in temporal lobe epilepsy: An index of interictal behaviour syndrome. *Journal of Neurology, Neurosurgery, and Psychiatry* 44:358–360, 1981.

Scherer, C. Psychological theories of emotion. In J. C. Borod, Ed. *The Neuropsychology of Emotion*. New York: Oxford University Press, 2000, pp. 137–162.

Shammi, P., and D. T. Stuss. Humour appreciation: A role of the right frontal lobe. *Brain* 122:657–666, 1999.

Suomi, S. J., H. F. Harlow, and J. K. Lewis. Effect of bilateral frontal lobectomy on social preferences of rhesus monkeys. *Journal of Comparative and Physiological Psychology* 70:448–453, 1970.

Terzian, H. Behavioral and EEG effects of intracarotid sodium amytal injection. *Acta Neurochirurgica* 12:230–239, 1964.

Thorne, B. M. Brain lesions and affective behavior in primates: A selected review. *Journal of General Psychology* 86:153–162, 1972.

Tompkins, C. A., and C. A. Mateer. Right hemisphere appreciation of intonational and linguistic indications of affect. *Brain and Language* 24:185–203, 1985.

Tucker, D. M., D. Derryberry, and P. Lau. Anatomy and physiology of human emotion: Vertical integration of brainstem, limbic, and cortical systems. In J. C. Borod, Ed. *The Neuropsychology of Emotion*. New York: Oxford University Press, 2000, pp. 56–79.

Tucker, D. M., R. T. Watson, and K. M. Heilman. Discrimination and evocation of affectively intoned speech in patients with right parietal disease. *Neurology* 27:947–950, 1977.

Waxman, S. G., and N. Geschwind. Hypergraphia in temporal lobe epilepsy. *Neurology* 24:629–636, 1974.

Wittling, W., and R. Roschmann. Emotion-related hemisphere asymmetry: Subjective emotional responses to laterally presented films. *Cortex* 29:431–438, 1993.

Young, A. W., F. Newcombe, E. H. de Haan, M. Small, and D. C. Hay. Face perception after brain injury: Selective impairments affecting identity and expression. *Brain* 116:941–959, 1993.

21

Spatial Behavior

Whenever he left his room in the hospital, he had trouble in finding the way back, because at any chosen point of the route he did not know whether to go right, left, downstairs, or upstairs (on one occasion, he walked from the main floor down to the basement, instead of going up to the first floor, where his bed was located). When he eventually arrived in front of his own room, he did not recognize it unless he chanced to see some distinguishing feature, such as the black beard of his roommate or a particular object on the bedside table. . . .

When taken to sections of the city he knew before his illness and required to lead the way, he tried hard to find familiar landmarks, such as a signboard, the name of a street, the tramcar numbers, etc., but this information, though effectively indicating to him he was near his home, failed to provide clues for choosing the right direction. . . .

Required to provide verbal information concerning routes or places well known before the disease, he performed fairly well as long as he could rely on purely verbal knowledge. Thus he was able to give the names of the intermediate stations on the railway line he used daily or the location of the main building of the city. Yet, he met with considerable difficulty when the way had to be retraced from spatial memory; for instance, when required to tell how he would walk between two sites chosen at random in the city, he could only say the initial street and then he became confused. . . .

He grossly mislocated cities and states on a map of his country as well as of Europe, a task with which he was familiar, since he had been a post office clerk. (Adolph Meyer's patient, summarized by de Renzi, 1982, p. 213)

The patient just described was originally examined by Adolph Meyer in the early 1900s and is but one of many patients whose impairments can be sources of insight into one of our most complex behaviors—spatial behavior. Our bodies occupy space, move through space, and interact with other entities in space; our brains mentally rotate and manipulate representations of space.

Other objects also occupy space and maintain relations in space with one another and with us. Philosophers have asked whether objects exist without space or, conversely, whether space exists without objects. They also ask whether space is a feature of the universe or merely a creation of our brains. And how do we acquire concepts of space? The spatial experiences of small animals, such as dogs and cats, or of children must be very different from those of airline pilots. Further complicating these questions is that many of the elements that we think of as aspects of "space" and spatial behavior—sensory perceptions, memory, attention processes, and motor behaviors, to name a few—fit equally well into other domains.

In this chapter, we present an overview of spatial behavior, along with a number of contemporary spatial theories and a survey of various models used to study spatial behavior. We also examine the roles of the temporal, parietal, and frontal lobes in spatial behavior and some of the factors that seem to affect individual performance on spatial tests.

The Organization of Spatial Behavior

The term *spatial behavior* refers to all of the behaviors with which we and other animals guide all or parts of our bodies through space. It also includes thought processes concerning space. The ability to move through space from one place to another is sometimes referred to as **topographic memory,** in recognition of the idea that the movements take place between or in relation to points or objects that are spatially distinct, such as the points on a map ("topography" refers to map making). The mental representations that we have of space are frequently referred to as **cognitive maps,** on the assumption that we represent space with our brains in the same way that it is represented on a map.

For the purpose of neurological study, space is sometimes broken down into subspaces of various kinds (Figure 21.1). One of them is the surface of the body, on which things such as objects of clothing or contact with external objects can be localized. Another is the *grasping space* surrounding the body, and a third is *distal space* that the body moves into or out of. All these subspaces have their representations within the brain, which is able to assign locations to real or imagined objects on or within them. Space can also be thought of as having a time dimension of past and future, described as *time space*. The challenge to scientists studying spatial behavior is to discover *how* the kinds and properties of space are represented. In this section of the chapter, after a brief historical overview of spatial function, we consider three theoretical approaches to understanding spatial behavior: spatial-navigation theories, cognitive-mapping theories, and the two-stream theory of spatial-information processing.

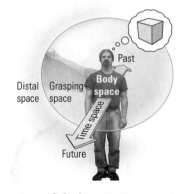

Figure 21.1 A conceptual model of the compartments of space.

Historical Background

Modern accounts of cerebral organization describe spatial processing in humans as a special function of the right hemisphere. This view has had an irregular history. John Hughlings-Jackson was the first to propose that the right hemisphere might have some special perceptual function to complement the language functions of the left hemisphere. In his 1874 paper, titled "On the Nature of the Duality of the Brain," he predicted that a person with damage restricted to the posterior part of the right hemisphere would have a distinctive syndrome:

> The patient would have difficulty in recognizing things; he would have difficulty in relating what had occurred, not from lack of words, but from a prior inability to revive images of persons, objects and places, of which the words are symbols. . . . He could not put before himself ideal images of places one after another; could not re-see where he had been, and could not therefore tell of it in words. (Jackson, 1932, p. 14)

Hughlings-Jackson was proposing a spatial–perceptual function for the right hemisphere, although he admitted that the evidence for his position was not strong. Between 1876 and 1905, a number of investigators described various cases of spatial–perceptual difficulties in a series of papers, confirming Hughlings-Jackson's prediction that such disorders exist; but most of the patients described in these papers appeared to have bilateral damage, rather than right-hemisphere damage. Nevertheless, Hughlings-Jackson's view of the special role of the right hemisphere persisted through the turn of the century.

Experiences with brain injury in soldiers during World War I (1914–1918) led to advances in the understanding of spatial disturbances, but the possibility of a special association between spatial deficits and right-hemisphere damage was largely ignored. Even as late as 1950, although a large number of spatial deficits had been described, the asymmetrical representation of spatial function in the two hemispheres did not attract neuropsychologists' notice, perhaps because most of the published reports were of single-case studies, which could be easily discounted. The more systematic work of Zangwill and of Hécaen and their coworkers in the 1950s forced a reexamination of the role of the right hemisphere in spatial performance. There now is little doubt that the right hemisphere has a special role in spatial behavior, although sometimes spatial impairments are also observed in people with damage to the left hemisphere.

Topographic Disorientation

There are many clinical reports of patients suffering from **topographic disorientation,** a gross disability in finding their way about, even in environments with which they were familiar before the onset of their injuries. Many of these reports are difficult to interpret because the patients also experienced other spatial deficits, such as left–right confusion, contralateral neglect, deficits in sensory spatial analysis, impairments in face recognition, impairments in color recognition, and visual-field defects. The first report of a topographic memory disorder was written by Hughlings-Jackson in 1876 and described a patient with a glioma in her right temporal lobe. This patient reported having difficulty finding her way in a park near her home. In 1890, Otfrid Foerster provided a more extensive description of a 44-year-old postal clerk who developed blindness on the right side of the visual field (a right hemianopia), followed a few days later by blindness on the left side of the visual field (a left hemianopia), a situation that left him with a small, central area of vision. This patient's most striking disability, however, was impairment in remembering where objects were located and in building up a picture of a route. When blindfolded, he was unable to point toward furniture in his room or to remember the location of a toilet that was a few steps away from his room. His amnesia was retrograde, extending back to things he knew before the onset of his disability. He could not describe or draw the spatial arrangement of his office or home or of well-known places in his city. He also could not draw general maps of the world or the city, although he could express some geographical ideas verbally.

In subsequent studies, a number of variations in the symptoms of topographic disorientation have been described. Some patients are unable to name buildings or landmarks that were formerly familiar to them. Others retain this ability. Some patients can describe routes and draw maps but become disoriented when they actually visit the locations, because they cannot identify familiar buildings or landmarks. Other patients can navigate routes but cannot describe or draw maps of them. Some patients can navigate in familiar places but become disoriented in new places, and others can eventually learn to navigate in new places by painstakingly memorizing buildings and landmarks and the routes from one to another.

Paterson and Zangwill attempted to sort out these complex clusters of symptoms by identifying subcomponents that may prove to have different anatomical loci. They suggested that topographic disorders be subdivided into two different impairments: topographic agnosia and topographic amnesia. **Topographic agnosia** is defined as a failure to identify individual landmarks, such as specific buildings, but retaining the ability to identify and recognize classes of objects, such as hills, office buildings, or churches. A person may recognize a building as a church but not recognize that it is the church of which he or she is a member. **Topographic amnesia** refers to an inability to remember topographic relations between landmarks that can be identified individually. A person may recognize a church as his or her own but may not know where it is located. In both conditions, it is necessary to distinguish between anterograde and retrograde impairments. People who lose the ability to navigate in environments that were familiar before their injuries have *retrograde spatial amnesia*. People who retain the ability to navigate in environments that were familiar before their injuries but who cannot navigate in novel environments have *anterograde spatial amnesia*. Patients may display both conditions, losing all topographic ability. Finally, it is necessary to identify patients who have true topographic disorders but compensate by using other strategies.

Although it is important to recognize that topographic disorientation can take a number of forms, some skepticism is in order concerning the precise disabilities described in the various case reports. Many of the case descriptions are compelling, but until quite recently none of the reports provided much experimental detail.

Brain Regions Compromised in Spatial Disorientation

Aguirre and D'Esposito reviewed the literature on spatial disorientation for the purpose of relating deficits to brain regions. They proposed five different kinds of deficits, each of which can be traced to a specific region of the posterior neocortex and limbic system (Figure 21.2).

Figure **21.2** Relation between brain injuries and spatial deficits in human subjects. Arrows show dorsal stream and ventral stream, which are described later in this chapter (note that both hemispheres shown are the right hemisphere).

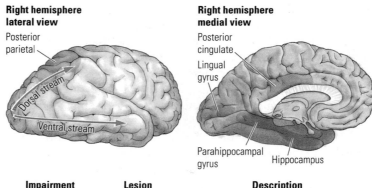

Right hemisphere lateral view

Posterior parietal

Dorsal stream

Ventral stream

Right hemisphere medial view

Posterior cingulate

Lingual gyrus

Parahippocampal gyrus

Hippocampus

Impairment	Lesion	Description
Egocentric disorientation	Posterior parietal	Unable to represent the location of objects with respect to self
Heading disorientation	Posterior cingulate	Unable to represent direction of orientation with respect to environment
Landmark agnosia	Lingual gyrus	Unable to represent appearance of prominent landmarks
Anterograde disorientation	Parahippocampal gyrus	Unable to learn new representations of environmental information
Spatial-mapping or memory deficit	Hippocampus	Anterograde and retrograde amnesia, especially for rich spatial details

1. Patients described as having **egocentric disorientation** have difficulty perceiving the relative location of objects with respect to the self. They have either unilateral or bilateral injuries located in the posterior parietal cortex. Although they are able to gesture toward objects as long as their eyes are open, this ability is completely lost when their eyes are closed. Their performance is impaired on a wide range of visuospatial tasks, including mental rotation (the ability to visualize the appearance of three-dimensional objects from different perspectives) and the ability to judge distances between objects. These patients are uniformly impaired in way-finding tasks both in formerly familiar and in novel environments. A case reported by Levine exemplifies the condition:

> The most striking abnormalities were visual and spatial. . . . He could not reach accurately for visual objects, even those he identified, whether they were presented in central or peripheral visual fields. When shown two objects, he made frequent errors in stating which was nearer or farther, above or below, or to the right or left. . . . He could not find his way about. At four months after the hemorrhages, he frequently got lost in his own house and never went out without a companion. . . . Spatial imagery was severely impaired. He could not say how to get from his house to the corner grocery store, a trip he had made several times a week for more than 5 years. In contrast he could describe the store and its proprietor. (Levine et al., 1985)

2. Patients said to have **heading disorientation** are unable to set a course to where they want to go, even though they are able to recognize landmarks, to recognize their own locations in relation to landmarks, and to describe where they want to go. In short, they have no "sense of direction." This condition is associated with injury in the right posterior cingulate cortex. A patient described by Takahashi is representative:

> [A]s he was driving his taxi in the same city [in which he had worked for years], he suddenly lost his understanding of the route to his destination. As he could quickly recognize the buildings and landscapes around him, he was able to determine his current location. However, he could not determine in which direction he should proceed. He stopped taking passengers and tried to return to the main office, but didn't know the appropriate direction in which to drive. Using the surrounding buildings, scenery, and road signs, he made several mistakes along the way. He remembered, during this time, passing the same places over and over again. (Takahashi et al., 1997)

3. Patients described as having **landmark agnosia** are unable to use prominent environmental features for the purposes of orientation. They can recognize churches, houses, and other landmarks—they do not have a deficit in the perception of environmental information—but they cannot use a particular church or house to guide their movement. They frequently use specific details as clues to help them recognize particular objects; for example, a patient may recognize his or her own house because of the car in the driveway or the tree in the yard. The lesion sites reported to produce landmark agnosia are either bilateral or on the right side of the medial aspect of the occipital lobe, affecting the lingual and fusiform gyri and sometimes the parahippocampal gyrus. A patient identified as A. H., described by Pallis, is an example:

> He complained a lot of his inability to recognize places. "In my mind's eye I know exactly where places are, what they look like. I can visualize R . . . Square without difficulty, and the streets that come into it. . . . I can draw you a plan of the roads from Cardiff to the Rhondda Valley. . . . It's when I'm out that the trouble starts. My reason tells me I must be in a certain place and yet I don't recognize it. It all has to be worked out each time." His topographic memory was good, as could be inferred from his accurate descriptions of paths, roads, the layout of the mineshafts [the patient was an engineer] and from his excellent performance in drawing maps of places familiar to him before his illness. (Pallis, 1955)

4. In **anterograde disorientation,** patients have no problem navigating in formerly familiar environments but experience difficulty in novel environments because of an inability to learn about unfamiliar objects by looking at them. If shown a novel object, they are not likely to be able to select it from an array of objects a short while later. In contrast, they *are* able to recall auditory and tactile information that is novel. Damage in the parahippocampal gyrus of the inferior ventral cortex on the right side is associated with this condition. Ross describes a patient with this kind of disorientation:

> The major problem he noted, besides a complete inability to recognize faces, was severe spatial disorientation. In order to find his way around the college campus or to walk to and from school, he was constantly

forced to consult maps and written notes. . . . The patient had no difficulty in accurately reaching for objects in space. . . . He was never able to learn the spatial organization of the neurology wing during the entire month he spent in the hospital. . . . When asked to construct a map of the neurology wing, he was able to do this task if allowed to walk through the ward but was unable to do it from memory. . . . [T]he patient also appeared spatially disoriented in the three-room apartment where he had been living for six months. In striking contrast, however, when he stayed at his parents' house, in which he grew up, there was no observable difficulty with spatial orientation. (Ross, 1980)

5. A very extensive literature implicates the hippocampus in **spatial learning,** but there is considerable controversy about the precise nature of the deficits caused by damage there. One theory proposes that the hippocampus has a direct and specific role in spatial navigation; another claims that, on the contrary, the hippocampus has a general role in memory and that anterograde spatial deficits arise as part of a general anterograde memory impairment. The results of recent brain-imaging studies suggest that the right hippocampus has a special role in complex spatial abilities (see the Snapshot on page 553). E. P.'s case, reported by Teng and Squire, is an illustration of the possible role of the hippocampus in spatial memory.

E. P. was a 76-year-old former laboratory technician who became amnesic in 1992, after an episode of herpes simplex encephalitis. He had extensive bilateral damage to the hippocampus and surrounding areas, including the parahippocampal gyrus. The experimenters identified five individuals who had attended E. P.'s high school and who had since moved away, as had E. P. The subjects were asked to describe how they would navigate from their homes to different locations in the area served by the school, how they would navigate between different locations in the area, and how they would navigate if the most logical routes were blocked off. E. P. scored as well as the control subjects on these tests. In contrast, when E. P. was asked to describe how he would navigate in his present environs, a location to which he had moved after his brain injury, he was unable to provide any responses to any questions. (Teng and Squire, 1999)

Teng and Squire suggest that E. P.'s spatial impairments are part of general anterograde memory impairment. It is worth noting, however, that, because parahippocampal injury by itself is reported to produce anterograde disorientation, it is by no means certain that E. P.'s anterograde spatial-memory deficit is due principally to the damage to his hippocampus.

In their study of K. C., a patient with a similar hippocampal plus parahippocampal gyrus lesion, Rosenbaum and colleagues report that, although the patient could produce what they called a "schematic cognitive map" of the environment in which he had lived before his injury, his memory of that environment's rich contextual details was impaired. For example, when shown a photograph of the neighborhood in which he had lived before his brain injury, he had difficulty identifying the viewpoint from which the photograph was taken, and he was unable to describe the surrounding environment that was not visible in the photograph. Rosenbaum and colleagues agree with Teng and

SNAPSHOT

Imaging the Hippocampi of London Taxi Drivers

To examine brain regions associated with topographic memory, Maguire and colleagues used licensed London taxi drivers as subjects. Official London taxi drivers must train for as long as 3 years and pass stringent examinations of spatial knowledge before receiving a license. The fact that all of these subjects had such an extensive knowledge of London meant that all of them could be tested with the same stimuli: the city's topography. The taxi drivers were given a number of tasks, two of which required topographic knowledge: (1) they were given a starting and destination point in the greater London area and asked to describe overtly, while undergoing a PET scan, the shortest legal route between the two points; and (2) they were required to recall and describe the appearance of individual world-renowned landmarks that were not in London and that they had never visited. A control task for the driving-sequence test was the recall of the plot of a film. As a control for the renowned-building test, the subjects were asked to describe individual frames from a film. The PET-scan images were superimposed onto the MRI reconstructions of each subject's brain. The brain areas that were activated during the first (spatial) test included the occipitotemporal areas, medial parietal cortex, posterior cingulate cortex, parahippocampal gyrus, and right hippocampus. The second (nonspatial) tasks did not activate the right hippocampus.

In a second study using London taxi drivers, Maguire and colleagues imaged the hippocampus by using MRI. Sixteen taxi drivers with 1.5 to 14.3 years of experience were scanned and compared with sixteen age-matched control subjects. Over successive MRI images, the entire cross-sectional area of the hippocampus was measured. The only increases in gray-matter volume (neurons) were in the right and left hippocampi; no increases were seen in other parts of the brain. The analysis of hippocampal volume indicated no overall differences between the taxi drivers and the control subjects, but measures in posterior and anterior hippocampal regions indicated that the control subjects had larger anterior hippocampal areas and

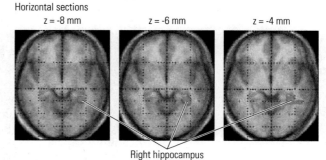

Horizontal sections

z = -8 mm   z = -6 mm   z = -4 mm

Right hippocampus

The location of activation seen in PET scans superimposed onto MRI brain images of taxi drivers as they recalled a complex route between two points in London. The peak activation is seen in the right hippocampus. (From Maguire et al., 2000.)

the taxi drivers had larger posterior hippocampal areas. In addition, the measures indicated that only the right posterior hippocampus increased in size as a function of years spent as a taxi driver.

As a result of these studies, Maguire and coworkers suggest that the "mental map" of London used by the taxi drivers in delivering their passengers is located in the right posterior hippocampus. Furthermore, they propose that this region of the hippocampus expands to accommodate the map. It is well established that new cells migrate from the ventricular zone into the hippocampus and join the granular layer of the hippocampus. The survival of these new cells conjointly with the use of the map may underlie the expansion of the right hippocampus.

(E. A. Maguire, R. S. J. Frackowiak, and C. D. Frith. Recalling routes around London: Activation of the right hippocampus in taxi drivers. *Journal of Neuroscience* 17:7103–7110, 1997.
E. A. Maguire, D. G. Gadian, I. S. Johnsrude, C. D. Good, J. Ashburner, R. S. J. Frackowiak, and C. D. Frith. Navigation-related structural change in the hippocampi of taxi drivers. *Proceedings of the National Academy of Sciences of the United States of America* 97:4398–4403, 2000.)

Squire that patients with hippocampal damage have some retrograde sparing of spatial abilities, but they also suggest that there is substantial retrograde amnesia for the richer contextual features of space.

Aguirre and D'Esposito conclude that the hippocampus may play a role in spatial behavior, but they note that there are no clinical reports of unilateral lesions producing real-life impairments. All such reports are instead mainly anecdotal and seldom include an actual measurement of real-life spatial navigation. An interesting contribution is made by Astur and coworkers, however, who presented a virtual navigation spatial problem to control subjects and to subjects with unilateral left- or right-hippocampal damage. The participants used a joystick to move around in a virtual three-dimensional swimming pool, trying to escape from the water, by finding a platform hidden just beneath the surface of the water, as quickly as possible. The computer gave them both auditory and visual feedback when they had succeeded. The view on the screen was a 60-° first-person field of view, approximately the same as seen by the human eye. When participants pushed the joystick to the right, the view on the screen would pan to the right, and so on. Each participant was given 20 trials, each of which might start from any of the four different starting locations around the edge of the pool. After that, the participants were each given a probe trial in which the escape platform was removed from the pool, and the time that the subject spent searching for the hidden platform at its former location was measured. The hippocampal subjects had brain lesions in the cortex overlying the hippocampus as well as having had unilateral removal of hippocampus and amygdala. Astur and colleagues report that both left- and right-hippocampal groups were severely impaired in solving the spatial navigation task and in searching for the platform at a location where it had formerly been hidden. Although it is unclear that the deficit can be ascribed to the hippocampal damage alone, because the overlying cortex and amygdala also were damaged, the results do suggest that the use of such lifelike tasks to study spatial abilities holds considerable promise.

The Dorsal and Ventral Streams

We have previously encountered Milner and Goodale's idea that there are at least two neural systems for processing the information used to represent objects in visual space: the posterior parietal cortex and the temporal cortex. Both receive information over pathways that begin in the visual cortex. A dorsal pathway, called the *dorsal stream*, projects to the posterior parietal cortex. A ventral pathway, called the *ventral stream*, projects to the inferior temporal cortex. Both the posterior parietal cortex and the inferior temporal cortex send projections to the frontal cortex, to guide the movements of looking, reaching, and locomotion. A component of the dorsal stream may project to the cingulate cortex and from there to the hippocampus.

A number of theories associate different aspects of spatial behavior with these two neural systems. In one proposal, the dorsal stream mediates "vision for action" and guides unconscious actions made with respect to objects. The ventral stream mediates "vision for recognition" and guides conscious actions made with respect to objects. Because spatial navigation has a large visual component, it seems logical to attribute two forms of spatial behavior and two forms of visual behavior to these streams and the parietal and temporal lobes, respectively.

The dorsal stream mediates egocentric spatial behavior, that which moves the body toward objects or in relation to objects whose identity is unimportant except that they provide spatial guidance. Recall that patients with egocentric disorientation are impaired in way-finding in both familiar and novel environments, yet they have no difficulty recognizing people or objects. By the same token, perhaps the ventral stream mediates allocentric spatial behavior—that which moves the body toward objects or in relation to objects whose identity is known.

Thus in regard to dorsal-stream damage, a person may recognize objects while being unable to use them for guidance; whereas, in regard to ventral-stream damage, a person may not recognize objects and so cannot use them for guidance. The impairments are related to topographic agnosia and topographic amnesia, respectively, identified by Paterson and Zangwill.

The Temporal Lobes and Spatial Behavior

A number of experimental approaches using animals have provided information that may be of use for understanding spatial navigation in humans. Much of this research focuses on the role of the hippocampus. As already noted, the clinical literature casts some doubt on whether the hippocampus is important in human spatial behavior. Thus, we do not yet know the extent to which the information summarized herein may apply to the spatial deficits displayed by human subjects with brain injury. The following sections describe research into two forms of spatial navigation: spatial mapping and dead reckoning.

The Hippocampus As a Cognitive Map

Much research in the past 50 years on how the brain controls spatial behavior has been driven by O'Keefe and Nadel's cognitive-mapping theory, which is summarized in their book titled *The Hippocampus As a Cognitive Map*. The theory has two parts. The first part proposes that, as animals travel through their environment, they create a brain representation of that environment in the form of a map, called a cognitive map. This map is then used to guide new trips through the same environment. The idea that animals use a cognitive map for spatial navigation has considerable appeal because maps provide a very simple way of storing a large amount of data. Look at the map of Napoleon's military campaign in Russia (Figure 21.3). The map vividly records his losses on his disastrous trip to Moscow and back to France. To describe the losses in words would require substantially more space than is taken up by the map. The second part of the theory is that the map is in the hippocampus. Although both the idea that animals use maps and the idea that the hippocampus is central to spatial behavior are questioned by many theoreticians, the theory has unquestionably stimulated an enormous amount of research.

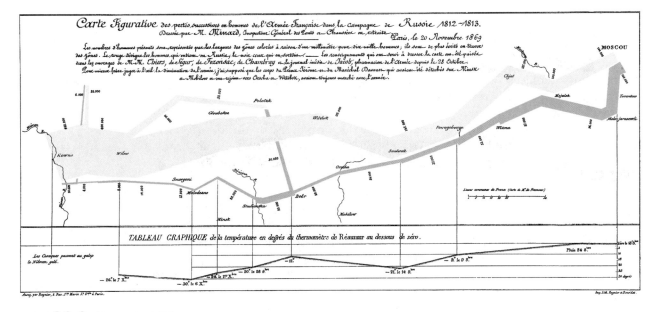

Figure 21.3 Maps can represent large amounts of information, as does this map drawn by Charles Joseph Minard, which portrays the losses suffered by Napoleon's army in the Russian campaign of 1812. Beginning at the left on the Polish–Russian border near the Niemen, the thick band shows the size of the army (422,000 men) as it invaded Russia. The width of the band indicates the size of the army at each position. In September, the army reached Moscow with 100,000 men. The path of Napoleon's retreat from Moscow in the bitterly cold winter is depicted by the dark lower band, which is tied to temperature and time scales. The remains of the Grande Armee struggled out of Russia with 10,000 men. (It may well be the best statistical graph ever drawn.) (E. J. Marey, *La Methode Graphique,* Paris, 1885.)

The idea that mapping and the hippocampus play a role in spatial behavior originated with a report on the activity of eight hippocampal cells by O'Keefe and Dostrovsky in 1971. These cells fired when rats were in certain locations on a testing platform and facing in a certain direction. On the basis of the activity of these cells, now called **place cells,** the authors proposed that the hippocampus is a map that represents features of the world and can anticipate spatial relations that are a consequence of the animal's movements. As speculative as this initial proposal seemed at first, it has been substantiated by the results of many studies of the activity of single hippocampal cells. Best and coworkers give the following summary of some of the remarkable properties of place cells.

1. The results of single-cell recording studies demonstrate that, within a short time of a rat's being placed in a novel environment, hippocampal cells begin to discharge when the animal is in certain places in that environment. For some cells it does not seem to matter whether the rat walks there itself or is carried there by the experimenter. Other cells encode not only the rat's location but also the direction and speed of the rat's voluntary movement. (If the rat is walking on a straight path, the active cells are more likely to code direction as well as location.)

2. If the lights are turned off after the animals have explored the new environment, the place cells maintain their activity relative to the previously visualized location of cues. If a rat is removed temporarily and then returned after the cues in the environment have been changed, then the cells will modify their activity to represent the new environment. If the rat is present when a cue is removed, the cells are more likely to maintain their original firing relations.

3. Moving a few visual cues has little effect on the pattern of activity displayed by the cells, but, if all room cues are rotated, the cells will then discharge with respect to the new location of the cues.

4. If a rat is exploring a T-maze for food, some place cells will discharge when the rat is in a particular part of the maze. Moreover, these cells may discharge, say, only if the rat is intending to make a left turn and not if it is intending to make a right turn.

5. Place cells seem to prefer visual cues, although they can also be influenced by olfactory, vestibular, tactile, and auditory cues. For example, place cells in animals that are blind will respond to cues that the animals discover by touch.

6. If one of a number of cups in an apparatus contains water, some place cells will fire in relation to that cup. If the cup is moved, the preferred firing location for those place cells changes with the cup.

7. If an animal is placed in an environment in which there is only one visual cue, then this single cue will determine where place cells discharge. If the single cue is removed, the cells continue to discharge, but the location at which they discharge begins to drift. If a visual cue that influences the firing of a place cell is moved about unpredictably relative to other cues, then the place cells eventually stop responding to that cue.

8. When numerous cells are recorded concurrently, many that are active in one environment will not be active when the rat is placed in another environment.

9. Place-cell activity is closely linked to an animal's ability to move; so, if a rat is restrained, the cells stop discharging.

Place cells can be recorded in places other than the hippocampus, but only hippocampal cells appear to have the special versatility that allows them to change activity in response to changes in environmental cues. In sum, the activity of place cells seems consistent with the idea that the cells are coding an animal's location and movement in space relative to surrounding cues.

The theory that the hippocampus has a role in spatial behavior has also been supported by the results of many studies of the effect of damage to the hippocampus. In general, they show that damaging the hippocampus disrupts the ability of an animal to navigate through its environment. O'Keefe and Nadel reviewed an extensive literature on maze learning by animals with hippocampal damage and concluded that the loss of a cognitive map could account for many of the impairments displayed by the animals.

Figure 21.4 illustrates a number of tasks used for studying the spatial navigation strategies of the rat. Figure 21.4D shows a typical research room, containing a rich array of visual cues, such as cupboards, pictures, and windows. In the center of the room is a swimming pool used in the Morris water task (named after its inventor, Richard Morris). In this test of spatial abilities, a rat must escape from the water onto a platform, which can be visible or hidden. If the platform is visible and thus serves as a landmark, the rat can swim directly to it, a response called a *cue response*, without needing to learn to use room cues

Figure 21.4 Tasks used to study spatial behavior in rodents. (A) The radial-arm maze was designed as a test of foraging behavior in animals. A rat must learn which alleys contain food and which alleys have been visited on a given day. (B) In the T-maze, a rat has to differentiate right and left. (C) The Grice box is a test of left–right differentiation. The food is placed in one alley until the animal has learned its location, then the food is placed in the other alley instead. (D) The swimming-pool task requires an animal to learn the location of a submerged, hidden platform. The only cue to the position of the platform is its spatial relation to cues about the room. Usually, these various tasks are presented in open rooms, and the animals can use the many surrounding cues as aids to orientation.

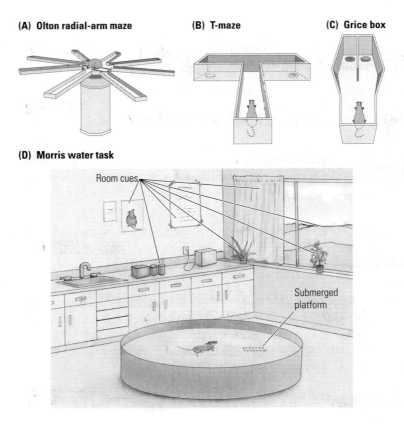

(A) Olton radial-arm maze

(B) T-maze

(C) Grice box

(D) Morris water task

Room cues

Submerged platform

to find it. If the platform is hidden, however, the rat will use more-distant room cues (termed distal cues) to locate the platform, a response called a *place response.* (Rats are well suited to this task. They are excellent swimmers, but their small size puts them at risk of losing normal body temperature if they stay in the water for long; so they are highly motivated to escape from the pool.) The various mazes illustrated in Figure 21.4A through C are used in other laboratory tests of spatial navigation.

A few findings from swimming-pool experiments demonstrate how a spatial problem can be solved by using a cognitive map. In a typical experiment, a rat is placed in a swimming pool that also contains an escape platform hidden just below the surface of the water (see Figure 21.4D). On the first trial, after having been put into the pool at a particular starting location, the rat swims almost randomly around the pool until it accidentally bumps into the platform. The rat is then given another trial, beginning at another starting location, and this time it finds the platform a little more quickly. Within a dozen trials or so, the rat swims directly to the platform from any starting location. Because the platform is not visible, the only way that the rat can find it is to know that the platform is in a specific location with respect to cues in the surrounding room. Thus, the rat must somehow "represent"—that is, create an internal image of—the location of the platform in relation to the room cues. According to O'Keefe and Nadel's cognitive-mapping theory, the animal creates an internal map of the room by using the prominent cues within the room, and it places the hidden platform on this map at the appropriate location relative to these cues. Similarly, a rat solves a maze problem by representing parts of the maze in its cognitive map.

If the hippocampus or the pathways leading into it or out of it are damaged in a rat, the animal is impaired in locating the platform. This impairment is not a general learning impairment: if a visible platform is placed in the pool, the rat quickly learns to swim directly to it; if the platform is again hidden, the rat is again impaired. That the rat is impaired in solving a place task is taken as evidence that the hippocampus must guide the animal's swim to the platform by using surrounding room cues. In experimental animals, neurotoxins can be used to selectively damage the cells of the hippocampus while sparing nonhippocampal structures, especially cortical structures. That animals treated in this way demonstrate impaired spatial behavior seems to provide strong support for the idea that the hippocampus plays some role in spatial behavior.

The Hippocampus and Food Finding in Birds

Stimulated by O'Keefe and Nadel's theory that the hippocampus plays a central role in spatial behavior, other researchers, using other species and other testing methods, have produced a number of new lines of supporting evidence. One line of evidence, summarized by Sherry and Duff, is based on food-caching behavior in birds.

Many bird species will take pieces of food—sunflower seeds, for example—and hide them for later consumption. Some birds can hide many hundreds of items and find them later. A particularly large body of research concerns the abilities of birds in two major families, the chickadee and tit family (Paridae) and the jay and nutcracker family (Corvidae). Chickadees store insect prey and seeds in scattered sites that typically include furrows in tree bark, conifer needle clusters, moss, and other natural hiding places. A small number of food items, often only one, are stored at each site, and cache sites are not reused. Cache sites may be scattered throughout a number of acres. Estimates of the number of items cached in a year number in the thousands. The items are left for periods ranging from hours to weeks before the bird returns to retrieve them.

The birds appear to use distal spatial cues rather than local landmarks to recall the location of their caches. Distal spatial cues are objects that are at some distance away from a cache site, and landmarks are cues that are in close proximity to the cache site. If landmarks in the vicinity of a food item are disturbed, the bird's ability to find the food is not disturbed. Similarly, if an artificial cue, such as a colored object, is moved from a cache site, the bird is not prevented from retrieving the food at that location. If more-distal cues are displaced, however, the bird's search in a location is displaced to same degree. If the caches on one side of an aviary are pilfered, the bird learns to avoid that side of the aviary. If cache sites marked by certain colored tapes are pilfered, but cache sites marked by different-colored tapes are not, the birds do not learn to differentiate between the colors, even though independent tests show that the birds can easily tell one color from another. The results of these experiments and many similar ones indicate that the birds are using distal spatial cues rather than local landmarks to mark the location of their cached food.

Figure 21.5 Size of the hippocampus relative to the forebrain in families and subfamilies of food-storing (black dots) and non-food-storing (blue dots) passerine birds (the order to which chickadees and sparrows belong). Both axes are logarithmic. The chickadee is an example of a caching bird, and the sparrow is an example of a noncaching bird. (After Sherry and Duff, 1996.)

• Caching birds • Noncaching birds

Chickadee   House sparrow

The results of studies comparing birds that cache food with birds that do not cache food indicate that the hippocampus is considerably larger in the birds that cache (Figure 21.5). If the hippocampus was damaged in birds that cached food, they continued to cache but were unable to retrieve the food. In a slightly different paradigm, female brown-headed cowbirds, which search for host nests in which to lay their eggs and thus must retain a memory of many potential host nests, were found to have a larger hippocampus than male cowbirds, which do not participate in searching for nests.

Clayton reports additional evidence based on a seasonal pattern of neurogenesis in black-capped chickadees. Precursor cells migrate into the hippocampus and differentiate into new neurons during the season in which birds are storing food. Food storing in chickadees reaches its maximum in autumn, continues through the winter, and decreases in spring and summer. Both hippocampal neurogenesis and hippocampal size reach a maximum in autumn and decrease in spring. Food-storing experience also correlates with hippocampal size. If a food-storing marsh tit is prevented from storing food early in development, the relative size of its hippocampus lags behind that of age-matched controls.

Taken together, findings in these studies showing that food-storing birds can remember hundreds of locations at which food is stored, use distal spatial cues to locate food, and require the hippocampus to do so suggest that the hippocampus plays an important role in spatial behavior.

Dead Reckoning

Dead reckoning—derived from the phrase "deduced reckoning"—is a form of navigation that depends on cues generated by an animal's own movement. It refers to the ability of an animal to know how far it has traveled and where in relation to a starting point, to monitor its speed and travel time, and to change direction as necessary. Dead reckoning was an early form of navigation used by sailors and is believed to have been used by Columbus on his journeys between Europe and Central America (Figure 21.6). Using a compass to monitor direction, the sailors calculated speed by throwing a piece of wood overboard at a certain point on the bow. As the ship moved past the piece of wood, a sailor chanted until the wood had passed a certain point on the stern. The chant was written in such a way that the last word spoken corresponded to a specific speed. If sailors could additionally tell time, they could locate their position. In other words, knowing direction, speed, and travel time allowed sailors to make an accurate record of a trip. This record could then be used to guide their return journey. Dead reckoning is still used today when fog interferes with the use of visual beacons; all a sailor needs is a speedometer, watch, and compass.

(A)

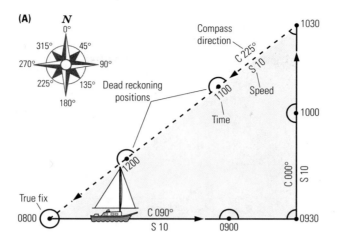

(B)

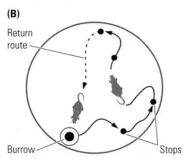

Return route

Burrow

Stops

Figure 21.6 Dead reckoning by sailors and rats. (A) An example of dead reckoning in which a ship starts from a known location, arrives at a destination, and returns to the starting point without the use of external cues. The starting point is at 0800 hours; the direction (C stands for compass) is 90°; and the speed (S) is 10 knots. Time, direction, and speed are noted at each directional change, and dead reckoning location is calculated and recorded each hour. Note that the return trip (dashed line) can be calculated from the plots made on the outward trip. (B) A rat foraging for a piece of food makes a number of turns and stops before finding the food and, on finding the food, returns directly home. The rat does not have a clock, compass, or speedometer and so must have internal processes for dead reckoning.

Nonhuman animals do not have mechanical ways of measuring speed, time, and direction when they navigate by dead reckoning. Instead, they must derive cues from their own movement, which are collectively called **idiothetic cues.** In principle, cues from a number of sensory systems, including proprioceptive and vestibular systems, can provide the necessary information. For example, sensory flow, including optical flow, gradients of sound and odors, and even wind resistance, provides idiothetic information about speed and direction of movement. In addition, an animal may monitor its movements by using the efferent copy of movement commands. That is, when an animal voluntarily decides to travel to a certain location, it can copy the instructions that it sends to its muscles. This efferent, or output, copy can be used to infer how far it has traveled and the direction that it has taken. Using these cues to compute velocity and direction over time, an animal can keep track of its location in relation to a starting point. Then, by reversing these computations, the animal is able to return to that starting point. Such behavior is useful when the starting point is a home to which the animal can carry food or to which it can escape from a predator. Dead reckoning is especially useful if an animal is traveling about in the dark, is in a new place where the environmental cues are unfamiliar, or is in a place where the visual cues often change. Charles Darwin was the first to suggest that animals could use dead reckoning to navigate. Subsequently, many researchers have confirmed that they do so. When we speak of an animal or

Figure 21.7 A rat's head-direction cells are located in various parts of the limbic system. In this drawing, the head-direction cell's preferred direction is when the rat is facing the top of the page. Each of the eight traces of neural activity shows the cell's relative rate of firing when the rat's face is turned toward the direction indicated by the corresponding arrow. Head-direction cells help inform the rat about its location in space.

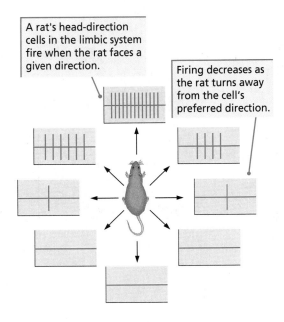

A rat's head-direction cells in the limbic system fire when the rat faces a given direction.

Firing decreases as the rat turns away from the cell's preferred direction.

person having a "sense of direction" or "sense of distance," most likely we are describing a conscious awareness of spatial location that is derived from the brain's unconscious skill at dead reckoning.

Taube summarized an extensive body of research suggesting that there are cells in the limbic system that indicate direction. Cells of this type are called **head-direction cells** (Figure 21.7).

1. A head-direction cell discharges whenever a rat points its head in a particular direction. Different cells have different preferred directions. For example, one cell might discharge whenever the rat points its head to the west, whereas another cell will discharge whenever the rat points its head to the south.

2. The firing of head-direction cells is not related to the position of the animal's trunk and does not depend significantly on whether the rat is still or moving. Furthermore, head-direction cells do not adapt over time but maintain their rate of discharge as long as the rat's head is pointing in the preferred direction. A head-direction cell is not activated by the presence of a particular *object* in the environment. Rather, such a cell is responsive to direction itself and so is like the needle of a compass that continues to point north when the compass is moved.

3. Nevertheless, surrounding cues influence head-direction cells. If a rat is taken to a novel environment, its head-direction cells will quickly develop a preferred orientation there. If the rat is then removed from that environment while the cues are rotated and is subsequently returned, the head-direction cells' preferences will rotate with the cues. If the cues are rotated *while* the rat is in the environment, the preferred direction of head-direction cells is not as greatly influenced.

4. If the lights are turned off, head-direction cells maintain their tuning for many minutes.

5. When a rat is allowed to explore two environments connected by a tunnel, its head-direction cells will maintain the same preferred direction in both environments; but, if the cues in one environment are rotated while the rat is absent and then the rat is returned to that environment, the head-direction cells' preferences will again rotate with the cues. When the rat enters the tunnel and crosses to the second environment, the head-direction cells revert to their former orientation.

6. Head-direction cells are not limited to orienting the animal in a horizontal plane; they maintain their directional tuning when the animal climbs vertically up or down as well.

7. Head-direction cells continue to discharge when the rat is restrained, unlike place cells, which stop firing in such a situation.

8. Whereas place cells may fire in one environment and not in another and at different rates on different occasions, every head-direction cell is locked into a network that is constantly active, depending only on head direction.

The regions of the limbic system in which head-direction cells are found are largely different from regions in which place cells are found. Figure 21.8 shows that head-direction cells are recorded in the lateral mammillary, anterior thalamus, cingulate cortex, and postsubicular regions of the hippocampus, whereas place cells are recorded in the entorhinal cortex, subiculum, and hippocampus. This anatomical organization suggests that there are two navigation systems. The place system allows an animal to navigate by using the relations between environmental cues, as proposed by the spatial-mapping theory. The head-direction system allows an animal to navigate in relation to its own spatial position. Perhaps another way of picturing the difference is to say that the place-cell system tells a rat where *things* are in the world and the head-direction system tells the rat where the rat itself is.

The results of a number of experiments have demonstrated that rats can navigate in situations in which place cells are deprived of all sensory cues so that only the head-direction system is operating. One of us (Whishaw) and colleagues described a testing situation in which rats emerge from a hidden burrow to forage on a circular table for large food pellets. When a rat finds a food pellet, it carries the pellet back to its refuge for eating. The outward trip made by a rat as it is looking for food is circuitous, but the homeward trip is direct. When foraging in the light, a rat is able to use both place-cell information and head-direction-cell information. If the rat is tested in the dark and all olfactory and auditory cues are removed, the rat can return home only if it can access a record of the body movements made on the outward trip to calculate the homeward trip. It must dead reckon and presumably rely on the head-direction system. Normal rats are very accurate at returning home in both the light and the dark. If the hippocampus or cingulate cortex is damaged, however, the rats are accurate in the light but not in the dark. The finding that damage to the hippocampus disrupts dead reckoning as well as some forms of spatial mapping may mean that the hippocampus participates in both forms of spatial navigation.

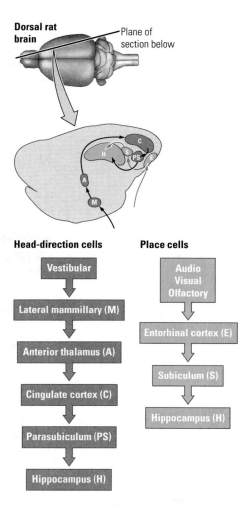

Figure 21.8 Locations in the brain where place cells and head-direction cells have been recorded in rats (sagittal section). The relation between the two systems is not well understood, but the place-cell system and the head-direction system may prove to be two circuits that mediate spatial behavior and project to the hippocampus.

Two Systems for Spatial Navigation

In our description of topographic dysfunction in human subjects, we mentioned the possibility that there are two systems for spatial behavior, one implicating the dorsal stream through the lateral parietal cortex and the other implicating the ventral stream through the temporal cortex. We suggested that the former system may utilize egocentric cues, or cues from the body's own movement, whereas the latter may utilize allocentric cues, or cues coming from the surroundings. It is tempting to conclude that the head-direction system has a role in egocentric movements, whereas the place-cell system controls allocentric movements. Unfortunately, few attempts have been made to record place or head-direction cells in primates or humans to test this hypothesis. Rats are small enough to move freely through complex environments while attached to electrodes; humans and monkeys are not. Rolls reports, however, that place cells are much less likely than head-direction cells to be recorded in monkeys, which instead seem to possess many "view cells"—cells that discharge when a monkey looks in particular directions. It seems possible; therefore, that place cells and head-direction cells may be closely linked to eye movements in primates and to body movements in rats.

Similarly, although there have been many tests of allocentric spatial behavior in brain-damaged humans, there have been few tests of dead reckoning. However, Worsley and coworkers examined the performance of neurosurgical patients with left or right temporal lobectomies on tests of dead reckoning. The patients were walked away from their homes in one direction for a while and then turned and walked in another direction. At this point, they were asked to return home. Patients with right-temporal lobectomies had difficulty returning to their homes. The right-temporal-lobectomy patients also had trouble when asked to walk in a given direction, make a turn of a certain size, and turn and walk for a certain distance again.

A Word of Caution

Despite the substantial body of evidence suggesting that the hippocampus, through its connections with the temporal lobe, plays some role in spatial behavior, there is other evidence that is somewhat inconsistent with that idea. Zola-Morgan and coworkers favor the idea that the hippocampus has a role in memory and that spatial memory is but one kind of memory. They describe R. B., who displayed general anterograde amnesia. He was a male postal worker who, at 52 years of age, suffered a temporary shortage of arterial blood to the brain secondary to a coronary bypass operation. In the next 5 years, until his death, R. B. exhibited marked anterograde amnesia. A postmortem examination revealed a bilateral loss of all cells in CA1, a restricted part of the hippocampus. R. B.'s case seems to suggest that general anterograde amnesia can follow hippocampal damage, which would be inconsistent with the idea that the hippocampus is selectively engaged in spatial behavior. One hypothesis consistent both with R. B.'s case and with much of the spatial evidence is that the hippocampus plays a *general* role in memory acquisition and does not exclusively or selectively control spatial behavior. Even the findings in studies on birds, although seemingly consistent with a special role of the hippocampus in spatial behavior, are amenable to a memory interpretation. If birds are given especially tasty or perishable items to store, they are likely to retrieve those items before retrieving other ones. Their spatial memories appear therefore to include important nonspatial information as well.

The Parietal Lobe

Not surprisingly, considering that the region forms part of the dorsal stream, damage to the parietal cortex results in spatial impairments. Disorders of visuospatial exploration stemming from such damage were described by Balint and are generally referred to as Balint's syndrome. Researchers now recognize about eight different defects of visual exploration that in most known instances have resulted from bilateral lesions of the parietal cortex but do not all coincide in every such case (Table 21.1). Perhaps the most dramatic symptoms are those first described by Balint.

Balint's patient had bilateral damage to the occipital and parietal cortex that included parts of the dorsal temporal lobes. He also had a zone of unilateral damage to the dorsal parietal and motor cortex (Figure 21.9). He had come to Balint's attention after suffering a stroke, and his condition remained unchanged for 6 years. This man had complete visual fields, was reported to be capable of eye movements, and recognized and named colors, objects, and pictures. When presented with visual stimuli, he directed his gaze from 35° to 40° to the right of them and saw only what was in his direct line of sight. Only after prompting would he look to the left and notice that the stimuli were there. After his attention had been directed to an object, he noticed nothing else—a response that was true for objects of all sizes, from a pin to a human figure. The patient would not look over a picture or scene but fastened on the first item that he saw in it. The impairment resulted in a reading defect, because he focused on a single letter and only with difficulty could work backward through a word to decode it. The patient was also impaired in reaching. If asked to grasp an object or point to a target, he groped and hit the target only by chance. Misreaching extended to lighting a cigar, which he would attempt to light in the middle. The patient was also unable to estimate distance and could not tell which of two objects was closer.

Gordon Holmes described a group of patients who had suffered penetrating missile wounds to the brain. Their most notable symptoms were various kinds of impairment in eye movement. They had difficulty in looking at a stimulus, whether it was presented visually or aurally, in maintaining visual fixation, in following a moving target, in keeping the eyes focused on an approaching object, and in blinking in response to a visual threat. These patients also failed to comprehend the spatial features of a stimulus at which they were looking and could recognize. That is, they had trouble judging the location of objects in space, estimating distance, discriminating length and size, and evaluating depth and thickness. As a result, they ran into objects when walking and had difficulty in reading and in counting scattered objects. The patients also sometimes failed to notice objects placed before them and, like Balint's patient, did not notice anything else once their attention had been attracted by a stimulus.

Since these early reports, there have been many accounts of patients with similar problems, although the precise symptoms have varied, depending on how an injury was acquired, whether it was bilateral, and where it was located.

Table 21.1 Deficits in visuospatial exploration

Displaced visual attention
Inability to perceive more than one stimulus
Defective visual control of movement (optic ataxia)
Inability to follow a moving target
Defective accommodation and convergence
Inability to maintain fixation
Inability to voluntarily direct gaze to targets (gaze apraxia)
Abnormal visual search

Figure 21.9 Balint's drawing of the areas of softening in his patient's brain. (After de Renzi, 1982.)

Left hemisphere

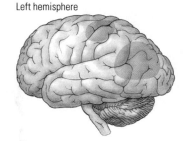

Right hemisphere

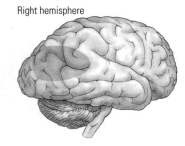

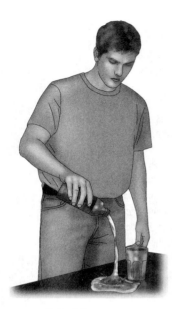

Figure **21.10** A patient with Balint's syndrome demonstrates a visuospatial deficit in his attempt to pour fluid into a glass. (After Allison et al., 1969.)

Figure 21.10 illustrates misjudgment by a patient studied by Allison and his colleagues who had bilateral posterior cortical lesions resulting in small lower-temporal-quadrant-field defects, accompanied by dramatic deficits in the visual control of reaching and other movements (so-called optic ataxia) and by deficits in eye movements.

> A manifestation of visual disorientation noted by the nursing staff five months after operation was when he attempted to light a cigarette. He took it out of the packet and put it in his mouth, then clumsily took a match out of the matchbox and lit it, afterwards directing the flame towards his lower lip, missing the cigarette. . . . He could not pour fluid from a bottle into a glass but spilled it on the tablecloth. He was unable to shake hands without first groping for the proffered hand. It could be demonstrated that visual memory was intact and did not contribute to his errors. When an object (e.g., a matchbox) was held up either above his head, to the right, or to the left and he was asked to note its position, close his eyes for a moment, and then point in the general direction in which he had seen the object, he did this correctly. Therefore, it appeared that his ability to remember the position of an object in space was not impaired. (Allison et al., 1969, pp. 324–326)

To differentiate the many deficits that such patients suffer, investigators have focused on two aspects of visual function: **visual localization** and **depth perception.** For example, to demonstrate a disorder of spatial localization independent of a disorder of reaching or pointing, Hannay and coworkers projected one or two dots on a screen for 300 ms. Two seconds later, an array of numbers was projected, and the subjects were asked to pick the number (or numbers) located in the same position (or positions) as the dot (or dots). Patients with right-hemisphere lesions were impaired at this task in comparison with control subjects and subjects with left-hemisphere lesions. This deficit is not simply a manifestation of neglect, because errors were distributed equally in the left and right visual fields. It is not surprising that a person who is unable to receive a sense impression of the location of points in space would have a hard time directing his or her movements, resulting in an apparent spatial deficit.

Depth is an important cue to the spatial location of objects. You can understand its importance when you try to catch a ball with one eye closed. Patients with severe impairments in depth perception have been described as far back as Balint's work of the early twentieth century, but a significant problem of interpretation arises when an impairment of depth perception is assumed on the basis of misreaching, because misreaching can be caused by any of a variety of deficits. Nonetheless, there is now good evidence that depth perception can be markedly abnormal in the presence of good visual acuity. A study by Carmon and Bechtoldt provides a compelling example. These researchers designed an experiment using random dot stereograms to study the cues necessary to perceive depth. Looking into eyepieces, their subjects saw an apparently random array of dots. When viewed with one eye alone, the array had no contour or depth and looked rather like a complex crossword puzzle with black and white boxes. However, when the array was viewed as a stereogram—both eyes open and each looking independently at left-eye and right-eye views of the same image—a striking figure–background contour suddenly appeared (a figure appeared to float in front of a background), because of slight disparities between the images shown to the left and right eye. Most normal subjects and patients with left-hemisphere damage easily perceived the contour, but most patients with right-hemisphere damage did very badly at this test, illustrating a defect in depth perception. The result supports the idea that at least some part of the mechanism for depth perception is more strongly represented in the right hemisphere.

Many of the deficits described in the preceding paragraphs appear to be related to parietal-cortex damage. In these cases, the dorsal stream, which projects through the parietal cortex, may be implicated. The function of the parietal cortex is to provide a coordinate system of visual space and to locate objects in this space. In the absence of this system, a patient will still see an object but will not be able to direct eye or hand movements toward it accurately. Various investigators have identified neurons in the monkey posterior parietal cortex that respond to stimuli presented within a monkey's grasping space. It is likely that these cells—or some of them—project to the motor system to guide the limbs in moving voluntarily toward targets in various spatial locations. The parietal cortex also contains neurons that appear to have a role in directing hand and eye movements toward stimuli presented in grasping space, providing further evidence that the parietal cortex has a special role in directing movements to visual targets.

The Frontal Lobe

The frontal cortex, too, is important for spatial discriminations. The most dramatic demonstration is from experiments by Nakamura and his coworkers. They spared all the visual areas of the posterior cortex while removing the entire cortex anterior to it in monkeys. The monkeys failed to show any signs of vision, but recordings of single-cell activity in the visual areas revealed that the cells were functioning normally. Thus, removal of the frontal cortex renders animals chronically blind and unable to navigate even though the visual system is functioning. Findings in a number of studies have demonstrated that more-selective impairments follow more-restricted lesions in the visual cortex. Haaxma and Kuypers demonstrated that, if the finger area of the motor cortex is disconnected from the visual centers, a monkey can no longer pick up food by using the pincer grasp.

It is difficult to distinguish impairments in the detection of objects from impairments in spatial behavior. Some features of object-detection impairments, however, do suggest that the underlying cause is a spatial impairment. Goldman-Rakic and coworkers, using rhesus monkeys with small lesions in the frontal cortex along the principal sulcus, report such an experiment. The monkeys had been trained to fixate on a spot of light in the center of a television monitor. A second dot of light was flashed briefly in a monkey's visual field. The monkeys were reinforced with food for waiting until the fixation spot disappeared before directing their gaze to the new visual target. Monkeys with unilateral lesions failed to direct their gaze to the new target after even very short delays. If there was no delay, however, they performed normally. Varying the location of the lesion produced selective deficits associated with different parts of the visual field. These findings demonstrate that the principal sulcus contains a mechanism for guiding responses on the basis of stored information in the absence of external cues. They also suggest that the memory for the location of objects may be mapped in visuospatial coordinates. There is a parallel to these eye-movement results in experiments that require monkeys to reach toward a target. If a monkey with lesions in the principal sulcus is given a delayed-response task in which the object's location is the relevant variable, impairments are observed after short delays (see Figure 16.11A). Other discrimination tasks that do not require memory for spatial location are not impaired by these lesions.

Passingham also reports memory impairments in a less-artificial task in rhesus monkeys with principal sulcus lesions. In this experiment, the monkeys were trained to retrieve peanuts from behind 25 different doors in the shortest number of trials, without returning to a door a second time. This task tested each monkey's spatial memory for doors that it had already opened. The monkeys with lesions were severely impaired in their performance. Petrides and Milner report a somewhat analogous deficit in people with frontal-lobe damage. These patients were presented with a set of pages that each contained an array of the same visual stimuli but with the stimuli presented in a different order on each page. They were asked to point to one of the stimuli on each page but to do so without pointing to the same page location twice. Thus, the patients had to remember the locations of the selections that they had made previously. The frontal-lobe patients displayed impairments at this task.

Because the frontal cortex has important connections with the basal ganglia, researchers hypothesized that spatial-memory impairments of a similar kind would be found subsequent to basal ganglia lesions. Ingle and Hoff report the results of an interesting experiment with frogs, indicating that just such impairment can be obtained. A visible barrier was placed beside a frog and then removed. After a delay, a large dark object was moved toward the frog, causing the frog to leap away. Normal frogs avoided leaping into the barrier's previous location or leaped in such a way that they landed behind its previous location, indicating that they remembered the location. Frogs with basal ganglia lesions behaved as if they failed to remember the barrier's previous location, although they avoided the barrier quite well when it was present.

Individual Differences in Spatial Abilities

Sex-Related Differences

Adult males tend to perform better than adult females on certain spatial tests. This male advantage in spatial ability is generally contrasted with a female advantage in language skills, fine-motor movements, and perceptual speed; however, the female advantage in these areas is conceded to be quite small in statistical terms, about a 0.2 standard deviation, whereas the male advantage in spatial performance is thought to be large, about a 0.5 standard deviation. In the tests of virtual water–maze learning described earlier, Astur and coworkers reported one of the largest sex differences favoring males. Maguire and colleagues, however, compiled evidence that females are more likely to navigate by using landmarks, whereas males are more likely to use spatial-mapping procedures; in the Astur task, landmarks were not prominent.

The study of spatial abilities dates to the early part of the twentieth century, in association with studies designed to predict mechanical aptitude. As interest in spatial abilities developed, studies eventually began to include mixed age and sex groups, from which the generalization that adult males perform better than adult females gradually emerged. When Maccoby and Jacklin reviewed this literature in 1974, the idea that this sex difference emerges in adolescence and is due to environmental influences became a dominant view. Subsequently, the results of many studies have demonstrated sex differences in much younger children. Part of the difficulty in ascertaining the validity of observed age and sex differences in spatial abilities stems from the large number of different kinds of tests that have been used and the diversity of the populations tested. In a 1982 review, however, Newcombe interpreted the evidence as suggesting that small sex differences are present in childhood and increase slightly with age.

The research suggests that females and males differ in their abilities at such skills as chess, mathematics, music, and art. Mathematical aptitude has received the closest scrutiny. Findings in a large number of studies have shown that males outperform females on tests of quantitative ability. In the United States, scores on the Scholastic Aptitude Test and the Johns Hopkins University mathematical talent search indicate that these differences become apparent in adolescence and are more evident at the high end of the performance scale. Among top scorers on the College Board aptitude tests, males outnumber females by about 17 to 1.

The existence of sex differences, however small, is of great interest to students of spatial function. On the practical side, they must be considered when tests of brain function are developed, standardized, and administered. They must also be considered in interpreting the consequences of brain damage. More important, they provide a key to understanding brain organization and function. Apart from environmental influences, the number of possible explanations for the differences between males and females is limited; therefore, the discovery of relevant factors through the use of the scientific method is a real possibility. The differences may be genetic, in which case they are sex linked and are probably determined by a recessive gene on the X chromosome. Alternatively, they may be hormonally produced, emerging as a result of the action of hormones on neural organization and function.

Genetic Contributions to Sex-Based Differences

The usual explanation of a genetic basis for male and female differences in spatial ability goes something like this. During the formative period of the evolution of modern humans, a differentiation of roles in food gathering was adaptive. A primary occupation of males was hunting, which required an ability to find one's way about a large area. Hunting also required the ability to throw spears and aim arrows, both of which are spatial skills. Males endowed with these abilities would be more successful than those who were not and consequently would be "selected" in the Darwinian sense. It is quite irrelevant that those skills are no longer needed today; if they are encoded in sex-linked genes, males will tend to get them anyway.

McGee suggests that spatial skills are heritable through an X-linked, recessive gene. Females have two X chromosomes, and males have one. Thus, traits that are thought to be carried by a single gene on the X chromosome are said to be sex linked: if such a gene is recessive, more males than females will be affected. Under this arrangement, according to the usual estimates, 50% of males and 25% of females will carry the gene and have enhanced spatial abilities. In other words, about one-fourth of females will score above the male median on tests of spatial abilities, a finding obtained in most studies. The recessive-gene hypothesis has been put to a number of tests, but it has not emerged unscathed. According to the hypothesis, certain correlations should emerge in the offspring of different families, but these correlations have not been obtained. Another problem concerns the tests used to obtain scores for correlations. Studies using different tests have obtained different correlations, raising the possibility that there may be different kinds of spatial abilities. The results suggest either that alternative inheritance models should be considered or that sex-related differences have other explanations.

Hormonal Influences on Sex-Based Differences

Three lines of evidence suggest that hormones influence sex differences in spatial abilities: (1) findings from developmental studies, (2) findings from studies of persons with chromosomal–hormonal abnormalities, and (3) findings from studies investigating the relation between androgenicity and spatial abilities.

As noted earlier, sex differences in spatial performance are found more reliably in adults than in prepubescent children, suggesting that such differences may be partly attributable to hormonal changes during puberty. Prenatal or early postnatal sex-related hormonal influences could account for differences obtained with prepubescent children. This hypothesis seems to be supported by the results of studies of patients with **Turner's syndrome,** a disorder found in females born with a single X chromosome rather than the normal XX pair. Their intelligence and verbal abilities are distributed throughout the normal range, but their spatial abilities are impaired. They get extremely low scores on tests of mental rotation, the block-design test of the Wechsler Adult Intelligence Scale, the spatial subtest of the Primary Mental Abilities Test, the Road-and-Map Test of Direction Sense, and tests of imaginary movements and direct rotation. The results are counterintuitive and at variance with the recessive-gene hypothesis, which would predict that females with a single X chromosome ought to be similar to males, who also have one X chromosome. Because females with Turner's syndrome produce no gonadal hormones, the suggestion is that gonadal hormones influence spatial abilities. Studies examining this hypothesis now propose that levels of androgens (masculinizing hormones) or the balance between estrogen and androgens might determine spatial abilities. Some researchers have even argued that the more androgens females receive, the better their spatial abilities. For males, who are already receiving a high level of androgens, more might be too much, and spatial and other abilities might be impaired. Consequently, females receiving large amounts of androgen and males receiving moderate amounts would be expected to have enhanced spatial skills.

The mechanisms that hormones are thought to influence in modulating spatial abilities are in the brain. Presumably, they are the same neural systems that are responsible for spatial abilities in general. How these mechanisms might work is not known. Early in life, hormones may influence neural connections, neural growth, and cell death, thus sculpting a spatial-neural system that is quite different in some persons (who therefore have enhanced spatial abilities) from that in others. On the other hand, hormones might selectively modulate neural function in these systems through still unknown mechanisms.

Handedness and Spatial Ability

It is often proposed that left-handedness might confer a special spatial advantage. For example, Leonardo da Vinci and Michelangelo were left-handed, left-handedness is common in tennis players and baseball pitchers, and there are reports that left-handers are disproportionately represented in faculties of engineering and architecture.

Harshman and colleagues reported results suggesting that the relations between cognitive functioning and handedness may be complex. Harshman's group administered an extensive battery of tests to three large samples, representing three different populations, defined by the investigators as a "high-reasoning population," a "low-reasoning population," and a randomly selected control group. Overall, males performed better on spatial tests than females, as was expected. In some of the populations, left-handedness in males was associated with lower spatial scores, but it was associated with higher spatial scores in females. In an attempt to find out why this effect existed only in certain populations, Harshman's group examined the effects of other variables and found that sex, handedness, and reasoning ability were all related to spatial scores. Among what he defined as a high-reasoning group, left-handed males had lower spatial scores and left-handed females had higher spatial scores than right-handed comparison groups. Among low-reasoning groups, the relation was reversed: left-handed males had high spatial scores and left-handed females had low spatial scores in relation to their comparison groups. In a retrospective analysis of previous studies, Harshman suggests that differences in the groups sampled could account for the contradictory results obtained in previous work. That is, if a sample group was a university population, high spatial scores might be expected from left-handed females and low spatial scores from left-handed males. If a sample population was more heterogeneous, the opposite pattern of results might be obtained.

Neuropsychological Spatial Tests

A surprising number of tests have been devised for measuring spatial abilities. A noteworthy example is the test used in Smith and Milner's studies of patients who had undergone elective surgery to remove the hippocampus as a treatment for epilepsy. These researchers employed 16 small toys as stimulus objects, spread out over a table. The subject was told that the purpose of the test was to measure the ability to estimate prices and that the task consisted of estimating the average price of a real object represented by the toy. The subject was told to point to a toy, name it, and think of a price. After 10 seconds, the price was asked for and the subject was instructed to move on to another toy, and so on. Then the subject was moved away from the table and was asked to recall the objects that had been on it. After this test of object recall, a sheet of brown paper the same size as the original table was placed before the subject, and he or she was asked to place the toys on it in their original arrangement. The two recall tests were then repeated 24 hours later. The object array is illustrated in Figure 21.11A. Scores were given for the recall of the objects' names; in addition, the researchers measured the distances between the objects original locations and the patient's immediate recollection of where the objects had been, as well as between the original locations and the patient's delayed recollection of where the objects had been. On the measure of name recall, both patients with right-hippocampus damage and patients with left-hippocampus damage were moderately impaired, with the left-hippocampal patients having lower scores than the right-hippocampal patients. The results for the spatial component of the experiment are shown in Figure 21.11B, indicating a selective participation of the right hippocampus in spatial memory. Scores for the left-temporal group were comparable to scores for the control group, but scores for the right-temporal group were extremely low on both immediate and delayed recall tests.

Visualization tests evaluate the ability to manipulate, rotate, twist, or invert two- or three-dimensional stimulus objects mentally. The underlying ability seems to entail a process of recognition, retention, and recall of a configuration whose parts move and change place, as when an object is manipulated in three-dimensional space or a flat pattern is folded and unfolded (Figure 21.12A). McGee suggests that visualization is important to two aspects of mental functioning: imagery and mathematical ability, especially for the understanding of geometry and algebra.

Orientation tests evaluate comprehension of the arrangement of elements within a visual stimulus pattern and the aptitude to remain unconfused by the changing orientation in which a spatial configuration may be presented (Figure 21.12B). McGee suggests that orientation ability is related to field independence—the ability to orient an object accurately while ignoring the background against which it is viewed.

Figure 21.11 Test of spatial memory and its results. (A) In this test of spatial memory for objects, showing a typical arrangement of 16 toys in 16 fixed locations, subjects are required to point to the objects and estimate their individual prices. The objects are then removed, and the subjects are asked to indicate where each object had been located within the array. (B) Graph of the performances of left-temporal and right-temporal patients and of controls on the recall of absolute location. (After Smith and Milner, 1981.)

(A) Test of spatial memory

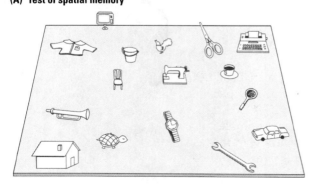

(B) Results

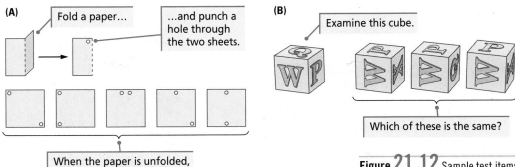

Figure 21.12 Sample test items similar to those used to measure visualization and orientation spatial abilities. (A) For visualization test, imagine folding and unfolding a piece of paper. After the paper has been folded as shown, a hole is punched, as indicated in the drawing, through all of the thicknesses. Which figure correctly shows the appearance of the paper when it is once again unfolded? (B) For orientation test, compare the three cubes on the right with the one on the left. No letter appears on more than one face of a given cube. Which of the three cubes on the right could be a different view of the cube on the left? (After Halpern, 1986.)

There is a growing consensus among researchers that two-dimensional paper-and-pencil tests may not tap the same spatial abilities that are exercised in the real-life process of way finding. Just as it is difficult to subject brain-injured patients to real-life tests of navigating through novel and familiar environments, it is not possible to perform brain scans on subjects as they perform real-life tasks. Consequently, the use of computer-based virtual spatial tasks has increased in the hope that these tasks can evaluate the same abilities as those used in a real spatial world.

Summary

There are a number of kinds of spatial abilities. Evidence obtained from brain-injured people suggests that the right hemisphere plays a special role in spatial behavior. Damage to the right hemisphere produces a number of different kinds of impairment in spatial abilities, depending on the location of the damage. Damage to dorsal parietal cortex and cingulate cortex impairs egocentric spatial behavior in which body position plays a central role. Damage to the lingual gyrus and parahippocampal gyrus impairs the use of external cues in spatial behavior. The role of the hippocampus is debated, but the results of imaging studies suggest that the right hemisphere plays a central role in complex navigation, such as that used by taxi drivers in traveling between two locations. The results of studies of spatial-navigation abilities in rodents suggest that there may also be an allocentric system in which place cells play a central role and an egocentric system in which head-direction cells play a central role. The former type of cell may be used in spatial mapping and the latter in dead reckoning. Damage to the parietal cortex results in a number of impairments affecting the accuracy with which eye movements or hand movements are directed toward objects. Damage to the frontal cortex impairs the memory process employed in directing the eyes to a target. Several lines of evidence suggest that sex and handedness influence human spatial abilities. Thus, the sex hormones and cortical organization can influence spatial behavior. Tests of spatial abilities are useful in indicating both the site and the side of damage in humans.

References

Aguirre, G. K., and M. D'Esposito. Topographical disorientation: A synthesis and taxonomy. *Brain* 122:1613–1628, 1999.

Allison, R. S., L. J. Hurwitz, J. G. White, and T. J. Wilmot. A follow-up study of a patient with Balint's syndrome. *Neuropsychologia* 7:319–333, 1969.

Astur, R. S., M. L. Oriitz, and R. J. Sutherland. A characterization of performance by men and women in a virtual Morris water task: A large and reliable sex difference. *Behavioural Brain Research* 93:185–190, 1998.

Astur, R. S., L. B. Taylor, A. N. Mamelak, L. Philpott, and R. J. Sutherland. Humans with hippocampus damage display severe spatial memory impairments in a virtual Morris water task. *Behavioural Brain Research* 132:77–84, 2002.

Balint, R. Seelenlahmung des Schauens, optische Ataxie, raumlielie Storung der Aufmerksamkeit, Mschr. *Psychiatry and Neurology* 25:51–81, 1909.

Benton, A. L. *Right-Left Discrimination and Finger Localization.* New York: Hoeber-Harper, 1959.

Benton, A. L. Visuoperceptive, visuospatial, and visuoconstructive disorders. In K. M. Heilman and E. Valenstein, Eds. *Clinical Neuropsychology.* New York: Oxford University Press, 1979.

Benton, A. L., N. R. Varney, and K. deS. Hamsher. Visuospatial judgment: A clinical test. *Archives of Neurology* 35:364–367, 1978.

Best, P. J., A. M. White, and A. Minai. Spatial processing in the brain: The activity of hippocampal place cells. *Annual Review of Neuroscience* 24:459–486, 2001.

Brain, W. R. Visual disorientation with special reference to lesions of the right cerebral hemisphere. *Brain* 64:244–272, 1941.

Carmon, A., and H. P. Bechtoldt. Dominance of the right cerebral hemisphere for stereopsis. *Neuropsychologia* 7:29–39, 1969.

Clayton, N. S. Memory and the hippocampus in food-storing birds: A comparative approach. *Neuropharmacology* 37:441–452, 1998.

Corballis, M. C. Mental rotation: Anatomy of a paradigm. In M. Potegal, Ed. *Spatial Abilities: Development and Physiological Foundations.* New York: Academic Press, 1982.

Corkin, S. Tactually-guided maze-learning in man: Effects of unilateral cortical excisions and bilateral hippocampal lesions. *Neuropsychologia* 3:339–351, 1965.

Corkin, S. The role of different cerebral structures in somaesthetic perception. In E. C. Carterette and M. P. Friedman, Eds. *Handbook of Perception,* vol. 6. New York: Academic Press, 1978.

Darwin, C. On the origin of certain instincts. *Nature* 7:417–418, 1873.

de Renzi, E. *Disorders of Space Exploration and Cognition.* New York: Wiley, 1982.

Goldman-Rakic, P. S. Circuitry of primate prefrontal cortex and regulation of behavior by representational memory. In V. B. Mountcastle, F. Plum, and S. R. Geiger, Eds. *Handbook of Physiology,* vol. 5, *Higher Functions of the Brain.* Bethesda, MD: American Physiological Society, 1987.

Grusser, O. J. The multimodal structure of the extrapersonal space. In A. Hein and M. Jeannerod, Eds. *Spatially Oriented Behavior.* New York: Springer, 1987.

Haaxma, R., and H. G. J. M. Kuypers. Intrahemispheric cortical connections and visual guidance of hand and finger movements in the rhesus monkey. *Brain* 98:239–260, 1975.

Halpern, D. F. *Sex Differences in Cognitive Abilities.* Hillsdale, NJ: Lawrence Erlbaum, 1986.

Hannay, H. J., N. R. Varney, and A. L. Benton. Visual localization in patients with unilateral brain disease. *Journal of Neurology, Neurosurgery and Psychiatry* 39:307–313, 1976.

Harshman, R. A., E. Hampson, and S. A. Berenbaum. Individual differences in cognitive abilities and brain organization I: Sex and handedness differences in ability. *Canadian Journal of Psychology* 37:144–192, 1983.

Head, H. *Studies in Neurology.* London: Oxford University Press, 1920.

Hécaen, H., J. de Ajuriaguerra, and J. Massonet. Les troubles visuoconstructifs par lesions parieto-occipitales droites: Role des perturbations vestibulaires. *Encephale* 1:122–179, 1951.

Hécaen, H., C. Tzortzis, and M. C. Masure. Troubles de l'orientation spatiale dans une pereuve de recherce d'itineraire lors des lesions corticales unilaterales. *Perception* 1:325–330, 1972.

Hécaen, H., C. Tzortzis, and P. Rondot. Loss of topographical memory with learning deficits. *Cortex* 16:525–542, 1980.

Holmes, G. Disturbances of visual space perception. *British Medical Journal* 2:230–233, 1919.

Holmes, G., and G. Horax. Disturbances of spatial orientation and visual attention, with loss of stereoscopic vision. *Archives of Neurology and Psychiatry* 1:385–407, 1919.

Ingle, D., and K. S. Hoff. Neural mechanisms of short-term memory in frogs. *Society for Neuroscience Abstracts* 14:692, 1988.

Jackson, J. H. On the nature of duality of the brain. *Brain* 38:80–103, 1915.

Levine, D. N., J. Warach, and M. J. Farah. Two visual systems in mental imagery: Dissociation of "what" and "where" in imagery disorders due to bilateral posterior cerebral lesions. *Neurology* 35:1010–1015, 1985.

Maccoby, E. E., and C. N. Jacklin. *The Psychology of Sex Differences.* Stanford, CA: Stanford University Press, 1974.

Maguire, E. A., N. Burgess, and J. O'Keefe. Human spatial navigation: Cognitive maps, sexual dimorphism, and neural substrates. *Current Opinion in Neurobiology* 9:171–177, 1999.

McFie, J., and O. L. Zangwill. Visual-constructive disabilities associated with lesions of the left hemisphere. *Brain* 83:243–260, 1960.

McGee, M. G. Human spatial abilities: Psychometric studies and environmental, genetic, hormonal, and neurological influences. *Psychological Bulletin* 86:889–918, 1979.

Milner, A. D., and M. A. Goodale. *The Visual Brain in Action.* Oxford: Oxford University Press, 1995.

Milner, B. Visually-guided maze learning in man: Effects of bilateral hippocampal, bilateral frontal, and unilateral cerebral lesions. *Neuropsychologia* 3:317–338, 1965.

Milner, B. Interhemispheric differences in the localization of psychological processes in man. *British Medical Bulletin* 27:272–277, 1971.

Milner, B., S. Corkin, and H.-L. Teuber. Further analysis of the hippocampal amnesic syndrome: 14-year follow-up study of H. M. *Neuropsychologia* 6:215–234, 1968.

Morris, R. G. M., P. Garrud, J. Rawlings, and J. O'Keefe. Place navigation impaired in rats with hippocampal lesions. *Nature* 297:681–683, 1982.

Nakamura, R. K., S. J. Schein, and R. Desimone. Visual responses from cells in striate cortex of monkeys rendered chronically "blind" by lesions of nonvisual cortex. *Experimental Brain Research* 63:185–190, 1986.

Newcombe, N. Sex-related differences in spatial ability: Problems and gaps in current approaches. In M. Potegal, Ed. *Spatial Abilities: Development and Physiological Foundations.* New York: Academic Press, 1982.

O'Keefe, J., and J. Dostrovsky. The hippocampus as a spatial map: Preliminary evidence from unit activity in the freely-moving rat. *Brain Research* 34:171–175, 1971.

O'Keefe, J., and L. Nadel. *The Hippocampus As a Cognitive Map.* New York: Clarendon Press, 1978.

Oxbury, J. M., D. C. Campbell, and S. M. Oxbury. Unilateral spatial neglect and impairments of spatial analysis and visual perception. *Brain* 97:551–564, 1974.

Pallis, C. A. Impaired identification of faces and places with agnosia for colors. *Journal of Neurology, Neurosurgery and Psychiatry* 18:218–224, 1955.

Parkinson, J. K., E. A. Murray, and M. Mishkin. A selective mnemonic role for the hippocampus in monkeys: Memory for the location of objects. *Journal of Neuroscience* 8:4159–4167, 1988.

Passingham, R. E. Memory of monkeys (*Maccaca mulatta*) with lesions in prefrontal cortex. *Behavioral Neuroscience* 99:3–21, 1985.

Paterson, A., and O. L. Zangwill. Disorders of visual space perception associated with lesions of the right cerebral hemisphere. *Brain* 67:331–358, 1944.

Petrides, M., and S. K. Iversen. Restricted posterior parietal lesions in the rhesus monkey and performance on visuospatial tasks. *Brain Research* 161:63–77, 1979.

Petrides, M., and B. Milner. Deficits on subject-ordered tasks after frontal- and temporal-lobe lesions in man. *Neuropsychologia* 20:249–292, 1982.

Posner, M. I., and M. E. Raichle. *Images of Mind.* New York: Scientific American Library, 1994.

Rolls, E. T. Spatial view cells and the representation of place in the primate hippocampus. *Hippocampus* 9:467–480, 1999.

Ross, E. D. Sensory-specific and fractional disorders of recent memory in man I: Isolated loss of visual recent memory. *Archives of Neurology* 37:193–200, 1980.

Semmes, J. A non-tactual factor in astereognosis. *Neuropsychologia* 3:295–315, 1965.

Shankweiler, D. Performance of brain damaged patients on two tests of sound localization. *Journal of Comparative and Physiological Psychology* 54:375–381, 1951.

Sherry, D. F., and S. J. Duff. Behavioural and neural bases of orientation in food-storing birds. *Journal of Experimental Biology* 199:165–172, 1996.

Smith, M. L., and B. Milner. The role of the right hippocampus in the recall of spatial location. *Neuropsychologia* 19:781–793, 1981.

Takahashi, N., M. Kawamura, J. Shiota, N. Kasahata, and K. Hirayama. Pure topographic disorientation due to a right retrosplenial lesion. *Neurology* 49:464–469, 1997.

Taube, J. S. Head direction cells and the neurophysiological basis for a sense of direction. *Progress in Neurobiology* 55:225–256, 1998.

Teng, E., and L. R. Squire. Memory for places learned long ago is intact after hippocampal damage. *Science* 400:675–677, 1999.

Tyler, H. R. Abnormalities of perception and defective eye movements (Balint's syndrome). *Cortex* 4:15–171, 1968.

Whishaw, I. Q., D. J. Hines, and D. G. Wallace. Dead reckoning (path integration) requires the hippocampal formation: Evidence from spontaneous exploration and spatial learning tasks in light (allothetic) and dark (idiothetic) tests. *Behavioural Brain Research* 127, 49–70, 2001.

Worsley, C. L., M. Recce, H. J. Spiers, J. Marley, C. E. Polkey, and R. G. Morris. Path integration following temporal lobectomy in humans. *Neuropsychologia* 39:452–464, 2001.

Zangwill, O. L. *Cerebral Dominance and Its Relation to Psychological Function.* Edinburgh: Oliver & Boyd, 1960.

Zola-Morgan, S., L. Squire, and D. G. Amaral. Human amnesia and the medial temporal region: Enduring memory impairment following a bilateral lesion limited to field CA1 of the hippocampus. *Journal of Neuroscience* 6:2950–2967, 1986.

Attention, Mental Images, and Consciousness

After returning from a trip abroad at age 28, R. P. developed a terrible headache and flu-like aches and fever. The flu symptoms disappeared after a few days, but the headache remained for several weeks. During this time, she noticed that she was unusually clumsy and started having difficulty recognizing people's faces.

We first met R. P. 2 years later. Among a variety of visual-perceptual problems, she presented especially severe deficits in facial recognition, a mental neglect of the left side of space, and constructional apraxia.

- The face-recognition deficit was so severe that R. P. was unable to recognize her identical twin sister except by movement and voice.

- The mental neglect was particularly intriguing. Before her illness, R. P. had earned a master's degree in library science. She was also an excellent cook, and one of her joys in life was having friends over for supper. She now found it impossible to entertain in the same way, however, because she could not remember where items were located in the kitchen, especially items on her left side.

- R. P.'s apraxia was not severe, but she had become unable to assemble things such as a bookshelf unit that she had bought. In fact, R. P. noted that she could not even imagine how the shelf could be put together.

Imaging studies found abnormally low blood flow in the superior parietal regions in both hemispheres and throughout the right temporal lobe, but the causes of R. P.'s symptoms were never really understood. It seems likely that a viral infection caused her symptoms and the abnormal blood flow.

R. P. had one other persisting symptom: her social cognition was impaired. She had been duped on two occasions by con artists who tricked her into giving them money for bogus projects. She complained that she did not seem to be able to tell when people were not trustworthy.

Attention, images, and consciousness are properties of the nervous system that direct complex actions of body and brain. They are not epiphenomena—properties that emerge simply because the brain is complex. R. P. showed deficits in attention and visual guidance of movements, in imaging movements, in recognizing faces, and in identifying the intentions of others. These deficits are among the topics of this chapter. At the chapter's end, we address questions about the neural basis of consciousness and why we are conscious.

Defining Attention and Consciousness

Donald Hebb and others have argued that the central question in neuropsychology is the relation between the mind and the brain. The question is easy to ask, yet it is not so easy to grasp what it is that we need to explain. One needed explanation is how we select information on which to act. Another is how we select behaviors.

Animals such as simple worms have a limited sensory capacity and an equally limited repertoire of behaviors. Animals such as dogs have a much more sophisticated sensory capacity and a corresponding increase in behavioral options. Primates, including humans, have even further developed sensory capacity and behavioral complexity.

Thus, as sensory and motor capacities increase, so does the problem of selection both of information and of behavior. Furthermore, as the brain expands, memory increases, providing an internal variable in both stimulus interpretation and response selection. Finally, as the number of sensory channels increases, the need to correlate the different inputs to produce a single "reality" arises. We first encountered this problem in Chapter 10 when we examined the binding problem.

One way to consider these evolutionary changes is to posit that, as the brain expands to increase sensorimotor capacity, so does some other process (or processes) having a role in sensory and motor selection. One proposed process for selective awareness and response to stimuli is attention.

The concept of attention implies that somehow we focus a "mental spotlight" on certain sensory inputs, motor programs, memories, or internal representations. This spotlight might be unconscious, in that we are not aware of the process, or it might be conscious, such as when we scan our memories for someone's name. The development of language should increase the likelihood of conscious attention, but it is unlikely that all conscious processing is verbal. One can speculate, for example, that the "Eureka" insight of Archimedes entailed conscious processing that was more than just verbal.

The point is that, as sensorimotor capacities expand, so do the processes of attention and consciousness. In broad terms, consciousness is, at a primary level, synonymous with awareness and, at a secondary level, with awareness of awareness. The clear implication is that consciousness is not a dichotomous phenomenon; rather, a gradual evolutionary increase in consciousness is correlated with the ability to organize sensory and motor capacities. The most evolved organizer is language, which implies an increased capacity for the processes of attention.

You encountered problems of attention and conscious awareness earlier. Recall, for example, the concepts of blindsight and blind touch discussed in Chapters 13 and 14. Patients can describe the location of sensory information for which they have no conscious awareness. Similarly, amnesic patients can show evidence of procedural memory even when they have no conscious recollection of having even been in a room before, let alone having learned a task.

People, such as R. P., with right posterior parietotemporal lesions show hemispatial neglect: they behave as though the left side of the world were not present. That this is not an input problem was illustrated beautifully in the experiments showing that patients have a cognitive hemispatial neglect, too. Thus, when asked to imagine a familiar scene from a particular perspective, patients neglected the left side; but, when asked to imagine the same scene from a perspective 180° removed, they described the previously neglected regions and this time neglected the previously described regions.

Attention

The concept of attention has an uneven history in psychology. Periods when attentional processes were simply assumed to be present contrast with periods when the need for specific attentional systems was rejected. For example, the behaviorist view held that a full account of behavior is possible in strictly physiological terms, with no reference to cognitive concepts such as attention or even consciousness. The emergence of cognitive science led to a reevaluation of this perspective. Investigators in both cognitive science and neuroscience have returned to the position first espoused by William James in the late 1800s: "Everyone knows what attention is. It is the taking possession by the mind, in clear and vivid form, of one out of what seems several simultaneously possible objects or trains of thought."

Renewed interest in such concepts as attention has led to the establishment of distinct subcultures among students of attention. Perhaps the biggest division is between investigators interested in the automatic processes taking part in attention and those interested in the conscious selection of sensory information. There has been less interest in the question of motor attention, which could be defined as the process of selecting behaviors. In addition, some researchers are interested in imagination (or imagery) and the role that it plays in behavioral selection.

Automatic Versus Conscious Processing

One area of agreement in cognitive psychology is that certain behaviors can be performed with little, if any, focused attention, whereas others are highly sensitive to the allocation of attention. Automatic processes direct behavior that occurs without intention, involuntarily, without conscious awareness, and without producing interference with ongoing activities. Automatic processing may be an innate property of the way in which sensory information is processed or it can be produced by extended training. (For more details, see reviews by Logan and by Bargh and Ferguson.)

Operations that are not automatic have been referred to by various terms, including controlled, effortful, attentive, and conscious. Conscious operations differ fundamentally from automatic processing in that they require focused attention. One way to look at the difference is to consider the automatic processes as bottom-up processing and the conscious processes as top-down processing. A person stopping at a red light is an example of bottom-up processing, whereas a person actively searching for a street at which to turn is an example of top-down processing.

Remember from the discussion of memory in Chapter 18 that bottom-up processing is data driven; that is, it relies almost exclusively on the stimulus information being presented in the environment. In contrast, top-down processing is conceptually driven. It relies on the use of information already in memory, including whatever expectation might exist regarding the task at hand. Viewed in this way, automatic and conscious processing can reasonably be presumed to require at least some different cortical circuits. One hypothesis is that whatever unique cortical circuits are recruited in attentive processing must include processes of consciousness.

Another way to examine the difference between automatic and conscious processing is to try it yourself. Consider the following experiment. Anne Treisman and her colleagues presented subjects with boxed arrays of stimuli such as the four shown in Figure 22.1. The task in each case is to identify the target that is different from all the others. Try it now.

Did you find some targets easier to find than others? Treisman's subjects did as well. Response time differs dramatically, depending upon the nature of the stimulus. When the task requires the identification of a target with an *extra* line, as at the upper left in Figure 22.1, search time is independent of the number of detractors. Apparently, the target visually "pops out" of the display. But, when the task requires the subject to find a target distinguished by the *lack* of a feature present in the other items, as on the upper right, the time taken to find the target varies directly with the number of detractors. Evidently, we must subject the items in the display to a serial search.

The result of Treisman's experiment is not intuitive. After all, each case requires the same discrimination between the same two stimuli. Thus we can infer that:

- certain aspects of visual processing are automatic. We need not focus attention on any particular aspect of the visual field. Analysis requires only a specific visual feature, such as a vertical line (the popouts in Figure 22.1), to locate the target.

- other aspects of visual processing depend on focused attention to locate the conjunction—the combinations of features, such as circles and lines—that leads to the target. Conjunction search is a serial process, as if a mental spotlight were scanning from one location to another. In the lower panels of Figure 22.1, for example, the conjunction of shading and form identifies the target.

In principle, it should be possible to develop feature processing with practice. Treisman and her colleagues have studied this possibility intensively, but they conclude that, although practice can speed up feature processing, it remains dependent on specific

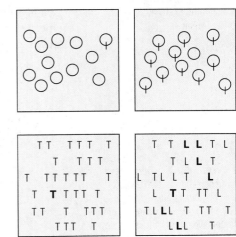

Figure 22.1 Visual processing tasks. (Left) Feature search. Here the ○ and the **T** "pop out" of the display automatically. (Right) Serial search. You must scan from symbol to symbol to locate the ○ and the **T** in each display. (Bottom) Conjunction. With focused attention, the combination of line weight and form identifies the target. (After Treisman and Gormican, 1986.)

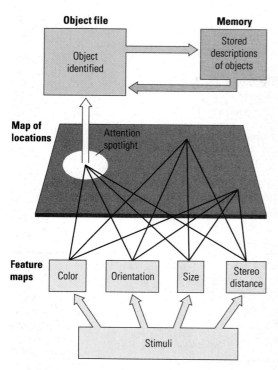

Object file → **Memory**

Object identified → Stored descriptions of objects

Map of locations

Attention spotlight

Feature maps

| Color | Orientation | Size | Stereo distance |

Stimuli

Figure 22.2 Treisman's model of feature search. Beginning at the bottom of the illustration, early vision encodes some simple and useful properties of a scene in a number of feature maps, which may preserve the spatial relations of the visual world but do not themselves make spatial information available to subsequent processing stages. Instead, focused attention selects and integrates the features present at particular locations. At later stages, the integrated information serves to create and update recognition "files" on perceptual objects. In turn, the file contents are compared with descriptions stored in a recognition network (memory). (After Treisman, 1986.)

automatic neural associations between features and on serial-processing pathways. Feature processing appears to be innate to the visual system.

Treisman has explained her results with a perceptual model of feature search, illustrated in Figure 22.2. A stimulus is registered in area V1 and is broken down into separate feature maps (see Chapter 13 for more details). This information is then serially processed in parallel pathways (for example, to area V3, V4, or V5). A characteristic of the later processing is that, at some point, different features of the object are integrated or conjoined. Because no single visual area specifically does this job, bits of the visual world must be processed serially, presumably by using some sort of reentry process (see Chapter 10).

Thus, the idea is that attention is directed to each location in turn and that features present in the same "fixation" of attention are combined to form a single object. Posner and Raichle suggest that, in a sense, the attentional process provides the "glue" that integrates features into a unitary object. When the features have been put together, the object can be perceived and held in memory as a unit.

A clear prediction from Treisman's theory is that neurons in the visual areas outside area V1 and probably outside area V2 should respond differentially, depending on whether attention is focused on the corresponding receptive field. In the next section, we consider evidence that these neurons do indeed respond differentially.

A question that arises from the results of the feature-detector research is, What constitutes a feature? Treisman presumes that features are the properties that cells in the visual system are coded to detect. But features may perhaps be biologically significant stimuli, as illustrated in an experiment by Eastwood and colleagues. You can try this one out, too. The researchers presented subjects with displays of schematic faces similar to those shown in Figure 22.3. The task was to identify the odd face, which could be a happy face in a sea of sad ones or visa versa. Before you try to do so, turn your book upside down.

Subjects were faster at detecting sad faces, whether they were upside down or right side up. Furthermore, when Eastwood and colleagues redid the experiment with abstract targets that signified either a happy or a sad state, subjects still found the sad-related feature faster.

Figure 22.3 Feature-search demonstration. Visual displays in which subjects must detect happy or sad faces. Subjects detect sad faces faster, even if presented upside down. (After Eastwood et al., 2001.)

Given that the features should be equally conspicuous in the happy and sad conditions, it follows that there is something biologically more important to detecting sad (negative) than happy (positive) stimuli. As mentioned in Chapter 20, certain cells in the amygdala are especially tuned to fear-related stimuli, and so it appears that negative stimuli (potentially dangerous or threatening features as well as sad ones) are attended to very efficiently and demand attention more than do targets for more-positive features. From an evolutionary perspective, favoring the nervous system that attends to stimuli that can make a difference to an animal's survival makes sense. The evolution of biological targets is likely more important to survival than are the simpler targets detected by cells in area V1.

Neurophysiological Evidence of Attention

Any experiment purporting to demonstrate that the focus of attention determines the responses of neurons must meet one important criterion. The *same stimulus* must activate a neuron at one time and not at another. This condition rules out the possibility that the changes in neural activity are somehow related to the actual features of the stimulus target. Consider the following experiment.

Moran and Desimone trained a monkey to hold a bar while it gazed at a fixation point on a screen. A sample stimulus (for instance, a vertical blue bar) appeared briefly at one location in the receptive field, followed about 500 ms later by two stimuli: one at the same location and another in a separate one, as illustrated in Figure 22.4. The key point is that both targets were in the cell's receptive field, but only one target was in the correct location. When the test stimulus was identical with the sample and in the same location, the animal was rewarded if it released the bar immediately. In this way, the same visual stimulus could be presented to different regions of the neurons' receptive fields, but the importance of the information varied with its location.

Figure 22.4 A monkey performing an attentional task demonstrating that, even though a given neuron normally responds to a stimulus in many locations, the neuron can adapt to attend selectively to information in a specific region of its receptive field. (After Moran and Desimone, 1985.)

Procedure

Monkeys were trained to release a bar when a certain stimulus was presented in a certain location. The monkeys learned to ignore stimuli in all other locations.

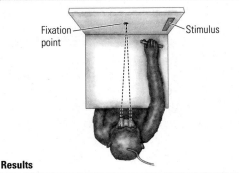

Fixation point

Stimulus

Results

In the performance of this task, researchers recorded the firing of neurons in visual area V4, which are sensitive to color and form. Stimuli were presented in either rewarded or unrewarded locations.

Pretraining recordings:

Rewarded location — Strong response

Unrewarded location — Strong response

Before training, neurons responded to stimuli in all locations.

Posttraining recordings:

Rewarded location — Strong response

Unrewarded location — Baseline response

After training, neurons responded only when the visual stimuli were in the rewarded location.

Conclusion

Neurons can respond selectively to information in their receptive field.

As the animals performed the task, the researchers recorded the firing of cells in area V4. Cells in area V4 are color and form sensitive; so different neurons responded to different conjunctions of features. Thus, a given cell might respond to one stimulus (for example, a horizontal green bar) and not to another (for example, a vertical red bar). These stimuli were presented either in the correct location or in an incorrect location for predicting reward, as illustrated in Figure 22.4.

The critical result is the behavior of the neuron in response to the effective target stimulus. When the effective stimulus was presented in the correct location, the cell was highly active. When the *same stimulus* was presented in an incorrect location, however, the cell was not responsive. It appears that, when attention is focused on a place in the visual world, the cell responds only to stimuli appropriate to that place.

Ineffective stimuli remained so regardless of where they were in the visual field. Moran and Desimone considered the possibility that visual areas activated earlier (V1) or later (TE) in visual processing might also show attentional effects. Cells in area V1 did not show attentional effects, whereas cells in area TE did. Presumably the features detected in area V1 were too simple to direct attention, whereas those in area TE could.

Moran and Desimone's results are also theoretically important to the general matter of space. The cells showing constraints in spatial attention were in areas V4 and TE, both parts of the object-recognition stream. Thus, neurons in this system are coding spatial location. This spatial coding in the ventral stream is consistent with Milner and Goodale's idea that both the dorsal and the ventral streams of visual processing play a role in perceiving space, but their roles are different (Chapter 13).

Note that Moran and Desimone's monkey did not have to make a movement in space. If it did, we would predict that cells in the posterior parietal cortex would be sensitive to attentional demands. In fact, Mountcastle and his colleagues reported just such results. They found that posterior parietal cells are active when animals reach to obtain an object, such as food, but are not active when the same movements are made for other reasons. Notice that these cells are responding not to the features of the stimuli but rather to the movements needed to get to them. Thus, there appear to be two types of visual attention, one related to the selection of stimuli and the other to the selection and direction of movements.

Attention can affect neurons in other ways as well. Kahneman noted that perceptual systems do not always work at peak efficiency. One explanation for their failure to do so is that we can process only so much information at once, and, if we are overloaded, there is a "bottleneck" in processing. Kahneman proposed that the capacity to perform mental activity is limited and that this limited capacity must be allocated among concurrent activities.

Thus, for Kahneman, one aspect of attention is the amount of effort that is directed toward a particular task. If a task is routine (such as driving on a road without much traffic), little attentional focus is used, and the driver can carry on a conversation. When the driver is turning across traffic at a busy intersection, however, attention must be focused on the task, and the conversation is briefly interrupted. You may have noticed that, when you attempt a difficult maneuver with a car, such as parking in a tight spot, you turn down your car radio. Some process must be active to shift and focus attention in response to changes in task demands.

Spitzer, working with Moran and Desimone, wondered if cells in area V4 might vary their firing characteristics in accord with the amount of effort needed to solve a particular visual problem. They trained monkeys much as was done in the Moran and Desimone experiment, except that they varied the difficulty of the task. They took advantage of the fact that cells respond to a range of stimuli (Figure 22.5A). Thus, a given cell responds optimally to a given orientation and color. This tuning is not precise, however, and the cell will respond to orientations and colors that approximate the preferred range.

Spitzer and colleagues reasoned that it should be easy for a cell to discriminate between a stimulus within its preferred orientation or color and a stimulus outside this orientation or color. For example, an easy discrimination would be one in which the test stimulus is orthogonal (oriented at 90°) to the sample (Figure 22.5B). In contrast, a difficult discrimination would be one in which both stimuli are within the range of a cell's preferred orientations—say, if the difference in orientation were only 22.5°, which is within the acceptable range for most cells (Figure 22.5C). They trained animals to make this discrimination, and the animals' performance confirmed that the finer discrimination was more difficult: 93% of their responses were correct under the easy conditions compared with 73% under the difficult conditions.

The change in response characteristics of the area V4 cells is intriguing. First, under the difficult condition, the cells increased their firing rate by an average of about 20%. Second, the tuning characteristics of the cells changed. Thus, whereas the cells tolerated an orientation difference of about 81° under the easy condition, the same cells became more selective about the stimuli to which they would respond under the difficult condition, the orientation range having been reduced to 53°. The more difficult task appears to have required increased attention to the differences between the stimuli, as manifested in a change in the stimulus selectivity of neurons in area V4. Stated differently, both the behavioral and the electrophysiological results indicate that increasing the amount of effort needed to perform a perceptual task can affect how information is processed in the visual system.

It is not known *how* this attentional effect can alter the cell's activity. One possibility is that a signal from the thalamus plays some role. The results of studies using monkeys have led to the idea that the critical region may be the pulvinar, which is a thalamic nucleus that projects to secondary visual areas in the tectopulvinar system (see Figure 8.8). Thus, cells in the pulvinar also respond to visual stimuli in a way that implies some type of selection process.

Petersen and his colleagues found that neurons in the pulvinar respond more vigorously to stimuli that are targets of behavior than they do to the same stimuli when they are not targets of behavior. That is, when a visual stimulus is present but has no meaning for the animal, the cells have a low firing rate. When the same stimulus now signifies a reward, the cells become more active.

Because the pulvinar complex projects to the posterior parietal cortex, temporal cortex, and prefrontal cortex, it may play some role in directing Treisman's "spotlight" to different parts of space. Petersen and his colleagues tested this predication by finding that disrupting the pulvinar does disrupt spatial attention. The pulvinar receives visual input from the colliculus, which is known to play a role in orienting to visual information; so it may be a collicular-pulvinar spotlight that is at work.

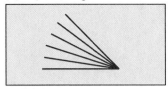

(A) Preferred range

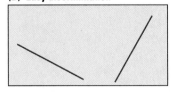

(B) Easy discrimination

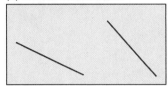

(C) Difficult discrimination

Figure 22.5 Effort and attention. (A) Range of line orientations to which a given cell will respond. (B) Easy condition. The left line is within the orientation preference of the cell, but the right line is outside this range. (C) Difficult condition. Both line orientations fall within the cell's preferred range of response. (Spitzer et al., 1988.)

We are still left with the problem of how the collicular-pulvinar spotlight is turned on. At present, we must be satisfied with the observation that knowledge of the task demands can somehow alter the activity of neurons in the visual system—the essence of a top-down process.

Functional Imaging and Attention

One place to start in our search for neural correlates of attention in normal humans is to look at attentional processes in the visual system that parallel those already studied in monkeys. Corbetta and colleagues designed the experiment illustrated in Figure 22.6A. A row of boxes streamed across a screen viewed by subjects who fixated on another box located just above the row. The task required subjects to maintain fixation on the upper box and to do one of two things: (1) to shift attention as a light moved from box to box across the row or (2) to maintain fixation on the central box and to ignore the movement of the light. Thus, as in the Moran and Desimone study of monkeys, the stimuli presented were identical, but the attentional requirements were different.

The results were clear. Relative to the fixed-attention task, attending to the moving light increased activation in the posterior parietal cortex (Figure 22.6B). Furthermore, if the moving light was presented to the left visual field, only the right parietal cortex was activated; whereas, if the moving light was presented to the right visual field, both the left and the right parietal cortexes were activated. In other words, the right parietal cortex was active when the stimulus was either in the left or in the right visual field, but the left parietal cortex was active only when the stimulus was in the contralateral (right) visual field.

In addition, there were two distinct foci of activation in the right parietal lobe, one corresponding to the left visual field and one to the right. These findings may explain why patients with right posterior parietotemporal lesions show more-pronounced contralateral neglect than do patients with left-hemisphere lesions. In the absence of the left parietal cortex, there is still a rep-

Figure 22.6 Shifting attention compared with fixed attention. (A) Experimental setups for the shifting and fixed conditions. (B) A summary of PET scans for the shifting-attention task reveals that activation of the parietal cortex increases compared with the fixed-attention task and is more extensive in the right parietal lobe. (After Corbetta et al., 1993.)

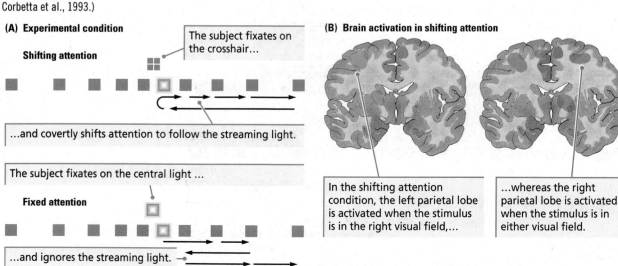

(A) Experimental condition

Shifting attention

The subject fixates on the crosshair...

...and covertly shifts attention to follow the streaming light.

The subject fixates on the central light ...

Fixed attention

...and ignores the streaming light.

(B) Brain activation in shifting attention

In the shifting attention condition, the left parietal lobe is activated when the stimulus is in the right visual field,...

...whereas the right parietal lobe is activated when the stimulus is in either visual field.

resentation of the right visual field, which is in the right parietal cortex. In the absence of the right parietal cortex, there is no representation of the left visual field in the parietal cortex, and the region is neglected, as we saw in R. L.'s case at the beginning of this chapter.

An intriguing aspect of this study is that there was no activation in area V4, as might be predicted from the results of electrophysiological studies of monkeys. An explanation is that the task did not require an integration of different stimulus properties; rather, it simply required a record of where something was. This possibility was confirmed in a parallel study by the same researchers.

In this case, Corbetta and colleagues presented the subjects with a screen with a small white spot in the center (Figure 22.7). Each target stimulus, frame 1, for example, was a spatially random distribution of 30 elements, all of identical shape and color and moving horizontally as a coherent sheet to the left or right. The shape, color, or speed of movement or all three might be changed in the second stimulus (frame 2). A stimulus was presented for 400 ms, followed by a second stimulus 200 ms later.

A subject had two different tasks. In the "selective attention" task, the subject was to report if the two sets of stimuli differed for a specific stimulus feature (for example, color). In the "divided attention" task, the subject was to indicate if there had been a change in *any* feature. The fundamental difference between the two tasks is that the selective task requires the adoption of a specific mental set for a specific feature, whereas the divided task does not.

The researchers posited that the selective task would require more-focused attention and the divided task would require more memory. Therefore, they predicted a different pattern of cortical activation in the two tasks.

PET measurements showed that the selective-attention task activated specific visual regions, the region varying with the feature detected. Thus, attention to color activated a region probably corresponding to area V4, whereas attention to shape activated regions corresponding to areas V3 and TE. The selective task also activated the insula, the posterior thalamus (probably pulvinar), the superior colliculus, and the orbital frontal cortex.

In contrast, the divided-attention task activated a mutually exclusive set of areas. Thus, although there was no activation of visual areas beyond the activation on passive presentation of the stimuli, there was activation of the anterior cingulate and dorsolateral prefrontal cortex. The important point is that the stimuli were identical in the two conditions, even though the tasks were different. The selective-attention task led to increased activation of visual areas that presumably were recruited to solve the task.

Taken together, the results of the Corbetta studies show that different cortical areas are activated in different attentional tasks:

• The parietal cortex is activated for attention to location; the occipital-temporal cortex is activated for attention to features such as color and form.

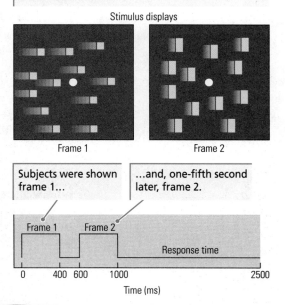

Selective-attention task: Were objects moving at different speeds in the two frames?

Divided-attention task: Was any feature of the two frames different?

Stimulus displays

Frame 1   Frame 2

Subjects were shown frame 1...   ...and, one-fifth second later, frame 2.

Frame 1   Frame 2

Response time

0   400 600   1000   2500

Time (ms)

Figure 22.7 Selective-attention compared with divided-attention tasks. Frames 1 and 2 model stimulus displays in the study by Corbetta and colleagues. The selective-attention task is to determine if there is a change from frame 1 to frame 2 in a particular feature (color, shape, speed of movement). In the divided-attention task, subjects report a change in any of the features. The bottom panel shows the timing of the frame presentations. (After Corbetta et al., 1991.)

- The anterior cingulate and prefrontal areas show activation during both visual tasks. Thus attention appears to generally require the activation of anterior cingulate and some prefrontal areas in addition to the activation of specific sensory areas related to a particular sensory modality, such as vision or touch.

Do these activations outside the visual areas indicate the existence of some general attentional system or are they specific to visual attention? And what about other sensory systems? One way to answer these questions is to examine attentional processes in other sensory systems. For example, the somatosensory system also must select stimuli for processing; so we can reasonably ask whether it has an attentional organization that parallels the visual system.

Burton and his colleagues thus conducted a PET study in which subjects had to direct their attention either to the roughness or the length of tactile stimuli. Note that the same stimulus was used, but the feature that was attended to varied. In control conditions, the subjects were stimulated but did not attend to any particular feature. As one would predict, tactile stimulation activated areas S1 and S2, but in addition, during the attentional task, there was activation in the posterior parietal cortex, likely in Brodmann's area 7. This activation did not overlap foci seen in studies of visual attention. Thus, distinct regions in the posterior parietal cortex appear to have roles in attention to different types of sensory inputs.

Networks of Attention

Let us recap what we have learned so that we can put our observations together. Our goal is to build a framework for a unifying theory of an attentional network in the brain.

- The electrophysiological evidence from monkeys shows four different attentional mechanisms: (1) a mechanism in the parietal cortex enhances spatial attention, (2) one in the visual and posterior temporal cortex selects object features, (3) one in the inferior temporal region selects objects themselves, and (4) one in the frontal eye fields selects movements.

- PET studies show parallel results in human subjects.

- The results of many studies show that regions of the frontal lobe also are activated during response selection. In particular, there is activation of the anterior cingulate cortex in divided-attention tasks (see the preceding section), as well as in tasks requiring response selection (see Chapter 16) or verb generation (see Chapter 19).

- There is activation of the premotor and prefrontal regions in specific tasks. Recall that Corbetta's divided-attention task activated the dorsolateral prefrontal cortex.

- In PET studies performed during verb-generation tasks (see Chapter 19), investigators found that verb generation activates the inferior frontal cortex.

Posner and Raichle suggest a model featuring two attentional spotlights. The first highlights a place in the world to analyze, and the second selects specific features for analysis. Posner proposes that, when we search for objects in the world, our focus of attention shifts from one location to another. To do so, attention must disengage from the current object of interest, move to a new object, and engage it. In an environment that is visually cluttered, another system that inhibits or filters out irrelevant information may be required.

The posterior parietal system may function to disengage, move, or engage attention. Indeed, damage to the posterior parietal cortex impairs performance on any task that requires this ability (see Chapter 14). In contrast, the focusing of attention on features of the object engaged may be a function of the posterior temporal regions. Damage to these regions produces agnosias, which must indicate, in part, a deficit in attending to specific features of stimuli.

Posner and Petersen proposed a second type of attentional system in addition to the posterior spotlights. This type is based in the frontal lobe and is closely related to the short-term-memory functions of the frontal lobe. Posner and Petersen cite four lines of evidence for an anterior attentional system:

1. Various frontal-lobe sites, especially the anterior cingulate, are active in a variety of tasks, both those entailing perceptual demands and those entailing response selection. Consider the divided-attention task described earlier. A subject must detect a feature and then respond. This task requires a working memory of what the features are and a recognition that one of the features has been detected. Posner and Raichle emphasize the importance of feature detection in response selection. Frontal-lobe patients are notorious for doing one thing and saying another, as though they do not detect the incongruity.

2. The involvement of frontal-lobe structures is proportional to the attentional effort. Thus, as the number of targets in a target-monitoring task increases, the involvement of frontal-lobe regions increases.

3. The frontal-lobe involvement in response selection is inversely related to practice. For example, in Chapter 19, we considered a verb-generation task in which subjects had to generate an action word in response to a noun (for instance, "cake-eat"). If subjects had practiced on specific nouns before the test, the insular cortex was active but the frontal areas were not.

4. Evidence from studies in both human patients and laboratory animals confirm that the frontal lobe has an important role in working (temporal) memory for both sensory events and movements.

Posner and Petersen call their frontal-lobe attentional system an "executive attentional system" and make the bold proposal that the contents of consciousness at any moment consist of the information being operated on by this executive system. In their view, the frontal lobe has charge of programming mental operations. Thus, it must play a major role in the activation of the selective-attention systems of the posterior cortex.

The direct evidence in favor of the Posner and Petersen model is not overwhelming, but their proposal does provide an interesting way to think about the brain systems engaged in consciousness. One feature of cortical evolution is that, as each new sensory channel was added, there was a corresponding development of the frontal lobe. It may very well be that this increase is necessary for the brain to operate on the sensory world and make sense of it. In the absence of frontal-lobe structures or in the event of dysfunction (such as schizophrenia), behavior would become muddled because conscious awareness of what the overwhelming sensory inputs mean and how they relate one to another would be lacking.

Mechanisms of Attention

One problem with the Posner and Petersen model is that it does not specify how the executive attentional system might influence neuronal activity in sensory areas. That is, how does the spotlight choose important events from among all the ongoing sensory information? Although several mechanisms are possible, one of them that is generating increasing interest is that the attentional system induces synchrony across a population of neurons that assess some sensory signal.

Figure 22.8 illustrates how a change in synchrony across a population of neurons can be affected by shifting the temporal positions of action potentials slightly so that two inputs to a given neuron arrive together. When this happens, the excitatory postsynaptic potentials (EPSPs) are summed and thus more likely to initiate an action potential in the postsynaptic neuron.

Crick and Koch proposed that the neural basis of attention is the change in synchrony of neural activity in cells that are within the focus of attention. Neiber and his colleagues proposed that this synchrony can be induced by sending simultaneous action potentials to all neurons in a given population. Each neuron that receives the simultaneous input is nudged toward a threshold to fire, which would enhance the synchrony of firing of all neurons receiving the synchronous input. Although what the optimal signal for inducing synchrony might be is not entirely clear, many researchers believe it to be a signal of about 40 Hz. We will return to the idea of synchrony in cognitive processing in a discussion of consciousness and the binding problem at the end of this chapter.

Unattended condition

| Asynchronous outputs from neurons 1 and 2 arrive on neuron 3,... | ...resulting in small EPSPs that do not lead to action potentials. |

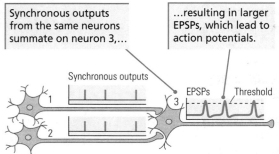

Attended condition

| Synchronous outputs from the same neurons summate on neuron 3,... | ...resulting in larger EPSPs, which lead to action potentials. |

Figure 22.8 How synchrony may modify the representation of attended stimuli. Neibur and colleagues suggest that, in the unattended condition, outputs arrive asynchronously on neuron 3 and are unlikely to lead to action potentials. In the attended condition, neural outputs that are in synchrony and thus summate on neuron 3 are more likely to lead to action potentials. (After Neibur et al., 2002)

Inattention

Each year more than 40,000 people are killed and more than 3 million are injured in automobile accidents in the United States. Most traffic accidents are due to human error, with inattention being one of the biggest villains. It is commonplace to hear of accidents in which one driver seemed not to see another and made a left-hand turn directly into the path of the oncoming vehicle.

On the surface, such errors seem incomprehensible. Understanding failures of attention is obviously important and is complementary to the study of how attention facilitates perception. Most studies of inattention are based either on demonstrations of inattention in cognitive-science laboratories or on observations of sensory neglect in patients. We consider each separately.

The Absence of Visual Attention

Three of the most popular tasks for demonstrating what Chun and Marois refer to as the "dark side of attention" are inattentional blindness, change blindness, and attentional blink.

Inattentional blindness occurs when a subject fails to notice an event that occurs during the performance of another task. A simple example is a failure to notice a dot flashed on a computer screen while performing a visual task. Perhaps the most stunning example of inattentional blindness was shown in an experiment by Simons and Chabris. Subjects were shown a film clip in which people were passing a basketball back and forth. The task was to count the number of passes. After about 45 seconds, a person wearing a gorilla suit walked across the display and exited the other side 5 seconds later. Remarkably, on average, more than 70% of the subjects did not see the gorilla. (Shortened versions of the displays can be downloaded from www.wjh.harvard.edu/~viscog/lab/demos.html.)

Subjects are often shocked when shown the clip again and asked to look for the gorilla, sometimes even exclaiming, "I missed *that?*" Importantly, when subjects have been alerted to expect unusual events, they readily detect them. In many ways, the failure to see the gorilla is like the failure to see an oncoming car. If a person is focussed on something else, such as reading a street sign, fiddling with the radio, or talking on a cell phone, the perception of other visual events that would normally be obvious is suppressed.

Change blindness refers to a failure to detect changes in the presence, identity, or location of objects in scenes. Like inattention blindness, change blindness is most likely to occur when people do not expect changes. Simons conducted an experiment in which about 50% of real-world observers failed to note a change in the identity of a person with whom they were conversing when the change consisted of a brief occlusion when a worker carried a door between the conversing people.

This type of inattention seems as preposterous as that in the gorilla experiment, but similar results can be shown in laboratory experiments, too. For example, subjects may take seconds to notice that an item is appearing and disappearing from a scene on a video screen. Again, when subjects have been told to expect change, they notice it more quickly.

Finally, *attentional blink* refers to a phenomenon in which subjects fail to detect a second visual target if it is presented within 500 ms of the first one. Attention to the first target prevents awareness of the second one, even if it is extremely conspicuous. Subjects have no difficulty in detecting the second target if they are told to ignore the first one. Presumably the visual system is taxed to the limit by requiring subjects to process so much information in such a short time.

These three paradigms of inattention are similar in that each shows a failure to attend to stimuli that are quite detectable. The visual system must be filtering the information out, but when? That is, does the information get filtered out during an early stage of processing or is it kept at an unconscious level?

The latter appears to be correct. Clever imaging experiments have shown, for example, that, in change-blindness experiments, the changing stimulus activates ventral-stream regions; in attentional-blink experiments, there is ERP evidence that the second stimulus was processed. But why do the unattended stimuli remain outside of conscious awareness? One reason would be that the executive attentional system, in conjunction with the posterior parietal engagement system, functions to selectively activate areas in the ventral stream.

Note that this reason implies not that the conscious perception takes place in the frontal-parietal network but that the activity in the network acts to filter information. A prediction from this conclusion is that people with damage to this network should have deficits in conscious perception, an example of which is sensory neglect.

Sensory Neglect

We first encountered the problem of neglect in a discussion of the effects of parietal-cortex lesions in Chapter 14, and it turned up again in R. P.'s case. Patients with lesions at the junction of the parietotemporal cortex (see Figure 14.6) behave as if the left side of the surrounding space had ceased to exist. As noted earlier, the results of imaging studies have shown that the right parietal region is engaged when attended stimuli are in the right or left visual fields, whereas the left parietal region is engaged only for stimuli in the right visual field. When the right parietal region is damaged, there is no backup system for the left side of space, and it is not brought into conscious awareness. Recall, too, that, when patients are presented with two stimuli simultaneously, they show extinction and ignore the stimulus on the left side (see Figure 14.5).

Rossetti and his colleagues wondered whether it is possible to modify the attentional system to attend to left-side information. In the 1960s, Richard Held and others performed experiments by fitting prisms to the eyes of laboratory animals and humans. Whatever the subject saw was displaced to one side or another. Such manipulations were initially disrupting, but, after the prisms had been worn for a few hours, the distortions diminished and subjects performed acts, such as reaching for objects, normally.

Rossetti placed prisms that induced a 10° shift of the visual field to the right on patients with contralateral neglect. Unlike the Held experiments, however, the subjects wore the prisms only for about 5 minutes each day. In the course of the prism adaptation, the subjects made 50 pointing movements to stimuli presented 10° to the left or right of the midline.

The results were stunning. The neglect patients showed an immediate reduction in the field defect, as illustrated in Figure 22.9. This improvement was surprisingly long lived, lasting for at least 2 hours after prism removal, and in F. D.'s case performance was even better after 2 hours.

There are two likely explanations for the prism effect. One explanation is that the activity in either the normal left or the remaining right parietal regions was recruited to deal with the distorted visual inputs. The other explanation is that a cerebellar or frontal region was recruited. Recall from Chapter 9 that cerebellar lesions impair the adaptation to prisms; so the activity in the cerebellum is likely important for motor aspects of the adaptation. The frontal lobe may have a complementary role that is related to attention more than to direct motor control.

Bossom showed that frontal, but not parietal or temporal, lesions in monkeys disrupted prism adaptation. The frontal lobe's role in prism adaptation in the Rosetti study may have been through the executive attentional system, which became activated as the subjects adapted to the sensory distortion. The role of the frontal lobe need not be strictly attentional, however. As noted in Chapter 16, the frontal lobe plays a central role in controlling movements

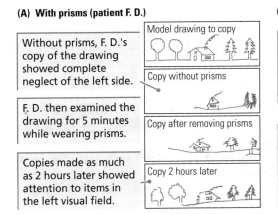

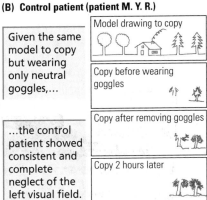

Figure 22.9 The prism effect. Two patients with contralateral neglect were asked to copy the same drawing. Both displayed complete neglect of the left side. Patient F. D. then wore prisms for 5 minutes. Control patient M. Y. R. wore neutral goggles. In both the immediate postprism test and 2 hours later, F. D.'s drawings (A) show attention to items in the left visual field, whereas M. Y. R.'s drawings (B) show no change. (After Rossetti et al., 1998.)

through corollary discharge, which is the signal from the motor system to the sensory system signaling what movement has been produced.

The role of the frontal lobe in directing attention leads us to wonder whether frontal-lobe lesions would also produce a neglect syndrome. Although not as common as neglect in parietal patients, neglect in both humans and laboratory animals with frontal injuries—especially injuries in area 6, the premotor cortex—has been reported on numerous occasions. The neglect in frontal-lobe patients is quite unlike that seen in parietal patients, however, because it tends to be directed only to the region of the perception of grasping space, leaving the perception of distant space intact.

Berti and Frassinetti describe a patient who, after a right frontal stroke, exhibited a selective neglect of peripersonal space. The neglect was apparent in a line-bisection task in which the patient used a light pen to bisect near or distant lines: bisecting the near lines showed neglect, but bisecting the distant lines did not. Curiously, when the patient acted on far lines by using a stick to touch the lines, the impairment appeared in distant space. The use of the stick apparently extended personal space so as to include all the space between the body and the stimulus. Evidently, the frontal attentional system can influence the way in which space is perceived.

Mental Images

When freestyle ski jumpers stand at the starting position, they spend some time going through contortions, moving their feet and their arms. They seem to be rehearsing the upcoming jump. Divers, in contrast, stand very still and then jump. Because they are going to make similar movements and their style is evaluated from the time they arrive on the diving board, they presumably must rehearse without making movements.

What is going on in the brains of these athletes? (See the Snapshot in Chapter 9 for mental images of real versus imagined movements.) They describe their activities as preparing, focusing, and rehearsing. Are they examining the layout of the jump or dive visually? Are they practicing the movements? Are they comparing the movements that they are going to make with the conditions of the moment? An early theory of what takes place during this preparation is that people, in their heads, adjust sensory and motor events so that the right outcome will occur. Although people may report that making this adjustment is exactly what they are doing, psychologists invariably argue that there is no little person in their heads to do such adjusting.

To escape the problem of the "little person in the head," various proposals have been advanced and abandoned in the past 200 years. The theory of afference suggested that sensations, presumably arising from the environment and the act of moving, guide behavior. The source of this theory was the idea that the brain is a passive recipient of impulses and is not capable of generating spontaneous activity. The theory of efference, which replaced the afference theory, suggested that the sensations of movement arise from the perception of the nervous system's activity in generating a movement.

The problem with both theories is the difficulty that they had in explaining how errors of movement are corrected. The problem can be seen more clearly in the strength of the theory that replaced them, the theory of reafference, which was referred to earlier as corollary discharge. According to this theory, when a movement is initiated, it leaves a trace or record of what the intended movement should be. As the movement is performed, it generates a second record that can be compared with the first. If the movement is not performed correctly, the error can be detected by comparing the two records and then making an adjustment on the next attempt.

The theory of reafference was generated separately by Roger Sperry and Eric von Holst. Sperry rotated the eyes of frogs so that the perceived location of an object was in a direction opposite that of its true location. The rotation caused the frogs to move in a direction opposite that of the real location of the object. Von Holst asked how an animal could disentangle its own movement from the movements of objects around it; that is, how does one distinguish self-movement from object movement? Both Sperry's experiments and von Holst's questions led to the conclusion that, to move successfully, an animal must generate a record of its movement and use this record as a reference to locate or plot the movements of other objects.

The idea that an animal generates a record of its movements, separate from the activity that generates the movement or the sensory information generated by the movement, suggests a central mental process or representation that contains schemas of movements. The function of sensations produced by movements is to update and correct the central representation, much as in the prism adaptation studies described earlier. People can correct for massive distortions produced by prisms, including left–right reversals and dorsal–ventral reversals. The important point is that, even though sensory information is grossly misleading, the system that represents and instructs movements is very good at compensating for the sensory distortions.

There have been a number of attempts to characterize the properties of central representations or images. That is, what do they look like? Experiments designed to answer this question examine whether the formation and topography of representations, as well as changes in them, match similar features of the real world. For example, a person asked to take one die of a pair of dice and rotate it so that the numbers that are visible match those of its mate will manipulate it several times until the two are matched. The manipulation consists of a number of movements and takes a certain amount of time.

When asked to perform the same task mentally, the person appears to require the same number of mental movements and to take about the same amount of time. Similarly, if people are asked to imagine walking a certain distance, they take about the same amount of time and make the same number of steps as they would to walk the same distance in reality. Such experiments suggest that mental images have very much the same features as real movements.

A criticism of equating the real dimensions of movements with those of representations on the basis of the these experiments is that subjects have some knowledge of the tasks and so can generate appropriate mental parallels. This criticism does not seem to be entirely valid, because, when subjects are given tasks that contain answers unknown to them in advance, similar results are obtained. For example, when people reach for an object that is close by or for one that is farther away, they take the same length of time. When they write their names in small script and in large script, the times are again equivalent. A priori, most subjects do not know that the times are equal and, if asked, will say that the times required for the tasks are different. Nevertheless, when people are asked to imagine reaching different distances or writing their names in letters of different sizes, the times that they report for the tasks are similar to the times actually required to perform those tasks. This result strengthens the idea that such features as the time and topography of movement images parallel those of actual movements.

The Neural Basis of Images

Where are mental images located? There are three possibilities:

1. The very same structures that produce movements could produce images.
2. Only a part of the structures that produce movements could produce images.
3. Movements and images are produced by completely independent areas of the brain.

Surprisingly, whereas it once might have been thought that the third possibility was most likely, at present most of the debate concerning these three possibilities considers only the first two serious options.

Roland performed one of the first experiments in which imagined movements and real movements were compared while regional cerebral blood flow (rCBF) was monitored (see Figure 9.3). When subjects imagined a series of finger movements, the premotor cortex was active. When they performed the movements, both the premotor cortex and the motor cortex were active.

The results of this experiment demonstrated that imagined and real movements are represented in the premotor cortex. They also favor the second possibility: that only a part of an area engaged in making a movement is engaged in forming images of that movement. Similar results favoring this position are obtained from case studies of patients with visual system lesions, including one study of a patient who could recognize visual patterns but could not form visual images of them. Other favorable results, as described by Behrmann and coworkers, are of patients who have severe trouble identifying real objects but have preserved visual imagery. These case studies suggest that earlier cortical visual levels (for example, areas V1 through V5) are engaged in perception, whereas only later visual levels (for example, area TE) form images.

Roland and Gulyas presented further evidence that the higher-level cortexes take part in both memory and images. They presented auditory, motor, and a variety of visual tasks to subjects and measured rCBF. In all their experiments, the areas activated were in the association cortexes of the temporal, parietal, and frontal lobes. Neither lower-level sensory areas nor primary motor areas were activated.

Roland and Gulyas favor the idea that the higher-level areas form a distributed system whose function is also to represent memory. The memories do not contain the dimensions of time and space, but the simultaneous activation of a number of regions could generate these properties. For Roland and Gulyas, mental images are activated memories.

There is also evidence against this view. Three lines of evidence from studies of the visual system favor the idea that the same structures participating in perception take part in forming images in the absence of visual stimulation. This position does not disagree that higher visual areas are engaged in imagery but argues that lower areas of the visual system also take part. Thus, in normal viewing, visual stimulation successively excites lower visual areas and then higher visual areas; whereas, in imagining, higher visual areas activate lower visual areas through reentrant fibers and so the same sets of neurons are activated in both perception and imaging. Here is the evidence:

1. Farah describes patient M. G. S., before and after the occipital cortex was unilaterally removed as a treatment for epilepsy. M. G. S. was asked to imagine walking toward an object, such as a mouse or a dog, or to imagine an approaching car. She was to indicate when the object completely filled the visual field (which would occur when M. G. S. was closer to the mouse than to the dog). Before surgery, her response was similar to that of control subjects. After surgery, the visual angle was reduced significantly relative both to that of the normal subjects and to her preoperative results (the objects now filled her visual field when she was farther away from them, presumably because her visual field was smaller). This finding is consistent with the idea that images have a topographical organization in the visual areas and that the area available to contain an image is reduced after loss of the primary visual cortex.

2. A number of rCBF studies find activation in primary visual areas during imagining (see the Snapshot in Chapter 13).

3. Evidence that could be taken to support the commonality of structures engaged in perception and imagining comes from studies of eye movements. In viewing, the eyes make saccades in a typical way to catch key elements of the stimulus. Norton and Stark reported that the same kinds of eye movements are made when looking at an object and in later imagining of the same object.

At present, research cannot distinguish between the position that only higher-level structures take part in imagining and the position that the same set of structures controlling viewing also control imagining. The disagreement between studies using rCBF may be related to differences in the kinds of tasks presented to the subjects, differences in the methods used to subtract baseline blood-flow activity in control conditions and test conditions, or even differences in subject populations.

With respect to the last point, we were surprised to learn from a colleague, who is internationally known for his work in visual perception, that he has no idea what visual imagery is, because he is unable to experience it. We both asserted, to his surprise, that we had no difficulty forming visual images. An additional problem with studies comparing perception and imaging relates to quantifying what it is that is seen. When two viewers look at a scene, they can come to reasonable agreement about what they are seeing. When they compare their mental images of the same scene, they have no reliable way to confirm that they are imagining the same thing.

Kinds of Images

Is there more than one type of mental image? If we return to our ski jumpers, we can see that they can imagine their jump in at least two different ways. They can use a process referred to as internal imagery—a first-person process in which they imagine that they themselves are making the movement. Alternatively, they can use what is called external imagery, in which they see some person, perhaps themselves or perhaps someone else, making the jump.

In the first case, the imagery is of the movements that they themselves will make; the anticipatory movements that they make in the imagery presumably correspond to the movements that they will make when they jump. This process is somewhat like practicing a golf swing before hitting the ball, without actually making the swing. In the second case, they are imagining themselves or some other person. They see that person, they see the jump, and they see the surrounding area. Furthermore, the view can change at will. It is as though they are actually watching some other person jump or are watching a jump on television.

The properties of internal and external images are quite different, although both are images of movement and both can represent the upcoming jump. Jeannerod refers to internal imagery as motor imagery; it is the self in action. External imagery is really the imagery of objects: a jumper, a jump, the surrounding area.

To gain an idea of how the two differ, consider the following example. A coach demonstrates a basketball shot to a player. The player watches and forms an image of the movements that the coach has made. The player then tries the shot. As the player does so, the coach (mentally, and perhaps with a little muscle tensing and grimacing) makes the same shot along with the player. If the player succeeds, the coach gives a little cheer, and, if the player misses, the coach groans and they begin again.

The two kinds of imagery differ in another way. When the player imagines the coach's movements, the image is created without muscle tension, effort, or exertion. When the coach imagines the player's shot, the image includes tension, effort, and exertion, as if the coach were actually taking the shot.

Images of the movements used in sports are relatively simple. They are movements that the participant has practiced and viewed hundreds of times. People form other images as well, images that are more complex and that can be unique in some way. Consider the following example. You need a book on bats. You look up the catalogue number on your computer and then set off to the library to get the book. On the way to the library, you meet a friend who wants to know where you are going. You explain. You both talk about bats, and then you continue on your way. When you get to the library, you find that you have forgotten the catalogue number. You look it up. When you get to the stacks, you find that the book is not there. The librarian tells you that the book is checked out, and it is impossible to get it back.

In this example, you have an image of a goal but no image of the movements that you must make or the terrain that you must traverse to reach the goal and certainly no image of where the book might be located. A goal image is very flexible in that it allows the incorporation of a variety of actions and subgoals. Other images that we have include thoughts, which are usually verbal images. That is, we talk to ourselves and hear the sounds of words, but we do not make sounds or movements. We also hum tunes and sing little songs to ourselves.

If we consider all the different kinds of images that we can form, it becomes clear that they closely parallel the things that we do. If we postulate that the images are formed by the same brain areas that produce actions, then each kind of image maps onto its own brain area. Thus, verbal images or thinking to one-self use language phonemic circuitry in the left hemisphere, whereas images of music or spatial events use right-hemisphere structures that normally subserve those events.

A dramatic example of the interplay between image and movement comes from the studies of mirror neurons (see Figure 9.13). In humans, the mirror neurons are found not only in area 6 but also in area 44, which is Broca's area. Rizzolatti and his colleagues reviewed the literature on this subject and make the unexpected conclusion that the results of brain-imaging studies have shown that activity in area 44 is related to the imaging of hand movements or mental rotation of objects by hand. Thus, area 44 participates not only in the generation of verbs that describe movements (see Chapter 19), which presumably entails a form of imagery, but also in the imagining of the movements represented by the verbs.

The parts of the brain engaged in internal versus external imagery are not known, but it seems unlikely that the same brain regions produce both kinds of images. Internal imagery of movements may use the object-location system (parietofrontal cortex system, or dorsal stream), and external imagery of movements in relation to objects may use the object-recognition system (inferior temporofrontal cortex system, or ventral stream). Images are probably also closely related to memories, as Roland suggests, in that they are in some ways active memories. Thus, each brain system is responsible for a triumvirate of functions: action, memory, and imagining.

Apraxia

How we view the relation among perceptions, actions, and images, which has some consequences for how we interpret various symptoms of brain damage. For example, if the same neural structures represent perception and images, then damage to those structures will have equivalent effects on perception and images. If the same structures represent movements and their images, then brain damage will have equivalent effects on actions and their images. If, on the other hand, images are formed in only a part of the circuitry or in some other location, then the effects of damage to the structures that control images will differ from those of damage to structures that control perception or action. Traditional attempts to categorize the effects of brain damage on movements are based on the view that perceptions, memories, and images are distinct.

Although the symptoms of apraxia had been described earlier by others, Hugo Liepmann began the first detailed analysis of apraxic symptoms. In 1900, he reported the case of an aphasic man who was unable to carry out hand movements when asked to do so. Curiously, he could follow directions if the required movement was a whole-body movement, such as sitting down, and he could make *spontaneous* hand movements.

Liepmann's patient was an imperial councilor, 48 years of age, hospitalized on a psychiatry service for "dementia." He displayed a motor aphasia, but he also manipulated objects in a peculiar fashion, and the difficulty that he had was limited to his right arm. This arm was not paralyzed, its muscular power was preserved, and it performed most of the movements required of daily life.

In contrast, when the patient was asked to use his right hand to point to his nose, make a fist, or show how to use a harmonica or a brush, he failed completely. Even though he made movements indicating that he understood the instructions, he could not make the appropriate movements. If the right arm was held by the observer, all the movements were carried out by the left arm. When the gesture required the coordinated use of both hands, the right hand prohibited the execution of the gesture, even while the left hand was responding correctly. For example, when the patient attempted to pour water into a glass, the left hand took the pitcher in order to pour while the right hand was bringing the glass to the mouth.

Because neither the comprehension of the instructions nor the motor execution itself was defective, the difficulty that produced the apraxia had to be located at another level. Liepmann placed it between the sensory memories (which understood instructions) and the motor memories (which allowed the patient to transform the instructions into an action). Liepmann offered the hypothesis that the disconnection must entail not only the association pathways in the interior of the left hemisphere but also the corpus callosum connecting the two hemispheres. The death of the imperial councilor allowed the hypothesis to be verified by autopsy.

In the ensuing years, Liepmann studied many patients with this unusual movement problem, and in 1920 he proposed his now-classic theory of apraxia, of which two important points are that

1. apraxia results from lesions of the left hemisphere or of the corpus callosum, and

2. there are several different types of apraxia, each most likely resulting from damage to a specific locus in the left hemisphere.

Strictly defined, apraxia means no action (Greek *praxis* means "action"). The term apraxia, however, is hardly ever used in this strict sense today. Rather, it is used to describe all sorts of missing or inappropriate actions that cannot be clearly attributed to paralysis, paresis, or other more primary motor deficits, on the one hand, or to lack of comprehension or motivation, on the other.

The modern concepts have their origins in Joseph Dejerine's reinterpretation of Liepmann's work. Because movements can be conceived as consisting of a goal, a series of subgoals, and a series of movements, different kinds of apraxia should be related to impairments in subcomponents of the actions. Consider the following patient:

> A woman with a biparietal lesion had worked for years as a fish-filleter. With the development of her symptoms, she began to experience difficulty in carrying on with her job. She did not seem to know what to do with her knife. She would stick the point in the head of a fish, start the first stroke, and then come to a stop. In her own mind she knew how to fillet fish, but yet she could not execute the maneuver. The foreman accused her of being drunk and sent her home for mutilating fish.
>
> This same patient also showed another unusual phenomenon which might possibly be apraxic in nature. She could never finish an undertaking. She would begin a job, drop it, start another, abandon that one, and within a short while would have four or five uncompleted tasks on her hands. This would cause her to do such inappropriate actions as putting the sugar bowl in the refrigerator, and the coffee pot inside the oven. (Critchley, 1953, pp. 158–159)

If the fish filleter could not conceive of the goal of filleting fish, she would perform the actions of filleting, but they would be haphazard (as was the case). She would be classified as having ideational apraxia. (In the example of going to the library for a book on bats, ideational apraxia would prevent the formation of this goal.)

On the other hand, the fish filleter might be able to form the goal of filleting a fish but not be able to form the subgoals of making the appropriate steps of filleting. In this case, she would be classified as having ideomotor apraxia. (In the library example, one might set off for the library but never arrive there because of an inability to make appropriate course adjustments along the way.)

Finally, if the fish filleter could form the goal and know the movement sequence but not execute the movement, she would be classified as having motor apraxia. (In the library example, one could not get the catalogue number of the book, because the fingers would not produce the movements to operate the keys of the computer, and possibly one would not be able to execute the walking movements.)

The classification of apraxia in this way is both a strength and a weakness. The classification appears to allow some obvious distinctions between knowing what to do and being able to do it, which is diagnostically useful. But this distinction is difficult to make. For example, which kind of apraxia does the fish filleter really have? When she stabs at the fish, is her problem not knowing what she wants to do or not knowing how to do it?

The several standard clinical tests often used to assess apraxia have similar weaknesses. For example, a patient might be asked to demonstrate the use of a particular object in its absence—to comb the hair or to hammer a nail. An apraxic person's response might be to do nothing or to use a part of the body as if it were the implement—to stroke a finger through the hair as if it were a comb or to hit the table with a fist as though it were a hammer. A normal person would pretend to hold the comb or hammer. Another test of apraxia might be to ask a person to perform such symbolic movements as saluting or waving goodbye; the person might remain still or respond by making an unrecognizable movement.

Although these tests are useful for on-the-spot assessments of apraxia, they do not permit objective quantification or more-penetrating analysis. Clinical description presents a further difficulty in that classifications of apraxia tend to be arbitrary. In addition, new types of apraxia tend to proliferate not because actual new symptoms are discovered but because new questions are put to the patients or new ways of assessing the responses are developed. Finally, slight variations in lesion location might be used as justification that one apraxia differs from another.

Asymmetry in Movement Control

One of the most important proposals in Liepmann's theory of apraxia is that the left hemisphere plays a special role not shared by the right hemisphere in the control of movement. Another line of evidence supporting Liepmann's left-hemisphere proposal is from a study by Milner and her colleagues. They taught patients a complex series of arm movements before intracarotid sodium amobarbital injections. After the injections, the patients were required to perform the movements. Only injections into the speaking hemisphere disrupted the movements, even though the movements were to be performed with the ipsilateral limb (controlled by the contralateral motor cortex that had not received an injection). Thus, the results of sodium amobarbital testing support the results of lesion studies in confirming a special role for the left hemisphere in the control of movement.

Given the left hemisphere's special control of many types of movement, one might ask whether the right hemisphere also might control certain other types of movements. In fact, a group of movements can be selectively disrupted by right-hemisphere lesions. These movements are used in tasks in which a variety of components must be assembled to form an object. Examples include (1) assembling pieces of a jigsaw puzzle to form a picture, (2) drawing a clock face or map, (3) copying a design composed of sticks of various lengths, (4) building bridges and towers with blocks, and (5) copying designs made up of differently colored blocks. Deficits on such tests are sometimes called constructional apraxias, which was a symptom exhibited by R. P., whose case is presented at the beginning of this chapter.

What is special about these constructional tasks? All require that objects be ordered in extrapersonal space. Dealing with the spatial relations of objects is believed to be a function of the right hemisphere, especially of the right parietal cortex. Although left parietal lesions also can produce some similar deficits, these deficits may have a different cause: left-hemisphere deficits may result from an affected person's inability to adjust the parts of his or her own body, rather than from an inability to adjust the position of an external object. This theoretically interesting proposition has yet to be clearly tested experimentally.

Social Cognition

We humans are social animals living in large groups. To thrive in such an environment requires a kind of social intelligence that allows us to make sense of another person's actions and intentions. This ability is often referred to as theory of mind—the ability to attribute mental states to self and others and to predict and understand people's behavior on the basis of their mental states. But what is entailed in developing a sense of other people's intentions?

In Chapter 15, we considered biological motion—movements that have particular relevance to a species, which for humans includes movements of our eyes, face, mouth, hands, and body (see the review by Langton et al.). These movements can have social meanings and presumably contribute to our impressions of the mental states of others. Cells in the superior temporal sulcus code such movements, and thus we can infer that the superior temporal sulcus must be a part of any neural network that controls social cognition. The Snapshot on page 601 describes an fMRI study illustrating that activity in the superior temporal sulcus is related to a subject's ability to detect the trustworthiness of faces. Recall that R. P. had been duped by con artists and complained that she seemed unable to detect people who were not trustworthy. She also had reduced blood flow in the right temporal lobe.

There is more to social cognition than the activity of the superior temporal sulcus, however. As described in Chapter 20, damage to the ventral prefrontal areas (including both the orbital cortex and the more ventral medial cortex) consistently produces personality changes characterized by impaired social judgment. Stuss and his colleagues devised a task to examine the ability to infer visual experience from others (see also a study by Rowe et al.).

In the Stuss task, a subject was presented with two Styrofoam cups, one of which had an object hidden under it. The test subject was not permitted to watch the placement of the objects, but, in one test condition, an assistant of the experimenter was able to watch the object (a 25-cent coin) placement. The subject kept the money for correct choices, and the assistant kept it for incorrect responses made by the subject.

The patient knew that the assistant was aware of the location of the object and that the assistant stood to gain by the patient making an error. On each trial, the assistant pointed to the wrong cup, the one without the money, and the subject then made his or her choice. This condition continued for 14 trials or until the subject made five consecutive correct responses. Ventral medial frontal lesions, particularly on the right, impaired the detection of deception. Remarkably, the patients in this study did not appear to realize that the assistant was trying to deceive them.

The results of a number of imaging studies provide corroborating evidence of the role of the frontal lobe in social cognition. For example, Fletcher and colleagues asked subjects to reflect on the thoughts and feelings of characters in comparison with control tasks in which thoughts and feelings were irrelevant and found specific medial frontal activation (see also Gallagher et al.).

Just as the orbitofrontal cortex is critical for social cognition, so is the amygdala. Fine and coworkers describe patient B. M., who had selective congenital left amygdala damage. The patient had an average IQ and performed within nor-

S N A P S H O T

Brain Activation in Social Cognition

Successful social interaction depends partly on the accurate judgments of the intentions of others. Facial appearance is a powerful stimulus for social judgments. An analysis of a face includes not only facial expression and direction of gaze but also an intangible feeling of trustworthiness in a face.

Winston and coworkers used fMRI to examine the neural substrates mediating this type of evaluative social judgment (see the illustration). Photographs of male faces were selected in a pilot study in which subjects rated the trustworthiness of the faces. During the scanning, the subjects were asked to judge either whether a face was that of a high-school or university student or whether the face was trustworthy.

The left and right amygdala and right insula were activated in response to faces judged to be untrustworthy, regardless of whether the subjects were judging trustworthiness or age. The amygdala activation is consistent with a role of the amygdala in judgments of facial expression. The insular activation is hypothesized to result from a response to changes in bodily states that form a "gut feeling" about something.

In contrast with the amygdala and insular activation, activation of the superior temporal sulcus and orbitofrontal cortex was task dependent. The right superior temporal sulcus showed enhanced activity only when subjects were making explicit judgments about trustworthiness. The orbitofrontal cortex showed activation when subjects made explicit judgments about trustworthiness, with greater activation in response to faces deemed trustworthy. In con-

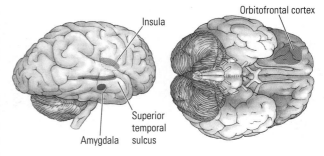

Areas of the brain activated when subjects evaluated faces. The amygdala and insula were activated regardless of whether there was an explicit instruction to evaluate trustworthiness, whereas the superior temporal sulcus and orbital frontal cortex was activated only when there was an instruction to make judgments about trustworthiness. (After Winston et al., 2002.)

trast, when judging age, this region showed greater activation in response to untrustworthy faces.

Winston and colleagues believe that activation of the superior temporal sulcus is the critical one in making judgments specifically about the intentions of others.

(J. S. Winston, B. A. Strange, J. O'Doherty, and R. J. Dolan. Automatic and intentional brain responses during evaluation of trustworthiness of faces. *Nature Neuroscience* 5:277–283, 2002.)

mal limits in most neuropsychological tests. In contrast, however, B. M. did very poorly on theory-of-mind tests. On one test, for example, B. M. was given 20 cartoons: 10 "mental state" cartoons and 10 "physical state" cartoons. For example, a mental-state cartoon might show a person surprised by winning a draw, whereas a physical-state cartoon would depict a person stubbing his toe. B. M. was unable to infer the mental state of the cartoon characters (scoring 1 of 10), but he had no difficulty identifying the physical state of the characters (scoring 9 of 10). B. M. has a significant deficit in inferring the mental state of others.

Few cases of specific amygdala damage are reported in the literature, but there is accumulating evidence that autistic people have consistent abnormalities in the cell density of the amygdala (for a review, see Courchesne). Autistic people consistently fail theory-of-mind tasks, and Baron-Cohen theorized that the extreme abnormalities in social cognition in autism result from an abnormality in an amygdala-prefrontal circuit.

To conclude, social cognition entails a vast set of abilities that allow people to live in large, complex social groups. The neural structures underlying social cognition have likely expanded significantly in human brain evolution, although in precisely which regions is still unclear. Nonetheless, there is good evidence that the prefrontal cortex, the amygdala, and the superior temporal sulcus must be a part of any network underlying social cognition (see the Snapshot on page 601). To this list, we might add the insular cortex, considered in the discussion of emotion in Chapter 20. The insular cortex would provide the source of "gut feelings" about information, which Adolphs has emphasized as being important both in emotional processing and in social cognition.

Consciousness

Conscious experience is probably the most familiar mental process that we know, yet its workings remain mysterious. Everyone has a vague idea of what is meant by being conscious, but consciousness is easier to identify than to define. Definitions of consciousness range from the view that it merely refers to complex thought processes to the more slippery implication that it is the subjective experience of awareness or of "inner self." Nonetheless, there is general agreement that whatever conscious experience is, it is a process.

Recall that one of the first modern theories of consciousness was proposed by Descartes. He proposed that being able to remember past events and being able to speak were the primary abilities that enabled consciousness. In preceding chapters, we encountered people who have lost the ability to remember and have lost the ability to speak. Those who knew these patients would not have described them as no longer being conscious. In fact, consciousness is probably not a single process but a collection of many processes, such as those associated with seeing, talking, thinking, emotion, and so on.

Consciousness is also not always the same. A person at different ages of life is not thought to be equally conscious at each age; young children and demented adults are usually not considered to experience the same type of consciousness as healthy adults do. Indeed, part of the process of maturation is becoming fully conscious. And consciousness varies across the span of a day as we pass through various states of sleep and waking.

Most definitions of consciousness exclude the conditions of simply being responsive to sensory stimulation or simply being able to produce movement. Thus, animals whose behavior is simply reflexive are not conscious. Similarly, the isolated spinal cord, although a repository for many reflexes, is not conscious. Machines that are responsive to sensory events and are capable of complex movements are not conscious. Many of the functions of normal humans, such as the beating of the heart, are not conscious processes. Similarly, many processes of the nervous system, including simple sensory processes and motor actions, are not conscious. Consciousness requires processes that differ from all of the aforementioned.

Some people have argued that certain processes are much more important for consciousness than others. Language is often argued to be essential to consciousness because language makes a fundamental change in the nature of human consciousness. Recall that Gazzaniga (Chapter 11) suggested that language acts as an interpreter, which he felt led to an important difference between the functions of the hemispheres. People who are aphasic are not considered to have lost conscious awareness, however; nor are people who have their right hemispheres removed. Patient H. M., whom we met in Chapter 18, has a dense amnesia, yet he is quite conscious and can engage in intelligent conversations. In sum, although language may alter the nature of our conscious experience, it seems unlikely that any one brain structure can be equated with consciousness. Rather, it makes more sense to view consciousness as a product of all cortical areas, their connections, and their cognitive operations.

Why Are We Conscious?

The simplest explanation of why we are conscious is that consciousness provides adaptive advantage. In other words, either our creation of the sensory world or our selection of behavior is enhanced by being conscious. Consider visual consciousness as an example. Crick and Koch noted that an animal such as a frog acts a bit like a zombie when it responds to visual input. Frogs respond to small, preylike objects by snapping and respond to large, looming objects by jumping. These responses are controlled by different visual systems and are best thought of as being reflexive rather than conscious. But these visual systems work well for the frog; so why do we need to add consciousness?

Crick and Koch suggest that reflexive systems are fine when the number of such systems are few but, as the number grows, such a reflexive arrangement becomes inefficient, especially if systems are in conflict. When the amount of information about some event increases, it is better to produce a single but complex representation and make it available for a sufficient amount of time to the parts of the brain (such as the frontal lobe) that make a choice among many different but possible plans for action.

We still need the ability to respond quickly and, presumably, unconsciously. In the human brain, the ventral stream is conscious, but the dorsal stream, which acts more rapidly, is not. The action of the unconscious, on-line dorsal stream can be seen anecdotally in many athletes. To hit a baseball or a tennis ball traveling at more than 90 miles per hour is believed to require athletes to swing before they are consciously aware of actually seeing the ball. The conscious awareness of the ball comes just after an athlete hits it.

The results of a series of experiments by Jeannerod's group have shown a similar dissociation between behavior and awareness in normal volunteers making grasping movements. Figure 22.10 illustrates the results of a representative experiment. Subjects were required to move one hand and grasp one of three rods as quickly as possible. The correct target on any given trial was determined by the illumination of a light on the target.

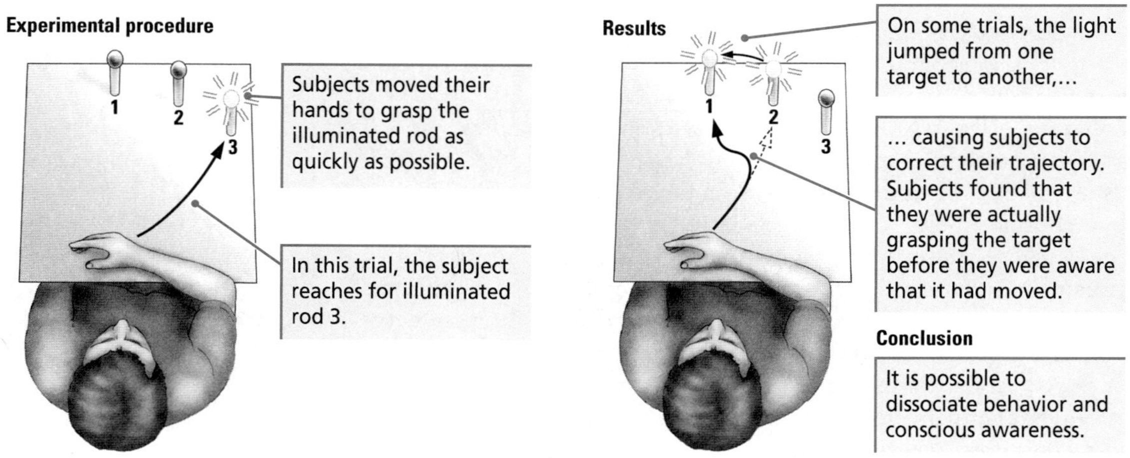

Experimental procedure

Subjects moved their hands to grasp the illuminated rod as quickly as possible.

In this trial, the subject reaches for illuminated rod 3.

Results

On some trials, the light jumped from one target to another,...

... causing subjects to correct their trajectory. Subjects found that they were actually grasping the target before they were aware that it had moved.

Conclusion

It is possible to dissociate behavior and conscious awareness.

Figure 22.10 Dissociation of behavior and conscious awareness. The paths that the hand follows to grasp the illuminated rod are indicated by the arrows. On some trials, the light switched unexpectedly from one target to another. The switch elicited a smooth and rapid movement correction. Subjects were asked to give a vocal response to indicate that they were aware of the target switch. On some trials, there was a dissociation between motor and vocal responses such that, to their surprise, subjects had already grasped the target some 300 milliseconds before they emitted the vocal response. (After Frith et al., 1999.)

On some trials, unbeknown to the subjects, the light jumped from one target to another. Subjects were asked to indicate if such a jump had occurred. As shown in Figure 22.10, subjects were able to make the trajectory correction on line but, to the surprise of many subjects, on some trials the subjects were actually grasping the target before they were aware that it had moved. Like baseball players, the conscious awareness of the stimulus event occurred after the movement had taken place. Clearly, no thought was required to make the movement, just as frogs appear to catch flies without thinking about the task.

Such movements contrast, however, with movements that must be directed toward a specific object. If we are reaching toward a bowl to grasp a jelly bean of a specific color, we must be aware of the difference between red, green, and yellow jelly beans, and we must direct our reach toward the desired color. Thus, the action of the conscious ventral stream is needed when we must discriminate and respond differentially to particular stimuli. Consciousness allows us to select behaviors that correspond to an understanding of the nuances of sensory inputs.

The Neural Basis of Consciousness

As stated earlier, consciousness must be a function of numerous interacting systems, presumably including sensory areas, memory structures, and perhaps structures underlying other processes such as emotion and executive functions. The problem for a theory of the neural basis of consciousness is to explain how all these systems can be integrated. We have returned to the binding problem that we first encountered in Chapter 10. Recall that Jerison suggested that one solution to the binding problem within the sensory domain was temporal integration. Crick and Koch have gone further and propose that binding is the solution to consciousness.

Before examining this idea more closely, we need to examine processes that are believed to be prerequisites of consciousness. Most investigators agree that at least four processes must take part:

1. *Arousal*, the waking up of the brain by nonspecific modulatory systems

2. *Perception*, the detection and binding of sensory features

3. *Attention*, the selection of a restricted sample of all available information

4. *Working memory*, the short-term storage of ongoing events

Engel and Singer propose that all these processes either require or modify the operation of an overall binding process and that binding is implemented by the transient and precise synchronization of neural discharges in diffuse neural networks. The general idea is that neurons that represent the same object or event fire their action potentials in a temporal synchrony with a precision of milliseconds. No such synchronization should take place between cells that are part of different cellular networks. Recall that the idea of synchrony was proposed earlier as a mechanism of attention. Taken further, it is proposed that without attention to an input there is no awareness of it (see Taylor for more on this point).

But what produces the synchrony? Neuronal groups exhibit a wide range of synchronous oscillations (6–80 Hz) and can shift from a desynchronized state to a rhythmic state in milliseconds. Thus we can predict that, when we become consciously aware of some event, there should be evidence of synchronous activity between widely separated brain regions.

Figure 22.11 illustrates this process in terms of synchronous activity in the gamma range (roughly 40 Hz) recorded when subjects viewed Mooney faces either right side up or upside down. When viewed upright, faces can be found but, when viewed inverted, it is impossible to find the face. The subject's task was to find the face and push one of two buttons to signify the presence or absence of a face.

Figure 22.11 shows a marked difference in neural activity in the two conditions. About 200 ms after the stimulus presentation (Figure 22.11A), there was synchrony in the left hemisphere in the upright-face condition inasmuch as electrodes in all lobes showed synchronous activity (Figure 22.11B) followed by a period of asynchrony in most of both hemispheres (Figure 22.11C). Such desynchronization is postulated to

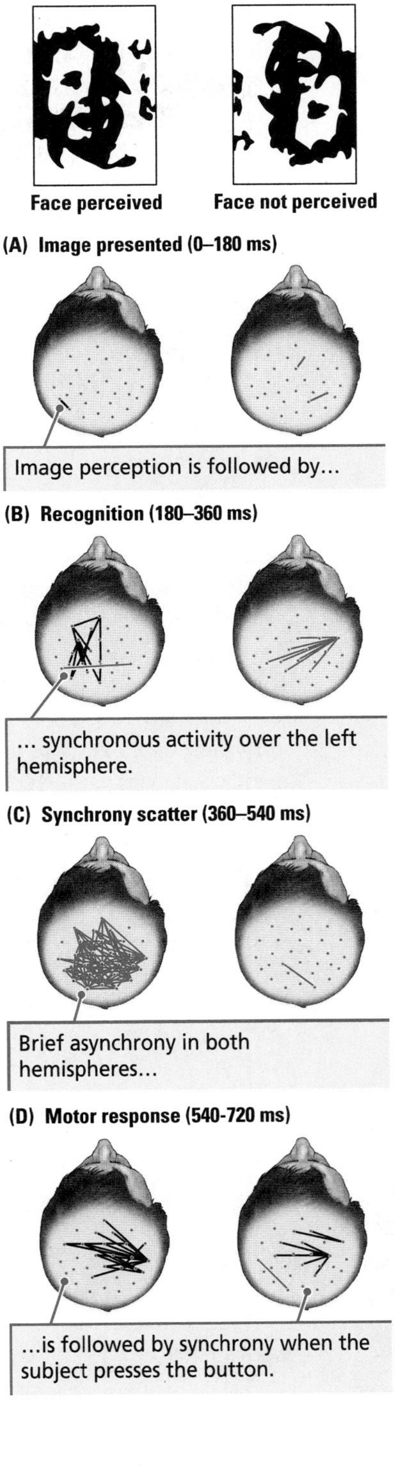

Face perceived   **Face not perceived**

(A) Image presented (0–180 ms)

Image perception is followed by...

(B) Recognition (180–360 ms)

... synchronous activity over the left hemisphere.

(C) Synchrony scatter (360–540 ms)

Brief asynchrony in both hemispheres...

(D) Motor response (540-720 ms)

...is followed by synchrony when the subject presses the button.

Figure 22.11 The shadow of a perception: Average scalp distribution of phase synchrony in EEG recorded from electrodes on the scalp marked by dots. The black lines show synchrony and the blue lines show asynchrony. (A) When subjects were shown an upright Mooney figure, they were able to perceive a face; whereas, when shown the figure inverted, they did not perceive a face. Synchrony is correlated with recognition of the face (B) and the motor response (D). Motor activity is preceded by a period of asynchrony (C). (After Rodriguez et al., 1999.)

be necessary, because there is a shift between synchrony in different neural assemblies. Finally, a return of synchrony coincided with the subject's button pressing (Figure 22.11D). Notice that, in the inverted condition, there was no synchrony during the analysis of the stimulus, as shown in Figure 22.11A and B, but there was during the motor response shown in Figure 22.11D.

Thompson and Varella reviewed the evidence on synchrony and consciousness and conclude that phase synchrony acts not only to bind the sensory attributes but also to bind all dimensions of the cognitive act, including associative memory, emotional tone, and motor planning. The problem, however, is that all studies to date are correlative. There is no direct evidence that changes in synchrony lead to changes in either behavior or consciousness. A search for such evidence is likely to be the direction of studies on consciousness in both laboratory animals and human subjects in the coming decade.

Summary

Attention, mental images, and consciousness are not epiphenomena resulting from the complexities of the brain. They are properties of the nervous system that direct complex actions of body and brain. Neuropsychologists have not quantified attention, imagery, or consciousness. Still, it is possible to theorize that they are functions of one or another brain region. It is also possible to create theories of how brain processes produce these phenomena. Attention allows the nervous system to focus on aspects of the world and on aspects of the brain itself. The processes of attention can be demonstrated by using behavioral, neurophysiological, and imaging techniques. The neural mechanisms underlying attention are extensive and are best thought of as a network of structures including sensory regions as well as the parietal, prefrontal, and anterior cingulate cortex. Inattention ("the dark side of attention") is a necessary fallout from the focusing of attention on specific information. The process of imagining allows the nervous system to represent places and objects so that the individual can reach those places and obtain those objects. Social cognition is a learned consciousness (theory of mind) that allows us to make sense of another person's actions and intentions. Consciousness, a property of complex brains, binds diverse aspects of sensory information into a single event that we experience as reality.

References

Adophs, R. Social cognition and the human brain. *Trends in Cognitive Sciences* 3:469–479, 1999.

Bargh, J. A., and M. J. Ferguson. Beyond behaviorism: On the automaticity of higher mental processes. Psychological Bulletin 126:925–945, 2000.

Baron-Cohen, S. *Mindblindness: An Essay on Autism and Theory of Mind*. Cambridge, MA: MIT Press, 1995.

Behrmann, M., M. Moscovitch, and G. Winocur. Intact visual imagery and impaired visual perception in a patient with visual agnosia. *Journal of Experimental Psychology: Human Perception and Performance* 20:1068–1087, 1994.

Berti, A., and F. Frassinetti. When far becomes near: Remapping of space by tool use. *Journal of Cognitive Neuroscience* 12:415–420, 2000.

Bossom, J. The effect of brain lesions on adaptation in monkeys. *Psychonomic Science* 2:45–46, 1965.

Burton, H., N. S. Abend, A.-M. K. MacLeod, R. J. Sinclair, A. Z. Snyder, and M. E. Raichle. Tactile attention tasks enhance activation in somatosensory regions of parietal cortex: A positron emission tomography study. *Cerebral Cortex* 9:662–674, 1999.

Chelazzi, L., E. K. Miller, J. Duncan, and R. Desimone. A neural basis for visual search in inferior temporal cortex. *Nature* 363:345–347, 1993.

Chun, M. M., and R. Marois. The dark side of visual attention. *Current Opinion in Neurobiology* 12:184–189, 2002.

Corbetta, M., F. M. Miezin, S. Dobmeyer, G. L. Shulman, and S. E. Petersen. Selective and divided attention during visual discrimination of shape, color, and speed: Functional anatomy by positron emission tomography. *Journal of Neuroscience* 11:2383–2402, 1991.

Corbetta, M., F. M. Miezin, G. L. Shulman, and S. E. Petersen. A PET study of visuospatial attention. *Journal of Neuroscience* 13:1202–1226, 1993.

Courchesne, E. Brainstem, cerebellar and limbic neuroanatomical abnormalities in autism. *Current Opinion in Neurobiology* 7:269–278, 1997.

Crick, F., and C. Koch. The problem of consciousness. *Scientific American* 267:152–159, 1992.

Crick, F., and C. Koch.. Consciousness and neuroscience. *Cerebral Cortex* 8:97–107, 1998.

Critchley, M. *The Parietal Lobes.* London: Arnold, 1953.

Eastwood, J. D., D. Smilek, and P. M. Merikle. Differential attentional guidance by unattended faces expressing positive and negative emotion. *Perception and Psychophysics* 63:1004–1013, 2001.

Engel, A. K., and W. Singer. Temporal binding and the neural correlates of sensory awareness. *Trends in Cognitive Sciences* 5:16–25, 2001.

Farah, M. J. *Visual Agnosia.* Cambridge, MA: MIT Press, 1990.

Fine, C., J. Lumsden, and R. J. R. Blair. Dissociation between "theory of mind" and executive functions in a patient with early left amygdala damage. *Brain* 124:287–298, 2001.

Fletcher, P. C., F. Happe, U. Frith, S. C. Baker, R. J. Dolan, and R. S. Frakowiak. Other minds in the brain: A functional imaging study of "theory of mind" in story comprehension. *Cognition* 57:109–128, 1995.

Frith, C., R. Perry, and E. Lumer. The neural correlates of conscious experience. *Trends in Cognitive Sciences* 3:105–114, 1999.

Gallagher, H. L., F. Happe, N. Brunswick, P. C. Fletcher, U. Frith, and C. D. Frith. Reading the mind in cartoons and stories: An fMRI study of "theory of mind" in verbal and nonverbal tasks. *Neuropsychologia* 38:11–21, 2000.

Geschwind, N. The apraxias: Neural mechanisms of disorders of learned movement. *American Scientist* 63:188–195, 1975.

Hebb, D. O. *Essay on Mind.* Hillsdale, NJ: Lawrence Earlbaum, 1980.

Jeannerod, M. The representing brain: Neural correlates of motor intention and imagery. *Behavioral and Brain Sciences* 17:187–245, 1994.

Jenkins, I. H., D. J. Brooks, P. D. Nixon, R. S. J. Frackowiak, and R. E. Passingham. Motor sequence learning: A study with positron emission tomography. *Journal of Neuroscience* 14:3775–3790, 1994.

Kahneman, D. *Attention and Effort.* Englewood Cliffs, N J: Prentice-Hall, 1973.

Karnath, H.-O., S. Ferber, and M. Himmelbach. Spatial awareness is a function of the temporal not the posterior parietal lobe. *Nature* 411:950–953, 2001.

Kastner, S., P. De Weerd, R. Desimone, and L. G. Ungerleider. Mechanisms of directed attention in the human extrastriate cortex as revealed by functional MRI. *Science* 282:108–112, 2001.

Kimura, D. Left-hemisphere control of oral and brachial movements and their relation to communication. *Philosophical Transactions of the Royal Society of London* B298:135–149, 1982.

Kimura, D. *Neuromotor Mechanisms in the Evolution of Human Communication.* New York: Oxford University Press, 1993.

Langton, S. R., R. J. Watt, and V. Bruce. Do the eyes have it? Cues to the direction of social attention. *Trends in Cognitive Sciences* 4:50–59, 2000.

Liepmann, H. *Die linke Hemisphare und das Handeln: Drei Aufsatze aus dem Apraxiegebiet.* Berlin: Springer, 1908.

Logan, G. D. Attention and preattention in theories of automaticity. *American Journal of Psychology* 105:317–340, 1992.

Milner, B. Hemispheric asymmetry in the control of gesture sequences. *Proceedings of XXI International Congress of Psychology.* Paris, 1976, p. 149.

Moran, J., and R. Desimone. Selective attention gates visual processing in the extrastriate cortex. *Science* 229:782–784, 1985.

Mountcastle, V. B. The parietal system and some higher brain functions. *Cerebral Cortex* 5:377–390, 1995.

Naatanen, T. *Attention and Brain Function.* Hillsdale, NJ: Lawrence Erlbaum, 1992.

Niebur, E., S. S. Hsiao, and K. O. Johnson. Synchrony: A neuron mechanism for attentional selection? *Current Opinion in Neurobiology* 12:190–194, 2002.

Norton, D., and L. Stark. Eye movements and visual perception. In R. Held and W. Richards, Eds. *Perception: Mechanisms and Models.* Readings from *Scientific American.* San Francisco: W. H. Freeman and Company, 1972.

Petersen, S. E., D. L. Robinson, and J. D. Morris. Contributions of the pulvinar to visual spatial orientation. *Neuropsychologia* 25:97–106, 1987.

Posner, M. I., and S. E. Petersen. The attention system of the brain. *Annual Review of Neuroscience* 13:25–42, 1990.

Posner, M. I., and M. E. Raichle. *Images of Mind.* New York: Scientific American Library, 1993.

Rizzolatti, G., L. Fogassi, and V. Gallese. Motor and cognitive functions of the ventral premotor cortex. *Current Opinion in Neurobiology* 12:149–154, 2002.

Rodriguez, E., N. George, J. P. Lachaux, J. Martinerie, B. Renault, and F. J. Varela. Perception's shadow: Long-distance synchronization of human brain activity. *Nature* 397:430–433, 1999.

Roland, P. E. *Brain Activation.* New York: Wiley, 1993.

Roland, P. E., and B. Gulyas. Visual imagery and visual representation. *Trends in Neuroscience* 17:281–287, 1994.

Rossetti, Y., G. Rode, L. Pisella, A. Farne, L. Li, D. Boisson, and M.-T. Perenin. Prism adaptation to a rightward optical deviation rehabilitates left hemispatial neglect. *Nature* 395:166–169, 1998.

Rowe, A. D., P. R. Bullock, C. E. Polkey, and R. G. Morris. "Theory of mind" impairments and their relationship to executive functioning following frontal lobe excisions. *Brain* 124:600–616, 2001.

Schall, J. D., and D. P. Hanes. Neural basis of saccade target selection in frontal eye field during visual search. *Nature* 366:467–469, 1993.

Simons, D. J. Attentional capture and inattentional blindness. *Trends in Cognitive Sciences* 4:147–155, 2000.

Simons, D. J., and C. F. Chabris. Gorillas in our midst: Sustained inattentional blindness for dynamic events. *Perception* 28:1059–1074, 1999.

Spitzer, H., R. Desimone, and J. Moran. Increased attention enhances both behavioral and neuronal performance. *Science* 240:338–340, 1988.

Stuss, D. T., G. G. Gallup, and M. P. Alexander. The frontal lobes are necessary for "theory of mind." *Brain* 124:279–286, 2001.

Taylor, J. G. Paying attention to consciousness. *Trends in Cognitive Sciences* 6:206–210, 2002.

Thompson, E. and F. J. Varela. Radical embodiment: Neural dynamics and consciousness. *Trends in Cognitive Sciences* 5:418–425, 2001.

Treisman, A. Features and objects in visual processing. *Scientific American* 254(11):114–124, 1986.

Treisman, A., and S. Gormican. Feature analysis in early vision. *Psychological Review* 95:15–30, 1988.

Brain Development and Plasticity

Alex had a congenital condition known as Sterge-Weber syndrome affecting his left hemisphere. Vargha-Khadem and colleagues report that by age 8 he had failed to develop speech, and his comprehension of single words and simple commands was equivalent to an average 3-year-old's. At 8½ years, his left hemisphere was removed to alleviate his poorly controlled seizure condition, allowing discontinuation of anticonvulsant medication by the time he was 9. At that time, Alex unexpectedly began to acquire speech and language. By age 15, he had the expressive and receptive language capacities of a 10-year-old, which is remarkable given that he had no expressive language at all when he was 9.

Although Alex still has severe cognitive difficulties compared with average children his age, he appears to have suffered little disadvantage from his protracted period of mutism and limited language comprehension. Thus, in contrast with the widely held view that early childhood is a particularly critical period for the acquisition of speech and language, including phonology, grammar, prosody, and semantics, Alex's case suggests that it is possible to develop clearly articulated, well structured, and appropriate language for the first time as late as age 9 and with the right hemisphere alone. Alex thus provides an unusually good example of brain plasticity during development.

Alex's case raises the question of why the brain in early life appears to be so flexible in compensating for injury. A parallel question is whether one kind of environment is more likely than others to stimulate plastic changes in the damaged or indeed even the normal brain. To answer such questions, we need to examine the normal development of the brain and how it influences behavior.

Approaches to Studying Development

Behavioral changes resulting from neural function can be examined in three ways. The first approach is to look at nervous system maturation and correlate it with the development of specific behaviors. For example, we can link the development of certain brain structures to the development of, say, grasping or crawling in infants. As the brain structures develop, their functions emerge and are manifested in behaviors that we can observe. Thus, structures that develop quickly exhibit their functions sooner than structures that develop more slowly; and, because the human brain continues to develop well into adolescence, it is not surprising that some behavioral abilities do not emerge until that time. For example, the frontal lobes continue to develop well into adolescence, reaching maturity when a child is about 16 to 18 years of age. Accordingly, certain behaviors controlled by the frontal lobes are slow to develop.

The second approach, the converse of the first, is to look at a growing child's behavior and then make inferences about neural maturation. For example, as language emerges in the young child, we expect to find corresponding changes in the neural structures that control language. In fact, such changes are what we do find. At birth, children do not speak, and even extensive speech training would not enable them to do so. The neural structures that enable people to speak are not yet mature enough. As language emerges, we can conclude that the speech-related structures in the brain are undergoing the necessary maturation. The same reasoning can be applied to frontal-lobe development. As frontal-lobe structures mature in adolescence, we look for related changes in behavior, but we can also do the reverse: because we observe new abilities emerging in the teenage years, we infer that they must be controlled by late-maturing neural structures.

The third approach to studying the relation between brain and behavioral development is to identify and study factors that influence both. From this perspective, the mere emergence of a certain brain structure is not enough; we must also know the experiences that shape how the structure functions and that therefore lead to the production of certain kinds of behaviors. Some of the experiences that influence brain function are related to the effects of hormones, injuries, and abnormal genes. Logically, if behavior is influenced by one of these experiences, then structures in the brain that are changed by that experience are responsible for the behavioral outcomes. For example, we might study how an abnormal secretion of a hormone affects both a certain brain structure and a certain behavior. We can then infer that, because the observed behavioral abnormality results from the abnormal functioning of the brain structure, that structure must normally play some role in controlling the behavior. In the following sections, we will consider some of the findings obtained by using these different approaches to studying brain development and plasticity.

The Development of the Human Brain

At the time that an egg is fertilized by a sperm, a human embryo consists of just a single cell. But this cell soon begins to divide; and, by the 14th day, the embryo consists of several sheets of cells with a raised area in the middle and looks something like a fried egg. The raised area is the primitive body. By 3 weeks after conception, it possesses a primitive brain, which is essentially a sheet of cells at one end of the embryo. This sheet of cells rolls up to form a

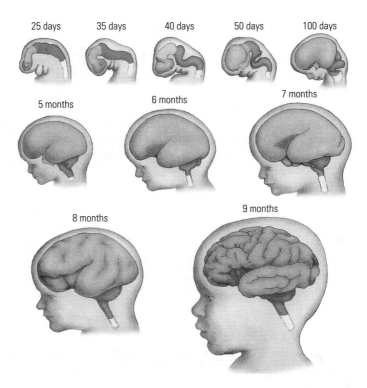

Figure 23.1 Embryonic and fetal stages of development of the human brain. Gray, forebrain; light blue, midbrain; blue, hindbrain. (After W. M. Cowan. Copyright © 1979 by Scientific American, Inc. All rights reserved.)

structure called the **neural tube,** much as a flat sheet of paper can be curled to make a cylinder.

The body and the nervous system change rapidly in the next 3 weeks of development. By 7 weeks (49 days), the embryo begins to resemble a miniature person, and, as Figure 23.1 shows, by about 100 days after conception, the brain looks distinctly human; however, it does not begin to form gyri and sulci until about 7 months. By the end of the 9th month, the brain has the gross appearance of the adult human organ, even though its cellular structure is different.

The results of research into the development of the child's brain have identified a series of changes that take place in a relatively fixed sequence, as summarized in Table 23.1. This program of development has two extraordinary features. First, subcomponents of the nervous system are formed from cells whose destination and function are largely predetermined before they migrate from the ventricular wall where they originate. Second, development is marked by an initial abundance of cells, branches, and connections, with an important part of subsequent maturation consisting of cell death or pruning back of the initial surfeit.

Deficits in the genetic program, intrauterine trauma, the influence of toxic agents, or other factors may lead to peculiarities or errors in development that contribute to obvious and severe deformities, such as those listed in Table 23.2. Less-pronounced deficits may lead to such problems as learning disabilities or may appear only as subtle changes in behavior.

Table 23.1 Stages of brain development

1. Cell birth (neurogenesis; gliogenesis)
2. Cell migration
3. Cell differentiation
4. Cell maturation (dendrite and axon growth)
5. Synaptogenesis (formation of synapses)
6. Cell death and synaptic pruning
7. Myelogenesis (formation of myelin)

Table 23.2 Types of abnormal development

Type	Symptom
Anencephaly	Absence of cerebral hemispheres, diencephalon, and midbrain
Holoprosencephaly	Cortex forms as a single undifferentiated hemisphere
Lissencephaly	Brain fails to form sulci and gyri and corresponds to a 12-week embryo
Micropolygyria	Gyri are more numerous, smaller, and more poorly developed than normal
Macrogyria	Gyri are broader and less numerous than normal
Microencephaly	Development of the brain is rudimentary and the person has low-grade intelligence
Porencephaly	Symmetrical cavities in the cortex, where cortex and white matter should be
Heterotopia	Displaced islands of gray matter appear in the ventricular walls or white matter, caused by aborted cell migration
Agenesis of the corpus callosum	Complete or partial absence of the corpus callosum
Cerebellar agenesis	Parts of the cerebellum, basal ganglia, or spinal cord are absent or malformed

Generating Neurons

The neural tube is the nursery for the brain. The cells lining it are known as **neural stem cells,** a stem cell being a cell with an extensive capacity for self-renewal. When a stem cell divides, it produces two stem cells, of which one dies and the other lives to divide again. This process is repeated over and over throughout a person's lifetime. In an adult, the neural stem cells line the ventricles, forming what is called the **ventricular zone.**

If this were all that stem cells did throughout a human life span, they would seem like an odd kind of cell to possess. But stem cells have another function: they give rise to so-called **progenitor** (precursor) **cells.** These progenitor cells also can divide, but, as shown in Figure 23.1, they eventually produce nondividing cells known as **neuroblasts** and **glioblasts,** which mature into neurons and glia. Neural stem cells, then, are the cells that give rise to all the many specialized cells of the brain and spinal cord. Stem cells continue to produce neurons and glia not just into early adulthood, but even in an aging brain, at least in the olfactory bulb and hippocampus. The fact that neurogenesis can continue into adulthood and even into senescence is important because it means that, when injury or disease causes neurons to die in an adult, perhaps the brain could be induced to replace those neurons. Unfortunately, we do not yet know how to instruct stem cells to carry out this replacement process. Consequently, injury to central nervous system tissue usually remains permanent.

A contentious question concerns what the new neurons might be doing in adult brains (see Gould et al.). The production of new neurons continuously throughout the life span suggests that perhaps old neurons are dying. They are. In fact, given the balance of cell generation and death in the olfactory bulb and hippocampus, we might speculate that the addition of new neurons and consequently their novel contribution to neural circuits could play a role in the formation of new memories, whereas the death of neurons and the subsequent loss of neural circuits could be related to the loss of old memories. The survival of new neurons in the hippocampus does appear to be related to experience: animals that learn tasks requiring activation of the hippocampus retain more of the newly formed neurons than do animals trained on tasks that do not require hippocampal circuitry. This question is far from settled, however, and is bound to remain controversial for some time (see Rakic for a provocative review).

Cell Migration and Differentiation

The production of neuroblasts destined to form the cerebral cortex is largely complete by the middle of gestation (4½ months), whereas the migration of cells to various regions continues for a number of months, even postnatally, with some regions not completing migration until about 8 months after birth. During the last 4½ months of gestation, the brain is especially delicate and is extremely vulnerable to injury or trauma, including asphyxia. Apparently, the brain can more easily cope with injury during neuron generation than it can during cell migration and differentiation. One reason may be that, after general neurogenesis has stopped, it does not naturally start again. If neurogenesis is still progressing, however, the brain may be able to replace its own injured cells or perhaps allocate existing healthy cells differently.

Cell migration begins shortly after the first neurons are generated, but it continues for weeks after neurogenesis is complete. At the completion of general neurogenesis, cell differentiation begins, the process in which neuroblasts become specific types of neurons. Cell differentiation is essentially complete at birth, although neuron maturation, which includes the growth of dendrites, axons, and synapses, continues for years and, in some parts of the brain, may continue into adulthood.

As seen throughout this book, the cortex is organized into various areas that differ from one another in their cellular makeup. How are different areas created in the course of development? Pasko Rakic and his colleagues argue that the ventricular zone contains a primitive map of the cortex that predisposes cells born in a certain ventricular region to migrate to a certain cortical location. For example, one region of the ventricular zone may produce cells destined to migrate to the visual cortex, whereas another region produces cells destined to migrate to the frontal lobes.

But how do the cells know where these different parts of the cortex are located? The answer is that they travel along "roads" made of cells known as **radial glial cells**, each of which has a fiber extending from the ventricular zone to the surface of the cortex, as illustrated in Figure 23.2. The cells from a given region of the ventricular zone need only follow the glial road and they will end up in the right location. The advantage of this system is that, as the brain grows, the glial fibers stretch, but they still go to the same place. Figure 23.2 also shows a cell that is migrating perpendicularly to the radial glial fibers. Although most cortical neurons follow the radial glial fibers, a small number of them appear to migrate by following some type of chemical signal. We do not yet know why some neurons function in this different way.

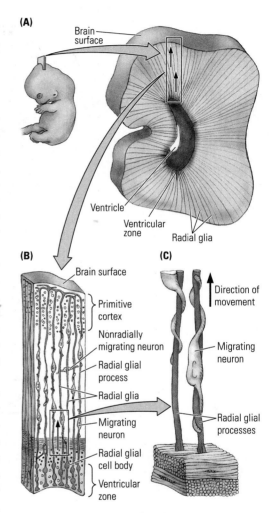

Figure 23.2 Development of cortical maps. (A) The map for the cortex is hypothesized to be represented in the ventricular zone. (B) Radial glial fibers extend from the ventricular zone to the cortical surface. (C) Neurons migrate along the radial glial fibers, which take them from the protomap in the ventricular zone to the corresponding region in the cortex. (After P. Rakic, *Science* 183:425, 1974.)

A curious feature of neuronal migration in the cerebral cortex is that the layers develop from the inside out, like layers being added to a ball. The neurons of layer VI, the innermost layer, migrate to their locations first, followed by those destined for layer V, and so on. In this way, successive waves of neurons pass earlier-arriving neurons to assume progressively more exterior positions in the cortex. The formation of the cortex is a bit like building the ground floor of a house first, then the second floor, and so on, until you reach the roof. The materials needed to build higher floors must pass through lower floors to get to their destinations.

Migration can stop prematurely, leaving a group of cells that belong in an outer layer scattered instead among inner layers of cells. Caviness and Sidman have made a major study of disturbed cell migration in the cerebellar cortex of a genetically mutant mouse called the reeler mouse. In this animal, the first cells to be generated lie near the surface and those generated last lie deepest, creating a cortical organization that is inverted compared with that of a normal mouse. Despite their aberrant position, the cells receive and send out appropriate connections, but the mice exhibit an abnormal, reeling movement. Failed or incomplete cell migration in humans also has been described, although the consequences differ from those in the reeler mouse, the most common effect in humans being disorders such as dyslexia or epilepsy.

Neural Maturation

After neurons have migrated to their final destinations and differentiated into specific neuron types, they must begin the process of growing dendrites to provide the surface area for synapses with other cells. They must also extend their axons to appropriate targets to initiate the formation of other synapses. These processes are part of neural maturation.

Two events take place in the development of a dendrite: (1) dendritic *arborization*, or branching, and (2) the growth of dendritic spines. As illustrated in Figure 23.3, dendrites begin as simple, individual processes protruding from the cell body. Later, they develop increasingly complex extensions that look much like the branches of trees visible in winter. This event is arborization. The dendritic branches then begin to form spines, on which most dendritic synapses take place.

Although dendritic development begins prenatally in humans, it continues for a long time after birth (Figure 23.3). In contrast with the development of axons, which grow at the rate of a millimeter per day, dendritic growth proceeds at a

Figure 23.3 Postnatal differentiation of the human cerebral cortex around Broca's area. The neurons first display simple dendritic fields. These fields become progressively more complex until a child reaches about 2 years of age. (After E. Lenneberg, *Biological Foundations of Language.* New York: Wiley, 1967, pp. 160–161.)

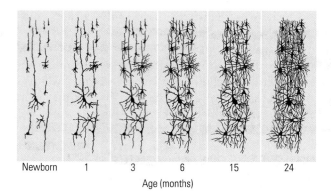

Newborn   1   3   6   15   24

Age (months)

relatively slow rate, measurable in micrometers per day. The disparity between the developmental rates of axons and dendrites is important, allowing the faster-growing axon to contact its target cell before the dendrites of that cell are completely formed and enabling the axon to play a role in dendritic differentiation.

A major enigma in developmental neurobiology is the mechanism that initiates and guides axonal growth. Axons have specific targets that they must reach if the neuron is to survive and become functional. Some axons seem to grow by being pulled from their cell bodies by a structure that is growing away from the region, such as a muscle growing away from the spinal cord early in development. Other axons traverse enormous distances and cope with such obstacles as being moved to another location, having their cell bodies rotated, or having their targets moved. Some axons follow an electrical or chemical gradient or a particular physical substrate. Some send out many branches or shoots and, when one of them reaches an appropriate target, the others follow. Several such mechanisms possibly operate simultaneously or sequentially.

The formation of appropriate neural pathways can be disrupted in a number of ways. An axon may fail to reach its target if its way is blocked, as can happen after scarring from head trauma in the early months of life. The development of axons can also be disrupted by anoxia, the ingestion of toxic materials, malnutrition, or some other disturbance. Several reports of anomalous fiber systems in mutant strains of mice suggest that abnormalities can also have a genetic basis. There have been mouse strains in which the corpus callosum is of abnormal size or is absent and mouse strains in which the fiber pathways in the hippocampal system are abnormal. In a number of albino animal species and possibly also in human albinos, the ipsilateral optic pathway is reduced in size and area of distribution.

Axonal development can also be disrupted if the axonal system's target is damaged, in which case the system may degenerate or may connect with an inappropriate target. Should the latter occur, the behavior supported by the invaded area may be affected, too. In a well-documented study of abnormal fiber growth, Schneider showed that, if the optic tectum in a hamster is removed on one side at birth, the fibers that should normally project to it project instead to the opposite side. This aberrant pathway is functional, but in a curious way. If a visual stimulus is presented to the eye contralateral to the damaged tectum, the hamster turns in the direction opposite that of the stimulus. The message has traveled from the eye to the tectum that would ordinarily receive input from the opposite side of the world. The abnormalities of posture and movement seen in children with certain kinds of athetosis (slow involuntary movement) and dystonia (imbalances in muscle tone) may arise because fiber systems meant to support posture and movement have connected to the wrong target.

To some extent, axons appear to be capable of overcoming obstacles to reach their targets. For example, if the spinal cord is partly sectioned, pyramidal tract axons that should pass through the damaged part of the cord may cross over to the undamaged side of the cord and then complete their journey to the appropriate target by recrossing the cord. Axons may also substitute for other axons. If the pyramidal cells of one hemisphere of the cortex are destroyed early in life, the axons of pyramidal cells from the other hemisphere will occupy the targets of the missing cells. There are many ways that a developing brain can adjust its growth to achieve functional connections if its normal development is hindered.

Synapse Formation and Pruning

The number of synapses in the human cerebral cortex is staggering, on the order of 10^{14}. Our genetic program could not possibly produce this huge number of connections by assigning each synapse a specific location. It is more likely that only the general outlines of neural connections in the brain are predetermined. The vast array of specific synaptic contacts are then guided into place by a variety of cues and signals.

Bourgeois outlined five distinct phases of synapse formation in the cerebral cortex of primates, as illustrated in Figure 23.4A for the macaque. The first two phases take place in early embryonic life and are characterized by the generation of low-density synapses represented by the areas of shading in the vertical bars below the graph. The synapses formed in phases 1 and 2 differ in their origin, but both groups are thought to be generated independently of experience.

In phase 3, the number of synapses grows rapidly. The rate in the macaque peaks at about 40,000 synapses per second. This phase begins before birth and continues until nearly 2 years of age in humans. Phase 4 is characterized by an initial plateau in synapse number followed by a rapid elimination of synapses that continues through puberty. The rate of loss may be maximal during puberty, although it is not shown in Figure 23.4. The reduction in synapses is dramatic; they may fall to 50% of the number present at age 2. And, just as synapses can be formed very rapidly during development, they may be lost at a rate of as many as 100,000 per second in adolescence. It should not surprise us that teenagers are so moody when their brains are undergoing such rapid changes in organization.

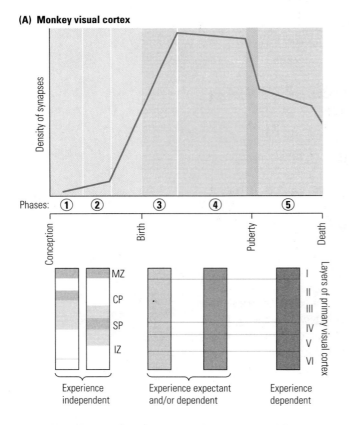

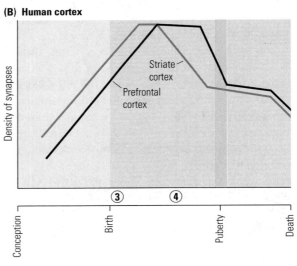

Figure 23.4 Phases of synapse formation and pruning. (A) Five different phases of synaptogenesis are identified between conception and death. The shading in the vertical bars indicates the areas of synapse formation during each phase. (B) Changes in the relative density of synapses in the visual cortex (blue line) and prefrontal cortex (black line) as a function of days after conception. (After Bourgeois, 2001.)

In phases 3 and 4, synapses are formed both by experience-expectant and by experience-dependent mechanisms. *Experience expectant* means that the synaptic development depends on the presence of certain sensory experiences for the organization of cortical circuits. For example, in the visual cortex, the synapses depend on exposure to features such as line orientation, color, and movement. The general pattern of these synapses is presumed to be common to all members of a species—provided that the individual members receive the appropriate experience. *Experience dependent* refers to the generation of synapses that are unique to an individual organism, because they are produced in response to experiences that are unique and personal. For example, in the visual system, these synapses can correspond to the learning of specific visual information such as the features of a particular face.

Phase 5 is characterized by a plateau in synapse number through middle age, followed by a slow, steady decline in the density of synapses with advancing age and a final rapid drop during senescence before death. All phase 5 synapses are experience dependent.

As Figure 23.4B illustrates, synapse loss is not the same all over the cortex, and synapse loss in primary sensory areas such as area V1 likely precedes synapse loss in the prefrontal cortex. One perplexing puzzle concerns the static, even slightly declining number of synapses in adulthood. After all, we continue to learn throughout adulthood, and presumably the formation of memories requires the formation of new synapses; so why don't we see an increase in synapse number corresponding to the formation of neural circuits underlying new memories? The only simple conclusion is that experience modifies existing circuits, and the generation of new synapses is somehow balanced by the loss of old ones. But we are still left with the problem of how we maintain so many memories for so long.

Glial Development

The birth of glial cells (both astrocytes and oligodendrocytes) begins after most neurons are born and continues throughout life. Although axons can function before they are encased by myelin, normal adult function is attained only after myelination is complete. Consequently, myelination is useful as a rough index of cerebral maturation.

In the early 1920s, Paul Flechsig noticed that myelination of the human cortex begins just after birth and continues until nearly 18 years of age. He also noticed that some cortical regions are myelinated by 3 to 4 years of age, whereas others show virtually no myelination at that time. Figure 23.5 shows one of Flechsig's maps of the brain, with areas shaded according to the age at which myelination takes place. Flechsig hypothesized that the areas maturing earliest control relatively simple movements or sensory analyses, whereas the late-myelinating areas control the highest mental functions. Investigators currently use MRI analyses to look at myelin development. In the next decade, interest in such approaches to correlating cognitive and anatomic development will likely increase.

The light-colored zones are very late to myelinate.

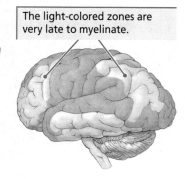

Figure 23.5 Progress of myelination in the human cortex. The fact that the light-colored zones are very late to myelinate led Flechsig to propose that they are qualitatively different in function from those that mature earlier.

Imaging Studies of Brain Development

Until recently, the use of functional imaging techniques in developmental studies has been limited, owing largely to the reliance of these techniques on the use of harmful radiation and the potential vulnerability of the developing brain to such exposure. In the past decade, however, MRI and fMRI techniques, which do not expose the subject to radiation, have been adapted for use with children and thus have the ability to revolutionize the study of human brain development. Few studies published to date, although two groups (Casey and colleagues; Rapoport and colleagues) have begun to publish intriguing data.

In one study, Casey and coworkers recorded cortical activity while children and adults performed a task of response inhibition that is presumed to entail the prefrontal cortex. The area of prefrontal activation was nearly four times as large in the children as it was in the adults, suggesting that, with age, cortical areas may become more specific in their participation in particular tasks. Another interpretation could be that the task was more difficult for the children, and thus to perform the task required more activation in the child's brain than in the adult's brain.

MRI and fMRI have been used in another way as well. Rapoport and his colleagues have been making repeated MRI scans of large numbers of children for nearly a decade, thus documenting the volumetric changes exhibited by their developing brains. Some of the children have had specific behavioral problems, and the researchers were also able to correlate the brain development of these children with the emergence of their behavioral anomalies. For example, they have documented the development of brain abnormalities in children with attention deficit hyperactivity disorder (ADHD) and childhood onset schizophrenia.

Attention deficit hyperactivity disorder is characterized by a slightly smaller (by 4%) total brain volume (both white and gray matter), abnormalities of the basal ganglia, and a striking (15%) decrease in the volume of a restricted region of the posterior cerebellum. These structural abnormalities do not progress with age, however. In contrast, patients with childhood-onset schizophrenia have smaller brain volume because of a 10% decrease in cortical gray volume. Moreover, they exhibit a progressive loss of regional gray volume, particularly in frontal and temporal regions, in adolescence. This loss of gray matter correlates with the emergence of more-severe psychiatric symptoms. In sum, although research has just begun to use functional imaging in developmental studies, MRI and fMRI promise to transform our current understanding of both normal and abnormal brain development.

The Development of Problem-Solving Ability

It seems reasonable to assume that, as a particular brain area matures, a person will exhibit behaviors corresponding to the maturation of that brain structure. The strongest advocate of this view has been Eric Lenneberg, who, in 1967, published a seminal book titled *Biological Foundations of Language*. A principal theme of the book is that children's acquisition of language is tied to the development of critical language areas in the cerebral cortex. This idea immediately stimulated debate about the merits of correlating brain and behavioral development. Today, the relation between brain development and behavior is widely accepted, although the influence of experience and learning on behavior is still considered critical. Psychologists believe that behaviors cannot emerge until the neural machinery for them has developed; however, when the machinery is in place, related behaviors develop quickly and are shaped significantly by experience. We use the development of problem solving as an example.

The first person to try to identify stages of cognitive development was Swiss psychologist Jean Piaget. He realized that the behavior of children could be used to make inferences about their understanding of the world. For example, a baby who lifts a cloth to retrieve a hidden toy is showing an understanding that objects continue to exist even when out of sight, a behavior that is said to correspond to the concept of *object permanence*. An absence of understanding also can be seen in children's behavior, as illustrated by a very young child's difficulty in grasping the principle of *conservation of liquid volume*, which is not displayed until about age 7. In a typical example, a child might watch a colored fluid being poured from a short fat beaker into a tall cylindrical one. Because the second beaker is taller, young children do not understand that the amount of liquid remains constant despite the difference in appearance.

By studying children's performances on such tasks, Piaget concluded that cognitive development is a continuous process. Children's strategies for exploring the world and their understanding of it are constantly changing. These changes are not simply the result of acquiring specific pieces of knowledge. Rather, at certain points in development, fundamental changes take place in the organization of a child's apparatus for learning about the world, and with these changes come new understandings.

Piaget identified four major stages of cognitive development, which are summarized in Table 23.3. Stage 1 is the sensorimotor period, from birth to about 18 to 24 months of age. In this period, babies learn to distinguish between themselves and the external world, they come to realize that objects exist even when out of sight, and they gain some understanding of cause-and-effect relations. In stage 2, the preoperational period, roughly from ages 2

Table 23.3 Piaget's stages of cognitive development

Typical age range	Description of the stage	Developmental phenomena
Birth to 18–24 months	*Stage 1: Sensorimotor* Experiences the world through senses and actions (looking, touching, mouthing)	Object permanence Stranger anxiety
About 2–6 years	*Stage 2: Preoperational* Represents things with words and images but lacks logical reasoning	Pretend play Egocentrism Language development
About 7–11 years	*Stage 3: Concrete operational* Thinks logically about concrete events; grasps concrete analogies and performs arithmetic operations	Conservation Mathematical transformations
About 12+ years	*Stage 4: Formal operational* Reasons abstractly	Abstract logic Potential for mature moral reasoning

Source: After D.G. Myers, *Psychology,* 5th ed. (New York: Worth Publishers, 1998), p. 89.

to 6 years, children acquire the ability to form mental representations of things in their world and to represent those things in words and drawings. Stage 3 is the period of concrete operations, from about 7 to 11 years of age. Now children are able to mentally manipulate concrete ideas such as volumes of liquid and dimensions of objects. Finally, stage 4 is the period of formal operations, which is usually reached after age 11. The child is now able to reason in the abstract, not just in concrete terms.

If we take Piaget's stages as rough approximations of qualitative changes that take place in children's thinking as they grow older, we can ask what changes in the brain might produce them. One place to look for brain changes is in the relative rate of brain growth. After birth, the brain does not grow uniformly but instead tends to increase in mass during irregularly occurring periods commonly called **growth spurts.** In an analysis of brain-to-body weight ratios, Epstein found consistent spurts in brain growth from 3 to 10 months (accounting for an increase of 30% in brain weight by the age of 1½ years), as well as between ages 2 and 4, 6 and 8, 10 and 12, and 14 and 16+ years. Brain weight increased by about 5% to 10% in each of these 2-year periods. The brain growth takes place without a concurrent increase in the number of neurons; so it is most likely due to the growth of glial cells and synapses. Although synapses themselves would be unlikely to add much weight to the brain, the growth of synapses is accompanied by increased metabolic demands, which causes neurons to become larger, new blood vessels to form, and new astrocytes to be produced.

We would expect such an increase in the complexity of the cortex to generate more complex behaviors; so we might predict that there would be significant, perhaps qualitative changes in cognitive function during each of the growth spurts. The first four brain-growth spurts coincide nicely with the four main stages of cognitive development described by Piaget. This correspondence suggests that significant alterations in neural functioning accompany the onset of each of Piaget's stages. At the same time, differences in the rate of brain development or perhaps in the rate at which specific groups of neurons mature may account for individual differences in the age at which the various cognitive advances identified by Piaget emerge. Although Piaget did not identify a fifth stage of cognitive development in later adolescence, the presence of a growth spurt during that time implies that there may in fact be one.

A difficulty in linking brain-growth spurts to cognitive development is that growth spurts are superficial measures of changes taking place in the brain. We need to know what neural events are contributing to brain growth and just where they are taking place. A way to find out is to observe children's attempts to solve specific problems that are diagnostic of damage to discrete brain regions in adults. If children perform a particular task poorly, then whatever brain region is engaged in that task in adults must not yet be mature in children. Similarly, if children can perform one task but not another, the tasks apparently require different brain structures and these structures mature at different rates.

Overman and Bachevalier used this logic to study the development of forebrain structures participating in learning and memory in young children and monkeys. Figure 23.6 shows the test situations that they presented to their subjects. The first task was simply to learn to displace an object to obtain a food reward. After the subjects learned this task, they were trained on two more tasks that are believed to measure the functioning of the temporal lobes and the basal ganglia, respectively.

Procedures

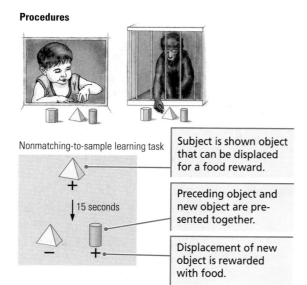

Nonmatching-to-sample learning task

Subject is shown object that can be displaced for a food reward.

Preceding object and new object are presented together.

Displacement of new object is rewarded with food.

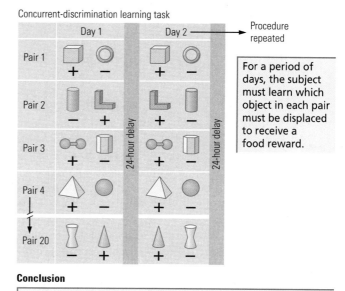

Concurrent-discrimination learning task

For a period of days, the subject must learn which object in each pair must be displaced to receive a food reward.

Conclusion

Both human and monkey infants learn the concurrent-discrimination task at a younger age than the nonmatching-to-sample task, implying that the neural structures underlying the former task mature sooner than those underlying the latter.

In the first of these two additional tasks, the subjects were shown an object that they could displace to receive a food reward. After a brief (15-s) delay, two objects were presented: the original object and a novel object. The subjects now had to displace the novel object to obtain the food reward. This *nonmatching-to-sample* task is thought to measure object recognition, which is a function of the temporal lobes. The subject can find the food only by recognizing the original object and *not* displacing it.

In the second of the two additional tasks, the subjects were presented with a pair of objects and had to learn that one object in that pair was always associated with a food reward, whereas the other object was never rewarded. The researchers made the task more difficult by sequentially giving the subjects 20 different object pairs. Each day the subjects were given one trial per pair. This task, called *concurrent discrimination*, is thought to measure trial-and-error learning of specific object information, which is a function of the basal ganglia.

Adults easily perform both tasks but describe the concurrent task as more difficult because it requires remembering far more information than does the nonmatching-to-sample task. The key question developmentally is whether there is a difference in the age at which children (or monkeys) can solve these two tasks. It turns out that children can solve the concurrent task by about 12 months of age, but not until about 18 months of age can they solve what most adults believe to be the easier task. These results imply that the basal ganglia, which are the critical site for the concurrent task, mature more quickly than the temporal lobe, which is the critical region for the nonmatching-to-sample task.

Figure 23.6 An experiment designed to show the order in which forebrain structures participating in learning and memory mature. In these versions of the Wisconsin General Test Apparatus, the subject's task is to displace an object to reveal a food reward. The nonmatching-to-sample task requires maturation of the temporal lobe; the other task, a concurrent-discrimination task, requires maturation of the basal ganglia. (After W. H. Overman, J. Bachevalier, M. Turner, and A. Peuster, 1992.)

Environmental Effects on Brain Development

The environment in which development takes place can greatly influence behavior. Singh and Zingg report that children raised by wolves behave like wolves and are difficult to socialize. But Skeels reports that children removed from substandard orphanages and placed in a mental institution developed normal intelligence by adulthood, whereas those who were not removed remained retarded. The children in the mental institution apparently received attention from the patients; such attention was not given to those who remained in the orphanages. The results of recent studies of the fate of the wave of Romanian orphans adopted into families after the fall of the Romanian communist regime show that, although the children were severely developmentally impaired, many of them, but not all, showed spectacular recovery (see Chapter 24; see also papers by Ames, by Gunnar, and by Rutter).

The key factor in predicting recovery was age at adoption. In a study by Ames, the Romanian orphans that were adopted before 4 months of age had average IQs, whereas those adopted at an average age of 19 months had lower IQs and brain imaging showed them to have smaller-than-normal brains. Thus the brain appears to be able to recover from a brief period of deprivation, but periods of deprivation longer than 6 months appear to produce significant abnormalities in brain development that cannot be completely repaired. Recall Genie, whom we met in Chapter 12. Genie, who experienced severe social and experiential deprivation as well as chronic malnutrition, showed severe retardation in cognitive, especially language, development.

How do the conditions of a person's early environment affect nervous system development? The brain is pliable, like plastic, as suggested by the term **brain plasticity,** which neuroscientists use to describe the constantly accruing changes in the structure of the brain that accompany experience: at least at the microscopic level, the structure can be molded into different forms. Brains exposed to different environmental experiences—not only external ones but also events taking place within a person's body—are molded in different ways. Internal events include the effects of hormones, injury, and abnormal genes. Early in life, the developing brain is especially responsive to these internal factors, which in turn alter the way that the brain reacts to external experiences. In this section, we explore a whole range of environmental influences—both external and internal—on brain development. We start with the question of exactly how experience alters brain structure.

Environmental Influences on Brain Organization

The simplest way of measuring the effects of environment on the nervous system is by documenting differences in brain size. The results of studies of animal brain size have shown that certain cortical areas are as much as 10% to 20% smaller in domestic animals than in animals of the same species and strain raised in the wild. These differences are apparently related to factors encountered early in life, because animals born in the wild and later domesticated have brains the same size as those of animals raised in the wild. The part of the brain that seems to be most affected by a domestic upbringing is the occipital cortex, which is reduced in size by as much as 35% in some animals. This reduction may be related to smaller eye and retina size.

Exposure to a complex versus impoverished environment increases brain size, most noticeably of the neocortex, with the greatest increase being in the occipital neocortex. Related to increased size are increases in the density of glial cells, the length of dendrites, the density of spines (the location of most excitatory synapses), and the size of synapses. Curiously, although many have assumed that the young brain will show greater changes in response to experience than an older brain will, there is evidence that the young and adult brain may actually respond differently to the same experience. One of us (Kolb) and his colleagues have shown, for example, that, whereas housing animals in complex environments with changing objects to play with increases the length of dendrites of pyramidal cells in the cortexes of both young and older animals, spine density *decreases* in young animals and *increases* in the older animals (Figure 23.7). Both young and old animals show similar functional benefits, however, performing better than their impoverished counterparts on a number of tests of skilled motor behavior as well as on tests of learning and memory.

We can speculate that the qualitative differences in experience-dependent synaptic changes at these different times in life must have some functional implications. One possibility is that an animal whose brain is stimulated in development may more easily change its brain in response to experience later in life. An example might be children who are exposed to different languages in development and who then learn additional languages later in life more quickly than do peers whose early experience was unilingual.

The fact that very early experience can alter brain structure and behavior in adulthood leads to the question whether prenatal experiences—those occurring during phase 1, 2, or early phase 3 synaptogenesis—also might alter brain development. The results of several studies show that newborns can identify the maternal voice that they heard in utero; so it seems possible that prenatal experience *can* influence brain development. Gibb and her colleagues manipulated prenatal experience in rats either by placing the pregnant dams in complex environments or by giving them daily tactile stimulation. This experience resulted in larger brains in the offspring, a result that could be due either to increased numbers of neurons or glia or both or to increased numbers of synapses. The larger-brained offspring then showed superior performance on both cognitive and motor tasks, just like animals raised in complex environments postnatally.

Experience and Neural Connectivity

Disturbances of the optics of the eye early in life (for example, cataracts and astigmatism) cause long-lasting impairments of vision even after the optical defects are corrected. Adults who have had lifelong cataracts removed to allow light to finally reach the retina have difficulty learning the identity of objects by looking at them. These visual impairments, called **amblyopia**—deficits of vision without obvious impairment of the eye—are thought to be caused by changes in the central nervous system. The results of behavioral studies have shown that amblyopia can be produced in animals; the process has been analyzed extensively in studies of cats and monkeys.

Hubel and Wiesel approached the problem by asking how the functional organization of the visual system of kittens might be altered by elimination of the visual input to one eye. The researchers were aware that inputs from each eye go to adjacent, alternating columns, called ocular dominance columns, in area V1 (in each column the alternate eye is dominant, as shown in Figure 23.8). This alternating arrangement of inputs from the two eyes presumably plays an important role in merging the images from each eye.

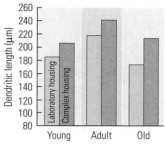

(A) Dendritic length

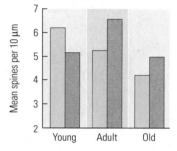

(B) Spine density

Figure 23.7 A comparison of the effects of 3 months of complex housing, beginning at different ages, on dendritic length (A) and spine density (B) in rats. Although all three age groups show similar increases in dendritic length, there is a qualitative difference in spine density: juveniles show a drop in spine density, whereas adults show an increase in density. (After Kolb, Gibb, and Gorny, 2003.)

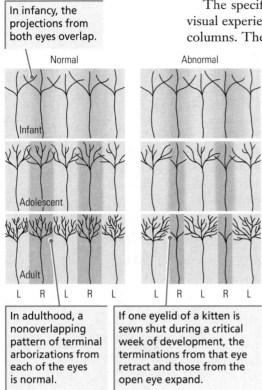

In infancy, the projections from both eyes overlap.

Normal   Abnormal

Infant

Adolescent

Adult

L R L R L   L R L R L

In adulthood, a nonoverlapping pattern of terminal arborizations from each of the eyes is normal.

If one eyelid of a kitten is sewn shut during a critical week of development, the terminations from that eye retract and those from the open eye expand.

Figure 23.8 Critical periods in development. In the postnatal development of ocular dominance columns in the cat, axons enter the cortex, where they grow large terminal arborizations. L, left eye; R, right eye.

The specific question asked by Hubel and Wiesel was whether restricting visual experience to one eye might alter the structure of the ocular dominance columns. They discovered that, if one eye is sewn shut for a time in early life, the eye appears to be essentially blind for a period of weeks after opening, although its function does improve somewhat with time. The results of cell-recording studies show that either stimulation in the deprived eye cannot activate cells in the cortex or, in those few cases in which it can, the cells are highly abnormal. The results also show that, the earlier the deprivation takes place, the shorter the length of deprivation required to produce effects and the more severe the effects.

These results confirm that environmental deprivation can retard development and that early deprivation is the most damaging. Findings from later studies by other researchers have shown that one reason for the abnormal functioning of the deprived eye is that the connections from that eye have been weakened by the lack of visual experience, as illustrated in Figure 23.8. Apparently, visual experience is necessary to validate (that is, to reinforce) functional connections in the brain. In the absence of activity, the synapses are lost. This principle of "use it or lose it" can be applied to the nervous system in general, although the effect of experience is not always as severe as that seen in the example of the deprived eye.

Can the visual system be changed by manipulation that is less drastic than complete sensory deprivation? Hirsch and Spinelli fitted kittens with lenses that brought a set of horizontal stripes into focus on one retina and a set of vertical stripes into focus on the other. After later removal of the lenses, they found that the eye that had seen horizontal stripes during the exposure period responded only to a stimulus oriented close to the horizontal, and the eye that had seen vertical stripes responded only to a stimulus oriented close to the vertical. These findings have been confirmed for kittens raised in an environment of stripes only or spots only or in one organized to be devoid of movement. In fact, work by Blakemore and Mitchell indicates that 1 hour of exposure on day 28 after birth is sufficient to bias a cortical unit to respond to a particular pattern.

Overall, this work suggests that the visual system is genetically programmed to make normal connections and normal responses, but it can lose much of this capacity if it is not exercised during the early months of life. When part of the system is deprived, some degree of capacity is lost. Moreover, the deprived part of the system is inhibited by the remaining functional areas, and so the defect is reinforced. Even so, removal of the inhibition can permit some degree of recovery. Finally, if the environment is so arranged that the system is exposed to stimuli of one type, the cells in the system develop a preference for those stimuli.

Plasticity of Representational Zones in the Developing Brain

The tendency for cortical organization to be influenced by experience can be seen not only in the brain subjected to restricted experience but also in the brain subjected to enriched experience. Consider, for example, the effect of practicing some skill, such as playing a musical instrument, for hours a day for many years in childhood. Elbert and colleagues studied stringed-instrument players as a model for how experience can alter the organization of the sensorimotor maps of the hand. The second through fifth digits of the left hand are continuously engaged in fingering the strings, whereas the thumb, which grasps the neck of the instrument, is less active. The right hand moves the bow, which also requires much less finger movement.

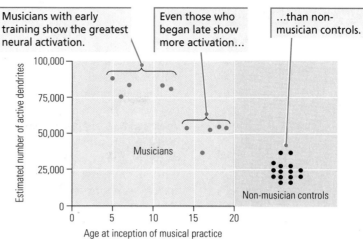

Musicians with early training show the greatest neural activation.

Even those who began late show more activation...

...than non-musician controls.

Figure 23.9 Effects of enrichment. This graph plots the age at which subjects began practicing on stringed instruments against the amount of neural activation that they showed in response to tactile stimulation of the fifth digit of the left hand. (After Elbert et al., 2001.)

Neuroimaging showed not only that representation of the fingers of the left hand occupied more space than did the thumb or the fingers of the right hand, but also that the amount of change was proportional to the age at which musical training began, as illustrated in Figure 23.9. The representational zone of the left-hand fingers was largest in subjects who had begun regular practice before age 13—that is, before puberty. But, even if training began later in life, the representation of the relevant digits still exceeded the representation seen in subjects without musical training. A later study found similar effects on the representation of piano-music frequencies in the auditory cortexes of piano players.

A characteristic of human speech perception is that adults are skilled at distinguishing speech sounds in their native language but often have difficulties making sound distinctions in other languages. For example, the difficulty that Japanese or Korean speakers have in making the distinction between "r" and "l" in English is well known. Werker and Tees compared the ability of infants to discriminate speech sounds taken from widely disparate languages, such as English, Hindi (from India), and Salish (a Native American language). Their results showed that young infants can discriminate between the speech sounds of different languages without previous experience, but their ability to do so declines over the first year of life.

In studies by others, event-related potentials have been used to examine this phenomenon, with the use of what is known as mismatch negativity (MMN). If a repeated speech sound, such as "l, l, l, . . ." is played to an infant and embedded in the middle is a different sound, such as "r," the ERP will show a negative deflection—a mismatch negativity—if the difference in the sound is detected by the auditory system, as illustrated in Figure 23.10. In studies by various groups (see reviews by Elbert et al. and by Kuhl), MMNs were detected for language-specific speech sounds in infants at 6 months of age, but 12-month-old infants no longer made many of the distinctions. These results imply

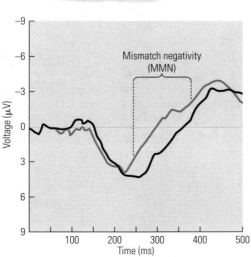

Figure 23.10 An infant in an ERP recording cap. On the left is an example of the mismatch negativity signal. One wave comes from a standard signal from one sound, and the other comes from a deviant signal. The MMN is the difference between the waves. If the brain detects that two signals are different, there will be a mismatch, but, if the brain does not discriminate between the signals, there will be no difference. (After Kuhl, 1999.)

that the auditory representation of sounds is altered by each infant's linguistically biased environment.

Knowledge of how experience reorganizes the cortex can be used to treat cognitive deficits in children. For example, some preschool children with no apparent psychiatric or neurological impairment have great difficulty learning language, in which case their condition is referred to as a *specific language impairment*. One theory suggests that such impairments may be caused by an abnormal representation of speech sounds in the auditory system. If so, then specific training ought to produce improvement. It does (see Chapter 24 for more details.)

Brain Injury and Plasticity

By 1868, Cotard—who knew that damage to the left frontal cortex could abolish speech—had observed children with left frontal lesions who nevertheless developed normal adult language functions. This observation was the origin of the idea that brain injury has milder and more short-lived effects if it is sustained in childhood. Then, in the 1930s, Margaret Kennard compared the effects of unilateral motor-cortex lesions on infant and adult monkeys and found that the impairments in the infant monkeys seemed milder than those in the adults.

The generalization that sparing of function follows infant lesions became known as the *Kennard principle*. For a time the idea received wide acceptance, but neuroscientists began to realize that earlier may not always be better and can sometimes be worse. Donald Hebb, for example, showed that children who incur prefrontal injuries in infancy or early childhood have very poor outcomes. The ultimate effect of a brain injury depends on the behavior affected, the extent and location of the damage, and the precise age at which the injury occurs. With respect to cognitive function in humans, it is clear that speech survives early brain damage, but some elements of syntax and some nonlanguage functions may not survive, and general intellectual ability may decline.

The Effects of Age

Age is an important determinant of the effects of early lesions. Three critical age divisions have been identified: before 1 year of age, between 1 and 5 years, and older than 5 years. Lesions incurred before the age of 1 tend to produce disproportionately greater impairments than do those incurred later. Lesions incurred between 1 and 5 years of age are followed by some reorganization of brain function, including rescuing of language functions. Lesions incurred later than age 5 permit little or no sparing of function. For example, in a comparison of the effects of lesions incurred before and after age 1, Riva and Cazzaniga found that earlier lesions reduced IQ more than did later lesions. An implication of the age-related effects of injury on language development is that the brain's manner of acquiring languages differs at different times in development. Further evidence for this hypothesis is described in the Snapshot on page 627.

Distinct Cortical Areas for Second Languages

Children generally find it easier than adults to acquire more than one language and to speak each one with a native accent. Kim and colleagues, asking whether the age at language acquisition might influence the way in which the language is represented in the brain, used fMRI to determine the spatial relation between native and second languages in the cortex.

Bilingual subjects were instructed to describe in their minds, without speaking aloud, the events that had taken place during a certain period of the preceding day (for example, the morning). On different scans, they used different languages. Some subjects had learned a second language as children, whereas others learned a second language as adults. As would be expected in a sentence-generation task, both Broca's and Wernicke's areas were activated. There was a difference between childhood and adult acquisition of the second language in the activation in Broca's area but not in Wernicke's area.

As shown in the illustration, activation in Broca's area overlapped virtually completely for the childhood-acquisition subjects, but there was an anatomical separation of the two languages in the adulthood-acquisition group. This spatial separation of the two languages in Broca's area suggests that language acquisition may alter the functional organization of Broca's area. Thus, as human infants learn languages, Broca's area undergoes modification according to the nature of the languages being learned. When modified, the region appears to resist subsequent modification, which necessitates the utilization of adjacent cortical areas for the second language learned as an adult.

(K. H. S. Kim, N. R. Relkin, K. Young-Min Lee, and J. Hirsch. Distinct cortical areas associated with native and second languages. *Nature* 388:171–174, 1997.)

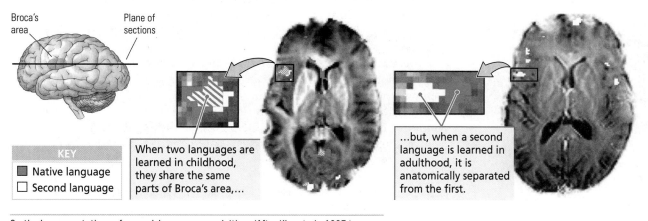

Broca's area

Plane of sections

KEY
- ■ Native language
- □ Second language

When two languages are learned in childhood, they share the same parts of Broca's area,...

...but, when a second language is learned in adulthood, it is anatomically separated from the first.

Cortical representations of second-language acquisition. (After Kim et al., 1997.)

The Effect of Brain Damage on Language

Language deficits resulting from cerebral injury in young children are usually short lived, and an injured child usually seems to nearly fully recover. This is the case even though language disorders subsequent to right-hemisphere damage are more frequent in children than in adults, the incidence being about 8%

Table 23.4 Summary of studies of aphasia resulting from unilateral lesions

Study	Age range of subjects	Number of cases	Percentage with right-hemisphere lesions
Childhood Lesions			
Guttman, 1942	2–14	15	7
Alajouanine and Lhermitte, 1965	6–15	32	0
McCarthy, 1963	After language acquisition	114	4
Basser, 1962	Before 5	20	35
Hécaen, 1976	3½–15	17	11
Total	2–15	198	8
Adult Lesions			
Russell and Espir, 1961	—	205	3
Hécaen, 1976	—	232	0.43
Total	—	437	1.6

Source: After Krashen, 1973, and Hécaen, 1976.

in children and 2% in adults (Table 23.4). The Basser study, which describes 35% of young children with right-hemisphere lesions as suffering from aphasia, is thought to be inaccurate, because many of the subjects may have had bilateral lesions.

Alajouanine and Lhermitte studied 32 cases of childhood aphasia, finding writing deficits in all and reading deficits in about half the children, in addition to their difficulty in speaking. Six months after injury, the researchers observed total recovery of spontaneous language in about a third of these subjects, and significant improvement was noted in all the others. When reexamined 1 year or more after injury, 24 of the 32 children had normal or almost normal language, although 14 still had some degree of dysgraphia; 22 of the children were eventually able to return to school.

Similarly, Hécaen followed postinjury recovery from aphasia and related symptoms in 15 children with left-hemisphere unilateral lesions, as summarized in Table 23.5. Besides disorders of speech, nearly all the children had dis-

Table 23.5 Frequency of different symptoms in 15 cases caused by left-hemisphere lesions in childhood

Symptom	Number of cases	Percentage	Evolution of symptoms
Mutism	9	60	From 5 days to 30 months
Articulatory disorders	12	80	Persistent in 4 cases
Auditory verbal comprehension disorders	6	40	Persistent in 1 case
Naming disorders	7	46	Persistent in 3 cases
Paraphasia	1	7	Disappearance
Reading disorders	9	60	Persistent in 3 cases
Writing disorders	13	86	Persistent in 7 cases
Facial apraxia	2	—	Transient
Acalculia	11	—	(Not reported)

Source: After Hécaen, 1976.

orders of writing and calculation. Of these 15 children, 5 showed complete recovery within 6 weeks to 2 years. Most of the remaining children showed considerable improvement; in many cases, the only remaining deficit was a mild difficulty in writing, a finding similar to that of Alajouanine and Lhermitte.

Woods and Teuber studied about 50 patients with prenatal or early postnatal brain damage to either the left or the right hemisphere. Using normal siblings as controls, they came to the following conclusions:

1. Language survives after early left-hemisphere injury.

2. Much of this survival seems attributable to appropriation of a potential language zone in the right hemisphere.

3. This shift of language location has a price: specifically, some kinds of visuospatial orientation are impaired.

4. Early lesions of the right hemisphere produce deficits similar to those produced by such lesions in adulthood.

In other words, if a child sustains a lesion of the left hemisphere that produces right hemiplegia, language functions are recovered to a remarkably greater degree than after a comparable lesion in an adult, presumably because some or all of the language abilities move to the right hemisphere. Presumably, language crowds into the right hemisphere at the expense of visuospatial functions. On the other hand, a lesion of the right hemisphere, which produces left hemiplegia, does not impair language ability.

A summary of this pattern of results, obtained from verbal and performance scores of the Wechsler Adult Intelligence Scale, is shown in Figure 23.11. Left-hemisphere lesions depress both verbal and performance scores. Right-hemisphere lesions depress only performance scores. In a subsequent study, Woods examined the effects of lesions incurred earlier than age 1. The main finding was that right-hemisphere lesions impaired both verbal and performance IQ. Riva and Cazzaniga confirmed these results and note that lesions incurred before 1 year of age produce more-severe overall impairments than do those incurred after age 1.

Not all aspects of language function are spared after lesions incurred between the ages of 1 and 5. Woods found that, on a speech-shadowing task, which requires a person to repeat passages of speech as they are read, adult right- and left-hemisphere lesions produce equal impairments. Virtually identical impairments are observed subsequent to early-childhood lesions, even though speech is significantly spared by the early left-hemisphere lesions.

The Reorganization of Language

The evidence that language is spared after early brain damage because the control of language is transferred to the opposite hemisphere raises three questions. What actual language functions are transferred? What type of brain damage causes them to be transferred? What is the age range during which transfer can take place? The first two questions have been addressed experimentally by Rasmussen and Milner, but the third has not yet been answered completely.

Using carotid sodium amobarbital injection and dichotic listening tests (see Chapter 11), Rasmussen and Milner localized language in a large number of patients who had suffered left-hemisphere injury early in life and had

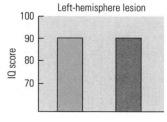

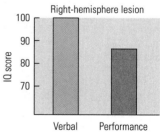

Figure 23.11 IQ scores on subtests of the Wechsler Adult Intelligence Scale. In infancy, these adults suffered a lesion of the left or the right hemisphere, as determined by the occurrence of hemiparesis. Note that both verbal and performance scores are depressed by left-hemisphere lesions, whereas only performance scores are depressed by right-hemisphere lesions (average IQ is 100). The results suggest that, if language moves to the right hemisphere, its usual functions are sacrificed to accommodate the shift. The results also suggest that right-hemisphere functions do not shift sufficiently to interfere with language. (After Teuber, 1975.)

Table 23.6 Changes in hemispheric speech representation after early brain damage

| | | PERCENTAGE WITH SPEECH REPRESENTATION | | |
	Handedness	Left	Bilateral	Right
No early damage	Right	96	0	4
	Left or mixed	70	15	15
Early damage	Right	81	7	12
	Left or mixed	28	19	53

Source: After Rasmussen and Milner, 1975, pp. 248–249.

Figure 23.12 Relations between early brain damage and hemisphere changes in language organization. (A) Anterior and posterior lesions (dark gray) after which language remained in the left hemisphere. The blue shading in the top figure shows the location of language zones. (B) An anterior–posterior lesion that causes all language to move to the right hemisphere. (C) An anterior lesion that causes the anterior speech zone to shift to the right hemisphere. (D) A posterior lesion that causes the posterior speech zone to shift to the right hemisphere. (After Rasmussen and Milner, 1977.)

(A) No shift in language

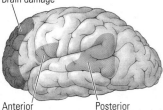

Brain damage

Anterior language area (Broca's area) Posterior language area (Wernicke's area)

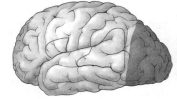

(B) Complete shift of language

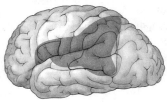

(C) Shift of anterior speech functions

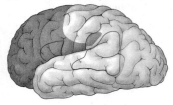

(D) Shift of posterior speech functions

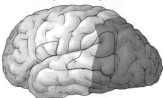

returned to the hospital years later because of complications. They found that the patients assorted into three groups, as shown in Table 23.6. In the first group, speech was in the left hemisphere; in the second group, it was represented bilaterally; and, in the third group, it was in the right hemisphere. The patients who had speech in the left hemisphere were found to have damage that did not invade the anterior speech zone (Broca's area) or the posterior speech zone (Wernicke's area).

Examples of brain damage that did not produce a shift in language lateralization are shown in Figure 23.12A. Both exemplar lesions are large, yet the dichotic listening test showed a right-ear advantage (a sign that a person's speech is localized in the left hemisphere). In the sodium amobarbital tests, the patients were mute both on naming tasks (for example, identifying objects as an experimenter holds each up and asks "What is this?") and on repetition tasks (for example, "Name the days of the week in order.") after left-hemisphere injection. The blue shading in the upper part of Figure 23.12A shows the locations of the anterior and posterior speech zones.

An example of a lesion that produced a complete shift of language to the right hemisphere is illustrated in Figure 23.12B. This patient showed a left-ear advantage on the dichotic listening test and was mute for naming and repetition after right-hemisphere sodium amobarbital injection. Note that the lesion invaded both the anterior and the posterior speech zones, which was typical for patients who developed right-hemisphere speech after early left-hemisphere lesions.

Examples of the lesions in patients who had bilateral speech are shown in Figure 23.12C and D. The patient whose lesion is shown in Figure 23.12C incurred a large left-frontal-lobe lesion at 6 years of age that included the anterior language zone. At age

18, the patient was right-handed and had a right-ear advantage for digits and a left-ear advantage for melodies. On the sodium amobarbital tests, a left-hemisphere injection produced a disturbance in series repetition (counting, reciting the days of the week forward or backward, or oral spelling), but naming was less disturbed. A right-hemisphere injection produced a disturbance in both series repetition and naming.

Because it is assumed that the right-ear advantage for digits is an indication of left-hemisphere speech and that the absence of series repetition after left-hemisphere sodium amobarbital injection is an indication of intact speech in the left posterior speech zone, it can be concluded that the lesion did not cause a complete shift of speech from the posterior left speech zone. Because naming was disturbed after a right-hemisphere injection of sodium amobarbital, the left-hemisphere speech functions of the anterior zone are assumed to have shifted to the right hemisphere.

The patient whose lesion is shown in Figure 23.12D had a large posterior lesion that was incurred at 2½ years of age. Testing at age 16 showed that she was left-handed and had a left-ear advantage for both digits and melodies. Sodium amobarbital tests showed that naming was disturbed by both left- and right-hemisphere injections, whereas series repetition was performed competently after the left but not the right hemisphere was injected. In this case, the large posterior lesion incurred early in life seems to have caused speech functions of the posterior zone to shift to the right, whereas the anterior speech zone still retained some speech function.

The results described so far, particularly those of Rasmussen and Milner, show that speech has a strong affinity for the left hemisphere and will not abandon it unless an entire center is destroyed, and even then it might shift only partly to the other hemisphere. This affinity is thought to be based on the special innate anatomical organization of the left hemisphere. In examining their patients with early left-hemisphere lesions, Rasmussen and Milner also noted that childhood injuries to the left hemisphere after 5 years of age rarely caused a change in speech patterns, from which they inferred that recovery after about age 6 is not due to transfer to the other hemisphere but to intrahemispheric reorganization, possibly with intact surrounding zones acquiring some control over speech. Further evidence comes from Woods and Teuber's study. Recall from Figure 23.11 that left- but not right-hemisphere lesions cause a decline in both verbal and performance IQ scores, a result that argues against the idea that the right hemisphere has equal potential for language.

Although the evidence supports the left-for-speech hypothesis, there is reason to believe that functional validation is still required; that is, practice with language is necessary to establish left-hemisphere preeminence. Woods reported that, if left-hemisphere lesions occur before the first birthday, both verbal and performance IQ are severely depressed. If left-hemisphere lesions occur after 1 year of age, neither verbal nor performance IQ is affected. Right-hemisphere lesions at any age lower only performance IQ. It seems likely that the effects of lesions before age 1 might be due to a disruption of verbal functions that had not yet been sufficiently validated or that perhaps were disrupted by the invasion of performance functions. We must note, however, that this suggestion is speculative, that IQ score is at best an imprecise measure of language, and that a more systematic study of these patients—one using linguistic tests—is called for.

The Absence of Language after Bilateral Lesions

Bilateral cortical lesions in children are rare. Nevertheless, a number of reports suggest that, when bilateral lesions do occur, the plasticity required for the acquisition or reacquisition of language subsequent to injury is not present. Vargha-Khadem and coworkers report such a case.

A. C. was born after a normal pregnancy, but the delivery was difficult and forceps were used. The next day, A. C. began to have epileptic seizures. He was given anticonvulsants and, after a couple weeks of treatment, was seizure free. When he began to walk, he had left hemiparesis that affected the left limbs. His language development was very delayed and did not advance beyond primitive speech consisting of a few two-word utterances. His rare attempts to make sentences could not be understood. Although he could follow instructions, suggesting a relatively preserved capacity for comprehension, he did poorly on the token test, which evaluates the ability to follow a number of sequentially presented instructions, and very poorly on most other tests of language ability. At the same time, his performance on the nonverbal parts of IQ tests suggested that he had at least normal intelligence.

A CT scan performed at age 6½ indicated that he had a lesion largely restricted to Broca's area in the left hemisphere and another lesion restricted to the middle part of the sensorimotor cortex on the right side. Thus, even though A. C. had a spared Broca's area on the right and spared posterior speech zones on both the left and the right, he failed to acquire language as he might be expected to have done had he received only a unilateral left-hemisphere lesion. The reason that A. C. failed to show sufficient plasticity to develop more-normal language is not known, but this case history strongly suggests that, for some reason, plasticity depends on at least one intact hemisphere.

Experimental Approaches to Studying Plasticity after Early Brain Injury

The mechanisms mediating the recovery of function after injury sustained in infancy can be studied experimentally by systematically varying the age at injury and the location of injury in laboratory animals. We consider first the behavioral effects of injury and then look at what the anatomical correlates might be.

The Effects of Early Brain Lesions on Behaviors Later in Life

We have already considered the relation between age at injury and functional outcome in human infants. One might expect to see a similar phenomenon in laboratory animals, and in fact, as mentioned earlier, Kennard showed that motor-cortex lesions in infant monkeys allow better functional outcome than do similar lesions in adulthood. This view was presumed to be correct until the 1970s, when contradictory findings began to emerge from laboratory studies. As in all fields of science, reality has proved much more complex than our original descriptions of it, and we now know that many factors influence the general dependability of the Kennard principle. These factors include the brain region injured, the precise developmental stage at injury, the age at assessment, the type of behavior measured, and exposure to gonadal hormones (for a review, see Kolb).

In the past 20 years, we (the authors) have removed virtually every region of the rat cortical mantle at varying ages, ranging from embryonic day 18 to adolescence (see Kolb and Gibb for a review). Our general finding is that recovery varies with the precise embryological age at which the removal took place (Table 23.7). If the cortex is injured bilaterally during neurogenesis, there is virtually complete functional recovery.

The ability of the brain to compensate for injury during the time of neurogenesis is remarkable. Sam Hicks demonstrated as much 40 years ago when he found that, if the developing brain was treated with X-radiation at the early stages of cortical neurogenesis (which effectively killed all of the cerebrum), the brain compensated by regenerating a substantial proportion of the lost cells. In short, the cerebrum was destroyed by the treatment, and the stem cells responded by overproducing new cortical neurons that rebuilt about 50% of what was lost. In contrast, however, if a rat's cortex is injured in the first few days after birth, which is a time of neural migration and cell differentiation, the effect is functionally devastating: the animal shows much more severe effects of injury than would be expected even if it had been aged at the time of injury.

This poor outcome is not a function of lesion size or of damage to particular cortical areas. Rather, something about the cortex during this developmental time makes it especially vulnerable. For example, damage at this time may disturb the process of synaptogenesis or may even alter stem-cell activity in some way. When this phase of development is over, however, the brain is especially able to compensate for injury. Rats incurring cortical injuries at 7 to 12 days of age show behavioral capacities in adulthood that exceed those of animals receiving similar lesions at any other time. In fact, on some behavioral tests, these animals show recovery that is virtually complete. Importantly, far more extensive recovery is seen in the ability to perform cognitive tasks, such as learning how to solve various spatial-navigation problems, than is seen in the performance of tests of species-typical behaviors such as nest building.

This difference is likely due to the relative ease of reorganizing cortical circuitry compared with connections in other parts of the brain. We must emphasize, too, that the extent of functional recovery also depends on the specific locations of cortical lesions. The most-extensive recovery is associated with lesions of the frontal areas, and the least-extensive recovery is associated with damage to the primary sensory areas. For example, rats with occipital lesions show no recovery of visually guided behaviors. In contrast, they do show an enhanced somatosensory capacity that is not observed in rats receiving similar lesions on day 4. This finding is consistent with the general idea that there is something special about the recovery from injuries received at about 10 days of age.

Table 23.7 Summary of the effects of frontal cortical injury at different ages in the rat

Age at injury	Behavioral result	Anatomical result
E18	Functional recovery	Gross anomalies in structure Brain size close to normal
P1–P5	Dismal functional outcome	Small brain, dendritic atrophy Abnormal connectivity
P7–P12	Functional recovery	Neurogenesis; astrogenesis Increased synapse number
P120	Partial return of function	Dendritic atrophy, then regrowth

Abbreviations: E18, embryonic day 18; P followed by number, postnatal day.
Source: After Kolb et al., 2001.

These findings are further complicated when we increase the lesion size to remove all of the cortex (decortication) or all of the cortex of one hemisphere (hemidecortication). Totally decorticated rats show no functional recovery regardless of the age at injury, suggesting that the plastic changes underlying recovery from focal cortical lesions are likely taking place in the remaining cortex and not in subcortical structures. Hemidecortication produces a quite different outcome: the earlier the removal, the greater the extent of functional recovery, although there are no data on the effects of prenatal hemidecortications.

Thus, rats with hemidecortication on the day of birth have a far better functional outcome than do animals with later hemidecortications. One explanation for this result is that the lesion does not interfere with migration and differentiation in the intact hemisphere, which is presumably where the recovery is being mediated. We have tested this hypothesis by making very small lesions in the intact hemispheres of hemidecorticated neonates and have seen that recovery is substantially compromised. This connection between unilateral injury and increased likelihood of recovery is reminiscent of the effects of cortical injuries on language in human infants. Recall the studies in which infants with bilateral injuries were shown to be at risk for permanent aphasia.

The only other laboratory species normally used for studies of early brain injury are cats and rhesus monkeys. In comparing these species with rats, one must take care to remember that rats, cats, and monkeys are not born at the same developmental age. Rats are born in a more immature state than are cats, and cats at birth are much more immature than monkeys. Both rats and kittens are helpless at birth, and some time elapses before their eyes are mature enough even to open, let alone to process visual information. In contrast, monkeys are relatively mature at birth; they are developmentally older than human newborns as well. Figure 23.13 compares the approximate relative ages at birth of the different species. Villablanca emphasizes the age-at-birth confound and concludes that, like newborn rats, kittens with prenatal injuries are functionally better off than kittens receiving lesions slightly later, during the time of synaptogenesis, as would be predicted from Figure 23.13.

The importance of the site of injury in the developing brain is shown nicely in studies by Bachevalier and Mishkin, who have varied the size and location of temporal lobe injury in infant monkeys. In their first studies, they examined the effects of neonatal visual-system lesions on the performance of the delayed nonmatching-to-sample task illustrated in Figure 23.6. In adult monkeys, lesions of the medial temporal cortex and of more laterally placed neocortex (area TE) severely impair performance on the task, especially when the intervals between presentations of the objects are increased. The researchers removed these areas in monkeys that were from 1 to 2 weeks old and then tested them on the nonmatching task, beginning at 10 months of age. The monkeys with medial temporal lesions were nearly as impaired as monkeys that received lesions as adults, whereas the monkeys that received

Figure 23.13 Developmental age. This diagram compares the developmental ages of the brains of the rat and human at various times after conception. Note that the day of birth is not related to the stage of neural development.

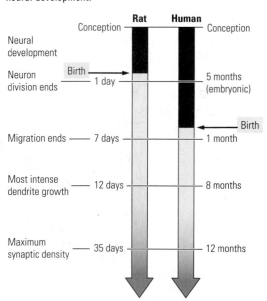

TE lesions in infancy performed much better than monkeys that received lesions as adults.

These results suggest that functional recovery may be better after some brain injuries than others. In further studies, Bachevalier and Mishkin examined the social behavior of monkeys that received lesions of the medial temporal area as infants. As they develop, these monkeys shun social contact with other monkeys and display stereotypical behavior, excessive self-directed behavior, and a lack of facial expression. In short, these animals appear autistic. If the temporal lobe lesions are restricted to the amygdala and entorhinal cortex, the autistic behavior is present but is not as severe. If the lesion is restricted to the parahippocampal gyrus and hippocampus, the autistic behavior emerges only in adulthood. Monkeys that receive damage to TE neonatally are not autistic but are hyperactive. Their behavior is annoying to adult monkeys, who do not like to interact with them.

The Effects of Early Brain Lesions on Brain Structure Later in Life

In principle, there are three ways in which the brain could show plastic changes that might support recovery after early injury:

1. *Changes in the organization of the remaining, intact circuits in the brain.* The general idea is that the brain could reorganize in some way "to do more with less." It is unlikely that a complexly integrated structure such as the cerebral cortex could undergo a wholesale reorganization of cortical connectivity; instead, recovery from cortical injury would be most likely to result from a change in the intrinsic organization of local cortical circuits in regions directly or indirectly disrupted by the injury. Although it might be possible to produce significant reorganization of cortical connectivity in the young brain, the overwhelming evidence in experimental animals is that such reorganization is rare and, as we shall see, just as likely to be associated with abnormal functioning as with recovery.

2. *Generation of new circuitry.* We have already seen that cerebral reorganization can be stimulated by experience in the normal brain, and it seems reasonable to expect that experience or some other treatment, such as a drug, could influence reparative processes in the remaining brain or could enhance the production of new circuitry. Once again, it seems most likely that the induced neuronal changes would take place in the intrinsic organization of the cortex rather than throughout the brain as a whole.

3. *Generation of neurons and glia to replace at least some lost neurons.* As stated earlier, the stem cells that give rise to the neurons and glia of the brain remain active in the subventricular zone throughout life. Thus perhaps neurogenesis could be stimulated after injury, especially in development, and these new neurons could replace those lost to injury or disease (see, for example, Weiss et al.).

Evidence exists that supports all three of these possible explanations for cerebral plasticity after early injury. We begin with the most obvious changes in the early-injured brain and then consider more-subtle changes.

Figure 23.14 Effects of neonatal lesions on brain weight and cell structure. (A) Brain weights of control rats and rats that received frontal lesions (top) as adults or at 1, 5, and 10 days of age. (B) Drawings of cortical pyramidal cells from the parietal cortex. Note the very low brain weights (A) and the poorly developed dendritic arbor on the cells (B) subsequent to the day-1 lesions. (After Kolb and Whishaw, 1989.)

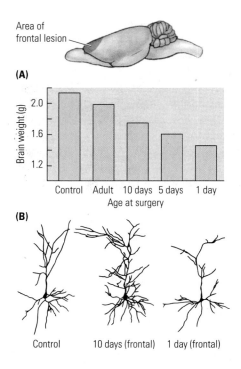

Area of frontal lesion

(A)

(B)

Control 10 days (frontal) 1 day (frontal)

Figure 23.15 Summary of the CT scan results from a subject who had a birth-related injury in the right posterior cortex. Note that in these horizontal sections the right hemisphere is smaller at every scan plane. (After Kolb and Whishaw, 1989.)

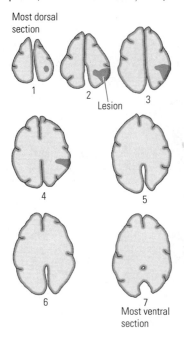

Most dorsal section

Lesion

Most ventral section

Brain Size

A dramatic consequence of brain damage in infancy is that it causes the brain to be smaller in adulthood. Furthermore, the earlier the lesion occurs, the smaller the brain's ultimate size. For example, as shown in Figure 23.14, the brains of rats with neonatal lesions were reduced in size by as much as 25%, whereas the brains of rats that were operated on as adults shrank by less than 12%. This size reduction, which in humans would be the equivalent of about 200 g, was due not to a proportionately larger lesion in the young brain but to shrinkage of the entire neocortex. No systematic analysis of this phenomenon has been made in monkeys or humans, but the same result is likely produced in humans. Figure 23.15 shows the results from a CT-scan of a 16 year-old woman who had suffered an injury to the right parietal cortex at birth. It is clear from the scan that her entire right hemisphere is smaller than the left.

Neuronal Morphology

To examine why lesions might cause the brain to shrink, one of us (Kolb) and his coworkers examined the structure of cells in the neocortex. With very early lesions, given to rats on their day of birth, the cells showed reduced complexity compared with adult cells. If the lesions were produced at 10 days of age, the cells had more-extensive dendritic fields than seen in controls; whereas, if the lesions were produced at 1 day of age, the cells had less-extensive dendritic fields (see Figure 23.14). The difference in dendritic fields leads to differences in the number of synapses: the more space for synapses, the more synapses there are.

In addition to differences in synapse number, there is a parallel difference in the number of astrocytes. Rats given lesions on day 10 have a markedly higher number of astrocytes than do controls, whereas rats given lesions on day 1 are no different from controls in that respect. The astrocyte difference may explain the increased synapse number, because one function of astrocytes is to produce **neurotrophic factors.** These factors are compounds that support growth and differentiation in developing neurons and may act to keep neurons alive in adulthood. One neurotrophic factor, basic fibroblast growth factor (bFGF), has been shown to be elevated after day-10 lesions but not after day-1 lesions. Furthermore, the administration of bFGF can attenuate the effects of day-1 lesions.

Cortical Connectivity

Contrary to what might be expected, the best functional outcome does not appear to be correlated with the most extensive rewiring of the cerebrum. In one series of studies, one of us (Kolb) and colleagues compared cortical–cortical, cortical–striatal, and certain subcortical–cortical connections after the production of frontal or parietal lesions on postnatal days 1 or 10. The general finding was that adult rats with day-1 lesions had abnormalities in all types of connections examined. For example, there were aberrant thalamic–cortical connections, such as projections from the medial geniculate (which should project to auditory cortex) to the visual cortex in the frontal-lesion animals.

These abnormal connections were probably not formed after the lesions, however, because results of the studies also showed that newborn animals had the same connections. Instead, these connections appear to be pruned off by day 7 or so in normal animals but not in the brain-injured rats. In contrast, rats with day-10 lesions had no obvious abnormalities in these connections. Hence, the day-1 animals had the worst functional outcomes, which were associated with the most-extensive abnormalities in connectivity, whereas the day-10 animals had the best functional outcomes, which were associated with no obvious abnormalities. It is reasonable to hypothesize that the abnormal connections were interfering with the normal functioning of the remaining brain, presumably owing to the fact that these connections are pathological and are normally eliminated in the course of development. After early cortical injury, the pruning of these connections appears to decrease or perhaps even stop.

Not all abnormal connections are harmful. It has been known for some time that both rats and cats with unilateral lesions of the motor cortex or complete hemidecortications show an expansion of corticospinal projections from the normal hemisphere to the ipsilateral side, and this expansion is correlated with improved function (see the Snapshot in Chapter 11 on page 275). These connections are particularly extensive in hemidecorticates and include anomalous projections from the intact hemisphere to the striatum on the injured side. Thus, abnormal connections are perhaps not always detrimental and may in fact be beneficial. In contrast with the abnormal connections seen in animals with early frontal lesions, the abnormalities in the corticospinal projections are not present in normal infants and must therefore indicate the growth of de novo connections.

Neurogenesis after Early Cortical Injury

The results of studies in adult animals have shown a small number of new neurons to be generated after cortical injury, but because of the small number they are unlikely to provide any functional benefit. Given that Hicks showed that impressive neurogenesis could be stimulated after prenatal cerebral injury, it seems reasonable to wonder if there is a way to restart neurogenesis after cerebral injury at other times during development.

Damage to the anterior midline telencephalon (olfactory bulb or anterior midline cortex) at about 10 days of age leads to the generation of significant numbers of new neurons, enough to fill the lesion cavities. The results of our studies have shown that these cells are functional and that they establish appropriate connections with the intact regions of the brain (although the tissue is not completely normal and the neurogenesis replaces only about 65% of the lost tissue). However, lesions earlier or later in life or lesions in other cortical areas do not stimulate neurogenesis; so there appears to be something special about the midline tissue at about 10 days of age. Nonetheless, the results do show that neurogenesis is possible after cortical injury at a time that cortical neurogenesis is normally complete. (For a review of this work, see Kolb, Gibb, and Gonzalez).

Although there are no reports of neurogenesis after early lesions in other species, it may occur in kittens with early frontal lesions. Villablanca and his group found that a kitten's striatum is unusually large after an early cortical lesion. These researchers suggest no explanation for this result, but one possibility is that the lesion stimulates the genesis of new striatal neurons.

Factors Influencing Plasticity after Early Cortical Injury

As already mentioned, the normal brain is affected by a wide variety of factors, ranging from general sensory experience to gonadal hormones and neurotrophic factors (for a review, see Kolb and Whishaw, 1998). It is reasonable to suppose that these factors will also influence the damaged brain. Although virtually all of the research to date has been done in rats, the evidence is compelling that a wide range of factors can facilitate functional recovery (Table 23.8).

Table 23.8 Summary of the effects of factors on plasticity after early cortical lesions

Treatment	Behavioral result	Anatomical result
Tactile stimulation	Recovery after P4 frontal, motor, or parietal lesions	Dendritic growth, bFGF increased, acetylcholine increased
Handling	No effect	Synaptic pruning
Prenatal tactile stimulation of dam	Recovery after P4 frontal lesions	Dendritic growth
Complex rearing from weaning	Recovery after P4 frontal or parietal lesions	Dendritic growth
Nicotine	Recovery after P3 frontal lesions	Acetylcholine increased Dendritic change?
Choline supplement	Enhanced recovery after P4 lesions	Increased dendritic growth
Hormone depletion	Blocks recovery after P7 frontal lesions	Blocks dendritic changes
Noradrenaline depletion	Blocks recovery after P7 frontal lesions	Blocks dendritic hypertrophy

Abbreviation: P followed by number, postnatal day.
Source: After Kolb and Gibb, 2001, and Kolb et al., 2001.

Perhaps one of the most potent treatments is tactile stimulation. A series of studies by Gibb and her colleagues have shown that stroking infant rats with a soft brush for 15 minutes, three times a day, for 10 days after a perinatal lesion of the frontal, parietal, or motor cortex can stimulate significant functional recovery in adulthood. The tactile stimulation promotes synaptogenesis in the remaining cortex, possibly because the treatment increases bFGF and acetylcholine levels in the cortex. Even more interesting is Gibb's finding that tactile stimulation of pregnant dams with a child's hairbrush for 15 minutes, three times a day, throughout the pregnancy not only can alter the synaptic organization of the as yet unborn progeny's brain in adulthood but can also facilitate recovery from cortical injury incurred in infancy. The mechanism of this behavioral effect is not yet known, although we can speculate that it may be related to the increased production of one or more neurotrophic factors.

Summary

The process of brain maturation in humans is long, lasting through ages 16 to 18 years. Neurons, the elementary components of the brain, are born, migrate, and, as their processes elaborate, establish connections with other neurons. Because the brain contains such a large number of cells and an even larger number of connections, the newborn brain possesses more neurons and connections than it needs and prunes them back to a stable adult level. The process of pruning is influenced by a variety of factors, especially sensory experience and gonadal hormones.

Behavioral and cognitive capacities follow parallel sequences of development, from the rudimentary to the complex. Stages of cognitive development identified by Piaget correlate with growth spurts in the brain. Similarly, neuropsychological measures of cognitive development correlate with changes in brain structure in the basal ganglia and cerebral cortex. Development does not take place without sensory input, however; experience has major effects on normal brain development. These effects can be seen not only in the morphology of the cerebral cortex and patterns of cortical connectivity but also in the representational maps.

Just as "normal" experiences shape brain development, abnormal experiences alter brain structure and behavior. Further, perturbations of the brain in the course of development can significantly alter brain development and result in severe behavioral abnormalities. The sensitivity of the brain to experience or injury varies with time, because there are periods in the course of development during which different brain regions are particularly sensitive to different events. Functional recovery after early injury may result from the modification of remaining circuits, the generation of new (abnormal) circuits, or the generation of neurons and glia. Various factors can influence recovery from early cortical injury, including experience, hormones, and neurotrophic factors.

References

Alajouanine, T., and F. Lhermitte. Acquired aphasia in children. *Brain* 88:653–662, 1965.

Ames, E. *The Development of Romanian Orphanage Children Adopted to Canada.* (Final report to the National Welfare Grants Program: Human Resources Development Canada). Burnaby, British Columbia: Simon Fraser University, 1997.

Basser, L. Hemiplegia of early onset and the faculty of speech with special reference to the effects of hemispherectomy. *Brain* 85:427–460, 1962.

Bachevalier, J. Neural bases of memory development: Insights from neuropsychological studies in primates. In C. A. Nelson and M. Luciana, Eds. *Handbook of Developmental Cognitive Neuroscience.* Cambridge, MA: MIT Press, 2001, pp. 365–380.

Bachevalier J., L. Malkova, and M. Mishkin. Effects of selective neonatal temporal lobe lesions on socioemotional behavior in infant rhesus monkeys (*Macaca mulatta*). *Behavioral Neuroscience* 115:545–559, 2001.

Bachevalier, J., and M. Mishkin. Effects of selective neonatal temporal lobe lesions on visual recognition memory in rhesus monkeys. *Journal of Neuroscience* 14:2128–2139, 1994.

Blakemore, C., and D. E. Mitchell. Environmental modification of the visual cortex and the neural basis of learning and memory. *Nature* 241:467–468, 1973.

Bourgeois, J.-P. Synaptogenesis in the neocortex of the newborn: The ultimate frontier for individuation? In C. A. Nelson and M. Luciana, Eds. *Handbook of Developmental Cognitive Neuroscience.* Cambridge, MA: MIT Press, 2001.

Casey, B. J., K. M. Thomas, and B. McCandliss. Applications of magnetic resonance imaging to the study of development. In C. A. Nelson and M. Luciana, Eds. *Handbook of Developmental Cognitive Neuroscience.* Cambridge, MA: MIT Press, 2001, pp. 137–147.

Caviness, V. S., Jr., and R. L. Sidman. Time of origin of corresponding cell classes in the cerebral cortex of normal and reeler mutant mice: An autoradiographic analysis. *Journal of Comparative Neurology* 148:141–152, 1973.

Crowley, J. C., and L. C. Katz. Ocular dominance development revisited. *Current Opinion in Neurobiology* 12:104–114, 2002.

Elbert, T., S. Heim, and B. Rockstroh. Neural plasticity and development. In C. A. Nelson and M. Luciana, Eds. *Handbook of Developmental Cognitive Neuroscience.* Cambridge, MA: MIT Press, 2001, pp. 191–204.

Epstein, H. T. Growth spurts during brain development: Implications for educational policy and practice. In J. S. Chard and A. F. Mirsky, Eds. *Education and the Brain.* Chicago: University of Chicago Press, 1978.

Flechsig, P. *Anatomie des menschlichen Gehirns und Ruckenmarks.* Leipzig: Georg Thieme, 1920.

Fuchs, E., and E. Gould. Mini-review—In vivo neurogenesis in the adult brain: Regulation and functional implications. *European Journal of Neuroscience* 12:2211–2214, 2000.

Gibb, R., C. R. Gonzalez, and B. Kolb. Prenatal enrichment leads to improved functional recovery following perinatal frontal cortex injury: Effects of maternal complex housing. *Society for Neuroscience Abstracts* 27:476.4, 2001.

Goldman, P. S. Functional development of the prefrontal cortex in early life and the problem of neuronal plasticity. *Experimental Neurology* 32:366–387, 1971.

Goldman, P. S., and T. W. Galkin. Prenatal removal of frontal association cortex in the fetal rhesus monkey: Anatomical and functional consequences in postnatal life. *Brain Research* 152:451–485, 1978.

Gould E., P. Tanapat, N. B. Hastings, and T. J. Shors. Neurogenesis in adulthood: A possible role in learning. *Trends in Cognitive Science* 3:186–192, 1999.

Gunnar, M. E. Effects of early deprivation: Findings from orphanage-reared infants and children. In C. A. Nelson and M. Luciana, Eds. *Developmental Cognitive Neuroscience.* Cambridge, MA: MIT Press, 2001, pp. 617–629.

Guttman, E. Aphasia in children. *Brain* 65:205–219, 1942.

Hécaen, H. Acquired aphasia in children and the ontogenesis of hemispheric functional specialization. *Brain and Language* 3:114–134, 1976.

Hicks, S. P., and C. J. D'Amato. Effects of ionizing radiation on developing brain and behavior. In *Studies on the Development of Behavior and the Nervous System.* New York: Academic Press, 1973, pp. 35–72.

Hirsch, H. V. B., and D. N. Spinelli. Modification of the distribution of receptive field orientation in cats by selective visual exposure during development. *Experimental Brain Research* 13:509–527, 1971.

Hubel, D. H., and T. N. Wiesel. Receptive fields of cells in striate cortex of very young, visually inexperienced kittens. *Journal of Neurophysiology* 26:994–1002, 1963.

Jacobsen, M. *Developmental Neurobiology*, 3d ed. New York, Plenum, 1991.

Kolb, B. *Brain Plasticity and Behavior.* Mahwah, NJ: Lawrence Erlbaum, 1995.

Kolb, B., and R. Gibb. Early brain injury, plasticity, and behavior. In C. A. Nelson and M. Luciana, Eds. *Developmental Cognitive Neuroscience.* Cambridge, MA: MIT Press, 2001, pp. 175–190.

Kolb, B., R. Gibb, and C. R. Gonzalez. Cortical injury and neural plasticity during brain development. In C. A. Shaw and J. C. McEachern, Eds. *Toward a Theory of Neuroplasticity.* Philadelphia: Taylor and Francis, 2001, pp. 223–243.

Kolb, B., R. Gibb, and G. Gorny. Experience-dependent changes in dendritic arbor and spine density in neocortex vary with age and sex. *Neurobiology of Learning and Memory* 79:1–10, 2003.

Kolb, B., and I. Q. Whishaw. Plasticity in the neocortex: Mechanisms underlying recovery from early brain damage. *Progress in Neurobiology* 32:235–276, 1989.

Kolb, B., and I. Q. Whishaw. Brain plasticity and behavior. *Annual Review of Psychology* 49:43–64, 1998.

Kornhuber, H. H., D. Bechinger, H. Jung, and E. Sauer. A quantitative relationship between the extent of localized cerebral lesions and the intellectual and behavioural deficiency in children. *European Archives of Psychiatry and Neurological Sciences* 235:129–133, 1985.

Krashen, S. D. Lateralization, language learning, and the critical period: Some new evidence. *Language Learning* 23:63–74, 1973.

Kuhl, P. K. The role of early experience in early language development: Linguistic experience alters the perception and production of speech. In N. A. Fox, L. A. Leavitt, and J. G. Warhol, Eds. *The Role of Early Experience in Infant Development*. Johnson & Johnson Consumer Companies, 1999, p. 120.

Kuhl, P. K., F. M. Tsao, H. M. Liu, Y. Zhang, and B. De Boer. Language/culture/mind/brain: Progress at the margins between disciplines. *Annals of the New York Academy of Sciences* 935:136–174, 2001.

McCarthy, G., 1963. Quoted in Krashen, S. D. Lateralization, language learning, and the critical period: Some new evidence. *Language Learning* 23:63–74, 1973.

Milner, B. Psychological aspects of focal epilepsy and its neurological management. *Advances in Neurology* 8:299–321, 1975.

Overman, W. H., and J. Bachevalier. Inferences about functional development of neural systems in children via the application of animal tests of cognition. In C. A. Nelson and M. Luciana, Eds. *Developmental Cognitive Neuroscience*. Cambridge, MA: MIT Press, 2001, pp. 109–124.

Piaget, J. *Biology and Knowledge*. Chicago: University of Chicago Press, 1971.

Price, B. H., K. R. Daffner, R. M. Stowe, and M. M. Mesulam. The compartmental learning disabilities of early frontal lobe damage. *Brain* 113:1383–1393, 1990.

Rakic, P. Neurogenesis in adult primate neocortex: An evaluation of the evidence. (Nature Reviews) *Neuroscience* 3:65–71, 2002.

Rasmussen, T., and B. Milner. Clinical and surgical studies of the cerebral speech areas in man. In K. J. Zulch, O. Creutzfeldt, and G. C. Galbraith, Eds. *Cerebral Localization*. Berlin and New York: Springer, 1975.

Rasmussen, T., and B. Milner. The role of early left-brain injury in determining lateralization of cerebral speech functions. *Annals of the New York Academy of Sciences* 299:355–369, 1977.

Rapoport J. L., F. X. Castellanos, N. Gogate, K. Janson, S. Kohler, and P. Nelson. Imaging normal and abnormal brain development: New perspectives for child psychiatry. *Australia and New Zealand Journal of Psychiatry* 35:272–281, 2001.

Riva, D., and L. Cazzaniga. Late effects of unilateral brain lesions sustained before and after age one. *Neuropsychologia* 24:423–428, 1986.

Russell, R., and M. Espir. *Traumatic Aphasia*. Oxford: Oxford University Press, 1961.

Rutter, M. Developmental catch-up, and deficit, following adoption after severe global early privation. *Journal of Child Psychology and Psychiatry* 39:465–476, 1998.

Schneider, G. E. Early lesions of superior colliculus: Factors affecting the formation of abnormal retinal projections. *Brain Behavior and Evolution* 8:73–109, 1973.

Singh, J. A. L., and R. M. Zingg. *Wolf Children and Feral Man*. New York: Harper, 1940.

Skeels, H. M. Adult status of children with contrasting early life experiences. *Monographs of the Society for Research in Child Development* 31:1–65, 1966.

Teuber, H.-L. Recovery of function after brain injury in man. In *Outcomes of Severe Damage to the Nervous System*, Ciba Foundation Symposium 34. Amsterdam: Elsevier-North Holland, 1975.

Vargha-Khadem, F., L. J. Carr, E. Brett, C. Adams, and M. Mishkin. Onset of speech after left hemispherectomy in a nine-year-old boy. *Brain* 120:159–182, 1997.

Vargha-Khadem, F., and G. V. Watters. Development of speech and language following bilateral frontal lesions. *Brain and Language* 25:167–183, 1985.

Villablanca, J. R., D. A. Hovda, G. F. Jackson, and C. Infante. Neurological and behavioral effects of a unilateral frontal cortical lesion in fetal kittens II: Visual system tests, and proposing a "critical period" for lesion effects. *Behavioral Brain Research* 57:79–92, 1993.

Weiss, S., B. A. Reynolds, A. L. Vescovi, C. Morshead, C. G. Craig, and D. van der Kooy. Is there a neural stem cell in the mammalian forebrain? *Trends in Neuroscience* 19:387–393, 1996.

Werker, J. F., and R. C. Tees. Developmental changes across childhood in the perception of non-native speech sounds. *Canadian Journal of Psychology* 37:278–286, 1983.

Werker, J. F., and A. Vouloumanos. Speech and language processing in infancy: A neurocognitive approach. In C. A. Nelson and M. Luciana, Eds. *Developmental Cognitive Neuroscience*. Cambridge, MA: MIT Press, 2001, pp. 269–280.

Woods, B. T. The restricted effects of right-hemisphere lesions after age one: Wechsler test data. *Neuropsychologia* 18:65–70, 1980.

Woods, B. T. Impaired speech shadowing after early lesions of either hemisphere. *Neuropsychologia* 25:519–525, 1987.

Woods, B. T., and H.-L. Teuber. Early onset of complementary specialization of cerebral hemispheres in man. *Transactions of the American Neurological Association* 98:113–117, 1973.

24

Developmental Disorders

Ms. P., a 19-year-old woman, was referred to us by a friend. She was working as a nurse's aide and had found her work so enjoyable that she was considering entering a nursing program. Because she had not completed high school and generally had a poor academic record, she came to us for guidance in deciding whether she could handle such a program. Ms. P. had particular difficulty with language skills, and her reading was so bad that she was unable to pass the written examination for a driver's license. In view of Ms. P.'s interest in furthering her nursing education, we decided to test her reading abilities and to administer a complete neuropsychological battery. The results showed an overall IQ of 85 on the Wechsler Adult Intelligence Scale, but there was a 32-point difference between her verbal IQ of 74 and her performance (nonverbal) IQ of 106. Specific tests of left-hemisphere function confirmed this discrepancy: although her verbal memory, verbal fluency, spelling, reading, and arithmetic scores were extremely low, her spatial skills were good, as were her nonverbal memory and her performance on tests such as the Wisconsin Card-Sorting Test and the Semmes Body-Placing Test. In short, her language skills were those of a 6-year-old, although she had attended school for 11 years, but her other abilities were normal for a person of her age.

In view of her deficient language skills, we concluded that Ms. P. was currently not capable of handling a nursing program. We also felt that she was unlikely to be able to develop the necessary language skills, especially because—as we inadvertently discovered—none of her five brothers and sisters could read either. We explained to Ms. P. that she was by no means retarded but that, just as some people had poor musical ability, she had poor verbal ability. (We were able to arrange an aural administration of the driver's test, which she passed.) Finally, we explained Ms. P.'s problem to her husband, a well-educated man with a master's degree. In the short time that they had been married, he had become totally frustrated with her inability to balance the bank account, read recipes, and so forth, and he was beginning to believe that his wife was either "crazy or retarded." They now had an understanding of the problem, which we hoped would help them work out domestic routines to minimize its effect.

The case of Ms. P. illustrates one type of a *developmental disorder*, a disorder that seems to have its origin in some abnormality in the way in which the brain develops. Hers was a relatively restricted difficulty with language skills that nevertheless must have made school an arduous and frustrating experience and that was clearly continuing to cause problems for her as an adult. In this chapter, we will survey a number of developmental disorders, including disorders of learning, attention, social behavior, and general intellectual functioning.

Learning Disabilities

Large numbers of children enter schools in which they are required to master a core curriculum. Some of them are completely unable to meet any demands of the school system that they enter; some learn, but only with great difficulty; some have to repeat one or more grades; some graduate but fail to master certain subject areas; and some even graduate without mastering basic knowledge in any area. For those who fail, the educational experience often leaves emotional and attitudinal scars that are carried throughout life.

The difficulties that children encounter in school can have any of a number of causes. A child may be disturbed by an unhappy home life, be bored by school, dislike school, dislike a teacher, have no aptitude for school, have low "intelligence," or have a physical handicap or the child may have brain dysfunction or brain damage. Some school systems may be equipped to assess and deal with these kinds of problems. Most have no resources for either assessment or remediation. Even when a school is not equipped to deal with learning problems, neuropsychology now receives enough publicity that, if a child is not learning effectively, the question whether the cause is brain damage or dysfunction or something else will probably arise.

Historical Background

Learning disability is an umbrella term used for a wide variety of school-related problems. Formal definitions of learning disabilities describe these diagnoses as applying to people who have adequate intelligence, opportunity to learn, instruction, and home environment, yet still do not succeed in acquiring certain scholastic abilities. These features are illustrated by the World Federation of Neurology's definition of dyslexia:

> A disorder manifested by difficulty in learning to read despite conventional instruction, adequate intelligence, and sociocultural opportunity. It is dependent upon fundamental cognitive disabilities which are frequently of constitutional origin.

Nevertheless, every key word of this definition and similar ones has been disputed. For example, why should a learning disability be called a disorder? What is meant by conventional instruction? What is meant by adequate intelligence? And so on. To comprehend the difficulty of arriving at satisfactory definitions, knowing some of the history of ideas about learning disabilities can be helpful. Our encapsulation of that history will focus on **dyslexia** (*dys*, "poor function," and *lexia*, "read"), an inability to read properly, because reading is central to many aspects of formal schooling as well as to other aspects of modern life.

Critchley points out that the term *dyslexia* emerged within the context of aphasia, the partial or complete loss of speech, and so it was thought of as being due to damage that occurred at an early age in brain areas responsible for language. In the late 1890s, when James Hinshelwood, a Glasgow eye surgeon, and Pringle Morgan, a Seaford general practitioner, first observed students who could not learn to read, they assumed that their reading failed to develop because the prerequisite brain areas were absent or abnormal. It seemed logical to conclude that **developmental dyslexia**—dyslexia acquired before birth or during early postbirth years—is similar in nature to **acquired dyslexia**—dyslexia due to brain damage after reading has been achieved. Developmental deficits in other spheres, such as mathematics, also would be due to some underlying brain problem.

In the 1920s and 1930s, Samuel T. Orton proposed that dyslexia is due to delayed function, not anatomical absence. Orton, the director of a medical clinic in Iowa, noted that dyslexia was correlated with left-handedness and with tendencies to reverse or invert letters and words when learning to read or write. He termed such dyslexia **strephosymbolia** (from the Greek, meaning "twisted symbols"). Orton thought that the nondominant hemisphere, usually the right hemisphere, which he postulated had a reversed image of things, was excessively dominant or not sufficiently controlled. He suggested that, if an instructor was clever or persevering, education could establish normal dominance of reading in the left hemisphere, and the problem would be resolved.

When sociologists and educational psychologists became interested in learning disabilities, they supposed that environmental explanations, rather than neurological ones, would account for learning impairments. This stance may perhaps have been motivated by the belief, or hope, that environmental causes could be reversed more easily than neurological ones.

The term "learning disability" had its origins in an address given by Samuel A. Kirk in 1963. Kirk argued for better descriptions of children's school problems, but he excluded children with sensory handicaps and mental retardation from the group that he called learning-disabled. The members of his audience who later joined together to form the Association for Children with Learning Disabilities were influenced both by his address and by his definition and further popularized the label that he had coined.

The search for causes of learning disabilities has resulted in a proliferation of terms whose purpose seems to be to dissociate the learning-disabled from the retarded and brain damaged. Fry published a tongue-in-cheek "Do-It-Yourself Terminology Generator," shown in Table 24.1 (from which about 2000 terms can be constructed), to emphasize the overabundance of terms currently flooding the field and the consequent increase in confusion and inaccuracy. Frequently, terms that are widely used take on a pejorative connotation and are then dropped in favor of a new term.

Table 24.1 "Do-it-yourself terminology generator"

Secondary	Nervous	Deficit
Minimal	Brain	Dysfunction
Mild	Cerebral	Damage
Minor	Neurological	Disorder
Chronic	Neurologic	Desynchronization
Diffuse	CNS	Handicap
Specific	Language	Disability
Primary	Reading	Retardation
Developmental	Perceptual	Deficiency
Disorganized	Impulsive	Impairment
Organic	Visual-motor	Pathology
Clumsy	Behavior	Syndrome
Functional	Psychoneurologic	Complex

Directions: Select any word from first column, add any word from second and third columns. If you don't like the result, try again. It will mean about the same thing.
Source: Fry, 1968. Reprinted with the permission of Edward Fry and the International Reading Association.

Incidence of Learning Disabilities

Most estimates of the number of students needing special training to overcome learning disabilities range from 10% to 15% of the school-age population, although only about 2% actually receive special education.

One problem that complicates the calculation of prevalence estimates is that a learning disability is an emerging condition. When children enter the first grade, few of them qualify as being learning-disabled, largely because a popular method of defining a learning disability is to apply a 2-year cutoff criterion: if an person is 2 years behind in academic progress as determined by a standard test, then that person is learning-disabled. When this criterion is used, fewer than 1% of 6-year-olds are disabled, 2% of 7-year-olds are disabled, and so on, until, at age 19, 25% qualify as being disabled. This pattern of emerging incidence develops because the learning-disabled are falling behind at a rate that is proportional to their degree of impairment.

Further complicating the process of calculating and utilizing prevalence rates is the variation in scholastic achievement from one school system to another. Achievement tests are often used to determine grade-equivalent performance, but even nondisabled school populations do not all display equivalent performance. Prevalence rates might be obtained by asking teachers to report the number of children in their class who are receiving special help, but many schools cannot provide such information, because they have no resources for special education.

Types of Learning Disabilities

The classification and incidence of learning disabilities correspond to the emphasis placed on self-control and on certain academic specialties in the public school system. Good behavior, reading, arithmetic, and spelling are emphasized, and learning-disability classification reflects this focus. Although art, music, and physical education are taught in many schools, referrals for failure in these areas are uncommon. If art, rather than reading, were the core subject in the early years of school, we suspect that current catalogues of types of disabilities would be different. Nevertheless, there *are* disabilities that interfere with the acquisition of reading, spatial orientation, mathematics, and social skills.

In summarizing the syndromes seen in a 2-year period at a clinic specializing in learning disabilities, Denckla reports that, of 484 children aged 6 to 16 years, 76% were classified as primarily dyslexic, with or without some associated problems, and 18% were classified as hyperactive. Thus, reading and behavior problems were the most common reasons for referral. The American Psychiatric Association's *Diagnostic and Statistical Manual of Mental Disorders* (DSM-IV) recognizes a number of categories of disorders arising in childhood, including mental retardation and mental disorders; disorders in reading, arithmetic, and motor activity; and certain mixed classifications. The U.S. Department of Health, Education, and Welfare lists 10 characteristics most often cited by various authors as being associated with a learning disability: (1) hyperactivity; (2) perceptual–motor impairments; (3) emotional lability; (4) general coordination deficits; (5) disorders of attention (short attention span, distractibility, perseveration); (6) impulsivity; (7) disorders of memory and thinking; (8) specific learning disabilities, including, especially, those of reading (dyslexia), arithmetic, writing, and spelling; (9) disorders of speech and hearing; and (10) equivocal neurological signs and irregular EEG. Not all learning-disabled children exhibit all these symptoms. For example, for every learning-disabled child with coordination problems, there is a learning-disabled child whose coordination is better than normal.

Reading Disabilities

Reading requires letter-identification skills, phonological skills (converting letters into sounds by using certain rules), grapheme association skills (using the visual gestalt of a word to access a previously learned sound), sequencing skills (in which a number of sounds are analyzed and combined in sequence), and short-term-memory skills (to retain pieces of information as they are sequentially extracted from written material). Acquired information also is important, including knowledge of words in the form of a **lexicon.** A dictionary-like store of words in the brain, a lexicon contains their meanings, knowledge of the way in which they can be combined, and information about the ideas with which they can be associated. Thus, reading is a multiprocess and multistage behavior. As such, one would expect that it could be disrupted in many different ways. In the following sections, we will describe (1) types of reading, (2) the role of sensory detection in reading, (3) other deficits that correlate with deficits in reading, and (4) the role of neuropsychological evaluation in reading.

Types of Reading

Reading can be accomplished in either of two ways. Consider the following example. Imagine that you are reading a novel about a man named Fzylx from Worcester. Let us assume that you have never encountered either the man's name or his hometown before. When you read the names, you presumably attempt to sound out the sequences of letters to arrive at a satisfactory pronunciation of the words. Suppose that the next day you overhear two people discussing a novel about a man named Fzylx from Worcester. At first, you might be struck by the similarity between the plot of your book and theirs, until you confront them and find out they are actually discussing Felix from Wooster! What has happened? When you read Fzylx and Worcester, you encountered two common problems in reading English. First, you had to read a name that is not English and so you had no rules by which to read it. Even so, you may have felt comfortable with your pronunciation, inasmuch as it allowed you to read the name. Second, you encountered an irregular word; that is, a word that is not pronounced the way that it is spelled. The only way to pronounce this type of word correctly is to memorize it. This type of reading is called **graphemic reading** (or sometimes *lexical reading*). It can be used for regular words as well, but it *must* be used for irregular words or words that are not found in English. It is also the way Arabic numerals (such as 4) and international symbolic road and direction signs must be read. The other way to read is to do what you tried to do with Fzylx and Worcester. You simply convert a letter or group of letters into sounds (phonemes) that will provide the clue to the meaning of the words. Stated differently, the sounds that you get by analyzing letter groups will lead you to a pronunciation, and you will be able to access your memory, or lexicon, for the meaning and connection of the word. This is known as **phonological reading.**

Bradley and Bryant suggest that the phonological procedure is used by beginning readers but that, as reading skill is attained, the graphemic procedure becomes more important. They suggest that the transition takes place between 6 and 10 years of age. Thus, normal reading initially requires phonological skills and later becomes dependent on grapheme skills. This progression may explain why many people have difficulty in finding typographical errors when they proofread. Rather than reading phonologically, they read graphemically and, practiced at graphemic reading, they need to read only part of a word before recognizing its meaning and shifting attention to the next word. If the spelling error is not within the part of the word actually read, it will not be noticed. As we shall see shortly, there is evidence that phonological reading may be a function of the left hemisphere and grapheme reading a function of the right. In some school systems, instruction begins with grapheme reading, skipping the phonological stage, a procedure that has ignited considerable controversy regarding the appropriate way to teach reading.

Given the differences between these two reading processes, we should find at least two different kinds of reading impairments, which, moreover, could arise at different ages. A child who is incompetent in the phonological procedure will have difficulty in the early stages of reading. A child who is competent in the phonological procedure but incompetent in the grapheme procedure will have difficulty later on. Frith demonstrated just such types of age-related disabilities among poor readers. It may also follow that a child who is impaired at the first type will be hampered in making the transition to the second type.

We should note here that these types of impairments would not by any means exhaust the classifications of poor readers. People with a poor short-term auditory memory may not make proper sense of written material, because they quickly forget the words and phrases as they proceed. This type of disability may be particularly obvious at older ages, when reading material becomes more complex. People with poor long-term memory may not understand the sense of words despite good decoding skills, simply because they do not have much information about the meaning of the words. This is similar to the situation of a person who speaks only English trying to read Italian. The person would be able to sound out the words by using general phonetic rules but would not understand what he or she was reading, not knowing what the words meant. In fact, people who are demented are often just like this. They can read, but they understand nothing.

The Role of Sensory Detection in Reading

Impairments in language and reading may stem from difficulties that children have with sounds. Bradley and Bryant tested the sound-categorization ability of children who had not yet started to read. The tests consisted of giving a child three or four words and asking him or her to pick out the word that does not have a sound (phoneme) in common with the others. For example, in the series "hill, pig, pin," "hill" would be the correct choice; in the series "cot, pot, hat," "hat" would be the correct choice, and in the series "pin, bun, gun," "pin" would be the correct choice. Bradley and Bryant found that, when the same children were older and had started to learn to read, those who were initially weak at sound categorization were the ones who later fell behind in reading and spelling. They argue that the initial insensitivity to rhyme and alliteration causes subsequent reading impairment, because, if the children who were initially impaired were given special training in rhyme and alliteration, their reading was far less impaired after training in reading began. In short, according to Bradley and Bryant, at least one cause of reading deficiency is a basic deficiency in phonological, or sound, awareness.

It is possible that children who are at risk for learning disabilities could be detected still earlier. Frith suggested that the babbling of babies may give clues about those who are at risk. Werker and Tees reported that young infants can detect differences between all known speech sounds, but, as they acquire language, their detection abilities become restricted to only those sounds used in their own language, to which they are exposed daily. Impairments in this refining of their detection abilities could lead to language difficulties.

Tallal and her coworkers examined the sensory detection abilities of children with learning disabilities and found that they are impaired in detecting sensory events that take place in rapid succession. If two sensory stimuli, such as two tones, are presented in succession very quickly, they will be heard as one tone. If the interval between the tones is gradually increased, a point will be reached at which they are heard as two tones. For most people, a separation of tens of milliseconds, from about 10 to 40 ms, is required before the two tones are discriminated. For people with language impairments, a much greater separation is needed (Figure 24.1). The relevance of this finding to language impairments is that stop consonants ("ba," "da," "ga," "pa," and "ta") contain a transition period in which the sounds (called formants) change very rapidly, usually within 40 ms. When stop consonants are used as stimuli, language-impaired people have difficulty in differentiating one such consonant from another, whereas they have no difficulty in detecting vowels. They also have no difficulty in detecting stop consonants if the transition period is lengthened. When this difficulty is detected in infants, it is predictive of later language impairment.

Tallal and coworkers suggest that the left hemisphere is specialized for making these rapid sensory discriminations and movements. Thus, it has the requisite capacity to become dominant for language. It follows that impairments of the left hemisphere will impair discrimination abilities that are important for both the acquisition and the production of language.

This idea points to possible strategies for remediation. Tallal and coworkers suggest that remediation of language-related disorders should focus on training in discrimination rather than on more generalized training in language-related skills. For example, they reason that, if a child has difficulty in discriminating "da" from "de" when the sounds are presented

Figure 24.1 Percentage of trials in which controls and language-impaired subjects discriminate two tones separated by different interstimulus intervals. (After Tallal et al., 1993.)

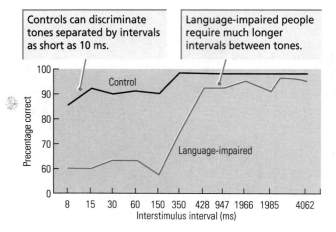

Controls can discriminate tones separated by intervals as short as 10 ms.

Language-impaired people require much longer intervals between tones.

at a normal rate, then slowing the presentation down so that the duration of the sounds is dragged out would make discrimination easier. They constructed computer games in which the subjects, rewarded each time that they made a correct discrimination (either between verbal or between nonverbal stimuli), gradually worked their way from simple to more-complex discrimination problems. They also designed computerized listening exercises that taught phonological discrimination through the use of acoustically modified speech. The computer-based exercises measured each subject's initial performance level and then led the subject through extensive daily training for a number of weeks, after which the subject's performance level was found to be closer to normal.

Training in sound-processing rates resulted in improvement in temporal integration on the discrimination tasks. The training also resulted in improvement in language comprehension abilities as assessed with the use of independent tests. In follow-up tests given approximately 6 months after training, the improvements were found to have endured. A group of subjects that received equivalent training in which natural rather than modified sounds were used showed no equivalent improvement (see the Snapshot on page 650).

The efficacy of this program—called Fast ForWord—has been tested in a large-scale trial conducted in 35 educational settings in the United States and Canada. A total of 500 children were trained for about 2 hours a day for as long as 2 months. The results indicated that the children improved in discrimination ability as a result of the training; they also improved in language skills as measured by independent tests. These findings suggest that improvement in sound discrimination can lead to improvement in language abilities.

Analysis of Correlated Deficits

It would be helpful if reading deficits displayed themselves in a straightforward manner, but unfortunately, they do not. People with dyslexia exhibit a wide range of different symptom clusters, as well as considerable individual variation. We cannot consider each of the many symptoms here, but they include deficits in attention, eye movement, development, memory, coordination, spatial abilities, movement sequencing, map reading, and visuospatial processing. The reason that language disorders are associated with so many kinds of symptoms is that language has a high-level role in managing our mental processes and thus affects many different kinds of behavior.

Impairments in separating stimuli have been found in all sensory modalities in dyslexic persons, as have impairments in the production of movements. Thus, language-impaired persons may require longer intervals between stimuli before they can detect two separate lights or two separate touches, and they may be impaired in producing rapid movements. They may also be impaired in sound-frequency discriminations and in detecting a target sound obscured by background noise. Hari and Renvall, in reviewing the many sensory and motor deficits associated with dyslexia, suggest that the central problem could be "sluggish attention shifting." In other words, when the attention of these dyslexic subjects is engaged, it cannot easily be disengaged, and vice versa. They suggest that the problem arises in the associational areas of the parietal lobe, which receive input from all sensory systems and then initiate movements. A

SNAPSHOT

Imaging Sound Perception in Normal and Dyslexic Subjects

Developmental dyslexia—difficulty in learning to read—affects between 5% and 20% of the population, yet its neural basis is not known. One hypothesis is that dyslexics are impaired in an aspect of phonological processing known as phonemic awareness, defined as the ability to consciously *decompose* words into their constituent speech sounds. Phonemic awareness develops as children learn to read, specifically as they learn to map written words onto existing representations of spoken language within their brains. The results of some research suggest that phonological processing deficits are indications of a more fundamental deficit in processing rapidly changing acoustical signals, an ability that is necessary for language comprehension. This hypothesis, known as the *rapid processing hypothesis,* led to the proposal that subjects given training in the discrimination of rapidly changing acoustical signals would improve in their ability to discriminate between the signals and in their comprehension of auditory language.

Temple and colleagues tested 8 adult subjects with a history of developmental dyslexia and 10 matched control subjects on their discrimination of rapid acoustical signals, while obtaining functional magnetic resonance images of the subjects' brain activity. The images revealed a specific disruption of the neural responses to transient, rapidly changing acoustical stimuli in the adults with developmental dyslexia. The largest activation in the control subjects was in the left prefrontal region, between the middle and superior frontal gyri in Brodmann's areas 46-10-9. Analysis of the dyslexic readers revealed no increase in left frontal response to the rapid relative to the slow stimuli. The illustration shows examples of rapid and slowed nonspeech acoustical signals (A) and examples of normal and dyslexic subjects' fMRI responses to rapid auditory stimuli (B). Note the greater activation of the left prefrontal cortex in normal readers.

Three of the dyslexic subjects then underwent a training program designed to improve rapid processing, after which they were again examined with the use of fMRI. The training consisted of computer exercises—100 minutes a day, 5 days a week, for 33 days—designed to improve rapid processing of linguistic and nonlinguistic stimuli. After training, two of the subjects improved on tests of rapid auditory processing and auditory language comprehension, and their fMRIs showed significantly increased activity in the left prefrontal cortex. The third subject showed no in-

problem there, they believe, could lead to an inability to switch attention that would affect many sensory domains as well as the production of movements.

It is important to emphasize that none of the theories concerning the underlying causes of reading impairments is uncontroversial. An understanding of learning disorders is fraught with complexity, as can be illustrated with a brief account of the magnocellular theory (a complete discussion of which would be far beyond the scope of this book). This theory states that reading disorders stem from problems in the magnocellular part of the visual system, which in normal function responds to rapidly changing stimuli. If a child's detection of visual motion is disturbed because of a dysfunction there, the child may have difficulty in reading because the words on the page appear to jump around. The theory also suggests that, if reading is done through a color filter or with only one eye, the perception of word movement can be reduced and reading can be improved. Skottum, in reviewing both the theory and its sup-

(A) Sound signals

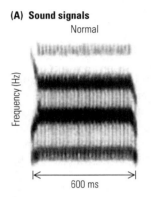

Normal

Slowed

(B) fMRI responses

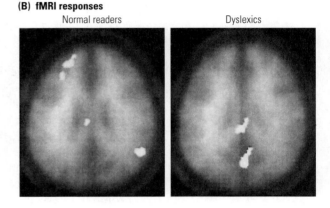

Normal readers   Dyslexics

crease in left frontal activity and no behavioral improvement. These results not only suggest a role for the left prefrontal cortex in processing nonlinguistic rapidly changing acoustical stimuli but also indicate that fMRI can be used for the diagnosis and treatment of reading disorders.

(E. Temple. Brain mechanisms in normal and dyslexic readers. *Current Opinion in Neurobiology* 12:178–183, 2002.)

Analyzing sound perception in normal and dyslexic readers. (A) Rapid and slowed nonspeech acoustic signals used as test stimuli and in training. (B) fMRI responses to rapid auditory stimuli in normal readers and dyslexic subjects. (From E. Temple, R. A. Poldrack, A. Protopapas, S. Nagarajan, T. Salz, P. Tallal, M. M. Merzenich, and J. D. Gabrieli. Disruption of the neural response to rapid acoustic stimuli in dyslexia: Evidence from functional MRI. *Proceedings of the National Academy of Sciences of the United States of America* 97:13907–13912, 2000.)

port, finds that, apart from problems with the theory itself, of 22 studies examining the theory, 4 were in agreement with it, 11 disagreed with it, and 7 were consistent with an alternative explanation. The mixed nature of these results stems from the complexities of the theory, inconsistencies in the choice and diagnosis of subjects, and methodological differences in the various lines of research used to test the theory.

Neuropsychological Evaluation

Neuropsychological approaches to assessing dyslexia generally rest on the following assumptions: (1) the disability may affect only one or a few spheres of endeavor; (2) a specific skill or lack of that skill can be detected through a neuropsychological testing procedure; (3) if one method or strategy of instruction is unsuccessful, another might be more successful; and (4) the neuropsychological test results should suggest a possible strategy for remediation of the learning disability. Although none of these assumptions has yet received anything like adequate scientific support, the neuropsychological testing strategy does provide a comprehensive evaluation of a person that is useful for counseling, as illustrated in Ms. P.'s case at the beginning of this chapter.

Neuropsychological testing assesses performance on a wide range of tasks, providing feedback on all areas of brain function. Most learning-disabled children are not dyslexic or dyscalculic (can't do math) alone but have a number of associated symptoms of which teachers and parents are usually unaware. The discovery of these associated deficits often helps the adults in the child's life to understand the difficulties with which the child is struggling. Neuropsychological tests can also help distinguish between children who have central reading impairments and those whose problems have emotional or social causes.

Many studies have focused on the IQ test results of learning-disabled children. These analyses attempt to correlate learning impairments with performance on the subtests of the Wechsler Intelligence Scale for Children. Rugel compiled the results from studies in which, collectively, a total of 1521 reading-disabled children and 554 control children were tested and compared. Figure 24.2 presents a graphic summary of these results. The dyslexic group displays low scores on four subtests: arithmetic, coding, information, and digit span. This profile, typical of many such studies, is referred to as the ACID profile. Dyslexic children characteristically have an overall IQ score that averages about 7 points lower than the same score attained by control children, but their mean IQ is roughly 100. We (Whishaw and Kolb) report that children above the age of 8 show the ACID profile, whereas those younger than 8 may not show a deficit in the information or arithmetic subscales. This finding suggests that ACID deficits in older children and adults are secondary to the underlying impairment that produces dyslexia. Although the deficits in digit span and coding are commonly seen with dyslexia, there is no agreement that they are necessarily related to a disability in reading.

Many researchers have commented on the large differences between verbal IQ and performance IQ in dyslexic persons. Some experts believe that two types of dyslexics can be identified on the basis of these scores. Generally speaking, however, a dyslexic child's subscores will vary greatly (the child will score in the high range on some subtests, in the low range on others, and in the average range on still others). Nevertheless, for an experienced counselor, the pattern displayed by any child may be meaningful.

In comparing the performance of a dyslexic group with that of the control group on other sections of their composite test battery, we (Whishaw and Kolb) found that the tests did discriminate between the two groups but that their doing so depended in part

Figure 24.2 Intelligence test profiles of developmentally dyslexic subjects and controls. Note the low scores on arithmetic, coding, information, and digit span, referred to as the ACID profile. (From Rugel, 1974; after Whishaw and Kolb, 1984.)

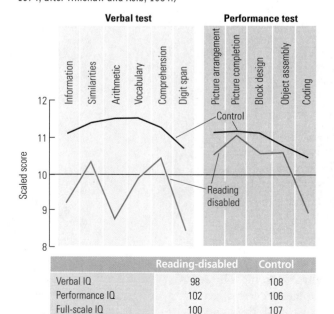

	Reading-disabled	Control
Verbal IQ	98	108
Performance IQ	102	106
Full-scale IQ	100	107
Number of subjects	1521	554

on the person's age. This age dependence was particularly evident in three tests. In the test of left–right differentiation (Figure 24.3), neither dyslexic children nor age-matched controls could score above chance if they were younger than 8 years old. After the age of 8, the control children performed well, whereas the dyslexic children continued to perform at chance. A different kind of emerging difference was found on tests of word fluency (for example, "Give as many words beginning with the letter 'S' as you can"), in which dyslexic and control scores were similar in children younger than 8 years but diverged increasingly in older age groups, suggesting that the fluency performance in the control group improved with age, whereas the dyslexic group remained almost static. A

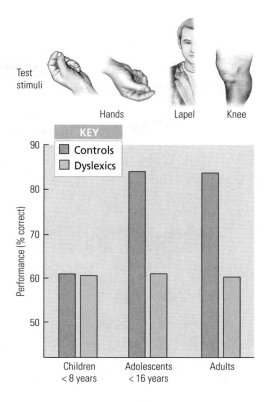

Figure 24.3 Performance on Semmes's left–right discrimination test by control subjects and dyslexic subjects. Stars signify significant group differences. (After Whishaw and Kolb, 1984.)

third pattern was obtained on the Semmes Body-Placing Test. Here (a test of left–right discrimination) significant group differences emerged only in adults, and these differences seemed to depend on the fact that adult control subjects displayed virtually perfect performance on the tests. These observations suggest to us that, although the tests can be applied with some success to children, they must be interpreted with caution in regard to younger children, and retesting at different ages is worthwhile.

Nonlanguage Learning Disabilities

In the six nonlanguage learning disabilities described in this section—that is, (1) hyperactivity, (2) cerebral palsy, (3) hydrocephalus, (4) autism, (5) fragile-X syndrome, and (6) fetal alcohol syndrome—children have difficulty in comprehending aspects of their environment, in pretending and anticipating, in interpreting the facial and emotional gestures of others, and in performing skilled movements.

Hyperactivity

Hyperactive child syndrome is distinguished from other types of learning disabilities in that an affected child is a behavioral problem in school, and all aspects of school performance are usually disrupted. This syndrome is sometimes called attention deficit disorder (ADD) or attention deficit hyperactivity disorder (ADHD). Hyperactive children may have specific learning disabilities in addition to the hyperactivity, and these disabilities possibly contribute to it. A number of diagnostic labels have been given to this disorder, including *minimal brain dysfunction*, *hyperkinetic child syndrome*, and *hyperkinetic impulsive disorder*. The DSM-IV lists the following diagnostic criteria:

1. *Excessive general hyperactivity or motor restlessness for the child's age.* In preschool and early school years, there may be incessant haphazard, impulsive running, climbing, or crawling. During middle childhood or adolescence, marked inability to sit still, up and down activity, and fidgeting are characteristic. The activity differs from the norms for the age both in quality and in quantity.

2. *Difficulty in sustaining attention, such as inability to complete tasks initiated or a disorganized approach to tasks.* The child frequently "forgets" demands made or tasks assigned and shows poor attention in unstructured situations or when demands are made for independent, unsupervised performance.

3. *Impulsive behavior.*

4. *Duration of at least 1 year.*

In infancy, hyperactive children are thought to exhibit poor and irregular sleep, colic, and feeding problems and to not like being cuddled or held still for long. Later, they are described as learning to run rather than to walk and as being driven to handle and play with everything. By the time they reach kindergarten, they are demanding, do not listen, and do not play well with other children. People outside the home may begin to reject a hyperactive child because of his or her behavior. By the time the child enters school, his or her high level of activity, low tolerance for frustration, poor concentration, and poor self-esteem lead to a referral for assessment. By adolescence, many of these children are failing in school, and from 25% to 50% of them have begun to encounter problems with the law. Their behavior remains restless, they withdraw from school, and they fail to develop social relations and maintain steady employment.

The hyperactive syndrome is described by Weiss and Hechtman as the most common behavioral disturbance among children. Estimates of its incidence vary because of different definitions and cultural differences in tolerance of hyperactive behavior. Estimates of the ratio of boys to girls range from 5:1 to 9:1. In the Isle of Wight study conducted by Rutter, an overall population incidence of 1 in 1000 was reported, but, in North America, where tolerance of hyperactive behavior seems lower, estimates of incidence are as high as 6 in 100. It does seem that North American parents' and teachers' estimates of what constitutes normal behavior may be unrealistic, because Weiss and Hechtman note that, in surveys of parents and teachers in North America, as many as 50% of children are reported as being hyperactive.

The suggested causes of hyperactivity include brain damage, encephalitis, genetics, food allergies, high lead concentrations, and various home and school environments. A single cause is unlikely to be responsible for all cases. Therapy includes counseling for the child and parents and careful structuring of the home and school environments. Beginning in the 1960s and continuing to the present, treatment with amphetamine-like stimulant drugs such as Ritalin has been popular, although the effectiveness of Ritalin or other drug treatment as a long-term solution is doubtful. When Ritalin *is* effective, it may be because, as a stimulant, it allows the person to concentrate on the task at hand. The drug may also have a general sedating effect on children.

Cerebral Palsy

Cerebral palsy is a disorder primarily of motor function caused by brain trauma in the course of fetal development or birth. Any simple definition is difficult, however, because (1) the motor symptoms take many forms, (2) there can be various kinds of accompanying cognitive impairments, and (3) the causes are diverse. In consequence, cerebral palsy cannot be accurately called a disease, a syndrome, or even a condition; it will take a different form in each person, depending on the nature of the brain damage. The term "cerebral palsy" is therefore most useful in an administrative sense, as a category of persons who are handicapped in many different ways by motor disorders due to nonprogressive brain abnormalities. Because brain damage is the underlying cause, cerebral palsy is not curable, but it often is amenable to therapy and training.

Cerebral palsy was first described in the medical literature in 1853 by London physician William Little. He recognized that the motor abnormalities of some babies are a result of abnormal parturition, difficult labor, premature birth, or asphyxia. He also recognized the permanence of the disabilities and their associated intellectual impairments; effects on personality (such as irritability and temper tantrums); and epilepsy. More important, he pointed out that the problems could be severely aggravated by subsequent improper training and education.

The incidence of cerebral palsy is estimated at about 6 per 1000 births. The numbers of males and females afflicted are about equal. Estimates of the degree of impairment suggest that about 10% of afflicted persons require no special services, 65% need services on an occasional basis, and about 25% need special schooling or custodial care. When cases of cerebral palsy are categorized by motor symptoms, about 50% of persons with the disorder are spastic (their limbs resist being moved), about 25% are athetoid (they make slow involuntary movements), about 10% are afflicted with rigidity (muscles around joints are stiff), and about 10% are ataxic (have difficulty making voluntary movements). As noted earlier, cerebral palsy has many causes, the most frequent of which are listed in Table 24.2. Nearly 50% of all cases are due to birth injury or injury suffered during development, 9% are secondary to convulsions, and 8% are due to prematurity. Smaller numbers result from other diverse causes. Incidence is also related to the mother's ability to carry a baby to term and to factors such as her body size, health habits, and weight gain during pregnancy.

Lesions of the corticospinal tracts, basal ganglia, brainstem, and cerebellum are presumed to be responsible for the disorders, but it has been difficult to establish clear-cut relations between lesions and clinical findings.

Table 24.2 Potential causes of cerebral palsy

Hereditary

Static—familial athetosis, familial paraplegia, familial tremor

Progressive—demyelinating diseases of viral or undetermined origin (chromosomal breakages are rare in cerebral palsy, as are disorders of metabolism)

Congenital (acquired in utero)

Infectious rubella, toxoplasmosis, cytomegalic inclusions, herpes simplex, and other viral or infectious agents

Maternal anoxia, carbon monoxide poisoning, strangulation, anemia, hypotension associated with spinal anesthesia, placental infarcts, placenta abruptio

Prenatal cerebral hemorrhage, maternal toxemia, direct trauma, maternal bleeding, diathesis

Prenatal anoxia, twisting or kinking of the cord

Miscellaneous toxins, drugs

Perinatal (obstetrical)

Mechanical anoxia—respiratory obstruction, narcotism due to oversedation with drugs, placenta previa or abruptio, hypotension associated with spinal anesthesia, breech delivery with delay of the after-coming head

Trauma—hemorrhage associated with dystocia, disproportions and malpositions of labor, sudden pressure changes, precipitate delivery, caesarean delivery

Complications of birth—"small for date" babies, prematurity, immaturity, dysmaturity, postmaturity, hyperbilirubinemia and isoimmunization factors (kernicterus due to Rh factor, ABO incompatibility), hemolytic disorders, "respiratory distress" disorders, syphilis, meningitis, and other infections, drug addiction reactions, hypoglycemic reactions, hypocalcemic reactions

Postnatal–Infancy

Trauma—subdural hematoma, skull fracture, cerebral contusion

Infectious—meningitis, encephalitis, brain abscess

Vascular accidents—congenital cerebral aneurism, thrombosis, embolism, hypertensive encephalopathy, sudden pressure changes

Toxins—lead, arsenic, coal-tar derivatives

Anoxia—carbon monoxide poisoning, strangulation, high-altitude and deep-pressure anoxia, hypoglycemia

Neoplastic and late neurodevelopmental defects—tumor, cyst, progressive hydrocephalus

Source: E. Denhoff, Medical aspects. In W. M. Cruickshank, Ed. *Cerebral Palsy.* Syracuse, NY: Syracuse University Press, 1976, p. 33. Reprinted with permission.

Hydrocephalus

Characterized by an increase in the volume of the cerebrospinal fluid (CSF), **hydrocephalus** can be caused in two ways. In one way, more likely to develop in adults, enlarged ventricles can be a secondary result of shrinkage or atrophy of surrounding brain tissue. In the second, more typical cause of hydrocephalus—and more typical in infants—obstruction of the flow of CSF results in a buildup of pressure in one or more ventricles that eventually causes their expansion. It is not certain that a simple overproduction of CSF is ever a cause of hydrocephalus.

Figure 24.4 is a drawing made from a cast of the lateral ventricles in a normal brain. In a living brain, the ventricles are filled with CSF. The usual amount in an adult is only about 130 cm³, of which about one-third is in the spinal cord's great lumbar cistern. As described in Chapter 3, CSF is made by the choroid plexus in the ventricles, most of it in the lateral ventricles. From there it flows through the interventricular foramina (windows) of Monro into the third ventricle, through the cerebral aqueduct, and then into the fourth ventricle. It finally escapes through three little holes in the roof of the fourth ventricle. These holes are the two laterally located foramina of Luschka and the medial foramen of Magendie. (The mnemonic is: lateral, Luschka; medial, Magendie.) The fluid then enters the subarachnoid space—the space beneath the arachnoid covering of the brain and spinal cord. It is absorbed into the veins and carried away by the bloodstream.

The circulation in the ventricles can be blocked at either of the interventricular foramina, causing an increase in pressure followed by expansion of either lateral ventricle. It can also be blocked at the level of the cerebral aqueduct (causing hydrocephalus of the first three ventricles) or by closure of the foramina in the roof of the fourth ventricle (producing hydrocephalus of the entire ventricular system). Any sudden obstruction of CSF flow will cause a rapid rise in intracranial pressure, ventricular dilation, and finally coma. A gradual obstruction, such as by a tumor, causes a less-rapid increase in pressure and consequent dilation, and the symptoms may include the gradual appearance of visual disturbances, palsies, dementia, and so on.

Infant hydrocephalus, characterized by a conspicuous enlargement of the head, usually develops during the first few months of life. As many as 27 of 100,000 newborn babies may suffer from it. In about 14% of these cases, a malformation impedes CSF circulation; most other cases are produced by inflammation or trauma, although about 4% are due to tumors. As the ventricles distend, they push the cerebral hemispheres into a balloon shape. Because the skull bones of an infant are not yet fused, continued pressure causes the expansion of the head in all directions. If expansion damages the cortex, intelligence may be impaired and dementia may result; but, if the cortex is not damaged, intelligence may be unimpaired even after the cortex has been stretched into a sheet of tissue less than a centimeter thick. Hydrocephalus can be treated with some success by the insertion into one lateral ventricle of a valve and a tube that passes into a jugular vein to drain into the cardiac atrium. Untreated, it often causes death or severe mental or motor disabilities.

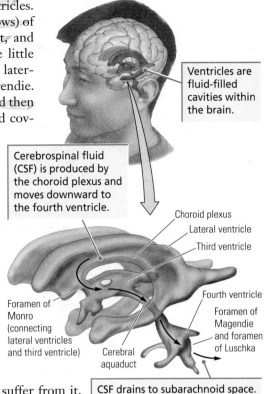

Ventricles are fluid-filled cavities within the brain.

Cerebrospinal fluid (CSF) is produced by the choroid plexus and moves downward to the fourth ventricle.

Choroid plexus
Lateral ventricle
Third ventricle
Fourth ventricle
Foramen of Magendie and foramen of Luschka
Foramen of Monro (connecting lateral ventricles and third ventricle)
Cerebral aquaduct

CSF drains to subarachnoid space.

Figure 24.4 Drawing of a cast of the ventricular system of the brain as seen from the side. The arrows indicate the direction of flow of cerebrospinal fluid. A blockage of the flow in the narrower parts of the ventricles (for example, the cerebral aqueduct) can cause the symptoms of hydrocephalus.

Autism

The term **autism** was first used by Kanner and Asperger in the 1940s to describe individual children without obvious signs of focal cerebral disease and with the symptoms of severely impaired social interaction, a bizarre and narrow range of interests, language and communication abnormalities, and, in some cases, preserved intellect. In summary, children with autism have a hard time communicating with others and functioning in the world outside the home. Autism is estimated to affect as many as 1 in 500 children, is four times as prevalent in boys as in girls, and has no known racial, ethnic, or social boundaries.

Many autistic infants are odd from birth, avoiding physical contact with caregivers by arching their backs or becoming limp when held. Approximately one-third of autistic children develop normally until between 1 and 3 years of age, when the autistic symptoms begin to emerge. Common characteristics are a failure to interact socially and an insistence on sameness. One possible reason for the latter may be an inability to understand and cope with novel situations. Autistic persons may exhibit repeated body movements (hand flapping, rocking), have unusual responses to people or unusual attachments to objects, and resist any changes in routine. In some cases, aggressive or self-injurious behavior or both behaviors are seen as well. Some autistic people are severely impaired, others can function on their own, and still others have exceptional abilities in some areas, such as music, art, or mathematics.

Autism has no known specific cause. There is some indication of a genetic influence, however: autism is more likely to develop in two identical twins than in two fraternal twins. There is also evidence that a virus can cause autism: women have an increased risk of having an autistic child after exposure to rubella in the first trimester of pregnancy. There is some suspicion that autism can be caused by industrial toxins, but the evidence for this cause is uncertain. In addition, the results of research reviewed by Bauman and Kempor suggest that brain abnormalities of various types—especially in the temporal lobes and cerebellum—might correlate with the degree of impairment displayed by an autistic person. In that case, impairments in explicit memories (memories for daily events) might be related to the temporal lobe abnormalities, whereas impairments in implicit memory (skills and conditioned responses) might be related to the cerebellar abnormalities. Evidence that the cerebellum controls conditioned responses suggests that the desire for sameness and the avoidance of novelty also may be related to cerebellar abnormality. One feature of conditional learning is habituation, or learning to ignore irrelevant or repeated stimuli. In the absence of an ability to habituate to ongoing events, a person may find such stimuli especially noxious and so avoid them in favor of maintaining sameness. This theory could explain why autistic people report that the sound of traffic, to which most people quickly habituate, remains for them frighteningly loud.

Roder suggests that one cause of autism may be an abnormality in the expression of genes that play a central role in the development of the brainstem. She finds that an area of the brainstem in the caudal part of the pons is small in autistic subjects and that several nuclei in this area, including the facial nucleus, which controls facial musculature, are small or missing (Figure 24.5). In addition, many autistic children have subtle facial abnormalities that may be due to abnormalities of the facial nerve. Perhaps mutation of the *HOSA1* gene, which plays a role in the development of the brainstem, or interference in the expression of this gene is responsible for many cases of autism.

A less-severe condition of withdrawal in children is referred to as **Asperger's syndrome.** These children, although withdrawn, exhibit early speech and good grammar, but they also exhibit narrow repetitive play, poor peer relations, and a need for routine and sameness. They, too, may excel in some aspect of behavior, such as reading, calculations, music, or art. **Hyperlexia** is a term describing unusual reading ability in otherwise cognitively impaired persons, such as children with Asperger's syndrome. It is marked by a precocious development of reading abilities between the ages of 3 and 5 years. Very often the children teach themselves to read. In Asperger's syndrome, hyperlexia is often accompanied by exceptional memory abilities, such as an unusual ability to remember words, television shows, names of streets, the weather, birthdays, and so forth. Reading may not be completely fluid, because there are often articulatory defects and prosodic abnormalities of intonation and rate of speech. Generally, comprehension of reading is impaired, and the children show emotional withdrawal, occasional echolalia (repeating words that they hear), and autistic symptoms.

Related to Asperger's syndrome is the **savant syndrome,** or *idiot savant syndrome,* first described by John Langdon Down in 1887. Since then, several hundred cases have been reported in the literature. The affected persons are remarkably similar in that they have a narrow range of special abilities and a common symptomatic triad of retardation, blindness, and musical genius. *Idiot savant* was coined by combining the word *idiot,* at one time an accepted name for a subcategory of mental retardation, with *savant,* which means a knowledgeable person. The term has endured despite its now pejorative connotation.

Savants are characterized by mental handicaps, resulting from a developmental disability or mental illness, combined with a talent that far exceeds their other abilities (talented savants) or the abilities of the general population (prodigious savants). The syndrome is estimated to affect males about six times as frequently as females. The special skill can appear quite suddenly and disappear equally quickly. Skills commonly displayed by savants include calendar calculations (some can tell the day of a person's birthday in any year of a 1000-year period); mathematical ability; musical ability, including the ability to play new pieces of music after hearing them once; sculpting; drawing; and peculiar feats of memory, such as memory of what the weather was like on every day of the savant's life, retention of the names of all visitors ever received by the savant and the dates of their visits, and the date of every burial in a parish in a 35-year time span as well as the names of all the attendees.

The causes of precocious abilities displayed by cognitively impaired children are not known. Some suggestions are that these children have islands capable of normal function in an otherwise impaired brain, that through some developmental abnormality they are overdeveloped in some brain areas and underdeveloped in others, or that they are using otherwise adequate brains in a functionally unusual manner. Because reasoning is generally poor, the left hemisphere is suggested to be impaired and the right hemisphere intact.

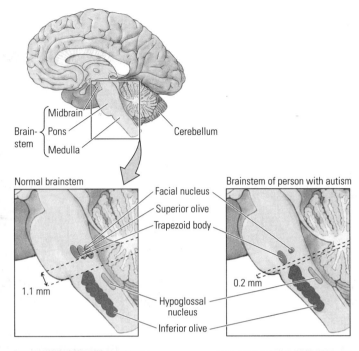

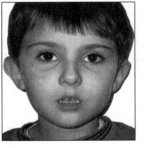

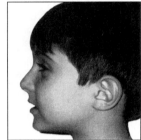

Figure 24.5 Effects of autism. Autism's effects include changes to the brainstem in which the posterior part of the pons is reduced in size. Several nuclei in this region, including the facial nucleus, superior olive, and trapezoid body, are either smaller than normal or missing. A child with autism is normal in appearance but may have some physical anomalies characteristic of the disorder. The corners of the mouth may be unusually low in relation to the upper lip, the tops of the ears may flop over (left), and the ears may be a bit lower than normal and have an almost square shape (right). (Drawings after Roder, © 2000 by Scientific American, Inc., all rights reserved; photographs courtesy of Susan L. Hyman.)

Fragile-X Syndrome

Fragile-X syndrome is the most common inherited cause of mental impairment. It affects about 1 in 2000 males and 1 in 4000 females. About 1 in 259 women and 1 in 800 men carry the fragile-X gene and could pass it on to their children. Fragile-X syndrome is characterized by mental handicaps and facial abnormalities. The mental impairment ranges from subtle learning disabilities to severe mental retardation and is associated with attention deficits, hyperactivity, anxiety and unstable mood, and autistic-like behaviors. The physical abnormalities include a long face, large ears, flat feet, and hyperextensible joints, especially fingers. Boys are typically more severely affected than girls in that most boys with fragile-X syndrome are typically retarded, whereas only about one-third of girls are retarded.

Fragile-X syndrome is caused by an abnormality of the *FMR1* gene, which is located on the long arm of the X chromosome. When functional, this gene encodes a protein (called fragile-X protein) that plays a role in the translation of mRNA into protein in neurons and that plays a role in synapse formation and elimination. The mutation occurs in a stretch of CGG repeats in the DNA. It is a sequence that is prone to increase in length as it is passed from generation to generation. When the number of repeats exceeds a critical level of about 100, the gene no longer makes a functional protein. Examination of neurons in affected persons at autopsy shows that dendritic spines are poorly formed and more numerous. Thus, the protein encoded by the *FMR1* gene may be required for the normal development and elimination of synapses. MRI scans of children with fragile-X syndrome show thinning of the cortex, an unusually small caudate, and an increase in ventricular size. The increase in ventricular size suggests a general loss of brain cells.

The symptoms of females are generally less severe than those of males because females have two X chromosomes; if one chromosome is abnormal, the other is usually able to manufacture the necessary protein. This difference suggests that—in theory at least—if a normal copy of the *FMR1* gene could be inserted into brain cells, neuronal abnormalities could be reduced. Gene insertion has been achieved in neurons cultured in a dish and in a mouse that had previously lacked the fragile-X gene. Another investigational approach to developing a treatment is based on the fact that the gene is capable of producing the protein but is turned off by the excessive number of CGG repeats. Researchers are exploring the possibility of restoring the gene's function without introducing any new genetic material.

Fetal Alcohol Syndrome

The term **fetal alcohol syndrome** (FAS) was coined by Jones and Smith in 1973 to describe a pattern of physical malformation and mental retardation observed in children born of alcoholic mothers. Children with FAS may have abnormal facial features, such as unusually wide spacing between the eyes (Figure 24.6). They also have a range of brain abnormalities, from small brains with abnormal gyri to brains of normal size with abnormal clusters of cells and misaligned cells in the cortex. Related to these anatomical abnormalities are certain behavioral symptoms common to FAS children. They have varying degrees of learning disability and lowered intelligence scores, as well as hyperactivity and other social problems. They have other physical symptoms, too, including small size and a tendency to be thin.

The recognition of FAS stimulated widespread interest in the effects of alcohol consumption by pregnant women. Pronounced FAS is found in the offspring of approximately 6% of alcoholic mothers. The incidence of it in different geographic regions varies widely, depending largely on the pattern and degree of alcohol abuse in those locations. Streissguth and Connor suggest that about 1 in 700 to 1 in 100 newborns have FAS.

Fetal alcohol syndrome is not an "all or none" diagnosis. Alcohol-induced abnormalities can range from hardly noticeable physical and psychological effects to the full-blown FAS syndrome. The severity is thought to be related to when, how much, and how frequently alcohol is consumed in a pregnancy. Apparently, the effects are the worst if drinking takes place in the first 3 months, which unfortunately may be a time when many women do not realize that they are pregnant. Severe FAS is also more likely to be caused by binge drinking, which produces high blood-alcohol levels. Other factors related to a more severe outcome are poor nutritional health of the mother and the mother's use of other drugs, including cigarettes.

A major question raised by FAS is how much alcohol is too much to drink during pregnancy. The matter is complex because the effects of alcohol on a fetus depend on so many factors. To be completely safe, it is best not to drink at all in the months preceding pregnancy and during it. This conclusion is supported by findings that as little as one drink of alcohol per day during pregnancy can lead to a decrease in intelligence test scores of children.

Fetal alcohol syndrome in both its full-blown and milder forms has important lessons to teach us. Alcohol is a widely used drug. It poses risks when used inappropriately but, when taken in moderation, is thought to have some health benefits. Even so, it should be avoided completely by women who are pregnant. A major problem is that women who are most at risk for bearing FAS babies are poor and not well educated, with alcohol-consumption problems that predate pregnancy and little access to prenatal care. Often they are unaware of the dangers that alcohol poses to a fetus and do not understand the need to abstain from drinking while they are pregnant.

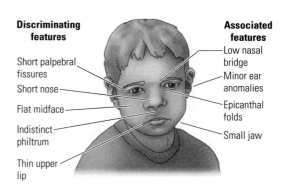

Discriminating features

Short palpebral fissures
Short nose
Flat midface
Indistinct philtrum
Thin upper lip

Associated features

Low nasal bridge
Minor ear anomalies
Epicanthal folds
Small jaw

Figure 24.6 Diagram of the characteristics of fetal alcohol syndrome in the face of a young child. Discriminating features, which indicate that the child has fetal alcohol syndrome, can be accompanied by associated features. (After Streissguth and Connor, 2001.)

Developmental Influences on Learning Disabilities

Six factors are most often cited as possible influences on the incidence of learning disabilities: (1) structural damage and toxic effects, (2) hormonal effects, (3) abnormal cerebral lateralization, (4) maturational lag, (5) environmental deprivation, and (6) genetic influences.

Structural Damage and Toxic Effects

When a childhood learning disability resembles a symptom seen in brain-damaged adults (dyslexia is an example), it is only natural to wonder whether the learning disability was caused by structural damage of a similar nature, perhaps resulting from birth trauma, encephalitis, anoxia, or an early-childhood accident. This is no doubt the case for a small minority of children, but many of the neurological symptoms associated with brain damage in adults are not typically observed in children, suggesting that structural damage is not likely to be the cause of most childhood learning disorders. For example, children with developmental dyslexia do not have hemianopsia (blindness in half of the visual field) or scotomas (blind spots in the visual field), symptoms present in a large percentage of brain-damaged adults with dyslexia. Furthermore, the results of EEG and CT-scan studies do not support a structural-damage hypothesis: abnormal EEGs similar to those correlated with known brain damage are not consistently correlated with learning disabilities.

Other possible causal factors include poor nutrition, drug use, and exposure to environmental contaminants. For example, Pihl and Parkes, analyzing specimens of hair from normal children and from learning-disabled children, found significant differences between the groups in the levels of sodium, cadmium, cobalt, lead, manganese, chromium, and lithium. When levels of these same elements were measured in hair taken from a second sample of children, the researchers were able to identify 98% of those who had been diagnosed as being learning-disabled. Although Pihl and Parkes could not identify the cause of the abnormal levels of trace elements, their success in diagnosing learning-disabled children leads to serious consideration of biochemical factors as causal factors in learning disabilities.

The Geschwind-Galaburda Theory

The Geschwind-Galaburda hypothesis proposes that hormones may affect brain development and learning. The seed of this hypothesis lies in Geschwind's observation that the planum temporale (an area thought to represent speech in the left hemisphere) is asymmetrical, being larger on the left and smaller on the right in most right-handers. This asymmetry is thought to be the basis of the underlying neural asymmetry that gives rise to the left hemisphere's dominant role in language. Because males are thought to show greater deviance from this asymmetrical pattern, the possibility that testosterone plays a role is suggested. During embryonic development, the male fetal gonads produce high levels of testosterone, comparable to the levels in adult males. The Geschwind-Galaburda hypothesis proposes that the embryonic surges of testosterone delay the development of the left hemisphere, allowing the right hemisphere both space and time for greater development. Thus, males in general have some comparatively better developed areas in the right hemisphere, which would presumably endow them with excellent spatial skills. If the testosterone-induced asymmetry produces some particularly large right-hemisphere areas, perhaps special abilities, such as precocious mathematical reasoning ability, may result. On the other hand, perhaps testosterone also produces some casualties, characterized by brain abnormalities and learning disabilities. An additional aspect of the hypothesis is that it explains the high incidence of autoimmune disorders (migraines, allergies, asthma, thyroid disorders, ulcerative colitis, and so forth) both among males in general and among males with exceptional abilities. The hypothesis proposes that testosterone also affects the development of the immune system, with a consequent increase in susceptibility to autoimmune disorders.

The appeal of the Geschwind-Galaburda hypothesis is that it can account for the general observation that females tend to do better than males at language-related tasks and males tend to do better than females at spatial tasks. It also accounts for the high incidence both of precocity and of learning disabilities among males. Furthermore, the proposed shift in cerebral dominance suggests an explanation for the high incidence of left-handedness among the precocious and among the learning-disabled. And, because the effects of testosterone on the brain will in some ways parallel its effects on the immune system, the hypothesis accounts for the high incidence of autoimmune disease in the precocious and learning-disabled male populations. Additionally, the theory allows for deviations in hormonal functions to produce increased incidences of learning disabilities, precociousness, left-handedness, and autoimmune disorders in females. Another appealing aspect is that the hypothesis is testable and can be explored by using animal models.

The first dissection of the brain of a person with a reading disability was performed by Drake, who examined the brain of a 12-year-old boy who died of cerebral hemorrhage. The boy's intelligence had been normal, but in school he had been impaired in arithmetic, writing, and reading. The autopsy revealed atypical gyral patterns in the parietal lobes, an atrophied corpus callosum, and neurons in the underlying white matter that should have migrated to the cortex.

Later Galaburda's group examined the brain of a 20-year-old man who had had a reading disability despite average intelligence. Visual inspection showed nothing abnormal, but microscopic examination revealed several abnormalities. Polymicrogyria (numerous small convolutions) and other architectonic abnormalities were found in the left frontal and parietal cortex. The locations of abnormal brain regions are shown in Figure 24.7. Subcortical abnormalities in the medial geniculate nucleus and the lateral posterior nucleus of the thalamus were discovered, as well. Since the original study, this group has reported similar findings in other cases.

Abnormal Cerebral Lateralization

A variety of theories rest on Orton's premise that learning disabilities result from slowed cerebral lateralization. This premise is based on the assumption that, because language is lateralized in the left hemisphere of most adults, such lateralization must be advantageous and acquired with language acquisition, and its slowed development would be deleterious to the acquisition of language skills. In the past 20 years, dozens of studies have examined dichotic and visual-field asymmetries, but the data are far from unequivocal. Satz concludes:

> One might ask what light laterality studies shed, if any, on the problem of cerebral dominance and reading disability. The answer should be— not much. The reason for this somewhat discouraging view lies in the numerous methodological and conceptual problems that continue to plague research efforts in this area. (Satz, 1976, p. 288)

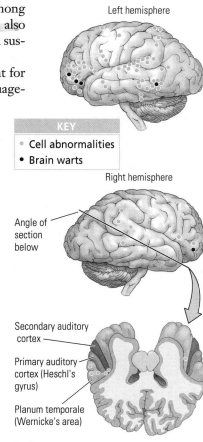

Figure 24.7 Drawings of the two hemispheres, showing the locations of cell abnormalities in the brain of a person who was diagnosed as being reading-disabled. The horizontal section illustrates the asymmetrical pattern of the planum temporale in which the dots, showing areas of cortical anomalies, indicate that the involvement is asymmetrical. (After Geschwind and Galaburda, 1985.)

Maturational Lag

The maturational-lag hypothesis postulates that the cognitive functions producing language, reading, and other complex behaviors are organized hierarchically and that the levels of the hierarchy develop sequentially in the course of ontogeny. Should one level of the hierarchy be slow to develop, the development of all subsequent levels will be delayed, inasmuch as higher functions depend on the integrity of lower ones. The original delay in maturation could result from a variety of factors. Two possibilities are delayed myelinization of a particular region and slow development of cortical connections.

Although the results of some studies do suggest that various functions in learning-disabled children are slow in maturing, the type of study needed for a definitive test of this hypothesis is a careful longitudinal analysis of children tested on a large number of perceptual, motor, and cognitive skills for a period of 10 to 15 years. When learning-disabled children *have* been reexamined in adulthood, they have been found to retain their characteristic impairments even though maturation should have been complete. For example, Frauenheim studied 40 adults who had been diagnosed as dyslexic in childhood and found that, on test performance and on self-report evaluations, they were essentially unchanged from the original diagnosis. This result does not support the maturational-lag hypothesis.

Environmental Deprivation

It is well known that environmental deprivation can have long-lasting consequences for physical and intellectual function. Children raised in orphanages with adequate physical care but without adequate social stimulation fail to thrive. They fall below age norms in both physical and intellectual development. A recent example is that of Romanian orphans. In the 1970s, the communist regime then governing Romania outlawed all forms of birth control and abortion. The result was hundreds of thousands of unwanted pregnancies, with children placed in orphanages, where the conditions were appalling. After the Communist government fell and the outside world was able to intervene, hundreds of these children were placed in adoptive homes throughout the world. There have been several studies of the fate of these children. Initially malnourished and small in size, they improved spectacularly in their adoptive homes. Their average height and weight became almost normal, and most achieved normal motor and cognitive development. A significant number were retarded, however, and many had psychosocial problems—difficulty in developing relations with peers and in developing secure attachments with adults. Children who were adopted before 6 months of age had significantly better outcomes than did those adopted at older ages.

People in developed countries continue to adopt children from developing countries—children who have been subjected to various degrees of deprivation. In addition, many children in even the most advanced countries suffer various degrees of deprivation and abuse. Accordingly, environmental deprivation continues to be a leading cause of learning disabilities.

The Birthday Effect

A subtle variant of the deprivation hypothesis is called the **birthday effect.** One perspective on this hypothesis comes from studies undertaken by Barnsley and colleagues of birthdays of North American hockey players. In senior hockey leagues, there is a negative relation between birth month and number of players. More than 30% of players have birth dates in the first quarter of the year (16% in January), whereas fewer than 15% have birth dates in the last quarter of the year (5% in December). Furthermore, a disproportionate number of the superstars have first-quarter birthdays. This birth discrepancy is not present in beginning leagues but emerges progressively as players are promoted through the leagues. The explanation appears to be straightforward. Players enter the most junior league according to age—children must be 8 years old between January 1 and December 31 of the year in which they enter Mite hockey. Equal numbers of children born in each month enter. But children born in December enter hockey almost a year earlier than children born in January, who in effect have had to wait a year. The younger, smaller children are at a developmental disadvantage from the outset. They receive less playing time and reinforcement and are more likely to drop out.

Research on the effects of relative age on educational achievement produces similar results. Children entering school at a younger age perform at a significantly lower level than do their older classmates. Both Diamond and Maddux found that children entering first grade at an early age were more likely than their older classmates to be classified as learning-disabled later in their school career. Furthermore, Maddux and coworkers found that, among children who are classified as gifted, a larger population entered school late than entered school early. This effect may last into later grades and even into university. The rather simple birthday effect stands in sharp contrast with the brain-based hypotheses and should inspire sober reflection in neuropsychologists who are making diagnoses.

Genetic Bases of Learning Disabilities

Any consideration of the possibility that learning disorders have a genetic basis must recognize some of the obstacles to demonstrating such a hypothesis. First, the environment can affect development in many ways. Consequently, it is extremely difficult to separate environmental influences from genetic effects in any kind of research. Second, learning disabilities take many forms. At present, criteria for categorizing types of learning disabilities are poorly developed, which makes it difficult for researchers to correlate specific types of disabilities with specific causes. Third, the incidence of learning disabilities is related to the quality of schooling. The average length of schooling and the demands made by schools on students have changed greatly in the past two generations; so it is difficult to compare the reading abilities of children with those of their parents. Fourth, learning-disabled children are typically of average intelligence, as are their parents (that is, their overall IQs are about 100), and people with strictly average IQs generally find school difficult, even when no specific disability exists. Fifth, the ability to read is itself probably inherited, making it difficult to sort out the contribution made by inherited reading skill from that made by a supposedly inherited causal factor underlying a disability.

Despite the difficulties of obtaining meaningful research results, the possibility of genetic causes has been raised repeatedly. Since the early twentieth century, many authors have referred to the high incidence of learning disabilities within certain families, and studies of twins have found a higher incidence of dyslexia in identical compared with fraternal twins. Asherson and Curran note that many genes are likely implicated in learning disorders. The results of different studies of families with a high incidence of reading disabilities suggest that there may be genes on chromosomes 1, 2, 6, and 15 related to the disorder. As our understanding of genes and their influence advances, it is quite possible that hundreds rather than just a few genetic abnormalities will prove to be associated with learning disabilities.

The Adult Outcome of Learning Disabilities

There are a variety of views about the outcome of children with learning disabilities. In the most optimistic outcome study, reported by Critchley, 20 dyslexic boys attended a private school and received special instruction using training methods. As adults, two of the boys became medical doctors, two college professors, one a lawyer, two research scientists, six owners or managers of businesses, one a school principal, three teachers, one an actor, one a factory foreman, and one a skilled laborer. There are also reports in the popular press of similar, though perhaps not so absolute, successes at various private schools for learning-disabled children. Most studies do not report such optimistic outcomes, however, and the most thorough of them reaches frankly pessimistic conclusions concerning academic outcome. Spreen examined the progress of 203 learning-disabled people over a long period, deriving the following findings from assessments, personal interviews, parental interviews, and other observations and data:

1. Persons in all but the control group suffered through a miserable and usually short school career and then experienced a miserable social life full of disappointments and failures. They also had a relatively poor chance of obtaining advanced training and skilled employment. They did not, however, have a higher incidence of juvenile delinquency or psychiatric problems.

2. Interviewed separately, subjects and their parents were largely in agreement concerning factual information, but parents tended to regard the learning disabilities as having had more serious effects on the well-being, happiness, and social interaction of their children than were reported by the children themselves. The affected children also had less-detailed memories of their childhood than the control children did. As the subjects aged, they developed firmer plans for their future and made better occupational adjustments, but they also gave increasingly negative descriptions of their school experiences. The eventual social adjustments of the females were worse than those of the males.

3. Although the learning-disabled eventually managed to make personal adjustments and find jobs, their dislike of school and dissatisfaction with it persisted.

Weiss and Hechtman reported that the prognosis for hyperactive children is relatively poor. Their behavior continues to be impulsive, and their lives are often characterized by frequent relocations, accidents, problems with the law, and so forth. As adults, their major problems may be low self-esteem and poor social skills, but they are not regarded as hyperactive by their employers, and they do not become mentally disturbed or commit crimes.

We end this section by emphasizing the importance of careful assessment in evaluating the particular cognitive deficits of each learning-disabled child. After problem areas have been identified, specialized teaching programs can be devised to circumvent handicaps. There may be little point in trying to teach a given child a particular skill that he or she is clearly not capable of learning. Perhaps the educational program for that child should instead be directed toward the acquisition of skills that can be used to gain employment. Counseling is an important part of the educational process both for the learning-disabled child and for the parents. It should focus not only on overcoming negative attitudes toward the educational system but also on understanding the child's unique handicaps and on devising strategies for circumventing some of them.

Summary

A variety of disorders appear in childhood and interfere with progress in school and in social adjustments. The acquisition of reading is central in school and so disorders that result in impairments in reading are understandably an obstacle to satisfactory academic progress. Although reading is a complex activity that can be disrupted in many different ways, a growing body of evidence suggests that an ability to make rapid discriminations and attentional shifts is particularly important for acquiring literacy. Procedures that specifically train subjects in stimulus discrimination have therefore proved helpful.

A number of common nonverbal disabilities lead to academic and social difficulties. Many of these conditions are associated with general diffuse damage that varies from case to case. A variety of environmental conditions also can influence brain function and developmental success, including brain injury, toxins, drugs, and environmental deprivation. Even somewhat more subtle influences such as the age at which a child begins school can have a surprisingly large effect on school success.

References

Asherson, P. J., and S. Curran. Approaches to gene mapping in complex disorders and their application in child psychiatry and psychology. *British Journal of Psychiatry* 179:122–128, 2001.

Barnsley, R. H., A. H. Thompson, and P. E. Barnsley. Hockey success and birth date: The relative age effect. *Canadian Association of Health, Physical Education, and Recreation*, 23–27, November–December, 1985.

Bauman, M. L., and T. L. Kempor. *The Neurobiology of Autism.* Baltimore: Johns Hopkins University Press, 1994.

Benton, A. *Right-Left Discrimination and Finger Localization.* New York: Hoeber-Harper, 1959.

Bradley, L., and P. E. Bryant. Categorizing sounds and learning to read: A causal connection. *Nature* 301:419–421, 1983.

Cobrinik, L. Unusual reading ability in severely disturbed children. *Journal of Autism and Childhood Schizophrenia* 4:163–175, 1974.

Critchley, M. *Developmental Dyslexia.* Springfield, IL: Charles C Thomas, 1964.

Cruickshank, W. M., Ed. *Cerebral Palsy.* Syracuse, NY: Syracuse University Press, 1976.

Defries, J. C., and S. N. Decker. Genetic aspects of reading disability: A family study. In R. N. Malatesha and P. G. Aaron, Eds. *Reading Disorders: Varieties and Treatments.* New York: Academic Press, 1982.

Denckla, M. B. Critical review of "electroencephalographic and neurophysiological studies in dyslexia." In A. L. Benton and D. Pearl, Eds. *Dyslexia: An Appraisal of Current Knowledge.* New York: Oxford University Press, 1978.

Denhoff, E. Medical aspects. In W. M. Cruickshank, Ed. *Cerebral Palsy.* Syracuse, NY: Syracuse University Press, 1976.

Diamond, G. H. The birthdate effect: A maturational effect? *Journal of Learning Disabilities* 16:161–164, 1983.

Douglas, V. I. Perceptual and cognitive factors as determinants of learning disabilities: A review chapter with special emphasis on attentional factors. In R. M. Knights and D. J. Bakker, Eds. *The Neuropsychology of Learning Disorders.* Baltimore: University Park Press, 1976.

Drake, W. Clinical and pathological findings in a child with a developmental learning disability. *Journal of Learning Disabilities* 1:468–475, 1968.

Frank, J., and H. H. Levinson. Dysmetric dyslexia and dyspraxia. *Academic Therapy* 11:133–143, 1976.

Frauenheim, J. G. Academic achievement characteristics of adult males who were diagnosed as dyslexic in childhood. *Journal of Learning Disabilities* 11:476–483, 1978.

Frith, U. Experimental approaches to developmental dyslexia. *Psychological Research* 43:97–109, 1981.

Fry, E. A do-it-yourself terminology generator. *Journal of Reading* 11:428–430, 1968.

Gaddes, W. H. *Learning Disabilities and Brain Function.* New York: Springer, 1980.

Galaburda, A. M., J. Corsiglia, G. D. Rosen, and G. F. Sherman. Planum temporale asymmetry: Reappraisal since Geschwind and Levitsky. *Neuropsychologia* 25:853–868, 1987.

Geschwind, N., and A. M. Galaburda. *Cerebral Lateralization.* Cambridge, MA: MIT Press, 1985.

Gould, S. J. *The Mismeasure of Man.* New York: Norton, 1981.

Hari, R., and H. Renvall. Impaired processing of rapid stimulus sequences in dyslexia. *Trends in Cognitive Sciences* 15:525–532, 2001.

Huelsman, C. B. The WISC syndrome for disabled readers. *Perceptual and Motor Skills* 30:535–550, 1970.

Hynd, G. W., and M. Semrud-Clikeman. Dyslexia and brain morphology. *Psychological Bulletin* 106:447–482, 1989.

Johnson, D. J., and H. R. Myklebust. *Learning Disabilities.* New York: Grune & Stratton, 1967.

Jones, K. L., and D. W. Smith. Fetal alcohol syndrome. *Teratology* 12:1–10, 1973.

Jorm, A. F. The cognitive and neurological basis of developmental dyslexia: A theoretical framework and review. *Cognition* 7:19–33, 1979.

Kinsbourne, M., and M. Hiscock. Does cerebral dominance develop? In S. J. Segalowitz and F. A. Gruber, Eds. *Language Development and Neurological Theory.* New York: Academic Press, 1977.

Langmore, S. E., and G. J. Canter. Written spelling deficit of Broca's aphasics. *Brain and Language* 18:293–314, 1983.

Leonard, C. M., et al. Anomalous cerebral structure in dyslexia revealed with magnetic resonance imaging. *Archives of Neurology* 50:461–469, 1993.

Levinson, H. N. *Dyslexia.* New York: Springer, 1980.

Little, W. J. *Deformities of the Human Frame.* London: Longmans, 1853.

Lorber, J. The results of early treatment of extreme hydrocephalus. *Developmental Medicine and Child Neurology Supplement* 16:21–29, 1968.

Lovegrove, W. J., M. Heddle, and W. Slaghuis. Reading disability: Spatial frequency specific deficits in visual information store. *Neuropsychologia* 18:111–115, 1980.

Lyle, J. G., and J. D. Goyen. Performance of retarded readers on the WISC and educational tests. *Journal of Abnormal Psychology* 74:105–112, 1969.

Lyle, J. G., and J. D. Goyen. Effect of speed of exposure and difficulty of discrimination on visual recognition of retarded readers. *Journal of Abnormal Psychology* 84:673–676, 1975.

Maccario, M., S. J. Hefferen, S. J. Keblusek, and K. A. Lipinski. Developmental dysphasia and electroencephalographic abnormalities. *Developmental Medicine and Child Neurology* 24:141–155, 1982.

Maddux, C. D. First-grade entry age in a sample of children labeled learning disabled. *Learning Disability Quarterly* 3:79–83, 1980.

Maddux, C. D., D. Stacy, and M. Scott. School entry age in a group of gifted children. *Gifted Child Quarterly* 25:180–184, 1981.

Malatesha, R. N., and D. R. Dougan. Clinical subtypes of developmental dyslexia: Resolution to an irresolute problem. In R. N. Malatesha and P. G. Aaron, Eds. *Reading Disorders.* New York: Academic Press, 1982.

Merzenich, M. M., C. Schreiner, W. Jenkins, and X. Wang. Neural mechanisms underlying temporal integration, segmentation, and input sequence representation: Some implications for the origin of learning disabilities. In P. Tallal, A. M. Galaburda, R. R. Llinas, and C. von Euler, Eds. *Temporal Information Processing in the Nervous System.* New York: New York Academy of Sciences, 1993.

Money, J. Child abuse: Growth failure, IQ deficit, and learning disability. *Journal of Learning Disabilities* 15:579–582, 1982.

Orton, S. T. *Reading, Writing, and Speech Problems in Children.* New York: Norton, 1937.

Pavlidis, G. T. Do eye movements hold the key to dyslexia? *Neuropsychologia* 19:57–64, 1981.

Pihl, R. O., and M. Parkes. Hair element content in learning disabled children. *Science* 198:204–206, 1977.

Reed, J. C. Reading achievement as related to differences between WISC verbal and performance I. Q.'s. *Child Development* 38:835–840, 1967.

Rosensweig, M. R., D. Krech, E. L. Bennett, and M. C. Diamond. Effects of environmental complexity and training on brain chemistry and anatomy: A replication and extension. *Journal of Comparative and Physiological Psychology* 55:427–429, 1962.

Roder, P. M. The early origins of autism. *Scientific American* 282(2):56–63, 2000.

Rourke, B. P. Neuropsychological assessment of children with learning disabilities. In S. B. Filskov and T. J. Boll, Eds. *Handbook of Clinical Neuropsychology.* New York: Wiley, 1981.

Rugel, R. P. WISC subtest scores of disabled readers: A review with respect to Bannatyne's categorization. *Journal of Learning Disability* 17:48–55, 1974.

Rutter, M., and W. Yule. The concept of specific reading retardation. *Journal of Child Psychology and Psychiatry* 16:181–197, 1975.

Satz, P. Cerebral dominance and reading disability: An old problem revisited. In R. M. Knights and D. J. Bakker, Eds. *The Neuropsychology of Learning Disorders.* Baltimore: University Park Press, 1976.

Semrud-Clikeman, M., and G. W. Hynd. Right hemispheric dysfunction in nonverbal learning disabilities: Social, academic, and adaptive functioning in adults and children. *Psychological Bulletin* 107:196–209, 1990.

Skottum, B.C. The magnocellular deficit theory of dyslexia: Evidence from contrast sensitivity. *Vision Research* 40:111–127, 2000.

Spreen, O. *Learning Disabled Children Growing Up.* New York: Oxford University Press, 1988.

Streissguth, A. P., and P. D. Connor. Fetal alcohol syndrome and other effects of prenatal alcohol: Developmental cognitive neuroscience implications. In C. A. Nelson and M. Luciana, Eds. *Handbook of Developmental Cognitive Neuroscience.* Cambridge, MA: MIT Press, 2001, pp. 505–518.

Tallal, P., S. Miller, and R. H. Fitch. Neurobiological basis of speech: A case for the preeminence of temporal processing. In P. Tallal, A. M. Galaburda, R. R. Llinas, and C. von Euler, Eds. *Temporal Information Processing in the Nervous System.* New York: New York Academy of Sciences, 1993.

Tallal, P., M. M. Merzenich, S. Miller, and W. Jenkins. Language learning impairments: Integrating basic science, technology, and remediation. *Experimental Brain Research* 123:210–219, 1998.

Treffert, D. A. The idiot savant: A review of the syndrome. *American Journal of Psychiatry* 145:563–572, 1988.

U.S. Department of Health, Education and Welfare. Minimal brain dysfunction in children. *National Institute of Neurological Diseases Monograph* 3:1–18, 1966.

Vellutino, F. R. Toward an understanding of dyslexia: Psychological factors in specific reading disability. In A. L. Benton and D. Pearl, Eds. *Dyslexia: An Appraisal of Current Knowledge.* New York: Oxford University Press, 1978.

Weiss, G., and L. Hechtman. The hyperactive child syndrome. *Science* 205:1348, 1979.

Werker, J. F., and R. C. Tees. Influences on infant speech processing: Toward a new synthesis. *Annual Review of Psychology* 50:509–535, 1999.

Whishaw, I. Q., and B. Kolb. Neuropsychological assessment of children and adults with developmental dyslexia. In R. N. Malatesha and H. A. Whitaker, Eds. *Dyslexia: A Global Issue.* The Hague: Martinus Nijhoff, 1984.

Witelson, S. F. Early hemisphere specialization and interhemispheric plasticity: An empirical and theoretical review. In S. J. Segalowitz and F. A. Gruber, Eds. *Language Development and Neurological Theory.* New York: Academic Press, 1977.

Zaidel, E. The split and half brains as models of congenital language disability. In C. L. Ludlow and M. E. Doran-Quine, Eds. *The Neuropsychological Basis of Language Disorders in Children.* Bethesda, MD: National Institute of Neurological and Communicative Disorders and Stroke, 1978.

Zangwill, O. L., and C. Blakemore. Dyslexia: Reversal of eye-movements during reading. *Neuropsychologia* 10:371–373, 1972.

Plasticity, Recovery, and Rehabilitation of the Adult Brain

In the battle of Smolensk in 1943, a bullet fractured the skull of soldier Lyova Saletsky, injuring the brain within. The damage was centered in the posterior left-hemisphere intersections of the occipital, temporal, and parietal cortex. Alexander Luria first examined Saletsky 3 months after the injury and then at 3-week intervals for the next 26 years, after which Luria wrote a wonderful little book, *The Man with a Shattered World.* In the 26 years, Saletsky painfully and slowly recovered the ability to read and write, in the process compiling a diary that gives a moving account of his initial deficits, slow recovery, and residual problems. The following excerpt is an example of what Saletsky had to say about his condition:

> I remember nothing, absolutely nothing! Just separate bits of information that I sense have to do with one field or another. But that's all! I have no real knowledge of any subject. My past has just been wiped out! Before my injury I understood everything people said and had no trouble learning any of the sciences. Afterwards I forgot everything I learned about science. All my education was gone.
>
> I know that I went to elementary school, graduated with honors from the middle school, completed three years of courses at the Tula Polytechnic Institute, did advanced work in chemistry, and before the war, finished all these requirements ahead of time. I remember that I was on the western front, was wounded in the head in 1943 when we tried to break through the Germans' defense in Smolensk, and that I've never been able to put my life together again. But I can't remember what I did or studied, the sciences I learned, subjects I took. I've forgotten everything. Words like *trigonometry, solid geometry, chemistry, algebra,* etc., come to mind, but I have no idea what they mean. (Luria, 1972, pp. 140–142)

Saletsky improved considerably in the 26 years of Luria's study, but he could never return to his original level of functioning. Luria sums up Saletsky's problems nicely when he says, "The damaged areas of the cerebral cortex could not be restored. Hence when he tried to think, his mind had to detour around these scorched areas and employ other faculties with which to learn and try to recover some lost skills" (Luria, 1972, p. 158).

Saletsky's case vividly illustrates the difficulty of stimulating functional recovery after brain injury. After a healthy brain has been injured, it will always be coping with damaged circuits. Nonetheless, there is often some restitution of function, in part because of the plastic properties of the brain and in part because brain-injured people learn to compensate, or, as Luria put it, "detour around these scorched areas." In this chapter, we begin by considering the nature of plasticity in the normal adult brain. We then examine how the brain responds to injury and, lastly, how various forms of rehabilitation may be used to stimulate change in the brain.

Cortical Plasticity in the Intact Adult Brain

The nervous system is not a static system but rather one that changes with time. This capacity to change, one of the system's most basic characteristics, can be seen in even the simplest of organisms, such as the tiny worm *Caenorhabditis elegans*, which has only 302 neurons (for a comprehensive survey of plasticity, see Shaw and McEachern). The results of studies by Morrison and van der Kooy showed, for example, that *C. elegans* can learn to make associations between sensory events, such as smells, and consequences, such as mild shocks. For the animal to learn such associations, the nervous system must undergo some type of change that can code this association. Thus, as a general rule, we can say that behavioral changes, described (depending on the circumstances) as learning, memory, addiction, maturation, recovery, and so on, are accompanied by corresponding changes in the nervous system. To understand processes such as memory and addiction, it is therefore necessary to understand the nature of the brain's plasticity.

Neural plasticity can be studied at many levels, from observable behavioral changes to cerebral maps, synaptic organization, physiological organization, molecular structure, and mitosis. We consider each level in turn.

Inferring Plasticity from Changes in Behavior

Learning and remembering new information must entail some kind of change in the cells of the nervous system. Such changes are presumed to constitute the neural record of the learned information. A comprehensive survey of what the study of behavioral change has contributed to the research on nervous system plasticity is beyond the scope of this discussion, but an example will serve to illustrate how such research is done.

Humans show a remarkable ability to adapt to a visually rearranged world. For example, Wolfgang Kohler fitted subjects with special glasses made of prisms that inverted the visual field and reversed left and right so that the subjects saw the world upside down and backward. For the first few days of constantly wearing these glasses, a subject's struggle to navigate an upside-down world was confusing and debilitating, but within a few days the world seemed to right itself, and the subject was once again able to dress, eat, walk about, and perform other daily activities with ease. Eventually, subjects could even perform complex activities such as skiing and riding a bicycle. When the glasses were finally removed, the subjects again needed time to adjust, because the world again appeared distorted to them, just as when they had first been fitted with the prisms.

Sugita emphasized that the adaptation of Kohler's subjects to the transformed visual world included several behavioral changes, each associated with changes in certain regions of the brain. One of these regions is the premotor cortex. If normal monkeys are fitted with adapting prisms, the monkeys adapt to the change just as the human subjects did; but, if a monkey's premotor cortex has been inactivated, the animal has great difficulty adapting. Another locus of change is the posterior parietal cortex. Clower and colleagues used PET to locate changes in regional blood flow in subjects adapting to prisms and found that, when the subjects used their eyes to guide them in reaching for objects, activation in the posterior parietal cortex greatly increased. Sugita also found that the properties of cells in the visual cortex change as monkeys adapt to prisms. Normally, cells in area V1 would respond only to cells in the contralateral visual field, but, with adaptation, the cells began to respond to stimuli in the ipsilateral field as well. These changes disappeared soon after the prisms were removed. Parallel changes were also seen in other ventral-stream pathways, such as area V4.

Whatever the plastic changes are that support prism adaptation, they presumably correspond to changes in synaptic organization, although the consistency and dependability of adaptation in both humans and monkeys suggest that the connections necessary for the adaptation are already in place. If so, adaptation would be a matter of enhancing the efficiency of these connections relative to the connections used for seeing the "normal" visual world.

Much remains to be learned about the nature of the plastic changes in the visually adapting brain, but it should be clear that, by studying novel situations in which behavior changes in dramatic ways, researchers are able to make inferences about the plastic properties of the nervous system. An understanding of such processes not only is of general interest with respect to how the normal brain functions but can also be a source of insight into ways of stimulating functional recovery after injury. Recall, for example, that Gainotti used prism adaptation as a way of stimulating recovery from contralateral neglect in stroke patients (see Chapter 22).

Plasticity in Cortical Maps

As described in Chapters 8 and 10, each sensory system has multiple maps providing topographic representations of the external world. The homunculi in the motor and somatosensory cortices serve as excellent examples of these representations (see Chapter 8). The size and organization of motor maps can be determined by stimulating the cortex either directly, with microelectrodes, or transcranially, by using magnetic stimulation to induce movements or by using functional imaging to map the areas activated when subjects are engaged in different behaviors. The results of studies in rats, monkeys, and humans have shown that specific motor training can increase the size of different components of the motor maps. Recall from Chapter 23 that the motor maps of violinists have a larger representation of the digits of the left hand than do the motor maps of nonmusicians. Nudo and his colleagues used a direct method to examine motor-map changes in squirrel monkeys that they trained to retrieve food objects from either small or large wells. To obtain food from the small wells, the animals had to use a pincer grasp of the digits; to obtain food from

(A) **Difficult task**

A group of monkeys was trained to retrieve food from a small well.

Simple task

Another group of monkeys was trained to retrieve food from a large well.

(B)

The motor representation of digit, wrist, and arm was mapped.

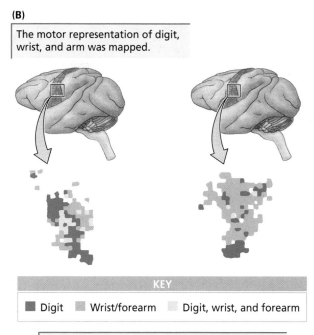

KEY		
■ Digit	■ Wrist/forearm	■ Digit, wrist, and forearm

A larger digit representation in the brain of the animal with the more difficult task corresponds to the neuronal changes for the acquired skill.

Figure 25.1 Differential effects of motor-skill acquisition and motor use on the functional organization of the squirrel monkey motor cortex. (A) The training procedures consisted of practice retrieving small pellets from either a small or a large well. The monkey is able to insert the entire hand into the large well but only one or two fingers into the small well. (B) Maps of brain activity during forelimb movements were produced by microelectrode stimulation of the cortex. The maps showed systematic changes in the animals trained with the small well but not with the large one. (After Nudo et al., 1997.)

the large wells, they used gross movements of the whole hand and wrist. As illustrated in Figure 25.1, when the researchers mapped the motor cortex with microelectrodes, they found that the area representing the digits was increased in the animals making digit movements, whereas no similar change took place in animals making larger movements.

Like motor maps, sensory maps are modified by experience. For example, Pantev and colleagues used MEG to show a 25% increase in the cortical representation for the musical scale in musicians compared with nonmusicians. This enlargement correlated with the age at which the musicians began to practice music. Rauschecker, who notes that early blindness results in an expansion of the auditory-responsive areas in the parietal and occipital lobes (areas that would not have auditory functions in sighted people), goes as far as to claim that this finding lends credibility to the generalization that blind people have greater musical abilities.

Plasticity in somatosensory representations has been extensively studied by Merzenich and colleagues, who showed that the organization of the maps can be changed by the manipulation of afferent inputs to the cortex. For example, if the afferent nerve from one or more digits is cut, the representation of the remaining digits expands, presumably allowing greater sensitivity in those digits. Furthermore, if two digits are sewn together, a single digit area replaces the two formerly separate digit areas on the map. A similar fusion of digit representation has been found in humans born with webbed fingers; if the digits are then separated surgically, the map reorganizes to produce a separate field for each, as found by Moligner and colleagues. In the same vein, Sterr and colleagues, studying Braille readers, found that extensive stimulation of one or more digits can increase the relative representation of those digits.

Such changes are not always adaptive. Focal hand dystonia, the loss of motor control of one or more digits, can result from repetitive synchronous movements of the digits, such as those made by musicians in a lifetime of playing. Elbert and colleagues studied the somatosensory maps of musicians with focal hand dystonia and found that they contained smaller-than-normal distances between the representations of the digits, much as in people with webbed fingers. Presumably, the musical training inadvertently caused the mapped representations of the digits to fuse. A logical extrapolation of this finding is that it should be possible to treat dystonia by training affected persons to make

(A)

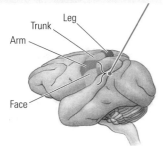

In the control monkey, this area of the somatosensory cortex represents the arm and face.

This normal pattern is illustrated by a normal face.

(B)

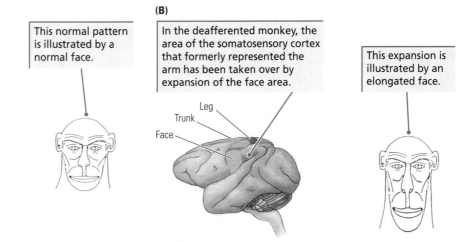

In the deafferented monkey, the area of the somatosensory cortex that formerly represented the arm has been taken over by expansion of the face area.

This expansion is illustrated by an elongated face.

Figure 25.2 Somatosensory cortex (as mapped by electrical recordings) of (A) a control monkey and (B) a monkey that has undergone arm deafferentation. (The face representations are shown right side up for simplicity.) Only the lower portion of the face area has expanded. (After Pons et al., 1991.)

independent asynchronous finger movements. Indeed, Candia and colleagues found such to be the case.

One of the best-known examples of somatosensory plasticity is described repeatedly in the extensive literature concerning studies of people and monkeys with amputations. In a classic study, Pons and his colleagues mapped the somatosensory representation of monkeys that had been deprived of somatosensory input to one limb by a nerve transection 12 years earlier. The researchers found that the denervated hand and arm area responded to tactile stimulation of the face on the affected side of the body. What was most surprising, however, was that the changes in the map were very large—covering more than 1 cm—as shown in Figure 25.2. The major change was an expansion of the face area to invade the denervated limb area. Parallel studies have been done in people and have similar results (see review by Elbert et al.). But what happens to the original map? Ramachandran demonstrated that the original maps are still present and can be detected by lightly stimulating the face (Figure 25.3). Studies by others have documented similar rearrangements of sensory maps subsequent to the amputation of other body parts. Aglioti found that, in women who have undergone bilateral mastectomies, the nipples, interestingly enough, seem to relocate to the ear lobes.

Figure 25.3 Mapping an amputated hand. (A) When an amputee is stroked lightly on the face with a cotton swab, he or she experiences the sensation of the missing hand being lightly touched. (B) Touching different parts of the face and noting what part of the hand each touch evokes allow a representation of the hand to be mapped on the face. As in the normal somatosensory cortex map, the area representing the thumb is disproportionately large. (After Ramachandran, 1993.)

(A)

(B)

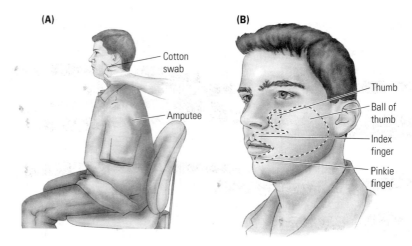

Cotton swab

Amputee

Thumb

Ball of thumb

Index finger

Pinkie finger

Plasticity in Synaptic Organization

Synaptic organization has been studied by using Golgi-type stains to reveal dendritic arborization and by using electron microscope technology to inspect synapse number and size. Inasmuch as both these approaches require postmortem tissue, the number of studies of synaptic changes in human brains has necessarily been limited. In one series of human synapse studies, Jacobs and colleagues examined the dendritic structure of neurons in different cortical regions taking part in different computational tasks. They were looking for a relation between the complexity of dendritic arborization in a given area and the nature of the computational task performed there. For example, when they compared the structure of neurons from the somatosensory representation of the trunk with the structure of neurons from the somatosensory representation of the fingers, they found greater complexity in the latter group of cells. They reasoned that the computational challenge to cortical neurons by somatosensory inputs from receptive fields on the chest wall must be less than that from the inputs from the fingers, and so the neurons representing the chest are less complex (Figure 25.4). Similarly, when they compared the cells in the finger area with those in the supramarginal gyrus, a region of the parietal lobe associated with higher cognitive processes (that is, with thinking), they found the neurons in the supramarginal gyrus to be more complex. A second hypothesis was that dendritic trees in all regions are subject to experience-dependent change. As a result, they predicted, predominant life experiences, such as a person's occupation, should alter the structure of dendritic trees. Although they did not test this hypothesis directly, they did make an interesting observation. In comparing cells in the trunk area, finger area, and supramarginal gyrus, they found curious individual differences. For example, especially large differences in trunk and finger neurons were found in the brains of people who had achieved a high level of finger dexterity and maintained it for long periods (as would a typist). In contrast, no trunk–finger difference was found in the brain of a person whose career as a sales representative did not require a high degree of specialized finger use and thus made less-complex demands on the finger neurons.

The results of Golgi-type studies of the brain tissue of laboratory animals support these conclusions. Experience-dependent changes have been seen in every species of animal tested, from fruit flies and bees to rats, cats, and monkeys (for a review, see Kolb and Whishaw).

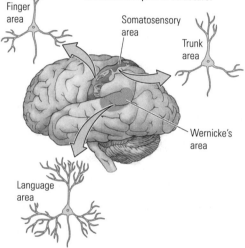

Figure 25.4 Evidence of Jacob and Scheibel's hypothesis that cell complexity is related to the computational demands on the cell. Cells that represent the trunk area of the body perform less-demanding computations than are performed by cells representing the finger region and therefore are less complex in structure. In contrast, cells engaged in higher-level cognitive functions (such as language, in Wernicke's area) perform more-demanding computations than are performed by cells engaged in finger functions and are more complex in structure.

Finger area

Somatosensory area

Trunk area

Wernicke's area

Language area

Plasticity in Physiological Organization

The general hypothesis tested in physiological studies of brain plasticity is that the nervous system can be changed by electrical stimulation. Two primary examples of such change are long-term potentiation and kindling.

Bliss and Lomo reported in 1973 that a brief, high-frequency electrical stimulation applied to the hippocampus resulted in a long-term change in the efficiency of the synapses that were activated by the stimulation, a phenomenon called **long-term potentiation** (LTP) or **long-term enhancement** (LTE).

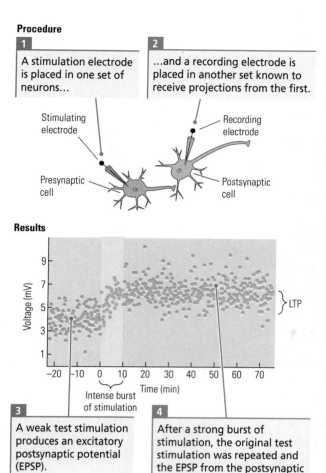

Procedure

1 A stimulation electrode is placed in one set of neurons...

2 ...and a recording electrode is placed in another set known to receive projections from the first.

Stimulating electrode

Recording electrode

Presynaptic cell

Postsynaptic cell

Results

3 A weak test stimulation produces an excitatory postsynaptic potential (EPSP).

4 After a strong burst of stimulation, the original test stimulation was repeated and the EPSP from the postsynaptic cell was recorded. Long-term potentiation (LTP) had resulted.

Figure 25.5 Demonstration of long-term changes in physiological response to stimulation. Each dot represents the size of an EPSP in response to a single test stimulus.

Brief pulses of current were delivered to a neuron for a period of a few seconds, and the magnitude of the response was recorded from neurons known to receive projections from the stimulated neuron (Figure 25.5). After a stable baseline of response (the excitatory postsynaptic potential, or EPSP) to the stimulation was established, the stimulation was changed to a burst of high frequency, driving the system very hard. (The high-frequency stimulation can be thought of as a "training stimulus.") After a brief rest period, the original test pulse was presented again, and this time the magnitude of the response (that is, the EPSP) was greater than before. Under optimal experimental conditions, this enhanced response can persist indefinitely and can be shown to correlate with changes in dendritic length and spine density in the postsynaptic neuron. This synaptic change has been adopted by many as a general model of how simple learning (if not more complex forms of learning) might take place, although it has also been viewed with skepticism by many others. In any case, LTP remains an important example of synaptic plasticity, is now known to be a characteristic of cells in the cerebral neocortex and hippocampus, and has been shown to correlate with various molecular changes as well as changes in dendritic morphology (see reviews by Cain and by Teyler).

Kindling refers to the development of persistent seizure activity after repeated exposure to an initially subconvulsant stimulus. This phenomenon was first described by Graham Goddard, who inadvertently discovered that repeated stimulation of the amygdala, though initially having little behavioral effect, would eventually produce epileptic seizures. Goddard chose the name kindling as an analogy to starting a fire with an initially ineffective bit of fuel. Like LTP, kindling is presumed to activate mechanisms similar to those activated for at least some kinds of learning. It can be demonstrated in most forebrain structures and, like LTP, is associated with a change in synaptic organization and with a variety of molecular-level events, such as the production of growth factors (for a review, see Teskey).

Both LTP and kindling have been studied for more than three decades, leading to a substantial body of literature on both. Their connection with behavior, however, is still a matter of some conjecture, although both techniques have begun to be used to study functional plasticity after cerebral injury.

Plasticity in Molecular Structure

The studies using maps, Golgi stains, or physiological techniques to show that the brain changes in response to experience are phenomenological; they describe and classify but do not explain. If we wish to know why the brain changes or understand how, we need to look at the mechanisms by which synaptic change is actually produced. In the final analysis, we must look at how different proteins are produced, which ultimately means looking at the effects of experience on genes. The development of new techniques of genetic screening—for example, *gene-chip arrays*—has allowed researchers to take bits of brain tissue and use them to analyze which genes have been affected by a particular experience. In these techniques, a miniature grid (on a chip about 1 cm in diameter) that can identify as many as 10,000 genes, each in a different location on the grid, is exposed to a homogenate of tissue. If certain genes are present in the tissue, they will react with a substance at one of the locations on the chip. Such techniques are undoubtedly powerful, providing a lot of information about which genes change when, for example, an animal is housed in a complex rather than a deprived environment; but, as yet, what the changes actually tell us about brain function is far from clear. Rampon and colleagues, for example, placed rats in complex environments for different lengths of time and found a significant increase in the activity of more than 100 genes (of 11,000 genes screened) in response to the experience.

In short, knowing that genes change is only the start. The real question is what the changes mean. Nonetheless, the effort to understand how genes are altered by experience is an important step in understanding how to enhance (or reduce) plastic changes in the brain, especially the changes that take place after injury.

Mitotic Activity

A real surprise of the late 1990s was the discovery that not only is the adult brain capable of manufacturing new neurons and glia but the generation of new cells is affected by experience. Both the olfactory bulbs and the hippocampus of mammals, including humans, incorporate new neurons into their existing circuitry. The olfactory-bulb cells are generated by mitosis of stem cells along the wall of the lateral ventricles, in the subventricular zone. The olfactory precursor cells migrate from the anterior part of the subventricular zone along a pathway known as the rostral migratory stream until they reach the olfactory bulb, where they differentiate into neurons. In contrast, the precursor cells in the hippocampus are located between the granule cell layer and the hilus, as illustrated in Figure 25.6.

The vigorous debate about whether new neurons are produced in the cerebral cortex of the normal, noninjured brain was mentioned in Chapter 23. New neurons *are* produced in small numbers in the injured cortex, which has led to the idea that a treatment for cortical injury might be to increase the number of cortical cells produced. If neurons are produced in the intact cerebral cortex, however, they are clearly produced in rather small numbers. Rakic noted that evolution appears to have gone to great

Figure 25.6 Neurogenesis in the hippocampus displayed over time course of cell division and maturation. (A) Section through the hippocampus illustrates the dentate gyrus, with a granule cell extending its dendrites upward and sending an axon to a pyramidal cell. (B) Precursor cells differentiate into immature neurons, migrate to the appropriate location, and grow mature connections. (After Ormerod and Galea, 2001.)

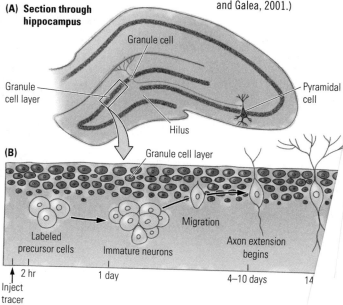

(A) **Section through hippocampus**

Granule cell

Granule cell layer

Pyramidal cell

Hilus

(B)

Granule cell layer

Migration

Labeled precursor cells

Immature neurons

Axon extension begins

2 hr

Inject tracer

1 day

4–10 days

14

lengths to prevent the production of new neurons in most of the adult brain. He observes that, although tumors made up of astrocytes (astrocytomas), for example, are common in the adult brain, there are virtually no neuron tumors (neuromas) in the adult brain, a fact that indicates the rarity of the production of new neurons in adults. Indeed, Rakic even suggests that, if we could understand why neurons are not produced more often, we might know how to stop tumorous growths of other types of body cells, including astrocytes.

The newly generated neurons in the olfactory bulb and hippocampus are assumed to have some function, but the nature of that function is not yet known. Certain possibilities are suggested by the principle that, if new neurons are being produced, room must be made for them or the brain cavity will fill up. Therefore, either the new neurons are being generated to replace lost ones or they somehow stimulate the death of old neurons or the new neurons themselves may be destined to be short-lived.

New neurons likely do replace old ones; however, the survival of new neurons is not certain and can be affected by many types of experience. Table 25.1 summarizes some of the factors that influence neuron generation and neuron survival in the hippocampus. Note especially that, when animals engage the hippocampus to solve some type of neuropsychological problem, the survival of new granule cells is enhanced. We can speculate that the cell survival is related to the successful acquisition of the task. If so, the implication is that learning could be compromised if cell proliferation or survival of both were compromised. Note, too, that stress is correlated with decreases in hippocampal cell proliferation and survival, which is interesting in light of the evidence that stress reduces mental efficiency and may especially impair some forms of memory. Perhaps even more interesting is that chronic stress is related to depression, and antidepressants that stimulate serotonin production (that is, the SSRIs such as fluoxitine) also increase neuron generation in the hippocampus. These observations suggest that the therapeutic activity of antidepressants may

Table 25.1 Effects of various factors on cell proliferation and hippocampal granule neuron survival

Factor	Effect on proliferation	Effect on survival
Adrenal steroids	Down	No change
Aging (rats)	Down	Down?
Adrenalectomy	Up	Up
Dentate gyrus lesions	Up	Up
Running-wheel activity	Up	Unknown
High levels of estradiol	Up	Up
Serotonin agonists (e.g., Prozac)	Up	Unknown
Hippocampal-dependent learning	No change	Up
Season (reduced daylight)	Up	Up
Kindling	Up	No change
Exposure to stress	Down	Down?

Source: After Ormerod and Galea, 2001.

be related to their ability to stimulate neurogenesis, which in turn may alter mental activity (for a further discussion, see Chapter 27). Just how this sequence of events might happen is still unknown.

In sum, neurogenesis is a selective form of plasticity that may be important for both olfactory- and hippocampal-related behaviors, although the precise role of cell generation and survival is largely a matter of speculation at this point. No doubt the study of neurogenesis in the adult brain will remain a rich broth of controversy for some time to come.

Can Plasticity Support Functional Recovery after Injury?

Clinical neurologists have long known that some recovery of function is possible after injury to the nervous system, but the nature and mechanisms of the mediating processes are still poorly understood. A significant problem is the lack of a generally accepted definition of what constitutes "recovery." The word could mean a complete return of function, a marked improvement in function, or indeed any degree of improvement. Another problem is a lack of knowledge concerning what plastic changes might take place in the nervous system after injury. The nature of these changes will influence how we conceptualize the processes related to recovery. Let us explore these problems briefly before considering the topic of brain plasticity and behavior after injury.

Compensation Compared with Recovery

We like to call the question of compensation "the problem of the three-legged cat." When cats are struck by automobiles, they commonly suffer severe injury to one of the back legs. The usual veterinary treatment is to remove the affected leg. Initially, the cats have a great deal of difficulty getting around, leading their owners to wonder, in despair, whether the cats wouldn't be better off dead. Fortunately, cats are resilient, and in a few weeks they seem as agile as before the amputation. This restoration of mobility is often so complete that an observer may not even realize that a leg is missing. In short, the cat has regained lost functions but has *not* recovered its lost leg. Rather, the cat has compensated for its difficulties and developed new behavioral strategies for locomoting through the world.

Many would argue that it is exactly what happens after brain injury. People do not actually recover the lost behaviors or capacities; instead, they develop a new way of functioning to compensate. Consider two cases that we have already encountered. Lyova Saletsky, who was introduced at the beginning of this chapter, had severe cognitive deficits with which he eventually learned to cope, but he clearly did not recover his lost abilities. Similarly, in Chapter 13 we encountered B. K., who had suffered a stroke that left him with a left-upper-field defect in which one quarter of the fovea was devoid of pattern vision. He was initially unable to read and was seriously impaired at recognizing faces. With the passage of time, he regained both these abilities, but not because his lost visual functions were somehow magically restored. Instead, B. K. learned to direct his vision so that parts of words that once disappeared into the scotoma are now captured in the lower visual fields. Similarly, when looking at a face, he directs his gaze to the person's right eye, a shift that places most of the face in the functioning part of his visual field and allows him to recognize who the person is. It is important to note that B. K. did not set out consciously to learn these strategies. They developed spontaneously. Thus, although he had "recovered" the ability to read and recognize faces, the original behaviors did not return.

Is all post-brain-injury improvement compensation or do some improvements actually constitute functional restitution? As stated in Chapter 23, some functional recovery is clearly possible in the infant brain, the best example being the partial return of language functions after left hemispherectomy. But even this "recovery" is not complete and obviously includes compensation in the sense that the right hemisphere now controls talking, a function that develops at the expense of some of the usual right-hemisphere functions. The extreme view is that actual restitution of function is possible only if the injured brain can be replaced and stimulated to function like the original brain—a tall order that seems unlikely to be an option for the adult brain in the near future.

A goal for those studying rehabilitation, therefore, is to find ways of stimulating plastic responses in the brain to provide the best possible compensation. We have seen, for example, that cortical maps can change in response to experience, including amputation. Is it not reasonable, then, to suppose that, if the brain itself is injured, there may be a way to encourage its maps to reorganize? However, we might find that plastic changes after cerebral injury could actually make functional outcome worse. Consider a hypothetical example in which, instead of a limb being amputated, the cortical representation of a limb was damaged by stroke (which could be thought of as "amputation" of the arm representation in the brain). If the arm representation were to reappear in the face area, the person's arm movements might improve, but his or her facial movements could be compromised. If such a change interfered with speech, the problem would not be trivial. Fortunately, deleterious effects of plastic changes are not common.

What Happens When a Brain Is Injured?

Although we may be able to point to a specific immediate cause of brain injury (stroke is such a cause), the damage that is then wrought on the brain is not the result of a single causative event. Rather, the initial event is followed by a cascade of cellular events that can seriously compromise not only the injured part of the brain but other brain regions as well. Consider what happens after a stroke, in which there is an interruption of the blood supply to one of the cerebral arteries. The lack of blood, called *ischemia*, results in a sequence of events that progresses even if the blood flow is restored. In the first seconds to minutes, as illustrated in Figure 25.7, there are changes in the ionic balance of the affected regions, including changes in pH and properties of the cell membrane. These ionic changes result in a variety of pathological events, such as the release of massive amounts of glutamate and the prolonged opening of calcium channels. The open calcium channels in turn allow toxic levels of calcium to enter the cell, not only producing direct toxic effects but also instigating various second-messenger pathways that can prove harmful to the neurons. In the ensuing minutes to hours, mRNA is stimulated, altering the production of proteins in the neurons and possibly proving toxic to the cells. Next, the tissues become inflamed and swollen, threatening the integrity of cells that may be relatively far removed from the site of injury. Finally, a form of neural shock—von Monakow called it **diaschisis**—occurs. As von Monakow noted, after the brain is injured, not only are localized neural tissue and its function lost, but areas related to the damaged region suffer a sudden withdrawal of excitation or inhibition. Such sudden changes in input can lead to a temporary loss of function, both in areas adjacent to an injury and in regions that may be quite distant.

A stroke may also be followed by changes in the metabolism or in the glucose utilization of the injured hemisphere or in both—changes that may persist for days. Like diaschisis, these metabolic changes can have severe effects on the functioning of otherwise normal tissue. After a cortical stroke, for example, metabolic rate throughout the rest of the hemisphere has been shown to decrease by about 25%.

Treatments for cerebral injury are directed at various targets in the postinjury cascade. For example, drugs called *neuroprotectants* can be used to block calcium channels or prevent ionic imbalance, in the hope that they will protect neurons from the cascade of toxic events that follow an ischemic episode. Other drugs can be used to reduce swelling or to enhance metabolic activity. The effects of neuroprotectants and anti-inflammatory drugs are obviously quite different from the effect of treatments aimed at stimulating plasticity and functional compensation.

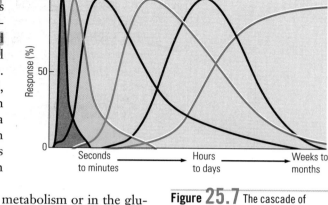

Figure 25.7 The cascade of changes taking place after a stroke. In the first seconds to minutes, ionic changes are followed by changes in second messengers and RNA production. These changes are followed by changes in protein production and inflammation, which slowly resolves in hours to days. Recovery follows and takes from weeks to months or years.

Examples of Functional Restitution

The return of function is seldom sudden. An examination of the stages of functional restitution and their associated behaviors often reveals a slow reemergence of restored functions that resembles the sequence of developmental stages in infants. We will consider two common examples of functional restoration after cortical stroke: recovery of movement and recovery of language. We will then examine some of the characteristics of functional improvement in two particular populations: soldiers with head injuries and neurosurgical cases. Finally, we will look at patients' prospects of returning to work and having a "normal" life after cerebral injury.

Recovery from Motor-Cortex Damage

Twitchell described recovery from hemiplegia (inability to move the contralateral limbs) produced by thrombosis, embolism, or stroke of the middle cerebral artery in humans. The recovery sequence closely parallels the development of reaching and of the grasp response described by Twitchell in infants. The hemiplegia, which appeared immediately after the damage occurred, was marked by complete flaccidity of the muscles and loss of all reflexes and voluntary movements. Recovery took place over a period of days or weeks and followed a relatively orderly sequence: (1) return of reflexes; (2) development of rigidity; (3) grasping that was facilitated by or occurred as part of other movements; and (4) development of voluntary grasping (which entailed recovery of movement sequentially in the shoulder, elbow, wrist, and hand—first in the flexor musculature and then in the extensor musculature). Voluntary grasping continued to improve until independent movements of the fingers were well developed. Complete recovery of use of the arms, when it occurred, appeared between 23 and 40 days after the lesion. About 30% of patients reached the last stage of recovery; the others showed arrested recovery at one of the preceding stages.

Recovery from Aphasia

Kertesz reviewed the prospects of recovery from aphasia and used the case histories of his own patients as examples. Figure 25.8 graphs the recovery of an example patient from each of his subgroups. (The "aphasia quotients" were derived from the patients' scores on the Western Aphasia Battery, which tests spontaneous speech content, fluency, comprehension, repetition, and so forth). Kertesz makes the following generalizations: First, posttrauma (head-injury) patients showed the most rapid and often almost complete recovery, whereas recovery in stroke patients was less pronounced and in some groups was almost absent. Second, initial deficits were the least severe in anomic patients (that is, people who are unable to generate the names for common objects) and the most severe in global aphasics, with intermediate severity seen in other groups. The actual rate of recovery, given initial impairments, was often quite similar in all groups. Third, when recovery occurred, patients tended to progress to one of the other stages, but recovery usually stopped with anomic aphasia. Fourth, most recovery occurred in the first 3 months (illustrated only for the posttrauma patient in Figure 25.8), with some recovery occurring in the next 6 months and less recovery occurring in the fol-

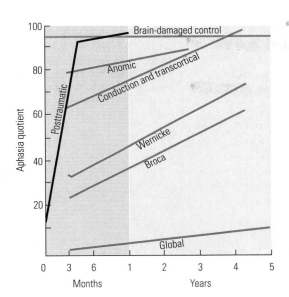

Figure 25.8 Initial deficits and recovery in stroke patients with different language disorders (blue lines) and in a posttrauma patient (black line). Each line is a representative patient. (After Kertesz, 1979.)

lowing 6 months. Thereafter, little or no recovery occurred. Fifth, there was some evidence that younger patients showed better recovery; the effects of intelligence, occupation, and sex in those patients were slight if present. Sixth, the language components that were most resistant to brain damage were naming, oral imitation, comprehension of nouns, and yes–no responses, functions that may be partly mediated by the right hemisphere.

Recovery from Traumatic Lesions

Teuber described the deficits of war veterans as assessed in tests given 1 week after injury and 20 years later. These patients are excellent candidates for study for a number of reasons: they underwent standardized testing after induction into the army, they were young at the time of injury, the immediate aftermath of the injury is documented, and the kind and extent of recovery can be documented through prolonged follow-up examinations by veterans' services.

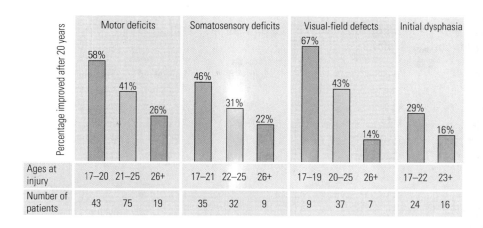

Figure 25.9 Estimated improvement, based on initial examination (no later than 1 week after injury) and follow-up examination (20 years later), for some body regions (extremities, sides of face) for which symptoms were recorded (reflex changes, paralysis, weakness) in the motor system; for noted sensory losses in the somatosensory system; for the visual field (diminution in number of quadrants known to be affected); and in symptoms interpreted as dysphasia. Note the advantage of younger age at the time of wounding. (After Teuber, 1975.)

Teuber's results, summarized in Figure 25.9, reveal that 4% of the veterans showed some recovery from motor defects, 36% showed some recovery from somatosensory defects, 43% showed some recovery from visual defects, and 24% showed some recovery from initial dysphasia.

Two comments should be made about Teuber's analysis. First, it must be noted that more than half the patient population showed no recovery at all, and the failure of more than 75% of patients to show recovery from dysphasia is not encouraging. The latter percentage is in line with Luria's report that 66% of his dysphasic patients showed no recovery. Second, the usefulness of the analysis is limited by the fact that the assessments are not quantitative; there is no estimate of the degree of recovery.

A study of a larger population of veterans, of the Vietnam War, was undertaken by Mohr and his coworkers. In general, their results are consistent with those of Teuber in that a great deal of recovery of function is seen subsequent to penetrating brain injury. In fact, Mohr reports more-extensive recovery from aphasia (34%) than does Teuber and reports that the recovery continued for years after injury.

More recently, Zihl and Cramon reported that practice in locating lights led to an increase in the visual field of partly blind patients, an improvement that would not have occurred without the practice. What effect specific therapy might have had on the patients reported in the veteran studies is not known.

Recovery from Surgical Lesions

Surgery to remove brain tumors or relieve epilepsy often damages parts of the brain that were intact and functional before the operation. Assessment tests have been administered to patients within days of tumor surgery and as long as 20 years after to evaluate such damage and gauge recovery. Unfortunately, recovery seems to have been so infrequent that the breakdown of data at different test–retest intervals is not reported. Table 25.2 summarizes the results from some studies in which tests were given a few days before surgery, within 20 days after surgery, and from 1 to 20 years after surgery. These results show that: after dorsolateral frontal lesions, there was no recovery in card sorting; after right temporal lesions, there was no recovery in recall of the Rey figure; and after parietal lesions, there was no recovery in finger-position sense or arm-movement copying.

Table **25.2** **Presurgical, postsurgical, and follow-up performance on neuropsychological tests by patients with cortical lesions**

Test	Lesion	Preop	Postop	Follow-up	Control	Reference
Card-sorting categories	Frontal	3.3	1.4	1.3	4.6	Milner, 1963
Card-sorting errors	Frontal	54.9	73.2	78.2	37.7	Milner, 1963
Rey-figure copy score	Right temporal	31.2	30.6	29.8	34.9	Taylor, 1969
Rey-figure recall score	Right temporal	15.4	15.3	13.8	24.2	Taylor, 1969
Finger-position sense Incidence of deficit (%)	Central					
Ipsilateral		24	14	6	—	Taylor, 1969
Contralateral		36	43	65	—	
Arm-movement copying	Left parietal		73	75.8	90.2	Kolb and Milner, 1981

The finding of no recovery is also reported in some other studies. Jones-Gottman and Milner tested patient groups within 2 weeks of surgery and 1 or more years later on spontaneous drawing tasks. The subjects were told to draw as many unnamable objects as they could within 5 minutes. Although all patient groups showed some reduction in performance level relative to control groups, patients with right frontal lesions were the most impaired, and there were no differences in performance between patients tested shortly after surgery and those tested more than a year after it.

There also seems to be little or no recovery in memory after bilateral medial-temporal-lobe removal. In a 14-year follow-up, Milner and colleagues report that the amnesic patient H. M. had a presurgical IQ of 104, a 2-year follow-up IQ of 112, and a 9-year follow-up IQ of 118, yet, despite this improvement in intelligence score, his anterograde amnesia remained essentially unchanged.

In some studies of patients with long-standing lesions, a degree of recovery has been noted on some tests. Milner reported in 1975 that patients with left temporal lesions had preoperative memory scores of 12, early postoperative scores of 4.4, and 5- to 20-year follow-up scores of 8. This improvement is significant. There are a number of possible explanations for the improvements observed on this test. First, the score is a composite of logical memory (recall of stories) and paired-associates learning (learning pairs of words, such as "frog" and "flower," and remembering one when given the other). Which component of the test showed recovery is not clear. Blakemore and Falconer studied paired-associates learning in 86 temporal lobectomy patients for as long as 10 years after surgery. They found that the deficit lasted for 2 to 3 years, after which they saw progressive recovery, provided the patients were young. Thus, the recovery observed by Milner could have been due to improvement in one facet of the task. Second, Jones-Gottman showed that, if left-temporal-lobe patients are taught to use imagery (for example, they imagine an elephant with a bouquet of flowers in its trunk for the associate word pair "bouquet-elephant"), they show substantial improvement in memory. Hence recovery may have been due to the development of alternative memory strategies. Third, the temporal cortex must have rather special properties to allow rapid memory storage. Those properties probably also make it especially prone to epilepsy. It is possible that, if any of the temporal cortex remains intact, it retains a special capacity for plasticity that is not characteristic of other brain areas.

In summary, we think that the results from some of the studies reported here are sources of important insight into the question of recovery of function. The results imply that, if the test is specific for certain brain areas and if the lesions destroy or disable the entire area, recovery will not occur. What makes this position particularly persuasive is that the surgical patients had tumors or epilepsy at the site of the lesions, which could have encouraged the function to move elsewhere. Nevertheless there is little or no evidence in the test results to suggest that any such transfer took place.

Return to Daily Life

A person's capacity to work and earn a living clearly depends on many behavioral abilities and configurations of abilities. Brain damage may affect some of them more than others, but people can compensate for brain damage in many ways. The results of studies by Dresser and his coworkers show that, when gainful employment is used as a measure of recovery, as was done for veterans injured in the Korean War, the resulting rates of recovery are quite high: approximately 80%. This measure gives the highest rate of recovery of any that we have found in the literature and strongly suggests that some factor such as behavioral compensation is operating. This high rate of recovery does not minimize the difficulties of the 20% who were not employed. Furthermore, it does not take into consideration the quality of employment. In fact, Oddy and Humphrey suggest that work is not a sensitive index of recovery. Of their 54 patients with closed-head injuries, 48 were back at work within 2 years, but many were restricted in their work activity and reported that they had not regained their full working capacity. Other aspects of their lives also suffered, because they had not fully resumed their leisure activities and social contacts. Interestingly, of all aspects of social relations, those with siblings suffered most. Oddy and Humphrey emphasize that therapy should be directed not only toward returning to work but also toward pursuing leisure activities and social relations.

One way to examine the chronic effects of brain damage and how those affected cope is to study the self-reports of people who have been brain damaged. Generally, very little attention is given to these reports, but they can be sources of valuable insight into questions of recovery. Fredrick Linge, a clinical psychologist, described the changes that he underwent after suffering brain damage in an automobile accident. He was in a coma for the first week after the accident and was not expected to recover significantly. Nevertheless, he did manage to return to a relatively demanding clinical practice about a year after his accident; but, even so, he was changed by the brain damage and had to make adjustments in life style and work routine to cope. He describes his adjustments in the following way:

> In learning to live with my brain damage, I have found through trial and error that certain things help greatly and others hinder my coping. In order to learn and retain information best, I try to eliminate as many distractions as possible and concentrate all my mental energy on the task at hand. . . . In the past I enjoyed a rather chaotic life style, but I now find that I want "a place for everything and everything in its place." When remembering is difficult, order and habit make the minutiae of daily living much easier.

> I cannot cope with anger as well as I was able to do before my accident. . . . [O]nce I become angry, I find it impossible to "put the brakes on" and I attribute this directly to my brain damage. It is extremely frightening to me to find myself in this state, and I still have not worked out a truly satisfactory solution, except insofar as I try to avoid anger-provoking situations or try to deal with them before they become too provoking.
>
> My one-track mind seems to help me to take each day as it comes without excessive worry and to enjoy the simple things of life in a way that I never did before. As well, I seem to be a more effective therapist, since I stick to the basic issues at hand and have more empathy with others than I did previously. (Linge, 1980, pp. 6–7)

This self-report by Linge shows that assessments of recovery cannot be limited to measures such as reemployment or even levels of renewed social contacts. Such measures may fail to indicate the ways in which a person has changed and the coping mechanisms that he or she has learned to employ. It is noteworthy that Linge was a professional psychologist who lived in a social milieu in which people were willing to help him reestablish himself. Many people who do not have similar support systems and resources will have a much more difficult time recovering. Linge's comments also demonstrate that the brain-damaged person must change not only the external environment but the internal environment as well.

Plasticity in the Injured Brain

Just as plasticity in the normal brain can be investigated at different levels, so too can plasticity in the injured brain. To date, most work has focused on changes in maps, determined either by functional imaging or by brain stimulation. We consider each method in turn.

Functional Imaging after Cerebral Injury

The functional changes observed after stroke provide an excellent window into cerebral plasticity. If patients can recover from stroke, despite having lost significant areas of cerebral cortex, then we can conclude that some type of change has taken place in the remaining parts of the brain. Functional imaging techniques, especially PET, fMRI, and TMS, can be used repeatedly in the weeks and months after stroke to document changes in cerebral activation that might correlate with functional improvement. Several recent reviews of such studies have led us to the following conclusions (see, especially, reviews by Cramer and Bastings and by Rijntjes and Weiller):

1. If the primary sensorimotor cortex survives a stroke, some functional improvement is likely to occur with the passage of time, even if hemiparesis immediately follows the stroke. Although the efferent fiber tracts may be damaged, thus causing the hemiparesis, the remaining cortex may yet become activated. Functional improvement is correlated with the appearance of this activation.

2. Activation of the motor areas during limb movements recruits cortical areas along the rim of cortical injury. In addition, larger areas of the motor cortex are often activated by particular movements. For example, hand or limb movements often activate regions of the face area, possibly because of intact pyramidal tract fibers leaving the face area.

3. The motions of stroke patients activate much larger areas of cortex, especially parietal and premotor areas, than do similar movements by control subjects. These regions of activation are extended both for language and for motor functions.

4. Reorganization is not restricted to one hemisphere; instead, similar changes take place bilaterally. Thus, although the performance of a unilateral motor task largely activates only the contralateral cortex, the brains of stroke victims show a marked increase in bilateral activation. The increased activation in the contralateral hemisphere is especially notable in patients with disturbances of language in which regions opposite the language areas (so-called homologous areas) show activation, a result that is illustrated in the Snapshot on page 688.

5. The capacity for reorganization declines with increasing size of stroke and increasing age. The relation to stroke size is likely due to the fact that the presence of incompletely damaged regions, such as Wernicke's area, is a good predictor of functional improvement. Recall that the severity of the initial deficit in aphasia correlates with later outcome (see Figure 25.8). Presumably, the extent of the initial deficit is related to the extent of injury.

6. There is considerable variability among stroke victims. This variability is probably related to differences in the degree of prestroke activations and is particularly true of language. People who show the greatest bilateral activation for language functions after stroke are probably those who already had some bilateral activation before the stroke, as occurs in left-handers. Rijntjes and Weiller note that the extent of activation of the right hemisphere during language tasks is highly variable and that the pattern of activation in people who have exhibited recovery from Wernicke's aphasia is remarkably similar to the maximal areas of right-hemisphere activation seen in normal brains.

In conclusion, functional improvement after stroke corresponds to a change in functional organization of the remaining brain, as shown in functional imaging studies. We hasten to point out, however, that such studies are usually reported only for patients who show good recovery; even so, the studies typically provide little information about the details of treatments that the patients might have received.

Physiological Mapping after Cerebral Injury

Nudo and his coworkers mapped the hand and digit areas of the motor cortex of squirrel monkeys. When they subsequently removed a part of the digit area, they found that use of the contralateral hand was reduced. When they then remapped the motor cortex, they found that the monkeys were unable to produce movements of the lower part of the arm, wrist, and digits, as illustrated in

SNAPSHOT

Using Imaging to Study Recovery and Compensation

Case LF1 was a right-handed 72-year-old retired professional who was taken to the hospital after waking up with speech difficulties and general confusion. MRI revealed a stroke damaging parts of the left inferior frontal cortex, including much of the anterior speech cortex. On examination a month after the stroke, LF1 was described as having a nonfluent aphasia in which he showed little spontaneous speech but could respond to simple questions. He could repeat words, read words, and name most objects. He performed poorly on speech production tasks, however, such as the Thurstone Word-Fluency Test, a task requiring the generation of multiple words beginning with a single letter (see Chapter 15).

LF1 was especially impaired at tasks that in normal subjects are known to activate the left prefrontal cortex—tasks such as generating verbs when given nouns, nouns when given verbs, or synonyms. Nonetheless, he was able to do some tasks that normally do activate the left inferior frontal cortex. One example is a word-completion task that would normally be impaired by a left inferior frontal lesion. For example, when he was given a part of a word, such as "Cou" or "Hou," he was able to use it to produce a complete word, such as "Couple" and "House." The presence of some intact language abilities led Buckner and his colleagues to use PET imaging on LF1 and 16 control subjects while they performed such tasks. The adjoining PET scans show that, unlike the control subjects, LF1 (bottom right) showed activation in the right-hemisphere region homologous to the left-hemisphere region activated in the control subjects (top right). This finding suggests that a pathway similar to the one activated in the normal subjects was activated in LF1 except that, in LF1, the activation was in the right hemisphere. The researchers conclude that LF1's compensatory pathway allowed him to recall and use words, but only in a limited manner, thus explaining his partial recovery. The compensatory pathway seems unlikely to have been formed after the stroke, because his functional improvement occurred within the first month after his stroke. Instead, some inhibitory process acting on the right-hemisphere connections seems more

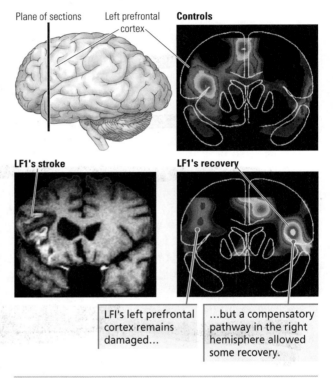

PET scans showing activation in LF1's right hemisphere (bottom right) and control subjects' left hemisphere (top right) when performing language tasks. (After Buckner et al., 1996.)

likely to have been released by the stroke, leading to his functional improvement. The right-hemisphere region is presumably used for other kinds of tasks in normal subjects but has the capacity to accomplish limited speech function in the damaged brain.

(R. L. Buckner, M. Corbetta, J. Schatz, M. E. Raichele, and S. E. Petersen. Preserved speech abilities and compensation following prefrontal damage. *Proceedings of the National Academy of Sciences of the United States of America* 93:1249–1253, 1996.)

Figure 25.10. In other words, the hand area had disappeared from the cortical map, and only a stump of the upper arm remained. They subjected additional animals to the same procedure, except that after surgery they provided therapy for the affected limb. The therapy consisted of substantial forced use in which the good limb was bound so that the monkey was forced to use the affected limb. When the researchers examined the motor maps of these monkeys again, the hand and digit area was present, except for the area that had originally been removed. Nevertheless, the therapy brought about some recovery of the use of the digits represented by the missing area. Presumably, the movements made by the digits that had lost their cortical representation were mediated by the representations of the remaining digits.

The importance of therapy is the significant feature of the Nudo experiments. Therapy is necessary to maintain the functions of the undamaged cortex and the movements that it represents. Therapy can also promote compensation for the affected body parts.

The form of plasticity described by Nudo and coworkers may explain the recovery in the following case reported by Bucy and coworkers. They studied a man with a pyramidal tract sectioned in the lower brainstem as a treatment for involuntary movements. During the first 24 hours after surgery, he had complete flaccid hemiplegia, followed by a slight return of voluntary movement in his extremities. By the 10th day, he could stand alone and walk with assistance. By the 24th day, he could walk unaided. Within 7 months, maximum recovery seemed to have been reached, and he could move his feet, hands, fingers, and toes with only slight impairment. At autopsy, 2½ years later, about 17% of his pyramidal tract fibers were found to be intact. The recovery of his ability to move his toes and fingers seems attributable to that remaining 17%, which did the job formerly done by the entire tract. We venture to observe that, if the man had been discouraged from using the afflicted limbs, his recovery would have been lessened.

Variables Affecting Recovery

Many variables in addition to lesion size affect the rate of recovery from brain damage. These variables are not fully discussed in many papers for the following reasons: measurements are difficult to make; patient groups are often small, which lessens the validity of any statistics derived from them; or, simply, a particular researcher may not think they are important. These variables include age, sex, handedness, intelligence, and personality. Overall, recovery from brain damage seems likely to be best if the patient is a young, intelligent, optimistic, left-handed female.

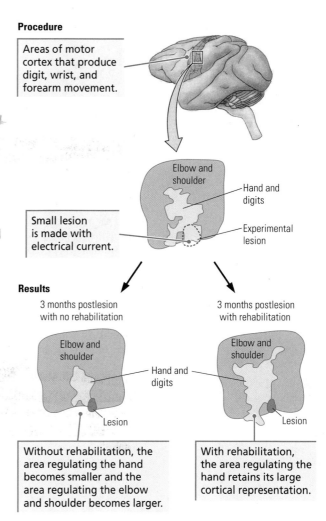

Procedure

Areas of motor cortex that produce digit, wrist, and forearm movement.

Elbow and shoulder

Hand and digits

Small lesion is made with electrical current.

Experimental lesion

Results

3 months postlesion with no rehabilitation

3 months postlesion with rehabilitation

Elbow and shoulder

Hand and digits

Lesion

Elbow and shoulder

Lesion

Without rehabilitation, the area regulating the hand becomes smaller and the area regulating the elbow and shoulder becomes larger.

With rehabilitation, the area regulating the hand retains its large cortical representation.

Rehabilitation prevents both a loss of movement in the hand and a decrease in the hand's cortical representation.

Figure 25.10 The effect of experience on the cortical representation of the forelimb in the motor cortex of a monkey after brain damage. The cortical representation of the digit, wrist, and forearm is mapped by using microstimulation. A small lesion is then made in the area indicated by the dashed lines. When the cortex is remapped months later, the map has decreased in size much beyond the area of the lesion. Furthermore, the new map has a larger representation of the elbow and shoulder than that of the preinjury map. In monkeys that underwent rehabilitative therapy, the hand area maintained its size. (After Nudo et al., 1996.)

Youth is one of the easier variables to measure. Teuber and coworkers found that, on a number of tests, recovery by soldiers from head injuries is greater in the 17-to-20 age group than in the 21-to-25 age group, which in turn is greater than in the age group 26+ (see Figure 25.9). Milner reports that patients older than 40 who have removals near the posterior temporal speech zone in the left hemisphere show less recovery than do younger patients. It is noteworthy that age does not always appear as a significant factor in studies of recovery, as reported by Kertesz.

An analysis of age effects is complicated by the fact that age is a contributing factor to the onset of many kinds of brain damage; that is, strokes and other kinds of brain abnormality are common in older people, who are more likely in any case to be declining in motor and cognitive function owing to the normal processes of aging. Thus, recovery may tend to be obscured by aging.

Handedness and sex, both for much the same reason, may influence the outcome of brain damage. Recall from Chapter 12 that a number of theories argue that female and male brains differ in both anatomy and functional organization, with imaging studies revealing less functional lateralization in the female. Considering the imaging evidence in brain-injured patients discussed earlier, if females have more bilateral functional activation, then they should show more functional recovery. Likewise, familial left-handers appear to be less lateralized in function than right-handers, again providing an advantage for recruiting undamaged regions after brain injury.

People with superior intelligence are generally believed to have better recovery than are those with lower intelligence. There is no clear reason for this difference, although whatever neural properties allow for higher intelligence may also provide an advantage after injury. For example, people of higher intelligence may have more-plastic brains and thus respond better to injury, although this possibility is not easy to prove. Alternatively, people of higher intelligence may be able to generate more strategies to solve problems than less intelligent people can. A complication is that, although the ultimate recovery of a very intelligent person may be excellent in relation to the recovery of others, the actual residual deficit may be equal simply because the very intelligent person would normally function at a higher level. Thus, in our experience, highly intelligent people generally complain more about the negative effects of residual deficits on quality of life.

The role of personality in recovery is difficult to evaluate, but optimistic, extroverted, and easygoing people are widely thought to have a better prognosis after brain injury. One reason could be that people who are more optimistic about recovering are more likely to comply with rehabilitation programs. Unfortunately, brain damage may have a negative influence on personality. For example, patients may develop postinjury depression and, as a result, would be expected to show poor or at least slow recovery.

Therapeutic Approaches to Brain Damage

Three major experimental therapeutic approaches to brain damage are: (1) rehabilitation procedures, which consist of a variety of behavioral and psychological therapies; (2) pharmacological therapies, which are intended to promote recovery in the immediate postsurgery period; (3) brain-tissue transplants and stem-cell-induction techniques, which are being developed in the hope of restoring normal brain function. Rehabilitation procedures are used widely, with mixed results; pharmacological and implantation techniques are in the animal-experimentation stage.

Rehabilitation

It would seem logical that people with brain injuries should be placed in a rehabilitation program of some sort. Surprisingly, however, neuroscientists as yet have little information concerning the value of different kinds of rehabilitation programs, the optimal timing for the initiation of a rehabilitation program, or even the optimal duration of rehabilitative therapy. Although both speech and physiotherapies are often assumed to be effective, the role of any specific therapy (the kinds of changes that it brings about and how or why they take place) is a matter of debate. Consider, for example, that patients undergoing speech therapy not only receive speech training but also have daily contact with a therapist. Much of this interaction is social and not strictly related to language. The importance of this type of stimulation cannot be overstated. For example, there is growing evidence that patients who are placed in a dedicated stroke unit, rather than treated as an outpatient, are likely to have a better outcome. Such a unit has a variety of professional rehabilitation therapists working together and providing stimulation for much of the waking day.

The results of studies of laboratory animals have consistently shown that the single most successful treatment strategy for optimizing functional recovery is placing animals in complex, stimulating environments (see studies by Johansson and her colleagues). But these results do not suggest that rehabilitation therapies are not useful. Indeed, the results of laboratory studies showing that specific types of training can alter motor maps suggest otherwise. Consider two examples.

Taub and his colleagues developed a therapy referred to as *constraint-induced movement therapy.* They based it on the observation that, after stroke, many patients have initial hemiparesis, develop strategies to use the unimpaired, opposite limb, and in so doing fail to attempt to use the impaired limb. The goal of constraint-induced therapy is to induce patients to use the affected limb for several hours a day for a period of weeks. This induced use is accomplished by placing the unaffected limb in a sling and forcing the patient to perform daily activities with the impaired limb. Additionally, patients are given various tasks to practice with the affected limb, tasks such as picking up objects or turning the pages of magazines. This therapy is effective in stimulating sometimes dramatic improvement in the affected limb. An explanation for the improvement is that the motor training stimulates plastic changes in the brain, leading to an enlargement of the motor representation of the affected arm and hand.

Liepert and colleagues measured this increase by using TMS both before and after 12 days of constraint-induced therapy. They found that the training stimulated a dramatic increase in the area of the cortex representing the paretic hand (a 50% increase in map size after 12 days of training and still present 6 months later). The location of the map expansion varied from patient to patient, presumably because the precise area of injury varied from person to person. As already mentioned, parallel studies on monkeys by Nudo yielded similar results, as illustrated in Figure 25.10.

The most critical problems faced by many brain-injured people are not strictly sensory or motor but more-complex cognitive problems. Consider, for example, the problems of patients with different forms of memory disturbances or spatial disorientation. For these patients, some form of cognitive rehabilitation is needed, and several cognitive programs are now available (see books by Sohlberg and Mateer and by Prigatano). A broader matter, however, is the difficulty of coping with residual cognitive deficits outside the clinic. For example, a person with spatial disorientations might benefit somewhat from practicing various paper-and-pencil tasks, but in the end the patient may continue to struggle with the real-world problem of finding his or her way home. Thus, therapy for brain damage often requires creativity and initiative on the part of the therapist trying to develop techniques that are relevant to an individual patient. We were once asked to recommend a therapy for a depressed motorcycle racer who had suffered extensive brain damage after crashing a hang glider. We half seriously suggested a tricycle, which his caregivers then had constructed for him. His attitude improved dramatically, and he was soon racing the tricycle around the hospital grounds and taking trips to town. The exercise and attitude change helped him tackle other tasks that furthered his recovery.

Substitution systems may be useful for some patients. For example, visual information can be recorded with a video camera and transformed into a tactile message presented on the skin as a partial substitute for vision. Various machines, especially computers, can be used to perform specific tasks.

Pharmacological Therapies

There has been a long-standing interest in the use of pharmacological therapies for ameliorating the effects of brain damage. The general idea is to use compounds that will facilitate plastic changes in the brain. For example, psychomotor stimulants such as amphetamine or nicotine are known to stimulate changes in cortical and subcortical circuits in the normal brain. It is hoped that the use of such compounds in the injured brain can stimulate synaptic changes that might facilitate functional recovery (see review by Feeney). Research results suggest that the rate of recovery can be increased if pharmacological treatments and experience are combined shortly after brain damage. The success of such treatments in the laboratory has led to the initiation of clinical trials using amphetamine with stroke patients, with promising results.

Psychomotor stimulants not only increase transmitter levels but also stimulate the production of various growth factors. For instance, Flores and Stewart showed that amphetamine stimulates an increase in the production of basic fibroblast growth factor (bFGF). This factor acts to enhance synaptogenesis in the brain and, presumably, could stimulate functional improvement after injury. Because the production of growth factors is stimulated not only by drugs but also by behavioral treatments, such as placing animals in complex environments, we may find that combinations of growth factors and behavioral therapies are more beneficial than the use of either modality alone.

Brain-Tissue Transplants and Stem-Cell Induction

The idea of transplanting neural tissue in mammals and the techniques for doing so date to the first decade of the twentieth century. Yet, until recently, the possibility that neural transplantation could have a practical application was viewed as rather remote. In the 1980s, researchers discovered that, if fetal tissue containing immature cells was extracted from particular brain regions and then inserted into the appropriate region of a recipient animal, the fetal tissue would grow and integrate into the host brain. Such a procedure would be impractical for repairing damage to a complex circuit such as the neocortex, but perhaps transplantation of specific cell types, such as dopaminergic cells from the brainstem, could be beneficial to patients missing those cells, such as Parkinson patients. More than 100 Parkinson patients have now received transplants. Improvements have been reported in some cases, but a large study by Fried and colleagues is not encouraging. By and large, the relief from symptoms has been minor or only short-lived. Perhaps the transplants do not grow sufficiently in the large human brain, are not adequately incorporated into brain circuitry, or are affected by the same disease process that is causing the original loss of dopamine cells.

Another approach to transplanting fetal tissue is to stimulate stem cells within the host brain by using growth factors. Knowing that the brain is capable of making new neurons even in adulthood, researchers hypothesize that it ought to be possible to potentiate the production of new neurons after injury. If these new neurons can then be induced to migrate to the site of injury and integrate into that part of the brain, they may be able restore some level of functioning there. An alternate approach is to take stem cells from a patient's brain or perhaps even from some other part of a patient's body (such as bone marrow), culture the cells to form thousands or millions of neurons of a particular type (such as dopaminergic cells), and then place these cells into the injured part of the brain, where they will differentiate and become integrated into the circuitry. Findings from preliminary studies suggest that both of these procedures are workable, at least in principle.

Summary

The brain is not a static organ but is constantly changing, a property known as plasticity. Brain plasticity can be studied at several levels, including the analysis of behavioral change, the measurement of cortical maps by using imaging or physiological techniques, the measurement of synaptic change by using Golgi or electron-microscopic techniques, the measurement of molecular changes (including genetic changes), and the demonstration of the generation of new neurons or glia or both.

Brain damage is a major cause of loss of function. When the brain is injured, a cascade of damaging molecular events unfolds within the first 48 hours after an injury, followed by an extended period of repair that may last years. The brain can compensate for injury, but true recovery of function is probably impossible without regenerating the lost brain tissues and restoring the original connections. The practical definition of restitution of function must be based on the extent to which the patient regains an acceptable daily life. Functional improvement is affected by a variety of factors, including age, handedness, sex, intelligence, and treatment. Therapy for brain injury currently includes (1) rehabilitation emphasizing the repeated use of affected limbs or cognitive processes and (2) pharmacological treatments designed to stimulate brain plasticity. In some special cases, such as Parkinson's disease, brain-cell transplantation or stem-cell induction may prove to be beneficial, likely in conjunction with rehabilitation or pharmacological treatments or both.

References

Aglioti, S. "Anomalous" representations and perceptions. In J. Grafman and Y. Christen, Eds. *Neuronal Plasticity: Building a Bridge from the Laboratory to the Clinic*. New York: Springer, 1999, pp.79–91.

Bach-y-Rita, P., Ed. *Recovery of Function: Theoretical Considerations for Brain Injury Rehabilitation*. Bern, Switzerland: Hyuber, 1980.

Blakemore, C. B., and M. A. Falconer. Long-term effects of anterior temporal lobectomy on certain cognitive functions. *Journal of Neurology, Neurosurgery, and Psychiatry* 30:364–367, 1967.

Bliss, T. V. P., and T. Lomo. Long lasting potentiation of synaptic transmission in the dentate area of the anesthetized rabbit following stimulation of the perforant path. *Journal of Physiology* 232:331–356, 1973.

Buckner, R. L., M. Corbetta, J. Schatz, M. E. Raichele, and S. E. Petersen. Preserved speech abilities and compensation following prefrontal damage. *Proceedings of the National Academy of Sciences of the United States of America* 93:1249–1253, 1996.

Bucy, P. C., J. E. Keplinger, and E. B. Siqueira. Destruction of the "pyramidal tract" in man. *Journal of Neurosurgery* 21:385–398, 1964.

Cain, D. P. Synaptic models of neuroplasticity: What is LTP? In C. A. Shaw and J. C. McEachern, Eds. *Toward a Theory of Neuroplasticity*. Lillington, NC: Taylor & Francis, 2001, pp. 118–129.

Candia, V., T. Elbert, E. Altenmuller, H. Rau, T. Schafer, and E. Taub. Constraint-induced movement therapy for focal hand dystonia in musicians. *Lancet* 353:42, 1999.

Clower, D. M., J. M. Hoffman, J. R. Voraw, T. L. Faber, R. P. Woods, and G. E. Alexander. Role of posterior parietal cortex in the recallibration of visually-guided reaching. *Nature* 383:618–621, 1996.

Cramer, S. C., and E. P. Bastings. Mapping clinically relevant plasticity after stroke. *Neuropharmacology* 39:842–851, 2000.

Dresser, A. C., A. M. Meirowsky, G. H. Weiss, M. L. McNeel, A. G. Simon, and W. F. Caveness. Gainful employment following head injury. *Archives of Neurology* 29:111–116, 1973.

Elbert, T., S. Heim, and B. Rockstroh. Neural plasticity and development. In C. A. Nelson and M. Luciana, Eds. *Handbook of Developmental Cognitive Neuroscience*. Cambridge: MIT Press, 2001, pp. 191–204.

Feeney, D. M. From laboratory to clinic: Noradrenergic enhancement of physical therapy for stroke or trauma patients. *Advances in Neurology* 73:383–394, 1997.

Flores, C., and J. Stewart. Basic fibroblast growth factor as a mediator of the effects of glutamate in the development of long-lasting sensitization to stimulant drugs: Studies in the rat. *Psychopharmacology (Berlin)* 151:152–165, 2000.

Freed, C. R., P. E. Greene, R. E. Breeze, W. Y. Tsai, W. DuMouchel, R. Kao, S. Dillon, H. Winfield, S. Culver, J. Q. Trojanowski, D. Eidelberg, and S. Fahn. Transplantation of embryonic dopamine neurons for severe Parkinson's disease. *New England Journal of Medicine* 344:710–719, 2001.

Jacobs, B., M. Schall, and A. B. Scheibel. A quantitative dendritic analysis of Wernicke's area in humans II: Gender, hemispheric, and environmental factors. *Journal of Comparative Neurology* 327:97–111, 1993.

Jacobs, B., and A. B. Scheibel. A quantitative dendritic analysis of Wernicke's area in humans I: Lifespan changes. *Journal of Comparative Neurology* 327:83–96, 1993.

Jenkins, W. M., M. M. Merzenich, M. T. Ochs, T. Allard, and E. Guic-Robles. Functional reorganization of primary somatosensory cortex in adult owl monkeys after behaviorally controlled tactile stimulation. *Journal of Neurophysiology* 63:82–104, 1990.

Johansson, B. B., and P. V. Belichenko. Neuronal plasticity and dendritic spines: Effect of environmental enrichment on intact and postischemic rat brain. *Journal of Cerebral Blood Flow and Metabolism* 22:89–96, 2002.

Jones, M. K. Imagery as a mnemonic aid after left temporal lobectomy: Contrast between material-specific and generalized memory disorders. *Neuropsychologia* 12:21–30, 1974.

Jones-Gottman, M., and B. Milner. Design fluency: The invention of nonsense drawings after focal cortical lesions. *Neuropsychologia* 15:653–674, 1977.

Kertesz, A. *Aphasia and Associated Disorders.* New York: Grune & Stratton, 1979.

Kohler, I. The formation and transformation of the perceptual world. *Psychological Issues* 3:1–173, 1964.

Kolb, B., and B. Milner. Performance of complex arm and facial movements after focal brain lesions. *Neuropsychologia* 19:491–503, 1981.

Kolb, B., and I. Q. Whishaw. Brain plasticity and behavior. *Annual Review of Psychology* 49:43–64, 1998.

Linge, F. What does it feel like to be brain-damaged? *Canada's Mental Health* 28:4–7, 1980.

Luria, A. R. *The Man with a Shattered World.* New York: Basic Books, Jonathan Cape, Ltd., 1972.

Merzenich, M. M., and W. M. Jenkins. Reorganization of cortical representations of the hand following alterations of skin inputs induced by nerve injury, skin island transfers, and experience. *Journal of Hand Therapy* 6:89–104, 1993.

Milner, B. Effect of different brain lesions on card sorting. *Archives of Neurology* 9:90–100, 1963.

Milner, B. Psychological aspects of focal epilepsy and its neurosurgical management. *Advances in Neurology* 8:299–321, 1975.

Milner, B., S. Corkin, and H.-L. Teuber. Further analysis of the hippocampal amnesic syndrome: 14-year follow-up study of H. M. *Neuropsychologia* 6:215–234, 1968.

Mohr, J. P., G. H. Weiss, W. F. Caveness, J. D. Dillon, J. P. Kistler, A. M. Meirowsky, and B. L. Rish. Language and motor disorders after penetrating head injury in Viet Nam. *Neurology* 30:1273–1279, 1980.

Moligner, A. J., A. I. Grossman, U. Ribary, M. Joliot, J. Volkmann, D. Rapaport, R. W. Beasley, and R. R. Llinas. Somatosensory cortical plasticity in adult humans revealed by magnetoencephalography. *Proceedings of the National Academy of Sciences of the United States of America* 90:3593–3597, 1993.

Morrison, G. E., and D. van der Kooy. A mutation in the AMPA-type glutamate receptor, glr-1, blocks olfactory associative and nonassociative learning in *Caenorhabditis elegans. Behavioral Neuroscience* 115:640–649, 2001.

Nudo, R. J., E. J. Plautz, and S. B. Frost. Role of adaptive plasticity in recovery of function after damage to motor cortex. *Muscle and Nerve* 24:1000–1019, 2001.

Nudo, R. J., E. J. Plautz, and G. W. Millikan. Adaptive plasticity in primate motor cortex as a consequence of behavioral experience and neuronal injury. *Seminars in Neuroscience* 9:13–23, 1997.

Nudo, R. J., B. M. Wise, F. SiFuentes, and G. W. Milliken. Neural substrates for the effects of rehabilitative training on motor recovery after ischemic infarct. *Science* 272:1793, 1996.

Oddy, M., and M. Humphrey. Social recovery during the year following severe head injury. *Journal of Neurology, Neurosurgery, and Psychiatry* 43:798–802, 1980.

Ormerod, B. K., and L. A. M. Galea. Mechanism and function of adult neurogenesis. In C. A. Shaw and J. C. McEachern, Eds. *Toward a Theory of Neuroplasticity.* Lillington, NC: Taylor & Francis, 2001, pp. 85–100.

Pantev, C., R. Oostenveld, A. Engelien, B. Ross, L. E. Roberts, and M. Hoke. Increased auditory cortical representation in musicians. *Nature* 392:811–814, 1998.

Pons, T. P., P. E. Garraghty, A. K. Ommaya, J. H. Kaas, E. Taum, and M. Mishkin. Massive cortical reorganization after sensory deafferentation in adult macaques. *Science* 272:1857–1860, 1991.

Prigatano, G. P. *Principles of Neuropsychological Rehabilitation.* New York: Oxford University Press, 2001.

Rakic, P. Adult neurogenesis in mammals: An identity crisis. *Journal of Neuroscience* 22:614–618, 2002.

Ramachandran, V. S., and W. Hirstein. The perception of phantom limbs: The D. O. Hebb lecture. *Brain* 121:1603–1630, 1998.

Rampon C., C. H. Jiang, H. Dong, Y. P. Tang, D. J. Lockhart, P. G. Schultz, J. Z. Tsien, and Y. Hu. Effects of environmental enrichment on gene expression in the brain. *Proceedings of the National Academy of Sciences of the United States of America* 97:12880–12884, 2000.

Rauschecker, J. P. Cortical plasticity and music. *Annals of the New York Academy of Sciences* 930:330–336, 2001.

Reynolds, B. A., and S. Weiss. Generation of neurons and astrocytes from isolated cells of the adult mammalian central nervous system. *Science* 255:1613–1808, 1992.

Rijntjes, M., and C. Weiller. Recovery of motor and language abilities after stroke: The contribution of functional imaging. *Progress in Neurobiology* 66:109–122, 2002.

Shaw, C. A., and J. C. McEachern, Eds. *Toward a Theory of Neuroplasticity.* Philadelphia: Taylor & Francis, 2001.

Sohlberg, M. M., and C. A. Mateer *Introduction to Cognitive Rehabilitation.* New York: Guilford Press, 1989.

Sterr, A., M. Muller, T. Elbert, B. Rockstroh, and E. Taub. Development of cortical reorganization in the somatosensory cortex of adult Braille students. *Electroencephalography and Clinical Neurophysiology Supplement* 49:292–298, 1999.

Sugita, Y. Global plasticity of adult visual system. In C. A. Shaw and J. C. McEachern, Eds. *Toward a Theory of Neuroplasticity.* Philadelphia: Taylor & Francis, 2001, pp. 44–50.

Taub, E., and D. M. Morris. Constraint-induced movement therapy to enhance recovery after stroke. *Current Atherosclerosis Reports* 3:279–286, 2001.

Taylor, L. B. Localization of cerebral lesions by psychological testing. *Clinical Neurosurgery* 16:269–287, 1969.

Teskey, G. C. Using kindling to model the neuroplastic changes associated with learning and memory, neuropsychiatric disorders, and epilepsy. In C. A. Shaw and J. C. McEachern, Eds. *Toward a Theory of Neuroplasticity.* Lillington, NC: Taylor & Francis, 2001, pp. 347–358.

Teuber, H.-L. Recovery of function after brain injury in man. In *Outcome of Severe Damage to the Nervous System: Ciba Foundation Symposium 34*. Amsterdam: Elsevier North-Holland, 1975.

Teyler, T. J. LTP and the superfamily of synaptic plasticities. In C. A. Shaw and J. C. McEachern, Eds. *Toward a Theory of Neuroplasticity*. Lillington, NC: Taylor & Francis, 2001, pp. 101–117.

Twitchell, T. E. The restoration of motor function following hemiplegia in man. *Brain* 74:443–480, 1951.

Twitchell, T. E. The automatic grasping response of infants. *Neuropsychologia* 3:247–259, 1965.

von Monakow, C. V. Lokalization der Hirnfunktionen. *Journal fur Psychologie and Neurologie* 17:185–200, 1911. Reprinted in G. von Bonin. *The Cerebral Cortex*. Springfield, IL: Charles C Thomas, 1960.

Zihl, J., and D. von Cramon. Visual field rehabilitation in the cortically blind? *Journal of Neurology, Neurosurgery, and Psychiatry* 49:965–967, 1986.

chapter

26

Neurological Disorders

On the afternoon of June 16, 1783, Dr. Samuel Johnson, the famed English lexicographer, sat for his portrait in the studio of Miss Frances Reynolds, the sadly untalented sister of Sir Joshua Reynolds. Despite his 73 years and marked obesity, Johnson afterwards walked the considerable distance from the studio to his home. He went to sleep at his usual hour in the evening and awoke according to his account around 3 a.m. on June 17. To his surprise and horror, he found that he could not speak. He immediately tested his mental faculties by successfully composing a prayer in Latin verse. Next he tried to loosen his powers of speech by drinking some wine, violating his recently acquired habits of temperance. The wine only put him back to sleep. Upon reawakening after sunrise, Johnson still could not speak. He found, however, that he could understand others and that he could write. His penmanship and composition were somewhat defective. . . . Johnson proceeded to summon his physicians, Drs. Brocklesby and Heberden, who came and examined him. They prescribed blisters on each side of the throat up to the ear, one on the head, and one on the back, along with salts of hartshorn [ammonium carbonate]. Heberden, who was one of London's leading doctors, predicted a speedy recovery. His confidence proved quite justified: the therapeutic regimen was so efficacious that Johnson's speech began returning within a day or two. Recovery proceeded smoothly over the next month, and even the mild disorders in writing lessened. Johnson finally was left with a slight but stable dysarthria [difficulty articulating words] until he succumbed to other causes later in the next year. (Rosner, 1974, p. 1)

D r. Johnson's case has been described and discussed a number of times because he was an interesting and celebrated person, the author of the first English dictionary, and because his transitory illness was never fully explained. His aphasia provides an example of almost complete loss of a specific function (speech) and seemingly rapid and almost complete recovery. The story also contains a testimony to the knowledge and insight of his doctors, because their prediction of the outcome was correct. There are, however, many questions that the critical reader may wish to ask. How much weight should self-testimony be accorded? Did Johnson in fact experience a stroke or some other brain disorder? His claiming to have discovered, when alone in the middle of the night, that he could not speak is not unreasonable, because he was known to have the habit of talking to himself. But, because he *was* an eccentric, we might also wonder if the speechlessness was faked for some purpose or if its cause was psychological. If his disorder was real, what was it and *where* was it? Some neurologists have thought that the lesion must have been very small or was only a transitory blood clot. Others have speculated that, because he could not speak for a time but could still think, compose Latin verse, and write, he might normally have had the functions of speech in both hemispheres. Obviously, Dr. Johnson's case provides substance for much speculation.

In this chapter we will describe the examination given to a patient by a neurologist, and then we will survey a number of common neurological disorders, including vascular disorders, epilepsy, tumors, headaches, infections, and disorders of the spinal cord.

The Neurological Examination

People suspected of having some disorder of the nervous system are usually examined by a neurologist, a physician specializing in the treatment of such disorders. The neurologist takes a history from the patient, makes a general assessment of the patient's condition, and perhaps recommends additional tests (for example, an EEG or a brain scan) that seem to be indicated by the history or the initial examination. At the end of this initial assessment, the neurologist writes a case summary.

The Patient's History

The neurologist's first step is to ask the patient about the problem. Information is also collected about the patient's background, with particular attention paid to any history of disease, accidents, and the occurrence of symptoms such as headache, loss of consciousness, and sleep disturbances. Family background is reviewed as well, because many diseases, such as epilepsy, have a high familial incidence.

While the history is being taken, the neurologist observes the patient's behavior, assessing mental status, watching facial features for abnormalities or asymmetries, listening for speech abnormalities, and observing posture. The patient's state of awareness is described with adjectives such as *alert, drowsy, stuporous, confused,* and so forth. Any evidence of delusions and hallucinations is reported. Facial expression and behavior reveal whether the patient is agitated, anxious, depressed, apathetic, or restless. The neurologist may test some simple aspects of memory by reciting a series of digits and asking the patient to repeat it. In addition, the neurologist may look to see whether the patient is left- or right-handed and ask about the history of handedness in the family, because handedness can be a clue to which hemisphere controls speech. A number of simple tests for speech may be given, such as asking the meaning of words, having rhymes or words repeated (for example, "la-la," "ta-ta"), having objects named, and having the patient read and write.

The Physical Examination

The neurologist uses a number of tools in the course of the physical examination. They include (1) a measuring tape to measure head and body size, the size of skin lesions, and so on; (2) a stethoscope to listen to the sounds of the heart and blood vessels and an otoscope to examine the auditory canal and eardrum; (3) a flashlight to elicit pupillary reflexes; (4) tongue blades to elicit the gag reflex and abdominal and plantar reflexes; (5) a vial of coffee to assess smell and vials of salt and sugar to assess taste; (6) a 256-Hz tuning fork to test vibratory sensation and hearing; (7) a cotton wisp to elicit the corneal reflex and to test sensitivity to light touch, plastic tubes to test temperature sensations, and pins to test pain sensation; (8) a hammer to elicit muscle stretch reflexes, such as the knee-jerk reflex; (9) some coins and keys to test the recognition of objects through touch; and (10) a blood-pressure cuff to measure blood pressure.

One of the most important parts of the neurological examination is the study of the head. Its general features such as size and shape are assessed, and a detailed examination is made of the sensory and motor functioning of its 12 sets of cranial nerves. Cranial-nerve malfunctions discovered in this part of the examination can be important clues to the location and nature of nervous system damage.

The motor system in other parts of the body is examined to assess muscle bulk, tone, and power; to test for the occurrence of involuntary muscle movements, such as shaking and tremors; and to assess the status of reflexes. In addition, coordination is examined by having a patient perform such tasks as walking heel to toe in a straight line, touching the neurologist's finger and his or her own nose repeatedly, making rapid alternating movements of the fingers, tapping the foot as rapidly as possible, and so on. Generally, all the muscles of the body are tested in head-to-foot order, and the status of each is recorded on a standard chart.

A sensory examination includes an investigation of sensitivity to painful stimulation, to touch, and to temperature, as well as an analysis of vibration sense, joint-position sense, two-point discrimination, tactile localization, identification of objects, and the ability to identify numbers or letters traced on the skin with a blunt object. These sensory tests allow the functions of individual sensory systems to be assessed and provide information about the location of possible dysfunctions.

Vascular Disorders

The normal functioning of the central nervous system can be affected by a number of vascular problems, because blood-vessel disease or damage can greatly—even totally—reduce the flow of oxygen and glucose to a brain region. If such interference lasts longer than 10 minutes, all cells in the affected region die. Most disease of the cerebral vascular system develops in the arterial system; disease of venous drainage is uncommon in the central nervous system. Cerebral vascular diseases are among the most common causes of death and chronic disability in the Western world.

A common term used in a discussion of cerebral vascular disorder is stroke, also known as **cerebral vascular accident. A stroke** is the sudden appearance of neurological symptoms as a result of interruption of blood flow. Stroke can result from a wide variety of vascular disorders, but not all vascular disorders produce stroke. The onset of dysfunction can be insidious, spanning months or even years. Stroke often produces an **infarct,** an area of dead or dying tissue resulting from an obstruction of the blood vessels normally supplying the area. As you read this paragraph, someone in the United States will suffer a vascular accident.

If the flow through small blood vessels, such as capillaries, is interrupted, the effects are more limited than the often-devastating consequences of damage to large vessels. If a stroke or other cerebral vascular disorder occurs in one restricted part of a vessel (and other parts of the system are relatively healthy), the prognosis can be rather good, because vessels in the surrounding areas can often supply blood to at least some of the deprived area. On the other hand, if a stroke affects a region supplied largely by weak or diseased vessels, the effects can be much more serious, because there is no possibility of compensation. In addition, the surrounding weak zones themselves may be at increased risk of stroke. In the long run, a small vascular lesion in a healthy brain will have a good prognosis for substantial recovery of function. In the event of preexisting vascular lesions, the effects of the new lesions may be extremely variable. The lesions can be cumulative and obliterate a functional zone of brain tissue, producing serious consequences. As with other lesions, the behavioral symptoms subsequent to vascular lesions depend on the location of damage.

Of the numerous vascular disorders that affect the central nervous system, the most common are ischemia, migraine stroke, cerebral hemorrhage, angiomas, and arteriovenous aneurysms.

Cerebral Ischemia

Ischemia refers to any of a group of disorders in which the symptoms are caused by vessel blockage preventing a sufficient supply of blood to the brain. In **thrombosis,** for example, some of the blood in a vessel has coagulated to form a plug or clot that has remained at the place of its formation. An **embolism** is a clot or other plug brought through the blood from a larger vessel and forced into a smaller one, where it obstructs circulation. An embolism can be a blood clot, a bubble of air, a deposit of oil or fat, or a small mass of cells detached from a tumor. Curiously, embolisms most often affect the middle cerebral artery of the left side of the brain. Reduction in blood flow can also result from other kinds of factors that narrow the vessel. The most common example of such narrowing is a condition marked by thickening and hardening of the arteries, called **cerebral arteriosclerosis.** When ischemia is temporary, it may be termed **cerebral vascular insufficiency** or **transient ischemia,** indicating the variable nature of the disorder with the passage of time. The onset of transient attacks is often abrupt; in many cases, they are experienced as fleeting sensations of giddiness or impaired consciousness.

Migraine Stroke

Since the late 1800s, physicians have recognized that migraine attacks may lead to infarcts and permanent neurological deficits. Such **migraine strokes** are relatively rare compared with other types, but they are believed to account for a significant proportion of strokes in young people (under 40 years of age), especially women. The immediate cause of these strokes is probably some form of vasospasm—constriction of blood vessels—but the underlying cause of the vasospasm remains a mystery.

The classic migraine stroke is experienced as a transient ischemic attack with a variety of neurological symptoms, including impaired sensory function (especially vision), numbness of the skin (especially in the arms), difficulties in moving, and aphasia. The precise symptoms depend on the vessels affected; however, the posterior cerebral artery is most commonly affected.

Cerebral Hemorrhage

Cerebral hemorrhage is a massive bleeding into the substance of the brain. The most frequent cause is high blood pressure, or *hypertension*. Other causes include congenital defects in cerebral arteries, blood disorders such as leukemia, and toxic chemicals. The onset of cerebral hemorrhage is abrupt, and the bleeding may quickly prove fatal. It usually occurs when a person is awake, presumably because the person is more active and thus has higher blood pressure. Prognosis is poor in cerebral hemorrhage, especially if the patient is unconscious for more than 48 hours.

Angiomas and Aneurysms

Angiomas are congenital collections of abnormal vessels that divert the normal flow of blood. These capillary, venous, or **arteriovenous** (A-V) **malformations** are masses of enlarged and tortuous cortical vessels that are supplied by one or more large arteries and are drained by one or more large veins, most often in the field of the middle cerebral artery. Because they create abnormalities in the amount and pattern of blood flow and are inherently weak, angiomas may lead to stroke or to an inadequate distribution of blood in the regions surrounding the vessels. In some cases, they cause arterial blood to flow directly into veins after only briefly, or sometimes not at all, servicing the surrounding brain tissue.

Aneurysms are vascular dilations resulting from localized defects in the elasticity of a vessel. They can be visualized as balloonlike expansions of vessels that are usually weak and prone to rupture. Although aneurysms are usually due to congenital defects, they may also develop from hypertension, arteriosclerosis, embolisms, or infections. A characteristic symptom of an aneurysm is severe headache, which may be present for years, because the aneurysm is exerting pressure on the dura mater, which is richly endowed with pain receptors.

Treatment of Vascular Disorders

Most vascular disorders have no specific treatment, although the most common remedies include drug therapy and surgery. Supportive therapies are useful if they are delivered within 3 hours after a vascular emergency. They include such drugs as anticoagulants to dissolve clots or prevent clotting, vasodilators to dilate the vessels, drugs to reduce blood pressure, and salty solutions or steroids to reduce cerebral **edema** (the accumulation of fluid in and around damaged tissue). Treatment with anticoagulants is effective only if they are given soon after a blood vessel is blocked. If treatment is delayed more than 3 hours, it is unlikely to be helpful. Surgical techniques have improved greatly in recent years but are not always practical. For example, the only certain cure for an aneurysm is total removal, which is usually not feasible. Aneurysms are sometimes painted with various plastic substances to prevent them from rupturing. In regard to cerebral hemorrhage, it may be necessary to perform surgery to relieve the pressure of the blood from the ruptured vessel on the rest of the brain.

Traumatic Head Injuries

Brain injury is a common result of automobile and industrial accidents; cerebral trauma or injury from a blow to the head is the most common form of brain damage in people under the age of 40; and, in one telephone survey in Sweden, cerebral concussion (injury resulting from a violent blow or shock) producing at least brief unconsciousness was reported by 5% of those interviewed. In addition, another 5% or so of the general population are likely to have suffered concussion without obvious unconsciousness, although they would have experienced some confusion about the events surrounding the blow to the head. The two most important factors in the incidence of head injury are age and sex. Children and elderly people are more likely to suffer head injuries from falls than are others, and males between 15 and 30 years of age are very likely to incur brain injuries, especially from automobile and motorcycle accidents (Figure 26.1). A child's chance of suffering significant closed-head injury before he or she is old enough to drive is 1 in 30.

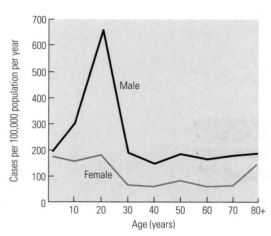

Figure 26.1 Incidence rates of head trauma in Olmsted County, Minnesota, 1965–1974. (After Annegers et al., 1980.)

Head injury can affect brain function by causing direct damage to the brain; by disrupting blood supply; by inducing bleeding, leading to increased intracranial pressure; by causing swelling, leading to increased intracranial pressure; by opening the brain to infection; and by producing scarring of brain tissue (the scarred tissue becomes a focus for later epileptic seizures). There are two main types of head injury: open-head injury and closed-head injury.

Open-Head Injuries

Open-head injuries are traumatic brain injuries in which the skull is penetrated, as in gunshot or missile wounds, or in which fragments of bone penetrate the brain substance. In many cases, the injury does not cause the victim to lose consciousness.

Open-head injuries tend to produce distinctive symptoms that may undergo 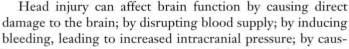 rapid and spontaneous recovery. The neurological signs may be highly specific, and the effects of the injuries often closely resemble those of surgical excision of a small area of cortex. The specificity of neurological symptoms subsequent to open-head injuries makes such patients especially good research subjects. Three thorough investigations of World War II (1939–1945) veterans with open-head injuries have been published—by Newcombe, by Luria, and by Teuber and coworkers.

Closed-Head Injuries

Closed-head injuries result from a blow to the head, which can subject the brain to a variety of mechanical forces. First, there is damage at the site of the blow, a bruise (contusion) called a **coup.** Coups are incurred where the brain has been compacted by the bone's pushing inward, even when the skull is not fractured. Second, the pressure that produces the coup may push the brain against the opposite side of the skull, producing an additional bruise, known as a **countercoup** (Figure 26.2). Third, the movement of the brain may cause a twisting or shearing of fibers, producing microscopic lesions. These lesions may occur throughout the brain but are most common in the frontal and temporal lobes. In addition, the twisting and shearing may damage the major fiber tracts of the brain, especially those crossing the midline, such as the corpus callosum and anterior commissure. As a result, connection between the two sides of the brain may be disrupted, leading to a disconnection syndrome. Fourth, the bruises and strains caused by the impact may produce bleeding (hemorrhage). Because the blood is trapped within the skull, it acts as a growing mass (hematoma), exerting pressure on surrounding structures. Finally, as with blows to other parts of the body, blows to the brain produce edema, another source of pressure on the brain tissue. Closed-head injuries resulting from traffic accidents are particularly severe because the head is moving when the blow is struck, thereby increasing the velocity of the impact, and multiplying the number and severity of small lesions throughout the brain. Computerized tomographic scans of accident victims suffering prolonged **coma** (a loss of consciousness) show diffuse brain injury and enlarged ventricles, signs associated with poor outcomes.

Closed-head injuries are commonly accompanied by coma. According to Lezak, the duration of unconsciousness can serve as a measure of the severity of damage, because it correlates directly with mortality, intellectual impairment, and deficits in social skills. The longer the coma lasts, the greater the possibility of serious impairment and death.

Two kinds of behavioral effects result from closed-head injuries: (1) discrete impairment of the specific functions mediated by the cortex at the site of the coup or countercoup lesion and (2) more generalized impairments from widespread trauma throughout the brain. Discrete impairment is most commonly associated with damage to the frontal and temporal lobes, which are the areas most susceptible to closed-head injuries. More general impairment, resulting from minute lesions and lacerations scattered throughout the brain and from tears due to movement of the hemispheres in relation to each other, is characterized by a loss of complex cognitive functions, including reductions in mental speed, concentration, and overall cognitive efficiency. The patients generally

Figure 26.2 Regions of the brain most frequently damaged in closed-head injury (indicated by gray and blue shading). A blow can produce a contusion both at the site of impact and at the opposite side of the brain, owing to compression of the brain against the front (A) or the back (B) of the skull.

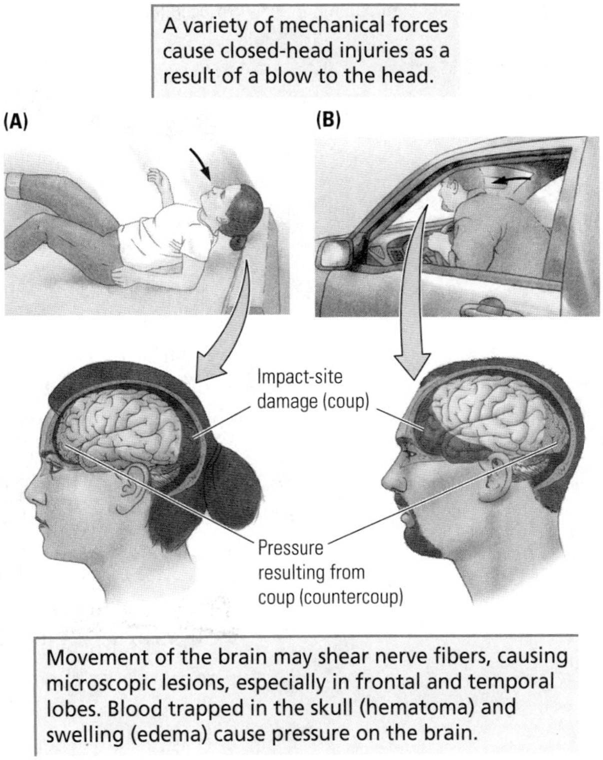

A variety of mechanical forces cause closed-head injuries as a result of a blow to the head.

(A)　　　(B)

Impact-site damage (coup)

Pressure resulting from coup (countercoup)

Movement of the brain may shear nerve fibers, causing microscopic lesions, especially in frontal and temporal lobes. Blood trapped in the skull (hematoma) and swelling (edema) cause pressure on the brain.

Table 26.1 Primary and secondary brain injury after closed-head trauma

Primary (Immediate on Impact) Brain Injuries
  Macroscopic lesions
    Contusions underlying the site of impact (coup)
    Countercoup contusion, frequently in the
      undersurfaces of the frontal lobes and the tips of
      the temporal lobes
    Laceration of the brain from depressed skull fracture
  Microscopic lesions
    Widespread shearing or stretching of fibers
Secondary Consequences of Brain Injury
  Intracranial hemorrhage
  Edema in white matter adjacent to focal mass lesions
  Diffuse brain swelling—hyperemia
  Ischemic brain damage
  Raised intracranial pressure
  Brain shift and herniation
Secondary Insult from Extracerebral Events
  Effects of multiple or systemic injury or both
    Hypoxia
    Fat embolism
Delayed Effects
  Degeneration of white matter
  Disturbed flow of cerebrospinal fluid—hydrocephalus

Source: After Levin et al., 1982.

complain of an inability to concentrate or to do things as well as they could before the accident, even though their intelligence rating may still be well above average. In fact, in our experience, it seems that bright people are the most affected by closed-head injuries because they are acutely aware of any loss of cognitive skill that prevents them from returning to their former competence level.

Closed-head injuries that damage the frontal and temporal lobes also tend to have significant effects on personality and social behavior. According to Lezak, relatively few victims of traffic accidents who have sustained severe head injuries ever resume their studies or return to gainful employment; if they do reenter the work force, they do so at a level lower than that before their accidents.

Often, the chronic effects of closed-head injuries are not accompanied by any obvious neurological signs, and the patients may therefore be referred for psychiatric evaluation. Thorough psychological assessments are especially useful in these cases for uncovering seriously handicapping cognitive deficits that have not yet become apparent. The pathological effects of closed-head injury are summarized in Table 26.1.

People who once sustain head injuries are more likely to sustain subsequent head injuries, and there is a strong suggestion in the literature that the effects of even very mild head injuries may be cumulative. For example, it is well established that a boxer will sustain a significant level of brain injury—culminating in a condition called *traumatic encephalopathy* (known more commonly as the "punch-drunk syndrome")—even though the periods of unconsciousness experienced by the boxer may have been few and of short duration.

Behavioral Assessment in Head Injury

Although neuroradiological measures can provide objective indicators of neural status after head injury, behavior is the most important measure of the integrity of the nervous system. In the immediate postinjury period, the two most obvious behavioral symptoms are coma and amnesia. Clinical judgment of the depth of coma was largely subjective and unreliable until the Glasgow Coma Scale (Table 26.2) was designed to provide an objective indicator of the degree of unconsciousness and of recovery from unconsciousness. In this scale, three indices of wakefulness are evaluated: eye opening, motor response, and verbal response. A score of 8 or less is often used as a criterion for severe closed-head injury, with a score ranging from 9 to 12 being a criterion for moderate injury. A shortcoming of the scale as a measure of the severity of brain injury is that as many as 50% of brain injury victims admitted to hospitals have scores ranging from 13 to 15, indicating an absence of coma, and yet later such patients may suffer many of the consequences of head injury.

Table 26.2 The Glasgow Coma Scale

Response	Points	Index of wakefulness
		Eye Opening (E)
None	1	Not attributable to ocular swelling
To pain	2	Pain stimulus is applied to chest or limbs
To speech	3	Nonspecific response to speech or shout, does not imply that the patient obeys command to open eyes
Spontaneous	4	Eyes are open; does not imply intact awareness
		Motor Response (M)
No response	1	Flaccid
Extension	2	"Decerebrate," adduction, internal rotation of shoulder, and pronation of the forearm
Abnormal flexion	3	"Decorticate," abnormal flexion, adduction of the shoulder
Withdrawal	4	Normal flexor response; withdraws from pain stimulus with abduction of the shoulder
Localizes pain	5	Pain stimulus applied to supraocular region or fingertip causes limb to move to attempt to avoid it
Obeys commands	6	Follows simple commands
		Verbal Response (V)
No response	1	(Self-explanatory)
Incomprehensible	2	Moaning and groaning, but no recognizable words
Inappropriate	3	Intelligible speech (e.g., shouting or swearing), but no sustained or coherent conversation
Confused	4	Patient responds to questions in a conversational manner, but the responses indicate varying degrees of disorientation and confusion
Oriented	5	Normal orientation to time, place, and person

Note: The summed Glasgow Coma Scale is equal to E + M + V (3–15 points).
Source: After B. Teasdale and B. Jennett, 1974.

Figure 26.3 Acute alterations in memory after closed-head injury. (A) A diagram showing the sequence of alterations. The period of coma and anterograde amnesia are often called the period of posttraumatic amnesia (PTA), although by some definitions PTA is limited to the anterograde amnesia. (B) Histograms showing the distribution of individual scores of story recall by patients in three groups distinguished by the period of PTA. Scores represent recall of the second of two stories. (Part A after Levin et al., 1982; part B after Newcombe, 1987.)

The length of posttraumatic amnesia is an alternative measure of severity of injury. Even though definitions of posttraumatic amnesia vary (some include the period of coma, whereas others are restricted to the period of anterograde amnesia), there is good evidence that the duration of amnesia is correlated (imperfectly) with later memory disturbance, as illustrated in Figure 26.3. A commonly used scale is as follows: amnesia lasting less than 10 minutes corresponds to very mild injury; amnesia lasting 10 to 60 minutes corresponds to mild injury; amnesia lasting 1 to 24 hours corresponds to moderate injury; amnesia lasting 1 to 7 days corresponds to severe injury; amnesia lasting more than 7 days corresponds to very severe injury. One problem with using amnesia as a measure is that there is no consistent method of measuring it. Researchers evaluate it, variously, by retrospective questioning, by measures of disorientation, or by neuropsychological assessment, and each method yields a different estimate of the severity of amnesia and hence of the extent of injury.

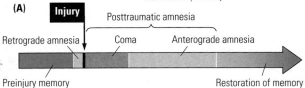

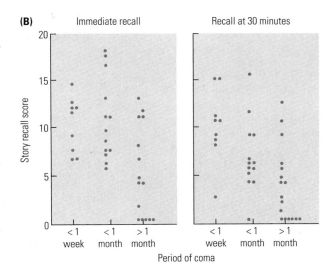

Recovery from Head Injury

Although it is often stated that recovery from head trauma may continue for 2 to 3 years, there is little doubt that the bulk of the cognitive recovery takes place in the first 6 to 9 months. Recovery of memory functions appears to be somewhat slower than recovery of general intelligence, and the final level of memory performance is lower than that of other cognitive functions. Levin and his colleagues suggested that people with brainstem damage, as inferred from oculomotor disturbance, have a poorer cognitive outcome, and it is probably true of people with initial dysphasias or hemipareses as well. Although the prognosis for significant recovery of cognitive functions is good, there is less optimism about the recovery of social skills or normal personality, areas that often change significantly. The results of numerous studies support the conclusion that the quality of life—in regard to social interactions, perceived stress levels, and enjoyment of leisure activities—is significantly reduced after closed-head injury and that this reduction is chronic. There have been few attempts to develop tools to measure changes in psychosocial adjustment in brain-injured people; so we must rely largely on subjective descriptions and self-reports, which provide little information about the specific causes of these problems.

Table **26.3** Factors that may precipitate seizures in susceptible persons

Hyperventilation
Sleep
Sleep deprivation
Sensory stimuli
  Flashing lights
  Reading, speaking, coughing
  Laughing
  Sounds: music, bells
Trauma
Hormonal changes
  Menses
  Puberty
  Adrenal steroids
  Adrenocorticotrophic hormone (ACTH)
Fever
Emotional stress
Drugs
  Phenothiazines
  Analeptics
  Tricyclic antidepressants
  Alcohol
  Excessive anticonvulsants

Source: After Pincus and Tucker, 1974.

Epilepsy

In epilepsy, a person suffers recurrent seizures of various types that register on an electrogram and are associated with disturbances of consciousness. Epileptic episodes have been called convulsions, seizures, fits, and attacks, but none of these terms on its own is entirely satisfactory, because the character of the episodes can vary greatly. Epileptic seizures are common; 1 person in 20 will experience at least one seizure in his or her lifetime. The prevalence of multiple seizures is much lower, however—about 1 in 200. Epileptic seizures are classified as **symptomatic seizures** if they can be identified with a specific cause, such as infection, trauma, tumor, vascular malformation, toxic chemicals, very high fever, or other neurological disorders. They are called **idiopathic seizures** if they appear to arise spontaneously and in the absence of other diseases of the central nervous system. Table 26.3 summarizes the great variety of circumstances that appear to be able to precipitate seizures. Although the range of these circumstances is striking, a consistent feature is that the brain is most epileptogenic when it is relatively inactive and the patient is sitting still.

Although epilepsy has long been known to run in families, its incidence is lower than a one-gene genetic model would predict. What is more likely is that certain genotypes have a predisposition to seizure problems given certain environmental circumstances. The most remarkable clinical feature of epileptic disorders is the widely varying length of intervals between attacks—from minutes to hours to weeks or even years. In fact, it is almost impossible to describe a basic set of symptoms to be expected in all or even most people with the disorder. At the same time, three particular symptoms *are* found in many types of epilepsy:

1. *An aura, or warning, of impending seizure.* This aura may take the form of a sensation—an odor or a noise—or it may simply be a "feeling" that the seizure is going to occur.

2. *Loss of consciousness.* Ranging from complete collapse in some people to simply staring off into space in others, loss of consciousness is often accompanied by amnesia in which the victim forgets the seizure itself and the period of lost consciousness.

3. *Movement.* Seizures commonly have a motor component, although the characteristics vary considerably. Some people shake during an attack; others exhibit automatic movements, such as rubbing the hands or chewing.

A diagnosis of epilepsy is usually confirmed by EEG. In some epileptics, however, seizures are difficult to demonstrate in this way except under special circumstances (for example, in an EEG recorded during sleep). Moreover, not all persons with an EEG suggestive of epilepsy actually have seizures. In fact, some estimates suggest that as many as 4 people in 20 have abnormal EEG patterns, which is many more than the number of people thought to suffer from epilepsy. Several schemes for classifying epilepsy have been published through the years. Four commonly recognized types of seizures are: focal seizures, generalized seizures, and akinetic and myoclonic seizures.

Focal Seizures

A **focal seizure** begins in one place and then spreads. In a **Jacksonian focal seizure,** for example, the attack begins with jerking movements in one part of the body (for example, a finger, a toe, or the mouth) and then spreads to adjacent parts. If the attack begins with a finger, the jerks might spread to other fingers, then the hand, the arm, and so on, producing the so-called Jacksonian march. Hughlings Jackson hypothesized in 1870 that such seizures probably originate from the point (focus) in the neocortex representing the region of the body where the movement is first seen. He was later proved correct.

Complex partial seizures, another type of focal seizure, originate most commonly in the temporal lobe and somewhat less frequently in the frontal lobe. Complex partial seizures are characterized by three common manifestations: (1) subjective experiences that presage the attack such as forced, repetitive thoughts, sudden alterations in mood, feelings of déjà vu, or hallucinations; (2) **automatisms,** which are repetitive stereotyped movements such as lip smacking or chewing or activities such as undoing buttons; and (3) postural changes, as when the person assumes a catatonic, or frozen, posture.

Generalized Seizures

Generalized seizures are bilaterally symmetrical without focal onset. One subtype, the **grand mal attack,** is characterized by loss of consciousness and by stereotyped motor activity. This kind of seizure typically comprises three stages: (1) a tonic stage, in which the body stiffens and breathing stops; (2) a clonic stage, in which there is rhythmic shaking; and (3) a postseizure, also called **postictal,** depression, during which the patient is confused. About 50% of these seizures are preceded by an aura.

The **petit mal attack** is a loss of awareness during which there is no motor activity except for blinking, turning the head, or rolling the eyes. These attacks are of brief duration, seldom exceeding about 10 seconds. The EEG recording of a petit mal seizure has a typical pattern known as the three-per-second spike and wave.

Akinetic and Myoclonic Seizures

Akinetic seizures are ordinarily seen only in children. Usually an affected child collapses suddenly and without warning. These seizures are often of very short duration, and the child may get up after only a few seconds. The fall can be dangerous, however, and it is commonly recommended that the children wear football helmets until the seizures can be controlled by medication. **Myoclonic spasms** are massive seizures that basically consist of a sudden flexion or extension of the body and often begin with a cry.

Treatment of Epilepsy

The treatment of choice for epilepsy is an anticonvulsant drug such as diphenylhydantoin (DPH, Dilantin), phenobarbital, or one of several others. Although the mechanism by which these drugs act is uncertain, they presumably inhibit the discharge of abnormal neurons by stabilizing the neuronal membrane. If medication fails to alleviate the seizure problem satisfactorily, surgery can be performed to remove the focus of abnormal functioning in patients with focal seizures.

Tumors

A **tumor,** or neoplasm, is a mass of new tissue that persists and grows independently of its surrounding structures and has no physiological use. Brain tumors grow from glia or other support cells rather than from neurons. The rate at which tumors grow varies widely, depending on the type of cell that gave rise to them. Tumors account for a relatively high proportion of neurological disease; after the uterus, the brain is the most common site for them. Tumors that are not likely to recur after removal are called benign, and tumors that *are* likely to recur after removal—often progressing and becoming a threat to life—are called malignant. Although there are good reasons for distinguishing between benign and malignant tumors, the benign tumor may be as serious as the malignant one, because benign tumors in the brain are often inaccessible to the surgeon. The brain is affected by many types of tumors, and no region of the brain is immune to tumor formation.

Tumors can affect behavior in a number of ways. A tumor may develop as a distinct entity in the brain, a so-called encapsulated tumor, and put pressure on the other parts of the brain (Figure 26.4). Encapsulated tumors are also sometimes cystic, which means that they produce a fluid-filled cavity in the brain, usually lined with the tumor cells. Because the skull is of fixed size, any increase in its contents compresses the brain, resulting in dysfunctions. In contrast with encapsulating tumors, so-called infiltrating tumors are not clearly marked off

Figure 26.4 Frontal section showing a meningioma arising in the dura mater and compressing the right cerebral hemisphere. Notice that the tumor has not infiltrated the brain. (From Zacks, © 1971; reprinted with permission.)

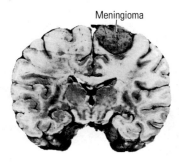

Meningioma

from the surrounding tissue; they may either destroy normal cells and occupy their place or surround existing cells (both neurons and glia) and interfere with their normal functioning (Figure 26.5). The general symptoms of brain tumors, which result from increased intracranial pressure, include headache, vomiting, swelling of the optic disk (papilledema), slowing of the heart rate (bradycardia), mental dullness, double vision (diplopia), and, finally, convulsions, as well as functional impairments due to damage to the brain where the tumor is located.

Brain tumors are distinguished on the basis of where they originate: they can be gliomas, meningiomas, or metastatic tumors. **Glioma** is a general term for the roughly 45% of brain tumors that arise from glial cells and infiltrate the brain substance. Gliomas, ranging from the relatively benign to the highly malignant, vary considerably in their response to treatment.

Meningiomas are growths attached to the meninges, the protective outer layer of the brain. They grow entirely outside the brain, are well encapsulated, and are the most benign of all brain tumors. But, even though meningiomas do not invade the brain, they are often multiple and disturb brain function by putting pressure on the brain, often producing seizures as a symptom. Although most meningiomas lie over the hemispheres, some develop between them and are therefore more difficult to remove. If meningiomas are removed completely, they tend not to recur. When they are present, however, it is not uncommon for these tumors to erode the overlying bone of the skull.

Metastasis is the transfer of disease from one organ or part to another not directly connected with it. Thus, a **metastatic tumor** in the brain is one that has become established by a transfer of tumor cells from some other region of the body, most often a lung or a breast. Indeed, it is not uncommon for the first indication of lung cancer to be evidence of a brain tumor. Metastases to the brain are usually multiple, making treatment complicated, and prognosis poor.

The most straightforward treatment of brain tumors is surgery, which is also the only way to make a definite histological diagnosis. If feasible, tumors are removed, but, as with tumors elsewhere in the body, success depends on early diagnosis. Radiation therapy is useful for treating certain types of tumors. Chemotherapy has not yet been very successful in the treatment of brain tumors, partly because of the difficulty of getting drugs to pass the blood–brain barrier and enter the tumor.

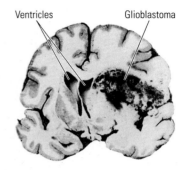

Ventricles | Glioblastoma

Figure 26.5 Frontal section showing a glioblastoma (a malignant type of glia-derived tumor) in the right cerebral hemisphere. Note the displacement of the ventricular system and the invasion of brain tissue (dark area). (From Bannister, © 1978; reprinted with permission.)

Headaches

Headache is so common among the general population that rare indeed is the person who has never suffered one. Headache may constitute a neurological disorder in itself, as in migraine; it may be secondary to neurological disease such as tumor or infection; or it may result from psychological factors, especially stress, as in tension headaches. The pain-sensitive structures within the skull that can produce the headache include the dura mater; the large arteries of the brain; the venous sinuses; and the branches of the 5th, 9th, and 10th cranial nerves and the 1st and 3rd cervical nerves. Pain can be elicited in these structures by pressure, displacement, or inflammation. There are a number of different kinds of headache, including migraine, headache associated with neurological disease, muscle-contraction headaches, and nonmigrainous vascular headaches.

Migraine

Migraine (derived from the Greek *hemi* and *kranion*, meaning "half of skull") is perhaps the most common neurological disorder, afflicting some 5% to 20% of the population at some time in their lives. The World Federation of Neurology defines migraine as a "familial disorder characterized by recurrent attacks of headache widely variable in intensity, frequency, and duration. Attacks are commonly unilateral and are usually associated with anorexia, nausea, and vomiting. In some cases they are preceded by, or associated with, neurological and mood disturbances." There are several types of migraine, including classic migraine, common migraine, cluster headache, and hemiplegic and ophthalmologic migraine. **Classic migraine** is probably the most interesting form, occurring in about 12% of migraine sufferers, because it begins with an aura, which usually lasts for 20 to 40 minutes. Karl Lashley, arguably the first neuropsychologist, suffered from classic migraine and carefully described his visual aura, which turned out to be common to many migraine sufferers (Figure 26.6).

The aura is thought to occur because constriction of one or more cerebral arteries has produced ischemia of the occipital cortex. The results of PET studies have shown that, during the aura, there is a reduction in blood flow in the posterior cortex, and this reduction spreads at the rate of about 2 mm/min, without regard to its location with respect to major blood vessels. Why the reduction in blood flow should spread independently of the major vessels is not known, but its doing so suggests that the vascular changes are secondary to changes in neural function. The actual headache begins as the vasoconstriction reverses (ending the neurological disturbance) and vasodilation takes place. The headache is experienced as an intense pain localized in one side of the head, although it often spreads on that side and sometimes extends to the opposite side as well. A severe headache can be accompanied by nausea and vomiting, and it may last for hours or even days. A significant number of people considered to have classic migraine never suffer the headache but experience the aura.

Common migraine is the most frequent type of migraine, occurring in more than 80% of migraine sufferers. There is no clear aura as there is in classic migraine, but there may be a gastrointestinal or other "signal" that an attack is pending. **Cluster headache** is a unilateral pain in the head or face that rarely lasts longer than 2 hours but recurs repeatedly for a period of weeks or even months before disappearing. Sometimes long periods pass between one series of cluster headaches and the next. The remaining two types of migraine, **hemiplegic migraine** and **ophthalmologic migraine,** are relatively rare and include loss of movement of the limbs and eyes, respectively.

The frequency of migraine attacks varies from as often as once a week to as seldom as once in a lifetime. In cases in which migraine is frequent, the occur-

Figure 26.6 The development of a migraine scotoma as described by Karl Lashley. A person first sees a small patch of lines in the center of the visual field, as shown near the small "x" in the center of the left-hand photograph. Information from the world is no longer visible in that part of the visual field. The striped area spreads progressively outward, leaving a white area where the stripes had been before. Within 15 to 20 minutes, the visual field is almost completely blocked by the scotoma. Normal vision returns shortly thereafter.

X = Fixation point

rence generally decreases with age and usually ceases in middle age. Migraine was generally believed to be rare before adolescence, but in recent years it has been recognized to afflict children as well, although the actual incidence in this population is uncertain.

Headache Associated with Neurological Disease

Headache is a symptom of many nervous system disorders, usually resulting from the distortion of pain-sensitive structures. Common disorders producing headache include tumor, head trauma, infection, vascular malformations, and severe hypertension (high blood pressure). The characteristics and locations of these headaches vary according to the underlying cause. For example, headache from a brain tumor is almost always located on the same side of the head as the tumor, particularly in the early stages of tumor growth. Headaches induced by brain tumors have no characteristic severity; they may vary from mild to excruciating. Likewise, hypertension headache, although it is nearly always located in the occipital region, is highly variable in severity.

Muscle-Contraction Headache

The most common headaches are **muscle-contraction headaches,** also known as tension or nervous headaches. They result from sustained contraction of the muscles of the scalp and neck caused by constant stress and tension, especially if poor posture is maintained for any time. Patients describe their pain as steady, nonpulsing, tight, squeezing, or pressing or as the feeling of having the head in a vise. Some patients complain of a crawling sensation. The headaches may be accompanied by anxiety, dizziness, and bright spots in front of the eyes. In some people, caffeine may exacerbate the headaches, presumably because it exacerbates anxiety.

Nonmigrainous Vascular Headaches

Headache associated with dilation of the cranial arteries can be induced by a wide variety of diseases and conditions. The most common causes are fever, anoxia (lack of oxygen), anemia, high altitude, physical effort, hypoglycemia (low blood sugar), foods, and chemical agents. In addition, headache may result from congestion and edema of the nasal membranes, often termed vasomotor rhinitis, which is assumed to be a localized vascular reaction to stress.

Treatment of Headaches

Migraine is treated by specific drugs at the time of an attack and by preventive measures between attacks. In an acute attack, **ergotamine** compounds, often given in conjunction with caffeine, are useful in alleviating the headache, probably because they produce constriction of the cerebral arteries, thus reducing dilation, which is the source of the pain. In addition, most migraine sufferers find that the headache is reduced in a totally dark room.

The most obvious treatment for headache arising from neurological disease is to treat the disease itself. Tension headaches can be relieved by muscle-relaxant drugs, minor tranquilizers, the application of heat to the affected muscles, and improvement of posture. They can also be prevented by avoiding the life situations that give rise to stress.

Infections

Infection is the invasion of the body by disease-producing (pathogenic) microorganisms and the reaction of the tissues to their presence and to the toxins generated by them. Because the central nervous system can be invaded by a wide variety of infectious agents—including viruses, bacteria, fungi, and metazoan parasites—the diagnosis and treatment of infection are important components of clinical neurology. Although infections of the nervous system usually spread from infection elsewhere in the body—especially the ears, nose, and throat—they also may be introduced directly into the brain as a result of head trauma, skull fractures, or surgery. Infections of the nervous system are particularly serious because the affected neurons and glia usually die, leaving permanent lesions.

There are a number of processes by which infections kill neural cells. First, infections may interfere with the blood supply to neurons, thus producing thrombosis, hemorrhaging of capillaries, or even the complete choking of larger blood vessels. Second, an infection may disturb glucose or oxygen metabolism in brain cells severely enough to kill them. Third, an infection may alter the characteristics of neural-cell membranes, thus changing the electrical properties of the neurons, or it may interfere with the basic enzymatic processes of neurons, producing any number of abnormal conditions. Fourth, infection leads to the formation of *pus*, a by-product of the body's defense against infection. Pus is a fluid composed basically of white blood cells, their by-products, by-products of the infectious microorganisms, and a thin fluid called liquor puris. Pus impairs neuronal functioning in at least two ways: it changes the composition of the extracellular fluids surrounding a neuron, thus altering neuronal function; and its presence increases pressure on the brain, disturbing normal functioning. Fifth and finally, infection often causes edema, which leads to compression of the brain tissues, again resulting in dysfunction.

Many infections of the nervous system are secondary to infections elsewhere in the body and are accompanied by symptoms of those other infections, including lowered blood pressure and other changes in blood circulation, fever, general malaise, headache, and delirium. In addition, symptoms of cerebral infections include both generalized symptoms of increased intracranial pressure—such as headache, vertigo, nausea, convulsions, and mental confusion—and symptoms specifically associated with the disturbance of particular brain functions.

Diagnostic tests for infection include CSF studies in addition to conventional methods of infection identification, such as smear and culture studies. Additionally, CT and other brain scans may be used to diagnose and locate some infectious disorders. Four types of infection can affect the central nervous system: viral infections, bacterial infections, mycotic (fungal) infections, and parasitic infestations.

Viral Infections

A **virus** is an encapsulated aggregate of nucleic acid that may be made of either DNA or RNA. Some viruses, such as those causing poliomyelitis and rabies, are called **neurotropic viruses,** because they have a special affinity for cells of the central nervous system. In contrast, **pantropic viruses** (such as those that cause mumps and herpes simplex) attack other body tissues in addition to the central nervous system. Most viral infections of the nervous system produce nonspecific lesions affecting widespread regions of the brain, such as lesions due to St. Louis encephalitis, rabies, and poliomyelitis.

Bacterial Infections

Bacterium is a loose generic name for any microorganism (typically one-celled) that has no chlorophyll and multiplies by simple division. Bacterial infections of the central nervous system result from an infestation of these organisms, usually through the bloodstream. The most common neurological disorders resulting from bacterial infection are meningitis and brain abscess. In **meningitis,** the meninges are infected by any of a variety of bacteria. **Brain abscesses** also are produced by a variety of bacteria, secondary to infection elsewhere in the body. An abscess begins as a small focus of purulent (pus-producing) bacteria that cause necrosis (death) of cells in the affected region. As the bacteria multiply and destroy more brain cells, the abscess behaves like an expanding mass (one that is often hollow in the center), producing increasing intracranial pressure.

Mycotic Infections

Invasion of the nervous system by a fungus is known as a **mycotic infection.** A fungus is any member of a large group of lower plants (in some taxonomic schemes) that lack chlorophyll and subsist on living or dead organic matter; the fungi include yeasts, molds, and mushrooms. Ordinarily the central nervous system is highly resistant to mycotic infections, but fungi may invade a brain whose resistance has been reduced by diseases such as cancer or tuberculosis.

Parasitic Infestations

A **parasite** is an organism that lives on or within another living organism—the host—at the host's expense. Several kinds of parasites invade the central nervous system and produce diseases, the most important of which are amebiasis and malaria. **Amebiasis** (also known as amebic dysentery), caused by an infestation of the protozoan ameba *Entamoeba histolytica* (protozoa are one-celled animals), results in encephalitis and brain abscesses. **Malaria** is caused by protozoa of the genus *Plasmodium*, which are transmitted by the bites of infected mosquitoes. Cerebral malaria arises when the plasmodia infect the capillaries of the brain, producing local hemorrhages and the subsequent degeneration of neurons.

Treatment of Infections

Treatment varies with the type of infection. Viral infections are extremely difficult to treat because there are no specific antidotes, and the only option is to let the disease run its course. Sedatives are sometimes administered to make the patient more comfortable. The important exception to this general rule is the treatment of rabies. When a person has had contact with a rabid animal, antirabies vaccine is administered over a period of 2 to 4 weeks to produce immunity before the disease actually develops. Once the disease does develop, rabies is fatal.

Bacterial cerebral infections have become less common with the introduction of antibiotic drugs, the usual treatment for these infections. In some cases, it may be necessary to drain abscesses to relieve intracranial pressure or to do spinal taps to remove cerebral spinal fluid and thus reduce the pressure of edema or a buildup of pus. Neither mycotic nor parasitic infections can be treated satisfactorily, although antibiotics are often used to treat associated disorders.

Disorders of Motor Neurons and the Spinal Cord

A number of movement disorders are produced by damage either to the spinal cord or to cortical projections to the spinal cord. These disorders include myasthenia gravis, a disorder of the muscle receptors; poliomyelitis, a disorder of the motor-neuron cell bodies; multiple sclerosis, a disorder of myelinated motor fibers; paraplegia and Brown-Sequard syndrome, caused by complete transection or hemitransection of the spinal cord, respectively; and hemiplegia, caused by cortical damage. Table 26.4 lists some of the medical terms used in describing movement disorders.

Table 26.4 Commonly used terms for movement disorders

Apraxia. Inability to carry out purposeful movements or movements on command in the absence of paralysis or other motor or sensory impairments. Usually follows damage to neocortex.

Ataxia. Failure of muscular coordination or an irregularity of muscular action. Commonly follows cerebellar damage.

Athetosis. A condition in which ceaseless slow, sinuous writhing movements occur, especially in the hands. Due to abnormal function of the extrapyramidal system.

Catalepsy. A condition marked by muscular rigidity in which voluntary movements are reduced or absent but posture is maintained. A feature of Parkinson's disease due to dopamine loss.

Cataplexy. Complete loss of movement and posture during which muscle tone is absent but consciousness is spared.

Chorea. Literally means dance but refers to the ceaseless occurrence of a wide variety of jerky movements that appear to be well coordinated but are performed involuntarily.

Hemiplegia. Complete or partial paralysis to one half of the body. Usually follows damage to the contralateral motor cortex.

Palsy. A paralysis of movement that usually refers to persisting movement disorders due to brain damage acquired perinatally.

Paralysis. Complete loss of movement or sensation (but more commonly movement) in a part of the body. Usually permanent after damage to motor neurons; temporary after damage to motor cortex (area 4).

Paraplegia. Paralysis or paresis of the lower torso and legs. Follows spinal-cord damage.

Spasticity. Increase in the tone of certain muscle groups that maintain posture against the force of gravity. If the limb is moved against the rigidity, resistance will initially increase, but then tone will suddenly melt (clasp-knife reflex). Thought to be produced by damage to the extrapyramidal motor fibers.

Tardive dyskinesia. Slow, persistent movements, particularly of the mouth and tongue. Usually follows long-term treatment with antipsychotic drugs.

Myasthenia Gravis

Myasthenia gravis (severe muscle weakness) is characterized by muscular fatigue in the wake of very little exercise. It may be apparent after a short period of exercise or work, toward the end of a long conversation, or sometimes even after a few repetitions of a movement. Rest brings a feeling of recovery. The rapid onset of weakness after exercise has begun distinguishes myasthenia gravis from other disorders such as depression or general fatigue. There are no visible signs of muscle pathology. Although myasthenia can affect people of any age, it is most likely to begin in the third decade of life and is more common in women than in men. All the muscles of the body may be affected, but those supplied by the cranial nerves are usually affected first. In this case, the initial symptoms are diplopia (double vision), ptosis (drooping of the eyelid), weakness of voice, and difficulty in chewing and swallowing or holding up the head. In some people, only the limbs are affected. Usually the symptoms are most apparent at the end of the day and are relieved after sleep. The severity of the disease varies from a mild unilateral ptosis in some people to an incapacitating generalized weakness, threatening death by respiratory paralysis, in others.

The muscular weakness is caused by a failure of normal neuromuscular transmission due to a paucity of muscle receptors for acetylcholine. These receptors may have been attacked by antibodies from the patient's own immune system. Treatment for myasthenia gravis has two objectives. First, acetylcholine therapy is used to relieve the symptoms. Second, thymectomy (surgical removal of the thymus to reduce antibody formation) and immunosuppressive drug treatment are used in the hope of arresting the disease's further progress. With these recent advances in treatment, mortality is currently very low.

Poliomyelitis

Poliomyelitis is an acute infectious disease caused by a virus that has a special affinity for the motor neurons of the spinal cord and sometimes for the motor neurons of the cranial nerves. Loss of these motor neurons causes paralysis and wasting of the muscles. If the motor neurons of the respiratory centers are attacked, death can result from asphyxia. The occurrence of the disease was sporadic and sometimes epidemic in North America until the Salk and Sabin vaccines were developed in the 1950s and 1960s. Since then, poliomyelitis has been well controlled. Why the virus has a special affinity for motor neurons is not known.

Multiple Sclerosis

Multiple sclerosis (MS; *sclerosis*, from Greek, meaning "hardness") is a disease characterized by the loss of myelin, largely in motor tracts but also in sensory tracts. The loss of myelin is not uniform; rather, it is lost in patches—small, hard, circumscribed scars, called **sclerotic plaques** (see the Snapshot on page 716) in which the myelin sheath and sometimes the axons are destroyed. Remissions and relapses are a striking feature of the disease; in many cases, the early signs are initially followed by improvement. The course varies, running from a few years to as long as 50 years. Its classic feature, however, is paraplegia, which may eventually confine the affected person to bed.

S N A P S H O T

The Use of Imaging to Diagnose Multiple Sclerosis

Multiple sclerosis produces strange symptoms that usually appear first in adulthood. The initial symptoms may be loss of sensation in the face, limbs, or body; blurring of vision; or loss of sensation and control in one or more limbs. Often these early symptoms go into remission, after which they may not appear again for years. In some forms, however, the disease may progress rapidly in just a few years until an affected person is limited to bed care.

Although neurologists in the nineteenth century were able to recognize the symptoms of multiple sclerosis, the immediate cause of the symptoms could be ascertained only when the patient died. Autopsy revealed hard patches of tissue in the spinal cord and in the brain. Histological analysis of the areas of hardening showed that the myelin surrounding axons there had degenerated, producing the sclerotic plaques. The cause of the disease itself—of the degeneration of myelin—is still unknown.

When the cause of the symptoms was known, measures of the conduction velocities of nervous system tracts could be used to diagnose multiple sclerosis, because the speed of conduction is reduced in the damaged nerve fibers. Today, brain-imaging techniques, such as MRI, are additional diagnostic tools that allow areas of sclerosis to be identified in the spinal cord and brain, as shown in the adjoining illustration. With these techniques, neurologists are less dependent on behavioral assessments for arriving at a diagnostic conclusion.

In spite of its value in diagnosing multiple sclerosis, however, MRI does a poor job of revealing the extent of the damage to myelin and axons and the damage with the passage of time. If the damage is mild, recovery may take place; if severe, recovery is unlikely. Fortunately, as described by Filippi, new imaging techniques are allowing neurologists to distinguish mild damage from severe damage. Additionally, imaging methods are being improved so that the course of sclerosis formation can be studied.

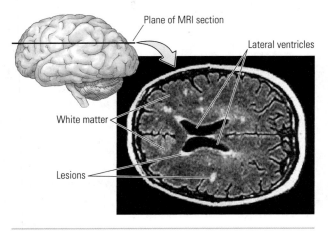

Discrete multiple sclerosis lesions around the ventricles and in the white matter of the brain. (After Ciccarelli et al., 2000.)

Another shortcoming of MRI, as described by Ciccarelli and colleagues, is that it has not helped neurologists correlate the brain lesions of multiple sclerosis with specific behavioral impairments. This lack of correlation is due in part to the fact that the sclerotic lesions are scattered throughout the white matter. It is also due in part to the fact that people not only vary greatly in their responses to brain damage but also have a propensity and ability to adjust their behavior to compensate for brain injury. Thus, even though brain imaging is useful in neurological diagnoses, it is unlikely to ever fully replace behavioral assessments.

(O. Ciccarelli, P. A. Brex, A. J. Thompson, and D. H. Miller. Disability and lesion load in MS: A reassessment with MS functional composite score and 3D fast Flair. *Journal of Neurology* 249:18–24, 2000.
M. Filippi. In-vivo tissue characterization of multiple sclerosis and other white matter diseases using magnetic resonance based techniques. *Journal of Neurology* 248:1019–1029, 2001.)

The cause of MS is still not known. Proposed causes include bacterial infection, a virus, environmental factors, and an immune response of the central nervous system. Often a number of cases will be seen in a single family, but there is no clear evidence that it is inherited or that it is transmitted from one person to another. Multiple sclerosis is most prevalent in northern Europe, somewhat less prevalent in North America, and rare in Japan and in more southerly or tropical countries. Where it is prevalent, its incidence of 50 per 100,000 makes it one of the most common structural diseases of the nervous system. Only Parkinson's disease is equally common. Multiple sclerosis has a female-to-male ratio of about 3 to 2, and its progress is often more rapid in females than in males.

Paraplegia

Paraplegia (from the Greek *para*, "alongside of," and *plegia*, "stroke") is a condition in which both lower limbs are paralyzed (**quadriplegia** is the paralysis of all four extremities). It is a direct consequence of complete transection of the spinal cord. Immediately after the cord has been severed, all activity ceases in the part distal to the cut, and all movement, sensation, and reflexes distal to the cut disappear. Owing to the loss of reflex activity, thermoregulatory control is absent (ending perspiration and leaving the skin cool and dry), as is bladder control (necessitating drainage of the bladder to prevent urinary retention). This condition, called *spinal shock*, lasts from 4 days to about 6 weeks. Gradually, some spinal reflexes return until, after a year or so, a stabilized condition is reached. A pinprick, for example, may again elicit a withdrawal reflex such as the triple response, which consists of flexion of the hip, knee, and ankle. No sensations, voluntary movements, or thermoregulatory control ever reappears below the lesion. Eventually, extensor activity may become sufficiently strong that weight can be supported briefly, but spinal circuits are too dependent on brain facilitation to permit prolonged standing in its absence.

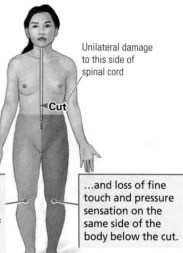

Figure 26.7 The differing effects of unilateral damage to the spinal cord on fine touch and pressure and on pain and temperature sensations.

Unilateral damage to this side of spinal cord

Cut

Unilateral damage causes loss of pain and temperature sensation on the opposite side of the body below the cut...

...and loss of fine touch and pressure sensation on the same side of the body below the cut.

Brown-Sequard Syndrome

Brown-Sequard syndrome refers to the consequences of a unilateral section through the spinal cord (Figure 26.7). Because some of the ascending and descending pathways cross the spinal cord and others do not, different symptoms appear on the two sides of the body below the cut. Contralateral to the side of the section, there is a loss of pain and temperature sensation because these pathways cross at the point at which they enter the cord. Sensations of fine touch and pressure are preserved there, however, because their pathways do not cross until they reach the caudal medulla. Fine touch and pressure sensation, but not pain and temperature sensation, is lost ipsilateral to the section, as are sensation and voluntary movements of distal musculature. Walking ability is recovered within 2 to 3 days, because control of this activity is bilateral.

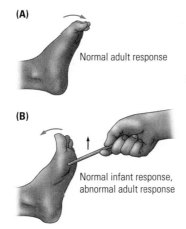

(A)

Normal adult response

(B)

Normal infant response,
abnormal adult response

Figure 26.8 Responses to stimulation of the lateral plantar surface of the left foot. (A) The normal adult response. (B) The normal infant and abnormal adult response, known as the Babinski sign. (After Gardner, 1968.)

Hemiplegia

The characteristics of **hemiplegia** (again, *hemi* means "half") are loss of voluntary movements on one side of the body, changes in postural tone, and changes in the status of various reflexes. Hemiplegia results from damage to the neocortex and basal ganglia contralateral to the motor symptoms. In infancy, such damage may result from birth injury, epilepsy, or fever. (Infant hemiplegia is usually discussed under the umbrella of cerebral palsy.) In young adults, hemiplegia is usually caused by rupture of a congenital aneurysm or by an embolism, a tumor, or a head injury. Most cases of hemiplegia, however, are found in middle-aged to elderly people and are usually due to hemorrhaging as a consequence of high blood pressure and degeneration of the blood vessels.

The damage that produces hemiplegia also affects a number of reflexes that are diagnostically important. In normal subjects, scratching the sole of the foot with a dull object produces a downward flexion of all toes. A person with hemiplegia, in contrast, responds with an upward flexion, especially of the big toe, and an outward fanning of the toes (Figure 26.8). This response, called the **Babinski sign** or **extensor plantar response,** is caused by the activation of flexor muscles and is often accompanied by flexion of the leg at the knee and hip. It is one of a family of flexion responses subsequent to motor-cortex or pyramidal-tract damage. Two reflexes are absent in hemiplegia: the **abdominal reflex,** which in normal people causes the abdominal muscles to retract when stroked, and the **cremasteric reflex,** which in normal males causes retraction of the testicles when the inner thigh is stroked.

There is a great deal of variation in the amount of recovery after hemiplegia, and treatment may have one or a combination of objectives. A patient may be trained to use the unaffected side, to use the affected side as much as spasticity and residual abilities allow, or to make movements that lessen spasticity and maximize voluntary control. The last strategy, described in detail by Bobath, is based on the fact that the strength of spasticity is related to posture. Bending over lessens spasticity and, if the arm is extended and the head is turned toward the arm, flexion spasticity is lessened. Such knowledge may enable some patients to make considerable use of their affected limbs.

Disorders of Sleep

The need for sleep varies considerably from one person to another, as well as in the same person at different stages of life. We have all been told that we need 8 hours of sleep each night for good health. In fact, there are both long and short sleepers. Some people can stay healthy on as little as an hour of sleep per day, whereas others may need to sleep as much as 10 to 12 hours. The definition of what constitutes adequate sleep must be decided within the context of a person's sleep history.

Sleep consists of at least two states that alternate periodically in the course of a complete sleep session. One state is a characterized by vivid dreaming, during which the subjects display rapid eye movements, or REMs. This state is called REM sleep, and the other is called non-REM (NREM) sleep. Typically, centers in the brainstem produce a condition of muscular paralysis during REM sleep, and so, apart from REMs and short bursts of twitches in the fingers, toes and other body parts, the body remains largely motionless. Even so, EEGs taken during dreams resemble the patterns seen when subjects are awake. NREM sleep is characterized by large movements, such as tossing and turning, and by a slow-wave EEG of various amplitudes. NREM is generally divided into four stages: stage 1 has the least amount of slow-wave activity and stage 4 has the most, with stages 2 and 3 falling between the two. REM and NREM occur in a typical alternating pattern, as illustrated in Figure 7.7.

Disorders of sleep are generally divided into two major groups: (1) **narcolepsy,** which is characterized by excessive sleep or brief inappropriate episodes of sleep, often associated with other symptoms; and (2) **insomnia,** which is characterized by an inadequate amount of sleep, an inability to fall asleep, or frequent inconvenient arousals from sleep. In addition to these two groups of disorders, other behaviors during sleep are disturbing to the afflicted person. These behaviors include night terrors, sleepwalking, grinding of the teeth, and myoclonic jerks (sudden vigorous movements). They are usually too transitory, too infrequent, or not sufficiently disruptive to be called sleep disorders. Some people display involuntary leg movements, a disorder called restless-leg syndrome.

Narcolepsy

Narcolepsy is defined as an inappropriate attack of sleep. The affected person has an overwhelming impulse to fall asleep or simply collapses into sleep at inconvenient times. The attacks may be infrequent or may occur many times a day. Narcolepsy disorders are surprisingly common; estimates suggest that as much as 0.02% of the population may suffer from them. Males and females seem equally affected. Although there is a high incidence of narcolepsy in the families of afflicted persons, no genetic causality has been demonstrated. Symptoms usually appear when people are between the ages of 10 and 20, and, once sleep attacks develop, they continue throughout life. Amphetamine-like stimulants and tricyclic antidepressants have been found to be useful in treatment.

The narcolepsies include (1) sleep attacks, (2) cataplexy, (3) sleep paralysis, and (4) hypnagogic hallucinations. Although these disorders do not generally exist at the same time or in the same person, they are present together often enough to be considered interrelated.

Sleep attacks are brief, often irresistible, episodes of sleep—probably slow-wave, NREM, naplike sleep—that last about 15 minutes and can occur at any time. Their approach is sometimes recognizable, but they can also occur without warning. The episodes are most apt to occur in times of boredom or after meals, but they can also occur in such activities as sexual intercourse, scuba diving, or baseball games. After a brief sleep attack, the affected person may awaken completely alert and remain attack free for a number of hours. **Cataplexy** (Greek *cata*, meaning "down," and *plexy*, meaning "strike") is a complete loss of muscle tone or a sudden paralysis that results in "buckling" of the knees or complete collapse. The attack may be so sudden that the fall results in injury, particularly because the loss of muscle tone and of reflexes prevents an affected person from making any motion that would break the fall. During the attack, the person remains conscious and, if the eyelids stay open or are opened, can recall seeing events that took place during the attack. In contrast with sleep attacks, cataplexic attacks usually occur at times of emotional excitement, such as when a person is laughing or angry. If emotions are held under tight control, the attacks can be prevented. Cataplexy is probably an attack of REM, or dream, sleep.

Sleep paralysis is an episode of paralysis in the transition between wakefulness and sleep. The period of paralysis is usually brief but can last as long as 20 minutes. Sleep paralysis has been experienced by half of all people, if classroom surveys are a true indication of its frequency. In contrast with cataplexy, the paralyzed person can be easily aroused by being touched or called by name and, if experienced with the attacks, can terminate them by grunting or using some other strategy that shakes off the sleep. What appears to happen in sleep paralysis is that the person wakes up but is still in the state of paralysis associated with dream sleep.

Hypnagogic hallucinations (Greek *hypnos*, meaning "sleep," and *gogic*, meaning "enter into") are episodes of auditory, visual, or tactile hallucination during sleep paralysis as an affected person is falling asleep or waking up. The hallucinations are generally frightening; the person may feel that a monster or something equally terrifying is lurking nearby. The same kinds of hallucinations can occur during episodes of cataplexy. A curious feature of the hallucinations is that the person is conscious and often aware of things that are actually happening, and so the hallucinations are even more bizarre because they can become intermixed with real events. These hallucinations may actually be dreams that a person is having while still conscious.

Insomnia

The results of studies of people who claim that they do not sleep, do not sleep well, or wake up frequently from sleep show that their insomnia can have many causes. Rechtschaffen and Monroe recorded EEGs from poor sleepers before and during sleep and found that they exaggerated the length of time that it took them to get to sleep. But the poor sleepers did have decreased dream sleep, moved more during sleep, and went through more transitions between sleep stages than normal people do. Moreover, when awakened from slow-wave sleep, they claimed that they had not been sleeping. The investigators concluded that, even though these poor sleepers did sleep by EEG criteria, they did not seem to benefit completely from the restorative properties of sleep. Surveys suggest that as many as 14% of people claim to suffer from insomnia, but the causes are diverse and include general factors such as anxiety, depression, fear of sleeping, environmental disturbances, and travel into new time zones (jet lag). Insomnia may be associated with nightmares and night terrors, sleep apnea (arrested breathing during sleep), restless-leg syndrome (a disorder characterized by frequent involuntary leg movements), myoclonus (involuntary muscle contraction), use of certain kinds of drugs, and certain kinds of brain damage.

Nightmares are intense, frightening dreams that lead to waking. Less common are *night terrors*, attempts to fight or flee accompanied by panic and screams or similar utterances. Nightmares occur during dream sleep, but night terrors occur during NREM sleep. Night terrors are usually brief (1 or 2 min) and usually forgotten on waking. Both phenomena are more common in children than in adults, perhaps because adults have had more experience with disturbing dreams and so are less easily awakened by them. Both can be sufficiently disturbing to disrupt sleep and lead to insomnia.

Sleep apnea (from the Greek for "not breathing") is a periodic cessation of respiration during sleep and ranges in length from about 10 seconds to 3 minutes. There are two types of sleep apnea. **Obstructive sleep apnea** occurs mainly during dream sleep and seems to be caused by a collapse of the oropharynx during the paralysis of dream sleep. Patients with this problem invariably have a history of loud snoring—sounds produced as a consequence of the difficulty of breathing through the constricted air passage. The obstruction can be reduced through surgical intervention. **Central sleep apnea** stems from a central nervous system disorder. It primarily affects males and is characterized by a failure of the diaphragm and accessory muscles to move. All-night recording sessions are needed to detect and diagnose both types of sleep apnea. Both types interrupt sleep, because an affected person is awakened partly or fully by the oxygen deprivation. Even so, the person may be unaware of the apnea and only be aware of suffering chronic daytime fatigue.

Most psychoactive drugs, whether stimulants or sedatives, eventually lead to insomnia. Hypnotics and sedatives may promote sleep at first, but only until habituation sets in. Furthermore, when drugs do induce sleep, it is not dream sleep, and so the user continues to feel deprived of sleep. Stimulants directly reduce sleep, but they may have their greatest effect on slow-wave sleep. Withdrawal from the drug usually puts an end to drug-induced insomnia.

Summary

A number of nervous system disorders are typically diagnosed by a neurologist, including closed- and open-head injuries, infections, migraines, tumors, motor disorders, and sleep disorders. Despite their diversity, the disorders are relatively common, which is unfortunate because they disrupt normal living. Neuropsychological analysis is helpful in evaluating the behavioral abilities of patients with these disorders and contributes to counseling and therapy.

References

Albuquerque, E. X., J. E. Rash, R. F. Myer, and J. R. Satterfield. An electrophysiological and morphological study of the neuromuscular junction in patients with myasthenia gravis. *Experimental Neurology* 51:536–563, 1976.

Annegers, J. F., J. D. Grabow, R. V. Groover, E. R. Laws, L. R. Elveback, and L. T. Kurland. Seizures after head trauma: A population study. *Neurology* 30:683–689, 1980.

Bakal, D. A. Headache: A biopsychological perspective. *Psychological Bulletin* 82:369–382, 1975.

Bannister, R. *Brain's Clinical Neurology*, 5th ed. New York: Oxford University Press, 1978.

Bobath, B. *Adult Hemiplegia: Evaluation and Treatment*. London: Heinemann Medical Books, 1970.

Bond, M. R. Neurobehavioral sequelae of closed head injury. In I. Grant and K. M. Adams, Eds. *Neuropsychological Assessment of Neuropsychiatric Disorders*. New York: Oxford University Press, 1986.

Brooks, N., L. Campsie, C. Symington, A. Beattie, and W. McKinlay. The five year outcome of severe blunt head injury: A relative's view. *Journal of Neurology, Neurosurgery, and Psychiatry* 49:764–770, 1986.

Changeux, J.-P., M. Kasai, and C.-Y. Lee. The use of a snake venom toxin to characterize the cholinergic receptor protein. *Proceedings of the National Academy of Sciences of the United States of America* 67:1241–1247, 1970.

Courville, C. B. *Pathology of the Nervous System*, 2d ed. Mountain View, CA: Pacific Press, 1945.

Dement, W., and N. Kleitman. Cyclic variations in EEG during sleep and their relation to eye movements, body motility and dreaming. *Electroencephalography and Clinical Neurophysiology* 9:673–690, 1957.

Fortuny, L. A., M. Briggs, F. Newcombe, G. Radcliffe, and C. Thomas. Measurement of the duration of post-traumatic amnesia. *Journal of Neurology, Neurosurgery, and Psychiatry* 43:377–379, 1980.

Gardner, H. *Fundamentals of Neurology*. Philadelphia: Saunders, 1968.

Hartmann, E. *The Biology of Dreaming*. Springfield, IL: Charles C Thomas, 1967.

Klonoff, P. S., W. G. Snow, and L. D. Costa. Quality of life in patients 2 to 4 years after closed head injury. *Neurosurgery* 19:735–743, 1986.

Lashley, K. S. Patterns of cerebral integration indicated by the scotomas of migraine. *Archives of Neurology and Psychiatry* 46:331–339, 1941.

Levin, H. S., A. L. Benton, and R. G. Grossman. *Neurobehavioral Consequences of Closed Head Injury*. New York: Oxford University Press, 1982.

Levin, H. S., H. E. Gary, W. M. High, S. Mattis, R. M. Ruff, H. M. Eisenberg, L. F. Marshall, and K. Tabaddor. Minor head injury and the postconcussional syndrome: Methodological issues in outcome studies. In H. S. Levin, J. Grafman, and H. M. Eisenberg, Eds. *Neurobehavioral Recovery from Head Injury*. New York: Oxford University Press, 1987.

Lezak, M. D. *Neuropsychological Assessment*, 2d ed. New York: Oxford University Press, 1983.

Luria, A. R. *The Working Brain*. New York: Penguin, 1973.

McNeil, E. B. *The Psychoses*. Englewood Cliffs, NJ: Prentice-Hall, 1970.

Marinkovic, S. V., M. M. Milisavljevic, V. Lolic-Draganic, and M. S. Kovacevic. Distribution of the occipital branches of the posterior cerebral artery: Correlation with occipital lobe infarcts. *Stroke* 18:728–732, 1987.

Moruzzi, G., and H. W. Magoun. Brainstem reticular formation and activation of the EEG. *Electroencephalography and Clinical Neurophysiology* 1:455–473, 1949.

Nathan, P., and M. Smith. Effects of two unilateral cordotomies on the mobility of the lower limbs. *Brain* 96:471–494, 1973.

Nauta, W. J. H. Hypothalamic regulation of sleep in rats: An experimental study. *Journal of Neurophysiology* 9:285–316, 1946.

Newcombe, F. *Missile Wounds of the Brain*. London: Oxford University Press, 1969.

Newcombe, F. Psychometric and behavioral evidence: Scope, limitations, and ecological validity. In H. S. Levin, J. Grafman, and H. M. Eisenberg, Eds. *Neurobehavioral Recovery from Head Injury*. New York: Oxford University Press, 1987.

Oppenheimer, D. R. Microscopic lesions in the brain following head injury. *Journal of Neurology, Neurosurgery, and Psychiatry* 31:299–306, 1968.

Patrick, J., and J. Lindstrom. Autoimmune response to acetylcholine receptor. *Science* 180:871–872, 1973.

Pincus, J. H., and G. J. Tucker. *Behavioral Neurology*. New York: Oxford University Press, 1974.

Pompeiano, O. Mechanisms of sensorimotor integration during sleep. In E. Stellar and L. Sprague, Eds. *Progress in Physiological Psychology*, vol. 3. New York: Academic Press, 1970.

Raichle, M. E., C. D. de Vivo, and J. Hanaway. Disorders of cerebral circulation. In S. G. Eliasson, A. L. Prensky, and W. B. Hardin, Eds. *Neurological Pathophysiology*, 2d ed. New York: Oxford University Press, 1978.

Rasmussen, T. Cortical resection in the treatment of focal epilepsy. *Advances in Neurology* 8:139–154, 1975.

Rechtschaffen, A., and W. Dement. Studies on the relation of narcolepsy, cataplexy, and sleep with low voltage random EEG activity. *Research Publications: Association for Research in Neurons and Mental Disease* 45:488–498, 1967.

Rechtschaffen, A., and L. J. Monroe. Laboratory studies of insomnia. In A. Kales, Ed. *Sleep: Physiology and Pathology*. Philadelphia: Lippincott, 1969.

Rosner, B. B. Recovery of function and localization of function in a historical perspective. In D. G. Stein, J. J. Rosen, and N. Butters, Eds. *Plasticity and Recovery of Function in the Central Nervous System*. New York: Academic Press, 1974.

Teasdale, G., and B. Jennett. The Glasgow Coma Scale. *Lancet* 2:81–84, 1974.

Terry, R. D., and P. Davies. Dementia of the Alzheimer type. *Annual Review of Neuroscience* 3:77–95, 1980.

Teuber, H.-L., W. S. Battersby, and M. B. Bender. *Visual Field Defects after Penetrating Wounds of the Brain*. Cambridge, MA: Harvard University Press, 1960.

Twitchell, T. E. The restoration of motor function following hemiplegia in man. *Brain* 74:443–480, 1951.

Webb, W. B. *Sleep: the Gentle Tyrant*. Englewood Cliffs, NJ: Prentice-Hall, 1975.

Wilberger, J. E., Z. Deeb, and W. Rothfus. Magnetic resonance imaging in cases of severe head injury. *Neurosurgery* 20:571–576, 1987.

Zacks, S. I. *Atlas of Neuropathology*. New York: Harper & Row, 1971.

chapter

27

Psychiatric and Related Disorders

When Mrs. T. was 16 years old, she began to experience her first symptom of schizophrenia: a profound feeling that people were staring at her. These bouts of self-consciousness soon forced her to end her public piano performances. Her self-consciousness led to withdrawal, then to fearful delusions that others were speaking of her, and finally to suspicions that they were plotting to harm her. At first Mrs. T.'s illness was intermittent, and the return of her intelligence, warmth, and ambition between episodes allowed her to complete several years of college, to marry, and to rear three children. She had to enter a hospital for the first time at 28, after the birth of her third child, when she began to hallucinate.

Now, at 45, Mrs. T. is never entirely well. She has seen dinosaurs on the street and live animals in her refrigerator. While hallucinating, she speaks and writes in an incoherent, but almost poetic, way. At other times, she is more lucid, but even then her voices sometimes lead her to do dangerous things, such as driving very fast down the highway in the middle of the night, dressed only in a nightgown. . . . At other times and without any apparent stimulus, Mrs. T. has bizarre visual hallucinations. For example, she saw cherubs in the grocery store. These experiences leave her preoccupied, confused and frightened, unable to perform such everyday tasks as cooking or playing the piano. (Gershon and Rieder, 1992, p. 127)

This chapter focuses on behavioral disorders, those characterized by dramatic abnormalities in cognitive functioning absent obvious lesions to the brain. We begin with the disorders commonly regarded as mental illness (schizophrenia and affective disorders) and then consider the history of psychosurgery. A survey of the physical and mental aspects of motor disorders (for example, Parkinson's disease) follows, and a discussion of dementias related to aging concludes the chapter.

The Brain and Behavior

Throughout the centuries since Descartes first posed the mind–body problem, the contrast between psychological and biological views of mental disorders has mirrored the debate between dualists and monists. Like these polar philosophical views, the mind–body problem is with us still.

Religion and poetry have viewed madness as an affliction of the spirit. Madness is central to classic as well as to contemporary fiction, for example. Think of Shakespeare's *Macbeth* and *Othello* or *The Idiot* by Dostoyesky. In contrast, medicine has explained madness as a disorder of various bodily humors and organs, although in most cases without much evidence or success.

In the past three decades, it has become clear that psychiatric, or behavioral, disorders have biochemical, anatomical, and genetic bases. It has also become clear that the distinction between behavioral disorders often referred to as mental illness, such as schizophrenia, and those described as motor disorders, such as Parkinson's disease, is not as clear-cut as it once seemed.

Schizophrenia

Schizophrenia is an extraordinary disorder. It has always been easier to identify schizophrenic behavior than to define what schizophrenia is. Perhaps the one universally accepted criterion for diagnosing schizophrenia is by eliminating the presence of other neurological disturbance or affective disorder—a definition by default.

The fourth edition of the *Diagnostic and Statistical Manual of the American Psychiatric Association* (DSM-IV) lists five symptoms of schizophrenia:

1. Delusions, or beliefs that distort reality, such as Mrs. T.'s suspicions that people were plotting against her

2. Hallucinations, or altered perceptions, such as hearing voices

3. Disorganized speech, such as incoherent statements or senseless rhyming

4. Disorganized, or excessively agitated, behavior

5. Various "negative" symptoms, such as blunted emotions, or loss of interest and drive, all of which are characterized by the absence of some normal response

Not all patients will exhibit all symptoms; rather, the symptoms observed in different patients are heterogeneous, which suggests that the biological correlates also will be heterogeneous.

Although schizophrenia was once believed to be characterized by a progressively deteriorating course with a dismal final outcome, this view is probably incorrect. Most patients appear to stay at a fairly stable level after the first few years of the disease, with little evidence of a decline in neuropsychological functioning. The symptoms come and go, much as in Mrs. T.'s case, but the severity is relatively constant after the first few years.

Structural Abnormalities in Schizophrenic Brains

Numerous studies have looked at the gross morphology of the brains of schizophrenics, both in tissue obtained at autopsy and in MRI and CT scans. Although the results are variable, most researchers agree that schizophrenic brains weigh less than normal brains and that the ventricles are enlarged. Schizophrenics have also been suggested to have smaller frontal lobes or at least a reduction in the number of neurons in the prefrontal cortex, as well as thinner parahippocampal gyri. The results of studies of cellular structure have shown abnormalities in both the prefrontal cortex and the hippocampus. The prefrontal cells have a simple dendritic organization, indicating fewer synapses than normal, whereas the pyramidal neurons in the hippocampus have a haphazard orientation, as illustrated in Figure 27.1.

It seems unlikely that disorientation of the hippocampal neurons can develop at any time except during embryogenesis, which suggests some developmental abnormality in the hippocampus. Lipska, Weinberger, and their colleagues proposed that the early hippocampal abnormality may be at least partly responsible for the abnormalities in the structure and function of the prefrontal cortex. They developed an intriguing animal model in which rats with perinatal hippocampal injuries develop abnormal dopaminergic organization in the prefrontal cortex. Not only do the animals have symptoms of prefrontal dysfunction but, like schizophrenia patients, the rats also have reduced synaptic space in the prefrontal pyramidal cells.

Investigators are using neuroimaging to study brain activation in schizophrenics during tasks such as the Wisconsin Card-Sorting Test (see Figure 16.8). For example, the results of experiments by Weinberger and his colleagues show that normal control subjects exhibit significant activation of the prefrontal cortex during card-sorting performance. Patients with schizophrenia do not. In one intriguing report, Berman and Weinberger studied identical twins who were discordant for schizophrenia (that is, only one was schizophrenic). PET scans showed differences between the twins during resting or control conditions, but, during card sorting, every schizophrenic twin's brain was hypofrontal compared with the well twin. This result is consistent with the hypothesis that the prefrontal cortex of schizophrenia patients is abnormal in both structure and function.

(A) Normal brain (organized)

(B) Schizophrenic brain (disorganized)

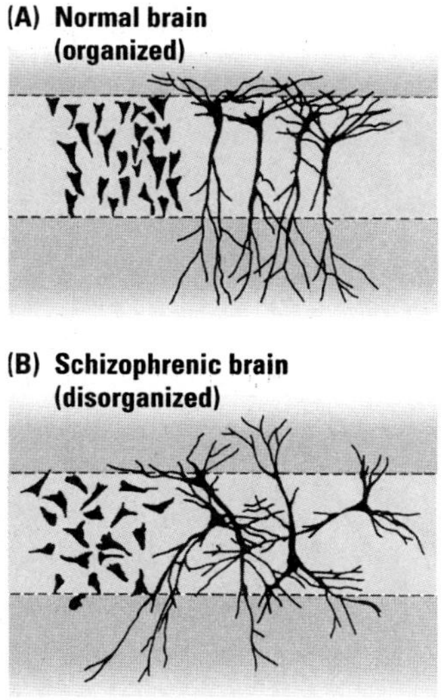

Figure 27.1 Examples of pyramidal cell orientation from the hippocampus of (A) a normal (organized) and (B) a schizophrenic (disorganized) brain. Note the haphazard orientations of these cells. (After Kovelman and Scheibel, 1984.)

Biochemical Abnormalities in Schizophrenic Brains

An important pathway in the prefrontal cortex is its dopaminergic input from the tegmental area. Interference with dopaminergic function disturbs the performance of cognitive tasks in laboratory animals, and so it is reasonable to infer that an abnormality in dopamine activity in the frontal lobe could be responsible for at least some symptoms of schizophrenia.

Perhaps the strongest evidence favoring a role for dopamine in schizophrenia comes from studies of the action of antipsychotic drugs (also called neuroleptic drugs). These drugs act on the dopamine synapse, and dopamine agonists (such as cocaine, amphetamine, and L-dopa) that enhance the action of dopamine can induce psychotic symptoms that are almost indistinguishable from those of classic paranoid schizophrenia. Moreover, if a schizophrenic takes amphetamine, the schizophrenic symptoms are heightened.

Although dopamine abnormalities are most commonly emphasized in schizophrenia, other chemical abnormalities have been found. Table 27.1 summarizes

Table 27.1 Biochemical changes in schizophrenia

Decreased dopamine metabolites in cerebrospinal fluid

Increased striatal D_2 receptors

Decreased expression of D_3 and D_4 mRNA in specific cortical regions

Decreased cortical glutamate

Increased cortical glutamate receptors

Decreased glutamate uptake sites in cingulate cortex

Decreased mRNA for the synthesis of GABA in prefrontal cortex

Increased $GABA_A$-binding sites in cingulate cortex

Abbreviations: D, dopamine; GABA, γ-aminobutyric acid.
Source: Byne et al., 1999, p. 242.

some major neurochemical changes associated with schizophrenia. In particular, in addition to the abnormalities in dopamine and dopamine receptors, there are abnormalities in glutamate and glutamate receptors and in GABA and GABA-binding sites. There appears to be considerable variation in the degree of the different abnormalities in individual patients, and how the neurochemical variations might be related to specific symptoms is not yet known.

Types of Schizophrenia?

The variability in both brain abnormalities and behavioral symptomatology led Timothy Crow to propose two distinct pathological syndromes in schizophrenia:

- Type I, equivalent to acute schizophrenia, is characterized by positive symptoms, meaning those that consist of behavioral excess, such as delusions and hallucinations. Type I is hypothesized to result from a dopaminergic dysfunction, and Type I schizophrenics are expected to be more responsive to neuroleptic drugs.

- Type II, equivalent to chronic schizophrenia, is characterized by negative symptoms including flattened affect and poverty of speech. Type II is characterized by structural abnormalities in the brain and poor response to antipsychotic drugs.

Crow's analysis had a major effect on clinical thinking about schizophrenia, although a major difficulty is that as many as 30% of schizophrenia patients show a pattern of mixed type I and type II symptoms. The type I and type II groupings may actually represent opposite end points on a continuum of biological and behavioral manifestations.

Neuropsychological Assessment

Schizophrenics do poorly on neuropsychological tests, although the nature of the neuropsychological impairment in schizophrenia is controversial. Overall, schizophrenics perform poorly on tests of long-term verbal and nonverbal memory as well as on tests sensitive to frontal lobe function. Performance on tests of visual discrimination, spatial orientation, and short-term verbal and nonverbal memory appears to be less affected. These results are concordant with the view that schizophrenia primarily affects frontal and temporal lobe structures. (We must caution, however, that people who have been chronically institutionalized for schizophrenia may not perform normally on *any* test, rendering their test assessments futile.)

Mood Disorders

Although the DSM-IV identifies many types of mood disorders, the ones of principal interest here are depression and mania, disorders that represent the extremes on a continuum of affect. The main symptoms of **clinical depression** are prolonged feelings of worthlessness and guilt, disruption of normal eating habits, sleep disturbances, a general slowing of behavior, and frequent thoughts of suicide. **Mania,** in contrast, is characterized by excessive euphoria, in which an affected person often formulates grandiose plans and behaves with uncontrollable hyperactivity. Periods of mania often switch, sometimes abruptly, into states of depression and back again; hence the condition is called **bipolar disorder.**

Neurochemical Aspects of Depression

A source of insight into the neurobiological basis of depression was the observation that patients given reserpine for high blood pressure often became severely depressed. Reserpine depletes monoamines, which include norepinephrine, dopamine, and serotonin. This observation led to the idea that monoamines might be reduced in depression, and postmortem studies of suicide victims supported this hypothesis.

Research in the past decade has complicated the picture, because it is now clear that many different receptors exist for each monoamine and that specific monoamine receptors may be disrupted in depression. An added complication is that no clear unifying theory accounts for the action of antidepressant medications to treat depression. It appears, for example, that neurotrophic (that is, growth-supporting) factors may play a role in the action of antidepressants. Brain-derived neurotrophic factor (BDNF) is upregulated by antidepressant medication and is downregulated by stress. Given that BDNF acts to enhance the growth and survival of neurons and synapses, BDNF dysfunction may adversely affect monoamine systems through the loss of either neurons or synapses.

The possible role of stress in altering the production of BDNF is important because it has become increasingly clear that monoamines modulate the secretion of hormones by the hypothalamic–adrenal system, as illustrated in Figure 27.2. The best-established abnormality in the hypothalamic–adrenal system (known as the **HPA axis**) is an oversecretion of the hormone hydrocortisone (cortisol). Cortisol, which is secreted by the adrenal glands, is associated with stress reactions.

When you are stressed, the hypothalamus secretes corticotropin-releasing hormone, which stimulates the pituitary to produce adrenocorticotropin (ACTH). The ACTH circulates through the blood and stimulates the adrenal gland to produce cortisol. The hypothalamic neurons that begin this cascade are regulated by norepinephrine neurons in the locus coeruleus. The possibility that the body's stress reaction is abnormal in depression has important implications, because stress-related hormones and transmitters have a widespread influence on cerebral functioning.

The recent development of fluoxitine (for example, Prozac) as a major drug for treating depression has an interesting story related to neurotrophic factors. Fluoxitine is a selective serotonin reuptake blocker (see Chapter 6) that effectively increases the amount of serotonin in the cortex. But fluoxitine may also have actions that are important to the hippocampus independent of serotonin.

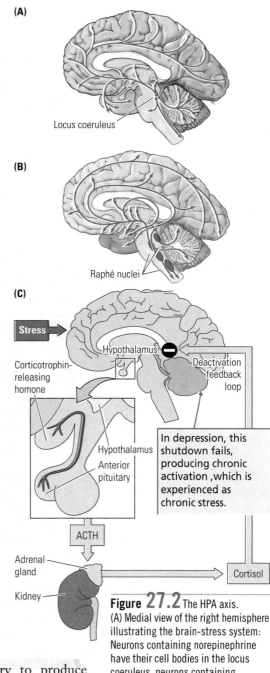

Figure 27.2 The HPA axis. (A) Medial view of the right hemisphere illustrating the brain-stress system: Neurons containing norepinephrine have their cell bodies in the locus coeruleus, neurons containing corticotrophin-releasing hormone are in the hypothalamus, and neurons containing dopamine have their cell bodies in the ventral tegmentum. (B) Medial view illustrating the serotonin cell bodies in the Raphé nuclei and their projections to the rest of the brain. (C) When activated, this system affects mood, thought, and, indirectly, the secretion of cortisol by the adrenal glands. Deactivation normally begins when cortisol binds to hypothalamic receptors.

The sustained elevation of stress-related hormones, the glucocorticoids, results in the death of granule cells in the hippocampus. This cell death could be a result of the lowered BDNF production. Fluoxitine stimulates both BDNF production and neurogenesis in the hippocampus, resulting in a net increase in the number of granule cells. The effects of fluoxitine on depression may therefore tell us a great deal about the relation between the HPA axis and behavior.

Blood Flow and Metabolic Abnormalities in Depression

The general symptoms of depression might lead us to predict a diffuse reduction in cerebral activity in depression, which was the general finding in the early PET studies looking at depressives. Striking regional differences have become clear, however, especially within the frontal lobe.

In their review of the literature, Drevets and his coworkers concluded that, whereas dorsolateral and medial prefrontal areas show decreased blood flow and metabolism, the orbital regions actually show an abnormal increase in these measures (see the Snapshot on page 729). Similarly, there is an increase in metabolism in the amygdala and medial thalamus, two structures intimately related to the prefrontal cortex in the control of emotional behavior (see Chapter 20). When depressives are imaged both before and during effective antidepressant treatment, the activity in the orbital cortex and amygdala decreases. If antidepressant medication is unsuccessful, PET studies fail to find a decrease in activity.

What do the observed changes in blood flow and metabolism mean for our understanding of depression? The increased activity in the amygdala may hold the key to answering this question. An abnormal increase in resting activity in the amygdala is specific to mood disorders and is the only structure in which the severity of the symptoms positively correlates with the increase in glucose metabolism. Recall from Chapter 20 that the amygdala acts to assign emotional significance to stimuli. In addition, the amygdala activity stimulates cortisol release, suggesting that amygdala activity may increase HPA-axis activity in depression. The increased activity in the orbital cortex could correspond to an attempt to modulate or inhibit amygdala activity.

Drevets and colleagues report that, in contrast with a positive relation between amygdala activity and depression, there is actually a negative relation for the orbital cortex. That is, higher activity appears to reduce depressive symptoms. Thus, the high activity in the orbital cortex may correspond to an attempt to break perseverative patterns of negative thought and emotion, which in turn result from overactivity in the amygdala.

Although speculative, the Drevets hypothesis is intriguing and worth watching in future studies. A question not addressed in the hypothesis, however, is why drugs, such as fluoxitine, that increase serotonin would reduce the overactivity in the amygdala. The answer is not entirely clear, although Drevets points out that reducing serotonin levels by diet actually increases amygdala activity, suggesting that serotonin may act to decrease amygdala activity.

But what is the significance of the decreased activity in the dorsolateral prefrontal cortex? Dolan and his colleagues suggest that the lowered activity relates to the reduced memory and attentional processing in depression. The cause of the lowered activity is not clear but may result from the increased activation related to emotional processing or depressive ruminations.

Cortical Metabolic and Anatomical Abnormalities in Mood Disorders

Disorders of mood may follow either a "unipolar" course consisting only of depression or a "bipolar" course in which normal affect alternates with episodes of both depression and mania. Drevets and colleagues collected PET images of cerebral blood flow from unmedicated unipolar and bipolar subjects (both groups were in a depressive phase and had a familial history of mood disorder) and from control subjects. The brain area with the largest difference between control and depressive groups was the medial frontal region lying immediately below the most anterior region of the corpus callosum (a region referred to as subgenual prefrontal cortex), which showed about a 12% decrease in blood flow (see the adjoining illustration).

In a follow-up series, the researchers compared control subjects with bipolar subjects who were in a manic phase and found a significant increase in activity in the same subgenual area. In a study done on one bipolar patient, they found that she had decreased blood flow during the depressive phase and increased blood flow during the manic phase.

Because the decreased blood flow in depressives could be due to changes either in synaptic activity or in tissue volume, the investigators collected MRI images in mood-disordered and control subjects in a parallel set of studies. The gray-matter volume of the left subgenual prefrontal cortex was reduced by about 39% in both the unipolar and the bipolar groups. This reduced volume was present regardless of the mood state. The Drevets group concludes that the reduction in gray-matter volume in mood disor-

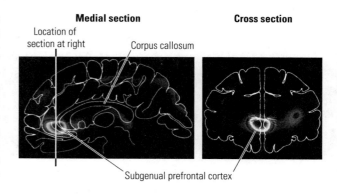

Reduced PET activation in depression. There is an area of reduced metabolism and blood flow in a region just below the corpus callosum (subgenual prefrontal cortex). (From Drevets, Gadde, and Krishman, 1999.)

ders could correspond either to an abnormality of brain development related to the tendency to develop mood episodes or to a degenerative change resulting from the illness.

(W. C. Drevets, J. L. Price, J. R. Simpson, R. D. Todd, T. Reich, M. Vannier, and M. E. Riachle. Subgenual prefrontal cortex abnormalities in mood disorders. *Nature* 386:824–827, 1997.)

Because serotonin is thought to play a key role in the sleep–wake cycle, EEG studies might be expected to reveal cortical abnormalities in this cycle. Kupfer and Thase found that slow-wave sleep is abnormal and that the onset of paradoxical sleep (REM sleep, or dreaming) is more rapid in depressed people. The researchers believe this measure to be a sensitive clinical test for depression. Further, they believe that the prognosis for the effectiveness of any particular antidepressant agent is likely to appear in the EEG before it does so clinically.

Finally, some depressed people might be predicted to exhibit only regional reduction in cortical activity because of some local disruption of neurotransmitter levels, and thus there might be different types of depressions characterized by different patterns of cerebral dysfunction. One possibility is that decreased thyroid-hormone production (hypothyroidism) may influence mood. The addition of thyroid hormone to antidepressant drug regimes for example, is known to potentiate and hasten the effectiveness of the drugs. To our knowledge, there have not yet been imaging studies of people with hypothyroid conditions, however.

Neurobiological Aspects of Bipolar Disorder

It has been much harder to find consistent changes in the brains of bipolar patients than in depressives. When positive results have been found, the effects are typically similar to those observed in depression, although there appears to be less consistency across patients. Post and Weiss hypothesize that mood-disorder episodes are often initially precipitated by psychosocial stressors but that the episodes begin to recur spontaneously and unrelated to external stressors in predisposed people. These episodes can become very rapid, with cycling occurring daily. Bipolar episodes may also be triggered by pharmacological agents such as antidepressants or in postpartum manic and depressive episodes and then develop an autonomous course. When bipolar disorders have begun an autonomous course, unrelated to external events, medication appears to become increasingly less effective.

What causes the autonomous recurrence of bipolar episodes? One possibility is that the brain of the bipolar patient is especially sensitive to the effects of stressors or drugs and that episodes of mood disorder actually change the brain. One model of such change is drug- or stress-induced sensitization, which we shall consider briefly. (For a more extensive discussion, see Post and Weiss.)

If animals are subjected to stress or are given psychomotor stimulants repeatedly, behavioral responsivity progressively increases. This increased responsivity is correlated with changes both in neurochemistry and in the morphology of neurons in dopamine-recipient regions—especially the prefrontal cortex. Recently, Kolb and Robinson discovered that drugs of abuse have different effects on the medial and orbital prefrontal regions, a finding reminiscent of the differences in blood flow and metabolism found in the homologous areas in human depressives. Thus, in predisposed people, an episode of some kind may sensitize the brain and produce changes in brain morphology.

Three factors make this **sensitization model** intriguing for understanding bipolar disorder:

1. There are large individual differences in the degree of sensitization and drug effects in laboratory animals and people. Genetically predisposed individuals may be especially sensitive and produce faster and likely larger neuronal changes in response to stressors.

2. The abuse of psychomotor stimulants such as cocaine is associated with full-blown manic episodes, suggesting a link between psychomotor stimulant-induced neuronal change and mania.

3. Bipolars are at high risk for substance abuse, suggesting that they are especially sensitive to drug effects.

The sensitization model of bipolar disorder is still largely hypothetical, but it does explain a disorder that has proved so difficult to understand and to treat. A challenge for researchers is to find a treatment that can effectively reverse the effects of sensitization.

Psychosurgery

Before the development of drugs for treating schizophrenia and affective disorders, few treatments were available. One that emerged in the 1930s was surgical (see Chapter 20). Although psychosurgery is no longer commonly used, it is worth reviewing in the context of schizophrenia and depression. For an excellent discussion of psychosurgery and its history, we recommend two books by Eliot Valenstein: *The Psychosurgery Debate* and *Great and Desperate Cures*.

Psychosurgery is the destruction of some region in the brain to alleviate severe and otherwise intractable psychiatric disorders. To distinguish current psychosurgical techniques from earlier and cruder lobotomy operations, the term *psychiatric surgery* has been suggested as a substitute, although the term refers to the same procedures. Brain surgery intended to repair damage to alleviate symptoms resulting from known neurological disease is not considered psychosurgery, even if the patient has severe behavioral and emotional symptoms. Brain surgery to alleviate intractable pain is normally considered psychosurgery because the operations are performed on normal brain tissue and because serious emotional disturbances often accompany chronic pain.

The belief that mental aberrations are related to disturbances of brain function dates to primitive times. The practice of opening the skull (trephining) for magical-medical purposes was apparently performed extensively dating to at least about 2000 B.C. (see Figure 1.10). Modern psychosurgery is usually traced to Portuguese neurologist Egas Moniz, who started the prefrontal procedures in 1935.

On the basis of studies of a small sample of chimpanzees by Carlyle Jacobsen, Moniz reasoned that destruction of the frontal lobe of psychiatrically ill people might be beneficial. Although he initially used alcohol injected into the frontal lobes to induce a frontal lesion, he soon switched to a technique in which nerve fibers were cut with a special knife called a *leukotome* (from the Greek *leuko*, meaning "white," here in reference to nerve fibers, and *tome*, meaning "cutting instrument"). The procedure consisted of drilling holes over the white matter to sever the frontal connections. Later modifications in the procedure were made in the United States by Walter Freeman and James Watts, including the Freeman-Watts procedure of drilling holes in the temples and Freeman's lateral transorbital procedure in which the leukotome was inserted through the bony orbit above the eyeball. It is impossible to estimate accurately how many psychosurgical procedures were performed worldwide, although Valenstein thinks that the best estimate for the United States between 1936 and 1978 is 35,000.

The introduction of antipsychotic drugs in the mid-1950s led to a sharp reduction in the number of psychosurgical operations, but there were still a significant number of psychiatric patients who were not helped by the drugs. Thus, there has been a continuing interest in surgical intervention to change behavior but, since the 1960s, the psychosurgical procedures employed have

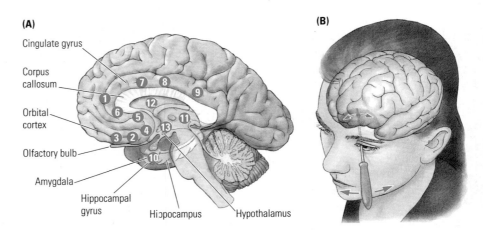

Figure 27.3 Targets for psychosurgery. (A) Approximate targets of psychosurgical operations currently in use include frontal lobe procedures and disconnection of the cingulate gyrus, amygdala, thalamus, and hypothalamus. *Frontal lobe procedures:* (1) bimedial leukotomy; (2) yttrium lesions in subcortical white matter; (3) orbital undercutting; (4) bifrontal stereotaxic subcaudate tractotomy; (5) anterior capsulotomy (destruction of fibers of internal capsule); (6) mesoloviotomy (similar to rostral cingulotomy, but lesion invades the genu, or "knee," of the corpus callosum). *Cingulotomies:* (7) anterior cingulotomy; (8) midcingulotomy; (9) posterior cingulotomy. *Amygdalectomy:* (10) amygdalectomy or amygdalotomy. *Thalamotomies:* (11) thalamotomy of the dorsomedial, centromedian, or parafascicular nuclei; (12) anterior thalamotomy. *Hypothalamotomy:* (13) section of the posterior, ventromedial, or lateral hypothalamus. (B) In the procedure for a transorbital leukotomy, a leukotome is inserted through the bone of the eye socket and the inferior frontal cortex is disconnected from the rest of the brain. (Part A after Valenstein, 1980.)

changed, in part because of advances in the neurosciences. There are currently about 13 different targets of psychosurgical operations, which are summarized in Figure 27.3A.

These procedures generally produce smaller lesions than did the original lobotomy-type procedures, and today they are rarely performed. The major reason for the end of the psychosurgery era is that the development of new generations of psychiatric drugs has meant that virtually everybody is responsive to some form of psychoactive medication. We note, parenthetically, that the most common form of psychosurgery—namely, frontal leukotomy (Figure 27.3B)—disconnected regions of the prefrontal cortex from the rest of the brain, and we have seen that abnormalities in the prefrontal cortex are associated with both schizophrenia and depression. The difficulty with psychosurgery, however, is that, although the abnormal activity of the prefrontal regions was removed, it was not replaced by normalized activity. The goal of drug treatment is to do just that.

Motor Disorders

The group of diseases comprising motor disorders has clinical symptoms marked by abnormalities in movement and posture that are referable to dysfunctions of the basal ganglia. Although the most obvious symptom is the motor affliction, all produce cognitive changes as well, changes that become especially marked as the diseases progress. Indeed, many patients with motor disorders develop symptoms similar to those of schizophrenia. Clinically, two groups of symptoms are distinguished: (1) a loss of movement, which is referred to as a hypokinetic-rigid syndrome (for example, Parkinson's disease); and (2) an increase in motor activity, which is known as a hyperkinetic-dystonic syndrome (for example Huntington's chorea and Gilles de la Tourette syndrome).

Hyperkinetic Disorders

Huntington's chorea (from the Greek *choreia*, meaning "dance") is a genetic disorder that results in intellectual deterioration and abnormal movements as an afflicted person reaches certain ages. George Huntington was 8 years old when he first saw people with "that disorder," as it was then called. He was driving with his father in his native New York when they came upon two women who were tall and thin and were twisting and grimacing. No doubt the disorder was familiar to his father and grandfather, both of whom were physicians.

Nevertheless, the sight of these women left such a profound impression on young George that he studied the disease when he later became a physician. In 1872, when he was 22, he wrote the first complete description of the disease. Its history in the United States can be traced to the village of Bures in England in 1630. At that time, whole families in Bures and its vicinity were branded and tried as witches. Some family members, who had or carried the disease, sailed to America among the 700 passengers of the John Winthrop fleet in 1630. In 1653, Ellin Wilkie (name fictitious), who had arrived with Winthrop, apparently had the disorder, because she was tried and hanged for witchcraft. Her granddaughter was later tried and pardoned in 1692.

Part of the early history of establishing the genetic basis for the disease entailed tracing the family backgrounds of afflicted persons whose ancestors were among the Winthrop passengers and settled in various parts of the United States. In other countries colonized by Europeans, similar family histories have been constructed that trace the disease to one or a few immigrants. Huntington's chorea is quite rare, with death rates of 1.6 per million people worldwide per year. It is most common among white Europeans and their descendants; it is rare among Asian and African racial groups. The number of people who will develop the disease is likely on the decline because of advances in genetic counseling.

Huntington's chorea, or hereditary chorea, is a progressive degenerative disease. The first symptom is usually a reduction of activity and restriction of interest. The first restless and involuntary movements may be attributed to an anxiety disorder (for example, hysteria in earlier times).

The first movements usually appear within a year of the onset of the behavioral symptoms. The involuntary movements are initially slight and consist of little more than continual fidgeting, but they slowly increase until they are almost incessant. The movements never entail single muscles but include whole limbs or parts of a limb. They are also irregular and follow no set pattern.

A reliable marker is that a sustained muscular contraction is not possible: when an object is held, the grip fluctuates; in addition, the tongue cannot be held protruded. Eventually, the movements become uncontrollable and affect the head, face, trunk, and limbs—impeding speech, swallowing, walking, writing, and other voluntary movements. Sometimes an afflicted person attempts to mask the abnormal movements with purposeful ones.

There are emotional and personality changes, impairments of recent memory, defective ability to manipulate acquired knowledge, and slowing of information processing. Apraxia, aphasia, and agnosias, which result from certain cortical diseases such as Alzheimer's disease, do not develop, however. The emotional changes include anxiety, depression, mania, and schizophrenia-like psychoses. Suicide is not uncommon in younger patients.

The first symptoms usually appear in people from 30 to 50 years of age. About 5% of cases begin before age 20 and are sometimes called "juvenile chorea." In contrast with adults, juveniles may exhibit muscle rigidity and slow movements, somewhat similar to those in Parkinson's disease, and they may

Normal transmitter system

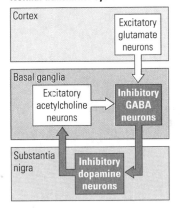

Huntington's chorea

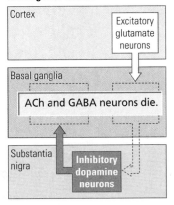

Figure 27.4 Model of neurotransmitter systems in Huntington's chorea. Acetylcholine (ACh) and γ-aminobutyric acid (GABA) neurons in the basal ganglia are thought to die, and, as a result, dopamine cells are released from GABA inhibition and become hyperactive, thus producing abnormal movements. The death of GABA cells may be caused by excessive activity of the glutamate pathway.

endure muscle spasms, tremor, disturbances of eye movement, and epilepsy. Adult patients live an average of 12 years after disease onset, but the progress of the disease is far more rapid in the juvenile cases.

Huntington's chorea is transmitted genetically as an autosomal dominant with complete penetrance, meaning that half the offspring of an affected person will develop the disease. The approximate location of the gene is now known, and a marker can be used before symptoms appear to determine whether a family member (even in utero) will develop the disease. Applying recombinant DNA procedures on a population in Venezuela, Gusella and colleagues narrowed the locus of the gene to a part of the short arm of chromosome 4 and detected a marker linked with this gene.

At autopsy, the brains of people with Huntington's chorea show shrinkage and thinning of the cerebral cortex. The basal ganglia are grossly atrophied and show a marked loss of intrinsic neurons. A dominant explanation of the disease is an imbalance among the various neurotransmitter systems of the basal ganglia. A simplified model of the these transmitter systems is shown in Figure 27.4. They include:

1. a glutamate projection from the cortex to the basal ganglia,

2. a γ-aminobutyric acid (GABA) projection from the basal ganglia to the substantia nigra,

3. a dopamine (DA) projection from the substantia nigra to the basal ganglia, and

4. acetylcholine (ACh) neurons in the basal ganglia.

Researchers postulate that the intrinsic neurons of the basal ganglia (GABA and ACh neurons) die in the course of the disease, leaving a largely intact nigrostriatal DA pathway. As a result of the decrease in inhibition of the DA cells by the GABA pathway, DA release in the basal ganglia increases. The hyperactivity of the dopamine system is believed to produce the characteristic abnormal movements, although exactly how is not clear.

The results of extensive neuropsychological studies by Fedio and colleagues and by Wexler show that Huntington patients are impaired in a broad range of memory tests, as well as in visual, auditory, and tactile perceptual tests. In addition, patients are especially poor at performing various frontal lobe tests (for example, the Chicago Word-Fluency Test and the stylus–maze test). People who have at least one parent with the disease and can thus be considered at risk appear to perform poorly only on the frontal lobe tests, suggesting that these tests might be useful as predictors of the disease. The effectiveness of these tests as predictors will be seen in the coming years as the subjects in these studies either begin to display other symptoms or do not do so.

Tourette's syndrome was described by Georges Gilles de la Tourette in 1885. In most important ways, his description of the disorder is still remarkably good. Until his review, this syndrome was seen either as an undifferentiated chorea or as a symptom of hysteria, and it had a variety of names, depending on where it had been observed.

The symptoms tend to evolve and to become more elaborate with age. Gilles de la Tourette described three stages of the syndrome. In the first stage, only multiple tics (twitches of the face, limbs, or the whole body) occur. In the second stage, inarticulate cries are added to the multiple tics. In the third stage, the emission of articulate words with **echolalia** (repeating what others have said, as well as repeating actions) and **coprolalia** (from the Greek *copro*, meaning "dung," but its current meaning is obscene or lewd, and *lalia*, meaning "speech") are added to the multiple tics and inarticulate cries.

The following case history, reported by Gilles de la Tourette, illustrates most of the major features of the syndrome:

> Miss X., 15 years old, spent several months at the Longchamps hydrotherapy institution at Bordeaux in the winter of 1883, where she was treated for convulsive attacks of chorea and ejaculations of loud vulgar and obscene words. Miss X. was very intelligent, she learned the lessons given her by her teacher with the greatest ease, and she played the piano well. She was tall and largely built. She was not well disciplined.
>
> When 9, Miss X. began having violent and irregular choreiform tics of the face, arms, and legs. At the same time she occasionally uttered a few vulgar words. After a few months the attacks disappeared. A year later they came back again. The tics first reappeared in the shoulders, then in the arms, and then in the face, where they were accompanied by loud guttural sounds. These indistinct sounds became very clearly articulated when she was 13. At that time her most frequent words were "get away, go away, imbecile." A little later her words became more frequent and much clearer, and were rough and lewd. She remained that way until the present.
>
> Miss X. belonged to an upper-class family. Her education was excellent. She never left her mother, who surrounded her in continuous, tender loving care. One had to wonder how and where she picked up the words she continually uttered: for example, "In God's name, fuck, shit, et cetera." When she is in her calm, normal state such words never pass her lips. (Gilles de la Tourette, 1885, pp. 41–42; translated by Lorna Whishaw)

Gilles de la Tourette recognized that people with the syndrome could be intelligent and productive and were not neurotic or psychotic. He also noted that the syndrome, or parts of it, ran in families and thus seemed hereditary. He pointed out that there was no treatment (although the symptoms lessened or disappeared during fevers), and so the symptoms were likely to be with the person for life.

Recent renewed interest in Tourette's syndrome is largely through the work of the Tourette Society in North America. Many patients with Tourette's syndrome have been misdiagnosed as troublemakers, hysterics, schizophrenics, and more—no doubt because they seem intelligent yet display bizarre behavior. Such diagnoses are now changing, and there is great interest in trying to understand the cause of the disorder in relation to brain function.

The incidence of Tourette's syndrome is less than 1 in 100,000, but the incidence can vary with the degree of professional knowledge about the disorder. In southern Alberta, Canada, which has a population base of about 100,000, a child psychiatrist interested in the disorder diagnosed more than 10 cases in 10 years. Thus, the actual incidence may be somewhat higher than the estimated incidence.

The average age of onset ranges between 2 and 15 years, with a median of 7 years; by 11 years of age, symptoms have appeared in 97% of cases. The most frequent symptoms are tics of the eye, head, or face (97%), upper limbs (81%), and lower limbs and body (55%). Complex movements including touching, hitting, and jumping appear in between 30% and 40% of cases.

Coprolalia may develop in as many as 60% of cases and then disappear in a third of them. As already noted, Tourette's syndrome is not associated with neuroses, psychoses, or other disorders. Electroencephalographic activity is often normal, although some patients may display abnormalities. The results of evoked-potential studies show that the premovement potentials associated with willed, voluntary movements do not occur with the tics in Tourette's syndrome patients, which confirms that these movements are involuntary.

Tourette's syndrome is presumed to have a subcortical origin, likely in the basal ganglia. There have been very few autopsy examinations of the brains of Tourette's syndrome patients, and, of those that have been done, only one reports an excessive number of small cells in the basal ganglia; others report that the cells there are normal. To date, the most consistent improvements are obtained with antidopaminergic agents such as haloperidol; thus it is thought that there may be some abnormality in the dopamine system in the basal ganglia. Clonidine, a norepinephrine receptor agonist, also is reported to be effective in some cases.

In general, the results of neuropsychological studies suggest abnormalities in some cognitive functions usually supported by the right hemisphere. For example, Sutherland and colleagues gave a composite test battery to a large sample of children and adults with Tourette's syndrome and found that the patients were especially bad at drawing and remembering complex geometric figures. The poor performance of these patients on the Rey Complex-Figure Test was particularly striking, because even patients with superior verbal IQ scores performed very poorly compared with control children or schizophrenic patients (Figure 27.5). The visuospatial difficulties observed in the Rey figure may have a real-world analogue as well: many Tourette's syndrome patients complain of having difficulty in remembering the locations of things in their daily lives.

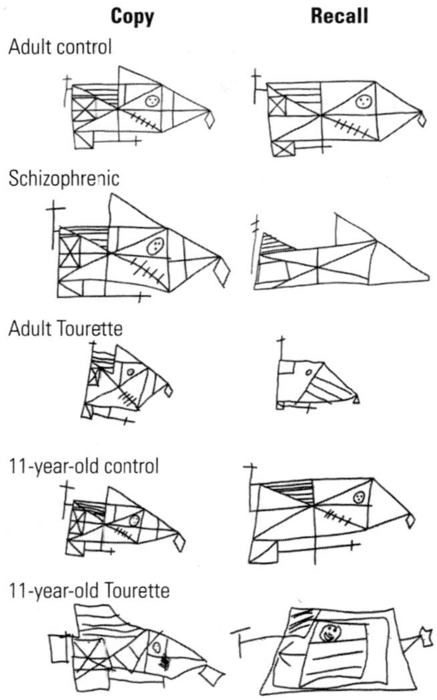

Figure 27.5 Representative performance by a normal adult control, a schizophrenic patient, an adult Tourette patient, a normal child, and a child Tourette patient on the Rey Complex-Figure Test: copying and recall. The Tourette patients are impaired at both the copying and the recall; the schizophrenic patient is impaired only at recall. (After Sutherland et al., 1982.)

Hypokinetic Disorders

In 1817, James Parkinson, a London physician, published an essay in which he argued that several different motor symptoms could be considered together as a group forming a distinctive condition that he referred to as the shaking palsy. His observations are interesting not only because his conclusion was correct but also because he made his observations in part at a distance, by watching the movements of victims in the streets of London. French neurologist Jean Charcot suggested that the disease be renamed to honor James Parkinson's recognition of its essential nature.

Parkinson's disease is fairly common; estimates of its incidence vary from 0.1% to 1.0% of the population worldwide, and the incidence rises sharply in old age. In view of the increasingly aging population in Western Europe and North America, the incidence of Parkinson's disease is certain to rise in the coming decades. It is also of interest for a number of other reasons:

- Parkinson's disease seems to be related to the degeneration of the **substantia nigra** and to the loss of the neurotransmitter dopamine, which is produced by cells of this nucleus. The disease, therefore, is an important source of insight into the role of this brainstem nucleus and its neurotransmitter in the control of movement.

- Because a variety of pharmacological treatments for Parkinson's disease relieve different features of its symptoms to some extent, the disease provides a model for understanding pharmacological treatments of motor disorders more generally.

- Although Parkinson's is described as a disease entity, the symptoms vary enormously among people, thus illustrating the complexity with which the components of movement are organized to produce fluid motion.

- Many symptoms of Parkinson's disease strikingly resemble changes in motor activity that take place as a consequence of aging. Thus the disease is an indirect source of insight into the more general problems of neural changes in aging.

The four major symptoms of Parkinson's disease are tremor, rigidity, akinesia, and disturbances of posture; each symptom may be manifested in different body parts in different combinations. Because some of the symptoms are the acquisition of abnormal behaviors (positive symptoms) and others the loss of normal behaviors (negative symptoms), we will consider the symptoms in these two major categories. Positive symptoms are behaviors not seen in normal people or seen only so rarely, and then in such special circumstances, that they can be considered abnormal. Negative symptoms are marked not by any particular behavior but rather by the absence of a behavior or by the inability to engage in an activity.

Positive Symptoms

Because positive symptoms are common in Parkinson's disease, they are thought to be held in check, or inhibited, in normal people but released from inhibition in the process of the disease. The most common positive symptoms are:

1. *Tremor at rest.* Tremor consists of alternating movements of the limbs when they are at rest; these movements stop during voluntary movements or during sleep. The tremors of the hands often have a "pill rolling" quality, as if a pill were being rolled between the thumb and forefinger.

2. *Muscular rigidity.* Muscular rigidity consists of simultaneously increased muscle tone in both extensor and flexor muscles. It is particularly evident when the limbs are moved passively at a joint; movement is resisted, but, with sufficient force, the muscles yield for a short distance and then resist movement again. Thus, complete passive flexion or extension of a joint is in a series of steps, giving rise to the term *cogwheel rigidity*. The rigidity may be severe enough to make all movements difficult. One man less severely afflicted by rigidity was moved to comment to us, "The slowness of

movement is conscious but not willed. That is, I form a plan in my mind; for instance, I wish to uncork that bottle. Then I deliberately invoke the effort that sets the muscles in motion. I'm aware of the slowness of the process; I'm unable to increase [its speed], but I always get the bottle open."

3. *Involuntary movements.* These movements may consist of continual changes in posture, sometimes to relieve tremor and sometimes to relieve stiffness, but often for no apparent reason. These small movements or changes in posture, sometimes referred to as **akathesia** or *cruel restlessness*, may be concurrent with general inactivity. Other involuntary movements are distortions of posture, such as those during *oculogyric crisis* (involuntary turns of the head and eyes to one side), which last for periods of minutes to hours.

Because the positive symptoms are actions, they are caused by the activity of some brain area. Before drug therapy became common, one treatment used to stop the positive symptoms was to localize the source of the symptom in the brain and make a lesion there. For example, tremor was treated by lesions made in the ventral lateral thalamus. This treatment was abandoned because improvement was only temporary. Recently, improvements in how the lesions are made and in their accurate placement has led to a resurgence of this therapy. Additionally, the best results have been obtained with lesions to the internal part of the globus pallidus (which eventually projects to the ventral lateral thalamus).

Negative Symptoms

After detailed analysis of negative symptoms, J. P. Martin divided patients severely affected with Parkinson's disease into five groups:

1. *Disorders of posture.* These disorders include disorders of fixation and of equilibrium. A *disorder of fixation* consists of an inability to maintain or difficulty in maintaining a part of the body (head, limbs, and so forth) in its normal position in relation to other parts. Thus, a person's head may droop forward or a standing person may gradually bend forward until he or she ends up on the knees. *Disorders of equilibrium* consist of difficulties in standing or even sitting unsupported. In less-severe cases, patients may have difficulty standing on one leg or, if pushed lightly on the shoulders, they may fall passively without taking corrective steps or attempting to catch themselves.

2. *Disorders of righting.* These disorders consist of difficulty in achieving a standing position from a supine position. Many advanced patients have difficulty even in rolling over.

3. *Disorders of locomotion.* Normal locomotion requires support of the body against gravity, stepping, balancing while the weight of the body is transferred from one limb to another, and pushing forward. Parkinson patients have difficulty initiating stepping, and, when they do walk, they shuffle with short footsteps on a fairly wide base of support because they have trouble maintaining equilibrium when shifting weight from one limb to the other. Often, Parkinson patients who have begun to walk demonstrate **festination:** they take faster and faster steps and end up running forward.

4. *Disturbances of speech*. One of the symptoms most noticeable to relatives is the almost complete absence of tone (prosody) in the speaker's voice.

5. *Akinesia*. A poverty or slowness of movement may also manifest itself in a blankness of facial expression or a lack of blinking, swinging of the arms when walking, spontaneous speech, or normal movements of fidgeting. It is also manifested in difficulty in making repetitive movements, such as tapping, even in the absence of rigidity. People who sit motionless for hours show akinesia in its most striking manifestation.

The symptoms of Parkinson's disease begin insidiously, often with a tremor in one hand and with slight stiffness in the distal parts of the limbs. Movements may then slow, the face becoming masklike with loss of eye blinking and poverty of emotional expression. Thereafter the body may become stooped, and gait becomes a shuffle with the arms hanging motionless at the sides. Speech may become slow and monotonous, and difficulty in swallowing saliva may result in drooling.

Although the disease is progressive, the rate at which the symptoms worsen is variable, and only rarely is progression so rapid that a person becomes disabled within 5 years; usually from 10 to 20 years elapse before symptoms cause incapacity. A most curious aspect of Parkinson's disease is its on-again–off-again quality: symptoms may appear suddenly and disappear just as suddenly. Partial remission may also occur in response to interesting or stimulating situations. Oliver Sacks recounts an incident in which a Parkinson patient leaped from his wheelchair at the seaside and rushed into the breakers to save a drowning man, only to fall back into his chair immediately afterward and become inactive again. Although remission of some symptoms in activating situations is common, remission is not usually as dramatic as in this case.

Causes of Parkinsonism

The three major types of Parkinson's disease are idiopathic, postencephalitic, and drug induced. Parkinson's disease may also result from arteriosclerosis, syphilis, the development of tumors poisoning by carbon monoxide, or manganese intoxication.

As suggested by its name, the cause of *idiopathic* Parkinson's disease is not known. Its origin may be familial or it may be part of the aging process, but it is also widely thought to have a viral origin. This type most often develops in people older than 50 years of age.

The *postencephalitic* form originated in the sleeping sickness (*encephalitis lethargica*) that appeared in the winter of 1916–1917 and vanished by 1927. Although the array of symptoms was bewilderingly varied, such that hardly any two patients seemed alike, Constantin von Economo demonstrated a unique pattern of brain damage—namely, the death of cells in the substantia nigra. Although many people seemed to recover completely from the encephalitis, most subsequently developed neurological or psychiatric disorders and parkinsonism. The latency between the initial and subsequent occurrences of the disease has never been adequately explained. Specific searches for viral particles or virus-specific products in Parkinson patients without encephalitis have revealed no evidence of viral cause, although it is still believed to be likely.

Drug-induced Parkinson's disease developed most recently and is associated with ingestion of various drugs, particularly major tranquilizers that include reserpine and several phenothiazine and butyrophenone derivatives. The symptoms are usually reversible, but they are difficult to distinguish from those of the genuine disorder.

External agents can cause Parkinson's symptoms quite rapidly. Langston and coworkers report that a contaminant, MPTP, of synthetic heroin is converted into MPP$^+$, which is extremely toxic to dopamine cells. A number of young drug users were found to display a complete parkinsonian syndrome shortly after using contaminated drugs. This finding suggests that other substances might cause similar effects. The results of demographic studies of patient admission in the cities of Vancouver and Helsinki show an increase in the incidence of patients getting the disease at ages younger than 40. This finding suggests that water and air might contain environmental toxins that work in a fashion similar to MPTP.

The cells of the substantia nigra are the point of origin of fibers that go to the frontal cortex and basal ganglia and to the spinal cord. The neurotransmitter at the synapses of these projections is dopamine. Bioassay of the brains of deceased Parkinson patients and analysis of the major metabolite of dopamine—homovanallic acid, which is excreted in the urine—have demonstrated that the amount of dopamine in the brain is reduced by more than 90% and is often reduced to undetectable amounts. Thus, the cause of Parkinson's disease has been identified with some certainty as a lack of dopamine or, in drug-induced cases, as a lack of dopamine action. Dopamine depletion may not account for the whole problem in some people, however, because decreases in norepinephrine have been recorded, and a number of results show that cells in some of the nuclei in the basal ganglia may degenerate as well.

Treatment of Parkinson's Disease

No known cure for Parkinson's disease exists, and none will be in sight until the factors that produce the progressive deterioration of the substantia nigra are known. Thus, treatment is symptomatic and directed toward support and comfort. The major symptoms of parkinsonism are influenced by psychological factors, a person's outcome being affected by how well he or she copes with the disability. As a result, patients should be counseled early regarding the meaning of symptoms, the nature of the disease, and the potential for most of them to lead long and productive lives. Physical therapy should consist of simple measures such as heat and massage to alleviate painful muscle cramps and training and exercise to cope with the debilitating changes in movement.

Pharmacological treatment has two main objectives: first, increase the activity in whatever dopamine synapses remain and, second, suppress the activity in structures that show heightened activity in the absence of adequate dopamine action. Drugs such as L-dopa, which is converted into dopamine in the brain, amantadine, amphetamine, monoamine oxidase inhibitors, and tricyclic antidepressants are used to enhance effective dopamine transmission. Naturally occurring anticholinergic drugs, such as atropine and scopolamine, and synthetic anticholinergics, such as benztropine (Cogentin), and trihexyphenidyl (Artane), are used to block the cholinergic systems of the brain that seem to show heightened activity in the absence of adequate dopamine activity.

One promising treatment is to try to increase the number of dopamine-producing cells. The simplest way to do so is to transplant embryonic dopamine cells into the basal ganglia; in the 1980s and 1990s, this treatment was used with varying degrees of success. A newer course of treatment proposes to increase the number of dopamine cells either by transplanting stem cells, which could then be induced to adopt a dopaminergic phenotype, or by stimulating endogenous stem cells to be produced and migrate to the basal ganglia. Both treatments are still highly experimental.

Psychological Aspects of Parkinson's Disease

Psychological symptoms in Parkinson patients are as variable as the motor symptoms. Nonetheless, a significant percentage of patients have cognitive symptoms that mirror their motor symptoms. Sacks, for example, reports the negative effects of the disease on cognitive function. There is an impoverishment of feeling, libido, motive, and attention; people may sit for hours, apparently lacking the will to enter or continue any course of activity. In our experience, thinking seems generally to be slowed and is easily confused with dementia because patients do not appear to be processing the content of conversations. In fact, they are simply processing very slowly.

The results of neuropsychological studies confirm that Parkinson patients often show cognitive symptoms similar to those shown by people with frontal lobe or basal ganglia lesions, such as deficits on the Wisconsin Card-Sorting Test. This association is not surprising, because there are close relations between the functions of the basal ganglia and the frontal cortex and because dopamine projections into the frontal cortex might be expected to degenerate in the same way as those of the basal ganglia degenerate. Test performance is not noticeably improved by drug therapy.

The cognitive slowing in Parkinson patients has some parallels to changes of Alzheimer's disease, and findings in postmortem studies show clear evidence of Alzheimer-like abnormalities in most patients, even if they did not have obvious signs of dementia. Neuropsychological investigations of other populations confirm the possibility of a general cognitive deterioration in Parkinson patients. For example, in their extensive study, Pirozzolo and coworkers found Parkinson patients significantly impaired—relative to age-matched controls—on several subtests of the Wechsler Adult Intelligence Scale, including information, digit span, digit symbol, and block design, and on measures of verbal memory (logical stories and paired associates). Finally, Boller and his colleagues found Parkinson patients impaired on a wide array of visuospatial tests, independent of intellectual impairment.

Dementia

Demographic structures such as those now developing in North America and Europe have never been experienced before. Since 1900, the percentage of older people has been steadily increasing. In 1900, about 4% of the population had attained 65 years of age. By 2030, about 20% of the population will be over

65—about 50 million people in the United States alone. Dementia affects between 1% and 6% of the population over the age of 65 and between 10% and 20% over the age of 80. Furthermore, Larrabee and Crook estimate that, for every demented person, several others suffer cognitive impairments that affect the quality of their lives.

In the next 35 years, projections estimate that between 10 million and 20 million elderly people will have mild to severe cognitive impairments in the United States. When this projection is extended across the rest of the developed world, the social and economic costs are truly staggering. Not every person who becomes old also becomes depressed, forgetful, or demented. Some people live to very old age and enjoy active, healthy, productive lives. The question for most of us is how to ensure that we are in this group, but at present there are depressingly few answers.

Dementia refers to an acquired and persistent syndrome of intellectual impairment. The DSM-IV defines the two essential diagnostic features of dementia as (1) memory and other cognitive deficits and (2) impairment in social and occupational functioning. Kaufer and DeKosky divide dementias into two broad categories: degenerative and nondegenerative (Table 27.2).

Degenerative dementias are pathological processes that are primarily intrinsic to the nervous system and tend to affect certain neural systems selectively. Many degenerative dementias are presumed to have a degree of genetic transmission. *Nondegenerative dementias* are a heterogeneous group of disorders with diverse etiologies, including vascular, endocrine, inflammatory, nutritional deficiency, and toxic conditions.

The most prevalent form of dementia is **Alzheimer's disease,** which accounts for about 65% of all dementias and is named for German physician Alois Alzheimer, who published a case study in 1906. The patient was a 51-year-old woman for whom Alzheimer described a set of clinical and neuropathological findings.

Table 27.2 Degenerative and nondegenerative dementias

Degenerative	Nondegenerative
Alzheimer's disease	Vascular dementias
Extrapyramidal syndromes:	e.g., multi-infarct dementia
e.g., progressive supernuclear palsy	Infectious dementia
Wilson's disease	e.g., AIDS dementia
Huntington's disease	Neurosyphillis
Parkinson's disease	Posttraumatic dementia
Frontotemporal dementia	Demyelinating dementia
corticobasal degeneration	e.g., multiple sclerosis
Leukodystrophies	Toxic or metabolic disorders
e.g., adrenoleukodystrophy	e.g., vitamin deficiencies (B_{12}, niacin)
Prion-related dementias	Chronic alcohol or drug abuse
e.g., Creutzfeld-Jakob disease	e.g., Korsakoff syndrome

Source: After Kaufer and De Kosky, 1999.

Anatomical Correlates of Alzheimer's Disease

Until the 1990s, the only way to identify and to study Alzheimer's disease was to study postmortem pathology. This approach was less than ideal, however, because it was impossible to determine which changes came early in the disease and which followed as a result of the early changes. Nonetheless, it became clear that there are widespread changes in the neocortex and limbic cortex and associated changes in a number of neurotransmitter systems, none of which alone can be correlated simply with the clinical symptoms. Interestingly, most of the brainstem, cerebellum, and spinal cord are spared the major ravages.

Neuritic (Amyloid) Plaques

Neuritic plaques, also known as senile plaques, are found chiefly in the cerebral cortex. Their increased concentration in the cortex has been correlated with the magnitude of cognitive deterioration. The plaques consist of a central core of homogeneous protein material known as *amyloid,* surrounded by degenerative cellular fragments (Figure 27.6). These fragments include axonal and dendritic processes and other components of neural cells. Neuritic plaques are generally considered nonspecific phenomena in that they can be found in non-Alzheimer patients and in dementias caused by other known events.

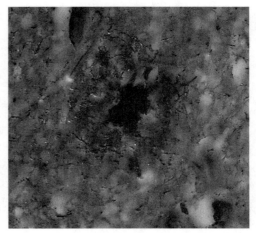

Figure 27.6 Neuritic plaque, which is often found in the cerebral cortexes of Alzheimer patients. The amyloid core (the dark spot in the center) is surrounded by the residue of degenerate cells. (Cecil Fox/Science Source/Photo Researchers.)

Paired Helical Filaments

Also known as neurofibrillary tangles, paired helical filaments are found in both the cerebral cortex and the hippocampus. The posterior half of the hippocampus is affected more severely than the anterior half. Light-microscopic examination has shown that the filaments have a double-helical configuration. They have been described mainly in human tissue and have also been observed in patients with Down syndrome, patients with Parkinson's disease, and patients with other dementias.

Neocortical Changes

These changes are not uniform. Although the cortex shrinks or atrophies, losing as much as one-third of its volume as the disease progresses, some areas are relatively spared. Figure 27.7 shows lateral and medial views of the human brain; shading indicates the areas of degeneration. The darker the blue, the more severe the degeneration.

As is clearly shown in Figure 27.7, the primary sensory and motor areas of the cortex, especially the visual cortex and the sensorimotor cortex, are spared. The frontal lobes are less affected than the posterior cortex, but the areas of most extensive change are the posterior parietal areas, inferior temporal cortex, and limbic cortex.

Figure 27.7 Distribution and severity of degeneration on (A) lateral and (B) medial aspects of the brain in an average Alzheimer case. The darker the area, the more pronounced the degeneration. White areas are spared, with only basic change discernible. (After Brun, 1983.)

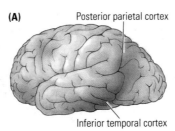

(A) Posterior parietal cortex

Inferior temporal cortex

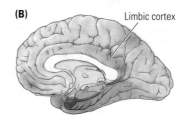

(B) Limbic cortex

(A) Cortical pyramidal cells

Normal adult pattern | Early Alzheimer's disease | Advanced Alzheimer's disease | Terminal Alzheimer's disease

(B) Hippocampal neurons

Middle age (50s) | Older (70s) | Very old (90s) | Alzheimer's disease

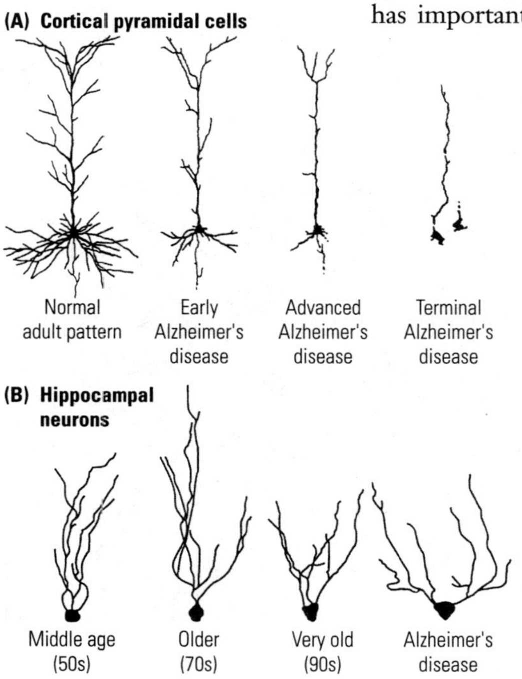

Figure 27.8 Neuronal pathology in Alzheimer's disease. (A) Sequence of changes in a cortical pyramidal cell in the course of the development of Alzheimer's dementia (from left to right): normal adult pattern; early stages of disease marked by patchy spine loss and thinning out of the dendritic tree, especially horizontally oriented branches; advanced stage with almost complete loss of basilar dendrites; and terminal stage. (B) Comparison of dendritic length of hippocampal neurons drawn from brain specimens of healthy persons in their 50s, 70s, and 90s and from a patient with Alzheimer's disease. The average length of dendrites increases from middle age into old age, decreasing only in late old age. Dendrites in brains with Alzheimer's disease do not show the age-related growth. (Part A drawn from Golgi-stained sections of human prefrontal cortex; after Scheibel, 1983. Part B after Selkoe, 1992.)

Paralimbic Cortex Changes

The limbic system undergoes the most severe degenerative changes in Alzheimer's disease and, of the limbic structures, the entorhinal cortex is affected earliest and most severely (see Figure 27.7). A number of investigators agree that the entorhinal cortex shows the clearest evidence of cell loss, which has important implications for understanding some of the disease symptoms.

The entorhinal cortex is the major relay through which information from the neocortex gets to the hippocampus and related structures and is then sent back to the neocortex. Damage to the entorhinal cortex is associated with memory loss. Given that memory loss is an early and enduring symptom of the disease, it is most likely caused by the degenerative changes that take place in this area of the cortex.

Cell Changes

Many studies describe loss of cells in the cortexes of Alzheimer patients, but this loss is disputed. There seems to be a substantial reduction in large neurons, but these cells may shrink rather than disappear. The more widespread cause of cortical atrophy, however, appears to be a loss of dendritic arborization, as illustrated in Figure 27.8.

The cause of these changes is not known. It is worth noting, however, that the degradation is not simply typical of aging. Coleman and Flood demonstrated that normal people actually show increases in dendritic arborization between their 50s and 70s (see Figure 27.8). Only in very old age does the pattern of degeneration begin to look like the neural cells typical of Alzheimer's disease.

Neurotransmitter Changes

In the 1970s, it was believed that a treatment for Alzheimer's could be found to parallel L-dopa treatment of Parkinson's disease, and the prime candidate neurotransmitter was acetylcholine. Unfortunately, the disease has proved far more complex, because other transmitters are clearly changed as well. Noradrenaline, dopamine, and serotonin are reduced and the NMDA and AMPA receptors for glutamate also are reduced.

The most interesting feature of the neurotransmitter changes is not the absolute decreases in any individual patient but the pattern of decreases. Although age-matched controls also show reductions in transmitter levels, when the pattern of reductions in all transmitter substances is plotted, the Alzheimer patients distinguish themselves from the control groups by showing greater reductions in two or more neurotransmitters.

Putative Causes of Alzheimer's Disease

At present, the cause of Alzheimer's disease is unknown. Given the increasing population of elderly people and thus of those with Alzheimer's disease, a good deal of research is being directed toward several potential causes, summarized in the following sections.

Genetics

There is an increased frequency of Alzheimer's disease in families that have had a member with Alzheimer's disease. The risk increases to 3.8% if a sibling has had the disease and to 10 in 100 if a parent has had the disease.

The application of molecular genetic methods has led to the discovery of three Alzheimer's disease susceptibility genes; they encode β-amyloid precursor protein (B-APP), presenilin 1, and presenilin 2. These susceptibilities were discovered by examining families with an unusually high incidence of Alzheimer's disease. The B-APP gene maps on chromosome 21, the chromosome found to be abnormal in Down syndrome. People with Down syndrome almost invariably develop dementia by age 40.

How an abnormality in the B-APP gene produces dementia is not know, but the abnormality is believed to cause the formation of amyloid plaques and neurofibrillary tangles. The presenilin genes have been found only recently, and they, too, appear to contribute to the production of amyloid, although the mechanism is not yet known (for a review, see Sherrington et al.).

Trace Metals

Early studies with animals identified neurofibrillary degeneration, similar to that in Alzheimer's disease, after the animals were given aluminum salts. Research that followed up this hint found increases ranging from 10 to 30 times the normal concentration of aluminum in Alzheimer patients' brains. At present, the reason for the accumulation of aluminum is not known; nor is whether taking action to reduce the accumulation would be helpful.

Immune Reactions

Some researchers think that, in old age, the immune system loses its ability to recognize a person's own body. As a result, it develops antibrain antibodies that then cause neuronal degeneration. In other words, the body actually begins to kill its own neurons, which in turn leads to dementia.

Slow Viruses

There is no direct evidence of a slow virus in Alzheimer's disease, but another degenerative dementia, **Creutzfeldt-Jakob disease,** appears to be caused by slow viruses and can pass among species, including between animals and humans (see Table 27.2). Indeed, the mad cow disease panic in Europe in the late 1990s was related to a slow virus.

The existence of slow viruses was suggested by the results of studies on a Papua New Guinea tribe in which the women engaged in ritual cannibalism by eating the brains of its deceased members. Years later, the women of the tribe became ataxic with a disease called *kurul*. After they died and their brains were ingested by others, the disease—apparently caused by a virus that takes years to produce symptoms—was passed on to those women.

Blood Flow

Historically, Alzheimer's disease was attributed to poor circulation. The results of PET studies confirm an extreme reduction in the amount of blood delivered to the brain and the amount of glucose extracted from the blood by neural tissue.

In normal people, blood flow to the brain declines by more than 20% between the ages of 30 and 60, but the brain compensates by more-efficient oxygen uptake. In Alzheimer's disease, the decline is enhanced, but there are no compensatory mechanisms. The greatest decreases in blood flow are found in those areas of the brain in which the most degenerative change is seen (see Figure 27.7). What is not known is whether the declines in blood flow and glucose metabolism are causal or secondary to degenerative brain changes. At least one pharmacological attempt to treat Alzheimer's disease stimulates brain blood flow.

Abnormal Proteins

The three main pathological changes associated with Alzheimer's disease—plaques, neurofibrillary tangles, and granulovacuolar bodies (small vacules about 3 μm in diameter, each containing a small granule)—consist of an accumulation of protein that is not seen in normal brains. This abnormal accumulation has led to the suggestion that unusual proteins are being produced and are accumulating, thus disrupting normal protein production and use. The increased protein accumulation in the brain of an Alzheimer patient may be the brain's attempt to repair itself, but for some reason the reparative processes go awry.

Clinical Symptoms and the Progression of Alzheimer's Disease

The most insidious feature of Alzheimer's disease is its slow onset and steady progress, which gradually rob a person, first, of recent memory, then, of more remote memory, and, finally, of the abilities to recognize family members and to function independently. An adaptation of Reisberg's detailed description of the stages of the disease and clinical symptoms appears in Table 27.3. As Reisberg points out, the disease progress is gradual, and patients spend from several months to several years in each stage. Reisberg also describes levels of impairment in five measures of cognitive function (concentration, recent and past memory, orientation, social functioning, and self-care) that are descriptive parallels of the stages shown in Table 27.3.

In view of the distinctive pattern of anatomical changes in the disease, one might expect a distinctive pattern of cognitive changes. Finding such a pattern would be important, because the symptoms displayed by Alzheimer patients are often confused with those seen in other disorders, such as depression or a series of small strokes. In view of the distinctly different approaches to managing depressed patients and Alzheimer patients, differential diagnosis would be very useful.

Fuld has used IQ subtest scales from the Wechsler Adult Intelligence Scale to distinguish the impairment patterns of Alzheimer's disease from those produced by cerebrovascular disease. Alzheimer patients are marked by the striking deficits that they show on digit symbol and block design, with successively milder impairments on object assembly, similarities and digit span, and information and vocabulary. Other Alzheimer's-sensitive tests include backward digits, telling the time on clocks without numbers, and object naming. Additionally, Alzheimer patients typically show deficits on tests of both left- and right-hemisphere function, and the impairments are not marked by sudden onset.

Table 27.3 Scale of behavioral change in Alzheimer's disease

Degree of cognitive decline	Symptoms
None	No subjective complaints of memory deficit. No memory deficit evident on clinical interview.
Very mild	Complaints of memory deficit, most often in (1) forgetting where one has placed familiar objects and (2) forgetting names that one formerly knew well. No objective evidence of memory deficit on clinical interview. No objective deficits in employment or social situations. Appropriate concern with respect to symptomatology.
Mild	Earliest clear-cut deficits. Manifestations in more than one of the following areas: (1) patient may get lost when traveling to an unfamiliar location; (2) coworkers become aware of patient's relatively poor performance; (3) patient may read a passage or a book and retain little material; (4) patient may demonstrate decreased facility in remembering names when introduced to new people; (5) patient may have lost or misplaced an object of value; (6) concentration deficit may be evident on clinical testing. Objective evidence of memory deficit obtained only with formal tests. Decreased performance in demanding employment and social settings. Denial begins to set in, and mild to moderate anxiety is displayed.
Moderate	Clear-cut deficit in clinical interview in (1) decreased knowledge of current and recent events; (2) memory of personal history; (3) concentration deficit in serial subtractions; (4) decreased ability to travel, handle finances, etc. Inability to perform complex tasks. Denial is dominant defense mechanism. Flattening of affect and withdrawal from challenging situations.
Moderately severe	Cannot function without some assistance. Unable to recall a major relevant aspect of current life, such as address or telephone number, names of close family members, name of schools attended. Frequent disorientation to date, day, season, and place. An educated person may have difficulty counting backward by fours from 40 and by twos from 20.
Severe	May occasionally forget name of spouse. Largely unaware of all recent events and experiences. Retains some knowledge of past life though sketchy. May have difficulty counting backward or forward from 10. Requires some assistance with activities of daily living (e.g., may become incontinent, requires travel assistance but occasionally displays ability to travel to familiar locations). Diurnal rhythm often disturbed. Can recall own name and distinguish familiar from unfamiliar persons in the environment. Changes in personality and emotional aspects, including delusional behavior, obsessive symptoms, anxiety, or loss of purposeful behavior.
Very severe	All verbal abilities are lost. Often there is no speech at all—only grunting; incontinent of urine; requires assistance in toileting and feeding. Loses basic psychomotor skill (e.g., ability to walk). The brain appears no longer to be able to tell the body what to do.

Source: After Reisburg, 1983.

Perhaps the most striking impairment in Alzheimer patients is related to memory performance. Virtually every neuropsychological test of memory reveals impairments relative to age-matched controls. Alzheimer patients are particularly prone to difficulties in producing the names of objects and in distinguishing among objects within a category.

Huff and colleagues conclude that the anomia deficit is characterized by a loss of information about specific objects and their names, rather than by a simple difficulty in retrieving information. The difficulties in naming are likely not simply due to difficulties with memory, because Alzheimer patients have a variety of language impairments that are most obvious as the complexity of the cognitive processing required increases. Thus, when engaging in simple conversations about the weather and so on, the patients appear to have normal language functioning but, if they are required to engage in more-complex discussions, their difficulty with language becomes more apparent.

Summary

Historically, psychiatry and neurology were the same field, and only recently have two separate specialties emerged. For many patients, however, the distinction is arbitrary. Diseases of the brain can produce severe psychological disturbances, and the causes are only beginning to be understood. Schizophrenia is a disease that emerges in the course of development, usually in late adolescence, and is associated especially with abnormalities in the structure and function of the dorsolateral prefrontal cortex and medial temporal region. Schizophrenia is likely not a single disorder but rather a continuum of disorders varying in the degree of positive and negative symptoms. The primary disorders of mood are depression and bipolar disorder. Both are related to abnormalities in the brain's response to stress through the HPA axis. Depression is associated with abnormally high activity in the orbital frontal cortex and amygdala. The action of antidepressants is to reduce amygdala activity, likely by increasing monoamine levels. Bipolar disorder may be a result of the brain's oversensitive response to stressors, including drugs, which in turn alters the chemistry and morphology of cells, especially in the orbital cortex or the amygdala or both. Motor disorders have been thought of traditionally as neurological, but these disorders can produce significant psychological abnormalities, likely because of an imbalance of neurotransmitter systems, especially the catecholamines and acetylcholine. These changes appear to have significant effects on frontal and temporal lobe function, leading to a variety of behavioral disturbances. Dementias are an increasing problem for society, owing to changing demographics. The most common dementia is Alzheimer's disease, which is associated with a variety of pathological changes in the forebrain. The cause or causes are not known, although research in molecular genetics has identified at least three genes that predispose people to the disease.

References

Becker, J. T., F. Boller, J. Saxton, and K. L. McGonigle-Gibson. Normal rates of forgetting of verbal and non-verbal material in Alzheimer's disease. *Cortex* 23: 59–72, 1987.

Benes, F. M., J. Davidson, and E. D. Bird. Quantitative cytoarchitectural studies of the cerebral cortex of schizophrenics. *Archives of General Psychiatry* 43:31–35, 1986.

Berman, K. F., and D. R. Weinberger. Regional cerebral blood flow in monozygotic twins concordant and discordant for schizophrenia. *Archives of General Psychiatry* 49:927–934, 1992.

Boller, F., D. Passafiume, M. C. Keefe, K. Rogers, L. Morrow, and Y. Kim. Visuospatial impairment in Parkinson's disease: Role of perceptual and motor factors. *Archives of Neurology* 41:485–490, 1984.

Bowen, F. P. Behavioral alterations in patients with Parkinson's disease. In M. D. Yahr, Ed. *The Basal Ganglia*. New York: Raven Press, 1976.

Bowles, N. L., L. K. Obler, and M. L. Albert. Naming errors in healthy aging and dementia of the Alzheimer type. *Cortex* 23:519–524, 1987.

Brown, R., N. Colter, J. A. Corsellis, T. J. Crow, C. D. Frith, R. Jagoe, and E. C. Johnstone. Postmortem evidence of structural brain changes in schizophrenia. *Archives of General Psychiatry* 43:35–42, 1986.

Brun, A. An overview of light and electron microscopic changes. In B. Reisberg, Ed. *Alzheimer's Disease*. New York: The Free Press, 1983.

Byne, W., E. Kemegther, L. Jones, V. Harouthunian, and K. L. Davis. The neurochemistry of schizophrenia. In D. S. Charney, E. J. Nestler, and B. S. Bunney, Eds. *The Neurobiology of Mental Illness*. New York: Oxford University Press, 1999, pp. 236–245.

Carlsson, M., and A. Carlsson. Interactions between gluatamatergic and monoaminergic systems within the basal ganglia: Implications for schizophrenia and Parkinson's disease. *Trends in Neurosciences* 13:272–276, 1990.

Charney, D. S., E. J. Nestler, B. S. Bunney, Eds. *The Neurobiology of Mental Illness*. New York: Oxford University Press, 1999.

Chase, T. N., N. S. Wexler, and A. Barbeau, Eds. *Advances in Neurology*, vol. 23, *Huntington's Disease*. New York: Raven Press, 1979.

Coleman, P. D., and D. G. Flood. Neuron numbers and dendritic extent in normal aging and Alzheimer's disease. *Neurobiology of Aging* 8:521–545, 1987.

Crow, T. J., and E. C. Johnstone. Schizophrenia: Nature of the disease process and its biological correlates. In F. Plum, Ed. *Handbook of Physiology*, vol. 5. Bethesda, MD: American Physiological Society, 1987.

Dolan, R. J., C. J. Bench, R. G. Brown, L. C. Scott, and R. S. J. Frackowiak. Neuropsychological dysfunction in depression: The relationship to regional cerebral BF. *Psychological Medicine* 24:849–857.

Drevets, W. C., K. M. Gadde, and R. R. Krishman. Neuroimaging studies of mood disorders. In D. S. Charney, E. J. Nestler, and B. S. Bunney, Eds. *The Neurobiology of Mental Illness*. New York: Oxford University Press, 1999, pp. 394–418.

Fedio, P., C. S. Cox, A. Neophytides, G. Canal Frederick, and T. N. Chase. Neuropsychological profile of Huntington's disease: Patients and those at risk. *Advances in Neurology* 23:239–256, 1979.

Friedhoff, A. J., and T. N. Chase, Eds. *Advances in Neurology*, vol. 35, *Gilles de la Tourette Syndrome*. New York: Raven Press, 1982.

Fuld, P. A. Psychometric differentiation of the dementias: An overview. In B. Reisberg, Ed. *Alzheimer's Disease*. New York: The Free Press, 1983.

Gilles de la Tourette, G. Étude sur un affection, nerveuse characterisee par l'incoordination motrice accompanagnee d'echolalie et de copralalie (jumping, latah, myriachit). *Archives of Neurology* 9:19–42, 158–200, 1885.

Gershon, E. S., and R.O. Reider. Major disorders of mind and brain. *Scientific American* 267(3):126–133.

Grady, C. L., J. B. Haxby, B. Horowitz, G. Berg, and S. I. Rapoport. Neuropsychological and cerebral metabolic function in early vs. late onset dementia of the Alzheimer type. *Neuropsychologia* 25:807–815, 1987.

Grant, I., and K. M. Adams, Eds. *Neuropsychological Assessment of Neuropsychiatric Disorders*. New York: Oxford University Press, 1986.

Gusella, J. F., M. E. MacDonald, C. M. Ambrose, and M. P. Duyao. Molecular genetics of Huntington's disease (Review). *Archives of Neurology* 50:1157–1163, 1993.

Healy, D. Rhythm and blues: Neurochemical, neuropharmacological and neuropsychological implications of a hypothesis of circadian rhythm dysfunction in the affective disorders. *Psychopharmacology* 93:271–285, 1987.

Heaton, R. K., L. E. Badde, and K. L. Johnson. Neuropsychological test results associated with psychiatric disorders in adults. *Psychological Bulletin* 85:141–162, 1978.

Heaton, R. K., and T. J. Crowley. Effects of psychiatric disorders and their somatic treatments on neuropsychological test results. In S. B. Gilskov and G. J. Boll, Eds. *Handbook of Clinical Neuropsychology*. New York: Wiley, 1981.

Huff, F. J., S. Corkin, and J. H. Growdon. Semantic impairment and anomia in Alzheimer's disease. *Brain and Language* 28:235–249, 1986.

Kaufer, D. I., and S. T. De Kosky. Diagnostic classifications: Relationship to the neurobiology of dementia. In D. S. Charney, E. J. Nestler, and B. S. Bunney, Eds. *The Neurobiology of Mental Illness*. New York: Oxford University Press, 1999, pp. 641–649.

Kolb, B., and T. E. Robinson. Plasticity in the prefrontal cortex: Some surprises and relation to behavioral disorders. *Synapse* (in press).

Kovelman, J. A., and A. B. Scheibel. A neurohistologic correlate of schizophrenia. *Biological Psychiatry* 19:1601–1621, 1984.

Kupfer, D. J., and M. E. Thase. The use of the sleep laboratory in the diagnosis of affective disorders. *Psychiatric Clinics of North America* 6:3–25, 1983.

Langston, J. W., P. Ballard, J. W. Tegrud, and I. Irwin. Chronic parkinsonism in humans due to a product of meperidine-analog synthesis. *Science* 219:979–980, 1983.

Larrabee, G. J., and T. H. Crook. Estimated prevalence of age-associated memory impairment derived from standardized tests of memory function. *International Psychogeriatrics* 6:945–1004, 1994.

Lipska, B. K., Z. Z. Khaing, C. S. Weickert, and D. R. Weinberger. BDNF mRNA expression in rat hippocampus and prefrontal cortex: Effects of neonatal ventral hippocampal damage and antipsychotic drugs. *European Journal of Neuroscience* 14:135–144, 2001.

Loring, D. W., and J. W. Largen. Neuropsychological patterns of presenile and senile dementia of the Alzheimer type. *Neuropsychologia* 23:351–357, 1985.

Martin, A., C. Cox, P. Brouwers, and P. Fedio. A note on different patterns of impaired and preserved cognitive abilities and their relation to episodic memory deficits in Alzheimer's patients. *Brain and Language* 25:181–198, 1985.

Martin, J. P. *The Basal Ganglia and Posture*. London: Ritman Medical Publishing, 1967.

Murdoch, B. E., H. J. Chenery, V. Wilks, and R. S. Boyle. Language disorders in dementia of the Alzheimer type. *Brain and Language* 31:122–137, 1987.

Parkinson, J. Essay on the shaking palsy. Reprinted in M. Critchley, Ed. *James Parkinson*. London: Macmillan, 1955.

Pirozzolo, F. J., E. C. Hansch, J. A. Mortimer, D. D. Webster, and M. A. Kuskowski. Dementia in Parkinson's disease: A neuropsychological analysis. *Brain and Cognition* 1:71–83, 1982.

Post, R. M., and S. R. B. Weiss. Neurobiological models of recurrence in mood disorder. In D. S. Charney, E. J. Nestler, and B. S. Bunney, Eds. *The Neurobiology of Mental Illness*. New York: Oxford University Press, 1999, pp. 365–384.

Randolph, C., T. E. Goldberg, and D. Weinberger. The neuropsychology of schizophrenia. In K. M. Heilman and E. Valenstein, Eds. *Clinical Neuropsychology*, 3d ed. New York: Oxford University Press, 1993.

Reisberg, B. Clinical presentation, diagnosis, and symptomatology of age-associated cognitive decline and Alzheimer's disease. In B. Reisberg, Ed. *Alzheimer's Disease*. New York: The Free Press, 1983.

Sacks, O. *Awakenings*. New York: Doubleday, 1973.

Scheibel, A. B. Dendritic changes. In B. Reisberg, Ed. *Alzheimer's Disease*. New York: The Free Press, 1983.

Selkoe, D. J. Aging brain, aging mind. *Scientific American* 267(3):135–142.

Sherrington, R., P. St. George Hyslop, M. Hutton, J. Perez-Tur, and J. Hardy. The molecular biology of Alzheimer's disease. In D. S. Charney, E. J. Nestler, and B. S. Bunney. Eds. *The Neurobiology of Mental Illness*. New York: Oxford University Press, 1999, pp. 650–658.

Spinnler, H., and S. Della Sala. The role of clinical neuropsychology in the neurological diagnosis of Alzheimer's disease. *Journal of Neurology* 235:258–271, 1988.

Sutherland, R. J., B. Kolb, W. M. Schoel, I. Q. Whishaw, and D. Davies. Neuropsychological assessment of children and adults with Tourette's syndrome: A comparison with learning disabilities and schizophrenia. *Advances in Neurology* 35:311–322, 1982.

Valenstein, E. S., Ed. *The Psychosurgery Debate*. San Francisco: W. H. Freeman and Company, 1980.

Valenstein, E. S. *Great and Desperate Cures*. New York: Basic Books, 1986.

Weinberger, D. R., K. F. Berman, R. L. Suddath, and E. F. Torrey. Evidence for dysfunction of a prefrontal-limbic network in schizophrenia: An MRI and regional cerebral blood flow study of discordant monozygotic twins. *American Journal of Psychiatry* 149:890–897, 1992.

Wexler, N. S. Perceptual-motor, cognitive, and emotional characteristics of persons at risk for Huntington's disease. *Advances in Neurology* 23:257–272, 1979.

chapter

28

Neuropsychological Assessment

R. L. was a 32-year-old nurse and mother of four. Driving home from work one afternoon, she stopped at a red light and was rear-ended by another vehicle. R. L.'s head snapped back and struck the head rest and then the side window as she bounced forward. She blacked out for a few minutes, but, when the emergency vehicles arrived, she was conscious, although disoriented and dysphasic, in addition to having severe pain in her back and neck from the whiplash.

R. L. spent about a week in the hospital, where neither CT nor MRI scans identified any cerebral injury, although several vertebrae were damaged. An accomplished musician, she could still play the piano well from memory, but she could no longer read music. In addition, her oral language skills remained impaired and she was completely unable to read.

R. L.'s difficulties did not abate, and she had spells of apraxia. For example, she often found herself unable to figure out how to put on her makeup; she would stare at her lipstick and have no idea how to use it. When R. L. came to us, she was depressed because, although the neurologists could find no reason for her impairments, she continued to have significant difficulties. Our neuropsychological evaluation revealed a woman of above-average intelligence who had a significant loss of verbal fluency and verbal memory, as well as severe dyslexia even a year after the accident. Now nearly 10 years later, she is still unable to read music and reads text only with great difficulty.

R. L.'s case illustrates one of the remaining problems in clinical neurology. People with closed-head injuries often have no sign of cerebral injury visible on neuroimaging but still have significant cognitive deficits, often so severe that they cannot resume their preinjury life styles. For many, the only evidence of neurological disorder comes from neuropsychological tests.

The 1980s were the heyday of neuropsychological assessment. Clinically trained neuropsychologists were in demand and neuropsychological evaluation was regarded as an essential tool in neurological assessment. The role of neuropsychological assessment has changed radically, however, and it has begun to develop a new face that is likely to continue changing for some time. In this chapter, we describe this changing role for neuropsychological assessment, consider the rationale behind assessment, and present summaries of six actual case assessments.

The Changing Face of Neuropsychological Assessment

The roots of neuropsychological assessment lie in neurology and psychiatry. Clinician Kurt Goldstein, for example, was expert in neurology, psychology, and psychiatry. The psychological basis of assessment began to diverge from medicine in the 1940s. The first neuropsychological tests were designed to identify people suffering from cerebral dysfunction attributable to some type of organic disease process (brain pathology), rather than to "functional disorders" linked to behavior.

Although test designers originally believed that it would be possible to construct a single test for brain damage and to establish a cutoff point that separated the brain-damaged from the non-brain-damaged patient, the task proved to be impossible. Gradually, more-sophisticated testing procedures were developed, largely in a few locations in Europe and North America, including Cambridge (Oliver Zangwill), Oxford (Freda Newcombe), Moscow (Alexander Luria), Montreal (Brenda Milner and Laughlin Taylor), Boston (Edith Kaplan and Hans-Leukas Teuber), and Iowa City (Arthur Benton).

By the early 1980s, neuropsychology was no longer confined to a few elite laboratories, and the new field of clinical neuropsychology blossomed in clinics and hospitals. Since that time, three factors have enhanced the rate of change in neuropsychological assessment: functional imaging, cognitive neuroscience, and managed health care. We consider each briefly.

Functional Imaging

Perhaps the biggest change in both neurology and neuropsychology in the past 25 years has been the development of functional imaging. Indeed, we have emphasized the importance of functional imaging in the Snapshots in Chapters 6 through 27. Thus, whereas in earlier eras the effects of cerebral injury or disease often had to be inferred from behavioral symptoms, neuroimaging has allowed investigators to identify changes in cerebral functioning in a wide variety of disorders, including most of the neurological and behavioral disorders discussed in Chapters 26 and 27.

The main role of the clinical neuropsychologist therefore has changed from one of diagnosis to one of participating in rehabilitation, especially in cases of chronic disease such as stroke and head injury. An important point to bear in mind, however, is that even the most sophisticated functional imaging techniques often do not predict the extent of behavioral disturbance observed in people with certain types of brain injury, especially in head trauma, as R. L.'s case illustrates. For people with closed-head injury, the only way to document the nature and extent of their disabilities is by a thorough neuropsychological assessment (see Christensen and Uzzell).

Cognitive Neuroscience

One effect of the growth of clinical neuropsychology is the diversification of methods used by individual neuropsychologists, the choice of tests varying with the disorder being investigated. Indeed, there are now two texts that summarize the various tests available (one by Lezak and the other by Spreen and Strauss).

From the early 1950s through the early 1980s, batteries of tests were developed, each with a different focus (Table 28.1). Many of these test batteries, such as the Halstead-Reitan Battery, retained the concept of cutoff scores, although this assumption presents difficulties because performance below a particular level cannot always be taken as being indicative of brain damage. For one thing, cerebral organization varies with such factors as sex, handedness, age, education, and experience. Furthermore, test problems can be solved by using different strategies and can thus entail different cortical regions. Symptoms of cortical injury can be highly specific (recall the color-blind painter's case described in Chapter 13). Finally, because many tests require problem solving of various kinds, we might expect task performance to vary with intelligence. All these factors make the use of cutoff scores difficult to justify.

A serious handicap in the development of test batteries was the absence of theory in test construction or use. Knowledge of brain function was based largely on clinical observation, and few clinicians other than Alexander Luria had tried to formulate a general theory of how the brain functions to produce cognition.

The emergence of cognitive neuroscience in the 1990s produced a dramatic change in the theoretical understanding of brain and cognition. Case studies once again became popular, each directed by sophisticated cognitive theory and assisted by structural and functional imaging technologies (see Shallice). These more-cognitive approaches also use multivariate statistical methods such as structural equation modeling to attempt to understand the way in which neural networks are disrupted in both individual cases and in groups. Test design has begun to incorporate this knowledge, but the emerging field of cognitive neuroscience will certainly change the way in which neuropsychological assessment is conducted in the future.

Perhaps the area most influenced to date is in understanding the functions of the right frontal lobe (see a review by Stuss and Levine). Historically, the right frontal lobe proved remarkably unresponsive to neuropsychological assessment. The combination of functional imaging and neuropsychological test development has now led to an understanding of the role of the right frontal lobe in previously inaccessible functions such as social cognition (see Chapter 22).

Table 28.1 Overview of neuropsychological test batteries

Test battery	Type	Basic reference
Benton's neuropsychological investigation	Composite	Benton et al., 1983
Boston Process Approach	Composite	Kaplan, 1988
Oxford neuropsychological procedures	Composite	Newcombe, 1969
Montreal Neurological Institute approach	Composite	Taylor, 1979
Frontal lobe assessment	Composite	Stuss and Levine, 2002
Western Ontario procedures	Composite	Kimura and McGlone, 1983
Halstead-Reitan Battery	Standardized	Reitan and Davison, 1974
Luria's neuropsychological investigation	Standardized	Christensen, 1975
Luria-Nebraska	Standardized	Golden, 1981
CanTab	Computerized	Robbins et al., 1998

Managed Care

Perhaps economics is the greatest challenge faced by practicing psychologists in the past decade. In the era of managed health care, clinicians are pressured to reduce the time and money spent on neuropsychological services. In particular, there is sometimes unreasonable pressure to reduce the number of tests given to individual patients, especially in view of the perception that medical imaging can provide faster and more accurate assessments of cerebral dysfunction.

As already noted, imaging has changed the way in which neuropsychological assessment will be used, but, in cases of head trauma, as R. L.'s case demonstrates, neuropsychological assessment is often the only way to document cognitive disturbances. Groth-Marnat suggests that psychologists must develop and promote assessment procedures that

- focus on diagnostic matters that are most clearly linked to treatment choice and outcomes;
- identify conditions that are likely to result in cost savings;
- are time efficient; and
- integrate treatment planning, progress monitoring, and outcome evaluation.

It is clear that clinical assessment will have to change if it is to survive the challenge of managed health care.

Rationale Behind Neuropsychological Assessment

By the 1990s, neuropsychologists had an impressive array of tests from which to choose, as summarized in Table 28.1. At one end of the spectrum are standardized test batteries with fixed criteria for organicity. These tests have in common the advantage of straightforward administration, scoring, and interpretation. There is little need to understand the theoretical bases of the tests or the nuances of cerebral organization to administer the tests, although such understanding is necessary for interpretation. Examples include the Halstead-Reitan Battery and the Luria-Nebraska Battery. More recently, Robbins and his colleagues at Cambridge University devised a computerized version of a standardized battery (CanTab) that has the advantage of being administered in a highly structured manner.

At the other end of the spectrum are individualized test batteries that require particular theoretical knowledge to administer and interpret. These assessments are more qualitative than quantitative. The testing of each patient is tailored to that person's etiology and by the qualitative nature of the performance on each test. An example is Luria's neurological approach, which is not really so much a test battery as a strategy for examining patients. (The Luria-Nebraska Battery was an attempt to make Luria's procedure more structured and quantitative but, in doing so, the Luria-Nebraska Battery became a completely different analysis.)

There is a middle ground, too, represented by composite batteries in which each test is given in a formalized way and may have comparison norms, but the qualitative performance on tests and the pattern of test results are considered. An example is the Boston Process Approach (Table 28.2). Other examples are described by Benton and colleagues, by Lezak, by McKenna and Warrington, by Milberg and colleagues, by Newcombe, by Smith, and by Taylor.

Across this spectrum, each battery is constantly changing in response to test revisions and developments, as well as to the clinical population being evaluated. One constraint on the choice of any test, however, is the training of clinical neuropsychologists. The use of tests that are based on theory requires an understanding of the theory of cerebral organization. It is not possible to take weekend workshops and emerge qualified to administer, evaluate or interpret such tests.

Factors Affecting Test Choice

Throughout this book, we have seen that circumscribed lesions in different cortical regions can produce discrete behavioral changes. Thus, working backward from this knowledge to localize unknown brain damage would seem reasonable. That is, given a particular behavioral change, one should be able to predict the site or sites of the disturbance most likely to be causing the change.

There are problems in working backward in such a manner, however. Research patients are often chosen for specific reasons. For example, whereas patients with rapidly expanding tumors would not be chosen for research, because their results are so difficult to interpret, neurosurgical patients are ideal research subjects, because the extent of their damage is known. Therefore, differences in the etiology of the neurological disorder might be expected to make assessment difficult. Indeed, people with diffuse dysfunction, as in head trauma, would seem likely to perform very differently from people with surgical removals.

Even after the practitioner has chosen tests that are appropriate for the etiology in question, significant questions must be resolved. First, how sensitive are the tests? If a large region of the brain is dysfunctioning, the assessment test need not be particularly sensitive to demonstrate the dysfunction. If the lesion is small, on the other hand, the behavioral effect may be rather specific. As we have seen, for example, a lesion in the right somatosensory representation of the face may produce very subtle sensory changes, and, unless specific tests of nonverbal fluency are used (see Chapter 16), the cognitive changes may go unnoticed, even with dozens of tests.

A related problem is that various factors may interact with brain pathology to make interpretation of test results difficult. Tests are seldom developed for subjects older than 60 or from ethnic or cultural backgrounds that differ from those subjects on whom the tests were developed. Therefore, as noted earlier, test scores cannot be interpreted with strict cutoff criteria.

Furthermore, intelligence alters an investigator's expectations of performance on tests: someone with an IQ score of 130 may be relatively impaired on a test of verbal memory but may appear normal compared with someone with a score of 90. Thus, unlike standard, quantitative psychometric assessment,

Table 28.2 Representative sample of the tests used in the Boston Process Approach to neuropsychological assessment

Intellectual and Conceptual Functions
Wechsler Adult Intelligence Scale III
Raven's Standard Progressive Matrices
Shipley Institute of Living Scale
Wisconsin Card-Sorting Test
Proverbs test

Memory Functions
Wechsler Memory Scale III
Rey Auditory Verbal Learning Test
Rey Complex-Figure Test
Benton Visual-Recognition Test
Consonant trigrams test
Cowboy Story-Reading Memory Test

Language Functions
Narrative writing sample
Tests of verbal fluency
Visual-perceptual functions
Cow-and-circle experimental test
Automobile puzzle
Parietal lobe battery
Hooper Visual Organization Test

Academic Skills
Wide Range Achievement Test

Self-Control and Motor Functions
Proteus Maze Test
Stroop Color-Word Interference Test
Luria Three-Step Motor Program
Finger tapping

neuropsychological assessment must be flexible. This flexibility makes interpretation difficult and requires extensive training in fundamental neuropsychology and neurology as well as in neuropsychological assessment.

Finally, we have seen in several earlier discussions that significant differences in test performance are related to factors such as sex and handedness. In addition, test performance is often biased by demographics. For example, in one three-city study of the effects of head trauma, investigators found that normal subjects in one city performed as poorly as brain-damaged subjects in another. Significant demographic differences influenced the test performance and thus had to be considered in the interpretation of the results.

Goals of Neuropsychological Assessment

The goal of assessment in general clinical psychology is the diagnosis of the disorder for the purpose of changing behavior. For example, intelligence and achievement tests may be given to schoolchildren to try to identify particular problem areas (poor short-term memory, for example, or slow reading) as an aid in teaching. Similarly, personality tests are used with an eye toward defining and curing a behavioral disorder, such as an anxiety disorder. The goals of clinical neuropsychology are different in some respects:

- Assessment aims to diagnose the presence of cortical damage or dysfunction and to localize it where possible. In doing so, there is an attempt to provide an accurate and unbiased estimate of a person's cognitive capacity.

- Assessment is used to facilitate patient care and rehabilitation. Serial assessments can provide information about the rate of recovery and the potential for resuming a previous lifestyle.

- Neuropsychological assessment can identify the presence of mild disturbances in cases in which other diagnostic studies have produced equivocal results. Examples are the effects of head trauma or the early symptoms of a degenerative disease.

- A related goal is to identify unusual brain organization that may exist in lefthanders or in people who have suffered childhood brain injury. This information is particularly valuable to surgeons, who would not want, for example, to inadvertently remove primary speech zones while performing surgery. Such information is likely to be obtained only from behavioral measures.

- In disorders such as focal epilepsy, the primary evidence corroborating an abnormal EEG may emerge from behavioral assessment, because radiological procedures often fail to specifically identify the abnormal brain tissue giving rise to the seizures.

- Because some recovery of function may be expected after brain injury, this recovery must be documented not only with rehabilitation in mind but also to determine the effectiveness of any medical treatment, particularly for neoplasms (tumors) or vascular abnormalities.

- Assessment assists a patient and the patient's family in understanding the patient's possible residual deficits so that realistic life goals and rehabilitation programs can be planned.

Intelligence Testing in Neuropsychological Assessment

Most neuropsychological assessments begin with a measure of general intelligence, most often one of the Wechsler scales, the most recent version being the Wechsler Adult Intelligence Scale–Third Edition (WAIS-III). The Wechsler scales have proved invaluable in determining a base level of cognitive functioning. These scales provide the distinct advantage of producing separate scores for verbal and performance subtests, as well as an overall IQ score.

The WAIS-III has seven subtests for evaluating verbal and performance scales. The verbal score is a measure of acquired knowledge, verbal reasoning, and comprehension of verbal information. The performance score provides an indication of a person's nonverbal reasoning, spatial processing skills, attentiveness to detail, and visuomotor integration.

Although the verbal and performance subtests were not designed to measure left- and right-hemisphere functions, respectively, the subtests have proved useful as a rough measure of left- and right-hemisphere function, respectively. The IQ scores obtained on both the verbal and the performance sections have a mean of 100 and a standard deviation of 15. A difference of more than 10 points between the verbal and the performance scores is usually taken as a clinically significant difference, although statistically this interpretation is liberal.

The results of a number of studies have demonstrated that well-defined left-hemisphere lesions produce a relatively low verbal IQ score compared with performance score, whereas well-defined right-hemisphere lesions produce a relatively low performance score. Diffuse damage, on the other hand, tends to produce a low performance score, leading to the erroneous belief that the verbal–performance IQ difference is not diagnostically useful. Although a reduced performance score is not definitive, it is rare to obtain a relatively low verbal IQ, and its appearance should not be ignored.

An evaluation of the WAIS subscales and IQ values was performed by Warrington and her colleagues, who did a retrospective study of 656 unselected patients with unilateral brain damage. Overall, their results showed that lesions of the left hemisphere depressed verbal IQs, whereas lesions of the right hemisphere depressed performance IQs, the exception in both cases being that of occipital lesions. However, the verbal–performance discrepancy score was less than 10 points in 53% of left-hemisphere cases and in 43% of right-hemisphere cases. A small number of cases had discrepancy scores greater than 10 points in the opposite direction: 6% with left-hemisphere lesions and 3% with right-hemisphere lesions. (It is curious that the patients with left parietal or temporoparietal lesions did not show a large drop in IQ, considering that one would expect them to be dysphasic. Because language skills were not mentioned in the Warrington study, her analysis could have excluded aphasic subjects. In our experience, dysphasic patients have very depressed verbal IQs, as would be expected.)

Warrington also analyzed a subset of WAIS subtests, including four verbal instruments (arithmetic, similarities, digit span, and vocabulary) and three nonverbal (picture completion, block design, and picture arrangement). Overall, left-hemisphere frontal, temporal, and parietal patients performed significantly more poorly on the four verbal tests. There were no differences between these left-hemisphere groups on the tests, however. The performance tests were less predictive of lesion side, because only the right parietal patients were significantly poorer on block design and picture arrangement.

One difficulty with postinjury intelligence testing is that a premorbid estimate of intellectual level must exist. A relatively low IQ score cannot be ascribed to a brain injury unless there is some idea of what the IQ was before the injury. This estimate is usually informal and based on a patient's education, occupation, and socioeconomic background. Wilson and colleagues describe a statistical procedure for estimating premorbid IQ scores.

Case Histories

Having surveyed the basic principles of neuropsychological theory and assessment, we now apply the tests and theory to a sample of clinical problems. In this section, we consider the test results and case histories of six patients. These case histories illustrate the use of neuropsychological tests in neuropsychological assessment.

Because of our affiliation with the Montreal Neurological Institute, our composite assessment battery is based on the tests derived from the study of neurosurgical patients by Brenda Milner, Laughlin Taylor, and their colleagues. Most of the tests have been discussed elsewhere in the text, especially in Chapters 14 through 16 in relation to neuropsychological assessment of parietal, temporal and frontal lobe function. Cases 1 and 2 are borrowed from Laughlin Taylor.

Case 1

This 33-year-old man had a history of seizures beginning 4 years before his admission to the hospital. His neurological examination on admission was negative, but he was having increasingly frequent seizures, characterized by his head and eyes turning to the right, a pattern that suggests supplementary motor cortex involvement.

Figure 28.1 Psychological test results before and after surgery in two cases.

The results of radiological and EEG studies suggested a left-frontal-lobe lesion (Figure 28.1), which was confirmed at surgery when a poorly differenti-

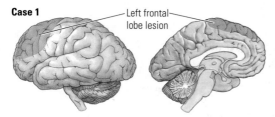

Case 1

Left frontal lobe lesion

	Preop	Postop
Full-scale IQ	115	102
Verbal IQ	111	103
Performance IQ	117	99
Memory quotient	118	108
Verbal recall	20	14
Nonverbal recall	10.5	10
Card sorting	1 cat.[a]	1 cat.[a]
Finger-position sense	Left Right	Left Right
	60/60 60/60	60/60 60/60
Drawings: Copy	36/36	35/36
Recall	21/36	24/36

[a] Significantly low score.

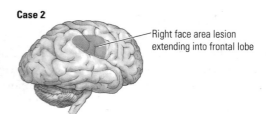

Case 2

Right face area lesion extending into frontal lobe

	Preop	Postop
Full-scale IQ	97	97
Verbal IQ	100	106
Performance IQ	94	88[a]
Memory quotient	94	92
Verbal recall	13.5	14.0
Nonverbal recall	3.5[a]	7.0
Card sorting	0 cat.[a]	1 cat.[a]
Finger-position sense	Left Right	Left Right
	55/60[a] 59/60	54/60[a] 60/60
Drawings: Copy	28/36[a]	26.5/36[a]
Recall	4/36[a]	9.5/36[a]

[a] Significantly low score.

ated astrocytoma was removed. The only difficulty that the patient experienced before surgery was in doing the Wisconsin Card-Sorting Test, where he made numerous perseverative errors and sorted only one category correctly. Two weeks after surgery, all the intelligence ratings, memory quotients, and delayed verbal-recall scores decreased, but these scores remained in essentially the same ratio to one another. Other tests were unchanged, the only significantly low score again being on the sorting test.

If this patient were like other patients with similar lesions, on follow-up a year after surgery, his intelligence ratings and memory scores would likely have returned to the preoperative level, although his card sorting would be unlikely to show any improvement.

Case 2

This 26-year-old man had an 8-year history of seizures dating to an episode of meningitis in which he was thought to have an intracerebral abscess. Subsequently, he developed seizures beginning in the left side of his face and left hand, and he was referred as a candidate for surgery because his seizures were uncontrolled by medication.

Before surgery, the patient scored within normal limits on tests of intelligence and general memory, although he did have difficulty with delayed recall of verbal material. He had slight defects of finger-position sense on the left hand, which together with some weakness in the left arm and leg pointed to damage in the right central area of the cortex. In addition, he had difficulty copying and recalling the Rey Complex Figure and was unable to perform the Wisconsin Card-Sorting Test, which suggested that his lesion might extend into the frontal and temporal areas as well.

The right facial area and a region extending into the right frontal lobe were removed at surgery (see Figure 28.1). After this removal, some residual epileptiform abnormality in both the frontal lobe and the superior temporal gyrus remained. Postoperative testing showed improvement in both verbal IQ and long-term verbal memory, but the patient had persistent difficulties on the card-sorting test, with finger-position sense on the left hand, and on the copy and recall of the Rey Complex Figure. His performance IQ score also declined.

The difficulty with finger position would be expected in such a case, but the continuing difficulties with card sorting and the Rey Complex Figure imply that areas in his right hemisphere are still dysfunctioning. This dysfunction is seen in residual abnormalities in the EEG recordings from the frontal and temporal regions.

Case 3

This right-handed woman, age 28, underwent emergency surgery subsequent to the bursting of an aneurysm in the right temporal lobe. Surgical reports indicated that parts of the right temporal and parietal cortex were damaged, and she had a left quadrantic hemianopia, indicating that the lesion extended posteriorly into the visual cortex. She was referred to us 2 years after the incident, at which time she was in good health and attending a university, but she was having social problems as well as difficulty with mathematics.

The results of her neuropsychological assessment are summarized in Table 28.3, where she can be seen to have several deficits consistent with right

Table **28.3** Examples of neuropsychological assessments of neurological patients

Test	Normal control	Case 3: Right temporal aneurysm	Case 4: Left temporal epilepsy	Case 5: Left-hemisphere stroke	Case 6: Traffic accident
Speech Lateralization, Dichotic					
Words					
Left ear	25	18	2*	F	16
Right ear	46	50	15	F	25
Handedness	R	R	R	R	R
General Intelligence					
Full-scale IQ	107	113	104	F	115
Verbal IQ	109	117	95*	F	127
Performance IQ	105	107*	111	108	96*
Visual Perceptual					
Mooney faces (abbreviated)	18/19	12/19*	16/19	16/19	17/19
Rey Complex Figure—copy	32/36	24/36*	31/36	30/36	34/36
Memory					
Wechsler Memory quotient	107	115	87*	F	100*
Rey Complex Figure—recall	22/36	11/36*	18/36*	17/36*	13/36*
Delayed recall of stories and					
paired associates	13	17	7*	—	23
Delayed recall of drawings	12	6*	10	9	2*
Spatial					
Right–left differentiation	52/60	48/60	43/60	51/60	35/60*
Semmes Body Placing	32/35	30/35	30/35	—	35/35
Language					
Reading	12	12	7*	F	20
Object naming	23/36	20/26	14/26*	F	—
Frontal Lobe					
Wisconsin Card Sorting	6.0 cat.	5.8 cat.	4.0 cat.	3.0 cat.	2.4 cat.*
Chicago Word Fluency	62	50	38	F	52
Motor Function					
Complex arm	92%	94%	89%	72%*	82%*
Face	88%	90%	89%	20%*	30%*

Abbreviations: F, could not be assessed because of dysphasia; R, right-handed; cat., categories.
*Abnormally poor score.

posterior damage. Her performance IQ score was 10 points lower than her verbal score, she had difficulty with the Mooney Closure Test, and her recall of visual material was well below the level expected for a woman of her age and intelligence. In contrast, she performed within expected limits on tests of left-hemisphere and frontal lobe function.

Case 4

A 22-year-old woman was referred to us by a clinical psychologist to assess the possibility of organic dysfunction. On several occasions, she had engaged in bizarre behaviors such as undressing in public and urinating on other people;

on one occasion, she attacked her roommate. After these episodes, she was confused and amnesic about her behavior, as well as about the periods just preceding the outbursts.

Her neuropsychological test results indicated that her left temporal lobe was abnormal, because her verbal memory, reading, and object naming were impaired, and she had a very low recall of dichotic words (see Table 28.3). Our diagnosis of temporal lobe epilepsy with a left-side focus was partly confirmed by a neurologist when EEG results showed left-hemisphere abnormality. As is often the case with epilepsy, a CT scan failed to reveal any unusual features, and nothing in the woman's history accounts for the epilepsy. The seizures are completely controlled with Dilantin, but her neuropsychological deficits remain.

Case 5

This 60-year-old woman suffered a stroke that, according to her CT scan, appeared to be localized in the cortical facial area and in Broca's area on the left. She was referred to us a year after the stroke because of her poor progress in regaining her speech through speech therapy. In view of her marked dysphasia, we first administered a token test.

Although this woman appeared to understand much of what was said to her, she was severely dysphasic and therefore obtained a very poor score on the token test. In view of this result, we gave her only a modified battery, designed to answer the referral question of what could be expected if she were to continue speech therapy.

Her test results, which are summarized in Table 28.3, showed that she was of average intelligence when measured with a nonverbal test, and she performed normally on all nonverbal tests of memory and perception that we administered. In contrast, she had a great deal of difficulty in copying movements, even though she had no hemiparesis. Indeed, she was totally unable to copy sequences of facial movements, although she could manage individual facial movements with some difficulty.

These results led us to conclude that this woman was aphasic and had a facial apraxia. We were pessimistic about her chances for further recovery of speech functions.

Case 6

This 37-year-old man had been in a traffic accident some 15 years earlier. He was in a coma for 6 weeks and suffered secondary injury from brain infection. At the time of his accident, he was a student in a graduate program in journalism, having previously obtained a bachelor's degree with honors in English literature.

When we first met him, he had severe motor problems, used canes to walk, and was both apraxic and ataxic. He had great difficulty in pronouncing words, especially when hurried or stressed, but careful language testing on the token test revealed no aphasic symptoms; his language problems were entirely due to a difficulty in coordinating the muscles of the mouth (that is, anarthria).

Since the time of his accident, this man lived at home with his parents and had not learned the social skills necessary to cope with his handicap. In short, he was being treated as though he were retarded and was being completely looked after by his family. Indeed, the patient himself believed he was retarded and was very reluctant to attempt rehabilitation.

At the urging of his family, we gave him a thorough assessment to evaluate his potential. His results were surprising, even to us. As summarized in Table 28.3, his intellect was superior (WAIS verbal IQ score of 127) and, although he had deficits on some tests, especially those requiring motor skills, his performance on most tests was average or above average. Despite his obvious motor handicaps, this man was clearly not retarded.

One significant cognitive loss, however, was his nonverbal memory, which was very poor. Armed with our test results, we were able to show him—and his family—that he could look after himself and should seek occupational therapy.

Summary

Neurology and clinical neuropsychology have changed radically in the past 25 years. Significant developments in functional and structural imaging have had a significant effect on the field of clinical neuropsychology. Whereas neuropsychological assessment had promised a way to localize focal cerebral injury, it has now been largely replaced in this function by medical imaging techniques. Not all neurological disease can be detected by imaging. The most sensitive measure of cerebral integrity is behavior, and behavioral analysis consistently finds dysfunction that is not seen in MRI, especially in cases of closed-head injury and epilepsy.

The tests used in neuropsychological assessment have changed in recent decades, owing in part to the dramatic development of cognitive neuroscience. And the use of test results has changed. Rather than being largely diagnostic, test results are becoming an integral part of rehabilitation. This changing role has economic implications as managed health care challenges the use of extensive neuropsychological evaluations, especially when adequate imaging data are available, regardless of its effectiveness. A wide range of clinical neuropsychological assessment tools are now available, the choice varying with the particular clinical question being asked. Analysis of the test results must consider a range of variables including age, sex, cultural background, and IQ score.

Case histories demonstrate that, despite technological advances, neuropsychological assessment is still an important tool for demonstrating functional localization after discrete functional injury and for assisting in planning for rehabilitation.

References

Benton, A. L. Neuropsychological assessment. *Annual Review of Psychology* 45:1–23, 1994.

Benton, A. L., D. de S. Hamsher, N. R. Varney, and O. Spreen. *Contributions to Neuropsychological Assessment: A Clinical Manual.* New York: Oxford University Press, 1983.

Christensen, A.-L. *Luria's Neuropsychological Investigation.* New York: Spectrum, 1975.

Christensen, A.-L., and B. P. Uzzell. *International Handbook of Neuropsychological Rehabilitation.* New York: Plenum, 2000.

Damasio, H., and A. R. Damasio. *Lesion Analysis in Neuropsychology.* New York: Oxford University Press, 1989.

Golden, C. J. A standardized version of Luria's neuropsychological tests. In S. Filskov and T. J. Boll, Eds.

Handbook of Clinical Neuropsychology. New York: Wiley Interscience, 1981.

Groth-Marnat, G. Financial efficacy of clinical assessment: Rationale guidelines and issues for future research. *Journal of Clinical Psychology* 55:813–824, 1999.

Kaplan, E. A process approach to neuropsychological assessment. In T. Boll and B. K. Bryant, Eds. *Clinical Neuropsychology and Brain Function: Research, Development, and Practice.* Washington, DC: American Psychological Association, 1988, pp. 129–167.

Kimura, D., and J. McGlone. *Neuropsychology Test Procedures.* Manual used at the University Hospital, London, Ontario, Canada, 1983.

Levin, H. S., and A. L. Benton. Neuropsychologic assessment. In A. B. Baker and R. J. Joynt, Eds. *Clinical Neurology,* vol. 1. New York: Harper & Row, 1986.

Lezak, M. D. *Neuropsychological Assessment,* 3d ed. New York: Oxford University Press, 1995.

McFie, J. *Assessment of Organic Intellectual Impairment.* New York: Wiley, 1975.

McKenna, P., and E. K. Warrington. The analytical approach to neuropsychological assessment. In I. Grant and K. M. Adams, Eds. *Assessment of Neuropsychiatric Disorders.* New York: Oxford University Press, 1986.

Milberg, W. P., N. Hebben, and E. Kaplan. The Boston Process Approach to neuropsychological assessment. In I. Grant and K. M. Adams, Eds. *Assessment of Neuropsychiatric Disorders.* New York: Oxford University Press, 1986.

Newcombe, F. *Missile Wounds of the Brain.* London: Oxford University Press, 1969.

Owen, A. M., A. C. Roberts, C. E. Polkey, B. J. Sahakian, and T. W. Robbins. Extradimensional versus intradimensional set shifting performance following frontal lobe excisions, temporal lobe excisions or amygdalo-hippocampectomy in man. *Neuropsychologia* 29:993–1006, 1991.

Reitan, R. M., and L. A. Davison. *Clinical Neuropsychology: Current Status and Application.* New York: Wiley, 1974.

Robbins, T. W., M. James, A. M. Owen, B. J. Sahakian, A. D. Lawrence, L. McInnes, and P. M. Rabbitt. A study of performance on tests from the CANTAB battery sensitive to frontal lobe dysfunction in a large sample of normal volunteers: Implications for theories of executive functioning and cognitive aging. Cambridge Neuropsychological Test Automated Battery. *Journal of the International Neuropsychology Society* 4:474–490, 1998.

Shallice, T. From neuropsychology to mental structure. Cambridge, UK: Cambridge University Press, 1988.

Smith, A. Principles underlying human brain functions in neuropsychological sequelae of different neuropathological processes. In S. B. Filskov and T. J. Boll, Eds. *Handbook of Clinical Neuropsychology.* New York: Wiley-Interscience, 1981.

Spreen, O., and E. Strauss. *A Compendium of Neuropsychological Tests.* New York: Oxford University Press, 1991.

Stuss, D. T., and B. Levine. Adult clinical neuropsychology: Lessons from studies of the frontal lobes. *Annual Review of Psychology* 53:401–433, 2002.

Taylor, L. B. Psychological assessment of neurosurgical patients. In T. Rasmussen and R. Marino, Eds. *Functional Neurosurgery.* New York: Raven Press, 1979.

Walsh, K. W. *Understanding Brain Damage,* 2d ed. London: Churchill Livingstone, 1991.

Warrington, E. K., M. James, and C. Maciejewski. The WAIS as a lateralizing and localizing diagnostic instrument: A study of 656 patients with unilateral cerebral excisions. *Neuropsychologia* 24:223–239, 1986.

Wilson, R. S., G. Rosenbaum, and G. Brown. The problem of premorbid intelligence in neuropsychological assessment. *Journal of Clinical Neuropsychology* 1:49–56, 1979.

Wood, J. M., H. N. Garb, S. O. Lilienfeld, and M. T. Nezworski. Clinical assessment. *Annual Review of Psychology* 53:519–543, 2002.

Glossary

ablation. Intentional destruction or removal of parts of the brain or spinal cord; brain lesion.

abdominal reflex. Contraction of the abdominal muscles in response to stroking the abdomen.

absence attack. Temporary loss of consciousness in some forms of epilepsy.

absolutely refractory. Refers to the period in an action potential during which a new action potential cannot be elicited, because of the closing of gate 2 of voltage-sensitive sodium channels.

acalculia. Inability to perform mathematical operations.

accessory cells. Cells that originate from germinal cells (spongioblasts) and contribute to the support, nourishment, conduction, and repair of neurons; occasionally the origins of tumors. Accessory cells are the astrocytes; the oligodendrocytes; and the ependymal, microglial, and Schwann cells.

achromatopsia. Inability to distinguish different hues despite the presence of normally pigmented cells in the retina. Sometimes called *cortical color blindness.*

acopia. Inability to copy a geometric design.

acquired dyslexia. Inability to read caused by brain damage in a person who could read formerly; distinguished from *developmental dyslexia*, which is a failure to learn to read.

action potential. Brief electrical impulse by which information is conducted along an axon; results from brief changes in the membrane's permeability to potassium and sodium ions.

active-transport system. Pump specialized for the transport of a particular substance across a membrane.

addiction. Physiological or psychological dependence on an agent (for example, alcohol, drug), with a tendency to increase its use.

adenosine triphosphate (ATP). Molecule important to cellular energy metabolism. The conversion of ATP into ADP (adenosine diphosphate) liberates energy. ATP can also be converted into cyclic AMP (adenosine monophosphate), which serves as an intermediate messenger in the production of postsynaptic potentials by some neurotransmitters and in the mediation of the effects of polypeptide hormones.

affect. Freudian term for the feeling of pleasantness or unpleasantness evoked by a stimulus; also the emotional complex associated with a mental state; the feeling experienced in connection with an emotion.

afference theory. States that all behavior is driven by sensory events. Compare **efference theory.**

afferent. Conducting toward the central nervous system or toward its higher centers.

afferent paresis. Loss of kinesthetic feedback that results from lesions to the postcentral gyrus (areas 1, 2, 3) and produces clumsy movements.

afterdischarge. Abnormal discharges from neurons subsequent to an epileptic seizure or brain stimulation.

agenesis of the corpus callosum. Condition in which the corpus callosum fails to develop.

agnosia. Partial or complete inability to recognize sensory stimuli, unexplainable by a defect in elementary sensation or by a reduced level of alertness.

agonist. A muscle that, in contracting to move a part, is opposed by another muscle (its antagonist).

agraphia. Decline in the ability to write or its loss.

akathesia. Condition of motor restlessness, ranging from a feeling of inner disquiet to an inability to sit or lie quietly.

akinesia. Absence or poverty of movement.

akinetic seizures. Seizures producing temporary paralysis of muscles, characterized by a sudden collapse without warning; most common in children.

alcohol. Any organic compound containing a hydroxyl group.

alcohol myopia. Behavior displayed after the consumption of alcohol in which local and immediate cues become prominent.

alexia. Inability to read.

allesthesia. Sensation of touch experienced at a point remote from the place touched.

allocentric space. Space made up of the relations of objects, independent of the perspective of the observer.

alpha rhythm. Regular (approximately 10 Hz) wave pattern in an electroencephalogram; found in most people when they are relaxed with eyes closed.

Alzheimer's disease. Degenerative brain disorder that first appears as a progressive memory loss and later develops into a generalized dementia. The origin of the disease is unknown, but cholinergic cells in the basal forebrain and cells in the entorhinal cortex appear to degenerate first.

amativeness. Inclination to love; localized by the phrenologists in the nape of the neck.

amblyopia. Dimness of vision without obvious impairment of the eye itself.

amebiasis. Infection due to amebas, especially *Entamoeba histolytica*, the causative agent of amebic dysentery.

amines. Class of compounds, including neurotransmitters. An amine has a component that is formed from ammonia by the replacement of one or more hydrogen atoms and that thus has an NH group attached.

amino acids. Class of biologically active compounds containing an NH_2 chemical group.

Ammon's horn. Part of the hippocampus.

amnesia. Partial or total loss of memory.

amnesic aphasia. Aphasic syndrome characterized by the inability to name objects and the production of unintended syllables, words, or phrases while speaking.

amphetamine. Synthetic powerful central nervous system stimulant; abuse may lead to dependence.

amusia. Inability to produce (motor) or to comprehend (sensory) musical sounds.

amygdala. Set of nuclei in the base of the temporal lobe; part of the limbic system.

anarthria. Incoordination of the musculature of the mouth, resulting in speechlessness.

anastomosis. Connection between parallel blood vessels that allows them to communicate their blood flows.

aneurysm. Vascular dilation resulting from a localized defect in vascular elasticity. A sac is formed by the dilation of the walls of an artery or a vein and is filled with blood.

angiography. Radiographic imaging of blood vessels filled with a contrast medium.

angioma. Collections of abnormal blood vessels, including capillary, venous, and arteriovenous malformations, resulting in abnormal blood flow.

angular gyrus. Gyrus in the parietal lobe corresponding roughly to Brodmann's area 39; important in language functions.

anion. Negatively charged ion.

anomia. Difficulty in finding words, especially those naming objects.

anomic aphasia. Inability to name objects.

anopia. Loss of vision.

anosmia. Absence of the sense of smell.

anosodiaphoria. Indifference to illness.

anosognosia. Loss of ability to recognize or to acknowledge an illness or bodily defect; usually associated with right parietal lesions.

antagonist. A muscle that counteracts the action of another muscle, its agonist; also a drug that blocks or reduces the effect of a neurotransmitter.

anterior cerebral artery. Originates from the carotid artery and services the orbital frontal and dorsolateral frontal regions, the anterior cingulate cortex, the corpus callosum, and the striatum.

anterior commissure. Fiber tract that connects the temporal lobes.

anterograde amnesia. Inability to remember events subsequent to a disturbance of the brain such as head injury, electroconvulsive shock, or certain degenerative diseases.

anterograde degeneration. Degeneration of the parts of a nerve cell that lie distal to damage to the cell, with the cell body used as reference; for example, when an axon is cut, anterograde degeneration occurs in the section from the cut to the synaptic terminals. Also called *Wallerian degeneration*.

anterograde disorientation. Impairment in spatial orientation that persists after a brain injury.

anterograde transport. Transport by a neuron, usually along axons, of substances in a direction that is away from the cell body.

antianxiety agent. Drug that reduces anxiety; benzodiazepines and sedative-hypnotic agents are of this type.

anvil. The middle of the three ossicles of the ear. In turn with the stapes and malleus, the anvil conducts vibrations from the tymponic membrane to the inner ear. Also called the *incus*.

aphagia. Inability to eat or chew.

aphasia. Defect or loss of power of expression by speech, writing, or signs or of comprehending spoken or written language due to injury or disease of the brain.

apoptosis. Cell death that is genetically programmed.

apperceptive agnosia. Broad category of visual agnosia in which elementary sensory functions appear to be relatively intact but a perceptual deficit that prevents recognition of an object is present.

apraxia. Inability to make voluntary movements in the absence of paralysis or other motor or sensory impairment; especially an inability to make proper use of an object.

aprosodia. Condition in which there is a loss of production or comprehension of the meaning of different tones of voice.

arachnoid. Thin sheet of delicate collagenous connective tissue that follows the contours of the brain.

archicortex. Part of the cerebral cortex that develops in association with the olfactory cortex and is phylogenetically older than the neopallium and lacks its layered structure. Also called *archipallium*, *allocortex*, or *olfactory cortex*. Corresponds to the dentate gyrus and hippocampal gyrus in mature mammals.

area postrema. Nucleus in the brainstem that is sensitive to blood-borne toxins and causes vomiting.

arcuate fasciculus. Long bundle of fibers connecting Wernicke's and Broca's areas.

Argyll-Robertson pupil. Constriction of the pupil of the eye to accommodation but not to light; used to diagnose damage to the midbrain relays of the third cranial (oculomotor) nerve.

arteriovenous (A-V) malformation. Abnormality of both the arterial and the venous blood flow, which often appears as a mass of vessels that are intertwined and lie on the surface of the cortex.

ascending activating systems. Group of neurons, each of which contains a common neurotransmitter, that have their cell bodies located in a nucleus in the basal forebrain or brainstem and their axons distributed to a wide region of the brain.

asomatognosia. Loss of knowledge or sensory awareness of one's own body and bodily condition; may be on one or both sides of the body; most commonly results from damage to the right parietal lobe.

Asperger's syndrome. Disorder in which a person has relatively good verbal communication but has unusual difficulty with social communication. Sometimes called *high-functioning autism.*

aspiny neurons. Class of inhibitory neurons that do not have dendritic spines.

association cell layers. Layers II and III of the cerebral cortex.

association cortex. All cortex that is not specialized motor or sensory cortex (the term survives from an earlier belief that inputs from the different senses meet and become associated). *See also* **prefrontal cortex** and **tertiary area.**

associative agnosia. Form of agnosia in which there is an object-identification deficit in the context of a preserved ability to copy or match stimuli presented in the affected modality.

associative learning. Form of learning in which two or more unrelated stimuli become associated with one another so that any one of them can elicit the same behavioral response.

astereognosis. Inability, with no defect in elementary tactile sensation, to recognize familiar objects by touch.

astrocyte. Type of glial cell. *See also* **accessory cells.**

astrocytoma. Slow-growing brain tumor resulting from the growth of astrocytes.

asymbolia. Inability to employ a conventional sign to stand for another object or event.

asymbolia for pain. Inability to understand the meaning of pain.

ataxia. Failure of muscular coordination; any of various irregularities of muscular action.

athetosis. Motor disorder marked by involuntary movements or slow writhing movements, especially in the hands.

attention. Hypothetical process that either allows a selective awareness of a part or aspect of the sensory environment or allows selective responsiveness to one class of stimuli.

attentional dyslexia. Disorder in which naming a letter is more difficult when it is accompanied by a second letter.

auditory agnosia. Impaired capacity to identify nonverbal acoustical stimuli.

auditory flow. Change in sound heard as a person moves past a sound source or as a sound source moves past a person.

aura. Subjective sensation, perceptual experience, or motor phenomenon that precedes and marks the onset of an epileptic seizure or migraine.

autism. Condition in which a person is dominated by self-centered thoughts or behaviors that are not subject to change by external stimulation. In children, the condition is often called *infantile autism* and is characterized by a failure to relate normally to people or external stimulation. Such children generally have severe language disorders and exhibit repetitive behaviors such as rocking.

autoimmune disease. Immune reaction directed against one's own body.

automatic behaviors. Stereotyped units of behavior linked in a fixed sequence—for example, grooming and chewing. Also called *reflexive, consummatory,* or *respondent behaviors. See also* **automatism.**

automatic movements. Spontaneous or involuntary movements.

automatism. Performance of nonreflex acts without conscious volition. Also called *automatic behavior.*

autonoetic awareness. Awareness of one's self, or self-knowledge.

autonomic nervous system. The part of the nervous system that controls the functions of all the parts of the body, with the exception of the skeletal muscles, so that the body and its organs are prepared for rest or for vigorous activity.

autopagnosia. Inability to localize and name the parts of one's own body—for example, finger agnosia.

autoradiography. Process by which radiolabeled substances are injected into the bloodstream, incorporated into cells, and transported along the cells' processes. When the tissue is exposed to a photographic film, it "takes its own picture" and reveals the route taken by the radiolabeled substance.

autoreceptor. Receptor in the membrane of a neuron that responds to the transmitter released by that neuron.

axoaxonic synapse. Synapse between two axons.

axodendritic synapse. Synapse between an axon and a dendrite.

axoextracellular synapse. Synapse that releases its neurotransmitter chemical into the extracellular space.

axomuscular synapse. Synapse between an axon and a muscle.

axon. Thin neuronal process that transmits action potentials away from the cell body to other neurons (or to muscles or glands).

axon collateral. Branch of an axon.

axon hillock. Site of origin of a nerve impulse.

axosecretory synapse. Synapse between an axon and a blood vessel in which the transmitter substance is passed into the bloodstream as a hormone.

axosomatic synapse. Synapse between an axon and the cell body of a neuron.

axosynaptic synapse. Synapse between an axon and another synapse.

Babinski sign (extensor plantar response). Abnormal response to stimulation on the sole of the foot in which there is an upward, extensor movement of the big toe; indicative of a corticospinal-tract lesion.

bacterium. Any prokaryotic organism.

Balint's syndrome. Agnosic syndrome that results from large bilateral parietal lesions and is composed of three deficits: (1) paralysis of eye fixation with inability to look voluntarily into the peripheral visual field, (2) optic ataxia, and (3) disturbance of visual attention such that the peripheral field is neglected.

balloonist theories. State that muscles move as they are filled with a substance such as a fluid or air.

barbiturates. Drugs used for their hypnotic and sedative effects.

basal ganglia. Group of large nuclei in the forebrain, including the caudate nucleus, putamen, globus pallidus, claustrum, and amygdala.

basilar membrane. In the cochlea, the receptor surface that transduces sound waves into neural activity.

behavioral compensation. Mechanism of recovery from brain injury in which behavior is modified to compensate for lost functions. Neither the recovered behavior nor the area that mediates recovery are the same as those that are lost.

Bell-Magendie law. Law, named after its cofounders, stating that the dorsal roots of the spinal cord are sensory and the ventral roots of the spinal cord are motor.

benzodiazepines. Any of a group of minor tranquilizers, having a common molecular structure and similar pharmacological activities, such as antianxiety, muscle relaxing, and sedative and hypnotic effects.

β-endorphin. Endogenous peptide that has actions similar to those of ingested opium.

beta rhythm. Irregular electroencephalographic activity of 13 to 30 Hz, generally associated with an alert state.

bilateral. Applying to both sides of the body.

binding problem. Theoretical problem with the integration of sensory information. Because a single sensory event is analyzed by multiple parallel channels that do not converge on a single region, there is said to be a problem in binding together the segregated analyses into a single sensory experience.

binocular deprivation. Removal of visual stimulation from both eyes by raising an animal in the dark, bandaging the eyes, or a similar technique.

biochemical techniques. Techniques that measure biologically relevant chemicals in tissue, including various types of assay procedures for determining the presence or concentration of different compounds.

biogenic amines. Group of neurotransmitters that includes norepinephrine, dopamine, and serotonin.

bipolar cells. Neurons having processes at both poles; characteristic especially of retinal cells.

bipolar disorder. Affective disorder in which a person alternates from periods of depression to periods of mania.

birthdate effect. Effect of birthdate on subsequent success at sports or school (some entrants are older and others are younger than average, producing differential advantages due to age).

bitemporal hemianopia. Loss of vision in both temporal fields due to damage to the medial region of the optic chiasm.

black widow spider venom. Poison, produced by the black widow spider, that promotes the release of aacetylcholine from the synapse.

blast. Immature neuron or glial cell.

blindsight. Ability to make better-than-chance decisions about the nature of visual stimuli that are not consciously perceived by patients with visual-field defects.

blood–brain barrier. Functional barrier, produced by the glial cells and by cells in the walls of the capillaries in the brain, that prevents the passage of many substances into the brain.

botulinum toxin. Toxin, associated with food poisoning, that blocks the release of acetylcholine from the synapse; used clinically to block unwanted activity in muscles.

brain. Encephalon; the part of the central nervous system contained within the cranium, comprising the forebrain, midbrain, and hindbrain, and developed from the anterior part of the embryonic neural tube.

brain abscess. Localized collection of pus in the brain; formed from tissues that have disintegrated as a result of infection.

brain hypothesis. Idea that the brain, rather than some other body organ such as the heart, produces behavior.

brain plasticity. Ability of the brain to change its structure in response to experience, drugs, hormones, or injury.

brain scan. *See* **radioisotope scan.**

brainstem. Hypothalamus, midbrain, and hindbrain. (Some authorities also include the thalamus and basal ganglia.)

Broca's aphasia. Expressive, or nonfluent, aphasia that is chiefly a defect of speech; results from a lesion to Broca's area.

Broca's area. Region of the left frontal lobe (frontal operculum) believed to take part in the production of language. Damage to this area results in Broca's aphasia.

Brodmann's map. Map of the cerebral cortex devised by Brodmann. It is based on cytoarchitectonic structure, and anatomical areas are identified by number. (It conforms remarkably closely to functional areas identified by the results of lesion and recording studies.)

Brown-Sequard syndrome. Condition of unilateral paralysis and loss of joint sensation and contralateral loss of pain and temperature sensation caused by damage to one half of the spinal cord.

butyrophenones. Class of drugs that block dopamine receptors.

caffeine. Central nervous system stimulant. Coffee and tea contain caffeine.

calcification. Accumulation of calcium in various brain regions after brain damage.

calmodulin. Protein that, on stimulation by Ca^{2+}, plays a role in undocking vesicles containing a neurotransmitter so that the neurotransmitter can be released into the synaptic cleft.

carbon monoxide (CO). Gas that acts as a chemical neurotransmitter.

cataplexy. Condition in which a person collapses owing to the loss of all muscle activity or tone; often triggered by an emotional stimulus such as mirth, anger, or fear, among others, and often associated with narcolepsy.

catecholamines. Class of neurotransmitters that includes epinephrine, norepinephrine, and dopamine.

caudate nucleus. Nucleus of the basal ganglia. Sometimes referred to as the *caudate putamen.*

caudate putamen. *See* **caudate nucleus.**

cell assembly. Hypothetical collection of neurons that become functionally connected; proposed by Hebb to be the basis of ideation, perception, and memory.

cell body. The part of the cell containing the nucleus and other organelles for making proteins.

cellular tolerance. Adjustments in the activities of brain cells so as to minimize the effects of alcohol in the blood; explains why the behavioral signs of intoxication may be very low despite a relatively high blood-alcohol level.

central nervous system. The part of the nervous system that is encased in the bones and includes the brain and spinal cord.

central sleep apnea. Sleep disturbance in which breathing stops when a person falls into deep sleep; may be associated with muscle relaxation during dream sleep.

central sulcus. Fissure running from the dorsal border of the hemisphere near its midpoint and obliquely downward and forward until it nearly meets the lateral fissure, dividing the frontal and parietal lobes. Also called *fissure of Rolando.*

cerebellum. Major structure of the hindbrain specialized for motor coordination.

cerebral arteriosclerosis. Condition marked by loss of elasticity and by thickening and hardening of the arteries; eventually results in dementia.

cerebral compression. Contraction of the brain substance due to an injury that has caused hemorrhage and the development of a hematoma.

cerebral contusion. Vascular injury resulting in bruising and edema and in hemorrhaging of capillaries.

cerebral cortex. Layer of gray matter on the surface of the cerebral hemispheres and composed of neurons and their synaptic connections, which form four to six sublayers.

cerebral hemorrhage. Bleeding into the brain.

cerebral hypoxia. Deficiency in the amount of oxygen getting into the brain through the bloodstream.

cerebral ischemia. Deficiency in the amount of blood getting to the brain; may be restricted to limited regions and may be caused by an obstruction or constriction of cerebral arteries.

cerebral laceration. Contusion severe enough to breach the brain substance.

cerebral palsy. Group of disorders that result from brain damage acquired prenatally.

cerebral trauma. Injury to the brain, usually resulting from a blow to the head.

cerebral vascular accident. *See* **stroke.**

cerebral vascular insufficiency. Deficiency in the amount of blood getting to the brain.

cerebrospinal fluid (CSF). Clear solution of sodium chloride and other salts that fills the ventricles inside the brain and circulates around the brain beneath the arachnoid layer in the subarachnoid space.

channel. Narrow passageway across the neuron membrane that allows the passage of different ions, which subsequently influence the membrane potential; different channels are opened by different ions or by voltage changes in the membrane.

chemical neurotransmitter. Chemical that binds to a receptor site of a membrane protein.

choroid plexus. Tissue that lines the cerebral ventricles and produces cerebrospinal fluid.

chromatolysis. Loss of protein in a damaged cell resulting in loss of its ability to absorb stain; literally, the breakdown of its ability to be colored.

chromosome. Strands of DNA combined with protein in the nucleus of each cell that contain the genetic code determining the structure and function of each individual organism.

cingulate cortex. Strip of limbic cortex lying just above the corpus callosum along the medial walls of the cerebral hemispheres.

cingulate sulcus. Cortical sulcus located on the medial wall of the cerebral hemisphere just above the corpus callosum.

cladogram. Phylogenetic tree that branches repeatedly, suggesting a classification of organisms based on the time sequence in which evoluntionary branches arise.

class-common behaviors. Behaviors and behavioral capacities common to all members of a phylogenetic class.

classical (Pavlovian) conditioning. Form of unconscious learning in which a neutral stimulus is paired with a stimulus that evokes behavior.

classic migraine. Symptom complex of periodic headaces, usually temporal and unilateral. *See also* **common migraine.**

clinical depression. Serious mood disorder characterized by persistent periods of depression that normally require some type of clinical treatment for remission.

cluster headache. Migrainelike disorder marked by attacks of unilateral intense pain over the eye and forehead, with flushing and watering of the eyes and nose. Attacks last about an hour and occur in clusters.

cocaine. Alkaloid obtained from the leaves of various species of *Erytroxylon* (coca plants) or produced synthetically; used as a local anethetic.

cochlea. Spiral tube forming part of the inner ear, which is the essential organ of hearing.

codeine. Alkaloid obtained from opium or prepared from morphine by methylation; used as a narcotic analgesic and as an antitussive agent.

cognition. General term for the processes of thinking.

cognitive map. Hypothetical map of some cognitive process such as spatial localization.

cognitive set. Tendency to approach a problem with a particular bias in thought; for example, when searching for a mailbox, one will have a cognitive set for mailboxes but not for, say, cats.

cognitive space. Space or time about which a person has knowledge.

collaterals. Side branches of axons that may be necessary for neuron survival (essential collateral) or may be secondary and not essential (sustaining collateral).

color agnosia. Inability to associate particular colors with objects or objects with colors.

color amnesia. Inability to remember the colors of common objects.

color anomia. Inability to name colors; generally associated with other aphasic symptoms. Also called *color aphasia.*

column. Hypothetical unit of cortical organization; believed to represent a vertically organized intracortical connectivity that is assumed to be a single functional unit. Sometimes used as a synonym for a *module.*

coma. State of deep unconsciousness due to brain injury or disease.

commissure. Bundle of fibers connecting corresponding points on the two sides of the central nervous system.

commissurotomy. Surgical disconnection of the two hemispheres by cutting the corpus callosum.

common descent. Refers to individual organisms or families that descend from the same ancestor.

common migraine. Symptom complex of periodic headaches, usually temporal and unilateral, often accompanied by irritability, nausea, vomiting, constipation or diarrhea, and photo-phobia; preceded by constriction of the cranial arteries, usually with resultant prodromal sensory symptoms and commencing symptoms, and commencing with the vasodilation that follows.

comparative approach. Method of study in which similarities and differences in morphology or behavior across different species are emphasized as a means to understanding the organization of brain and behavior.

complex partial seizure. Focal seizure that most commonly originates in the temporal lobe; characterized by subjective feelings, automatisms, and motor symptoms. Sometimes referred to as a *temporal-lobe seizure.*

computerized tomography (CT) scan. X-ray procedure in which a computer draws a map from the measured densities of the brain; superior to a conventional X-ray because it provides a three-dimensional representation of the brain. Also called *EMI-Scan,* a trade name.

computerized transaxial tomography. Technique by which a series of brain X-rays are used to construct a three-dimensional representation of the brain.

concentration gradient. Difference in the concentrations of an ion on the two sides of a membrane.

concussion. Condition of widespread paralysis of the functions of the brain that arises immediately after a blow to the head.

conduction aphasia. Type of fluent aphasia in which, despite alleged normal comprehension of spoken language, words are repeated incorrectly.

cones. Highly specialized conical or flask-shaped cells in the retina that are maximally sensitive to light of particular wavelengths; are the basis of color vision.

confabulation. The recitation of imaginary experiences to fill gaps in memory.

conjunction search. Concept in attentional theory that assumes the existence of a mechanism with which the sensory system searches for particular combinations of sensory information.

consciousness. The state of being conscious; responsiveness of the mind to impressions made by the senses.

consolidation of memories. Process through which short-term memories are converted into long-term memories.

constructional apraxia. Inability to perform well-rehearsed and familiar sequences of movements when making or preparing something. The deficit is not attributable to an inability to move or to perform the individual acts required for the task.

contralateral. Residing in the side of the body opposite the reference points.

contralateral neglect. Neglect of part of the body or space contralateral to a lesion.

contrast X-ray. Radiographic procedure using the injection of radiopaque dye or air into the ventricles, or of dye into the arteries, for purposes of diagnosis.

conventional radiography. X-ray.

convergent thinking. Form of thinking in which there is a search for a single answer to a question (for example, 2 + 2 = ?), in contrast with *divergent thinking*, in which multiple solutions are sought.

coprolalia. The utterance of obscene words, especially words relating to feces.

corollary discharge. Transmission by one area of the brain to another, informing the latter area of the former's actions; commonly used more specifically for a signal from the motor system to the sensory system that a particular movement is being produced.

corollary discharge theory. States that, when an individual initiates a movement, the nervous system keeps a record of the intended movement with which it compares the actual movement. The intended movement is the corollary discharge. Also known as *reafference theory*.

corpus callosum. Fiber system connecting the homotopic areas of the two hemispheres. A split-brain patient is one whose corpus callosum has been severed.

cortex. External layer of the brain; in this book, synonymous with *neocortex. See also* **neocortex.**

cortical quotient (CQ). Measure of the relative size of the cortex; analogous to *encephalization quotient* but applied only to the cortex.

corticobulbar fibers. Traditionally, refers to connections between the cerebral cortex and the medulla oblongata; in more common usage, refers to connections between the cerebral cortex and the lower brainstem.

corticobulbar tracts. Descending tracts from the neocortex that innervate facial motor neurons; are initially part of the corticospinal tracts.

corticospinal fibers. Connect the cerebral cortex and the spinal cord.

corticospinal pathway. Motor pathway originating in layer V of the cerebral cortex and ending in the spinal cord.

corticospinal tract. Bundle of fibers directly connecting the cerebral cortex to the spinal cord.

countercoup. Brain injury suffered by tissue at the end of the skull opposite the region striking an object.

coup. Brain injury suffered by tissue underlying the region of skull striking an object.

cranial nerves. Set of 12 pairs of nerves conveying sensory and motor signals to and from the head.

cranioscopy. Technique of measuring the skull to determine the location of bumps and depressions for phrenological analysis.

cremasteric reflex. Retraction of testicles in response to stroking the inner thigh.

Creutzfeldt-Jakob disease. Form of senile dementia in which there is generalized cortical atrophy. The cause is unknown, but a prion is suspected.

crossed aphasia. Aphasia that results from damage to the right hemisphere.

cross-modal matching. Ability to match sensory characteristics of objects across sensory modalities—for example, the ability to visually recognize an object that was previously perceived by touch.

cross-tolerance. Form of tolerance in which the response to a novel drug is reduced because of tolerance developed in response to a related drug.

cue response. Navigational behavior in which an animal locomotes to a position on the basis of its location relative to a single cue. Distinguished from *place* or *position response*.

curare. A drug, obtained from a South American plant, that blocks acetylcholine receptors.

cytoarchitectonic analysis. An analysis of cytoarchitectonic maps.

cytoarchitectonic map. Map of the cortex based on the organization, structure, and distribution of the cells.

cytochrome oxidase. Enzyme made in mitochondria. Increased enzyme activity is thought to correspond to heightened neural activity; tissue can be stained for this enzyme to estimate which areas of the brain display high levels of activity.

dead reckoning. Ability to monitor one's movement by using cues generated by the movement.

deafferentation. Process of removing the afferent input to a structure or region of the nervous system.

decerebrate. Elimination of cerebral function by transecting the brainstem just above the superior colliculi; an animal so prepared is said to be decerebrate.

decerebrate rigidity. Excessive tone in all muscles, producing extension of the limbs and dorsoflexion of the head because antigravity musculature overpowers other muscles; caused by brainstem or cerebellar lesions.

decerebration. Disconnection of the cerebral hemispheres from the brainstem, resulting in deprivation of sensory input and the ability to affect behavior.

declarative memory. Type of memory illustrated by the ability to recount the details of events, including time, place, and circumstances, compared with the ability to perform some act or behavior. Literally, it refers to the ability to recount what one knows, which is lost in many types of amnesia.

decortication. Removal of the cortex of the brain.

decussation. Crossing of pathways from one side of the brain to the other.

deep dyslexia. Reading impairment characterized by a peculiar constellation of errors, suggesting that the reading is being performed by the nondominant hemisphere.

degeneration. Death of neurons or neuronal processes in response to injury in the degenerating neuron or, in some cases, in other neurons.

delayed nonmatching-to-sample task. Behavioral task in which a subject is presented with a sample stimulus and then, after some delay, is presented with the same stimulus and another, novel stimulus. The subject's task is to choose the novel stimulus to obtain reward.

delta (δ) wave. Rhythmic electroencephalographic waveform with a frequency ranging from 0 to 3 Hz that can be recorded from the scalp of a subject who is sleeping.

delusion. Belief opposed to reality but firmly held despite evidence of its falsity; characteristic of some types of psychotic disorders.

dememtia. Organic loss of intellectual function.

dendrite. Treelike process at the receiving end of the neuron.

dendritic spine. Protuberence on the dendrites of excitatory neurons; the location of most synapses on such neurons.

dendrodendritic synapses. Synapse between two endrites.

denervation supersensitivity. Condition of increased susceptibility to drugs, resulting from the proliferation of receptors after denervation (removal of terminations) of an area.

dentate gyrus. A region of the hippocampal formation.

2-deoxyglucose. Sugar that interferes with the metabolism of glucose. A radioactive marker (such as ^{14}C) can be attached to 2-deoxyglucose. When this compound is taken up by the blood, it is transported to the brain and will stay in the brain regions that have been most active, which provides a method for measuring metabolic activity.

deoxyribonucleic acid (DNA). Long, complex macromolecule consisting of two interconnected helical strands. Strands of DNA, which contain an organism's genetic information, and their associated proteins constitute the chromosomes.

dependence. State in which doses of a drug are required to prevent the onset of abstinence (that is, withdrawal) symptoms.

dependency hypothesis. Drug-addiction hypothesis that postulates that drug use is maintained to prevent withdrawal symptoms.

depolarization. Inward transfer of positive ions, erasing a difference of potential between the inside and the outside of the neuron.

depression. Hollow or depressed area; downward or inward displacement.

depth-of-processing effect. Improvement in subsequent recall of an object about which a person has given thought to its meaning or shape. A structure deep in the brain is presumed to improve the memory of the object.

depth perception. Ability to perceive three-dimensionality in visual stimuli.

dermatome. Area of skin supplied with afferent nerve fibers by a single spinal dorsal root.

desynchronization. Change in electroencephalographic activity from a high-amplitude slow pattern to a low-amplitude fast pattern.

developmental approach. Method of study in which changes in the brain and behavior across different ages is used as a way to understand relations between the brain and behavior.

developmental dyslexia. Inability to learn adequate reading skills even when opportunity and appropriate instruction are given.

diaschisis. Special kind of shock subsequent to brain damage in which areas connected to the damaged area show a transitory arrest of function.

dichaptic test. Procedure for simultaneously presenting different objects to each hand to determine which hand is most effective at identifying the objects.

dichotic listening. Procedure for simultaneously presenting a different auditory input to each ear through stereophonic earphones.

diencephalic. Pertaining to the diencephalon. A diencephalic animal is one in which the diencephalon is the highest functioning region.

diencephalon. Region of the brain that includes the hypothalamus, thalamus, and epithalamus.

diffusion. Process of becoming diffused, or widely spread.

diplopia. Perception of two images of a single object; double vision.

disconnection. Severing, by damage or by surgery, of the fibers that connect two areas of the brain such that the two areas can no longer communicate; the condition that results.

disconnection syndrome. Behavioral syndrome resulting from the disconnection of two or more brain regions rather than from damage to a specific brain region.

discourse. Highest level of language processing. In discourse, sentences are strung together to form a meaningful narrative.

disengagement. The process whereby attention is shifted from one stimulus to another.

disinhibition. Removal of inhibition from a system.

disinhibition theory. Theory to explain the effects of alcohol in which intoxication is associated with the loss of moral and social values in favor of instinctual behaviors.

disorientation. Loss of proper bearings, or a state of mental confusion concerning time, place, or identity.

dissolution. According to an unproved theory, the condition in which disease or damage in the highest levels of the brain would produce not loss of function but rather a repertory of simpler behaviors seen in animals that have not evolved that particular brain structure.

distal. Being away from, or distant to, some point.

distributed systems. Mediation of behavior by neurons and connections between neurons that are located in different areas of the brain.

divergent thinking. Form of thinking in which there is a search for multiple solutions to a problem (for example, how many ways one can use a pen?), in contrast with *convergent thinking*, in which a single solution is sought.

dopamine (DA). Monoamine formed in the body by the decarboxylation of L-dopa. An intermediate product in the synthesis of norepinephrine, dopamine acts as a neurotrasmitter in the central nervous system.

dopamine hypothesis of schizophrenia. Proposes that schizophrenic symptoms are due to excess activity of the neurotransmitter dopamine.

dorsal column. Cells in the dorsal spinal cord, which, in upright humans, can be thought of as forming a column from the bottom to the top of the spinal cord, in contrast with *ventral column.*

dorsal root. Nerve, composed of fibers carrying sensory information, that enters each segment of the dorsal (posterior in humans) part of the spinal cord.

dorsal-root ganglion. Protuberance produced by the aggregation of cell bodies of the sensory fibers, which are located adjacent to the part of the spinal cord into which their axons enter.

dorsal stream. Visual processing pathway that orginates in the visual cortex; controls the visual guidance of movement.

dorsomedial thalamus. Thalamic nucleus providing a major afferent input to the prefrontal cortex; degenerates in Korsakoff's disease, leading to a severe amnesic syndrome.

double dissociation. Experimental technique by which two areas of neocortex are functionally dissociated by two behavioral tests, each test being affected by a lesion in one zone and not the other.

dream sleep. Stage of sleep in which muscles are paralyzed, sensory input to the brain is blocked, and the brain shows a waking state of activity, during which vivid dreaming takes place. *See also* **REM (rapid eye movement) sleep.**

D₂ receptor. A receptor for the neurotransmitter dopamine; target for major tranquilizers.

drug. Any medicinal substance.

dualism. Theory that there are two distinct stem cells for blood-cell formation: one for the lymphatic cells and the other for the myeloid cells.

dura mater. Tough, double layer of collagenous fiber enclosing the brain in a kind of loose sac.

dysarthria. Difficulty in speech production caused by incoordination of the speech apparatus.

dyscalculia. Difficulty in performing arithmetical operations.

dyseidetic. Refers to difficulty in recognizing words by their visual configurations.

dyskinesia. Any disturbance of movement.

dyslexia. Difficulty in reading.

dysphagia. Impairment of speech caused by damage to the central nervous system.

dysphonetic. Refers to the inability to decode words or to recognize them by using phonic or sound principles.

dystonia. Abnormality of muscle tone; usually excessive muscle tone.

echolalia. Condition in which a person repeats words or noises that he or she hears.

edema. An abnormal acculmation of fluid in intercellular spaces of the body.

efference theory. States that the sensations produced by an act provide the conscious perception of the act.

efferent. Conducting away from higher centers in the central nervous system and toward muscle or gland.

egocentric disorientation. Difficulty in determining one's location in space.

egocentric space. Space that is relative to a person's perspective. Compare **allocentric space.**

electroconvulsive shock therapy (ECT). Application of a massive electrical shock across the brain as a treatment for affective disorders.

electroencephalogram (EEG). Electrical potentials recorded by placing electrodes on the scalp or in the brain.

electromyogram (EM). Recording of electrical activity of the muscles as well as the electrical response of the peripheral nerves.

electron microscope. Microscope that creates images of very small objects by bouncing electrons off the object and creating a picture through the object's resistance to electrons.

electrooculogram (EOG). Electroencephalographic tracings made while moving the eyes a constant distance between two fixation points.

electrostatic gradient. Gradient between an area of low electrical charge and an area of high electrical charge; develops across the membrane of a cell or between two parts of the same cell.

embolism. Sudden blocking of an artery or a vein by a blood clot, bubble of air, deposit of fat, or small mass of cells deposited by the blood current.

emotion. State of mental excitement characterized by alteration of feeling tone and by physiological and behavioral changes.

encephalitis. Inflammation of the central nervous system as a result of infection.

encephalization. Process by which higher structures, such as the cerebral cortex, take over the functions of lower centers; may imply either a phylogenetic or an ontogenetic shift of function. Also called *encorticalization.*

encephalization quotient (EQ). Ratio of actual brain size to expected brain size for a typical mammal of a particular body size.

encephalomalacia. Softening of the brain, resulting from vascular disorders caused by inadequate blood flow.

encephalopathy. Chemical, physical, allergic, or toxic inflammation of the central nervous system.

encorticalization. *See* **encephalization.**

end foot. Terminal part of an axon; conveys information to other neurons.

endoplasmic reticulum (ER). Extensive internal membrane system in the cytoplasm. Ribosomes attach to part of the ER to form what is known as the *rough ER.*

endorphins. Any of a group of endogenous polypeptide brain substances that bind to opiate receptors in various areas of the brain and thereby raise the pain threshold.

endothelial cells. Cells that form blood vessels.

entorhinal cortex. Cortex found on the medial surface of the temporal lobe; provides a major route for neocortical input to the hippocampal formation; often shows degeneration in Alzheimer's disease.

ependymal cells. Glial cells forming the lining of the ventricles; some produce cerebrospinal fluid.

epilepsy. Condition characterized by recurrent seizures of various types associated with a disturbance of consciousness.

epinephrine (EP). Neurotransmitter found in the sympathetic nervous system; mobilizes the body for fight or flight.

episodic memory. Memory containing autobiographical events that took place in specifiable temporal and spatial contexts.

epithalamus. Collection of nuclei forming the phylogenetically most primitive region of the thalamus; includes the habenulae, pineal body, and stria medullaris.

equipotentiality. Hypothesis that each part of a given area of the brain is able to encode or produce the behavior normally controlled by the entire area.

ergotamine. Drug used in the treatment of migraine and tension headaches that acts by constricting cerebral arteries.

ethology. Study of the natural behavior of animals.

Euclidean space. Real space, with three dimensions, according to the laws of Euclid.

event-related potential (ERP). Complex electroencephalographic waveform that is related in time to a specific sensory event; composed of a series of specific subunits that are related to specific aspects of cerebral processing (for example, P_3).

evoked potential. Short train of large, slow waves recorded from the scalp and corresponding to dendritic activity.

excitatory neurotransmitter. Transmitter substance that decreases a cell's membrane potential and increases the likelihood that the cell will fire.

excitatory postsynaptic potential (EPSP). Small change in the membrane potential of a cell that leads to depolarization and increased likelihood that the cell will fire.

exocytosis. Discharge from a cell of particles that are too large to diffuse through the wall.

explicit memory. Memory in which subjects can retrieve an item and indicate that they know the item (that is, conscious memory). Compare **implicit memory.**

expressive aphasia. Disturbance of language in which there is a severe deficit in producing language.

extension. Movement by which a limb is straightened.

extensor muscle. Muscle that acts to straighten a limb.

extensor plantar response. Extensor movement of the foot toward a surface that the foot touches.

extensor reflex. Advancement of a limb to contact a stimulus in response to tactile stimuli that activate fine touch and pressure receptors. The response is mediated by a multisynaptic spinal reflex circuit.

external imagery. Third-person imagery in which a person engaging in an act imagines that it is another person doing so.

exteroceptive. Sherrington's term in reference to the external surface field of distribution of receptor organs—for example, the skin and mucous membranes.

exteroceptive receptor. Receptor that functions to identify events that take place outside the body.

extinction. Term used in learning theory for the decreased probability that a behavior will occur if reinforcement is withheld.

extracellular fluid. Fluid and its contents that surround a neuron or glial cell.

face amnesia. Inability to remember faces.

factor analysis. Statistical procedure designed to determine if the variability in scores can be related to one or more factors that are reliably influencing performance.

fasciculation. Small local contraction of muscles, visible through the skin, representing a spontaneous discharge of a number of fibers innervated by a single motor-nerve filament.

feature search. Cognitive strategy in which sensory stimuli are scanned for a specific feature, such as color.

festination. Tendency to engage in behavior at faster and faster speeds; usually refers to walking but can include other behaviors such as talking and thinking.

fetal alcohol syndrome (FAS). Disorder characterized by mental retardation as well as stunted growth and congenital defects of the face and head; caused by excessive alcohol intake by the mother during pregnancy.

fimbria-fornix. Anatomical pathway running from the septal region to the hippocampus.

finger agnosia. Inability to distinguish fingers.

fissure. Cleft, produced by folds of the neocortex, that extends to the ventricles.

flexion. Movement by which a limb is bent at the joint, bringing the limb toward the body.

flexor muscle. Muscle that acts to bend a limb at a joint.

flocculus. Small mass on the lower side of each cerebral hemisphere and continuous with the nodule of the vermis.

fluent aphasia. Speech disorder in which a person articulates words in a languagelike fashion, but what is said actually makes little sense; usually results from damage to the left posterior cortex. *See also* **Wernicke's aphasia.**

fMRI. *See* **functional magnetic resonance imaging.**

focal seizure. Seizure that begins locally and then spreads—for example, from one finger to the whole body.

folia. Narrow folds of the cerebellum.

forebrain. Cerebral hemispheres, basal ganglia, thalamus, amygdala, hippocampus, and septum.

formant. Group of sound waves specific to each vowel sound.

fovea. Region at the center of the retina that is specialized for high acuity. Its receptive fields are at the center of the eye's visual field.

fragile-X syndrome. Form of mental retardation caused by an abnormality in a fragile section of the X chromosome.

frontal lobes. All the neocortex forward of the central sulcus.

frontal operculum. Upper region of the inferior frontal gyrus.

fugue state. Transient disturbance of consciousness in which a person performs purposeful acts but has no conscious recollection of those actions.

functional analysis. Analysis of brain organization based on studying the effects of brain damage, stimulating areas of the brain chemically or electrically, or recording the activity of cells in relation to behavior.

functional magnetic resonance imaging (fMRI). Magnetic resonance imaging in which changes in elements such as iron or oxygen are measured during the performance of a specific behavior; used to measure brain activity during rest or behavior. *See also* **magnetic resonance imaging (MRI).**

functional map. Map of the cortex constructed by stimulating areas of the brain electrically and noting elicited behavior or by recording electrical activity during certain behaviors; relates specific behaviors to brain areas.

functional validation. According to theory, a neural system requires sensory stimulation to become fully functional.

GABA$_A$ receptor. Gamma-aminobutyric acid receptor on which sedative hypnotics and antianxiety drugs act.

gamma-aminobutyric acid (GABA). Amino acid neurotransmitter that inhibits neurons.

ganglion cells. Cells of the retina that give rise to the optic nerve.

gated channel. Membrane channel that allows the passage of specific ions when the gate is open and prevents such passage when the gate is closed.

generalized seizure. Seizure that spreads from a starting point to encompass large regions of the brain; usually results in gross motor movements.

general mover theory. Theory of evolutionary change that argues that genetic movement is driven simultaneously by multiple factors rather than by a specific factor.

generator. Something that produces or causes to exist.

geniculostriate pathway. Visual pathway from the eye to the lateral geniculate nucleus of the thalamus to the primary visual cortex (striate cortex).

geniculostriate system. Consists of projections from the retina of the eye to the lateral geniculate nucleus of the thalamus, then to areas 17, 18, and 19, and then to areas 20 and 21; controls the perception of form, color, and pattern.

genu. Bulbous part of the anterior part of the corpus callosum.

germinal cells. Cells from which particular tissues are formed in the course of development.

Gerstmann syndrome. Collection of symptoms due to left parietal lesion; alleged to include finger agnosia, right–left confusion, acalculia, and agraphia (a source of some controversy).

gestural theory. Theory of language evolution stating that language developed from gestures used for communication.

glia. One of two classes of cells in the nervous system, the other one being neurons; provide insulation, nutrients, and support for neurons.

glial cells. Supportive cells of the central nervous system. *See also* **glia.**

glial sheath. Glial cells, such as oligodendrocytes and Schwann cells, that wrap themselves around the axons of neurons, thus forming a sheath.

glioblast. Progenitor cell that gives rise to different types of glial cells.

glioblastoma. Highly malignant, rapidly growing brain tumor; most common in adults over 35 years of age; results from the sudden growth of spongioblasts.

glioma. Any brain tumor that arises from glial cells.

gliosis. Migration and proliferation of glial cells in areas of neural tissue that have undergone damage. Their presence serves as a sign of tissue damage.

globus pallidus. Part of the basal ganglia that receives projections from the caudate nucleus and sends projections to the ventral lateral nucleus of the thalamus; literally, pale globe or sphere.

glutamate. An excitatory amino acid transmitter.

glycoproteins. Class of proteins. A glycoprotein is a protein with an attached carbohydrate group.

Golgi apparatus. Complex of parallel membranes in the cytoplasm that wraps the product of a secretory cell or a protein manufactured by a nerve cell.

Golgi body. Membrane in neurons that covers proteins made in neurons.

graded potential. Electrical potential in a neuron or receptor cell that changes with the intensity of the stimulus. Also known as a *generator potential*.

grand mal attack. Seizure characterized by loss of consciousness and stereotyped, generalized convulsions.

grand mal epilepsy. Often preceded by an aura, in which a sudden loss of conciousness is immediately followed by generalized convulsions.

granule cells. Neurons that are round in appearance, in contrast with *pyramidal cells*, which have pyramidal-shaped cell bodies.

granulovacuolar bodies. Abnormal structures in the brain characterized by granules (small beadlike masses of tissue) and vacuoles (small cavities in the protoplasm of cells).

grapheme. Refers to the pictorial qualities of a written word that permit it to be understood without being sounded out; a group of letters that conveys a meaning.

graphemic reading. Reading in which the meaning of a word is derived from the picture that it makes as a whole rather than by sounding out the syllables.

graphesthesia. Ability to identify numbers or letters traced on the skin with a blunt object.

gray matter. Any brain area composed predominantly of cell bodies.

growth spurt. Sudden growth in development that lasts for a finite time.

guanyl nucleotide-binding protein (G protein). Protein that carries a message from a metabotropic receptor to other receptors or to second messengers.

gyrus (pl. gyri). Convolution of the cortex of the cerebral hemispheres.

habituation. Gradual quantitative decrease in a response after repeated exposure to a stimulus.

hallucination. Perception for which there is no appropriate external stimulus; characteristic of some types of psychotic disorders.

hammer. Ossicle in the middle ear.

head-direction cell. Neuron in the hippocampus that discharges when an animal faces in a particular direction.

heading disorientation. Inability to move or guide one's movements in a direction appropriate to the perceived cues.

Hebb synapse. Hypothetical synapse formed when two neurons are concurrently in the same state of activity; named after Donald Hebb, who postulated such a mechanism in 1949.

hebephrenic schizophrenia. Form of schizophrenia characterized by silly behavior and mannerisms, giggling, and shallow affect.

hedonic hypothesis. Proposes that people abuse drugs because the drugs make them feel good.

hematoma. Local swelling or tumor filled with effused blood.

heme group. Nonprotein, insoluble, iron protoporphyrin constituent of hemoglobin, a constituent of blood.

hemianopia. Loss of pattern vision in either the left or the right visual field.

hemiballism. Motor disorder characterized by sudden involuntary movements of a single limb.

hemiparesis. Muscular weakness affecting one side of the body.

hemiplegia. Paralysis of one side of the body.

hemiplegic migraine. Migraine that leads to paralysis of one side of the body.

hemisphere. In the brain, either of the pair of structures constituting the telencephalon; sometimes also used to refer to either side of the cerebellum.

hemispherectomy. Removal of a cerebral hemisphere.

heroin. Diacetylmorphine, a highly addictive morphine derivative.

Heschl's gyrus. Gyrus of the human temporal lobe that is roughly equivalent to auditory area I. Also known as the *transverse temporal gyrus*.

hierarchical organization. Principle of cerebral organization in which information is processed serially, with each level of processing assumed to represent the elaboration of some hypothetical process.

high decerebrate. Preparation in which an animal has an intact midbrain, hindbrain, and spinal cord. *See also* **decerebrate** and **decerebration**.

high decerebration. Injury to the brainstem in which the highest intact functioning structure is the midbrain.

higher-order area. Brain area that is of more recent evolutionary origin and receives its inputs from older (lower) areas.

hindbrain. Region of the brain that consists primarily of the cerebellum, medulla oblongata, pons, and fourth ventricle.

hippocampus. Primitive cortical structure lying in the anterior medial region of the temporal lobe.

histochemical techniques. Various techniques that rely on chemical reactions in cells to mark features of a cell for microscopic visualization.

histofluorescent technique. Literally, cell fluorescence, a technique in which a fluorescent compound is used to label cells.

homeostasis. Maintenance of a chemically and physically constant internal environment.

hominid. General term referring to primates that walk upright, including all forms of humans, living and extinct.

homonymous hemianopia. Total loss of vision due to complete cuts of the optic tract, lateral geniculate body, or area 17.

homotopic. At the same place on the body.

homotopic areas. Corresponding points in the two hemispheres of the brain that are related to the midline of the body.

homunculus. Representation of the human body in the sensory or motor cortex; any topographical representation of the body by a neural area.

horseradish peroxidase (HRP). Compound that, when introduced into a cell, is then distributed to all its parts, allowing the cell to be visualized.

HPA axis. The hypothalamic-pituitary-adrenal circuit controlling hormone production.

Huntington's chorea. Hereditary disease characterized by chorea (ceaseless, involuntary, jerky movements) and progressive dementia, ending in death.

hydrocephalus. Condition characterized by abnormal accumulation of fluid in the cranium, accompanied by enlargement of the head, prominence of the forehead, atrophy of the brain, mental deterioration, and convulsions.

6-hydroxydopamine (6-OHDA). Chemical selectively taken up by axons and terminals of norepinephrinergic or dopaminergic neurons that acts as a poison, damaging or killing the neurons.

hyperactive child syndrome. Characterized by low attention span and poor impulse control, which results in disruptive behavior.

hyperactivity. More activity than normally expected.

hyperkinesia. Condition in which movements of a part or all of the body increase.

hyperkinetic symptom. Symptom of brain damage; consists of involuntary excessive movements.

hyperlexia. Condition in which a person is given to excessive reading or is a precocious reader, often without understanding the meaning of what is read.

hypermetamorphosis. Tendency to attend and react to every visual stimulus, leading to mental distraction and confusion.

hyperpolarization. Process by which a nerve membrane becomes more resistant to the passage of sodium ions and consequently more difficult to excite with adequate stimulation; during hyperpolarization, the electrical charge on the inside of the membrane relative to that on the outside becomes more negative.

hypnogogic hallucination. Dreamlike event at the beginning of sleep.

hypothalamus. Collection of nuclei located below the thalamus; controls nearly all behavior including movement, feeding, sexual activity, sleeping, emotional expression, temperature regulation, and endocrine regulation.

ideational apraxia. Vague term used to describe a disorder of gestural behavior in which the overall conception of how a movement is carried out is lost; emerges when a person is required to manipulate objects.

ideomotor apraxia. Inability to use and understand nonverbal communication such as gesture and pantomime.

idiopathic seizure. Seizure disorder that appears to arise spontaneously and in the absence of other diseases of the central nervous system.

idiothetic cue. Derives from the self; a cue generated by one's own movement.

illusion. False or misinterpreted sensory impression of a real sensory image.

immunohistochemical staining. Antibody-based label that, when applied to tissue postmortem, reveals the presence of a specific molecule or close relatives of that molecule.

implicit memory. Memory in which subjects can demonstrate knowledge but cannot explicitly retrieve the information (for example, a motor skill). Compare **explicit memory.**

incentive salience. Refers to cues that, after having been associated with drug use, become sought.

incentive-sensitization theory. Holds that, when a drug has been used in association with certain cues, the cues themselves will elicit desire for the drug.

infantile amnesia. Inability to remember events from early infancy or early childhood.

infarct. Area of dead or dying tissue resulting from an obstruction of the blood vessels normally supplying the area.

infection. Invasion and multiplication of microorganisms in body tissues.

inferior colliculus. Nucleus of the tectum of the midbrain that receives auditory projections and takes part in whole-body orientation to auditory stimuli.

inhibitory neurotransmitter. Increases the membrane polarity of a cell, making an action potential less likely.

inhibitory postsynaptic potential (IPSP). Small localized change that increases a membrane's potential, making an action potential less likely.

input cell layers. Layers of tissue that receive inputs, such as layer 4 in the cerebral cortex.

insomnia. Inability to sleep.

intelligence quotient (IQ). Defined originally as the ratio of mental age to chronological age multiplied by 100. On contemporary intelligence tests, the average performance for a given age is assigned a value of 100 and a person's intelligence quotient is expressed relative to 100.

intermediate zone. Layer of cells in the spinal cord that lies immediately above the motor neurons of the ventral horn.

internal carotid artery. Branch of the carotid artery that is a major source of blood to the brain.

internal imagery. First-person imagery in which a person imagines that it is himself or herself who engages in an act.

interneuron. Any neuron lying between a sensory neuron and a motor neuron.

interoceptive. Sherrington's term referring to the internal sensory receptors, such as those in the viscera.

interoceptive receptor. Receptor that responds to information originating inside the body.

intracellular fluid. Fluid and its contents found within neurons and glial cells.

invariance hypothesis. Suggests that the structure of each cerebral hemisphere ensures that the hemisphere will develop a set of specialized functions; for example, the left hemisphere is specialized at birth for language.

ionotropic receptor. Receptor that has two parts: a binding site for a neurotransmitter and a pore that regulates ion flow.

ipsilateral. Residing in the same side of the body as the point of reference.

ischemia. Deficiency of blood due to functional constriction or actual obstruction of a blood vessel.

isolation syndrome. *See* **transcortical aphasia.**

Jacksonian focal seizure. Seizure that has consistent sensory or motor symptoms such as a twitching in the face or hand.

Kennard principle. Idea that early brain damage produces less-severe behavioral effects than does brain damage incurred later in life; coined after Margaret Kennard reported this phenomenon in a series of papers on the study of neonatally brain-damaged monkeys.

kindling. Production of epilepsy by repeated stimulation—for example, by an electrode in the brain.

kinesthesis. Perception of movement or position of the limbs and body; commonly used to refer to the perception of changes in the angles of joints.

Klüver-Bucy syndrome. Group of symptoms resulting from bilateral damage to the temporal lobes; characterized especially by hypersexuality, excessive oral behavior, and visual agnosia.

Korsakoff's syndrome. Group of symptoms resulting from degeneration of the dorsomedial thalamic nucleus and produced by chronic alcoholism; metabolic disorder of the central nervous system due to a lack of vitamin B_1 (thiamine) and often associated with chronic alcoholism. Also called *Korsakoff-Wernicke disease.*

landmark agnosia. Loss of the ability to know one's location or guide one's movement in relation to a building or landmark that had once been familiar.

landmark test. Behavioral test in which the subject must learn the association between a specific cue (the landmark) and the location of reward.

larynx. Organ of voice; the air passage between the lower pharynx and trachea, containing the vocal cords and formed by nine cartilages: the thyroid, cricoid, and epiglottis and the paired arytenoid, corniculate, and cuneiform cartilages.

lateral corticospinal tract. In the lateral spinal cord, a pathway that carries information instructing movement.

lateral fissure. Deep cleft on the basal surface of the brain that extends laterally, posteriorly, and upward, thus separating the temporal and parietal lobes. Also called *Sylvian fissure.*

laterality. Refers to the side of the brain that controls a given function. Hence, studies of laterality are undertaken to determine which side of the brain controls various functions.

lateralization. Process by which functions become located primarily on one side of the brain.

lateral system. One of the two major motor groups of tracts in the motor system; includes the lateral corticospinal tract, which originates in the neocortex, and the rubrospinal tract, which originates in the red nucleus in the brainstem.

learned tolerance. Experience in performing a behavior under the influence of a drug results in improved performance of the behavior when subsequently under the influence of the drug.

learning disability. Generally defined by work performance in a specific school subject that falls significantly below average; for example, a reading disability is sometimes defined as reading 2 years below the class average.

lesion. Any damage to the nervous system.

letter-by-letter reading. Reading in which the meaning of a text is determined by extracting information from each letter, one letter at a time.

Leu-enkephalin. Peptide neurotransmitter that produces some of the effects of opioid drugs.

lexicon. Dictionary (that is, memory store) in the brain that contains words and their meanings.

light microscope. Microscope that relies on shining light through tissue to visualize that tissue through an eyepiece.

limbic lobe. Term coined by Paul Broca to refer to the structures between the brainstem and the telencephalon; in modern usage, equivalent to the limbic system, which includes the hippocampus, septum, cingulate cortex, hypothalamus, and amygdala.

limbic system. Elaboration of the structures of the limbic lobe to form a hypothetical functional system originally believed to be important in controlling affective behavior; neural systems that line the inside wall of the neocortex.

limb-kinetic apraxia. Form of apraxia in which a person is unable to make voluntary movements of the limbs in response to verbal commands; presumed to result from a disconnection of the motor program from language.

lipofuscin granule. Dark-pigmented substance that accumulates in brain cells as they age.

localization of function. Hypothetically, the control of each kind of behavior by a different specific brain area.

longitudinal fissure. Divides the two hemispheres. Also known as the *sagittal fissure.*

long-term enhancement (LTE). Long-lasting change in the postsynaptic response of a cell that results from previous experience with a high-frequency stimulation. Also known as *enhancement* or *long-term potentiation (LTP).*

long-term memory. Form of memory postulated by Broadbent in which information is assumed to be stored for longer than about 15 minutes.

long-term potentiation (LTP). *See* **long-term enhancement (LTE).**

low decerebrate. Preparation in which both the hindbrain and spinal cord of an animal remain intact. *See also* **decerebrate** and **decerebration.**

lysergic acid diethylamide (LSD). Drug that produces visual hallucinations, presumably by influencing the serotonin system.

lysosome. Small body containing digestive enzymes seen with the use of an electron microscope in many types of cells.

macular sparing. Condition in which the central region of the visual field is not lost, even though temporal or nasal visual fields are lost.

magnetic resonance imaging (MRI). Imaging procedure in which a computer draws a map from the measured changes in the magnetic resonance of atoms in the brain; allows the production of a structural map of the brain without actually opening the skull. Also known as *magnetic resonance spectroscopy* and *nuclear magnetic resonance (NMR). See also* **functional magnetic resonance imaging (fMRI).**

magnetoencephalogram (MEG). Magnetic potentials recorded from detectors placed outside the skull.

magnocellular layer. Layer of neurons composed of large cells.

major tranquilizer. Drug that blocks the dopamine 2 (D_2) receptor and used mainly for treating schizophrenia. Also called a *neuroleptic drug.*

malaria. Infectious febrile disease caused by protozoa of the genus *Plasmodium*, which are parasitc in red blood cells; transmitted by *Anopheles* mosquitoes and marked by attacks of chills, fever, and sweating occurring at intervals that depend on the time required for the devlopment of a new generation of parasites in the body.

mania. Disordered mental state of extreme excitment; specifically, the manic type of manic-depressive psychosis.

mass-action hypothesis. Proposes that the entire neocortex participates in every behavior.

massa intermedia. Mass of gray matter that connects the left and right thalami across the midline.

materialism. Philosophical position that holds that behavior can be explained as a function of the nervous system without explanatory recourse to the mind.

maturation hypothesis. Argues that both hemispheres initially have roles in language but the left hemisphere gradually becomes more specialized for language control.

maturational-lag hypothesis. Explains a disability by suggesting that a system is not yet mature or is maturing slowly.

medial longitudinal fissure. Fissure that separates the two hemispheres.

median eminence. Pathway connecting the two sides of the thalamus.

medulla oblongata. Part of the hindbrain immediately rostral to the spinal cord.

medulloblastoma. Highly malignant brain tumor found almost exclusively in the cerebellums of children; results from the growth of germinal cells that infiltrate the cerebellum.

meninges. Three layers of protective tissue—the dura mater, arachnoid, and pia mater—that encase the brain and spinal cord.

meningioma. Encapsulated brain tumor growing from the meninges.

meningitis. Inflammation of the meninges.

mental level. Measure of intelligence in which ability is expressed as a level of performance that is average for a given age.

mental rotation. Ability to make a mental image of an object and imagine it in a new location relative to its background.

mescaline. Poisonous alkaloid from the flowering heads of a Mexican cactus; produces an intoxication with delusions of color and sound.

mesencephalon. Middle brain; term for the middle one of the three primary embryonic vesicles, which subsequently comprises the tectum and tegmentum.

mesolimbic dopamine system. Dopamine neurons in the midbrain that project to the nucleus accumbens and to medial parts of the basal ganglia, limbic system, and neocortex.

messenger RNA(mRNA). Type of ribonucleic acid synthesized from DNA (deoxyribonucleic acid); attaches to ribosomes to specify the sequences of amino acids that form proteins.

metabolic tolerance. Reduced sensitivity to a substance that results from the increased ability of cells to metabolize the substance.

metabotropic receptor. Receptor linked to a G protein (guanyl nuleotide-binding protein); can affect other receptors or act with second messengers to affect other cellular processes.

metastasis. Transfer of a disease from one part of the body to another; common characteristic of malignant tumors.

metastatic tumor. Tumor that arises through the transfer of tumor cells from elsewhere in the body.

metencephalon. Anterior part of the rhombencephalon; composed of the cerebellum and pons.

Met-enkephalin. Peptide neurotransmitter that produces some of the effects of opioid drugs.

mGluR4. Receptor on the tongue; sensitive to glutamate.

microfilaments. Small tubelike processes in cells. Their function is uncertain, but it may be to control the shape, movement, or fluidity of the cytoplasm or substances within the cell.

microtubules. Fiberlike substances in the soma and processes of nerve cells; transport substances from the soma to the distal elements of the cell or from distal parts of the cell to the soma.

midbrain. Short segment between the forebrain and hindbrain, including the tectum and tegmentum.

middle cerebral artery. Runs along the length of the Sylvian fissure and sends blood to the ventral part of the frontal lobe, most of the parietal lobe, and the temporal lobe.

migraine. Type of headache characterized by an aching, throbbing pain, often unilateral; may be preceded by a visual aura presumed to result from ischemia of the occipital cortex induced by vasoconstriction of cerebral arteries.

migraine stroke. Condition in which a cerebral vessel constricts, cutting off the blood supply to a cortical region. If the constriction is severe enough and lasts more than a few minutes, neuronal death may occur, leading to an infarct.

millisecond. One thousandth of a second.

millivolt. One thousandth of a volt.

mind. The psyche; the faculty, or brain function, by which one is aware of one's surroundings and by which one experiences feeling, emotions, and desires and is able to attend, reason, and make decisions.

mind–body problem. Problem of how to explain how a nonmaterial mind can command a material body.

miniature postsynaptic potential (MPP). Small excitatory or inhibitory graded potential, the amplitude of which is related to the number of quanta of neurotransmitter released at the synapse.

mitochondrion. Complex cellular organelle that produces most of a cell's energy through a number of processes.

module. Hypothetical unit of cortical organization, believed to represent a vertically organized intracortical connectivity that is assumed to correspond to a single functional unit. Sometimes used as a synonym for *column*.

monists. People who believe that the mind and body are one.

monoamine oxidase (MAO) inhibitor. Chemical that blocks MAO from degrading neurotransmitters such as dopamine, noradrenaline, and serotonin.

monoamines. Group of neurotransmitters, including norepinephrine and dopamine, that have an amine (NH_2) group.

monoclonal antibody. Antibody that is cloned or derived from a single cell.

monocular blindness. Blindness in one eye caused by the destruction of its retina or optic nerve.

monocular deprivation. Removal of visual stimulation to one eye by closure or bandaging.

morpheme. Smallest meaningful unit of speech.

morphine. Principal and most active alkaloid of opium. Its hydrochloride and sulfate salts are used as narcotic analgesics.

morphological reconstruction. Reconstruction of the body of an animal, often from only skeletal remains.

motoneuron. Sherrington's term for the unit formed by motor neurons and the muscle fiber to which their axon terminations are connected.

motor aphasia. Disorder in which an affected person is unable to make the correct movements of the mouth and tongue to form words, in contrast with *sensory aphasia*, in which speech is fluent but without content; a form of nonfluent aphasia.

motor apraxia. Inability, in the absence of paralysis, to execute the voluntary movements needed to perform a goal-oriented action.

motor cortex. Region of the cerebral cortex that, when stimulated electrically, produces muscle movements.

motor neuron. Neuron that has its cell body in the spinal cord and projects to muscles.

motor pathway. Anatomical pathway from the brain to the spinal cord and muscles.

motor program. Hypothetical neural circuit so arranged that it produces a certain type of movement—for example, walking.

movement. Act of moving; motion.

multimodal cortex. Receives sensory inputs from more than one sensory modality—for example, vision and audition.

multiple sclerosis (MS). Disease of unknown cause in which there are patches of demyelination in the central nervous system; may lead to motor weakness or incoordination, speech disturbance, and sometimes to other cognitive symptoms.

muscle-contraction headache. Caused by prolonged contraction of the muscles on the skull.

mutation. Permanent transmissible change in the genetic material.

myasthenia gravis. Condition of fatigue and weakness of the muscular system without sensory disturbance or atrophy;

results from a reduction in acetylcholine available at the synapse.

mycotic infection. Invasion of the nervous system by a fungus.

myelencephalon. Posterior part of the rhombencephalon, including the medulla oblongata and fourth ventricle.

myelin. Lipid substance forming an insulating sheath around certain nerve fibers; formed by oligodendroglia in the central nervous system and by Schwann cells in the peripheral nervous system.

myelination. Formation of myelin on axons; sometimes used as an index of maturation.

myelin stains. Dyes that stain glial cells, particularly those that wrap themselves around axons.

myoclonic spasms. Massive seizures consisting of sudden flexions or extensions of the body and often beginning with a cry.

nalorphine. Semisynthetic congener of morphine; used as an antagonist to morphine and related narcotics and in the diagnosis of narcotic addiction.

naloxone. Narcotic antagonist structurally related to oxymorphone; used as an antidote to narcotic overdosage.

narcolepsy. Condition in which a person is overcome by uncontrollable, recurrent, brief episodes of sleep.

narcotic analgesic. Drug that has sedative and pain-relieving properties.

nasal hemianopia. Loss of vision of one nasal visual field due to damage to the lateral region of the optic chiasm.

natural selection. Proposition in the theory of evolution that animals with certain adaptive characteristics will survive in certain environments and pass on their genetic characteristics to their offspring, whereas less-fortunate animals, lacking those characteristics, die off.

necrosis. Tissue death, usually as individual cells, groups of cells, or in small localized areas.

negative symptoms. The absence of behaviors; contrasts with *positive symptoms*, which indicate the presence of abnormal behaviors.

neglect dyslexia. Misreading errors usually confined to a single half of a word.

neocortex. Newest layer of the brain, forming the outer layer, or "new bark"; has from four to six layers of cells; in this book, synonymous with *cortex*.

neotony. Fact that newly evolved species often resemble the young of their ancestors.

nerve. Macroscopic, cordlike structure comprising a collection of nerve fibers that convey impulses between a part of the central nervous system and some other body region.

nerve fiber. As part of a neuron, a long process that carries information from the neuron to other neurons; also a collection of nerve fibers.

nerve growth factor (NGF). Protein that plays a role in maintaining the growth of a cell.

nerve impulse. Movement or propagation of an action potential along the length of an axon; begins at a point close to the cell body and travels away from it.

nerve net hypothesis. Idea that the brain is composed of a continuous network of interconnected fibers.

neural stem cells. Cells that gives rise to all neurons in the nervous system.

neural tube. Structure in the early stage of brain development from which the brain and spinal cord develop.

neuritic plaques. Areas of incomplete necrosis that are often seen in the cortexes of people with senile dementias such as Alzheimer's disease.

neuroblast. Any embryonic cell that develops into a neuron.

neuroendocrine. Refers to the interaction of the neural and endocrine (hormonal) systems.

neurofibril. Any of numerous fibrils making up part of the internal structure of a neuron; may be active in transporting precursor chemicals for the synthesis of neurotransmitters.

neurohumoral. Refers in general to the action of hormones on the brain.

neuroleptic drug. Drug that has an antipsychotic action principally affecting psychomotor activity and that is generally without hypnotic effects.

neurologist. Physician specializing in the treatment of disorders of the nervous system.

neurology. Branch of medical science dealing with the nervous system, both normal and diseased.

neuron. Basic unit of the nervous system; the nerve cell; includes the cell body (soma), many processes called dendrites, and an axon. Its function is to transmit and store information.

neuron hypothesis. Idea that the functional units of the brain are neurons.

neuropsychology. Study of the relations between brain function and behavior.

neuroscience. Embryology, anatomy, physiology, biochemistry, and pharmacology of the nervous system.

neurotoxin. Any substance that is poisonous or destructive to nerve tissue; for example, 6-hydroxydopamine, placed in the ventricles of the brain, will selectively destroy the norepinephrine and dopamine systems.

neurotransmitter. Chemical that is released from a synapse in response to an action potential and acts on postsynaptic receptors to change the resting potential of the receiving cell; transmits information chemically from one neuron to another.

neurotransmitter substance. Substance that meets four criteria: (1) it must be present in neurons; (2) when released, it must produce a response in a target cell; (3) the same response must be obtained when the chemical is experimentally placed on the target; and (4) there must be a mechanism for the removal of the substance.

neurotrophic factors. Class of compounds that act to support growth and differentiation in developing neurons and may act to keep certain neurons alive in adulthood.

neurotropic viruses. Viruses having a strong affinity for cells of the central nervous system. *See also* **pantropic viruses.**

nicotine. Poisonous alkaloid, obtained from tobacco or produced synthetically; used as an agricultural insecticide and, in veterinary medicine, as an external parasiticide.

nightmares. Terrifying dreams.

Nissl stain. Used to stain neurons for microscopic examination.

Nissl substance. Large granular body that stains with basic dyes; collectively forms the substance of the reticulum of the cytoplasm of a nerve cell.

nitric oxide (NO). Gas that acts as a chemical neurotransmitter in many cells.

node of Ranvier. Space separating the Schwann cells that form the covering (or myelin) on a nerve axon; because the nerve impulse jumps from one node to the next, its propagation is accelerated.

nonfluent aphasia. Impairment of speech subsequent to brain damage, particularly to the frontal part of the hemisphere dominant for speech; characterized by difficulty in articulating words.

non-REM (NREM) sleep. All segments of sleep excluding REM sleep.

norepinephrine. Chemical neurotransmitter in the brain; found in one of the nonspecific ascending systems.

norepinephrinergic neuron. Neuron that contains norepinephrine in its synapses or uses norepinephrine as its neurotransmitter.

nuclear magnetic resonance (NMR). *See* **magnetic resonance imaging (MRI).**

nuclear membrane. Surrounds the nucleus of a cell.

nucleolus. Organelle within the nucleus of a cell; produces ribosomes.

nucleus. Spherical structure in the soma of a cell; contains DNA and is essential to cell function; also, a group of cells forming a cluster that can be identified histologically.

nystagmus. Constant, tiny involuntary eye movements that have a variety of causes.

object constancy. Perceptual experience in which objects are identified as being the same regardless of the angle of view.

object recognition. Ability to identify the characteristics of objects including their name and function.

obstructive sleep apnea. Constriction of the breathing apparatus that results in loss of breath during sleep; thought to be a major cause of snoring.

occipital horns. Most posterior projections of the lateral ventricles that protrude into the occipital lobe.

occipital lobe. General area of the cortex lying in the back part of the head.

olfaction. Sense of smell or the act of smelling.

oligodendrocytes. Specialized support, or glial, cells in the brain that form a covering of myelin on nerve cells to speed the nerve impulse. Also called *oligodendroglia.*

ophthalmologic migraine. Migraine affecting vision.

opium. Crude resinous extract from the opium poppy.

optic ataxia. Deficit in the visual control of reaching and other movements and in eye movements.

optic chiasm. Point at which the optic nerve from one eye partly crosses to join the other, forming a junction at the base of the brain.

optic flow. Apparent motion of visual information when an animal is in motion.

orbital frontal cortex. Lies adjacent to the cavity containing the eye but, anatomically defined, receives projections from the dorsomedial nucleus of the thalamus.

organic brain syndrome. General term for behavioral disorders that result from brain malfunction attributable to known or unknown causes.

organicity. General term (of limited value in neuropsychology) used to refer to abnormal behavior that is assumed to have a biological (organic) basis.

organ of Corti. Organ lying against the basilar membrane in the cochlear duct; contains special sensory receptors for hearing and consists of neuroepithelial hair cells and several types of supporting cells.

organophosphate. Organic ester of phosphoric or thiophosphoric acid.

orientation. Direction.

orienting reaction. Process by which an animal's attention is engaged by a novel stimulus.

oscilloscope. Instrument that displays a visual representation of electrical variations on the fluorescent screen of a cathode-ray tube.

otolith organs. Bodies in the inner ear that provide vestibular information.

output cell. Cell that conveys information away from a circuit; motor neuron that conveys information to a muscle.

output cell layers. Cell layers that send efferent connections to other parts of the nervous system; layers 5 and 6 in the cerebral cortex.

oval window. Region in the inner ear where the ossicles amplify and convey vibrations that subsequently stimulate the basilar membrane.

paired helical filaments. Two spiral filaments made of chains of amino acids.

paleocortex. Part of the cerebral cortex forming the pyriform cortex and parahippocampal gyrus. Also called the *paleopallium*.

pantropic viruses. Viruses that attack any body tissue. *See also* **neurotropic viruses.**

papilledema. Swelling of the optic disc caused by increased pressure from cerebrospinal fluid; used as a diagnostic indicator of tumors or other swellings in the brain.

paragraphia. Writing of incorrect words or perseveration in writing the same word.

paralimbic cortex. Area of three-layered cortex that is adjacent to the classically defined limbic cortex and has a direct connection with the limbic cortex—for example, the cingulate cortex.

parallel-development hypothesis. Proposes that both hemispheres, by virtue of their anatomy, play special roles, one for language and one for space.

paraphasia. Production of unintended syllables, words, or phrases during speech.

paraplegia. Paralysis of the legs due to spinal-cord damage.

parasite. Plant or animal that lives on or within another living organism at whose expense it obtains some advantage.

paresis. General term for loss of physical and mental ability due to brain disease, particularly from syphilitic infection; a term for slight or incomplete paralysis.

parietal lobe. General region of the brain lying beneath the parietal bone.

parieto-occipital sulcus. Sulcus in the occipital cortex.

Parkinson's disease. Disease of the motor system that is correlated with a loss of dopamine in the brain and is characterized by tremors, rigidity, and reduction in voluntary movement.

pars opercularis. Part of the inferior frontal lobe adjacent to the parietal lobe and overhanging the insula.

parvocellular layer. Layer of neurons containing small cells.

peptide. Any member of a class of compounds of low molecular weight that yield two or more amino acids on hydrolysis. Peptides form the consistent parts of proteins.

perception. Cognition resulting from the activity of cells in the various sensory regions of the neocortex beyond the primary sensory cortex.

perforant pathway. Large anatomical pathway connecting the entorhinal cortex and subiculum with the hippocampal formation.

peripheral nerves. Nerves that lie outside the spinal cord and the brain.

peripheral nervous system. Collective name for all of the neurons in the body that are located outside the brain and spinal cord.

perseveration. Tendency to emit repeatedly the same verbal or motor response to varied stimuli.

petit mal attack. Seizure characterized by a loss of awareness during which there is no motor activity except blinking of the eyes or turning of the head and rolling of the eyes; of brief duration (typically 10 seconds).

petit mal epilepsy. Epilepsy seen especially in children, in which there is sudden momentary unconsciousness with only minor myoclonic jerks.

phagocytes. Cells that engulf microorganisms, other cells, and foreign particles as part of the lymphatic system's defenses.

phenothiazines. Group of major tranquilizers (for example, chlorpromazine) that are similar in molecular structure to the compound phenothiazine.

pheromone. Substance produced by one individual that is perceived (as an odor) by a second individual of the same species and that leads to a specific behavioral reaction in the second individual; acts as a chemical signal between animals of the same species.

phoneme. Unit of sound that forms a word or part of a word.

phonological. Refers to sound, as in theories of reading that emphasize the role of sound in decoding the meaning of words.

phonological reading. Reading that relies on sounding out the parts of words.

phrenology. Long-discredited study of the relation between mental faculties and the skull's surface features.

physical dependence. Indicated by the display of withdrawal symptoms on cessation of drug use.

pia mater. Moderately tough connective tissue that clings to the surface of the brain.

piloerection. Erection of the hair.

pineal body. Asymmetrical structure in the epithalamus, thought by Descartes to be the seat of the soul, but now thought to take part in circadian rhythms.

pinna. Auricle; the part of the ear outside the head.

pituitary gland. Collection of neurons at the base of the hypothalamus.

place cells. Cells that are maximally responsive to specific locations in the world.

place response. Navigational behavior in which an animal locomotes to a position on the basis of its location relative to multiple cues. Compare **cue response** and **position response.**

place task. Task in which an animal must find a place that it cannot see by using the relation between two or more cues in its surroundings.

planum temporale. Cortical area just posterior to the auditory cortex (Heschl's gyrus) within the Sylvian fissure.

plasmodium. Genus of sporozoa parasitic in the red blood cells of animals and humans; the malarial parsite.

plasticity. According to theory, the ability of the brain to change in various ways to compensate for loss of function due to damage.

pneumoencephalography. X-ray technique in which the cerebrospinal fluid is replaced by air introduced through a lumbar puncture.

poliomyelitis. Acute viral disease characterized by involvement of the nervous system and possibly paralysis. There may be atrophy of the affected muscles, leading to a permanent deformity.

polygraph. Apparatus for simultaneously recording blood pressure, pulse, and respiration, as well as variations in electrical resistance of the skin. Popularly known as a *lie detector.*

polymodal cortex. Cortex that receives sensory inputs from more than one sensory modality—for example, vision and audition.

polypeptide chain. Peptide containing more than two amino acids linked by peptide bonds.

polyribosome. Structure formed by the combination of mRNA and ribosomes that serves as the site for protein synthesis.

polysensory neuron. Neuron that responds to information from more than one sensory modality.

pons. Part of the hindbrain; composed mostly of motor-fiber tracts going to such areas as the cerebellum and spinal tract.

position response. Navigational behavior in which an animal locomotes to a position on the basis of movements (for example, left or right) previously made to arrive at the same location. Compare **cue response** and **place response.**

positive symptoms. Occurrence of abnormal behaviors. Compare **negative symptoms.**

positron-emission tomography (PET). Imaging technique in which a subject is given a radioactively labeled compound such as glucose, which is metabolized by the brain, and the radioactivity is later recorded by a special detector.

postconcussional syndrome. Constellation of somatic and psychological symptoms including headache, dizziness, fatigue, diminished concentration, memory deficit, irritability, anxiety, insomnia, hypochondriacal concern, and hypersensitivity to noise and light, all of which are typical after suffering a brief period of disturbed consciousness, usually after a blow to the head.

posterior cerebral artery. Cerebral artery that supplies blood to the posterior part of the cerebral hemispheres, including the occipital lobe and hippocampal formation.

posterior parietal cortex. Nonspecific expression referring to tissue beyond the primary somatosensory areas; usually includes areas PE, PF, and PG.

postictal. Subsequent to a seizure.

postictal depression. State of reduced affect subsequent to a seizure.

postsynaptic membrane. Membrane lying adjacent to a synaptic connection across the synaptic space from the terminal.

posttraumatic psychosis. Psychotic reaction after head trauma.

praxis. Action, movement, or series of movements.

preadaption. Behavior that evolves for one purpose but then becomes useful for another purpose.

precentral gyrus. Gyrus lying in front of the central sulcus.

precession. Act of preceding.

preferred cognitive mode. Use of one type of thought process in preference to another—for example, visuospatial instead of verbal; sometimes attributed to the assumed superior function of one hemisphere over the other.

prefrontal cortex. Cortex lying in front of the primary and secondary motor cortex and thus the association, or tertiary, cortex in the frontal lobe.

premotor cortex. Cerebral cortex lying immediately anterior to the motor cortex; includes several functional areas, especially the supplementary motor area and Broca's area.

presynaptic membrane. Terminal membrane adjacent to the subsynaptic space.

primary motor cortex. Neocortical area corresponding to Brodmann's area 4; forms the major source of the corticospinal tract.

primary projection area. Area of the brain that first receives a connection from another system.

primary sensory cortex. Neocortical areas that receive the projections of the principal thalamic regions for each sensory modality; corresponds to Brodmann's areas 17 (vision), 41 (audition), and 3-1-2 (somatosensation).

primary zones. Areas of the cortex that first receive projections from sensory systems or that project most directly to muscles. Also known as *primary sensory areas.*

prime mover theories. Theories that explain brain size in regard to a single factor.

priming. Experimental technique by which a stimulus is used to sensitize the nervous system to a later presentation of the same or a similar stimulus.

priming task. Task in which subjects are presented with information that will subsequently influence their behavior but that they may not subsequently consciously recall; for example, given a list of words, a subject may be more likely to subsequently use a word on the list than some other word that also would be appropriate.

proactive interference. Interference of something already experienced with the learning of new information.

procedural memory. Memory for certain ways of doing things or for certain movements; this memory system is thought to be independent of declarative memory (that is, memory used to "tell about" some event).

progenitor cell. Cell that is derived from a stem cell and acts as a precursor cell that migrates and produces a neuron or glial cell.

projection map. Map of the cortex made by tracing axons from the sensory systems into the brain and from the neocortex to the motor systems of the brainstem and spinal cord.

proprioception. Perception of the position and movement of the body, limbs, and head.

proprioceptive. Refers to sensory stimuli coming from the muscles and tendons.

prosencephalon. Front brain; term for the most anterior part of the embryonic brain, which subsequently evolves into the telencephalon and diencephalon.

prosody. Variation in stress, pitch, and rhythm of speech by which different shades of meaning are conveyed.

prosopagnosia. Inability, not explained by defective visual acuity or reduced consciousness or alertness, to recognize familiar faces; rare in pure form and thought to be secondary to right parietal lesions.

protein. Any of a group of complex organic compounds containing carbon, hydrogen, oxygen, nitrogen, and sulfur. Proteins, the principal constituents of the protoplasm of all cells, are of high molecular weight and consist of α-amino acids connected by peptide linkages.

proximal. Being close to something.

pseudodepression. Condition of personality subsequent to frontal-lobe lesion in which apathy, indifference, and loss of initiative are apparent symptoms but are not accompanied by a patient's sense of depression.

pseudopsychopathy. Condition of personality subsequent to frontal-lobe lesion in which immature behavior, lack of tact and restraint, and other behaviors symptomatic of psychopathology are apparent but are not accompanied by the equivalent mental or emotional components of psychopathology.

psilocybin. Psychedelic drug obtained from the mushroom *Psilocybe mexicana.*

psychedelic drug. Any drug that induces behavior characterized by visual hallucinations, intensified perception, and, sometimes, behavior similar to that observed in psychosis.

psychoactive drug. Any chemical substance that alters mood or behavior by altering the functions of the brain.

psychology. Science dealing with the mind and mental processes, especially in relation to human and animal behavior.

psychometrics. Science of measuring human abilities.

psychomotor activation. Increase in cognitive or motor behavior often seen in response to a stimulant drug.

psychosis. Major mental disorder of organic or emotional origin in which a person's ability to think, respond emotionally, remember, communicate, interpret reality, and behave appropriately is sufficiently impaired that the ordinary demands of life cannot be met; applicable to conditions having a wide range of severity and duration—for example, schizophrenia or depression.

psychosurgery. Surgical intervention to sever fibers connecting one part of the brain to another or to remove or destroy brain tissue with the intent of modifying or altering disturbances of behavior, thought content, or mood for which no organic pathological cause can be demonstrated by established tests and techniques (for example, lobotomy).

ptosis. Drooping of the upper eyelid from paralysis of the third nerve (oculomotor).

pulvinar. Thalamic nucleus that receives projections from the visual cortex and superior colliculus and sends connections to the secondary and tertiary temporal and parietal cortex.

pump. Protein in the cell membrane that actively transports a substance across the membrane. Also called a *transporter.*

punctate evolution. Evolution that appears to occur suddenly, rather than in gradual steps; sometimes referred to as *punctuated evolution.*

punctuated evolution. *See* **punctate evolution.**

pure aphasia. Aphasia in the absence of other language disorders such as alexia or agraphia.

putamen. Nucleus of the basal ganglia complex.

putative transmitters. Chemicals strongly suspected of being neurotransmitters but not conclusively proved to be so.

pyramid. Pointed or cone-shaped structure or part.

pyramidal cells. Cells that have pyramid-shaped cell bodies; they usually send information from one region of the cortex to some other brain area.

pyramidalis area. Brodmann's area 4.

pyramidal tract. Pathway from the pyramidal cells of the fifth and sixth layers of the neocortex to the spinal cord.

pyriform cortex. Old cortex; subserves olfactory functions.

quadrantanopia. Defective vision or blindness in one-fourth of the visual field.

quadriplegia. Paralysis of the legs and arms due to spinal cord damage.

quantum. Unit of measure in quantum theory.

quasi-evolutionary sequence. Hypothetical ancestral lineage of a contemporary species; comprises the currently living species that most closely resemble the ancestors; for example, the ancestral lineage for humans would include hedgehogs, tree shrews, bush babies, rhesus monkeys, and chimpanzees.

radial glial cells. Cells that form miniature "highways" that provide pathways for migrating neurons to follow to their appropriate destinations.

radioisotope scan. Scanning of the cranial surface with a Geiger counter, after an intravenous injection of a radioisotope has been given, to detect tumors, vascular disturbances, atrophy, and so forth.

rapidly adapting receptor. Body sensory receptor that responds briefly to the onset of a stimulus on the body.

rate-limiting factor. Any enzyme that is in limited supply and so limits the rate at which a chemical can be produced.

readiness potential. Evoked potential that occurs just before a movement.

reading disabled. Refers to the inability to read, irrespective of the cause.

reafference. Confirmation by one part of the nervous system of the activity in another. *See also* **corollary discharge.**

reafference theory. *See* **corollary discharge theory.**

real space. Space that one sees around oneself; three-dimensional space.

receptive field. Area from which a stimulus can activate a sensory receptor.

receptor. Protein on a cell membrane to which another molecule can attach.

reciprocal inhibition. Activation of one muscle group with inhibition of its antagonists.

red nucleus. Nucleus in the anterior part of the tegmentum that is the source of a major motor projection.

reentry. Process by which cortical regions send projections back to regions from which they receive afferents; proposed as a mechanism for solving the binding problem.

referred pain. Pain that is felt in a body part other than that in which the cause that produced it is situated.

regeneration. Process by which neurons damaged by trauma regrow connections to the area that they innervated before the trauma.

relatively refractory. Refers to the later phase of an action potential during which increased electrical current is required to produce another action potential; a phase during which potassium channels are still open.

REM (rapid eye movement) sleep. Part of sleep during which rapid eye movements occur; associated with loss of muscle tone and vivid dreams.

resting potential. Normal voltage across a nerve-cell membrane; varies between 60 and 90 mV in the cells of various animals.

reticular activating system. Diffuse neural system located in the brainstem that functions to arouse the forebrain.

reticular formation. Mixture of nerve cells and fibers in the lower and ventral part of the brainstem, extending from the spinal cord to the thalamus and giving rise to important ascending and descending systems. Also known as the *reticular activating system.*

reticular matter. Area of the nervous system composed of intermixed cell bodies and axons; has a mottled gray and white, or netlike, appearance.

retrograde amnesia. Inability to remember events that took place before the onset of amnesia.

retrograde degeneration. Degeneration of a nerve cell between the site of damage and the cell body, including the cell body and all its remaining processes.

retrograde transport. Transport of material by a neuron from its axon back to the cell body. Labels or dyes can be placed at the termination of an axon, picked up by the axonal arborization, and transported to the cell body, which makes it possible to trace pathways.

rhinencephalon. Alternative term for the limbic system; literally, smell brain.

rhombencephalon. Hindmost posterior embryonic part of the brain, which divides into the metencephalon and myelencephalon.

ribonucleic acid (RNA). Complex macromolecule composed of a sequence of nucleotide bases attached to a sugar–phosphate backbone. Messenger RNA delivers genetic information from DNA to a ribosome (ribosomal RNA), where the appropriate molecules of transfer RNA assemble the appropriate amino acids to produce the polypeptide encoded by the DNA.

ribosome. Large complex of enzymes and RNA (ribonucleic acid) molecules that catalyzes reactions in the formation of proteins.

righting reflex. Reflex by which an animal placed in an inverted posture returns to upright; survives low decerebration and hence a reflex.

rods. Light-sensitive retinal receptor cells that contain rhodopsin; together with cones, they form the receptor layer of the retina.

roentgenography. Photography in which X-rays are used.

rubrospinal tract. Pathway from the red nucleus to the spinal cord; has a role in the control of the limbs.

saccade. Series of involuntary, abrupt, and rapid small movements or jerks of both eyes simultaneously in changing the point of fixation.

saccule. One of two vestibular receptors of the middle ear; stimulated when the head is oriented normally; maintains head and body in an upright position.

saltatory conduction. Propagation of a nerve impulse on a myelinated axon; characterized by its leaping from one node of Ranvier to another.

savant syndrome. Characterized by various degrees of retardation, along with some special, sometimes supranormal, skill.

scanning electron microscope. Electron microscope that can produce three-dimensional images of an object.

schizophrenia. Type of psychosis characterized by disordered cognitive functioning and poor social adjustment; literally, splitting of thought and emotive processes; probably due to brain malfunction.

Schwann cells. Glial cells that form myelin in the peripheral nervous system.

sclera. Tough white outer coat of the eyeball.

sclerotic plaque. Decribes the hardening or inflammation of connective tissue or blood vessels. Sclerotic plaques are often seen in brains of people with Alzheimer's disease.

scotoma. Small blind spot in the visual field caused by small lesions, an epileptic focus, or migraines of the occipital lobe.

secondary area. Cortical region that receives inputs from the primary areas and is thought to participate in more complex sensory and perceptual or motor functions.

secondary cortex. Cortex that Paul Fleshig found to develop after the primary motor and sensory regions. Alexander Luria proposed that these regions have roles in perception (secondary sensory) and in the organization of movements (secondary motor).

secondary projection area. Area of the cortex that receives projections from a primary projection area or sends projections to it.

second-generation antidepressant. Antidepressant thought to be more selective than a first-generation antidepressant in its action on serotonin reuptake transporters.

second messengers. Diffusible molecules that may influence a variety of cellular constituents, including ion channels. When a transmitter is released and binds to a receptor, an intermediate protein (a G protein), which is bound to the receptor, releases the second-messenger molecule.

sedative-hypnotic. Any drug that acts to depress neural activity (and behavior) by either decreasing noradrenergic activity or increasing GABAergic activity.

selective serotonin uptake blocker. Drug that acts to selectively prevent the reuptake of serotonin at the synapse, resulting in a relative increase in the action of serotonin on the postsynaptic membrane.

semantic memory. Memory of world knowledge that is stored independently of the time and place that it was acquired.

semantics. Study of meaning in language.

semicircular canals. Structures in the middle ear that are open on one side and act as part of the receptor unit for balance.

sensation. Result of activity of receptors and their associated afferent pathways to the corresponding primary sensory neocortical areas.

sensitization. Condition in which subsequent exposures to a drug (or other agent) induce a stronger behavioral response than did the original exposure.

sensitization model. Model of bipolar illness that proposes that the brain of the bipolar patient is especially sensitive to the effects of stressors or drugs and that episodes of mood disorder actually change the brain.

sensory aphasia. *See* **Wernicke's aphasia.**

sensory neglect. Condition in which an individual does not respond to sensory stimulation.

sensory pathway. Conveys sensory information to the brain.

sensory receptor. Cell that transduces sensory information into nervous activity.

septum. Nucleus in the limbic system that, when lesioned in rats, produces sham rage and abolishes the theta EEG waveform.

serial lesion effect. Effect in which slowly acquired lesions or lesions acquired in stages tend to have less-severe symptoms than those of lesions of equivalent size that are acquired at one time.

serotonin uptake blocker. Drug that selectively blocks the reuptake of serotonin into the terminal.

sex-related differences. Behavioral differences between males and females that are related to experience, genes, or hormones, or some combination of them.

sexual selection. Mechanism of evolution in which the processes of determining who mates with whom also determine the characteristics of the offspring that will be produced.

short-term memory. Form of memory postulated by Broadbent in which information is assumed to be stored for no more than about 15 minutes.

silent synapses. Synapses that do not appear to be functional until other, dominant synapses are removed.

simultagnosia. Symptom in which a person is unable to perceive more than one object at a time.

simultaneous extinction. Second stage of recovery from contralateral neglect; characterized by response to stimuli on the neglected side as if there were a simultaneous stimulation on the contralateral side.

single-photon emission computerized tomography (SPECT). Imaging technique in which a subject is given a radioactively labeled compound such as glucose, which is metabolized by the brain. The radioactivity is later recorded by a special detector. Similar to positron-emission tomography, but less accurate, SPECT has the advantage of not requiring a cyclotron to produce the isotopes.

skull. The cranium; the bony framework of the head, composed of the cranial and facial bones.

sleep apnea. Condition in which breathing stops when a person falls into deep sleep.

sleep attack. Sudden loss of consciousness.

sleep paralysis. Inability to move on awakening from sleep.

slowly adapting receptor. Body sensory receptor that responds as long as a sensory stimulus is on the body.

slow-wave sleep. Stage of sleep characterized by an electroencephalogram dominated by large-amplitude slow waves.

small-molecule transmitters. Class of neurotransmitters made in the synapse from products derived from the diet.

sodium–potassium pump. Pumplike mechanism that shunts sodium out of the cell and potassium into it.

soma. Cell body, including the cell membrane, nucleus, and cytoplasm.

somatic muscles. Muscles of the body that are attached to the skeleton.

somatosensory system. Neural system pertaining to the tactile senses, including touch, kinesthesia, pain, and proprioception.

somatosensory threshold. Threshold for detecting different tactile sensations.

somatosensory zone. Any region of the brain responsible for analyzing sensations of fine touch and pressure and possibly of pain and temperature.

somnolence. Sleepiness; excessive drowsiness.

sparing. Phenomenon by which some brain functions are saved from disruption after the occurrence of a lesion early in life, usually before the particular function has developed.

spatial learning. Learning spatial information such as the location of a goal object.

spatial summation. Tendency of two adjacent events to add. Hence, two adjacent postsynaptic potentials add or subtract.

specifically reading retarded. Refers to people who have adequate intelligence to be able to read but cannot read.

spinal cord. Part of the nervous system enclosed in the vertebral column.

spinal reflex. Response obtained when only the spinal cord is functioning.

spiny neurons. Class of neurons that have dendritic spines; most are excitatory.

splenium. Generally, a bandlike structure; used in reference to the posterior rounded end of the corpus callosum.

spongioblasts. Immature cells that develop into glial cells.

spreading depression. Condition in which a wave of depolarization spreads across the cortical surface, leading to a period in which the tissue is functionally blocked.

sprouting. Phenomenon subsequent to partial damage in which the remaining neurons or parts of a neuron sprout terminations to connect to the previously innervated area.

SQUID (superconducting quantum interferance device). Machine used to measure small magnetic fields produced by neurons in the brain.

stellate cell. Nerve cell characterized by having a star-shaped cell body. Such cells serve largely as association cells whose processes remain within the region of the brain in which the cell body is located.

stem cell. Supporting cell structure comparable to the stalk of a plant.

stereognosis. Recognition of objects through the sense of touch.

stimulation. Act of applying a stimulus or an irritant to something; the occurrence of such a stimulus or irritant.

stimulus. Irritant or event that causes a change in action of some brain area.

stimulus gradient. Gradient along which the intensity of a cue increases or decreases; for example, odors get stronger as the source is approached.

storage granules. Vesicles in the terminal that are presumed to store neurotransmitters.

stirrup. One of the ossicle bones of the middle ear. Also known as the *stapes*.

strephosymbolia. Disorder of perception in which objects seem reversed, as in a mirror; disability in which there is confusion between similar but oppositely oriented letters (for example, *b* and *d*) or words and a tendency to reverse direction in reading or writing.

stretch reflex. Contraction of a muscle to resist stretching; mediated through a muscle spindle, a special sensory receptor system in the muscle.

striate cortex. The primary visual cortex in the occipital lobe; has a striped appearance when stained, which gives it its name.

stroke. Sudden appearance of neurological symptoms as a result of severe interruption of blood flow.

study-test modality shift. Process by which subjects, when presented with information in one modality (reading) and tested in another modality (aurally), display poorer performance than when they are instructed and tested in the same modality.

subarachnoid space. Space between the arachnoid layer and the pia mater of the meninges.

subcortical loop. Anatomical pathway in which information goes from a subcortical structure, such as the amygdala, to the cortex and then back to the originating structure.

substance abuse. Use of a drug for the psychological and behavioral changes that it produces aside from its possible therapeutic effects.

substance dependence. Desire for a drug manifested by frequent use of the drug.

substantia gelatinosa. Gelatinous-appearing cap forming the dorsal part of the posterior horn of the spinal cord.

substantia nigra. Nucleus area in the midbrain containing the cell bodies of axons containing dopamine. In freshly prepared human tissue, the region appears black; hence the name (Latin, meaning "black substance").

sulcus (pl. sulci). Small cleft produced by folding of the cortex.

superior colliculus. Nucleus of the tectum in the midbrain that receives visual projections and controls whole-body reflexes to visual stimuli.

supplementary motor cortex. Small region of the cortex that lies outside the primary motor cortex but will produce movements when stimulated.

surface dyslexia. Inability to read words on the basis of their pictographic or graphemic representations, although the ability to read by using phonological, or sounding-out, procedures is retained.

Sylvian fissure. *See* **lateral fissure.**

symptomatic seizures. Seizures that have specific symptoms that may aid in localizing the seizure origin.

synapse. Point of contact between two cells. Classically, synapse refers to the junction between an axonal terminal and another cell, but other types of contacts also are found.

synaptic cleft. Space between the end foot of a neuron and the cell to which it connects.

synaptic knob. Also called *bouton termineau, end foot, synapsis, synapse,* or *terminal knob. See* **synapse.**

synaptic vesicles. Small vesicles visible in electron micrographs of terminals; believed to contain neurotransmitters.

Syndenham's chorea. Acute childhood disorder characterized by involuntary movements that gradually become severe, affecting virtually all movements including speech. Also known as St. Vitus's dance.

synesthesia. Ability to perceive a stimulus of one sense as a sensation of a different sense, as when sound produces a sensation of color.

syntax. Way in which words are put together, following the rules of grammar, to form phrases, clauses, or sentences; proposed as a unique characteristic of human language.

tachistoscope. Mechanical apparatus consisting of projector, viewer, and screen by which visual stimuli can be presented to selective parts of the visual field.

tactile. Refers to the sense of touch.

tactile form recognition. Recognition of the shape of objects by touch.

tardive dyskinesia. Slow, abnormal limb or body-part movements.

tectopulvinar pathway. Visual pathway from the eye to the tectum to the pulvinar (thalamus) to the secondary visual areas.

tectopulvinar system. Part of the visual system that functions to locate visual stimuli; includes the superior colliculus, posterior thalamus, and areas 20 and 21.

tectum. Area of the midbrain above the cerebral aqueduct (the roof); consists of the superior and inferior colliculi, which mediate whole-body response to visual and auditory stimuli, respectively.

tegmentum. Area of the midbrain below the cerebral aqueduct (the floor); contains sensory and motor tracts and a number of nuclei.

telencephalon. Endbrain; includes the cortex, basal ganglia, limbic system, and olfactory bulbs.

teleodendria. Fine terminal branches of an axon.

temporal lobe. Area of the cortex found laterally on the head, below the lateral sulci adjacent to the temporal bones.

temporal memory. Memory for the order of events in time.

temporal summation. Tendency of two events related in time to add. Hence, two temporally related postsynaptic potentials add or subtract.

terminal degeneration. Degeneration of the terminals of neurons; can be detected by selective tissue staining.

tertiary area. Area of the cortex that receives projections from a secondary projection area or sends projections to it. *See also* **association cortex.**

thalamus. Group of nuclei of the diencephalon.

theory of mind. Ability to predict what others are thinking or planning to do.

thermoregulation. Ability to regulate body temperature.

theta rhythm. Brain rhythm with a frequency of 4 to 7 Hz.

threshold. Point at which a stimulus produces a response.

threshold potential. Voltage level of a neural membrane at which an action potential is triggered by the opening of sodium and potassium voltage-sensitive channels; about -50 millivolts.

thrombosis. Plug or clot in a blood vessel; formed by the coagulation of blood.

tight junction. Connection between cells when their membranes are fused. Normally, cells are separated by a small space.

time-dependent amnesia. Amnesia that lasts for a brief period.

tolerance. Ability to endure unusually large doses of a drug without ill effect as a result of continuing use of the drug.

tonotopic theory. Pertains to the organization of the auditory cortex in which different frequencies of sound are represented in different cortical regions.

topographic agnosia. Loss of knowledge about the organization of the space; inability to recognize one's location in space, such as a failure to recognize one's own neighborhood.

topographic amnesia. Inability to remember the location of things or places; difficulty in remembering one's way in one's environment.

topograhic disorientation. Confusion regarding one's location in space; likely due to topographic agnosia or amnesia.

topographic map. Map of the neocortex showing various features, projections, cell distributions, and so on.

topographic memory. Memory for the organization of the world.

topographic organization. A neural-spatial representation of the body or areas of the sensory world perceived by a sensory organ.

topographic representation. Representation of the auditory world in which sounds are located in a systematic fashion in a progression from lower to higher frequencies.

Tourette's syndrome. Disease characterized by involuntary movements of body parts and involuntary utterance of words and sounds.

tract. Large collection of axons coursing together within the central nervous system.

transcortical aphasia. Aphasia in which a person can repeat and understand words and name objects but cannot speak spontaneously or can repeat words but cannot comprehend them.

transcranial magnetic stimulation (TMS). Procedure in which a magnetic coil is placed over the skull to stimulate the underlying brain; can be used either to induce behavior or to disrupt ongoing behavior.

transcranially. Across the skull.

transcription. Synthesis of RNA with the use of a DNA template and catalyzed by RNA polymerase; the base sequences of the RNA and DNA are complementary.

transient global amnesia. Short-lived neurological disturbance characterized by memory loss; may result from transient episodes of ischemia.

transient ischemia. Short-lived condition of inadequate supply of blood to a brain area.

translation. Synthesis of a polypeptide with the use of messenger RNA as a template.

transmitter-activated receptor. In the membrane of a cell, a receptor that has a binding site for a neurotransmitter.

transmitter substance. Allows neurons to communicate with one another and with glands, muscles, and other body organs.

transneuronal degeneration. Degeneration of a cell that synapses with a damaged cell or a cell onto which a damaged cell synapses; for example, sectioning of optic tracts results in the degeneration of lateral geniculate body cells.

transporter. Protein molecule that pumps a substance across a membrane.

traumatic encephalopathy. Degenerative disease of the brain brought on by a head trauma.

trephining. Removing a circular disc of bone, chiefly from the skull.

tricyclic antidepressant. Antidepressant that blocks the serotonin reuptake transporter.

tubules. Variety of kinds of thin rods of material in cells that provide structure, aid in movement, and serve as pathways for the transport of material within a cell.

tumor. Mass of new tissue that persists and grows independently; a neoplasm; surrounds tissue and has no physiological use.

Turner's syndrome. Genetic condition in which a female has only a single X chromosome. Women with Turner's syndrome have severe spatial deficits.

two-point discrimination. Ability to discriminate two individual points on the skin. The two-point threshold is the minimum distance apart that two points must be placed to be perceived as two points rather than one point.

uncinate fasciculus. Fiber tract connecting the temporal and frontal cortex; a hooked or curved tract.

unconscious inference. Decision or judgment made without knowing the source of the information leading to the judgment.

unilateral visual neglect. Neglect of all sensory events of one or more modalities of stimulation when the stimulation is restricted to one half of the world as defined by the central axis of the body.

unit activity. Electrical potential of a single cell.

utricle. Largest of the subdivisions of the labyrinth of the middle ear; major organ of the vestibular system, which provides information about the position of the head.

ventral corticospinal tract. Pathway from the cortx to the spinal cord carrying instructions for the movement of the trunk. This pathway does not cross over to the opposite side of the brainstem at the pyramidal protrusion.

ventral root. Tract of fibers leaving the spinal cord; on the ventral part of an animal's spinal cord and on the anterior part of a human's spinal cord.

ventral stream. Visual pathway from the primary visual cortex to the temporal cortex; primarily responsible for the conscious identification of visual stimuli.

ventricle. Cavity of the brain that contains cerebral spinal fluid.

ventricular zone. Zone in which stem cells reside that surrounds the ventricles.

ventriculography. X-ray technique by which the contours of the ventricles are highlighted by using an opaque medium introduced into the ventricle through a cannula inserted through the skull.

ventromedial system. One of the two major groups of tracts in the motor system; made up of the vestibulospinal tract, reticulospinal tract, and tectospinal tract, which originate in the brainstem, and the ventral corticospinal tract, which originates in the neocortex.

vertebral artery. Major artery supplying blood to the hindbrain and spinal cord.

vesicle. Small bladder or sac containing liquid.

vestibular system. Sensory system with receptors in the middle ear that respond to body position and movement.

virus. One of a group of minute infectioius agents characterized by a lack of independent metabolism and by the ability to replicate only within living host cells.

visual agnosia. Inability to combine visual impressions into complete patterns and therefore an inability to recognize objects; inability to perceive objects and to draw or copy them.

visualization. Ability to form a mental image of an object.

visual localization. Identification of a place in visual space.

vocal cords. Folds of mucous membrane in the larynx that are attached to the vocal muscles.

vocal fold. Vocal cord.

voltage gradient. Difference in voltage between two regions that allows a flow of current if the two regions are connected.

voltage-sensitive channel. Narrow passageway across the neuron membrane that is opened and closed in response to changes in the voltage across the membrane.

voltage-sensitive potassium channel. Voltage-sensitive channel that allows the passage of potassium.

voltage-sensitive sodium channel. Voltage-sensitive channel that allows the passage of sodium.

volume conducted. Electrical potential recorded in tissue at some distance away from its source.

voluntary movement. Any movement that takes an animal from one place to another; can be elicited by lower-level sensory input or executed through lower-level postural support and reflex systems. Also called *appetitive, instrumental, purposive,* or *operant movement.*

voxel. Area from which a measurement is taken, thus defining the resolution of an MRI measurement.

Wallerian degeneration. *See* **anterograde degeneration.**

Wernicke-Geschwind model. Theoretical model of the neurological organization of language in which there is a serial passage of information from the auditory cortex to the posterior speech zone to the anterior speech zone.

Wernicke's aphasia. Inability to comprehend speech or to produce meaningful speech; subsequent to lesions to the posterior cortex. Also called sensory aphasia. *See also* **fluent aphasia.**

Wernicke's area. Posterior part of the superior temporal gyrus, roughly equivalent to area 22.

white matter. Areas of the nervous system rich in axons covered with glial cells.

Wilson's disease. Genetic disease characterized by the failure to metabolize copper, which is concentrated in the brain.

withdrawal reflex. Withdrawal of a limb in response to applied stimuli that activate pain and temperature fibers. The reflex is mediated by a multisynaptic pathway in the spinal cord.

withdrawal symptom. A behavior displayed by a user when drug use ends.

word salad. Refers to fluent aphasia in which a person produces intelligible words that appear to be strung together randomly.

working memory. Short-term memory; memory for information just received and necessary for the "on line" performance of a task.

Name Index

Subject Index

Note: Page numbers followed by f indicate figures; those followed by t indicate tables.